LIQUIDITY RATIOS

Ratio	Formula	Description	Reference
Current ratio	$\frac{\text{Current Assets}}{\text{Current Liabilities}}$	Measures short-term debt-paying ability	Chapter 5, LO5
Quick ratio	$\frac{\text{Cash + Marketable Securities + Receivables}}{\text{Current Liabilities}}$	Measures short-term debt-paying ability	Chapter 17, LO3
Receivable turnover	$\frac{\text{Net Sales}}{\text{Average Accounts Receivable}}$	Average number of times receivables are turned into cash during an accounting period	Chapter 8, LO1
Days' sales uncollected	$\frac{\text{Days in Year}}{\text{Receivable Turnover}}$	Average number of days a company must wait to receive payment for credit sales or to collect accounts receivable	Chapter 8, LO 1
Inventory turnover	$\frac{\text{Costs of Goods Sold}}{\text{Average Inventory}}$	Number of times a company's average inventory is sold during an accounting period	Chapter 7, LO1
Days' inventory on hand	$\frac{\text{Days in Year}}{\text{Inventory Turnovers}}$	Average number of days taken to sell inventory on hand	Chapter 7, LO1
Payables turnover	$\frac{\text{Costs of Goods Sold +/– Change in Inventory}}{\text{Average Accounts Payable}}$	Average number of times a company pays its accounts payable in an accounting period	Chapter 9, LO1
Days' payable	$\frac{\text{Days in Year}}{\text{Payables Turnover}}$	Average number of days a company takes to pay accounts payable	Chapter 9, LO1

PROFITABILITY RATIOS

Ratio	Formula	Description	Reference
Profit margin	$\frac{\text{Net Income}}{\text{Net Sales}}$	Percentage of each sales dollar that contributes to net income	Chapter 5, LO5
Asset turnover	$\frac{\text{Net Sales}}{\text{Average Total Assets}}$	How efficiently assets are used to produce sales	Chapter 5, LO5
Return on assets	$\frac{\text{Net Income}}{\text{Average Total Assets}}$	How efficiently a company uses its assets to produce income, or the amount earned on each dollar of assets invested	Chapter 5, LO5
Return on equity	$\frac{\text{Net Income}}{\text{Average Owner's Equity}}$	Relates the amount earned by a business to the owner's investment in the business	Chapter 5, LO5

LONG-TERM SOLVENCY RATIOS

Ratio	Formula	Description	Reference
Debt to equity ratio	$\frac{\text{Total Liabilities}}{\text{Owner's Equity}}$	Proportion of a company's assets financed by creditors and the p[illegible]ion financed by the owner	Chapter 5, LO5
Interest coverage ratio	$\frac{\text{Income Before Income Taxes + Interest Expense}}{\text{Interest Expense}}$	Degree of protectio[illegible] default on interest p[illegible]	[illegible]ter 13, LO1

CASH FLOW ADEQUACY RATIOS

Ratio	Formula	Description	Reference
Cash flow yield	$\frac{\text{Net Cash Flows from Operating Activities}}{\text{Net Income}}$	Measures a company's ability to generate operating cash flows in relation to net income	[illegible]apter 15, LO2
Cash flows to sales	$\frac{\text{Net Cash Flows from Operating Activities}}{\text{Net Sales}}$	Ratio of net cash flows from operating activities to sales	Chapter 15, LO2
Cash flows to assets	$\frac{\text{Net Cash Flows from Operating Activities}}{\text{Average Total Assets}}$	Measures the ability of assets to generate operating cash flows	Chapter 15, LO2
Free cash flow	Net Cash Flows from Operating Activities – Dividends – Net Capital Expenditures	Measures the amount of cash that remains after deducting the funds a company must commit to continue operating at its planned level	Chapter 11, LO1

MARKET STRENGTH RATIOS

Ratio	Formula	Description	Reference
Price/earnings ratio	$\frac{\text{Market Price per Share}}{\text{Earnings per Share}}$	Measures investors' confidence in a company's future; a means of comparing stock values	Chapter 12, LO1
Dividends yield	$\frac{\text{Dividends per Share}}{\text{Market Price per Share}}$	Measures a stock's current return to an investor or stockholder	Chapter 12, LO1

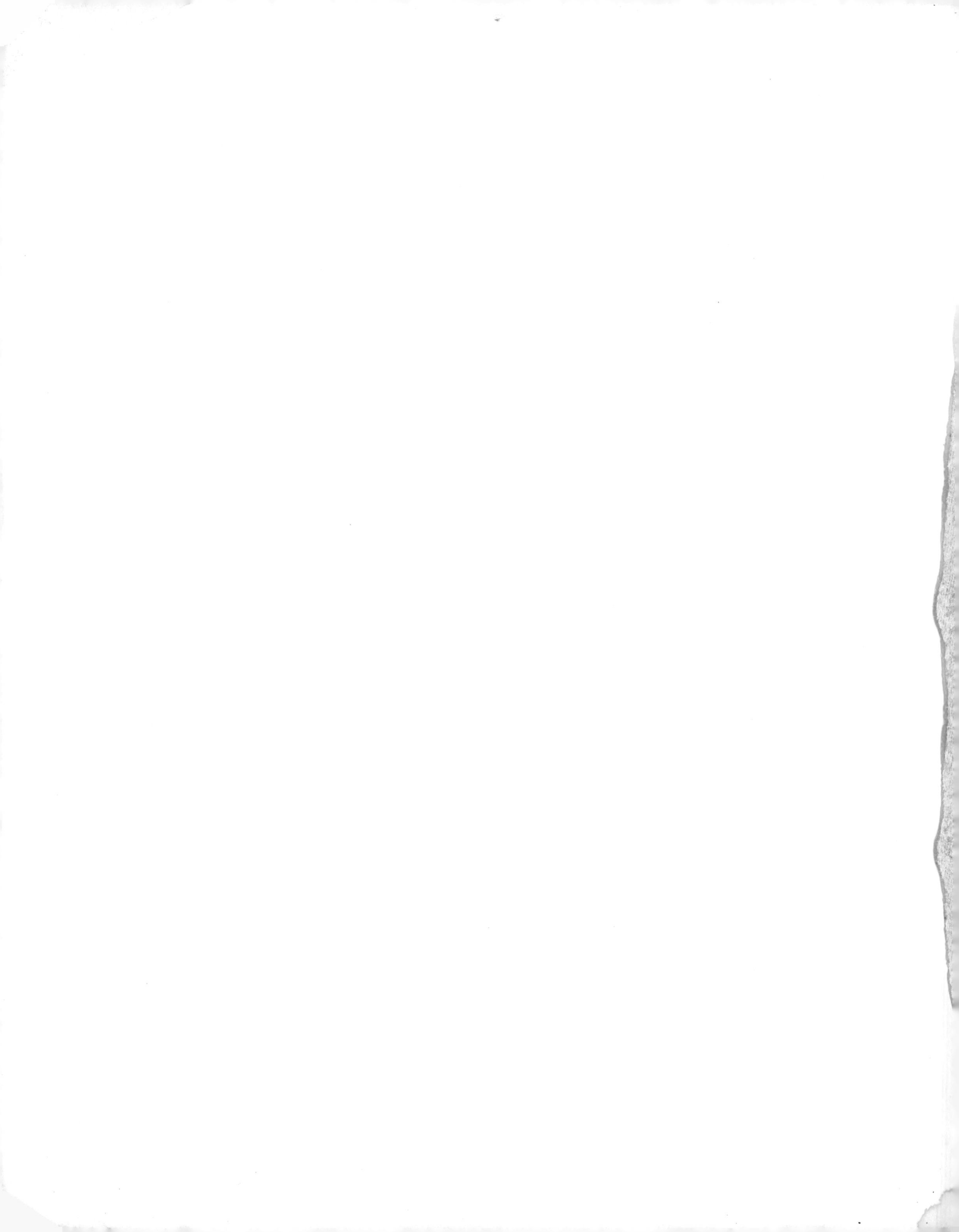

Principles of Financial Accounting

Selected Chapters

Belverd E. Needles, Jr. | Marian Powers

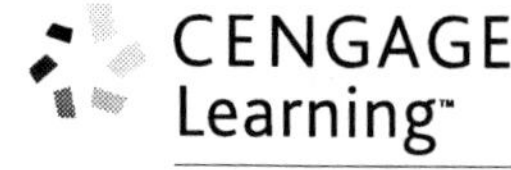

Australia • Brazil • Japan • Korea • Mexico • Singapore • Spain • United Kingdom • United States

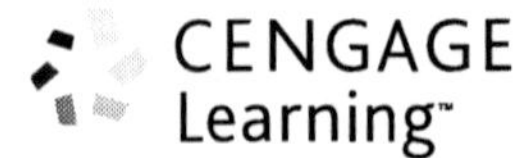

Principles of Financial Accounting: Selected Chapters

Executive Editors:
Maureen Staudt
Michael Stranz

Senior Project Development Manager:
Linda deStefano

Marketing Specialist:
Courtney Sheldon

Senior Production/Manufacturing Manager:
Donna M. Brown

PreMedia Manager:
Joel Brennecke

Sr. Rights Acquisition Account Manager:
Todd Osborne

Cover Image:
Getty Images*

*Unless otherwise noted, all cover images used by Custom Solutions, a part of Cengage Learning, have been supplied courtesy of Getty Images with the exception of the Earthview cover image, which has been supplied by the National Aeronautics and Space Administration (NASA).

Principles of Financial Accounting, 11th Edition
Belverd E. Needles | Marian Powers

ISBN-13: 978-1-111-46699-2

ISBN-10: 1-111-46699-8

Cengage Learning
5191 Natorp Boulevard
Mason, Ohio 45040
USA
Cengage Learning is a leading provider of customized learning solutions with office locations around the globe, including Singapore, the United Kingdom, Australia, Mexico, Brazil, and Japan. Locate your local office at:
international.cengage.com/region.

Cengage Learning products are represented in Canada by Nelson Education, Ltd.
For your lifelong learning solutions, visit **www.cengage.com/custom.**
Visit our corporate website at **www.cengage.com.**

Printed in the United States of America

Brief Contents

Principles of Financial Accounting

ELEVENTH EDITION

CHAPTER

1

Uses of Accounting Information and the Financial Statements

Making a Statement

INCOME STATEMENT

Revenues

– Expenses

= Net Income

STATEMENT OF OWNER'S EQUITY

Beginning Balance

+ Net Income

– Withdrawals

= Ending Balance

BALANCE SHEET

Assets	Liabilities
	Owner's Equity

A = L + OE

STATEMENT OF CASH FLOWS

Operating activities

+ Investing activities

+ Financing activities

= Change in Cash

+ Beginning Balance

= Ending Cash Balance

Financial statements measure how well a business is run.

Today, more people than ever before recognize the importance of accounting information and the profound effect that unethical and misleading financial reports can have on a business, its owners, its employees, its lenders, and the financial markets. In this chapter, we discuss the importance of ethical financial reporting, the uses and users of accounting information, and the financial statements that accountants prepare. We end the chapter with a discussion of generally accepted accounting principles.

LEARNING OBJECTIVES

LO1 Define *accounting* and describe its role in making informed decisions, identify business goals and activities, and explain the importance of ethics in accounting. (pp. 4–10)

LO2 Identify the users of accounting information. (pp. 10–13)

LO3 Explain the importance of business transactions, money measure, and separate entity. (pp. 13–15)

LO4 Identify the three basic forms of business organization. (pp. 15–16)

LO5 Define *financial position*, and state the accounting equation. (pp. 17–19)

LO6 Identify the four basic financial statements. (pp. 19–23)

LO7 Explain how generally accepted accounting principles (GAAP) and international financial reporting standards (IFRS) relate to financial statements and the independent CPA's report, and identify the organizations that influence GAAP. (pp. 24–27)

DECISION POINT ▶ A USER'S FOCUS KEEP-FIT CENTER

On January 1, 2010, Lilian Jackson, an experienced fitness coach, started a business called Keep-Fit Center, which offers classes and private instruction in aerobics, yoga, and Pilates. By December 31, 2010, the center had generated fees of $375,500, and its clients were giving it high marks for excellent service. Lilian is therefore now considering expanding the business. To do so, she would need a bank loan, and to qualify for one, both she and the bank would have to use various financial measures to determine the business's profitability and liquidity (i.e., its ability to repay the loan).

Whether a business is small like Keep-Fit Center or large like **CVS**, the same financial measures are used to evaluate it. In this chapter, as you learn more about accounting and the business environment, you will become familiar with these financial measures and be able to answer questions such as those on the right.

- ▶ Is Keep-Fit Center meeting its goal of profitability?
- ▶ As owner of Keep-Fit Center, what financial knowledge does Lilian Jackson need to measure progress toward the company's goals?
- ▶ In deciding whether to make a loan to Keep-Fit Center, what financial knowledge would a bank need to evaluate the company's financial performance?

Accounting as an Information System

LO1 Define *accounting* and describe its role in making informed decisions, identify business goals and activities, and explain the importance of ethics in accounting.

Accounting is an information system that measures, processes, and communicates financial information about an economic entity.[1] An economic entity is a unit that exists independently, such as a business, a hospital, or a governmental body. Although the central focus of this book is on business entities, we include other economic units at appropriate points in the text and end-of-chapter assignments.

Accountants focus on the needs of decision makers who use financial information, whether those decision makers are inside or outside a business or other economic entity. Accountants provide a vital service by supplying the information decision makers need to make "reasoned choices among alternative uses of scarce resources in the conduct of business and economic activities."[2] As shown in Figure 1-1, accounting is a link between business activities and decision makers.

1. Accounting measures business activities by recording data about them for future use.
2. The data are stored until needed and then processed to become useful information.
3. The information is communicated through reports to decision makers.

In other words, data about business activities are the input to the accounting system, and useful information for decision makers is the output.

Business Goals, Activities, and Performance Measures

A **business** is an economic unit that aims to sell goods and services to customers at prices that will provide an adequate return to its owners. The list that follows contains the names of some well-known businesses and the principal goods or services that they sell.

FIGURE 1-1
Accounting as an Information System

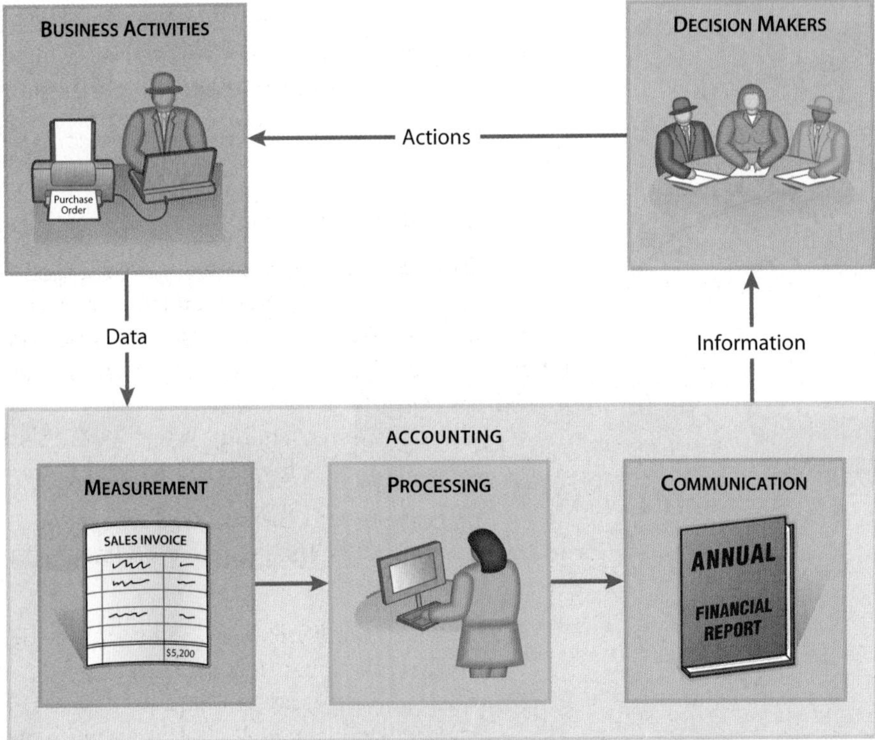

FIGURE 1-2
Business Goals and Activities

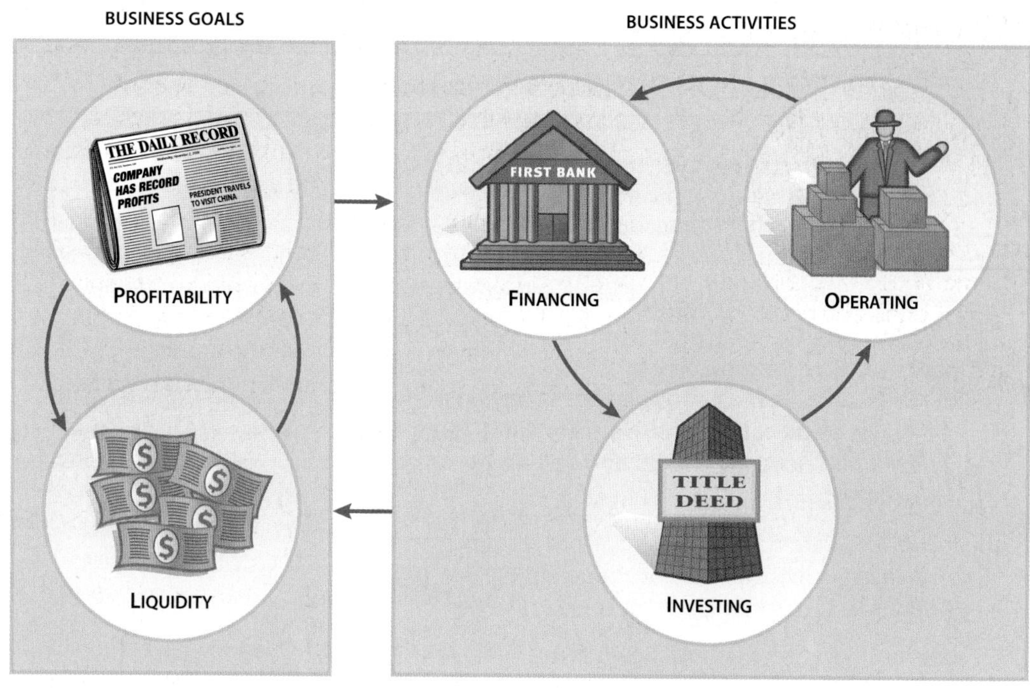

Wal-Mart Corp.	Comprehensive discount store
Reebok International Ltd.	Athletic footwear and clothing
Best Buy Co.	Consumer electronics, personal computers
Wendy's International Inc.	Food service
Starbucks Corp.	Coffee
Southwest Airlines Co.	Passenger airline

Despite their differences, these businesses have similar goals and engage in similar activities, as shown in Figure 1-2.

The two major goals of all businesses are profitability and liquidity.

- **Profitability** is the ability to earn enough income to attract and hold investment capital.
- **Liquidity** is the ability to have enough cash to pay debts when they are due.

> **Study Note**
> Users of accounting information focus on a company's profitability and liquidity. Thus, more than one measure of performance is of interest to them. For example, lenders are concerned primarily with cash flow, and owners are concerned with earnings and withdrawals.

For example, **Toyota** may meet the goal of profitability by selling many cars at a price that earns a profit, but if its customers do not pay for their cars quickly enough to enable Toyota to pay its suppliers and employees, the company may fail to meet the goal of liquidity. If a company is to survive and be successful, it must meet both goals.

All businesses, including Lilian Jackson's Keep-Fit Center, pursue their goals by engaging in operating, investing, and financing activities.

- **Operating activities** include selling goods and services to customers, employing managers and workers, buying and producing goods and services, and paying taxes.
- **Investing activities** involve spending the capital a company receives in productive ways that will help it achieve its objectives. These activities include buying land, buildings, equipment, and other resources that are needed to operate the business and selling them when they are no longer needed.

FOCUS ON BUSINESS PRACTICE

What Does CVS Have to Say About Itself?

CVS, a major drug store chain, describes the company's progress in meeting its major business objectives as follows:

Liquidity: "Along with our strong free cash flow generation, . . . we faced virtually none of the liquidity issues that sent shockwaves across so much of the business landscape in 2008. CVS Caremark has a solid balance sheet and an investment grade credit rating, and we maintain a commercial paper program currently backed by $4 billion in committed bank facilities."

Profitability: "CVS Caremark generated record revenue and earnings, achieved industry-leading same-store sales growth, and continued to gain share across our businesses."[3]

CVS's main business activities are shown at the right.

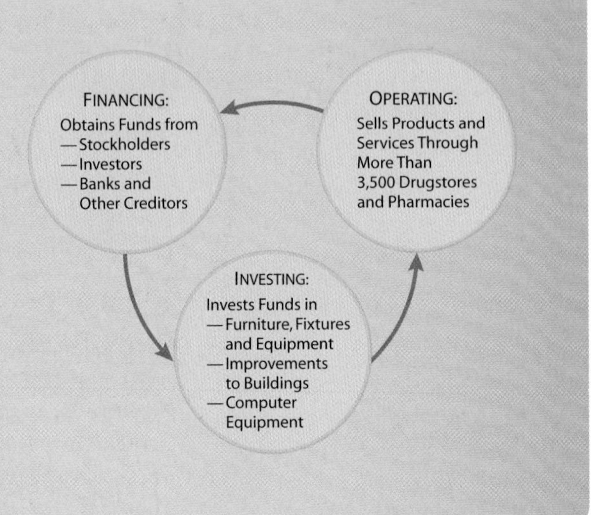

- **Financing activities** involve obtaining adequate funds, or capital, to begin operations and to continue operating. These activities include obtaining capital from creditors, such as banks and suppliers, and from owners. They also include repaying creditors and paying a return to the owners.

An important function of accounting is to provide **performance measures**, which indicate whether managers are achieving their business goals and whether the business activities are well managed. The evaluation and interpretation of financial statements and related performance measures is called **financial analysis**. For financial analysis to be useful, performance measures must be well aligned with the two major goals of business—profitability and liquidity.

Profitability is commonly measured in terms of earnings or income, and cash flows are a common measure of liquidity. In 2008, the drug and pharmacy chain **CVS** projected earnings of $3.5 billion and cash flows from operating activities of $4.5 billion in 2009. These figures indicate that CVS was achieving both profitability and liquidity in difficult financial times.[4] Not all companies were so fortunate in 2008. For instance, **General Motors** reported that it would have to curtail spending on new auto and truck models because its earnings (or profitability) and cash flows were negative; in fact, they were the largest in the history of the U.S. auto industry. Clearly, General Motors was not meeting either its profitability or liquidity goals to such an extent that management had to go to the government for a bailout in the billions of dollars. In spite of the bailout, the company was forced to declare bankruptcy in 2009.

Although it is important to know the amounts of earnings and cash flows in any given period and whether they are rising or falling, ratios of accounting measures are also useful tools of financial analysis. For example, to assess Keep-Fit Center's profitability, it would be helpful to consider the ratio of its earnings to total assets, and for liquidity, the ratio of its cash flows to total assets. In addition, ratios of accounting measures allow for comparisons from one period to another and from one company to another.

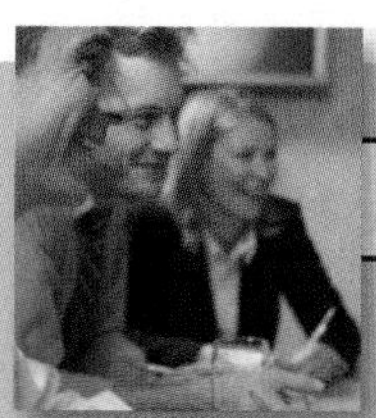

FOCUS ON BUSINESS PRACTICE

Cash Bonuses Depend on Accounting Numbers!

Nearly all businesses use the amounts reported in their financial statements as a basis for rewarding management. Because managers act to achieve these accounting measures, selecting measures that are not easily manipulated is important. Equally important is maintaining a balance of measures that reflect the goals of profitability and liquidity.[5]

Financial and Management Accounting

Accounting's role of assisting decision makers by measuring, processing, and communicating financial information is usually divided into the categories of management accounting and financial accounting. Although the functions of management accounting and financial accounting overlap, the two can be distinguished by the principal users of the information they provide.

Management accounting provides *internal* decision makers, who are charged with achieving the goals of profitability and liquidity, with information about operating, investing, and financing activities. Managers and employees who conduct the activities of the business need information that tells them how they have done in the past and what they can expect in the future. For example, **The Gap**, a retail clothing business, needs an operating report on each outlet that tells how much was sold at that outlet and what costs were incurred, and it needs a budget for each outlet that projects the sales and costs for the next year.

Financial accounting generates reports and communicates them to *external* decision makers so they can evaluate how well the business has achieved its goals. These reports are called **financial statements**. **CVS**, whose stock is traded on the New York Stock Exchange, sends its financial statements to its owners (called *stockholders*), its banks and other creditors, and government regulators. Financial statements report directly on the goals of profitability and liquidity and are used extensively both inside and outside a business to evaluate the business's success. It is important for every person involved with a business to understand financial statements. They are a central feature of accounting and a primary focus of this book.

Processing Accounting Information

It is important to distinguish accounting from the ways in which accounting information is processed by bookkeeping, computers, and management information systems.

Accounting includes the design of an information system that meets users' needs, and its major goals are the analysis, interpretation, and use of information. **Bookkeeping**, on the other hand, is mechanical and repetitive; it is the process of recording financial transactions and keeping financial records. It is a small—but important—part of accounting.

Today, computers collect, organize, and communicate vast amounts of information with great speed. They can perform both routine bookkeeping chores and complex calculations. Accountants were among the earliest and most enthusiastic users of computers, and today they use computers in all aspects of their work.

Study Note

Computerized accounting information is only as reliable and useful as the data that go into the system. The accountant must have a thorough understanding of the concepts that underlie accounting to ensure the data's reliability and usefulness.

Computers make it possible to create a management information system to organize a business's many information needs. A **management information system (MIS)** consists of the interconnected subsystems that provide the information needed to run a business. The accounting information system is the most important subsystem because it plays the key role of managing the flow of economic data to all parts of a business and to interested parties outside the business.

Ethical Financial Reporting

Ethics is a code of conduct that applies to everyday life. It addresses the question of whether actions are right or wrong. Actions—whether ethical or unethical, right or wrong—are the product of individual decisions. Thus, when an organization acts unethically by using false advertising, cheating customers, polluting the environment, or treating employees unfairly, it is not the organization that is responsible—it is the members of management and other employees who have made a conscious decision to act in this manner.

Ethics is especially important in preparing financial reports because users of these reports must depend on the good faith of the people involved in their preparation. Users have no other assurance that the reports are accurate and fully disclose all relevant facts.

The intentional preparation of misleading financial statements is called **fraudulent financial reporting.**[6] It can result from the distortion of records (e.g., the manipulation of inventory records), falsified transactions (e.g., fictitious sales), or the misapplication of various accounting principles. There are a number of motives for fraudulent reporting—for instance, to cover up financial weakness to obtain a higher price when a company is sold; to meet the expectations of investors, owners, and financial analysts; or to obtain a loan. The incentive can also be personal gain, such as additional compensation, promotion, or avoidance of penalties for poor performance.

Whatever the motive for fraudulent financial reporting, it can have dire consequences, as the accounting scandals that erupted at **Enron Corporation** and **WorldCom** attest. Unethical financial reporting and accounting practices at those two major corporations caused thousands of people to lose their jobs, their investment incomes, and their pensions. They also resulted in prison sentences and fines for the corporate executives who were involved.

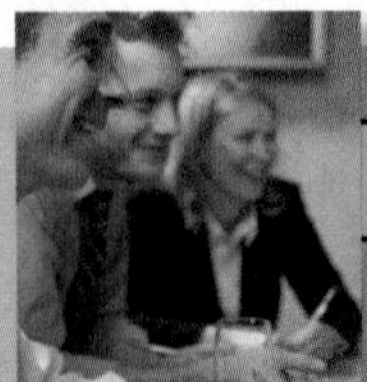

FOCUS ON BUSINESS PRACTICE

How Did Accounting Develop?

Accounting is a very old discipline. Forms of it have been essential to commerce for more than 5,000 years. Accounting, in a version close to what we know today, gained widespread use in the 1400s, especially in Italy, where it was instrumental in the development of shipping, trade, construction, and other forms of commerce. This system of double-entry bookkeeping was documented by the famous Italian mathematician, scholar, and philosopher Fra Luca Pacioli. In 1494, Pacioli published his most important work, *Summa de Arithmetica, Geometrica, Proportioni et Proportionalita*, which contained a detailed description of accounting as practiced in that age. This book became the most widely read book on mathematics in Italy and firmly established Pacioli as the "Father of Accounting."

Unethical accounting practices at Enron led to the collapse of the company and the loss of thousands of jobs and pensions. This photograph shows the former Enron building in Houston, Texas.

Courtesy of Paul S. Wolf, 2009/Used under license from Shutterstock.com.

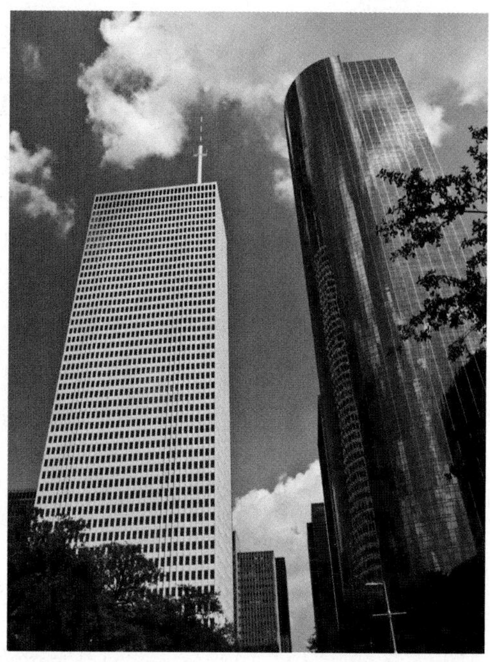

In 2002, Congress passed the **Sarbanes-Oxley Act** to regulate financial reporting and the accounting profession, among other things. This legislation ordered the Securities and Exchange Commission (SEC) to draw up rules requiring the chief executives and chief financial officers of all publicly traded U.S. companies to swear that, based on their knowledge, the quarterly statements and annual reports that their companies file with the SEC are accurate and complete. Violation can result in criminal penalties. A company's management expresses its duty to ensure that financial reports are not false or misleading in the management report that appears in the company's annual report. For example, **Target Corporation**'s management report includes the following statement:

> Management is responsible for the consistency, integrity and presentation of the information in the Annual Report.[7]

However, it is accountants, not management, who physically prepare and audit financial reports. To meet the high ethical standards of the accounting profession, they must apply accounting concepts in such a way as to present a fair view of a company's operations and financial position and to avoid misleading readers of their reports. Like the conduct of a company, the ethical conduct of a profession is a collection of individual actions. As a member of a profession, each accountant has a responsibility—not only to the profession but also to employers, clients, and society as a whole—to ensure that any report he or she prepares or audits provides accurate, reliable information.

The high regard that the public has historically had for the accounting profession is evidence that an overwhelming number of accountants have upheld the ethics of the profession. Even as the Enron and WorldCom scandals were making headlines, a Gallup Poll showed an increase of 28 percent in the accounting profession's reputation between 2002 and 2005, placing it among the most highly rated professions.[8]

Accountants and top managers are, of course, not the only people responsible for ethical financial reporting. Managers and employees at all levels must be conscious of their responsibility for providing accurate financial information to the people who rely on it.

STOP & APPLY >

Match the terms below with the definitions (some answers may be used more than once):

	Terms	Definitions
_____	1. Management accounting	a. An unethical practice
_____	2. Liquidity	b. A business goal
_____	3. Financial accounting	c. Engaged in by all businesses
_____	4. Investing activities	d. Major function of accounting
_____	5. Operating activities	
_____	6. Financing activities	
_____	7. Profitability	
_____	8. Fraudulent financial reporting	

SOLUTION

1. d; 2. b; 3. d; 4. c; 5. c; 6. c; 7. b; 8. a

Decision Makers: The Users of Accounting Information

LO2 Identify the users of accounting information.

As shown in Figure 1-3, the people who use accounting information to make decisions fall into three categories:

1. Those who manage a business
2. Those outside a business enterprise who have a direct financial interest in the business
3. Those who have an indirect financial interest in a business

These categories apply to governmental and not-for-profit organizations as well as to profit-oriented ventures.

Management

Study Note

Managers are internal users of accounting information.

Management refers to the people who are responsible for operating a business and meeting its goals of profitability and liquidity. In a small business, management may consist solely of the owners. In a large business, managers must decide what to do, how to do it, and whether the results match their original plans. Successful managers consistently make the right decisions based on timely and valid information.

FIGURE 1-3
The Users of Accounting Information

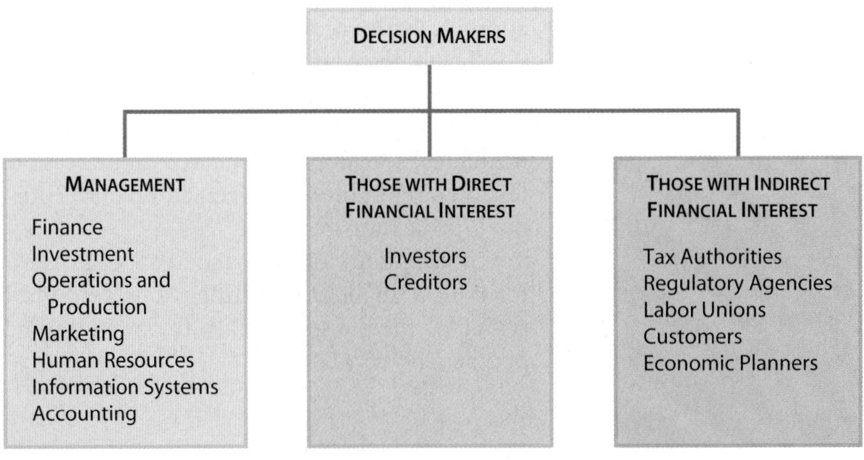

To make good decisions, Lilian Jackson and other owners and managers need answers to such questions as:

- What were the company's earnings during the past quarter?
- Is the rate of return to the owners adequate?
- Does the company have enough cash?
- Which products or services are most profitable?

Because so many key decisions are based on accounting data, management is one of the most important users of accounting information.

In its decision-making process, management performs functions that are essential to the operation of a business. The same basic functions must be performed in all businesses, and each requires accounting information on which to base decisions. The basic management functions are:

Financing the business: obtaining funds so that a company can begin and continue operating

Investing resources: investing assets in productive ways that support a company's goals

Producing goods and services: managing the production of goods and services

Marketing goods and services: overseeing how goods or services are advertised, sold, and distributed

Managing employees: overseeing the hiring, evaluation, and compensation of employees

Providing information to decision makers: gathering data about all aspects of a company's operations, organizing the data into usable information, and providing reports to managers and appropriate outside parties. Accounting plays a key role in this function.

Users with a Direct Financial Interest

Another group of decision makers who need accounting information are those with a direct financial interest in a business. They depend on accounting to measure and report information about how a business has performed. Most businesses periodically publish a set of general-purpose financial statements that report their success in meeting the goals of profitability and liquidity. These statements show what has happened in the past, and they are important indicators of what will happen in the future. Many people outside the company carefully study these financial reports. The two most important groups are investors (including owners) and creditors.

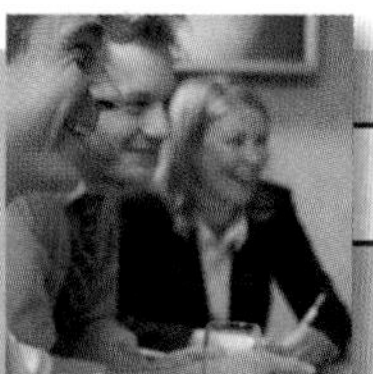

FOCUS ON BUSINESS PRACTICE

What Do CFOs Do?

According to a survey, the chief financial officer (CFO) is the "new business partner of the chief executive officer" (CEO). CFOs are increasingly required to take on responsibilities for strategic planning, mergers and acquisitions, and tasks involving international operations, and many of them are becoming CEOs of their companies. Those who do become CEOs are finding that "a financial background is invaluable when they're saddled with the responsibility of making big calls."[9]

Study Note

The primary external users of accounting information are investors and creditors.

Investors Those such as Lilian Jackson, owner of the Keep-Fit Center, and **CVS**'s stockholders who may invest in a business and acquire a part ownership in it are interested in its past success and its potential earnings. A thorough study of a company's financial statements helps potential investors judge the prospects for a profitable investment. After investing, they must continually review their commitment, again by examining the company's financial statements.

Creditors Most companies borrow money for both long- and short-term operating needs. Creditors, those who lend money or deliver goods and services before being paid, are interested mainly in whether a company will have the cash to pay interest charges and to repay the debt at the appropriate time. They study a company's liquidity and cash flow as well as its profitability. Banks, finance companies, mortgage companies, securities firms, insurance firms, suppliers, and other lenders must analyze a company's financial position before they make a loan.

Users with an Indirect Financial Interest

In recent years, society as a whole, through governmental and public groups, has become one of the largest and most important users of accounting information. Users who need accounting information to make decisions on public issues include tax authorities, regulatory agencies, and various other groups.

Tax Authorities Government at every level is financed through the collection of taxes. Companies and individuals pay many kinds of taxes, including federal, state, and city income taxes; Social Security and other payroll taxes; excise taxes; and sales taxes. Each tax requires special tax returns and often a complex set of records as well. Proper reporting is generally a matter of law and can be very complicated. The Internal Revenue Code, for instance, contains thousands of rules governing the preparation of the accounting information used in computing federal income taxes.

Regulatory Agencies Most companies must report periodically to one or more regulatory agencies at the federal, state, and local levels. For example, all publicly traded corporations must report periodically to the **Securities and Exchange Commission (SEC)**. This body, set up by Congress to protect the public, regulates the issuing, buying, and selling of stocks in the United States. Companies listed on a stock exchange also must meet the special reporting requirements of their exchange.

Other Groups Labor unions study the financial statements of corporations as part of preparing for contract negotiations; a company's income and costs often play an important role in these negotiations. Those who advise investors and creditors—financial analysts, brokers, underwriters, lawyers, economists, and the financial press—also have an indirect interest in the financial performance and prospects of a business. Consumer groups, customers, and the general public have become more concerned about the financing and earnings of corporations as well as the effects that corporations have on inflation, the environment, social issues, and the quality of life. And economic planners, among them the President's Council of Economic Advisers and the Federal Reserve Board, use aggregated accounting information to set and evaluate economic policies and programs.

Governmental and Not-for-Profit Organizations

More than 30 percent of the U.S. economy is generated by governmental and not-for-profit organizations (hospitals, universities, professional organizations, and charities). The managers of these diverse entities perform the same functions as managers of businesses, and they therefore have the same need for accounting information and a knowledge of how to use it. Their functions include raising funds from investors (including owners), creditors, taxpayers, and donors and deploying scarce resources. They must also plan how to pay for operations and to repay creditors on a timely basis. In addition, they have an obligation to report their financial performance to legislators, boards, and donors, as well as to deal with tax authorities, regulators, and labor unions. Although most of the examples in this text focus on business enterprises, the same basic principles apply to governmental and not-for-profit organizations.

STOP & APPLY >

Match the terms below with the type of user of accounting information (some answers may be used more than once):

_____	1. Tax authorities	a. Internal user
_____	2. Investors	b. Direct external user
_____	3. Management	c. Indirect user
_____	4. Creditors	
_____	5. Regulatory agencies	
_____	6. Labor unions and consumer groups	

SOLUTION

1. c; 2. b; 3. a; 4. b; 5. c; 6. c

Accounting Measurement

LO3 Explain the importance of business transactions, money measure, and separate entity.

In this section, we begin the study of the measurement aspects of accounting—that is, what accounting actually measures. To make an accounting measurement, the accountant must answer four basic questions:

1. What is measured?
2. When should the measurement be made?
3. What value should be placed on what is measured?
4. How should what is measured be classified?

Accountants in industry, professional associations, public accounting, government, and academic circles debate the answers to these questions constantly, and the answers change as new knowledge and practice require. But the basis of today's accounting practice rests on a number of widely accepted concepts and conventions, which are described in this book. We begin by focusing on the first question: What is measured? We discuss the other three questions (recognition, valuation, and classification) in the next chapter.

Every system must define what it measures, and accounting is no exception. Basically, financial accounting uses money to gauge the impact of business transactions on separate business entities.

Business Transactions

Business transactions are economic events that affect a business's financial position. Businesses can have hundreds or even thousands of transactions every day. These transactions are the raw material of accounting reports.

A transaction can be an exchange of value (a purchase, sale, payment, collection, or loan) between two or more parties. A transaction also can be an economic event that has the same effect as an exchange transaction but that does not involve an exchange. Some examples of "nonexchange" transactions are losses from fire, flood, explosion, and theft; physical wear and tear on machinery and equipment; and the day-by-day accumulation of interest.

To be recorded, a transaction must relate directly to a business entity. Suppose a customer buys toothpaste from **CVS** but has to buy shampoo from a competing store because CVS is out of shampoo. The transaction in which the toothpaste was sold is entered in CVS's records. However, the purchase of the shampoo from the competitor is not entered in CVS's records because even though it indirectly affects CVS economically, it does not involve a direct exchange of value between CVS and the customer.

Money Measure

All business transactions are recorded in terms of money. This concept is called **money measure**. Of course, nonfinancial information may also be recorded, but it is through the recording of monetary amounts that a business's transactions and activities are measured. Money is the only factor common to all business transactions, and thus it is the only unit of measure capable of producing financial data that can be compared.

Study Note

The common unit of measurement used in the United States for financial reporting purposes is the dollar.

The monetary unit a business uses depends on the country in which the business resides. For example, in the United States, the basic unit of money is the dollar. In Japan, it is the yen; in Europe, the euro; and in the United Kingdom, the pound. In international transactions, exchange rates must be used to translate from one currency to another. An **exchange rate** is the value of one currency in terms of another. For example, a British person purchasing goods from a U.S. company like **CVS** and paying in U.S. dollars must exchange British pounds for U.S. dollars before making payment. In effect, currencies are goods that can be bought and sold.

Table 1-1 illustrates the exchange rates for several currencies in dollars. It shows the exchange rate for British pounds as \$1.49 per pound on a particular date. Like the prices of many goods, currency prices change daily according to supply and demand. For example, a year earlier, the exchange rate for British pounds was \$1.98. Although our discussion in this book focuses on dollars, some examples and assignments involve foreign currencies.

TABLE 1-1
Examples of Foreign Exchange Rates

Country	Price in \$U.S.	Country	Price in \$U.S.
Australia (dollar)	0.72	Hong Kong (dollar)	0.13
Brazil (real)	0.46	Japan (yen)	0.011
Britain (pound)	1.49	Mexico (peso)	0.07
Canada (dollar)	0.85	Russia (ruble)	0.03
Europe (euro)	1.35	Singapore (dollar)	0.68

Source: The Wall Street Journal, January 7, 2009.

Separate Entity

Study Note

For accounting purposes, a business is *always* separate and distinct from its owners, creditors, and customers.

For accounting purposes, a business is a **separate entity**, distinct not only from its creditors and customers but also from its owners. It should have its own set of financial records, and its records and reports should refer only to its own affairs.

For example, Just Because Flowers Company should have a bank account separate from the account of Holly Sapp, the owner. Holly Sapp may own a home, a car, and other property, and she may have personal debts, but these are not the resources or debts of Just Because Flowers. Holly Sapp may own another business, say a stationery shop. If she does, she should have a completely separate set of records for each business.

STOP & APPLY >

Match the terms below with the type of user of accounting information:

_____	1. Requires an exchange of value between two or more parties	a. Business transaction
_____	2. Requires a separate set of records for a business	b. Money measure
_____	3. An amount associated with a business transaction	c. Separate entity

SOLUTION

1. a; 2. c; 3. b

The Forms of Business Organization

LO4 Identify the three basic forms of business organization.

The three basic forms of business organization are the sole proprietorship, the partnership, and the corporation. Accountants recognize each form as an economic unit separate from its owners. Legally, however, only the corporation is separate from its owners. The characteristics of corporations make them very efficient in amassing capital, which enables them to grow extremely large. As Figure 1-4 shows, even though corporations are fewer in number than sole proprietorships and partnerships, they contribute much more to the U.S. economy in monetary terms. For example, in 2007, **Exxon Mobil** generated more revenues than all but 30 of the world's countries. Here, we point out the most important features of each form of business.

Characteristics of Corporations, Sole Proprietorships, and Partnerships

Study Note

A key disadvantage of a partnership is the unlimited liability of its owners. Unlimited liability can be avoided by organizing the business as a corporation or, in some states, by forming what is known as a limited liability partnership (LLP).

A **sole proprietorship** is a business owned by one person.* The owner takes all the profits or losses of the business and is liable for all its obligations. As Figure 1-4 shows, sole proprietorships represent the largest number of businesses in the United States, but typically they are the smallest in size.

A **partnership** is like a sole proprietorship in most ways, but it has two or more owners. The partners share the profits and losses of the business according to a prearranged formula. Generally, any partner can obligate the business

*Accounting for a sole proprietorship is simpler than accounting for a partnership or corporation. For that reason, we focus on the sole proprietorship in the early part of this book. At critical points, however, we call attention to the essential differences between accounting for a sole proprietorship and accounting for a partnership or corporation.

FIGURE 1-4
Number and Receipts of U.S. Proprietorships, Partnerships, and Corporations

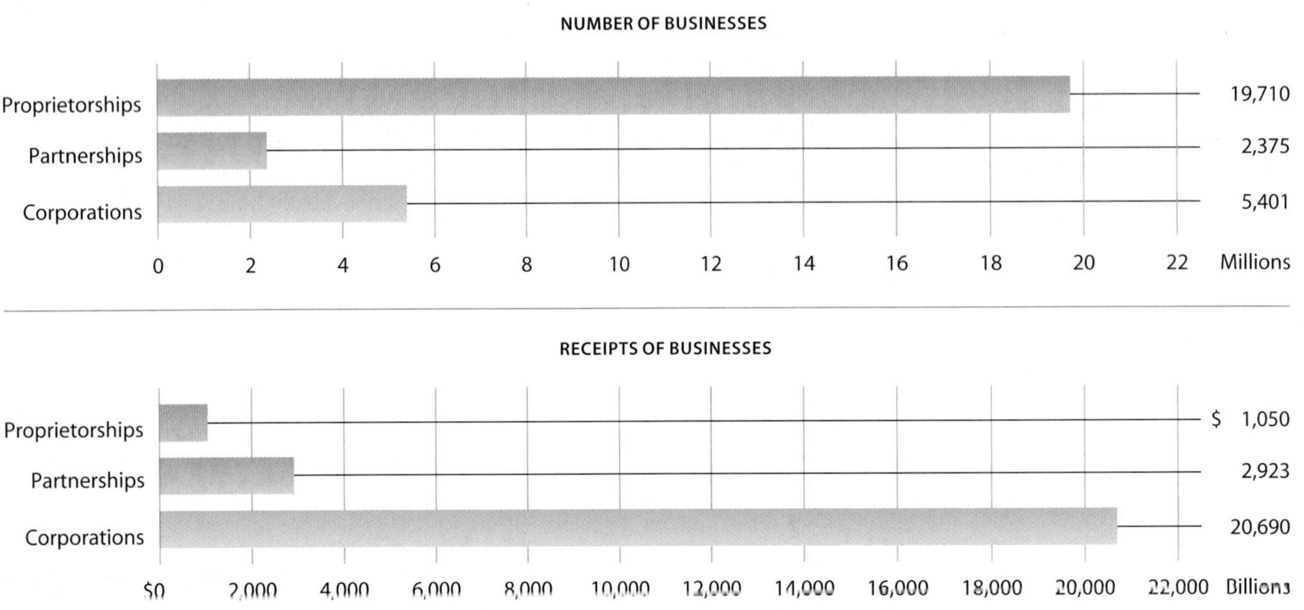

Source: U.S. Treasury Department, Internal Revenue Service, Statistics of Income Bulletin, Winter 2006.

to another party, and the personal resources of each partner can be called on to pay the obligations. A partnership must be dissolved if the ownership changes, as when a partner leaves or dies. If the business is to continue as a partnership after this occurs, a new partnership must be formed.

Both the sole proprietorship and the partnership are convenient ways of separating the owners' commercial activities from their personal activities. Legally, however, there is no economic separation between the owners and the businesses. A **corporation**, on the other hand, is a business unit chartered by the state and legally separate from its owners (the stockholders). The stockholders, whose ownership is represented by shares of stock, do not directly control the corporation's operations. Instead, they elect a board of directors to run the corporation for their benefit. In exchange for their limited involvement in the corporation's operations, stockholders enjoy *limited liability*; that is, their risk of loss is limited to the amount they paid for their shares. Thus, stockholders are often willing to invest in risky, but potentially profitable, activities. Also, because stockholders can sell their shares without dissolving the corporation, the life of a corporation is unlimited and not subject to the whims or health of a proprietor or a partner.

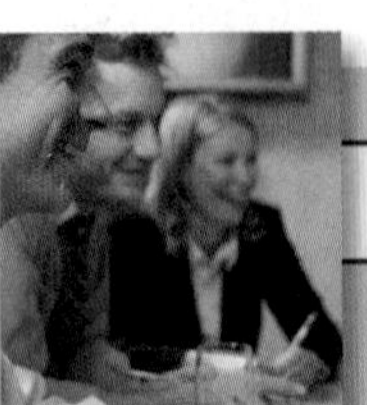

FOCUS ON BUSINESS PRACTICE

Are Most Corporations Big or Small Businesses?

Most people think of corporations as large national or global companies whose shares of stock are held by thousands of people and institutions. Indeed, corporations can be huge and have many stockholders. However, of the approximately 4 million corporations in the United States, only about 15,000 have stock that is publicly bought and sold. The vast majority of corporations are small businesses privately held by a few stockholders. Illinois alone has more than 250,000 corporations. Thus, the study of corporations is just as relevant to small businesses as it is to large ones.

STOP & APPLY >

Match the descriptions on the left with the forms of business enterprise on the right:

_____ 1. Pays dividends
_____ 2. Owned by only one person
_____ 3. Multiple co-owners
_____ 4. Management appointed by board of directors
_____ 5. Most numerous but usually small in size
_____ 6. Biggest segment of the economy

a. Sole proprietorship
b. Partnership
c. Corporation

SOLUTION
1. c; 2. a; 3. b; 4. c; 5. a; 6. c

Financial Position and the Accounting Equation

LO5 Define *financial position*, and state the accounting equation.

Financial position refers to a company's economic resources, such as cash, inventory, and buildings, and the claims against those resources at a particular time. Another term for claims is *equities.*

Every company has two types of equities: creditors' equities, such as bank loans, and owner's equity. The sum of these equities equals a company's resources:

Economic Resources = Creditors' Equities + Owner's Equity

In accounting terminology, economic resources are called *assets* and creditors' equities are called *liabilities.* So the equation can be written like this:

Assets = Liabilities + Owner's Equity

This equation is known as the **accounting equation**. The two sides of the equation must always be equal, or "in balance," as shown in Figure 1-5. To evaluate the financial effects of business activities, it is important to understand their effects on this equation.

FIGURE 1-5
The Accounting Equation

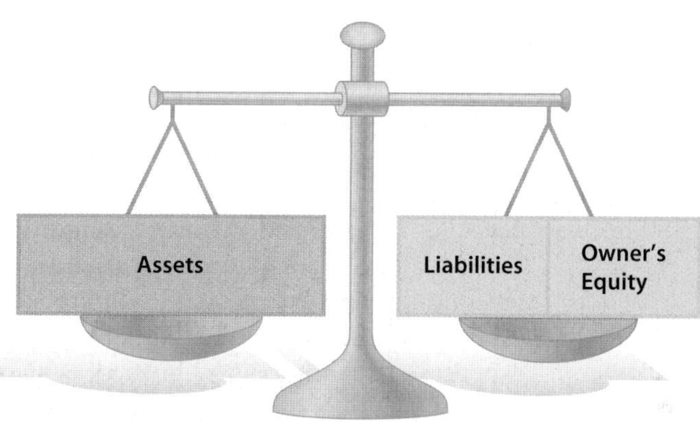

Assets

Assets are the economic resources of a company that are expected to benefit the company's future operations. Certain kinds of assets—for example, cash and money that customers owe to the company (called *accounts receivable*)—are monetary items. Other assets—inventories (goods held for sale), land, buildings, and equipment—are nonmonetary, physical items. Still other assets—the rights granted by patents, trademarks, and copyrights—are nonphysical.

Liabilities

Liabilities are a business's present obligations to pay cash, transfer assets, or provide services to other entities in the future. Among these obligations are amounts owed to suppliers for goods or services bought on credit (called *accounts payable*), borrowed money (e.g., money owed on bank loans), salaries and wages owed to employees, taxes owed to the government, and services to be performed.

As debts, liabilities are claims recognized by law. That is, the law gives creditors the right to force the sale of a company's assets if the company fails to pay its debts. Creditors have rights over owners and must be paid in full before the owners receive anything, even if payment of the debt uses up all the assets of the business.

Owner's Equity

Owner's equity represents the claims by the owner of a business to the assets of the business. Theoretically, owner's equity is what would be left if all liabilities were paid, and it is sometimes said to equal **net assets.** By rearranging the accounting equation, we can define owner's equity this way:

$$\text{Owner's Equity} = \text{Assets} - \text{Liabilities}$$

Owner's equity is affected by the owner's investments in and withdrawals from the business and by the business's revenues and expenses. Owner's investments are assets that the owner puts into the business (e.g., by transferring cash from a personal bank account to the business's bank account). In this case, the assets (cash) of the business increase, and the owner's equity in those assets also increases. Owner's withdrawals are assets that the owner takes out of the business (e.g., by transferring cash from the business's bank account to a personal bank account). In this case, the assets of the business decrease, as does the owner's equity in the business.

Simply stated, **revenues** and **expenses** are the increases and decreases in owner's equity that result from operating a business. For example, the amount a customer pays (or agrees to pay in the future) to **CVS** for a product or service is a revenue for CVS. CVS's assets (cash or accounts receivable) increase, as does its stockholders' (owner's) equity in those assets. On the other hand, the amount CVS must pay out (or agree to pay out) so that it can provide a product or service is an expense. In this case, the assets (cash) decrease or the liabilities (accounts payable) increase, and the owner's equity decreases.

Generally, a company is successful if its revenues exceed its expenses. When revenues exceed expenses, the difference is called **net income**. When expenses exceed revenues, the difference is called **net loss**. It is important not to confuse expenses and withdrawals, both of which reduce owner's equity. In summary, owner's equity is the accumulated net income (revenues − expenses) less withdrawals over the life of the business.

STOP & APPLY

Johnson Company had assets of $140,000 and liabilities of $60,000 at the beginning of the year, and assets of $200,000 and liabilities of $70,000 at the end of the year. During the year, $20,000 was invested in the business, and withdrawals of $24,000 were made. What amount of net income did the company earn during the year?

Beginning of the year

Assets	=	Liabilities	+	Owner's Equity
$140,000	=	$60,000	+	**$ 80,000**

During year

		Investment	+	20,000
		Withdrawals	−	24,000
		Net income		?

End of year

$200,000	=	$70,000	+	**$130,000**

SOLUTION

Net income = $54,000

Start by finding the owner's equity at the beginning of the year. (Check: $140,000 − $60,000 = $80,000)

Then find the owner's equity at the end of the year. (Check: $200,000 − $70,000 = $130,000)

Then determine net income by calculating how the transactions during the year led to the owner's equity amount at the end of the year. (Check: $80,000 + $20,000 − $24,000 + $54,000 = $130,000)

Financial Statements

LO6 Identify the four basic financial statements.

Study Note

Businesses use four basic financial statements to communicate financial information to decision makers.

Financial statements are the primary means of communicating important accounting information about a business to those who have an interest in the business. These statements are models of the business enterprise in that they show the business in financial terms. As is true of all models, however, financial statements are not perfect pictures of the real thing. Rather, they are the accountant's best effort to represent what is real. Four major financial statements are used to communicate accounting information about a business: the income statement, the statement of owner's equity, the balance sheet, and the statement of cash flows.

Income Statement

The **income statement** summarizes the revenues earned and expenses incurred by a business over an accounting period (see Exhibit 1-1). Many people consider it the most important financial report because it shows whether a business achieved its profitability goal—that is, whether it earned an acceptable income. Exhibit 1-1 shows that Weiss Consultancy had revenues of $14,000 from consulting. From this amount, total expenses of $5,600 were deducted (equipment rental expense of $2,800, wages expense of $1,600, and utilities expense of $1,200) to arrive at net income of $8,400. To show the period to which the statement applies, it is dated "For the Month Ended December 31, 2011."

EXHIBIT 1-1
Income Statement for Weiss Consultancy

Weiss Consultancy
Income Statement
For the Month Ended December 31, 2011

Revenues		
Consulting fees earned		$14,000
Expenses		
Equipment rental expense	$2,800	
Wages expense	1,600	
Utilities expense	1,200	
Total expenses		5,600
Net income		$ 8,400

Statement of Owner's Equity

The **statement of owner's equity** shows the changes in owner's equity over an accounting period. In Exhibit 1-2, beginning owner's equity is zero because Weiss Consultancy began operations in this accounting period. During the month, the owner, James Weiss, invested $200,000 in the business, and the company earned an income (as shown on the income statement) of $8,400. Deducted from this amount are $2,400 of withdrawals that the owner made during the month, leaving an ending balance of $206,000 of capital in the business.

The Balance Sheet

Study Note
The date on the balance sheet is a single date, whereas the dates on the other three statements cover a period of time, such as a month, quarter, or year.

The purpose of a **balance sheet** is to show the financial position of a business on a certain date, usually the end of the month or year (see Exhibit 1-3). For this reason, it often is called the *statement of financial position* and is dated as of a specific date. The balance sheet presents a view of the business as the holder of resources, or assets, that are equal to the claims against those assets. The claims consist of the company's liabilities and the owner's equity in the company. Exhibit 1-3 shows that Weiss Consultancy has several categories of assets, which total $208,400. These assets equal the total liabilities of $2,400 (accounts payable) plus the ending balance of owner's equity of $206,000. Notice that the amount of the owner's Capital account on the balance sheet comes from the ending balance on the statement of owner's equity.

EXHIBIT 1-2
Statement of Owner's Equity for Weiss Consultancy

Weiss Consultancy
Statement of Owner's Equity
For the Month Ended December 31, 2011

J. Weiss, Capital, December 1, 2011	$ 0
Investment by J. Weiss	200,000
Net income for the month	8,400
Subtotal	$208,400
Less withdrawals	2,400
J. Weiss, Capital, December 31, 2011	$206,000

EXHIBIT 1-3
Balance Sheet for Weiss Consultancy

Weiss Consultancy Balance Sheet December 31, 2011			
Assets		**Liabilities**	
Cash	$ 62,400	Accounts payable	$ 2,400
Accounts receivable	4,000	Total liabilities	$ 2,400
Supplies	2,000		
Land	40,000	**Owner's Equity**	
Buildings	100,000	J. Weiss, Capital	206,000
Total assets	$208,400	Total liabilities and owner's equity	$208,400

Statement of Cash Flows

Study Note

The statement of cash flows explains the change in cash in terms of operating, investing, and financing activities over an accounting period. It provides valuable information that cannot be determined in an examination of the other financial statements.

Whereas the income statement focuses on a company's profitability, the **statement of cash flows** focuses on its liquidity (see Exhibit 1-4). **Cash flows** are the inflows and outflows of cash into and out of a business. Net cash flows are the difference between the inflows and outflows.

As you can see in Exhibit 1-4, the statement of cash flows is organized according to the three major business activities described earlier in the chapter.

- **Cash flows from operating activities:** The first section of Exhibit 1-4 shows the cash produced by business operations. Weiss's operating activities produced net cash flows of $4,800 (liquidity) compared to net income of $8,400 (profitability). The company used cash to increase accounts receivable and supplies. However, by borrowing funds, it increased accounts payable. This is not a good trend, which Weiss should try to reverse in future months.
- **Cash flows from investing activities:** Weiss used cash to expand by purchasing land and a building.
- **Cash flows from financing activities:** Weiss obtained most of its cash from the owner, who then made a small cash withdrawal.

Study Note

Notice the sequence in which these statements are prepared: Income statement, statement of owner's equity, balance sheet, and finally, the statement of cash flows.

Overall, Weiss had a net increase in cash of $62,400, due in large part to the investment by the owner. In future months, Weiss must generate more cash through operations.

The statement of cash flows is related directly to the other three financial statements. Notice that net income comes from the income statement and that withdrawals come from the statement of owner's equity. The other items in the statement represent changes in the balance sheet accounts: accounts receivable, supplies, accounts payable, land, and buildings. Here we focus on the importance and overall structure of the statement. Its construction and use are discussed in a later chapter.

Relationships Among the Financial Statements

Exhibit 1-5 illustrates the relationships among the four financial statements by showing how they would appear for Weiss Consultancy. The period covered is the month of December 2011. Notice the similarity of the headings at the top of each statement. Each identifies the company and the kind of statement. The income statement, the statement of owner's equity, and the statement of cash flows indicate the period to which they apply; the balance sheet gives the specific date to which it applies. Much of this book deals with developing, using, and interpreting more complete versions of these statements.

EXHIBIT 1-4

Statement of Cash Flows for Weiss Consultancy

Weiss Consultancy
Statement of Cash Flows
For the Month Ended December 31, 2011

Cash flows from operating activities		
Net income		$ 8,400
Adjustments to reconcile net income to net cash flows from operating activities		
(Increase) in accounts receivable	($ 4,000)	
(Increase) in supplies	(2,000)	
Increase in accounts payable	2,400)	(3,600)
Net cash flows from operating activities		$ 4,800
Cash flows from investing activities		
Purchase of land	($ 40,000)	
Purchase of building	(100,000)	
Net cash flows from investing activities		(140,000)
Cash flows from financing activities		
Investments by owner	$ 200,000	
Withdrawals	(2,400)	
Net cash flows from financing activities		197,600
Net increase (decrease) in cash		$ 62,400
Cash at beginning of month		0
Cash at end of month		$ 62,400

Note: Parentheses indicate a negative amount.

EXHIBIT 1-5
Income Statement, Statement of Owner's Equity, Balance Sheet, and Statement of Cash Flows for Weiss Consultancy

Weiss Consultancy
Statement of Cash Flows
For the Month Ended December 31, 2011

Cash flows from operating activities		
Net income		$ 8,400
Adjustments to reconcile net income to net cash flows from operating activities		
(Increase) in accounts receivable	($ 4,000)	
(Increase) in supplies	(2,000)	
Increase in accounts payable	2,400	(3,600)
Net cash flows from operating activities		$ 4,800
Cash flows from investing activities		
Purchase of land	($ 40,000)	
Purchase of building	(100,000)	
Net cash flows from investing activities		(140,000)
Cash flows from financing activities		
Investments by owner	$200,000	
Withdrawals	(2,400)	
Net cash flows from financing activities		197,600
Net increase (decrease) in cash		$ 62,400
Cash at beginning of month		0
Cash at end of month		$ 62,400

Weiss Consultancy
Income Statement
For the Month Ended December 31, 2011

Revenues		
Consulting fees		$14,000
Expenses		
Equipment rental expense	$2,800	
Wages expense	1,600	
Utilities expense	1,200	
Total expenses		5,600
Net income		$ 8,400

Weiss Consultancy
Statement of Owner's Equity
For the Month Ended December 31, 2011

J. Weiss, Capital, December 1, 2011	$ 0
Investment by J. Weiss	200,000
Net income for the month	8,400
Subtotal	$208,400
Less withdrawals	2,400
J. Weiss, Capital, December 31, 2011	$206,000

Weiss Consultancy
Balance Sheet
December 31, 2011

Assets		**Liabilities**	
Cash	$ 62,400	Accounts payable	$ 2,400
Accounts receivable	4,000	Total liabilities	$ 2,400
Supplies	2,000		
Land	40,000	**Owner's Equity**	
Buildings	100,000	J. Weiss, Capital	206,000
Total assets	$208,400	Total liabilities and owner's equity	$208,400

STOP & APPLY >

Complete the following financial statements by determining the amounts that correspond to the letters. (Assume no new investments by owners.)

Income Statement

Revenues	$2,775
Expenses	(a)
Net income	$ (b)

Statement of Owner's Equity

Beginning balance	$7,250
Net income	(c)
Less withdrawals	500
Ending balance	$7,500

Balance Sheet

Total assets	$ (d)
Liabilities	$4,000
Owner's equity	
L. Buckman, capital	(e)
Total liabilities and owner's equity	$ (f)

SOLUTION

Net income links the income statement and the statement of owner's equity. The ending balance of owner's equity links the statement of owner's equity and the balance sheet.

Thus, start with (c), which must equal $750 (check: $7,250 + $750 – $500 = $7,500). Then, (b) equals (c), or $750. Thus, (a) must equal $2,025 (check: $2,775 – $2,025 = $750). Because (e) equals $7,500 (ending balance from the statement of owner's equity), (f) must equal $11,500 (check: $4,000 + $7,500 = $11,500). Now, (d) equals (f), or $11,500.

Generally Accepted Accounting Principles

LO7 Explain how generally accepted accounting principles (GAAP) and international financial reporting standards (IFRS) relate to financial statements and the independent CPA's report, and identify the organizations that influence GAAP.

To ensure that financial statements are understandable to their users, a set of practices, called **generally accepted accounting principles (GAAP)**, has been developed to provide guidelines for financial accounting. "Generally accepted accounting principles encompass the conventions, rules, and procedures necessary to define accepted accounting practice at a particular time."[10] In other words, GAAP arise from wide agreement on the theory and practice of accounting at a particular time. These "principles" are not like the unchangeable laws of nature in chemistry or physics. They evolve to meet the needs of decision makers, and they change as circumstances change or as better methods are developed.

In this book, we present accounting practice, or GAAP, as it is today, and we try to explain the reasons or theory on which the practice is based. Both theory and practice are important to the study of accounting. However, accounting is a discipline that is always growing, changing, and improving. Just as years of research are necessary before a new surgical method or lifesaving drug can be introduced, it may take years for new accounting discoveries to be implemented. As a result, you may encounter practices that seem contradictory. In some cases, we point out new directions in accounting. Your instructor also may mention certain weaknesses in current theory or practice.

TABLE 1-2
Large International Certified Public Accounting Firms

Firm	Home Office	Some Major Clients
Deloitte & Touche	New York	General Motors, Procter & Gamble
Ernst & Young	New York	Coca-Cola, McDonald's
KPMG	New York	General Electric, Xerox
PricewaterhouseCoopers	New York	Exxon Mobil, IBM, Ford

GAAP and the Independent CPA's Report

Because financial statements are prepared by management and could be falsified for personal gain, all companies that sell shares of their stock to the public and many companies that apply for sizable loans have their financial statements audited by an independent **certified public accountant (CPA)**. *Independent* means that the CPA is not an employee of the company being audited and has no financial or other compromising ties with it. CPAs are licensed by all states for the same reason that lawyers and doctors are—to protect the public by ensuring the quality of professional service. The firms listed in Table 1-2 employ about 25 percent of all CPAs.

An **audit** is an examination of a company's financial statements and the accounting systems, controls, and records that produced them. The purpose of the audit is to ascertain that the financial statements have been prepared in accordance with generally accepted accounting principles. If the independent CPA is satisfied that this standard has been met, his or her report contains the following language:

> In our opinion, the financial statements . . . present fairly, in all material respects . . . in conformity with generally accepted accounting principles . . .

This wording emphasizes that accounting and auditing are not exact sciences. Because the framework of GAAP provides room for interpretation and the application of GAAP necessitates the making of estimates, the auditor can render only an opinion about whether the financial statements *present fairly* or conform *in all material respects* to GAAP. The auditor's report does not preclude minor or immaterial errors in the financial statements. However, a favorable report from

Study Note

The audit lends credibility to a set of financial statements. The auditor does not attest to the absolute accuracy of the published information or to the value of the company as an investment. All he or she renders is an opinion, based on appropriate testing, about the fairness of the presentation of the financial information.

FOCUS ON BUSINESS PRACTICE **IFRS**

IFRS: The Arrival of International Financial Reporting Standards in the United States

Over the next few years, international financial reporting standards (IFRS) will become much more important in the United States and globally. The International Accounting Standards Board (IASB) has been working with the Financial Accounting Standards Board (FASB) and similar boards in other nations to achieve identical or nearly identical standards worldwide. IFRS are now required in many parts of the world, including Europe. The Securities and Exchange Commission (SEC) recently voted to allow foreign registrants in the United States. This is a major development because in the past, the SEC required foreign registrants to explain how the standards used in their statements differed from U.S. standards. This change affects approximately 10 percent of all public U.S. companies. In addition, the SEC may in the near future allow U.S. companies to use IFRS.[11]

the auditor does imply that, on the whole, investors (owners) and creditors can rely on the financial statements. Historically, auditors have enjoyed a strong reputation for competence and independence. The independent audit has been an important factor in the worldwide growth of financial markets.

Organizations That Issue Accounting Standards

Study Note

The FASB is the primary source of GAAP, but the IASB is increasing in importance.

Two organizations issue accounting standards that are used in the United States: the FASB and the IASB. The **Financial Accounting Standards Board (FASB)** is the most important body for developing rules on accounting practice. This independent body has been designated by the Securities and Exchange Commission (SEC) to issue *Statements of Financial Accounting Standards.*

With the growth of financial markets throughout the world, global cooperation in the development of accounting principles has become a priority. The **International Accounting Standards Board (IASB)** has approved more than 40 **international financial reporting standards (IFRS)**. Foreign companies may use these standards in the United States rather than having to convert their statements to U.S. GAAP as called for by the FASB standards.

Other Organizations That Influence GAAP

Many organizations directly or indirectly influence GAAP and so influence much of what is in this book.

Study Note

The PCAOB regulates audits of public companies registered with the Securities and Exchange Commission.

The **Public Company Accounting Oversight Board (PCAOB)**, a governmental body created by the Sarbanes-Oxley Act, regulates the accounting profession and has wide powers to determine the standards that auditors must follow and to discipline them if they do not.

The **American Institute of Certified Public Accountants (AICPA)**, the professional association of certified public accountants, influences accounting practice through the activities of its senior technical committees.*

Study Note

The AICPA is the primary professional organization of certified public accountants.

The **Securities and Exchange Commission (SEC)** is an agency of the federal government that has the legal power to set and enforce accounting practices for companies whose securities are offered for sale to the general public. As such, it has enormous influence on accounting practice.

The **Governmental Accounting Standards Board (GASB)**, which is under the same governing body as the FASB, issues accounting standards for state and local governments.

U.S. tax laws that govern the assessment and collection of revenue for operating the federal government also influence accounting practice. Because a major source of the government's revenue is the income tax, the tax laws specify the rules for determining taxable income. The **Internal Revenue Service (IRS)** interprets and enforces these rules. In some cases, the rules conflict with good accounting

*In May 2005, the AICPA passed a resolution to start working with the FASB to develop GAAP for privately held, for-profit companies, which would result in recognition, measurement, and disclosure differences, where appropriate, from current GAAP for public companies. If and when this resolution is acted upon, two sets of GAAP will exist: one for private companies and one for public companies.

practice, but they are nonetheless an important influence on practice. Cases in which the tax laws affect accounting practice are noted throughout this book.

Professional Conduct

The code of professional ethics of the American Institute of Certified Public Accountants (and adopted, with variations, by each state) governs the conduct of CPAs. Fundamental to this code is responsibility to clients, creditors, investors (owners), and anyone else who relies on the work of a CPA. The code requires CPAs to act with integrity, objectivity, and independence.

- **Integrity** means the accountant is honest and candid and subordinates personal gain to service and the public trust.
- **Objectivity** means the accountant is impartial and intellectually honest.
- **Independence** means the accountant avoids all relationships that impair or even appear to impair his or her objectivity.

The accountant must also exercise **due care** in all activities, carrying out professional responsibilities with competence and diligence. For example, an accountant must not accept a job for which he or she is not qualified, even at the risk of losing a client to another firm, and careless work is unacceptable. These broad principles are supported by more specific rules that public accountants must follow; for instance, with certain exceptions, client information must be kept strictly confidential. Accountants who violate the rules can be disciplined or even suspended from practice.

The **Institute of Management Accountants (IMA)** also has a code of professional conduct. It emphasizes that management accountants have a responsibility to be competent in their jobs, to keep information confidential except when authorized or legally required to disclose it, to maintain integrity and avoid conflicts of interest, and to communicate information objectively and without bias.[12]

Study Note

The IMA is the primary professional association of management accountants.

Corporate Governance

The financial scandals at **Enron**, **WorldCom**, and other companies highlighted the importance of **corporate governance,** which is the oversight of a corporation's management and ethics by its board of directors. Corporate governance is growing and is clearly in the best interests of a business. A survey of 124 corporations in 22 countries found that 78 percent of boards of directors had established ethical standards, a fourfold increase over a 10-year period. In addition, research has shown that, over time, companies with codes of ethics tend to have higher stock prices than those that have not adopted such codes.[13]

To strengthen corporate governance, a provision of the Sarbanes-Oxley Act requires boards of directors to establish an **audit committee** made up of independent directors who have financial expertise. This provision is aimed at ensuring that boards of directors are objective in evaluating management's performance. The audit committee is also responsible for engaging the corporation's independent auditors and reviewing their work. Another of the committee's functions is to ensure that adequate systems exist to safeguard the corporation's resources and that accounting records are reliable. In short, the audit committee is the front line of defense against fraudulent financial reporting.

STOP & APPLY >

Match the common acronym with its description:

____	1. GAAP	a. Sets U.S. accounting standards
____	2. IFRS	b. Audits financial statements
____	3. CPA	c. Established by the Sarbanes-Oxley Act
____	4. FASB	d. Sets international accounting standards
____	5. IASB	e. Established by the FASB
____	6. PCAOB	f. Established by the IASB
____	7. AICPA	g. Influences accounting standards through member CPAs
____	8. SEC	h. Receives audited financial statements of public companies

SOLUTION

1. c; 2. f; 3. b; 4. a; 5. d; 6. c; 7. g; 8. h

▸ KEEP-FIT CENTER: REVIEW PROBLEM

Preparation and Interpretation of Financial Statements

LO6

The Decision Point at the beginning of this chapter focused on Keep-Fit Center, an apparently successful new company. Although the firm generated commissions from sales of property, the owner, Lilian Jackson, had these questions:

- Is Keep-Fit Center meeting its goal of profitability?
- As owner of Keep-Fit Center, what financial knowledge does Lilian Jackson need to measure progress toward the company's goals?
- In deciding whether to make a loan to Keep-Fit Center, what financial knowledge would a bank need to evaluate the company's financial performance?

As you've learned in this chapter, managers and others with an interest in a business measure its profitability in financial terms such as *net sales*, *net income*, *total assets*, and *owner's equity* and liquidity in terms such as *cash flows*. Owners and managers report on the progress they have made toward their financial goals in their company's financial statements.

The following financial statement accounts and amounts are from the records of Keep-Fit Center for the year ended December 31, 2010, the company's first year of operations:

Accounts payable	$ 19,000
Accounts receivable	104,000
Cash	111,000
Equipment	47,000
Fees revenue	375,000
Investment by L. Jackson	100,000
Marketing expense	18,000
Salaries	172,000
Salaries payable	78,000
Studio and equipment rent expense	91,000
Supplies	2,000
Supplies expense	6,000
Utilities expense	11,000
Withdrawals	10,000

Required

1. Prepare an income statement, statement of owner's equity, and balance sheet for Keep-Fit Center. For examples, refer to Exhibit 1-5.
2. User insight: From the income statement and balance sheet, does it appear that Keep-Fit Center is profitable? Why or why not?

Answers to Review Problem

1. Preparation of financial statements

	A	B	C	D	E
1			**Keep-Fit Center**		
2			**Income Statement**		
3			**For the Year Ended April 30, 2010**		
4	Revenues:				
5		Fees revenues			$375,000
6					
7	Expenses:				
8		Marketing expense		$ 18,000	
9		Studio and equipment rent expense		91,000	
10		Salaries expense		172,000	
11		Supplies expense		6,000	
12		Utilities expense		11,000	
13	Total expenses				298,000
14	Net income				$ 77,000
15					

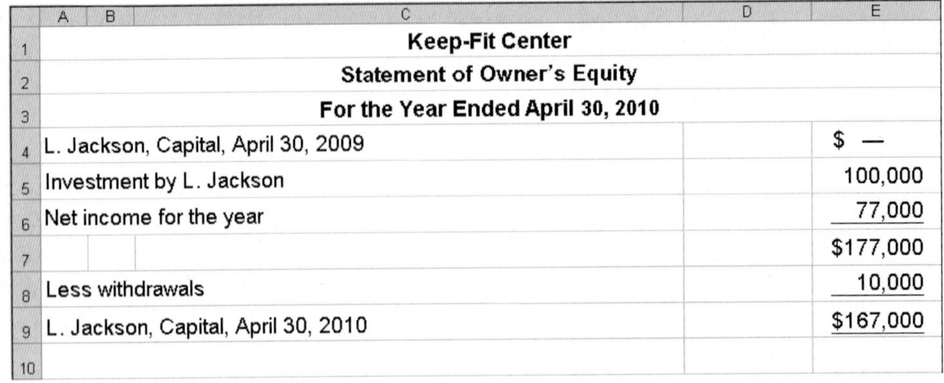

Keep-Fit Center			
Statement of Owner's Equity			
For the Year Ended April 30, 2010			
L. Jackson, Capital, April 30, 2009			$ —
Investment by L. Jackson			100,000
Net income for the year			77,000
			$177,000
Less withdrawals			10,000
L. Jackson, Capital, April 30, 2010			$167,000

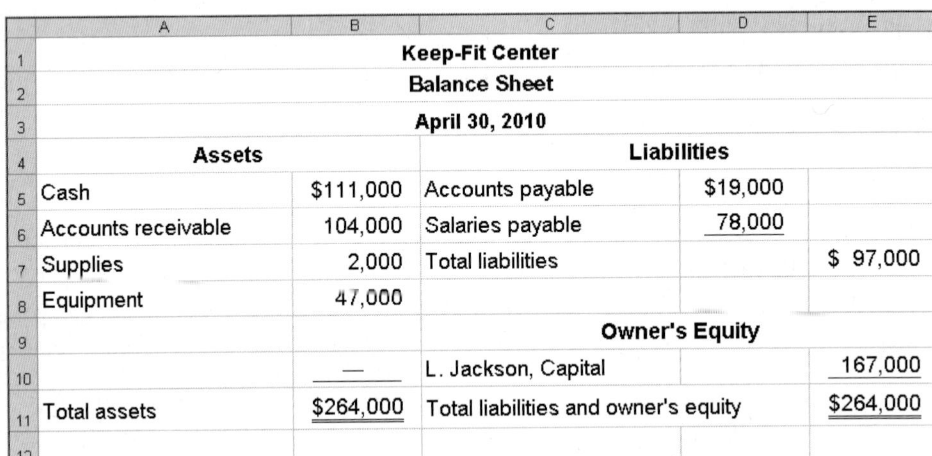

Keep-Fit Center				
Balance Sheet				
April 30, 2010				
Assets		Liabilities		
Cash	$111,000	Accounts payable	$19,000	
Accounts receivable	104,000	Salaries payable	78,000	
Supplies	2,000	Total liabilities		$ 97,000
Equipment	47,000			
		Owner's Equity		
	—	L. Jackson, Capital		167,000
Total assets	$264,000	Total liabilities and owner's equity		$264,000

2. Keep-Fit Center is profitable. The income statement shows that it earned $77,000 after expenses were deducted from fees revenue. Further, it may be observed that this $77,000 of net income is very good when compared to total assets of $264,000 and owner's equity on the balance sheet.

LO1 Define *accounting* and describe its role in making informed decisions, identify business goals and activities, and explain the importance of ethics in accounting.

Accounting is an information system that measures, processes, and communicates financial information about an economic entity. It provides the information necessary to make reasoned choices among alternative uses of scarce resources in the conduct of business and economic activities. A business is an economic entity that engages in operating, investing, and financing activities to achieve the goals of profitability and liquidity.

Management accounting focuses on the preparation of information primarily for internal use by management. Financial accounting is concerned with the development and use of reports that are communicated to those outside the business as well as to management. Ethical financial reporting is important to the well-being of a company; fraudulent financial reports can have serious consequences for many people.

LO2 Identify the users of accounting information.

Accounting plays a significant role in society by providing information to managers of all institutions and to individuals with a direct financial interest in those institutions, including present or potential investors (owners) and creditors. Accounting information is also important to those with an indirect financial interest in the business—for example, tax authorities, regulatory agencies, and economic planners.

LO3 Explain the importance of business transactions, money measure, and separate entity.

To make an accounting measurement, the accountant must determine what is measured, when the measurement should be made, what value should be placed on what is measured, and how to classify what is measured. The objects of accounting measurement are business transactions. Financial accounting uses money measure to gauge the impact of these transactions on a separate business entity.

LO4 Identify the three basic forms of business organization.

The three basic forms of business organization are the sole proprietorship, the partnership, and the corporation. Accountants recognize each form as an economic unit separate from its owners, although legally only the corporation is separate from its owners. A sole proprietorship is a business owned by one person. A partnership is like a sole proprietorship in most ways, but it has two or more owners. A corporation, on the other hand, is a business unit chartered by the state and legally separate from its owners (the stockholders).

LO5 Define *financial position*, and state the accounting equation.

Financial position refers to a company's economic resources and the claims against those resources at a particular time. The accounting equation shows financial position as Assets = Liabilities + Owner's Equity. Business transactions affect financial position by decreasing or increasing assets, liabilities, and owner's equity in such a way that the accounting equation is always in balance.

LO6 Identify the four basic financial statements.

The four basic financial statements are the income statement, the statement of owner's equity, the balance sheet, and the statement of cash flows. They are the primary means by which accountants communicate the financial condition and activities of a business to those who have an interest in the business.

LO7 Explain how generally accepted accounting principles (GAAP) and international financial reporting standards (IFRS) relate to financial statements and the independent CPA's report, and identify the organizations that influence GAAP.

Acceptable accounting practice consists of the conventions, rules, and procedures that make up generally accepted accounting principles at a particular time. GAAP are essential to the preparation and interpretation of financial statements and the independent CPA's report. Foreign companies registered in the United States may use international financial reporting standards (IFRS).

Among the organizations that influence the formulation of GAAP are the Public Company Accounting Oversight Board, the Financial Accounting Standards Board, the American Institute of Certified Public Accountants, the Securities and Exchange Commission, and the Internal Revenue Service.

All accountants are required to follow a code of professional ethics, the foundation of which is responsibility to the public. Accountants must act with integrity, objectivity, and independence, and they must exercise due care in all their activities.

The board of directors is responsible for determining corporate policies and appointing corporate officers. It is also responsible for corporate governance, the oversight of a corporation's management and ethics. The audit committee, which is appointed by the board and made up of independent directors, is an important factor in corporate governance.

REVIEW of Concepts and Terminology

The following concepts and terms were introduced in this chapter:

CHAPTER ASSIGNMENTS

BUILDING Your Basic Knowledge and Skills

Short Exercises

Short exercises are simple applications of chapter material for one or more learning objectives. If you need help locating the related text discussions, refer to the LO numbers in the margin.

LO1 **Accounting and Business Enterprises**

SE 1. Match the terms on the left with the definitions on the right:

___ 1. Accounting
___ 2. Profitability
___ 3. Liquidity
___ 4. Financing activities
___ 5. Investing activities
___ 6. Operating activities
___ 7. Financial accounting
___ 8. Management accounting
___ 9. Ethics
___ 10. Fraudulent financial reporting

a. The process of producing accounting information for the internal use of a company's management.
b. Having enough cash available to pay debts when they are due.
c. Activities management engages in to obtain adequate funds for beginning and continuing to operate a business.
d. The process of generating and communicating accounting information in the form of financial statements to decision makers outside the organization.
e. Activities management engages in to spend capital in ways that are productive and will help a business achieve its objectives.
f. The ability to earn enough income to attract and hold investment capital.
g. An information system that measures, processes, and communicates financial information about an identifiable economic entity.
h. The intentional preparation of misleading financial statements.
i. Activities management engages in to operate the business.
j. A code of conduct that addresses whether actions are right or wrong.

LO3 LO4 **Accounting Concepts**

SE 2. Indicate whether each of the following words or phrases relates most closely to (a) a business transaction, (b) a separate entity, or (c) a money measure:

1. Partnership
2. U.S. dollar
3. Payment of an expense
4. Sole proprietorship
5. Sale of an asset

LO4 Forms of Business Organization

SE 3. Match the descriptions on the left with the forms of business organization on the right:

_____	1. Most numerous	a. Sole proprietorship
_____	2. Commands most revenues	b. Partnership
_____	3. Has two or more co-owners	c. Corporation
_____	4. Has stockholders	
_____	5. Is owned by only one person	
_____	6. Has a board of directors	

LO5 The Accounting Equation

SE 4. Determine the amount missing from each accounting equation below.

Assets	=	Liabilities	+	Owner's Equity
1. ?		$50,000		$ 70,000
2. $156,000		$84,000		?
3. $292,000		?		$192,000

LO5 The Accounting Equation

SE 5. Use the accounting equation to answer each question below.

1. The assets of Aaron Company are $240,000, and the liabilities are $90,000. What is the amount of the owner's equity?
2. The liabilities of Oak Company equal one-fifth of the total assets. The owner's equity is $40,000. What is the amount of the liabilities?

LO5 The Accounting Equation

SE 6. Use the accounting equation to answer each question below.

1. At the beginning of the year, Fazio Company's assets were $45,000, and its owner's equity was $25,000. During the year, assets increased by $30,000 and liabilities increased by $5,000. What was the owner's equity at the end of the year?
2. At the beginning of the year, Gal Company had liabilities of $50,000 and owner's equity of $96,000. If assets increased by $40,000 and liabilities decreased by $30,000, what was the owner's equity at the end of the year?

LO5 The Accounting Equation and Net Income

SE 7. Carlton Company had assets of $280,000 and liabilities of $120,000 at the beginning of the year, and assets of $400,000 and liabilities of $140,000 at the end of the year. During the year, the owner invested an additional $40,000 in the business, and the company made withdrawals of $48,000. What amount of net income did the company earn during the year?

LO6 Preparation and Completion of a Balance Sheet

SE 8. Use the following accounts and balances to prepare a balance sheet with the accounts in proper order for Global Company at June 30, 2010, using Exhibit 1-3 as a model:

Accounts Receivable	$ 1,600
Wages Payable	700
Owner's Capital	28,700
Building	22,000
Cash	?

LO6

Preparation of Financial Statements

SE 9. Tarech Company engaged in activities during the first year of its operations that resulted in the following: service revenue, \$4,800; expenses, \$2,450; and withdrawals, \$410. In addition, the year-end balances of selected accounts were as follows: Cash, \$1,890; Other Assets, \$1,000; Accounts Payable, \$450; and Owner's Capital, \$500. In proper format, prepare the income statement, statement of retained earnings, and balance sheet for Tarech Company (assume the year ends on December 31, 2010). (**Hint:** You must solve for the beginning and ending balances of Owner's Equity for 2010.)

Exercises

Exercises are more complex applications of chapter concepts than short exercises.

LO1 LO2 LO3 LO4

Discussion Questions

E 1. Develop a brief answer to each of the following questions:

1. What makes accounting a valuable discipline?
2. Why do managers in governmental and not-for-profit organizations need to understand financial information as much as managers in profit-seeking businesses do?
3. Are all economic events business transactions?
4. Sole proprietorships, partnerships, and corporations differ legally; how and why does accounting treat them alike?

LO1 LO5 LO6 LO7

Discussion Questions

E 2. Develop a brief answer to each of the following questions:

1. How are expenses and withdrawals similar, and how are they different?
2. In what ways are **CVS** and **Southwest Airlines** comparable? Not comparable?
3. How do generally accepted accounting principles (GAAP) differ from the laws of science?
4. What are some unethical ways in which a business may do its accounting or prepare its financial statements?

LO1 LO2 LO3 LO7

The Nature of Accounting

E 3. Match the terms on the left with the descriptions on the right:

___ 1. Bookkeeping
___ 2. Creditors
___ 3. Money measure
___ 4. Financial Accounting Standards Board (FASB)
___ 5. Business transactions
___ 6. Financial statements
___ 7. Communication
___ 8. Securities and Exchange Commission (SEC)
___ 9. Investors
___ 10. Sarbanes-Oxley Act
___ 11. Management
___ 12. Management information system

a. The recording of all business transactions in terms of money
b. A process by which information is exchanged between individuals through a common system of symbols, signs, or behavior
c. The process of identifying and assigning values to business transactions
d. Legislation ordering CEOs and CFOs to swear that any reports they file with the SEC are accurate and complete
e. Shows how well a company is meeting the goals of profitability and liquidity
f. Collectively, the people who have overall responsibility for operating a business and meeting its goals

g. People who commit money to earn a financial return
h. The interconnected subsystems that provide the information needed to run a business
i. The most important body for developing and issuing rules on accounting practice, called *Statements of Financial Accounting Standards*
j. An agency set up by Congress to protect the public by regulating the issuing, buying, and selling of stocks
k. Economic events that affect a business's financial position
l. People to whom money is due

LO2 LO4 **Users of Accounting Information and Forms of Business Organization**

E 4. Gottlieb Pharmacy has recently been formed to develop a new type of drug treatment for cancer. Previously a partnership, Gottlieb has now become a corporation. Describe the various groups that will have an interest in the financial statements of Gottlieb. What is the difference between a partnership and a corporation? What advantages does the corporate form have over the partnership form of business organization?

LO3 **Business Transactions**

E 5. Velu owns and operates a minimart. Which of Velu's actions described below are business transactions? Explain why any other actions are not considered transactions.

1. Velu reduces the price of a gallon of milk in order to match the price offered by a competitor.
2. Velu pays a high school student cash for cleaning up the driveway behind the market.
3. Velu fills his son's car with gasoline in payment for his son's restocking the vending machines and the snack food shelves.
4. Velu pays interest to himself on a loan he made to the business three years ago.

LO3 LO4 **Accounting Concepts**

E 6. Financial accounting uses money measures to gauge the impact of business transactions on a separate business entity. Indicate whether each of the following words or phrases relates most closely to (a) a business transaction, (b) a separate entity, or (c) a money measure:

1. Corporation
2. Euro
3. Sales of products
4. Receipt of cash
5. Sole proprietorship
6. U.S. dollar
7. Partnership
8. Owner's investments
9. Japanese yen
10. Purchase of supplies

LO3 **Money Measure**

E 7. You have been asked to compare the sales and assets of four companies that make computer chips to determine which company is the largest in each category. You have gathered the following data, but they cannot be used for direct comparison because each company's sales and assets are in its own currency:

Company (Currency)	Sales	Assets
U.S. Chip (U.S. dollar)	2,750,000	1,300,000
Nanhai (Hong Kong dollar)	5,000,000	2,800,000
Tova (Japanese yen)	350,000,000	290,000,000
Holstein (Euro)	3,500,000	3,900,000

Assuming that the exchange rates in Table 1-1 are current and appropriate, convert all the figures to U.S. dollars and determine which company is the largest in sales and which is the largest in assets.

LO5 The Accounting Equation

E 8. Use the accounting equation to answer each question that follows. Show any calculations you make.

1. The assets of Rasche Company are $380,000, and the owner's equity is $155,000. What is the amount of the liabilities?
2. The liabilities and owner's equity of Lee Company are $65,000 and $79,500, respectively. What is the amount of the assets?
3. The liabilities of Hurka Company equal one-third of the total assets, and owner's equity is $180,000. What is the amount of the liabilities?
4. At the beginning of the year, Jahis Company's assets were $310,000, and its owner's equity was $150,000. During the year, assets increased $45,000 and liabilities decreased $22,500. What is the owner's equity at the end of the year?

LO5 LO6 Identification of Accounts

E 9.

1. Indicate whether each of the following accounts is an asset (A), a liability (L), or a part of owner's equity (OE):

   a. Cash
   b. Salaries Payable
   c. Accounts Receivable
   d. Owner's Capital
   e. Land
   f. Accounts Payable
   g. Supplies

2. Indicate whether each account below would be shown on the income statement (IS), the statement of owner's equity (OE), or the balance sheet (BS).

   a. Repair Revenue
   b. Automobile
   c. Fuel Expense
   d. Cash
   e. Rent Expense
   f. Accounts Payable
   g. Withdrawals

LO6 Preparation of a Balance Sheet

E 10. Listed in random order are some of the account balances for the Uptime Services Company as of December 31, 2011.

Accounts Payable	$ 25,000	Accounts Receivable	$31,250
Building	56,250	Cash	12,500
Owner's Capital	106,250	Equipment	25,000
Supplies	6,250		

Place the balances in proper order and prepare a balance sheet similar to the one in Exhibit 1-3.

LO6 Preparation and Integration of Financial Statements

E 11. Proviso Company had the following accounts and balances during 2010: Service Revenue, $26,400; Rent Expense, $2,400; Wages Expense, $16,680; Advertising Expense, $2,700; Utilities Expense, $1,800; and Withdrawals, $1,400. In addition, the year-end balances of selected accounts were as follows: Cash, $3,100; Accounts Receivable, $1,500; Supplies, $200; Land, $2,000; Accounts Payable, $900; Investment by Owner, $2,480; and beginning capital balance of $2,000.

In proper format, prepare the income statement, statement of owner's equity, and balance sheet for Proviso Company (assume the year ends on December 31, 2010). (**Hint:** You must solve for the beginning and ending balances of owner's equity for 2010.)

LO5 **Owner's Equity and the Accounting Equation**

E 12. The total assets and liabilities at the beginning and end of the year for Schupan Company are listed below.

	Assets	Liabilities
Beginning of the year	$180,000	$ 68,750
End of the year	275,000	150,500

Determine Schupan Company's net income or loss for the year under each of the following alternatives:

1. The owner made no investments in or withdrawals from the business during the year.
2. The owner made no investments in the business but withdrew $27,500 during the year.
3. The owner invested $16,250 in the business but made no withdrawals during the year.
4. The owner invested $12,500 in the business and withdrew of $29,000 during the year.

LO6 **Statement of Cash Flows**

E 13. Martin Service Company began the year 2010 with cash of $55,900. In addition to earning a net income of $38,000 and making cash withdrawals of $19,500, Martin Service borrowed $78,000 from the bank and purchased equipment with $125,000 of cash. Also, Accounts Receivable increased by $7,800, and Accounts Payable increased by $11,700.

Determine the amount of cash on hand at December 31, 2010, by preparing a statement of cash flows similar to the one in Exhibit 1–4.

LO4 LO5 LO6 **Statement of Owner's Equity**

E 14. Below is information from the statement of owner's equity of Mrs. Kitty's Cookies for a recent year.

Withdrawals	0
Net income	?
Owner's Equity, January 31, 2010	$159,490
Owner's Equity, January 31, 2009	$105,000

Prepare the statement of owner's equity for Mrs. Kitty's Cookies in good form. You will need to solve for the amount of net income. What is owner's equity? Why might the owner decide not to make any withdrawals from the company?

LO7 **Accounting Abbreviations**

E 15. Identify the accounting meaning of each of the following abbreviations: AICPA, SEC, PCAOB, GAAP, FASB, IRS, GASB, IASB, IMA, and CPA.

Problems

LO6 **Preparation and Interpretation of Financial Statements**

P 1. Below is a list of financial statement items.

____ Utilities expense	____ Equipment	____ Withdrawals
____ Building	____ Revenues	____ Fees earned
____ Owner's capital	____ Accounts receivable	____ Cash
____ Net income	____ Accounts payable	____ Supplies
____ Land	____ Rent expense	____ Wages expense

Required

1. Indicate whether each item is found on the income statement (IS), statement of owner's equity (OE), and/or balance sheet (BS).

User insight ▶ 2. Which statement is most closely associated with the goal of profitability?

LO6 **Integration of Financial Statements**

P 2. The following three independent sets of financial statements have several amounts missing:

	Set A	Set B	Set C
Income Statement			
Revenues	$5,320	$ 8,600	$ m
Expenses	a	g	2,010
Net income	$ 510	$ h	$ n
Statement of Owner's Equity			
Beginning balance	$1,780	$15,400	$ 200
Net income	b	i	450
Less withdrawals	c	1,000	o
Ending balance	$ d	$16,000	$ p
Balance Sheet			
Total assets	$ e	$ j	$1,900
Liabilities	$ f	$ 2,000	$1,300
Owner's equity			
Owner's capital	2,100	k	q
Total liabilities and owner's equity	$2,700	$ l	$ r

Required

1. Complete each set of financial statements by determining the amounts that correspond to the letters.

User insight ▶ 2. Why is it necessary to prepare the income statement prior to the balance sheet?

Curious if you got the right answer? Look at the Check Figures section that precedes Chapter 1.

LO1 LO6 **Preparation and Interpretation of Financial Statements**

P 3. Below are the financial accounts of Special Assets. The company has just completed its 10th year of operations ended December 31, 2011.

Accounts Payable	$ 3,600
Accounts Receivable	4,500
Cash	71,700
Commission Sales Revenue	400,000
Commissions Expense	225,000
Commissions Payable	22,700

Equipment	$59,900
Marketing Expense	20,100
Office Rent Expense	36,000
Owner's Capital, December 31, 2010	64,300
Supplies	700
Supplies Expense	2,600
Telephone and Computer Expenses	5,100
Wages Expense	32,000
Withdrawals	33,000

Required

1. Prepare the income statement, statement of owner's equity, and balance sheet for Special Assets. There were no investments by the owner during the year.

User insight ▶ 2. The owner is considering expansion. What other statement would be useful to the owner in assessing whether the company's operations are generating sufficient funds to support the expenses? Why would it be useful?

LO4 LO6 Preparation and Interpretation of Financial Statements

P 4. The following are the accounts of Unique Ad, an agency that develops marketing materials for print, radio, and television. The agency's first year of operations just ended on January 31, 2010.

Accounts Payable	$ 19,400
Accounts Receivable	24,900
Advertising Service Revenue	165,200
Cash	1,800
Equipment Rental Expense	37,200
Marketing Expense	6,800
Office Rent Expense	13,500
Owner's Capital	5,000*
Salaries Expense	86,000
Salaries Payable	1,300
Supplies	1,600
Supplies Expense	19,100
Withdrawals	0

*Represents the initial investment by the owner.

Required

1. Prepare the income statement, statement of owner's equity, and balance sheet for Unique Ad.

User insight ▶ 2. Review the financial statements and comment on the financial challenges Unique Ad faces.

LO1 LO6 LO7 Use and Interpretation of Financial Statements

P 5. The financial statements for the Oros Riding Club follow.

Oros Riding Club
Income Statement
For the Month Ended November 30, 2011

Revenues		
Riding lesson revenue	$4,650	
Locker rental revenue	1,450	
Total revenues		$6,100
Expenses		
Salaries expense	$1,125	
Feed expense	750	
Utilities expense	450	
Total expenses		2,325
Net income		$3,775

Oros Riding Club
Statement of Owner's Equity
For the Month Ended November 30, 2011

Owner's capital, October 31, 2011	$35,475
Investment by owner	6,000
Net income for the month	3,775
Subtotal	$45,250
Less withdrawals	2,400
Owner's capital, November 30, 2011	$42,850

Oros Riding Club
Balance Sheet
November 30, 2011

Assets		**Liabilities**	
Cash	$ 6,700	Accounts payable	$11,250
Accounts receivable	900	**Owner's Equity**	
Supplies	750	Owner's capital	42,850
Land	15,750		
Building	22,500		
Horses	7,500	Total liabilities and	
Total assets	$54,100	owner's equity	$54,100

Oros Riding Club
Statement of Cash Flows
For the Month Ended November 30, 2011

Cash flows from operating activities		
Net income		$3,775
Adjustments to reconcile net income to net cash flows from operating activities		
Increase in accounts receivable	$ (400)	
Increase in supplies	(550)	
Increase in accounts payable	400	(550)
Net cash flows from operating activities		$3,225
Cash flows from investing activities		
Purchase of horses	$2,000	
Sale of horses	(1,000)	
Net cash flows from financing activities		1,000
Cash flows from financing activities		
Investment by Owner	$6,000	
Cash withdrawals	(2,400)	
Net cash flows from financing activities		3,600
Net increase in cash		$7,825
Cash at beginning of month		475
Cash at end of month		$8,300

Required

User insight ▶ 1. Explain how the four statements for Oros Riding Club relate to each other.

User insight ▶ 2. Which statements are most closely associated with the goals of liquidity and profitability? Why?

User insight ▶ 3. If you were the owner of this business, how would you evaluate the company's performance? Give specific examples.

User insight ▶ 4. If you were a banker considering Oros Riding Club for a loan, why might you want the company to be audited by an independent CPA? What would the audit tell you?

Looking for more practice? Alternate problems have the same format and learning objectives as problems that appear earlier.

Alternate Problems

LO6 **Integration of Financial Statements**

P 6. Below are three independent sets of financial statements with several amounts missing.

Income Statement	**Set A**	**Set B**	**Set C**
Revenues	$1,200	$ g	$ 240
Expenses	a	5,000	m
Net income	$ b	$ h	$ 148
Statement of Owner's Equity			
Beginning balance	$2,900	$24,400	$ 340
Net income	c	1,600	n
Less withdrawals	200	i	o
Ending balance	$3,090	$ j	$ p
Balance Sheet			
Total assets	$ d	$30,000	$ q
Liabilities	$1,600	$ 5,000	$ r
Owner's equity			
Owner's capital	e	k	380
Total liabilities and owner's equity	$ f	$ l	$ 580

Required

1. Complete each set of financial statements by determining the amounts that correspond to the letters.

User insight ▶ 2. In what order is it necessary to prepare the financial statements and why?

LO1 LO6 **Preparation and Interpretation of Financial Statements**

P 7. Below are the financial accounts of Metro Labs. The company has just completed its third year of operations ended November 30, 2011.

Accounts Payable	$ 7,400
Accounts Receivable	51,900
Cash	115,750
Design Service Revenue	300,000
Marketing Expense	19,700
Office Rent Expense	50,000
Owner's Capital, November 30, 2010	70,400
Salaries Expense	96,000
Salaries Payable	2,700
Supplies	800
Supplies Expense	6,350
Withdrawals	40,000

Required

1. Prepare the income statement, statement of owner's equity, and balance sheet for Metro Labs. There were no investments by the owner during the year.

User insight ▶ 2. Evaluate the company's ability to meet its bills when they come due.

LO4 LO6 **Preparation and Interpretation of Financial Statements**

P 8. Below are the accounts of Giordano's Pizza. The company has just completed its first year of operations ended September 30, 2010.

Accounts Payable	$10,500
Accounts Receivable	13,200
Cash	2,600
Delivery Truck Rent Expense	7,200

Equipment	$ 6,300
Equipment Rental Expense	2,900
Marketing Expense	1,500
Owner's Capital	2,000*
Pizza Revenue	82,000
Salaries Expense	56,000
Salaries Payable	700
Supplies	400
Supplies Expense	4,100
Withdrawals	1,000

*Represents the initial investment by the owner

Required

1. Prepare the income statement, statement of owner's equity, and balance sheet for Giordano's Pizza.

User insight ▶ 2. Why would the owner of Giordano's Pizza set his business up as a sole proprietorship and not a partnership? Discuss the advantages of the two forms of business organizations.

LO6 Integration of Financial Statements

P 9. Below are three independent sets of financial statements with several amounts missing.

Income Statement	**Set X**	**Set Y**	**Set Z**
Revenues	$1,100	$ g	$240
Expenses	a	5,200	m
Net income	$ b	$ h	$ 80
Statement of Owner's Equity			
Beginning balance	$2,900	$24,400	$240
Net income	c	1,600	n
Less withdrawals	200	i	o
Ending balance	$3,000	$ j	$ p
Balance Sheetz			
Total assets	$ d	$31,000	$ q
Liabilities	$1,600	$ 5,000	$ r
Owner's equity			
Owner's capital	e	k	280
Total liabilities and owner's equity	$ f	$ l	$580

Required

1. Complete each set of financial statements by determining the amounts that correspond to the letters.

User insight ▶ 2. In what order is it necessary to prepare the financial statements and why?

LO6 Preparation and Interpretation of Financial Statements

P 10. Below are the financial accounts of Brad Realty. The company has just completed its 10th year of operations ended December 31, 2011.

Accounts Payable	$ 3,600
Accounts Receivable	4,500
Cash	91,600
Commission Sales Revenue	450,000
Commissions Expense	225,000
Commissions Payable	22,700

Equipment	$59,000
Marketing Expense	29,200
Office Rent Expense	36,000
Owner's Capital, December 31, 2010	50,300
Supplies	700
Supplies Expense	2,600
Telephone and Computer Expenses	5,100
Wages Expense	32,000
Withdrawals	40,000

Required

1. Prepare the income statement, statement of owner's equity, and balance sheet for Brad Realty. There were no investments by the owner during the year.

User insight ▶

2. The owner is considering expansion. What other statement would be useful to the owner in assessing whether the company's operations are generating sufficient funds to support expenses? Why would it be useful?

ENHANCING Your Knowledge, Skills, and Critical Thinking

LO1 LO2

Business Activities and Management Functions

C 1. **Costco Wholesale Corporation** is America's largest membership retail company. According to its letter to stockholders:

> Our mission is to bring quality goods and services to our members at the lowest possible price in every market where we do business. . . . A hallmark of Costco warehouses has been the extraordinary sales volume we achieve.[14]

To achieve its business goals, Costco must organize its management by functions that relate to the principal activities of a business. Discuss the three basic activities Costco will engage in to achieve its goals, and suggest some examples of each. What is the role of Costco's management? What functions must its management perform to carry out these activities?

LO5

Concept of an Asset

C 2. **Southwest Airlines Co.** is one of the most successful airlines in the United States. Its annual report contains this statement: "We are a company of People, not Planes. That is what distinguishes us from other airlines and other companies. At Southwest Airlines, People are our most important asset."[15] Are employees considered assets in the financial statements? Why or why not? Discuss in what sense Southwest considers its employees to be assets.

LO7

Generally Accepted Accounting Principles

C 3. **Fidelity Investments Company** is a well-known mutual fund investment company. It makes investments worth billions of dollars in companies listed on the New York Stock Exchange and other stock markets. Generally accepted accounting principles (GAAP) are very important for Fidelity's investment analysts. What are generally accepted accounting principles? Why are financial statements that have been prepared in accordance with GAAP and audited by an independent CPA useful for Fidelity's investment analysts? What organizations influence GAAP? Explain how they do so.

LO7 Professional Ethics

C 4. Discuss the ethical choices in the situations below. In each instance, describe the ethical dilemma, determine the alternative courses of action, and tell what you would do.

1. You are the payroll accountant for a small business. A friend asks you how much another employee is paid per hour.
2. As an accountant for the branch office of a wholesale supplier, you discover that several of the receipts the branch manager has submitted for reimbursement as selling expenses actually stem from nights out with his spouse.
3. You are an accountant in the purchasing department of a construction company. When you arrive home from work on December 22, you find a large ham in a box marked "Happy Holidays—It's a pleasure to work with you." The gift is from a supplier who has bid on a contract your employer plans to award next week.
4. As an auditor with one year's experience at a local CPA firm, you are expected to complete a certain part of an audit in 20 hours. Because of your lack of experience, you know you cannot finish the job within that time. Rather than admit this, you are thinking about working late to finish the job and not telling anyone.
5. You are a tax accountant at a local CPA firm. You help your neighbor fill out her tax return, and she pays you $200 in cash. Because there is no record of this transaction, you are considering not reporting it on your tax return.
6. The accounting firm for which you work as a CPA has just won a new client, a firm in which you own 200 shares of stock that you received as an inheritance from your grandmother. Because it is only a small number of shares and you think the company will be very successful, you are considering not disclosing the investment.

LO6 LO7 Analysis of Four Basic Financial Statements

C 5. Refer to the **CVS** annual report in the Supplement to Chapter 5 to answer the questions below. Keep in mind that every company, while following basic principles, adapts financial statements and terminology to its own special needs. Therefore, the complexity of CVS's financial statements and the terminology in them will differ somewhat from the financial statements in the text.

1. What titles does CVS give to its four basic financial statements? (Note that the word *consolidated* in the titles of the financial statements means that these statements combine those of several companies owned by CVS.)
2. Prove that the accounting equation works for CVS on December 31, 2008, by finding the amounts for the following equation: Assets = Liabilities + Shareholders' (Owner's) Equity.
3. What were the total revenues of CVS for the year ended December 31, 2008?
4. Was CVS profitable in the year ended December 31, 2008? How much was net income (loss) in that year, and did it increase or decrease from the year ended December 29, 2007?
5. Did the company's cash and cash equivalents increase from December 29, 2007, to December 31, 2008? If so, by how much? In what two places in the statements can this number be found or computed?
6. Did cash flows from operating activities, cash flows from investing activities, and cash flows from financing activities increase or decrease from 2007 to 2008?
7. Who is the auditor for the company? Why is the auditor's report that accompanies the financial statements important?

LO1 LO5 Performance Measures and Financial Statements

C 6. Refer to the **CVS** annual report and the financial statements of **Southwest Airlines Co.** in the Supplement to Chapter 5 to answer these questions:

1. Which company is larger in terms of assets and in terms of revenues? What do you think is the best way to measure the size of a company?
2. Which company is more profitable in terms of net income? What is the trend of profitability over the past three years for both companies?
3. Which company has more cash? Which increased its cash the most in the last year? Which has more liquidity as measured by cash flows from operating activities?

CHAPTER

2

Analyzing Business Transactions

Making a Statement

INCOME STATEMENT

Revenues

– Expenses

= Net Income

STATEMENT OF OWNER'S EQUITY

Beginning Balance

+ Net Income

– Withdrawals

= Ending Balance

BALANCE SHEET

Assets	**Liabilities**
	Owner's Equity

A = L + OE

STATEMENT OF CASH FLOWS

Operating activities
+ Investing activities
+ Financing activities
= Change in Cash
+ Beginning Balance
= Ending Cash Balance

Business transactions can affect all the financial statements.

All business transactions require the application of three basic accounting concepts: recording a transaction at the right time, placing the right value on it, and calling it by the right name. Most accounting frauds and mistakes violate one or more of these basic accounting concepts. What you learn in this chapter will help you avoid making such mistakes. It will also help you recognize correct accounting practices.

LEARNING OBJECTIVES

LO1 **Explain how the concepts of recognition, valuation, and classification apply to business transactions and why they are important factors in ethical financial reporting.** (pp. 50–53)

LO2 **Explain the double-entry system and the usefulness of T accounts in analyzing business transactions.** (pp. 54–57)

LO3 **Demonstrate how the double-entry system is applied to common business transactions.** (pp. 58–65)

LO4 **Prepare a trial balance, and describe its value and limitations.** (pp. 65–67)

LO5 **Show how the timing of transactions affects cash flows and liquidity.** (pp. 68–69)

SUPPLEMENTAL OBJECTIVE

SO6 **Define the *chart of accounts*, record transactions in the general journal, and post transactions to the ledger.** (pp. 70–75)

DECISION POINT ▶ A USER'S FOCUS PAWS AND HOOFS CLINIC

After graduating from veterinary school, Larry Cox started the Paws and Hoofs Clinic. On his second day of business, he received a standing order from Quarter Horse Stables to examine its horses on a monthly basis for one year. The fee for the service was to be $500 per visit, or $6,000 for the year. Confident that his agreement with Quarter Horse Stables will work out, Larry is thinking of including the $6,000 in his financial statements. He believes that doing so would be a good advertisement for his business, but he must answer the questions at right to determine if this is acceptable practice.

- ▶ Is there a difference between an economic event and a business transaction that should be recorded in the accounting records?
- ▶ Can a business transaction benefit a business even though no cash is received when the transaction takes place?
- ▶ What is the difference between an asset and an expense?

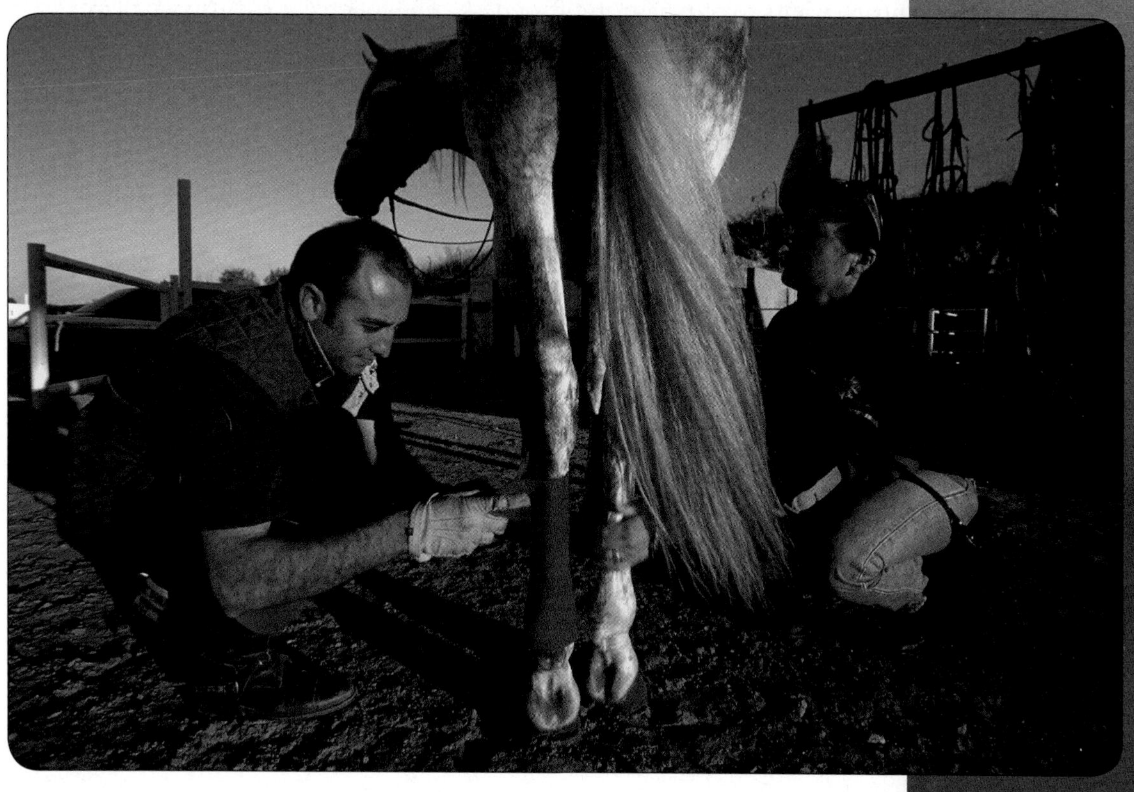

Measurement Issues

LO1 Explain how the concepts of recognition, valuation, and classification apply to business transactions and why they are important factors in ethical financial reporting.

Business transactions are economic events that affect a company's financial position. As shown in Figure 2-1, to measure a business transaction, you must decide when the transaction occurred (the recognition issue), what value to place on the transaction (the valuation issue), and how the components of the transaction should be categorized (the classification issue).

These three issues—recognition, valuation, and classification—underlie almost every major decision in financial accounting today. They are at the heart of accounting for pension plans, mergers of giant companies, and international transactions. In discussing these issues, we follow generally accepted accounting principles and use an approach that promotes an understanding of basic accounting concepts. Keep in mind, however, that measurement issues can be controversial and resolutions to them are not always as cut-and-dried as the ones presented here.

Recognition

Study Note

In accounting, *recognize* means to record a transaction or event.

The **recognition** issue refers to the difficulty of deciding *when* a business transaction should be recorded. The resolution of this issue is important because the date on which a transaction is recorded affects amounts in the financial statements.

To illustrate some of the factors involved in the recognition issue, suppose a company wants to purchase an office desk. The following events take place:

1. An employee sends a purchase requisition for the desk to the purchasing department.
2. The purchasing department sends a purchase order to the supplier.
3. The supplier ships the desk.
4. The company receives the desk.
5. The company receives the bill from the supplier.
6. The company pays the bill.

Study Note

A purchase should usually not be recognized (recorded) before title is transferred, because until that point, the vendor has not fulfilled its contractual obligation and the buyer has no liability.

According to accounting tradition, a transaction should be recorded when title to merchandise passes from the supplier to the purchaser and creates an obligation to pay. Thus, depending on the details of the shipping agreement for the desk, the transaction should be recognized (recorded) at the time of either event **3** or **4**. This is the guideline we generally use in this book. However, many small

FIGURE 2-1
The Role of Measurement Issues

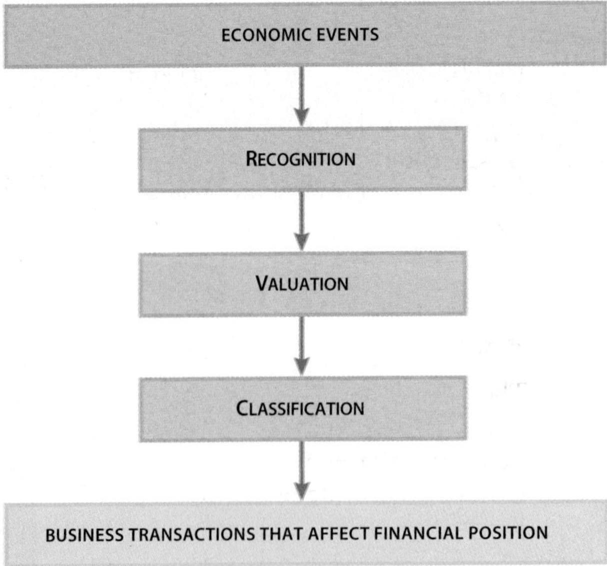

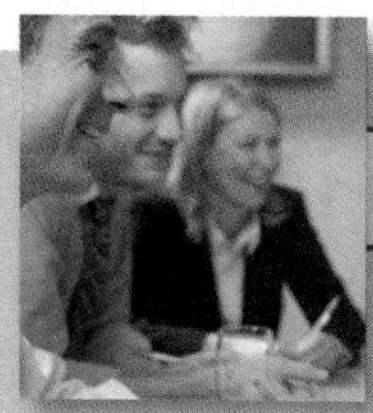

FOCUS ON BUSINESS PRACTICE

Accounting Policies: Where Do You Find Them?

The Boeing Company, one of the world's makers of airliners, takes orders for planes years in advance. Although it is an important economic event to both Boeing and the buyer, neither the buyer nor the seller would record the event as a transaction. So, how do you know when companies record sales or purchase transactions? The answer to this question and others about companies' accounting policies can be found in the Summary of Significant Accounting Policies in their annual reports. For example, in that section of its annual report, Boeing states: "We recognize sales for commercial airplane deliveries as each unit is completed and accepted by the customer."[1]

businesses that have simple accounting systems do not record a transaction until they receive a bill (event **5**) or pay it (event **6**), because these are the implied points of title transfer. The predetermined time at which a transaction should be recorded is the **recognition point.**

Although purchase requisitions and purchase orders (events **1** and **2**) are economic events, they do not affect a company's financial position, and they are not recognized in the accounting records. Even the most important economic events may not be recognized in the accounting records.

Here are some more examples of economic events that should and should not be recorded as business transactions:

Events That Are Not *Recorded as Transactions*	*Events That* Are *Recorded as Transactions*
A customer inquires about the availability of a service.	A customer buys a service.
A company hires a new employee.	A company pays an employee for work performed.
A company signs a contract to provide a service in the future.	A company performs a service.

The recognition issue can be difficult to resolve. Consider an advertising agency that is planning a major advertising campaign for a client. Employees may work on the plan several hours a day for a number of weeks. They add value to the plan as they develop it. Should this added value be recognized as the plan is being developed or at the time it is completed? Usually, the increase in value is recorded at the time the plan is finished and the client is billed for it. However, if a plan is going to take a long time to develop, the agency and the client may agree that the client will be billed at key points during its development. In that case, a transaction is recorded at each billing.

Valuation

> **Study Note**
> The value of a transaction usually is based on a business document—a canceled check or an invoice.

The **valuation** issue focuses on assigning a monetary value to a business transaction and accounting for the assets and liabilities that result from the business transactions. Generally accepted accounting principles state that all business transactions should be valued at *fair value* when they occur. **Fair value** is defined as the *exchange price* of an actual or potential business transaction between market participants.[2] This practice of recording transactions at exchange price at the

FOCUS ON BUSINESS PRACTICE

IFRS

The Challenge of Fair Value Accounting

The measurement of fair value is a major challenge in merging international financial reporting standards (IFRS) with U.S. GAAP. Both the International Accounting Standards Board (IASB) and the Financial Accounting Standards Board (FASB) are committed to this effort. Fair value is the price to sell an asset or transfer a liability in an orderly market by an arm's-length transaction. Fair value represents a hypothetical transaction that in many cases is difficult to measure: It represents the selling price of an asset or the payment price of a liability. It does not represent the price of acquiring the asset or assuming the liability. In practice, the potential selling price of equipment used in a factory or an investment in a private company for which no ready market exists may not be easy to determine.

point of recognition is commonly referred to as the **cost principle.** It is used because the cost, or exchange price, is verifiable. For example, when Larry Cox performs the service for Quarter Horse Stables described in the Decision Point at the beginning of this chapter, he and Quarter Horse Stables will record the transaction in their respective records at the price they have agreed on.

Normally, the value of an asset is held at its initial fair value or cost until the asset is sold, expires, or is consumed. However, if there is evidence that the fair value of the asset or liability has changed, an adjustment to the initial value may be required. There are different rules for the application of fair value to different classes of assets. For example, a building or equipment remains at cost unless there is convincing evidence that the fair value is less than cost. In this case, a loss should be recorded to reduce the value from its cost to fair value. Investments, on the other hand, are often accounted for at fair value, regardless of whether fair value is greater or less than cost. Because these investments are available for sale, the fair value is the best measure of the potential benefit to the company. In its annual report, **Intel Corporation** states: "Investments designated as available-for-sale on the balance sheet date are reported at fair value."[3]

FOCUS ON BUSINESS PRACTICE

No Dollar Amount: How Can That Be?

Determining the value of a sale or purchase transaction isn't difficult when the value equals the amount of cash that changes hands. However, barter transactions, in which exchanges are made but no cash changes hands, can make valuation more complicated. Barter transactions are quite common in business today. Here are some examples:

- A consulting company provides its services to an auto dealer in exchange for the loan of a car for a year.
- An office supply company provides a year's supply of computer paper to a local weekly newspaper in exchange for an advertisement in 52 issues of the newspaper.
- Two Internet companies each provide an advertisement and link to the other's website on their own websites.

Determining the value of these transactions is a matter of determining the fair value of the items being traded.

Classification

> **Study Note**
>
> If **CVS** buys paper towels to resell to customers, the cost would be recorded as an asset in the Inventory account. If the paper towels are used for cleaning in the store, the cost is an expense.

The **classification** issue has to do with assigning all the transactions in which a business engages to appropriate categories, or accounts. Classification of debts can affect a company's ability to borrow money, and classification of purchases can affect its income. One of the most important classification issues in accounting is the difference between an expense and an asset, both represented by debits in the accounts. To use the Decision Point case again as an example, if Larry Cox buys medicines that are used immediately, their cost is classified as an expense. If the medicines will be used in the future, they are classified as assets.

As we explain later in the chapter, proper classification depends not only on correctly analyzing the effect of each transaction on a business but also on maintaining a system of accounts that reflects that effect.

Ethics and Measurement Issues

Recognition, valuation, and classification are important factors in ethical financial reporting, and generally accepted accounting principles provide direction about their treatment. These guidelines are intended to help managers meet their obligation to their company's owners and to the public. Many of the worst financial reporting frauds over the past several years have resulted from violations of these guidelines.

- **Computer Associates** violated the guidelines for recognition when it kept its books open a few days after the end of a reporting period so revenues could be counted a quarter earlier than they should have been. In all, the company prematurely reported $3.3 billion in revenues from 363 software contracts. When the SEC ordered the company to stop the practice, Computer Associates' stock price dropped by 43 percent in a single day.
- Among its many other transgressions, **Enron Corporation** violated the guidelines for valuation when it valued assets that it transferred to related companies at far more than their actual value.
- By a simple violation of the guidelines for classification, **WorldCom** (now **MCI**) perpetrated the largest financial fraud in history, which resulted in the largest bankruptcy in history. Over a period of several years, the company recorded expenditures as expenses that should have been classified as assets; this had the effect of understating the company's expenses and overstating its income by more than $10 billion.

STOP & APPLY >

Four major issues underlie every accounting transaction: recognition, valuation, classification, and ethics. Match each of these issues to the statements below that are most closely associated with the issue. A company:

1. Records a piece of equipment at the price paid for it.
2. Records the purchase of the equipment on the day on which it takes ownership.
3. Records the equipment as an expense in order to show lower earnings.
4. Records the equipment as an asset because it will benefit future periods.

SOLUTION

1. valuation; 2. recognition; 3. ethics; 4. classification

Double-Entry System

LO2 Explain the double-entry system and the usefulness of T accounts in analyzing business transactions.

Study Note

Each transaction must include at least one debit and one credit, and the debit totals must equal the credit totals.

The double-entry system, the backbone of accounting, evolved during the Renaissance. The first systematic description of double-entry bookkeeping appeared in 1494, two years after Columbus discovered America, in a mathematics book by Fra Luca Pacioli. Goethe, the famous German poet and dramatist, referred to double-entry bookkeeping as "one of the finest discoveries of the human intellect." Werner Sombart, an eminent economist-sociologist, believed that "double-entry bookkeeping is born of the same spirit as the system of Galileo and Newton."

What is the significance of the double-entry system? The system is based on the *principle of duality*, which means that every economic event has two aspects—effort and reward, sacrifice and benefit, source and use—that offset, or balance, each other. In the **double-entry system,** each transaction must be recorded with at least one debit and one credit, and the total amount of the debits must equal the total amount of the credits. Because of the way it is designed, the whole system is always in balance. All accounting systems, no matter how sophisticated, are based on the principle of duality.

Accounts

Accounts are the basic storage units for accounting data and are used to accumulate amounts from similar transactions. An accounting system has a separate account for each asset, each liability, and each component of owner's equity, including revenues and expenses. Whether a company keeps records by hand or by computer, managers must be able to refer to accounts so that they can study their company's financial history and plan for the future. A very small company may need only a few dozen accounts; a multinational corporation may need thousands.

An account title should describe what is recorded in the account. However, account titles can be rather confusing. For example, *Fixed Assets, Plant and Equipment, Capital Assets,* and *Long-Lived Assets* are all titles for long-term assets. Moreover, many account titles change over time as preferences and practices change.

When you come across an account title that you don't recognize, examine the context of the name—whether it is classified in the financial statements as an asset, liability, or component of owner's equity—and look for the kind of transaction that gave rise to the account.

The T Account

Study Note

Many students have preconceived ideas about what *debit* and *credit* mean. They think *debit* means "decrease" (or implies something bad) and *credit* means "increase" (or implies something good). It is important to realize that *debit* simply means "left side" and *credit* simply means "right side."

The **T account** is a good place to begin the study of the double-entry system. Such an account has three parts: a title, which identifies the asset, liability, or owner's equity account; a left side, which is called the **debit** side; and a right side, which is called the **credit** side. The T account, so called because it resembles the letter *T*, is used to analyze transactions and is not part of the accounting records. It looks like this:

Title of Account	
Debit (left) side	Credit (right) side

Any entry made on the left side of the account is a debit, and any entry made on the right side is a credit. The terms *debit* (abbreviated Dr., from the Latin *debere*) and *credit* (abbreviated Cr., from the Latin *credere*) are simply the accountant's words for "left" and "right" (*not* for "increase" or "decrease"). We present a more formal version of the T account, the ledger account form, later in this chapter.

The T Account Illustrated

Suppose a company had several transactions during the month that involved the receipt or payment of cash. These transactions can be summarized in the Cash account by recording receipts on the left (debit) side of a T account and payments on the right (credit) side.

	CASH	
	Dr.	Cr.
	100,000	70,000
	3,000	400
		1,200
	103,000	**71,600**
Bal.	**31,400**	

The cash receipts on the left total $103,000. (The total is written in smaller, bold figures so that it cannot be confused with an actual debit entry.) The cash payments on the right side total $71,600. These totals are simply working totals, or **footings.** Footings, which are calculated at the end of each month, are an easy way to determine cash on hand. The difference in dollars between the total debit footing and the total credit footing is called the **balance,** or *account balance.* If the balance is a debit, it is written on the left side. If it is a credit, it is written on the right side. Notice that the Cash account has a debit balance of $31,400 ($103,000 − $71,600). This is the amount of cash the business has on hand at the end of the month.

Rules of Double-Entry Accounting

The two rules of the double-entry system are that every transaction affects at least two accounts and that total debits must equal total credits. In other words, for every transaction, one or more accounts must be debited, or entered on the left side of the T account, and one or more accounts must be credited, or entered on the right side of the T account, and the total dollar amount of the debits must equal the total dollar amount of the credits.

Look again at the accounting equation:

Assets = Liabilities + Owner's Equity

You can see that if a debit increases assets, then a credit must be used to increase liabilities or owner's equity because they are on opposite sides of the equal sign. Likewise, if a credit decreases assets, then a debit must be used to decrease liabilities or owner's equity. These rules can be shown as follows:

ASSETS		=	LIABILITIES		+	OWNER'S EQUITY	
Debit for increases (+)	Credit for decreases (−)		Debit for decreases (−)	Credit for increases (+)		Debit for decreases (−)	Credit for increases (+)

Study Note

Although withdrawals are a component of owner's equity, they normally appear only in the statement of owner's equity. They do not appear in the owner's equity section of the balance sheet or as an expense on the income statement.

1. Debit increases in assets to asset accounts. Credit decreases in assets to asset accounts.
2. Credit increases in liabilities and owner's equity to liability and owner's equity accounts. Debit decreases in liabilities and owner's equity to liability and owner's equity accounts.

One of the more difficult points to understand is the application of double-entry rules to the components of owner's equity. The key is to remember that withdrawals and expenses are deductions from owner's equity. Thus, transactions that *increase* withdrawals or expenses *decrease* owner's equity. Consider this expanded version of the accounting equation:

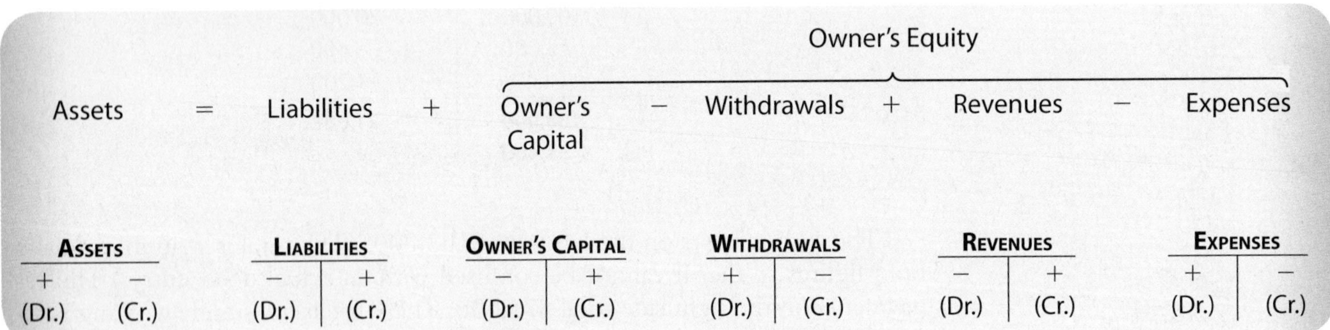

Normal Balance

The **normal balance** of an account is its usual balance and is the side (debit or credit) that increases the account. Table 2-1 summarizes the normal account balances of the major account categories. If you have difficulty remembering the normal balances and the rules of debit and credit, try using the acronym AWE: Asset accounts, Withdrawals, and Expenses are always increased by debits. All other normal accounts are increased by credits.

Owner's Equity Accounts

Figure 2-2 illustrates how owner's equity accounts relate to each other and to the financial statements. The distinctions among these accounts are important for both legal purposes and financial reporting.

TABLE 2-1
Normal Account Balances of Major Account Categories

	Increases Recorded by		Normal Balance	
Account Category	**Debit**	**Credit**	**Debit**	**Credit**
Assets	x		x	
Liabilities		x		x
Owner's equity:				
Owner's Capital		x		x
Withdrawals	x		x	
Revenues		x		x
Expenses	x		x	

FIGURE 2-2
Relationships of Owner's Equity Accounts

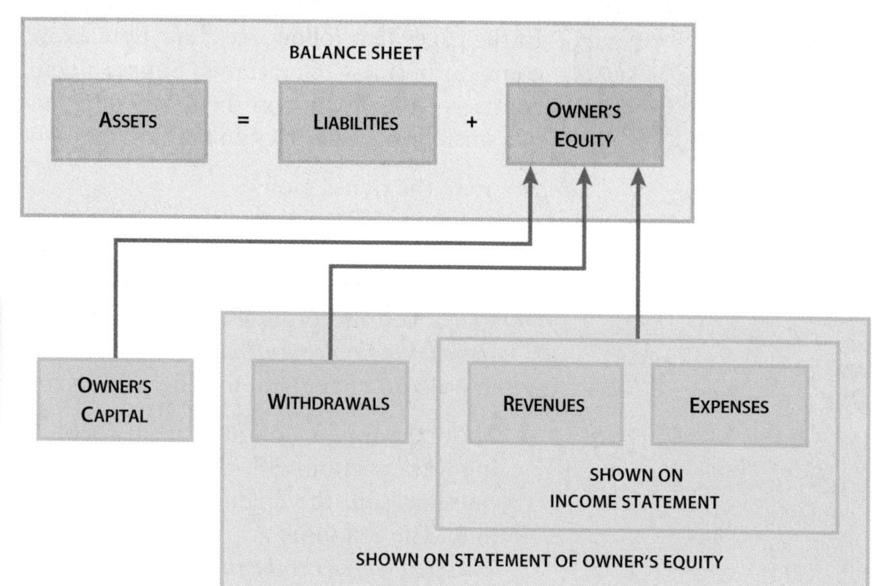

Study Note

Although revenues and expenses are components of owner's equity, they appear on the income statement, not in the owner's equity section of the balance sheet. Figure 2-2 illustrates this point.

STOP & APPLY >

You are given the following list of accounts with dollar amounts:

J. Morgan, Withdrawals	$ 75	Cash	$625
Accounts Payable	200	J. Morgan, Capital	400
Wages Expense	150	Fees Revenue	250

Insert the account title at the top of the corresponding T account that follows and enter the dollar amount as a normal balance in the account. Then show that the accounting equation is in balance.

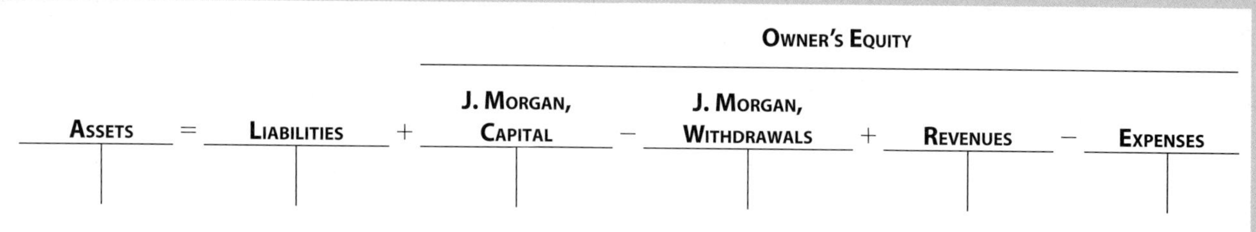

SOLUTION

Cash		Accounts Payable		J. Morgan, Capital		J. Morgan, Withdrawals		Fees Revenue		Wages Expense	
625			200		400	75			250	150	

Assets = Liabilities + Owner's Equity
$625 = $200 + ($400 − $75 + $250 − $150)
$625 = $200 + $425
$625 = $625

Business Transaction Analysis

LO3 Demonstrate how the double-entry system is applied to common business transactions.

In the pages that follow, we show how to apply the double-entry system to some common business transactions. **Source documents**—invoices, receipts, checks, or contracts—usually support the details of a transaction. We focus on the transactions of a small firm, Miller Design Studio. For each transaction, we follow these steps:

1. State the transaction.
2. Analyze the transaction to determine which accounts are affected.
3. Apply the rules of double-entry accounting by using T accounts to show how the transaction affects the accounting equation. It is important to note that *this step is not part of the accounting records* but is undertaken *before* recording a transaction in order to understand the effects of the transaction on the accounts.
4. Show the transaction in **journal form.** The journal form is a way of recording a transaction with the date, debit account, and debit amount shown on one line, and the credit account (indented) and credit amount on the next line. The amounts are shown in their respective debit and credit columns. *This step represents the initial recording of a transaction in the records* and takes the following form:

		Dr.	Cr.
Date	Debit Account Name	Amount	
	Credit Account Name		Amount

A series of transactions in this form results in a chronological record of the transactions called a *general journal.* Periodically, each debit and credit in an entry is transferred to its appropriate account in a list of accounts called the *general ledger.* We discuss the relationship of the general journal to the general ledger later in this chapter.

5. Provide a comment that will help you apply the rules of double entry.

The formal process of recording and posting of transactions in the records is illustrated under SO 6 at the end of this chapter. Chapters 3 and 4 cover other steps necessary to produce financial statements.

> **Study Note**
>
> T accounts are used to understand and visualize the double-entry effects of a transaction on the accounting equation. They help in then recording the journal entry in the general journal.

Owner's Investment to Form the Business

July 1: Joan Miller invests $40,000 in cash to form Miller Design Studio.

Analysis: An owner's investment in the business *increases* the asset account *Cash* with a debit and *increases* the owner's equity account *J. Miller, Capital* with a credit.

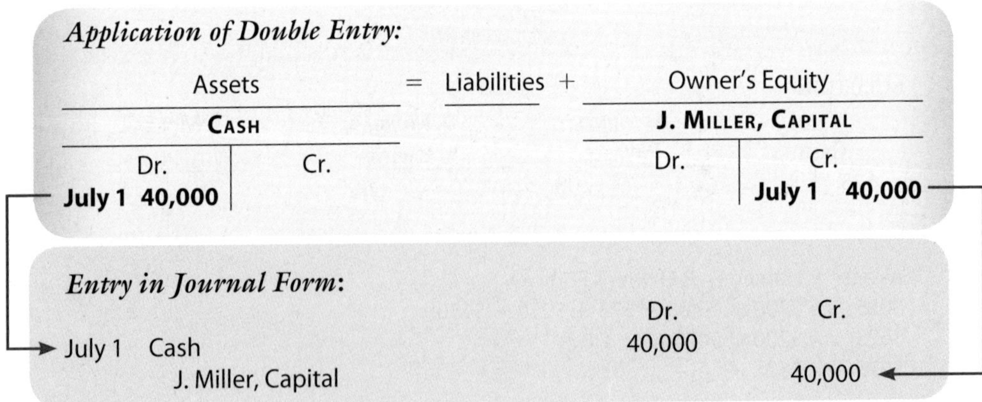

Comment: If Joan Miller had invested assets other than cash in the business, the appropriate asset accounts would be increased with a debit.

Economic Event That Is Not a Business Transaction

July 2: Orders office supplies, $5,200.

Comment: When an economic event does not constitute a business transaction, no entry is made. In this case, there is no confirmation that the supplies have been shipped or that title has passed.

Prepayment of Expenses in Cash

July 3: Rents an office; pays two months' rent in advance, $3,200.

Analysis: The prepayment of office rent in cash *increases* the asset account *Prepaid Rent* with a debit and *decreases* the asset account *Cash* with a credit.

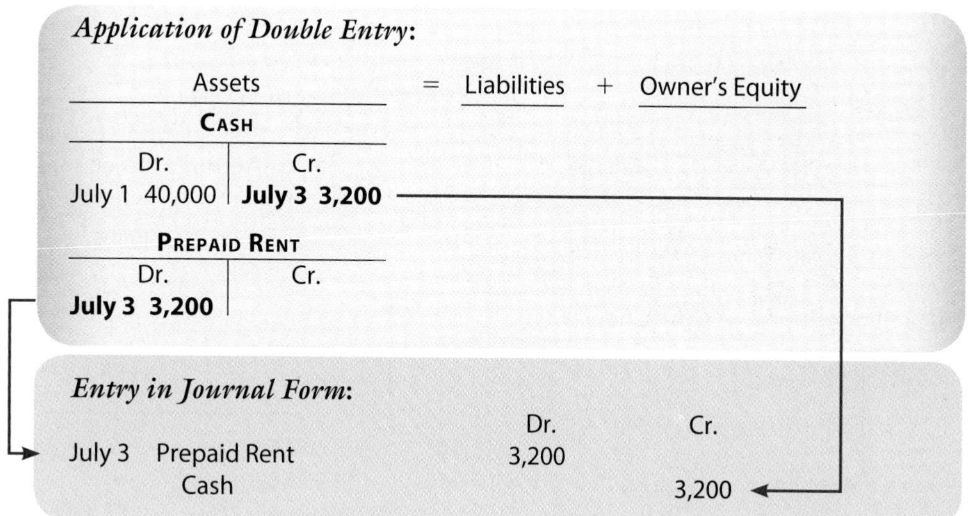

Comment: A prepaid expense is an asset because the expenditure will benefit future operations. This transaction does not affect the totals of assets or liabilities and owner's equity because it simply trades one asset for another asset. If the company had paid only July's rent, the owner's equity account *Rent Expense* would be debited because the total benefit of the expenditure would be used up in the current month.

Purchase of an Asset on Credit

July 5: Receives office supplies ordered on July 2 and an invoice for $5,200.

Analysis: The purchase of office supplies on credit *increases* the asset account *Office Supplies* with a debit and *increases* the liability account *Accounts Payable* with a credit.

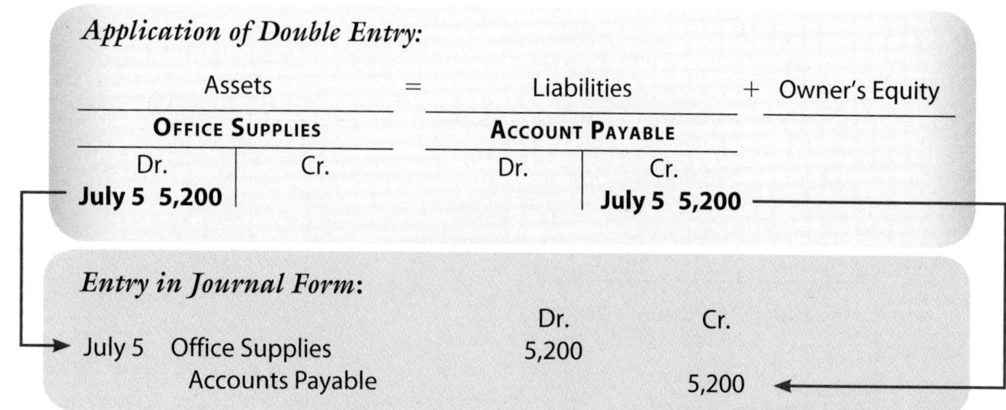

Comment: Office supplies are considered an asset (prepaid expense) because they will not be used up in the current month and thus will benefit future periods. Accounts Payable is used when there is a delay between the time of the purchase and the time of payment.

Purchase of an Asset Partly in Cash and Partly on Credit

July 6: Purchases office equipment, $16,320; pays $13,320 in cash and agrees to pay the rest next month.

Analysis: The purchase of office equipment in cash and on credit *increases* the asset account *Office Equipment* with a debit, *decreases* the asset account *Cash* with a credit, and *increases* the liability account *Accounts Payable* with a credit.

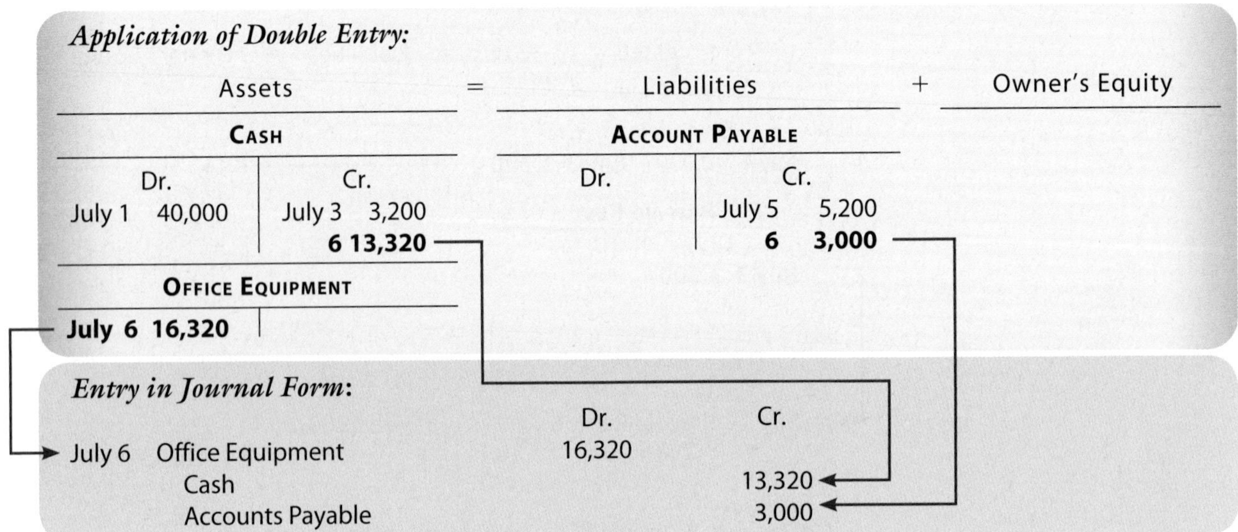

Comment: As this transaction illustrates, assets may be paid for partly in cash and partly on credit. When more than two accounts are involved in a journal entry, as they are in this one, it is called a **compound entry.**

Payment of a Liability

July 9: Makes a partial payment of the amount owed for the office supplies received on July 5, $2,600.

Analysis: A payment of a liability *decreases* the liability account *Accounts Payable* with a debit and *decreases* the asset account *Cash* with a credit.

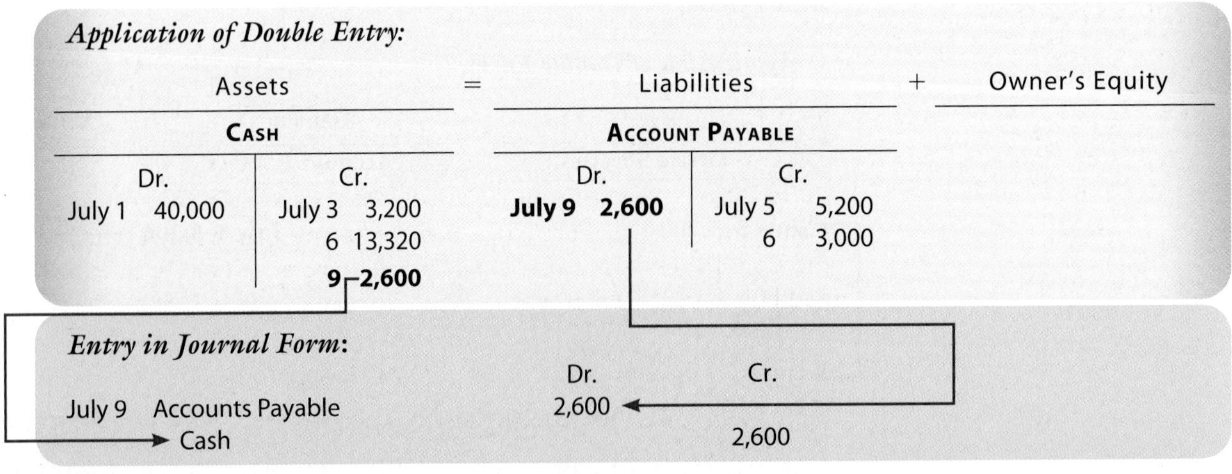

Comment: Note that the office supplies were recorded when they were purchased on July 5.

Revenue in Cash

July 10: Performs a service for an investment advisor by designing a series of brochures and collects a fee in cash, $2,800.

Analysis: Revenue received in cash *increases* the asset account *Cash* with a debit and *increases* the owner's equity account *Design Revenue* with a credit.

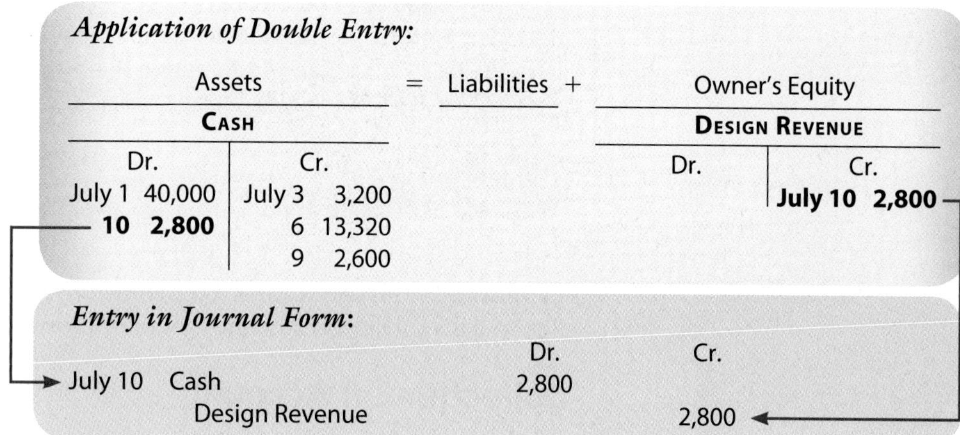

Entry in Journal Form:

		Dr.	Cr.
July 10	Cash	2,800	
	Design Revenue		2,800

Comment: For this transaction, revenue is recognized when the service is provided and the cash is received.

Revenue on Credit

July 15: Performs a service for a department store by designing a TV commercial; bills for the fee now but will collect the fee later, $9,600.

Analysis: A revenue billed to a customer *increases* the asset account *Accounts Receivable* with a debit and *increases* the owner's equity account *Design Revenue* with a credit. Accounts Receivable is used to indicate the company's right to collect the money in the future.

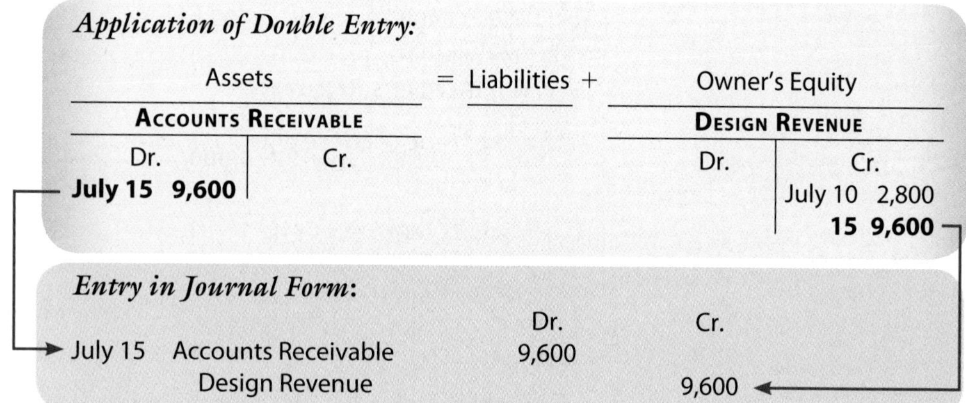

Entry in Journal Form:

		Dr.	Cr.
July 15	Accounts Receivable	9,600	
	Design Revenue		9,600

Comment: In this case, there is a delay between the time revenue is earned and the time the cash is received. Revenues are recorded at the time they are earned and billed regardless of when cash is received.

Revenue Collected in Advance

July 19: Accepts an advance fee as a deposit on a series of brochures to be designed, $1,400.

Analysis: Revenue received in advance *increases* the asset account *Cash* with a debit and *increases* the liability account *Unearned Design Revenue* with a credit.

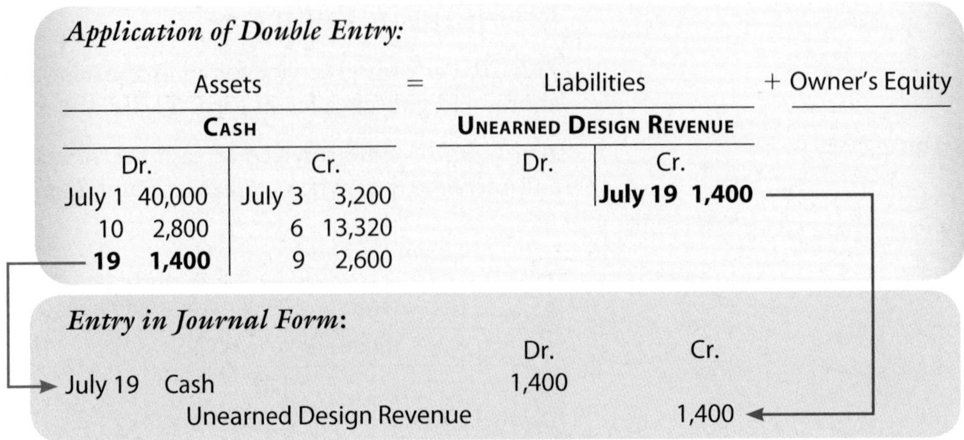

Comment: In this case, cash is received before the fees are earned. Unearned Design Revenue is a liability because the firm must provide the service or return the deposit.

Collection on Account

July 22: Receives cash from customer previously billed on July 15, $5,000.

Analysis: Collection of an account receivable from a customer previously billed *increases* the asset account *Cash* with a debit and *decreases* the asset account *Accounts Receivable* with a credit.

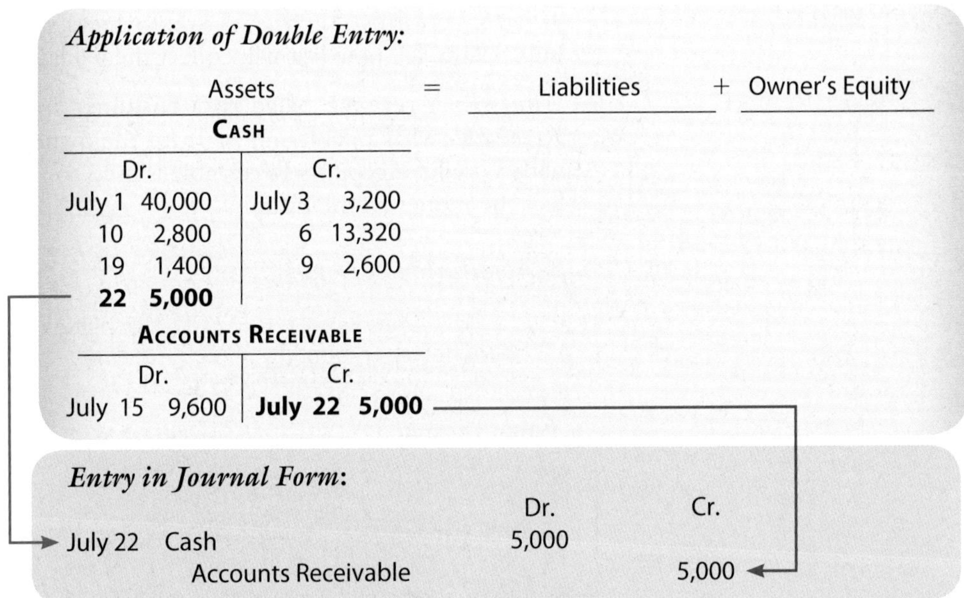

Comment: Note that the revenue related to this transaction was recorded on July 15. Thus, no revenue is recorded at this time.

Expense Paid in Cash

July 26: Pays employees four weeks' wages, $4,800.

Analysis: This cash expense *increases* the owner's equity account *Wages Expense* with a debit and *decreases* the asset account *Cash* with a credit.

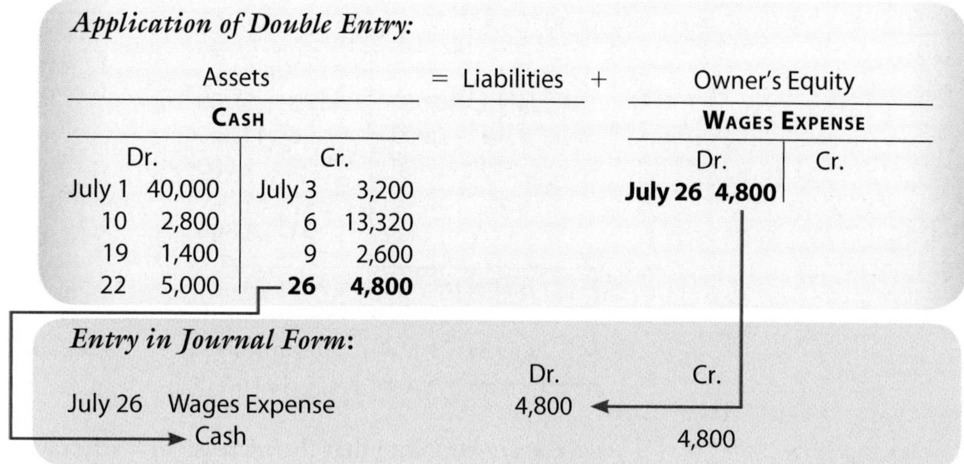

Comment: Note that the increase in Wages Expense will *decrease* owner's equity.

Expense to Be Paid Later

July 30: Receives, but does not pay, the utility bill that is due next month, $680.

Analysis: This cash expense *increases* the owner's equity account *Utilities Expense* with a debit and *increases* the liability account *Accounts Payable* with a credit.

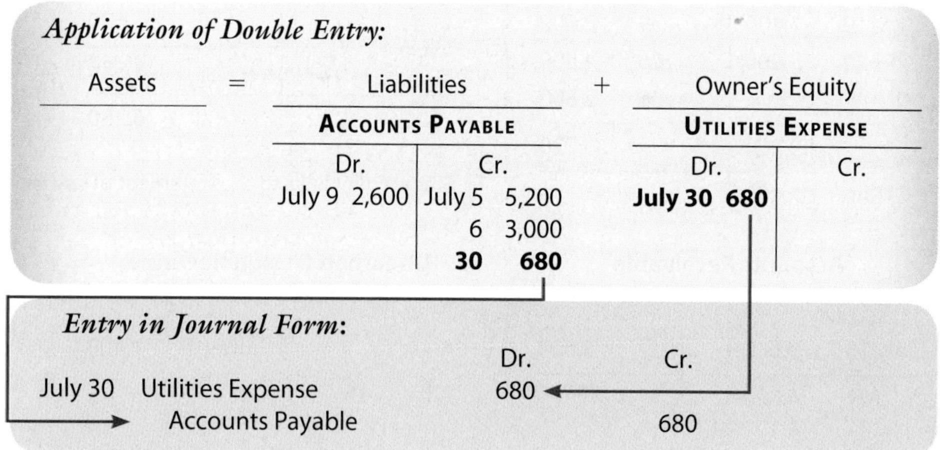

Comment: The expense is recorded if the benefit has been received and the amount is owed, even if the cash is not to be paid until later. Note that the increase in Utilities Expense will *decrease* owner's equity.

Withdrawals

July 31: Withdraws $2,800 in cash.

Analysis: A cash withdrawal *increases* the owner's equity account *Withdrawals* with a debit and *decreases* the asset account *Cash* with a credit.

Application of Double Entry:

Assets = Liabilities + Owner's Equity

CASH

Dr.		Cr.	
July 1	40,000	July 3	3,200
10	2,800	6	13,320
19	1,400	9	2,600
22	5,000	26	4,800
		31	**2,800**

J. MILLER, WITHDRAWALS

Dr.		Cr.	
July 31	**2,800**		

Entry in Journal Form:

		Dr.	Cr.
July 31	J. Miller, Withdrawals	2,800	
	Cash		2,800

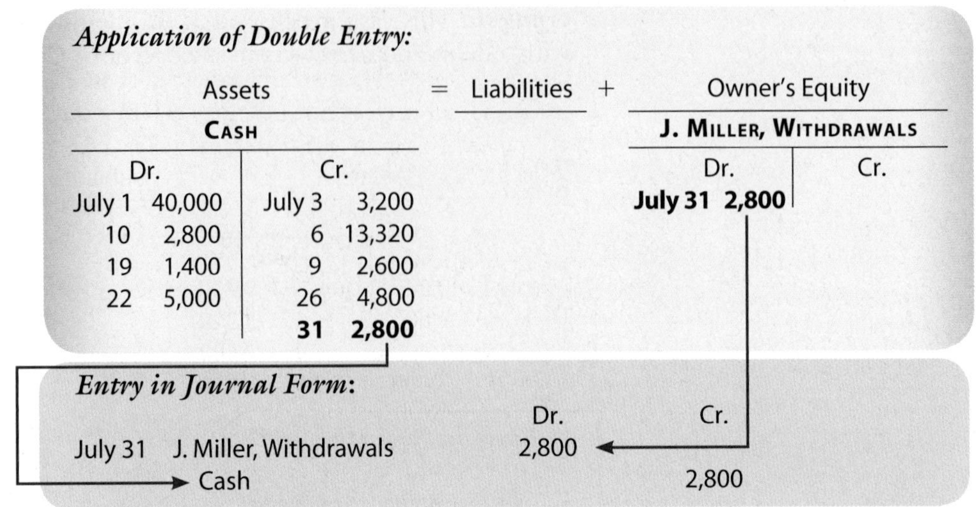

Comment: Note that the increase in Withdrawals will *decrease* owner's equity.

EXHIBIT 2-1 Summary of Transactions of Miller Design Studio

Assets = Liabilities + Owner's Equity

Cash

Dr.		Cr.	
July 1	40,000	July 3	3,200
10	2,800	6	13,320
19	1,400	9	2,600
22	5,000	26	4,800
		31	2,800
	49,200		26,720
Bal.	22,480		

This account links to the statement of cash flows.

Accounts Payable

Dr.		Cr.	
July 9	2,600	July 5	5,200
		6	3,000
		30	680
	2,600		8,880
		Bal.	6,280

J. Miller, Capital

Dr.		Cr.	
		July 1	40,000

J. Miller, Withdrawals

Dr.		Cr.	
July 31	2,800		

Accounts Receivable

Dr.		Cr.	
July 15	9,600	July 22	5,000
Bal.	4,600		

Unearned Design Revenue

Dr.		Cr.	
		July 19	1,400

Design Revenue

Dr.		Cr.	
		July 10	2,800
		15	9,600
		Bal.	12,400

Office Supplies

Dr.		Cr.	
July 5	5,200		

Wages Expense

Dr.		Cr.	
July 26	4,800		

Prepaid Rent

Dr.		Cr.	
July 3	3,200		

Utilities Expense

Dr.		Cr.	
July 30	680		

These accounts link to the income statement.

Office Equipment

Dr.		Cr.	
July 6	16,320		

Assets	=	Liabilities	+	Owner's Equity
$51,800	=	$7,680	+	$44,120

Summary of Transactions

Exhibit 2-1 uses the accounting equation to summarize the transactions of Miller Design Studio. Note that the income statement accounts appear under owner's equity and that the transactions in the Cash account will be reflected on the statement of cash flows.

STOP & APPLY >

The following accounts are applicable to Leona's Nail Salon, a company that provides manicures and pedicures:

1. Cash
2. Accounts Receivable
3. Supplies
4. Equipment
5. Accounts Payable
6. Services Revenue
7. Wages Expense
8. Rent Expense

For Leona's Nail Salon, enter the number corresponding to the proper account for each debit and credit for the following transactions:

	Debit	Credit
a. Made a rent payment for the current month.	8	1
b. Received cash from customers for current services.	____	____
c. Agreed to accept payment next month from a client for current services.	____	____
d. Purchased supplies on credit.	____	____
e. Purchased a new chair and table for cash.	____	____
f. Made a payment on accounts payable.	____	____

SOLUTION

	Debit	Credit
a. Made a rent payment for the current month.	8	1
b. Received cash from customers for current services.	1	6
c. Agreed to accept payment next month from a client for current services.	2	6
d. Purchased supplies on credit.	3	5
e. Purchased a new chair and table for cash.	4	1
f. Made a payment on accounts payable.	5	1

The Trial Balance

LO4 Prepare a trial balance, and describe its value and limitations.

For every amount debited, an equal amount must be credited. This means that the total of debits and credits in the T accounts must be equal. To test this, the accountant periodically prepares a **trial balance.** Exhibit 2-2 shows a trial balance for Miller Design Studio. It was prepared from the accounts in Exhibit 2-1.

Preparation and Use of a Trial Balance

Although a trial balance may be prepared at any time, it is usually prepared on the last day of the accounting period. The preparation involves these steps:

EXHIBIT 2-2
Trial Balance

Miller Design Studio
Trial Balance
July 31, 2011

Account	Debit	Credit
Cash	$22,480	
Accounts Receivable	4,600	
Office Supplies	5,200	
Prepaid Rent	3,200	
Office Equipment	16,320	
Accounts Payable		$ 6,280
Unearned Design Revenue		1,400
J. Miller, Capital		40,000
J. Miller, Withdrawals	2,800	
Design Revenue		12,400
Wages Expense	4,800	
Utilities Expense	680	
	$60,080	$60,080

Study Note

The trial balance is usually prepared at the end of an accounting period. It is an initial check that the accounts are in balance.

1. List each account that has a balance, with debit balances in the left column and credit balances in the right column. Accounts are listed in the order in which they appear in the financial statements.
2. Add each column.
3. Compare the totals of the columns.

Once in a while, a transaction leaves an account with a balance that isn't "normal." For example, when a company overdraws its bank account, its Cash account (an asset) will show a credit balance instead of a debit balance. The "abnormal" balance should be copied into the trial balance columns as it stands, as a debit or a credit.

The trial balance proves whether the accounts are in balance. *In balance* means that the total of all debits recorded equals the total of all credits recorded. But the trial balance does not prove that the transactions were analyzed correctly or recorded in the proper accounts. For example, there is no way of determining from the trial balance that a debit should have been made in the Office Supplies account rather than in the Office Equipment account. And the trial balance does not detect whether transactions have been omitted, because equal debits and credits will have been omitted. Also, if an error of the same amount is made in both a debit and a credit, it will not be evident in the trial balance. The trial balance proves only that the debits and credits in the accounts are in balance.

FOCUS ON BUSINESS PRACTICE

Are All Trial Balances Created Equal?

In computerized accounting systems, posting is done automatically, and the trial balance can be easily prepared as often as needed. Any accounts with abnormal balances are highlighted for investigation. Some general ledger software packages for small businesses list the trial balance amounts in a single column and show credit balances as minuses. In such cases, the trial balance is in balance if the total is zero.

Finding Trial Balance Errors

If the debit and credit balances in a trial balance are not equal, look for one or more of the following errors:

1. A debit was entered in an account as a credit, or vice versa.
2. The balance of an account was computed incorrectly.
3. An error was made in carrying the account balance to the trial balance.
4. The trial balance was summed incorrectly.

Other than simply adding the columns incorrectly, the two most common mistakes in preparing a trial balance are

1. Recording an account as a credit when it usually carries a debit balance, or vice versa. This mistake causes the trial balance to be out of balance by an amount divisible by 2.
2. Transposing two digits when transferring an amount to the trial balance (for example, entering $23,459 as $23,549). This error causes the trial balance to be out of balance by an amount divisible by 9.

So, if a trial balance is out of balance and the addition of the columns is correct, determine the amount by which the trial balance is out of balance and divide it first by 2 and then by 9. If the amount is divisible by 2, look in the trial balance for an amount that is equal to the quotient. If you find such an amount, chances are it's in the wrong column. If the amount is divisible by 9, trace each amount back to the T account balance, checking carefully for a transposition error. If neither of these techniques is successful in identifying the error, first recompute the balance of each T account. Then, if you still have not found the error, retrace each posting to the journal or the T account.

STOP & APPLY >

Prepare a trial balance from the following list of accounts (in alphabetical order) of the Jasoni Company as of March 31, 2011. Compute the balance of cash.

Accounts Payable	$ 9	Jasoni, Capital	$16
Accounts Receivable	5	Equipment	2
Building	10	Land	1
Cash	?	Inventory	3

SOLUTION

Jasoni Company
Trial Balance
March 31, 2011

Cash	$ 4	
Accounts Receivable	5	
Inventory	3	
Land	1	
Building	10	
Equipment	2	
Accounts Payable		$ 9
Jasoni, Capital		16
Totals	$25	$25

Cash Flows and the Timing of Transactions

LO5 Show how the timing of transactions affects cash flows and liquidity.

To avoid financial distress, a company must be able to pay its bills on time. Because the timing of cash flows is critical to maintaining adequate liquidity to pay bills, managers and other users of financial information must understand the difference between transactions that generate immediate cash and those that do not. Consider the transactions of Miller Design Studio shown in Figure 2-3. Most of them involve either an inflow or outflow of cash.

As you can see in Figure 2-3, Miller's Cash account has more transactions than any of its other accounts. Look at the transactions of July 10, 15, and 22:

- July 10: Miller received a cash payment of $2,800.
- July 15: The firm billed a customer $9,600 for a service it had already performed.
- July 22: The firm received a partial payment of $5,000 from the customer, but it had not received the remaining $4,600 by the end of the month.

Because Miller incurred expenses in providing this service, it must pay careful attention to its cash flows and liquidity.

One way Miller can manage its expenditures is to rely on its creditors to give it time to pay. Compare the transactions of July 3, 5, and 9 in Figure 2-3.

- July 3: Miller prepaid rent of $3,200. That immediate cash outlay may have caused a strain on the business.
- July 5: The firm received an invoice for office supplies in the amount of $5,200. In this case, it took advantage of the opportunity to defer payment.
- July 9: The firm paid $2,600, but it deferred paying the remaining $2,600 until after the end of the month.

Large companies face the same challenge, but often on a much greater scale. For example, it can take **Boeing** a number of years to plan and make the aircraft that customers order. At the end of 2008, Boeing had orders totaling $352 billion.[4] Think of the cash outlays Boeing must make before it delivers the planes and collects payment for them. To maintain liquidity so that Boeing can eventually reap the rewards of delivering the planes, Boeing's management must carefully plan the company's needs for cash.

> **Study Note**
>
> Recording revenues and expenses when they occur will provide a clearer picture of a company's profitability on the income statement. The change in cash flows will provide a clearer picture of a company's liquidity on the statement of cash flows.

FIGURE 2-3
Transactions of Miller Design Studio

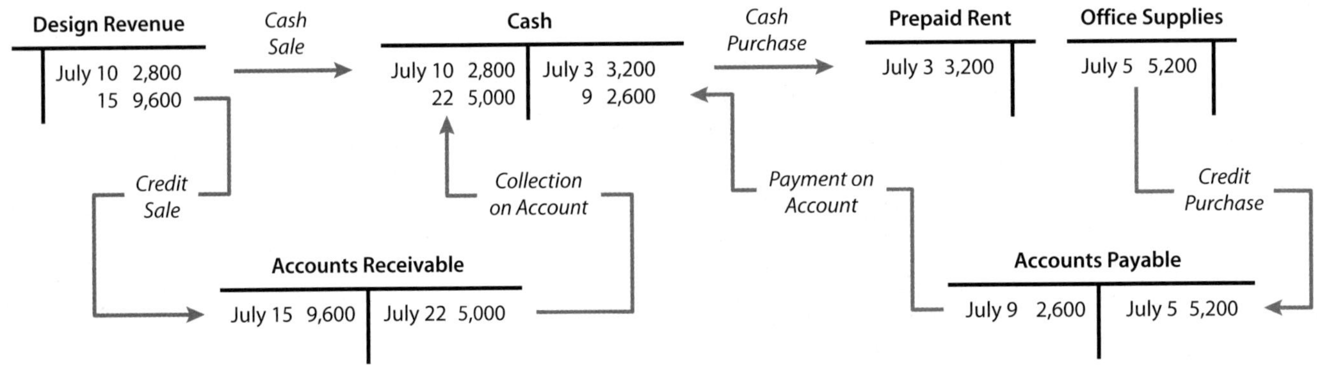

FOCUS ON BUSINESS PRACTICE

Should Earnings Be Aligned with Cash Flows?

Electronic Data Systems Corporation (EDS), the large computer services company, announced that it was reducing past earnings by $2.24 billion to implement a new accounting rule that would more closely align its earnings with cash flows. Analysts had been critical of EDS for recording revenue from its long-term contracts when the contracts were signed rather than when the cash was received. In fact, about 40 percent of EDS's revenue had been recognized well before the cash was to be received. Analysts' response to the change in EDS's accounting was very positive. "Finally, maybe, we'll see cash flows moving in line with earnings," said one.[5] Although there are natural and unavoidable differences between earnings and cash flows, it is best if accounting rules are not used to exaggerate these differences.

STOP & APPLY >

A company engaged in the following transactions:

Oct. 1 Performed services for cash, $1,050.
2 Paid expenses in cash, $550.
3 Incurred expenses on credit, $650.
4 Performed services on credit, $900.
5 Paid on account, $350.
6 Collected on account, $600.

Enter the correct titles in the following T accounts, and enter the transactions above in the accounts. Determine the cash balance after these transactions, the amount still to be received, and the amount still to be paid.

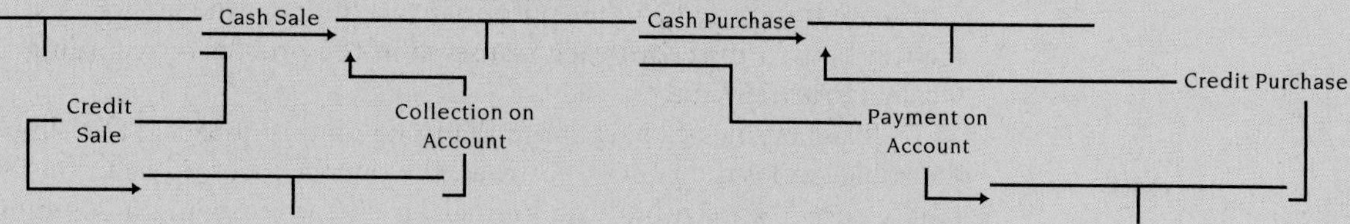

SOLUTION

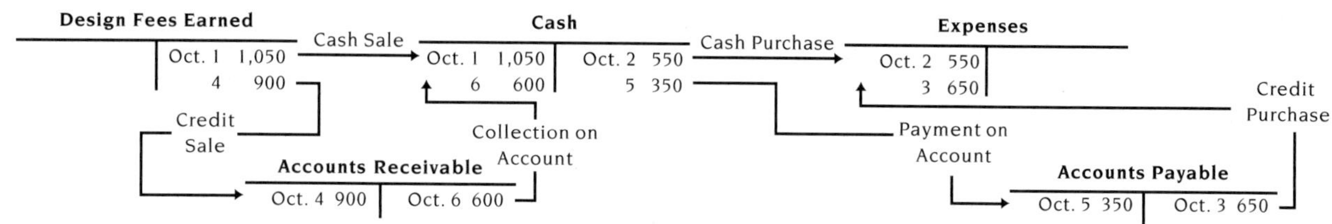

Cash balance after transactions: $1,050 + $600 − $550 − $350 = $750
Amount still to be received: $900 − $600 = $300
Amount still to be paid: $650 − $350 = $300

Recording and Posting Transactions

SO6 Define the *chart* of *accounts*, record transactions in the general journal, and post transactions to the ledger.

Earlier in the chapter, we described how transactions are analyzed according to the rules of double entry and how a trial balance is prepared. As Figure 2-4 shows, transaction analysis and preparation of a trial balance are the first and last steps in a four-step process. The two intermediate steps are recording the entry in the general journal and posting the entry to the ledger. In this section, we demonstrate how these steps are accomplished in a manual accounting system.

Chart of Accounts

In a manual accounting system, each account is kept on a separate page or card. These pages or cards are placed together in a book or file called the **general ledger.** In the computerized systems that most companies have today, accounts are maintained electronically. However, as a matter of convenience, accountants still refer to the group of company accounts as the *general ledger*, or simply the *ledger*.

> **Study Note**
> A chart of accounts is a table of contents for the ledger. Typically, it lists accounts in the order in which they appear in the ledger, which is usually the order in which they appear in the financial statements. The numbering scheme allows for some flexibility.

To help identify accounts in the ledger and make them easy to find, the accountant often numbers them. A list of these numbers with the corresponding account titles is called a **chart of accounts.** A very simple chart of accounts appears in Exhibit 2-3. The first digit in the account number identifies the major financial statement classification—that is, an account number that begins with the digit 1 means that the account is an asset account, an account number that begins with a 2 means that the account is a liability account, and so forth. The second and third digits identify individual accounts. The gaps in the sequence of numbers allow the accountant to expand the number of accounts.

General Journal

> **Study Note**
> The journal is a chronological record of events.

Although transactions can be entered directly into the ledger accounts, this method makes identifying individual transactions or finding errors very difficult because the debit is recorded in one account and the credit in another. The solution is to record all transactions chronologically in a **journal.** The journal is sometimes called the *book of original entry* because it is where transactions first enter the accounting records. Later, the debit and credit portions of each transaction are transferred to the appropriate accounts in the ledger. A separate **journal entry** is used to record each transaction; the process of recording transactions is called **journalizing.**

Most businesses have more than one kind of journal. The simplest and most flexible kind is the **general journal,** the one we focus on here. Businesses will also have several special-purpose journals, each for recording a common transaction, such as credit sales, credit purchases, cash receipts, and cash disbursements. At this

FIGURE 2-4
Analyzing and Processing Transactions

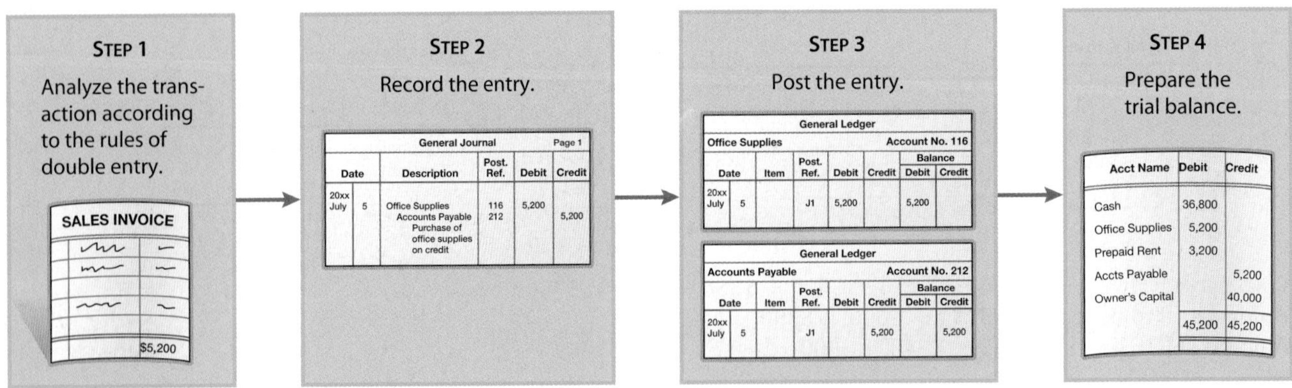

EXHIBIT 2-3 Chart of Accounts for a Small Business

Account Number	Account Name	Description
		Assets
111	Cash	Money and any medium of exchange (coins, currency, checks, money orders, and money on deposit in a bank)
112	Notes Receivable	Promissory notes (written promises to pay definite sums of money at fixed future dates) due from others
113	Accounts Receivable	Amounts due from others for revenues or sales on credit (sales on account)
116	Office Supplies	Prepaid expense; office supplies purchased and not used
117	Prepaid Rent	Prepaid expense; rent paid in advance and not used
118	Prepaid Insurance	Prepaid expense; insurance purchased and not expired
141	Land	Property owned for use in the business
142	Buildings	Structures owned for use in the business
143	Accumulated Depreciation–Buildings	Periodic allocation of the cost of buildings to expense; deducted from buildings
146	Office Equipment	Office equipment owned for use in the business
147	Accumulated Depreciation–Office Equipment	Periodic allocation of the cost of office equipment to expense; deducted from Office Equipment
		Liabilities
211	Notes Payable	Promissory notes due to others
212	Accounts Payable	Amounts due to others for purchases on credit
213	Unearned Design Revenue	Unearned revenue; advance deposits for design services to be provided in the future
214	Wages Payable	Amounts due to employees for wages earned and not paid
		Owner's Equity
311	Owner's Capital	Owner's investments in a company and claims against company assets derived from profitable operations
313	Withdrawals	Distributions of assets (usually cash) that reduce owner's capital
314	Income Summary	Temporary account used at the end of the accounting period to summarize the revenues and expenses for the period
		Revenues
411	Design Revenue	Revenues derived from design services
		Expenses
511	Wages Expense	Amounts earned by employees
512	Utilities Expense	Amounts for utilities, such as water, electricity, and gas, used
513	Telephone Expense	Amounts of telephone services used
514	Rent Expense	Amounts of rent on property and buildings used
515	Insurance Expense	Amounts for insurance expired
517	Office Supplies Expense	Amounts for office supplies used
518	Depreciation Expense–Buildings	Amount of buildings' cost allocated to expense
520	Depreciation Expense–Office Equipment	Amount of office equipment cost allocated to expense

EXHIBIT 2-4
The General Journal

A	=	L	+ OE
+ 3,200			
− 3,200			

A	=	L	+ OE
+ 5,200		+ 5,200	

General Journal — **Page 1**

Date		Description	Post. Ref.	Debit	Credit
2010					
July	3	Prepaid Rent		3,200	
		Cash			3,200
		Paid two months' rent in advance			
	5	Office Supplies		5,200	
		Accounts Payable			5,200
		Purchase of office supplies on credit			

point, we cover only the general journal. Exhibit 2-4, which displays two of the transactions of Miller Design Studio that we discussed earlier, shows the format for recording entries in a general journal. As you can see in Exhibit 2-4, the entries in a general journal include the following information about each transaction:

1. The date. The year appears on the first line of the first column, the month on the next line of the first column, and the day in the second column opposite the month. For subsequent entries on the same page for the same month and year, the month and year can be omitted.
2. The names of the accounts debited and credited, which appear in the Description column. The names of the accounts that are debited are placed next to the left margin opposite the dates; on the line below, the names of the accounts credited are indented.
3. The debit amounts, which appear in the Debit column opposite the accounts that are debited, and the credit amounts, which appear in the Credit column opposite the accounts credited.
4. An explanation of each transaction, which appears in the Description column below the account names. An explanation should be brief but sufficient to explain and identify the transaction.
5. The account numbers in the Post. Ref. column, if they apply.

At the time the transactions are recorded, nothing is placed in the Post. Ref. (posting reference) column. (This column is sometimes called LP or *Folio.*) Later, if the company uses account numbers to identify accounts in the ledger, the account numbers are filled in. They provide a convenient cross-reference from the general journal to the ledger and indicate that the entry has been posted to the ledger. If the accounts are not numbered, the accountant uses a checkmark (✓) to signify that the entry has been posted.

General Ledger

The general journal is used to record the details of each transaction. The general ledger is used to update each account.

The Ledger Account Form The **ledger account form,** which contains four columns for dollar amounts, is illustrated in Exhibit 2-5.

The account title and number appear at the top of the account form. As in the journal, the transaction date appears in the first two columns. The Item column

EXHIBIT 2-5
Accounts Payable in the General Ledger

General Ledger

Accounts Payable						**Account No. 212**	
						Balance	
Date		**Item**	**Post. Ref.**	**Debit**	**Credit**	**Debit**	**Credit**
2010							
July	5		J1		5,200		5,200
	6		J1		3,000		8,200
	9		J1	2,600			5,600
	30		J2		680		6,280

Study Note

A T account is a means of quickly analyzing a set of transactions. It is simply an abbreviated version of a ledger account. Ledger accounts, which provide more information, are used in the accounting records.

is rarely used to identify transactions because explanations already appear in the journal. The Post. Ref. column is used to note the journal page on which the original entry for the transaction can be found. The dollar amount is entered in the appropriate Debit or Credit column, and a new account balance is computed in the last two columns opposite each entry. The advantage of this account form over the T account is that the current balance of the account is readily available.

Posting After transactions have been entered in the journal, they must be transferred to the ledger. The process of transferring journal entry information from the journal to the ledger is called **posting.** Posting is usually done after several entries have been made—for example, at the end of each day or less frequently, depending on the number of transactions. As Exhibit 2-6 shows, in posting, each amount in the Debit column of the journal is transferred to the Debit column of the appropriate account in the ledger, and each amount in the Credit column of the journal is transferred to the Credit column of the appropriate account in the ledger. The steps in the posting process are as follows:

1. In the ledger, locate the debit account named in the journal entry.
2. Enter the date of the transaction in the ledger and, in the Post. Ref. column, the journal page number from which the entry comes.
3. In the Debit column of the ledger account, enter the amount of the debit as it appears in the journal.
4. Calculate the account balance and enter it in the appropriate Balance column.
5. Enter in the Post. Ref. column of the journal the account number to which the amount has been posted.
6. Repeat the same five steps for the credit side of the journal entry.

Notice that Step **5** is the last step in the posting process for each debit and credit. As noted earlier, in addition to serving as an easy reference between the journal entry and the ledger account, this entry in the Post. Ref. column of the journal indicates that the entry has been posted to the ledger.

Some Notes on Presentation

A ruled line appears in financial reports before each subtotal or total to indicate that the amounts above are added or subtracted. It is common practice to use a double line under a final total to show that it has been verified.

EXHIBIT 2-6
Posting from the General Journal to the Ledger

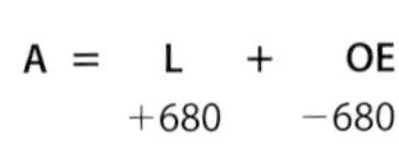

General Journal **Page 2**

Date		Description	Post. Ref.	Debit	Credit
2010					
July	30	Utilities Expense	512	680	
		Accounts Payable	212		680
		Received bill from utility company			

General Ledger

Accounts Payable **Account No. 212**

Date		Item	Post. Ref.	Debit	Credit	Balance Debit	Balance Credit
2010							
July	5		J1		5,200		5,200
	6		J1		3,000		8,200
	9		J1	2,600			5,600
	30		J2		680		6,280

General Ledger

Utilities Expense **Account No. 512**

Date		Item	Post. Ref.	Debit	Credit	Balance Debit	Balance Credit
2010							
July	30		J2	680		680	

Dollar signs ($) are required in all financial statements and on the trial balance and other schedules. On these reports, a dollar sign should be placed before the first amount in each column and before the first amount in a column following a ruled line. Dollar signs in the same column are aligned. Dollar signs are not used in journals and ledgers.

On normal, unruled paper, commas and decimal points are used when recording dollar amounts. On the paper used in journals and ledgers, commas and decimal points are unnecessary because ruled columns are provided to properly align dollars and cents. Commas, dollar signs, and decimal points are also unnecessary in electronic spreadsheets. In this book, because most problems and illustrations are in whole dollar amounts, the cents column usually is omitted. When accountants deal with whole dollars, they often use a dash in the cents column to indicate whole dollars rather than taking the time to write zeros.

Account names are capitalized when referenced in text or listed in work documents like the journal or ledger. In financial statements, however, only the first word of an account name is capitalized.

STOP & APPLY >

Record the following transactions in proper journal form and use the following account numbers—Cash, 111; Supplies 114; and Accounts Payable, 212—to show in the Post Ref. columns that the entries have been posted:

June 4 Purchased supplies for $40 on credit,
8 Paid for the supplies purchased on June 4

SOLUTION

Date		Description	Post. Ref.	Debit	Credit
June	4	Supplies	114	40	
		Accounts Payable	212		40
		Purchased supplies on credit			
	8	Accounts Payable	212	40	
		Cash	114		40
		Paid amount due for supplies			

▸ PAWS AND HOOFS CLINIC: REVIEW PROBLEM

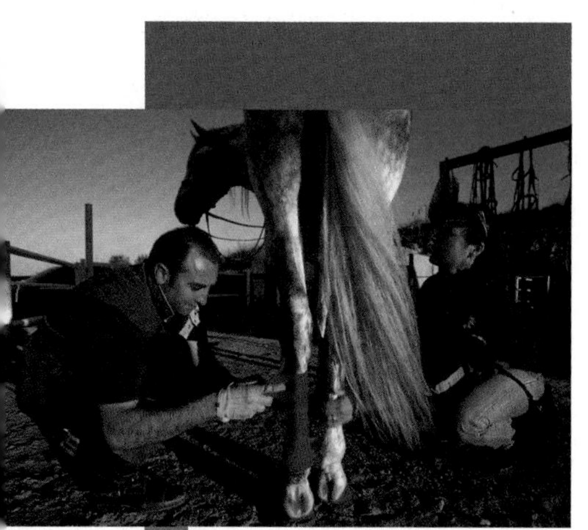

In the Decision Point at the beginning of the chapter, we described the standing order for monthly service that Quarter Horse Stables placed with Paws and Hoofs Clinic. We noted that Larry Cox, the owner of the clinic, was confident of receiving $6,000 in fees over the course of the year and that he was thinking of including the fees in his financial statements. We asked these questions:

- Is there a difference between an economic event and a business transaction that should be recorded in the accounting records?
- Can a business transaction benefit a business even though no cash is received when the transaction takes place?
- What is the difference between an asset and an expense?

Transaction Analysis, T Accounts, Journalizing, and the Trial Balance

LO1 LO3
LO4 SO6

Paws and Hoofs Clinic engaged in the following economic events during May 2010:

May 1 Larry Cox invested $20,000 in cash to form Paws and Hoofs Clinic.
2 Made an agreement to provide $6,000 in services over the next year to Quarter Horse Stables.
3 Paid $600 in advance for two months' rent of an office.
9 Purchased medical supplies for $400 in cash.
12 Purchased $4,000 of equipment on credit; made a 25 percent down payment.
15 Delivered a calf for a fee of $350 on credit.
18 Made a payment of $500 on the equipment purchased on May 12.
27 Paid a utility bill of $140.

Required

1. Identify the company's business transactions, and record them in journal form.
2. Post the transactions to the following T accounts: Cash, Accounts Receivable, Medical Supplies, Prepaid Rent, Equipment, Accounts Payable, L. Cox, Capital; Veterinary Fees Earned, and Utilities Expense.
3. Prepare a trial balance for the month of May.
4. User insight: Answer the following questions:
   a. How does the event on May 2 illustrate the difference between an economic event and a business transaction?
   b. How does the business transaction of May 15 benefit the business even though no cash was received?
   c. How do the transactions of May 9 and May 27 illustrate the difference between an asset and an expense?

Answers to Review Problem

1. Transactions recorded in journal form:

	A	B	C	D	E	F	G	H
1	May	1		Cash			20,000	
2					L. Cox, Capital			20,000
3						Issued $20,000 in cash		
4						to form Paws and Hoofs Clinic		
5		3		Prepaid Rent			600	
6					Cash			600
7						Paid two months' rent in advance		
8						for an office		
9		9		Medical Supplies			400	
10					Cash			400
11						Purchased medical supplies for cash		
12		12		Equipment			4,000	
13					Accounts Payable			3,000
14					Cash			1,000
15						Purchased equipment on credit,		
16						paying 25 percent down		
17		15		Accounts Receivable			350	
18					Veterinary Fees Earned			350
19						Fee on credit for delivery of a calf		
20		18		Accounts Payable			500	
21					Cash			500
22						Partial payment for equipment		
23						purchased May 12		
24		27		Utilities Expense			140	
25					Cash			140
26						Paid utility bill		
27								

2. Transactions posted to T accounts:

	A	B	C	D	E	F	G	H	I	J	K	L	M
1			**Cash**							**Accounts Payable**			
2	May	1	20,000	May	3	600		May	18	500	May	12	3,000
3					9	400					*Bal.*		2,500
4					12	1,000							
5					18	500				**L.Cox, Capital**			
6					27	140					May	1	20,000
7			20,000			2,640							
8	*Bal.*		17,360							**Veterinary Fees Earned**			
9											May	15	350
10			**Accounts Receivable**										
11	May	15	350							**Utilities Expense**			
12								May	27	140			
13			**Medical Supplies**										
14	May	9	400										
15													
16			**Prepaid Rent**										
17	May	3	600										
18													
19			**Equipment**										
20	May	12	4,000										
21													

3. Trial balance:

	A	B	C	D	E
1			**Paws and Hoofs Clinic**		
2			**Trial Balance**		
3			**May 31, 2010**		
4					
5	Cash			$17,360	
6	Accounts Receivable			350	
7	Medical Supplies			400	
8	Prepaid Rent			600	
9	Equipment			4,000	
10	Accounts Payable				$ 2,500
11	L. Cox, Capital				20,000
12	Veterinary Fees Earned				350
13	Utilities Expense			140	
14				$22,850	$22,850
15					

4. User insight:

a. Despite its importance as an economic event, the standing order on May 2 did not constitute a business transaction. Neither the buyer nor the seller should have recognized it in their accounting records. At the time of the

agreement, Larry Cox had provided no services. Even "firm" orders like this one may be changed or canceled sometime during the year.

b. Cox provided a service on May 15 and thus earned a revenue and added an asset to accounts receivable, which will provide cash for the business when the client pays the bill.

c. Although closely related and recorded by debits, assets and expenses are different in how they affect future operations. The supplies purchased on May 9 are classified as an asset because they will benefit future accounting periods. The payment for utilities is classified as an expense because it is used up and will not benefit future periods.

LO1 Explain how the concepts of recognition, valuation, and classification apply to business transactions and why they are important factors in ethical financial reporting.

To measure a business transaction, you must determine when the transaction occurred (the recognition issue), what value to place on the transaction (the valuation issue), and how the components of the transaction should be categorized (the classification issue). In general, recognition occurs when title passes, and a transaction is valued at the exchange price—the fair value or cost at the time the transaction is recognized. Classification refers to assigning transactions to the appropriate accounts. GAAP provide guidance about the treatment of these three basic measurement issues. Failure to follow these guidelines is a major reason some companies issue unethical financial statements.

LO2 Explain the double-entry system and the usefulness of T accounts in analyzing business transactions.

In the double-entry system, each transaction must be recorded with at least one debit and one credit, and the total amount of the debits must equal the total amount of the credits. Each asset, liability, and component of owner's equity, including revenues and expenses, has a separate account, which is a device for storing transaction data. The T account is a useful tool for quickly analyzing the effects of transactions. It shows how increases and decreases in assets, liabilities, and owner's equity are debited and credited to the appropriate accounts.

LO3 Demonstrate how the double-entry system is applied to common business transactions.

The double-entry system is applied by analyzing transactions to determine which accounts are affected and by using T accounts to show how the transactions affect the accounting equation. The transactions may be recorded in journal form with the date, debit account, and debit amount shown on one line, and the credit account (indented) and credit amount on the next line. The amounts are shown in their respective debit and credit columns.

LO4 Prepare a trial balance, and describe its value and limitations.

A trial balance is used to check that the debit and credit balances are equal. It is prepared by listing each account balance in the appropriate Debit or Credit column. The two columns are then added, and the totals are compared. The major limitation of a trial balance is that even when it shows that debit and credit balances are equal, it does not guarantee that the transactions were analyzed correctly or recorded in the proper accounts.

LO5 Show how the timing of transactions affects cash flows and liquidity.

Some transactions generate immediate cash. For those that do not, there is a holding period in either Accounts Receivable or Accounts Payable before the cash is received or paid. The timing of cash flows is critical to a company's ability to maintain adequate liquidity so that it can pay its bills on time.

Supplemental Objective

SO6 Define the *chart of accounts*, record transactions in the general journal, and post transactions to the ledger.

The chart of accounts is a list of account numbers and titles; it serves as a table of contents for the ledger. The general journal is a chronological record of all transactions; it contains the date of each transaction, the titles of the accounts involved, the amounts debited and credited, and an explanation of each entry. After transactions have been entered in the general journal, they are posted to the ledger. Posting is done by transferring the amounts in the Debit and Credit columns of the general journal to the Debit and Credit columns of the corresponding account in the ledger. After each entry is posted, a new balance is entered in the appropriate Balance column.

REVIEW of Concepts and Terminology

The following concepts and terms were introduced in this chapter:

Accounts 54 (LO2)

Balance 55 (LO2)

Chart of accounts 70 (SO6)

Classification 53 (LO1)

Compound entry 60 (LO3)

Cost principle 52 (LO1)

Credit 54 (LO2)

Debit 54 (LO2)

Double-entry system 54 (LO2)

Fair value 51 (LO1)

Footings 55 (LO2)

General journal 70 (SO6)

General ledger 70 (SO6)

Journal 70 (SO6)

Journal entry 70 (SO6)

Journal form 58 (LO3)

Journalizing 70 (SO6)

Ledger account form 72 (SO6)

Normal balance 56 (LO2)

Posting 73 (SO6)

Recognition 50 (LO1)

Recognition point 51 (LO1)

Source documents 58 (LO3)

T account 54 (LO2)

Trial balance 65 (LO4)

Valuation 51 (LO1)

CHAPTER ASSIGNMENTS

BUILDING Your Basic Knowledge and Skills

Short Exercises

Short exercises are simple applications of chapter material for one or more learning objectives. If you need help locating the related text discussions, refer to the LO numbers in the margin.

LO1 **Recognition**

SE 1. Which of the following events would be recognized and entered in the accounting records of Kazuo Company? Why?

Jan. 10 Kazuo Company places an order for office supplies.
Feb. 15 Kazuo Company receives the office supplies and a bill for them.
Mar. 1 Kazuo Company pays for the office supplies.

LO1 LO3 **Recognition, Valuation, and Classification**

SE 2. Tell how the concepts of recognition, valuation, and classification apply to this transaction:

Cash	
Dr.	Cr.
	June 1 1,000

Supplies	
Dr.	Cr.
June 1 1,000	

LO1 **Classification of Accounts**

SE 3. Tell whether each of the following accounts is an asset, a liability, a revenue, an expense, or none of these:

a. Accounts Payable
b. Supplies
c. Withdrawals
d. Fees Earned
e. Supplies Expense
f. Accounts Receivable
g. Unearned Revenue
h. Equipment

LO2 **Normal Balances**

SE 4. Tell whether the normal balance of each account in **SE 3** is a debit or a credit.

LO3 **Transaction Analysis**

SE 5. Leon Bear started a computer programming business, Bear's Programming Service. For each transaction that follows, indicate which account is debited and which account is credited.

May 2 Leon Bear invested $5,000.
5 Purchased a computer for $2,500 in cash.
7 Purchased supplies on credit for $300.
19 Received cash for programming services performed, $500.
22 Received cash for programming services to be performed, $600.
25 Paid the rent for May, $650.
31 Billed a customer for programming services performed, $250.

LO3 **Recording Transactions in T Accounts**

SE 6. Set up T accounts and record each transaction in **SE 5**. Determine the balance of each account.

LO4 **Preparing a Trial Balance**

SE 7. From the T accounts created in **SE 6**, prepare a trial balance dated May 31, 2010.

LO5 **Timing and Cash Flows**

SE 8. Use the T account for Cash below to record the portion of each of the following transactions, if any, that affect cash. How do these transactions affect the company's liquidity?

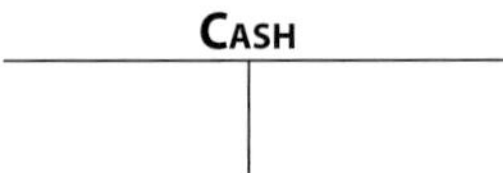

Jan. 2 Provided services for cash, $1,200
4 Paid expenses in cash, $700
8 Provided services on credit, $1,100
9 Incurred expenses on credit, $800

SO6 **Recording Transactions in the General Journal**

SE 9. Prepare a general journal form like the one in Exhibit 2-4 and label it Page 4. Record the following transactions in the journal:

Sept. 6 Billed a customer for services performed, $3,800.
16 Received partial payment from the customer billed on Sept. 6, $1,800.

SO6 **Posting to the Ledger Accounts**

SE 10. Prepare ledger account forms like the ones in Exhibit 2-5 for the following accounts: Cash (111), Accounts Receivable (113), and Service Revenue (411). Post the transactions that are recorded in **SE 9** to the ledger accounts for 2011, at the same time making the proper posting references. Also prepare a trial balance.

SO6 **Recording Transactions in the General Journal**

SE 11. Record the transactions in **SE 5** in the general journal for 2011.

Exercises

LO1 LO2 LO3 **Discussion Questions**

E 1. Develop a brief answer to each of the following questions.

1. Which is the most important issue in recording a transaction: recognition, valuation, or classification?
2. What is an example of how a company could make false financial statements through a violation of the recognition concept?
3. How are assets and expenses related, and why are the debit and credit effects for assets and expenses the same?
4. In what way are unearned revenues the opposite of prepaid expenses?

LO4 LO5 SO6 **Discussion Questions**

E 2. Develop a brief answer to each of the following questions.

1. Which account would be most likely to have an account balance that is not normal?

2. A company incurs a cost for a part that is needed to repair a piece of equipment. Is the cost an asset or an expense? Explain.
3. If a company's cash flows for expenses temporarily exceed its cash flows from revenues, how might it make up the difference so that it can maintain liquidity?
4. How would the asset accounts in the chart of accounts for Miller Design Studio differ if it were a retail company that sold promotional products instead of a service company?

LO1 Recognition

E 3. Which of the following events would be recognized and recorded in the accounting records of Villa Company on the date indicated?

Jan. 15	Villa Company offers to purchase a tract of land for $140,000. There is a high likelihood that the offer will be accepted.
Feb. 2	Villa Company receives notice that its rent will increase from $500 to $600 per month effective March 1.
Mar. 29	Villa Company receives its utility bill for the month of March. The bill is not due until April 9.
June 10	Villa Company places an order for new office equipment costing $21,000.
July 6	The office equipment Villa Company ordered on June 10 arrives. Payment is not due until August 1.

LO1 Application of Recognition Point

E 4. Torez Flower Shop uses a large amount of supplies in its business. The following table summarizes selected transaction data for supplies that Torez Flower Shop purchased:

Order	Date Shipped	Date Received	Amount
a	June 26	July 5	$300
b	July 10	15	750
c	16	22	400
d	23	30	600
e	27	Aug. 1	750
f	Aug. 3	7	500

Determine the total purchases of supplies for July alone under each of the following assumptions:

1. Torez Flower Shop recognizes purchases when orders are shipped.
2. Torez Flower Shop recognizes purchases when orders are received.

LO2 T Accounts, Normal Balance, and the Accounting Equation

E 5. You are given the following list of accounts with dollar amounts:

Rent Expense	$ 450
Cash	1,725
Service Revenue	750
M. Powell, Withdrawals	375
Accounts Payable	600
M. Powell, Capital	1,200

Insert each account name at the top of its corresponding T account and enter the dollar amount as a normal balance in the account. Then show that the accounting equation is in balance.

Assets	= Liabilities	+ M. Powell, Capital	− M. Powell, Withdrawals	+ Revenues	− Expenses
		Owner's Equity			

LO2 Classification of Accounts

E 6. The following ledger accounts are for the Tuner Service Company:

a. Cash
b. Wages Expense
c. Accounts Receivable
d. R. Shuckman, Capital
e. Service Revenue
f. Prepaid Rent
g. Accounts Payable
h. Investments in Securities
i. Land
j. Supplies Expense
k. Prepaid Insurance
l. Utilities Expense
m. Fees Earned
n. R. Shuckman, Withdrawals
o. Wages Payable
p. Unearned Revenue
q. Office Equipment
r. Rent Payable
s. Notes Receivable
t. Interest Expense
u. Notes Payable
v. Supplies
w. Interest Receivable
x. Rent Expense

Complete the following table, using X's to indicate each account's classification and normal balance (whether a debit or a credit increases the account).

	Type of Account						Normal Balance (increases balance)	
			Owner's Equity					
Item	**Asset**	**Liability**	**R. Shuckman, Capital**	**R. Shuckman, Withdrawals**	**Revenue**	**Expense**	**Debit**	**Credit**
a.	X						X	

LO3 Transaction Analysis

E 7. Analyze transactions **a–g**, following the example below.

a. Sarah Lopez invested $2,500 in cash to establish Sarah's Beauty Parlor.
b. Paid two months' rent in advance, $1,680.
c. Purchased supplies on credit, $120.
d. Received cash for barbering services, $700.
e. Paid for supplies purchased in **c**.
f. Paid utility bill, $72.
g. Withdrew $100 in cash.

Example

a. The asset account Cash was increased. Increases in assets are recorded by debits. Debit Cash $2,500. A component of owner's equity, S. Lopez, Capital, was increased. Increases in owner's capital are recorded by credits. Credit S. Lopez, Capital $2,500.

LO3 **Transaction Analysis**

E 8. The following accounts are applicable to Dale's Lawn Service, a company that maintains condominium grounds:

1. Cash
2. Accounts Receivable
3. Supplies
4. Equipment
5. Accounts Payable
6. Lawn Services Revenue
7. Wages Expense
8. Rent Expense

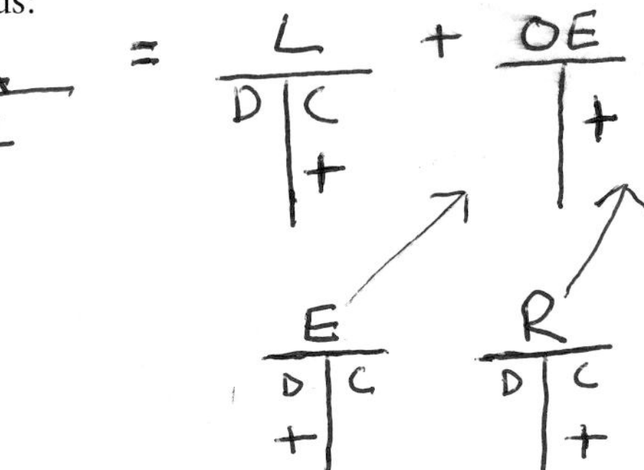

Dale's Lawn Service completed the following transactions:

	Debit	Credit
a. Paid for supplies purchased on credit last month.	5	1
b. Received cash from customers billed last month.		
c. Made a payment on accounts payable.		
d. Purchased supplies on credit.		
e. Billed a client for lawn services.		
f. Made a rent payment for the current month.		
g. Received cash from customers for lawn services.		
h. Paid employee wages.		
i. Ordered equipment.		
j. Received and paid for the equipment ordered in **i**.		

Analyze each transaction and show the accounts affected by entering the corresponding numbers in the appropriate debit or credit columns as shown in transaction **a**. Indicate no entry, if appropriate.

LO3 **Recording Transactions in T Accounts**

E 9. Open the following T accounts: Cash; Repair Supplies; Repair Equipment; Accounts Payable; T. Ornega, Capital; Withdrawals; Repair Fees Earned; Salaries Expense; and Rent Expense. Record the following transactions for the month of June directly in the T accounts; use the letters to identify the transactions in your T accounts. Determine the balance in each account.

a. Tony Ornega opened Ornega Repair Service by investing $4,300 in cash and $1,600 in repair equipment.
b. Paid $800 for the current month's rent.
c. Purchased repair supplies on credit, $1,100.
d. Purchased additional repair equipment for cash, $600.
e. Paid salary to a helper, $900.
f. Paid $400 of amount purchased on credit in **c**.
g. Accepted cash for repairs completed, $3,720.
h. Withdrew $1,000 in cash.

LO4 **Trial Balance**

E 10. After recording the transactions in **E 9**, prepare a trial balance in proper sequence for Ornega Repair Service as of June 30, 2011.

LO3 **Analysis of Transactions**

E 11. Explain each transaction (**a–h**) entered in the following T accounts:

Cash

a.	20,000	b.	7,500
g.	750	e.	1,800
h.	450	f.	2,250

Accounts Receivable

c.	4,000	g.	750

Equipment

b.	7,500	h.	450
d.	4,500		

Accounts Payable

f.	2,250	d.	4,500

B. Caldwell, Capital

		a.	20,000

Service Revenue

		c.	4,000

Wages Expense

e.	1,800		

LO4 **Preparing a Trial Balance**

E 12. The list that follows presents the accounts (in alphabetical order) of the Dymarski Company as of March 31, 2011. The list does not include the amount of Accounts Payable.

Accounts Payable	?
Accounts Receivable	$ 2,800
Building	20,400
Cash	5,400
K. Dymarski, Capital	18,870
Equipment	7,200
Land	3,120
Notes Payable	10,000
Prepaid Insurance	660

Prepare a trial balance with the proper heading (see Exhibit 2-2) and with the accounts listed in the chart of accounts sequence (see Exhibit 2-3). Compute the balance of Accounts Payable.

LO4 **Effects of Errors on a Trial Balance**

E 13. Which of the following errors would cause a trial balance to have unequal totals? Explain your answers.

a. A payment to a creditor was recorded as a debit to Accounts Payable for $129 and as a credit to Cash for $102.
b. A payment of $150 to a creditor for an account payable was debited to Accounts Receivable and credited to Cash.
c. A purchase of office supplies of $420 was recorded as a debit to Office Supplies for $42 and as a credit to Cash for $42.
d. A purchase of equipment for $450 was recorded as a debit to Supplies for $450 and as a credit to Cash for $450.

LO4 **Correcting Errors in a Trial Balance**

E 14. The trial balance for Marek Services at the end of July 2011 appears at the top of the opposite page. It does not balance because of a number of errors. Marek's accountant compared the amounts in the trial balance with the ledger, recomputed the account balances, and compared the postings. He found the following errors:

a. The balance of Cash was understated by $800.
b. A cash payment of $420 was credited to Cash for $240.
c. A debit of $120 to Accounts Receivable was not posted.
d. Supplies purchased for $60 were posted as a credit to Supplies.
e. A debit of $180 to Prepaid Insurance was not posted.

Marek Services
Trial Balance
July 31, 2011

Cash	$ 3,440	
Accounts Receivable	5,660	
Supplies	120	
Prepaid Insurance	180	
Equipment	7,400	
Accounts Payable		$ 4,540
T. Marek, Capital		10,560
T. Marek, Withdrawals		700
Revenues		5,920
Salaries Expense	2,600	
Rent Expense	600	
Advertising Expense	340	
Utilities Expense	26	
	$20,366	$21,720

f. The Accounts Payable account had debits of $5,320 and credits of $9,180.
g. The Notes Payable account, with a credit balance of $2,400, was not included on the trial balance.
h. The debit balance of T. Marek, Withdrawals was listed in the trial balance as a credit.
i. A $200 debit to T. Marek, Withdrawals was posted as a credit.
j. The actual balance of Utilities Expense, $260, was listed as $26 in the trial balance.

Prepare a corrected trial balance.

LO5 Cash Flow Analysis

CASH FLOW

E 15. A company engaged in the following transactions:

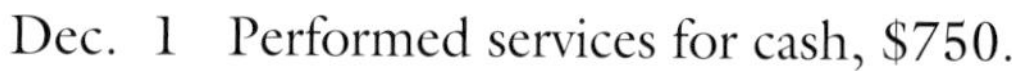

Dec. 1 Performed services for cash, $750.
1 Paid expenses in cash, $550.
2 Performed services on credit, $900.
3 Collected on account, $600.
4 Incurred expenses on credit, $650.
5 Paid on account, $350.

Enter the correct titles on the following T accounts and enter the above transactions in the accounts. Determine the cash balance after these transactions, the amount still to be received, and the amount still to be paid.

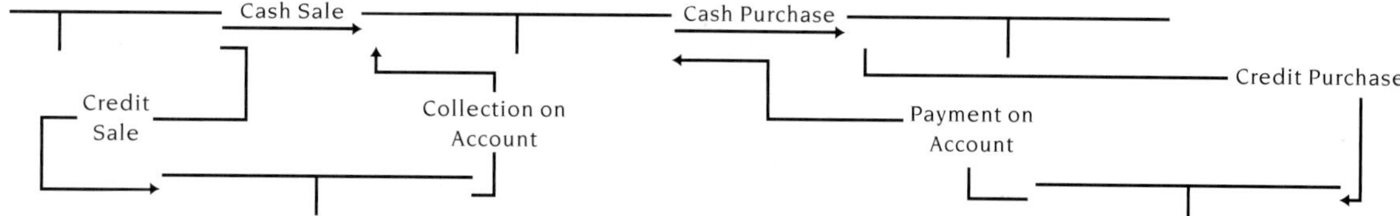

SO6 Recording Transactions in the General Journal

E 16. Record the transactions in E 9 in the general journal.

LO3 SO6 **Analysis of Unfamiliar Transactions**

E 17. Managers and accountants often encounter transactions with which they are unfamiliar. Use your analytical skills to analyze and record in journal form the following transactions, which have not yet been discussed in the text.

May	1	Purchased merchandise inventory on account, $1,200.
	2	Purchased marketable securities for cash, $3,000.
	3	Returned part of merchandise inventory purchased for full credit, $250.
	4	Sold merchandise inventory on account, $800 (record sale only).
	5	Purchased land and a building for $300,000. Payment is $60,000 cash, and there is a 30-year mortgage for the remainder. The purchase price is allocated as follows: $100,000 to the land and $200,000 to the building.
	6	Received an order for $12,000 in services to be provided. With the order was a deposit of $3,500.

SO6 **Recording Transactions in the General Journal and Posting to the Ledger Accounts**

E 18. Open a general journal form like the one in Exhibit 2-4, and label it Page 10. After opening the form, record the following transactions in the journal:

Dec.	14	Purchased equipment for $6,000, paying $2,000 as a cash down payment.
	28	Paid $3,000 of the amount owed on the equipment.

Prepare three ledger account forms like the one shown in Exhibit 2-5. Use the following account numbers: Cash, 111; Office Equipment, 146; and Accounts Payable, 212. Then post the two transactions from the general journal to the ledger accounts, being sure to make proper posting references. Assume that the Cash account has a debit balance of $8,000 on the day prior to the first transaction.

Problems

LO2 **T Accounts, Normal Balance, and The Accounting Equation**

P 1. Delux Design Company creates radio and television advertising for local businesses in the twin cities. The following alphabetical list shows Delux Design's account balances as of January 31, 2011:

Accounts Payable	$ 3,210
Accounts Receivable	39,000
Cash	9,200
Design Revenue	105,000
Equipment	?
J. Smith, Capital	37,000
J. Smith, Withdrawals	18,000
Loans Payable	5,000
Rent Expense	5,940
Telephone Expense	480
Unearned Revenue	9,000
Wages Expense	62,000

Required

Insert the account title at the top of its corresponding T account and enter the dollar amount as a normal balance in the account. Determine the balance of Equipment and then show that the accounting equation is in balance.

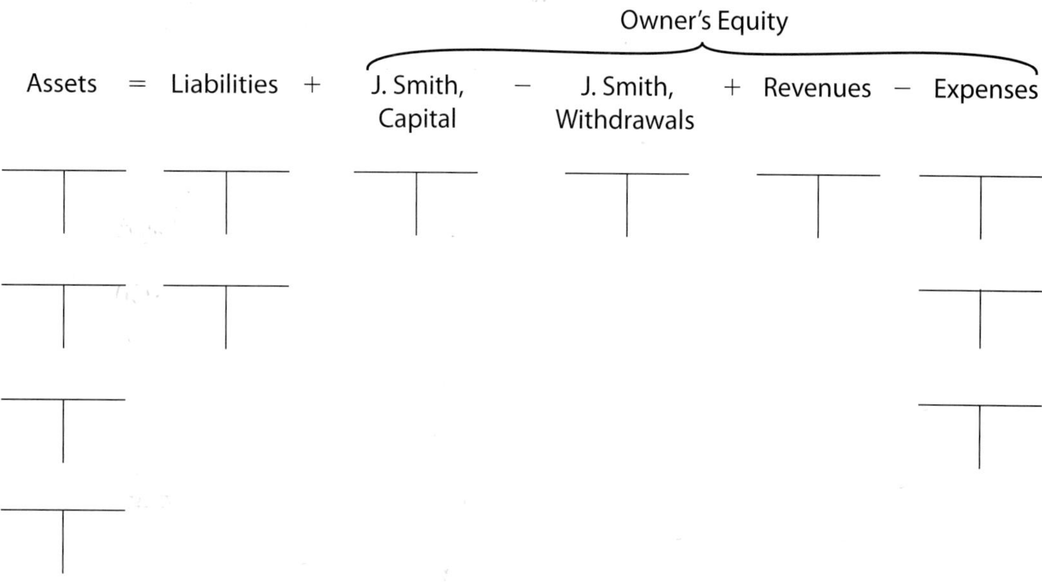

LO3 Transaction Analysis

P 2. The following accounts are applicable to Tom's Warehouse Sweeps:

1. Cash
2. Accounts Receivable
3. Supplies
4. Prepaid Insurance
5. Equipment
6. Notes Payable
7. Accounts Payable
8. T. Henzel, Capital
9. T. Henzel, Withdrawals
10. Service Revenue
11. Rent Expense
12. Repair Expense

Tom's Warehouse Sweeps completed the following transactions:

	Debit	Credit
a. Paid for supplies purchased on credit last month.		
b. Billed customers for services performed.		
c. Paid the current month's rent.		
d. Purchased supplies on credit.		
e. Received cash from customers for services performed but not yet billed.		
f. Purchased equipment on account.		
g. Received a bill for repairs.		
h. Returned part of the equipment purchased in f for a credit.		
i. Received payments from customers previously billed.		
j. Paid the bill received in g.		
k. Received an order for services to be performed.		
l. Paid for repairs with cash.		
m. Made a payment to reduce the principal of the note payable.		
n. Made a cash withdrawal.		

Required

Analyze each transaction and show the accounts affected by entering the corresponding numbers in the appropriate debit or credit column as shown in transaction **a**. Indicate no entry, if appropriate.

LO3 LO4 LO5

Transaction Analysis, T Accounts, and Trial Balance

P 3. Carmen Dahlen opened a secretarial school called Star Office Training.

a. Dahlen contributed the following assets to the business:

Cash	$5,700
Computers	5,000
Office Equipment	3,600

b. Found a location for her business and paid the first month's rent, $260.
c. Paid for an advertisement announcing the opening of the school, $190.
d. Received applications from three students for a four-week secretarial program and two students for a ten-day keyboarding course. The students will be billed a total of $1,300.
e. Purchased supplies on credit, $330.
f. Billed the enrolled students, $2,040.
g. Purchased a second-hand computer, $480, and office equipment, $380, on credit.
h. Paid for the supplies purchased on credit in **e**, $330.
i. Paid cash to repair a broken computer, $40.
j. Received partial payment from students previously billed, $1,380.
k. Paid the utility bill for the current month, $90.
l. Paid an assistant one week's salary, $440.
m. Made a cash withdrawal of $300.

Required

1. Set up the following T accounts: Cash; Accounts Receivable; Supplies; Computers; Office Equipment; Accounts Payable; C. Dahlen, Capital; C. Dahlen, Withdrawals; Tuition Revenue; Salaries Expense; Utilities Expense; Rent Expense; Repair Expense; and Advertising Expense.
2. Record the transactions directly in the T accounts, using the transaction letter to identify each debit and credit.
3. Prepare a trial balance using today's date.

User insight ▶

4. Examine transactions **f** and **j**. What were the revenues, and how much cash was received from the revenues? What business issues might you see arising from the differences in these numbers?

LO1 LO3 LO4

Transaction Analysis, Journal Form, T Accounts, and Trial Balance

P 4. Melvin Patel bid for and won a concession to rent bicycles in the local park during the summer. During the month of June, Patel completed the following transactions for his bicycle rental business:

June	2	Began business by placing $7,200 in a business checking account in the name of the company.
	3	Purchased supplies on account for $150.
	4	Purchased 10 bicycles for $2,500, paying $1,200 down and agreeing to pay the rest in 30 days.

June 5 Paid $2,900 in cash for a small shed to store the bicycles and to use for other operations.
8 Paid $400 in cash for shipping and installation costs (considered an addition to the cost of the shed) to place the shed at the park entrance.
9 Hired a part-time assistant to help out on weekends at $7 per hour.
10 Paid a maintenance person $75 to clean the grounds.
13 Received $970 in cash for rentals.
17 Paid $150 for the supplies purchased on June 3.
18 Paid a $55 repair bill on bicycles.
23 Billed a company $110 for bicycle rentals for an employee outing.
25 Paid the $100 fee for June to the Park District for the right to operate the bicycle concession.
27 Received $960 in cash for rentals.
29 Paid the assistant $240.
30 Made a cash withdrawal of $500.

Required

1. Prepare entries to record these transactions in journal form.
2. Set up the following T accounts and post all the journal entries: Cash; Accounts Receivable; Supplies; Shed; Bicycles; Accounts Payable; M. Patel, Capital; M. Patel, Withdrawals; Rental Revenue; Wages Expense; Maintenance Expense; Repair Expense; and Concession Fee Expense.
3. Prepare a trial balance for Patel Rentals as of June 30, 2011.

User insight ▶ 4. Compare and contrast how the issues of recognition, valuation, and classification are settled in the transactions of June 3 and 10.

LO3 LO4 LO5 SO6

Transaction Analysis, General Journal, Ledger Accounts, and Trial Balance

P 5. Alpha Pro Company is a marketing firm. The company's trial balance on July 31, 2011, appears below.

Alpha Pro Company
Trial Balance
July 31, 2011

Cash (111)	$10,590	
Accounts Receivable (113)	5,500	
Office Supplies (116)	610	
Office Equipment (146)	4,200	
Accounts Payable (212)		$ 2,600
K. Yating, Capital (311)		18,300
	$20,900	$20,900

During the month of August, the company completed the following transactions:

Aug.	2	Paid rent for August, $650.
	3	Received cash from customers on account, $2,300.
	7	Ordered supplies, $380.
	10	Billed customers for services provided, $2,800.
	12	Made a payment on accounts payable, $1,300.
	14	Received the supplies ordered on August 7 and agreed to pay for them in 30 days, $380.
	17	Discovered some of the supplies were not as ordered and returned them for full credit, $80.
	19	Received cash from a customer for services provided, $4,800.
	24	Paid the utility bill for August, $250.
	26	Received a bill, to be paid in September, for advertisements placed in the local newspaper during the month of August to promote Alpha Pro Company, $700.
	29	Billed a customer for services provided, $2,700.
	30	Paid salaries for August, $3,800.
	31	Made a cash withdrawal of $1,200.

Required

1. Open accounts in the ledger for the accounts in the trial balance plus the following accounts: K. Yating, Withdrawals (313); Marketing Fees (411); Salaries Expense (511); Rent Expense (514); Utilities Expense (512); and Advertising Expense (516).
2. Enter the July 31, 2011, account balances from the trial balance.
3. Enter the August transactions in the general journal (Pages 22 and 23).
4. Post the journal entries to the ledger accounts. Be sure to make the appropriate posting references in the journal and ledger as you post.
5. Prepare a trial balance as of August 31, 2011.

User insight ▶

6. Examine the transactions for August 3, 10, 19, and 29. What were the revenues, and how much cash was received from the revenues? What business issues might you see arising from the differences in these numbers?

Alternate Problems

LO2 T Accounts, Normal Balance, and the Accounting Equation

P 6. The Stewart Construction Company builds foundations for buildings and parking lots. The following alphabetical list shows Stewart Construction's account balances as of April 30, 2011:

A. Stewart, Capital	$20,000
A. Stewart, Withdrawals	3,500
Accounts Payable	1,950
Accounts Receivable	5,060
Cash	?
Equipment	13,750
Notes Payable	10,000
Revenue Earned	8,700
Supplies	3,250
Supplies Expense	3,600
Utilities Expense	210
Wages Expense	4,400

Required

Insert the account at the top of its corresponding T account, and enter the dollar amount as a normal balance in the account. Determine the balance of cash and then show that the accounting equation is in balance.

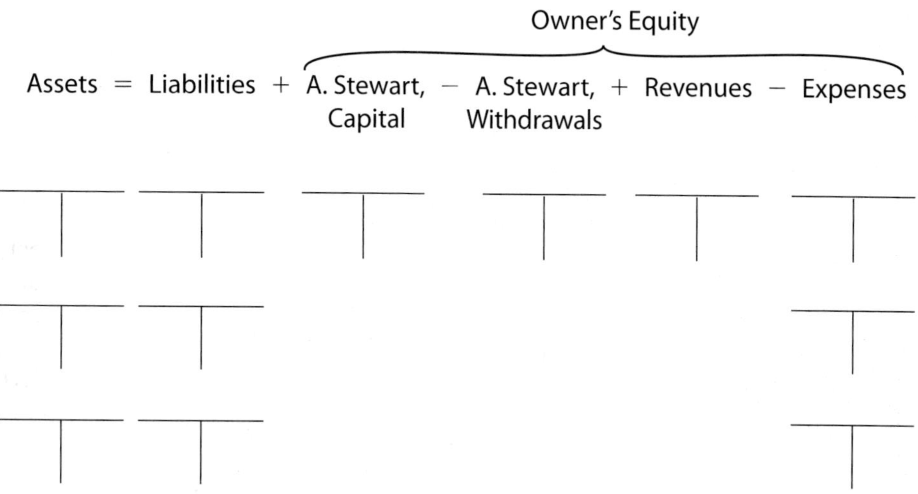

LO1 LO3 LO4 **Transaction Analysis, T Accounts, and Trial Balances**

P 7. Brad Cupello began an upholstery cleaning business on October 1 and engaged in the following transactions during the month:

Oct.	1	Began business by depositing $15,000 in a bank account in the name of the company.
	2	Ordered cleaning supplies, $3,000.
	3	Purchased cleaning equipment for cash, $2,800.
	4	Made two months' van lease payment in advance, $1,200.
	7	Received the cleaning supplies ordered on October 2 and agreed to pay half the amount in 10 days and the rest in 30 days.
	9	Paid for repairs on the van with cash, $1,080.
	12	Received cash for cleaning upholstery, $960.
	17	Paid half the amount owed on supplies purchased on October 7, $1,500.
	21	Billed customers for cleaning upholstery, $1,340.
	24	Paid cash for additional repairs on the van, $80.
	27	Received $600 from the customers billed on October 21.
	31	Made a cash withdrawal of $700.

Required

1. Set up the following T accounts: Cash; Accounts Receivable; Cleaning Supplies; Prepaid Lease; Cleaning Equipment; Accounts Payable; B. Cupello, Capital; B. Cupello, Withdrawals; Cleaning Revenue; and Repair Expense.
2. Record transactions directly in the T accounts. Identify each entry by date.
3. Prepare a trial balance for Cupello Upholstery Cleaning as of October 31, 2011.

User insight ▶

4. Compare and contrast how the issues of recognition, valuation, and classification are settled in the transactions of October 7 and 9.

LO3 LO4 LO5 SO6

Transaction Analysis, General Journal, Ledger Accounts, and Trial Balance

P 8. The Golden Nursery School Company provides baby-sitting and child-care programs. On January 31, 2011, the company had the following trial balance:

Golden Nursery School Company
Trial Balance
January 31, 2011

Cash (111)	$ 2,070	
Accounts Receivable (113)	1,700	
Equipment (146)	1,040	
Buses (148)	17,400	
Notes Payable (211)		$15,000
Accounts Payable (212)		1,640
T. Kuo, Capital (311)		5,570
	$22,210	$22,210

During the month of February, the company completed the following transactions:

Feb. 2 Paid this month's rent, $400.
3 Received fees for this month's services, $650.
4 Purchased supplies on account, $85.
5 Reimbursed the bus driver for gas expenses, $40.
6 Ordered playground equipment, $1,000.
8 Made a payment on account, $170.
9 Received payments from customers on account, $1,200.
10 Billed customers who had not yet paid for this month's services, $700.
11 Paid for the supplies purchased on February 4.
13 Purchased and received playground equipment ordered on February 6 for cash, $1,000.
17 Purchased equipment on account, $290.
19 Paid this month's utility bill, $145.
22 Received payment for one month's services from customers previously billed, $500.
26 Paid part-time assistants for services, $460.
27 Purchased gas and oil for the bus on account, $325.
28 Made a cash withdrawal of $200.

Required

1. Open accounts in the ledger for the accounts in the trial balance plus the following ones: Supplies (116); T. Kuo, Withdrawals (313); Service Revenue (411); Rent Expense (514); Gas and Oil Expense (510); Wages Expense (511); and Utilities Expense (512).
2. Enter the January 31, 2011, account balances from the trial balance.
3. Enter the above transactions in the general journal (Pages 17 and 18).
4. Post the entries to the ledger accounts. Be sure to make the appropriate posting references in the journal and ledger as you post.
5. Prepare a trial balance as of February 28, 2011.

User insight ▶

6. Examine the transactions for February 3, 9, 10, and 22. What were the revenues, and how much cash was received from the revenues? What business issue might you see arising from the differences in these numbers?

LO3 **Transaction Analysis**

P 9. The following accounts are applicable to Walter's Chimney Sweeps:

1. Cash
2. Accounts Receivable
3. Supplies
4. Prepaid Insurance
5. Equipment
6. Notes Payable
7. Accounts Payable
8. W. Norman, Capital
9. W. Norman, Withdrawals
10. Service Revenue
11. Rent Expense
12. Repair Expense

Walter's Chimney Sweeps completed the following transactions:

	Debit	**Credit**
a. Paid for supplies purchased on credit last month.	7	1
b. Billed customers for services performed.	___	___
c. Paid the current month's rent.	___	___
d. Purchased supplies on credit.	___	___
e. Received cash from customers for services performed but not yet billed.	___	___
f. Purchased equipment on account.	___	___
g. Received a bill for repairs.	___	___
h. Returned part of the equipment purchased in **f** for a credit.	___	___
i. Received payments from customers previously billed.	___	___
j. Paid the bill received in **g**.	___	___
k. Received an order for services to be performed.	___	___
l. Paid for repairs with cash.	___	___
m. Made a payment to reduce the principal of the note payable.	___	___
n. Made a cash withdrawal.	___	___

Required

Analyze each transaction and show the accounts affected by entering the corresponding numbers in the appropriate debit or credit column as shown in transaction **a**. Indicate no entry, if appropriate.

LO3 LO4 LO5 **Transaction Analysis, T Accounts, and Trial Balance**

P 10. Bob Lutz opened a secretarial school called Best Secretarial Training.

a. Lutz contributed the following assets to the business:

Cash	$5,700
Computers	4,300
Office Equipment	3,600

b. Found a location for his business and paid the first month's rent, $260.
c. Paid for an advertisement announcing the opening of the school, $190.
d. Received applications from three students for a four-week secretarial program and two students for a ten-day keyboarding course. The students will be billed a total of $1,300.
e. Purchased supplies on credit, $330.
f. Billed the enrolled students, $1,740.

g. Purchased a second-hand computer, $480, and office equipment, $380, on credit.
h. Paid for the supplies purchased on credit in **e**, $330.
i. Paid cash to repair a broken computer, $40.
j. Received partial payment from students previously billed, $1,080.
k. Paid the utility bill for the current month, $90.
l. Paid an assistant one week's salary, $440.
m. Made a cash withdrawal of $300.

Required

1. Set up the following T accounts: Cash; Accounts Receivable; Supplies; Computers; Office Equipment; Accounts Payable; B. Lutz, Capital; B. Lutz, Withdrawals; Tuition Revenue; Salaries Expense; Utilities Expense; Rent Expense; Repair Expense; and Advertising Expense.
2. Record the transactions directly in the T accounts, using the transaction letter to identify each debit and credit.
3. Prepare a trial balance using today's date.
4. User insight ▶ Examine transactions **f** and **j**. What were the revenues and how much cash was received from the revenues? What business issues might you see arising from the differences in these numbers?

ENHANCING Your Knowledge, Skills, and Critical Thinking

LO1 Valuation Issue

C 1. Nike, Inc. manufactures athletic shoes and related products. In one of its annual reports, Nike made this statement: "Property, plant, and equipment are recorded at cost."[6] Given that the property, plant, and equipment undoubtedly were purchased over several years and that the current value of those assets is likely to be very different from their original cost, what authoritative basis is there for carrying the assets at cost? Does accounting generally recognize changes in value after the purchase of property, plant, and equipment? Assume you are an accountant for Nike. Write a memo to management explaining the rationale underlying Nike's approach.

LO5 Cash Flows

C 2. You have been promoted recently and now have access to the firm's monthly financial statements. Business is good. Revenues are increasing rapidly, and income is at an all-time high. The balance sheet shows growth in receivables, and accounts payable have declined. However, the chief financial officer is concerned about the firm's cash flows from operating activities because they are decreasing. What are some reasons why a company with a positive net income may fall short of cash from its operating activities? What could be done to improve this situation?

LO1 Recognition Point and Ethical Considerations

C 3. Jerry Hasbrow, a sales representative for Penn Office Supplies Company, is compensated on a commission basis and receives a substantial bonus if he meets his annual sales goal. The company's recognition point for sales is the day of shipment. On December 31, Hasbrow realizes he needs sales of $2,000 to reach his sales goal and receive the bonus. He calls a purchaser for a local insurance company, whom he knows well, and asks him to buy $2,000 worth of copier paper today. The purchaser says, "But Jerry, that's more than a year's supply for us." Hasbrow says, "Buy it today. If you decide it's too much, you can return however much you want for full credit next month." The purchaser says, "Okay, ship it." The paper is shipped on December 31 and recorded as a sale. On January 15, the purchaser returns $1,750 worth of paper for full credit (approved by Hasbrow) against the bill. Should the shipment on December 31 be recorded as a sale? Discuss the ethics of Hasbrow's action.

LO1 LO3 Valuation and Classification Issues for Dot-Coms

C 4. The dot-com business has raised many issues about accounting practices, some of which are of great concern to both the SEC and the FASB. Important ones relate to the valuation and classification of revenue transactions. Many dot-com companies seek to report as much revenue as possible because revenue growth is seen as a key performance measure for these companies. **Amazon.com** is a good example. Consider the following situations:

a. An Amazon.com customer orders and pays $28 for a video game on the Internet. Amazon sends an email to the company that makes the product, which sends the video game to the customer. Amazon collects $28 from the customer and pays $24 to the other company. Amazon never owns the video game.
b. Amazon agrees to place a banner advertisement on its website for another dot-com company. Instead of paying cash for the advertisement, the other company agrees to let Amazon advertise on its website.
c. Assume the same facts as in situation **b** except that Amazon agrees to accept the other company's common stock in this barter transaction. Over the next six months, the price of that stock declines.

Divide the class into three groups. Assign each group one of the above situations. Each group should discuss the valuation and classification issues that arise in the assigned situation, including how Amazon should account for each transaction.

LO1 Recognition, Valuation, and Classification

C 5. Refer to the Summary of Significant Accounting Policies in the notes to the financial statements in the **CVS Corporation** annual report at the end of Chapter 5 to answer these questions:

1. How does the concept of recognition apply to advertising costs?
2. How does the concept of valuation apply to inventories?
3. How does the concept of classification apply to cash and cash equivalents?

Revenue Recognition

C 6. Refer to the financial statements of **CVS** and **Southwest Airlines Co.** in the Supplement to Chapter 5. What is the total revenue for CVS and Southwest on the respective income statements? How do you think the nature of each business will affect revenue recognition for prescriptions filled for CVS versus airline tickets for Southwest? When do you think cash is received and revenues are earned for each company?

CHAPTER

3 Measuring Business Income

Making a Statement

INCOME STATEMENT

Revenues

– Expenses

= Net Income

STATEMENT OF OWNER'S EQUITY

Beginning Balance

+ Net Income

– Withdrawals

= Ending Balance

BALANCE SHEET

Assets	**Liabilities**
	Owner's Equity

A = L + OE

STATEMENT OF CASH FLOWS

Operating activities

+ Investing activities

+ Financing activities

= Change in Cash

+ Beginning Balance

= Ending Cash Balance

Adjusting entries affect the balance sheet and income statement but not the statement of cash flows.

Income, or earnings, is the most important measure of a company's success or failure. Thus, the incentive to manage, or misstate, earnings by manipulating the numbers can be powerful, and because earnings are based on estimates, manipulation can be easy. For these reasons, ethical behavior is extremely important when measuring business income.

LEARNING OBJECTIVES

LO1 Define *net income*, and explain the assumptions underlying income measurement and their ethical application. (pp. 100–104)

LO2 Define *accrual accounting*, and explain how it is accomplished. (pp. 104–106)

LO3 Identify four situations that require adjusting entries, and illustrate typical adjusting entries. (pp. 107–116)

LO4 Prepare financial statements from an adjusted trial balance. (pp. 116–119)

LO5 Use accrual-based information to analyze cash flows. (pp. 119–120)

DECISION POINT ▸ A USER'S FOCUS RELIABLE ANSWERING SERVICE

Reliable Answering Service takes telephone messages for doctors, lawyers, and other professionals and relays them immediately when they involve an emergency. At the end of any accounting period, Reliable has many transactions that will affect future periods. Examples appear in the company's trial balance on the following page. They include *office supplies* and *prepaid expenses*, which, though paid in the period just ended, will benefit future periods and are therefore recorded as assets. Another example is *unearned revenue*, which represents receipts for services the company will not perform and earn until a future period. If prepaid expenses and unearned revenue are not accounted for properly at the end of a period, the company's income will be misstated. Similar misstatements can occur when a company fails to record (accrue) expenses that it incurred or revenue that it has earned but not yet received. Knowing the answers to the questions at right will help prevent such misstatements.

- ▸ What assumptions must Reliable Answering Service make to account for transactions that span accounting periods?
- ▸ How does Reliable assign its revenues and expenses to the proper accounting period so that net income is properly measured?
- ▸ Why are the adjustments that these transactions require important to Reliable's financial performance?

1	Reliable Answering Service			
2	Trial Balance			
3	December 31, 2011			
4				
5	Cash		$2,160	
6	Accounts Receivable		1,250	
7	Office Supplies		180	
8	Prepaid Insurance		240	
9	Office Equipment		3,400	
10	Accumulated Depreciation--Office Equipment			$ 600
11	Accounts Payable			700
12	Unearned Revenue			460
13	S. Goldstein, Capital			4,870
14	S. Goldstein, Withdrawals		400	
15	Answering Service Revenue			2,900
16	Wages Expense		1,500	
17	Rent Expense		400	
18			$9,530	$9,530
19				

Profitability Measurement: Issues and Ethics

LO1 Define *net income,* and explain the assumptions underlying income measurement and their ethical application.

As you know, profitability and liquidity are the two major goals of a business. For a business to succeed, or even to survive, it must earn a profit. **Profit,** however, means different things to different people. Accountants prefer to use the term **net income** because it can be precisely defined from an accounting point of view as the *net increase in owner's equity that results from a company's operations.*

Net income is reported on the income statement, and management, owners, and others use it to measure a company's progress in meeting the goal of profitability. Readers of income statements need to understand what net income means and be aware of its strengths and weaknesses as a measure of a company's performance.

Net Income

Net income is accumulated in the owner's Capital account. In its simplest form, it is measured as the difference between revenues and expenses when revenues exceed expenses:

$$\text{Net Income} = \text{Revenues} - \text{Expenses}$$

When expenses exceed revenues, a **net loss** occurs.

Study Note

The essence of revenue is that something has been *earned* through the sale of goods or services. That is why cash received through a loan does not constitute revenue.

Revenues are *increases in owner's equity* resulting from selling goods, rendering services, or performing other business activities. When a business delivers a product or provides a service to a customer, it usually receives cash or is promised that it will receive cash in the near future. The amount of cash promised is recorded in either Accounts Receivable or Notes Receivable. The total of these accounts and the total cash received from customers in an accounting period are the company's revenues for that period.

Study Note

The primary purpose of an expense is to generate revenue.

Expenses are *decreases in owner's equity* resulting from the cost of selling goods or rendering services and the cost of the activities necessary to carry on a business, such as attracting and serving customers. In other words, expenses are the cost of the goods and services used in the course of earning revenues. Examples include salaries expense, rent expense, advertising expense, utilities expense, and depreciation (allocation of cost) of a building or office equipment. These expenses are often called the *cost of doing business* or *expired costs.*

Not all increases in owner's equity arise from revenues, nor do all decreases in owner's equity arise from expenses. Owner's investments increase owner's equity but are not revenues, and withdrawals decrease owner's equity but are not expenses.

Income Measurement Assumptions

Users of financial reports should be aware that estimates and assumptions play a major role in the measurement of net income and other key indicators of performance. The management of **Netflix**, the online movie rental company, acknowledges this in its annual report, as follows:

> The preparation of . . . financial statements in conformity with generally accepted accounting principles in the United States requires management to make estimates and assumptions that affect the reported amounts of assets and liabilities, . . . and the reported amount of revenues and expenses.[1]

The major assumptions made in measuring business income have to do with continuity, periodicity, and matching.

Continuity Measuring business income requires that certain expense and revenue transactions be allocated over several accounting periods. Choosing the number of accounting periods raises the issue of **continuity.** What is the expected life of the business? Many businesses last less than five years, and in any given year, thousands of businesses go bankrupt. The majority of companies present annual financial statements on the assumption that the business will continue to operate indefinitely—that is, that the company is a **going concern.** The continuity assumption is as follows:

> Unless there is evidence to the contrary, the accountant assumes that the business will continue to operate indefinitely.

Justification for all the techniques of income measurement rests on the assumption of continuity. Consider, for example, the value of assets on the balance sheet. The continuity assumption allows the cost of certain assets to be held on the balance sheet until a future accounting period, when the cost will become an expense on the income statement.

When a firm is facing bankruptcy, the accountant may set aside the assumption of continuity and prepare financial statements based on the assumption that the firm will go out of business and sell all of its assets at liquidation value—that is, for what they will bring in cash.

Periodicity Measuring business income requires assigning revenues and expenses to a specific accounting period. However, not all transactions can be easily assigned to specific periods. For example, when a company purchases a building, it must estimate the number of years the building will be in use. The portion of the cost of the building that is assigned to each period depends on this estimate and requires an assumption about **periodicity.** The assumption is as follows:

> Although the lifetime of a business is uncertain, it is nonetheless useful to estimate the business's net income in terms of accounting periods.

FOCUS ON BUSINESS PRACTICE

Fiscal Years Vary

The fiscal years of many schools and governmental agencies end on June 30 or September 30. The table at the right shows the last month of the fiscal year of some well-known companies.

Company	*Last Month of Fiscal Year*
Apple Computer	September
Caesars World	July
Fleetwood Enterprises	April
H.J. Heinz	March
Kelly Services	December
MGM-UA Communications	August
Toys "R" Us	January

Study Note

Accounting periods are of equal length so that one period can be compared with the next.

Financial statements may be prepared for any time period, but generally, to make comparisons easier, the periods are of equal length. A 12-month accounting period is called a **fiscal year;** accounting periods of less than a year are called **interim periods.** The fiscal year of many organizations is the calendar year, January 1 to December 31. However, retailers often end their fiscal years during a slack season, and in this case, the fiscal year corresponds to the yearly cycle of business activity.

Matching To measure net income adequately, revenues and expenses must be assigned to the accounting period in which they occur, regardless of when cash is received or paid. This is an application of the **matching rule:**

> Revenues must be assigned to the accounting period in which the goods are sold or the services performed, and expenses must be assigned to the accounting period in which they are used to produce revenue.

In other words, expenses should be recognized in the same accounting period as the revenues to which they are related. However, a direct cause-and-effect relationship between expenses and revenues is often difficult to identify. When there is no direct means of connecting expenses and revenues, costs are allocated in a systematic way among the accounting periods that benefit from the costs. For example, a building's cost is expensed over the building's expected useful life, and interest on investments is recorded as income even though it may not have been received.

The **cash basis of accounting** differs from the matching rule in that it is the practice of accounting for revenues in the period in which cash is received and for expenses in the period in which cash is paid. Some individuals and businesses use this method to account for income taxes. With this method, taxable income is calculated as the difference between cash receipts from revenues and cash payments for expenses.

Although the cash basis of accounting works well for some small businesses and many individuals, it does not meet the needs of most businesses.

Ethics and the Matching Rule

As shown in Figure 3-1, applying the matching rule involves making assumptions. It also involves exercising judgment. Consider the assumptions and judgment involved in estimating the useful life of a building. The estimate should be based

FIGURE 3-1
Assumptions and the Matching Rule

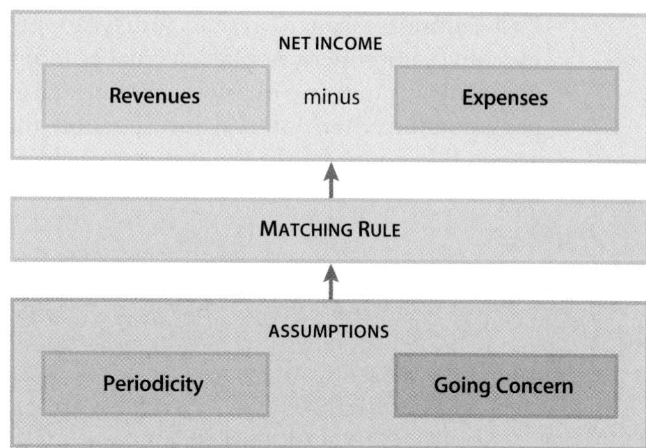

on realistic assumptions, but management has latitude in making that estimate, and its judgment will affect the final net income that is reported.

The manipulation of revenues and expenses to achieve a specific outcome is called **earnings management.** Research has shown that companies that manage their earnings are much more likely to exceed projected earnings targets by a little than to fall short by a little. Why would management want to manage earnings to keep them from falling short? It may want to

- Meet a previously announced goal and thus meet the expectations of the market.
- Keep the company's stock price from dropping.
- Meet a goal that will enable it to earn bonuses.
- Avoid embarrassment.

Earnings management, though not the best practice, is not illegal. However, when the estimates involved in earnings management begin moving outside a reasonable range, the financial statements become misleading. For instance, net income is misleading when revenue is overstated or expenses are understated by significant amounts. As noted earlier in the text, the preparation of financial statements that are intentionally misleading constitutes fraudulent financial reporting.

Most of the enforcement actions that the Securities and Exchange Commission has brought against companies in recent years involve misapplications of the matching rule resulting from improper accrual accounting. For example,

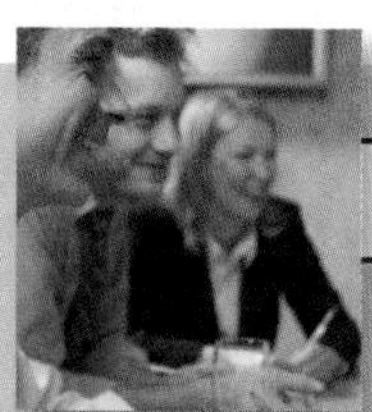

FOCUS ON BUSINESS PRACTICE

Are Misstatements of Earnings Always Overstatements?

Not all misstatements of earnings are overstatements. For instance, privately held companies, which do not have to be concerned about the effect of their earnings announcements on owners or investors, may understate income to reduce or avoid income taxes. In an unusual case involving a public company, the SEC cited and fined **Microsoft** for understating its income. Microsoft, a very successful company, accomplished this by overstating its unearned revenue on the balance sheet. The company's motive in trying to appear less successful than it actually was may have been that it was facing government charges of being a monopoly.[2]

Dell Computer had to restate four years of its financial results because senior executives improperly applied accrual accounting to give the impression that the company was meeting quarterly earnings targets. After the SEC action, the company conducted an internal investigation that resulted in many changes in its accounting controls.[3] In the rest of this chapter, we focus on accrual accounting and its proper application.

STOP & APPLY

Match the assumptions or actions with the concepts below:

_____ 1. Increases in owner's equity resulting from selling goods, rendering services, or performing other business activities

_____ 2. Manipulation of revenues and expenses to achieve a specific change in owner's equity

_____ 3. Increase in owner's equity that results from a company's operations.

_____ 4. Decreases in owner's equity resulting from the cost of selling goods, rendering services, and other business activities.

a. Net income b. Revenues c. Expenses d. Earnings management

SOLUTION

1. b; 2. d; 3. a; 4. c

Accrual Accounting

LO2 Define *accrual accounting,* and explain how it is accomplished.

Accrual accounting encompasses all the techniques accountants use to apply the matching rule. In accrual accounting, revenues and expenses are recorded in the periods in which they occur rather than in the periods in which they are received or paid.

Accrual accounting is accomplished in the following ways:

1. Recording revenues when they are earned.
2. Recording expenses when they are incurred.
3. Adjusting the accounts.

Recognizing Revenues

As you may recall, the process of determining when revenue should be recorded is called **revenue recognition.** The Securities and Exchange Commission requires that all the following conditions be met before revenue is recognized:[4]

- Persuasive evidence of an arrangement exists.
- A product or service has been delivered.
- The seller's price to the buyer is fixed or determinable.
- Collectibility is reasonably assured.

For example, suppose Miller Design Studio has created a brochure for a customer and that the transaction meets the SEC's four criteria: Miller and the

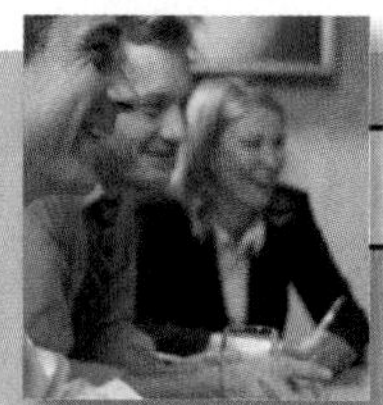

FOCUS ON BUSINESS PRACTICE

Revenue Recognition: Principles Versus Rules

Revenue recognition highlights the differences between international and U.S. accounting standards. Although U.S. standards are referred to as generally accepted accounting *principles*, the FASB has issued extensive *rules* for revenue recognition in various situations and industries. The IASB, on the other hand, has one broad IFRS for revenue recognition and leaves it to companies and their auditors to determine how to apply the broad *principle*. As a result, revenue recognition is an issue that will provide a challenge to achieving international convergence of accounting practices.

customer agree that the customer owes for the service, the service has been rendered, both parties understand the price, and there is a reasonable expectation that the customer will pay the bill. When Miller bills the customer, it records the transaction as revenue by debiting Accounts Receivable and crediting Design Revenue. Note that revenue can be recorded even though cash has not been collected; all that is required is a reasonable expectation that cash will be received.

Recognizing Expenses

Expenses are recorded when there is an agreement to purchase goods or services, the goods have been delivered or the services rendered, a price has been established or can be determined, and the goods or services have been used to produce revenue. For example, when Miller Design Studio receives its utility bill, it recognizes the expense as having been incurred and as having helped produce revenue. Miller records this transaction by debiting Utilities Expense and crediting Accounts Payable. Until the bill is paid, Accounts Payable serves as a holding account. Note that recognition of the expense does not depend on the payment of cash.

Adjusting the Accounts

Accrual accounting also involves adjusting the accounts. Adjustments are necessary because the accounting period, by definition, ends on a particular day. The balance sheet must list all assets and liabilities as of the end of that day, and the income statement must contain all revenues and expenses applicable to the period ending on that day. Although operating a business is a continuous process, there must be a cutoff point for the periodic reports. Some transactions invariably span the cutoff point, and some accounts therefore need adjustment.

Study Note

Even though certain revenues and expenses theoretically change during the period, there usually is no need to adjust them until the end of the period, when the financial statements are prepared.

As you can see in Exhibit 3-1, some of the accounts in Miller Design Studio's trial balance as of July 31 do not show the correct balances for preparing the financial statements. The trial balance lists prepaid rent of $3,200. At $1,600 per month, this represents rent for the months of July and August. So, on July 31, one-half of the $3,200 represents rent expense for July, and the remaining $1,600 represents an asset that will be used in August. An adjustment is needed to reflect the $1,600 balance in the Prepaid Rent account on the balance sheet and the $1,600 rent expense on the income statement.

As you will see, several other accounts in Miller Design Studio's trial balance do not reflect their correct balances. Like the Prepaid Rent account, they need to be adjusted.

EXHIBIT 3-1
Trial Balance

Miller Design Studio Trial Balance July 31, 2011		
Cash	$22,480	
Accounts Receivable	4,600	
Office Supplies	5,200	
Prepaid Rent	3,200	
Office Equipment	16,320	
Accounts Payable		$ 6,280
Unearned Design Revenue		1,400
J. Miller, Capital		40,000
J. Miller, Withdrawals	2,800	
Design Revenue		12,400
Wages Expense	4,800	
Utilities Expense	680	
	$60,080	$60,080

Adjustments and Ethics

Accrual accounting can be difficult to understand. The account adjustments take time to calculate and enter in the records. Also, adjusting entries do not affect cash flows in the current period because they never involve the Cash account. You might ask, "Why go to all the trouble of making them? Why worry about them?" For one thing, the SEC has identified issues related to accrual accounting and adjustments as an area of utmost importance because of the potential for abuse and misrepresentation.[5]

All adjustments are important because of their effect on performance measures of profitability and liquidity. Adjusting entries affect net income on the income statement, and they affect profitability comparisons from one accounting period to the next. They also affect assets and liabilities on the balance sheet and thus provide information about a company's *future* cash inflows and outflows. This information is needed to assess management's performance in achieving sufficient liquidity to meet the need for cash to pay ongoing obligations. The potential for abuse arises because considerable judgment underlies the application of adjusting entries. When this judgment is misused, performance measures can be misleading.

STOP & APPLY >

Four conditions must be met before revenue can be recognized. Identify which of these conditions applies to the following actions:

a. Determines that the firm has a good credit rating.
b. Agrees to a price for services before it performs them.
c. Performs services.
d. Signs a contract to perform services.

SOLUTION

a. Collectibility is reasonably assured.
b. The seller's price to the buyer is fixed or determinable.
c. A product or service has been delivered.
d. Persuasive evidence of an arrangement exists.

The Adjustment Process

LO3 Identify four situations that require adjusting entries, and illustrate typical adjusting entries.

When transactions span more than one accounting period, accrual accounting requires the use of **adjusting entries.** Figure 3-2 shows the four situations in which adjusting entries must be made. Each adjusting entry affects one balance sheet account and one income statement account. As we have already noted, adjusting entries never affect the Cash account.

The four types of adjusting entries are as follows:

Type 1. Allocating recorded costs between two or more accounting periods. Examples of these costs are prepayments of rent, insurance, and supplies and the depreciation of plant and equipment. The adjusting entry in this case involves an asset account and an expense account.

Type 2. Recognizing unrecorded, incurred expenses. Examples of these expenses are wages and interest that have been incurred but are not recorded during an accounting period. The adjusting entry involves an expense account and a liability account.

Type 3. Allocating recorded, unearned revenues between two or more accounting periods. Examples include cash received in advance and deposits made on goods or services. The adjusting entry involves a liability account and a revenue account.

Type 4. Recognizing unrecorded, earned revenues. An example is revenue that a company has earned for providing a service but for which it has not billed or collected a fee by the end of the accounting period. The adjusting entry involves an asset account and a revenue account.

> **Study Note**
>
> Adjusting entries provide information about past or future cash flows but never involve an entry to the Cash account.

Adjusting entries are either deferrals or accruals.

- A **deferral** is the postponement of the recognition of an expense already paid (Type 1 adjustment) or of revenue received in advance (Type 3 adjustment). The cash payment or receipt is recorded before the adjusting entry is made.
- An **accrual** is the recognition of a revenue (Type 4 adjustment) or expense (Type 2 adjustment) that has arisen but not been recorded during the accounting period. The cash receipt or payment occurs in a future accounting period, after the adjusting entry has been made.

Type 1 Adjustment: Allocating Recorded Costs (Deferred Expenses)

Companies often make expenditures that benefit more than one period. These costs are debited to an asset account. At the end of an accounting period, the

FIGURE 3-2
The Four Types of Adjustments

INCOME STATEMENT \ BALANCE SHEET	Asset	Liability
Expense	1. Allocating recorded costs between two or more accounting periods.	2. Recognizing unrecorded, incurred expenses.
Revenue	4. Recognizing unrecorded, earned revenues.	3. Allocating recorded, unearned revenues between two or more accounting periods.

When transactions span more than one accounting period, an adjusting entry is necessary. Depreciation of plant and equipment, such as that found in this warehouse, is a type of transaction that requires an adjusting entry. In this case, the adjusting entry involves an asset account and an expense account.

Courtesy of Timothy Babasade/ istockphoto.com.

amount of the asset that has been used is transferred from the asset account to an expense account. Two important adjustments of this type are for prepaid expenses and the depreciation of plant and equipment.

Study Note

The expired portion of a prepayment is converted to an expense; the unexpired portion remains an asset.

Prepaid Expenses Companies customarily pay some expenses, including those for rent, supplies, and insurance, in advance. These costs are called **prepaid expenses.** By the end of an accounting period, a portion or all of prepaid services or goods will have been used or have expired. The required adjusting entry reduces the asset and increases the expense, as shown in Figure 3-3. The amount of the adjustment equals the cost of the goods or services used or expired.

FIGURE 3-3
Adjustment for Prepaid (Deferred) Expenses

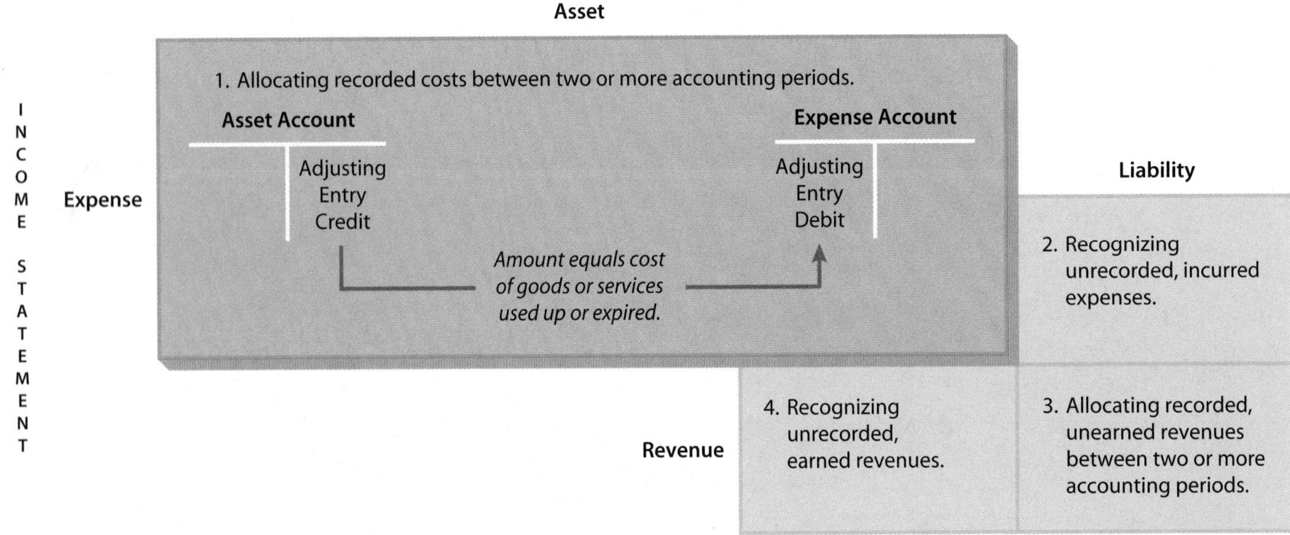

If adjusting entries for prepaid expenses are not made at the end of an accounting period, both the balance sheet and the income statement will present incorrect information. The company's assets will be overstated, and its expenses will be understated. Thus, owner's equity on the balance sheet and net income on the income statement will be overstated.

To illustrate this type of adjusting entry and the others discussed below, we refer again to the transactions of Miller Design Studio.

At the beginning of July, Miller Design Studio paid two months' rent in advance. The advance payment resulted in an asset consisting of the right to occupy the office for two months. As each day in the month passed, part of the asset's cost expired and became an expense. By July 31, one-half of the asset's cost had expired and had to be treated as an expense. The adjustment is as follows:

Adjustment for Prepaid Rent

July 31: Expiration of one month's rent, $1,600.

Analysis: Expiration of prepaid rent *decreases* the asset account *Prepaid Rent* with a credit and *increases* the owner's equity account *Rent Expense* with a debit.

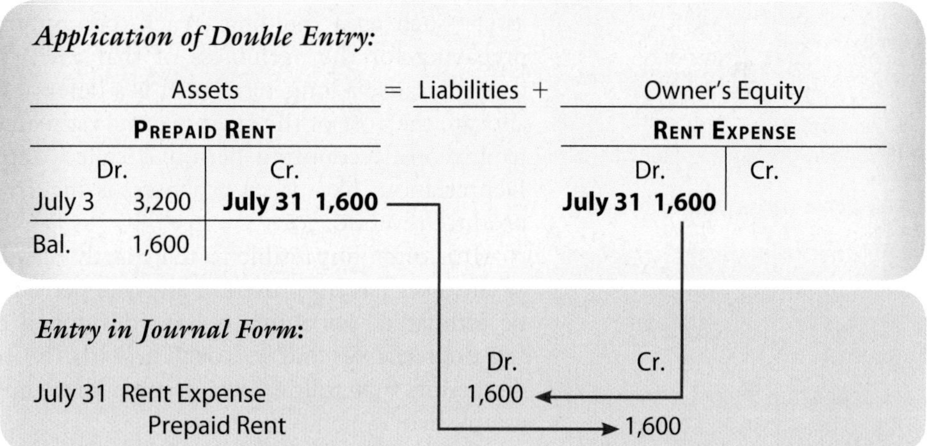

Comment: The Prepaid Rent account now has a balance of $1,600, which represents one month's rent that will be expensed during August. The logic in this analysis applies to all prepaid expenses.

Miller Design Studio purchased $5,200 of office supplies in early July. A careful inventory of the supplies is made at the end of the month. It records the number and cost of supplies that have not yet been consumed and are thus still assets of the company. Suppose the inventory shows that office supplies costing $3,660 are still on hand. This means that of the $5,200 of supplies originally purchased, $1,540 worth were used (became an expense) in July. The adjustment is as follows:

Adjustment for Supplies

July 31: Consumption of supplies, $1,540

Analysis: Consumption of office supplies *decreases* the asset account *Office Supplies* with a credit and *increases* the expense account *Office Supplies Expense* with a debit.

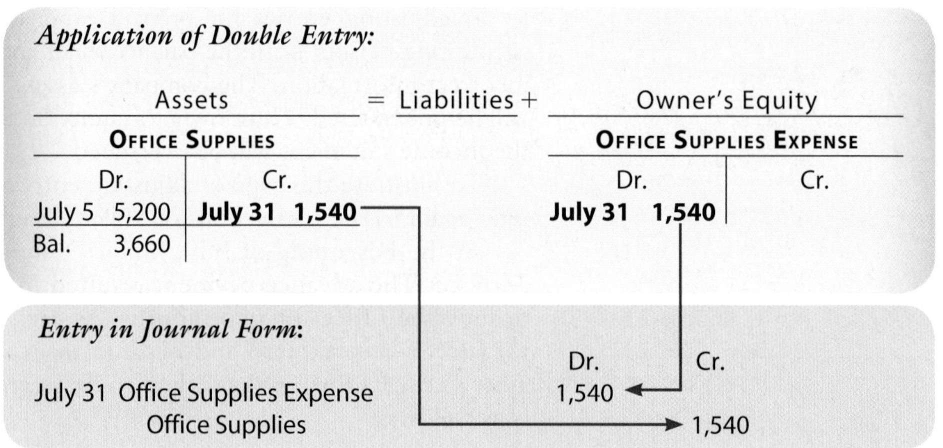

Comment: The asset account Office Supplies now reflects the correct balance of $3,660 of supplies yet to be consumed. The logic in this example applies to all kinds of supplies.

> **Study Note**
> In accounting, depreciation refers only to the *allocation* of an asset's cost, not to any decline in the asset's value.

> **Study Note**
> The difficulty in estimating an asset's useful life is further evidence that the net income figure is, at best, an estimate.

Depreciation of Plant and Equipment When a company buys a long-term asset—such as a building, truck, computer, or store fixture—it is, in effect, prepaying for the usefulness of that asset for as long as it benefits the company. Because a long-term asset is a deferral of an expense, the accountant must allocate the cost of the asset over its estimated useful life. The amount allocated to any one accounting period is called **depreciation,** or *depreciation expense.* Depreciation, like other expenses, is incurred during an accounting period to produce revenue.

It is often impossible to tell exactly how long an asset will last or how much of the asset has been used in any one period. For this reason, depreciation must be estimated. Accountants have developed a number of methods for estimating depreciation and for dealing with the related complex problems. (In the discussion that follows, we assume that the amount of depreciation has been established.)

To maintain historical cost in specific long-term asset accounts, separate accounts—called **Accumulated Depreciation accounts**—are used to accumulate the depreciation on each long-term asset. These accounts, which are deducted from their related asset accounts on the balance sheet, are called *contra accounts.* A **contra account** is a separate account that is paired with a related account—in this case, an asset account. The balance of a contra account is shown on a financial statement as a deduction from its related account. The net amount is called the **carrying value,** or *book value,* of the asset. As the months pass, the amount of the accumulated depreciation grows, and the carrying value of the asset declines.

Adjustment for Plant and Equipment

July 31: Depreciation of office equipment, $300

Analysis: Depreciation *decreases* the asset account *Office Equipment* by *increasing* the contra account *Accumulated Depreciation–Office Equipment* with a credit and *increasing* the owner's equity account *Depreciation Expense–Office Equipment* with a debit.

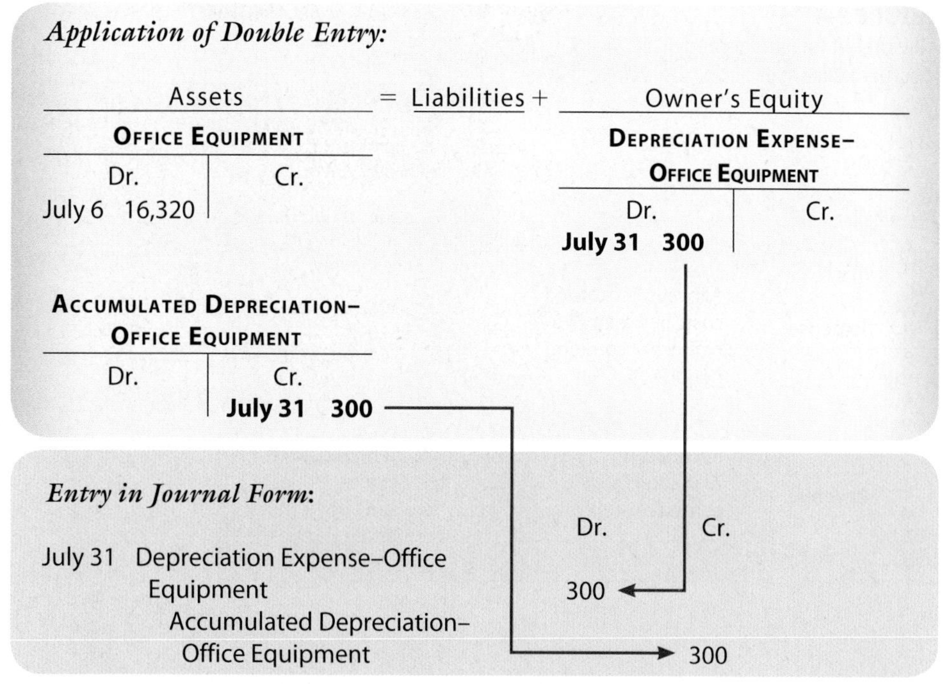

Comment: The carrying value of Office Equipment is $16,020 ($16,320 − $300) and is presented on the balance sheet as follows:

Property, Plant, and Equipment		
Office equipment	$16,320	
Less accumulated depreciation	300	$16,020

Application to Netflix, Inc. **Netflix** has prepaid expenses and property and equipment similar to those in the examples we have presented. Among Netflix's prepaid expenses are payments made in advance to movie companies for rights to DVDs. By paying in advance, Netflix is able to negotiate lower prices. These fixed payments are debited to Prepaid Expense. When the movies produce revenue, the prepaid amounts are transferred to expense through adjusting entries.[6]

Type 2 Adjustment: Recognizing Unrecorded, Incurred Expenses (Accrued Expenses)

Study Note

Remember that in accrual accounting, an expense must be recorded in the period in which it is incurred regardless of when payment is made.

Usually, at the end of an accounting period, some expenses incurred during the period have not been recorded in the accounts. These expenses require adjusting entries. One such expense is interest on borrowed money. Each day, interest accumulates on the debt. As shown in Figure 3-4, at the end of the accounting period, an adjusting entry is made to record the accumulated interest, which is an expense of the period, and the corresponding liability to pay the interest. Other common unrecorded expenses are wages and utilities. As the expense and the corresponding liability accumulate, they are said to *accrue*—hence, the term **accrued expenses.**

To illustrate how adjustments are made for unrecorded, incurred wages, suppose Miller Design Studio has two pay periods a month rather than one. In July, its pay periods end on the 12th and the 26th, as indicated in the calendar on the next page.

FIGURE 3-4
Adjustment for Unrecorded (Accrued) Expenses

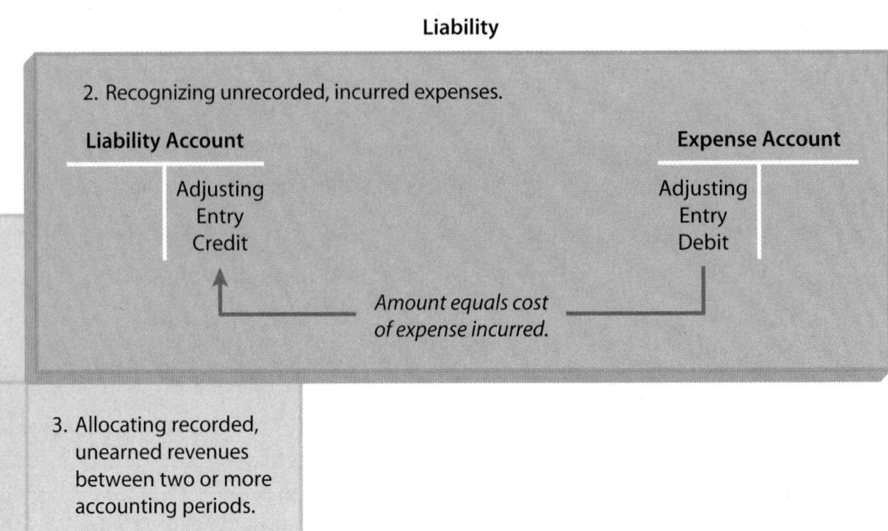

JULY

SUN	M	T	W	TH	F	SAT
	1	2	3	4	5	6
7	8	9	10	11	**12**	13
14	15	16	17	18	19	20
21	22	23	24	25	**26**	27
28	29	30	31			

By the end of business on July 31, Miller's assistant will have worked three days (Monday, Tuesday, and Wednesday) beyond the last pay period. The employee has earned the wages for those days but will not be paid until the first payday in August. The wages for these three days are rightfully an expense for July, and the liabilities should reflect that the company owes the assistant for those days. Because the assistant's wage rate is \$2,400 every two weeks, or \$240 per day (\$2,400 ÷ 10 working days), the expense is \$720 (\$240 × 3 days).

Adjustment for Unrecorded Wages

July 31: Accrual of unrecorded wages, \$720

Analysis: Accrual of wages *increases* the owner's equity account *Wages Expense* with a debit and *increases* the liability account *Wages Payable* with a credit.

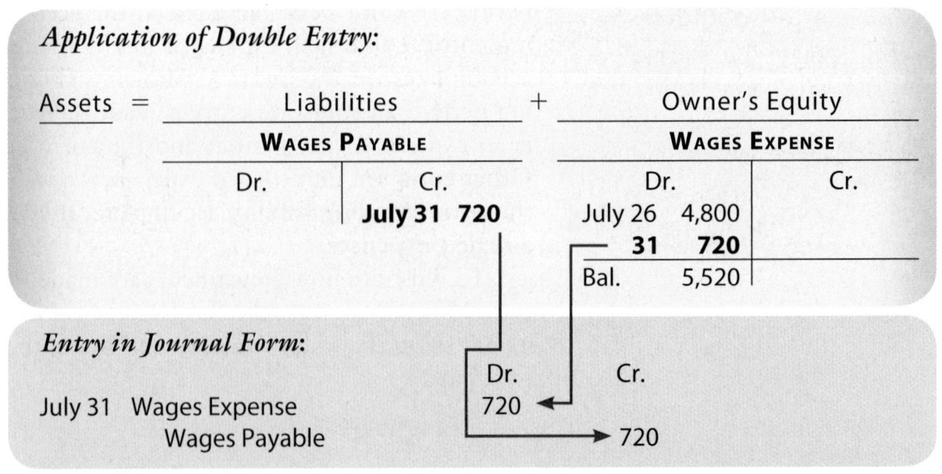

Comment: Note that the increase in Wages Expense will *decrease* owner's equity and that total wages for the month are $5,520, of which $720 will be paid next month.

Application to Netflix, Inc. In 2008, **Netflix** had accrued expenses of $31,394,000.[7] If the expenses had not been accrued, Netflix's liabilities would be significantly understated, as would the corresponding expenses on Netflix's income statement. The end result would be an overstatement of the company's earnings.

Type 3 Adjustment: Allocating Recorded, Unearned Revenues (Deferred Revenues)

> **Study Note**
>
> Unearned revenue is a liability because there is an obligation to deliver goods or perform a service, or to return the payment. Once the goods have been delivered or the service performed, the liability is transferred to revenue.

Just as expenses can be paid before they are used, revenues can be received before they are earned. When a company receives revenues in advance, it has an obligation to deliver goods or perform services. **Unearned revenues** are therefore shown in a liability account.

For example, publishing companies usually receive cash in advance for magazine subscriptions. These receipts are recorded in a liability account, Unearned Subscriptions. If the company fails to deliver the magazines, subscribers are entitled to their money back. As the company delivers each issue of the magazine, it earns a part of the advance receipts. This earned portion must be transferred from the Unearned Subscriptions account to the Subscription Revenue account, as shown in Figure 3-5.

During July, Miller Design Studio received $1,400 from another firm as advance payment for a series of brochures. By the end of the month, it had completed $800 of work on the brochures, and the other firm had accepted the work.

Adjustment for Unearned Revenue

July 31: Performance of services for which cash was received in advance, $800

Analysis: Performing the services for which cash was received in advance *increases* the owner's equity account *Design Revenue* with a credit and *decreases* the liability account *Unearned Design Revenue* with a debit.

FIGURE 3-5
Adjustment for Unearned (Deferred) Revenues

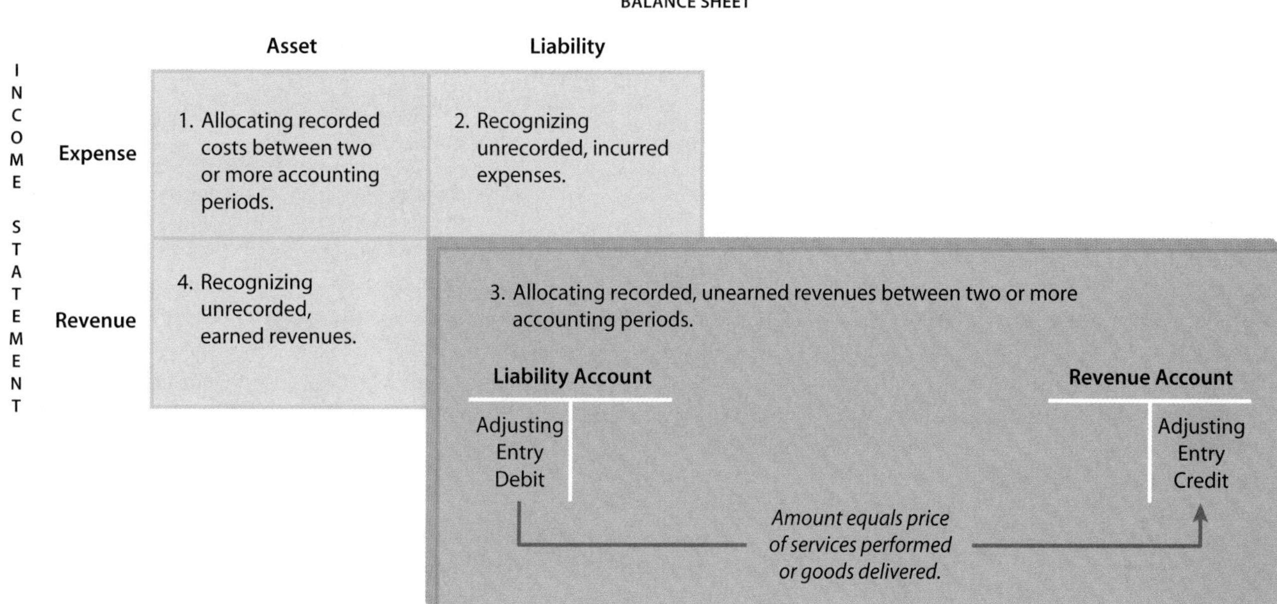

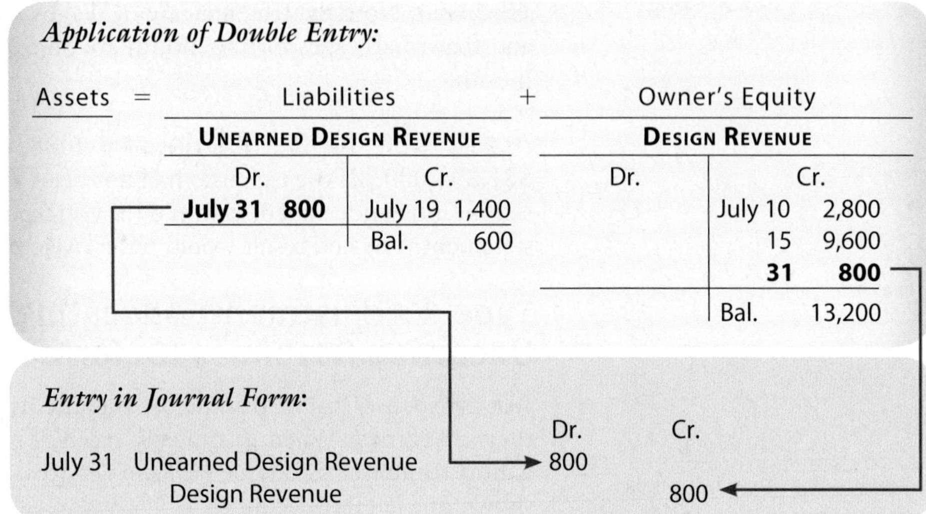

Comment: Unearned Design Revenue now reflects the amount of work still to be performed, $600.

Application to Netflix, Inc. **Netflix** has a current liability account called Deferred (Unearned) Revenue. Deferred revenue consists of subscriptions (monthly payments) billed in advance to customers for which revenues have not yet been earned. Subscription revenues are recognized by prorating them over each subscriber's monthly subscription period. As time passes and customers use the service, the revenue is transferred from Netflix's Deferred Revenue account to its Subscription Revenue account.

Type 4 Adjustment: Recognizing Unrecorded, Earned Revenues (Accrued Revenues)

Accrued revenues are revenues that a company has earned by performing a service or delivering goods but for which no entry has been made in the accounting records. Any revenues earned but not recorded during an accounting period require an adjusting entry that debits an asset account and credits a revenue account, as shown in Figure 3-6. For example, the interest on a note

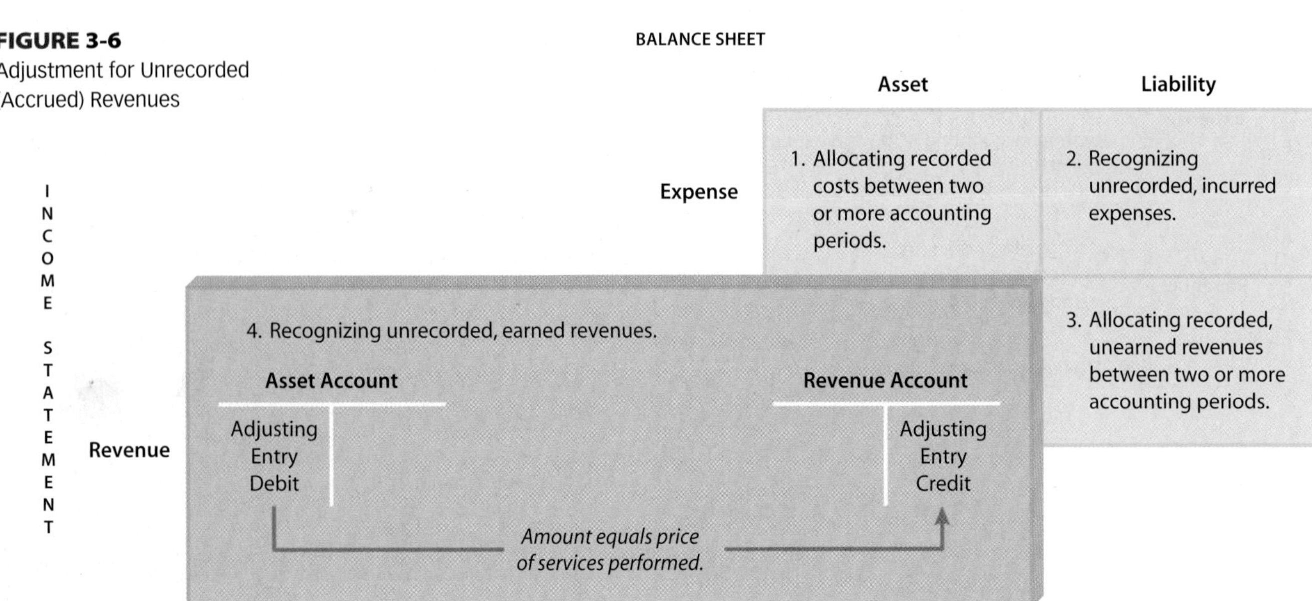

FIGURE 3-6
Adjustment for Unrecorded (Accrued) Revenues

receivable is earned day by day but may not be received until another accounting period. The Interest Receivable account should be debited and the Interest Income account should be credited for the interest accrued at the end of the current period.

When a company earns revenue by performing a service—such as designing a series of brochures or developing marketing plans—but will not receive the revenue for the service until a future accounting period, it must make an adjusting entry. This type of adjusting entry involves an asset account and a revenue account.

During July, Miller Design Studio agreed to create two advertisements for Maggio's Pizza Company. It also agreed that the first advertisement would be finished by July 31. By the end of the month, Miller had earned $400 for completing the first advertisement. The client will not be billed until the entire project has been completed.

Adjustment for Design Revenue

July 31: Accrual of unrecorded revenue, $400

Analysis: Accrual of unrecorded revenue *increases* the owner's equity account *Design Revenue* with a credit and *increases* the asset account *Accounts Receivable* with a debit.

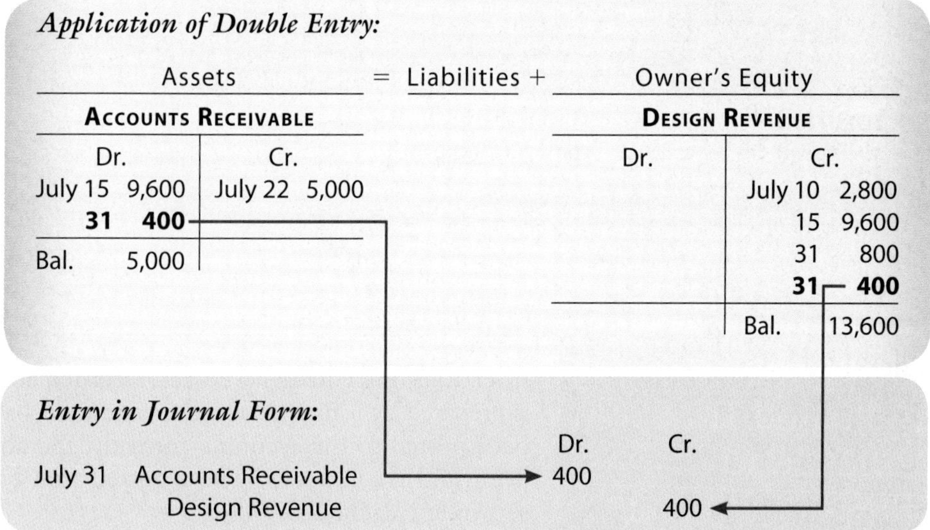

Comment: Design Revenue now reflects the total revenue earned during July, $13,600. Some companies prefer to debit an account called Unbilled Accounts Receivable. Other companies simply flag the transactions in Accounts Receivable as "unbilled." On the balance sheet, they are usually combined with accounts receivable.

Application to Netflix, Inc. Since **Netflix**'s subscribers pay their subscriptions in advance by credit card, Netflix does not need to bill customers for services provided but not paid. The company is in the enviable position of having no accounts receivable and thus a high degree of liquidity.

A Note About Journal Entries

Thus far, we have presented a full analysis of each journal entry. The analyses showed you the thought process behind each entry. By now, you should be fully aware of the effects of transactions on the accounting equation and the rules of debit and credit. For this reason, in the rest of the book, we present journal entries without full analysis.

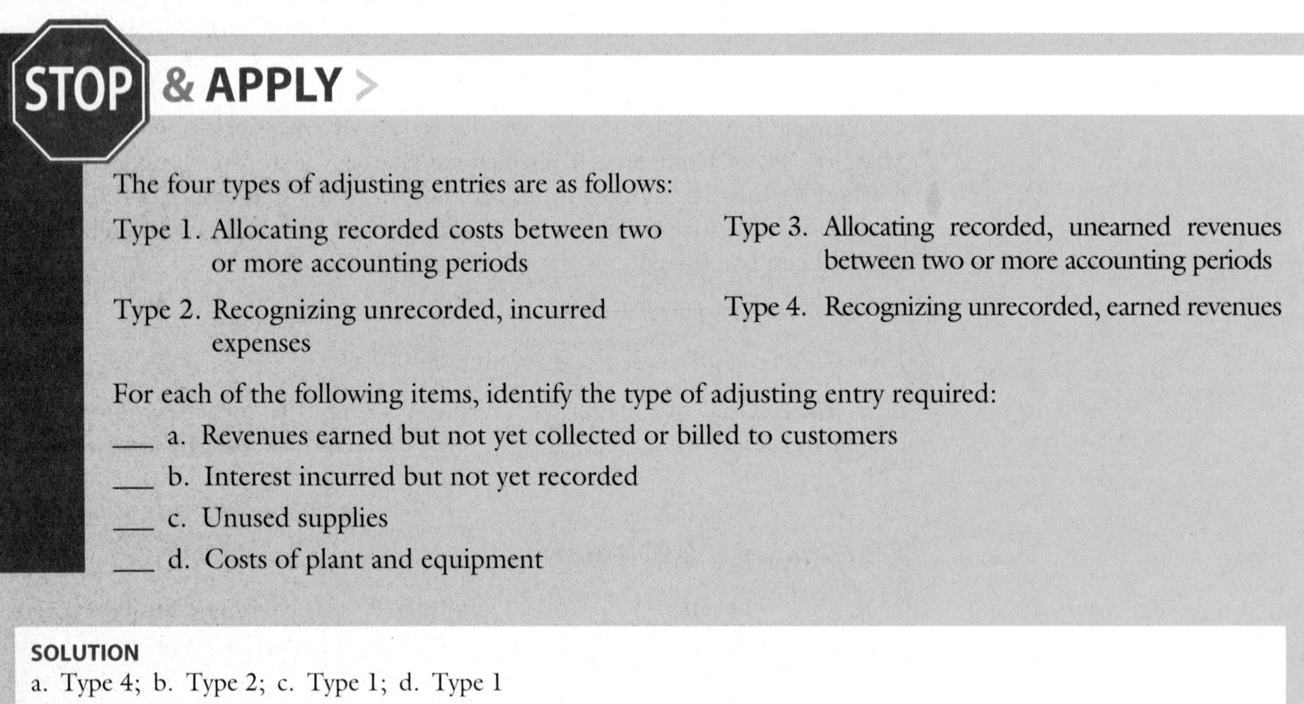

STOP & APPLY >

The four types of adjusting entries are as follows:

Type 1. Allocating recorded costs between two or more accounting periods

Type 2. Recognizing unrecorded, incurred expenses

Type 3. Allocating recorded, unearned revenues between two or more accounting periods

Type 4. Recognizing unrecorded, earned revenues

For each of the following items, identify the type of adjusting entry required:

___ a. Revenues earned but not yet collected or billed to customers

___ b. Interest incurred but not yet recorded

___ c. Unused supplies

___ d. Costs of plant and equipment

SOLUTION

a. Type 4; b. Type 2; c. Type 1; d. Type 1

Using the Adjusted Trial Balance to Prepare Financial Statements

LO4 Prepare financial statements from an adjusted trial balance.

After adjusting entries have been recorded and posted, an **adjusted trial balance** is prepared by listing all accounts and their balances. If the adjusting entries have been posted to the accounts correctly, the adjusted trial balance will have equal debit and credit totals. The adjusted trial balance for Miller Design Studio is shown in Exhibit 3-2.

Some accounts in Exhibit 3-2, such as Cash and Accounts Payable, have the same balances as in the trial balance in Exhibit 3-1 because no adjusting entries affected them. The balances of other accounts, such as Office Supplies and Prepaid Rent, differ from those in the trial balance because adjusting entries did affect them. The adjusted trial balance also has some new accounts, such as depreciation accounts and Wages Payable, that are not in the trial balance.

The adjusted trial balance facilitates the preparation of the financial statements. As shown in Exhibit 3-2, the revenue and expense accounts are used to prepare the income statement.

EXHIBIT 3-2 Relationship of the Adjusted Trial Balance to the Income Statement

Miller Design Studio
Adjusted Trial Balance
July 31, 2011

Cash	$22,480	
Accounts Receivable	5,000	
Office Supplies	3,660	
Prepaid Rent	1,600	
Office Equipment	16,320	
Accumulated Depreciation–Office Equipment		$ 300
Accounts Payable		6,280
Unearned Design Revenue		600
Wages Payable		720
J. Miller, Capital		40,000
J. Miller, Withdrawals	2,800	
Design Revenue		13,600
Wages Expense	5,520	
Utilities Expense	680	
Rent Expense	1,600	
Office Supplies Expense	1,540	
Depreciation Expense–Office Equipment	300	
	$61,500	$61,500

Miller Design Studio
Income Statement
For the Month Ended July 31, 2011

Revenues		
Design revenue		$13,600
Expenses		
Wages expense	$5,520	
Utilities expense	680	
Rent expense	1,600	
Office supplies expense	1,540	
Depreciation expense–office equipment	300	
Total expenses		9,640
Net income		$ 3,960

Study Note

The net income figure from the income statement is needed to prepare the statement of owner's equity, and the bottom-line figure of that statement is needed to prepare the balance sheet. This dictates the order in which the statements are prepared.

Study Note

The adjusted trial balance is a second check that the ledger is still in balance. Because it reflects updated information from the adjusting entries, it is used in preparing the formal financial statements. It does not mean there are no accounting errors.

Then, as shown in Exhibit 3-3, the statement of owner's equity and the balance sheet are prepared. Notice that the net income from the income statement is combined with the Withdrawals account on the statement of owner's equity to give the net change in the J. Miller, Capital account.

The resulting balance of J. Miller, Capital at July 31 is used in preparing the balance sheet, as are the asset and liability account balances in the adjusted trial balance.

EXHIBIT 3-3 Relationship of the Adjusted Trial Balance to the Balance Sheet and Statement of Owner's Equity

Miller Design Studio
Adjusted Trial Balance
July 31, 2011

Cash	$22,480	
Accounts Receivable	5,000	
Office Supplies	3,660	
Prepaid Rent	1,600	
Office Equipment	16,320	
Accumulated Depreciation–Office Equipment		$ 300
Accounts Payable		6,280
Unearned Design Revenue		600
Wages Payable		720
J. Miller, Capital		40,000
J. Miller, Withdrawals	2,800	
Design Revenue		13,600
Wages Expense	5,520	
Utilities Expense	680	
Rent Expense	1,600	
Office Supplies Expense	1,540	
Depreciation Expense–Office Equipment	300	
	$61,500	$61,500

Miller Design Studio
Balance Sheet
July 31, 2011

Assets

Cash		$22,480
Accounts receivable		5,000
Office supplies		3,660
Prepaid rent		1,600
Office equipment	$16,320	
Less accumulated depreciation	300	16,020
Total assets		$48,760

Liabilities

Accounts payable	$ 6,280
Unearned design revenue	600
Wages payable	720
Total liabilities	$ 7,600

Owner's Equity

J. Miller, Capital	41,160
Total liabilities and owner's equity	$48,760

Miller Design Studio
Statement of Owner's Equity
For the Month Ended July 31, 2011

J. Miller, Capital, July 1, 2011	$ 0
Investment by J. Miller	40,000
Net income	3,960
Subtotal	$43,960
Less withdrawals	2,800
J. Miller, Capital, July 31, 2011	$41,160

The adjusted trial balance for Carroll Company on December 31, 2010, contains the following accounts and balances: D. Carroll, Capital, $300; D. Carroll, Withdrawals, $100; Service Revenue, $1,000; Rent Expense, $300; Wages Expense, $400; and Telephone Expense, $100. Compute net income and prepare a statement of owner's equity in proper form for the month of December.

SOLUTION

Net income = $1,000 − $300 − $400 − $100
= $1,000 − $800
= $200

Carroll Company
Statement of Owner's Equity
For the Month Ended December 31, 2010

D. Carroll, Capital, Dec. 1, 2010	$ 300
Net income	200
Subtotal	$ 500
Less withdrawals	100
D. Carroll, Capital, Dec. 31, 2010	$ 400

Cash Flows from Accrual-Based Information

LO5 Use accrual-based information to analyze cash flows.

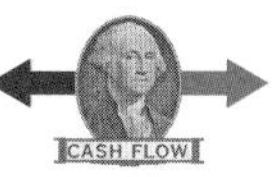

Study Note

Income as determined by accrual accounting is important to a company's profitability. Cash flows are related to a company's liquidity. Both are important to a company's success.

Management has the short-range goal of ensuring that its company has sufficient cash to pay ongoing obligations—in other words, management must ensure the company's liquidity. To plan payments to creditors and assess the need for short-term borrowing, managers must know how to use accrual-based information to analyze cash flows.

Almost every revenue or expense account on the income statement has one or more related accounts on the balance sheet. For instance, Office Supplies Expense is related to Office Supplies, Wages Expense is related to Wages Payable, and Design Revenue is related to Unearned Design Revenue. As we have shown, these accounts are related by making adjusting entries, the purpose of which is to apply the matching rule to the measurement of net income.

The cash inflows that a company's operations generate and the cash outflows that they require can also be determined by analyzing these relationships. For example, suppose that after receiving the financial statements in Exhibits 3-2 and 3-3, management wants to know how much cash was expended for office supplies. On the income statement, Office Supplies Expense is $1,540, and on the balance sheet, Office Supplies is $3,660. Because July was the company's first month of operation, there was no prior balance of office supplies, so the amount of cash expended for office supplies during the month was $5,200 ($1,540 + $3,660 = $5,200).

Thus, the cash flow used in purchasing office supplies—$5,200—was much greater than the amount expensed in determining income—$1,540. In planning for August, management can anticipate that the cash needed may be less than the amount expensed because, given the large inventory of office supplies, the company will probably not have to buy office supplies in the coming month. Understanding these cash flow effects enables management to better predict the business's need for cash in August.

The general rule for determining the cash flow received from any revenue or paid for any expense (except depreciation, which is a special case not covered here) is to determine the potential cash payments or cash receipts and deduct the amount not paid or not received. As shown below, the application of the general rule varies with the type of asset or liability account:

Type of Account	*Potential Payment or Receipt Not Paid or Received*		*Result*
Prepaid Expense	Ending Balance + Expense for the Period − Beginning Balance	=	Cash Payments for Expenses
Unearned Revenue	Ending Balance + Revenue for the Period − Beginning Balance	=	Cash Receipts from Revenues
Accrued Expense	Beginning Balance + Expense for the Period − Ending Balance	=	Cash Payments for Expenses
Accrued Revenue	Beginning Balance + Revenue for the Period − Ending Balance	=	Cash Receipts from Revenues

For instance, suppose that on May 31, a company had a balance of $480 in Prepaid Insurance and that on June 30, the balance was $670. If the insurance expense during June was $120, the amount of cash expended on insurance during June can be computed as follows:

Prepaid Insurance at June 30	$670
Insurance Expense during June	120
Potential cash payments for insurance	$790
Less Prepaid Insurance at May 31	480
Cash payments for insurance during June	$310

The beginning balance is deducted because it was paid in a prior accounting period. Note that the cash payments equal the expense plus the increase in the balance of the Prepaid Insurance account [$120 + ($670 − $480) = $310]. In this case, the cash paid was almost three times the amount of insurance expense. In future months, cash payments are likely to be less than the expense.

STOP & APPLY >

Supplies had a balance of $400 at the end of May and $360 at the end of June. Supplies Expense was $550 for the month of June. How much cash was received for services provided during June?

SOLUTION

Supplies at June 30	$360
Supplies Expense during June	550
Potential cash payments for supplies	$910
Less Supplies at May 31	400
Cash payments for supplies during June	$510

▸ RELIABLE ANSWERING SERVICE: REVIEW PROBLEM

In the Decision Point at the beginning of the chapter, we noted that Reliable Answering Service has many transactions that span accounting periods. We asked these questions:

- What assumptions must Reliable Answering Service make to account for transactions that span accounting periods?
- How does Reliable assign its revenues and expenses to the proper accounting period so that net income is properly measured?
- Why are the adjustments that these transactions require important to Reliable's financial performance?

Two of the assumptions Reliable must make are that it will continue as a going concern for an indefinite time (the continuity assumption) and that it can make useful estimates of its income in terms of accounting periods (the periodicity assumption). These assumptions enable the company to apply the matching rule—that is, revenues are assigned to the accounting period in which goods are sold or services are performed, and expenses are assigned to the accounting period in which they are used to produce revenue. These adjustments are important in order to measure net income adequately.

Posting to T Accounts, Determining Adjusting Entries, and Using an Adjusted Trial Balance to Prepare Financial Statements
LO3 LO4

In addition to Reliable's trial balance, which appears at the beginning of the chapter, the following information is also available for the company on December 31, 2011:

- Why are the adjustments that these transactions require important to Reliable's financial performance?
  a. Insurance that expired during December amounted to $40.
  b. Office supplies on hand on December 31 totaled $75.
  c. Depreciation for December totaled $100.
  d. Accrued wages on December 31 totaled $120.
  e. Revenues earned for services performed in December but not billed by the end of the month totaled $300.
  f. Revenues received in December in advance of services yet to be performed totaled $160.

Required

1. Prepare T accounts for the accounts in the trial balance, and enter the balances.
2. Determine the required adjusting entries, and record them directly in the T accounts. Open new T accounts as needed.
3. Prepare an adjusted trial balance.
4. Prepare an income statement, a statement of owner's equity, and a balance sheet for the month ended December 31, 2011.
5. User insight: Which accounts on Reliable's income statement are potentially affected by adjusting entries? Which account on Reliable's balance sheet is never affected by an adjusting entry?

Answers to Review Problem

1. T accounts set up and amounts from trial balance entered
2. Adjusting entries recorded

	A	B	C	D	E	F	G	H	I	J	K	L	M	N
1	**Cash**					**Accounts Receivable**					**Office Supplies**			
2	Bal.	2,160				Bal.	1,250				Bal.	180	(b)	105
3						(e)	300				*Bal.*	*75*		
4						*Bal.*	*1,550*							
5											**Accumulated Depreciation--**			
6	**Prepaid Insurance**					**Office Equipment**					**Office Equipment**			
7	Bal.	240	(a)	40		Bal.	3,400						Bal.	600
8	*Bal.*	200											(c)	100
9													*Bal.*	*700*
10														
11	**Accounts Payable**					**Unearned Revenue**					**Wages Payable**			
12			Bal.	700		(f)	160	Bal.	460				(d)	120
13								*Bal.*	*300*					
14											**Answering**			
15	**S. Goldstein, Capital**					**S. Goldstein, Withdrawals**					**Service Revenue**			
16			Bal.	4,870		Bal.	400						Bal.	2,900
17													(e)	300
18													(f)	160
19													*Bal.*	*3,360*
20														
21	**Wages Expense**					**Rent Expense**					**Insurance Expense**			
22	Bal.	1,500				Bal.	400				(a)	40		
23	(d)	120												
24	*Bal.*	*1,620*												
25						**Depreciation Expense--**								
26	**Office Supplies Expense**					**Office Equipment**								
27	(b)	105				(c)	100							
28														

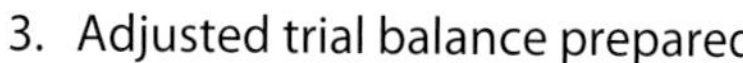

3. Adjusted trial balance prepared

Reliable Answering Service Adjusted Trial Balance December 31, 2011		
Cash	$ 2,160	
Accounts Receivable	1,550	
Office Supplies	75	
Prepaid Insurance	200	
Office Equipment	3,400	
Accumulated Depreciation--Office Equipment		$ 700
Accounts Payable		700
Unearned Revenue		300
Wages Payable		120
S. Goldstein, Capital		4,870
S. Goldstein, Withdrawals	400	
Answering Service Revenue		3,360
Wages Expense	1,620	
Rent Expense	400	
Insurance Expense	40	
Office Supplies Expense	105	
Depreciation Expense--Office Equipment	100	
	$10,050	$10,050

4. Financial statements prepared

Reliable Answering Service Income Statement For the Month Ended December 31, 2011		
Revenues		
Answering service revenue		$3,360
Expenses		
Wages expense	$1,620	
Rent expense	400	
Insurance Expense	40	
Office Supplies Expense	105	
Depreciation Expense--Office Equipment	100	
Total expenses		2,265
Net income		$1,095

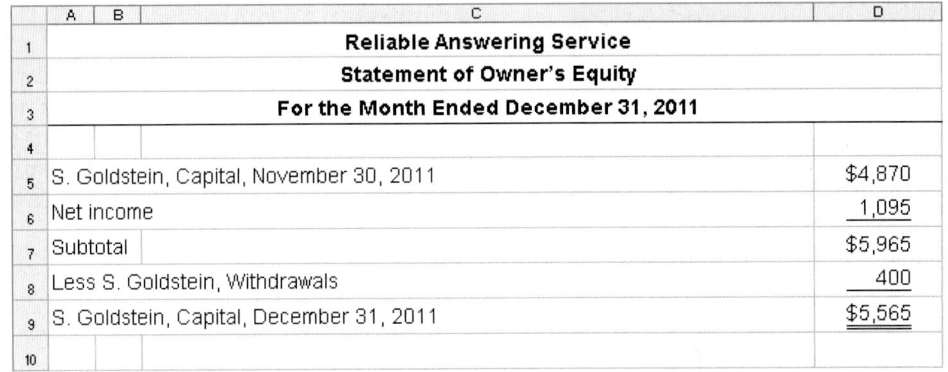

Reliable Answering Service	
Statement of Owner's Equity	
For the Month Ended December 31, 2011	
S. Goldstein, Capital, November 30, 2011	$4,870
Net income	1,095
Subtotal	$5,965
Less S. Goldstein, Withdrawals	400
S. Goldstein, Capital, December 31, 2011	$5,565

Reliable Answering Service		
Balance Sheet		
December 31, 2011		
Assets		
Cash		$2,160
Accounts receivable		1,550
Office supplies		75
Prepaid insurance		200
Office equipment	$3,400	
Less accumulated depreciation	700	2,700
Total assets		$6,685
Liabilities		
Accounts Payable		$ 700
Unearned Revenue		300
Wage Payable		120
Total liabilities		$1,120
Owner's Equity		
S. Goldstein, Capital, November 30, 2010	$5,565	
Total owner's equity		5,565
Total liabilities and owner's capital		$6,685

5. All accounts on the income statement are potentially affected by adjusting entries. Cash on the balance sheet is never affected by an adjusting entry.

LO1 Define *net income,* and explain the assumptions underlying income measurement and their ethical application.

Net income is the net increase in owner's equity that results from a company's operations. Net income equals revenues minus expenses; when expenses exceed revenues, a net loss results. Revenues equal the price of goods sold or services rendered during a specific period. Expenses are the costs of goods and services used in the process of producing revenues.

The continuity assumption recognizes that even though businesses face an uncertain future, without evidence to the contrary, accountants must assume that a business will continue to operate indefinitely. The periodicity assumption recognizes that although the lifetime of a business is uncertain, it is nonetheless useful to estimate the business's net income in terms of accounting periods. The matching rule holds that revenues must be assigned to the accounting period in which the goods are sold or the services performed, and expenses must be assigned to the accounting period in which they are used to produce revenue.

Because applying the matching rule involves making assumptions and exercising judgment, it can lead to earnings management, which is the manipulation of revenues and expenses to achieve a specific outcome. When the estimates involved in earnings management move outside a reasonable range, financial statements become misleading. Financial statements that are intentionally misleading constitute fraudulent financial reporting.

LO2 Define *accrual accounting,* and explain how it is accomplished.

Accrual accounting consists of all the techniques accountants use to apply the matching rule. It is accomplished by recognizing revenues when they are earned, by recognizing expenses when they are incurred, and by adjusting the accounts.

LO3 Identify four situations that require adjusting entries, and illustrate typical adjusting entries.

Adjusting entries are required when (1) recorded costs must be allocated between two or more accounting periods, (2) unrecorded expenses exist, (3) recorded, unearned revenues must be allocated between two or more accounting periods, and (4) unrecorded, earned revenues exist. The preparation of adjusting entries is summarized as follows:

	Type of Account		
Type of Adjusting Entry	**Debited**	**Credited**	**Examples of Balance Sheet Accounts**
1. Allocating recorded costs (previously paid, expired)	Expense	Asset (or contra-asset)	Prepaid rent Prepaid insurance Office supplies Accumulated depreciation–office equipment
2. Accrued expenses (incurred, not paid)	Expense	Liability	Interest payable Wages payable
3. Allocating recorded, unearned revenues (previously received, earned)	Liability	Revenue	Unearned design revenue
4. Accrued revenues (earned, not received)	Asset	Revenue	Accounts receivable Interest receivable

LO4 Prepare financial statements from an adjusted trial balance.

An adjusted trial balance is prepared after adjusting entries have been posted to the accounts. Its purpose is to test whether the adjusting entries have been posted correctly before the financial statements are prepared. The balances in the revenue and expense accounts in the adjusted trial balance are used to prepare the income statement. The balances in the asset and liability accounts in the adjusted trial balance and in the statement of owner's equity are used to prepare the balance sheet.

LO5 Use accrual-based information to analyze cash flows.

To ensure a company's liquidity, managers must know how to use accrual-based information to analyze cash flows. The general rule for determining the cash flow received from any revenue or paid for any expense (except depreciation) is to determine the potential cash receipts or cash payments and deduct the amount not received or not paid.

REVIEW of Concepts and Terminology

The following concepts and terms were introduced in this chapter:

Accrual 107 (LO3)
Accrual accounting 104 (LO2)
Accrued expenses 111 (LO3)
Accrued revenues 114 (LO3)
Accumulated Depreciation accounts 110 (LO3)
Adjusted trial balance 116 (LO4)
Adjusting entries 107 (LO3)
Carrying value 110 (LO3)
Cash basis of accounting 102 (LO1)
Continuity 101 (LO1)
Contra account 110 (LO3)
Deferral 107 (LO3)
Depreciation 110 (LO3)
Earnings management 103 (LO1)
Expenses 101 (LO1)
Fiscal year 102 (LO1)
Going concern 101 (LO1)
Interim periods 102 (LO1)
Matching rule 102 (LO1)
Net income 100 (LO1)
Net loss 100 (LO1)
Periodicity 101 (LO1)
Prepaid expenses 108 (LO3)
Profit 100 (LO1)
Revenue recognition 104 (LO2)
Revenues 100 (LO1)
Unearned revenues 113 (LO3)

CHAPTER ASSIGNMENTS

BUILDING Your Basic Knowledge and Skills

Short Exercises

LO1 LO2 **Accrual Accounting Concepts**

SE 1. Match the concepts of accrual accounting on the right with the assumptions or actions on the left:

___ 1. Assumes expenses should be assigned to the accounting period in which they are used to produce revenues	a. Periodicity
___ 2. Assumes a business will last indefinitely	b. Continuity
___ 3. Assumes revenues are earned at a point in time	c. Matching rule
___ 4. Assumes net income that is measured for a short period of time, such as one quarter, is a useful measure	d. Revenue recognition

LO3 **Adjustment for Prepaid Insurance**

SE 2. The Prepaid Insurance account began the year with a balance of $920. During the year, insurance in the amount of $2,080 was purchased. At the end of the year (December 31), the amount of insurance still unexpired was $1,400. Prepare the year-end entry in journal form to record the adjustment for insurance expense for the year.

LO3 **Adjustment for Supplies**

SE 3. The Supplies account began the year with a balance of $760. During the year, supplies in the amount of $1,960 were purchased. At the end of the year (December 31), the inventory of supplies on hand was $880. Prepare the year-end entry in journal form to record the adjustment for supplies expense for the year.

LO3 **Adjustment for Depreciation**

SE 4. The depreciation expense on office equipment for the month of March is $100. This is the third month that the office equipment, which cost $1,900, has been owned. Prepare the adjusting entry in journal form to record depreciation for March and show the balance sheet presentation for office equipment and related accounts after the March 31 adjustment.

LO3 **Adjustment for Accrued Wages**

SE 5. Wages are paid each Saturday for a six-day workweek. Wages are currently running $1,380 per week. Prepare the adjusting entry required on June 30, assuming July 1 falls on a Tuesday.

LO3 **Adjustment for Unearned Revenue**

SE 6. During the month of August, deposits in the amount of $2,200 were received for services to be performed. By the end of the month, services in the amount of $1,520 had been performed. Prepare the necessary adjustment for Service Revenue at the end of the month.

LO4 **Preparation of an Income Statement and Statement of Owner's Equity from an Adjusted Trial Balance**

SE 7. The adjusted trial balance for Shimura Company on December 31, 2010, contains the following accounts and balances: J. Shimura, Capital, $4,300; J. Shimura, Withdrawals, $175; Service Revenue, $1,300; Rent Expense, $200; Wages Expense, $450; Utilities Expense, $100; and Telephone Expense, $25. Prepare an income statement and statement of owner's equity in proper form for the month of December.

LO5 **Determination of Cash Flows**

SE 8. Unearned Revenue had a balance of $650 at the end of November and $450 at the end of December. Service Revenue was $2,550 for the month of December. How much cash was received for services provided during December?

Exercises

LO1 LO2 LO3 **Discussion Questions**

E 1. Develop a brief answer to each of the following questions.

1. When a company has net income, what happens to its assets and/or to its liabilities?
2. Is accrual accounting more closely related to a company's goal of profitability or liquidity?
3. Will the carrying value of a long-term asset normally equal its market value?

LO4 **Discussion Questions**

E 2. Develop a brief answer to each of the following questions.

1. If, at the end of the accounting period, you were looking at the T account for a prepaid expense like supplies, would you look for the amounts expended in cash on the debit or credit side? On which side would you find the amount expensed during the period?
2. Would you expect net income to be a good measure of a company's liquidity? Why or why not?

LO1 LO2 LO3 **Applications of Accounting Concepts Related to Accrual Accounting**

E 3. The accountant for Ronaldo Company makes the assumptions or performs the activities listed below. Tell which of the following concepts of accrual accounting most directly relates to each assumption or action: (a) periodicity, (b) continuity, (c) matching rule, (d) revenue recognition, (e) deferral, and (f) accrual.

1. In estimating the life of a building, assumes that the business will last indefinitely
2. Records a sale when the customer is billed
3. Postpones the recognition of a one-year insurance policy as an expense by initially recording the expenditure as an asset
4. Recognizes the usefulness of financial statements prepared on a monthly basis even though they are based on estimates
5. Recognizes, by making an adjusting entry, wages expense that has been incurred but not yet recorded
6. Prepares an income statement that shows the revenues earned and the expenses incurred during the accounting period

LO2 **Application of Conditions for Revenue Recognition**

E 4. Four conditions must be met before revenue should be recognized. In each of the following cases, tell which condition has *not* been met.

a. Company A accepts a contract to perform services in the future for $2,000.
b. Company B ships products worth $3,000 to another company without an order from the other company but tells the company it can return the products if it does not sell them.
c. Company C performs $10,000 of services for a firm with financial problems.
d. Company D agrees to work out a price later for services that it performs for another company.

LO3 **Adjusting Entry for Unearned Revenue**

E 5. Fargo Voice of Fargo, North Dakota, publishes a monthly magazine featuring local restaurant reviews and upcoming social, cultural, and sporting events. Subscribers pay for subscriptions either one year or two years in advance. Cash received from subscribers is credited to an account called Magazine Subscriptions Received in Advance. On December 31, 2009, the end of the company's fiscal year, the balance of this account is $840,000. Expiration of subscriptions revenue is as follows:

During 2009	$175,000
During 2010	415,000
During 2011	250,000

Prepare the adjusting entry in journal form for December 31, 2009.

LO3 **Adjusting Entries for Prepaid Insurance**

E 6. An examination of the Prepaid Insurance account shows a balance of $16,845 at the end of an accounting period, before adjustment. Prepare entries in journal form to record the insurance expense for the period under the following independent assumptions:

1. An examination of the insurance policies shows unexpired insurance that cost $8,270 at the end of the period.
2. An examination of the insurance policies shows insurance that cost $2,150 has expired during the period.

LO3 **Adjusting Entries for Supplies: Missing Data**

E 7. Each of the following columns represents a Supplies account:

	a	b	c	d
Supplies on hand at July 1	$264	$346	$196	$?
Supplies purchased during the month	113	?	174	1,928
Supplies consumed during the month	194	972	?	1,741
Supplies on hand at July 31	?	436	85	1,118

1. Determine the amounts indicated by the question marks.
2. Make the adjusting entry for column **a**, assuming supplies purchased are debited to an asset account.

LO3 **Adjusting Entry for Accrued Salaries**

E 8. Hugo Company has a five-day workweek and pays salaries of $35,000 each Friday.

1. Prepare the adjusting entry required on May 31, assuming that June 1 falls on a Wednesday.
2. Prepare the entry to pay the salaries on June 3, including the amount of salaries payable from requirement **1.**

LO3 Revenue and Expense Recognition

E 9. Optima Company produces computer software that Tech Company sells. Optima receives a royalty of 15 percent of sales. Tech Company pays royalties to Optima Company semiannually—on May 1 for sales made in July through December of the previous year and on November 1 for sales made in January through June of the current year. Royalty expense for Tech Company and royalty income for Optima Company in the amount of $6,000 were accrued on December 31, 2008. Cash in the amounts of $6,000 and $10,000 was paid and received on May 1 and November 1, 2009, respectively. Software sales during the July to December 2009 period totaled $150,000.

1. Calculate the amount of royalty expense for Tech Company and royalty income for Optima during 2009.
2. Record the adjusting entry that each company made on December 31, 2009.

LO4 Preparation of Financial Statements

E 10. Prepare the monthly income statement, monthly statement of owner's equity, and the balance sheet at August 31, 2011, for Alvin Cleaning Company from the data provided in the adjusted trial balance below. The owner made no investments during the period.

Alvin Cleaning Company
Adjusted Trial Balance
August 31, 2011

Cash	$ 4,750	
Accounts Receivable	2,592	
Prepaid Insurance	380	
Prepaid Rent	200	
Cleaning Supplies	152	
Cleaning Equipment	3,875	
Accumulated Depreciation–Cleaning Equipment		$ 320
Truck	7,200	
Accumulated Depreciation–Truck		720
Accounts Payable		420
Wages Payable		295
Unearned Janitorial Revenue		1,690
A. Wish, Capital		15,034
A. Wish, Withdrawals	2,000	
Janitorial Revenue		14,620
Wages Expense	5,680	
Rent Expense	1,350	
Gas, Oil, and Other Truck Expenses	580	
Insurance Expense	380	
Supplies Expense	2,920	
Depreciation Expense–Cleaning Equipment	320	
Depreciation Expense–Truck	720	
	$33,099	$33,099

LO3 **Adjusting Entries**

E 11. Prepare year-end adjusting entries for each of the following:

1. Office Supplies has a balance of $336 on January 1. Purchases debited to Office Supplies during the year amount to $1,660. A year-end inventory reveals supplies of $1,140 on hand.
2. Depreciation of office equipment is estimated to be $2,130 for the year.
3. Property taxes for six months, estimated at $1,800, have accrued but have not been recorded.
4. Unrecorded interest income on U.S. government bonds is $850.
5. Unearned Revenue has a balance of $1,800. Services for $750 received in advance have now been performed.
6. Services totaling $800 have been performed; the customer has not yet been billed.

LO3 **Accounting for Revenue Received in Advance**

E 12. Robert Shapiro, a lawyer, received $84,000 on October 1 to represent a client in real estate negotiations over the next 12 months.

1. Record the entries required in Shapiro's records on October 1 and at the end of the fiscal year, December 31.
2. How would this transaction be reflected on the income statement and balance sheet on December 31?

LO5 **Determination of Cash Flows**

E 13. After adjusting entries had been made, the balance sheets of Ramiro's Company showed the following asset and liability amounts at the end of 2009 and 2010:

	2010	2009
Prepaid insurance	$2,400	$2,900
Wages payable	1,200	2,200
Unearned fees	4,200	1,900

The following amounts were taken from the 2010 income statement:

Insurance expense	$ 3,800
Wages expense	19,500
Fees earned	8,900

Calculate the amount of cash paid for insurance and wages and the amount of cash received for fees during 2010.

LO5 **Relationship of Expenses to Cash Paid**

E 14. The income statement for Sahan Company included the following expenses for 2011:

Rent expense	$ 75,000
Interest expense	11,700
Salaries expense	121,000

Listed below are the related balance sheet account balances at year end for last year and this year.

	Last Year	This Year
Prepaid rent	—	$ 1,350
Interest payable	$1,500	—
Salaries payable	7,500	114,000

1. Compute the cash paid for rent during the year.
2. Compute the cash paid for interest during the year.
3. Compute the cash paid for salaries during the year.

Problems

LO3 **Determining Adjustments**

P 1. At the end of the first three months of operation, the trial balance of City Answering Service appears as shown below. Tim Bass, the owner of City Answering Service, has hired an accountant to prepare financial statements to determine how well the company is doing after three months. Upon examining the accounting records, the accountant finds the following items of interest:

a. An inventory of office supplies reveals supplies on hand of $150.
b. The Prepaid Rent account includes the rent for the first three months plus a deposit for April's rent.
c. Depreciation on the equipment for the first three months is $416.
d. The balance of the Unearned Answering Service Revenue account represents a 12-month service contract paid in advance on February 1.
e. On March 31, accrued wages total $105.

City Answering Service
Trial Balance
March 31, 2010

Cash	$ 3,582	
Accounts Receivable	4,236	
Office Supplies	933	
Prepaid Rent	800	
Equipment	4,700	
Accounts Payable		$ 2,673
Unearned Answering Service Revenue		888
T. Bass, Capital		5,933
T. Bass, Withdrawals	2,100	
Answering Service Revenue		9,102
Wages Expense	1,900	
Office Cleaning Expense	345	
	$18,596	$18,596

Required

All adjustments affect one balance sheet account and one income statement account. For each of the above situations, show the accounts affected, the amount of the adjustment (using a + or – to indicate an increase or decrease), and the balance of the account after the adjustment in the following format:

Balance Sheet Account	Amount of Adjustment (+ or −)	Balance After Adjustment	Income Statement Account	Amount of Adjustment (+ or −)	Balance After Adjustment

LO2 LO3 **Preparing Adjusting Entries**

P 2. On November 30, the end of the current fiscal year, the following information is available to assist Caruso Company's accountants in making adjusting entries:

a. Caruso Company's Supplies account shows a beginning balance of $2,350. Purchases during the year were $4,218. The end-of-year inventory reveals supplies on hand of $1,397.

b. The Prepaid Insurance account shows the following on November 30:

Beginning balance	$4,720
July 1	4,200
October 1	7,272

The beginning balance represents the unexpired portion of a one-year policy purchased in September of the previous year. The July 1 entry represents a new one-year policy, and the October 1 entry represents additional coverage in the form of a three-year policy.

c. The following table contains the cost and annual depreciation for buildings and equipment, all of which Caruso Company purchased before the current year:

Account	Cost	Annual Depreciation
Buildings	$298,000	$16,000
Equipment	374,000	40,000

d. On September 1, the company completed negotiations with a client and accepted an advance of $18,600 for services to be performed monthly in the next year. The $18,600 was credited to Unearned Services Revenue.

e. The company calculated that as of November 30, it had earned $7,000 on an $11,000 contract that would be completed and billed in January.

f. Among the liabilities of the company is a note payable in the amount of $300,000. On November 30, the accrued interest on this note amounted to $18,000.

g. On Saturday, December 2, the company, which is on a six-day workweek, will pay its regular employees their weekly wages of $15,000.

h. On November 29, the company completed negotiations and signed a contract to provide services to a new client at an annual rate of $23,000.

Required

1. Prepare adjusting entries for each item listed above.

User insight ▶ 2. Explain how the conditions for revenue recognition are applied to transactions **e** and **h**.

LO3 LO4 Determining Adjusting Entries, Posting to T Accounts, and Preparing an Adjusted Trial Balance

P 3. The trial balance for Prima Consultants Company on December 31, 2010, appears below. The following information is also available:

a. Ending inventory of office supplies, $97
b. Prepaid rent expired, $500
c. Depreciation of office equipment for the period, $720
d. Interest accrued on the note payable, $600
e. Salaries accrued at the end of the period, $230
f. Service revenue still unearned at the end of the period, $1,410
g. Service revenue earned but not billed, $915

Required

1. Open T accounts for the accounts in the trial balance plus the following: Interest Payable; Salaries Payable; Office Supplies Expense; Depreciation Expense–Office Equipment; and Interest Expense. Enter the account balances.
2. Determine the adjusting entries and post them directly to the T accounts.
3. Prepare an adjusted trial balance.

User insight ▶ 4. Which financial statements do each of the above adjustments affect? What financial statement is *not* affected by the adjustments?

Prima Consultants Company
Trial Balance
December 31, 2010

Cash	$ 13,786	
Accounts Receivable	24,840	
Office Supplies	991	
Prepaid Rent	1,400	
Office Equipment	7,300	
Accumulated Depreciation–Office Equipment		$ 2,600
Accounts Payable		1,820
Notes Payable		10,000
Unearned Service Revenue		2,860
M. Sirot, Capital		30,387
M. Sirot, Withdrawals	15,000	
Service Revenue		58,500
Salaries Expense	33,400	
Utilities Expense	1,750	
Rent Expense	7,700	
	$106,167	$106,167

LO3 LO4 **Determining Adjusting Entries and Tracing Their Effects to Financial Statements**

P 4. VIP Limo Service was organized to provide limousine service between the airport and various suburban locations. It has just completed its second year of business. Its trial balance is below.

VIP Limo Service
Trial Balance
June 30, 2010

Cash (111)	$ 9,812	
Accounts Receivable (113)	14,227	
Prepaid Rent (117)	12,000	
Prepaid Insurance (118)	4,900	
Prepaid Maintenance (119)	12,000	
Spare Parts (140)	11,310	
Limousines (148)	220,000	
Accumulated Depreciation–Limousines (149)		$ 35,000
Notes Payable (211)		45,000
Unearned Passenger Service Revenue (213)		30,000
A. Pham, Capital (311)		88,211
A. Pham, Withdrawals (313)	20,000	
Passenger Service Revenue (411)		428,498
Gas and Oil Expense (510)	89,300	
Salaries Expense (511)	206,360	
Advertising Expense (516)	26,800	
	$626,709	$626,709

The following information is also available:

a. To obtain space at the airport, VIP Limo paid two years' rent in advance when it began the business.
b. An examination of insurance policies reveals that $1,800 expired during the year.
c. To provide regular maintenance for the vehicles, VIP Limo deposited $12,000 with a local garage. An examination of maintenance invoices reveals charges of $10,944 against the deposit.
d. An inventory of spare parts shows $2,016 on hand.
e. VIP Limo depreciates all of its limousines at the rate of 12.5 percent per year. No limousines were purchased during the year.
f. A payment of $10,500 for one full year's interest on notes payable is now due.
g. Unearned Passenger Service Revenue on June 30 includes $17,815 for tickets that employers purchased for use by their executives but which have not yet been redeemed.

Required

1. Determine the adjusting entries and enter them in the general journal (Page 14).
2. Open ledger accounts for the accounts in the trial balance plus the following: Interest Payable (213); Rent Expense (514); Insurance Expense (515); Spare Parts Expense (516); Depreciation Expense–Limousines (517); Maintenance Expense (518); and Interest Expense (519). Record the balances shown in the trial balance.

3. Post the adjusting entries from the general journal to the ledger accounts, showing proper references.

User insight ▶ 4. Prepare an adjusted trial balance, an income statement, a statement of owner's equity, and a balance sheet. The owner made no investments during the period.

Alternate Problems

LO3 Determining Adjustments

P 5. At the end of its fiscal year, the trial balance for Andy's Cleaners appears as shown below:

Andy's Cleaners
Trial Balance
September 30, 2010

Cash	$ 11,788	
Accounts Receivable	26,494	
Prepaid Insurance	3,400	
Cleaning Supplies	7,374	
Land	18,000	
Building	186,000	
Accumulated Depreciation–Building		$ 45,600
Accounts Payable		18,400
Unearned Cleaning Revenue		1,700
Mortgage Payable		110,000
A. Kopec, Capital		56,560
A. Kopec, Withdrawals	9,000	
Cleaning Revenue		159,634
Wages Expense	101,330	
Cleaning Equipment Rental Expense	6,100	
Delivery Truck Expense	4,374	
Interest Expense	11,000	
Other Expenses	7,034	
	$391,894	$391,894

The following information is also available:

a. A study of the company's insurance policies shows ssssthat $680 is unexpired at the end of the year.
b. An inventory of cleaning supplies shows $1,150 on hand.
c. Estimated depreciation on the building for the year is $12,800.
d. Accrued interest on the mortgage payable is $1,000.
e. On September 1, the company signed a contract, effective immediately, with Hope County Hospital to dry clean, for a fixed monthly charge of $425, the uniforms used by doctors in surgery. The hospital paid for four months' service in advance.
f. Sales and delivery wages are paid on Saturday. The weekly payroll is $3,060. September 30 falls on a Thursday, and the company has a six-day pay week.

Required

All adjustments affect one balance sheet account and one income statement account. For each of the above situations, show the accounts affected, the amount of the adjustment (using a + or − to indicate an increase or decrease), and the balance of the account after the adjustment in the following format:

Balance Sheet Account	Amount of Adjustment (+ or −)	Balance After Adjustment	Income Statement Account	Amount of Adjustment (+ or −)	Balance After Adjustment

LO2 LO3 **Preparing Adjusting Entries**

P 6. On June 30, the end of the current fiscal year, the following information is available to Conti Company's accountants for making adjusting entries:

a. Among the liabilities of the company is a mortgage payable in the amount of $260,000. On June 30, the accrued interest on this mortgage amounted to $13,000.
b. On Friday, July 2, the company, which is on a five-day workweek and pays employees weekly, will pay its regular salaried employees $18,700.
c. On June 29, the company completed negotiations and signed a contract to provide monthly services to a new client at an annual rate of $7,200.
d. The Supplies account shows a beginning balance of $1,615 and purchases during the year of $4,115. The end-of-year inventory reveals supplies on hand of $1,318.
e. The Prepaid Insurance account shows the following entries on June 30:

Beginning balance	$1,620
January 1	2,900
May 1	3,366

The beginning balance represents the unexpired portion of a one-year policy purchased in April of the previous year. The January 1 entry represents a new one-year policy, and the May 1 entry represents the additional coverage of a three-year policy.

f. The following table contains the cost and annual depreciation for buildings and equipment, all of which were purchased before the current year:

Account	Cost	Annual Depreciation
Buildings	$170,000	$ 7,300
Equipment	218,000	20,650

g. On June 1, the company completed negotiations with another client and accepted an advance of $21,600 for services to be performed in the next year. The $21,600 was credited to Unearned Service Revenue.
h. The company calculates that as of June 30 it had earned $4,500 on a $7,500 contract that will be completed and billed in August.

Required

1. Prepare adjusting entries for each item listed above.

User insight ▶ 2. Explain how the conditions for revenue recognition are applied to transactions **c** and **h**.

LO3 Determining Adjusting Entries, Posting to T Accounts, and Preparing an Adjusted Trial Balance

P 7. The trial balance for Best Advisors Service on December 31, 2011, is as follows:

Best Advisors Service
Trial Balance
December 31, 2011

Cash	$ 18,500	
Accounts Receivable	8,250	
Office Supplies	2,662	
Prepaid Rent	1,320	
Office Equipment	9,240	
Accumulated Depreciation–Office Equipment		$ 1,540
Accounts Payable		5,940
Notes Payable		11,000
Unearned Service Revenue		2,970
M. Dabrowska, Capital		26,002
M. Dabrowska, Withdrawals	22,000	
Service Revenue		72,600
Salaries Expense	49,400	
Rent Expense	4,400	
Utilities Expense	4,280	
	$120,052	$120,052

The following information is also available:

a. Ending inventory of office supplies, $300
b. Prepaid rent expired, $610
c. Depreciation of office equipment for the period, $526
d. Accrued interest expense at the end of the period, $570
e. Accrued salaries at the end of the period, $330
f. Service revenue still unearned at the end of the period, $1,166
g. Service revenue earned but unrecorded, $3,100

Required

1. Open T accounts for the accounts in the trial balance plus the following: Interest Payable; Salaries Payable; Office Supplies Expense; Depreciation Expense–Office Equipment; and Interest Expense. Enter the balances shown on the trial balance.
2. Determine the adjusting entries and post them directly to the T accounts.
3. Prepare an adjusted trial balance.

User insight ▶

4. Which financial statements do each of the above adjustments affect? Which financial statement is *not* affected by the adjustments?

LO3 LO4 **Determining Adjusting Entries and Tracing Their Effects to Financial Statements**

P 8. Helen Ortega opened a small tax-preparation service. At the end of its second year of operation, Ortega Tax Service had the trial balance that appears below.

Ortega Tax Service
Trial Balance
December 31, 2010

Cash	$ 3,700	
Accounts Receivable	1,099	
Prepaid Insurance	240	
Office Supplies	780	
Office Equipment	7,100	
Accumulated Depreciation–Office Equipment		$ 770
Accounts Payable		635
Unearned Tax Fees		219
H. Ortega, Capital		6,939
H. Ortega, Withdrawals	6,000	
Tax Fees Revenue		21,926
Office Salaries Expense	8,300	
Advertising Expense	650	
Rent Expense	2,400	
Telephone Expense	220	
	$30,489	$30,489

The following information is also available:

a. Office supplies on hand, December 31, 2010, $225.
b. Insurance still unexpired, $100.
c. Estimated depreciation of office equipment, $795.
d. Telephone expense for December, $21; the bill was received but not recorded.
e. The services for all unearned tax fees had been performed by the end of the year.

Required

1. Open T accounts for the accounts in the trial balance plus the following: Office Supplies Expense; Insurance Expense; and Depreciation Expense–Office Equipment. Record the balances shown in the trial balance.
2. Determine the adjusting entries and post them directly to the T accounts.
3. Prepare an adjusted trial balance, an income statement, a statement of owner's equity, and a balance sheet. The owner made no investments during the period.
4. Why is it not necessary to show the effects of the above transactions on the statement of cash flows?

User insight ▶

ENHANCING Your Knowledge, Skills, and Critical Thinking

LO1 LO2 LO3

Importance of Adjustments

C 1. Never Flake Company, which operated in the northeastern part of the United States, provided a rust-prevention coating for the underside of new automobiles. The company advertised widely and offered its services through new car dealers. When a dealer sold a new car, the salesperson attempted to sell the rust-prevention coating as an option. The protective coating was supposed to make cars last longer in the severe northeastern winters. A key selling point was Never Flake's warranty, which stated that it would repair any damage due to rust at no charge for as long as the buyer owned the car.

For several years, Never Flake had been very successful in generating enough cash to continue operations. But in 2011, the company suddenly declared bankruptcy. Company officials said that the firm had only $5.5 million in assets against liabilities of $32.9 million. Most of the liabilities represented potential claims under the company's lifetime warranty. It seemed that owners were keeping their cars longer now than previously. Therefore, more damage was being attributed to rust. Discuss what accounting decisions could have helped Never Flake survive under these circumstances.

LO1

Earnings Management and Fraudulent Financial Reporting

C 2. In recent years, the Securities and Exchange Commission (SEC) has been waging a public campaign against corporate accounting practices that manage or manipulate earnings to meet the expectations of Wall Street analysts. Corporations engage in such practices in the hope of avoiding shortfalls that might cause serious declines in their stock price. For each of the following cases that the SEC challenged, tell why each is a violation of the matching rule and how it should be accounted for:

a. **Lucent Technologies** sold telecommunications equipment to companies from which there was no reasonable expectation of payment because of the companies' poor financial condition.
b. **America Online (AOL)** recorded advertising as an asset rather than as an expense.
c. **Eclipsys** recorded software contracts as revenue even though it had not yet rendered the services.
d. **KnowledgeWare** recorded revenue from sales of software even though it told customers they did not have to pay until they had the software.

LO2 LO3

Analysis of an Asset Account

C 3. The Walt Disney Company is engaged in the financing, production, and distribution of motion pictures and television programming. In Disney's 2008 annual report, the balance sheet contained an asset called "film and television costs." Film and television costs, which consist of the costs associated with producing films and television programs less the amount expensed, were $5,394,000,000. The estimated amount of film and television costs expensed (amortized) during the next year were $3,500,000,000. The amount estimated to be spent for new film productions was $2,900,000,000.

1. What are film and television costs, and why would they be classified as an asset?
2. Prepare an entry in T account form to record the amount the company spent on new film and television productions during 2010 (assume all expenditures are paid for in cash).

3. Prepare an adjusting entry in T account form to record the expense for film and television productions during 2009. Show the balance of the Film and Television Costs account at the end of the next year.
4. Suggest a method by which The Walt Disney Company might have determined the amount of the expense in 3 in accordance with the matching rule.

LO1 LO2 LO3 **Importance of Adjustments**

C 4. Main Street Service Co. has achieved fast growth in the St. Louis area by selling service contracts on large appliances, such as washers, dryers, and refrigerators. For a fee, Main Street agrees to provide all parts and labor on an appliance after the regular warranty runs out. For example, by paying a fee of $200, a person who buys a dishwasher can add two years (years 2 and 3) to the regular one-year (year 1) warranty on the appliance. In 2009, the company sold service contracts in the amount of $1.8 million, all of which applied to future years. Management wanted all the sales recorded as revenues in 2009, contending that the amount of the contracts could be determined and the cash had been received. Discuss whether you agree with this logic. How would you record the cash receipts? What assumptions do you think Main Street should make? Would you consider it unethical to follow management's recommendation? Who might be hurt or helped by this action?

LO3 **Real-World Observation of Business Activities**

C 5. Visit a company with which you are familiar and observe its operations. (The company can be where you work, where you eat, or where you buy things.) Identify at least two sources of revenue for the company and six types of expenses. For each type of revenue and each type of expense, determine whether it is probable that an adjusting entry is required at the end of the accounting period. Then specify the adjusting entry as a deferred revenue, deferred expense, accrued revenue, or accrued expense. Design a table with columns and rows that summarizes your results in an easy-to-understand format.

LO3 **Analysis of Balance Sheet and Adjusting Entries**

C 6. In **CVS Corporation**'s annual report in the Supplement to Chapter 5, refer to the balance sheet and the Summary of Significant Accounting Policies in the notes to the financial statements.

a. Examine the accounts in the current assets, property and equipment, and current liabilities sections of CVS's balance sheet. Which are most likely to have had year-end adjusting entries? Describe the nature of the adjusting entries. For more information about the property and equipment section, refer to the notes to the financial statements.
b. Where is depreciation (and amortization) expense disclosed in CVS's financial statements?
c. CVS has a statement on the "Use of Estimates" in its Summary of Significant Accounting Policies. Read this statement and tell how important estimates are to the determination of depreciation expense. What assumptions do accountants make that allow these estimates to be made?

CHAPTER

4 Completing the Accounting Cycle

Making a Statement

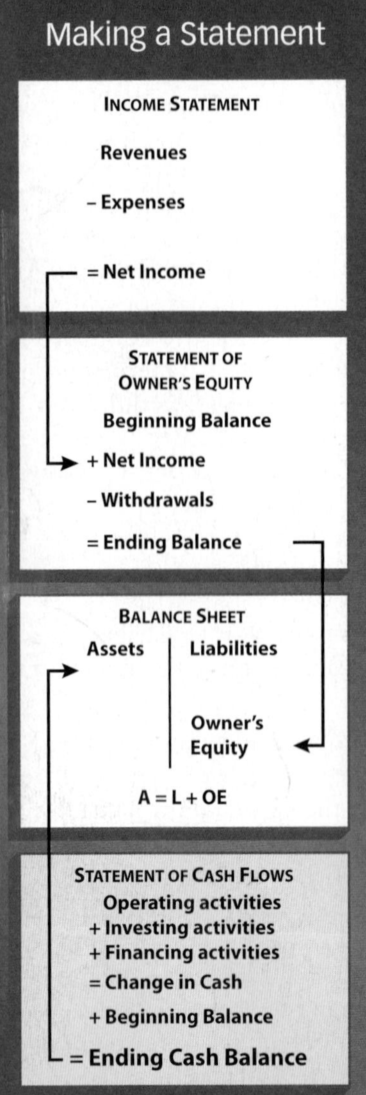

Closing entries set the accounts on the income statement to zero and transfer the resulting balance of net income or loss to the owner's Capital account on the balance sheet. Closing entries do not affect cash flows.

All companies prepare financial statements annually, and whether required by law or not, preparing them every quarter, or even every month, is a good idea because these interim reports give management an ongoing view of a company's financial performance. The preparation of financial statements requires not only adjusting entries, which we described in the last chapter, but also closing entries, which we explain in this chapter.

LEARNING OBJECTIVES

LO1 Describe the accounting cycle and the role of closing entries in the preparation of financial statements. (pp. 144–146)

LO2 Prepare closing entries. (pp. 147–151)

LO3 Prepare reversing entries. (pp. 152–153)

LO4 Prepare and use a work sheet. (pp. 154–158)

DECISION POINT ▸ A USER'S FOCUS WESTWOOD MOVERS

Westwood Movers provides moving and storage services for the local college and its students and employees. Westwood's business tends to be seasonal; its busiest times are generally in the late spring and early fall. Thus, to keep a careful eye on fluctuations in earnings and cash flows, Westwood prepares financial statements each quarter.

As you know from Chapter 3, before a company prepares financial statements, it must make adjusting entries to the income statement and owner's equity accounts. After those entries have been made, an adjusted trial balance listing all the accounts and balances is prepared. Accounts from the adjusted trial balance are then used to prepare the financial statements. For example, in preparing its income statement, Westwood Movers would use the revenue and expense accounts from its adjusted trial balance, which appear on the following page. (This adjusted trial balance is "partial" in that it omits all balance sheet accounts except the owner's equity accounts.) In addition, Westwood, like all other companies, must prepare its accounts for the next accounting period by making closing entries. Doing all this takes time and effort, but the results benefit both management and external users of the company's financial statements by providing important information about revenues and operating income.

To accomplish these tasks, Westwood Movers needs to be able to answer the questions on the right.

- ▸ What steps must a company follow to prepare its accounts for the next accounting period?
- ▸ After following these steps, how is the ending balance of the owner's Capital account determined?

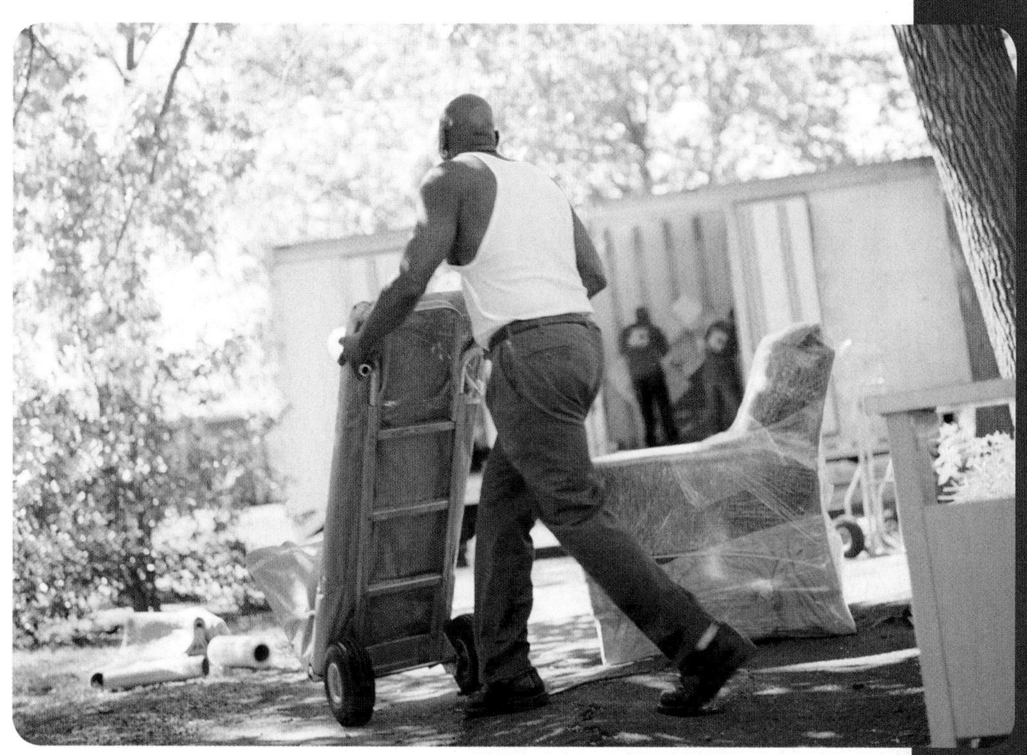

	A	B	C	D	E
1			Westwood Movers		
2			Partial Adjusted Trial Balance		
3			June 30, 2011		
4					
5	J. Thomas, Capital				$ 24,740
6	J. Thomas, Withdrawals			$ 18,000	
7	Moving Services Revenue				185,400
8	Driver Wages Expense			88,900	
9	Fuel Expense			19,000	
10	Other Wages Expense			14,400	
11	Packing Supplies Expense			6,200	
12	Office Equipment Rental Expense			3,000	
13	Utilities Expense			4,450	
14	Insurance Expense			4,200	
15	Interest Expense			5,100	
16	Depreciation Expense			10,040	
17					

From Transactions to Financial Statements

To interpret and analyze a company's performance requires an understanding of how transactions are recognized and eventually end up in financial statements. Two concepts that foster this understanding are the accounting cycle and closing entries.

LO1 Describe the accounting cycle and the role of closing entries in the preparation of financial statements.

The Accounting Cycle

As Figure 4-1 shows, the **accounting cycle** is a series of steps whose ultimate purpose is to provide useful information to decision makers. These steps are as follows:

1. *Analyze* business transactions from source documents.
2. *Record* the transactions by entering them in the general journal.
3. *Post* the journal entries to the ledger, and prepare a trial balance.
4. *Adjust* the accounts, and prepare an adjusted trial balance.
5. *Prepare* financial statements.
6. *Close* the accounts, and prepare a post-closing trial balance.

You are already familiar with Steps 1 through 5 from previous chapters. In the next section, we describe Step 6, which may be performed before or after Step 5.

Closing Entries

Balance sheet accounts, such as Cash and Accounts Payable, are considered **permanent accounts,** or *real accounts,* because they carry their end-of-period balances into the next accounting period. In contrast, revenue and expense accounts, such as Revenues Earned and Wages Expense, are considered **temporary accounts,** or *nominal accounts,* because they begin each accounting period with a zero balance, accumulate a balance during the period, and are then cleared by means of closing entries.

Closing entries are journal entries made at the end of an accounting period. They have two purposes:

1. They set the stage for the next accounting period by clearing revenue and expense accounts and the Withdrawals account of their balances.

FIGURE 4-1 Overview of the Accounting Cycle

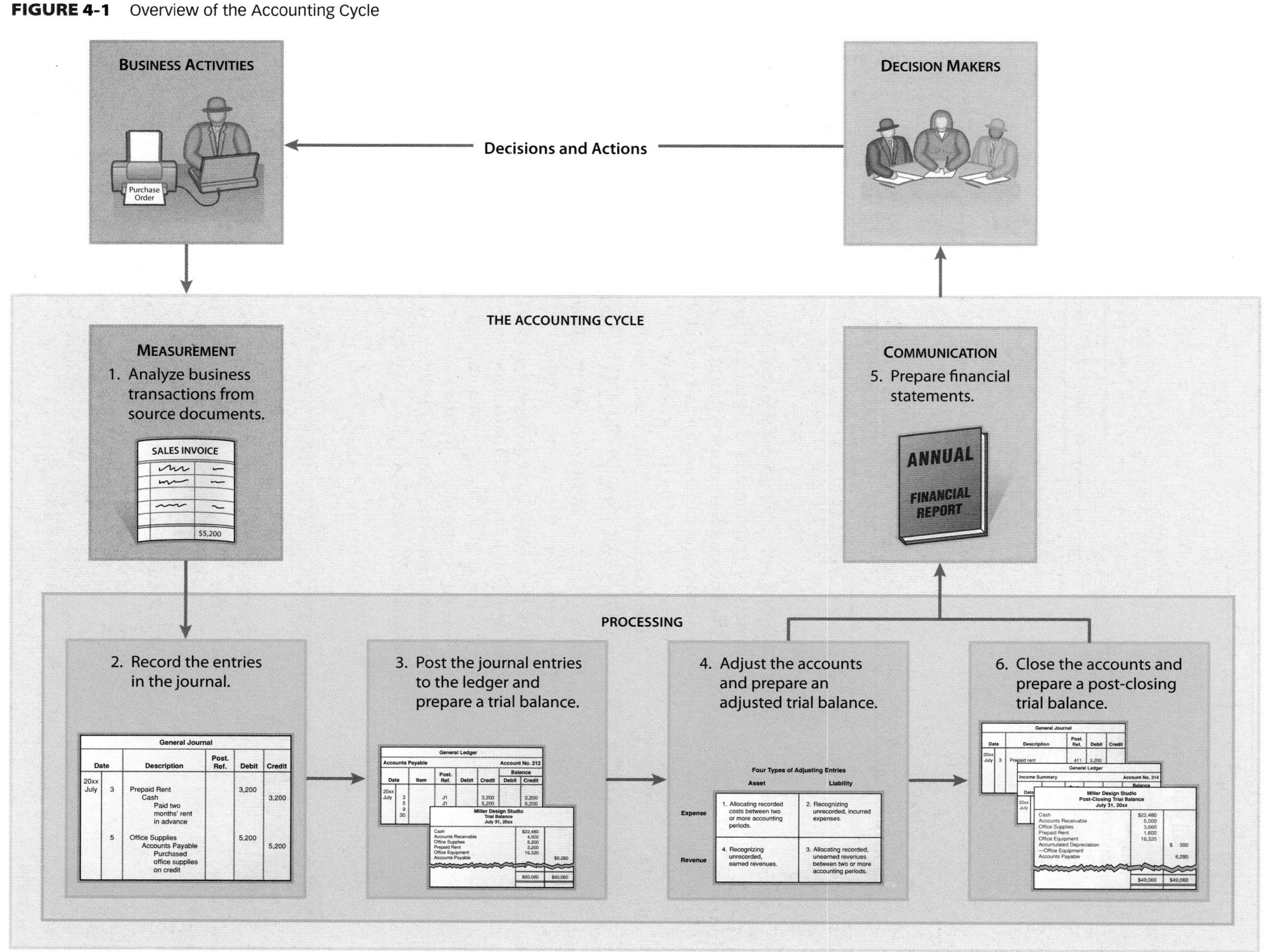

FIGURE 4-2 Overview of the Closing Process

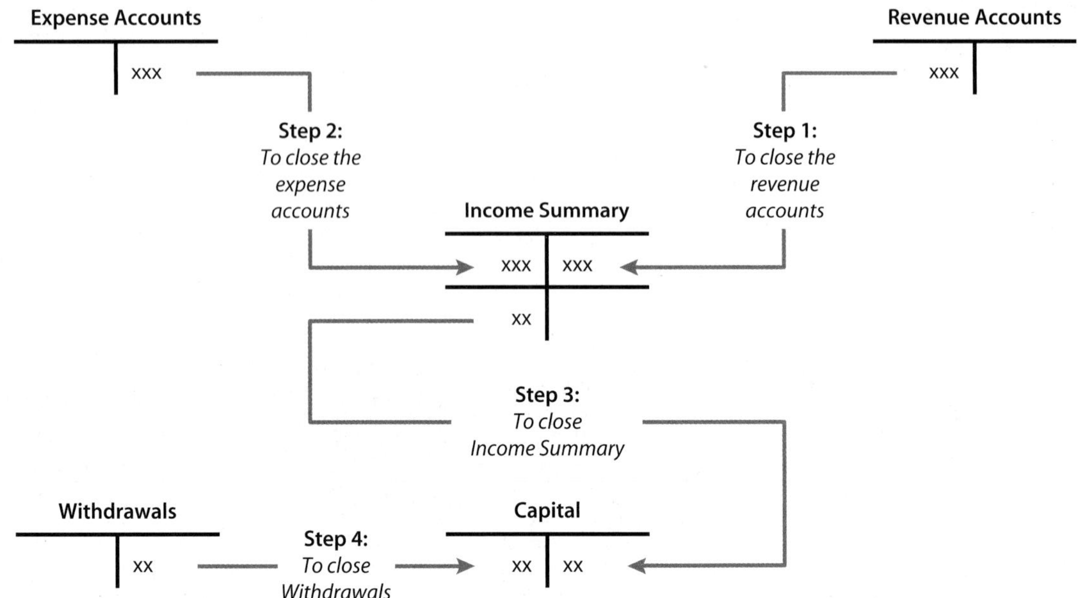

2. They summarize a period's revenues and expenses by transferring the balances of revenue and expense accounts to the Income Summary account. The **Income Summary account** is a temporary account that summarizes all revenues and expenses for the period. It is used only in the closing process—never in the financial statements. Its balance equals the net income or loss reported on the income statement. The net income or loss is then transferred to the owner's Capital account.

Figure 4-2 shows an overview of the closing process. The net income or loss is transferred from the Income Summary account to the owner's Capital account because even though revenues and expenses are recorded in individual accounts, they represent increases and decreases in owner's Capital. Closing entries transfer the net effect of increases (revenues) and decreases (expenses) to owner's Capital. For corporations like **Netflix**, the net income or loss is transferred from the Income Summary account to the Retained Earnings account, which is part of the stockholders' (owner's) equity of a corporation.

& APPLY >

In each of the following pairs of activities, tell which activity is done first in the accounting cycle:

1. Close the accounts or adjust the accounts
2. Analyze the transactions or post the entries to the ledger
3. Record the transactions in the journal or prepare the initial trial balance
4. Prepare the post-closing trial balance or prepare the adjusted trial balance

SOLUTION

1. Adjust the accounts
2. Analyze the transactions
3. Record the transactions in the journal
4. Prepare the adjusted trial balance

Preparing Closing Entries

LO2 Prepare closing entries.

> **Study Note**
> Although it is not absolutely necessary to use the Income Summary account when preparing closing entries, doing so simplifies the procedure.

The steps involved in making closing entries are as follows:

Step 1. Close the credit balances on the income statement accounts to the Income Summary account.

Step 2. Close the debit balances on the income statement accounts to the Income Summary account.

Step 3. Close the Income Summary account balance to the owner's Capital account.

Step 4. Close the Withdrawals account balance to the owner's Capital account.

As you will learn in later chapters, not all revenue accounts have credit balances and not all expense accounts have debit balances. For that reason, when referring to closing entries, we often use the term *credit balances* instead of *revenue accounts* and the term *debit balances* instead of *expense accounts.*

An adjusted trial balance provides all the data needed to record the closing entries. Exhibit 4-1 shows the relationships of the four kinds of closing entries to Miller Design Studio's adjusted trial balance.

Step 1: Closing the Credit Balances

> **Study Note**
> After Step 1 has been completed, the Income Summary account reflects the account balance of the Design Revenue account before it was closed.

On the credit side of the adjusted trial balance in Exhibit 4-1, Design Revenue shows a balance of $13,600. To close this account, a journal entry must be made debiting the account in the amount of its balance and crediting it to the Income Summary account. Exhibit 4-2 shows how the entry is posted. Notice that the entry sets the balance of the revenue account to zero and transfers the total revenues to the credit side of the Income Summary account.

Step 2: Closing the Debit Balances

Several expense accounts show balances on the debit side of the adjusted trial balance in Exhibit 4-1. A compound entry is needed to credit each of these expense accounts for its balance and to debit the Income Summary account for the total. Exhibit 4-3 shows the effect of posting the closing entry. Notice how the entry reduces the expense account balances to zero and transfers the total of the account balances to the debit side of the Income Summary account.

Step 3: Closing the Income Summary Account Balance

> **Study Note**
> After Step 3 has been completed, the credit balance of the Income Summary account ($3,960) represents net income—the key measure of performance. When a net loss occurs, debit the owner's Capital account (to reduce it) and credit the Income Summary account (to close it).

After the entries closing the revenue and expense accounts have been posted, the balance of the Income Summary account equals the net income or loss for the period. A credit balance in the Income Summary account represents a net income (i.e., revenues exceed expenses), and a debit balance represents a net loss (i.e., expenses exceed revenues).

At this point, the balance of the Income Summary account, whatever its nature, is closed to the owner's Capital account, as shown in Exhibit 4-1. Exhibit 4-4 shows how the closing entry is posted when a company has a net income. Notice the dual effect of closing the Income Summary account and transferring the balance to owner's Capital.

Step 4: Closing the Withdrawals Account Balance

The Withdrawals account shows the amount by which owner's Capital decreased during an accounting period. The debit balance of the Withdrawals account is closed to the owner's Capital account, as illustrated in Exhibit 4-1. Exhibit 4-5

EXHIBIT 4-1 Preparing Closing Entries from the Adjusted Trial Balance

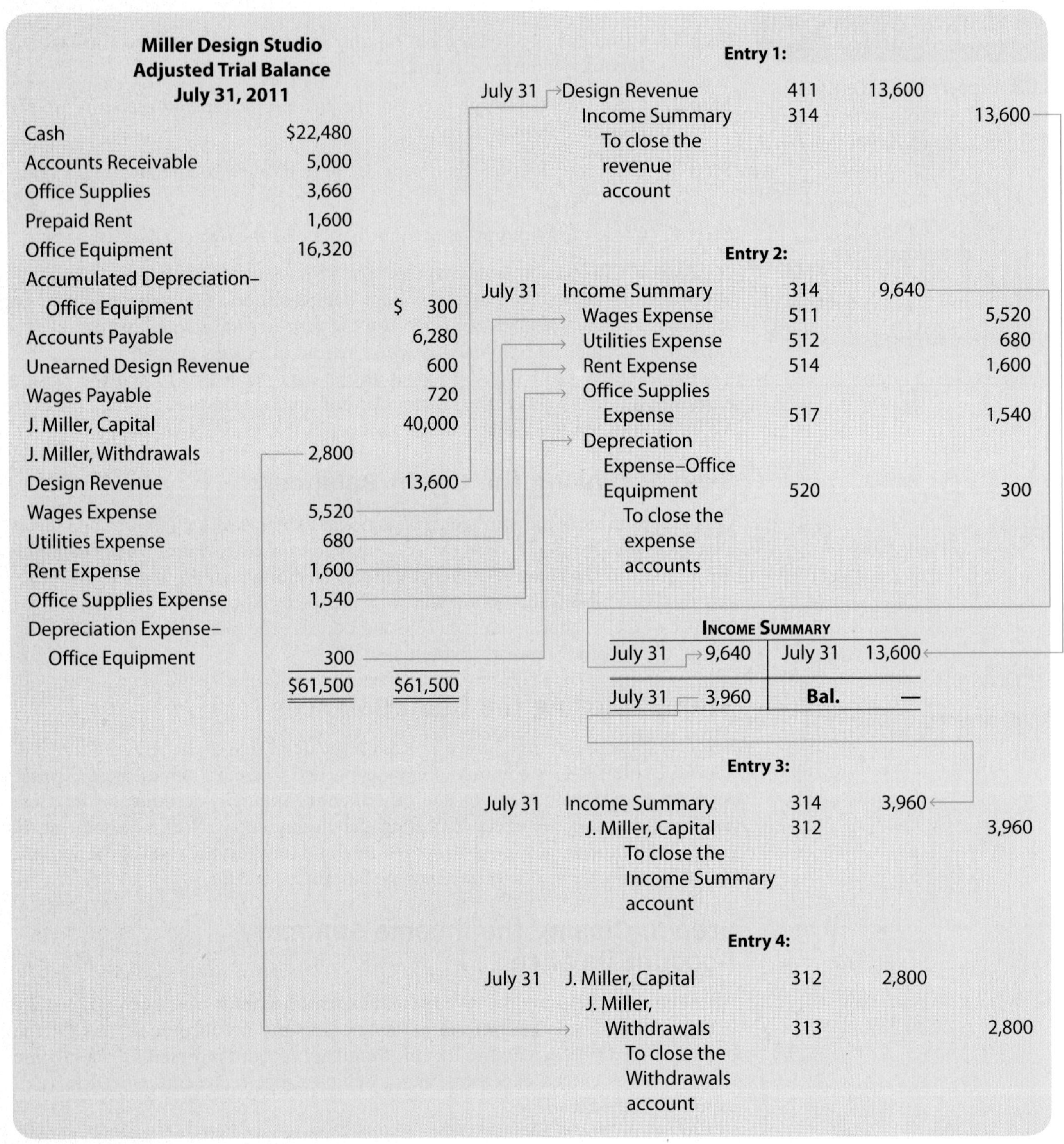

Miller Design Studio
Adjusted Trial Balance
July 31, 2011

Cash	$22,480	
Accounts Receivable	5,000	
Office Supplies	3,660	
Prepaid Rent	1,600	
Office Equipment	16,320	
Accumulated Depreciation–Office Equipment		$ 300
Accounts Payable		6,280
Unearned Design Revenue		600
Wages Payable		720
J. Miller, Capital		40,000
J. Miller, Withdrawals	2,800	
Design Revenue		13,600
Wages Expense	5,520	
Utilities Expense	680	
Rent Expense	1,600	
Office Supplies Expense	1,540	
Depreciation Expense–Office Equipment	300	
	$61,500	$61,500

Entry 1:

July 31	Design Revenue	411	13,600	
	Income Summary	314		13,600
	To close the revenue account			

Entry 2:

July 31	Income Summary	314	9,640	
	Wages Expense	511		5,520
	Utilities Expense	512		680
	Rent Expense	514		1,600
	Office Supplies Expense	517		1,540
	Depreciation Expense–Office Equipment	520		300
	To close the expense accounts			

Income Summary

July 31	9,640	July 31	13,600
July 31	3,960	**Bal.**	—

Entry 3:

July 31	Income Summary	314	3,960	
	J. Miller, Capital	312		3,960
	To close the Income Summary account			

Entry 4:

July 31	J. Miller, Capital	312	2,800	
	J. Miller, Withdrawals	313		2,800
	To close the Withdrawals account			

> **Study Note**
>
> Note that the Withdrawals account is closed to the owner's Capital account, not to the Income Summary account.

shows the posting of the closing entry and the transfer of the balance of the Withdrawals account to the owner's Capital account. In a corporation like **Netflix**, payments to owners are called *dividends*, and they are closed to the Retained Earnings account.

The Accounts After Posting

After all the steps in the closing process have been completed and all closing entries have been posted, everything is ready for the next accounting period.

EXHIBIT 4-2
Posting the Closing Entry of a Credit Balance to the Income Summary Account

Design Revenue — Account No. 411

Date	Item	Post. Ref.	Debit	Credit	Balance	
					Debit	Credit
July 10		J2		2,800		2,800
15		J2		9,600		12,400
31	Adj.	J3		800		13,200
31	Adj.	J3		400		13,600
31	Closing	J4	13,600			—

Income Summary — Account No. 314

Date	Item	Post. Ref.	Debit	Credit	Balance	
					Debit	Credit
July 31	Closing	J4		13,600		13,600

The revenue, expense, and Withdrawals accounts (temporary accounts) have zero balances. The owner's Capital account has been increased or decreased to reflect net income or net loss (net income in our example) and has been decreased for withdrawals. The balance sheet accounts (permanent accounts) show the correct balances, which are carried into the next period.

EXHIBIT 4-3 Posting the Closing Entry of Debit Balances to the Income Summary Account

Wages Expense — Account No. 511

Date	Item	Post. Ref.	Debit	Credit	Balance	
					Debit	Credit
July 26		J2	4,800		4,800	
31	Adj.	J3	720		5,520	
31	Closing	J4		5,520	—	

Utilities Expense — Account No. 512

Date	Item	Post. Ref.	Debit	Credit	Balance	
					Debit	Credit
July 30		J2	680		680	
31	Closing	J4		680	—	

Rent Expense — Account No. 514

Date	Item	Post. Ref.	Debit	Credit	Balance	
					Debit	Credit
July 31	Adj.	J3	1,600		1,600	
31	Closing	J4		1,600	—	

Office Supplies Expense — Account No. 517

Date	Item	Post. Ref.	Debit	Credit	Balance	
					Debit	Credit
July 31	Adj.	J3	1,540		1,540	
31	Closing	J4		1,540	—	

Depreciation Expense–Office Equipment — Account No. 520

Date	Item	Post. Ref.	Debit	Credit	Balance	
					Debit	Credit
July 31	Adj.	J3	300		300	
31	Closing	J4		300	—	

Income Summary — Account No. 314

Date	Item	Post. Ref.	Debit	Credit	Balance	
					Debit	Credit
July 31	Closing	J4		13,600		13,600
31	Closing	J4	9,640*			3,960

*Total of all credit closing entries to expense accounts is debited to the Income Summary account.

EXHIBIT 4-4 Posting the Closing Entry of the Income Summary Account Balance to the Owner's Equity Account

Income Summary — Account No. 314

Date	Item	Post. Ref.	Debit	Credit	Balance Debit	Balance Credit
July 31	Closing	J4		13,600		13,600
31	Closing	J4	9,640			3,960
31	Closing	J4	3,960			—

J. Miller, Capital — Account No. 312

Date	Item	Post. Ref.	Debit	Credit	Balance Debit	Balance Credit
July 1		J1		40,000		40,000
31	Closing	J4		3,960		43,960

EXHIBIT 4-5 Posting the Closing Entry of the Withdrawals Account Balance to the Owner's Capital Account

J. Miller, Withdrawals — Account No. 313

Date	Item	Post. Ref.	Debit	Credit	Balance Debit	Balance Credit
July 31		J2	2,800		2,800	
31	Closing	J4		2,800	—	

J. Miller, Capital — Account No. 312

Date	Item	Post. Ref.	Debit	Credit	Balance Debit	Balance Credit
July 1		J1		40,000		40,000
31	Closing	J4		3,960		43,960
31	Closing	J4	2,800			41,160

The Post-Closing Trial Balance

Because errors can be made in posting closing entries to the ledger accounts, it is necessary to prepare a **post-closing trial balance.** As you can see in Exhibit 4-6, a post-closing trial balance contains only balance sheet accounts because the income statement accounts and the Withdrawals account have been closed and now have zero balances. It is a final check that total debits equal total credits.

EXHIBIT 4-6
Post-Closing Trial Balance

Miller Design Studio
Post-Closing Trial Balance
July 31, 2011

Cash	$22,480	
Accounts Receivable	5,000	
Office Supplies	3,660	
Prepaid Rent	1,600	
Office Equipment	16,320	
Accumulated Depreciation–Office Equipment		$ 300
Accounts Payable		6,280
Unearned Design Revenue		600
Wages Payable		720
J. Miller, Capital		41,160
	$49,060	$49,060

Prepare the necessary closing entries from the following partial adjusted trial balance for Fountas Recreational Park, and compute the ending balance of the owner's Capital account. (Except for K. Fountas, Capital, balance sheet accounts have been omitted.)

Fountas Recreational Park
Partial Adjusted Trial Balance
June 30, 2010

K. Fountas, Capital		$93,070
K. Fountas, Withdrawals	$36,000	
Campsite Rentals		88,200
Wages Expense	23,850	
Insurance Expense	3,784	
Utilities Expense	1,800	
Supplies Expense	1,320	
Depreciation Expense–Building	6,000	

SOLUTION

Closing entries prepared:

June 30	Campsite Rentals	88,200	
	Income Summary		88,200
	To close the credit balance account		
30	Income Summary	36,754	
	Wages Expense		23,850
	Insurance Expense		3,784
	Utilities Expense		1,800
	Supplies Expense		1,320
	Depreciation Expense–Building		6,000
	To close the debit balance accounts		
30	Income Summary	51,446	
	K. Fountas, Capital		51,446
	To close the Income Summary account		
	$88,200 − $36,754 = $51,446		
30	K. Fountas, Capital	36,000	
	K. Fountas, Withdrawals		36,000
	To close the Withdrawals account		

Ending balance of the K. Fountas, Capital account computed:

K. Fountas, Capital

June 30	36,000	Beg. Bal.	93,070
		June 30	51,446
		End. Bal.	108,516

Reversing Entries: An Optional First Step

LO3 Prepare reversing entries.

Study Note

Reversing entries are the opposite of adjusting entries and are dated the first day of the new period. They apply only to certain adjusting entries and are never required.

A **reversing entry** is an optional journal entry made on the first day of an accounting period. It has the opposite effect of an adjusting entry made at the end of the previous period—that is, it debits the credits and credits the debits of an earlier adjusting entry. The sole purpose of reversing entries is to simplify routine bookkeeping procedures, and they apply only to certain adjusting entries. Deferrals should not be reversed because doing so would not simplify bookkeeping in future accounting periods. As used in this text, reversing entries apply only to accruals (accrued revenues and expenses).

To see how reversing entries can be helpful, consider this adjusting entry made in the records of Miller Design Studio to accrue wages expense:

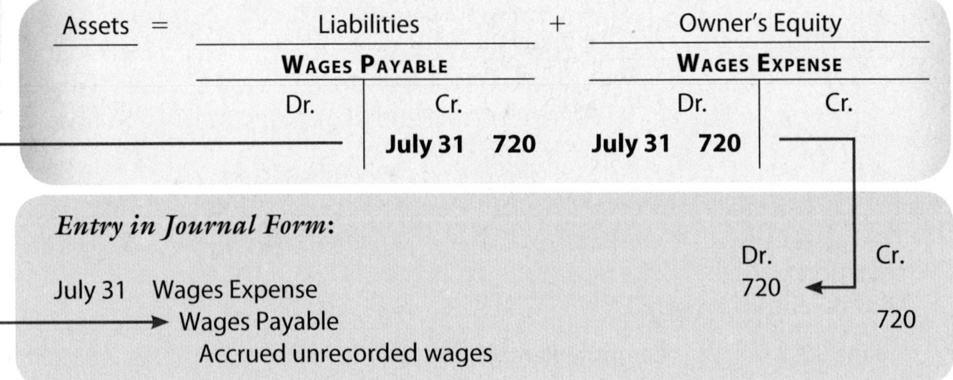

When the company pays its assistant on the next regular payday, its accountant would make this entry:

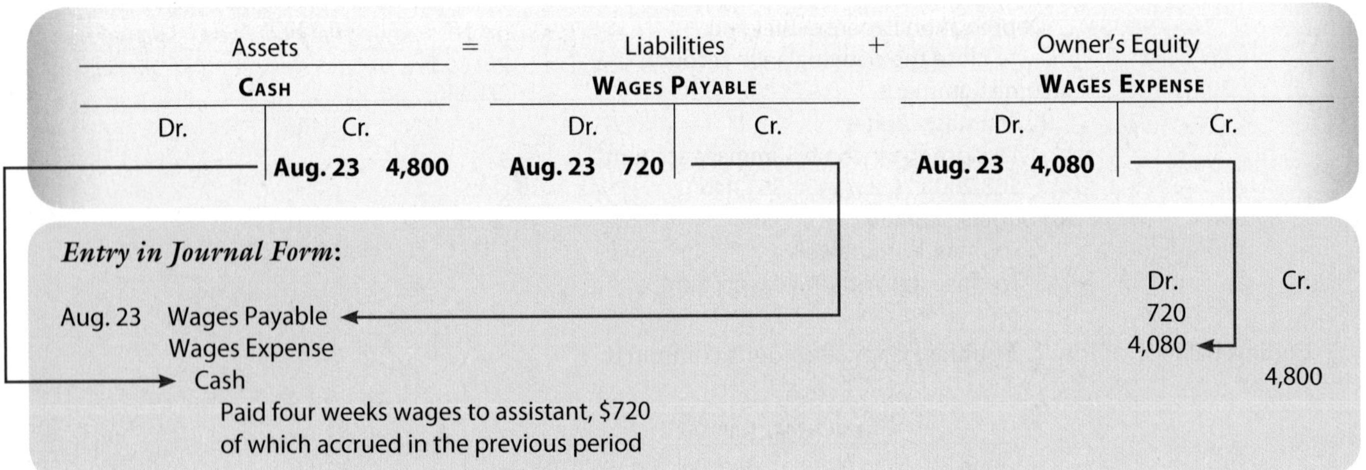

If no reversing entry is made at the time of payment, the accountant would have to look in the records to find out how much of the $4,800 applies to the current accounting period and how much applies to the previous period. That may seem easy in our example, but think how difficult and time-consuming it would be if a company had hundreds of employees working on different schedules. A reversing entry helps solve the problem of applying revenues and expenses to the correct accounting period.

For example, consider the following sequence of entries and their effects on the Wages Expense account:

		Dr.	Cr.
1. Adjusting Entry			
July 31	Wages Expense	720	
	Wages Payable		720
2. Closing Entry			
July 31	Income Summary	5,520	
	Wages Expense		5,520
3. Reversing Entry			
Aug. 1	Wages Payable	720	
	Wages Expense		720
4. Payment Entry			
Aug. 23	Wages Expense	4,800	
	Cash		4,800

Wages Expense **Account No. 511**

Date	Post. Ref.	Debit	Credit	Balance Debit	Balance Credit
July 26	J2	4,800		4,800	
31	J3	720		5,520	
31	J4		5,520	—	
Aug. 1	J5		720		720
23	J6	4,800		4,080	

Entry **1** adjusted Wages Expense to accrue $720 in the July accounting period.

Entry **2** closed the $5,520 in Wages Expense for July to Income Summary, leaving a zero balance.

Entry **3**, the reversing entry, set up a credit balance of $720 on August 1 in Wages Expense, which is the expense recognized through the adjusting entry in July (and also reduced the liability account Wages Payable to a zero balance). The reversing entry always sets up an abnormal balance in the income statement account and produces a zero balance in the balance sheet account.

Entry **4** recorded the $4,800 payment of wages as a debit to Wages Expense, automatically leaving a balance of $4,080, which represents the correct wages expense to date in August. The reversing entry simplified the process of making the payment entry on August 23.

Reversing entries apply to any accrued expenses or revenues. Miller Design Studio's only accrued expense was wages expense. An adjusting entry for the company's accrued revenue (Design Revenue) would require the following reversing entry:

		Dr.	Cr.
Aug. 1	Design Revenue	400	
	Accounts Receivable		400
	Reversed the adjusting entry for accrued revenue earned		

STOP & APPLY >

Which of the following accounts after adjustment will most likely require reversing entries:

a. Salaries Payable
b. Accumulated Depreciation
c. Interest Payable
d. Supplies
e. Taxes Payable

SOLUTION

a., c., and e.

The Work Sheet: An Accountant's Tool

LO4 Prepare and use a work sheet.

To organize data and avoid omitting important information that might affect the financial statements, accountants use **working papers**. Because working papers provide evidence of past work, they enable accountants to retrace their steps when they need to verify information in the financial statements.

A **work sheet** is a special kind of working paper. The work sheet is extremely useful when a company prepares financial statements on both an annual and seasonal basis, as **Netflix** does, and when an accountant must make numerous adjustments. It is often used as a preliminary step in preparing financial statements. Using a work sheet lessens the possibility of omitting an adjustment and helps the accountant check the arithmetical accuracy of the accounts. The work sheet is never published and is rarely seen by management. It is a tool for the accountant. Because preparing a work sheet is a mechanical process, many accountants use a computer for this purpose.

> **Study Note**
> The work sheet is not a financial statement, it is not required, and it is not made public.

Preparing the Work Sheet

A work sheet often has one column for account names and multiple columns with headings like the ones shown in Exhibit 4-7. A heading that includes the name of the company and the period of time covered (as on the income statement) identifies the work sheet. As Exhibit 4-7 shows, preparation of a work sheet involves five steps.

> **Study Note**
> The Trial Balance columns of a work sheet take the place of a trial balance.

Step 1. Enter and Total the Account Balances in the Trial Balance Columns The debit and credit balances of the accounts on the last day of an accounting period are copied directly from the ledger into the Trial Balance columns (the green columns in Exhibit 4-7). When accountants use a work sheet, they do not have to prepare a separate trial balance.

Step 2. Enter and Total the Adjustments in the Adjustments Columns The required adjustments are entered in the Adjustments columns of the work sheet (the purple columns in Exhibit 4-7). As each adjustment is entered, a letter is used to identify its debit and credit parts. For example, in Exhibit 4-7, the letter (**a**) identifies the adjustment made for the rent that Miller Design Studio prepaid on July 3, which results in a debit to Rent Expense and a credit to Prepaid Rent. These identifying letters may be used to reference supporting computations or documentation for the related adjusting entries and can simplify the recording of adjusting entries in the general journal.

A trial balance includes only accounts that have balances. If an adjustment involves an account that does not appear in the trial balance, the new account is added below the accounts listed on the work sheet. For example, Rent Expense has been added to Exhibit 4-7. Accumulated depreciation accounts, which have a zero balance only in the initial period of operation, are the sole exception to this rule. They are listed immediately after their associated asset accounts. For example, in Exhibit 4-7, the Accumulated Depreciation–Office Equipment account is listed immediately after Office Equipment.

When all the adjustments have been made, the two Adjustments columns must be totaled. This procedure proves that the debits and credits of the adjustments are equal, and it generally reduces errors in the work sheet.

Step 3. Enter and Total the Adjusted Account Balances in the Adjusted Trial Balance Columns The adjusted trial balance in the work sheet is prepared by combining the amount of each account in the Trial Balance columns with the corresponding amount in the Adjustments columns and entering each result in the Adjusted Trial Balance columns (the yellow columns in Exhibit 4-7).

Exhibit 4-7 contains examples of **crossfooting**, or adding and subtracting a group of numbers horizontally. The first line shows Cash with a debit balance

EXHIBIT 4-7 The Work Sheet

Miller Design Studio
Work Sheet
For the Month Ended July 31, 2011

	Trial Balance		Adjustments		Adjusted Trial Balance		Income Statement		Balance Sheet	
Account Name	**Debit**	**Credit**	**Debit**	**Credit**	**Debit**	**Credit**	**Debit**	**Credit**	**Debit**	**Credit**
Cash	22,480				22,480				22,480	
Accounts Receivable	4,600		(f) 400		5,000				5,000	
Office Supplies	5,200			(b) 1,540	3,660				3,660	
Prepaid Rent	3,200			(a) 1,600	1,600				1,600	
Office Equipment	16,320				16,320				16,320	
Accumulated Depreciation–Office Equipment				(c) 300		300				300
Accounts Payable		6,280				6,280				6,280
Unearned Design Revenue		1,400	(e) 800			600				600
J. Miller, Capital		40,000				40,000				40,000
J. Miller, Withdrawals	2,800				2,800				2,800	
Design Revenue		12,400		(e) 800 (f) 400		13,600		13,600		
Wages Expense	4,800		(d) 720		5,520		5,520			
Utilities Expense	680				680		680			
	60,080	60,080								
Rent Expense			(a) 1,600		1,600		1,600			
Office Supplies Expense			(b) 1,540		1,540		1,540			
Depreciation Expense–Office Equipment			(c) 300		300		300			
Wages Payable				(d) 720		720				720
			5,360	5,360	61,500	61,500	9,640	13,600	51,860	47,900
Net Income							3,960			3,960
							13,600	13,600	51,860	51,860

Note: The columns of the work sheet are prepared in the following order: (1) Trial Balance, (2) Adjustments, (3) Adjusted Trial Balance, and (4) Income Statement and Balance Sheet columns. In the fifth step, the Income Statement and Balance Sheet columns are totaled.

of $22,480. Because there are no adjustments to the Cash account, $22,480 is entered in the debit column of the Adjusted Trial Balance columns. On the second line, Accounts Receivable shows a debit of $4,600 in the Trial Balance columns. Because there is a debit of $400 from adjustment **f** in the Adjustments columns, it is added to the $4,600 and carried over to the debit column of the Adjusted Trial Balance columns at $5,000. On the next line, Office Supplies shows a debit of $5,200 in the Trial Balance columns and a credit of $1,540 from adjustment **b** in the Adjustments columns. Subtracting $1,540 from $5,200 results in a $3,660 debit balance in the Adjusted Trial Balance columns. This process is followed for all the accounts, including those added below the trial balance totals. The Adjusted Trial Balance columns are then *footed* (totaled) to check the accuracy of the crossfooting.

Step 4. Extend the Account Balances from the Adjusted Trial Balance Columns to the Income Statement or Balance Sheet Columns Every account in the adjusted trial balance is an income statement account or a balance sheet account. Each account is extended to its proper place as a debit or credit in either the Income Statement columns or the Balance Sheet columns (the blue columns in Exhibit 4-7). As shown in Exhibit 4-7, revenue and expense accounts are extended to the Income Statement columns, and asset, liability, Capital, and Withdrawals accounts are extended to the Balance Sheet columns.

To avoid overlooking an account, the accounts are extended line by line, beginning with the first line (Cash) and not omitting any subsequent lines. For instance, the Cash debit balance of $22,480 is extended to the debit column of the Balance Sheet columns; then, the Accounts Receivable debit balance of $5,000 is extended to the debit column of the Balance Sheet columns; and so forth.

Step 5. Total the Income Statement Columns and the Balance Sheet Columns. Enter the Net Income or Net Loss in Both Pairs of Columns as a Balancing Figure, and Recompute the Column Totals This fifth and last step, shown in the brown columns at the bottom of Exhibit 4-7, is necessary to compute net income or net loss and to prove the arithmetical accuracy of the work sheet.

Net income (or net loss) is equal to the difference between the total debits and credits of the Income Statement columns. It is also equal to the difference between the total debits and credits of the Balance Sheet columns.

Revenues (Income Statement credit column total)	$13,600
Expenses (Income Statement debit column total)	(9,640)
Net Income	$ 3,960

In this case, revenues (credit column) exceed expenses (debit column). Thus, Miller Design Studio has a net income of $3,960. The same difference occurs between the total debits and credits of the Balance Sheet columns.

The $3,960 is entered in the debit side of the Income Statement columns and in the credit side of the Balance Sheet columns to balance the columns. Remember that the excess of revenues over expenses (net income) increases owner's equity and that increases in owner's equity are recorded by credits.

When a net loss occurs, the opposite rule applies. The excess of expenses over revenues—net loss—is placed in the credit side of the Income Statement columns as a balancing figure. It is then placed in the debit side of the Balance Sheet columns because a net loss decreases owner's equity, and decreases in owner's equity are recorded by debits.

As a final check, the four columns are totaled again. If the Income Statement columns and the Balance Sheet columns do not balance, an account may have been extended or sorted to the wrong column, or an error may have been made in adding the columns. Of course, equal totals in the two pairs of columns are not absolute proof of accuracy. If an asset has been carried to the Income Statement debit column (or an expense has been carried to the Balance Sheet debit column) or a similar error with revenues or liabilities has been made, the work sheet will balance, but the net income figure will be wrong.

Study Note

Theoretically, adjusting entries can be recorded in the accounting records before the financial statements are prepared or even before the work sheet is completed. However, they always precede the preparation of closing entries.

Using the Work Sheet

Accountants use the completed work sheet in performing three principal tasks. These tasks are as follows:

1. **Recording the adjusting entries in the general journal.** Because the information needed to record the adjusting entries can be copied from the work sheet, entering the adjustments in the journal is an easy step, as shown in Exhibit 4-8. The adjusting entries are then posted to the general ledger.

EXHIBIT 4-8
Adjustments from the Work Sheet Entered in the General Journal

General Journal — **Page 3**

Date	Description	Post. Ref.	Debit	Credit
2011				
(a) July 31	Rent Expense	514	1,600	
	Prepaid Rent	117		1,600
	To recognize expiration of one month's rent			
(b) 31	Office Supplies Expense	517	1,540	
	Office Supplies	116		1,540
	To recognize office supplies used during the month			
(c) 31	Depreciation Expense–Office Equipment	520	300	
	Accumulated Depreciation–Office Equipment	147		300
	To record depreciation of office equipment for a month			
(d) 31	Wages Expense	511	720	
	Wages Payable	214		720
	To accrue unrecorded wages			
(e) 31	Unearned Design Revenue	213	800	
	Design Revenue	411		800
	To recognize payment for services not yet performed			
(f) 31	Accounts Receivable	113	400	
	Design Revenue	411		400
	To accrue design fees earned but unrecorded			

2. **Recording the closing entries in the general journal.** The Income Statement columns of the work sheet show all the accounts that need to be closed, except for the Withdrawals account. Exhibits 4-1 through 4-5 show how the closing entries are entered in the journal and posted to the ledger.
3. **Preparing the financial statements.** Once the work sheet has been completed, preparing the financial statements is simple because the account balances have been sorted into the Income Statement and Balance Sheet columns.

STOP & APPLY >

Place the following columns of a work sheet in the proper order:

a. Balance Sheet columns
b. Trial Balance columns
c. Income Statement columns
d. Adjusted Trial Balance columns
e. Adjustments columns

SOLUTION
b., e., d., c., a.

▸ WESTWOOD MOVERS: REVIEW PROBLEM

In the Decision Point at the beginning of the chapter, we pointed out that at the end of an accounting period, Westwood Movers, like all other companies, must prepare its accounts for the next accounting period. We posed these questions:

- What steps must a company follow to prepare its accounts for the next accounting period?
- After following these steps, how is the ending balance of the owner's Capital account determined?

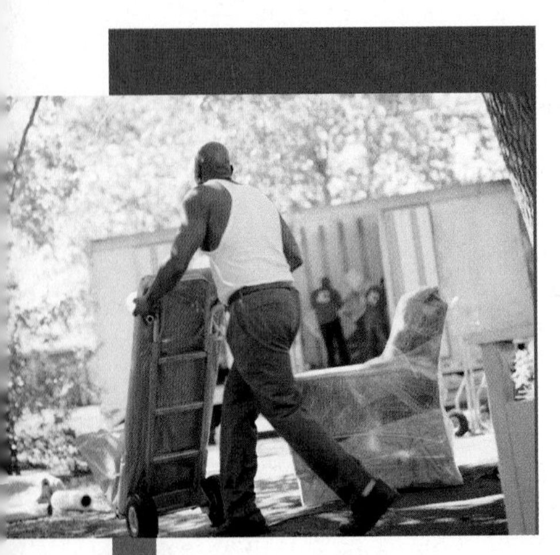

Preparation of Closing Entries LO2

1. Prepare the necessary closing entries from the partial adjusted trial balance for Westwood Movers that appears in the Decision Point. (As we noted earlier, this adjusted trial balance omits all balance sheet accounts except the owner's equity accounts.)
2. Compute the ending balance of the owner's Capital account.
3. User insight: In the closing process, why is it unnecessary to consider balance sheet accounts other than owner's equity accounts?

Answers to Review Problem

1. Closing entries prepared:

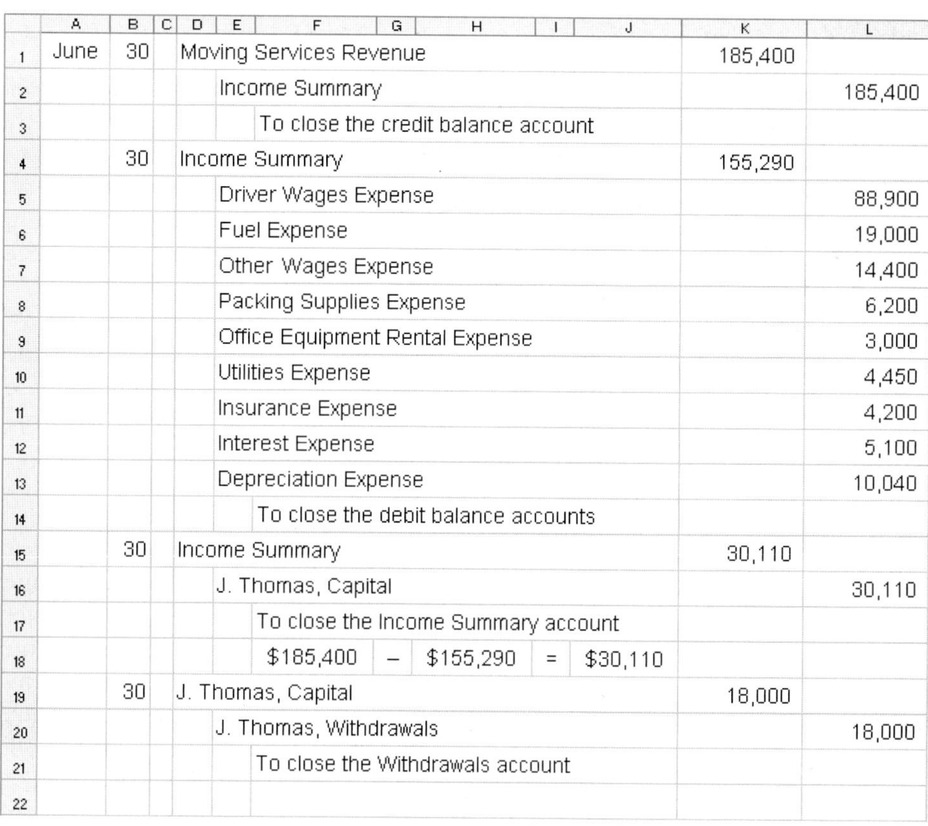

	A	B	C–J	K	L
1	June	30	Moving Services Revenue	185,400	
2			Income Summary		185,400
3			To close the credit balance account		
4		30	Income Summary	155,290	
5			Driver Wages Expense		88,900
6			Fuel Expense		19,000
7			Other Wages Expense		14,400
8			Packing Supplies Expense		6,200
9			Office Equipment Rental Expense		3,000
10			Utilities Expense		4,450
11			Insurance Expense		4,200
12			Interest Expense		5,100
13			Depreciation Expense		10,040
14			To close the debit balance accounts		
15		30	Income Summary	30,110	
16			J. Thomas, Capital		30,110
17			To close the Income Summary account		
18			$185,400 – $155,290 = $30,110		
19		30	J. Thomas, Capital	18,000	
20			J. Thomas, Withdrawals		18,000
21			To close the Withdrawals account		
22					

2. Ending balance of the J. Thomas, Capital account computed:

	A	B	C	D	E	F
1			**J. Thomas, Capital**			
2	June	30	18,000	Beg. Bal.		24,740
3				June	30	30,110
4				*End. Bal.*		*36,850*
5						

3. The reason other balance sheet accounts are not considered in the closing process is that the balances of all asset and liability accounts carry over to the next accounting period. Thus, they do not need to be set to zero, as do the income statements accounts and the Withdrawals account. Also, they do not need to be updated, as does the owner's Capital account.

STOP & REVIEW >

LO1 Describe the accounting cycle and the role of closing entries in the preparation of financial statements.

The steps in the accounting cycle are as follows: (1) analyze business transactions from source documents; (2) record the transactions by entering them in the general journal; (3) post the entries to the ledger, and prepare a trial balance; (4) adjust the accounts, and prepare an adjusted trial balance; (5) prepare financial statements; and (6) close the accounts, and prepare a post-closing trial balance. (Step 6 may occur before or after Step 5.)

Closing entries have two purposes: (1) They clear the balances of all temporary accounts (revenue, expense, and Withdrawals accounts) so that they have zero balances at the beginning of the next accounting period, and (2) they summarize a period's revenues and expenses in the Income Summary account so that the net income or loss for the period can be transferred as a total to owner's Capital.

LO2 Prepare closing entries.

The first two steps in preparing closing entries are to transfer the balances of the revenue and expense accounts to the Income Summary account. The balance of the Income Summary account is then transferred to the owner's Capital account. Finally, the balance of the Withdrawals account is transferred to owner's Capital. After the closing entries have been posted to the ledger accounts, a post-closing trial balance is prepared as a final check on the balance of the ledger and to ensure that all temporary (nominal) accounts have been closed.

LO3 Prepare reversing entries.

Reversing entries are optional journal entries made on the first day of an accounting period. Reversing entries have the opposite effect of adjusting entries made at the end of the previous period—that is, a reversing entry debits the credits and credits the debits of an earlier adjusting entry. The sole purpose of reversing entries is to simplify routine bookkeeping procedures, and they apply only to certain adjusting entries. As used in this text, reversing entries apply only to accruals.

LO4 Prepare and use a work sheet.

The five steps in preparing a work sheet are (1) enter and total the account balances in the Trial Balance columns; (2) enter and total the adjustments in the Adjustments columns; (3) enter and total the adjusted account balances in the Adjusted Trial Balance columns; (4) extend the account balances from the Adjusted Trial Balance columns to the Income Statement or Balance Sheet columns; and (5) total the Income Statement and Balance Sheet columns, enter the net income or net loss in both pairs of columns as a balancing figure, and recompute the column totals.

A work sheet is useful in recording both adjusting and closing entries and in preparing the financial statements. The income statement and balance sheet can be prepared directly from the Income Statement and Balance Sheet columns of the completed work sheet. The statement of owner's equity is prepared using owner's Withdrawals, net income, additional investments, and the beginning balance of the owner's Capital account.

REVIEW of Concepts and Terminology

The following concepts and terms were introduced in this chapter:

Accounting cycle 144 (LO1)

Closing entries 144 (LO1)

Crossfooting 154 (LO4)

Income Summary account 146 (LO1)

Permanent accounts 144 (LO1)

Post-closing trial balance 150 (LO2)

Reversing entry 152 (LO3)

Temporary accounts 144 (LO1)

Working papers 154 (LO4)

Work sheet 154 (LO4)

CHAPTER ASSIGNMENTS

BUILDING Your Basic Knowledge and Skills

Short Exercises

LO1 Accounting Cycle

SE 1. Resequence the following activities to indicate the usual order of the accounting cycle:

a. Close the accounts.
b. Analyze the transactions.
c. Post the entries to the ledger.
d. Prepare the financial statements.
e. Adjust the accounts.
f. Record the transactions in the journal.
g. Prepare the post-closing trial balance.
h. Prepare the initial trial balance.
i. Prepare the adjusted trial balance.

LO2 Closing Revenue Accounts

SE 2. Assume that at the end of the accounting period there are credit balances of $6,800 in Patient Services Revenues and $3,600 in Laboratory Fees Revenues. Prepare the required closing entry in journal form. The accounting period ends December 31.

LO2 Closing Expense Accounts

SE 3. Assume that debit balances at the end of the accounting period are $2,800 in Rent Expense, $2,200 in Wages Expense, and $1,000 in Other Expenses. Prepare the required closing entry in journal form. The accounting period ends December 31.

LO2 Closing the Income Summary Account

SE 4. Assuming that total revenues were $10,400 and total expenses were $6,000, prepare the entry in journal form to close the Income Summary account to the R. Shah, Capital account. The accounting period ends December 31.

LO2 Closing the Withdrawals Account

SE 5. Assuming that withdrawals during the accounting period were $1,600, prepare the entry in journal form to close the R. Shah, Withdrawals account to the R. Shah, Capital account. The accounting period ends December 31.

LO2 Posting Closing Entries

SE 6. Show the effects of the transactions in **SE 2, SE 3, SE 4,** and **SE 5** by entering beginning balances in appropriate T accounts and recording the transactions. Assume that the R. Shah, Capital account had a beginning balance of $1,300.

LO3 **Preparation of Reversing Entries**

SE 7. Below, indicated by letters, are the adjusting entries at the end of March.

Account Name	Debit	Credit
Prepaid Insurance		(a) 180
Accumulated Depreciation–Office Equipment		(b) 1,050
Salaries Expense	(c) 360	
Insurance Expense	(a) 180	
Depreciation Expense–Office Equipment	(b) 1,050	
Salaries Payable		(c) 360
	1,590	1,590

Prepare the required reversing entry in journal form.

LO3 **Effects of Reversing Entries**

SE 8. Assume that prior to the adjustments in **SE 7**, Salaries Expense had a debit balance of $1,800 and Salaries Payable had a zero balance. Prepare a T account for each of these accounts. Enter the beginning balance; post the adjustment for accrued salaries, the appropriate closing entry, and the reversing entry; and enter the transaction in the T accounts for a payment of $480 for salaries on April 3.

LO2 **Preparation of Closing Entries**

SE 9. The adjusted trial balance for Mendoza Company on December 31, 2011, contains the following accounts and balances: C. Mendoza, Capital, $4,300; C. Mendoza, Withdrawals, $175; Service Revenue, $1,300; Rent Expense, $200; Wages Expense, $450; Utilities Expense, $100; and Telephone Expense, $25. Prepare the closing entries.

LO2 LO4 **Preparation of Closing Entries from a Work Sheet**

SE 10. Prepare the required closing entries in journal form for the year ended December 31, using the following items from the Income Statement columns of a work sheet and assuming that withdrawals by the owner, T. Jameson, were $7,000:

Account Name	Debit	Credit
Repair Revenue		35,860
Wages Expense	13,260	
Rent Expense	2,800	
Supplies Expense	6,390	
Insurance Expense	1,370	
Depreciation Expense–Repair Equipment	3,020	
	26,840	35,860
Net Income	9,020	
	35,860	35,860

Exercises

LO1 LO2 Discussion Questions

E 1. Develop brief answers to each of the following questions:

1. Why is the accounting cycle called a "cycle"?
2. Could closing entries be made without using the Income Summary account?
3. Why does the post-closing trial balance contain only balance sheet accounts?

LO3 LO4 Discussion Questions

E 2. Develop brief answers to each of the following questions:

1. Why are reversing entries helpful?
2. Under what circumstances would the Income Statement and Balance Sheet columns on a work sheet balance when they are initially totaled?

LO2 Preparation of Closing Entries

E 3. The income statement accounts for the Monroe Realty Company at the end of its fiscal year are shown below. Prepare the required closing entries in journal form. Chris Ross is the owner.

Account Name	Debit	Credit
Commission Revenue		$26,620
Wages Expense	$9,110	
Rent Expense	1,300	
Supplies Expense	4,160	
Insurance Expense	915	
Depreciation Expense–Office Equipment	1,345	
Total Expenses		16,830
Net Income		$ 9,790

LO3 Reversing Entries

E 4. Selected September T accounts for Hubbord Company are presented below.

SUPPLIES

Dr.		Cr.	
9/1 Bal.	860	9/30 Adj.	1,280
Sept. purchases	940		
Bal.	520		

SUPPLIES EXPENSE

Dr.		Cr.	
9/30 Adj.	1,280	9/30 Closing	1,280
Bal.	—		

WAGES PAYABLE

Dr.		Cr.	
		9/30 Adj.	640
		Bal.	640

WAGES EXPENSE

Dr.		Cr.	
Sept. wages	3,940	9/30 Closing	4,580
9/30 Adj.	640		
Bal.	—		

1. In which of the accounts would a reversing entry be helpful? Why?
2. Prepare the appropriate reversing entry.
3. Prepare the entry to record a payment on October 25 for wages totaling $3,140. How much of this amount represents wages expense for October?

LO2 **Preparation of a Trial Balance**

E 5. The following alphabetical list presents the accounts and balances for Sally's Cleaners on June 30, 2011. All the accounts have normal balances.

Accounts Payable	$15,420
Accounts Receivable	7,650
Accumulated Depreciation–Office Equipment	1,350
Advertising Expense	1,800
Cash	7,635
Office Equipment	15,510
Prepaid Insurance	1,680
Rent Expense	7,200
Revenue from Commissions	57,900
S. Nash, Capital	30,630
S. Nash, Withdrawals	27,000
Supplies	825
Wages Expense	36,000

Prepare the trial balance by listing the accounts in the correct order, with the balances in the appropriate debit or credit column.

LO4 **Completion of a Work Sheet**

E 6. The following is a highly simplified alphabetical list of trial balance accounts and their normal balances for the month ended March 31, 2011:

Accounts Payable	$ 4
Accounts Receivable	7
Accumulated Depreciation–Office Equipment	1
Cash	4
J. Wells, Capital	12
J. Wells, Withdrawals	6
Office Equipment	8
Prepaid Insurance	2
Service Revenue	23
Supplies	4
Unearned Revenues	3
Utilities Expense	2
Wages Expense	10

1. Prepare a work sheet, entering the trial balance accounts in the order in which they would normally appear and entering the balances in the correct debit or credit column.
2. Complete the work sheet using the following information: expired insurance, $1; estimated depreciation on office equipment, $1; accrued wages, $1; and unused supplies on hand, $1. In addition, $2 of the unearned revenues balance had been earned by the end of the month.

LO4 **Preparation of Statement of Owner's Equity**

E 7. The Capital, Withdrawals, and Income Summary accounts for Eva's Hair Salon are shown in T account form at the top of the next page. The closing entries have been recorded for the year ended December 31, 2010.

E. Kristen, Capital

Dr.		Cr.	
12/31/10	4,500	12/31/09	13,000
		12/31/10	9,500
		Bal.	**18,000**

Income Summary

Dr.		Cr.	
12/31/10	21,500	12/31/10	31,000
12/31/10	9,500		
Bal.	—		

E. Kristen, Withdrawals

Dr.		Cr.	
4/1/10	1,500	12/31/10	4,500
7/1/10	1,500		
10/1/10	1,500		
Bal.	—		

Prepare a statement of owner's equity for Eva's Hair Salon.

LO3 LO4 Preparation of Adjusting and Reversing Entries from Work Sheet Columns

E 8. The items that appear below are from the Adjustments columns of a work sheet dated June 30, 2011.

Account Name	Adjustments Debit	Adjustments Credit
Prepaid Insurance		(a) 240
Office Supplies		(b) 630
Accumulated Depreciation–Office Equipment		(c) 1,400
Accumulated Depreciation–Store Equipment		(d) 2,200
Office Salaries Expense	(e) 240	
Store Salaries Expense	(e) 480	
Insurance Expense	(a) 240	
Office Supplies Expense	(b) 630	
Depreciation Expense–Office Equipment	(c) 1,400	
Depreciation Expense–Store Equipment	(d) 2,200	
Salaries Payable		(e) 720
	5,190	5,190

1. Prepare the adjusting entries in journal form.
2. Where required, prepare appropriate reversing entries in journal form.

LO2 LO4 Preparation of Closing Entries from the Work Sheet

E 9. The items that follow are from the Income Statement columns of the work sheet for Ben's Repair Shop for the year ended December 31, 2011. Prepare entries in journal form to close the revenue, expense, Income Summary, and Withdrawals accounts. The owner, Ben Junkus, withdrew $6,000 during the year.

Account Name	Income Statement Debit	Income Statement Credit
Repair Revenue		25,620
Wages Expense	8,110	
Rent Expense	1,200	
Supplies Expense	4,260	
Insurance Expense	915	
Depreciation Expense–Repair Equipment	1,345	
	15,830	25,620
Net Income	9,790	
	25,620	25,620

LO4 Adjusting Entries and Preparation of a Balance Sheet

E 10. In the partial work sheet for L. Wung Company that follows, the Trial Balance and Income Statement columns have been completed. All amounts are in dollars.

Account Name	Trial Balance Debit	Trial Balance Credit	Income Statement Debit	Income Statement Credit
Cash	14			
Accounts Receivable	24			
Supplies	22			
Prepaid Insurance	16			
Building	50			
Accumulated Depreciation–Building		16		
Accounts Payable		8		
Unearned Revenues		4		
L. Wung, Capital		64		
Revenues		88		92
Wages Expense	54		60	
	180	180		
Insurance Expense			8	
Supplies Expense			16	
Depreciation Expense–Building			4	
Wages Payable			—	—
			88	92
Net Income			4	
			92	92

1. Show the adjustments that have been made in journal form without giving an explanation.
2. Prepare a balance sheet for December 31, 2010.

Problems

LO1 LO2 Preparation of Closing Entries

P 1. Affordable Trailer Rental rents small trailers by the day for local moving jobs. This is its adjusted trial balance at the end of the current fiscal year:

Affordable Trailer Rental
Adjusted Trial Balance
June 30, 2011

Cash	$ 692	
Accounts Receivable	972	
Supplies	119	
Prepaid Insurance	360	
Trailers	12,000	
Accumulated Depreciation–Trailers		$ 7,200
Accounts Payable		271
Wages Payable		200
A. Tropp, Capital		5,694
A. Tropp, Withdrawals	7,200	
Trailer Rentals Revenue		45,546
Wages Expense	23,400	
Insurance Expense	720	
Supplies Expense	266	
Depreciation Expense–Trailers	2,400	
Other Expenses	10,782	
	$58,911	$58,911

Required

1. From the information given, record closing entries in journal form.

User insight ▶ 2. If closing entries were not prepared at the end of the accounting period, what problems would result in the next accounting period?

LO1 LO2 Closing Entries Using T Accounts and Preparation of Financial Statements

P 2. The adjusted trial balance for Settles Tennis Club at the end of the company's fiscal year appears at the top of the next page.

Required

1. Prepare T accounts and enter the balances for B. Settles, Capital; B. Settles, Withdrawals; Income Summary, and all revenue and expense accounts.
2. Enter the four required closing entries in the T accounts, labeling the components *a*, *b*, *c*, and *d*, as appropriate.
3. Prepare an income statement, a statement of retained earnings, and a balance sheet for Settles Tennis Club.
4. Explain why it is necessary to make closing entries at the end of an accounting period.

Settles Tennis Club
Adjusted Trial Balance
June 30, 2011

Cash	$ 26,200	
Prepaid Advertising	9,600	
Supplies	1,200	
Land	100,000	
Building	645,200	
Accumulated Depreciation–Building		$ 260,000
Equipment	156,000	
Accumulated Depreciation–Equipment		50,400
Accounts Payable		73,000
Wages Payable		9,000
Property Taxes Payable		22,500
Unearned Revenue–Locker Fees		3,000
B. Settles, Capital		471,150
B. Settles, Withdrawals	54,000	
Revenue from Court Fees		678,100
Revenue from Locker Fees		9,600
Wages Expense	351,000	
Maintenance Expense	51,600	
Advertising Expense	39,750	
Utilities Expense	64,800	
Supplies Expense	6,000	
Depreciation Expense–Building	30,000	
Depreciation Expense–Equipment	12,000	
Property Taxes Expense	22,500	
Miscellaneous Expense	6,900	6,900
	$1,576,750	$1,576,750

LO2 Preparation of Closing Entries

P 3. Robert Half International, Inc. is a global specialized staffing firm. Information adapted from the statement of earnings (in thousands, without earnings per share information) in its annual report for the year ended December 31, 2005, follows.[1] The firm reported distributing cash (dividends) in the amount of $47,781,000 to the owners in 2005.

Revenues	
Service revenues	$3,338,439
Interest income	10,948
Total revenues	$3,349,387
Expenses	
Employee compensation and benefits	$1,965,390
Selling, general, and administrative expenses	991,823
Income taxes	154,304
Total expenses	$3,111,517
Net income	$ 237,870

Required

1. Prepare in journal form the closing entries Robert Half would have made on December 31, 2005. Treat income taxes as an expense and cash distributions to owners as withdrawals.
2. Based on your handling of requirement 1 and the effect of expenses and cash distributions on owner's capital, what theoretical reason can you give for not including expenses and cash distributions in the same closing entry?

LO2 LO3 LO4 **Preparation of a Work Sheet, Financial Statements, and Adjusting, Closing, and Reversing Entries**

P 4. At the end of the fiscal year, the trial balance of Reed Delivery Service appeared as shown below.

Reed Delivery Service
Trial Balance
August 31, 2010

Cash	$ 10,072	
Accounts Receivable	29,314	
Prepaid Insurance	5,340	
Delivery Supplies	14,700	
Office Supplies	2,460	
Land	15,000	
Building	196,000	
Accumulated Depreciation–Building		$ 53,400
Trucks	103,800	
Accumulated Depreciation–Trucks		30,900
Office Equipment	15,900	
Accumulated Depreciation–Office Equipment		10,800
Accounts Payable		9,396
Unearned Lockbox Fees		8,340
Mortgage Payable		72,000
N. Reed, Capital		128,730
N. Reed, Withdrawals	30,000	
Delivery Service Revenue		283,470
Lockbox Fees Earned		28,800
Truck Drivers' Wages Expense	120,600	
Office Salaries Expense	44,400	
Gas, Oil, and Truck Repairs Expense	31,050	
Interest Expense	7,200	
	$625,836	$625,836

Required

1. Enter the trial balance amounts in the Trial Balance columns of a work sheet and complete the work sheet using the information that follows:
   a. Expired insurance, $3,060.
   b. Inventory of unused delivery supplies, $1,430.
   c. Inventory of unused office supplies, $186.
   d. Estimated depreciation on the building, $14,400.
   e. Estimated depreciation on the trucks, $15,450.
   f. Estimated depreciation on the office equipment, $2,700.
   g. The company credits the lockbox fees of customers who pay in advance to the Unearned Lockbox Fees account. Of the amount credited to this account during the year, $5,630 had been earned by August 31.

h. Lockbox fees earned but unrecorded and uncollected at the end of the accounting period, $816.
i. Accrued but unpaid truck drivers' wages at the end of the year, $1,920.

2. Prepare an income statement, a statement of owner's equity, and a balance sheet for the company. Assume the owner, Natalie Reed, made no additional investments.
3. Prepare adjusting, closing, and, when necessary, reversing entries from the work sheet.
4. Can the work sheet be used as a substitute for the financial statements? Explain your answer. (User insight ▶)

LO1 LO2 The Complete Accounting Cycle Without a Work Sheet: Two Months *(second month optional)*

P 5. On May 1, 2011, Conrad Sayer opened Conrad's Repair Service. During the month, he completed the following transactions for the company:

May	1	Began business by depositing $5,000 in a bank account in the name of the company.
	1	Paid the rent for the store for current month, $425.
	1	Paid the premium on a one-year insurance policy, $480.
	2	Purchased repair equipment from Chmura Company, $4,200. Terms were $600 down and $300 per month for one year. First payment is due June 1.
	5	Purchased repair supplies from Brown Company on credit, $468.
	8	Paid cash for an advertisement in a local newspaper, $60.
	15	Received cash repair revenue for the first half of the month, $400.
	21	Paid Brown Company on account, $225.
	31	Received cash repair revenue for the last half of May, $975.
	31	Made a withdrawal, $300.

Required for May

1. Prepare journal entries to record the May transactions.
2. Open the following accounts: Cash (111); Prepaid Insurance (117); Repair Supplies (119); Repair Equipment (144); Accumulated Depreciation–Repair Equipment (145); Accounts Payable (212); C. Sayer, Capital (311); C. Sayer, Withdrawals (313); Income Summary (314); Repair Revenue (411); Store Rent Expense (511); Advertising Expense (512); Insurance Expense (513); Repair Supplies Expense (514); and Depreciation Expense–Repair Equipment (515). Post the May journal entries to the ledger accounts.
3. Using the following information, record adjusting entries in the general journal and post to the ledger accounts:
   a. One month's insurance has expired.
   b. The remaining inventory of unused repair supplies is $169.
   c. The estimated depreciation on repair equipment is $70.
4. From the accounts in the ledger, prepare an adjusted trial balance. (*Note:* Normally, a trial balance is prepared before adjustments but is omitted here to save time.)
5. From the adjusted trial balance, prepare an income statement, a statement of owner's equity, and a balance sheet for May.
6. Prepare and post closing entries.
7. Prepare a post-closing trial balance.

(Optional)

During June, Conrad Sayer completed these transactions for Conrad's Repair Service:

June 1 Paid the monthly rent, $425.
1 Made the monthly payment to Chmura Company, $300.
6 Purchased additional repair supplies on credit from Brown Company, $863.
15 Received cash repair revenue for the first half of the month, $914.
20 Paid cash for an advertisement in the local newspaper, $60.
23 Paid Brown Company on account, $600.
30 Received cash repair revenue for the last half of the month, $817.
30 Recorded a withdrawal by owner, $300.

8. Prepare and post journal entries to record the June transactions.
9. Using the following information, record adjusting entries in the general journal and post to the ledger accounts:
   a. One month's insurance has expired.
   b. The inventory of unused repair supplies is $413.
   c. The estimated depreciation on repair equipment is $70.
10. From the accounts in the ledger, prepare an adjusted trial balance.
11. From the adjusted trial balance, prepare the June income statement, statement of owner's equity, and balance sheet.
12. Prepare and post closing entries.
13. Prepare a post-closing trial balance.

Alternate Problems

LO1 LO2 Preparation of Closing Entries

P 6. The adjusted trial balance for Patch Consultant Company at the end of its fiscal year is shown below.

Patch Consultant Company
Adjusted Trial Balance
December 31, 2011

Cash	$ 7,275	
Accounts Receivable	2,325	
Prepaid Insurance	585	
Office Supplies	440	
Office Equipment	6,300	
Accumulated Depreciation–Office Equipment		$ 765
Automobile	6,750	
Accumulated Depreciation–Automobile		750
Accounts Payable		1,700
Unearned Consulting Fees		1,500
S. Patch, Capital		14,535
S. Patch, Withdrawals	7,000	
Consulting Fees Earned		31,700
Office Salaries Expense	13,500	
Advertising Expense	2,525	
Rent Expense	2,650	
Telephone Expense	1,600	
	$50,950	$50,950

Required

1. Prepare the required closing entries.

User insight ▶ 2. Explain why closing entries are necessary at the end of the accounting period.

LO2 Preparation of Closing Entries

P 7. The adjusted trial balance for Greg Painting Company at December 31, 2011, is provided below. The owner made no investments during the period.

Greg Painting Company
Adjusted Trial Balance
December 31, 2011

Cash	$ 4,750	
Accounts Receivable	2,592	
Prepaid Insurance	380	
Prepaid Rent	200	
Painting Supplies	152	
Painting Equipment	3,875	
Accumulated Depreciation–Painting Equipment		$ 320
Truck	7,200	
Accumulated Depreciation–Truck		720
Accounts Payable		420
Wages Payable		295
Unearned Painting Revenue		1,690
G. Rak, Capital		15,034
G. Rak, Withdrawals	2,000	
Painting Revenue		14,620
Wages Expense	5,680	
Rent Expense	1,350	
Gas, Oil, and Other Truck Expenses	580	
Insurance Expense	380	
Supplies Expense	2,920	
Depreciation Expense–Painting Equipment	320	
Depreciation Expense–Truck	720	
	$33,099	$33,099

Required

Prepare in journal form the required closing entries.

LO2 LO4 Preparation of a Work Sheet, Financial Statements, and Adjusting and Closing Entries

P 8. Pierot Theater Company's trial balance at the end of its current fiscal year is shown at the top of the next page.

Pierot Theater Company
Trial Balance
June 30, 2010

Cash	$ 31,800	
Accounts Receivable	18,544	
Prepaid Insurance	19,600	
Office Supplies	780	
Cleaning Supplies	3,590	
Land	20,000	
Building	400,000	
Accumulated Depreciation–Building		$ 39,400
Theater Furnishings	370,000	
Accumulated Depreciation–Theater Furnishings		65,000
Office Equipment	31,600	
Accumulated Depreciation–Office Equipment		15,560
Accounts Payable		45,506
Gift Books Liability		41,900
Mortgage Payable		300,000
P. Rieu, Capital		312,648
P. Rieu, Withdrawals	60,000	
Ticket Sales Revenue		411,400
Theater Rental Revenue		45,200
Usher Wages Expense	157,000	
Office Wages Expense	24,000	
Utilities Expense	112,700	
Interest Expense	27,000	
	$1,276,614	$1,276,614

Required

1. Enter Pierot Theater Company's trial balance amounts in the Trial Balance columns of a work sheet and complete the work sheet using the following information:
   a. Expired insurance, $17,400.
   b. Inventory of unused office supplies, $244.
   c. Inventory of unused cleaning supplies, $468.
   d. Estimated depreciation on the building, $14,000.
   e. Estimated depreciation on the theater furnishings, $36,000.
   f. Estimated depreciation on the office equipment, $3,160.
   g. The company credits all gift books sold during the year to the Gift Books Liability account. A gift book is a booklet of ticket coupons that is purchased in advance as a gift. The recipient redeems the coupons at some point in the future. On June 30 it was estimated that $37,800 worth of the gift books had been redeemed.
   h. Accrued but unpaid usher wages at the end of the accounting period, $860.
2. Prepare an income statement, a statement of owner's equity, and a balance sheet. Assume no additional investments by the owner, Pierot Rieu.
3. Prepare adjusting and closing entries from the work sheet.

User insight ▶

4. Can the work sheet be used as a substitute for the financial statements? Explain your answer.

LO2 **Preparation of Closing Entries**

P 9. The adjusted trial balance for Burke Consultants Company at the end of its fiscal year is shown below.

Burke Consultants Company
Adjusted Trial Balance
December 31, 2010

Cash	$ 7,575	
Accounts Receivable	2,625	
Prepaid Insurance	585	
Office Supplies	440	
Office Equipment	6,300	
Accumulated Depreciation–Office Equipment		$ 765
Automobile	6,750	
Accumulated Depreciation–Automobile		750
Accounts Payable		1,700
Unearned Consulting Fees		1,500
D. Burke, Capital		14,535
D. Burke, Withdrawals	7,000	
Consulting Fees Earned		32,550
Office Salaries Expense	13,500	
Advertising Expense	2,525	
Rent Expense	2,650	
Telephone Expense	1,850	
	$51,800	$51,800

Required

Prepare in journal form the required closing entries for Burke Consultants Company.

LO2 **Preparation of Closing Entries**

P 10. The adjusted trial balance for Van Rental Service at the end of its fiscal year is shown on the next page.

Required

Prepare in journal form the required closing entries for Van Rental Service.

Van Rental Service
Adjusted Trial Balance
December 31, 2010

Cash	$ 10,215	
Accounts Receivable	12,100	
Prepaid Rent	13,000	
Prepaid Insurance	4,700	
Prepaid Maintenance	10,350	
Spare Parts	11,520	
Vans	310,000	
Accumulated Depreciation–Vans		$ 55,000
Notes Payable		48,730
Unearned Rental Revenue		35,500
R. Krazel, Capital		115,305
R. Krazel, Withdrawals	18,000	
Rental Revenue		523,498
Gas and Oil Expense	87,100	
Salaries Expense	202,710	
Advertising Expense	36,800	
Rent Expense	12,000	
Insurance Expense	1,800	
Spare Parts Expense	9,294	
Depreciation Expense–Vans	27,500	
Maintenance Expense	10,944	
	$778,033	$778,033

ENHANCING Your Knowledge, Skills, and Critical Thinking

LO1 **Interim Financial Statements**

C 1. Offshore Drilling Company provides services for drilling operations off the coast of Louisiana. The company has a significant amount of debt to Southern National Bank in Baton Rouge. The bank requires the company to provide it with quarterly financial statements. Explain what is involved in preparing financial statements every quarter.

LO1 **Purpose of Closing Entries**

C 2. Maury Jacobs, owner of Jacobs Furniture Company, notices the amount of time it takes the company's accountant to prepare closing entries. He suggests that the company could save time and money by not doing closing entries. He argues that only adjusting entries are needed to determine the company's earnings. Explain the purposes of closing entries and why they are worth doing.

LO1 **Accounting Efficiency**

C 3. Way Heaters Company manufactures industrial heaters used in making candy. It sells its heaters to some customers on credit with generous terms specifying payment six months after purchase and an interest rate based on current bank rates. Because the interest on the loans accrues a little every day but is not paid until the note's due date, an adjusting entry must be made at the end of each accounting period to debit Interest Receivable and credit Interest Income for the amount of the interest accrued but not received to date. The company prepares financial statements every month. Keeping track of what has been accrued in the past is time-consuming because the notes carry different dates and interest rates.

Form in-class groups to determine what the accountant can do to simplify the process of making the adjusting entry for accrued interest each month. Compare the groups' solutions in a class discussion.

LO1 **Ethics and Time Pressure**

C 4. James Bear, an accountant for Rosa Company, has made adjusting entries and is preparing the adjusted trial balance for the first six months of the year. Financial statements must be delivered to the bank by 5 P.M. to support a critical loan agreement. By noon, Bear has been unable to balance the adjusted trial balance. The figures are off by $1,320, so he increases the balance of the owner's Capital account by $1,320. He closes the accounts, prepares the statements, and sends them to the bank on time. Bear hopes that no one will notice the problem and believes that he can find the error and correct it by the end of next month. Are Bear's actions ethical? Why or why not? Did he have other alternatives?

LO1 **Fiscal Year, Closing Process, and Interim Reports**

C 5. Refer to the notes to the financial statements in the **CVS** annual report in the Supplement to Chapter 5. When does CVS end its fiscal year? For what reasons might it have chosen this date? From the standpoint of completing the accounting cycle, what advantage does this date have? Does CVS prepare interim financial statements? What are the implications of interim financial statements for the accounting cycle?

LO1 **Interim Financial Reporting and Seasonality**

C 6. Both **CVS** and **Southwest Airlines** provide quarterly financial information in their financial statements. Quarterly financial reports provide important information about the "seasonality" of a company's operations. *Seasonality* refers to how dependent a company is on sales during different seasons of the year, and how that affects a company's need to plan for cash flows and inventory. From the quarterly financial information for CVS in the Supplement to Chapter 5, determine the effects of seasons on CVS's net revenues and net earnings by calculating for the most recent year the percentage of quarterly net sales and net earnings to annual net sales and net earnings. Discuss the results. How do you think the effect of seasons might differ for Southwest's operating revenues and income?

COMPREHENSIVE Problem: Miller Design Studio

This comprehensive problem involving Miller Design Studio covers all the learning objectives in this chapter and in the chapters on measuring business transactions and measuring business income. To complete the problem, you may sometimes have to refer to this material.

The July 31, 2011, post-closing trial balance for the Miller Design Studio is on the next page.

Miller Design Studio
Post-Closing Trial Balance
July 31, 2011

Cash	$22,480	
Accounts Receivable	5,000	
Office Supplies	3,660	
Prepaid Rent	1,600	
Office Equipment	16,320	
Accumulated Depreciation–Office Equipment		$ 300
Accounts Payable		6,280
Unearned Design Revenue		600
Wages Payable		720
J. Miller, Capital		41,160
	$49,060	$49,060

During August, the studio engaged in these transactions:

Aug. 1 Received an additional investment of cash from J. Miller, $20,000.
2 Purchased additional office equipment with cash, $4,700.
7 Purchased additional office supplies for cash, $540.
8 Completed the series of designs that began on July 31 and billed for the total design services performed, including the accrued revenues of $800 that had been recognized in an adjusting entry in July, $1,400.
12 Paid the amount due for the office equipment purchased last month, $3,000.
13 Accepted an advance in cash for design work to be done, $2,400.
15 Performed design services and received a cash fee, $2,900.
16 Received payment on account for design services performed last month, $2,800.
19 Made a partial payment on the utilities bill that was received and recorded at the end of July, $140.
20 Performed design services for Rave Department Stores and agreed to accept payment next month, $3,200.
21 Performed design services for cash, $1,160.
22 Received and paid the utilities bill for August, $900.
23 Paid the assistant for four weeks' wages, $4,800.
26 Paid the rent for September in advance, $1,600.
30 Paid cash to J. Miller as a withdrawal for personal expenses, $2,800.

Required

1. Record entries in journal form and post to the ledger accounts the optional reversing entries on August 1 for Wages Payable and Accounts Receivable (see adjustment for unrecorded wages on page 116 and adjustment for design revenue on page 119). (Begin the general journal on page 5.)
2. Record the transactions for August in journal form.
3. Post the August transactions to the ledger accounts.
4. Prepare the Trial Balance columns of a work sheet.

5. Prepare adjusting entries and complete the work sheet using the information below.
   a. One month's prepaid rent has expired, $1,600.
   b. An inventory of supplies reveals $2,020 still on hand on August 31.
   c. Depreciation on equipment for August is calculated to be $300.
   d. Services performed for which payment had been received in advance totaled $1,300.
   e. Services performed that will not be billed until September totaled $580.
   f. Wages accrued by the end of August, $720.
6. From the work sheet, prepare an income statement, a statement of owner's equity, and a balance sheet for August 31, 2011.
7. Record the adjusting entries on August 31, 2011, in journal form, and post them to the ledger accounts.
8. Record the closing entries on August 31, 2011, in journal form, and post them to the ledger accounts.
9. Prepare a post-closing trial balance at August 31, 2011.

CHAPTER

5 Financial Reporting and Analysis

Making a Statement

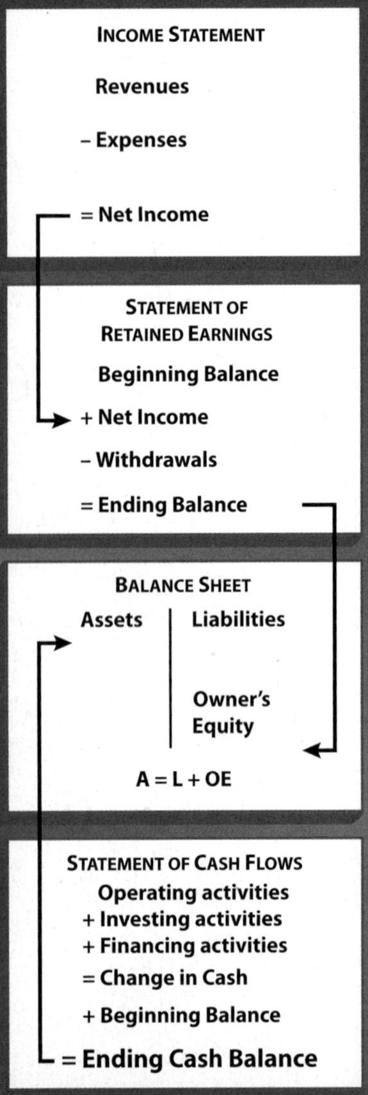

INCOME STATEMENT

Revenues

– Expenses

= Net Income

STATEMENT OF RETAINED EARNINGS

Beginning Balance

+ Net Income

– Withdrawals

= Ending Balance

BALANCE SHEET

Assets	**Liabilities**
	Owner's Equity

A = L + OE

STATEMENT OF CASH FLOWS

Operating activities
+ Investing activities
+ Financing activities
= Change in Cash
+ Beginning Balance
= Ending Cash Balance

Grouping like accounts on the balance sheet and income statement aids analysis.

Owners, creditors, and other interested parties rely on the integrity of a company's financial reports. A company's managers and accountants therefore have a responsibility to act ethically in the reporting process. However, what is often overlooked is that the users of financial reports also have a responsibility to recognize and understand the types of judgments and estimates that underlie these reports.

LEARNING OBJECTIVES

LO1 Describe the objective of financial reporting and identify the qualitative characteristics, conventions, and ethical considerations of accounting information. (pp. 182–185)

LO2 Define and describe the conventions of *consistency, full disclosure, materiality, conservatism,* and *cost-benefit.* (pp. 185–189)

LO3 Identify and describe the basic components of a classified balance sheet. (pp. 190–195)

LO4 Describe the features of multistep and single-step classified income statements. (pp. 196–200)

LO5 Use classified financial statements to evaluate liquidity and profitability. (pp. 201–208)

DECISION POINT ▶ A USER'S FOCUS FUN-FOR-FEET COMPANY

- ▶ How should the income statement be organized to provide the best information?
- ▶ What key measures best capture a company's financial performance?

Fun-For-Feet Company is a retailer of casual footwear for college students. It has two stores, and the owner, Jay Bonali, now wants to open a third. To obtain a loan so that he can open a third store, he will have to present the company's financial statements to his bank. Shown below is the kind of income statement Jay has always prepared in the past. He is concerned that this simple, single-step income statement may not provide the bank with adequate information about how the company generates its income, and he is also wondering how he can best show the bank that the company is profitable. In other words, he is looking for answers to the two questions that appear in the margin to the right.

Fun-For-Feet Company
Income Statement
For the Year Ended December 31, 2011

Revenues		
Net sales		$1,207,132
Interest income		5,720
Total revenues		$1,212,852
Costs and expenses		
Cost of goods sold	$787,080	
Selling expenses	203,740	
General and administrative expenses	100,688	
Interest expense	13,560	
Total costs and expenses		1,105,068
Net income		$ 107,784

Foundations of Financial Reporting

LO1 Describe the objective of financial reporting and identify the qualitative characteristics, conventions, and ethical considerations of accounting information.

By issuing stocks and bonds that are traded in financial markets, companies can raise the cash they need to carry out current and future business activities. Investors are interested mainly in returns from dividends and increases in the market value of their investment. Creditors want to know if the firm can repay a loan plus interest in accordance with specified terms. Very importantly, both investors and creditors need to know if the firm can generate adequate cash flows to maintain its liquidity. Financial statements are important to both groups in making that judgment. They offer valuable information that helps investors and creditors judge a company's ability to pay dividends or other distributions to owners and repay debts with interest.

In the following sections, we describe the objectives of financial reporting and the qualitative characteristics, accounting conventions, and ethical considerations that are involved. Figure 5-1 illustrates these factors.

Objective of Financial Reporting

The Financial Accounting Standards Board (FASB) emphasizes the needs of current and potential investors (owners) and creditors while recognizing the needs of other users when it defines the objective of financial reporting as follows:[1]

> To provide financial information about the reporting entity that is useful to present and potential equity investors, lenders, and other creditors in making decisions in their capacity as capital providers. Information that is decision-useful to capital providers may also be useful to other users of financial reporting who are not capital providers.

To be useful for decision making, financial reporting must enable the user to do the following:

- **Assess cash flow prospects.** Since the ultimate value of an entity and its ability to pay dividends, interest, and otherwise provide returns to capital providers depends on its ability to generate future cash flows, capital providers and other users need information to help make judgments about the entity's ability to generate cash flows.
- **Assess stewardship.** Since management is accountable for the custody and safekeeping of the entity's economic resources and for their efficient and profitable use, capital providers and others need information about the entity's resources (assets), claims against them (liabilities and owner's [stockholders'] equity), and changes in these resources and claims as impacted by transactions (earnings and cash flows) and other economic events.

Financial reporting includes the financial statements periodically presented to parties outside the business. The statements—the balance sheet, the income statement, the statement of owner's equity, and the statement of cash flows—are important outputs of the accounting system but not the only output. Management's explanations and other information, including underlying assumptions and significant uncertainties about methods and estimates used in the financial reports, constitute important components of financial reporting by an entity. Because of a potential conflict of interest between managers, who must prepare the statements, and investors or creditors, who invest in or lend money to the business, financial statements usually are audited by outside accountants to ensure their reliability.

Qualitative Characteristics of Accounting Information

Students in their first accounting course often get the idea that accounting is 100 percent accurate. Contributing to this perception is that introductory textbooks like this one present the basics of accounting in a simple form to help students understand them. All the problems can be solved, and all the numbers

FIGURE 5-1
Factors Affecting Financial Reporting

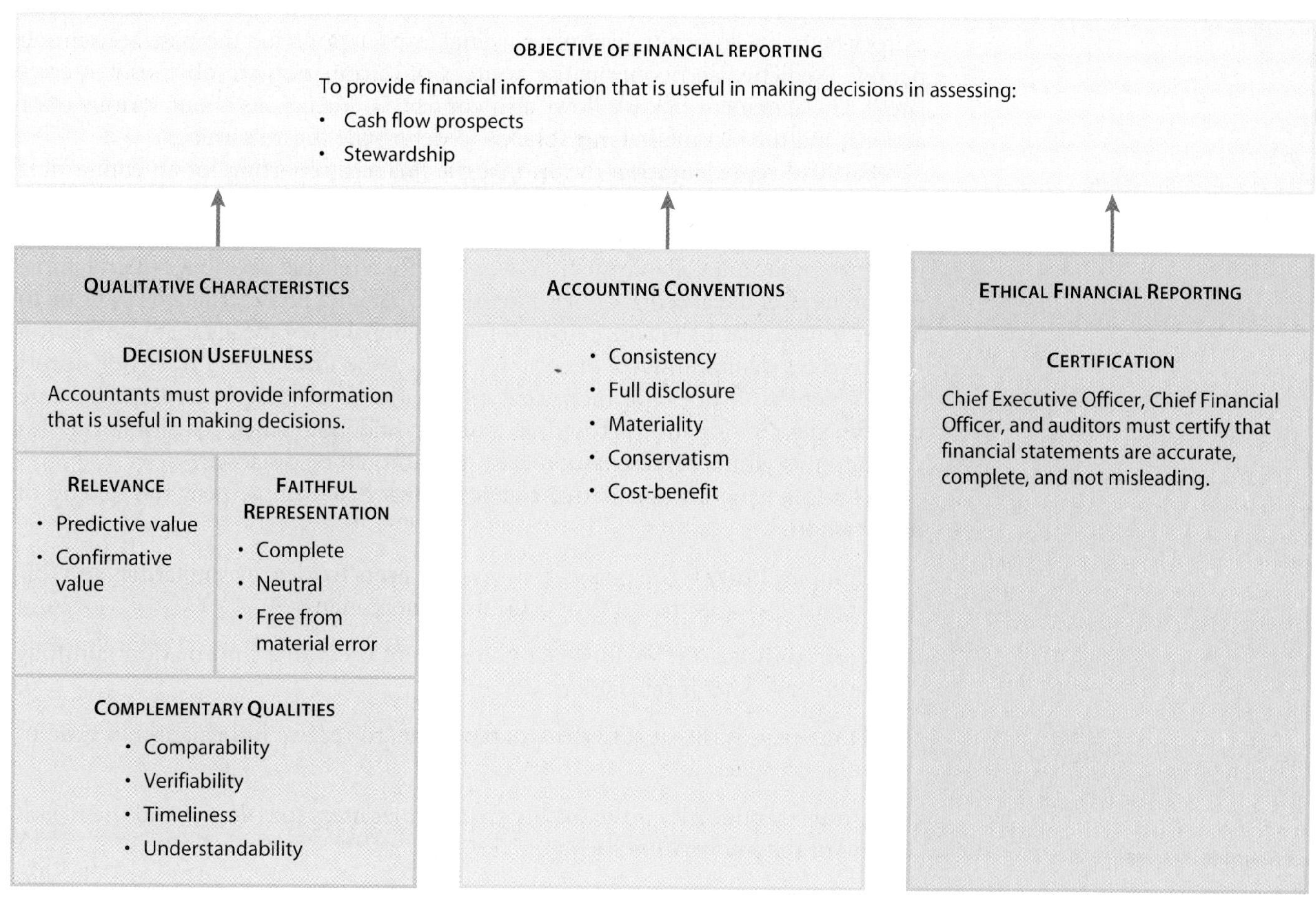

add up; what is supposed to equal something else does. Accounting seems very much like mathematics in its precision. In practice, however, accounting information is neither simple nor precise, and it rarely satisfies all criteria. The FASB emphasizes this fact in the following statement:

> The information provided by financial reporting often results from approximate, rather than exact, measures. The measures commonly involve numerous estimates, classifications, summarizations, judgments, and allocations. The outcome of economic activity in a dynamic economy is uncertain and results from combinations of many factors. Thus, despite the aura of precision that may seem to surround financial reporting in general and financial statements in particular, with few exceptions the measures are approximations, which may be based on rules and conventions, rather than exact amounts.[2]

The goal of generating accounting information is to provide data that different users need to make informed decisions for their unique situations. How this goal is achieved provides much of the interest and controversy in accounting. To facilitate interpretation of accounting information, the FASB has established standards, or **qualitative characteristics,** by which to judge the information.[3] The most important or fundamental qualitative characteristics are relevance and faithful representation.

Relevance means that the information has a direct bearing on a decision. In other words, if the information were not available, a different decision would be made. To be relevant, information must have *predictive value, confirmative value,* or both. Information has predictive value if it helps current and potential investors (owners) and creditors make decisions about the future. For example, the statement of cash flows can provide information as to whether the company has sufficient funds to expand or if it will need to raise funds from capital providers. Information has confirmative value if it provides the information needed to determine if expectations have been met. For example, the income statement provides information as to whether a company has met earnings expectations for the past accounting period. Predictive and confirmative sources of information are obviously interrelated. The statement of cash flows also confirms expectations about various prior actions, and the income statement helps to determine future earnings.

Faithful representation means that the financial reporting for an entity must be a reliable depiction of what it purports to represent. To be faithful, financial information must be *complete, neutral,* and *free from material error.* Complete information includes all information necessary for a reliable decision. Neutral information implies the absence of bias intended to attain a predetermined result or to induce a particular behavior. Freedom from material error means that information must meet a minimum level of accuracy so that the information does not distort what it depicts. It does not mean that information is absolutely accurate, because most financial information is based on estimates and judgments. If major uncertainties as to the faithful representation exist, they should be disclosed.

The following are qualitative characteristics that complement the quality of information:

- **Comparability** is the quality that enables users to identify similarities and differences between two sets of economic phenomena.
- **Verifiability** is the quality that helps assure users that information faithfully represents what it purports to depict.
- **Timeliness** is the quality that enables users to receive information in time to influence a decision.
- **Understandability** is the quality that enables users to comprehend the meaning of the information they receive.

Accounting Conventions

For accounting information to be understandable, accountants must prepare financial statements in accordance with accepted practices. But the decision maker also must know how to interpret the information; in making decisions, he or she must judge what information to use, how to use it, and what it means. Familiarity with the **accounting conventions,** or constraints on accounting, used in preparing financial statements enable the user to better understand accounting information. These conventions, which we discuss later in the chapter, affect how and what information is presented in financial statements.

Ethical Financial Reporting

As we noted earlier in the text, in 2002, in the wake of accounting scandals at **Enron** and **WorldCom**, Congress passed the Sarbanes-Oxley Act. One of the important outcomes of this legislation was that the Securities and Exchange Commission instituted rules requiring the chief executive officers and chief financial officers of all publicly traded companies to certify that, to their knowledge, the quarterly and annual statements that their companies file with the SEC are accurate and complete. Subsequently, an investigation by the audit committee of **Dell Computer**'s board of directors and management disclosed weaknesses in the company's controls and led to restatements of the financial statements for the prior four years. After extensive improvements in control and the restatements, the company's chief executive officer, Michael S. Dell, made the following certifying statement in the company's annual report to the SEC:

> Based on my knowledge, the financial statements, and other financial information included in this report, fairly present in all material respects the financial condition, results of operations and cash flows . . . for the periods represented in this report.[4]

The chief financial officer may sign a similar certification.

As the Enron and WorldCom scandals demonstrated, fraudulent financial reporting can have high costs for investors, lenders, employees, and customers. It can also have high costs for the people who condone, authorize, or prepare misleading reports—even those at the highest corporate levels. In March 2005, Bernard J. Ebbers, former CEO of WorldCom, was convicted of seven counts of filing false reports with the SEC and one count each of securities fraud and conspiracy.[5] In 2006, both Kenneth Lay, former chairman of Enron Corporation, and Jeffrey Skilling, Enron's former CEO, were convicted on charges similar to the ones of which Ebbers was convicted.

STOP & APPLY >

The lettered items below represent a classification scheme for the concepts of financial accounting. Match each numbered term in the list that follows with the letter of the category in which it belongs.

a. Decision makers (users of accounting information)
b. Objectives of accounting information
c. Accounting measurement considerations
d. Accounting processing considerations
e. Qualitative characteristics

1. Furnishing information that is useful in assessing cash flow prospects
2. Verifiability
3. Relevance
4. Assess stewardship
5. Faithful representation
6. Recognition
7. Investors
8. Predictive value
9. Management
10. Valuation
11. Internal accounting control
12. Furnishing information that is useful to investors and creditors

SOLUTION

1. b; 2. e; 3. e; 4. b; 5. e; 6. c; 7. a; 8. e; 9. a; 10. c; 11. d; 12. b

Accounting Conventions for Preparing Financial Statements

LO2 Define and describe the conventions of *consistency, full disclosure, materiality, conservatism,* and *cost-benefit.*

Financial statements are based largely on estimates and the application of accounting rules for recognition and allocation. To facilitate interpretation, accountants depend on five conventions, or rules of thumb, in recording transactions and preparing financial statements: consistency, full disclosure, materiality, conservatism, and cost-benefit.

Consistency

Consistent use of accounting measures and procedures is important in achieving comparability. The **consistency** convention requires that once a company

Like any other manufacturer, Goodyear must ensure that the quality of its products is consistent and that its accounting methods are as well. When a company changes an accounting method, it must inform users of its financial statements of the change. Such information is essential in making effective comparisons of a company's performance over several periods or in comparing its performance with that of other companies.

Courtesy of Zanskar/Dreamstime.

has adopted an accounting procedure, it must use it from one period to the next unless a note to the financial statements informs users of a change in procedure. Generally accepted accounting principles specify what the note must contain:

> The nature of and justification for a change in accounting principle and its effect on income should be disclosed in the financial statements of the period in which the change is made. The justification for the change should explain clearly why the newly adopted accounting principle is preferable.[6]

For example, in the notes to its financial statements, **Goodyear Tire & Rubber Company** disclosed that it had changed its method of accounting for inventories with the approval of its auditors because management felt the new method improved the matching of revenues and costs. Without such an acknowledgment, users of financial statements can assume that the treatment of a particular transaction, account, or item has not changed since the last period. For consistency, all years presented use this new method.

Full Disclosure (Transparency)

The convention of **full disclosure** (or transparency) requires that financial statements present all the information relevant to users' understanding of the statements. That is, the statements must be transparent so that they include any explanation needed to keep them from being misleading. Explanatory notes are therefore an integral part of the financial statements. For instance, as we have already mentioned, the notes should disclose any change that a company has made in its accounting procedures.

A company must also disclose significant events arising after the balance sheet date in the financial statements. Suppose a firm has purchased a piece of land for a future subdivision. Shortly after the end of its fiscal year, the firm is served papers to halt construction because the Environmental Protection Agency asserts that the land was once a toxic waste dump. This information, which obviously affects the users of the financial statements, must be disclosed in the statements for the fiscal year just ended.

Additional note disclosures required by the FASB and other official bodies include the accounting procedures used in preparing the financial statements and important terms of a company's debt, commitments, and contingencies. However, the statements can become so cluttered with notes that they impede rather than help understanding. Beyond the required disclosures, the application of the full-disclosure convention is based on the judgment of management and of the accountants who prepare the financial statements.

In recent years, investors and creditors also have had an influence on full disclosure. To protect them, independent auditors, the stock exchanges, and the SEC have made more demands for disclosure by publicly owned companies. The SEC has pushed especially hard for the enforcement of full disclosure. As a result, more and better information about corporations is available to the public today than ever before.

Study Note

Theoretically, a $10 stapler is a long-term asset and should therefore be capitalized and depreciated over its useful life. However, the convention of materiality allows the stapler to be expensed entirely in the year of purchase because its cost is small and writing it off in one year will have no effect on anyone's decision making.

Materiality

Materiality refers to the relative importance of an item or event. In general, an item or event is material if there is a reasonable expectation that knowing about it would influence the decisions of users of financial statements. Some items or events are so small or insignificant that they would make little difference to decision makers no matter how they are handled. Thus, a large company like **Dell Computer Corporation** may decide that expenditures for durable items of less than $500 should be charged as expenses rather than recorded as long-term assets and depreciated.

The materiality of an item normally is determined by relating its dollar value to an element of the financial statements, such as net income or total assets. As a rule, when an item is worth 5 percent or more of net income, accountants treat it as material. However, materiality depends not only on the value of an item but also on its nature. For example, in a multimillion-dollar company, a mistake of $5,000 in recording an item may not be important, but the discovery of even a small bribe or theft can be very important. Moreover, many small errors can add up to a material amount.

Study Note

The purpose of conservatism is not to produce the lowest net income and lowest asset value. It is a guideline for choosing among GAAP alternatives, and it should be used with care.

Conservatism

When accountants are uncertain about the judgments or estimates they must make, which is often the case, they look to the convention of **conservatism.** This

FOCUS ON BUSINESS PRACTICE

How Much Is Material? It's Not Only a Matter of Numbers

The materiality issue was long a pet peeve of the SEC, which contended that companies were increasingly abusing the convention to protect their stocks from taking a pounding when earnings did not reach their targets. In consequence, the SEC issued a rule that put stricter requirements on the use of materiality. In addition to providing quantitative guides, the rule includes qualitative considerations. The percentage assessment of materiality—the rule of thumb of 5 percent or more of net income that accountants and companies have traditionally used—is acceptable as an initial screening. However, the rule states that companies cannot decline to book items in the interest of meeting earnings estimates, preserving a growing earnings trend, converting a loss to a profit, increasing management compensation, or hiding an illegal transaction, such as a bribe.[7]

FOCUS ON BUSINESS PRACTICE

How Will Convergence of U.S. GAAP with IFRS Affect Accounting Conventions?

The FASB and the IASB are working toward converging U.S. generally accepted accounting principles (GAAP) with international financial reporting standards (IFRS). Their goal is "to increase the international comparability and the quality of standards used in the United States [which] is consistent with the FASB's obligation to its domestic constituents, who benefit from comparability across national borders."[8] In addition to the comparability convention being affected, other accounting conventions will also be affected by the adoption of IFRS. For instance, conservatism, which has been the bedrock of accounting practice for many decades, would no longer be part of the conceptual framework. The practice of writing up the value of a nonfinancial asset, such as inventory or equipment, that has increased in fair value and recording it as income under IFRS would be considered a violation of the conservatism convention under U.S. GAAP. Such changes will influence the way accountants in the United States analyze financial statements.

convention holds that when faced with choosing between two equally acceptable procedures, or estimates, accountants should choose the one that is least likely to overstate assets and income.

One of the most common applications of the conservatism convention is the use of the lower-of-cost-or-market method in accounting for inventories. Under this method, if an item's market value is greater than its original cost, the more conservative cost figure is used. If the market value is below the original cost, the more conservative market value is used. The latter situation often occurs in the computer industry.

Conservatism can be a useful tool in doubtful cases, but when it is abused, it can lead to incorrect and misleading financial statements. For example, there is no uncertainty about how a long-term asset of material cost should be treated. When conservatism is used to justify expensing such an asset in the period of purchase, income and assets for the current period will be understated, and income in future periods will be overstated. Its cost should be recorded as an asset and spread over the useful life of the asset, as explained in Chapter 3. Accountants therefore depend on the conservatism convention only when uncertain about which accounting procedure or estimate to use.

Cost-Benefit

The **cost-benefit** convention holds that the benefits to be gained from providing accounting information should be greater than the costs of providing it. Of course, minimum levels of relevance and reliability must be reached if accounting information is to be useful. Beyond the minimum levels, however, it is up to the FASB and the SEC, which stipulate the information that must be reported, and the accountant, who provides the information, to judge the costs and benefits in each case.

Firms use the cost-benefit convention for both accounting and nonaccounting decisions. Department stores could almost completely eliminate shoplifting if they hired five times as many clerks as they now have and assigned them to watching customers. The benefit would be reduced shoplifting. The cost would be reduced sales (customers do not like being closely watched) and increased wages expense. Although shoplifting is a serious problem for department stores, the benefit of reducing shoplifting in this way does not outweigh the cost.

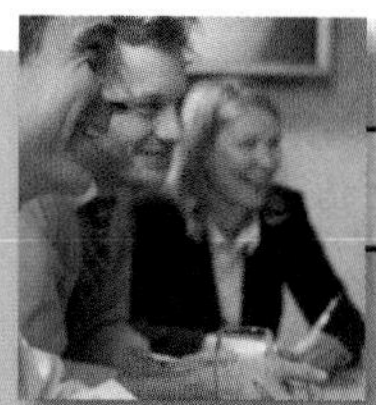

FOCUS ON BUSINESS PRACTICE

When Is "Full Disclosure" Too Much? It's a Matter of Cost and Benefits.

The large accounting firm of **Ernst & Young** reported that over a 20-year period, the total number of pages in the annual reports of 25 large, well-known companies increased an average of 84 percent, and the number of pages of notes increased 325 percent—from 4 to 17 pages. Management's discussion and analysis increased 300 percent, from 3 pages to 12.[9] Because some people feel that "these documents are so daunting that people don't read them at all," the SEC allows companies to issue to the public "summary reports" in which the bulk of the notes can be reduced.

Although more accessible and less costly, summary reports are controversial because many analysts feel that it is in the notes that one gets the detailed information necessary to understand complex business operations. One analyst remarked, "To banish the notes for fear they will turn off readers would be like eliminating fractions from math books on the theory that the average student prefers to work with whole numbers."[10] Where this controversy will end, nobody knows. Detailed reports still must be filed with the SEC, but more and more companies are providing summary reports to the public.

The costs and benefits of a requirement for accounting disclosure are both immediate and deferred. Judging the final costs and benefits of a far-reaching and costly requirement for accounting disclosure is difficult. For instance, the FASB allows certain large companies to make a supplemental disclosure in their financial statements of the effects of changes in consumer price levels. Most companies choose not to present this information because they believe the costs of producing and providing it exceed its benefits to the readers of their financial statements. Cost-benefit is a question that the FASB, the Securities and Exchange Commission, and all other regulators face. Even though there are no definitive ways of measuring costs and benefits, much of an accountant's work deals with these concepts.

STOP & APPLY >

Each of the five accounting conventions below is described in one of the statements in the numbered list that follows. Match each statement to the letter of the appropriate convention.

_____ a. Consistency
_____ b. Full disclosure
_____ c. Materiality
_____ d. Conservatism
_____ e. Cost-benefit

1. A note to the financial statements explains the company's method of revenue recognition.
2. Inventory is accounted for at its market value, which is less than its original cost.
3. A company uses the same method of revenue recognition year after year.
4. Several accounts are grouped into one category because the total amount of each account is small.
5. A company does not keep detailed records of certain operations because the information gained from the detail is not deemed useful.

SOLUTION

1. b; 2. d; 3. a; 4. c; 5. e

Classified Balance Sheet

LO3 Identify and describe the basic components of a classified balance sheet.

As you know, a balance sheet presents a company's financial position at a particular time. The balance sheets we have presented thus far categorize accounts as assets, liabilities, and owner's equity. Because even a fairly small company can have hundreds of accounts, simply listing accounts in these broad categories is not particularly helpful to a statement user. Setting up subcategories within the major categories can make financial statements much more useful. This format enables owners and creditors to study and evaluate relationships among the subcategories.

General-purpose external financial statements that are divided into subcategories are called **classified financial statements.** Figure 5-2 depicts the subcategories into which assets, liabilities, and owner's equity are usually broken down.

The subcategories of Cruz Company's classified balance sheet, shown in Exhibit 5-1, typify those used by most corporations in the United States. The subcategories under owner's equity would, of course, be different if Cruz Company was a corporation or partnership rather than a sole proprietorship.

Assets

As you can see in Exhibit 5-1, the classified balance sheet of a U.S. company typically divides assets into four categories:

1. Current assets
2. Investments
3. Property, plant, and equipment
4. Intangible assets

These categories are listed in the order of their presumed ease of conversion into cash. For example, current assets are usually more easily converted to cash than are property, plant, and equipment. For simplicity, some companies group investments, intangible assets, and other miscellaneous assets into a category called **other assets.**

Current Assets **Current assets** are cash and other assets that a company can reasonably expect to convert to cash, sell, or consume within one year or its *normal operating cycle,* whichever is longer. A company's **normal operating cycle** is the average time it needs to go from spending cash to receiving cash. For example, suppose a company uses cash to buy inventory and sells the inventory to a customer on credit. The resulting receivable must be collected in cash before the normal operating cycle ends.

The normal operating cycle for most companies is less than one year, but there are exceptions. For example, because of the length of time it takes **The Boeing Company** to build aircraft, its normal operating cycle exceeds one year. The inventory used in building the planes is nonetheless considered a current asset because the planes will be sold within the normal operating cycle. Another example is a company that sells on an installment basis. The payments for a television

FIGURE 5-2
Classified Balance Sheet

ASSETS	=	LIABILITIES
• Current assets • Investments • Property, plant, and equipment • Intangible assets		• Current liabilities • Long-term liabilities
		OWNER'S EQUITY
		• Capital

EXHIBIT 5-1
Classified Balance Sheet for Cruz Company

Cruz Company
Balance Sheet
December 31, 2010

Assets			
Current assets			
Cash		$ 41,440	
Short-term investments		28,000	
Notes receivable		32,000	
Accounts receivable		141,200	
Merchandise inventory		191,600	
Prepaid insurance		26,400	
Supplies		6,784	
Total current assets			$467,424
Investments			
Land held for future use			50,000
Property, plant, and equipment			
Land		$ 18,000	
Building	$ 82,600		
Less accumulated depreciation	34,560	48,040	
Equipment	$108,000		
Less accumulated depreciation	57,800	50,200	
Total property, plant, and equipment			116,240
Intangible assets			
Trademark			2,000
Total assets			$635,664
Liabilities			
Current liabilities			
Notes payable		$ 60,000	
Accounts payable		102,732	
Salaries payable		8,000	
Total current liabilities			$ 170,732
Long-term liabilities			
Mortgage payable			71,200
Total liabilities			$241,932
Owner's Equity			
M. Cruz, Capital		$393,732	
Total owner's equity			393,732
Total liabilities and owner's equity			$635,664

set or a refrigerator can extend over 24 or 36 months, but these receivables are still considered current assets.

Cash is obviously a current asset. Short-term investments, notes and accounts receivable, and inventory that a company expects to convert to cash within the next year or the normal operating cycle are also current assets. On the balance sheet, they are listed in order of their ease of conversion to cash.

Prepaid expenses, such as rent and insurance paid in advance, and inventories of supplies bought for use rather than for sale should be classified as current assets. These assets are current in the sense that if they had not been bought earlier, a current outlay of cash would be needed to obtain them.

In deciding whether an asset is current or noncurrent, the idea of "reasonable expectation" is important. For example, Short-Term Investments, also called *Marketable Securities*, is an account used for temporary investments, such as U.S. Treasury bills, of "idle" cash—that is, cash that is not immediately required for operating purposes. Management can reasonably expect to sell these securities as cash needs arise over the next year or within the company's current operating cycle. Investments in securities that management does not expect to sell within the next year and that do not involve the temporary use of idle cash should be shown in the investments category of a classified balance sheet.

Investments The **investments** category includes assets, usually long-term, that are not used in normal business operations and that management does not plan to convert to cash within the next year. Items in this category are securities held for long-term investment, long-term notes receivable, land held for future use, plant or equipment not used in the business, and special funds established to pay off a debt or buy a building. Also included are large permanent investments in another company for the purpose of controlling that company.

> **Study Note**
>
> For an investment to be classified as current, management must expect to sell it within the next year or the current operating cycle, so it must be readily marketable.

Property, Plant, and Equipment **Property, plant, and equipment** are tangible long-term assets used in a business's day-to-day operations. They represent a place to operate (land and buildings) and the equipment used to produce, sell, and deliver goods or services. They are therefore also called *operating assets* or, sometimes, *fixed assets*, *tangible assets*, *long-lived assets*, or *plant assets*. Through depreciation, the costs of these assets (except land) are spread over the periods they benefit. Past depreciation is recorded in the Accumulated Depreciation accounts.

To reduce clutter on the balance sheet, property, plant, and equipment are often combined—for example:

Property, plant, and equipment (net) $116,240

The company provides the details in a note to the financial statements.

The property, plant, and equipment category also includes natural resources owned by the company, such as forest lands, oil and gas properties, and coal mines, if they are used in the regular course of business. If they are not, they are listed in the investments category.

Intangible Assets **Intangible assets** are long-term assets with no physical substance whose value stems from the rights or privileges they extend to their owners. Some of these assets, such as patents and copyrights, are recorded at cost, which is spread over the expected life of the right or privilege. Others with indefinite lives, such as trademarks and brands, are recorded at cost and remain at that amount unless it becomes apparent that they have lost their value. Also, goodwill, which arises in an acquisition of another company, is an intangible asset that is recorded at cost but is not amortized. It is reviewed each year for possible loss of value, or impairment.

Liabilities

Liabilities are divided into two categories that are based on when the liabilities fall due: current liabilities and long-term liabilities.

Current Liabilities **Current liabilities** are obligations that must be satisfied within one year or within the company's normal operating cycle, whichever is longer. These liabilities are typically paid out of current assets or by incurring new short-term liabilities. They include notes payable, accounts payable, the current portion of long-term debt, salaries and wages payable, and customer advances (unearned revenues).

Study Note

The portion of a mortgage that is due during the next year or the current operating cycle would be classified as a current liability; the portion due after the next year or the current operating cycle would be classified as a long-term liability.

Long-Term Liabilities Debts that fall due more than one year in the future or beyond the normal operating cycle, which will be paid out of noncurrent assets, are **long-term liabilities.** Mortgages payable, long-term notes, bonds payable, employee pension obligations, and long-term lease liabilities generally fall into this category.

Owner's Equity

The terms *owner's equity, capital,* and *net worth* are used interchangeably. They all refer to the owner's interest in a company. The first two terms are preferred to *net worth* because most assets are recorded at original cost rather than at current value. For this reason, the ownership section will not represent "worth." It is really a claim against the assets of the company.

Although the form of business organization does not usually affect the accounting treatment of assets and liabilities, the equity section of the balance sheet differs depending on whether the business is a sole proprietorship, a partnership, or a corporation.

Study Note

The only difference in equity between a sole proprietorship and a partnership is the number of Capital accounts.

Sole Proprietorship You are already familiar with the owner's equity section of a sole proprietorship, like the one shown in the balance sheet for Cruz Company in Exhibit 5-1:

Owner's Equity	
M. Cruz, Capital	$393,732

Partnership The equity section of a partnership's balance sheet is called *partners' equity.* It might appear as follows:

Partners' Equity		
R. Hay, Capital	$ 168,750	
M. Cruz, Capital	224,982	
Total partners' equity		$393,732

Corporation Corporations are by law separate, legal entities that are owned by their stockholders. The equity section of a balance sheet for a corporation is called stockholders' equity and has two parts: contributed, or paid-in, capital and retained earnings. It might appear like this:

Stockholders' Equity		
Contributed capital		
Common stock, $10 par value, 20,000 shares authorized, issued, and outstanding	$200,000	
Additional paid-in capital	40,000	
Total contributed capital	$240,000	
Retained earnings	153,732	
Total stockholders' equity		393,732
Total liabilities and stockholders' equity		$635,664

Remember that owner's equity accounts show the sources of and claims on assets. Of course, the claims are not on any particular asset but on the assets as a whole. It follows, then, that a corporation's contributed and earned capital accounts measure its stockholders' claims on assets and also indicate the sources of the assets. The **contributed capital** (also called *paid-in capital*) accounts reflect the amounts of assets invested by stockholders. Generally, contributed capital is shown on corporate balance sheets by two amounts: (1) the face, or par, value of issued stock and (2) the amounts paid in, or contributed, in excess of the par value per share. In the illustration above, stockholders invested amounts equal to the par value of the outstanding stock of $200,000 plus $40,000 in additional paid-in capital for a total of $240,000.

The **Retained Earnings** account is sometimes called *Earned Capital* because it represents the stockholders' claim to the assets that are earned from operations and reinvested in corporate operations. Distributions of assets to shareholders, which are called *dividends*, reduce the Retained Earnings account balance just as withdrawals of assets by the owner of a business reduce the Capital account balance. Thus the Retained Earnings account balance, in its simplest form, represents the earnings of the corporation less dividends paid to stockholders over the life of the business.

Dell's Balance Sheets

Although balance sheets generally resemble the one shown in Exhibit 5-1 for Cruz Company, no two companies have financial statements that are exactly alike.

EXHIBIT 5-2 Classified Balance Sheet for Dell Computer Corporation

Dell Computer Corporation
Consolidated Statement of Financial Position
(in millions)

	January 30, 2009	February 1, 2008
Assets		
Current assets:		
Cash and cash equivalents	$ 8,352	$ 7,764
Short-term investments	740	208
Accounts receivable, net	4,731	5,961
Financing receivables, net	1,712	1,732
Inventories	867	1,180
Other	3,749	3,035
Total current assets	20,151	19,880
Property, plant, and equipment, net	2,277	2,668
Investments	454	1,560
Other non-current assets	3,618	3,453
Total assets	$26,500	$27,561
Liabilities and Stockholders' Equity		
Current liabilities:		
Short-term debt	$ 113	$ 225
Accounts payable	8,309	11,492
Accrued and other liabilities	6,437	6,809
Total current liabilities	14,859	18,526
Long-term debt	1,898	362
Other non-current liabilities	5,472	4,844
Total liabilities	22,229	23,732

EXHIBIT 5-2 Classified Balance Sheet for Dell Computer Corporation (continued)

	January 30, 2009	February 1, 2008
Stockholders' equity:		
Preferred stock and capital in excess of $.01 par value; shares issued and outstanding: none	—	—
Common stock and capital in excess of $.01 par value; shares authorized: 7,000; shares issued: 3,338* and 3,320,* respectively; shares outstanding: 1,944 and 2,060, respectively	11,189	10,589
Treasury stock, at cost; 919 and 785 shares, respectively	(27,904)	(25,037)
Retained earnings	20,677	18,199
Other comprehensive loss	309	(16)
Total stockholders' equity	4,271	3,735
Total liabilities and stockholders' equity	$ 26,500	$ 27,561

*Includes an immaterial amount of redeemable common stock.

Source: Adapted from Dell Computer Corporation, Form 10-K, 2009.

The balance sheet of **Dell Computer Corporation** is a good example of some of the variations. As shown in Exhibit 5-2, it provides data for two years so that users can evaluate the change from one year to the next. Note that its major classifications are similar, but not identical, to those of Cruz Company. For instance, Cruz has asset categories for investments and intangibles, and Dell has an asset category called "other non-current assets," which is a small amount of its total assets. Also note that Dell has a category called "other non-current liabilities." Because this category is listed after long-term debt, it represents longer-term liabilities, due more than one year after the balance sheet date.

STOP & APPLY >

The lettered items below represent a classification scheme for a balance sheet. The numbered items are account titles. Match each account with the letter of the category in which it belongs, or indicate that it does not appear on the balance sheet.

a. Current assets
b. Investments
c. Property, plant, and equipment
d. Intangible assets
e. Current liabilities
f. Long-term liabilities
g. Owner's Capital
h. Not on balance sheet

1. Trademark
2. Marketable Securities
3. Land Held for Future Use
4. Property Taxes Payable
5. Note Payable in Five Years
6. Investment by Owner
7. Land Used in Operations
8. Accumulated Depreciation
9. Accounts Receivable
10. Interest Expense
11. Unearned Revenue
12. Prepaid Rent

SOLUTION

1. d; 2. a; 3. b; 4. e; 5. f; 6. g; 7. c; 8. c; 9. a; 10. h; 11. e; 12. a

Forms of the Income Statement

LO4 Describe the features of multistep and single-step classified income statements.

In the income statements we have presented thus far, expenses have been deducted from revenue in a single step to arrive at net income. Here, we look at a multistep income statement and a single-step format more complex than the one we presented in earlier chapters.

Multistep Income Statement

A **multistep income statement** goes through a series of steps, or subtotals, to arrive at net income. Figure 5-3 compares the multistep income statement of a service company with that of a **merchandising company,** which buys and sells products, and a **manufacturing company,** which makes and sells products.

As you can see in Figure 5-3, in a service company's multistep income statement, the operating expenses are deducted from revenues in a single step to arrive at income from operations. In contrast, because manufacturing and merchandising companies make or buy goods for sale, they must include an additional step for the cost of goods sold. Exhibit 5-3 shows a multistep income statement for Cruz Company, a merchandising company.

Net Sales The first major part of a merchandising or manufacturing company's multistep income statement is **net sales,** often simply called *sales.* Net sales consist

FIGURE 5-3
The Components of Multistep Income Statements for Service and Merchandising or Manufacturing Companies

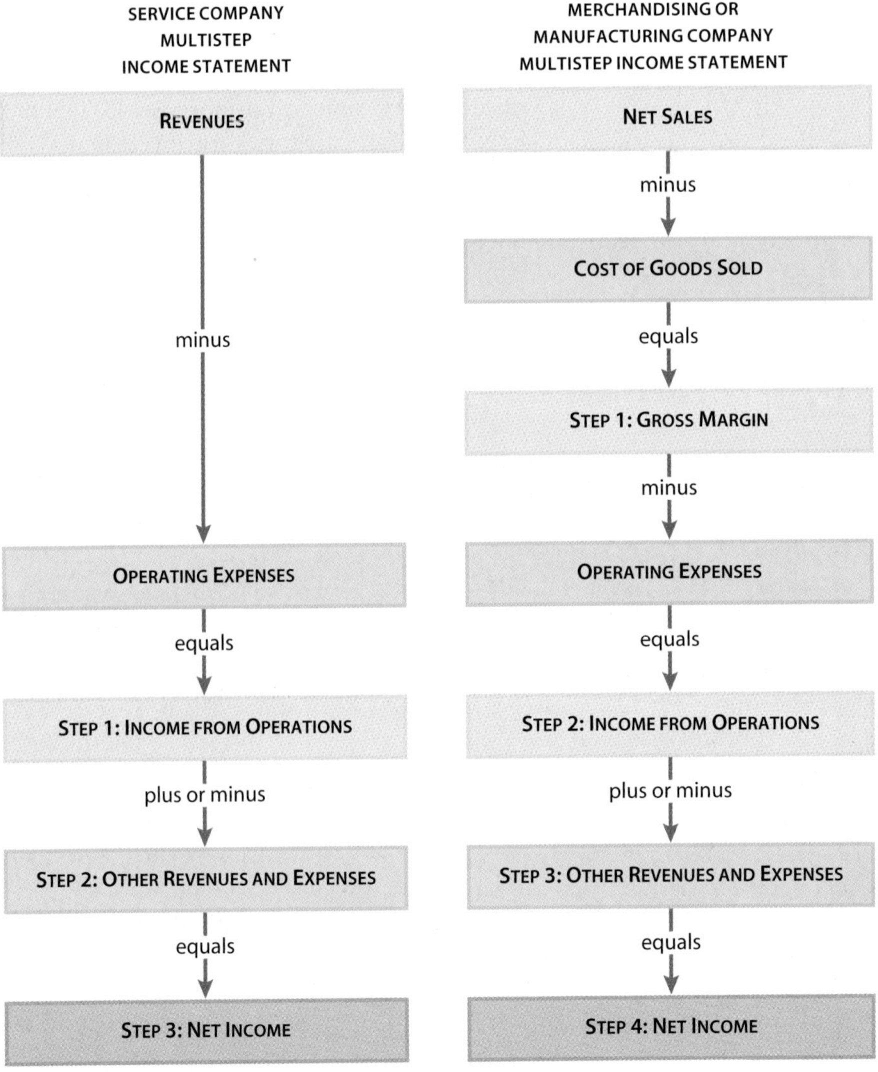

Study Note

The multistep income statement is a valuable analytical tool that is often overlooked. Analysts frequently convert a single-step statement into a multistep one because the latter separates operating sources of income from nonoperating ones. Owners want income to result primarily from operations, not from one-time gains or losses.

EXHIBIT 5-3 Multistep Income Statement for Cruz Company

	Cruz Company Income Statement For the Year Ended December 31, 2010		
Step 1	**Net sales**		$1,248,624
	Cost of goods sold		815,040
	Gross margin		$ 433,584
Step 2	**Operating expenses**		
	Selling expenses	$219,120	
	General and administrative expenses	138,016	
	Total operating expenses		357,136
	Income from operations		$ 76,448
Step 3	**Other revenues and expenses**		
	Interest income	$ 5,600	
	Less interest expense	10,524	
	Excess of other expenses over other revenues		4,924
Step 4	**Net income**		$ 71,524

of the gross proceeds from sales (gross sales) less sales returns and allowances and any discounts allowed.

- **Gross sales** consist of total cash sales and total credit sales during an accounting period. Even though the cash may not be collected until the following accounting period, under the revenue recognition rule, revenue is recorded as earned when title for merchandise passes from seller to buyer at the time of sale.
- **Sales returns and allowances** are cash refunds, credits on account, and discounts from selling prices made to customers who have received defective products or products that are otherwise unsatisfactory. If other discounts are given to customers, they also should be deducted from gross sales.

Managers, owners, and others often use the amount of sales and trends in sales as indicators of a firm's progress. To detect trends, they compare the net sales of different accounting periods. Increasing sales suggest growth; decreasing sales indicate the possibility of decreased future earnings and other financial problems.

Cost of Goods Sold The second part of a multistep income statement for a merchandiser or manufacturer is **cost of goods sold,** also called *cost of sales*. Cost of goods sold (an expense) is the amount a merchandiser paid for the merchandise it sold during an accounting period. For a manufacturer, it is the cost of making the products it sold during an accounting period.

Gross Margin The third major part of a multistep income statement for a merchandiser or manufacturer is **gross margin,** or *gross profit*, which is the difference between net sales and the cost of goods sold (Step 1 in Exhibit 5-3). To be successful, companies must achieve a gross margin sufficient to cover operating expenses and provide an adequate net income.

> Study Note
>
> Gross margin is an important measure of profitability. When it is less than operating expenses, the company has suffered a loss from operations.

Managers are interested in both the amount and percentage of gross margin. The percentage is computed by dividing the amount of gross margin by net sales. In the case of Cruz Company, the amount of gross margin is $433,584, and the percentage of gross margin is 34.7 percent ($433,584 ÷ $1,248,624).

This information is useful in planning business operations. For instance, management may try to increase total sales by reducing the selling price. Although this strategy reduces the percentage of gross margin, it will work if the total of items sold increases enough to raise the absolute amount of gross margin. This is the strategy followed by discount warehouse stores like **Sam's Club** and **Costco Wholesale Corporation**.

On the other hand, management may decide to keep a high gross margin from sales and try to increase sales and the amount of gross margin by increasing operating expenses, such as advertising. This is the strategy used by upscale specialty stores like **Neiman Marcus** and **Tiffany & Co.** Other strategies to increase gross margin from sales include using better purchasing methods to reduce cost of goods sold.

Operating Expenses **Operating expenses**—expenses incurred in running a business other than the cost of goods sold—are the next major part of a multistep income statement. Operating expenses are often grouped into the categories of selling expenses and general and administrative expenses.

- Selling expenses include the costs of storing goods and preparing them for sale; preparing displays, advertising, and otherwise promoting sales; and delivering goods to a buyer if the seller has agreed to pay the cost of delivery.
- General and administrative expenses include expenses for accounting, personnel, credit checking, collections, and any other expenses that apply to overall operations. Although occupancy expenses, such as rent expense, insurance expense, and utilities expense, are often classified as general and administrative expenses, they can also be allocated between selling expenses and general and administrative expenses.

Careful planning and control of operating expenses can improve a company's profitability.

Study Note

Many financial analysts use income from operations as a key measure of profitability.

Income from Operations **Income from operations,** or *operating income,* is the difference between gross margin and operating expenses (Step 2 in Exhibit 5-3). It represents the income from a company's main business. Income from operations is often used to compare the profitability of two or more companies or divisions within a company.

Other Revenues and Expenses **Other revenues and expenses,** also called *nonoperating revenues and expenses,* are not related to a company's operating activities (Step 3 in Exhibit 5-3). This section of a multistep income statement includes revenues from investments (such as dividends and interest on stocks, bonds, and savings accounts) and interest earned on credit or notes extended to customers. It also includes interest expense and other expenses that result from borrowing money or from credit extended to the company. If a company has other kinds of revenues and expenses not related to its normal business operations, they, too, are included in this part of the income statement.

An analyst who wants to compare two companies independent of their financing methods—that is, *before* considering other revenues and expenses—would focus on income from operations.

Income Taxes **Income taxes**, also called *provision for income taxes,* represent the expense for federal, state, and local taxes on corporate income. Income taxes do not appear on the income statements of sole proprietorships and partnerships because the persons who own these businesses are the tax-paying units; they pay income taxes on their share of the business income. Corporations, however, must report and pay income taxes on their earnings. Income taxes are shown as a separate item on a corporation's income statement. Usually, the word *expense* is not used on the statement.

Because federal, state, and local income taxes for corporations are substantial, they have a significant effect on business decisions. Current federal income tax rates for corporations vary from 15 percent to 35 percent depending on the amount of income before income taxes and other factors. Most other taxes, such as property and employment taxes, are included in operating expenses.

Net Income **Net income** is the final figure, or "bottom line," of an income statement. It is what remains of gross margin after operating expenses have been deducted and other revenues and expenses have been added or deducted (Step 4 in Exhibit 5-3).

Net income is an important performance measure because it represents the amount of earnings that accrue to owners. It is the amount transferred to owner's capital from all the income that business operations have generated during an accounting period. Both managers and owners often use net income to measure a business's financial performance over the past accounting period.

Dell's Income Statements

Like balance sheets, income statements vary among companies. You will rarely, if ever, find an income statement exactly like the one we have presented for Cruz Company. Companies use both different terms and different structures. For example, as you can see in Exhibit 5-4, in its multistep income statement, **Dell Computer Corporation** provided three years of data for purposes of comparison.

EXHIBIT 5-4 Multistep Income Statement for Dell Computer Corporation

Dell Computer Corporation
Consolidated Statement of Income
(in millions, except per share amounts)

	Fiscal Year Ended		
	January 30, 2009	**February 1, 2008**	**February 2, 2007**
Net revenue	$61,101	$61,133	$57,420
Cost of revenue	50,144	49,462	47,904
Gross margin	10,957	11,671	9,516
Operating expenses:			
Selling, general, and administrative	7,102	7,538	5,948
In-process research and development	2	83	—
Research, development, and engineering	663	610	498
Total operating expenses	7,767	8,231	6,446
Operating income	3,190	3,440	3,070
Investment and other income, net	134	387	275
Income before income taxes	3,324	3,827	3,345
Income tax provision	846	880	762
Net income	$ 2,478	$ 2,947	$ 2,583

Source: Dell Computer Corporation, Form 10-K, 2009.

EXHIBIT 5-5 Single-Step Income Statement for Cruz Company

Cruz Company
Income Statement
For the Year Ended December 31, 2010

Revenues		
Net sales		$1,248,624
Interest income		5,600
Total revenues		$1,254,224
Costs and expenses		
Cost of goods sold	$815,040	
Selling expenses	219,120	
General and administrative expenses	138,016	
Interest expense	10,524	
Total costs and expenses		1,182,700
Net income		$ 71,524

Single-Step Income Statement

Exhibit 5-5 shows a **single-step income statement** for Cruz Company. In this type of statement, net income is derived in a single step by putting the major categories of revenues in the first part of the statement and the major categories of costs and expenses in the second part. Both the multistep form and the single-step form have advantages: The multistep form shows the components used in deriving net income, and the single-step form has the advantage of simplicity.

Study Note

If you encounter income statement components not covered in this chapter, refer to the index at the end of the book to find the topic and read about it.

STOP & APPLY >

A classification scheme for a multistep income statement and a list of accounts appear below. Match each account with the category in which it belongs, or indicate that it is not on the income statement.

a. Net sales
b. Cost of goods sold
c. Selling expenses
d. General and administrative expenses
e. Other revenues and expenses
f. Not on income statement

1. Sales Returns and Allowances
2. Cost of Sales
3. Dividend Income
4. Delivery Expense
5. Office Salaries Expense
6. Wages Payable
7. Sales Salaries Expense
8. Advertising Expense
9. Interest Expense
10. Commissions Expense

SOLUTION

1. a; 2. b; 3. e; 4. c; 5. d; 6. f; 7. c; 8. c; 9. e; 10. c

Using Classified Financial Statements

LO5 Use classified financial statements to evaluate liquidity and profitability.

> **Study Note**
> Accounts must be classified correctly before the ratios are computed. If they are not classified correctly, the ratios will be incorrect.

Owners and creditors base their decisions largely on their assessments of a firm's potential liquidity and profitability, and in making those assessments, they often rely on ratios. As you will see in the following pages, ratios use the components of classified financial statements to reflect how well a firm has performed in terms of maintaining liquidity and achieving profitability.

Evaluation of Liquidity

Liquidity means having enough money on hand to pay bills when they are due and to take care of unexpected needs for cash. Two measures of liquidity are working capital and the current ratio.

Working Capital **Working capital** is the amount by which current assets exceed current liabilities. It is an important measure of liquidity because current liabilities must be satisfied within one year or one operating cycle, whichever is longer, and current assets are used to pay the current liabilities. Thus, the excess of current assets over current liabilities—the working capital—is what is on hand to continue business operations.

For Cruz Company, working capital is computed as follows:

Current assets	\$467,424
Less current liabilities	170,732
Working capital	\$296,692

Working capital can be used to buy inventory, obtain credit, and finance expanded sales. Lack of working capital can lead to a company's failure.

Current Ratio The current ratio is closely related to working capital. Many bankers and other creditors believe it is a good indicator of a company's ability to pay its debts on time. The **current ratio** is the ratio of current assets to current liabilities. For Cruz Company, it is computed like this:

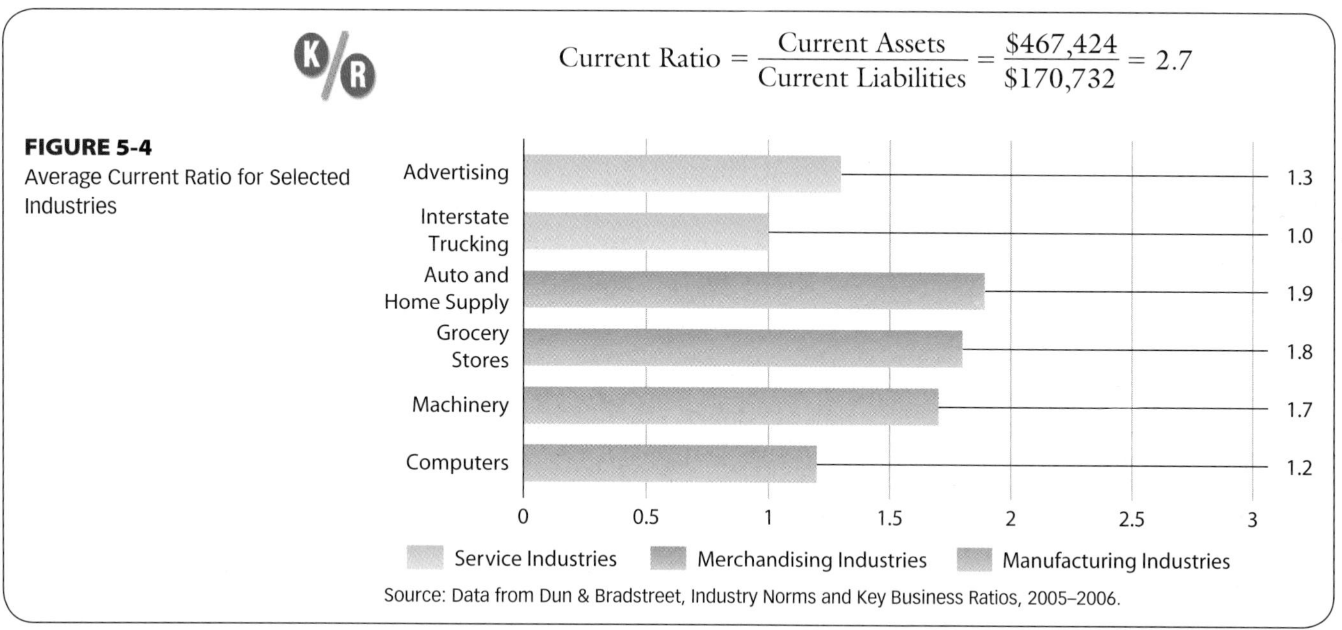

FIGURE 5-4
Average Current Ratio for Selected Industries

Source: Data from Dun & Bradstreet, Industry Norms and Key Business Ratios, 2005–2006.

Thus, Cruz Company has \$2.70 of current assets for each \$1.00 of current liabilities. Is that good or bad? The answer requires a comparison of this year's current ratio with ratios for earlier years and with similar measures for companies in the same industry, which for Cruz Company is auto and home supply.

As Figure 5-4 illustrates, the average current ratio varies from industry to industry. For the advertising industry, which has no merchandise inventory, the current ratio is 1.3. The auto and home supply industry, in which companies carry large merchandise inventories, has an average current ratio of 1.9. The current ratio for Cruz Company, 2.7, exceeds the average for its industry.

A very low current ratio, of course, can be unfavorable, indicating that a company will not be able to pay its debts on time. But that is not always the case. For example, **McDonald's** and various other successful companies have very low current ratios because they carefully plan their cash flows. A very high current ratio may indicate that a company is not using its assets to the best advantage. In other words, it could probably use its excess funds more effectively to increase its overall profit.

Evaluation of Profitability

Just as important as paying bills on time is *profitability*—the ability to earn a satisfactory income. As a goal, profitability competes with liquidity for managerial attention because liquid assets, although important, are not the best profit-producing resources. Cash, of course, means purchasing power, but a satisfactory profit can be made only if purchasing power is used to buy profit-producing (and less liquid) assets, such as inventory and long-term assets.

To evaluate a company's profitability, you must relate its current performance to its past performance and prospects for the future, as well as to the averages of other companies in the same industry. The following are the ratios commonly used to evaluate a company's ability to earn income:

1. Profit margin
2. Asset turnover
3. Return on assets
4. Debt to equity ratio
5. Return on equity

Profit Margin The **profit margin** shows the percentage of each sales dollar that results in net income. It should not be confused with gross margin, which is not a ratio but rather the amount by which revenues exceed the cost of goods sold. Cruz Company has a profit margin of 5.7 percent. It is computed as follows:

FOCUS ON BUSINESS PRACTICE IFRS

How Has the Goal of Convergence of U.S. GAAP and IFRS Made Financial Analysis More Difficult?

Although the SEC believes that the ideal outcome of a cooperative international accounting standard-setting process would be worldwide use of a single set of high-quality accounting standards for both domestic and cross-border financial reporting, the reality is that such consistency does not now exist and will be a challenge to implement.[11] For a period of time, users of financial statements will have difficulty comparing companies' performance. Profitability measures of foreign firms that file in the United States using IFRS will not be comparable to profitability measures of companies that file using U.S. GAAP. For instance, consider the reporting earnings of the following European companies under both standards in a recent year (earnings in millions of euros):

	IFRS Earnings	*GAAP Earnings*	*% Diff.*
Bayer AG	1,695	269	530.1%
Reed Elsevier	625	399	56.6
Benetton Group	125	100	25.0

Given that assets and equity for these companies are also likely to differ as well as the use of fair value in valuing assets and liabilities, all profitability ratios—profit margin, asset turnover, return on assets, debt to equity ratio, and return on equity—will be affected.

$$\text{Profit Margin} = \frac{\text{Net Income}}{\text{Net Sales}} = \frac{\$71{,}524}{\$1{,}248{,}624} = 0.057, \text{ or } 5.7\%$$

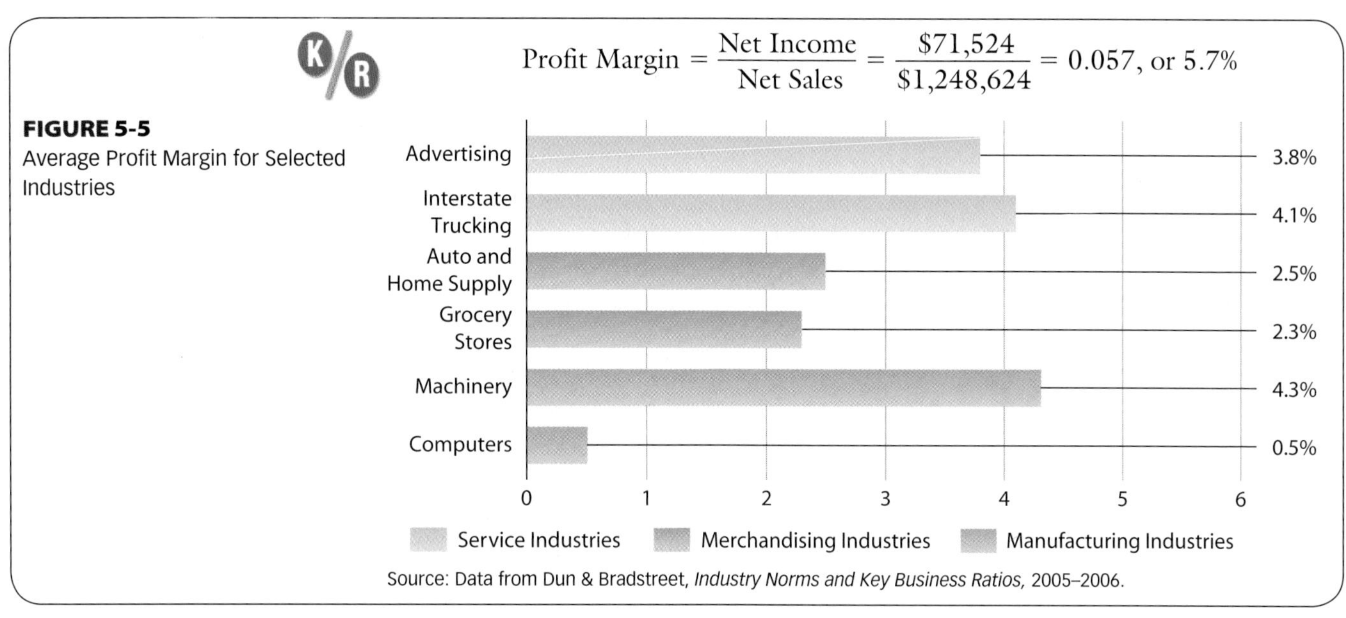

FIGURE 5-5
Average Profit Margin for Selected Industries

Source: Data from Dun & Bradstreet, *Industry Norms and Key Business Ratios*, 2005–2006.

Thus, on each dollar of net sales, Cruz Company makes 5.7 cents. A difference of 1 or 2 percent in a company's profit margin can be the difference between a fair year and a very profitable one.

Asset Turnover The **asset turnover** ratio measures how efficiently assets are used to produce sales. In other words, it shows how many dollars of sales are generated by each dollar of assets. A company with a higher asset turnover uses its assets more productively than one with a lower asset turnover.

The asset turnover ratio is computed by dividing net sales by average total assets. Average total assets are the sum of assets at the beginning of an accounting period and at the end of the period divided by 2. For example, if Cruz Company had assets of $594,480 at the beginning of the year, its asset turnover would be computed as follows:

$$\text{Asset Turnover} = \frac{\text{Net Sales}}{\text{Average Total Assets}}$$

$$= \frac{\$1{,}248{,}624}{(\$635{,}664 + \$594{,}480) \div 2} = \frac{\$1{,}248{,}624}{\$615{,}072} = 2.0 \text{ Times}$$

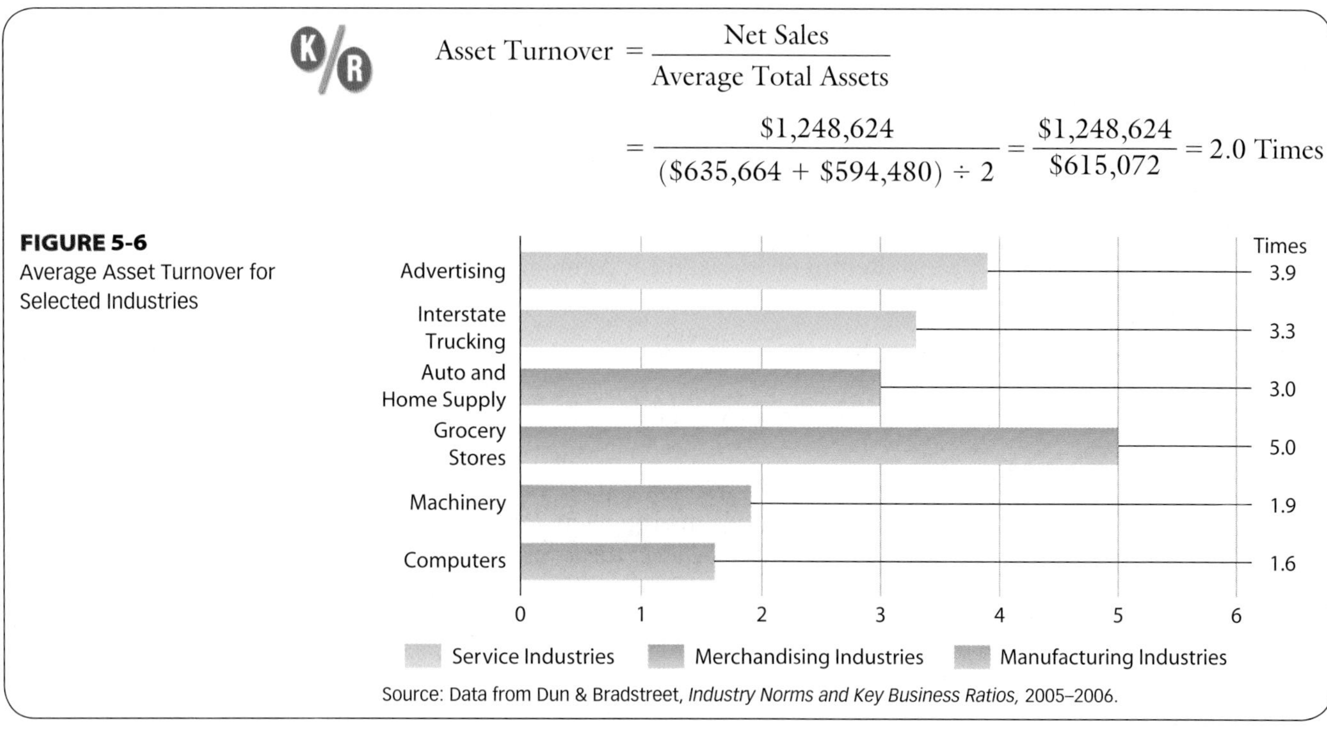

FIGURE 5-6
Average Asset Turnover for Selected Industries

Source: Data from Dun & Bradstreet, *Industry Norms and Key Business Ratios*, 2005–2006.

Thus, Cruz Company would produce $2.00 in sales for each dollar invested in assets. This ratio shows a relationship between an income statement figure (net sales) and a balance sheet figure (total assets).

> **Study Note**
> Return on assets is one of the most widely used measures of profitability because it reflects both the profit margin and asset turnover.

Return on Assets Both the profit margin and asset turnover ratios have limitations. The profit margin ratio does not consider the assets necessary to produce income, and the asset turnover ratio does not take into account the amount of income produced. The **return on assets** ratio overcomes these deficiencies by relating net income to average total assets. For Cruz Company, it is computed like this:

$$\text{Return on Assets} = \frac{\text{Net Income}}{\text{Average Total Assets}}$$

$$= \frac{\$71{,}524}{(\$635{,}664 + \$594{,}480) \div 2}$$

$$= \frac{\$71{,}524}{\$615{,}072} = 0.116, \text{ or } 11.6\%$$

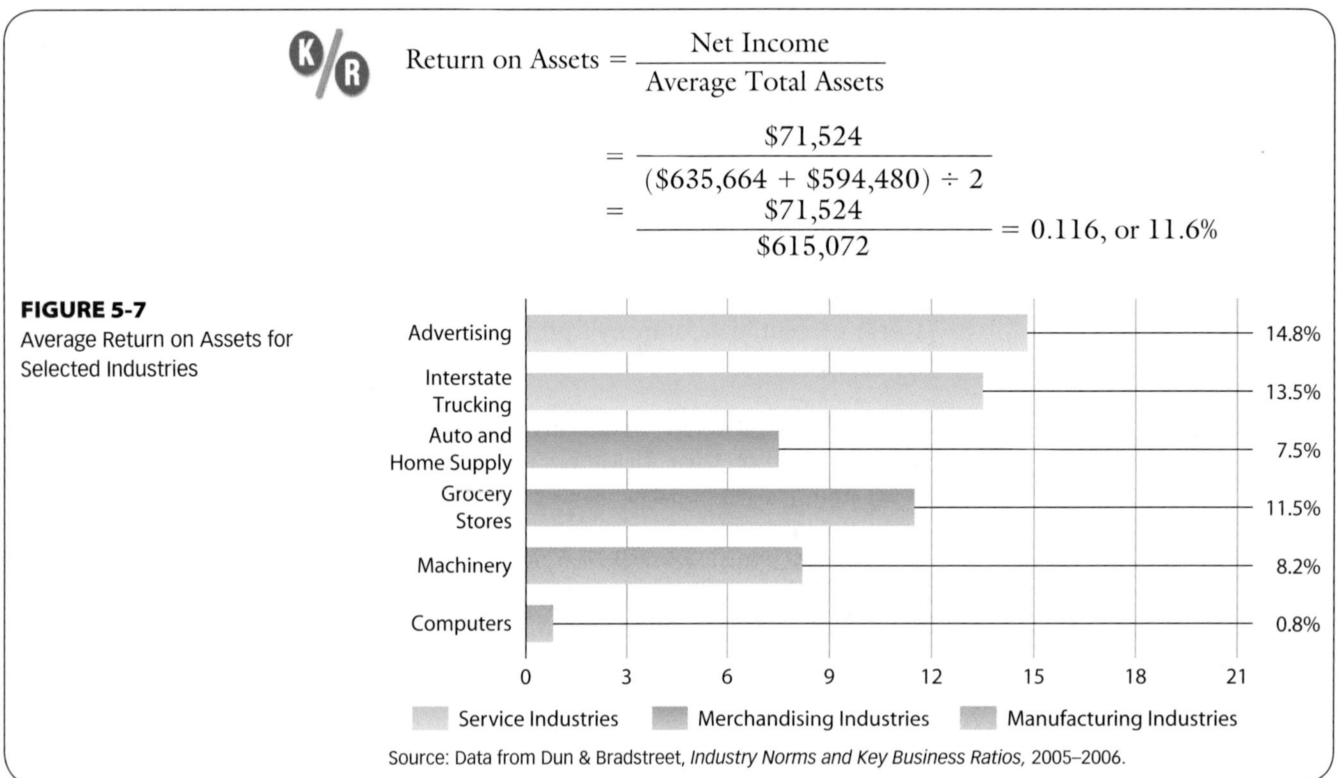

FIGURE 5-7
Average Return on Assets for Selected Industries

Source: Data from Dun & Bradstreet, *Industry Norms and Key Business Ratios*, 2005–2006.

For each dollar invested, Cruz Company's assets generate 11.6 cents of net income. This ratio indicates the income-generating strength (profit margin) of the company's resources and how efficiently the company is using all its assets (asset turnover).

Return on assets, then, combines profit margin and asset turnover:

$$\frac{\text{Net Income}}{\text{Net Sales}} \times \frac{\text{Net Sales}}{\text{Average Total Assets}} = \frac{\text{Net Income}}{\text{Average Total Assets}}$$

$$\text{Profit Margin} \times \text{Asset Turnover} = \text{Return on Assets}$$

$$5.7\% \times 2.00 \text{ Times} = 11.4\%^{*}$$

Thus, a company's management can improve overall profitability by increasing the profit margin, the asset turnover, or both. Similarly, in evaluating a company's overall profitability, a financial statement user must consider how these two ratios interact to produce return on assets.

*The slight difference between 11.4 and 11.6 percent is due to rounding.

By studying Figures 5-5, 5-6, and 5-7, you can see the different ways in which various industries combine profit margin and asset turnover to produce return on assets. For instance, by comparing the return on assets for grocery stores and computer companies, you can see how they achieve that return in very different ways. The grocery store industry has a profit margin of 2.3 percent, which when multiplied by an asset turnover of 5.0 times gives a return on assets of 11.5 percent. The auto and home supply industry has a higher profit margin, 2.5 percent, and a lower asset turnover, 3.0 times, and produces a return on assets of 7.5 percent.

Cruz Company's profit margin of 5.7 percent is well above the auto and home supply industry's average, but its asset turnover of 2.0 times lags behind the industry average. Cruz Company is sacrificing asset turnover to achieve a higher profit margin. This strategy is evidently working, because Cruz Company's return on assets of 11.4 percent exceeds the industry average of 7.5 percent.

Debt to Equity Ratio Another useful measure of profitability is the **debt to equity ratio,** which shows the proportion of a company's assets that is financed by creditors and the proportion that is financed by the owner. This ratio is computed by dividing total liabilities by owner's equity. The balance sheets of most companies do not show total liabilities; a short way of determining them is to deduct the total owner's equity from total assets.

A debt to equity ratio of 1.0 means that total liabilities equal owner's equity—that half of a company's assets are financed by creditors. A ratio of 0.5 means that one-third of a company's total assets are financed by creditors. A company with a high debt to equity ratio is at risk in poor economic times because it must continue to repay creditors. Owner's investments, on the other hand, do not have to be repaid, and withdrawals can be deferred when a company suffers because of a poor economy.

Cruz Company's debt to equity ratio is computed as follows:

$$\text{Debt to Equity Ratio} = \frac{\text{Total Liabilities}}{\text{Owner's Equity}} = \frac{\$241{,}932}{\$393{,}732} = 0.614, \text{ or } 61.4\%$$

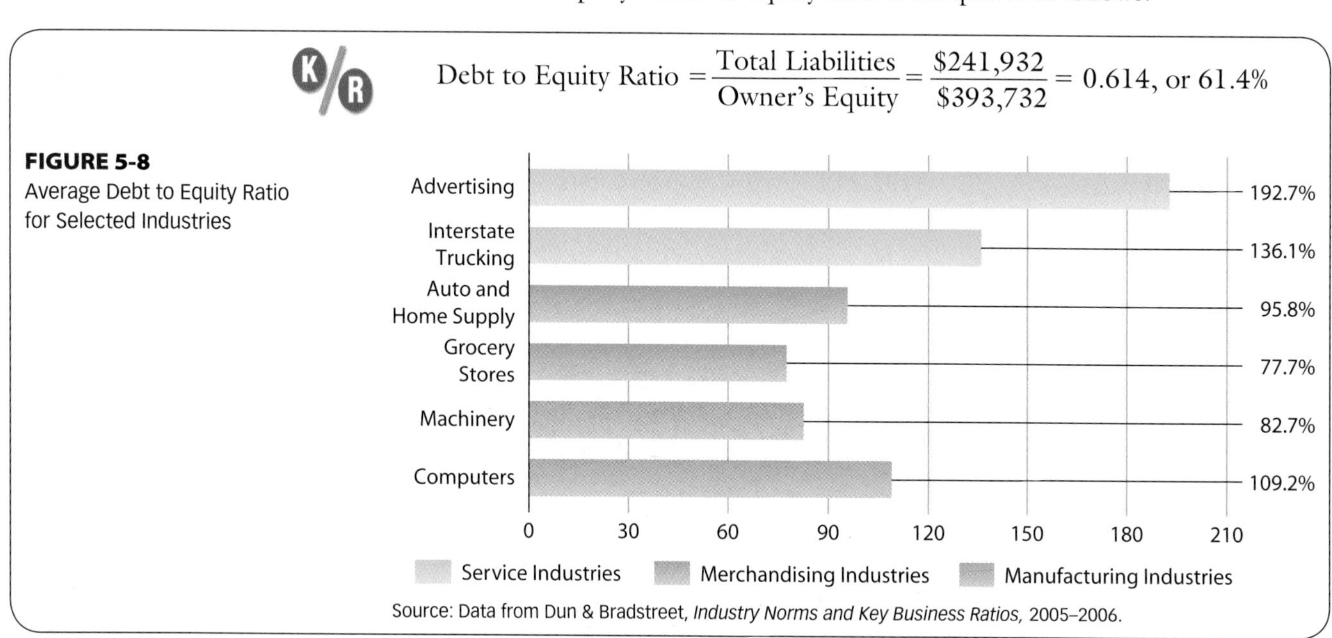

FIGURE 5-8
Average Debt to Equity Ratio for Selected Industries

Source: Data from Dun & Bradstreet, *Industry Norms and Key Business Ratios,* 2005–2006.

The debt to equity ratio of 61.4 percent means that Cruz Company receives less than half of its financing from creditors and that it receives more than half from the owner.

The debt to equity ratio does not fit neatly into either the liquidity or profitability category. It is clearly very important to liquidity analysis because

FOCUS ON BUSINESS PRACTICE

What Performance Measures Do Top Companies Use to Compensate Executives?

The boards of directors of public companies often use financial ratios to judge the performance of their top executives and to determine annual bonuses. Public companies must disclose the ratios or performance measures they use in creating these compensation plans. Studies show that the most successful companies over a sustained period of time, like Dell Computer, tend to focus the most on profitability measures. For instance, successful companies use earnings goals combined with sales growth 61 percent of the time compared to 43 percent for not-so-successful companies. Among the most common earnings goals are return on assets (19 percent for the best companies versus 5 percent for other companies) and return on equity (19 percent versus 7 percent). Clearly, successful companies set objectives that will provide incentives to management to increase profitability.[12]

it relates to debt and its repayment. It is also relevant to profitability for two reasons:

1. Creditors are interested in the proportion of the business that is debt-financed because the more debt a company has, the more profit it must earn to ensure the payment of interest to creditors.
2. Owners are interested in the proportion of the business that is debt-financed because the amount of interest paid on debt affects the amount of profit left to provide a return on the owner's investment.

The debt to equity ratio also shows how much expansion is possible through borrowing additional long-term funds.

Figure 5-8 shows that the debt to equity ratio in selected industries varies from a low of 77.7 percent in the grocery stores industry to a high of 192.7 percent in the advertising industry.

Return on Equity Of course, owners are interested in how much they have earned on their investment in the business. Their **return on equity** is measured by the ratio of net income to average owner's equity. Taking the ending owner's equity from the balance sheet and assuming that beginning owner's equity is \$402,212, Cruz Company's return on equity is computed as follows:

$$\text{Return on Equity} = \frac{\text{Net Income}}{\text{Average Owner's Equity}}$$

$$= \frac{\$71,524}{(\$393,732 + \$402,212) \div 2} = \frac{\$71,524}{\$397,972} = 0.180, \text{ or } 18.0\%$$

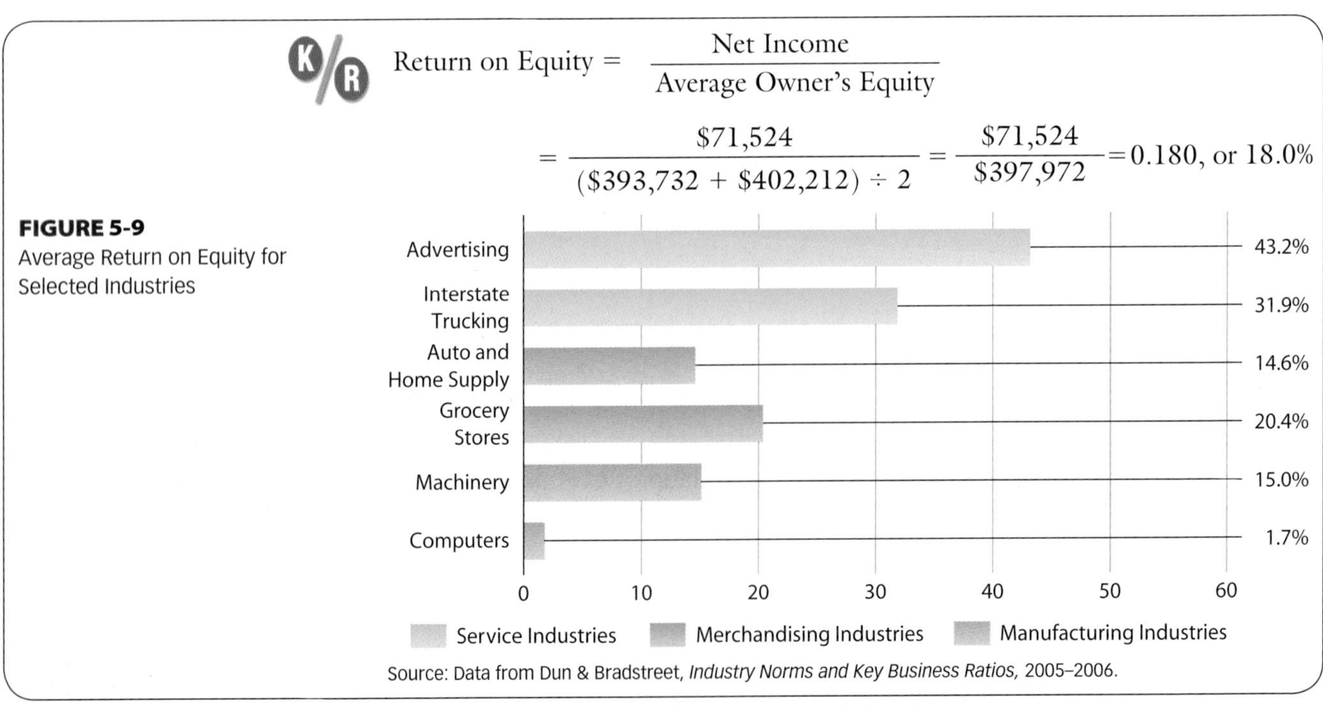

FIGURE 5-9
Average Return on Equity for Selected Industries

Source: Data from Dun & Bradstreet, *Industry Norms and Key Business Ratios*, 2005–2006.

Thus, Cruz Company earned 18.0 cents for every dollar invested by the owner. Whether this is an acceptable return depends on several factors, such as how much the company earned in previous years and how much other companies in the same industry earned. As measured by return on equity, the advertising industry is the most profitable of our sample industries, with a return on equity of 43.2 percent (see Figure 5-9). Cruz Company's average return on equity of 18.0 percent is better than the average of 14.6 percent for the auto and home supply industry.

STOP & APPLY >

Roth Company is considering applying for a bank loan. Various data from the classified financial statements of Roth Company are presented below.

	2011	2010		2011	2010
Current assets	$200,000	$170,000	Owner's equity	$ 640,000	$ 610,000
Total assets	880,000	710,000	Sales	1,200,000	1,050,000
Current liabilities	90,000	50,000	Net income	60,000	80,000
Long-term liabilities	150,000	50,000			

Its total assets and owner's equity at the beginning of 2010 were $690,000 and $590,000, respectively.

a. Use (1) liquidity analysis and (2) profitability analysis to document the Roth's financial position.

b. Discuss Roth's profitability and liquidity. Do you think it will qualify for a bank loan?

SOLUTION

a. (1)

	Current Assets	Current Liabilities	Working Capital	Current Ratio
2010	$170,000	$50,000	$120,000	3.40
2011	200,000	90,000	110,000	2.22
Decrease in working capital			$ 10,000	
Decrease in current ratio				1.18

(2) Profitability analysis

	Net Income	Sales	Profit Margin	Average Total Assets	Asset Turnover	Return on Assets	Average Owner's Equity	Return on Equity
2010	$80,000	$1,050,000	7.6%	$700,000[1]	1.50	11.4%	$600,000[3]	13.3%
2011	60,000	1,200,000	5.0%	795,000[2]	1.51	7.6%	625,000[4]	9.6%
Increase (decrease)	($20,000)	$ 150,000	(2.6)%	$ 95,000	0.01	(3.8)%	$ 25,000	(3.7)%

b. Liquidity and profitability discussed

Both working capital and the current ratio declined between 2010 and 2011 because the $40,000 increase in current liabilities ($90,000 − $50,000) was greater than the $30,000 increase in current assets.

Net income decreased by $20,000 despite an increase in sales of $150,000 and an increase in average total assets of $95,000. Thus, the profit margin fell from 7.6 percent to 5.0 percent, and return on assets fell from 11.4 percent to 7.6 percent. Asset turnover showed almost no change and so did not contribute to the decline

[1]($710,000 + $690,000) ÷ 2
[2]($880,000 + $710,000) ÷ 2
[3]($610,000 + $590,000) ÷ 2
[4]($640,000 + $610,000) ÷ 2

(continued)

in profitability. The decrease in return on equity, from 13.3 percent to 9.6 percent, was not as great as the decrease in return on assets because the growth in total assets was financed mainly by debt rather than by owner's equity, as shown in the capital structure analysis below.

	Total Liabilities	Owner's Equity	Debt to Equity Ratio
2010	$100,000	$610,000	16.4%
2011	240,000	640,000	37.5%
Increase	$140,000	$ 30,000	21.1%

Total liabilities increased by $140,000, while owner's equity increased by $30,000. Thus, the amount of the business financed by debt in relation to the amount financed by owner's equity increased between 2010 and 2011.

Both liquidity and profitability have declined. Roth will probably have to focus on improving current operations before expanding or getting a bank loan.

▸ FUN-FOR-FEET COMPANY: REVIEW PROBLEM

Multi-Step Income Statement and Profitability Ratios

LO4 LO5

In the Decision Point at the beginning of the chapter, we noted that Jay Bonali, owner of Fun-For-Feet Company, was seeking answers to the following questions:

- How should the income statement be organized to provide the best information?
- What key measures best capture a company's financial performance?

The multi-step form of the income statement provides more useful information than the single-step form because it enables the user to understand how the company generates its income. Further, the key ratios of asset turnover, profit margin, and return on assets are important measures of profitability.

1. Using the information in Fun-For-Feet's single-step income statement shown in the Decision Point, prepare a multi-step income statement.
2. Assuming average total assets are $1,000,000 and average total owner's equity is $400,000, compute the following profitability ratios: asset turnover, profit margin, and return on assets.
3. User insight: Explain why the multi-step income statement helps users understand the business better.

Answers to Review Problem

1. Multi-step income statement prepared

Fun-For-Feet Company
Income Statement
For the Year Ended December 31, 2011

Revenues		
Net sales		$1,207,132
Less cost of goods sold		787,080
Gross margin		$ 420,052
Operating expenses		
Selling expenses	$203,740	
General and administrative expenses	100,688	
Total operating expenses		304,428
Income from operations		$ 115,624

Other income and expense		
Interest income	$ 5,720	
Less interest expense	13,560	
Excess of other expenses over other revenues		7,780
Net Income		$ 107,784

2. Profitability ratios computed

   Asset turnover: Net sales/Average total assets

   $1,207,132/$1,000,000 = 1.2 times

   Profit margin: Net income/Net sales

   $107,784/$1,207,132 = 0.089, or 8.9%

   Return on assets: Net income/Average total assets

   $107,784/$1,000,000 = 0.1077, or 10.8%

3. Multi-step income statement discussed

   The multi-step income statement helps users understand the business better because it separates the operating (income from operations) part of the business from the investing (interest income) and financing (interest expense) parts of the business. It also shows the amount (gross margin) available to pay operating expenses on products sold.

LO1 Describe the objective of financial reporting and identify the qualitative characteristics, conventions, and ethical considerations of accounting information.

The objective of financial reporting is to provide financial information about the reporting entity that is useful to present and potential equity investors, lenders, and other creditors in making decisions in their capacity as capital providers. To be decision-useful, financial information must be useful in assessing cash flow prospects and stewardship. Because of the estimates and judgment that go into preparing financial information, such information must exhibit the qualitative characteristics of relevance and faithful representation. To be relevant, information must have predictive value, confirmative value, or both. To be faithful, financial information must be complete, neutral, and free from material error. Complementing the quality of information are the qualities of comparability, verifiability, timeliness, and understandability. It is also important for users to understand the constraints on financial information or accounting conventions used to prepare financial statements. Since the passage of the Sarbanes-Oxley Act in 2002, CEOs and CFOs have been required to certify to the accuracy and completeness of their companies' financial statements.

LO2 Define and describe the conventions of *consistency, full disclosure, materiality, conservatism,* and *cost-benefit.*

Because accountants' measurements are not exact, certain conventions are applied to help users interpret financial statements. Consistency requires the use of the same accounting procedures from period to period and enhances the comparability of financial statements. Full disclosure means including all relevant information in the financial statements. The materiality convention has to do with determining the relative importance of an item. Conservatism entails using the procedure that is least likely to overstate assets and income. The cost-benefit convention holds that the benefits to be gained from providing accounting information should be greater than the costs of providing it.

LO3 Identify and describe the basic components of a classified balance sheet.

The basic components of a classified balance sheet are as follows:

Assets	Liabilities	Owner's Equity
Current assets	Current liabilities	Owner's capital
Investments	Long-term liabilities	
Property, plant, and equipment		
Intangible assets		

Current assets are cash and other assets that a firm can reasonably expect to convert to cash or use up during the next year or the normal operating cycle, whichever is longer. Investments are assets, usually long-term, that are not used in the normal operation of a business. Property, plant, and equipment are tangible long-term assets used in day-to-day operations. Intangible assets are long-term assets with no physical substance whose value stems from the rights or privileges they extend to owners.

A current liability is an obligation due to be paid or performed during the next year or the normal operating cycle, whichever is longer. Long-term liabilities are debts that fall due more than one year in the future or beyond the normal operating cycle.

The equity section of a sole proprietorship's balance sheet differs from the equity section of a partnership's or corporation's balance sheet in that it does not have subcategories for contributed capital (the assets invested by stockholders) and retained earnings (stockholders' claim to assets earned from operations and reinvested in operations).

LO4 Describe the features of multistep and single-step classified income statements. Classified income statements for external reporting can be in multistep or single-step form. The multistep form arrives at net income through a series of steps; the single-step form arrives at it in a single step. A multistep income statement usually has a separate section for other revenues and expenses.

LO5 Use classified financial statements to evaluate liquidity and profitability. In evaluating a company's liquidity and profitability, investors (owners) and creditors rely on the data provided in classified financial statements. Two measures of liquidity are working capital and the current ratio. Five measures of profitability are profit margin, asset turnover, return on assets, debt to equity ratio, and return on equity. Industry averages are useful in interpreting these ratios.

REVIEW of Concepts and Terminology

The following concepts and terms were introduced in this chapter:

Accounting conventions 184 (LO1)
Classified financial statements 190 (LO3)
Comparability 184 (LO2)
Conservatism 187 (LO2)
Consistency 185 (LO2)
Contributed capital 194 (LO3)
Cost-benefit 188 (LO2)
Cost of goods sold 197 (LO4)
Current assets 190 (LO3)
Current liabilities 192 (LO3)
Faithful representation 184 (LO1)
Full disclosure 186 (LO2)
Gross margin 197 (LO4)
Gross sales 197 (LO4)
Income from operations 198 (LO4)
Income taxes 198 (LO4)
Intangible assets 192 (LO3)
Investments 192 (LO3)
Long-term liabilities 193 (LO3)
Manufacturing company 196 (LO4)
Materiality 187 (LO2)
Merchandising company 196 (LO4)
Multistep income statement 196 (LO4)
Net income 199 (LO4)
Net sales 196 (LO4)
Normal operating cycle 190 (LO3)
Operating expenses 198 (LO4)
Other assets 190 (LO3)
Other revenues and expenses 198 (LO4)
Property, plant, and equipment 192 (LO3)
Qualitative characteristics 183 (LO1)
Relevance 183 (LO1)
Retained Earnings 194 (LO3)
Sales returns and allowances 197 (LO4)
Single-step income statement 200 (LO4)
Timeliness 184 (LO1)
Understandability 184 (LO1)
Verifiability 184 (LO1)
Working capital 201 (LO5)

Key Ratios

Asset turnover 203 (LO5)
Current ratio 201 (LO5)
Debt to equity ratio 205 (LO5)
Profit margin 202 (LO5)
Return on assets 204 (LO5)
Return on equity 206 (LO5)

CHAPTER ASSIGNMENTS

BUILDING Your Basic Knowledge and Skills

Short Exercises

LO1 Objectives and Qualitative Characteristics

SE 1. Identify each of the following statements as related to either an objective (O) of financial information or as a qualitative (Q) characteristic of accounting information:

1. Information about business resources, claims to those resources, and changes in them should be provided.
2. Decision makers must be able to interpret accounting information.
3. Information that is useful in making investment and credit decisions should be furnished.
4. Accounting information must exhibit relevance and faithful representation.
5. Information useful in assessing cash flow prospects should be provided.

LO2 Accounting Conventions

SE 2. State which of the accounting conventions—consistency, full disclosure, materiality, conservatism, or cost-benefit—is being followed in each case described below.

1. Management provides detailed information about the company's long-term debt in the notes to the financial statements.
2. A company does not account separately for discounts received for prompt payment of accounts payable because few of these transactions occur and the total amount of the discounts is small.
3. Management eliminates a weekly report on property, plant, and equipment acquisitions and disposals because no one finds it useful.
4. A company follows the policy of recognizing a loss on inventory when the market value of an item falls below its cost but does nothing if the market value rises.
5. When several accounting methods are acceptable, management chooses a single method and follows that method from year to year.

LO3 Classification of Accounts: Balance Sheet

SE 3. Tell whether each of the following accounts is a current asset; an investment; property, plant, and equipment; an intangible asset; a current liability; a long-term liability; owner's equity; or not on the balance sheet:

1. Delivery Trucks
2. Accounts Payable
3. Note Payable (due in 90 days)
4. Delivery Expense
5. Owner's Capital
6. Prepaid Insurance
7. Trademark
8. Investment to Be Held Six Months
9. Factory Not Used in Business

LO3 Classified Balance Sheet

SE 4. Using the following accounts, prepare a classified balance sheet at year end, May 31, 20xx: Accounts Payable, $800; Accounts Receivable, $1,100; Accumulated Depreciation–Equipment, $700; Cash, $200; Owner's Investment, $1,000; Equipment, $3,000; Franchise, $200; Investments (long-term), $500; Merchandise Inventory, $600; Notes Payable (long-term), $400; Owner's

Capital, $?; Wages Payable, $100. Assume that this is the company's first year of operations.

LO4 **Classification of Accounts: Income Statement**

SE 5. Tell whether each of the following accounts is part of net sales, cost of goods sold, operating expenses, or other revenues and expenses, or is not on the income statement:

1. Delivery Expense
2. Interest Expense
3. Unearned Revenue
4. Sales Returns and Allowances
5. Cost of Sales
6. Depreciation Expense
7. Investment Income
8. Owner's Capital

LO4 **Single-Step Income Statement**

SE 6. Using the following accounts, prepare a single-step income statement at year end, May 31, 20xx: Cost of Goods Sold, $840; General Expenses, $450; Interest Expense, $210; Interest Income, $90; Net Sales, $2,400; Selling Expenses, $555.

LO4 **Multistep Income Statement**

SE 7. Using the accounts presented in **SE 6,** prepare a multistep income statement.

LO5 **Liquidity Ratios**

SE 8. Using the following accounts and balances taken from a year-end balance sheet, compute working capital and the current ratio:

Accounts Payable	$ 7,000
Accounts Receivable	10,000
Cash	4,000
Marketable Securities	2,000
Merchandise Inventory	12,000
Notes Payable in Three Years	13,000
Property, Plant, and Equipment	40,000
Owner's Capital	48,000

LO5 **Profitability Ratios**

SE 9. Using the following information from a balance sheet and an income statement, compute the (1) profit margin, (2) asset turnover, (3) return on assets, (4) debt to equity ratio, and (5) return on equity. (The previous year's total assets were $200,000, and owner's equity was $140,000.)

Total assets	$240,000
Total liabilities	60,000
Total owner's equity	180,000
Net sales	260,000
Cost of goods sold	140,000
Operating expenses	80,000

LO5 **Profitability Ratios**

SE 10. Assume that a company has a profit margin of 6.0 percent, an asset turnover of 3.2 times, and a debt to equity ratio of 50 percent. What are the company's return on assets and return on equity?

Exercises

LO1 LO2 Discussion Questions

E 1. Develop a brief answer to each of the following questions:

1. How do the four basic financial statements meet the stewardship objective of financial reporting?
2. What are some areas that require estimates to record transactions under the matching rule?
3. How can financial information be consistent but not comparable?
4. When might an amount be material to management but not to the CPA auditing the financial statements?

LO3 LO4 LO5 Discussion Questions

E 2. Develop a brief answer to each of the following questions:

1. Why is it that land held for future use and equipment not currently used in the business are classified as investments rather than as property, plant, and equipment?
2. Which is the better measure of a company's performance—income from operations or net income?
3. Why is it important to compare a company's financial performance with industry standards?
4. Is the statement "Return on assets is a better measure of profitability than profit margin" true or false and why?

LO1 LO2 Financial Accounting Concepts

E 3. The lettered items below represent a classification scheme for the concepts of financial accounting. Match each numbered term in the list that follows with the letter of the category in which it belongs.

a. Decision makers (users of accounting information)
b. Business activities or entities relevant to accounting measurement
c. Objective of accounting information
d. Accounting measurement considerations
e. Accounting processing considerations
f. Qualitative characteristics
g. Accounting conventions
h. Financial statements

1. Conservatism
2. Verifiability
3. Statement of cash flows
4. Materiality
5. Faithful representation
6. Recognition
7. Cost-benefit
8. Predictive value
9. Business transactions
10. Consistency
11. Full disclosure
12. Furnishing information that is useful to investors and creditors
13. Specific business entities
14. Classification
15. Management
16. Neutrality
17. Internal accounting control
18. Valuation
19. Investors
20. Completeness
21. Relevance
22. Furnishing information that is useful in assessing cash flow prospects

LO2 Accounting Concepts and Conventions

E 4. Each of the statements below violates a convention in accounting. State which of the following accounting conventions is violated: consistency, materiality, conservatism, full disclosure, or cost-benefit.

1. A series of reports that are time-consuming and expensive to prepare are presented to the owner each month, even though they are never used.
2. A company changes its method of accounting for depreciation.
3. The company in 2 does not indicate in the financial statements that the method of depreciation was changed; nor does it specify the effect of the change on net income.
4. A company's new office building, which is built next to the company's existing factory, is debited to the factory account because it represents a fairly small dollar amount in relation to the factory.
5. The asset account for a pickup truck still used in the business is written down to what the truck could be sold for, even though the carrying value under conventional depreciation methods is higher.

LO3 **Classification of Accounts: Balance Sheet**

E 5. The lettered items below represent a classification scheme for a balance sheet, and the numbered items in the list below are account titles. Match each account with the letter of the category in which it belongs.

a. Current assets
b. Investments
c. Property, plant, and equipment
d. Intangible assets
e. Current liabilities
f. Long-term liabilities
g. Owner's equity
h. Not on balance sheet

1. Patent
2. Building Held for Sale
3. Prepaid Rent
4. Wages Payable
5. Note Payable in Five Years
6. Building Used in Operations
7. Fund Held to Pay Off Long-Term Debt
8. Inventory
9. Prepaid Insurance
10. Depreciation Expense
11. Accounts Receivable
12. Interest Expense
13. Unearned Revenue
14. Short-Term Investments
15. Accumulated Depreciation
16. Owner's Capital

LO3 **Classified Balance Sheet Preparation**

E 6. The following data pertain to Branner Company: Accounts Payable, $10,200; Accounts Receivable, $7,600; Accumulated Depreciation–Building, $2,800; Accumulated Depreciation–Equipment, $3,400; Bonds Payable, $12,000; Building, $14,000; Cash, $6,240; Copyright, $1,240; Equipment, $30,400; Inventory, $8,000; Investment in Corporate Securities (long-term), $4,000; Investment in Six-Month Government Securities, $3,280; F. Branner, Capital, $47,640; Land, $1,600; Prepaid Rent, $240; and Revenue Received in Advance, $560.

Prepare a classified balance sheet at December 31, 2011. Assume that this is Branner Company's first year of operations.

LO4 **Classification of Accounts: Income Statement**

E 7. Using the classification scheme below for a multistep income statement, match each account with the letter of the category in which it belongs.

a. Net sales
b. Cost of sales
c. Selling expenses
d. General and administrative expenses
e. Other revenues and expenses
f. Not on income statement

1. Sales Discounts
2. Cost of Goods Sold
3. Dividend Income
4. Advertising Expense
5. Office Salaries Expense
6. Freight Out Expense
7. Prepaid Insurance
8. Utilities Expense
9. Sales Salaries Expense
10. Rent Expense
11. Depreciation Expense–Delivery Equipment
12. Interest Expense

LO4 **Preparation of Income Statements**

E 8. A company has the following data: net sales, \$202,500; cost of goods sold, \$110,000; selling expenses, \$45,000; general and administrative expenses, \$30,000; interest expense, \$2,000; and interest income, \$1,500.

1. Prepare a single-step income statement.
2. Prepare a multistep income statement.

LO4 **Multistep Income Statement**

E 9. A single-step income statement appears below. Present the information in a multistep income statement, and indicate what insights can be obtained from the multistep form as opposed to the single-step form.

Vision Company
Income Statement
For the Year Ended December 31, 2011

Revenues		
Net sales		$1,207,132
Interest income		5,720
Total revenues		$1,212,852
Costs and expenses		
Cost of goods sold	$787,080	
Selling expenses	203,740	
General and administrative expenses	100,688	
Interest expense	13,560	
Total costs and expenses		1,105,068
Net income		$ 107,784

LO5 **Liquidity Ratios**

E 10. The accounts and balances that follow are from the general ledger of Dimaz Company. Compute the (1) working capital and (2) current ratio.

Accounts Payable	$ 6,640
Accounts Receivable	4,080
Cash	600
Current Portion of Long-Term Debt	4,000
Long-Term Investments	8,320
Marketable Securities	5,040
Merchandise Inventory	10,160
Notes Payable (90 days)	6,000
Notes Payable (2 years)	16,000
Notes Receivable (90 days)	10,400
Notes Receivable (2 years)	8,000
Prepaid Insurance	160
Property, Plant, and Equipment	48,000
Property Taxes Payable	500
I. Dimaz, Capital	22,640
Salaries Payable	340
Supplies	140
Unearned Revenue	300

LO5 **Profitability Ratios**

E 11. The following end-of-year amounts are from the financial statements of Jang Company: total assets, $213,000; total liabilities, $86,000; owner's equity, $127,000; net sales, $391,000; cost of goods sold, $233,000; operating expenses, $94,000; and withdrawals, $20,000. During the past year, total assets increased by $37,500. Total owner's equity was affected only by net income and withdrawals. Compute the (1) profit margin, (2) asset turnover, (3) return on assets, (4) debt to equity ratio, and (5) return on equity.

LO5 **Liquidity and Profitability Ratios**

E 12. The simplified balance sheet and income statement for a company appear below.

Balance Sheet
December 31, 2011

Assets		**Liabilities**	
Current assets	$ 55,000	Current liabilities	$ 25,000
Investments	10,000	Long-term liabilities	30,000
Property, plant, and equipment	146,500	Total liabilities	$ 55,000
Intangible assets	18,500	**Owner's Equity**	
		Owner's capital	175,000
Total assets	$230,000	Total liabilities and owner's equity	$230,000

(continued)

Income Statement
For the Year Ended December 31, 2011

Net sales	$415,000
Cost of goods sold	250,000
Gross margin	$165,000
Operating expenses	130,000
Net income	$ 35,000

Total assets and owner's equity at the beginning of 2011 were $180,000 and $140,000, respectively. The owner made no investments or withdrawals during the year.

1. Compute the following liquidity measures: (a) working capital and (b) current ratio.
2. Compute the following profitability measures: (a) profit margin, (b) asset turnover, (c) return on assets, (d) debt to equity ratio, and (e) return on equity.

Problems

LO2 Accounting Conventions

P 1. In each case below, accounting conventions may have been violated.

1. After careful study, Lipski Company, which has offices in 40 states, has determined that its method of depreciating office furniture should be changed. The new method is adopted for the current year, and the change is noted in the financial statements.
2. In the past, Gomez Company has recorded operating expenses in general accounts (e.g., Salaries Expense and Utilities Expense). Management has determined that despite the additional recordkeeping costs, the company's income statement should break down each operating expense into its components of selling expense and administrative expense.
3. Param Company's auditor discovered that a company official had authorized the payment of a $1,200 bribe to a local official. Management argued that because the item was so small in relation to the size of the company ($1,700,000 in sales), the illegal payment should not be disclosed.
4. K&T Bookstore built a small addition to its main building to house a new computer games section. Because no one could be sure that the computer games section would succeed, the accountant took a conservative approach and recorded the addition as an expense.
5. Since it began operations ten years ago, Chang Company has used the same generally accepted inventory method. The company does not disclose in its financial statements what inventory method it uses.

Required

In each of these cases, identify the accounting convention that applies, state whether or not the treatment is in accord with the convention and generally accepted accounting principles, and briefly explain why.

LO4 **Forms of the Income Statement**

P 2. The income statements that follow are for Doug's Tools Corporation.

Doug's Tools Corporation
Income Statements
For the Years Ended July 31, 2012 and 2011

	2012	2011
Revenues		
Net sales	$464,200	$388,466
Interest income	1,420	750
Total revenues	$465,620	$389,216
Costs and expenses		
Cost of goods sold	$243,880	$198,788
Selling expenses	95,160	55,644
General and administrative expenses	90,840	49,286
Interest expense	5,600	1,100
Total costs and expenses	$435,480	$304,818
Net income	$ 30,140	$ 84,398

Required

1. From the information provided, prepare a multistep income statement for 2011 and 2012 showing percentages of net sales for each component.

User insight ▶ 2. Did income from operations increase or decrease between 2011 and 2012? Write a short explanation of why this change occurred.

LO3 LO5 **Classified Balance Sheet**

P 3. The following information is from the June 30, 2011, post-closing trial balance of Mike's Hardware Company.

Account Name	Debit	Credit
Cash	$ 32,000	
Short-Term Investments	33,000	
Notes Receivable	10,000	
Accounts Receivable	276,000	
Merchandise Inventory	145,000	
Prepaid Rent	1,600	
Prepaid Insurance	4,800	
Sales Supplies	1,280	
Office Supplies	440	
Deposit for Future Advertising	3,680	
Building, Not in Use	49,600	
Land	23,400	
Delivery Equipment	41,200	
Accumulated Depreciation–Delivery Equipment		$ 28,400
Trademark	4,000	
Accounts Payable		114,600
Salaries Payable		5,200
Interest Payable		840
Long-Term Notes Payable		80,000
M. Logan, Capital		396,960

Required

1. From the information provided, prepare a classified balance sheet for Mike's Hardware Company.
2. Compute Mike's Hardware's current ratio and debt to equity ratio.

User insight ▶ 3. As a user of the classified balance sheet, why would you want to know the current ratio or the debt to equity ratio?

LO5 Liquidity and Profitability Ratios

P 4. Arun Company has had poor operating results for the past two years. As the accountant for Arun Company, you have the following information available to you:

	2010	2009
Current assets	$ 22,500	$ 17,500
Total assets	72,500	55,000
Current liabilities	10,000	5,000
Long-term liabilities	10,000	—
Owner's equity	52,500	50,000
Net sales	131,000	100,000
Net income	8,000	5,500

Total assets and owner's equity at the beginning of 2009 were $45,000 and $40,000, respectively. The owner made no investments in 2009 or 2010.

Required

User insight ▶ 1. Compute the following measures of liquidity for 2009 and 2010: (a) working capital and (b) current ratio. Comment on the differences between the years.

2. Compute the following measures of profitability for 2009 and 2010: (a) profit margin, (b) asset turnover, (c) return on assets, (d) debt to equity ratio, and (e) return on equity. Comment on the change in performance from 2009 to 2010.

LO3 LO4 LO5 Classified Financial Statement Preparation and Analysis

P 5. Jimenez Company sells outdoor sports equipment. At the December 31, 2009, year end, the following financial information was available from the income statement: administrative expenses, $80,800; cost of goods sold, $350,420; interest expense, $22,640; interest income, $2,800; net sales, $714,390; and selling expenses, $220,200.

The following information was available from the balance sheet (after closing entries were made): accounts payable, $32,600; accounts receivable, $104,800; accumulated depreciation–delivery equipment, $17,100; accumulated depreciation–store fixtures, $42,220; cash, $28,400; delivery equipment, $88,500; inventory, $136,540; investment in securities (long-term), $56,000; investment in U.S. government securities (short-term), $39,600; long-term notes payable, $100,000; C. Jimenez, Capital, $359,300 (ending balance); notes payable (short-term), $50,000; prepaid expenses (short-term), $5,760; and store fixtures, $141,620.

Total assets and total owner's equity at December 31, 2008, were $524,400 and $376,170, respectively, and owner's withdrawals for the year were $60,000. The owner did not make any additional investments in the company during the year.

Required

1. From the information above, prepare (a) an income statement in single-step form, (b) a statement of owner's equity, and (c) a classified balance sheet.

2. From the statements you have prepared, compute the following measures: (a) working capital and current ratio (for liquidity); and (b) profit margin, asset turnover, return on assets, debt to equity ratio, and return on equity (for profitability).

User insight ▶ 3. Using the industry averages for the auto and home supply business in Figures 5-4 through 5-9 in this chapter, determine whether Jimenez Company needs to improve its liquidity or its profitability. Explain your answer, making recommendations as to specific areas on which Jimenez Company should concentrate.

Alternate Problems

LO2 Accounting Conventions

P 6. In each case below, accounting conventions may have been violated.

1. Rhonda's Manufacturing Company uses the cost method for computing the balance sheet amount of inventory unless the market value of the inventory is less than the cost, in which case the market value is used. At the end of the current year, the market value is $151,000 and the cost is $162,000. Rhonda's Manufacturing Company uses the $151,000 figure to compute the value of inventory because management believes it is the more cautious approach.
2. Goldman Company has annual sales of $10,000,000. It follows the practice of recording any items costing less than $250 as expenses in the year purchased. During the current year, it purchased several chairs for the executive conference room at $245 each, including freight. Although the chairs were expected to last for at least ten years, they were recorded as an expense in accordance with company policy.
3. Helman Company closed its books on October 31, 2010, before preparing its annual report. On November 3, 2010, a fire destroyed one of the company's two factories. Although the company had fire insurance and would not suffer a loss on the building, it seemed likely that it would suffer a significant decrease in sales in 2011 because of the fire. It did not report the fire damage in its 2010 financial statements because the fire had not affected its operations during that year.
4. Cure Drug Company spends a substantial portion of its profits on research and development. The company had been reporting its $6,000,000 expenditure for research and development as a lump sum, but management recently decided to begin classifying the expenditures by project, even though its recordkeeping costs will increase.
5. During the current year, Curt Nives Company (CNC) changed from one generally accepted method of accounting for inventories to another method.

Required

For each of these cases, identify the accounting convention that applies, state whether or not the treatment is in accord with the convention and GAAP, and briefly explain why.

LO4 **Forms of the Income Statement**

P 7. Oak Nursery Company's single-step income statements for 2011 and 2010 follow.

Oak Nursery Company
Income Statements
For the Years Ended April 30, 2011 and 2010

	2011	2010
Revenues		
Net sales	$525,932	$475,264
Interest income	1,800	850
Total revenues	$527,732	$476,114
Costs and expenses		
Cost of goods sold	$234,948	$171,850
Selling expenses	161,692	150,700
General and administrative expenses	62,866	42,086
Interest expense	3,600	1,700
Total costs and expenses	$463,106	$366,336
Net income	$ 64,626	$109,778

Required

1. From the information provided, prepare multistep income statements for 2010 and 2011 showing percentages of net sales for each component.
2. User insight ▶ Did income from operations increase or decrease from 2010 to 2011? Write a short explanation of why this change occurred.

LO5 **Liquidity and Profitability Ratios**

P 8. A summary of data from the income statements and balance sheets for Roman Construction Supply Company for 2011 and 2010 appears below.

	2011	2010
Current assets	$ 183,000	$ 155,000
Total assets	1,160,000	870,000
Current liabilities	90,000	60,000
Long-term liabilities	400,000	290,000
Owner's equity	670,000	520,000
Net sales	2,300,000	1,740,000
Net income	150,000	102,000

Total assets and owner's equity at the beginning of 2010 were $680,000 and $420,000, respectively.

Required

1. User insight ▶ Compute the following liquidity measures for 2010 and 2011: (a) working capital and (b) current ratio. Comment on the differences between the years.
2. User insight ▶ Compute the following measures of profitability for 2010 and 2011: (a) profit margin, (b) asset turnover, (c) return on assets, (d) debt to equity ratio, and (e) return on equity. Comment on the change in performance from 2010 to 2011.

LO3 LO4 LO5

Classified Financial Statement Preparation and Analysis

P 9. Wu Company sells outdoor sports equipment. At the December 31, 2010, year end, the following financial information was available from the income statement: administrative expenses, $161,600; cost of goods sold, $700,840; interest expense, $45,280; interest income, $5,600; net sales, $1,428,780; and selling expenses, $440,400.

The following information was available from the balance sheet (after closing entries were made): accounts payable, $65,200; accounts receivable, $209,600; accumulated depreciation–delivery equipment, $34,200; accumulated depreciation–store fixtures, $84,440; cash, $56,800; delivery equipment, $177,000; inventory, $273,080; investment in securities (long-term), $112,000; investment in U.S. government securities (short-term), $79,200; long-term notes payable, $200,000; Y. Wu, Capital, $718,600 (ending balance); notes payable (short-term), $100,000; prepaid expenses (short-term), $11,520; and store fixtures, $283,240.

Total assets and total owner's equity at December 31, 2009, were $1,048,800 and $752,340, respectively, and owner's withdrawals for the year were $120,000. The owner did not make any additional investments in the company during the year.

Required

1. From the information above, prepare (a) an income statement in single-step form, (b) a statement of owner's equity, and (c) a classified balance sheet.
2. From the statements you have prepared, compute the following measures: (a) working capital and current ratio (for liquidity); and (b) profit margin, asset turnover, return on assets, debt to equity ratio, and return on equity (for profitability).
3. Using the industry averages for the auto and home supply business in Figures 5-4 through 5-9 in this chapter, determine whether Wu Company needs to improve its liquidity or its profitability. Explain your answer, making recommendations as to specific areas on which Wu Company should concentrate.

User insight ▶

LO5

Liquidity and Profitability Ratios

P 10. Rollins Products Company has had poor operating results for the past two years. As the accountant for Rollins Products Company, you have the following information available to you:

	2011	2010
Current assets	$ 45,000	$ 35,000
Total assets	145,000	110,000
Current liabilities	20,000	10,000
Long-term liabilities	20,000	—
Owner's equity	105,000	100,000
Net sales	262,000	200,000
Net income	16,000	11,000

Total assets and owner's equity at the beginning of 2010 were $90,000 and $80,000, respectively. The owner made no investments in 2010 or 2011.

Required

1. Compute the following measures of liquidity for 2010 and 2011: (a) working capital and (b) current ratio. Comment on the differences between the years.
2. Compute the following measures of profitability for 2009 and 2010: (a) profit margin, (b) asset turnover, (c) return on assets, (d) debt to equity ratio, and (e) return on equity. Comment on the change in performance from 2010 to 2011.

ENHANCING Your Knowledge, Skills, and Critical Thinking

LO2 **Consistency and Full Disclosure**

C 1. City Parking, which operates a seven-story parking building in downtown Pittsburgh, has a calendar year end. It serves daily and hourly parkers, as well as monthly parkers who pay a fixed monthly rate in advance. The company traditionally has recorded all cash receipts as revenues when received. Most monthly parkers pay in full during the month prior to that in which they have the right to park. The company's auditors have said that beginning in 2009, the company should consider recording the cash receipts from monthly parking on an accrual basis, crediting Unearned Revenues. Total cash receipts for 2009 were $1,250,000, and the cash receipts received in 2009 and applicable to January 2010 were $62,500. Discuss the relevance of the accounting conventions of consistency, full disclosure, and materiality to the decision to record the monthly parking revenues on an accrual basis.

LO2 **Materiality**

C 2. Kubicki Company operates a chain of designer bags and shoes stores in the Houston area. This year the company achieved annual sales of $75 million, on which it earned a net income of $3 million. At the beginning of the year, management implemented a new inventory system that enabled it to track all purchases and sales. At the end of the year, a physical inventory reveals that the actual inventory was $120,000 below what the new system indicated it should be. The inventory loss, which probably resulted from shoplifting, is reflected in a higher cost of goods sold. The problem concerns management but seems to be less important to the company's auditors. What is materiality? Why might the inventory loss concern management more than it does the auditors? Do you think the amount of inventory loss is material?

LO5 **Comparison of Profitability**

C 3. Two of the largest chains of grocery stores in the United States are **Albertson's, Inc.**, and the **Great Atlantic & Pacific Tea Company (A&P)**. In a recent fiscal year, Albertson's had a net income of $765 million, and A&P had a net income of $14 million. It is difficult to judge which company is more profitable from those figures alone because they do not take into account the relative sales, sizes, and investments of the companies. Data (in millions) needed to complete a financial analysis of the two companies follow:[13]

	Albertson's	A&P
Net sales	$36,762	$10,151
Beginning total assets	15,719	3,335
Ending total assets	16,078	3,309
Beginning total liabilities	10,017	2,489
Ending total liabilities	10,394	2,512
Beginning stockholders' equity	5,702	846
Ending stockholders' equity	5,684	797

1. Determine which company was more profitable by computing profit margin, asset turnover, return on assets, debt to equity ratio, and return on equity for the two companies. Comment on the relative profitability of the two companies.
2. What do the ratios tell you about the factors that go into achieving an adequate return on assets in the grocery industry? For industry data, refer to Figures 5-4 through 5-9 in this chapter.
3. How would you characterize the use of debt financing in the grocery industry and the use of debt by these two companies?

LO1 **Qualitative Characteristics of Accounting Information**

C 4. Review the multistep income statement presented in Exhibits 5-3 and 5-4. In your group, discuss how this form of the income statement meets each of these qualitative characteristics of accounting information: understandability, usefulness, relevance, and reliability. Be prepared to present your conclusions in class.

LO3 LO4 **Classified Balance Sheet and Multistep Income Statement**

C 5. Refer to **CVS Corporation**'s annual report in the Supplement to Chapter 5 to answer the following questions.

1. Consolidated balance sheets:
   a. Did the amount of working capital increase or decrease from 2007 to 2008? By how much?
   b. Did the current ratio improve from 2007 to 2008?
   c. Does the company have long-term investments or intangible assets?
   d. Did the debt to equity ratio of CVS change from 2007 to 2008?
   e. What proportion of owners' (shareholders') equity is retained earnings?
2. Consolidated statements of operations:
   a. Does CVS use a multistep or single-step income statement?
   b. Is it a comparative statement?
   c. What is the trend of net earnings?
   d. How significant are income taxes for CVS?

LO5 **Financial Analysis**

C 6. Compare the financial performance of **CVS** and **Southwest Airlines Co.** on the basis of liquidity and profitability for 2008 and 2007. Use the following ratios: working capital, current ratio, debt to equity ratio, profit margin, asset turnover, return on assets, and return on equity. In 2006, total assets and total stockholders' equity for CVS were $20,574.1 million and $9,917.6 million, respectively. Southwest's total assets were $13,460 million, and total stockholders' equity was $6,449 million in 2006. Comment on the relative performance of the two companies. In general, how does Southwest's performance compare to CVS's with respect to liquidity and profitability? What distinguishes Southwest's profitability performance from that of CVS?

SUPPLEMENT TO CHAPTER 5

How to Read an Annual Report

More than 4 million corporations are chartered in the United States. Most of them are small, family-owned businesses. They are called *private* or *closely held corporations* because their common stock is held by only a few people and is not for sale to the public. Larger companies usually find it desirable to raise investment funds from many investors by issuing common stock to the public. These companies are called *public companies.* Although they are fewer in number than private companies, their total economic impact is much greater.

Public companies must register their common stock with the Securities and Exchange Commission (SEC), which regulates the issuance and subsequent trading of the stock of public companies. The SEC requires the management of public companies to report each year to stockholders on their companies' financial performance. This report, called an *annual report*, contains the company's annual financial statements and other pertinent data. Annual reports are a primary source of financial information about public companies and are distributed to all of a company's stockholders. They must also be filed with the SEC on a Form 10-K.

The general public may obtain an annual report by calling or writing the company or accessing the report online at the company's website. If a company has filed its 10-K electronically with the SEC, it can be accessed at *www.sec.gov/edgar.shtml.* Many libraries also maintain files of annual reports or have them available on electronic media, such as *Compact Disclosure.*

This supplement describes the major components of the typical annual report. We have included many of these components in the annual report of **CVS Caremark Corporation**, one of the country's most successful retailers. Case assignments in each chapter refer to this annual report. For purposes of comparison, the supplement also includes the financial statements and summary of significant accounting policies of **Southwest Airlines Co.**, one of the largest and most successful airlines in the United States.

The Components of an Annual Report

In addition to listing the corporation's directors and officers, an annual report usually contains a letter to the stockholders (also called *shareholders*), a multiyear summary of financial highlights, a description of the company, management's discussion and analysis of the company's operating results and financial condition, the financial statements, notes to the financial statements, a statement about management's responsibilities, and the auditors' report.

Letter to the Stockholders

Traditionally, an annual report begins with a letter in which the top officers of the corporation tell stockholders about the company's performance and prospects. In CVS's 2008 annual report, the chairman and chief executive officer wrote to the stockholders about the highlights of the past year, the key priorities for the new year, and other aspects of the business. He reported as follows:

> Today, we are the nation's largest pharmacy health care company. With U.S. health care costs expected to reach more than $4 trillion annually over the next decade, we are beginning to deliver healthy outcomes for patients and driving down costs in ways that no other company in our industry can.

Financial Highlights

The financial highlights section of an annual report presents key statistics for at least a five-year period but often for a ten-year period. It is often accompanied by graphs. CVS's annual report, for example, gives key figures for sales, operating profits, and other key measures. Note that the financial highlights section often includes nonfinancial data and graphs, such as the number of stores in CVS's case.

Description of the Company

An annual report contains a detailed description of the company's products and divisions. Some analysts tend to scoff at this section of the annual report because it often contains glossy photographs and other image-building material, but it should not be overlooked because it may provide useful information about past results and future plans.

Management's Discussion and Analysis

In this section, management describes the company's financial condition and results of operations and explains the difference in results from one year to the next. For example, CVS's management explains the effects of its strategy to relocate some of its stores:

> Total net revenues continued to benefit from our active relocation program, which moves existing in-line shopping center stores to larger, more convenient, freestanding locations. Historically, we have achieved significant improvements in customer count and net revenue when we do this. As of December 31, 2008, approximately 62% of our existing stores were freestanding, compared to approximately 64% and 61% at December 29, 2007 and December 30, 2006, respectively. During 2008, the decrease in the percentage of freestanding stores resulted from the addition of the Longs Drug Stores.

CVS's management also describes the increase in cash flows from investing activities:

> Net cash used in investing activities increased to $4.6 billion in 2008. This compares to $3.1 billion in 2007 and $4.6 billion in 2006. The increase in net cash used in investing activities during 2008 was primarily due to the Longs Acquisition. The $3.1 billion of net cash used in investing activities during 2007 was primarily due to the Caremark Merger. The increase in net cash used in investing activities during 2006 was primarily due to the Albertson's Acquisition.

Financial Statements

All companies present the same four basic financial statements in their annual reports, but the names they use may vary. As you can see in Exhibits S-1 to S-4, CVS presents statements of operations (income statements), balance sheets, statements of cash flows, and statements of shareholders' equity (includes retained earnings). (Note that the numbers given in the statements are in millions, but the last six digits are omitted. For example, $4,793,300,000 is shown as $4,793.3.)

The headings of CVS's financial statements are preceded by the word *consolidated*. A corporation issues *consolidated* financial statements when it consists of more than one company and has combined the companies' data for reporting purposes.

CVS provides several years of data for each financial statement: two years for the balance sheet and three years for the others. Financial statements presented in this fashion are called *comparative financial statements*. Such statements are in accordance with generally accepted accounting principles and help readers assess the company's performance over several years.

CVS's fiscal year ends on the Saturday nearest the end of December (December 31, 2008 in the latest year). Retailers commonly end their fiscal years during a slow period, usually the end of January, which is in contrast to CVS's choosing the end of December.

Income Statements CVS uses a multistep form of the income statement in that results are shown in several steps (in contrast to the single-step form illustrated in the chapter). The steps are gross profit, operating profit, earnings before income tax provision, and net earnings (see Exhibit S-1). The company also shows net earnings available to common shareholders, and it discloses the basic earnings per share and diluted earnings per share. Basic earnings per share is used for most analysis. Diluted earnings per share assumes that all rights that could be exchanged for common shares, such as stock options, are in fact exchanged. The weighted average number of shares of common stock, used in calculating the per share figures, are shown at the bottom of the income statement.

Balance Sheets CVS has a typical balance sheet for a retail company (see Exhibit S-2). In the assets and liabilities sections, the company separates out the current assets and the current liabilities. Current assets will become available as cash or will be used up in the next year; current liabilities will have to be paid or satisfied in the next year. These groupings are useful in assessing a company's liquidity.

Several items in the shareholders' equity section of the balance sheet may need explanation. Common stock represents the number of shares outstanding at par value. Capital surplus (additional paid-in capital) represents amounts invested by stockholders in excess of the par value of the common stock. Preferred stock is capital stock that has certain features that distinguish it from common stock. Treasury stock represents shares of common stock the company repurchased.

Statements of Cash Flows Whereas the income statement reflects CVS's profitability, the statement of cash flows reflects its liquidity (see Exhibit S-3). This statement provides information about a company's cash receipts, cash payments, and investing and financing activities during an accounting period.

The first major section of CVS's consolidated statements of cash flows shows cash flows from operating activities. It shows the cash received and paid for various items related to the company's operations. The second major section is cash flows from investing activities. Except for acquisitions in 2006, 2007, and 2008, the largest outflow in this category is additions for property and equipment. This figure demonstrates that CVS is a growing company. The third major section

EXHIBIT S-1
CVS's Income Statements

Consolidated means that data from all companies owned by CVS are combined.

CVS Caremark Corporation
Consolidated Statements of Operations

CVS's fiscal year ends on the Saturday closest to December 31.

(In millions, except per share amounts)	***Fiscal Year Ended*** **Dec. 31, 2008 (52 weeks)**	**Dec. 29, 2007 (52 weeks)**	**Dec. 30, 2006 (53 weeks)**
Net revenues	$87,471.9	$76,329.5	$43,821.4
Cost of revenues	69,181.5	60,221.8	32,079.2
Gross profit	18,290.4	16,107.7	11,742.2
Total operating expenses	12,244.2	11,314.4	9,300.6
Operating profit[1]	6,046.2	4,793.3	2,441.6
Interest expense, net[2]	509.5	434.6	215.8
Earnings before income tax provision	5,536.7	4,358.7	2,225.8
Loss from discontinued operations, net of income tax benefit of $82.4	(132)	—	—
Income tax provision	2,192.6	1,721.7	856.9
Net earnings[3]	3,212.1	2,637.0	1,368.9
Preference dividends, net of income tax benefit[4]	14.1	14.2	13.9
Net earnings available to common shareholders	$ 3,198.0	$ 2,622.8	$ 1,355.0
BASIC EARNINGS PER COMMON SHARE:[5]			
Net earnings	$ 2.23	$ 1.97	$ 1.65
Weighted average common shares outstanding	1,433.5	1,328.2	820.6
DILUTED EARNINGS PER COMMON SHARE:			
Net earnings	$ 2.18	$ 1.92	$ 1.60
Weighted average common shares outstanding	1,469.1	1,371.8	853.2
DIVIDENDS DECLARED PER COMMON SHARE:	$ 0.25800	$ 0.22875	$ 0.15500

1. This section shows earnings from ongoing operations.
2. CVS shows interest expense and income taxes separately.
3. The net earnings figure moves to the statements of shareholders' equity.
4. CVS shows the dividends distributed to preferred shareholders. This distribution is not an expense.
5. CVS discloses various breakdowns of earnings per share.

is cash flows from financing activities. You can see here that CVS's largest cash inflows are for borrowing of long-term and short-term debt.

At the bottom of the statements of cash flows, you can see a reconciliation of net earnings to net cash provided by operating activities. This disclosure is important to the user because it relates the goal of profitability (net earnings) to liquidity (net cash provided). Most companies substitute this disclosure for the operating activities at the beginning of their statement of cash flows, as illustrated in Chapter 1.

Statements of Shareholders' Equity Instead of a simple statement of retained earnings, CVS presents consolidated statements of shareholders' equity (see Exhibit S-4). These statements explain the changes in components of stockholders' equity, including retained earnings.

EXHIBIT S-2 CVS'S Balance Sheets

CVS Caremark Corporation
Consolidated Balance Sheets

(In millions, except shares and per share amounts)	Dec. 31, 2008	Dec. 29, 2007
ASSETS:		
Cash and cash equivalents	$ 1,352.4	$ 1,056.6
Short-term investments	—	27.5
Accounts receivable, net	5,384.3	4,579.6
Inventories	9,152.6	8,008.2
Deferred income taxes	435.2	329.4
Other current assets	201.7	148.1
Total current assets	$ 16,526.2	14,149.4
Property and equipment, net	$ 8,125.2	$ 5,852.8
Goodwill	25,493.9	23,922.3
Intangible assets, net	10,466.2	10,429.6
Deferred income taxes	—	—
Other assets	368.4	367.8
Total assets	$ 60,959.9	$ 54,721.9
LIABILITIES:		
Accounts payable	$ 3,800.7	$ 3,593.0
Claims and discounts payable	2,814.2	2,484.3
Accrued expenses	3,177.6	2,556.8
Short-term debt	3,044.1	2,085.0
Current portion of long-term debt	653.3	47.2
Total current liabilities	13,489.9	10,766.3
Long-term debt	8,057.2	8,349.7
Deferred income taxes	3,701.7	3,426.1
Other long-term liabilities	1,136.7	857.9
Commitments and contingencies (Note 11)		
SHAREHOLDERS' EQUITY:		
Preferred stock, $0.01 par value: authorized 120,619 shares; no shares issued or outstanding	—	—
Preference stock, series one ESOP convertible, par value $1.00: authorized 50,000,000 shares; issued and outstanding 3,798,000 shares at December 29, 2007 and 3,990,000 shares at December 30, 2006	191.5	203.0
Common stock, par value $0.01: authorized 3,200,000,000 shares; issued 1,590,139,000 shares at December 29, 2007 and 847,266,000 shares at December 30, 2006	16.0	15.9
Treasury stock, at cost: 153,682,000 shares at December 30, 2007 and 21,529,000 shares at December 30, 2006	(5,812.3)	(5,620.4)
Shares held in trust, 9,224,000 shares at December 29, 2007	(55.5)	(301.3)
Guaranteed ESOP obligation	—	(44.5)
Capital surplus	27,279.6	26,831.9
Retained earnings	13,097.8	10,287.0
Accumulated other comprehensive loss	(142.7)	(49.7)
Total shareholders' equity	34,574.4	31,321.9
Total liabilities and shareholders' equity	$ 60,959.9	$ 54,721.9

CVS categorizes certain assets as current assets.

These are noncurrent or long-term assets.

CVS categorizes certain liabilities as current liabilities.

These are noncurrent or long-term liabilities.

Balances in the shareholders' equity section are from the statements of shareholders' equity.

EXHIBIT S-3 CVS's Statements of Cash Flows

CVS Corporation
Consolidated Statements of Cash Flows

Cash flows are shown for operating activities, investing activities, and financing activities.

	Fiscal Year Ended		
(In millions)	Dec. 31, 2008 (52 weeks)	Dec. 29, 2007 (52 weeks)	Dec. 30, 2006 (53 weeks)
CASH FLOWS FROM OPERATING ACTIVITIES:			
Cash receipts from revenues	$69,493.7	$61,986.3	$43,273.7
Cash paid for inventory	(51,374.7)	(45,772.6)	(31,422.1)
Cash paid to other suppliers and employees	(11,832.0)	(10,768.6)	(9,065.3)
Interest and dividends received	20.3	33.6	15.9
Interest paid	(573.7)	(468.2)	(228.1)
Income taxes paid	(1,786.5)	(1,780.8)	(831.7)
NET CASH PROVIDED BY OPERATING ACTIVITIES	3,947.1	3,229.7	1,742.4
CASH FLOWS FROM INVESTING ACTIVITIES:			
Additions to property and equipment	(2,179.9)	(1,805.3)	(1,768.9)
Proceeds from sale-leaseback transactions	203.8	601.3	1,375.6
Acquisitions (net of cash acquired) and other investments	(2,650.7)	(1,983.3)	(4,224.2)
Cash outflow from hedging activities	—	—	(5.3)
Sale of short-term investments	27.5	—	—
Proceeds from sale or disposal of assets	18.7	105.6	29.6
NET CASH USED IN INVESTING ACTIVITIES	(4,580.6)	(3,081.7)	(4,593.2)
CASH FLOWS FROM FINANCING ACTIVITIES:			
Additions to/(reductions in) short-term debt	959.0	242.3	1,589.3
Repayment of debt assumed in acquisition	(352.8)	—	—
Additions to long-term debt	350.0	6,000.0	1,500.0
Reductions in long-term debt	(1.8)	(821.8)	(310.5)
Dividends paid	(383.0)	(322.4)	(140.9)
Proceeds from exercise of stock options	327.8	552.4	187.6
Excess tax benefits from stock based compensation	53.1	97.8	42.6
Repurchase of common stock	(23.0)	(5,370.4)	—
NET CASH PROVIDED BY (USED IN) FINANCING ACTIVITIES	929.3	377.9	2,868.1
Net increase in cash and cash equivalents	295.8	525.9	17.3
Cash and cash equivalents at beginning of year	1,056.6	530.7	513.4
CASH AND CASH EQUIVALENTS AT END OF YEAR	$ 1,352.4	$ 1,056.6	$ 530.7
RECONCILIATION OF NET EARNINGS TO NET CASH PROVIDED BY OPERATING ACTIVITIES			
Net earnings	$ 3,212.1	$ 2,637.0	$ 1,368.9
Adjustments required to reconcile net earnings to net cash provided by operating activities:	1,274.2	1,094.6	733.3
Depreciation and amortization Stock based compensation	92.5	78.0	69.9
Deferred income taxes and other non-cash items	(3.4)	40.1	98.2
Change in operating assets and liabilities providing/(requiring) cash, net of effects from acquisitions:			
Accounts receivable, net	(291.0)	279.7	(540.1)
Inventories	(448.1)	(448.0)	(624.1)
Other current assets	12.5	(59.2)	(21.4)
Other assets	19.1	(26.4)	(17.2)
Accounts payable	(63.9)	(181.4)	396.7
Accrued expenses	182.5	(168.2)	328.9
Other long-term liabilities	0.6	(16.5)	(50.7)
NET CASH PROVIDED BY OPERATING ACTIVITIES	$ 3,947.1	$ 3,229.7	$ 1,742.4

Cash and cash equivalents move to balance sheets.

This section explains the difference between net earnings and net cash provided by operating activities.

EXHIBIT S-4 CVS's Statements of Stockholders' Equity

Each component of shareholders' equity is explained.

CVS Caremark Corporation
Consolidated Statements of Shareholders' Equity

(In millions)	Shares			Dollars		
	Dec. 31, 2008	**Dec. 29, 2007**	**Dec. 30, 2006**	**Dec. 31, 2008**	**Dec. 29, 2007**	**Dec. 30, 2006**
PREFERENCE STOCK:						
Beginning of year	3.8	4.0	4.2	$ 203.0	$ 213.3	$ 222.6
Conversion to common stock	(0.2)	(0.2)	(0.2)	(11.5)	(10.3)	(9.3)
End of year	3.6	3.8	4.0	191.5	203.0	213.3
COMMON STOCK:						
Beginning of year	1,590.1	847.3	838.8	15.9	8.5	8.4
Common stock issued for Caremark Merger	—	712.7	—	—	7.1	—
Stock options exercised and awards	13.2	30.1	8.5	0.1	0.3	0.1
End of year	1,603.3	1,590.1	847.3	16.0	15.9	8.5
TREASURY STOCK:						
Beginning of year	(153.7)	(21.5)	(24.5)	(5,620.4)	(314.5)	(356.5)
Purchase of treasury shares	(6.5)	(135.0)	0.1	(33.0)	(5,378.7)	(0.1)
Transfer from Trust	(7.5)	—	—	(272.3)	—	—
Conversion of preference stock	1.0	0.9	0.8	35.2	24.7	11.7
Employee stock purchase plan issuance	2.2	1.9	2.1	78.2	48.1	30.4
End of year	(164.5)	(153.7)	(21.5)	(5,812.3)	(5,620.4)	(314.5)
GUARANTEED ESOP OBLIGATION:						
Beginning of year				(44.5)	(82.1)	(114.0)
Reduction of guaranteed ESOP Obligation				44.5	37.6	31.9
End of year				—	(44.5)	(82.1)
SHARES HELD IN TRUST:						
Beginning of year	(9.2)	—	—	(301.3)	—	—
Transfer to treasury stock	7.5	—	—	245.8	—	—
Shares acquired through Caremark Merger	—	(9.2)	—	—	(301.3)	—
End of year	(1.7)	(9.2)		(55.5)	(301.3)	—
CAPITAL SURPLUS:						
Beginning of year				26,831.9	2,198.4	1,922.4
Common stock issued for Caremark Merger, net of issuance costs				—	23,942.4	—
Conversion of shares held in Trust to treasury stock				26.5		
Stock option activity and awards				391.8	607.7	235.8
Tax benefit on stock options and awards				53.1	97.8	42.6
Conversion of preference stock				(23.7)	(14.4)	(2.4)
End of year				27,279.6	26,831.9	2,198.4
ACCUMULATED OTHER COMPREHENSIVE LOSS:						
Beginning of year				(49.7)	(72.6)	(90.3)
Recognition of unrealized gain/(loss) on derivatives, net of income tax				3.4	3.4	(0.3)
Pension liability adjustment				(96.4)	19.5	23.6
Pension liability adjustment to initially apply SFAS No. 158, net of tax benefit				—	—	(5.6)
End of year				(142.7)	(49.7)	(72.6)

EXHIBIT S-4 continued

RETAINED EARNINGS:			
Beginning of year	10,287.0	7,966.6	6,738.6
Net earnings ← Net earnings are from the income statement.	3,212.1	2,637.0	1,368.9
Common stock dividends	(369.7)	(308.8)	(127.0)
Preference stock dividends	(14.0)	(14.8)	(15.6)
Tax benefit on preference stock dividends	0.6	1.2	1.7
Adoption of EITF 06-04 and EITF 06-10	(18.2)	—	—
Adoption of FIN 48	—	5.8	—
End of year	13,097.8	10,287.0	7,966.6
TOTAL SHAREHOLDERS' EQUITY	$34,574.4	$31,321.9	$9,917.6
COMPREHENSIVE INCOME:			
Net earnings	$ 3,212.1	$ 2,637.0	$1,368.9
Recognition of unrealized gain/(loss) on derivatives, net of income tax	3.4	3.4	(0.3)
Pension liability, net of income tax	(96.4)	19.5	23.6
COMPREHENSIVE HOME	$ 3,119.1	$ 2,659.9	$1,392.2

Notes to the Financial Statements

To meet the requirements of full disclosure, a company must add notes to the financial statements to help users interpret some of the more complex items. The notes are considered an integral part of the financial statements. In recent years, the need for explanation and further details has become so great that the notes often take more space than the statements themselves. The notes to the financial statements include a summary of significant accounting policies and explanatory notes.

Summary of Significant Accounting Policies Generally accepted accounting principles require that the financial statements include a *Summary of Significant Accounting Policies.* In most cases, this summary is presented in the first note to the financial statements or as a separate section just before the notes. In this summary, the company tells which generally accepted accounting principles it has followed in preparing the statements. For example, in CVS's report, the company states the principles followed for revenue recognition:

> The RPS [Retail Pharmacy Segment] recognizes revenue from the sale of merchandise (other than prescription drugs) at the time the merchandise is purchased by the retail customer. Revenue from the sale of prescription drugs is recognized at the time the prescription is filled, which is or approximates when the retail customer picks up the prescription. Customer returns are not material. Revenue generated from the performance of services in the RPS' healthcare clinics is recognized at the time the services are performed. . . .The PSS [Pharmacy Services Segment] recognizes revenues from prescription drugs sold by its mail service pharmacies and under national retail pharmacy network contracts where the PSS is the principal using the gross method at the contract prices negotiated with its customers.

Explanatory Notes Other notes explain some of the items in the financial statements. For example, CVS describes its commitments for future lease payments as follows:

Following is a summary of the future minimum lease payments under capital and operating leases as of December 31, 2008:

(In millions)	Capital Leases	Operating Leases
2009	17.0	1,744.2
2010	17.2	1,854.4
2011	17.2	1,609.0
2012	17.6	1,609.0
2013	17.9	1,682.6
Thereafter	83.0	14,821.0
	$169.9	$23,294.6

Information like this is very useful in determining the full scope of a company's liabilities and other commitments.

Supplementary Information Notes In recent years, the FASB and the SEC have ruled that certain supplemental information must be presented with financial statements. Examples are the quarterly reports that most companies present to their stockholders and to the SEC. These quarterly reports, called *interim financial statements,* are in most cases reviewed but not audited by a company's independent CPA firm. In its annual report, CVS presents unaudited quarterly financial data from its 2008 quarterly statements. The quarterly data also includes the high and low price for the company's common stock during each quarter.

Reports of Management's Responsibilities

Separate statements of management's responsibility for the financial statements and for internal control structure accompany the financial statements as required by the Sarbanes-Oxley Act of 2002. In its reports, CVS's management acknowledges its responsibility for the consistency, integrity, and presentation of the financial information and for the system of internal controls.

Reports of Certified Public Accountants

The *registered independent auditors' report* deals with the credibility of the financial statements. This report, prepared by independent certified public accountants, gives the accountants' opinion about how fairly the statements have been presented. Because management is responsible for preparing the financial statements, issuing statements that have not been independently audited would be like having a judge hear a case in which he or she was personally involved. The certified public accountants add the necessary credibility to management's figures for interested third parties. They report to the board of directors and the stockholders rather than to the company's management.

In form and language, most auditors' reports are like the one shown in Figure S-1. Usually, such a report is short, but its language is very important. It normally has four parts, but it can have a fifth part if an explanation is needed.

1. The first paragraph identifies the financial statements that have been audited. It also identifies responsibilities. The company's management is responsible for the financial statements, and the auditor is responsible for expressing an opinion on the financial statements based on the audit.
2. The second paragraph, or *scope section,* states that the examination was made in accordance with standards of the Public Company Accounting Oversight Board (PCAOB). This paragraph also contains a brief description of the objectives and nature of the audit.

3. The third paragraph, or *opinion section*, states the results of the auditors' examination. The use of the word *opinion* is very important because the auditor does not certify or guarantee that the statements are absolutely correct. To do so would go beyond the truth, because many items, such as depreciation, are based on estimates. Instead, the auditors simply give an opinion about whether, overall, the financial statements "present fairly," in all material respects, the company's financial position, results of operations, and cash flows. This means that the statements are prepared in accordance with generally accepted accounting principles. If, in the auditors' opinion, the statements do not meet accepted standards, the auditors must explain why and to what extent.
4. The fourth paragraph identifies a new accounting standard adopted by the company.
5. The fifth paragraph says the company's internal controls are effective.

FIGURE S-1 Auditor's Report for CVS Caremark Corporation

Report of Independent Registered Public Accounting Firm
The Board of Directors and Shareholders

CVS Caremark Corporation

1. We have audited the accompanying consolidated balance sheets of CVS Caremark Corporation as of December 31, 2008 and December 29, 2007, and the related consolidated statements of operations, shareholders' equity and cash flows for the fiscal years ended December 31, 2008 and December 29, 2007. These financial statements are the responsibility of the Company's management. Our responsibility is to express an opinion on these financial statements based on our audits.
2. We conducted our audits in accordance with the standards of the Public Company Accounting Oversight Board (United States). Those standards require that we plan and perform the audit to obtain reasonable assurance about whether the financial statements are free of material misstatement. An audit includes examining, on a test basis, evidence supporting the amounts and disclosures in the financial statements. An audit also includes assessing the accounting principles used and significant estimates made by management, as well as evaluating the overall financial statement presentation. We believe that our audits provide a reasonable basis for our opinion.
3. In our opinion, the financial statements referred to above present fairly, in all material respects, the consolidated financial position of CVS Caremark Corporation at December 31, 2008 and December 29, 2007, and the consolidated results of its operations and its cash flows for the fiscal years ended December 31, 2008 and December 29, 2007, in conformity with U.S. generally accepted accounting principles.
4. As discussed in Note 1 to the consolidated financial statements, effective December 31, 2006, CVS Caremark Corporation adopted Financial Accounting Standards Board (FASB) Interpretation No. 48, *Accounting for Uncertainty in Income Taxes—an interpretation of FASB Statement No. 109* and effective December 30, 2007, CVS Caremark Corporation adopted Emerging Issues Task Force (EITF) No. 06-4, *Accounting for Deferred Compensation and Postretirement Benefit Aspects of Endorsement Split-Dollar Life Insurance Arrangements* and EITF No. 06-10, *Accounting for Collateral Assignment Split-Dollar Life Insurance Arrangements.*
5. We also have audited, in accordance with the standards of the Public Company Accounting Oversight Board (United States), CVS Caremark Corporation's internal control over financial reporting as of December 31, 2008, based on criteria established in *Internal Control—Integrated Framework* issued by the Committee of Sponsoring Organizations of the Treadway Commission and our report dated February 26, 2009 expressed an unqualified opinion thereon.

Ernst and Young LLP
Boston, Massachusetts
February 26, 2009

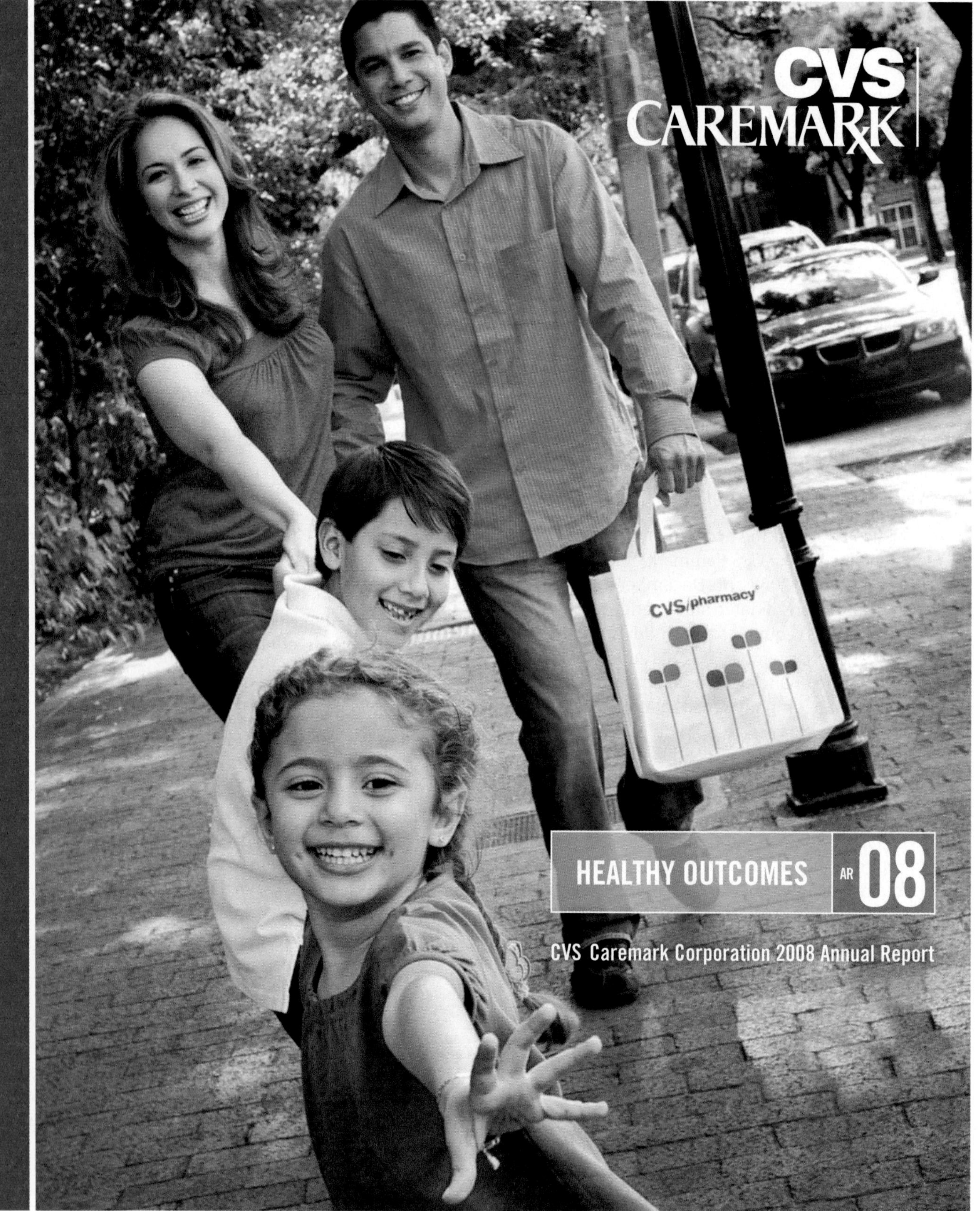
CVS
CAREMARK
CVS/pharmacy
HEALTHY OUTCOMES
AR 08
CVS Caremark Corporation 2008 Annual Report

Tom Ryan | Chairman of the Board, President & CEO

Dear Shareholder:

CVS Caremark Corporation posted strong results over the past year, and we moved swiftly to capitalize on the competitive advantage created through the landmark 2007 merger of CVS and Caremark.

Today, we are the nation's largest pharmacy health care company. With U.S. health care costs expected to reach more than $4 trillion annually over the next decade, we are beginning to deliver healthy outcomes for patients and driving down costs in ways that no other company in our industry can.

Here are just a few of the year's many accomplishments:

- CVS Caremark generated record revenue and earnings, achieved industry-leading same-store sales growth, and continued to gain share across our businesses.
- We introduced our Proactive Pharmacy Care offerings, which are designed to make pharmacy care more accessible and lower overall health care costs for patients and payors.
- Our PBM added more than 90 new clients during our latest selling season, which will generate approximately $7 billion in revenue for us in 2009.
- We completed the acquisition of Longs Drug Stores and its PBM, RxAmerica®, in October 2008 and also opened 317 new or relocated CVS/pharmacy stores.

Although we are not immune to the recession, we continued to enjoy strong growth in 2008. Total revenues rose 14.6 percent to $87.5 billion. Driven in part by record operating margins, net earnings increased 21.8 percent. A number of factors fueled our margin gains, with continued growth in generic drugs leading the way.

Along with our strong free cash flow generation, I'm happy to report that we faced virtually none of the liquidity issues that sent shockwaves across so much of the business landscape

"CVS Caremark is adding clients across the PBM spectrum – from large- and small-cap companies to government entities and private insurers. We're achieving this by offering payors and patients everything they have come to expect from a top-rated PBM; however, we're also offering plan design options and services that no standalone PBM can match."

in 2008. CVS Caremark has a solid balance sheet and an investment grade credit rating, and we maintain a commercial paper program currently backed by $4 billion in committed bank facilities.

As noted, the U.S. economy is definitely in a recession and it will likely last throughout 2009. We'll feel its effect to some degree, with growth in script utilization slowing industry-wide. Lower utilization, layoffs, and job loss will affect our PBM business; however, in a landscape where control of health care spending is urgently needed, our proven cost-reducing services and the cost-effective care offered through MinuteClinic should prove more valuable than ever.

Our share price certainly wasn't immune to the turmoil in the financial markets during the past year, but we still outperformed the broad market averages. Our shares fell 27.7 percent in 2008, compared with the 38.5 percent decline of the S&P 500 Index and the 33.8 percent drop in the Dow Jones Industrial Average (DJIA). Over the past five years, on average CVS Caremark shares returned 10.4 percent annually. The S&P 500 and DJIA had negative returns of 2.2 percent and 1.1 percent, respectively, over the same period.

Our Proactive Pharmacy Care Offerings Are Gaining Traction with PBM Clients

Looking at our PBM business, we're very pleased with the broad-based enthusiasm among customers for the groundbreaking new products and services we have brought to market. This was reflected in the number of sizable new contracts we won in the latest selling season.

CVS Caremark is adding clients across the PBM spectrum – from large- and small-cap companies to government entities and private insurers. We're achieving this by offering payors and patients everything they have come to expect from a top-rated PBM; however, we're also offering plan design options and services that no standalone PBM can match. Through the Proactive Pharmacy Care offerings we began rolling out in 2008, we're giving consumers easier access to their medications and to the counseling they need, whether it is through one of our mail pharmacies or at one of our more than 6,900 stores. By helping patients adhere to their drug therapies, we're lowering overall health care costs and improving outcomes.

You can read about specific Proactive Pharmacy Care offerings, such as Maintenance Choice and integrated specialty, elsewhere in this report. Let me note, though, how pleased we are that over 200 clients have already committed to offering Maintenance Choice to their more than 2 million covered lives.

Specialty pharmacy and our Medicare Part D Prescription Drug Plan (PDP) business are also part of our PBM segment. The past year marked our 30th anniversary in specialty pharmacy, our industry's fastest-growing sector. In fact, specialty pharmacy accounts for approximately 20 percent of the money spent on prescription drugs in the United States even though these medications are used by only a small fraction of the population. Payors need help managing these costs and CVS Caremark is the clear category leader. Based on prescriptions we fill or manage, we have a 27 percent share of the $38 billion specialty market addressable by PBMs and drug retailers. Still, we currently provide specialty services to only 60 percent of our PBM customers. The ability to cross sell to the remaining 40 percent represents an important opportunity for growth.

Medicare Part D continues to play a key role in ensuring that seniors can afford the prescriptions they need. We're a major factor in this arena through our SilverScript® and RxAmerica proprietary PDP plan offerings and as a provider of PBM services to these plans and to PDPs sponsored by others. Through our PDPs and related PBM activities, we expect to cover approximately 1.5 million lives in 2009.

PBM NET REVENUES*

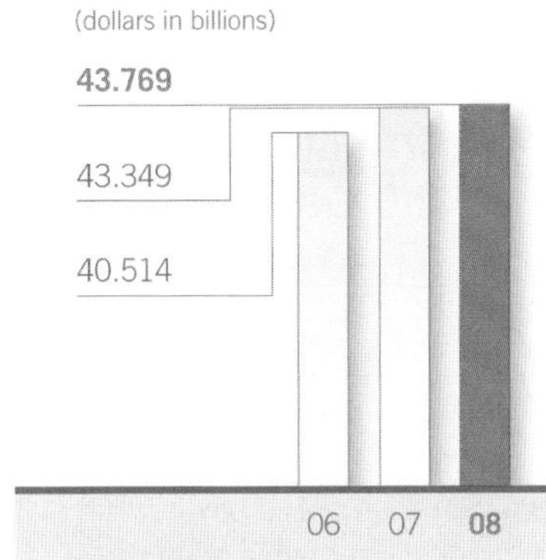

*Comparable data

STORE COUNT AT YEAR END

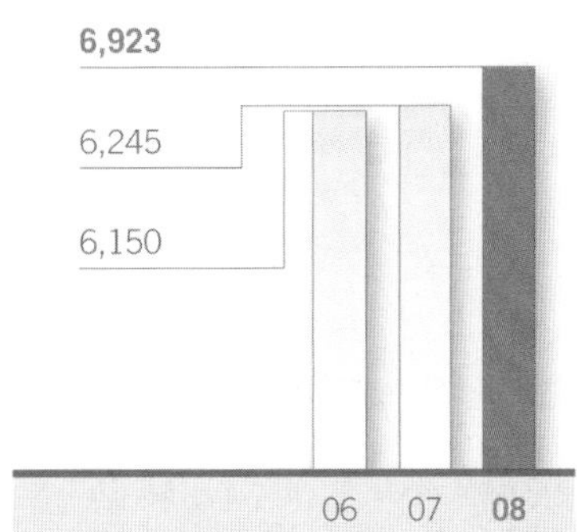

SAME-STORE SALES INCREASE

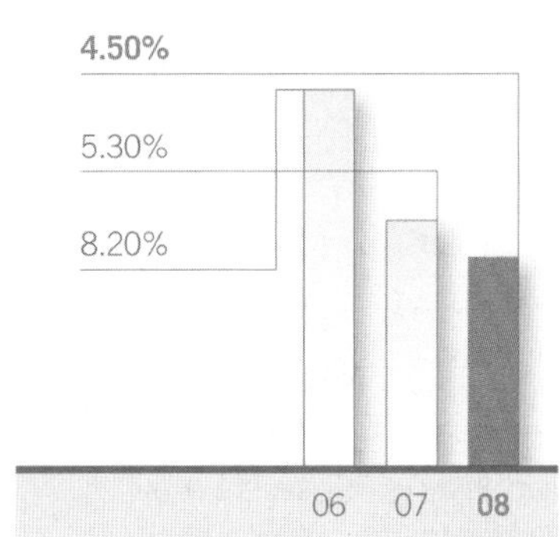

We're Moving Quickly to Integrate Longs Drug Stores and Improve Their Performance

In our retail business, I'm delighted to welcome over 20,000 Longs' colleagues to our company. The Longs acquisition has given us a high-quality network of more than 500 drugstores – primarily in Central and Northern California and Hawaii – as well as Longs' RxAmerica PBM. Commercial real estate values in California and Hawaii are among the highest in the country, and it would have taken at least a decade to assemble the prime locations we acquired had we instead opted exclusively for organic growth in these markets. We had only a modest presence in Central and Northern California and none in Hawaii. By acquiring Longs, we have become the leader in both markets virtually overnight. In fact, we now have over 800 stores in California, more than any other drugstore chain.

We've also begun to integrate RxAmerica – and its 8 million plan participants – with our PBM business. More importantly, our greater presence on the West Coast and in Hawaii plays an important strategic role for our PBM as it pursues new contracts. We can extend our Proactive Pharmacy Care offerings to plan sponsors with active or retired employees living in these markets.

I've often said that we don't acquire stores for growth. Rather, we acquire stores that we can grow. The Longs deal is no exception. Our existing stores outperform the Longs locations significantly in sales per square foot, gross margins, and other important measures. We intend to leverage our systems, our focus on private label and exclusive brands, our category mix, and the ExtraCare loyalty card to turn good stores into great ones. We recognize that the recession is impacting the California economy, and it may take us a while to accomplish this. When the economy rebounds, though, we will have outstanding, well-run assets in place.

We've had a lot of experience in making the most of the opportunities inherent in our acquisitions. Just take a look at the stores we acquired from JCPenney in 2004 and from Albertsons in 2006. We've been able to increase their sales per square foot considerably and have realized healthy margin gains as well. Moreover, we still see significant opportunities to improve the profitability of both acquisitions.

We Led the Industry in Same-Store Sales Growth In Both the Pharmacy and Front of the Store

Even as we completed the Longs acquisition, we continued to execute our organic growth strategy at retail. Retail square footage increased by 3.6 percent, in line with our annual target. We opened a total of 317 new or relocated stores. Factoring in closings, organic net unit growth increased by 150 stores.

Our CVS/pharmacy-Retail business had an outstanding year, with same-store sales rising an industry-leading 4.5 percent. Pharmacy same-store sales increased by 4.8 percent, even with the adoption of new generics. We're gratified by early consumer response to the Health Savings Pass for prescription drugs we introduced in November for the uninsured and underinsured. Given the current state of the economy, this is one of the ways in which we can help make health care more affordable for the general public. We are also in the process of rolling out our new pharmacy system, RxConnect™, which will reengineer the way pharmacists communicate and fill prescriptions.

"With strong execution across our businesses, we have good reason to feel optimistic about the future. We expect a number of long-term industry trends to work in our favor as well, including rising use of generic drugs and the aging of the U.S. population."

Same-store sales in the front of the store increased by 3.6 percent, and we gained share in 85 percent of our front-store categories. Since non-discretionary items account for the majority of front-end sales, that part of our business should prove relatively recession-resistant. And given the state of the economy, customers have been more willing to try our private-label and proprietary products. Sales of private-label and CVS-exclusive brands rose faster than in prior years to more than 16 percent of our front-end total at year-end. Much like generics in the pharmacy, these offerings also yield greater margins.

MinuteClinic's Expanded Offerings Bolster Our Health Care Strategy

As part of our broader health care strategy, we've continued to open MinuteClinic locations and expand their range of services. They now include wellness and prevention screenings, and a larger selection of vaccinations. We also launched pilot programs to incorporate MinuteClinic into our PBM offerings. For example, some of our PBM plan participants can now stop in for health assessments at convenient locations.

We've noted since MinuteClinic's acquisition that its competitive price can help us lower costs for health plans and self-insured employers. They have begun to embrace this model, and we've been able to contract with more payors as a result. In fact, visits paid for by third parties amounted to more than 70 percent of our total in 2008.

Our expanded health care focus can also be seen in the appointment of Troyen Brennan, M.D., in November 2008 to the newly created role of chief medical officer. Dr. Brennan, a practicing physician, former hospital administrator and, most recently, chief medical officer at Aetna, has assumed responsibility for MinuteClinic, Accordant Health Care, clinical and medical affairs, and our health care strategy.

Broad Industry Trends Will Contribute to Our Long-Term Performance

With strong execution across our businesses, we have good reason to feel optimistic about the future. We expect a number of long-term industry trends to work in our favor as well, including rising use of generic drugs and the aging of the U.S. population. Well over 60 percent of all drugs dispensed in 2008 across our industry were generics. That figure is likely to rise to 75 percent by 2012 as several blockbuster drugs lose patent protection.

Looking at the U.S. population, approximately 38 million people are 65 or older today. That number is projected to climb to 47 million by 2015, and prescription drug use is expected to rise substantially within this demographic. With leading market positions in California, Florida, and other sun-belt states, we stand to benefit from this trend to a greater extent than most other pharmacy players.

Other changes are likely to unfold in the coming years that should benefit CVS Caremark, patients, and payors alike. Among them, the Obama administration has already begun exploring ways in which health insurance can be broadened to cover a larger portion of the population. The resulting increase in access to prescription drugs would be good for CVS Caremark and good for the country. Legislation paving the way for a biogeneric approval process as well as growth in e-prescribing is also on the horizon. We look forward to working with the new administration on health care reform.

On behalf of the board of directors and CVS Caremark's 215,000 colleagues across the country, thank you for your confidence in our company and our vision. We are just beginning to realize the benefits of our broader pharmacy health care mission.

T. M. Ryan.

Thomas M. Ryan
Chairman of the Board,
President & CEO

Consolidated Statements of Operations

	Fiscal Year Ended		
In millions, except per share amounts	**Dec. 31, 2008**	Dec. 29, 2007	Dec. 30, 2006
Net revenues	**$ 87,471.9**	$ 76,329.5	$ 43,821.4
Cost of revenues	**69,181.5**	60,221.8	32,079.2
Gross profit	**18,290.4**	16,107.7	11,742.2
Total operating expenses	**12,244.2**	11,314.4	9,300.6
Operating profit	**6,046.2**	4,793.3	2,441.6
Interest expense, net	**509.5**	434.6	215.8
Earnings before income tax provision	**5,536.7**	4,358.7	2,225.8
Income tax provision	**2,192.6**	1,721.7	856.9
Earnings from continuing operations	**3,344.1**	2,637.0	1,368.9
Loss from discontinued operations, net of income tax benefit of $82.4	**(132.0)**	–	–
Net earnings	**3,212.1**	2,637.0	1,368.9
Preference dividends, net of income tax benefit	**14.1**	14.2	13.9
Net earnings available to common shareholders	**$ 3,198.0**	$ 2,622.8	$ 1,355.0
BASIC EARNINGS PER COMMON SHARE:			
Earnings from continuing operations	**$ 2.32**	$ 1.97	$ 1.65
Loss from discontinued operations	**(0.09)**	–	–
Net earnings	**$ 2.23**	$ 1.97	$ 1.65
Weighted average common shares outstanding	**1,433.5**	1,328.2	820.6
DILUTED EARNINGS PER COMMON SHARE:			
Earnings from continuing operations	**$ 2.27**	$ 1.92	$ 1.60
Loss from discontinued operations	**(0.09)**	–	–
Net earnings	**$ 2.18**	$ 1.92	$ 1.60
Weighted average common shares outstanding	**1,469.1**	1,371.8	853.2
Dividends declared per common share	**$ 0.25800**	$ 0.22875	$ 0.15500

See accompanying notes to consolidated financial statements.

Consolidated Balance Sheets

In millions, except shares and per share amounts	Dec. 31, 2008	Dec. 29, 2007
ASSETS:		
Cash and cash equivalents	$ 1,352.4	$ 1,056.6
Short-term investments	–	27.5
Accounts receivable, net	5,384.3	4,579.6
Inventories	9,152.6	8,008.2
Deferred income taxes	435.2	329.4
Other current assets	201.7	148.1
Total current assets	16,526.2	14,149.4
Property and equipment, net	8,125.2	5,852.8
Goodwill	25,493.9	23,922.3
Intangible assets, net	10,446.2	10,429.6
Other assets	368.4	367.8
Total assets	$ 60,959.9	$ 54,721.9
LIABILITIES:		
Accounts payable	$ 3,800.7	$ 3,593.0
Claims and discounts payable	2,814.2	2,484.3
Accrued expenses	3,177.6	2,556.8
Short-term debt	3,044.1	2,085.0
Current portion of long-term debt	653.3	47.2
Total current liabilities	13,489.9	10,766.3
Long-term debt	8,057.2	8,349.7
Deferred income taxes	3,701.7	3,426.1
Other long-term liabilities	1,136.7	857.9
Commitments and contingencies (Note 12)	–	–
SHAREHOLDERS' EQUITY:		
Preferred stock, $0.01 par value: authorized 120,619 shares; no shares issued or outstanding	–	–
Preference stock, series one ESOP convertible, par value $1.00: authorized 50,000,000 shares; issued and outstanding 3,583,000 shares at December 31, 2008 and 3,798,000 shares at December 29, 2007	191.5	203.0
Common stock, par value $0.01: authorized 3,200,000,000 shares; issued 1,603,267,000 shares at December 31, 2008 and 1,590,139,000 shares at December 29, 2007	16.0	15.9
Treasury stock, at cost: 164,502,000 shares at December 31, 2008 and 153,682,000 shares at December 29, 2007	(5,812.3)	(5,620.4)
Shares held in trust, 1,700,000 shares at December 31, 2008 and 9,224,000 shares at December 29, 2007	(55.5)	(301.3)
Guaranteed ESOP obligation	–	(44.5)
Capital surplus	27,279.6	26,831.9
Retained earnings	13,097.8	10,287.0
Accumulated other comprehensive loss	(142.7)	(49.7)
Total shareholders' equity	34,574.4	31,321.9
Total liabilities and shareholders' equity	$ 60,959.9	$ 54,721.9

See accompanying notes to consolidated financial statements.

Consolidated Statements of Cash Flows

	Fiscal Year Ended		
In millions	**Dec. 31, 2008**	Dec. 29, 2007	Dec. 30, 2006
CASH FLOWS FROM OPERATING ACTIVITIES:			
Cash receipts from revenues	**$ 69,493.7**	$ 61,986.3	$ 43,273.7
Cash paid for inventory	**(51,374.7)**	(45,772.6)	(31,422.1)
Cash paid to other suppliers and employees	**(11,832.0)**	(10,768.6)	(9,065.3)
Interest and dividends received	**20.3**	33.6	15.9
Interest paid	**(573.7)**	(468.2)	(228.1)
Income taxes paid	**(1,786.5)**	(1,780.8)	(831.7)
Net cash provided by operating activities	**3,947.1**	3,229.7	1,742.4
CASH FLOWS FROM INVESTING ACTIVITIES:			
Additions to property and equipment	**(2,179.9)**	(1,805.3)	(1,768.9)
Proceeds from sale-leaseback transactions	**203.8**	601.3	1,375.6
Acquisitions (net of cash acquired) and other investments	**(2,650.7)**	(1,983.3)	(4,224.2)
Cash outflow from hedging activities	**–**	–	(5.3)
Sale of short-term investments	**27.5**	–	–
Proceeds from sale or disposal of assets	**18.7**	105.6	29.6
Net cash used in investing activities	**(4,580.6)**	(3,081.7)	(4,593.2)
CASH FLOWS FROM FINANCING ACTIVITIES:			
Net additions to short-term debt	**959.0**	242.3	1,589.3
Repayment of debt assumed in acquisition	**(352.8)**	–	–
Additions to long-term debt	**350.0**	6,000.0	1,500.0
Reductions in long-term debt	**(1.8)**	(821.8)	(310.5)
Dividends paid	**(383.0)**	(322.4)	(140.9)
Proceeds from exercise of stock options	**327.8**	552.4	187.6
Excess tax benefits from stock-based compensation	**53.1**	97.8	42.6
Repurchase of common stock	**(23.0)**	(5,370.4)	–
Net cash provided by financing activities	**929.3**	377.9	2,868.1
Net increase in cash and cash equivalents	**295.8**	525.9	17.3
Cash and cash equivalents at beginning of year	**1,056.6**	530.7	513.4
Cash and cash equivalents at end of year	**$ 1,352.4**	$ 1,056.6	$ 530.7
RECONCILIATION OF NET EARNINGS TO NET CASH PROVIDED BY OPERATING ACTIVITIES:			
Net earnings	**$ 3,212.1**	$ 2,637.0	$ 1,368.9
Adjustments required to reconcile net earnings to net cash provided by operating activities:			
Depreciation and amortization	**1,274.2**	1,094.6	733.3
Stock-based compensation	**92.5**	78.0	69.9
Deferred income taxes and other non-cash items	**(3.4)**	40.1	98.2
Change in operating assets and liabilities providing/(requiring) cash, net of effects from acquisitions:			
Accounts receivable, net	**(291.0)**	279.7	(540.1)
Inventories	**(488.1)**	(448.0)	(624.1)
Other current assets	**12.5**	(59.2)	(21.4)
Other assets	**19.1**	(26.4)	(17.2)
Accounts payable	**(63.9)**	(181.4)	396.7
Accrued expenses	**182.5**	(168.2)	328.9
Other long-term liabilities	**0.6**	(16.5)	(50.7)
Net cash provided by operating activities	**$ 3,947.1**	$ 3,229.7	$ 1,742.4

See accompanying notes to consolidated financial statements.

Consolidated Statements of Shareholders' Equity

	Shares			Dollars		
In millions	**Dec. 31, 2008**	Dec. 29, 2007	Dec. 30, 2006	**Dec. 31, 2008**	Dec. 29, 2007	Dec. 30, 2006
PREFERENCE STOCK:						
Beginning of year	**3.8**	4.0	4.2	**$ 203.0**	$ 213.3	$ 222.6
Conversion to common stock	**(0.2)**	(0.2)	(0.2)	**(11.5)**	(10.3)	(9.3)
End of year	**3.6**	3.8	4.0	**191.5**	203.0	213.3
COMMON STOCK:						
Beginning of year	**1,590.1**	847.3	838.8	**15.9**	8.5	8.4
Common stock issued for Caremark Merger	**–**	712.7	–	**–**	7.1	–
Stock options exercised and awards	**13.2**	30.1	8.5	**0.1**	0.3	0.1
End of year	**1,603.3**	1,590.1	847.3	**16.0**	15.9	8.5
TREASURY STOCK:						
Beginning of year	**(153.7)**	(21.5)	(24.5)	**(5,620.4)**	(314.5)	(356.5)
Purchase of treasury shares	**(6.5)**	(135.0)	0.1	**(33.0)**	(5,378.7)	(0.1)
Conversion of preference stock	**1.0**	0.9	0.8	**35.2**	24.7	11.7
Transfer from Trust	**(7.5)**	–	–	**(272.3)**	–	–
Employee stock purchase plan issuance	**2.2**	1.9	2.1	**78.2**	48.1	30.4
End of year	**(164.5)**	(153.7)	(21.5)	**(5,812.3)**	(5,620.4)	(314.5)
GUARANTEED ESOP OBLIGATION:						
Beginning of year				**(44.5)**	(82.1)	(114.0)
Reduction of guaranteed ESOP obligation				**44.5**	37.6	31.9
End of year				**–**	(44.5)	(82.1)
SHARES HELD IN TRUST:						
Beginning of year	**(9.2)**	–	–	**(301.3)**	–	–
Transfer to treasury stock	**7.5**	–	–	**245.8**	–	–
Shares acquired through Caremark Merger	**–**	(9.2)	–	**–**	(301.3)	–
End of year	**(1.7)**	(9.2)		**(55.5)**	(301.3)	–
CAPITAL SURPLUS:						
Beginning of year				**26,831.9**	2,198.4	1,922.4
Common stock issued for Caremark Merger, net of issuance costs				**–**	23,942.4	–
Conversion of shares held in Trust to treasury stock				**26.5**	–	–
Stock option activity and awards				**391.8**	607.7	235.8
Tax benefit on stock options and awards				**53.1**	97.8	42.6
Conversion of preference stock				**(23.7)**	(14.4)	(2.4)
End of year				**27,279.6**	26,831.9	2,198.4

Consolidated Statements of Shareholders' Equity

	Shares			Dollars		
In millions	**Dec. 31, 2008**	Dec. 29, 2007	Dec. 30, 2006	**Dec. 31, 2008**	Dec. 29, 2007	Dec. 30, 2006
ACCUMULATED OTHER COMPREHENSIVE LOSS:						
Beginning of year				**(49.7)**	(72.6)	(90.3)
Recognition of unrealized gain/(loss) on derivatives, net of income tax				**3.4**	3.4	(0.3)
Pension liability adjustment, net of income tax				**(96.4)**	19.5	23.6
Pension liability adjustment to initially apply SFAS No.158, net of income tax				**–**	–	(5.6)
End of year				**(142.7)**	(49.7)	(72.6)
RETAINED EARNINGS:						
Beginning of year				**10,287.0**	7,966.6	6,738.6
Net earnings				**3,212.1**	2,637.0	1,368.9
Common stock dividends				**(369.7)**	(308.8)	(127.0)
Preference stock dividends				**(14.0)**	(14.8)	(15.6)
Tax benefit on preference stock dividends				**0.6**	1.2	1.7
Adoption of EITF 06-04 and EITF 06-10				**(18.2)**	–	–
Adoption of FIN 48				**–**	5.8	–
End of year				**13,097.8**	10,287.0	7,966.6
Total shareholders' equity				**$ 34,574.4**	$ 31,321.9	$ 9,917.6
COMPREHENSIVE INCOME:						
Net earnings				**$ 3,212.1**	$ 2,637.0	$ 1,368.9
Recognition of unrealized gain/(loss) on derivatives, net of income tax				**3.4**	3.4	(0.3)
Pension liability, net of income tax				**(96.4)**	19.5	23.6
Comprehensive income				**$ 3,119.1**	$ 2,659.9	$ 1,392.2

See accompanying notes to consolidated financial statements.

Notes to Consolidated Financial Statements

NO 1 SIGNIFICANT ACCOUNTING POLICIES

Description of business. CVS Caremark Corporation (the "Company") operates one of the largest pharmacy services businesses and the largest retail pharmacy business (based on revenues and store count) in the United States.

Pharmacy Services Segment (the "PSS"). The PSS provides a full range of prescription benefit management services including mail order pharmacy services, specialty pharmacy services, plan design and administration, formulary management and claims processing. The Company's customers are primarily employers, insurance companies, unions, government employee groups, managed care organizations and other sponsors of health benefit plans and individuals throughout the United States.

As a pharmacy benefits manager, the PSS manages the dispensing of pharmaceuticals through our mail order pharmacies and national network of approximately 60,000 retail pharmacies (which include our CVS/pharmacy® and Longs Drug® stores) to eligible participants in the benefits plans maintained by our customers and utilizes its information systems to perform, among other things, safety checks, drug interaction screenings and brand to generic substitutions.

The PSS's specialty pharmacies support individuals that require complex and expensive drug therapies. The specialty pharmacy business includes mail order and retail specialty pharmacies that operate under the Caremark® and CarePlus CVS/pharmacy™ names.

The PSS also provides health management programs, which include integrated disease management for 27 conditions, through our Accordant® health management offering.

In addition, through our SilverScript Insurance Company ("SilverScript") and Accendo Insurance Company ("Accendo") subsidiaries, the PSS is a national provider of drug benefits to eligible beneficiaries under the Federal Government's Medicare Part D program. The PSS acquired Accendo in the Longs Acquisition (see Note 2 later in this document), and, effective January 1, 2009, Accendo replaced RxAmerica® as the Medicare-approved prescription drug plan for the RxAmerica Medicare Part D drug benefit plans.

Our pharmacy services business generates net revenues primarily by contracting with clients to provide prescription drugs to plan participants. Prescription drugs are dispensed by our mail order pharmacies, specialty pharmacies and national network of retail pharmacies. Net revenues are also generated by providing additional services to clients, including administrative services such as claims processing and formulary management, as well as health care related services such as disease management.

The pharmacy services business operates under the Caremark Pharmacy Services®, Caremark®, CVS Caremark™, CarePlus CVS/pharmacy™, CarePlus™, RxAmerica®, Accordant Care™ and TheraCom® names. As of December 31, 2008, the Pharmacy Services Segment operated 58 retail specialty pharmacy stores, 19 specialty mail order pharmacies and 7 mail service pharmacies located in 26 states, Puerto Rico and the District of Columbia.

Retail Pharmacy Segment (the "RPS"). The RPS sells prescription drugs and a wide assortment of general merchandise, including over-the-counter drugs, beauty products and cosmetics, photo finishing, seasonal merchandise, greeting cards and convenience foods through our CVS/pharmacy and Longs Drug retail stores and online through CVS.com®.

The RPS also provides health care services through its MinuteClinic health care clinics. These health care clinics utilize nationally recognized medical protocols to diagnose and treat minor health conditions and are staffed by nurse practitioners and physician assistants.

As of December 31, 2008, our retail pharmacy business included 6,923 retail drugstores (of which 6,857 operated a pharmacy) located in 41 states and the District of Columbia operating primarily under the CVS/pharmacy® or Longs Drug® names, our online retail website, CVS.com® and 560 retail health care clinics operating under the MinuteClinic® name (of which 534 were located in CVS/pharmacy stores).

Basis of presentation. The consolidated financial statements include the accounts of the Company and its wholly-owned subsidiaries. All material intercompany balances and transactions have been eliminated.

Fiscal year change. On December 23, 2008, the Board of Directors of the Company approved a change in the Company's fiscal year end from the Saturday nearest December 31 of each year to December 31 of each year to better reflect the Company's position in the health care, rather than the retail industry. The fiscal year change was effective beginning with the fourth quarter of fiscal 2008. Prior to Board approval of this change, the Saturday nearest December 31, 2008 would have resulted in a 53-week fiscal year that would have ended January 3, 2009.

Following is a summary of the impact of the fiscal year change:

Fiscal Year	Fiscal Year-End	Fiscal Period	Fiscal Period Includes
2008	December 31, 2008	December 30, 2007 – December 31, 2008	368 days
2007	December 29, 2007	December 31, 2006 – December 29, 2007	364 days
2006	December 30, 2006	January 1, 2006 – December 30, 2006	364 days

Unless otherwise noted, all references to years relate to the above fiscal years.

Reclassifications. Certain reclassifications have been made to the consolidated financial statements of prior years to conform to the current year presentation.

Use of estimates. The preparation of financial statements in conformity with generally accepted accounting principles requires management to make estimates and assumptions that affect the reported amounts in the consolidated financial statements and accompanying notes. Actual results could differ from those estimates.

Cash and cash equivalents. Cash and cash equivalents consist of cash and temporary investments with maturities of three months or less when purchased.

Short-term investments. The Company's short-term investments consisted of auction rate securities with initial maturities of greater than three months when purchased. These investments, which were classified as available-for-sale, were carried at historical cost, which approximated fair value at December 29, 2007. The Company had no short-term investments at December 31, 2008.

Accounts receivable. Accounts receivable are stated net of an allowance for uncollectible accounts of $188.8 million and $107.8 million as of December 31, 2008 and December 29, 2007, respectively. The balance primarily includes amounts due from third party providers (e.g., pharmacy benefit managers, insurance companies and governmental agencies) and vendors as well as clients, participants and manufacturers.

Fair value of financial instruments. As of December 31, 2008, the Company's financial instruments include cash and cash equivalents, accounts receivable, accounts payable and short-term debt. Due to the short-term nature of these instruments, the Company's carrying value approximates fair value. The carrying amount and estimated fair value of long-term debt was $7.9 billion and $6.9 billion, respectively as of December 31, 2008. The carrying amount and estimated fair value of long-term debt was $8.2 billion as of December 29, 2007. The fair value of long-term debt was estimated based on rates currently offered to the Company for debt with similar terms and maturities. The Company had outstanding letters of credit, which guaranteed foreign trade purchases, with a fair value of $7.0 million as of December 31, 2008 and $5.7 million as of December 29, 2007. There were no outstanding investments in derivative financial instruments as of December 31, 2008 or December 29, 2007.

Inventories. Inventories are stated at the lower of cost or market on a first-in, first-out basis using the retail method of accounting to determine cost of sales and inventory in our CVS/pharmacy stores, average cost to determine cost of sales and inventory in our mail service and specialty pharmacies and the cost method of accounting to determine inventory in the Longs Drug Stores and our distribution centers. The Longs Drug Stores will be conformed to the retail method of accounting when their accounting systems are converted in 2009. Physical inventory counts are taken on a regular basis in each store and a continuous cycle count process is the primary procedure used to validate the inventory balances on hand in each distribution center to ensure that the amounts reflected in the accompanying consolidated financial statements are properly stated. During the interim period between physical inventory counts, the Company accrues for anticipated physical inventory losses on a location-by-location basis based on historical results and current trends.

Property and equipment. Property, equipment and improvements to leased premises are depreciated using the straight-line method over the estimated useful lives of the assets, or when applicable, the term of the lease, whichever is shorter. Estimated useful lives generally range from 10 to 40 years for buildings, building improvements and leasehold improvements and 3 to 10 years for fixtures and equipment. Repair and maintenance costs are charged directly to expense as incurred. Major renewals or replacements that substantially extend the useful life of an asset are capitalized and depreciated.

Following are the components of property and equipment:

In millions	**Dec. 31, 2008**	Dec. 29, 2007
Land	**$ 1,304.1**	$ 586.4
Building and improvements	**1,343.1**	896.0
Fixtures and equipment	**6,216.1**	4,947.4
Leasehold improvements	**2,581.3**	2,133.2
Capitalized software	**665.6**	474.6
Capital leases	**181.7**	181.7
	12,291.9	9,219.3
Accumulated depreciation and amortization	**(4,166.7)**	(3,366.5)
	$ 8,125.2	$ 5,852.8

Notes to Consolidated Financial Statements

The Company capitalizes application development stage costs for significant internally developed software projects. These costs are amortized over the estimated useful lives of the software, which generally range from 3 to 5 years. Unamortized costs were $70.0 million as of December 31, 2008 and $74.2 million as of December 29, 2007.

Goodwill. The Company accounts for goodwill and intangibles under Statement of Financial Accounting Standards ("SFAS") No. 142, "Goodwill and Other Intangible Assets." As such, goodwill and other indefinite-lived assets are not amortized, but are subject to impairment reviews annually, or more frequently if necessary. See Note 3 for additional information about goodwill.

Intangible assets. Purchased customer contracts and relationships are amortized on a straight-line basis over their estimated useful lives of up to 20 years. Purchased customer lists are amortized on a straight-line basis over their estimated useful lives of up to 10 years. Purchased leases are amortized on a straight-line basis over the remaining life of the lease. See Note 3 for additional information about intangible assets.

Impairment of long-lived assets. The Company accounts for the impairment of long-lived assets in accordance with SFAS No. 144, "Accounting for Impairment or Disposal of Long-Lived Assets." As such, the Company groups and evaluates fixed and finite-lived intangible assets excluding goodwill, for impairment at the lowest level at which individual cash flows can be identified. When evaluating assets for potential impairment, the Company first compares the carrying amount of the asset group to the individual store's estimated future cash flows (undiscounted and without interest charges). If the estimated future cash flows used in this analysis are less than the carrying amount of the asset group, an impairment loss calculation is prepared. The impairment loss calculation compares the carrying amount of the asset group to the asset group's estimated future cash flows (discounted and with interest charges). If required, an impairment loss is recorded for the portion of the asset group's carrying value that exceeds the asset group's estimated future cash flows (discounted and with interest charges).

Revenue Recognition:

Pharmacy Services Segment. The PSS sells prescription drugs directly through its mail service pharmacies and indirectly through its national retail pharmacy network. The PSS recognizes revenues from prescription drugs sold by its mail service pharmacies and under national retail pharmacy network contracts where the PSS is the principal using the gross method at the contract prices negotiated with its customers. Net revenue from the PSS includes: (i) the portion of the price the customer pays directly to the PSS, net of any volume-related or other discounts paid back to the customer (see "Drug Discounts" later in this document), (ii) the portion of the price paid to the PSS ("Mail Co-Payments") or a third party pharmacy in the PSS' national retail pharmacy network ("Retail Co-Payments") by individuals included in its customers' benefit plans and (iii) administrative fees for national retail pharmacy network contracts where the PSS is not the principal as discussed later in this document.

SEC Staff Accounting Bulletin 104, "Revenue Recognition, corrected copy" ("SAB 104") provides the general criteria for the timing aspect of revenue recognition, including consideration of whether: (i) persuasive evidence of an arrangement exists, (ii) delivery has occurred or services have been rendered, (iii) the seller's price to the buyer is fixed or determinable and (iv) collectability is reasonably assured. The Company has established the following revenue recognition policies for the PSS in accordance with SAB 104:

- Revenues generated from prescription drugs sold by mail service pharmacies are recognized when the prescription is shipped. At the time of shipment, the Company has performed substantially all of its obligations under its customer contracts and does not experience a significant level of reshipments.
- Revenues generated from prescription drugs sold by third party pharmacies in the PSS' national retail pharmacy network and associated administrative fees are recognized at the PSS' point-of-sale, which is when the claim is adjudicated by the PSS' online claims processing system.

The PSS determines whether it is the principal or agent for its national retail pharmacy network transactions using the indicators set forth in Emerging Issues Task Force ("EITF") Issue No. 99-19, "Reporting Revenue Gross as a Principal versus Net as an Agent" on a contract by contract basis. In the majority of its contracts, the PSS has determined it is the principal due to it: (i) being the primary obligor in the arrangement, (ii) having latitude in establishing the price, changing the product or performing part of the service, (iii) having discretion in supplier selection, (iv) having involvement in the determination of product or service specifications and (v) having credit risk. The PSS' obligations under its customer contracts for which revenues are reported using the gross method are separate and distinct from its obligations to the third party pharmacies included in its national retail pharmacy network contracts. Pursuant to these contracts, the PSS is contractually required to pay the third party pharmacies in its national retail pharmacy network for products sold, regardless of whether the PSS is paid by its customers. The PSS' responsibilities under its customer contracts typically include validating eligibility and coverage levels, communicating the prescription price and the co-payments due to the third party retail pharmacy, identifying possible adverse drug interactions for the pharmacist to address with the physician prior to dispensing, suggesting clinically appropriate generic alternatives where appropriate and approving the prescription for dispensing. Although the PSS does not have credit risk with respect to Retail Co-Payments, management believes that all of the other indicators of gross revenue reporting are present. For contracts under which the PSS acts as an agent, the PSS records revenues using the net method.

Drug Discounts. The PSS deducts from its revenues any discounts paid to its customers as required by EITF No. 01-9, "Accounting for Consideration Given by a Vendor to a Customer (Including a Reseller of the Vendor's Products)" ("EITF 01-9"). The PSS pays discounts to its customers in accordance with the terms of its customer contracts, which are normally based on a fixed discount per prescription for specific products dispensed or a percentage of manufacturer discounts received for specific products dispensed. The liability for discounts due to the PSS' customers is included in "Claims and discounts payable" in the accompanying consolidated balance sheets.

Medicare Part D. The PSS began participating in the Federal Government's Medicare Part D program as a Prescription Drug Plan ("PDP") on January 1, 2006. The PSS' net revenues include insurance premiums earned by the PDP, which are determined based on the PDP's annual bid and related contractual arrangements with the Centers for Medicare and Medicaid Services ("CMS"). The insurance premiums include a beneficiary premium, which is the responsibility of the PDP member, but is subsidized by CMS in the case of low-income members, and a direct premium paid by CMS. Premiums collected in advance are initially deferred in accrued expenses and are then recognized in net revenues over the period in which members are entitled to receive benefits.

In addition to these premiums, the PSS' net revenues include co-payments, deductibles and co-insurance (collectively, the "Member Co-Payments") related to PDP members' actual prescription claims in its net revenues. In certain cases, CMS subsidizes a portion of these Member Co-Payments and pays the PSS an estimated prospective Member Co-Payment subsidy amount each month. The prospective Member Co-Payment subsidy amounts received from CMS are also included in the PSS' net revenues. The Company assumes no risk for these amounts, which represented 1.3% and 0.8% of consolidated net revenues in 2008 and 2007, respectively. If the prospective Member Co-Payment subsidies received differ from the amounts based on actual prescription claims, the difference is recorded in either accounts receivable or accrued expenses.

The PSS accounts for CMS obligations and Member Co-Payments (including the amounts subsidized by CMS) using the gross method consistent with its revenue recognition policies for Mail Co-Payments and Retail Co-Payments (discussed previously in this document), which include the application of EITF 99-19. See Note 7 for additional information about Medicare Part D.

Retail Pharmacy Segment. The RPS recognizes revenue from the sale of merchandise (other than prescription drugs) at the time the merchandise is purchased by the retail customer. Revenue from the sale of prescription drugs is recognized at the time the prescription is filled, which is or approximates when the retail customer picks up the prescription. Customer returns are not material. Revenue generated from the performance of services in the RPS' health care clinics is recognized at the time the services are performed. See Note 13 for additional information about the revenues of the Company's business segments.

Cost of Revenues:

Pharmacy Services Segment. The PSS' cost of revenues includes: (i) the cost of prescription drugs sold during the reporting period directly through its mail service pharmacies and indirectly through its national retail pharmacy network, (ii) shipping and handling costs and (iii) the operating costs of its mail service pharmacies and customer service operations and related information technology support costs (including depreciation and amortization). The cost of prescription drugs sold component of cost of revenues includes: (i) the cost of the prescription drugs purchased from manufacturers or distributors and shipped to participants in customers' benefit plans from the PSS' mail service pharmacies, net of any volume-related or other discounts (see "Drug Discounts" previously in this document) and (ii) the cost of prescription drugs sold (including Retail Co-Payments) through the PSS' national retail pharmacy network under contracts where it is the principal, net of any volume-related or other discounts.

Retail Pharmacy Segment. The RPS' cost of revenues includes: the cost of merchandise sold during the reporting period and the related purchasing costs, warehousing and delivery costs (including depreciation and amortization) and actual and estimated inventory losses. See Note 13 for additional information about the cost of revenues of the Company's business segments.

Vendor Allowances and Purchase Discounts:

The Company accounts for vendor allowances and purchase discounts under the guidance provided by EITF Issue No. 02-16, "Accounting by a Customer (Including a Reseller) for Certain

Notes to Consolidated Financial Statements

Consideration Received from a Vendor," and EITF Issue No. 03-10, "Application of EITF Issue No. 02-16 by Resellers to Sales Incentives Offered to Consumers by Manufacturers."

Pharmacy Services Segment. The PSS receives purchase discounts on products purchased. The PSS' contractual arrangements with vendors, including manufacturers, wholesalers and retail pharmacies, normally provide for the PSS to receive purchase discounts from established list prices in one, or a combination of, the following forms: (i) a direct discount at the time of purchase, (ii) a discount for the prompt payment of invoices or (iii) when products are purchased indirectly from a manufacturer (e.g., through a wholesaler or retail pharmacy), a discount (or rebate) paid subsequent to dispensing. These rebates are recognized when prescriptions are dispensed and are generally calculated and billed to manufacturers within 30 days of the end of each completed quarter. Historically, the effect of adjustments resulting from the reconciliation of rebates recognized to the amounts billed and collected has not been material to the PSS' results of operations. The PSS accounts for the effect of any such differences as a change in accounting estimate in the period the reconciliation is completed. The PSS also receives additional discounts under its wholesaler contract if it exceeds contractually defined annual purchase volumes.

The PSS earns purchase discounts at various points in its business cycle (e.g., when the product is purchased, when the vendor is paid or when the product is dispensed) for products sold through its mail service pharmacies and third party pharmacies included in its national retail pharmacy network. In addition, the PSS receives fees from pharmaceutical manufacturers for administrative services. Purchase discounts and administrative service fees are recorded as a reduction of "Cost of revenues" as required by EITF 02-16.

Retail Pharmacy Segment. Vendor allowances received by the RPS reduce the carrying cost of inventory and are recognized in cost of revenues when the related inventory is sold, unless they are specifically identified as a reimbursement of incremental costs for promotional programs and/or other services provided. Funds that are directly linked to advertising commitments are recognized as a reduction of advertising expense (included in operating expenses) when the related advertising commitment is satisfied. Any such allowances received in excess of the actual cost incurred also reduce the carrying cost of inventory. The total value of any upfront payments received from vendors that are linked to purchase commitments is initially deferred. The deferred amounts are then amortized to reduce cost of revenues over the life of the contract based upon purchase volume. The total value of any upfront payments received from vendors that are not linked to purchase commitments is also initially deferred. The deferred amounts are then amortized to reduce cost of revenues on a straight-line basis over the life of the related contract. The total amortization of these upfront payments was not material to the accompanying consolidated financial statements.

Shares held in trust. As a result of the Caremark Merger (see Note 2 for additional information about the Caremark Merger), the Company maintains grantor trusts, which held approximately 1.7 million and 9.2 million shares of its common stock at December 31, 2008 and December 29, 2007, respectively. These shares are designated for use under various employee compensation plans. Since the Company holds these shares, they are excluded from the computation of basic and diluted shares outstanding.

Insurance. The Company is self-insured for certain losses related to general liability, workers' compensation and auto liability. The Company obtains third party insurance coverage to limit exposure from these claims. The Company is also self-insured for certain losses related to health and medical liabilities. The Company's self-insurance accruals, which include reported claims and claims incurred but not reported, are calculated using standard insurance industry actuarial assumptions and the Company's historical claims experience.

Store opening and closing costs. New store opening costs, other than capital expenditures, are charged directly to expense when incurred. When the Company closes a store, the present value of estimated unrecoverable costs, including the remaining lease obligation less estimated sublease income and the book value of abandoned property and equipment, are charged to expense. The long-term portion of the lease obligations associated with store closings was $398.6 million and $370.0 million in 2008 and 2007, respectively.

Advertising costs. Advertising costs are expensed when the related advertising takes place. Advertising costs, net of vendor funding, (included in operating expenses), were $323.8 million in 2008, $290.6 million in 2007 and $265.3 million in 2006.

Interest expense, net. Interest expense was $529.8 million, $468.3 million and $231.7 million, and interest income was $20.3 million, $33.7 million and $15.9 million in 2008, 2007 and 2006, respectively. Capitalized interest totaled $27.8 million in 2008, $23.7 million in 2007 and $20.7 million in 2006.

Accumulated other comprehensive loss. Accumulated other comprehensive loss consists of changes in the net actuarial gains and losses associated with pension and other post retirement benefit plans, unrealized losses on derivatives and an adjustment to initially apply SFAS No. 158. In accordance with SFAS No. 158, the amount included in accumulated other comprehensive income related to the Company's pension and post retirement plans was $216.9 million pre-tax ($132.3 million after-tax) as of December 31, 2008 and $58.7 million pre-tax ($35.9 million after-tax) as of December 29, 2007. The unrealized loss on derivatives totaled $16.6 million pre-tax ($10.5 million after-tax) and $21.9 million pre-tax ($13.8 million after-tax) as of December 31, 2008 and December 29, 2007, respectively.

Stock-based compensation. On January 1, 2006, the Company adopted SFAS No. 123(R), "Share-Based Payment," using the modified prospective transition method. Under this method, compensation expense is recognized for options granted on or after January 1, 2006 as well as any unvested options on the date of adoption. As allowed under the modified prospective transition method, prior period financial statements have not been restated. Prior to January 1, 2006, the Company accounted for its stock-based compensation plans under the recognition and measurement principles of Accounting Principles Board ("APB") Opinion No. 25, "Accounting for Stock Issued to Employees," and related interpretations. As such, no stock-based employee compensation costs were reflected in net earnings for options granted under those plans since they had an exercise price equal to the fair market value of the underlying common stock on the date of grant. See Note 10 for additional information about stock-based compensation.

Income taxes. The Company provides for federal and state income taxes currently payable, as well as for those deferred because of timing differences between reported income and expenses for financial statement purposes versus tax purposes. Federal and state tax credits are recorded as a reduction of income taxes. Deferred tax assets and liabilities are recognized for the future tax consequences attributable to differences between the carrying amount of assets and liabilities for financial reporting purposes and the amounts used for income tax purposes. Deferred tax assets and liabilities are measured using the enacted tax rates expected to apply to taxable income in the years in which those temporary differences are expected to be recoverable or settled. The effect of a change in tax rates is recognized as income or expense in the period of the change. See Note 11 for additional information about income taxes.

Loss from discontinued operations. In connection with certain business dispositions completed between 1991 and 1997, the Company continues to guarantee store lease obligations for a number of former subsidiaries, including Linens 'n Things. On May 2, 2008, Linens Holding Co. and certain affiliates, which operate Linens 'n Things, filed voluntary petitions under Chapter 11 of the United States Bankruptcy Code in the United States Bankruptcy Court for the District of Delaware. Pursuant to the court order entered on October 16, 2008, Linens Holding Co. is in the process of liquidating the entire Linens 'n Things retail chain. The Company's loss from discontinued operations includes $132.0 million of lease-related costs ($214.4 million, net of an $82.4 million income tax benefit), which the Company believes it will likely be required to satisfy pursuant to its Linens 'n Things lease guarantees. These amounts, which are expected to change as each lease is resolved, were calculated in accordance with SFAS No. 146, "Accounting for Costs Associated with Exit or Disposal Activities."

Earnings per common share. Basic earnings per common share is computed by dividing: (i) net earnings, after deducting the after-tax Employee Stock Ownership Plan ("ESOP") preference dividends, by (ii) the weighted average number of common shares outstanding during the year (the "Basic Shares").

When computing diluted earnings per common share, the Company assumes that the ESOP preference stock is converted into common stock and all dilutive stock awards are exercised. After the assumed ESOP preference stock conversion, the ESOP Trust would hold common stock rather than ESOP preference stock and would receive common stock dividends ($0.25800 per share in 2008, $0.22875 per share in 2007 and $0.15500 per share in 2006) rather than ESOP preference stock dividends (currently $3.90 per share). Since the ESOP Trust uses the dividends it receives to service its debt, the Company would have to increase its contribution to the ESOP Trust to compensate it for the lower dividends. This additional contribution would reduce the Company's net earnings, which in turn, would reduce the amounts that would be accrued under the Company's incentive compensation plans.

Diluted earnings per common share is computed by dividing: (i) net earnings, after accounting for the difference between the dividends on the ESOP preference stock and common stock and after making adjustments for the incentive compensation plans, by (ii) Basic Shares plus the additional shares that would be issued assuming that all dilutive stock awards are exercised and the ESOP preference stock is converted into common stock. Options to purchase 20.9 million, 10.7 million, and 4.7 million shares of common stock were outstanding as of December 31, 2008, December 29, 2007 and December 30, 2006, respectively, but were not included in the calculation of diluted earnings per share because the options' exercise prices were greater than the average market price of the common shares and, therefore, the effect would be antidilutive. See Note 8 for additional information about the ESOP.

Notes to Consolidated Financial Statements

New accounting pronouncements. In the first quarter of 2008, the Company adopted EITF Issue No. 06-4, "Accounting for Deferred Compensation and Postretirement Benefit Aspects of Endorsement Split-Dollar Life Insurance Arrangements" ("EITF 06-4"). EITF 06-4 requires the application of the provisions of SFAS No. 106, "Employers' Accounting for Postretirement Benefits Other Than Pensions" ("SFAS 106") (if, in substance, a postretirement benefit plan exists), or Accounting Principles Board Opinion No. 12 (if the arrangement is, in substance, an individual deferred compensation contract) to endorsement split-dollar life insurance arrangements. SFAS 106 requires the recognition of a liability for the discounted value of the future premium benefits that will be incurred through the death of the underlying insureds. The adoption of this statement did not have a material effect on the Company's consolidated results of operations, financial position and cash flows.

In the first quarter of 2008, the Company adopted EITF No. 06-10 "Accounting for Collateral Assignment Split-Dollar Life Insurance Agreements" ("EITF 06-10") effective fiscal 2008. EITF 06-10 provides guidance for determining a liability for the postretirement benefit obligation as well as recognition and measurement of the associated asset on the basis of the terms of the collateral assignment agreement. The adoption of this statement did not have a material effect on the Company's consolidated results of operations, financial position and cash flows.

In the first quarter of 2008, the Company adopted Financial Accounting Standards Board ("FASB") Staff Position No. FAS 157-3, "Determining the Fair Value of a Financial Asset When the Market for That Asset Is Not Active," which clarifies the application of SFAS No. 157 in a market that is not active. The adoption of this statement did not have a material impact on the Company's consolidated results of operations, financial position and cash flows.

In December 2007, the FASB issued SFAS No. 141 (revised 2007), Business Combinations ("SFAS 141R"), which replaces SFAS 141. SFAS 141R establishes the principles and requirements for how an acquirer recognizes and measures in its financial statements the identifiable assets acquired, the liabilities assumed, any noncontrolling interest in the acquiree and the goodwill acquired. The Statement also establishes disclosure requirements which will enable users to evaluate the nature and financial effects of business combinations. SFAS 141R is effective for fiscal years beginning after December 15, 2008.

been treated as an adjustment to the purchase price allocation if they had been recognized under SFAS 141. It is possible that a significant portion of these benefits will be recognized within the next twelve months. To the extent these benefits are recognized

they had been recognized under SFAS 141. It is possible that a significant portion of these benefits will be recognized within the next twelve months. To the extent these benefits are recognized after the adoption of SFAS 141R, their recognition would affect the Company's effective income tax rate rather than being treated as an adjustment to the purchase price allocation of the acquiree.

In February 2008, the FASB issued FASB Staff Position ("FSP") No. SFAS 157-2, "Effective Date of FASB Statement No. 157," which defers the effective date of SFAS 157 for nonfinancial assets and nonfinancial liabilities, except those that are recognized or disclosed at fair value in the financial statements on a recurring basis (at least annually), to fiscal years and interim periods within those fiscal years, beginning after November 15, 2008. The Company does not believe the adoption of this statement will have a material effect on its consolidated results of operations, financial position and cash flows.

In April 2008, the FASB issued FSP No. FAS 142-3, "Determining the Useful Life of Intangible Assets," which amends the factors an entity should consider in developing renewal or extension assumptions used in determining the useful lives of recognized intangible assets. This statement is effective for fiscal years beginning after December 15, 2008. The Company does not believe the adoption of this statement will have a material effect on its consolidated results of operations, financial position and cash flows.

In June 2008, the FASB reached consensus on EITF Issue No. 08-3, "Accounting by Lessees for Nonrefundable Maintenance Deposits" ("EITF 08-3"). Under EITF 08-3, lessees should account for nonrefundable maintenance deposits as deposit assets if it is probable that maintenance activities will occur and the deposit is therefore realizable. Amounts on deposit that are not probable of being used to fund future maintenance activities should be expensed. EITF 08-3 is effective for fiscal years beginning after December 15, 2008. Early application is not permitted. The Company does not believe the adoption of this statement will have a material effect on its consolidated results of operations, financial position and cash flows.

In December 2008, the FASB issued FSP No. FAS 132(R)-1, "Employers' Disclosures about Postretirement Benefit Plan Assets," which enhances the required disclosures about plan assets in an employer's defined benefit pension or other postretirement plan, including investment allocations decisions, inputs and valuations techniques used to measure the fair value of plan assets and significant concentrations of risks within plan assets. This statement is effective for financial statements issued for fiscal years ending after December 15, 2009. The Company is currently evaluating the potential impact the adoption of this statement may have on its consolidated financial statement disclosures.

Notes to Consolidated Financial Statements

NO 15 QUARTERLY FINANCIAL INFORMATION (UNAUDITED)

In millions, except per share amounts	First Quarter	Second Quarter	Third Quarter	Fourth Quarter	Fiscal Year
2008:[1]					
Net revenues	**$ 21,326.0**	**$ 21,140.3**	**$ 20,863.4**	**$ 24,142.2**	**$ 87,471.9**
Gross profit	**4,293.0**	**4,373.2**	**4,400.6**	**5,223.6**	**18,290.4**
Operating profit	**1,370.1**	**1,478.1**	**1,466.2**	**1,731.8**	**6,046.2**
Earnings from continuing operations	**748.5**	**823.5**	**818.8**	**953.3**	**3,344.1**
Loss from discontinued operations, net of income tax benefit	**–**	**(48.7)**	**(82.8)**	**(0.5)**	**(132.0)**
Net earnings	**748.5**	**774.8**	**736.0**	**952.8**	**3,212.1**
Earnings per share from continuing operations, basic	**0.52**	**0.57**	**0.57**	**0.66**	**2.32**
Loss per common share from discontinued operations	**–**	**(0.03)**	**(0.06)**	**–**	**(0.09)**
Net earnings per common share, basic	**0.52**	**0.54**	**0.51**	**0.66**	**2.23**
Earnings per common share from continuing operations, diluted	**0.51**	**0.56**	**0.56**	**0.65**	**2.27**
Loss per common share from discontinued operations	**–**	**(0.03)**	**(0.06)**	**–**	**(0.09)**
Net earnings per common share, diluted	**0.51**	**0.53**	**0.50**	**0.65**	**2.18**
Dividends per common share	**0.06000**	**0.06000**	**0.06900**	**0.06900**	**0.25800**
Stock price: (New York Stock Exchange)					
High	**41.53**	**44.29**	**40.14**	**34.90**	**44.29**
Low	**34.91**	**39.02**	**31.81**	**23.19**	**23.19**
2007:					
Net revenues	$ 13,188.6	$ 20,703.3	$ 20,495.2	$ 21,942.4	$ 76,329.5
Gross profit	3,303.2	4,158.5	4,195.2	4,450.8	16,107.7
Operating profit	736.5	1,309.8	1,271.1	1,475.9	4,793.3
Net earnings	408.9	723.6	689.5	815.0	2,637.0
Net earnings per common share, basic	0.45	0.48	0.47	0.56	1.97
Net earnings per common share, diluted	0.43	0.47	0.45	0.55	1.92
Dividends per common share	0.04875	0.06000	0.06000	0.06000	0.22875
Stock price: (New York Stock Exchange)					
High	34.93	39.44	39.85	42.60	42.60
Low	30.45	34.14	34.80	36.43	30.45

(1) On December 23, 2008, our Board of Directors approved a change in our fiscal year-end from the Saturday nearest December 31 of each year to December 31 of each year to better reflect our position in the health care, rather than the retail industry. The fiscal year change was effective beginning with the fourth quarter of fiscal 2008. Prior to Board approval of this change, the Saturday nearest December 31, 2008 would have resulted in a 53-week fiscal year that would have ended January 3, 2009. As you review our operating performance, please consider that fiscal years 2008 and 2007 and fiscal quarters 2008 and 2007 include 368 days, 364 days, 95 days and 91 days, respectively.

Five-Year Financial Summary

In millions, except per share amounts	2008[1]	2007[2]	2006	2005	2004
Statement of operations data:					
Net revenues	**$ 87,471.9**	$ 76,329.5	$ 43,821.4	$ 37,006.7	$ 30,594.6
Gross profit	**18,290.4**	16,107.7	11,742.2	9,694.6	7,915.9
Operating expenses[3][4]	**12,244.2**	11,314.4	9,300.6	7,675.1	6,461.2
Operating profit[5]	**6,046.2**	4,793.3	2,441.6	2,019.5	1,454.7
Interest expense, net	**509.5**	434.6	215.8	110.5	58.3
Income tax provision[6]	**2,192.6**	1,721.7	856.9	684.3	477.6
Earnings from continuing operations	**3,344.1**	2,637.0	1,368.9	1,224.7	918.8
Loss from discontinued operations, net of tax benefit[7]	**(132.0)**	–	–	–	–
Net earnings	**$ 3,212.1**	$ 2,637.0	$ 1,368.9	$ 1,224.7	$ 918.8
Per common share data:					
Basic earnings per common share:					
Earnings from continuing operations	**$ 2.32**	$ 1.97	$ 1.65	$ 1.49	$ 1.13
Loss from discontinued operations	**(0.09)**	–	–	–	–
Net earnings	**$ 2.23**	$ 1.97	$ 1.65	$ 1.49	$ 1.13
Diluted earnings per common share:					
Earnings from continuing operations	**$ 2.27**	$ 1.92	$ 1.60	$ 1.45	$ 1.10
Loss from discontinued operations	**(0.09)**	–	–	–	–
Net earnings	**$ 2.18**	$ 1.92	$ 1.60	$ 1.45	$ 1.10
Cash dividends per common share	**0.25800**	0.22875	0.15500	0.14500	0.13250
Balance sheet and other data:					
Total assets	**$ 60,959.9**	$ 54,721.9	$ 20,574.1	$ 15,246.6	$ 14,513.3
Long-term debt (less current portion)	**$ 8,057.2**	$ 8,349.7	$ 2,870.4	$ 1,594.1	$ 1,925.9
Total shareholders' equity	**$ 34,574.4**	$ 31,321.9	$ 9,917.6	$ 8,331.2	$ 6,987.2
Number of stores (at end of period)	**6,923**	6,301	6,205	5,474	5,378

(1) On December 23, 2008, our Board of Directors approved a change in our fiscal year-end from the Saturday nearest December 31 of each year to December 31 of each year to better reflect our position in the health care, rather than the retail industry. The fiscal year change was effective beginning with the fourth quarter of fiscal 2008. Prior to Board approval of this change, the Saturday nearest December 31, 2008 would have resulted in a 53-week fiscal year that would have ended January 3, 2009. As you review our operating performance, please consider that fiscal 2008 includes 368 days, compared to each of the remaining fiscal years presented, which include 364 days.

(2) Effective March 22, 2007, pursuant to the Agreement and Plan of Merger dated as of November 1, 2006, as amended (the "Merger Agreement"), Caremark Rx, Inc. was merged with and into a newly formed subsidiary of CVS Corporation, with the CVS subsidiary, Caremark Rx, L.L.C. ("Caremark"), continuing as the surviving entity (the "Caremark Merger"). Following the Caremark Merger, the name of the Company was changed to "CVS Caremark Corporation." By virtue of the Caremark Merger, each issued and outstanding share of Caremark common stock, par value $0.001 per share, was converted into the right to receive 1.67 shares of CVS Caremark's common stock, par value $0.01 per share. Cash was paid in lieu of fractional shares.

(3) In 2006, the Company adopted the Securities and Exchange Commission (SEC) Staff Accounting Bulletin ("SAB") No. 108, "Considering the Effects of Prior Year Misstatements when Qualifying Misstatements in Current Year Financial Statements." The adoption of this statement resulted in a $40.2 million pre-tax ($24.7 million after-tax) decrease in operating expenses for 2006.

(4) In 2004, the Company conformed its accounting for operating leases and leasehold improvements to the views expressed by the Office of the Chief Accountant of the Securities and Exchange Commission to the American Institute of Certified Public Accountants on February 7, 2005. As a result, the Company recorded a non-cash pre-tax adjustment of $65.9 million ($40.5 million after-tax) to operating expenses, which represents the cumulative effect of the adjustment for a period of approximately 20 years. Since the effect of this non-cash adjustment was not material to 2004, or any previously reported fiscal year, the cumulative effect was recorded in the fourth quarter of 2004.

(5) Operating profit includes the pre-tax effect of the charge discussed in Note (3) and Note (4) above.

(6) Income tax provision includes the effect of the following: (i) in 2006, a $11.0 million reversal of previously recorded tax reserves through the tax provision principally based on resolving certain state tax matters, (ii) in 2005, a $52.6 million reversal of previously recorded tax reserves through the tax provision principally based on resolving certain state tax matters, and (iii) in 2004, a $60.0 million reversal of previously recorded tax reserves through the tax provision principally based on finalizing certain tax return years and on a 2004 court decision relevant to the industry.

(7) In connection with certain business dispositions completed between 1991 and 1997, the Company continues to guarantee store lease obligations for a number of former subsidiaries, including Linens 'n Things. On May 2, 2008, Linens Holding Co. and certain affiliates, which operate Linens 'n Things, filed voluntary petitions under Chapter 11 of the United States Bankruptcy Code in the United States Bankruptcy Court for the District of Delaware. Pursuant to the court order entered on October 16, 2008, Linens Holding Co. is in the process of liquidating the entire Linens 'n Things retail chain. The loss from discontinued operations includes $132.0 million of lease-related costs ($214.4 million, net of an $82.4 million income tax benefit), which the Company believes it will likely be required to satisfy pursuant to its Linens 'n Things lease guarantees. These amounts, which are expected to change as each lease is resolved, were calculated in accordance with SFAS No. 146, "Accounting for Costs Associated with Exit or Disposal Activities."

Report of Independent Registered Public Accounting Firm

The Board of Directors and Shareholders
CVS Caremark Corporation

We have audited the accompanying consolidated balance sheets of CVS Caremark Corporation as of December 31, 2008 and December 29, 2007, and the related consolidated statements of operations, shareholders' equity and cash flows for the fiscal years ended December 31, 2008 and December 29, 2007. These financial statements are the responsibility of the Company's management. Our responsibility is to express an opinion on these financial statements based on our audits.

We conducted our audits in accordance with the standards of the Public Company Accounting Oversight Board (United States). Those standards require that we plan and perform the audit to obtain reasonable assurance about whether the financial statements are free of material misstatement. An audit includes examining, on a test basis, evidence supporting the amounts and disclosures in the financial statements. An audit also includes assessing the accounting principles used and significant estimates made by management, as well as, evaluating the overall financial statement presentation. We believe that our audits provide a reasonable basis for our opinion.

In our opinion, the financial statements referred to above present fairly, in all material respects, the consolidated financial position of CVS Caremark Corporation at December 31, 2008 and December 29, 2007, and the consolidated results of its operations and its cash flows for the fiscal years ended December 31, 2008 and December 29, 2007, in conformity with U.S. generally accepted accounting principles.

As discussed in Note 1 to the consolidated financial statements, effective December 31, 2006, CVS Caremark Corporation adopted Financial Accounting Standards Board (FASB) Interpretation No. 48, *Accounting for Uncertainty in Income Taxes – an interpretation of FASB Statement No. 109* and effective December 30, 2007, CVS Caremark Corporation adopted Emerging Issues Task Force (EITF) No. 06-4, *Accounting for Deferred Compensation and Postretirement Benefit Aspects of Endorsement Split-Dollar Life Insurance Arrangements* and EITF No. 06-10, *Accounting for Collateral Assignment Split-Dollar Life Insurance Arrangements.*

We also have audited, in accordance with the standards of the Public Company Accounting Oversight Board (United States), CVS Caremark Corporation's internal control over financial reporting as of December 31, 2008, based on criteria established in *Internal Control – Integrated Framework* issued by the Committee of Sponsoring Organizations of the Treadway Commission and our report dated February 26, 2009 expressed an unqualified opinion thereon.

Ernst & Young LLP

The Board of Directors and Shareholders
CVS Caremark Corporation

We have audited the accompanying consolidated statements of operations, shareholders' equity and cash flows of CVS Caremark Corporation (formerly CVS Corporation) and subsidiaries for the fiscal year ended December 30, 2006. These consolidated financial statements are the responsibility of the Company's management. Our responsibility is to express an opinion on these consolidated financial statements based on our audit.

We conducted our audit in accordance with the standards of the Public Company Accounting Oversight Board (United States). Those standards require that we plan and perform the audit to obtain reasonable assurance about whether the financial statements are free of material misstatement. An audit includes examining, on a test basis, evidence supporting the amounts and disclosures in the financial statements. An audit also includes assessing the accounting principles used and significant estimates made by management, as well as evaluating the overall financial statement presentation. We believe that our audit provides a reasonable basis for our opinion.

In our opinion, the consolidated financial statements referred to above present fairly, in all material respects, the results of operations and cash flows of CVS Caremark Corporation and subsidiaries for the fiscal year ended December 30, 2006, in conformity with U.S. generally accepted accounting principles.

KPMG LLP

KPMG LLP
Providence, Rhode Island
February 27, 2007

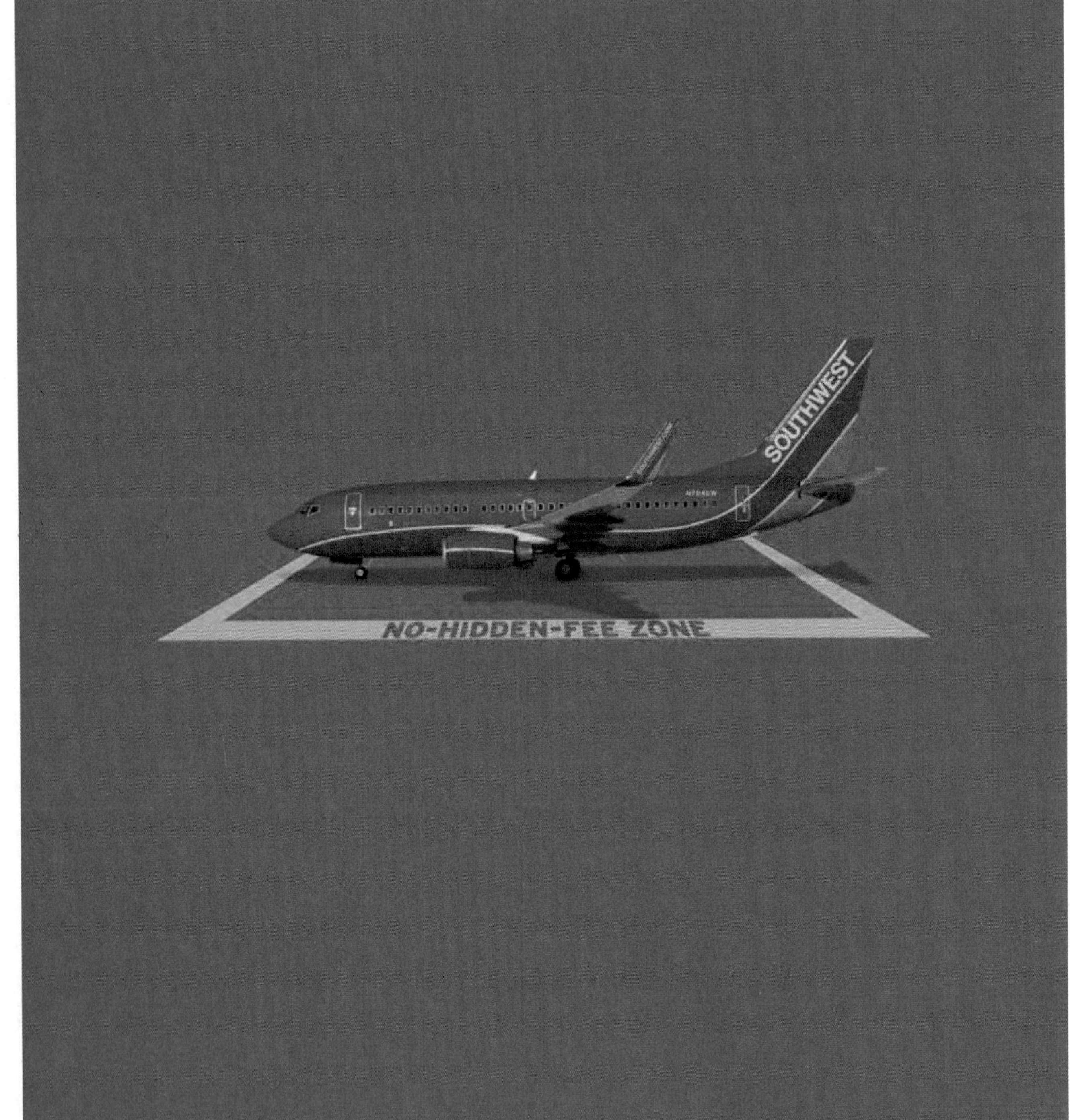

SOUTHWEST AIRLINES CO. 2008 ANNUAL REPORT

Item 8. ***Financial Statements and Supplementary Data***

SOUTHWEST AIRLINES CO.

CONSOLIDATED BALANCE SHEET

	December 31,	
	2008	**2007**
	(In millions, except share data)	
ASSETS		
Current assets:		
Cash and cash equivalents	**$ 1,368**	$ 2,213
Short-term investments	**435**	566
Accounts and other receivables	**209**	279
Inventories of parts and supplies, at cost	**203**	259
Fuel derivative contracts	**—**	1,069
Deferred income taxes	**365**	—
Prepaid expenses and other current assets	**3 13**	57
Total current assets	**2,893**	4,443
Property and equipment, at cost:		
Flight equipment	**13,722**	13,019
Ground property and equipment	**1,769**	1,515
Deposits on flight equipment purchase contracts	**380**	626
	15,871	15,160
Less allowance for depreciation and amortization	**4,831**	4,286
	11,040	10,874
Other assets	**375**	1,455
	$14,308	$16,772
LIABILITIES AND STOCKHOLDERS' EQUITY		
Current liabilities:		
Accounts payable	**$ 668**	$ 759
Accrued liabilities	**1,012**	3,107
Air traffic liability	**963**	931
Current maturities of long-term debt	**163**	41
Total current liabilities	**2,806**	4,838
Long-term debt less current maturities	**3,498**	2,050
Deferred income taxes	**1,904**	2,535
Deferred gains from sale and leaseback of aircraft	**105**	106
Other deferred liabilities	**1,042**	302
Commitments and contingencies		
Stockholders' equity:		
Common stock, $1.00 par value: 2,000,000,000 shares authorized; 807,611,634 shares issued in 2008 and 2007	**808**	808
Capital in excess of par value	**1,215**	1,207
Retained earnings	**4,919**	4,788
Accumulated other comprehensive income (loss)	**(984)**	1,241
Treasury stock, at cost: 67,619,062 and 72,814,104 shares in 2008 and 2007, respectively	**(1,005)**	(1,103)
Total stockholders' equity	**4,953**	6,941
	$14,308	$16,772

See accompanying notes.

SOUTHWEST AIRLINES CO.

CONSOLIDATED STATEMENT OF INCOME

	Years Ended December 31,		
	2008	**2007**	**2006**
	(In millions, except per share amounts)		
OPERATING REVENUES:			
Passenger	**$10,549**	$9,457	$8,750
Freight	**145**	130	134
Other	**329**	274	202
Total operating revenues	**11,023**	9,861	9,086
OPERATING EXPENSES:			
Salaries, wages, and benefits	**3,340**	3,213	3,052
Fuel and oil	**3,713**	2,690	2,284
Maintenance materials and repairs	**721**	616	468
Aircraft rentals	**154**	156	158
Landing fees and other rentals	**662**	560	495
Depreciation and amortization	**599**	555	515
Other operating expenses	**1,385**	1,280	1,180
Total operating expenses	**10,574**	9,070	8,152
OPERATING INCOME	**449**	791	934
OTHER EXPENSES (INCOME):			
Interest expense	**130**	119	128
Capitalized interest	**(25)**	(50)	(51)
Interest income	**(26)**	(44)	(84)
Other (gains) losses, net	**92**	(292)	151
Total other expenses (income)	**171**	(267)	144
INCOME BEFORE INCOME TAXES	**278**	1,058	790
PROVISION FOR INCOME TAXES	**100**	413	291
NET INCOME	**$ 178**	$ 645	$ 499
NET INCOME PER SHARE, BASIC	**$ .24**	$ .85	$ .63
NET INCOME PER SHARE, DILUTED	**$ .24**	$ .84	$ .61

See accompanying notes.

SOUTHWEST AIRLINES CO.

CONSOLIDATED STATEMENT OF STOCKHOLDERS' EQUITY

	Years Ended December 31, 2008, 2007, and 2006					
	Common Stock	Capital in excess of par value	Retained earnings	Accumulated other comprehensive income (loss)	Treasury stock	Total
	(In millions, except per share amounts)					
Balance at December 31, 2005	$802	$ 963	$4,018	$ 892	$ —	$ 6,675
Purchase of shares of treasury stock	—	—	—	—	(800)	(800)
Issuance of common and treasury stock pursuant to Employee stock plans	6	39	(196)	—	410	259
Tax benefit of options exercised	—	60	—	—	—	60
Share-based compensation	—	80	—	—	—	80
Cash dividends, $.018 per share	—	—	(14)	—	—	(14)
Comprehensive income (loss)						
Net income	—	—	499	—	—	499
Unrealized (loss) on derivative instruments	—	—	—	(306)	—	(306)
Other	—	—	—	(4)	—	(4)
Total comprehensive income						189
Balance at December 31, 2006	$808	$1,142	$4,307	$ 582	$ (390)	$ 6,449
Purchase of shares of treasury stock	—	—	—	—	(1,001)	(1,001)
Issuance of common and treasury stock pursuant to Employee stock plans	—	—	(150)	—	288	138
Tax benefit of options exercised	—	28	—	—	—	28
Share-based compensation	—	37	—	—	—	37
Cash dividends, $.018 per share	—	—	(14)	—	—	(14)
Comprehensive income (loss)						
Net income	—	—	645	—	—	645
Unrealized gain on derivative instruments	—	—	—	636	—	636
Other	—	—	—	23	—	23
Total comprehensive income						1,304
Balance at December 31, 2007	$808	$1,207	$4,788	$ 1,241	$(1,103)	$ 6,941
Purchase of shares of treasury stock	—	—	—	—	(54)	(54)
Issuance of common and treasury stock pursuant to Employee stock plans	—	—	(34)	—	152	118
Tax benefit of options exercised	—	(10)	—	—	—	(10)
Share-based compensation	—	18	—	—	—	18
Cash dividends, $.018 per share	—	—	(13)	—	—	(13)
Comprehensive income (loss)						
Net income	—	—	178	—	—	178
Unrealized (loss) on derivative instruments	—	—	—	(2,166)	—	(2,166)
Other	—	—	—	(59)	—	(59)
Total comprehensive income (loss)						(2,047)
Balance at December 31, 2008	**$808**	**$1,215**	**$4,919**	**$ (984)**	**$(1,005)**	**$ 4,953**

See accompanying notes.

SOUTHWEST AIRLINES CO.

CONSOLIDATED STATEMENT OF CASH FLOWS

	Years Ended December 31,		
	2008	**2007**	**2006**
		(In millions)	
CASH FLOWS FROM OPERATING ACTIVITIES:			
Net income	**$ 178**	$ 645	$ 499
Adjustments to reconcile net income to net cash provided by operating activities:			
Depreciation and amortization	**599**	555	515
Deferred income taxes	**56**	328	277
Amortization of deferred gains on sale and leaseback of aircraft	**(12)**	(14)	(16)
Share-based compensation expense	**18**	37	80
Excess tax benefits from share-based compensation arrangements	**—**	(28)	(60)
Changes in certain assets and liabilities:			
Accounts and other receivables	**71**	(38)	(5)
Other current assets	**(384)**	(229)	87
Accounts payable and accrued liabilities	**(1,853)**	1,609	(223)
Air traffic liability	**32**	131	150
Other, net	**(226)**	(151)	102
Net cash provided by (used in) operating activities	**(1,521)**	2,845	1,406
CASH FLOWS FROM INVESTING ACTIVITIES:			
Purchases of property and equipment, net	**(923)**	(1,331)	(1,399)
Purchases of short-term investments	**(5,886)**	(5,086)	(4,509)
Proceeds from sales of short-term investments	**5,831**	4,888	4,392
Debtor in possession loan to ATA Airlines, Inc.	**—**	—	20
Other, net	**—**	—	1
Net cash used in investing activities	**(978)**	(1,529)	(1,495)
CASH FLOWS FROM FINANCING ACTIVITIES:			
Issuance of long-term debt	**1,000**	500	300
Proceeds from credit line borrowing	**91**	—	—
Proceeds from revolving credit agreement	**400**	—	—
Proceeds from sale and leaseback transactions	**173**	—	—
Proceeds from Employee stock plans	**117**	139	260
Payments of long-term debt and capital lease obligations	**(55)**	(122)	(607)
Payments of cash dividends	**(13)**	(14)	(14)
Repurchase of common stock	**(54)**	(1,001)	(800)
Excess tax benefits from share-based compensation arrangements	**—**	28	60
Other, net	**(5)**	(23)	—
Net cash provided by (used in) financing activities	**1,654**	(493)	(801)
NET INCREASE (DECREASE) IN CASH AND CASH EQUIVALENTS	**(845)**	823	(890)
CASH AND CASH EQUIVALENTS AT BEGINNING OF PERIOD	**2,213**	1,390	2,280
CASH AND CASH EQUIVALENTS AT END OF PERIOD	**$ 1,368**	$ 2,213	$ 1,390
SUPPLEMENTAL DISCLOSURES			
Cash payments for:			
Interest, net of amount capitalized	**$ 100**	$ 63	$ 78
Income taxes	**$ 71**	$ 94	$ 15

See accompanying notes.

NOTES TO CONSOLIDATED FINANCIAL STATEMENTS
December 31, 2008

1. Summary of Significant Accounting Policies

Basis of Presentation

Southwest Airlines Co. (the Company) is a major domestic airline that provides point-to-point, low-fare service. The Consolidated Financial Statements include the accounts of the Company and its wholly owned subsidiaries. All significant intercompany balances and transactions have been eliminated. The preparation of financial statements in conformity with generally accepted accounting principles in the United States (GAAP) requires management to make estimates and assumptions that affect the amounts reported in the financial statements and accompanying notes. Actual results could differ from these estimates.

Certain prior period amounts have been reclassified to conform to the current presentation. In the Consolidated Statement of Income for the years ended December 31, 2007 and 2006, jet fuel sales taxes and jet fuel excise taxes are both presented as a component of "Fuel and oil" instead of being included in "Other operating expenses" as previously presented. For the years ended December 31, 2007 and 2006, the Company reclassified a total of $154 million and $146 million, respectively, in jet fuel sales taxes and jet fuel excise taxes as a result of this change in presentation. For the year ended December 31, 2008, "Fuel and oil" includes $187 million in jet fuel sales taxes and jet fuel excise taxes.

Cash and cash equivalents

Cash in excess of that necessary for operating requirements is invested in short-term, highly liquid, income-producing investments. Investments with maturities of three months or less are classified as cash and cash equivalents, which primarily consist of certificates of deposit, money market funds, and investment grade commercial paper issued by major corporations and financial institutions. Cash and cash equivalents are stated at cost, which approximates market value.

Short-term investments

Short-term investments consist of investments with maturities of greater than three months but less than twelve months. These are primarily money market funds and investment grade commercial paper issued by major corporations and financial institutions, short-term securities issued by the U.S. Government, and certain auction rate securities with auction reset periods of less than 12 months for which auctions have been successful or are expected to be successful within the following 12 months. All of these investments are classified as available-for-sale securities and are stated at fair value, except for $17 million in auction rate securities that are classified as trading securities as discussed in Note 11. For all short-term investments, at each reset period, the Company accounts for the transaction as "Proceeds from sales of short-term investments" for the security relinquished, and a "Purchase of short-investments" for the security purchased, in the accompanying Consolidated Statement of Cash Flows. Unrealized gains and losses, net of tax, are recognized in "Accumulated other comprehensive income (loss)" in the accompanying Consolidated Balance Sheet. Realized net gains on specific investments, which totaled $13 million in 2008, $17 million in 2007, and $17 million in 2006, are reflected in "Interest income" in the accompanying Consolidated Statement of Income.

The Company's cash and cash equivalents and short-term investments as of December 31, 2007 included $2.0 billion in collateral deposits received from a counterparty of the Company's fuel derivative instruments. As of December 31, 2008, the Company did not hold any cash collateral deposits from counterparties, but had $240 million of its cash on deposit with a counterparty. Although amounts provided or held are not restricted in any way, investment earnings from these deposits generally must be remitted back to the entity that provided the deposit. Depending on the fair value of the Company's fuel derivative instruments, the amounts of collateral deposits held or provided at any point in time can fluctuate significantly. Therefore, the Company generally excludes cash collateral deposits held, but includes deposits provided, in its decisions related to long-term cash planning and forecasting. See Note 10 for further information on these collateral deposits and fuel derivative instruments.

Accounts and other receivables

Accounts and other receivables are carried at cost. They primarily consist of amounts due from credit card companies associated with sales of tickets

NOTES TO CONSOLIDATED FINANCIAL STATEMENTS — (Continued)

for future travel and amounts due from counterparties associated with fuel derivative instruments that have settled. The amount of allowance for doubtful accounts as of December 31, 2008, 2007, and 2006 was immaterial. In addition, the provision for doubtful accounts and write-offs for 2008, 2007, and 2006 were immaterial.

Inventories

Inventories primarily consist of flight equipment expendable parts, materials, aircraft fuel, and supplies. All of these items are carried at average cost, less an allowance for obsolescence. These items are generally charged to expense when issued for use. The reserve for obsolescence was immaterial at December 31, 2008, 2007, and 2006. In addition, the Company's provision for obsolescence and write-offs for 2008, 2007, and 2006 was immaterial.

Property and equipment

Property and equipment is stated at cost. Depreciation is provided by the straight-line method to estimated residual values over periods generally ranging from 23 to 25 years for flight equipment and 5 to 30 years for ground property and equipment once the asset is placed in service. Residual values estimated for aircraft are generally 10 to 15 percent and for ground property and equipment range from zero to 10 percent. Property under capital leases and related obligations is recorded at an amount equal to the present value of future minimum lease payments computed on the basis of the Company's incremental borrowing rate or, when known, the interest rate implicit in the lease. Amortization of property under capital leases is on a straight-line basis over the lease term and is included in depreciation expense.

When appropriate, the Company evaluates its long-lived assets used in operations for impairment. Impairment losses would be recorded when events and circumstances indicate that an asset might be impaired and the undiscounted cash flows to be generated by that asset are less than the carrying amounts of the asset. Factors that would indicate potential impairment include, but are not limited to, significant decreases in the market value of the long-lived asset(s), a significant change in the long-lived asset's physical condition, and operating or cash flow losses associated with the use of the long-lived asset. Excluding the impact of cash collateral deposits with counterparties based on the fair value of the Company's fuel derivative instruments, the Company continues to experience positive cash flow associated with its aircraft fleet, and there have been no impairments of long-lived assets recorded during 2008, 2007, or 2006.

Aircraft and engine maintenance

The cost of scheduled inspections and repairs and routine maintenance costs for all aircraft and engines are charged to maintenance expense as incurred. Modifications that significantly enhance the operating performance or extend the useful lives of aircraft or engines are capitalized and amortized over the remaining life of the asset.

Intangible assets

Intangible assets primarily consist of leasehold rights to airport owned gates. These assets are amortized on a straight-line basis over the expected useful life of the lease, approximately 20 years. The accumulated amortization related to the Company's intangible assets at December 31, 2008, and 2007, was $12 million and $9 million, respectively. The Company periodically assesses its intangible assets for impairment in accordance with SFAS 142, *Goodwill and Other Intangible Assets*; however, no impairments have been noted.

Revenue recognition

Tickets sold are initially deferred as "Air traffic liability". Passenger revenue is recognized when transportation is provided. "Air traffic liability" primarily represents tickets sold for future travel dates and estimated refunds and exchanges of tickets sold for past travel dates. The majority of the Company's tickets sold are nonrefundable. Tickets that are sold but not flown on the travel date (whether refundable or nonrefundable) can be reused for another flight, up to a year from the date of sale, or refunded (if the ticket is refundable). A small percentage of tickets (or partial tickets) expire unused. The Company estimates the amount of future refunds and exchanges, net of forfeitures, for all unused tickets once the flight date has passed.

NOTES TO CONSOLIDATED FINANCIAL STATEMENTS — (Continued)

The Company is also required to collect certain taxes and fees from Customers on behalf of government agencies and remit these back to the applicable governmental entity on a periodic basis. These taxes and fees include U.S. federal transportation taxes, federal security charges, and airport passenger facility charges. These items are collected from Customers at the time they purchase their tickets, but are not included in Passenger revenue. The Company records a liability upon collection from the Customer and relieves the liability when payments are remitted to the applicable governmental agency.

Frequent flyer program

The Company records a liability for the estimated incremental cost of providing free travel under its Rapid Rewards frequent flyer program at the time an award is earned. The estimated incremental cost includes direct passenger costs such as fuel, food, and other operational costs, but does not include any contribution to overhead or profit.

The Company also sells frequent flyer credits and related services to companies participating in its Rapid Rewards frequent flyer program. Funds received from the sale of flight segment credits are accounted for under the residual value method. Under this method, the Company has determined the portion of funds received for sale of flight segment credits that relate to free travel, currently estimated at 81 percent of the amount received per flight segment credit sold. These amounts are deferred and recognized as "Passenger revenue" when the ultimate free travel awards are flown or the credits expire unused. The remaining 19 percent of the amount received per flight segment credit sold, which is assumed not to be associated with future travel, includes items such as access to the Company's frequent flyer program population for marketing/solicitation purposes, use of the Company's logo on co-branded credit cards, and other trademarks, designs, images, etc. of the Company for use in marketing materials. This remaining portion is recognized in "Other revenue" in the period earned.

Advertising

The Company expenses the costs of advertising as incurred. Advertising expense for the years ended December 31, 2008, 2007, and 2006 was $199 million, $191 million, and $182 million, respectively.

Share-based Employee compensation

The Company has share-based compensation plans covering the majority of its Employee groups, including a plan covering the Company's Board of Directors and plans related to employment contracts with the Chairman Emeritus of the Company. The Company accounts for share-based compensation utilizing the fair value recognition provisions of SFAS No. 123R, "Share-Based Payment." See Note 14.

Financial derivative instruments

The Company accounts for financial derivative instruments utilizing Statement of Financial Accounting Standards No. 133 (SFAS 133), "Accounting for Derivative Instruments and Hedging Activities," as amended. The Company utilizes various derivative instruments, including crude oil, unleaded gasoline, and heating oil-based derivatives, to attempt to reduce the risk of its exposure to jet fuel price increases. These instruments primarily consist of purchased call options, collar structures, and fixed-price swap agreements, and upon proper qualification are accounted for as cash-flow hedges, as defined by SFAS 133. The Company has also entered into interest rate swap agreements to convert a portion of its fixed-rate debt to floating rates and one floating-rate debt issuance to a fixed-rate. These interest rate hedges are accounted for as fair value hedges or as cash flow hedges, as defined by SFAS 133.

Since the majority of the Company's financial derivative instruments are not traded on a market exchange, the Company estimates their fair values. Depending on the type of instrument, the values are determined by the use of present value methods or standard option value models with assumptions about commodity prices based on those observed in underlying markets. Also, since there is not a reliable forward market for jet fuel, the Company must estimate the future prices of jet fuel in order to measure the effectiveness of the hedging instruments in offsetting changes to those prices, as required by SFAS 133. Forward jet fuel prices are estimated through utilization of a statistical-based regression

NOTES TO CONSOLIDATED FINANCIAL STATEMENTS — (Continued)

equation with data from market forward prices of like commodities. This equation is then adjusted for certain items, such as transportation costs, that are stated in the Company's fuel purchasing contracts with its vendors.

For the effective portion of settled hedges, as defined in SFAS 133, the Company records the associated gains or losses as a component of "Fuel and oil" expense in the Consolidated Statement of Income. For amounts representing ineffectiveness, as defined, or changes in fair value of derivative instruments for which hedge accounting is not applied, the Company records any gains or losses as a component of "Other (gains) losses, net", in the Consolidated Statement of Income. Amounts that are paid or received associated with the purchase or sale of financial derivative instruments (i.e., premium costs of option contracts) are classified as a component of "Other (gains) losses, net", in the Consolidated Statement of Income in the period in which the instrument settles or expires. All cash flows associated with purchasing and selling derivatives are classified as operating cash flows in the Consolidated Statement of Cash Flows, within "Changes in certain assets and liabilities." See Note 10 for further information on SFAS 133 and financial derivative instruments.

Software capitalization

The Company capitalizes certain costs related to the acquisition and development of software in accordance with Statement of Position 98-1, "Accounting for the Costs of Computer Software Developed or Obtained for Internal Use." The Company amortizes these costs using the straight-line method over the estimated useful life of the software which is generally five years.

Income taxes

The Company accounts for deferred income taxes utilizing Statement of Financial Accounting Standards No. 109 (SFAS 109), "Accounting for Income Taxes", as amended. SFAS 109 requires an asset and liability method, whereby deferred tax assets and liabilities are recognized based on the tax effects of temporary differences between the financial statements and the tax bases of assets and liabilities, as measured by current enacted tax rates. When appropriate, in accordance with SFAS 109, the Company evaluates the need for a valuation allowance to reduce deferred tax assets.

The Company's policy for recording interest and penalties associated with audits is to record such items as a component of income before taxes. Penalties are recorded in "Other (gains) losses, net," and interest paid or received is recorded in interest expense or interest income, respectively, in the statement of income. For the year ended December 31, 2008, the Company recorded no interest related to the settlement of audits for certain prior periods.

Concentration Risk

Approximately 77 percent of the Company's Employees are unionized and are covered by collective bargaining agreements. Historically, the Company has managed this risk by maintaining positive relationships with its Employees and its Employee's Representatives. The following Employee groups are under agreements that have become amendable and are currently in negotiations: Pilots, Flight Attendants, Ramp, Operations, Provisioning, and Freight Agents, Stock Clerks, and Customer Service and Reservations Agents. The Company reached a Tentative Agreement with its Mechanics during fourth quarter 2008, and the agreement was ratified by this group during January 2009. The Company's Aircraft Appearance Technicians and its Flight Dispatchers are subject to agreements that become amendable during 2009.

The Company attempts to minimize its concentration risk with regards to its cash, cash equivalents, and its investment portfolio. This is accomplished by diversifying and limiting amounts among different counterparties, the type of investment, and the amount invested in any individual security or money market fund.

To manage risk associated with financial derivative instruments held, the Company selects and will periodically review counterparties based on credit ratings, limits its exposure to a single counterparty, and monitors the market position of the program and its relative market position with each counterparty. The Company also has agreements with

NOTES TO CONSOLIDATED FINANCIAL STATEMENTS — (Continued)

counterparties containing early termination rights and/or bilateral collateral provisions whereby security is required if market risk exposure exceeds a specified threshold amount or credit ratings fall below certain levels. At December 31, 2008, the Company had provided $240 million in cash collateral deposits to one of its counterparties under these bilateral collateral provisions. The cash collateral provided to the counterparty has been recorded as a reduction to "Cash and cash equivalents" and an increase to "Prepaid expenses and other current assets." Cash collateral deposits serve to decrease, but not totally eliminate, the credit risk associated with the Company's hedging program. See Note 10 for further information.

The Company operates an all-Boeing 737 fleet of aircraft. If the Company was unable to acquire additional aircraft from Boeing, or Boeing was unable or unwilling to provide adequate support for its products, the Company's operations could be adversely impacted. However, the Company considers its relationship with Boeing to be excellent and believes the advantages of operating a single fleet type outweigh the risks of such a strategy.

CHAPTER

6

The Operating Cycle and Merchandising Operations

Making a Statement

INCOME STATEMENT

Revenues

– Expenses

= Net Income

STATEMENT OF OWNER'S EQUITY

Beginning Balance

+ Net Income

– Withdrawals

= Ending Balance

BALANCE SHEET

Assets	**Liabilities**
	Owner's Equity

A = L + OE

STATEMENT OF CASH FLOWS

Operating activities

+ Investing activities

+ Financing activities

= Change in Cash

+ Beginning Balance

= Ending Cash Balance

Merchandising transactions can affect all the financial statements.

Buying and selling goods and services is fundamental to the operation of retail and wholesale merchandising businesses. Managers who do not understand the dynamics of the cash flows of buying and selling merchandise and collecting from customers run the risk of putting their company in bankruptcy. Today's global environment, in which many goods are purchased and sold overseas, presents managers with additional challenges. In this chapter, we address the management of the operating cycle, the choice of inventory systems, merchandising income statements, and the recording of merchandising transactions.

LEARNING OBJECTIVES

LO1 Identify the management issues related to merchandising businesses. (pp. 268–272)

LO2 Describe the terms of sale related to merchandising transactions. (pp. 272–275)

LO3 Prepare an income statement and record merchandising transactions under the perpetual inventory system. (pp. 275–280)

LO4 Prepare an income statement and record merchandising transactions under the periodic inventory system. (pp. 281–286)

DECISION POINT ▶ A USER'S FOCUS FONG COMPANY

- ▶ How can merchandising transactions be recorded to reflect the company's performance?
- ▶ How can the company efficiently manage its cycle of merchandising operations?

Fong Company is a small but successful and fast-growing merchandising company that specializes in selling stylish, low-priced fashions to young people. Like all merchandisers, Fong has two key decisions to make: the price at which it will sell goods and the level of service it will provide. A department store may set the price of its merchandise at a relatively high level and provide a great deal of service. A discount store, on the other hand, may price its merchandise at a relatively low level and provide limited service. Fong Company is a discount merchandiser.

A list of Fong's transactions during a typical month appears on the next page. Such transactions make up the company's merchandising, or operating, cycle. Fong has to know how to record these transactions so that its financial statements give an accurate picture of the company's performance. Fong also has to know how to manage its merchandising cycle efficiently so that it has adequate cash on hand to maintain liquidity.

July 1	Sold merchandise to Pablo Lopez on credit, terms n/30, FOB shipping point, $2,100 (cost, $1,260).
2	Purchased merchandise on credit from Dorothy Company, terms n/30, FOB shipping point, $3,800.
2	Paid Custom Freight $290 for freight charges on merchandise received.
9	Purchased merchandise on credit from MNR Company, terms n/30, FOB shipping point, $3,600, including $200 freight costs paid by MNR Company.
11	Accepted from Pablo Lopez a return of merchandise, which was returned to inventory, $300 (cost, $180).
14	Returned for credit $600 of merchandise purchased on July 2.
16	Sold merchandise for cash, $1,000 (cost, $600).
22	Paid Dorothy Company for purchase of July 2 less return on July 14.
23	Received full payment from Pablo Lopez for his July 1 purchase, less return on July 11.

Managing Merchandising Businesses

LO1 Identify the management issues related to merchandising businesses.

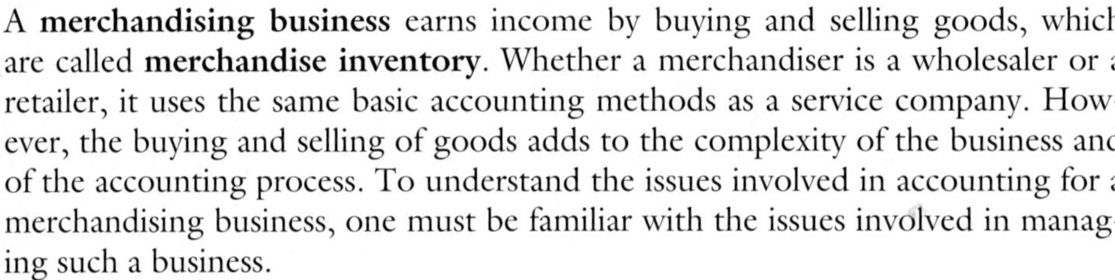

A **merchandising business** earns income by buying and selling goods, which are called **merchandise inventory**. Whether a merchandiser is a wholesaler or a retailer, it uses the same basic accounting methods as a service company. However, the buying and selling of goods adds to the complexity of the business and of the accounting process. To understand the issues involved in accounting for a merchandising business, one must be familiar with the issues involved in managing such a business.

Operating Cycle

> **Study Note**
> A company must provide financing for the average days' inventory on hand plus the average number of days to collect credit sales less the average number of days it is allowed to pay its suppliers.

Merchandising businesses engage in a series of transactions called the **operating cycle**. Figure 6-1 shows the transactions that make up this cycle. Some companies buy merchandise for cash and sell it for cash, but these companies are usually small companies, such as a produce market or a hot dog stand. Most companies buy merchandise on credit and sell it on credit, thereby engaging in the following four transactions:

1. Purchase of merchandise inventory for cash or on credit
2. Payment for purchases made on credit
3. Sales of merchandise inventory for cash or on credit
4. Collection of cash from credit sales

The first three transactions represent the time it takes to purchase inventory, sell it, and collect for it. Merchandisers must be able to do without the cash for this period of time either by relying on cash flows from other sources within the company or by borrowing. If they lack the cash to pay bills when they come due, they can be forced out of business. Thus managing cash flow is a critical concern.

The suppliers that sold the company the merchandise usually also sell on credit and thus help alleviate the cash flow problem by providing financing for a period of time before they require payment (transaction 4). However, this period is rarely as long as the operating cycle. The period between the time the supplier must be paid and the end of the operating cycle is sometimes referred to as the *cash gap*, and more formally as the financing period.

The **financing period**, illustrated in Figure 6-2, is the amount of time from the purchase of inventory until it is sold and payment is collected, less the amount

FIGURE 6-1
Cash Flows in the Operating Cycle

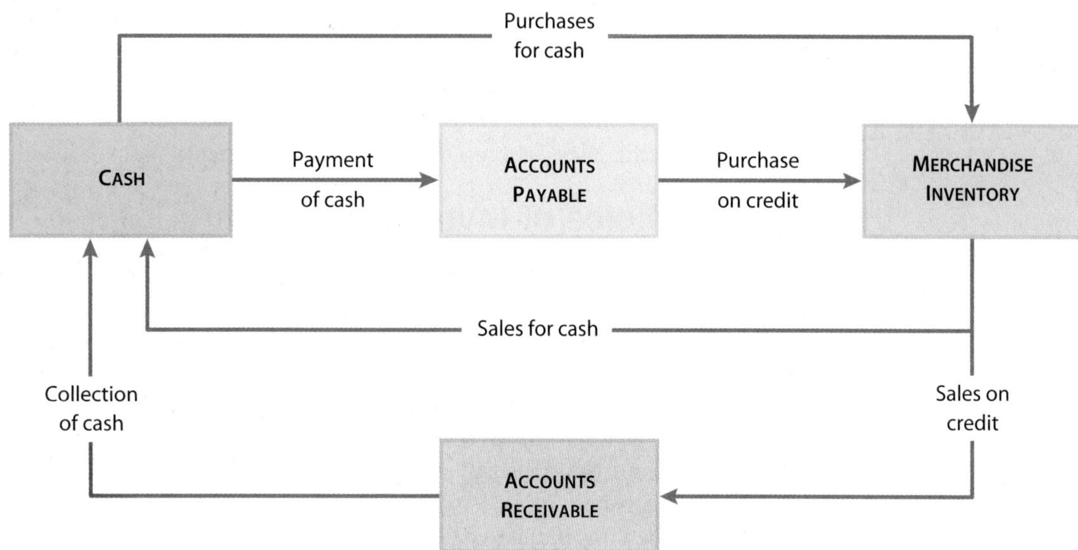

of time creditors give the company to pay for the inventory. Thus, if it takes 60 days to sell the inventory, 60 days to collect for the sale, and creditors' payment terms are 30 days, the financing period is 90 days. During the financing period, the company will be without cash from this series of transactions and will need either to have funds available internally or to borrow from a bank.

The type of merchandising operation in which a company engages can affect the financing period. For example, compare **Costco**'s financing period with that of a traditional discount store chain, **Target Corporation**:

	Target	*Costco*	*Difference*
Days' inventory on hand	56 days	31 days	(25) days
Days' receivable	34	4	(30)
Less days' payable	(59)	(31)	(28)
Financing period	**31 days**	**4 days**	**(27) days**

Costco has an advantage over Target because it holds its inventory for a shorter period before it sells it and collects receivables much faster. Its very short financing period is one of the reasons Costco can charge such low prices. Helpful ratios for calculating the three components of the financing period will be covered in subsequent chapters on inventories, receivables, and current liabilities.

By reducing its financing period, a company can improve its cash flow. Many merchandisers, including Costco, do this by selling as much as possible for cash.

FIGURE 6-2
The Financing Period

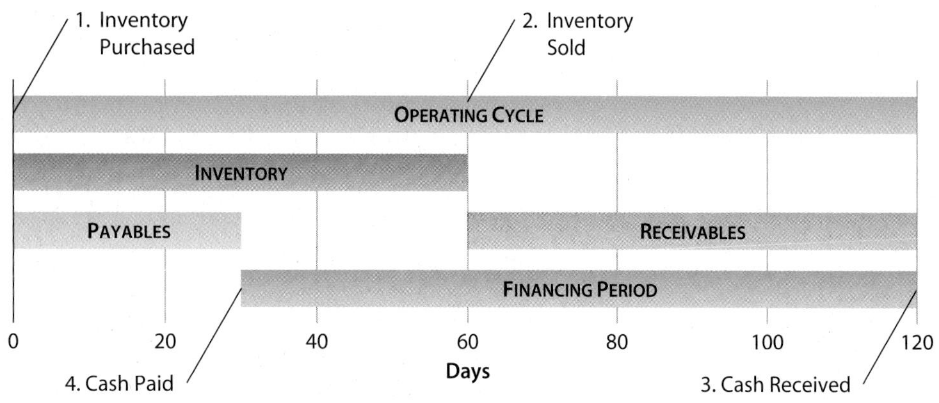

Study Note

A sale takes place when title to the goods transfers to the buyer.

Cash sales include sales made on bank *credit cards,* such as Visa or MasterCard, and on *debit cards,* which draw directly on the purchaser's bank account. They are considered cash sales because funds from them are available to the merchandiser immediately. Small retail stores may have mostly cash sales and very few credit sales, whereas large wholesale concerns may have almost all credit sales.

Choice of Inventory System

Another issue in managing a merchandising business is the choice of inventory system. Management must choose the system or combination of systems that best achieves the company's goals. The two basic systems of accounting for the many items in merchandise inventory are the perpetual inventory system and the periodic inventory system.

Study Note

Under the perpetual inventory system, the Merchandise Inventory account and the Cost of Goods Sold account are updated with every sale.

Under the **perpetual inventory system**, continuous records are kept of the quantity and, usually, the cost of individual items as they are bought and sold. Under this system, the cost of each item is recorded in the Merchandise Inventory account when it is purchased. As merchandise is sold, its cost is transferred from the Merchandise Inventory account to the Cost of Goods Sold account. Thus, at all times the balance of the Merchandise Inventory account equals the cost of goods on hand, and the balance in Cost of Goods Sold equals the cost of merchandise sold to customers.

Managers use the detailed data that the perpetual inventory system provides to respond to customers' inquiries about product availability, to order inventory more effectively and thus avoid running out of stock, and to control the costs associated with investments in inventory.

Study Note

The value of ending inventory on the balance sheet is determined by multiplying the quantity of each inventory item by its unit cost.

Under the **periodic inventory system**, the inventory not yet sold, or on hand, is counted periodically. This physical count is usually taken at the end of the accounting period. No detailed records of the inventory on hand are maintained during the accounting period. The figure for inventory on hand is accurate only on the balance sheet date. As soon as any purchases or sales are made, the inventory figure becomes a historical amount, and it remains so until the new ending inventory amount is entered at the end of the next accounting period.

Some retail and wholesale businesses use the periodic inventory system because it reduces the amount of clerical work. If a business is fairly small, management can maintain control over its inventory simply through observation or by using an offline system of cards or computer records. But for larger businesses, the lack of detailed records may lead to lost sales or high operating costs.

Because of the difficulty and expense of accounting for the purchase and sale of each item, companies that sell items of low value in high volume have traditionally used the periodic inventory system. Examples of such companies include drugstores, automobile parts stores, department stores, and discount stores. In contrast, companies that sell items that have a high unit value, such as appliances or automobiles, have tended to use the perpetual inventory system.

The distinction between high and low unit value for inventory systems has blurred considerably in recent years. Although the periodic inventory system is still widely used, computerization has led to a large increase in the use of the perpetual inventory system. It is important to note that the perpetual inventory system does not eliminate the need for a physical count of the inventory. A physical count of inventory should be taken periodically to ensure that the actual number of goods on hand matches the quantity indicated by the computer records.

Foreign Business Transactions

Most large merchandising and manufacturing firms and even many small ones transact some of their business overseas. For example, a U.S. manufacturer may expand by selling its product to foreign customers, or it may lower its product cost by buying a less expensive part from a source in another country. Such sales

FOCUS ON BUSINESS PRACTICE

How Have Bar Codes Influenced the Choice of Inventory Systems?

Most grocery stores, which traditionally used the periodic inventory system, now employ bar coding to update the physical inventory as items are sold. At the checkout counter, the cashier scans the electronic marking on each product, called a *bar code* or *universal product code* (UPC), into the cash register, which is linked to a computer that records the sale. Bar coding has become common in all types of retail companies, and in manufacturing firms and hospitals as well. It has also become a major factor in the increased use of the perpetual inventory system. Interestingly, some retail businesses now use the perpetual inventory system for keeping track of the physical flow of inventory and the periodic inventory system for preparing their financial statements.

and purchase transactions may take place in Japanese yen, British pounds, or some other foreign currency.

When an international transaction involves two different currencies, as most such transactions do, one currency has to be translated into another by using an exchange rate. As we noted earlier in the text, an *exchange rate* is the value of one currency stated in terms of another. We also noted that the values of other currencies in relation to the dollar rise and fall daily according to supply and demand. Thus, if there is a delay between the date of sale or purchase and the date of receipt of payment, the amount of cash involved in an international transaction may differ from the amount originally agreed on.

If the billing of an international sale and the payment for it are both in the domestic currency, no accounting problem arises. For example, if a U.S. maker of precision tools sells $160,000 worth of its products to a British company and bills the British company in dollars, the U.S. company will receive $160,000 when it collects payment. However, if the U.S. company bills the British company in British pounds and accepts payment in pounds, it will incur an **exchange gain or loss** if the exchange rate between dollars and pounds changes between the date of sale and the date of payment.

For example, assume that the U.S. company billed the sale of $200,000 at £100,000, reflecting an exchange rate of 2.00 (that is, $2.00 per pound) on the sale date. Now assume that by the date of payment, the exchange rate has fallen to 1.90. When the U.S. company receives its £100,000, it will be worth only $190,000 (£100,000 × $1.90 = $190,000). It will have incurred an exchange loss of $10,000 because it agreed to accept a fixed number of British pounds in payment for its products, and the value of each pound dropped before the payment was made. Had the value of the pound in relation to the dollar increased, the company would have made an exchange gain.

The same logic applies to purchases as to sales, except that the relationship of exchange gains and losses to changes in exchange rates is reversed. For example, assume that the U.S company purchases products from the British company for $200,000. If the payment is to be made in U.S. dollars, no accounting problem arises. However, if the British company expects to be paid in pounds, the U.S. company will have an exchange gain of $10,000 because it agreed to pay a fixed £100,000, and between the dates of purchase and payment, the exchange value of the pound decreased from $2.00 to $1.90. To make the £100,000 payment, the U.S. company has to expend only $190,000.

Exchange gains and losses are reported on the income statement. Because of their bearing on a company's financial performance, they are of considerable interest to managers and investors. Lack of uniformity in international accounting standards is another matter of which investors must be wary.

STOP & APPLY >

The management of SavRite Company made the decisions below. Indicate whether each decision pertains primarily to (a) cash flow management, (b) choice of inventory system, or (c) foreign transactions.

1. Decided to increase the credit terms offered to customers from 20 days to 30 days to speed up collection of accounts.
2. Decided to purchase goods made by a supplier in India.
3. Decided that sales would benefit if sales people knew the amount of each item of inventory that was on hand at any one time.
4. Decided to try to negotiate a longer time to pay suppliers than had been previously granted.

SOLUTION

1. a; 2. c; 3. b; 4. a

Terms of Sale

LO2 Describe the terms of sale related to merchandising transactions.

When goods are sold on credit, both parties should understand the amount and timing of payment as well as other terms of the purchase, such as who pays delivery charges and what warranties or rights of return apply. Sellers quote prices in different ways. Many merchants quote the price at which they expect to sell their goods. Others, particularly manufacturers and wholesalers, quote prices as a percentage (usually 30 percent or more) off their list or catalogue prices. Such a reduction is called a **trade discount.**

For example, if an article is listed at $1,000 with a trade discount of 40 percent, or $400, the seller records the sale at $600, and the buyer records the purchase at $600. The seller may raise or lower the trade discount depending on the quantity purchased. The list or catalogue price and related trade discount are used only to arrive at an agreed-on price; they do not appear in the accounting records.

> **Study Note**
> A trade discount applies to the list or catalogue price. A sales discount applies to the sales price.

Sales and Purchases Discounts

The terms of sale are usually printed on the sales invoice and thus constitute part of the sales agreement. Terms differ from industry to industry. In some industries, payment is expected in a short period of time, such as 10 or 30 days. In these cases, the invoice is marked "n/10" ("net 10") or "n/30" ("net 30"), meaning that the amount of the invoice is due either 10 days or 30 days after the invoice date. If the invoice is due 10 days after the end of the month, it is marked "n/10 eom."

In some industries, it is customary to give a discount for early payment. This discount, called a **sales discount**, is intended to increase the seller's liquidity by reducing the amount of money tied up in accounts receivable. An invoice that offers a sales discount might be labeled "2/10, n/30," which means that the buyer either can pay the invoice within 10 days of the invoice date and take a 2 percent discount or can wait 30 days and pay the full amount of the invoice. It is often advantageous for a buyer to take the discount because the saving of 2 percent over a period of 20 days (from the 11th day to the 30th day) represents an effective annual rate of 36.5 percent (365 days ÷ 20 days × 2% = 36.5%). Most companies would be better off borrowing money to take the discount. The practice of giving sales discounts has been declining because it is costly to the seller and because, from the buyer's viewpoint, the amount of the discount is usually very small in relation to the price of the purchase.

> **Study Note**
> Early collection also has the advantage of reducing the probability of a customer's defaulting.

Because it is not possible to know at the time of a sale whether the customer will pay in time to take advantage of a sales discount, the discounts are recorded only at the time the customer pays. For example, suppose Kloss Motor Company sells merchandise to a customer on September 20 for $600 on terms of 2/10, n/30. Kloss records the sale on September 20 for the full amount of $600. If the customer takes advantage of the discount by paying on or before September 30, Kloss will receive $588 in cash and will reduce its accounts receivable by $600. The difference of $12 ($600 × 0.02) will be debited to an account called *Sales Discounts*. Sales Discounts is a contra-revenue account with a normal debit balance that is deducted from sales on the income statement.

The same logic applies to **purchases discounts,** which are discounts that a buyer takes for the early payment of merchandise. For example, the buyer in the transaction described above will record the purchase on September 20 at $600. If the buyer pays on or before September 30, it will record cash paid of $588 and reduce its accounts payable by $600. The difference of $12 is recorded as a credit to an account called *Purchases Discounts*. The Purchases Discounts account reduces cost of goods sold or purchases depending on the inventory method used.

Transportation Costs

In some industries, the seller usually pays transportation costs and charges a price that includes those costs. In other industries, it is customary for the purchaser to pay transportation charges. Special terms designate whether the seller or the purchaser pays the freight charges.

FOB shipping point means that the seller places the merchandise "free on board" at the point of origin and the buyer bears the shipping costs. The title to the merchandise passes to the buyer at that point. For example, when the sales agreement for the purchase of a car says "FOB factory," the buyer must pay the freight from the factory where the car was made to wherever he or she is located, and the buyer owns the car from the time it leaves the factory. **FOB destination** means that the seller bears the transportation costs to the place where the

Shipping terms affect the financial statements. *FOB shipping point* means the buyer pays the freight charges; when relatively small, these charges are usually included in cost of goods sold on the buyer's income statement. *FOB destination* means the seller pays the freight charges; they are included in selling expenses on the seller's income statement.

Courtesy of Borilov/Dreamstime LLC.

merchandise is delivered. The seller retains title until the merchandise reaches its destination and usually prepays the shipping costs, in which case the buyer makes no accounting entry for freight. The effects of these special shipping terms are summarized as follows:

Shipping Term	*Where Title Passes*	*Who Pays the Cost of Transportation*
FOB shipping point	At origin	Buyer
FOB destination	At destination	Seller

When the buyer pays the transportation charge, it is called **freight-in,** and it is added to the cost of merchandise purchased. Thus, freight-in increases the buyer's cost of merchandise inventory, as well as the cost of goods sold after the product is sold. When freight-in is a relatively small amount, most companies include the cost in the cost of goods sold on the income statement rather than going to the trouble of allocating part of it to merchandise inventory.

Shipping terms affect the financial statements. *FOB shipping point* means the buyer pays the freight charges; when relatively small, these charges are usually included in cost of goods sold on the buyer's income statement. *FOB destination* means the seller pays the freight charges; they are included in selling expenses on the seller's income statement. When the seller pays the transportation charge, it is called **delivery expense**, or *freight-out.* Because the seller incurs this cost to facilitate the sale of its product, the cost is included in selling expenses on the income statement.

Terms of Debit and Credit Card Sales

Many retailers allow customers to use debit or credit cards to charge their purchases. Debit cards deduct directly from a person's bank account, whereas a credit card allows for payment later. Five of the most widely used credit cards are American Express, Discover Card, Diners Club, MasterCard, and Visa. The customer establishes credit with the lender (the credit card issuer) and receives a plastic card to use in making charges. If a seller accepts the card, the customer signs an invoice at the time of the sale. The sale is communicated to the seller's bank, resulting in a cash deposit in the seller's bank account. Thus, the seller does not have to establish the customer's credit, collect from the customer, or tie up money in accounts receivable. As payment, the lender, rather than paying the total amount of the credit card sales, takes a discount of 2 to 6 percent. The discount is a selling expense for the merchandiser. For example, if a restaurant makes sales of $1,000 on Visa credit cards and Visa takes a 4 percent discount on the sales, the restaurant would record Cash in the amount of $960 and Credit Card Expense in the amount of $40.

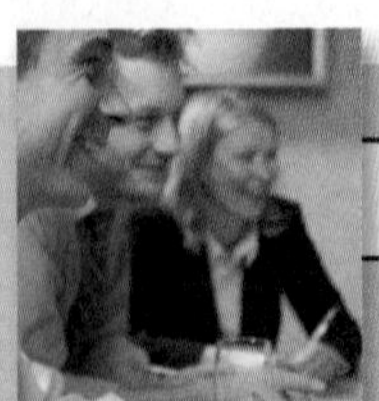

FOCUS ON BUSINESS PRACTICE

Are We Becoming a Cashless Society?

Are checks and cash obsolete? Do you "swipe it"? Most Americans do. About 75 percent of Americans use credit or debit cards rather than checks. Debit cards generate more than 16 billion transactions per year. It is estimated that electronic payments totaling more than $1 trillion outnumber the roughly 40 billion checks written each year. Consumers like the convenience. Retailers, like **McDonald's** and **Starbucks**, like the cards, even though there are fees, because use of cards usually increases the amount of sales.[1]

STOP & APPLY >

A local company sells refrigerators that it buys from the manufacturer.

a. The manufacturer sets a list or catalogue price of $1,200 for a refrigerator. The manufacturer offers its dealers a 40 percent trade discount.

b. The manufacturer sells the machine under terms of FOB shipping point. The cost of shipping is $120.

c. The manufacturer offers a sales discount of 2/10, n/30. Sales discounts do not apply to shipping costs.

What is the net cost of the refrigerator to the dealer, assuming it is paid for within 10 days of purchase?

SOLUTION

a. $1,200 − ($1,200 × 0.40) = $720

b. $720 + $120 = $840

c. $840 − ($720 × 0.02) = $825.60

Perpetual Inventory System

LO3 Prepare an income statement and record merchandising transactions under the perpetual inventory system.

Exhibit 6-1 shows how an income statement appears when a company uses the perpetual inventory system. The focal point of the statement is cost of goods sold, which is deducted from net sales to arrive at gross margin. Under the perpetual inventory system, the Merchandise Inventory and Cost of Goods Sold accounts are continually updated during the accounting period as purchases, sales, and other inventory transactions that affect these accounts occur.

Purchases of Merchandise

Figure 6-3 shows how transactions involving purchases of merchandise are recorded under the perpetual inventory system. As you can see, the focus of these journal entries is Accounts Payable. In this section, we present a summary of the entries made for merchandise purchases. (For a comparison of complete journal entries made under the perpetual and periodic inventory systems, see the Review Problem in this chapter.)

EXHIBIT 6-1
Income Statement Under the Perpetual Inventory System

Kloss Motor Company
Income Statement
For the Year Ended December 31, 2010

Net sales	$957,300
Cost of goods sold*	525,440
Gross margin	$431,860
Operating expenses	313,936
Net income	$117,924

*Freight-in has been included in cost of goods sold.

Study Note

On the income statement, freight-in is included as part of cost of goods sold, and delivery expense (freight-out) is included as an operating (selling) expense.

FIGURE 6-3 Recording Purchase Transactions Under the Perpetual Inventory System

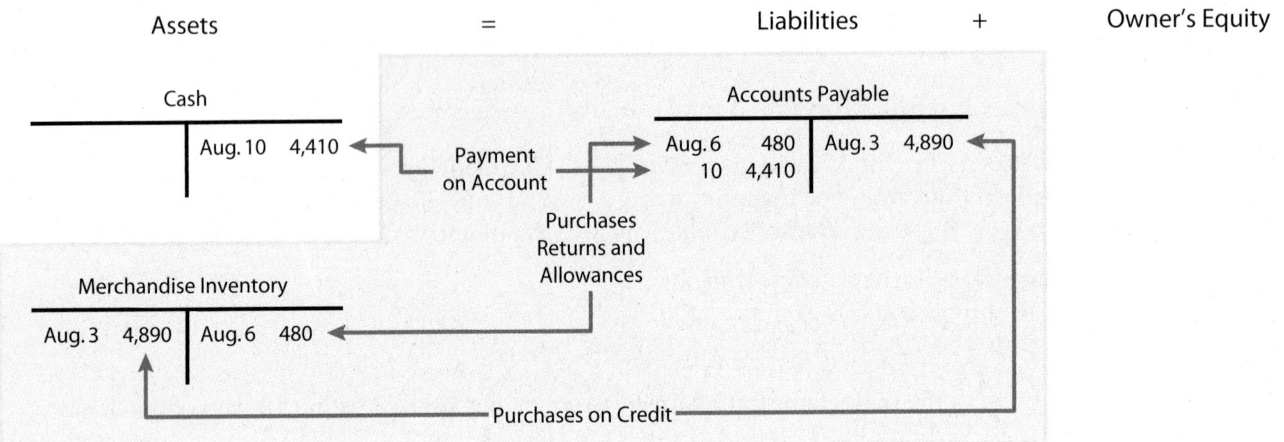

Study Note

The Merchandise Inventory account increases when a purchase is made.

Purchases on Credit

Aug. 3: Received merchandise purchased on credit, invoice dated Aug. 1, terms n/10, $4,890.

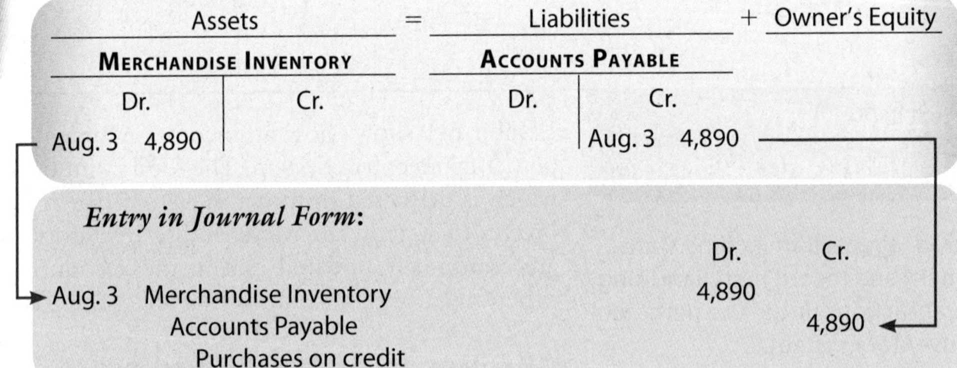

Comment: Under the perpetual inventory system, the cost of merchandise is recorded in the Merchandise Inventory account at the time of purchase. In the transaction described here, payment is due ten days from the invoice date. If an invoice includes a charge for shipping or if shipping is billed separately, it should be debited to Freight-In.

Purchases Returns and Allowances

Aug. 6: Returned part of merchandise received on Aug. 3 for credit, $480.

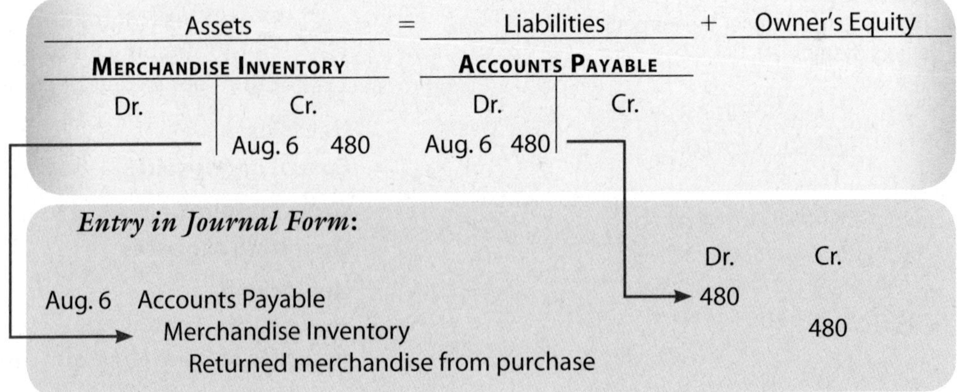

Comment: Under the perpetual inventory system, when a buyer is allowed to return all or part of a purchase or is given an allowance—a reduction in the amount to be paid—Merchandise Inventory is reduced, as is Accounts Payable.

Payments on Account

Aug. 10: Paid amount in full due for the purchase of Aug. 3, part of which was returned on Aug. 6, $4,410.

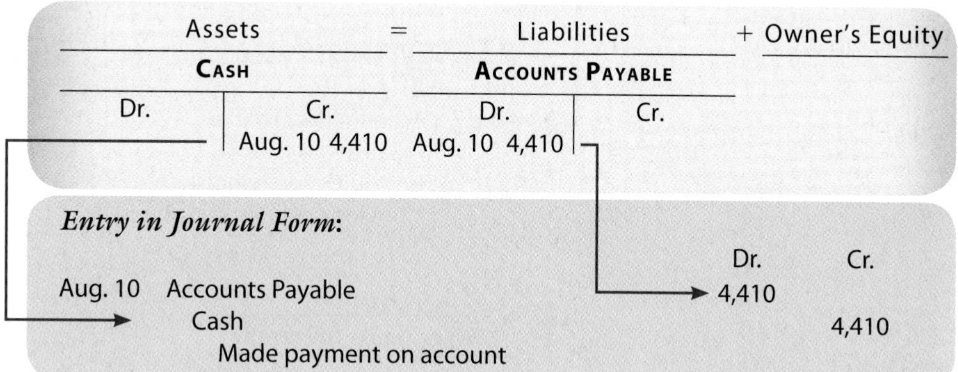

Comment: Payment is made for the net amount due of $4,410 ($4,890 − $480).

Study Note

The Cost of Goods Sold account is increased and the Merchandise Inventory account is decreased when a sale is made.

Sales of Merchandise

Figure 6-4 shows how transactions involving sales of merchandise are recorded under the perpetual inventory system. These transactions involve several accounts, including Cash, Accounts Receivable, Merchandise Inventory, Sales Returns and Allowances, and Cost of Goods Sold.

FIGURE 6-4 Recording Sales Transactions Under the Perpetual Inventory System

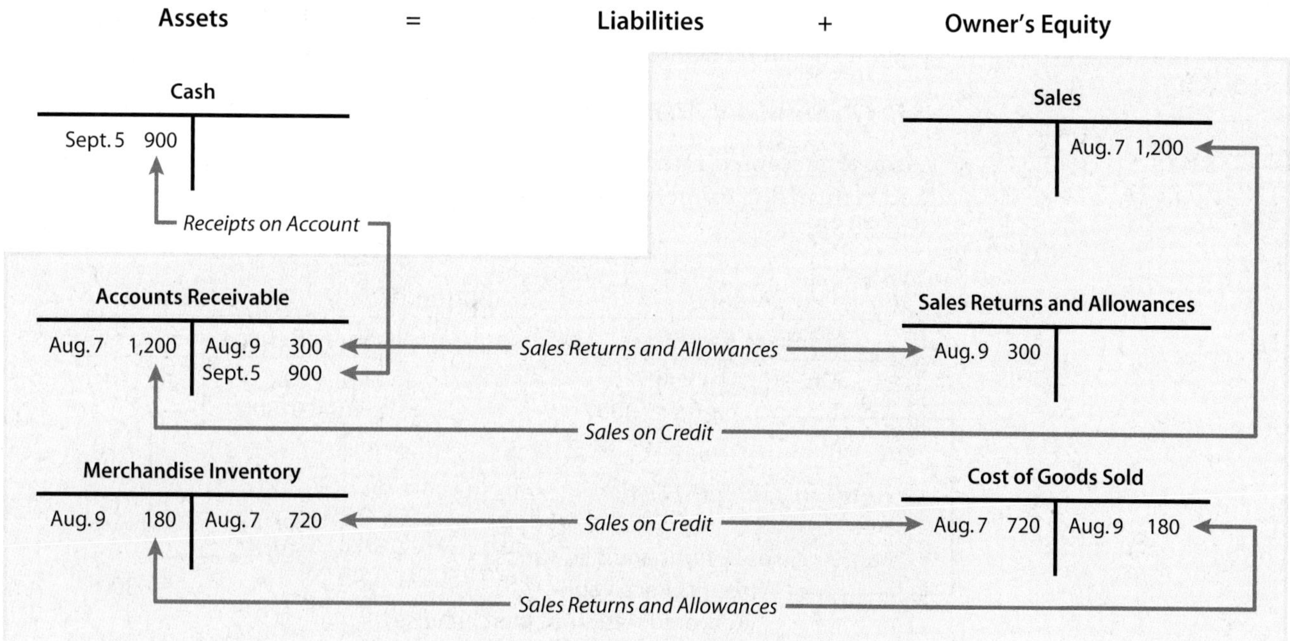

Sales on Credit

Aug. 7: Sold merchandise on credit, terms n/30, FOB destination, $1,200; the cost of the merchandise was $720.

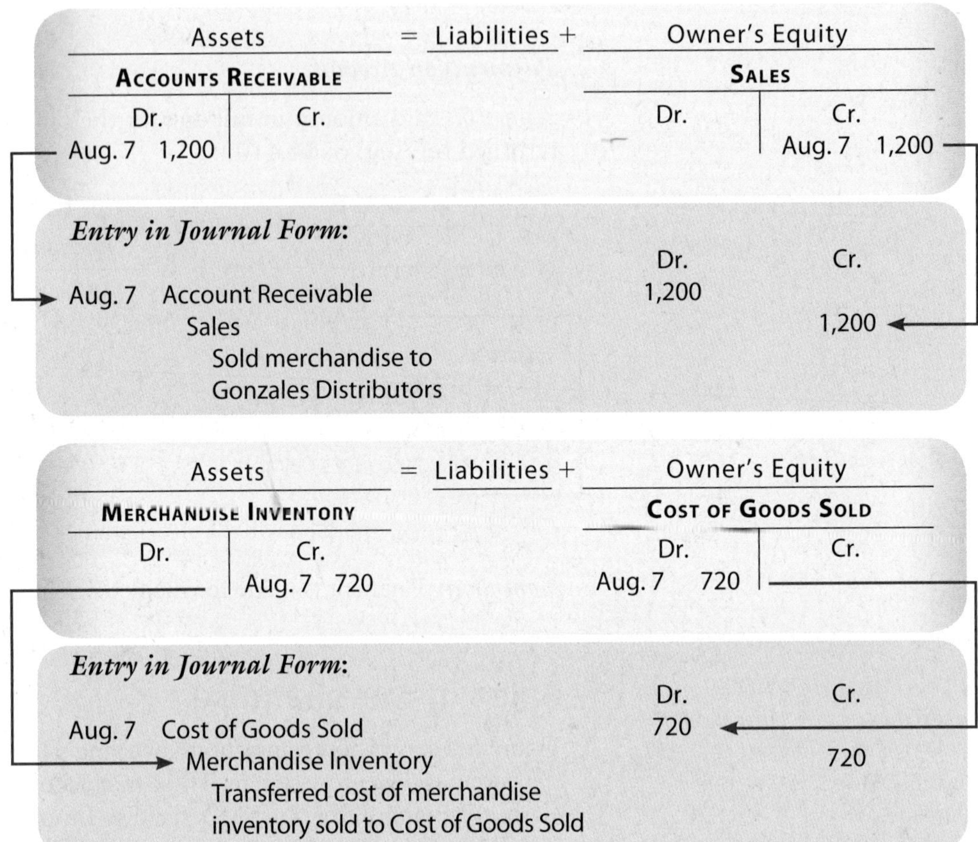

Comment: Under the perpetual inventory system, sales always require two entries, as shown in Figure 6-4. First, the sale is recorded by increasing Accounts Receivable and Sales. Second, Cost of Goods Sold is updated by a transfer from Merchandise Inventory. In the case of cash sales, Cash rather than Accounts Receivable is debited for the amount of the sale. If the seller pays for the shipping, it should be debited to Delivery Expense.

Sales Returns and Allowances

Aug. 9: Accepted return of part of merchandise sold on Aug. 7 for full credit and returned it to merchandise inventory, $300; the cost of the merchandise was $180.

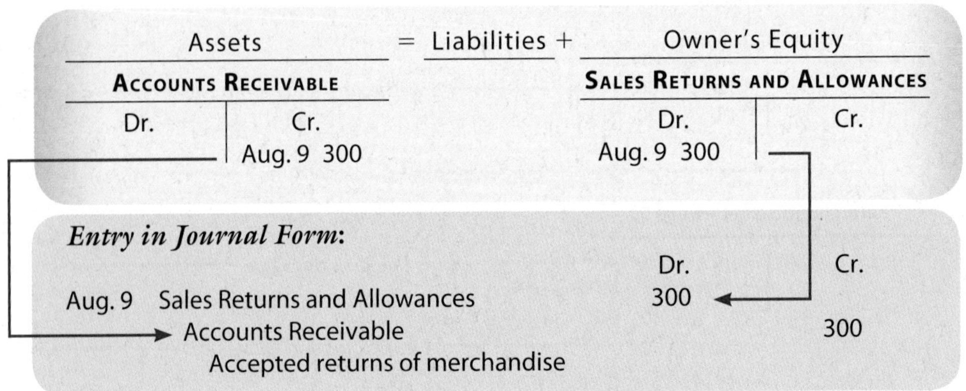

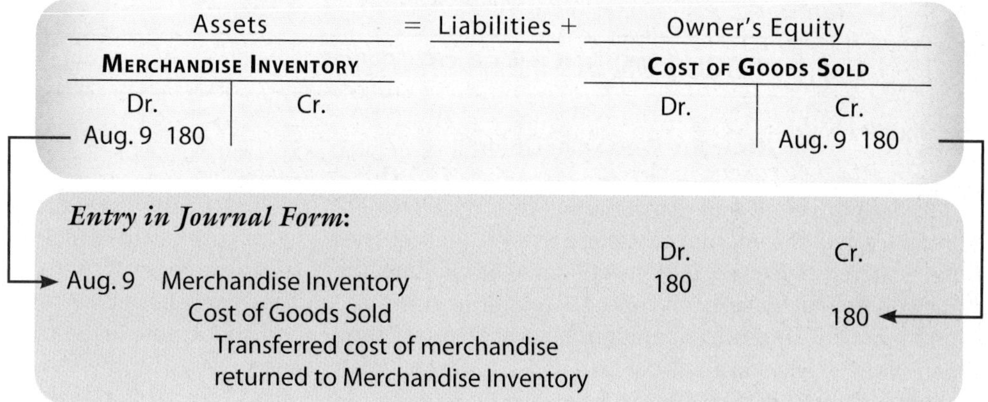

Study Note

Because the Sales account is established with a credit, its contra account, Sales Returns and Allowances, is established with a debit.

Comment: Under the perpetual inventory system, when a seller allows the buyer to return all or part of a sale or gives an allowance—a reduction in amount—two entries are again necessary. First, the original sale is reversed by reducing Accounts Receivable and debiting Sales Returns and Allowances. The **Sales Returns and Allowances** account gives management a readily available measure of unsatisfactory products and dissatisfied customers. It is a contra-revenue account with a normal debit balance and is deducted from sales on the income statement. Second, the cost of the merchandise must also be transferred from the Cost of Goods Sold account back into the Merchandise Inventory account. If the company makes an allowance instead of accepting a return, or if the merchandise cannot be returned to inventory and resold, this transfer is not made.

Receipts on Account

Sept. 5: Collected in full for sale of merchandise on Aug. 7, less the return on Aug. 9, $900.

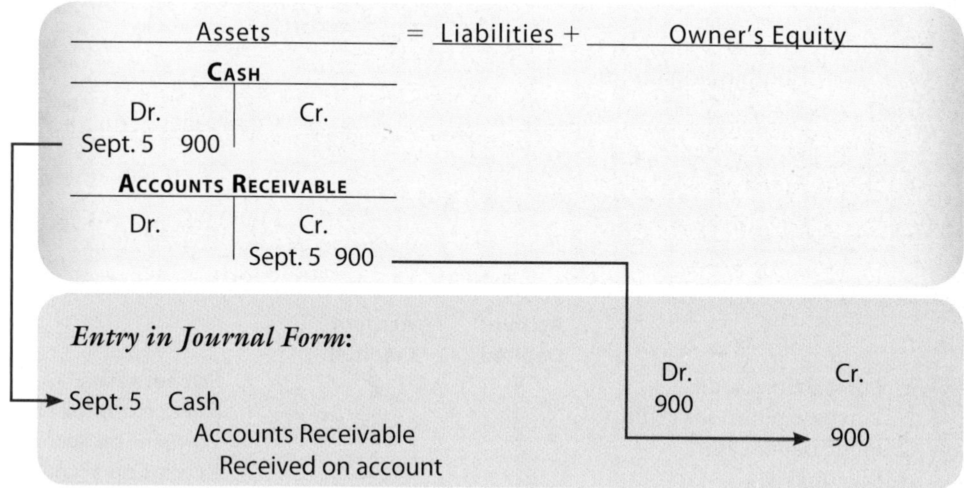

Comment: Collection is made for the net amount due of $900 ($1,200 − $300).

FOCUS ON BUSINESS PRACTICE

How Are Web Sales Doing?

In spite of the demise of many Internet retailers, merchandise sales over the Internet continue to thrive. Internet sales are expected to exceed $150 million in 2008.[2] To date, the companies that have been most successful in using the Internet to enhance their operations have been established mail-order retailers like **Lands' End** and **L.L. Bean**. Other retailers, such as **Office Depot**, have also benefited from their use of the Internet. Office Depot, which focuses primarily on business-to-business Internet sales, has set up customized web pages for tens of thousands of corporate clients. These websites allow customers to make online purchases and check store inventories. Although Internet transactions are recorded in the same way as on-site transactions, the technology adds a level of complexity to the transactions.

STOP & APPLY >

The numbered items that follow are account titles, and the lettered items are types of merchandising transactions. For each transaction, indicate which accounts are debited or credited by placing the account numbers in the appropriate columns.

1. Cash
2. Accounts Receivable
3. Merchandise Inventory
4. Accounts Payable
5. Sales
6. Sales Returns and Allowances
7. Cost of Goods Sold

	Account Debited	Account Credited		Account Debited	Account Credited
a. Purchase on credit	___	___	e. Sale for cash	___	___
b. Purchase return for credit	___	___	f. Sales return for credit	___	___
c. Purchase for cash	___	___	g. Payment on account	___	___
d. Sale on credit	___	___	h. Receipt on account	___	___

SOLUTION

	Account Debited	Account Credited		Account Debited	Account Credited
a. Purchase on credit	3	4	e. Sale for cash	1,7	3,5
b. Purchase return for credit	4	3	f. Sales return for credit	3,6	2,7
c. Purchase for cash	3	1	g. Payment on account	4	1
d. Sale on credit	2,7	3,5	h. Receipt on account	1	2

Periodic Inventory System

LO4 Prepare an income statement and record merchandising transactions under the periodic inventory system.

Exhibit 6-2 shows how an income statement appears when a company uses the periodic inventory system. A major feature of this statement is the computation of cost of goods sold. Cost of goods sold must be computed on the income statement because it is not updated for purchases, sales, and other transactions during the accounting period, as it is under the perpetual inventory system. Figure 6-5 illustrates the components of cost of goods sold.

It is important to distinguish between goods available for sale and cost of goods sold. **Cost of goods available for sale** is the total cost of merchandise that *could* be sold in the accounting period. Cost of goods sold is the cost of merchandise *actually* sold. The difference between the two numbers is the amount *not* sold, or the ending merchandise inventory. Cost of goods available for sale is the sum of the following two factors:

- The amount of merchandise on hand at the beginning of accounting period or beginning inventory.
- The net purchases during the period. (Net purchases consist of total purchases less any deductions such as purchases returns and allowances and freight-in.)

As you can see in Exhibit 6-2, Kloss Motor Company has cost of goods available for sale during the period of $718,640 ($211,200 + $507,440). The ending inventory of $193,200 is deducted from this figure to determine the cost of goods sold. Thus, the company's cost of goods sold is $525,440 ($718,640 − $193,200). Figure 6-5 illustrates these relationships in visual form.

An important component of the cost of goods sold section is **net cost of purchases.** As you can see in the income statement in Exhibit 6-2, net cost of purchases is the sum of net purchases and freight-in. **Net purchases** equal total purchases less any deductions, such as purchases returns and allowances and any discounts allowed by suppliers for early payment. Freight-in is added to net purchases because transportation charges are a necessary cost of receiving merchandise for sale.

EXHIBIT 6-2
Income Statement Under the Periodic Inventory System

Kloss Motor Company
Income Statement
For the Year Ended December 31, 2010

Net sales			$957,300
Cost of goods sold			
Merchandise inventory, December 31, 2009		$211,200	
Purchases	$505,600		
Less purchases returns and allowances	31,104		
Net purchases	$474,496		
Freight-in	32,944		
Net cost of purchases		507,440	
Cost of goods available for sale		$718,640	
Less merchandise inventory, December 31, 2010		193,200	
Cost of goods sold			525,440
Gross margin			$431,860
Operating expenses			313,936
Net income			$117,924

Study Note

Most published financial statements are condensed, eliminating the detail shown here under cost of goods sold.

FIGURE 6-5
The Components of Cost of Goods Sold

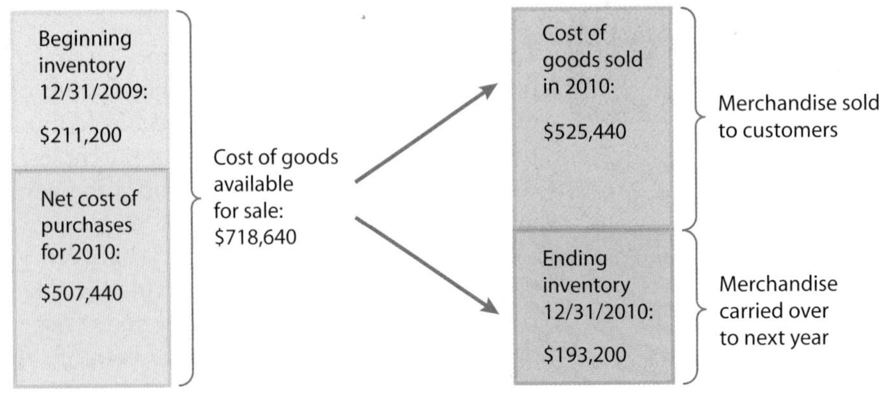

Purchases of Merchandise

Figure 6-6 shows how transactions involving purchases of merchandise are recorded under the periodic inventory system. A primary difference between the perpetual and periodic inventory systems is that in the perpetual inventory system, the Merchandise Inventory account is adjusted each time a purchase, sale, or other inventory transaction occurs, whereas in the periodic inventory system, the Merchandise Inventory account stays at its beginning balance until the physical inventory is recorded at the end of the period. The periodic system uses a Purchases account to accumulate purchases during an accounting period and a Purchases Returns and Allowances account to accumulate returns of and allowances on purchases.

Study Note

Purchases accounts and Purchases Returns and Allowances accounts are used only in conjunction with a periodic inventory system.

We will now illustrate how Kloss Motor Company would record purchase transactions under the periodic inventory system.

Purchases on Credit

Study Note

Under the periodic inventory system, the Purchases account increases when a company makes a purchase.

Aug. 3: Received merchandise purchased on credit, invoice dated Aug. 1, terms n/10, $4,890.

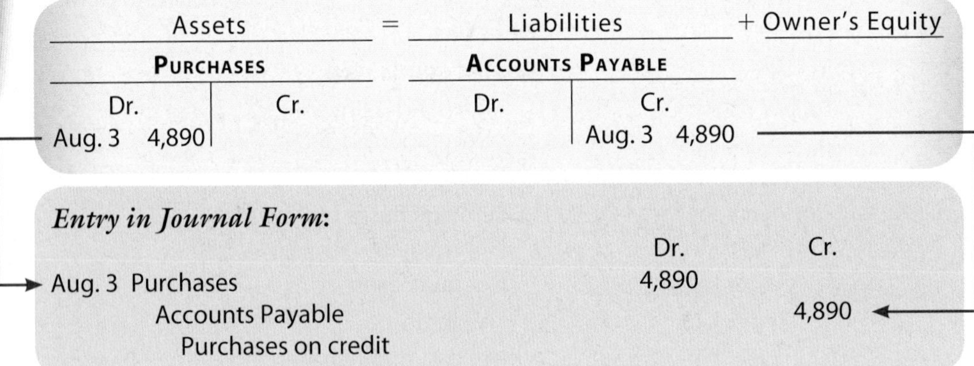

Comment: Under the periodic inventory system, the cost of merchandise is recorded in the **Purchases account** at the time of purchase. This account is a temporary one used only with the periodic inventory system. Its sole purpose is to accumulate the total cost of merchandise purchased for resale during an accounting period. (Purchases of other assets, such as equipment, are recorded in the appropriate asset account, not in the Purchases account.) The Purchases account does not indicate whether merchandise has been sold or is still on hand.

FIGURE 6-6 Recording Purchase Transactions Under the Periodic Inventory System

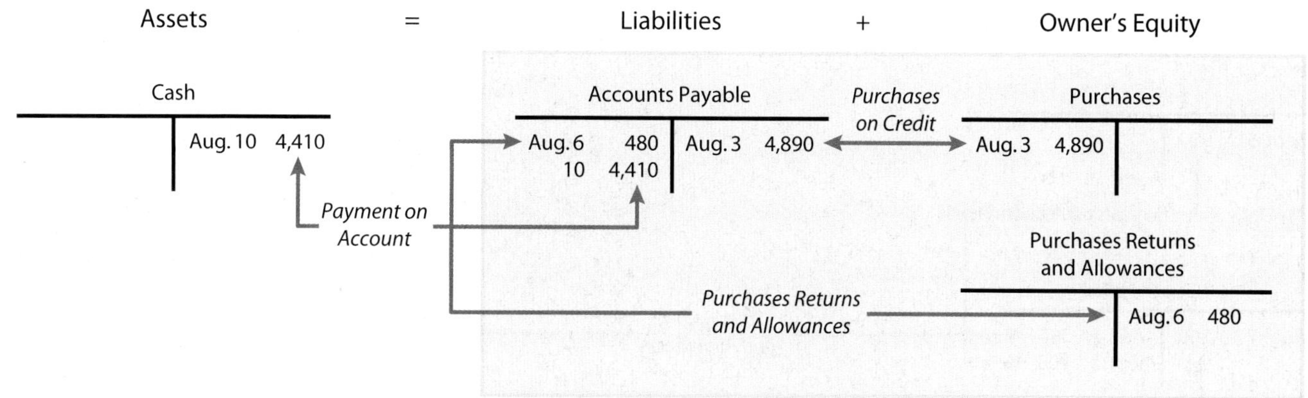

Purchases Returns and Allowances

Aug. 6: Returned part of merchandise received on Aug. 3 for credit, $480.

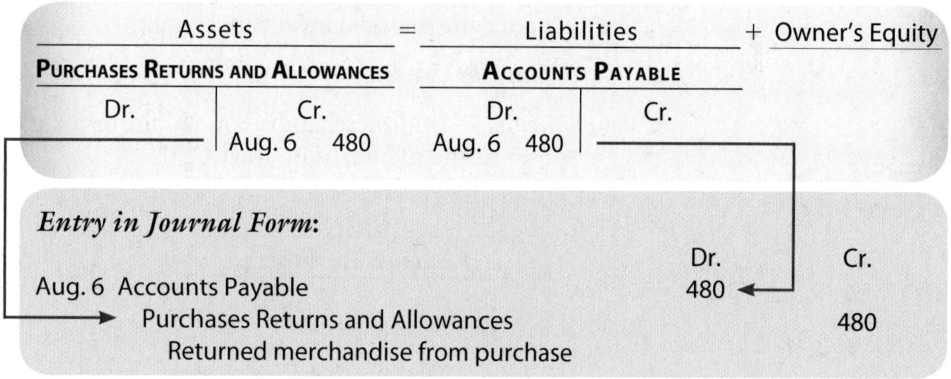

Comment: Under the periodic inventory system, the amount of a return or allowance is recorded in the **Purchases Returns and Allowances account**. This account is a contra-purchases account with a normal credit balance, and it is deducted from purchases on the income statement. Accounts Payable is also reduced.

Payments on Account

Aug. 10: Paid amount in full due for the purchase of Aug. 3, part of which was returned on Aug. 6, $4,410.

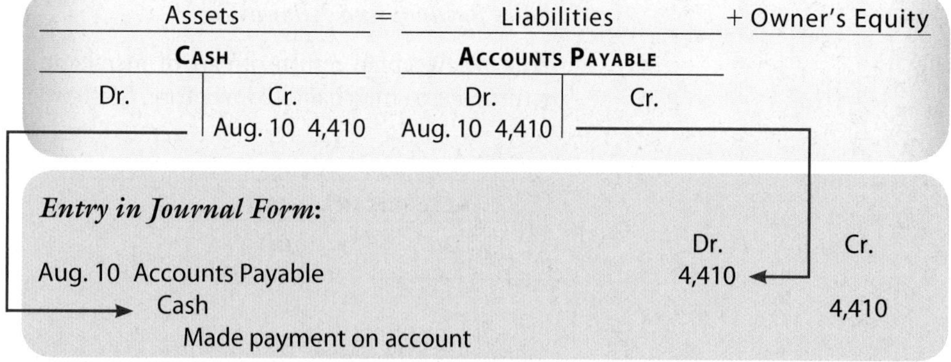

Comment: Payment is made for the net amount due of $4,410 ($4,890 − $480).

FIGURE 6-7 Recording Sales Transactions Under the Periodic Inventory System

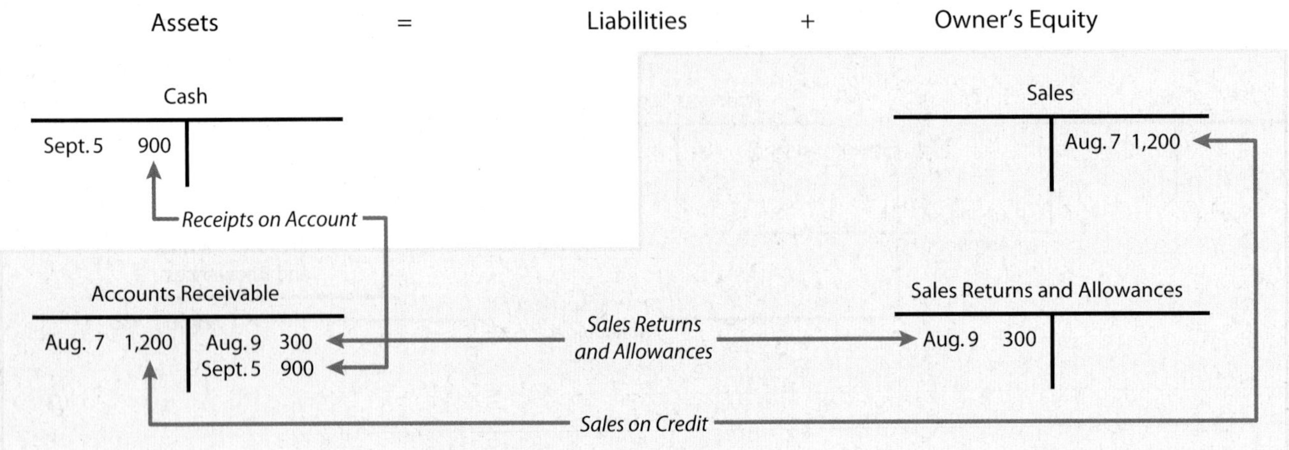

Sales of Merchandise

Figure 6-7 shows how transactions involving sales of merchandise are recorded under the periodic inventory system.

Sales on Credit

Aug. 7: Sold merchandise on credit, terms n/30, FOB destination, $1,200; the cost of the merchandise was $720.

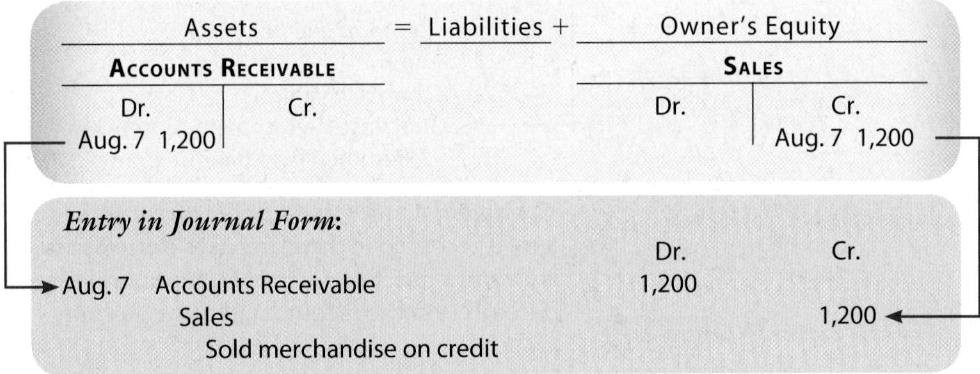

Comment: As shown in Figure 6-7, under the periodic inventory system, sales require only one entry to increase Sales and Accounts Receivable. In the case of cash sales, Cash rather than Accounts Receivable is debited for the amount of the sale. If the seller pays for the shipping, the amount should be debited to Delivery Expense.

Sales Returns and Allowances

Aug. 9: Accepted return of part of merchandise sold on Aug. 7 for full credit and returned it to merchandise inventory, $300; the cost of the merchandise was $180.

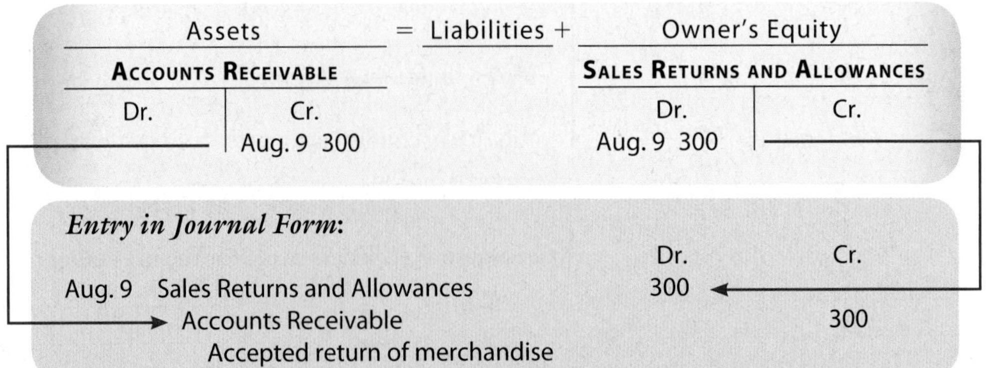

Comment: Under the periodic inventory system, when a seller allows the buyer to return all or part of a sale or gives an allowance, only one entry is needed to reduce Accounts Receivable and debit Sales Returns and Allowances. The Sales Returns and Allowances account is a contra-revenue account with a normal debit balance and is deducted from sales on the income statement.

Receipts on Account

Sept. 5: Collected in full for sale of merchandise on Aug. 7, less the return on Aug. 9, $900.

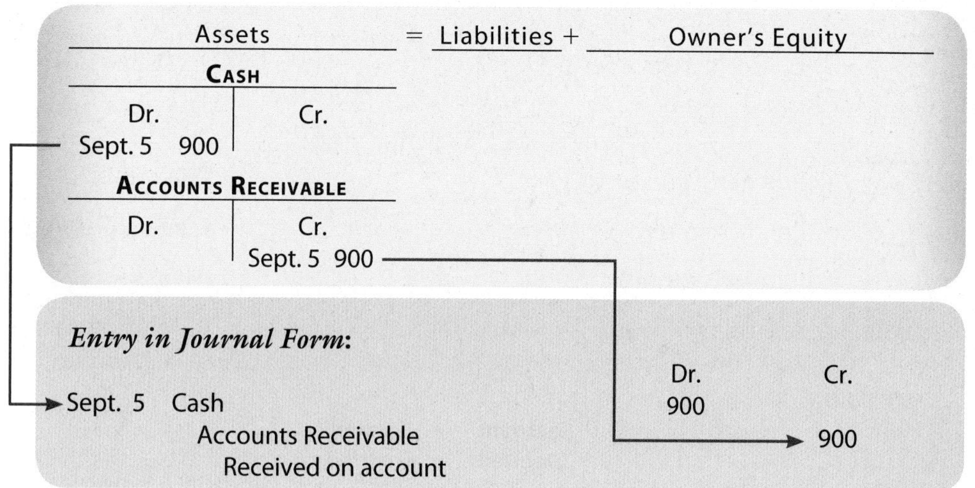

Comment: Collection is made for the net amount due of $900 ($1,200 – $300).

FOCUS ON BUSINESS PRACTICE

Are Sales Returns Worth Accounting For?

Some industries routinely have a high percentage of sales returns. More than 6 percent of all nonfood items sold in stores are eventually returned to vendors. This amounts to over $100 billion a year, or more than the gross national product of two-thirds of the world's nations.[3] Book publishers like **Simon & Schuster** often have returns as high as 30 to 50 percent because to gain the attention of potential buyers, they must distribute large numbers of copies to many outlets. Magazine publishers like **AOL Time Warner** expect to sell no more than 35 to 38 percent of the magazines they send to newsstands and other outlets.[4] In all these businesses, it pays management to scrutinize the Sales Returns and Allowances account for ways to reduce returns and increase profitability.

STOP & APPLY >

The numbered items below are account titles, and the lettered items are types of merchandising transactions. For each transaction, indicate which accounts are debited or credited by placing the account numbers in the appropriate columns.

1. Cash
2. Accounts Receivable
3. Merchandise Inventory
4. Accounts Payable
5. Sales
6. Sales Returns and Allowances
7. Purchases
8. Purchases Returns and Allowances

	Account Debited	Account Credited		Account Debited	Account Credited
a. Purchase on credit	___	___	e. Sale for cash	___	___
b. Purchase return for credit	___	___	f. Sales return for credit	___	___
c. Purchase for cash	___	___	g. Payment on account	___	___
d. Sale on credit	___	___	h. Receipt on account	___	___

SOLUTION

	Account Debited	Account Credited		Account Debited	Account Credited
a. Purchase on credit	7	4	e. Sale for cash	1	5
b. Purchase return for credit	4	8	f. Sales return for credit	6	2
c. Purchase for cash	7	1	g. Payment on account	4	1
d. Sale on credit	2	5	h. Receipt on account	1	2

▸ FONG COMPANY: REVIEW PROBLEM

In the chapter's opening Decision Point Fong Company, a merchandiser, engaged in several transactions shown in the Financial Highlights and faced these questions:

- How can merchandising transactions be recorded to reflect the company's performance?
- How can the company efficiently manage its cycle of merchandising operations?

Merchandising Transactions
LO2 LO3

Required

1. Record the transactions listed in the Decision Point in journal form, assuming that Fong Company uses (a) the perpetual inventory system and (b) the periodic inventory system.
2. User insight: Discuss how Fong Company can manage its operating cycle so that it has adequate cash to maintain liquidity.

Answers to Review Problem

1(a) and (b). Transactions recorded in journal form (accounts that differ under the two systems are in bold type)

	A	B	C	D	E	F	G	H	I	J	K	L	M	N
1	**1. Perpetual Inventory System**								**2. Periodic Inventory System**					
2	July	1		Accounts Receivable			2,100			Accounts Receivable			2,100	
3					Sales			2,100			Sales			2,100
4						Sold merchandise on						Sold merchandise on		
5						account to Pablo Lopez,						account to Pablo Lopez,		
6						terms n/30, FOB shipping						terms n/30, FOB shipping		
7						point						point		
8		1		**Cost of Goods Sold**			1,260							
9					**Merchandise Inventory**			1,260						
10						Transferred cost of								
11						merchandise sold to Cost								
12						of Goods Sold account								
13		2		**Merchandise Inventory**			3,800			**Purchases**			3,800	
14					Accounts Payable			3,800			Accounts Payable			3,800
15						Purchased merchandise						Purchased merchandise		
16						on account from Dorothy						on account from Dorothy		
17						Company, terms n/30, FOB						Company, terms n/30, FOB		
18						shipping point						shipping point		
19		2		Freight-In			290			Freight-In			290	
20					Cash			290			Cash			290
21						Paid freight on previous						Paid freight on previous		
22						purchase						purchase		
23		9		**Merchandise Inventory**			3,400			**Purchases**			3,400	
24				Freight-In			200			Freight-In			200	
25					Accounts Payable			3,600			Accounts Payable			3,600
26						Purchased merchandise on						Purchased merchandise on		
27						account from MNR Company,						account from MNR Company,		
28						terms n/30, FOB shipping						terms n/30, FOB shipping		
29						point, freight paid by supplier						point, freight paid by supplier		
30		11		Sales Returns and Allowances			300			Sales Returns and Allowances			300	
31					Accounts Receivable			300			Accounts Receivable			300
32						Accepted return of						Accepted return of		
33						merchandise from Pablo						merchandise from Pablo		
34						Lopez						Lopez		

(continued)

	A	B	C	D	E	F	G	H	I	J	K	L	M	N
1	**1. Perpetual Inventory System**								**2. Periodic Inventory System**					
2	July	11		**Merchandise Inventory**			180							
3					**Cost of Goods Sold**			180						
4						Transferred cost of								
5						merchandise returned to								
6						Merchandise Inventory								
7						account								
8		14		Accounts Payable			600			Accounts Payable			600	
9					**Merchandise Inventory**			600			**Purchases Returns and Allowances**			600
10						Returned portion of						Returned portion of		
11						merchandise purchased						merchandise purchased		
12						from Dorothy Company						from Dorothy Company		
13		16		Cash			1,000			Cash			1,000	
14					Sales			1,000			Sales			1,000
15						Sold merchandise for cash						Sold merchandise for cash		
16		16		**Cost of Goods Sold**			600							
17					**Merchandise Inventory**			600						
18						Transferred cost of								
19						merchandise sold to Cost of								
20						Goods Sold account								
21		22		Accounts Payable			3,200			Accounts Payable			3,200	
22					Cash			3,200			Cash			3,200
23						Made payment on account to						Made payment on account to		
24						Dorothy Company						Dorothy Company		
25						$3,800 − $600 = $3,200						$3,800 − $600 = $3,200		
26		23		Cash			1,800			Cash			1,800	
27					Accounts Receivable			1,800			Accounts Receivable			1,800
28						Received payment on						Received payment on		
29						account from Pablo Lopez						account from Pablo Lopez		
30						$2,100 − $300 = $1,800						$2,100 − $300 = $1,800		

2. Cycle of merchandising transactions discussed

Fong engages in all parts of the merchandising cycle. It buys goods on credit, which gives it time to carry the goods in inventory until customers buy them. It sells the goods both for cash and on credit. When it sells on credit, it must wait to collect payment. Thus, the company must arrange for short-term financing to ensure that it has enough cash on hand to maintain liquidity.

& REVIEW >

LO1 Identify the management issues related to merchandising businesses.

Merchandising companies differ from service companies in that they earn income by buying and selling goods. The buying and selling of goods adds to the complexity of the business and raises three issues that management must address. First, the series of transactions in which merchandising companies engage (the operating cycle) requires careful cash flow management. Second, management must choose whether to use the perpetual or the periodic inventory system. Third, if a company has international transactions, it must deal with changing exchange rates.

LO2 Describe the terms of sale related to merchandising transactions.

A trade discount is a reduction from the list or catalogue price of a product. A sales discount is a discount given for early payment of a sale on credit. Terms of 2/10, n/30 mean that the buyer can take a 2 percent discount if the invoice is paid within 10 days of the invoice date. Otherwise, the buyer is obligated to pay the full amount in 30 days. Discounts on sales are recorded in the Sales Discounts account, and discounts on purchases are recorded in the Purchases Discounts account. FOB shipping point means that the buyer bears the cost of transportation and that title to the goods passes to the buyer at the shipping origin. FOB destination means that the seller bears the cost of transportation and that title does not pass to the buyer until the goods reach their destination. To the seller, debit and credit card sales are similar to cash sales.

LO3 Prepare an income statement and record merchandising transactions under the perpetual inventory system.

Under the perpetual inventory system, the Merchandise Inventory account is continuously adjusted by entering purchases, sales, and other inventory transactions as they occur. Purchases increase the Merchandise Inventory account, and purchases returns decrease it. As goods are sold, their cost is transferred from the Merchandise Inventory account to the Cost of Goods Sold account.

LO4 Prepare an income statement and record merchandising transactions under the periodic inventory system.

When the periodic inventory system is used, the cost of goods sold section of the income statement must include the following elements:

Purchases − Purchases Returns and Allowances + Freight-in = Net cost of Purchases

Beginning Merchandise Inventory + Net Cost of Purchases = Cost of Goods Available for Sale

Cost of Goods Available for Sale − Ending Merchandise Inventory = Cost of Goods Sold

Under the periodic inventory system, the Merchandise Inventory account stays at the beginning level until the physical inventory is recorded at the end of the accounting period. A Purchases account is used to accumulate purchases of merchandise during the accounting period, and a Purchases Returns and Allowances account is used to accumulate returns of purchases and allowances on purchases.

REVIEW of Concepts and Terminology

The following concepts and terms were introduced in this chapter:

Cost of goods available for sale 281 (LO4)
Delivery expense 274 (LO2)
Exchange gain or loss 271 (LO1)
Financing period 268 (LO1)
FOB destination 273 (LO2)
FOB shipping point 273 (LO2)
Freight-in 274 (LO2)
Merchandise inventory 268 (LO1)
Merchandising business 268 (LO1)
Net cost of purchases 281 (LO4)
Net purchases 281 (LO4)
Operating cycle 268 (LO1)
Periodic inventory system 270 (LO1)
Perpetual inventory system 270 (LO1)
Purchases account 282 (LO4)
Purchases discounts 273 (LO2)
Purchases Returns and Allowances account 283 (LO4)
Sales discount 272 (LO2)
Sales Returns and Allowances account 279 (LO3)
Trade discount 272 (LO2)

CHAPTER ASSIGNMENTS

BUILDING Your Basic Knowledge and Skills

Short Exercises

LO1 Identification of Management Issues

SE 1. Identify each of the following decisions as most directly related to (a) cash flow management, (b) choice of inventory system, or (c) foreign merchandising transactions:

1. Determination of the amount of time from the purchase of inventory until it is sold and the amount due is collected
2. Determination of the effects of changes in exchange rates
3. Determination of policies governing sales of merchandise on credit
4. Determination of whether to use the periodic or the perpetual inventory system

LO1 Operating Cycle

SE 2. On average, Mason Company holds its inventory 40 days before it is sold, waits 25 days for customers' payments, and takes 33 days to pay suppliers. For how many days must it provide financing in its operating cycle?

LO2 Terms of Sale

SE 3. A dealer buys tooling machines from a manufacturer and resells them to its customers.

a. The manufacturer sets a list or catalogue price of $12,000 for a machine. The manufacturer offers its dealers a 40 percent trade discount.
b. The manufacturer sells the machine under terms of FOB shipping point. The cost of shipping is $700.
c. The manufacturer offers a sales discount of 2/10, n/30. The sales discount does not apply to shipping costs.

What is the net cost of the machine to the dealer, assuming it is paid for within 10 days of purchase?

LO2 Sales and Purchases Discounts

SE 4. On April 15, Meier Company sold merchandise to Curran Company for $5,000 on terms of 2/10, n/30. Assume a return of merchandise on April 20 of $850 and collection in full on April 25. What is the amount collected by Meier on April 25?

LO3 Purchases of Merchandise: Perpetual Inventory System

SE 5. Record in T account form each of the following transactions, assuming the perpetual inventory system is used:

Aug.	2	Purchased merchandise on credit from Indio Company, invoice dated August 1, terms n/10, FOB shipping point, $1,150.
	3	Received bill from Lee Shipping Company for transportation costs on August 2 shipment, invoice dated August 1, terms n/30, $105.
	7	Returned damaged merchandise received from Indio Company on August 2 for credit, $180.
	10	Paid in full the amount due to Indio Company for the purchase of August 2, part of which was returned on August 7.

LO4 **Purchases of Merchandise: Periodic Inventory System**

SE 6. Record in T account form the transactions in SE 5, assuming the periodic inventory system is used.

LO4 **Cost of Goods Sold: Periodic Inventory System**

SE 7. Using the following data and assuming cost of goods sold is $273,700, prepare the cost of goods sold section of a merchandising income statement (periodic inventory system). Include the amount of purchases for the month of October.

Freight-in	$13,800
Merchandise inventory, Sept. 30, 20xx	37,950
Merchandise inventory, Oct. 31, 20xx	50,600
Purchases	?
Purchases returns and allowances	10,350

LO4 **Sales of Merchandise: Periodic Inventory System**

SE 8. Record in T account form the following transactions, assuming the periodic inventory system is used:

Aug. 4	Sold merchandise on credit to Rivera Company, terms n/30, FOB destination, $5,040.
5	Paid transportation costs for sale of August 4, $462.
9	Part of the merchandise sold on August 4 was accepted back from Rivera Company for full credit and returned to merchandise inventory, $1,470.
Sept. 3	Collected in full the amount due from Rivera Company for merchandise sold on August 4, less the return on August 9.

Exercises

LO1 LO2 **Discussion Questions**

E 1. Develop a brief answer to each of the following questions:

1. Can a company have a "negative" financing period?
2. Suppose you sold goods to a company in Europe at a time when the exchange rate for the dollar was declining in relation to the euro. Would you want the European company to pay you in dollars or euros?
3. Which inventory system—the perpetual or periodic—is more useful to management? Why?

LO2 LO3 LO4 **Discussion Questions**

E 2. Develop a brief answer to each of the following questions:

1. Assume a large shipment of uninsured merchandise to your company is destroyed when the delivery truck has an accident and burns. Would you want the terms to be FOB shipping point or FOB destination?
2. Under the perpetual inventory system, the Merchandise Inventory account is constantly updated. What would cause it to have the wrong balance?
3. Why is a physical inventory needed under both the periodic and perpetual inventory systems?

LO1 **Management Issues and Decisions**

E 3. The management of Posad Cotton Company made the decisions that follow. Indicate whether each decision pertains primarily to (a) cash flow management, (b) choice of inventory system, or (c) foreign transactions.

1. Decided to reduce the credit terms offered to customers from 30 days to 20 days to speed up collection of accounts.
2. Decided that the benefits of keeping track of each item of inventory as it is bought and sold would exceed the costs of such a system.
3. Decided to purchase goods made by a Chinese supplier.
4. Decided to switch to a new cleaning service that will provide the same service at a lower cost with payment due in 30 days instead of 20 days.

LO1 **Foreign Merchandising Transactions**

E 4. Elm Company purchased a special-purpose machine from Ritholz Company on credit for €75,000. At the date of purchase, the exchange rate was $1.00 per euro. On the date of the payment, which was made in euros, the value of the euro was $1.25. Did Elm incur an exchange gain or loss? How much was it?

LO2 **Terms of Sale**

E 5. A household appliance dealer buys refrigerators from a manufacturer and resells them to its customers.

a. The manufacturer sets a list or catalogue price of $2,500 for a refrigerator. The manufacturer offers its dealers a 30 percent trade discount.
b. The manufacturer sells the machine under terms of FOB destination. The cost of shipping is $240.
c. The manufacturer offers a sales discount of 2/10, n/30. Sales discounts do not apply to shipping costs.

What is the net cost of the refrigerator to the dealer, assuming it is paid for within 10 days of purchase?

LO2 LO4 **Sales Involving Discounts: Periodic Inventory System**

E 6. Given the following transactions engaged in by Stanford Company, prepare journal entries and, assuming the periodic inventory system, determine the total amount received from Penkas Company.

Mar.	1	Sold merchandise on credit to Penkas Company, terms 2/10, n/30, FOB shipping point, $1,000.
	3	Accepted a return from Penkas Company for full credit, $400.
	10	Collected amount due from Penkas Company for the sale, less the return and discount.
	11	Sold merchandise on credit to Penkas Company, terms 2/10, n/30, FOB shipping point, $1,600.
	31	Collected amount due from Penkas Company for the sale of March 11.

LO2 LO3 **Purchases Involving Discounts: Perpetual Inventory System**

E 7. Lien Company engaged in the following transactions:

July	2	Purchased merchandise on credit from Jonak Company, terms 2/10, n/30, FOB destination, invoice dated July 1, $4,000.
	6	Returned some merchandise to Jonak Company for full credit, $500.
	11	Paid Jonak Company for purchase of July 2 less return and discount.
	14	Purchased merchandise on credit from Jonak Company, terms 2/10, n/30, FOB destination, invoice dated July 12, $4,500.
	31	Paid amount owed Jonak Company for purchase of July 14.

Prepare journal entries and, assuming the perpetual inventory system, determine the total amount paid to Jonak Company.

LO3 **Preparation of the Income Statement: Perpetual Inventory System**

E 8. Selected account balances at December 31, 2011, for Receptions, Etc., are listed below. Prepare an income statement for the year ended December 31, 2011. Show detail of net sales. The company uses the perpetual inventory system, and Freight-In has not been included in Cost of Goods Sold.

Account Name	Debit	Credit
Sales		$498,000
Sales Returns and Allowances	$ 23,500	
Cost of Goods Sold	284,000	
Freight-In	14,700	
Selling Expenses	43,000	
General and Administrative Expenses	87,000	

LO3 **Recording Purchases: Perpetual Inventory System**

E 9. The following transactions took place under the perpetual inventory system. Record each transaction in T account form.

a. Purchased merchandise on credit, terms n/30, FOB shipping point, $2,500.
b. Paid freight on the shipment in transaction **a**, $135.
c. Purchased merchandise on credit, terms n/30, FOB destination, $1,400.
d. Purchased merchandise on credit, terms n/30, FOB shipping point, $2,600, which includes freight paid by the supplier of $200.
e. Returned part of the merchandise purchased in transaction **c**, $500.
f. Paid the amount owed on the purchase in transaction **a.**
g. Paid the amount owed on the purchase in transaction **d.**
h. Paid the amount owed on the purchase in transaction **c** less the return in **e**.

LO3 **Recording Sales: Perpetual Inventory System**

E 10. On June 15, Palmyra Company sold merchandise for $5,200 on terms of n/30 to Lim Company. On June 20, Lim Company returned some of the merchandise for a credit of $1,200, and on June 25, Lim paid the balance owed. Give Palmyra's entries in T account form to record the sale, return, and receipt of cash under the perpetual inventory system. The cost of the merchandise sold on June 15 was $3,000, and the cost of the merchandise returned to inventory on June 20 was $700.

LO4 **Preparation of the Income Statement: Periodic Inventory System**

E 11. Using the selected year-end account balances at December 31, 2010, for the Morris General Store shown below, prepare a 2010 income statement. Show detail of net sales. The company uses the periodic inventory system. Beginning merchandise inventory was $28,000; ending merchandise inventory is $21,000.

Account Name	Debit	Credit
Sales		$309,000
Sales Returns and Allowances	$ 15,200	
Purchases	114,800	
Purchases Returns and Allowances		7,000
Freight-In	5,600	
Selling Expenses	56,400	
General and Administrative Expenses	37,200	

LO4 Merchandising Income Statement: Missing Data, Multiple Years

E 12. Determine the missing data for each letter in the following three income statements for Sampson Paper Company (in thousands):

	2011	2010	2009
Sales	$ p	$ h	$572
Sales returns and allowances	48	38	a
Net sales	q	634	b
Merchandise inventory, beginning	r	i	76
Purchases	384	338	c
Purchases returns and allowances	62	j	34
Freight-in	s	58	44
Net cost of purchases	378	k	d
Cost of goods available for sale	444	424	364
Merchandise inventory, ending	78	l	84
Cost of goods sold	t	358	e
Gross margin	284	m	252
Selling expenses	u	156	f
General and administrative expenses	78	n	66
Total operating expenses	260	256	g
Net income	v	o	54

LO4 Recording Purchases: Periodic Inventory System

E 13. Using the data in **E 9**, give the entries in T account form to record each of the transactions under the periodic inventory system.

LO4 Recording Sales: Periodic Inventory System

E 14. Using the relevant data in **E 10**, give the entries in T account form to record each of the transactions under the periodic inventory system.

Problems

LO1 LO3 Merchandising Income Statement: Perpetual Inventory System

P 1. At the end of the fiscal year, June 30, 2010, selected accounts from the adjusted trial balance for Barbara's Video Store were as follows:

Barbara's Video Store
Partial Adjusted Trial Balance
June 30, 2010

Sales		$870,824
Sales Returns and Allowances	$ 25,500	
Cost of Goods Sold	442,370	
Freight-In	20,156	
Store Salaries Expense	216,700	
Office Salaries Expense	53,000	
Advertising Expense	36,400	
Rent Expense	28,000	
Insurance Expense	5,600	
Utilities Expense	18,320	
Store Supplies Expense	3,328	
Office Supplies Expense	3,628	
Depreciation Expense–Store Equipment	3,600	
Depreciation Expense–Office Equipment	3,700	

Required

1. Prepare a multistep income statement for Barbara's Video Store. Freight-In should be combined with Cost of Goods Sold. Store Salaries Expense, Advertising Expense, Store Supplies Expense, and Depreciation Expense–Store Equipment are selling expenses. The other expenses are general and administrative expenses. The company uses the perpetual inventory system. Show details of net sales and operating expenses.

User insight ▶ 2. Based on your knowledge at this point in the course, how would you use the income statement for Barbara's Video Store to evaluate the company's profitability? What other financial statement should you consider and why?

LO3 **Merchandising Transactions: Perpetual Inventory System**

P 2. Vargo Company engaged in the following transactions in August 2011:

Aug.	7	Sold merchandise on credit to Ken Smith, terms n/30, FOB shipping point, $3,000 (cost, $1,800).
	8	Purchased merchandise on credit from Novak Company, terms n/30, FOB shipping point, $6,000.
	9	Paid Smart Company for shipping charges on merchandise purchased on August 8, $254.
	10	Purchased merchandise on credit from Mara's Company, terms n/30, FOB shipping point, $9,600, including $600 freight costs paid by Sewall.
	14	Sold merchandise on credit to Rose Milito, terms n/30, FOB shipping point, $2,400 (cost, $1,440).
	14	Returned damaged merchandise received from Novak Company on August 8 for credit, $600.
	17	Received check from Ken Smith for his purchase of August 7.
	19	Sold merchandise for cash, $1,800 (cost, $1,080).
	20	Paid Mara's Company for purchase of August 10.
	21	Paid Novak Company the balance from the transactions of August 8 and August 14.
	24	Accepted from Rose Milito a return of merchandise, which was put back in inventory, $200 (cost, $120).

Required

1. Prepare entries in journal form (refer to the Review Problem) to record the transactions, assuming use of the perpetual inventory system.

User insight ▶ 2. Receiving cash rebates from suppliers based on the past year's purchases is a common practice in some industries. If at the end of the year Vargo Company receives rebates in cash from a supplier, should these cash rebates be reported as revenue? Why or why not?

LO1 LO4 **Merchandising Income Statement: Periodic Inventory System**

P 3. Selected accounts from the adjusted trial balance for Louise's Gourmet Shop as of March 31, 2011, the end of the current fiscal year, appear on the next page. The merchandise inventory for Louise's Gourmet Shop was $38,200 at the beginning of the year and $29,400 at the end of the year.

Required

1. Using the information given, prepare a multistep income statement for Louise's Gourmet Shop. Store Salaries Expense, Advertising Expense, Store Supplies Expense, and Depreciation Expense–Store Equipment are selling expenses. The other expenses are general and administrative expenses. The company uses the periodic inventory system. Show details of net sales and operating expenses.

Louise's Gourmet Shop
Partial Adjusted Trial Balance
March 31, 2011

Sales		$168,700
Sales Returns and Allowances	$ 5,700	
Purchases	70,200	
Purchases Returns and Allowances		2,600
Freight-In	2,300	
Store Salaries Expense	33,125	
Office Salaries Expense	12,875	
Advertising Expense	23,800	
Rent Expense	2,400	
Insurance Expense	1,300	
Utilities Expense	1,560	
Store Supplies Expense	2,880	
Office Supplies Expense	1,075	
Depreciation Expense–Store Equipment	1,050	
Depreciation Expense–Office Equipment	800	

User insight ▶ 2. Based on your knowledge at this point in the course, how would you use the income statement for Louise's Gourmet Shop to evaluate the company's profitability? What other financial statements should you consider, and why?

LO4 Merchandising Transactions: Periodic Inventory System

P 4. Use the data in **P 2** for this problem.

Required

1. Prepare entries in journal form to record the transactions, assuming use of the periodic inventory system. (Use the Review Problem in this chapter as a model.)

User insight ▶ 2. Most companies call the first line of the income statement *net sales.* Other companies call it *sales.* Do you think these terms are equivalent and comparable? What would be the content of net sales? Why might a company use *sales* instead of *net sales?*

LO3 Merchandising Transactions: Perpetual Inventory System

P 5. Tattle Company engaged in the following transactions in October 2010:

Oct. 7 Sold merchandise on credit to Lina Ortiz, terms n/30, FOB shipping point, $6,000 (cost, $3,600).
8 Purchased merchandise on credit from Ruff Company, terms n/30, FOB shipping point, $12,000.
9 Paid Ruff Company for shipping charges on merchandise purchased on October 8, $508.
10 Purchased merchandise on credit from Sewall Company, terms n/30, FOB shipping point, $19,200, including $1,200 freight costs paid by Sewall.
14 Sold merchandise on credit to Peter Watts, terms n/30, FOB shipping point, $4,800 (cost, $2,880).

Oct. 14 Returned damaged merchandise received from Ruff Company on October 8 for credit, $1,200.
17 Received check from Lina Ortiz for her purchase of October 7.
19 Sold merchandise for cash, $3,600 (cost, $2,160).
20 Paid Sewall Company for purchase of October 10.
21 Paid Ruff Company the balance from the transactions of October 8 and October 14.
24 Accepted from Peter Watts a return of merchandise, which was put back in inventory, $400 (cost, $240).

Required

1. Prepare entries in journal form (refer to the Review Problem) to record the transactions, assuming use of the perpetual inventory system.

User insight ▶ 2. Receiving cash rebates from suppliers based on the past year's purchases is a common practice in some industries. If at the end of the year Tattle Company receives rebates in cash from a supplier, should these cash rebates be reported as revenue? Why or why not?

Alternate Problems

LO1 LO3 Merchandising Income Statement: Perpetual Inventory System

P 6. At the end of the fiscal year, August 31, 2010, selected accounts from the adjusted trial balance for Pasha's Patio Furniture were as follows:

Pasha's Patio Furniture
Partial Adjusted Trial Balance
August 31, 2010

Sales		$169,000
Sales Returns and Allowances	$ 9,000	
Cost of Goods Sold	61,400	
Freight-In	2,300	
Store Salaries Expense	32,825	
Office Salaries Expense	12,875	
Advertising Expense	24,100	
Rent Expense	2,400	
Insurance Expense	1,200	
Utilities Expense	1,560	
Store Supplies Expense	2,680	
Office Supplies Expense	1,175	
Depreciation Expense–Store Equipment	1,250	
Depreciation Expense–Office Equipment	800	

Required

1. Using the information given, prepare a multistep income statement for Pasha's Patio Furniture. Store Salaries Expense, Advertising Expense, Store Supplies Expense, and Depreciation Expense–Store Equipment are selling expenses. The other expenses are general and administrative expenses. The company uses the perpetual inventory system. Show details of net sales and operating expenses.

User insight ▶ 2. Based on your knowledge at this point in the course, how would you use the income statement for Pasha's Patio Furniture to evaluate the company's profitability? What other financial statement should be considered, and why?

LO3 **Merchandising Transactions: Perpetual Inventory System**

P 7. Sarah Company engaged in the following transactions in July 2010:

July 1 Sold merchandise to Chi Dong on credit, terms n/30, FOB shipping point, $2,100 (cost, $1,260).
3 Purchased merchandise on credit from Angel Company, terms n/30, FOB shipping point, $3,800.
5 Paid Speed Freight for freight charges on merchandise received, $290.
8 Purchased merchandise on credit from Expo Supply Company, terms n/30, FOB shipping point, $3,600, which includes $200 freight costs paid by Expo Supply Company.
12 Returned some of the merchandise purchased on July 3 for credit, $600.
15 Sold merchandise on credit to Tom Kowalski, terms n/30, FOB shipping point, $1,200 (cost, $720).
17 Sold merchandise for cash, $1,000 (cost, $600).
18 Accepted for full credit a return from Chi Dong and returned merchandise to inventory, $200 (cost, $120).
24 Paid Angel Company for purchase of July 3 less return of July 12.
25 Received check from Chi Dong for July 1 purchase less the return on July 18.

Required

1. Prepare entries in journal form to record the transactions, assuming use of the perpetual inventory system. (Use the Review Problem in this chapter as a model.)

User insight ▶ 2. Most companies call the first line of the income statement *net sales.* Other companies call it *sales.* Do you think these terms are equivalent and comparable? What would be the content of net sales? Why might a company use *sales* instead of *net sales?*

LO1 LO4 **Merchandising Income Statement: Periodic Inventory System**

P 8. Selected accounts from the adjusted trial balance of Daniel's Sports Equipment on September 30, 2010, the fiscal year end, appear at the top of the next page. The company's beginning merchandise inventory was $81,222 and ending merchandise inventory is $76,664 for the period.

Required

1. Prepare a multistep income statement for Daniels's Sports Equipment. Store Salaries Expense, Advertising Expense, Store Supplies Expense, and Depreciation Expense–Store Equipment are selling expenses. The other expenses are general and administrative expenses. The company uses the periodic inventory system. Show details of net sales and operating expenses.

User insight ▶ 2. Based on your knowledge at this point in the course, how would you use the income statement for Daniel's Sports Equipment to evaluate the company's profitability? What other financial statements should you consider and why?

Daniel's Sports Equipment
Partial Adjusted Trial Balance
September 30, 2010

Sales		$440,912
Sales Returns and Allowances	$ 18,250	
Purchases	221,185	
Purchases Returns and Allowances		30,238
Freight-In	10,078	
Store Salaries Expense	105,550	
Office Salaries Expense	26,500	
Advertising Expense	20,200	
Rent Expense	15,000	
Insurance Expense	2,200	
Utilities Expense	18,760	
Store Supplies Expense	464	
Office Supplies Expense	814	
Depreciation Expense–Store Equipment	1,800	
Depreciation Expense–Office Equipment	1,850	

LO4 **Merchandising Transactions: Periodic Inventory System**

P 9. Use the data in **P 7** for this problem.

Required

1. Prepare entries in journal form to record the transactions, assuming use of the periodic inventory system. (Use the Review Problem in this chapter as a model.)

User insight ▶ 2. Receiving cash rebates from suppliers based on the past year's purchases is common in some industries. If at the end of the year, Sarah Company receives rebates in cash from a supplier, should these cash rebates be reported as revenue? Why or why not?

LO4 **Merchandising Transactions: Periodic Inventory System**

P 10. Use the data in **P 5** for this problem.

Required

1. Prepare entries in journal form to record the transactions, assuming use of the periodic inventory system. (Use the Review Problem in this chapter as a model.)

ENHANCING Your Knowledge, Skills, and Critical Thinking

LO1 **Cash Flow Management**

C 1. Jewell Home Source has operated in Kansas for 30 years. The company has always prided itself on giving customers individual attention. It carries a large inventory so it can offer a good selection and deliver purchases quickly. It accepts credit cards and checks but also provides 90 days of credit to reliable customers who have purchased from the company in the past. It maintains good relations with suppliers by paying invoices quickly.

During the past year, the company has been strapped for cash and has had to borrow from the bank to pay its bills. An analysis of its financial statements reveals that, on average, inventory is on hand for 70 days before being sold, and receivables are held for 90 days before being collected. Accounts payable are paid, on average, in 20 days.

What are the operating cycle and the financing period? How long are Jewell's operating cycle and financing period? Describe three ways in which Jewell can improve its management of cash flow.

LO1 Periodic Versus Perpetual Inventory Systems

C 2. Books-For-All is a well-established chain of 20 bookstores in western Ohio. In recent years, the company has grown rapidly, adding five new stores in regional malls. The manager of each store selects stock based on the market in his or her region. Managers select items from a master list of available titles that the central office provides. Every six months, a physical inventory is taken, and financial statements are prepared using the periodic inventory system. At that time, books that have not sold well are placed on sale or, whenever possible, returned to the publisher.

Management has found that when selecting books, the new managers are not judging the market as well as the managers of the older, established stores. Thus, management is thinking about implementing a perpetual inventory system and carefully monitoring sales from the central office. Do you think Books Unlimited should switch to the perpetual inventory system or stay with the periodic inventory system? Discuss the advantages and disadvantages of each system.

LO1 LO3 Comparison of Traditional Merchandising with E-commerce

C 3. *E-commerce* is a word coined to describe business conducted over the Internet. E-commerce is similar in some ways to traditional retailing, but it presents new challenges. Go to the website of **Amazon.com**. Investigate and list the steps a customer takes to purchase an item on the site. How do these steps differ from those in a traditional retail store such as **Borders** or **Barnes & Noble**? What are some of the accounting challenges in recording Internet transactions? Be prepared to discuss your results in class.

LO1 LO2 Merchandise Accounting and Inventory Systems

C 4. Go to a retail business, such as a bookstore, clothing shop, gift shop, grocery store, hardware store, or car dealership, in your local shopping area or a shopping mall. Ask to speak to someone who is knowledgeable about the store's inventory methods. Your instructor will assign groups to find the answers to the following questions. Be prepared to discuss your findings in class.

1. **Merchandising Accounting** Is the company a part of a chain or is it a small business? Does the company sell only merchandise or a combination of merchandise and services? How are sales recorded? Does the company sell on credit? If so, who decides who gets credit and what are the typical terms? Does the company buy any merchandise or, in the case of a chain, does it order merchandise? If it purchases merchandise, how are purchases recorded?
2. **Inventory Systems** How is each item of inventory identified? Does the business have a computerized or a manual inventory system? Which inventory system, periodic or perpetual, is used? How often do employees take a physical inventory? What procedures are followed in taking a physical inventory? What kinds of inventory reports are prepared or received?

LO1 **Operating Cycle and Financing Period**

C 5. Refer to **CVS**'s annual report in the Supplement to Chapter 5 and to Figures 6-1 and 6-2 in this chapter. Assume that at any one time CVS has about 76 days of merchandise inventory available for sale, takes about 18 days to collect its receivables, and takes about 40 days to pay its creditors. Write a memorandum to your instructor briefly describing CVS's operating cycle and financing period. The memorandum should identify the most common transactions in CVS's operating cycle. It should also refer to the importance of accounts receivable, accounts payable, and merchandise inventory in CVS's financial statements. Complete the memorandum by explaining why the operating cycle and financing period are favorable to the company.

LO1 **Income Statement Analysis**

C 6. Refer to the **CVS** annual report in the Supplement to Chapter 5 and to the following data (in millions) for **Walgreens** in 2008: net sales, $59,034; cost of sales, $42,391; total operating expenses, $13,202; and inventories, $7,249. Determine which company—CVS or Walgreens—had more profitable merchandising operations in 2008 by preparing a schedule that compares the companies in terms of net sales, cost of sales, gross margin, total operating expenses, and income from operations as a percentage of sales. (*Hint:* Put the income statements in comparable formats.) In addition, for each company, compute inventory as a percentage of the cost of goods sold. Which company has the highest prices in relation to costs of sales? Which company is more efficient in its operating expenses? Which company manages its inventory better? Overall, on the basis of the income statement, which company is more profitable? Explain your answers.

SUPPLEMENT TO CHAPTER 6

Special-Purpose Journals

Special-purpose journals promote efficiency, economy, and control. Although manual special-purpose journals are used by companies that have not yet computerized their systems, the concepts that underlie these journals also underlie the programs that drive computerized general ledger accounting systems.

Most business transactions—90 to 95 percent—fall into one of four categories. Each kind of transaction can be recorded in a special-purpose journal.

Transaction	*Special-Purpose Journal*	*Posting Abbreviation*
Sale of merchandise on credit	Sales journal	S
Purchase on credit	Purchases journal	P
Receipt of cash	Cash receipts journal	CR
Disbursement of cash	Cash payments journal	CP

The general journal is used to record transactions that do not fall into any of these special categories. For example, purchase returns, sales returns, and adjusting and closing entries are recorded in the general journal. (When transactions are posted from the general journal to the ledger accounts, the posting abbreviation used is ***J.***)

Using special-purpose journals greatly reduces the work involved in entering and posting transactions in the general ledger. For example, in most cases, instead of posting every debit and credit for each transaction, only the total amounts of the transactions are posted. In addition, labor can be divided by assigning each journal to a different employee. This division of labor is important in establishing good internal control.

Sales Journal

The **sales journal** is designed to handle all credit sales. Cash sales are recorded in the cash receipts journal. Exhibit S6-1 illustrates a page from a typical sales journal and related ledger accounts. The

EXHIBIT S6-1
Sales Journal and Related Ledger Accounts

Study Note
The checkmarks indicate daily postings to the subsidiary accounts, which normally are listed in alphabetical or numerical order. Also, the column totals are posted to the appropriate general ledger accounts at the end of the month.

Sales Journal — **Page 1**

Date		Account Debited	Invoice Number	Terms	Post. Ref.	Amount (Debit/ Credit Accounts Receivable/Sales)
July	1	Peter Clark	721	2/10, n/30	√	750
	5	Georgetta Jones	722	2/10, n/30	√	500
	8	Eugene Cumberland	723	2/10, n/30	√	335
	12	Maxwell Gertz	724	2/10, n/30	√	1,165
	18	Peter Clark	725	1/10, n/30	√	1,225
	25	Michael Powers	726	2/10, n/30	√	975
						4,950
						(114/411)

Post total at end of month.

Accounts Receivable 114

Date		Post. Ref.	Debit	Credit	Balance Debit	Balance Credit
July	31	S1	4,950		4,950	

Sales 411

Date		Post. Ref.	Debit	Credit	Balance Debit	Balance Credit
July	31	S1		4,950		4,950

page records six sales transactions involving five customers. Notice how the sales journal saves time:

1. Only one line is needed to record each transaction. Each entry consists of a debit to a customer in Accounts Receivable. The corresponding credit to Sales is understood.
2. The account names do not have to be written out because each entry automatically is debited to Accounts Receivable and credited to Sales.
3. No explanations are necessary because the function of the sales journal is to record credit sales only.
4. Only one amount—the total credit sales for the month—has to be posted. It is posted twice: once as a debit to Accounts Receivable and once as a credit to Sales. You can see the time this saves for the six transactions listed in Exhibit S6-1. Imagine the time saved when there are hundreds of sales transactions.

Controlling Accounts and Subsidiary Journals Controlling accounts and subsidiary ledgers contain important details about the figures in special-purpose journals and other books of original entry. A **controlling account,** also called a *control account,* is an account in the general ledger that maintains the total of the individual account balances in a subsidiary ledger. A **subsidiary ledger** is a ledger separate from the general ledger that contains a group of related

EXHIBIT S6-2
Relationship of Sales Journal, General Ledger, and Accounts Receivable Subsidiary Ledger and the Posting Procedure

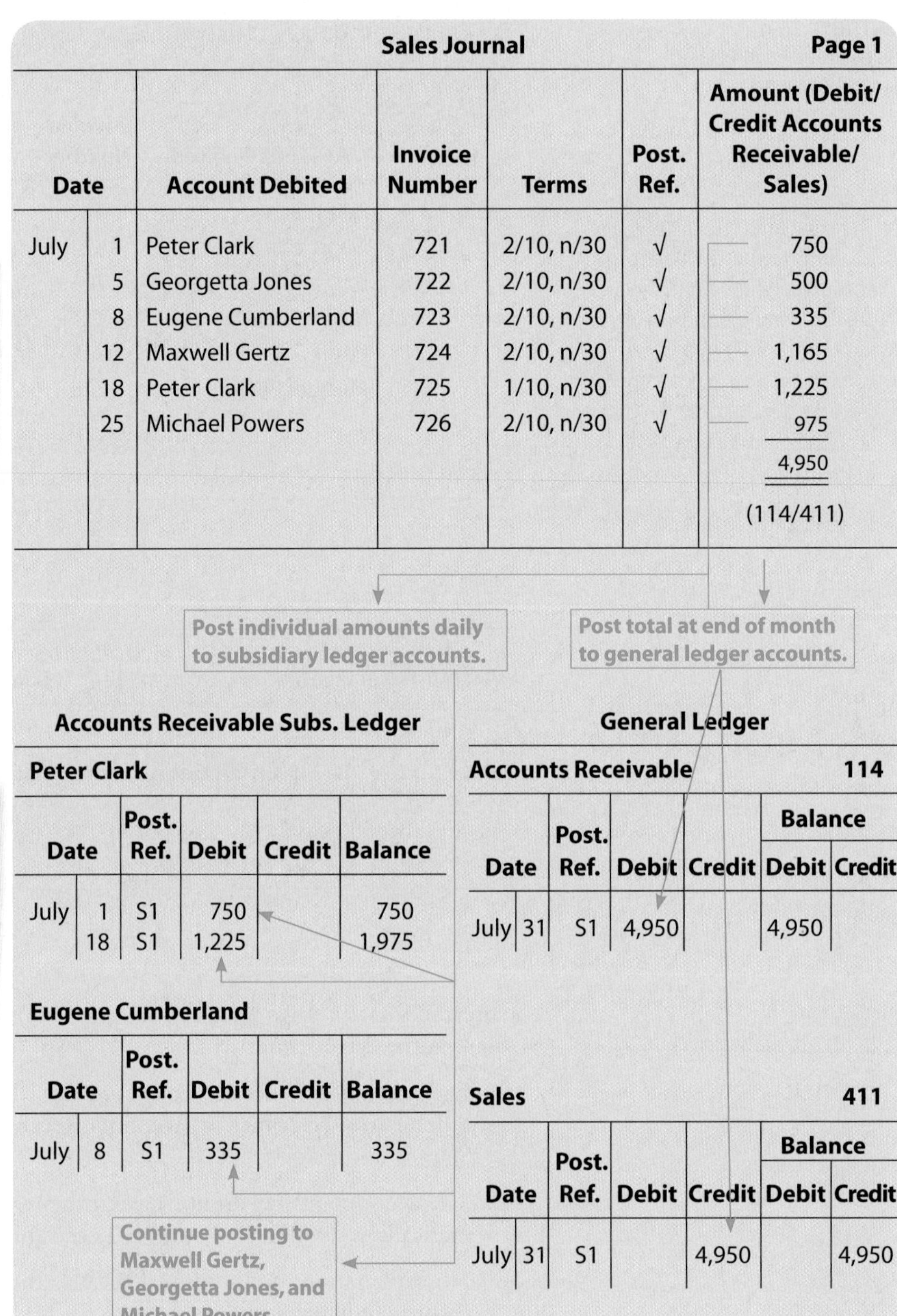

Sales Journal — **Page 1**

Date		Account Debited	Invoice Number	Terms	Post. Ref.	Amount (Debit/Credit Accounts Receivable/Sales)
July	1	Peter Clark	721	2/10, n/30	√	750
	5	Georgetta Jones	722	2/10, n/30	√	500
	8	Eugene Cumberland	723	2/10, n/30	√	335
	12	Maxwell Gertz	724	2/10, n/30	√	1,165
	18	Peter Clark	725	1/10, n/30	√	1,225
	25	Michael Powers	726	2/10, n/30	√	975
						4,950
						(114/411)

Accounts Receivable Subs. Ledger

Peter Clark

Date		Post. Ref.	Debit	Credit	Balance
July	1	S1	750		750
	18	S1	1,225		1,975

Eugene Cumberland

Date		Post. Ref.	Debit	Credit	Balance
July	8	S1	335		335

General Ledger

Accounts Receivable — **114**

Date		Post. Ref.	Debit	Credit	Balance Debit	Balance Credit
July	31	S1	4,950		4,950	

Sales — **411**

Date		Post. Ref.	Debit	Credit	Balance Debit	Balance Credit
July	31	S1		4,950		4,950

Study Note
Accounts in the subsidiary ledger are maintained in alphabetical order. If account numbers are used to identify customers, the accounts would be listed in account number order.

Study Note
Subsidiary accounts are posted daily to prevent customers from exceeding their credit limits and to have up-to-date balances for customers wishing to pay their accounts.

accounts. The total of the balances in the subsidiary ledger accounts equals or ties in with the balance in the corresponding controlling account.

For example, up to this point we've used a single Accounts Receivable account. However, a single entry in Accounts Receivable does not tell us how much each customer has bought and how much each customer has paid or still owes. In practice, almost all companies that sell to customers on credit keep an individual accounts receivable record for each customer. If the company has 6,000 credit customers, there are 6,000 accounts receivable. To include all these accounts in the general ledger with the other asset, liability, and owner's equity accounts would make it very bulky. Consequently, most companies place individual customers' accounts in a separate, subsidiary ledger. In the accounts receivable subsidiary ledger, customers' accounts are filed either alphabetically or numerically (if account numbers are used).

When a company puts individual customers' accounts in an accounts receivable subsidiary ledger, it still must maintain an Accounts Receivable account in the general ledger. This account controls in the sense that its balance must equal the total of the individual account balances in the subsidiary ledger. Transactions that involve accounts receivable, such as credit sales, must be posted to the individual customers' accounts daily. Postings to the controlling account in the general ledger are made at least once a month. When the amounts in the subsidiary ledger and the controlling account do not match, the accountant must find the error and correct it.

Most companies use an accounts payable subsidiary ledger as well. It is possible to use a subsidiary ledger for almost any account in the general ledger, such as Notes Receivable, Short-Term Investments, and Equipment, when management wants specific information on individual items.

Summary of the Sales Journal Procedure Exhibit S6-2 illustrates the procedure for using a sales journal:

1. Enter each sales invoice in the sales journal on a single line. Record the date, the customer's name, the invoice number, and the amount. No column is needed for the terms if the terms on all sales are the same.
2. At the end of each day, post each individual sale to the customer's account in the accounts receivable subsidiary ledger. As each sale is posted, place a check mark (or customer account number, if used) in the Post. Ref. (posting reference) column of the sales journal to indicate that it has been posted. In the Post. Ref. column of each customer's account, place an *S* and the sales journal page number (*S1* means Sales Journal—Page 1) to indicate the source of the entry.
3. At the end of the month, sum the Amount column in the sales journal to determine the total credit sales, and post the total to the general ledger accounts (debit Accounts Receivable and credit Sales). Place the numbers of the accounts debited and credited beneath the total in the sales journal to indicate that this step has been completed. In the general ledger, indicate the source of the entry in the Post. Ref. column of each account.
4. Verify the accuracy of the posting by adding the account balances of the accounts receivable subsidiary ledger and comparing the total with the balance of the Accounts Receivable controlling account in the general ledger. You can do this by listing the accounts in a schedule of accounts receivable, like the one in Exhibit S6-3, in the order in which the accounts

Study Note

In theory, the sum of the account balances from the subsidiary accounts must equal the balance in the related general ledger controlling account. In practice, however, the equality is verified only at the end of the month, when the general ledger is posted.

EXHIBIT S6-3
Schedule of Accounts Receivable

Mitchell's Used Car Sales
Schedule of Accounts Receivable
July 31, 2011

Peter Clark	$1,975
Eugene Cumberland	335
Maxwell Gertz	1,165
Georgetta Jones	500
Michael Powers	975
Total Accounts Receivable	$4,950

are maintained. This step is performed after posting collections on account in the cash receipts journal.

Study Note
Columns can be added to a special-purpose journal for accounts that are commonly used.

Sales Taxes Many cities and states require retailers to collect a sales tax from their customers and periodically remit the total collected to the city or state. In this case, an additional column is needed in the sales journal to record the credit to Sales Taxes Payable on credit sales. The form of the entry is shown in Exhibit S6-4.

Purchases Journal

Study Note
It is easy to forget that a cash purchase is entered into the cash payments journal, not into the purchases journal.

The **purchases journal** is used to record purchases on credit. It can take the form of either a single-column journal or a multicolumn journal. In the single-column journal shown in Exhibit S6-5, only credit purchases of merchandise for resale to customers are recorded. This kind of transaction is recorded with a debit to Purchases and a credit to Accounts Payable. When the single-column purchases journal is used, credit purchases of items other than merchandise are recorded in the general journal. Cash purchases are never recorded in the purchases journal; they are recorded in the cash payments journal, which we explain later.

Like the Accounts Receivable account, the Accounts Payable account in the general ledger is generally used as a controlling account. So that the company knows how much it owes each supplier, it keeps a separate account for each supplier in an accounts payable subsidiary ledger.

The procedure for using the purchases journal is much like that for using the sales journal:

1. Enter each purchase invoice in the purchases journal on a single line. Record the date, the supplier's name, the invoice date, the terms (if given), and the amount. It is not necessary to record the shipping terms in the terms column because they do not affect the payment date.

2. At the end of each day, post each individual purchase to the supplier's account in the accounts payable subsidiary ledger. As each purchase is posted, place a check mark in the Post. Ref. column of the purchases journal to show that it has been posted. Also place a *P* and the page number of the purchases journal (*P1* stands for Purchases Journal—Page 1) in the Post. Ref. column of each supplier's account to show the source of the entry.

3. At the end of the month, sum the Amount column in the purchases journal, and post the total to the general ledger accounts (a debit to Purchases and a credit to Accounts Payable). Place the numbers of the accounts debited and credited beneath the totals in the purchases journal to show that this step has

EXHIBIT S6-4 Section of a Sales Journal with a Column for Sales Taxes

Sales Journal — **Page 7**

Date		Account Debited	Invoice Number	Terms	Post. Ref.	Debit: Accounts Receivable	Credits: Sales Tax Payable	Credits: Sales
Sept.	1	Ralph P. Hake	727	2/10, n/30	√	206	6	200

EXHIBIT S6-5
Relationship of Single-Column Purchases Journal to the General Ledger and the Accounts Payable Subsidiary Ledger

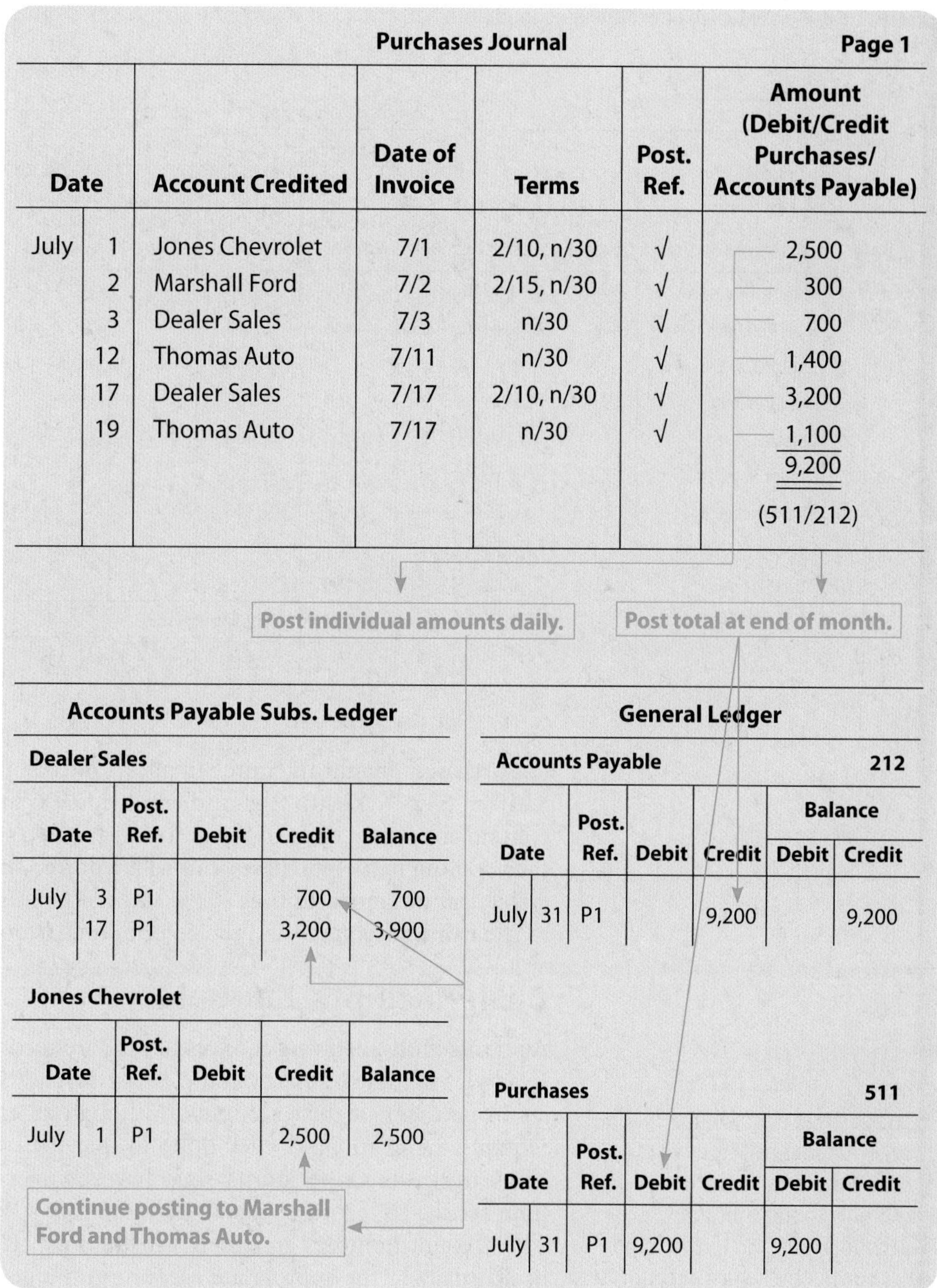

Purchases Journal — Page 1

Date		Account Credited	Date of Invoice	Terms	Post. Ref.	Amount (Debit/Credit Purchases/ Accounts Payable)
July	1	Jones Chevrolet	7/1	2/10, n/30	√	2,500
	2	Marshall Ford	7/2	2/15, n/30	√	300
	3	Dealer Sales	7/3	n/30	√	700
	12	Thomas Auto	7/11	n/30	√	1,400
	17	Dealer Sales	7/17	2/10, n/30	√	3,200
	19	Thomas Auto	7/17	n/30	√	1,100
						9,200
						(511/212)

Accounts Payable Subs. Ledger

Dealer Sales

Date		Post. Ref.	Debit	Credit	Balance
July	3	P1		700	700
	17	P1		3,200	3,900

Jones Chevrolet

Date		Post. Ref.	Debit	Credit	Balance
July	1	P1		2,500	2,500

General Ledger

Accounts Payable 212

Date		Post. Ref.	Debit	Credit	Balance Debit	Balance Credit
July	31	P1		9,200		9,200

Purchases 511

Date		Post. Ref.	Debit	Credit	Balance Debit	Balance Credit
July	31	P1	9,200		9,200	

been carried out. In the general ledger, indicate the source of the entry in the Post. Ref. column of each account.

4. Check the accuracy of the posting by adding the account balances of the accounts payable subsidiary ledger and comparing the total with the balance of the Accounts Payable controlling account in the general ledger. This step can be done by preparing a schedule of accounts payable from the subsidiary ledger.

> **Study Note**
> The multicolumn purchases journal can accommodate the purchase of anything on credit. Each column total (except the total of Other Accounts) must be posted at the end of the month.

The single-column purchases journal can be expanded to record credit purchases of items other than merchandise by adding separate debit columns for other accounts that are used often. For example, the multicolumn purchases journal in Exhibit S6-6 has columns for Freight In, Store Supplies, Office Supplies, and Other Accounts. Here, the total credits to Accounts Payable ($9,637) equal the total debits

EXHIBIT S6-6 A Multicolumn Purchases Journal

Purchases Journal **Page 1**

						Credit	Debits						
											Other Accounts		
Date		Account Credited	Date of Invoice	Terms	Post. Ref.	Accounts Payable	Purchases	Freight In	Store Supplies	Office Supplies	Account	Post. Ref.	Amount
July	1	Jones Chevrolet	7/1	2/10, n/30	√	2,500	2,500						
	2	Marshall Ford	7/2	2/15, n/30	√	300	300						
	2	Shelby Car Delivery	7/2	n/30	√	50		50					
	3	Dealer Sales	7/3	n/30	√	700	700						
	12	Thomas Auto	7/11	n/30	√	1,400	1,400						
	17	Dealer Sales	7/17	2/10, n/30	√	3,200	3,200						
	19	Thomas Auto	7/17	n/30	√	1,100	1,100						
	25	Osborne Supply	7/21	n/10	√	187			145	42			
	28	Auto Supply	7/28	n/10	√	200					Parts	120	200
						9,637	9,200	50	145	42			200
						(212)	(511)	(514)	(132)	(133)			(√)

to Purchases, Freight In, Store Supplies, Office Supplies, and Parts ($9,200 + $50 + $145 + $42 + $200). Again, the individual transactions in the Accounts Payable column are posted daily to the accounts payable subsidiary ledger, and the totals of each column in the purchases journal are posted monthly to the corresponding general ledger accounts. Entries in the Other Accounts column are posted individually to the named accounts, and the column total is not posted.

Cash Receipts Journal

All transactions involving receipts of cash are recorded in the **cash receipts journal.** Examples of these transactions are cash from cash sales and cash from credit customers in payment of their accounts. Although all cash receipts are alike in that they require a debit to Cash, they differ in that they require a variety of credit entries. Thus, the cash receipts journal must have several columns. The Other Accounts column is used to record credits to accounts not specifically represented by a column. The account numbers are entered in the Post. Ref. column, and the amounts are posted daily to the appropriate account in the general ledger. The Other Accounts column totals, therefore, are not posted at the end of the month. Only at the end of the month are the control account balances meaningful or correct.

Study Note

The cash receipts journal can accommodate all receipts of cash. Daily postings are made, not only to the subsidiary accounts, but also to the "other accounts." The Other Accounts column totals, therefore, are not posted at the end of the month. Only at the end of the month are the control account balances meaningful or correct.

The cash receipts journal shown in Exhibit S6-7 has three debit columns and three credit columns. The three debit columns are as follows:

1. **Cash:** Each entry must have an amount in this column because each transaction involves a receipt of cash.
2. **Sales discounts:** This company allows a 2 percent discount for prompt payment. Therefore, it is useful to have a column for sales discounts. Notice that in the transactions of July 8 and 28, the debits to Cash and Sales Discounts equal the credits to Accounts Receivable.
3. **Other accounts:** The Other Accounts column (sometimes called *Sundry Accounts*) is used for transactions that involve both a debit to Cash and a debit to some account other than Sales Discounts.

EXHIBIT S6-7 Relationship of the Cash Receipts Journal to the General Ledger and the Accounts Receivable Subsidiary Ledger

Cash Receipts Journal — Page 1

Date		Account Debited/Credited	Post. Ref.	Debits: Cash	Debits: Sales Discounts	Debits: Other Accounts	Credits: Accounts Receivable	Credits: Sales	Credits: Other Accounts
July	1	Henry Mitchell, Capital	311	20,000					20,000
	5	Sales		1,200				1,200	
	8	Georgetta Jones	√	490	10		500		
	13	Sales		1,400				1,400	
	16	Peter Clark	√	750			750		
	19	Sales		1,000				1,000	
	20	Store Supplies	132	500					500
	24	Notes Payable	213	5,000					5,000
	26	Sales		1,600				1,600	
	28	Peter Clark	√	588	12		600		
				32,528	22		1,850	5,200	25,500
				(111)	(412)		(114)	(411)	(√)

Post individual amounts in Accounts Receivable ledger columns daily.

Post totals at end of month.

Total not posted.

Post individual amounts in Other Accounts column daily.

General Ledger

Cash — 111

Date		Post. Ref.	Debit	Credit	Balance Debit	Balance Credit
July	31	CR1	32,528		32,528	

Accounts Receivable — 114

Date		Post. Ref.	Debit	Credit	Balance Debit	Balance Credit
July	31	S1	4,950		4,950	
	31	CR1		1,850	3,100	

Store Supplies — 132

Date		Post. Ref.	Debit	Credit	Balance Debit	Balance Credit
Bal.					500	
July	20	CR1		500	—	

Accounts Receivable Subsidiary Ledger

Peter Clark

Date		Post. Ref.	Debit	Credit	Balance
July	1	S1	750		750
	16	CR1		750	—
	18	S1	1,225		1,225
	28	CR1		600	625

Georgetta Jones

Date		Post. Ref.	Debit	Credit	Balance
July	5	S1	500		500
	8	CR1		500	—

Continue posting to Notes Payable and Henry Mitchell, Capital.

Continue posting to Sales and Sales Discounts.

These are the credit columns:

1. **Accounts receivable:** This column is used to record collections on account from customers. The name of the customer is written in the Account Debited/Credited column so that the payment can be entered in the corresponding account in the accounts receivable subsidiary ledger. Posting to the individual accounts receivable accounts is usually done daily so that each customer's balance is up-to-date.
2. **Sales:** This column is used to record all cash sales during the month. Retail firms that use cash registers would make an entry at the end of each day for the total sales from each cash register for that day. The debit, of course, is in the Cash debit column.
3. **Other accounts:** This column is used for the credit portion of any entry that is neither a cash collection from accounts receivable nor a cash sale. The name of the account to be credited is indicated in the Account Debited/Credited column. For example, the transactions of July 1, 20, and 24 involve credits to accounts other than Accounts Receivable or Sales. These individual postings should be done daily (or weekly if there are just a few of them). If a company finds that it consistently is crediting a certain account in the Other Accounts column, it can add another credit column to the cash receipts journal for that particular account.

The procedure for posting the cash receipts journal, as shown in Exhibit S6-7, is as follows:

1. Post the transactions in the Accounts Receivable column daily to the individual accounts in the accounts receivable subsidiary ledger. The amount credited to the customer's account is the same as that credited to Accounts Receivable. A check mark in the Post. Ref. column of the cash receipts journal indicates that the amount has been posted, and a *CR1* (Cash Receipts Journal—Page 1) in the Post. Ref. column of each subsidiary ledger account indicates the source of the entry.
2. Post the debits/credits in the Other Accounts columns daily, or at convenient short intervals during the month, to the general ledger accounts. Write the account number in the Post. Ref. column of the cash receipts journal as the individual items are posted to indicate that the posting has been done, and write *CR1* in the Post. Ref. column of the general ledger account to indicate the source of the entry.
3. At the end of the month, total the columns in the cash receipts journal, as shown below. The sum of the Debits column totals must equal the sum of the Credits column totals:

Debits Column Totals		*Credits Column Totals*	
Cash	$32,528	Accounts Receivable	$ 1,850
Sales Discounts	22	Sales	5,200
Other Accounts	0	Other Accounts	25,500
Total Debits	$32,550	Total Credits	$32,550

   This step is called *crossfooting*.
4. Post the Debits column totals as follows:

   a. *Cash* Posted as a debit to the Cash account.

   b. *Sales Discounts* Posted as a debit to the Sales Discounts account.

5. Post the Credits column totals as follows:
   a. *Accounts Receivable* Posted as a credit to the Accounts Receivable controlling account.
   b. *Sales* Posted as a credit to the Sales account.
6. Write the account numbers below each column in the cash receipts journal as they are posted to indicate that these steps have been completed. *CR1* is written in the Post. Ref. column of each account in the general ledger to indicate the source of the entry.
7. Notice that the total of the Other Accounts column is not posted because each entry was posted separately when the transaction occurred. The individual accounts were posted in Step 2. Place a check mark at the bottom of the column to show that postings in that column have been made and that the total is not posted.

Cash Payments Journal

Study Note

The cash payments journal can accommodate all cash payments. It functions like the cash receipts journal, although it uses some different general ledger accounts.

All transactions involving payments of cash are recorded in the **cash payments journal** (also called the *cash disbursements journal*). Examples of these transactions are cash purchases and payments of obligations resulting from earlier purchases on credit. The form of the cash payments journal is much like that of the cash receipts journal. The cash payments journal shown in Exhibit S6-8 has three credit columns and five debit columns.

The credit columns for the cash payments journal are as follows:

1. **Cash:** Each entry must have an amount in this column because each transaction involves a payment of cash.
2. **Purchases discounts:** When purchases discounts are taken, they are recorded in this column.
3. **Other accounts:** This column is used to record credits to accounts other than Cash or Purchases Discounts. Notice that the July 31 transaction shows a purchase of Land for $15,000, with a check for $5,000 and a note payable for $10,000.

The debit columns are as follows:

1. **Accounts payable:** This column is used to record payments to suppliers that have extended credit to the company. Each supplier's name is written in the Payee column so that the payment can be entered in the supplier's account in the accounts payable subsidiary ledger.
2. **Salary expense, advertising expense, and rent expense:** Continue posting the column total for any column that has an account title at the top. These are accounts for which there are usually multiple expenditures in a month. Placing the account number at the bottom of the column indicates the total has been posted to its respective account.
3. **Other accounts:** Cash can be expended for many reasons. Therefore, an Other Accounts or Sundry Accounts column is needed in the cash payments journal. The title of the account to be debited is written in the Account Credited/Debited column, and the amount is entered in the Other Accounts debit column. If a company finds that a particular account appears often in the Other Accounts column, it can add another debit column to the cash payments journal.

EXHIBIT S6-8 Relationship of the Cash Payments Journal to the General Ledger and the Accounts Payable Subsidiary Ledger

Cash Payments Journal **Page 1**

					Credits			Debits				
Date	**Ck. No.**	**Payee**	**Account Credited/ Debited**	**Post. Ref.**	**Cash**	**Purchases Discounts**	**Other Accounts**	**Accounts Payable**	**Salary Expense**	**Advertising Expense**	**Rent Expense**	**Other Accounts**
July 2	101	Sondra Tidmore	Purchases	511	400							400
6	102	Daily Journal			100					100		
8	103	Siviglia Agency			250						250	
11	104	Jones Chevrolet		√	2,450	50		2,500				
16	105	Charles Kuntz			600				600			
17	106	Marshall Ford		√	294	6		300				
24	107	Grabow & Company	Prepaid Insurance	119	480							480
27	108	Dealer Sales		√	3,136	64		3,200				
9		Daily Journal			100					100		
30	109	A&B Equipment Company	Office Equipment	144	900							400
			Service Equipment	146								500
31	110	Burns Real Estate	Notes Payable	213	5,000		10,000					
			Land	141								15,000
					13,710	120	10,000	6,000	600	200	250	16,780
					(111)	(512)	(√)	(212)	(611)	(612)	(613)	(√)

Post individual amounts in Other Accounts column daily.

Post individual amounts in Accounts Payable column daily.

Post totals at end of month.

Totals not posted.

General Ledger

Cash **111**

Date		Post. Ref.	Debit	Credit	Balance Debit	Balance Credit
July	31	CR1	32,528		32,528	
	31	CP1		13,710	18,818	

Prepaid Insurance **119**

Date		Post. Ref.	Debit	Credit	Balance Debit	Balance Credit
July	24	CP1	480		480	

Accounts Payable Subsidiary Ledger

Dealer Sales

Date		Post. Ref.	Debit	Credit	Balance
July	3	P1		700	700
	17	P1		3,200	3,900
	27	CP1	3,200		700

Jones Chevrolet

Date		Post. Ref.	Debit	Credit	Balance
July	1	P1		2,500	2,500
	11	CP1	2,500		—

Marshall Ford

Date		Post. Ref.	Debit	Credit	Balance
July	2	P1		300	300
	17	CP1	300		—

Continue posting to Land, Office Equipment, Service Equipment, Notes Payable, and Purchases.

Continue posting to Purchases Discounts and Accounts Payable, Salary Expense, Advertising Expense, and Rent Expense

The procedure for posting the cash payments journal, shown in Exhibit S6-8, is as follows:

1. Post the transactions in the Accounts Payable columns daily to the individual accounts in the accounts payable subsidiary ledger. Place a check mark in the Post. Ref. column of the cash payments journal to indicate that the posting has been made.
2. Post the debits/credits in the Other Accounts debit/credit columns to the general ledger daily or at convenient short intervals during the month. Write the account number in the Post. Ref. column of the cash payments journal as the individual items are posted to indicate that the posting has been completed and *CP1* (Cash Payments Journal-Page 1) in the Post. Ref. column of each general ledger account.
3. At the end of the month, the columns are footed and crossfooted. That is, the sum of the Credits column totals must equal the sum of the Debits column totals, as follows:

Credit Column Totals		*Debit Column Totals*	
Cash	$13,710	Accounts Payable	$ 6,000
Purchases Discounts	120	Salary Expense	600
Other Accounts	10,000	Advertising Expense	200
		Rent Expense	250
		Other Accounts	16,780
Total Credits	$23,830	Total Debits	$23,830

4. At the end of the month, post the column totals for Cash, Purchases Discounts, Accounts Payable, Salary Expense, Advertising Expense, and Rent Expense to their respective accounts in the general ledger. Write the account number below each column in the cash payments journal as it is posted to indicate that this step has been completed and *CP1* in the Post. Ref. column of each general ledger account. Place a check mark under the total of each Other Accounts column in the cash payments journal to indicate that the postings in the column have been made and that the total is not posted.

General Journal Adjusting and closing entries are recorded in the general journal. Transactions that do not involve sales, purchases, cash receipts, or cash payments should also be recorded in the general journal. Usually, there are only a few of these transactions. Two examples of entries that do not fit in a special-purpose journal are a return of merchandise bought on account and an allowance from a supplier for credit.

These entries are shown in Exhibit S6-9. Notice that the entries include a debit or a credit to a controlling account (Accounts Payable or Accounts Receivable). The name of the customer or supplier also is given here. When this kind of debit or credit is made to a controlling account in the general ledger, the entry must be posted twice: once to the controlling account and once to the individual account in the subsidiary ledger. This procedure keeps the subsidiary ledger equal to the controlling account. Notice that the July 26 transaction is posted by a debit to Sales Returns and Allowances in the general ledger (shown by the account number 413), a credit to the Accounts Receivable controlling account in the general ledger (account number 114), and a credit to the Maxwell Gertz account in the accounts receivable subsidiary ledger (check mark).

EXHIBIT S6-9
Transactions Recorded in the General Journal

Study Note

The general journal is used only to record transactions that cannot be accommodated by the special-purpose journals. Whenever a controlling account is recorded, it must be "double posted" to the general ledger and the subsidiary accounts. All general journal entries are posted daily; column totals are neither obtained nor posted.

General Journal **Page 1**

Date		Description	Post. Ref.	Debit	Credit
July	25	Accounts Payable, Thomas Auto	212/√	700	
		Purchases Returns and Allowances	513		700
		Returned used car for credit; invoice date 7/11			
	26	Sales Returns and Allowances	413	35	
		Accounts Receivable, Maxwell Gertz	114/√		35
		Allowance for faulty tire			

Problems

Cash Receipt and Cash Payments Journals

P 1. Kimball Company is a small retail business that uses a manual data processing system similar to the one described in the chapter. Among its special-purpose journals are multicolumn cash receipts and cash payments journals. These were the cash transactions for Kimball Company during the month of November:

Nov. 1 Paid November rent to R. Carello, $1,000, with check no. 782.
3 Paid Stavos Wholesale on account, $2,300 less a 2 percent discount, check no. 783.
4 Received payment on account of $1,000, within the 2 percent discount period, from J. Walker.
5 Cash sales, $2,632.
8 Paid Moving Freight on account, $598, with check no. 784.
9 The owner, Fred Kimball, invested an additional $10,000 in cash and a truck valued at $14,000 in the business.
11 Paid Escobedo Supply on account, $284, with check no. 785.
14 Cash sales, $2,834.
15 Paid Moving Freight $310 for the freight on a shipment of merchandise received today, with check no. 786.
16 Paid Ludman Company on account, $1,568 net a 2 percent discount, with check no. 787.
17 Received payment on account from P. Sivula, $120.
18 Cash sales, $1,974.
19 Received payment on a note receivable, $1,800 plus $36 interest.
20 Purchased office supplies from Escobedo Supply, $108, with check no. 788.
21 Paid a note payable in full to Kenington Bank, $4,100 including $100 interest, with check no. 789.
24 Cash sales, $2,964.

Nov. 25 Paid $500 less a 2 percent discount to Stavos Wholesale, with check no. 790.
26 Paid sales clerk Tracy Dye $1,100 for her monthly salary, with check no. 791.
27 Purchased equipment from Standard Corporation for $16,000, paying $4,000 with check no. 792 and signing a note payable for the difference.
30 Fred Kimball withdrew $1,200 from the business, using check no. 793.

Required

1. Enter these transactions in the cash receipts and cash payments journals.
2. Foot and crossfoot the journals.
3. If a manager wanted to know the total sales for the accounting period, where else would the manager need to refer to obtain the data needed?

Purchases and General Journals

P 2. Meloon Lawn Supply Company uses a multicolumn purchases journal and a general journal similar to those illustrated in the text. The company also maintains an accounts payable subsidiary ledger. The items below represent the company's credit transactions for the month of July.

July 2 Purchased merchandise from Diego Fertilizer Company, $2,640.
3 Purchased office supplies of $166 and store supplies of $208 from Laronne Supply, Inc.
5 Purchased cleaning equipment from Whitman Company, $1,856.
7 Purchased display equipment from Laronne Supply, Inc., $4,700.
10 Purchased lawn mowers from Brandon Lawn Equipment Company, for resale, $8,400 (which included transportation charges of $350).
14 Purchased merchandise from Diego Fertilizer Company, $3,444.
18 Purchased a lawn mower from Brandon Lawn Equipment Company to be used in the business, $950 (which included transportation charges of $70).
23 Purchased store supplies from Laronne Supply, Inc., $54.
27 Returned a defective lawn mower purchased on July 10 for full credit, $750.

Required

1. Enter the preceding transactions in the purchases journal and the general journal. Assume that all terms are n/30 and that invoice dates are the same as the transaction dates. Use Page 1 for all references.
2. Foot and crossfoot the purchases journal.
3. Open the following general ledger accounts: Store Supplies (116), Office Supplies (117), Lawn Equipment (142), Display Equipment (144), Cleaning Equipment (146), Accounts Payable (211), Purchases (611), Purchases Returns and Allowances (612), and Freight In (613). Open accounts payable subsidiary ledger accounts as needed. Post from the journals to the ledger accounts.

Comprehensive Use of Special-Purpose Journals

P 3. Ye Olde Book Store opened its doors for business on May 1. During May, the following transactions took place:

May 1 Linda Berrill began the business by depositing $42,000 in the new company's bank account.
3 Issued check no. C001 to Remax Rentals for one month's rent, $1,000.
4 Received a shipment of books from Chassman Books, Inc., invoice dated May 3, terms 5/10, n/60, FOB shipping point, $15,680.
5 Received a bill for freight from Menden Shippers for the previous day's shipment, terms n/30, $790.
6 Received a shipment from Lakeside Books, invoice dated May 6, terms 2/10, n/30, FOB shipping point, $11,300.
7 Issued check no. C002 to Pappanopoulos Freight for transportation charges on the previous day's shipment, $574.
8 Issued check no. C003 to Yun Chao Equipment Company for store equipment, $10,400.
9 Sold books to Midtown Center, terms 5/10, n/30, invoice no. 1001, $1,564.
10 Returned books to Chassman Books, Inc., for credit, $760.
11 Issued check no. C004 to WCAM for radio commercials, $235.
12 Issued check no. C005 to Chassman Books, Inc., for balance of amount owed less discount.
13 Cash sales for the first two weeks, $4,018. (For this problem, cash sales are recorded every two weeks, not daily as they are in actual practice.)
14 Issued check no. C006 to Lakeside Books, $6,000 less discount.
15 Signed a 90-day, 10 percent note for a bank loan and received $20,000 in cash.
15 Sold books to Steve Oahani, terms n/30, invoice no. 1002, $260.
16 Issued a credit memorandum to Midtown Center for returned books, $124.
17 Received full payment from Midtown Center of balance owed less discount.
18 Sold books to Missy Porter, terms n/30, invoice no. 1003, $194.
19 Received a shipment from Perspectives Publishing Company, invoice dated May 18, terms 5/10, n/60, $4,604.
20 Returned additional books purchased on May 4 to Chassman Books, Inc., for credit at gross price, $1,436.
21 Sold books to Midtown Center, terms 5/10, n/30, invoice no. 1004, $1,634.
23 Received a shipment from Chassman Books, Inc., invoice dated May 19, terms 5/10, n/60, FOB shipping point, $2,374.
24 Issued check no. C007 to Menden Shippers for balance owed on account plus shipping charges of $194 on previous day's shipment.
27 Cash sales for the second two weeks, $7,488.
29 Issued check no. C008 to Payroll for salaries for first four weeks of the month, $1,400.
30 Issued check no. C009 to WXAM for radio commercials, $235.
31 Cash sales for the last four days of the month, $554.

Required

1. Prepare a sales journal, a multicolumn purchases journal, a cash receipts journal, a cash payments journal, and a general journal. Use Page 1 for all journal references.
2. Open the following general ledger accounts: Cash (111); Accounts Receivable (112); Store Equipment (141); Accounts Payable (211); Notes Payable (212); Linda Berrill, Capital (311); Sales (411); Sales Discounts (412); Sales Returns and Allowances (413); Purchases (511); Purchases Discounts (512); Purchases Returns and Allowances (513); Freight In (514); Salaries Expense (611); Advertising Expense (612); and Rent Expense (613).
3. Open accounts receivable subsidiary ledger accounts for Midtown Center, Steve Oahani, and Missy Porter.
4. Open accounts payable subsidiary ledger accounts for Chassman Books, Inc.; Lakeside Books; Menden Shippers; and Perspectives Publishing Company.
5. Enter the transactions in the journals and post as appropriate.
6. Foot and crossfoot the journals, and make the end-of-month postings.
7. Prepare a trial balance of the general ledger and prove the control balances of Accounts Receivable and Accounts Payable by preparing schedules of accounts receivable and accounts payable.

CHAPTER

8 Inventories

Making a Statement

INCOME STATEMENT

Revenues

– Expenses

= Net Income

STATEMENT OF OWNER'S EQUITY

Beginning Balance

+ Net Income

– Withdrawals

= Ending Balance

BALANCE SHEET

Assets	**Liabilities**
	Owner's Equity

A = L + OE

STATEMENT OF CASH FLOWS

Operating activities
+ Investing activities
+ Financing activities
= Change in Cash
+ Beginning Balance
= Ending Cash Balance

Valuation of inventories affects the amount of inventories on the balance sheet and the cost of goods sold on the income statement.

For any company that makes or sells merchandise, inventory is an extremely important asset. Managing this asset is a challenging task. It requires not only protecting goods from theft or loss but also ensuring that operations are highly efficient. Further, as you will see in this chapter, proper accounting of inventory is essential because misstatements will affect net income in at least two years.

LEARNING OBJECTIVES

LO1 Explain the management decisions related to inventory accounting, evaluation of inventory level, and the effects of inventory misstatements on income measurement. (pp. 352–358)

LO2 Define *inventory cost*, contrast goods flow and cost flow, and explain the lower-of-cost-or-market (LCM) rule. (pp. 358–360)

LO3 Calculate inventory cost under the periodic inventory system using various costing methods. (pp. 361–364)

LO4 Explain the effects of inventory costing methods on income determination and income taxes. (pp. 365–367)

SUPPLEMENTAL OBJECTIVES

SO5 Calculate inventory cost under the perpetual inventory system using various costing methods. (pp. 367–370)

SO6 Use the retail method and gross profit method to estimate the cost of ending inventory. (pp. 370–372)

DECISION POINT ▸ A USER'S FOCUS SNUGS COMPANY

Snugs Company is a new store that sells a variety of stylish leather boots and bags. Because Snugs is a merchandising company, inventory is a very important component of its total assets, and the decisions that George Lopez, the company's owner, makes about how to account for inventory can have a significant impact on its operating results. As you will learn in this chapter, George has several decisions to make, including which inventory system and costing method to use, how to value inventory, and how much inventory to keep in stock.

- ▸ How should Snugs Company decide which inventory system and costing method to use?
- ▸ How do decisions about inventory evaluation and inventory levels affect operating results?

Managing Inventories

LO1 Explain the management decisions related to inventory accounting, evaluation of inventory level, and the effects of inventory misstatements on income measurement.

Inventory is considered a current asset because a company normally sells it within a year or within its operating cycle. For a merchandising company like **CVS** or **Walgreens**, inventory consists of all goods owned and held for sale in the regular course of business. Because manufacturing companies like **Toyota** are engaged in making products, they have three kinds of inventory:

- Raw materials (goods used in making products)
- Work in process (partially completed products)
- Finished goods ready for sale

In a note to its financial statements, Toyota showed the following breakdown of its inventories (figures are in millions):[1]

Inventories	*2008*	*2007*
Raw materials (includes supplies)	$ 2,990	$ 3,072
Work in process	2,395	2,006
Finished goods	12,093	10,203
Total inventories	$17,478	$15,281

The work in process and the finished goods inventories have three cost components:

- Cost of the raw materials that go into the product
- Cost of the labor used to convert the raw materials to finished goods
- Overhead costs that support the production process

Overhead costs include the costs of indirect materials (such as packing materials), indirect labor (such as the salaries of supervisors), factory rent, depreciation of plant assets, utilities, and insurance.

Inventory Decisions

Study Note

Management considers the behavior of inventory prices over time when selecting inventory costing methods.

The primary objective of inventory accounting is to determine income properly by matching costs of the period against revenues for the period. As you can see in Figure 8-1, in accounting for inventory, management must choose among different processing systems, costing methods, and valuation methods. These different systems and methods usually result in different amounts of reported net income. Thus, management's choices affect investors' and creditors' evaluations of a company, as well as internal evaluations, such as the performance reviews on which bonuses and executive compensation are based.

The consistency convention requires that once a company has decided on the systems and methods it will use in accounting for inventory, it must use them from one accounting period to the next unless management can justify a change. If a change is justifiable, the full disclosure convention requires that the notes to the financial statements clearly explain the change and its effects.

Because the valuation of inventory affects income, it can have a considerable impact on the amount of income taxes a company pays—and the amount of taxes it pays can have a considerable impact on its cash flows. Federal income tax regulations are specific about the valuation methods a company may use. As a result, management is sometimes faced with the dilemma of how to apply GAAP to income determination and still minimize income taxes.

FIGURE 8-1
Management Choices in Accounting for Inventories

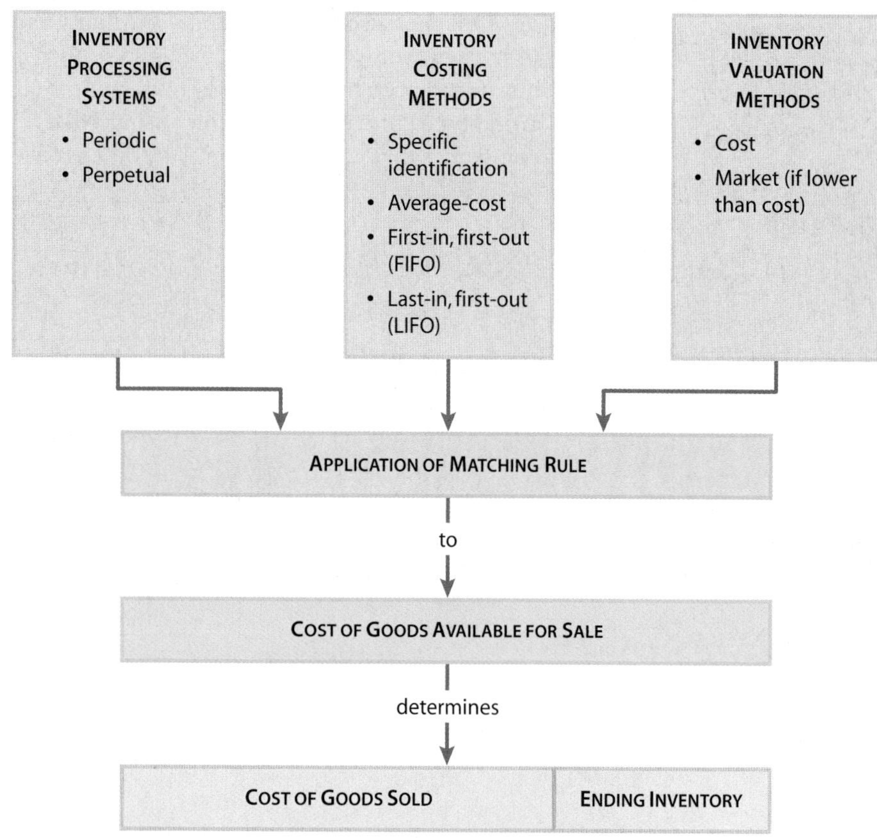

Evaluating the Level of Inventory

> **Study Note**
> Some of the costs of carrying inventory are insurance, property tax, and storage costs. Other costs may result from spoilage and employee theft.

The level of inventory a company maintains has important economic consequences. Ideally, management wants to have a great variety and quantity of goods on hand so that customers have a large choice and do not have to wait for an item to be restocked. But implementing such a policy can be expensive. Handling and storage costs and the interest cost of the funds needed to maintain high inventory levels are usually substantial. On the other hand, low inventory levels can result in disgruntled customers and lost sales.

FOCUS ON BUSINESS PRACTICE

A Whirlwind Inventory Turnover—How Does Dell Do It?

Dell Computer Corporation turns its inventory over every 5 days. How can it do this when other computer companies have inventory on hand for 60 days or even longer? Technology and good inventory management are a big part of the answer.

Dell's speed from order to delivery sets the standard for the computer industry. Consider that a computer ordered by 9 a.m. can be delivered the next day by 9 p.m. How can Dell do this when it does not start ordering components and assembling computers until a customer places an order? First, Dell's suppliers keep components warehoused just minutes from Dell's factories, making efficient, just-in-time operations possible. Another time and money saver is the handling of computer monitors. Monitors are no longer shipped first to Dell and then on to buyers. Dell sends an e-mail message to a shipper, such as **United Parcel Service**, and the shipper picks up a monitor from a supplier and schedules it to arrive with the PC. In addition to contributing to a high inventory turnover, this practice saves Dell about $30 per monitor in freight costs. Dell is showing the world how to run a business in the cyber age by selling more than $1 million worth of computers a day on its website.[2]

One measure that managers commonly use to evaluate inventory levels is **inventory turnover**, which is the average number of times a company sells its inventory during an accounting period. It is computed by dividing cost of goods sold by average inventory. For example, using **Nike**'s Annual Report we can compute the company's inventory turnover for 2009 as follows (figures are in millions):

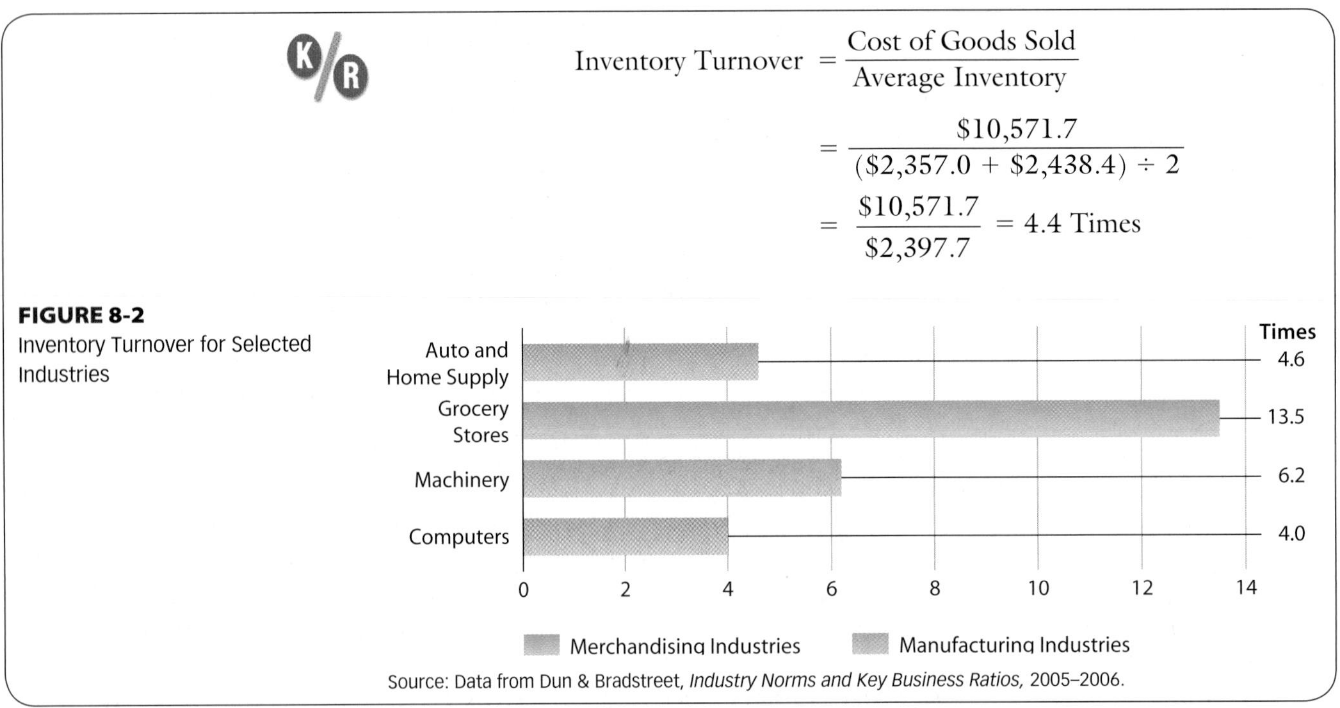

$$\text{Inventory Turnover} = \frac{\text{Cost of Goods Sold}}{\text{Average Inventory}}$$

$$= \frac{\$10{,}571.7}{(\$2{,}357.0 + \$2{,}438.4) \div 2}$$

$$= \frac{\$10{,}571.7}{\$2{,}397.7} = 4.4 \text{ Times}$$

FIGURE 8-2
Inventory Turnover for Selected Industries

Source: Data from Dun & Bradstreet, *Industry Norms and Key Business Ratios,* 2005–2006.

Another common measure of inventory levels is **days' inventory on hand**, which is the average number of days it takes a company to sell the inventory it has in stock. For Nike, it is computed as follows:

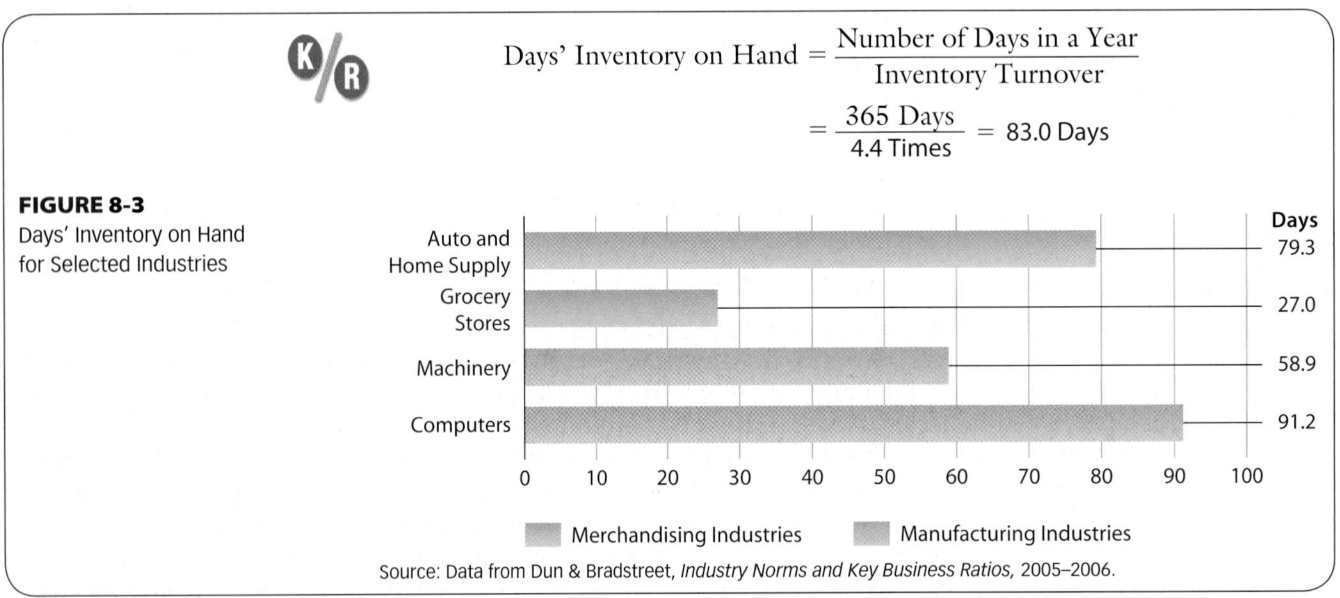

$$\text{Days' Inventory on Hand} = \frac{\text{Number of Days in a Year}}{\text{Inventory Turnover}}$$

$$= \frac{365 \text{ Days}}{4.4 \text{ Times}} = 83.0 \text{ Days}$$

FIGURE 8-3
Days' Inventory on Hand for Selected Industries

Source: Data from Dun & Bradstreet, *Industry Norms and Key Business Ratios,* 2005–2006.

Nike turned its inventory over 4.4 times in 2009 or, on average, every 83.0 days. Thus, it had to provide financing for the inventory for almost three months before it sold it.

To reduce their levels of inventory, many merchandisers and manufacturers use supply-chain management in conjunction with a just-in-time operating environment. With **supply-chain management**, a company uses the Internet to

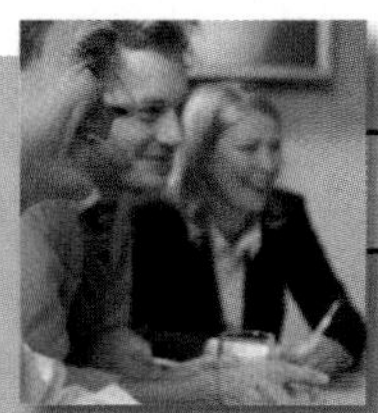

FOCUS ON BUSINESS PRACTICE

What Do You Do to Cure a Bottleneck Headache?

A single seat belt can have as many as 50 parts, and getting the parts from suppliers was once a big problem for **Autoliv, Inc.**, a Swedish maker of auto safety devices. Autoliv's plant in Indianapolis was encountering constant bottlenecks in dealing with 125 different suppliers. To keep the production lines going required high-priced, rush shipments on a daily basis. To solve the problem, the company began using supply-chain management, keeping in touch with suppliers through the Internet rather than through faxes and phone calls. This system allowed suppliers to monitor the inventory at Autoliv and thus to anticipate problems. It also provided information on quantity and time of recent shipments, as well as continuously updated forecasts of parts that would be needed in the next 12 weeks. With supply-chain management, Autoliv reduced inventory by 75 percent and rush freight costs by 95 percent.[3]

Study Note

Inventory turnover will be systematically higher if year-end inventory levels are low. For example, many merchandisers' year-end is in January when inventories are lower than at any other time of the year.

order and track goods that it needs immediately. A **just-in-time operating environment** is one in which goods arrive just at the time they are needed.

Nike uses supply-chain management to increase inventory turnover. It manages its inventory purchases through business-to-business transactions that it conducts over the Internet. It also uses a just-in-time operating environment in which it works closely with suppliers to coordinate and schedule shipments so that the shipments arrive exactly when needed. The benefits of using supply-chain management in a just-in-time operating environment are that Nike has less money tied up in inventory and its cost of carrying inventory is reduced.

Effects of Inventory Misstatements on Income Measurement

The reason inventory accounting is so important to income measurement is the way income is measured on the income statement. Recall that gross margin is the difference between net sales and cost of goods sold and that cost of goods sold depends on the portion of cost of goods available for sale assigned to ending inventory. These relationships lead to the following conclusions:

- The higher the value of ending inventory, the lower the cost of goods sold and the higher the gross margin.
- Conversely, the lower the value of ending inventory, the higher the cost of goods sold and the lower the gross margin.

Because the amount of gross margin has a direct effect on net income, the value assigned to ending inventory also affects net income. In effect, the value of ending inventory determines what portion of the cost of goods available for sale is assigned to cost of goods sold and what portion is assigned to the balance sheet as inventory to be carried over into the next accounting period.

The basic issue in separating goods available for sale into two components—goods sold and goods not sold—is to assign a value to the goods not sold, the ending inventory. The portion of goods available for sale not assigned to the ending inventory is used to determine the cost of goods sold. Because the figures for ending inventory and cost of goods sold are related, a misstatement in the inventory figure at the end of an accounting period will cause an equal misstatement in gross margin and income before income taxes in the income statement. The amount of assets and stockholders' equity on the balance sheet will be misstated by the same amount.

Inventory is particularly susceptible to fraudulent financial reporting. For example, it is easy to overstate or understate inventory by including end-of-the-year purchase and sales transactions in the wrong fiscal year or by simply misstating inventory. A misstatement can occur because of mistakes in the accounting process. It can also occur because of deliberate manipulation of operating results motivated by a desire to enhance the market's perception of the company, obtain bank financing, or achieve compensation incentives.

In one spectacular case, **Rite Aid Corporation**, the large drugstore chain, falsified income by manipulating its computerized inventory system to cover losses from shoplifting, employee theft, and spoilage. In another case, bookkeepers at **RentWay, Inc.**, a company that rents furniture to apartment dwellers, boosted income artificially over several years by overstating inventory in small increments that were not noticed by top management.

Whatever the causes of an overstatement or understatement of inventory, the three examples that follow illustrate the effects. In each case, beginning inventory, net cost of purchases, and cost of goods available for sale are stated correctly. In Example 1, ending inventory is correctly stated; in Example 2, it is overstated by $3,000; and in Example 3, it is understated by $3,000.

Example 1. Ending Inventory Correctly Stated at $5,000

Cost of Goods Sold for the Year		*Income Statement for the Year*	
Beginning inventory	$ 6,000	Net sales	$ 50,000
Net cost of purchases	29,000	Cost of goods sold	30,000
Cost of goods available for sale	$35,000	Gross margin	$ 20,000
Ending inventory	5,000	Operating expenses	16,000
Cost of goods sold	$30,000	Income before income taxes	$ 4,000

Example 2. Ending Inventory Overstated by $3,000

Cost of Goods Sold for the Year		*Income Statement for the Year*	
Beginning inventory	$ 6,000	Net sales	$ 50,000
Net cost of purchases	29,000	Cost of goods sold	27,000
Cost of goods available for sale	$35,000	Gross margin	$ 23,000
Ending inventory	8,000	Operating expenses	16,000
Cost of goods sold	$27,000	Income before income taxes	$ 7,000

Example 3. Ending Inventory Understated by $3,000

Cost of Goods Sold for the Year		*Income Statement for the Year*	
Beginning inventory	$ 6,000	Net sales	$ 50,000
Net cost of purchases	29,000	Cost of goods sold	33,000
Cost of goods available for sale	$35,000	Gross margin	$ 17,000
Ending inventory	2,000	Operating expenses	16,000
Cost of goods sold	$33,000	Income before income taxes	$ 1,000

In all three examples, the cost of goods available for sale was $35,000. The difference in income before income taxes resulted from how this $35,000 was divided between ending inventory and cost of goods sold.

Autoliv's use of supply-chain management is an example of how this system has benefited businesses. By using the Internet to order and track the numerous parts involved in the manufacture of the seat belts pictured here, Autoliv prevented delays in the shipments of parts by allowing its suppliers to monitor inventory and thus to anticipate problems. The firm also drastically reduced its inventory and freight costs.

Courtesy of Kathy Wynn/Dreamstime.

Study Note

A misstatement of inventory has the opposite effect in two successive accounting periods.

Because the ending inventory in one period becomes the beginning inventory in the following period, a misstatement in inventory valuation affects not only the current period but the following period as well. Over two periods, the errors in income before income taxes will offset, or counterbalance, each other. For instance, in Example 2, the overstatement of ending inventory will cause a $3,000 overstatement of beginning inventory in the following year, which will result in a $3,000 understatement of income. Because the total income before income taxes for the two periods is the same, it may appear that one need not worry about inventory misstatements. However, the misstatements violate the matching rule. In addition, management, creditors, and investors base many decisions on the accountant's determination of net income. The accountant has an obligation to make the net income figure for each period as useful as possible.

The effects of inventory misstatements on income before income taxes are as follows:

Year 1	*Year 2*
Ending inventory overstated	***Beginning inventory overstated***
Cost of goods sold understated	Cost of goods sold overstated
Income before income taxes overstated	Income before income taxes understated
Ending inventory understated	***Beginning inventory understated***
Cost of goods sold overstated	Cost of goods sold understated
Income before income taxes understated	Income before income taxes overstated

During 2010, Max's Sporting Goods had beginning inventory of $500,000, ending inventory of $700,000, and cost of goods sold of $2,100,000. Compute the inventory turnover and days' inventory on hand.

SOLUTION

Inventory Turnover = Cost of Goods Sold/Average Inventory

$$= \frac{\$2{,}100{,}000}{(\$700{,}000 + \$500{,}000)/2} = \frac{\$2{,}100{,}000}{\$600{,}000}$$

= 3.5 Times

Days' Inventory on Hand = 365/Inventory Turnover

= 365/3.5= 104.3 Days

Inventory Cost and Valuation

LO2 Define *inventory cost*, contrast goods flow and cost flow, and explain the lower-of-cost-or-market (LCM) rule.

The primary basis of accounting for inventories is cost, the price paid to acquire an asset. **Inventory cost** includes the following:

- Invoice price less purchases discounts
- Freight-in, including insurance in transit
- Applicable taxes and tariffs

Other costs—for ordering, receiving, and storing—should in principle be included in inventory cost. In practice, however, it is so difficult to allocate such costs to specific inventory items that they are usually considered expenses of the accounting period rather than inventory costs.

Inventory costing and valuation depend on the prices of the goods in inventory. The prices of most goods vary during the year. A company may have purchased identical lots of merchandise at different prices. Also, when a company deals in identical items, it is often impossible to tell which have been sold and which are still in inventory. When that is the case, it is necessary to make an assumption about the order in which items have been sold. Because the assumed order of sale may or may not be the same as the actual order of sale, the assumption is really about the *flow of costs* rather than the *flow of physical inventory.*

Goods Flows and Cost Flows

Goods flow refers to the actual physical movement of goods in the operations of a company. **Cost flow** refers to the association of costs with their *assumed* flow in the operations of a company. The assumed cost flow may or may not be the same as the actual goods flow. The possibility of a difference between cost flow and goods flow may seem strange at first, but it arises because several choices of assumed cost flow are available under generally accepted accounting principles. In fact, it is sometimes preferable to use an assumed cost flow that bears no relationship to goods flow because it gives a better estimate of income, which is the main goal of inventory valuation.

> **Study Note**
> The assumed flow of inventory costs does not have to correspond to the physical flow of goods.

Merchandise in Transit Because merchandise inventory includes all items that a company owns and holds for sale, the status of any merchandise in transit, whether the company is selling it or buying it, must be evaluated to see if the merchandise should be included in the inventory count. Neither the seller nor the buyer has *physical* possession of merchandise in transit. As Figure 8-4 shows, ownership is determined by the terms of the shipping agreement, which indicate when title

FIGURE 8-4
Merchandise in Transit

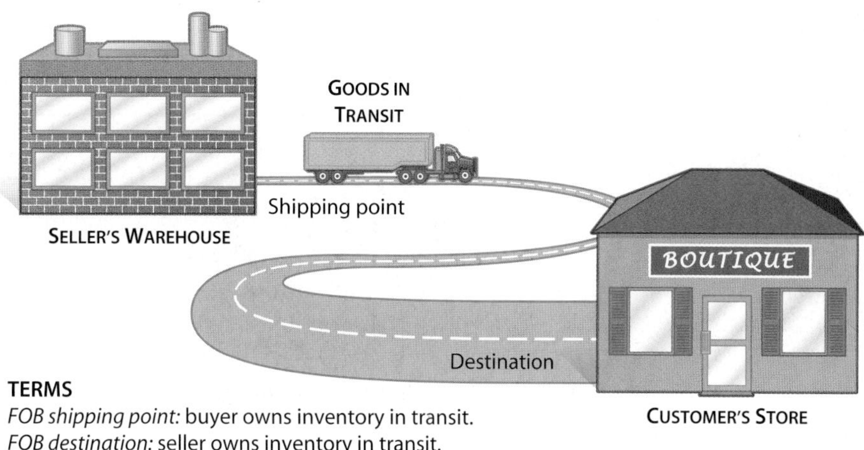

passes. Outgoing goods shipped FOB (free on board) destination are included in the seller's merchandise inventory, whereas those shipped FOB shipping point are not. Conversely, incoming goods shipped FOB shipping point are included in the buyer's merchandise inventory, but those shipped FOB destination are not.

Merchandise on Hand Not Included in Inventory At the time a company takes a physical inventory, it may have merchandise on hand to which it does not hold title. For example, it may have sold goods but not yet delivered them to the buyer, but because the sale has been completed, title has passed to the buyer. Thus, the merchandise should be included in the buyer's inventory, not the seller's. Goods held on consignment also fall into this category.

A **consignment** is merchandise that its owner (the consignor) places on the premises of another company (the consignee) with the understanding that payment is expected only when the merchandise is sold and that unsold items may be returned to the consignor. Title to consigned goods remains with the consignor until the consignee sells the goods. Consigned goods should not be included in the consignee's physical inventory because they still belong to the consignor.

> **Study Note**
> Cost must be determined by one of the inventory costing methods before it can be compared with the market value.

Lower-of-Cost-or-Market (LCM) Rule

Although cost is usually the most appropriate basis for valuation of inventory, inventory may at times be properly shown in the financial statements at less than its historical, or original, cost. If the market value of inventory falls below its historical cost because of physical deterioration, obsolescence, or decline in price level, a loss has occurred. This loss is recognized by writing the inventory down

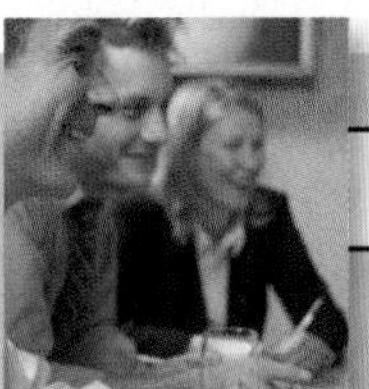

FOCUS ON BUSINESS PRACTICE

Lower of Cost or Market Can Be Costly

When the lower-of-cost-or-market rule comes into play, it can be an indication of how bad things are for a company. When the market for Internet and telecommunications equipment had soured, **Cisco Systems**, a large Internet supplier, found itself faced with probably the largest inventory loss in history. It had to write down to zero almost two-thirds of its $2.5 billion inventory, 80 percent of which consisted of raw materials that would never be made into final products.[4] In another case, through poor management, a downturn in the economy, and underperforming stores, **Kmart**, the discount department store, found itself with a huge amount of excess merchandise, including more than 5,000 truckloads of goods stored in parking lots, which it could not sell except at drastically reduced prices. The company had to mark down its inventory by $1 billion in order to sell it, which resulted in a debilitating loss.[5]

FOCUS ON BUSINESS PRACTICE

IFRS

Is "Market" the Same as Fair Value?

When the lower-of-cost-or-market rule is used, what does "market" mean? Under IFRS, market is determined to be fair value, which is understood to be the amount at which an asset can be sold. However, under U.S. standards, market in valuing inventory is normally considered to be replacement cost or the amount at which the asset can be purchased. The two "market" values, selling price and purchasing price, can often be quite different for the same asset. This is an issue that will have to be addressed if the U.S. and international standards are to achieve convergence.

to **market**—that is, to its current replacement cost. For a merchandising company, market is the amount that it would pay at the present time for the same goods, purchased from the usual suppliers and in the usual quantities.

When the replacement cost of inventory falls below its historical cost (as determined by an inventory costing method), the **lower-of-cost-or-market (LCM) rule** requires that the inventory be written down to the lower value and that a loss be recorded. This rule is an example of the application of the conservatism convention because the loss is recognized before an actual transaction takes place. Under historical cost accounting, the inventory would remain at cost until it is sold. According to an AICPA survey, approximately 80 percent of 600 large companies apply the LCM rule to their inventories for financial reporting.[6]

Disclosure of Inventory Methods

The full disclosure convention requires that companies disclose their inventory methods, including the use of LCM, in the notes to their financial statements, and users should pay close attention to them. For example, **Toyota** discloses that it uses the lower-of-cost-or-market method in this note to its financial statements:

> Inventories are valued at cost, not in excess of market, cost being determined on the "average cost" basis. . . .[7]

STOP & APPLY >

Match the letter of each item below with the numbers of the related items:

a. An inventory cost
b. An assumption used in the valuation of inventory
c. Full disclosure convention
d. Conservatism convention
e. Consistency convention
f. Not an inventory cost or assumed flow

____ 1. Cost of consigned goods
____ 2. A note to the financial statements explaining inventory policies
____ 3. Application of the LCM rule
____ 4. Goods flow
____ 5. Transportation charge for merchandise shipped FOB shipping point
____ 6. Cost flow
____ 7. Choosing a method and sticking with it
____ 8. Transportation charge for merchandise shipped FOB destination

SOLUTION

1. f; 2. c; 3. d; 4. b; 5. a; 6. f; 7. e; 8. f

Inventory Cost Under the Periodic Inventory System

LO3 Calculate inventory cost under the periodic inventory system using various costing methods.

The value assigned to ending inventory is the result of two measurements: quantity and cost. As you know, under the periodic inventory system, quantity is determined by taking a physical inventory; under the perpetual inventory system, quantities are updated as purchases and sales take place. Cost is determined by using one of the following methods, each based on a different assumption of cost flow:

1. Specific identification method
2. Average-cost method
3. First-in, first-out (FIFO) method
4. Last-in, first-out (LIFO) method

Study Note

If the prices of merchandise purchased never changed, there would be no need for inventory methods. It is price changes that necessitate some assumption about the order in which goods are sold.

The choice of method depends on the nature of the business, the financial effects of the method, and the cost of implementing the method.

To illustrate how each method is used under the periodic inventory system, we use the following data for April, a month in which prices were rising:

April	1	Inventory	160 units @ $10.00	$ 1,600
	6	Purchase	440 units @ $12.50	5,500
	25	Purchase	400 units @ $14.00	5,600
Goods available for sale			1,000 units	$12,700
Sales			560 units	
On hand April 30			440 units	

The problem of inventory costing is to divide the cost of the goods available for sale ($12,700) between the 560 units sold and the 440 units on hand.

Specific Identification Method

The **specific identification method** identifies the cost of each item in ending inventory. It can be used only when it is possible to identify the units in ending inventory as coming from specific purchases. For instance, if the April 30 inventory consisted of 100 units from the April 1 inventory, 200 units from the April 6 purchase, and 140 units from the April 25 purchase, the specific identification method would assign the costs as follows:

Periodic Inventory System—Specific Identification Method

100 units @ $10.00	$1,000	Cost of goods available	
200 units @ $12.50	2,500	for sale	$12,700
140 units @ $14.00	1,960	→ Less April 30 inventory	5,460
440 units at a cost of	$5,460	Cost of goods sold	$ 7,240

The specific identification method may appear logical, and it can be used by companies that deal in high-priced articles, such as works of art, precious gems, or rare antiques. However, most companies do not use it for the following reasons:

1. It is usually impractical, if not impossible, to keep track of the purchase and sale of individual items.

2. When a company deals in items that are identical but that it bought at different prices, deciding which items were sold becomes arbitrary. If the company were to use the specific identification method, it could raise or lower income by choosing the lower- or higher-priced items.

Average-Cost Method

Under the **average-cost method**, inventory is priced at the average cost of the goods available for sale during the accounting period. Average cost is computed by dividing the total cost of goods available for sale by the total units available for sale. This gives an average unit cost that is applied to the units in ending inventory.

In our illustration, the ending inventory would be $5,588, or $12.70 per unit, determined as follows:

Periodic Inventory System—Average-Cost Method

Cost of Goods Available for Sale ÷ Units Available for Sale = Average Unit Cost

$12,700 ÷ 1,000 units = $12.70

Ending inventory: 440 units @ $12.70 =	$ 5,588
Cost of goods available for sale	$12,700
Less April 30 inventory	5,588
Cost of goods sold	$ 7,112

The average-cost method tends to level out the effects of cost increases and decreases because the cost of the ending inventory is influenced by all the prices paid during the year and by the cost of beginning inventory. Some analysts, however, criticize this method because they believe recent costs are more relevant for income measurement and decision making.

First-In, First-Out (FIFO) Method

Study Note

Because of their perishable nature, some products, such as milk, require a *physical flow* of first-in, first-out. However, the inventory method used to account for them can be based on an assumed cost *flow* that differs from FIFO, such as average-cost or LIFO.

The **first-in, first-out (FIFO) method** assumes that the costs of the first items acquired should be assigned to the first items sold. The costs of the goods on hand at the end of a period are assumed to be from the most recent purchases, and the costs assigned to goods that have been sold are assumed to be from the earliest purchases. Any business, regardless of its goods flow, can use the FIFO method because the assumption underlying it is based on the flow of costs, not the flow of goods.

In our illustration, the FIFO method would result in an ending inventory of $6,100, computed as follows:

Periodic Inventory System—FIFO Method

400 units @ $14.00 from purchase of April 25	$ 5,600
40 units @ $12.50 from purchase of April 6	500
440 units at a cost of	$ 6,100
Cost of goods available for sale	$12,700
Less April 30 inventory	6,100
Cost of goods sold	$ 6,600

Thus, the FIFO method values ending inventory at the most recent costs and includes earlier costs in cost of goods sold. During periods of rising prices, FIFO yields the highest possible amount of net income because cost of goods sold shows the earliest costs incurred, which are lower during periods of inflation. Another reason for this is that businesses tend to raise selling prices as costs increase, even when they purchased the goods before the cost increase. In periods of declining prices, FIFO tends to charge the older and higher prices against

FOCUS ON BUSINESS PRACTICE

How Widespread Is LIFO?

Achieving convergence in inventory methods between U.S. and international accounting standards will be very difficult. As may be seen in Figure 8-6 (on page 366), LIFO is the second most popular inventory method in the United States. However, outside the United States, hardly any companies use LIFO because it is not allowed under international financial reporting standards (IFRS). Further, U.S. companies may use different inventory methods for different portions of their inventory as long as there is proper disclosure. International standards only allow this practice in very limited cases. Also, as noted earlier in the chapter, U.S. and international standards have different ways of measuring "market" value of inventories. Because these differences are so significant, there is no current effort to resolve them.[8]

revenues, thus reducing income. Consequently, a major criticism of FIFO is that it magnifies the effects of the business cycle on income.

Last-In, First-Out (LIFO) Method

Study Note

Physical flow under LIFO can be likened to the changes in a gravel pile as the gravel is sold. As the gravel on top leaves the pile, more is purchased and added to the top. The gravel on the bottom may never be sold. Although the physical flow is last-in, first-out, any acceptable cost flow assumption can be made.

The **last-in, first-out (LIFO) method** of costing inventories assumes that the costs of the last items purchased should be assigned to the first items sold and that the cost of ending inventory should reflect the cost of the goods purchased earliest. Under LIFO, the April 30 inventory would be $5,100:

Periodic Inventory System—LIFO Method

160 units @ $10.00 from April 1 inventory	$ 1,600
280 units @ $12.50 from purchase of April 6	3,500
440 units at a cost of	$ 5,100
Cost of goods available for sale	$12,700
Less April 30 inventory	5,100
Cost of goods sold	$ 7,600

Study Note

In inventory valuation, the flow of costs—and hence income determination—is more important than the physical movement of goods and balance sheet valuation.

The effect of LIFO is to value inventory at the earliest prices and to include the cost of the most recently purchased goods in the cost of goods sold. This assumption, of course, does not agree with the actual physical movement of goods in most businesses. There is, however, a strong logical argument to support LIFO. A certain size of inventory is necessary in a going concern—when inventory is sold, it must be replaced with more goods. The supporters of LIFO reason that the fairest determination of income occurs if the current costs of merchandise are matched against current sales prices, regardless of which physical units of merchandise are sold. When prices are moving either up or down, the cost of goods sold will, under LIFO, show costs closer to the price level at the time the goods are sold. Thus, the LIFO method tends to show a smaller net income during inflationary times and a larger net income during deflationary times than other methods of inventory valuation. The peaks and valleys of the business cycle tend to be smoothed out.

An argument can also be made against LIFO. Because the inventory valuation on the balance sheet reflects earlier prices, it often gives an unrealistic picture of the inventory's current value. Balance sheet measures like working capital and current ratio may be distorted and must be interpreted carefully.

FIGURE 8-5
The Impact of Costing Methods on the Income Statement and Balance Sheet Under the Periodic Inventory System

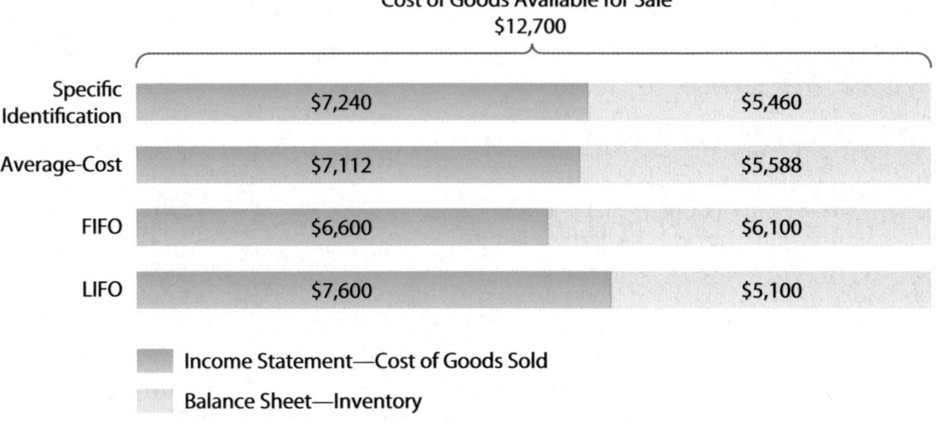

Summary of Inventory Costing Methods

Figure 8-5 summarizes how the four inventory costing methods affect the cost of goods sold on the income statement and inventory on the balance sheet when a company uses the periodic inventory system. In periods of rising prices, FIFO yields the highest inventory valuation, the lowest cost of goods sold, and hence a higher net income; LIFO yields the lowest inventory valuation, the highest cost of goods sold, and thus a lower net income.

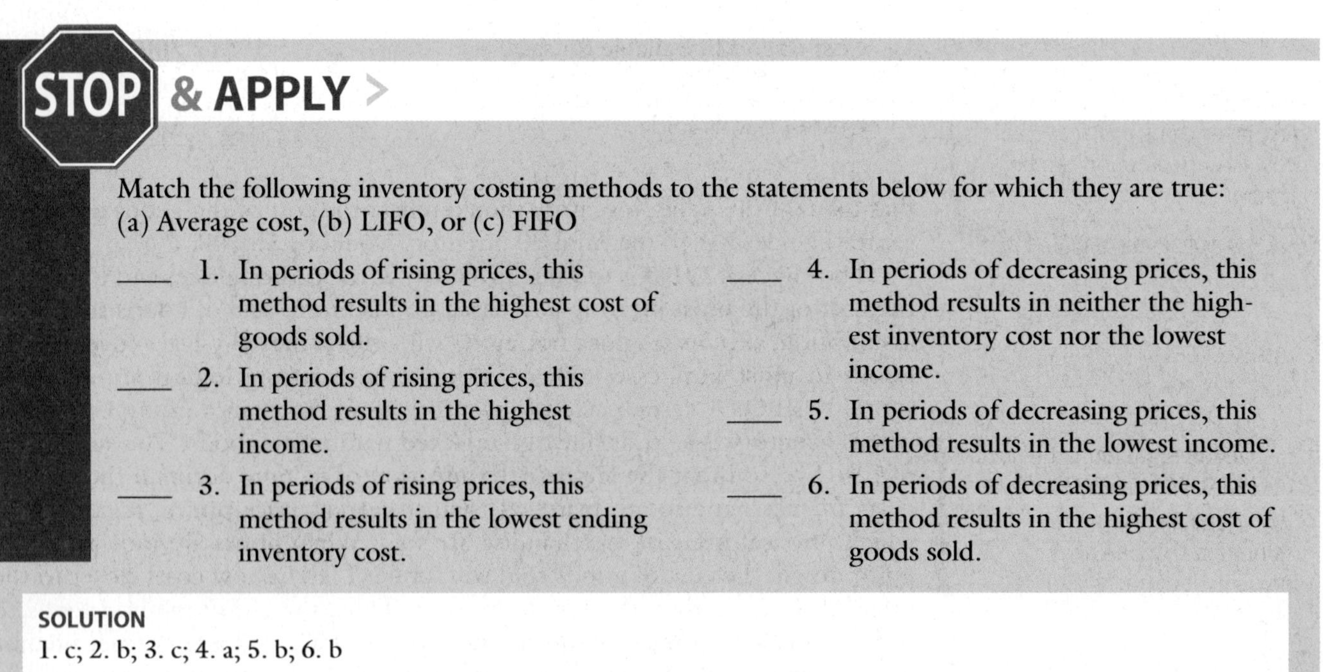

STOP & APPLY >

Match the following inventory costing methods to the statements below for which they are true: (a) Average cost, (b) LIFO, or (c) FIFO

____ 1. In periods of rising prices, this method results in the highest cost of goods sold.

____ 2. In periods of rising prices, this method results in the highest income.

____ 3. In periods of rising prices, this method results in the lowest ending inventory cost.

____ 4. In periods of decreasing prices, this method results in neither the highest inventory cost nor the lowest income.

____ 5. In periods of decreasing prices, this method results in the lowest income.

____ 6. In periods of decreasing prices, this method results in the highest cost of goods sold.

SOLUTION

1. c; 2. b; 3. c; 4. a; 5. b; 6. b

Impact of Inventory Decisions

LO4 Explain the effects of inventory costing methods on income determination and income taxes.

Table 8-1 shows how the specific identification, average-cost, FIFO, and LIFO methods of pricing inventory affect gross margin. The table uses the same data as in the previous section and assumes April sales of $10,000.

Keeping in mind that April was a period of rising prices, you can see in Table 8-1 that LIFO, which charges the most recent—and, in this case, the highest—prices to cost of goods sold, resulted in the lowest gross margin. Conversely, FIFO, which charges the earliest—and, in this case, the lowest—prices to cost of goods sold, produced the highest gross margin. The gross margin under the average-cost method falls between the gross margins produced by LIFO and FIFO, so this method clearly has a less pronounced effect.

During a period of declining prices, the LIFO method would produce a higher gross margin than the FIFO method. It is apparent that both these methods have the greatest impact on gross margin during prolonged periods of price changes, whether up or down. Because the specific identification method depends on the particular items sold, no generalization can be made about the effect of changing prices on gross margin.

Effects on the Financial Statements

As Figure 8-6 shows, the FIFO, LIFO, and average-cost methods of inventory costing are widely used. Each method has its advantages and disadvantages—none is perfect. Among the factors managers should consider in choosing an inventory costing method are the trend of prices and the effects of each method on financial statements, income taxes, and cash flows.

As we have pointed out, inventory costing methods have different effects on the income statement and balance sheet. The LIFO method is best suited for the income statement because it matches revenues and cost of goods sold. But it is not the best method for valuation of inventory on the balance sheet, particularly during a prolonged period of price increases or decreases. FIFO, on the other hand, is well suited to the balance sheet because the ending inventory is closest to current values and thus gives a more realistic view of a company's current assets. Readers of financial statements must be alert to the inventory methods a company uses and be able to assess their effects.

Study Note

In periods of rising prices, LIFO results in lower net income and thus lower taxes.

Effects on Income Taxes

The Internal Revenue Service governs how inventories must be valued for federal income tax purposes. IRS regulations give companies a wide choice of inventory

TABLE 8-1
Effects of Inventory Costing Methods on Gross Margin

	Specific Identification Method	Average-Cost Method	FIFO Method	LIFO Method
Sales	$ 10,000	$10,000	$10,000	$10,000
Cost of goods sold				
Beginning inventory	$ 1,600	$ 1,600	$ 1,600	$ 1,600
Purchases	11,100	11,100	11,100	11,100
Cost of goods available for sale	$ 12,700	$12,700	$12,700	$12,700
Less ending inventory	5,460	5,588	6,100	5,100
Cost of goods sold	$ 7,240	$ 7,112	$ 6,600	$ 7,600
Gross margin	$ 2,760	$ 2,888	$ 3,400	$ 2,400

FIGURE 8-6
Inventory Costing Methods Used by 600 Large Companies

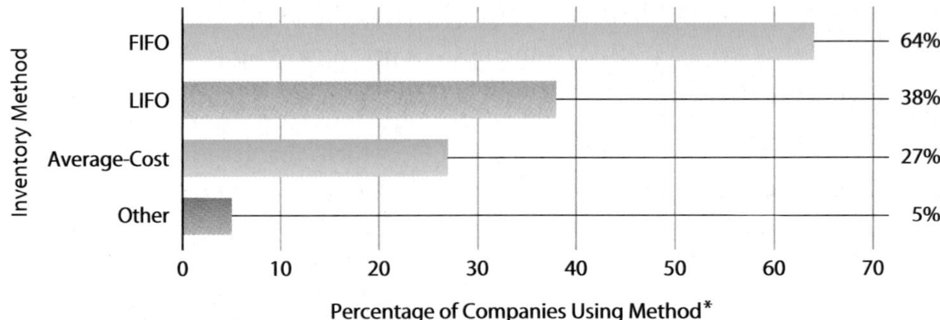

* Totals more than 100% due to use of more than one method.

Source: From "Accounting Trends & Techniques" (New York: AICPA, 2007). Copyright © 2007 by American Institute of Certified Public Accountants. Reprinted with permission.

costing methods, including specific identification, average-cost, FIFO, and LIFO, and, except when the LIFO method is used, it allows them to apply the lower-of-cost-or-market rule. However, if a company wants to change the valuation method it uses for income tax purposes, it must have advance approval from the IRS.* This requirement conforms to the consistency convention. A company should change its inventory method only if there is a good reason to do so. The company must show the nature and effect of the change in its financial statements.

Many accountants believe that using the FIFO and average-cost methods in periods of rising prices causes businesses to report more than their actual profit, resulting in excess payment of income tax. Profit is overstated because cost of goods sold is understated relative to current prices. Thus, the company must buy replacement inventory at higher prices, while additional funds are needed to pay income taxes. During periods of rapid inflation, billions of dollars reported as profits and paid in income taxes were believed to be the result of poor matching of current costs and revenues under the FIFO and average-cost methods. Consequently, many companies, believing that prices would continue to rise, switched to the LIFO inventory method.

When a company uses the LIFO method to report income for tax purposes, the IRS requires that it use the same method in its accounting records, and, as we have noted, it disallows use of the LCM rule. The company may, however, use the LCM rule for financial reporting purposes.

Over a period of rising prices, a business that uses the LIFO method may find that for balance sheet purposes, its inventory is valued at a figure far below what it currently pays for the same items. Management must monitor such a situation carefully, because if it lets the inventory quantity at year end fall below the level at the beginning of the year, the company will find itself paying higher income taxes. Higher income before taxes results because the company expenses the historical costs of inventory, which are below current costs. When sales have reduced inventories below the levels set in prior years, it is called a **LIFO liquidation**—that is, units sold exceed units purchased for the period.

Managers can prevent a LIFO liquidation by making enough purchases before the end of the year to restore the desired inventory level. Sometimes, however, a LIFO liquidation cannot be avoided because products are discontinued or supplies are interrupted, as in the case of a strike. In 2006, 26 out of 600 large companies reported a LIFO liquidation in which their net income increased due to the matching of historical costs with present sales dollars.[9]

*A single exception to this rule is that when companies change to LIFO from another method, they do not need advance approval from the IRS.

Effects on Cash Flows

Generally speaking, the choice of accounting methods does not affect cash flows. For example, a company's choice of average cost, FIFO, or LIFO does not affect what it pays for goods or the price at which it sells them. However, the fact that income tax law requires a company to use the same method for income tax purposes and financial reporting means that the choice of inventory method will affect the amount of income tax paid. Therefore, choosing a method that results in lower income will result in lower income taxes due. In most other cases where there is a choice of accounting method, a company may choose different methods for income tax computations and financial reporting.

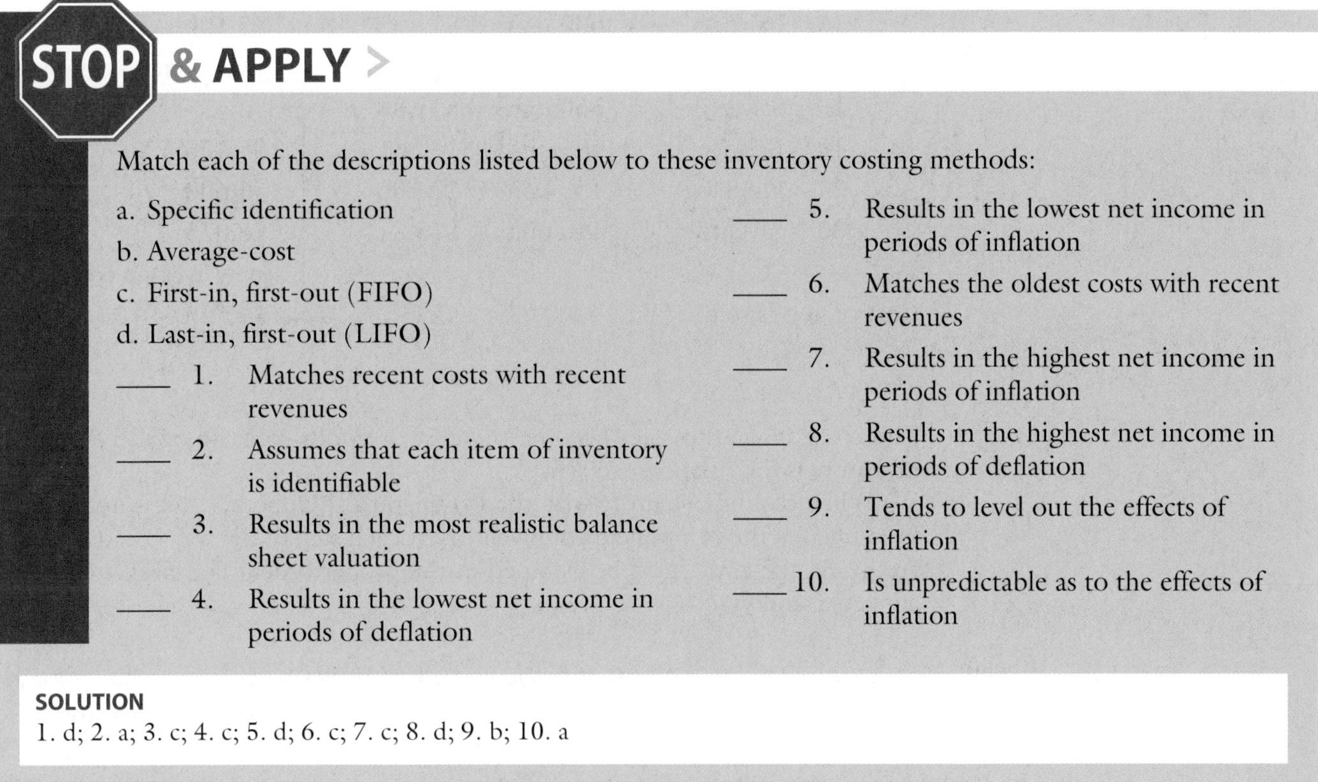

STOP & APPLY >

Match each of the descriptions listed below to these inventory costing methods:

a. Specific identification
b. Average-cost
c. First-in, first-out (FIFO)
d. Last-in, first-out (LIFO)

____ 1. Matches recent costs with recent revenues
____ 2. Assumes that each item of inventory is identifiable
____ 3. Results in the most realistic balance sheet valuation
____ 4. Results in the lowest net income in periods of deflation
____ 5. Results in the lowest net income in periods of inflation
____ 6. Matches the oldest costs with recent revenues
____ 7. Results in the highest net income in periods of inflation
____ 8. Results in the highest net income in periods of deflation
____ 9. Tends to level out the effects of inflation
____ 10. Is unpredictable as to the effects of inflation

SOLUTION
1. d; 2. a; 3. c; 4. c; 5. d; 6. c; 7. c; 8. d; 9. b; 10. a

Inventory Cost Under the Perpetual Inventory System

SO5 Calculate inventory cost under the perpetual inventory system using various costing methods.

Under the perpetual inventory system, cost of goods sold is accumulated as sales are made and costs are transferred from the Inventory account to the Cost of Goods Sold account. The cost of the ending inventory is the balance of the Inventory account. To illustrate costing methods under the perpetual inventory system, we use the following data:

Inventory Data—April 30

April	1	Inventory	160 units @ $10.00
	6	Purchase	440 units @ $12.50
	10	Sale	560 units
	25	Purchase	400 units @ $14.00
	30	Inventory	440 units

The specific identification method produces the same inventory cost and cost of goods sold under the perpetual system as under the periodic system because

Study Note

The costs of an automated perpetual system are considerable. They include the costs of automating the system, maintaining the system, and taking a physical inventory.

cost of goods sold and ending inventory are based on the cost of the identified items sold and on hand. The detailed records of purchases and sales maintained under the perpetual system facilitate the use of the specific identification method.

The average-cost method uses a different approach under the perpetual and periodic systems, and it produces different results. Under the periodic system, the average cost is computed for all goods available for sale during the period. Under the perpetual system, an average is computed after each purchase or series of purchases, as follows:

Perpetual Inventory System—Average-Cost Method

April	1	Inventory	160 units @ $10.00	$1,600
	6	Purchase	440 units @ $12.50	5,500
	6	Balance	600 units @ $11.83*	$7,100
				(new average computed)
	10	Sale	560 units @ $11.83*	(6,625)
	10	Balance	40 units @ $11.83*	$ 475
	25	Purchase	400 units @ $14.00	5,600
	30	Inventory	440 units @ $13.81*	$6,075
				(new average computed)
Cost of goods sold				$6,625

The costs applied to sales become the cost of goods sold, $6,625. The ending inventory is the balance, $6,075.

When costing inventory with the FIFO and LIFO methods, it is necessary to keep track of the components of inventory at each step of the way because as sales are made, the costs must be assigned in the proper order. The FIFO method is applied as follows:

Perpetual Inventory System—FIFO Method

April	1	Inventory	160 units @ $10.00		$1,600
	6	Purchase	440 units @ $12.50		5,500
	10	Sale	160 units @ $10.00	($1,600)	
			400 units @ $12.50	(5,000)	(6,600)
	10	Balance	40 units @ $12.50		$ 500
	25	Purchase	400 units @ $14.00		5,600
	30	Inventory	40 units @ $12.50	$ 500	
			400 units @ $14.00	5,600	$6,100
Cost of goods sold					$6,600

Note that the ending inventory of $6,100 and the cost of goods sold of $6,600 are the same as the figures computed earlier under the periodic inventory system. This will always occur because the ending inventory under both systems consists of the last items purchased—in this case, the entire purchase of April 25 and 40 units from the purchase of April 6.

*Rounded

FOCUS ON BUSINESS PRACTICE

More Companies Enjoy LIFO!

The availability of better technology may partially account for the increasing use of LIFO in the United States. Using the LIFO method under the perpetual inventory system has always been a tedious process, especially if done manually. The development of faster and less expensive computer systems has made it easier for companies that use the perpetual inventory system to switch to LIFO and enjoy that method's economic benefits.

The LIFO method is applied as follows:

Perpetual Inventory System—LIFO Method

April	1	Inventory	160 units @ $10.00		$1,600
	6	Purchase	440 units @ $12.50		5,500
	10	Sale	440 units @ $12.50	($5,500)	
			120 units @ $10.00	(1,200)	(6,700)
	10	Balance	40 units @ $10.00		$ 400
	25	Purchase	400 units @ $14.00		5,600
	30	Inventory	40 units @ $10.00	$ 400	
			400 units @ $14.00	5,600	$6,000
Cost of goods sold					$6,700

Notice that the ending inventory of $6,000 includes 40 units from the beginning inventory and 400 units from the April 25 purchase.

Figure 8-7 compares the average-cost, FIFO, and LIFO methods under the perpetual inventory system. The rank of the results is the same as under the periodic inventory system, but some amounts have changed. For example, LIFO has the lowest balance sheet inventory valuation regardless of the inventory system used, but the amount is $6,000 using the perpetual system versus $5,100 using the periodic system.

FIGURE 8-7
The Impact of Costing Methods on the Income Statement and Balance Sheet Under the Perpetual Inventory System

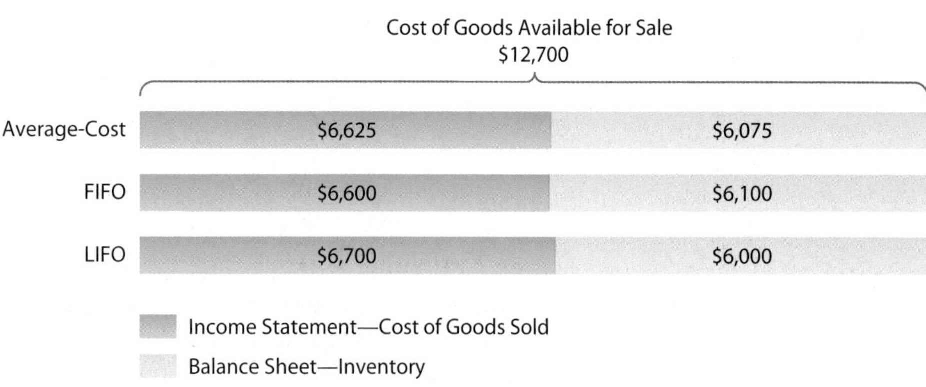

STOP & APPLY

Make the calculations asked for below given the following data:

		Inventory Data—April 30	
May	1	Inventory	100 units @ $4.00
	5	Purchase	200 units @ $5.00
	6	Sale	250 units

Using the perpetual inventory system, determine the cost of good sold associated with the sale on May 6 under the following methods: (a) average-cost, (b) FIFO, and (c) LIFO

SOLUTION

a. Average-cost method:

100 units × $4	$ 400
200 units × $5	1,000
300 units	$1,400

$1,400/300= $4.67 per unit

Cost of good sold = 250 units × $4.67 = $1,168*

b. FIFO method:

100 units × $4.00	$ 400
150 units × $5.00	750
Cost of goods sold	$1,150

c. LIFO method:

200 units × $5.00	$1,000
50 units × $4.00	200
Cost of goods sold	$1,200

*Rounded

Valuing Inventory by Estimation

SO6 Use the retail method and gross profit method to estimate the cost of ending inventory.

It is sometimes necessary or desirable to estimate the value of ending inventory. The retail method and gross profit method are most commonly used for this purpose.

Retail Method

The **retail method** estimates the cost of ending inventory by using the ratio of cost to retail price. Retail merchandising businesses use this method for two main reasons:

1. To prepare financial statements for each accounting period, one must know the cost of inventory; the retail method can be used to estimate the cost without taking the time or going to the expense of determining the cost of each item in the inventory.
2. Because items in a retail store normally have a price tag or a universal product code, it is common practice to take the physical inventory at retail from these price tags or codes and to reduce the total value to cost by using the retail method. The term *at retail* means the amount of the inventory at the marked selling prices of the inventory items.

Study Note

When estimating inventory by the retail method, the inventory need not be counted.

TABLE 8-2
Retail Method of Inventory Estimation

Study Note

Freight-in does not appear in the Retail column because retailers automatically price their goods high enough to cover freight charges.

	Cost	Retail
Beginning inventory	$ 80,000	$110,000
Net purchases for the period (excluding freight-in)	214,000	290,000
Freight-in	6,000	
Goods available for sale	$300,000	$400,000
Ratio of cost to retail price: $\frac{\$300,000}{\$400,000} = 75\%$		
Net sales during the period		320,000
Estimated ending inventory at retail		$ 80,000
Ratio of cost to retail	75%	
Estimated cost of ending inventory	$ 60,000	

When the retail method is used to estimate ending inventory, the records must show the beginning inventory at cost and at retail. They must also show the amount of goods purchased during the period at cost and at retail. The net sales at retail is the balance of the Sales account less returns and allowances. A simple example of the retail method is shown in Table 8-2.

Goods available for sale is determined at cost and at retail by listing beginning inventory and net purchases for the period at cost and at their expected selling price, adding freight-in to the cost column, and totaling. The ratio of these two amounts (cost to retail price) provides an estimate of the cost of each dollar of retail sales value. The estimated ending inventory at retail is then determined by deducting sales for the period from the retail price of the goods that were available for sale during the period. The inventory at retail is then converted to cost on the basis of the ratio of cost to retail.

The cost of ending inventory can also be estimated by applying the ratio of cost to retail price to the total retail value of the physical count of the ending inventory. Applying the retail method in practice is often more difficult than this simple example because of such complications as changes in retail price during the period, different markups on different types of merchandise, and varying volumes of sales for different types of merchandise.

Gross Profit Method

The **gross profit method** (also known as the *gross margin method*) assumes that the ratio of gross margin for a business remains relatively stable from year to year. The gross profit method is used in place of the retail method when records of the retail prices of beginning inventory and purchases are not available. It is a useful way of estimating the amount of inventory lost or destroyed by theft, fire, or other hazards; insurance companies often use it to verify loss claims. The gross profit method is acceptable for estimating the cost of inventory for interim reports, but it is not acceptable for valuing inventory in the annual financial statements.

As Table 8-3 shows, the gross profit method is simple to use. First, figure the cost of goods available for sale in the usual way (add purchases to beginning inventory). Second, estimate the cost of goods sold by deducting the estimated gross margin of 30 percent from sales. Finally, deduct the estimated cost of goods sold from the goods available for sale to arrive at the estimated cost of ending inventory.

TABLE 8-3
Gross Profit Method of Inventory Estimation

1.	Beginning inventory at cost		$100,000
	Purchases at cost (including freight-in)		580,000
	Cost of goods available for sale		$680,000
2.	Less estimated cost of goods sold		
	Sales at selling price	$800,000	
	Less estimated gross margin ($800,000 × 30%)	240,000	
	Estimated cost of goods sold		560,000
3.	Estimated cost of ending inventory		$120,000

STOP & APPLY >

Campus Jeans Shop had net retail sales of $195,000 during the current ayear. The following additional information was obtained from the company's accounting records:

	At Cost	*At Retail*
Beginning inventory	$ 40,000	$ 60,000
Net purchases (excluding freight-in)	130,000	210,000
Freight-in	10,000	

Using the retail method, estimate the company's ending inventory at cost. Assuming that a physical inventory taken at year end revealed an inventory on hand of $66,000 at retail value, what is the estimated amount of inventory shrinkage (loss due to theft, damage, etc.) at cost using the retail method?

SOLUTION

	Cost	Retail
Beginning inventory	$ 40,000	$ 60,000
Net purchases for the period (excluding freight-in)	130,000	210,000
Freight-in	10,000	
Goods available for sale	$180,000	$270,000
Ratio of cost to retail price: $\frac{\$180,000}{\$270,000} = 66.7\%$		
Net sales during the period		195,000
Estimated ending inventory at retail		$ 84,000
Ratio of cost to retail	66.7%	
Estimated cost of ending inventory	$ 56,000	

Estimated inventory loss = Estimated cost − (Retail inventory count × 2/3)
= $56,000 − ($66,000 × 2/3) = $56,000 − $44,000
= $12,000

▸ SNUGS COMPANY: REVIEW PROBLEM

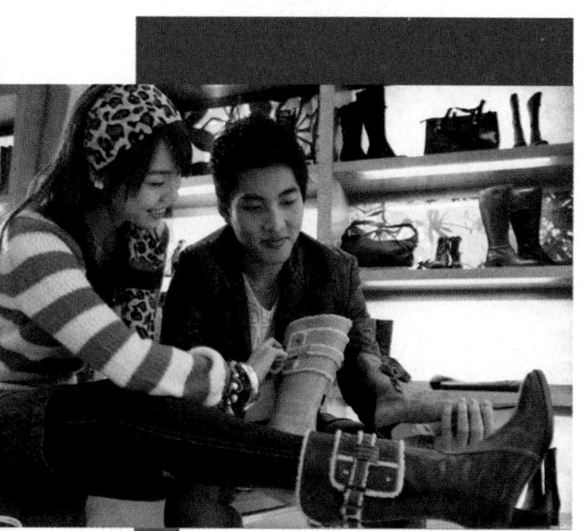

In this chapter's Decision Point, we posed the following questions:

- How should Snugs Company decide which inventory system and costing method to use?
- How do decisions about inventory evaluation and inventory levels affect operating results?

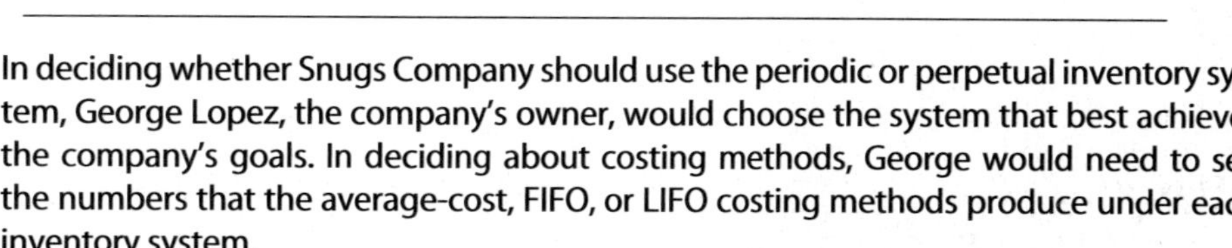

In deciding whether Snugs Company should use the periodic or perpetual inventory system, George Lopez, the company's owner, would choose the system that best achieves the company's goals. In deciding about costing methods, George would need to see the numbers that the average-cost, FIFO, or LIFO costing methods produce under each inventory system.

Periodic and Perpetual Inventory Systems and Inventory Ratios
LO1 LO3
SO5

As you know from having read this chapter, the decisions that George Lopez or any other manager makes about the evaluation of inventory affect a company's net income, the amount of taxes it pays, and its cash flows. Decisions about inventory levels also have important economic consequences: too low a level can result in disgruntled customers and too high a level can result in substantial storage, handling, and interest costs.

The table that follows summarizes Snug Company's beginning inventory, purchases, sales, and ending inventory in May:

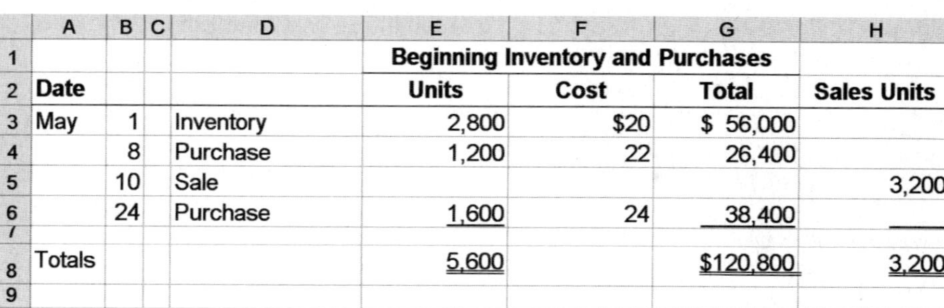

	A	B	C	D	E	F	G	H
1					Beginning Inventory and Purchases			
2	Date				Units	Cost	Total	Sales Units
3	May	1		Inventory	2,800	$20	$ 56,000	
4		8		Purchase	1,200	22	26,400	
5		10		Sale				3,200
6		24		Purchase	1,600	24	38,400	
7								
8	Totals				5,600		$120,800	3,200
9								

Required

1. Using the data for May and assuming that Snugs Company uses the periodic inventory system, compute the cost that should be assigned to ending inventory and to cost of goods sold using (a) the average-cost method, (b) the FIFO method, and (c) the LIFO method.
2. Using the same data and assuming that the company uses the perpetual inventory system, compute the cost that should be assigned to ending inventory and to cost of goods sold using (a) the average-cost method, (b) the FIFO method, and (c) the LIFO method.
3. Compute inventory turnover and days' inventory on hand under each of the inventory cost flow assumptions in 1. What conclusion can you draw from this comparison?

Answers to Review Problem

	Units	Amount
Beginning inventory	2,800	$ 56,000
Purchases	2,800	64,800
Available for sale	5,600	$120,800
Sales	3,200	
Ending inventory	2,400	

1. Periodic inventory system:

a. Average-cost method

Cost of goods available for sale	$120,800
Less ending inventory consisting of 2,400 units at $21.57*	51,768
Cost of goods sold	$ 69,032

*$120,800 ÷ 5,600 units = $21.57 (rounded)

b. FIFO method

Cost of goods available for sale		$120,800
Less ending inventory consisting of		
May 24 purchase (1,600 × $24)	$38,400	
May 8 purchase (800 × $22)	17,600	56,000
Cost of goods sold		$ 64,800

c. LIFO method

Cost of goods available for sale	$120,800
Less ending inventory consisting of beginning inventory (2,400 × $20)	48,000
Cost of goods sold	$ 72,800

2. Perpetual inventory system:

a. Average-cost method

Date			Units	Cost	Amount
May	1	Inventory	2,800	$20.00	$56,000
	8	Purchase	1,200	22.00	26,400
	8	Balance	4,000	20.60	$82,400
	10	Sale	(3,200)	20.60	(65,920)
	10	Balance	800	20.60	$16,480
	24	Purchase	1,600	24.00	38,400
	31	Inventory	2,400	22.87*	$54,880
Cost of goods sold					$65,920

*Rounded.

b. FIFO method

Date			Units	Cost	Amount
May	1	Inventory	2,800	$20	$56,000
	8	Purchase	1,200	22	26,400
	8	Balance	2,800	20	
			1,200	22	$82,400
	10	Sale	(2,800)	20	
			(400)	22	(64,800)
	10	Balance	800	22	$17,600
	24	Purchase	1,600	24	38,400
	31	Inventory	800	22	
			1,600	24	$56,000
Cost of goods sold					$64,800

c. LIFO method

Date			Units	Cost	Amount
May	1	Inventory	2,800	$20	$56,000
	8	Purchase	1,200	22	26,400
	8	Balance	2,800	20	
			1,200	22	$82,400
	10	Sale	(1,200)	22	
			(2,000)	20	(66,400)
	10	Balance	800	20	$16,000
	24	Purchase	1,600	24	38,400
	31	Inventory	800	20	
			1,600	24	$54,400
Cost of goods sold					$66,400

3. Ratios computed:

	Average-Cost	FIFO	LIFO
Cost of Goods Sold / Average Inventory	$\frac{\$69,032}{(\$51,768 + \$56,000) \div 2} =$	$\frac{\$64,800}{(\$56,000 + \$56,000) \div 2} =$	$\frac{\$72,800}{(\$48,000 + \$56,000) \div 2} =$
	$\frac{\$69,032}{\$53,884} = 1.3$	$\frac{\$64,800}{\$56,000} = 1.2$	$\frac{\$72,800}{\$52,000} = 1.4$
Inventory Turnover:	1.3 times	1.2 times	1.4 times
Days' Inventory on Hand:	(365 days ÷ 1.3 times)	(365 days ÷ 1.2 times)	(365 days ÷ 1.4 times)
	280.8 days	304.2 days	260.7 days

In periods of rising prices, the LIFO method will always result in a higher inventory turnover and lower days' inventory on hand than the other costing methods. When comparing inventory ratios for two or more companies, their inventory methods should be considered.

STOP & REVIEW >

LO1 Explain the management decisions related to inventory accounting, evaluation of inventory level, and the effects of inventory misstatements on income measurement.

The objective of inventory accounting is the proper determination of income through the matching of costs and revenues. In accounting for inventories, management must choose the type of processing system, costing method, and valuation method the company will use. Because the value of inventory affects a company's net income, management's choices will affect not only external and internal evaluations of the company but also the amount of income taxes the company pays and its cash flows.

The level of inventory a company maintains has important economic consequences. To evaluate inventory levels, managers commonly use inventory turnover and its related measure, days' inventory on hand. Supply-chain management and a just-in-time operating environment are a means of increasing inventory turnover and reducing inventory carrying costs.

If the value of ending inventory is understated or overstated, a corresponding error—dollar for dollar—will be made in income before income taxes. Furthermore, because the ending inventory of one period is the beginning inventory of the next, the misstatement affects two accounting periods, although the effects are opposite.

LO2 Define *inventory cost,* contrast goods flow and cost flow, and explain the lower-of-cost-or-market (LCM) rule.

Inventory cost includes the invoice price less purchases discounts; freight-in, including insurance in transit; and applicable taxes and tariffs. Goods flow refers to the actual physical flow of merchandise in a business, whereas cost flow refers to the assumed flow of costs. The lower-of-cost-or-market rule states that if the replacement cost (market cost) of the inventory is lower than the original cost, the lower figure should be used.

LO3 Calculate inventory cost under the periodic inventory system using various costing methods.

The value assigned to ending inventory is the result of two measurements: quantity and cost. Quantity is determined by taking a physical inventory. Cost is determined by using one of four inventory methods, each based on a different assumption of cost flow. Under the periodic inventory system, the specific identification method identifies the actual cost of each item in inventory. The average-cost method assumes that the cost of inventory is the average cost of goods available for sale during the period. The first-in, first-out (FIFO) method assumes that the costs of the first items acquired should be assigned to the first items sold. The last-in, first-out (LIFO) method assumes that the costs of the last items acquired should be assigned to the first items sold. The inventory method used may or may not correspond to the actual physical flow of goods.

LO4 Explain the effects of inventory costing methods on income determination and income taxes.

During periods of rising prices, the LIFO method will show the lowest net income; FIFO, the highest; and average-cost, in between. LIFO and FIFO have the opposite effects in periods of falling prices. No generalization can be made regarding the specific identification method. The Internal Revenue Service requires that if LIFO is used for tax purposes, it must be used for financial statements; it also does not allow the lower-of-cost-or-market rule to be applied to the LIFO method.

Supplemental Objectives

SO5 Calculate inventory cost under the perpetual inventory system using various costing methods. Under the perpetual inventory system, cost of goods sold is accumulated as sales are made and costs are transferred from the Inventory account to the Cost of Goods Sold account. The cost of the ending inventory is the balance of the Inventory account. The specific identification method and the FIFO method produce the same results under both the perpetual and periodic inventory systems. The results differ for the average-cost method because an average is calculated after each sale rather than at the end of the accounting period. Results also differ for the LIFO method because the cost components of inventory change constantly as goods are bought and sold.

SO6 Use the retail method and gross profit method to estimate the cost of ending inventory. Two methods of estimating the value of inventory are the retail method and the gross profit method. Under the retail method, inventory is determined at retail prices and is then reduced to estimated cost by applying a ratio of cost to retail price. Under the gross profit method, cost of goods sold is estimated by reducing sales by estimated gross margin. The estimated cost of goods sold is then deducted from the cost of goods available for sale to estimate the cost of ending inventory.

REVIEW of Concepts and Terminology

The following concepts and terms were introduced in this chapter:

Average-cost method 362 (LO3)
Consignment 359 (LO2)
Cost flow 358 (LO2)
First-in, first-out (FIFO) method 362 (LO3)
Goods flow 358 (LO2)
Gross profit method 371 (SO6)
Inventory cost 358 (LO2)
Just-in-time operating environment 355 (LO1)
Last-in, first-out (LIFO) method 363 (LO3)
LIFO liquidation 366 (LO4)
Lower-of-cost-or-market (LCM) rule 360 (LO2)
Market 360 (LO2)
Retail method 370 (SO6)
Specific identification method 361 (LO3)
Supply-chain management 354 (LO1)

Key Ratios

Days' inventory on hand 354 (LO1)
Inventory turnover 354 (LO1)

CHAPTER ASSIGNMENTS

BUILDING Your Basic Knowledge and Skills

Short Exercises

LO1 **Management Issues**

SE 1. Indicate whether each of the following items is associated with (a) allocating the cost of inventories in accordance with the matching rule, (b) assessing the impact of inventory decisions, (c) evaluating the level of inventory, or (d) engaging in an unethical practice.

1. Calculating days' inventory on hand
2. Ordering a supply of inventory to satisfy customer needs
3. Valuing inventory at an amount to achieve a specific profit objective
4. Calculating the income tax effect of an inventory method
5. Deciding the cost to place on ending inventory

LO1 **Inventory Turnover and Days' Inventory on Hand**

SE 2. During 2010, Gabriella's Fashion had beginning inventory of $960,000, ending inventory of $1,120,000, and cost of goods sold of $4,400,000. Compute the inventory turnover and days' inventory on hand.

LO3 **Specific Identification Method**

SE 3. Assume the following data with regard to inventory for Caciato Company:

Aug. 1	Inventory	40 units @ $10 per unit	$ 400
8	Purchase	50 units @ $11 per unit	550
22	Purchase	35 units @ $12 per unit	420
Goods available for sale		125 units	$1,370
Aug. 15	Sale	45 units	
28	Sale	25 units	
Inventory, Aug. 31		55 units	

Assuming that the inventory consists of 30 units from the August 8 purchase and 25 units from the purchase of August 22, calculate the cost of ending inventory and cost of goods sold.

LO3 **Average-Cost Method: Periodic Inventory System**

SE 4. Using the data in SE 3, calculate the cost of ending inventory and cost of goods sold according to the average-cost method under the periodic inventory system.

LO3 **FIFO Method: Periodic Inventory System**

SE 5. Using the data in SE 3, calculate the cost of ending inventory and cost of goods sold according to the FIFO method under the periodic inventory system.

LO3 **LIFO Method: Periodic Inventory System**

SE 6. Using the data in SE 3, calculate the cost of ending inventory and cost of goods sold according to the LIFO method under the periodic inventory system.

LO4 **Effects of Inventory Costing Methods and Changing Prices**

SE 7. Using Table 8-1 as an example, prepare a table with four columns that shows the ending inventory and cost of goods sold for each of the results from your calculations in **SE 3** through **SE 6**, including the effects of the different prices at which the merchandise was purchased. Which method(s) would result in the lowest income taxes?

SO5 Average-Cost Method: Perpetual Inventory System

SE 8. Using the data in **SE 3**, calculate the cost of ending inventory and cost of goods sold according to the average-cost method under the perpetual inventory system.

SO5 FIFO Method: Perpetual Inventory System

SE 9. Using the data in **SE 3**, calculate the cost of ending inventory and cost of goods sold according to the FIFO method under the perpetual inventory system.

SO5 LIFO Method: Perpetual Inventory System

SE 10. Using the data in **SE 3**, calculate the cost of ending inventory and cost of goods sold according to the LIFO method under the perpetual inventory system.

Exercises

LO1 LO2 Discussion Questions

E 1. Develop a brief answer to each of the following questions:

1. Is it good or bad for a retail store to have a large inventory?
2. Which is more important from the standpoint of inventory costing: the flow of goods or the flow of costs?
3. Why is misstatement of inventory one of the most common means of financial statement fraud?
4. Given that the LCM rule is an application of the conservatism convention in the current accounting period, is the effect of this application also conservative in the next period?

LO4 SO5 SO6 Discussion Questions

E 2. Develop a brief answer to each of the following questions:

1. Under what condition would all four methods of inventory pricing produce exactly the same results?
2. Under the perpetual inventory system, why is the cost of goods sold not determined by deducting the ending inventory from goods available for sale, as it is under the periodic method?
3. Which of the following methods do not require a physical inventory: periodic inventory system, perpetual inventory method, retail method, or gross profit method?

LO1 Management Issues

E 3. Indicate whether each of the following items is associated with (a) allocating the cost of inventories in accordance with the matching rule, (b) assessing the impact of inventory decisions, (c) evaluating the level of inventory, or (d) engaging in an unethical action.

1. Computing inventory turnover
2. Valuing inventory at an amount to meet management's targeted net income
3. Application of the just-in-time operating environment
4. Determining the effects of inventory decisions on cash flows
5. Apportioning the cost of goods available for sale to ending inventory and cost of goods sold

6. Determining the effects of inventory methods on income taxes
7. Determining the assumption about the flow of costs into and out of the company

LO1 **Inventory Ratios**

E 4. Just a Buck Discount Stores is assessing its levels of inventory for 2010 and 2011 and has gathered the following data:

	2011	2010	2009
Ending inventory	$ 96,000	$ 81,000	$69,000
Cost of goods sold	480,000	450,000	

Compute the inventory turnover and days' inventory on hand for 2010 and 2011 and comment on the results.

LO1 **Effects of Inventory Errors**

E 5. Condensed income statements for Kan-Du Company for two years are shown below.

	2011	2010
Sales	$504,000	$420,000
Cost of goods sold	300,000	216,000
Gross margin	$204,000	$204,000
Operating expenses	120,000	120,000
Income before income taxes	$ 84,000	$ 84,000

After the end of 2011, the company discovered that an error had resulted in a $36,000 understatement of the 2010 ending inventory.

Compute the corrected operating income for 2010 and 2011. What effect will the error have on operating income and owner's equity for 2012?

LO1 LO2 LO3 **Accounting Conventions and Inventory Valuation**

E 6. Turnbow Company, a telecommunications equipment company, has used the LIFO method adjusted for lower of cost or market for a number of years. Due to falling prices of its equipment, it has had to adjust (reduce) the cost of inventory to market each year for two years. The company is considering changing its method to FIFO adjusted for lower of cost or market in the future. Explain how the accounting conventions of consistency, full disclosure, and conservatism apply to this decision. If the change were made, why would management expect fewer adjustments to market in the future?

LO3 **Periodic Inventory System and Inventory Costing Methods**

E 7. Gary's Parts Shop recorded the following purchases and sales during the past year:

Jan. 1	Beginning inventory	125 cases @ $46	$ 5,750
Feb. 25	Purchase	100 cases @ $52	5,200
June 15	Purchase	200 cases @ $56	11,200
Oct. 15	Purchase	150 cases @ $56	8,400
Dec. 15	Purchase	100 cases @ $60	6,000
Goods available for sale		675	$36,550
Total sales		500 cases	
Dec. 31	Ending inventory	175 cases	

Assume that Gary's Parts Shop sold all of the June 15 purchase and 100 cases each from the January 1 beginning inventory, the October 15 purchase, and the December 15 purchase.

Determine the costs that should be assigned to ending inventory and cost of goods sold under each of the following assumptions: (1) costs are assigned by the specific identification method; (2) costs are assigned by the average-cost method; (3) costs are assigned by the FIFO method; (4) costs are assigned by the LIFO method. What conclusions can be drawn about the effect of each method on the income statement and the balance sheet of Gary's Parts Shop? Round your answers to the nearest whole number and assume the periodic inventory system.

LO3 Periodic Inventory System and Inventory Costing Methods

E 8. During its first year of operation, Deja Vu Company purchased 5,600 units of a product at $21 per unit. During the second year, it purchased 6,000 units of the same product at $24 per unit. During the third year, it purchased 5,000 units at $30 per unit. Deja Vu Company managed to have an ending inventory each year of 1,000 units. The company uses the periodic inventory system.

Prepare cost of goods sold statements that compare the value of ending inventory and the cost of goods sold for each of the three years using (1) the FIFO inventory costing method and (2) the LIFO method. From the resulting data, what conclusions can you draw about the relationships between the changes in unit price and the changes in the value of ending inventory?

LO3 Periodic Inventory System and Inventory Costing Methods

E 9. In chronological order, the inventory, purchases, and sales of a single product for a recent month are as follows:

		Units	Amount per Unit
June 1	Beginning inventory	150	$ 60
4	Purchase	400	66
12	Purchase	800	72
16	Sale	1,300	120
24	Purchase	300	78

Using the periodic inventory system, compute the cost of ending inventory, cost of goods sold, and gross margin. Use the average-cost, FIFO, and LIFO inventory costing methods. Explain the differences in gross margin produced by the three methods. Round unit costs to cents and totals to dollars.

LO4 Effects of Inventory Costing Methods on Cash Flows

E 10. Infinite Products, Inc., sold 120,000 cases of glue at $40 per case during 2010. Its beginning inventory consisted of 20,000 cases at a cost of $24 per case. During 2010, it purchased 60,000 cases at $28 per case and later 50,000 cases at $30 per case. Operating expenses were $1,100,000, and the applicable income tax rate was 30 percent.

Using the periodic inventory system, compute net income using the FIFO method and the LIFO method for costing inventory. Which alternative produces the larger cash flow? The company is considering a purchase of 10,000 cases at $30 per case just before the year end. What effect on net income and on cash flow will this proposed purchase have under each method? (**Hint:** What are the income tax consequences?)

SO5 Perpetual Inventory System and Inventory Costing Methods

E 11. Referring to the data provided in **E 9** and using the perpetual inventory system, compute the cost of ending inventory, cost of goods sold, and gross margin. Use the average-cost, FIFO, and LIFO inventory costing methods. Explain the reasons for the differences in gross margin produced by the three methods. Round unit costs to cents and totals to dollars.

LO3 SO5 Periodic and Perpetual Systems and Inventory Costing Methods

E 12. During July 2010, Tricoci, Inc., sold 250 units of its product Empire for $4,000. The following units were available:

	Units	Cost
Beginning inventory	100	$ 2
Purchase 1	40	4
Purchase 2	60	6
Purchase 3	150	9
Purchase 4	90	12

A sale of 250 units was made after purchase 3. Of the units sold, 100 came from beginning inventory and 150 came from purchase 3.

Determine cost of goods available for sale and ending inventory in units. Then determine the costs that should be assigned to cost of goods sold and ending inventory under each of the following assumptions: (1) Costs are assigned under the periodic inventory system using (a) the specific identification method, (b) the average-cost method, (c) the FIFO method, and (d) the LIFO method. (2) Costs are assigned under the perpetual inventory system using (a) the average-cost method, (b) the FIFO method, and (c) the LIFO method. For each alternative, show the gross margin. Round unit costs to cents and totals to dollars.

SO6 Retail Method

E 13. Olivia's Dress Shop had net retail sales of $125,000 during the current year. The following additional information was obtained from the company's accounting records:

	At Cost	At Retail
Beginning inventory	$20,000	$ 30,000
Net purchases (excluding freight-in)	70,000	110,000
Freight-in	5,200	

1. Using the retail method, estimate the company's ending inventory at cost.
2. Assume that a physical inventory taken at year end revealed an inventory on hand of $9,000 at retail value. What is the estimated amount of inventory shrinkage (loss due to theft, damage, etc.) at cost using the retail method?

SO6 Gross Profit Method

E 14. Chen Mo-Wan was at home when he received a call from the fire department telling him his store had burned. His business was a total loss. The insurance company asked him to prove his inventory loss. For the year, until the date of the fire, Chen's company had sales of $900,000 and purchases of $560,000. Freight-in amounted to $27,400, and beginning inventory was $90,000. Chen always priced his goods to achieve a gross margin of 40 percent. Compute Chen's estimated inventory loss.

Problems

LO1 LO3 **Periodic Inventory System and Inventory Costing Methods**

P 1. El Faro Company merchandises a single product called Smart. The following data represent beginning inventory and purchases of Smart during the past year: January 1 inventory, 34,000 units at $11.00; February purchases, 40,000 units at $12.00; March purchases, 80,000 units at $12.40; May purchases, 60,000 units at $12.60; July purchases, 100,000 units at $12.80; September purchases, 80,000 units at $12.60; and November purchases, 30,000 units at $13.00. Sales of Smart totaled 393,000 units at $20.00 per unit. Selling and administrative expenses totaled $2,551,000 for the year. El Faro Company uses the periodic inventory system.

Required

1. Prepare a schedule to compute the cost of goods available for sale.
2. Compute income before income taxes under each of the following inventory cost flow assumptions: (a) the average-cost method; (b) the FIFO method; and (c) the LIFO method.

User insight ▶

3. Compute inventory turnover and days' inventory on hand under each of the inventory cost flow assumptions listed in requirement 2. What conclusion can you draw?

LO1 LO3 **Periodic Inventory System and Inventory Costing Methods**

P 2. The inventory of Product PIT and data on purchases and sales for a two-month period follow. The company closes its books at the end of each month. It uses the periodic inventory system.

Apr.	1	Beginning inventory	50 units @ $204
	10	Purchase	100 units @ $220
	17	Sale	90 units
	30	Ending inventory	60 units
May	2	Purchase	100 units @ $216
	14	Purchase	50 units @ $224
	22	Purchase	60 units @ $234
	30	Sale	200 units
	31	Ending inventory	70 units

Required

1. Compute the cost of ending inventory of Product PIT on April 30 and May 31 using the average-cost method. In addition, determine cost of goods sold for April and May. Round unit costs to cents and totals to dollars.
2. Compute the cost of the ending inventory on April 30 and May 31 using the FIFO method. In addition, determine cost of goods sold for April and May.
3. Compute the cost of the ending inventory on April 30 and May 31 using the LIFO method. In addition, determine cost of goods sold for April and May.

User insight ▶

4. Do the cash flows from operations for April and May differ depending on which inventory costing method is used—average-cost, FIFO, or LIFO? Explain.

LO4 SO5 **Perpetual Inventory System and Inventory Costing Methods**

P 3. Use the data provided in **P 2**, but assume that the company uses the perpetual inventory system. (**Hint:** In preparing the solutions required below, it is helpful to determine the balance of inventory after each transaction, as shown in the Review Problem in this chapter.)

Required

1. Determine the cost of ending inventory and cost of goods sold for April and May using the average-cost method. Round unit costs to cents and totals to dollars.
2. Determine the cost of ending inventory and cost of goods sold for April and May using the FIFO method.
3. Determine the cost of ending inventory and cost of goods sold for April and May using the LIFO method.

User insight ▶

4. Assume that this company grows for many years in a long period of rising prices. How realistic do you think the balance sheet value for inventory would be and what effect would it have on the inventory turnover ratio?

SO6 **Retail Method**

P 4. Ptak Company operates a large discount store and uses the retail method to estimate the cost of ending inventory. Management suspects that in recent weeks there have been unusually heavy losses from shoplifting or employee pilferage. To estimate the amount of the loss, the company has taken a physical inventory and will compare the results with the estimated cost of inventory. Data from the accounting records of Ptak Company are as follows:

	At Cost	At Retail
August 1 beginning inventory	$102,976	$148,600
Purchases	143,466	217,000
Purchases returns and allowances	(4,086)	(6,400)
Freight-in	1,900	
Sales		218,366
Sales returns and allowances		(1,866)
August 31 physical inventory at retail		124,900

Required

1. Using the retail method, prepare a schedule to estimate the dollar amount of the store's month-end inventory at cost.
2. Use the store's cost to retail ratio to reduce the retail value of the physical inventory to cost.
3. Calculate the estimated amount of inventory shortage at cost and at retail.

User insight ▶

4. Many retail chains use the retail method because it is efficient. Why do you think using this method is an efficient way for these companies to operate?

SO6 **Gross Profit Method**

P 5. Rudy Brothers is a large retail furniture company that operates in two adjacent warehouses. One warehouse is a showroom, and the other is used to store merchandise. On the night of June 22, 2011, a fire broke out in the storage warehouse and destroyed the merchandise stored there. Fortunately, the fire did not reach the showroom, so all the merchandise on display was saved.

Although the company maintained a perpetual inventory system, its records were rather haphazard, and the last reliable physical inventory had been taken on December 31. In addition, there was no control of the flow of goods between the showroom and the warehouse. Thus, it was impossible to tell what goods should have been in either place. As a result, the insurance company required an independent estimate of the amount of loss. The insurance company examiners were satisfied when they received the following information:

Merchandise inventory on December 31, 2010	$363,700.00
Purchases, January 1 to June 22, 2011	603,050.00
Purchases returns, January 1 to June 22, 2011	(2,676.50)
Freight-in, January 1 to June 22, 2011	13,275.00
Sales, January 1 to June 22, 2011	989,762.50
Sales returns, January 1 to June 22, 2011	(7,450.00)
Merchandise inventory in showroom on June 22, 2011	100,740.00
Average gross margin	44%

Required

1. Prepare a schedule that estimates the amount of the inventory lost in the fire.

User insight ▶

2. What are some other reasons management might need to estimate the amount of inventory?

Alternate Problems

LO1 LO3

Periodic Inventory System and Inventory Costing Methods

P 6. The Jarmen Cabinet Company sold 2,200 cabinets during 2010 at $80 per cabinet. Its beginning inventory on January 1 was 130 cabinets at $28. Purchases made during the year were as follows:

February	225 cabinets @ $31.00
April	350 cabinets @ $32.50
June	700 cabinets @ $35.00
August	300 cabinets @ $33.00
October	400 cabinets @ $34.00
November	250 cabinets @ $36.00

The company's selling and administrative expenses for the year were $50,500. The company uses the periodic inventory system.

Required

1. Prepare a schedule to compute the cost of goods available for sale.
2. Compute income before income taxes under each of the following inventory cost flow assumptions: (a) the average-cost method, (b) the FIFO method, and (c) the LIFO method.

User insight ▶

3. Compute inventory turnover and days' inventory on hand under each of the inventory cost flow assumptions in requirement 2. What conclusion can you draw from this comparison?

LO1 LO3

Periodic Inventory System and Inventory Costing Methods

P 7. The inventory, purchases, and sales of Product CAT for March and April are listed below. The company closes its books at the end of each month. It uses the periodic inventory system.

Mar.	1	Beginning inventory	60 units @ $98
	10	Purchase	100 units @ $104
	19	Sale	90 units
	31	Ending inventory	70 units
Apr.	4	Purchase	120 units @ $106
	15	Purchase	50 units @ $108
	23	Sale	200 units
	25	Purchase	100 units @ $110
	30	Ending inventory	140 units

Required

1. Compute the cost of the ending inventory on March 31 and April 30 using the average-cost method. In addition, determine cost of goods sold for March and April. Round unit costs to cents and totals to dollars.
2. Compute the cost of the ending inventory on March 31 and April 30 using the FIFO method. Also determine cost of goods sold for March and April.
3. Compute the cost of the ending inventory on March 31 and April 30 using the LIFO method. Also determine cost of goods sold for March and April.
4. (User insight ▶) Do the cash flows from operations for March and April differ depending on which inventory costing method is used—average-cost, FIFO, or LIFO? Explain.

LO4 SO5 **Perpetual Inventory System and Inventory Costing Methods**

P 8. Use the data provided in **P 7**, but assume that the company uses the perpetual inventory system. (**Hint**: In preparing the solutions required below, it is helpful to determine the balance of inventory after each transaction, as shown in the Review Problem in this chapter.)

Required

1. Determine the cost of ending inventory and cost of goods sold for March and April using the average-cost method. Round unit costs to cents and totals to dollars.
2. Determine the cost of ending inventory and cost of goods sold for March and April using the FIFO method.
3. Determine the cost of ending inventory and cost of goods sold for March and April using the LIFO method.
4. (User insight ▶) Assume that this company grows for many years in a long period of rising prices. How realistic do you think the balance sheet value for inventory would be and what effect would it have on the inventory turnover ratio?

SO6 **Retail Method**

P 9. Fuentes Company operates a large discount store and uses the retail method to estimate the cost of ending inventory. Management suspects that in recent weeks there have been unusually heavy losses from shoplifting or employee pilferage. To estimate the amount of the loss, the company has taken a physical inventory and will compare the results with the estimated cost of inventory. Data from the accounting records of Fuentes Company are as follows:

	At Cost	At Retail
October 1 beginning inventory	$51,488	$ 74,300
Purchases	71,733	108,500
Purchases returns and allowances	(2,043)	(3,200)
Freight-in	950	
Sales		109,183
Sales returns and allowances		(933)
October 31 physical inventory at retail		62,450

Required

1. Using the retail method, prepare a schedule to estimate the dollar amount of the store's month-end inventory at cost.
2. Use the store's cost to retail ratio to reduce the retail value of the physical inventory to cost.

3. Calculate the estimated amount of inventory shortage at cost and at retail.

User insight ▶ 4. Many retail chains use the retail method because it is efficient. Why do you think using this method is an efficient way for these companies to operate?

SO6 Gross Profit Method

P 10. Oakley Sisters is a large retail furniture company that operates in two adjacent warehouses. One warehouse is a showroom, and the other is used to store merchandise. On the night of April 22, 2010, a fire broke out in the storage warehouse and destroyed the merchandise stored there. Fortunately, the fire did not reach the showroom, so all the merchandise on display was saved.

Although the company maintained a perpetual inventory system, its records were rather haphazard, and the last reliable physical inventory had been taken on December 31. In addition, there was no control of the flow of goods between the showroom and the warehouse. Thus, it was impossible to tell what goods should have been in either place. As a result, the insurance company required an independent estimate of the amount of loss. The insurance company examiners were satisfied when they received the following information:

Merchandise inventory on December 31, 2009	$ 727,400
Purchases, January 1 to April 22, 2010	1,206,100
Purchases returns, January 1 to April 22, 2010	(5,353)
Freight-in, January 1 to April 22, 2010	26,550
Sales, January 1 to April 22, 2010	1,979,525
Sales returns, January 1 to April 22, 2010	(14,900)
Merchandise inventory in showroom on April 22, 2010	201,480
Average gross margin	44%

Required

1. Prepare a schedule that estimates the amount of the inventory lost in the fire.

User insight ▶ 2. What are some other reasons management might need to estimate the amount of inventory?

ENHANCING Your Knowledge, Skills, and Critical Thinking

LO1 Evaluation of Inventory Levels

C 1. JCPenney, a large retail company with many stores, has an inventory turnover of 3.7 times. **Dell Computer Corporation**, an Internet mail-order company, has an inventory turnover of about 77.8. Dell achieves its high turnover through supply-chain management in a just-in-time operating environment. Why is inventory turnover important to companies like JCPenney and Dell? Why are comparisons among companies important? Are JCPenney and Dell a good match for comparison? Describe supply-chain management and a just-in-time operating environment. Why are they important to achieving a favorable inventory turnover?

LO4 LIFO Inventory Method

C 2. Seventy-six percent of chemical companies use the LIFO inventory method for the costing of inventories, whereas only 9 percent of computer equipment companies use LIFO.[10] Describe the LIFO inventory method. What effects does it have on reported income, cash flows, and income taxes during periods of price changes? Why do you think so many chemical companies use LIFO while most companies in the computer industry do not?

LO1 LO4

Inventories, Income Determination, and Ethics

C 3. Jazz, Inc., which has a December 31 year end, designs and sells fashions for young professional women. Lyla Hilton, president of the company, fears that the forecasted 2010 profitability goals will not be reached. She is pleased when Jazz receives a large order on December 30 from The Executive Woman, a retail chain of upscale stores for businesswomen. Hilton immediately directs the controller to record the sale, which represents 13 percent of Jazz's annual sales. At the same time, she directs the inventory control department not to separate the goods for shipment until after January 1. Separated goods are not included in inventory because they have been sold.

On December 31, the company's auditors arrive to observe the year-end taking of the physical inventory under the periodic inventory system. How will Hilton's actions affect Jazz's 2010 profitability? How will they affect Jazz's 2011 profitability? Were Hilton's actions ethical? Why or why not?

LO2 LO4

Retail Business Inventories

C 4. Your instructor will assign teams to various types of stores in your community—a grocery, clothing, book, music, or appliance store. Make an appointment to interview the manager for 30 minutes to discuss the company's inventory accounting system. The store may be a branch of a larger company. Ask the following questions, summarize your findings in a paper, and be prepared to discuss your results in class:

1. What is the physical flow of merchandise into the store, and what documents are used in connection with this flow?
2. What documents are prepared when merchandise is sold?
3. Does the store keep perpetual inventory records? If so, does it keep the records in units only, or does it keep track of cost as well? If not, what system does the store use?
4. How often does the company take a physical inventory?
5. How are financial statements generated for the store?
6. What method does the company use to cost its inventory for financial statements?

LO1 LO4
SO5 SO6

Inventory Costing Methods and Ratios

C 5. Refer to the note related to inventories in **CVS Corporation**'s annual report in the Supplement to Chapter 5 to answer the following questions: What inventory method(s) does CVS use? If LIFO inventories had been valued at FIFO, why would there be no difference? Do you think many of the company's inventories are valued at market? Few companies use the retail method, so why do you think CVS uses it? Compute and compare the inventory turnover and days' inventory on hand for CVS for 2008 and 2007. Ending 2006 inventories were $7,560.2 million.

LO1 **Inventory Efficiency**

C 6. Refer to **CVS**'s annual report in the Supplement to Chapter 5 and to the following data (in millions) for **Walgreens**: cost of goods sold, $42,391 and $38,518.1 for 2008 and 2007, respectively; inventories, $7,249, $6,790, $6,050 for 2008, 2007, and 2006, respectively. Ending inventories for 2006 for CVS were $7,560.2 million.

Calculate inventory turnover and days' inventory on hand for 2007 and 2008. If you did **C 5**, refer to your answer there for CVS. Has either company improved its performance over the past two years? What advantage does the superior company's performance provide to it? Which company appears to make the most efficient use of inventories? Explain your answers.

CHAPTER

Cash and Receivables

Making a Statement

INCOME STATEMENT

Revenues

– Expenses

= Net Income

STATEMENT OF OWNER'S EQUITY

Beginning Balance

+ Net Income

– Withdrawals

= Ending Balance

BALANCE SHEET

Assets	**Liabilities**
	Owner's Equity

A = L + OE

STATEMENT OF CASH FLOWS

Operating activities
+ Investing activities
+ Financing activities
= Change in Cash
+ Beginning Balance
= Ending Cash Balance

Estimation of uncollectible credit sales affects the amount of accounts receivable on the balance sheet and operating expenses on the income statement.

Cash and receivables require careful oversight to ensure that they are ethically handled. If cash is mismanaged or stolen, it can bring about the downfall of a business. Because accounts receivable and notes receivable require estimates of future losses, they can be easily manipulated to show improvement in reported earnings. Improved earnings can, of course, enhance a company's stock price, as well as the bonuses of its executives. In this chapter, we address the management of cash and demonstrate the importance of estimates in accounting for receivables.

LEARNING OBJECTIVES

LO1 Identify and explain the management and ethical issues related to cash and receivables. (pp. 392–399)

LO2 Define *cash equivalents*, and explain methods of controlling cash, including bank reconciliations. (pp. 399–403)

LO3 Apply the allowance method of accounting for uncollectible accounts. (pp. 403–411)

LO4 Define *promissory note*, and make common calculations for promissory notes receivable. (pp. 411–415)

DECISION POINT ► A USER'S FOCUS PENTE COMPUTER COMPANY

Pente Computer Company sells computer products for cash or on credit. The company's peak sales occur in August and September, when students are shopping for computers and computer-related supplies, and during the pre-holiday season in November and December. It is now January, and Andre Pente, the company's owner, has been reviewing the company's performance over the past two years. He has determined that in those years, approximately 1.5 percent of net sales have been uncollectible, and he is concerned that this year, the company may not have enough cash to cover operations before sales begin to increase again in late summer. In this chapter, we discuss concepts and techniques that would help Pente manage his cash and accounts receivable so that the company maintains its liquidity by answering the questions at the right.

- ► How can Pente Computer Company manage its cash needs?
- ► How can the company reduce the level of uncollectible accounts and increase the likelihood that accounts receivable will be paid on time?
- ► How can the company evaluate the effectiveness of its credit policies and the level of its accounts receivable?

Management Issues Related to Cash and Receivables

LO1 Identify and explain the management and ethical issues related to cash and receivables.

The management of cash and accounts and notes receivable is critical to maintaining adequate liquidity. These assets are important components of the operating cycle, which also includes inventories and accounts payable. In dealing with cash and receivables, management must address five key issues: managing cash needs, setting credit policies, evaluating the level of accounts receivable, financing receivables, and making ethical estimates of credit losses.

Cash Management

On the balance sheet, **cash** usually consists of currency and coins on hand, checks and money orders from customers, and deposits in checking and savings accounts. Cash is the most liquid of all assets and the most readily available to pay debts. It is central to the operating cycle because all operating transactions eventually use or generate cash.

Cash may include a *compensating balance*, an amount that is not entirely free to be spent. A **compensating balance** is a minimum amount that a bank requires a company to keep in its bank account as part of a credit-granting arrangement. Such an arrangement restricts cash; in effect, it increases the interest on the loan and reduces a company's liquidity. The Securities and Exchange Commission therefore requires companies that have compensating balances to disclose the amounts involved.

Most companies experience seasonal cycles of business activity during the year. During some periods, sales are weak; during others, they are strong. There are also periods when expenditures are high, and periods when they are low. For toy companies, college textbook publishers, amusement parks, construction companies, and manufacturers of sports equipment, the cycles are dramatic, but all companies experience them to some degree.

Seasonal cycles require careful planning of cash inflows, cash outflows, borrowing, and investing. Figure 9-1 shows the seasonal cycles typical of an athletic sportswear company like **Nike**. As you can see, cash receipts from sales are highest in the late spring and summer because that is when most people engage in outdoor sports. Sales are relatively low in the winter months. On the other hand, cash expenditures are highest in late winter and spring as the company builds up inventory for spring and summer selling. During the late summer, fall, and

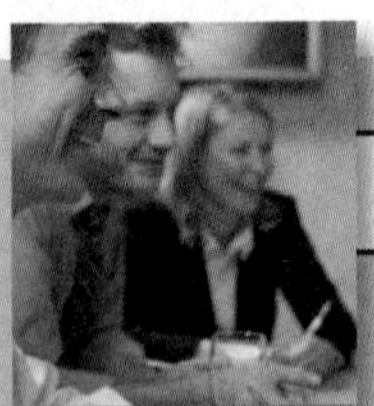

FOCUS ON BUSINESS PRACTICE

How Do Good Companies Deal with Bad Times?

Good companies manage their cash well even in bad times. When a slump in the technology market caused **Texas Instrument**'s sales to decline by more than 40 percent, resulting in a loss of nearly $120 million, this large electronics firm actually increased its cash by acting quickly to cut its purchases of plant assets by two-thirds. It also reduced its payroll and lowered the average number of days it had inventory on hand from 71 to 58.[1]

In similar circumstances, some companies have not reacted as quickly as Texas Instruments. For example, before 9/11, the Big Three automakers—**General Motors**, **Ford**, and **DaimlerChrysler**—were awash in cash. However, in little over a year, the three companies went through $28 billion in cash through various purchases, losses, dividends, and share buybacks. Then, with increasing losses from rising costs, big rebates, and zero percent financing, they were suddenly faced with a shortage of cash. As a result, Standard & Poor's lowered their credit ratings, which raises the interest cost of borrowing money. Perhaps the Big Three should have held on to some of that cash.[2] By 2009, GM and DaimlerChrysler were bankrupt and needed huge government bailouts in order to survive and emerge again as viable companies.

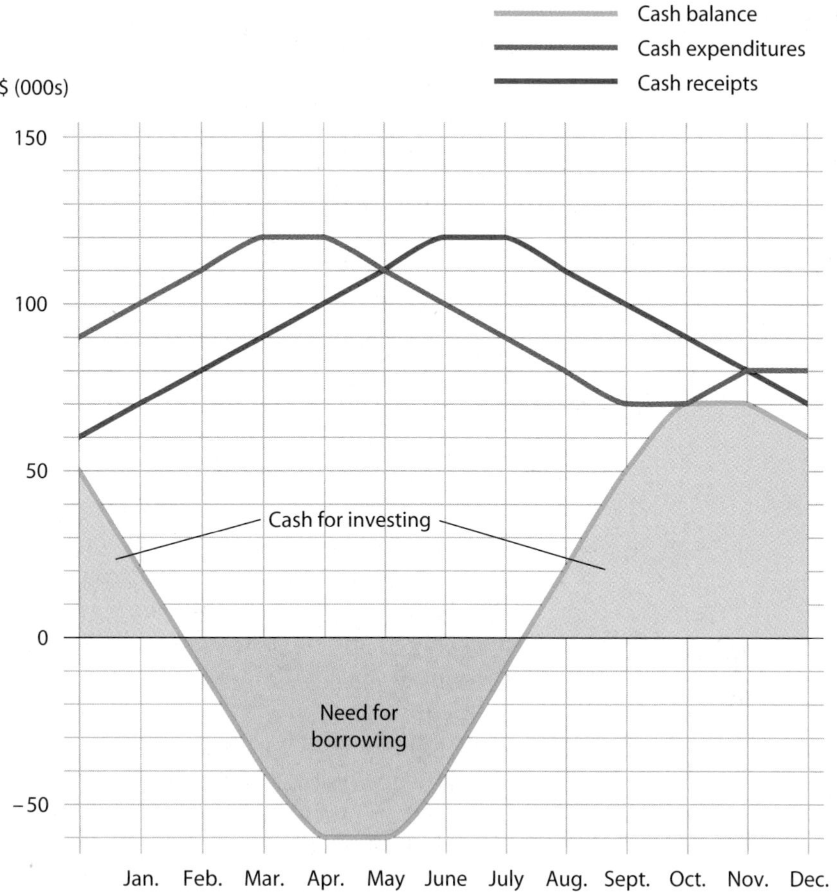

FIGURE 9-1
Seasonal Cycles and Cash Requirements for an Athletic Sportswear Company

winter, the company has excess cash on hand that it needs to invest in a way that will earn a return but still permit access to cash as needed. During spring and early summer, the company needs to plan for short-term borrowing to tide it over until cash receipts pick up later in the year.

Accounts Receivable and Credit Policies

Like cash, accounts receivable and notes receivable are major types of **short-term financial assets**. Both kinds of receivables result from extending credit to individual customers or to other companies. Retailers like **Sears** (now merged with **Kmart**) have made credit available to nearly every responsible person in the United States. Every field of retail trade has expanded by allowing customers to make payments a month or more after the date of sale. What is not so apparent is that credit has expanded even more among wholesalers and manufacturers like **Nike** than at the retail level. Figure 9-2 shows the levels of accounts receivable in selected industries.

As we have indicated, **accounts receivable** are the short-term financial assets of a wholesaler or retailer that arise from sales on credit. This type of credit is often called **trade credit**. Terms of trade credit usually range from 5 to 60 days, depending on industry practice. For some companies that sell to consumers, **installment accounts receivable**, which allow the buyer to make a series of time payments, constitute a significant portion of accounts receivable. Department stores, appliance stores, furniture stores, used car dealers, and other retail businesses often offer installment credit. The installment accounts receivable of retailers like **Sears** and **JCPenney** can amount to millions of dollars. Although the

FIGURE 9-2
Accounts Receivable as a Percentage of Total Assets for Selected Industries

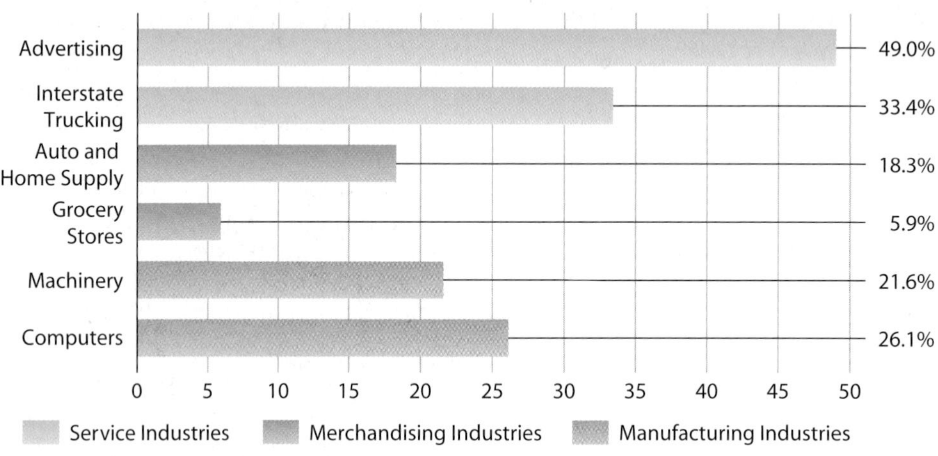

Source: Data from Dun & Bradstreet, *Industry Norms and Key Business Ratios,* 2005–2006.

payment period may be 24 months or more, installment accounts receivable are classified as current assets if such credit policies are customary in the industry.

On the balance sheet, *accounts receivable* designates amounts arising from credit sales made to customers in the ordinary course of business. Because loans or credit sales made to employees, officers, or owners of the corporation increase the risk of uncollectibility and conflict of interest, they appear separately on the balance sheet under asset titles like *receivables from employees.*

Normally, individual accounts receivable have debit balances, but sometimes customers overpay their accounts either by mistake or in anticipation of making future purchases. When these accounts show credit balances, the company should show the total credits on its balance sheet as a current liability. The reason for this is that if the customers make no future purchases, the company will have to grant them refunds.

Companies that sell on credit do so to be competitive and to increase sales. In setting credit terms, a company must keep in mind the credit terms of its competitors and the needs of its customers. Obviously, any company that sells on credit wants customers who will pay their bills on time. To increase the likelihood of selling only to customers who will pay on time, most companies develop control procedures and maintain a credit department. The credit department's responsibilities include examining each person or company that applies for credit and approving or rejecting a credit sale to that customer. Typically, the credit department asks for information about the customer's financial resources and debts. It may also check personal references and credit bureaus for further information. Then, based on the information it has gathered, it decides whether to extend credit to the customer.

Companies that are too lenient in granting credit can run into difficulties when customers don't pay. For example, **Sprint**, one of the weaker companies in the highly competitive cell phone industry, targeted customers with poor credit histories. It attracted so many who failed to pay their bills that its stock dropped by 50 percent, to $2.50, because of the losses that resulted.[3]

Evaluating the Level of Accounts Receivable

Two common measures of the effect of a company's credit policies are receivable turnover and days' sales uncollected. The **receivable turnover** shows how many times, on average, a company turned its receivables into cash during an accounting period. It reflects the relative size of a company's accounts receivable and the success of its credit and collection policies. It may also be affected by external factors, such as seasonal conditions and interest rates. **Days' sales uncollected** is a related measure that shows, on average, how long it takes to collect accounts receivable.

The receivable turnover is computed by dividing net sales by average accounts receivable (net of allowances). Theoretically, the numerator should be net credit sales, but the amount of net credit sales is rarely available in public reports, so investors use total net sales. Using data from **Nike**'s annual report, we can compute the company's receivable turnover in 2009 as follows (dollar amounts are in millions):

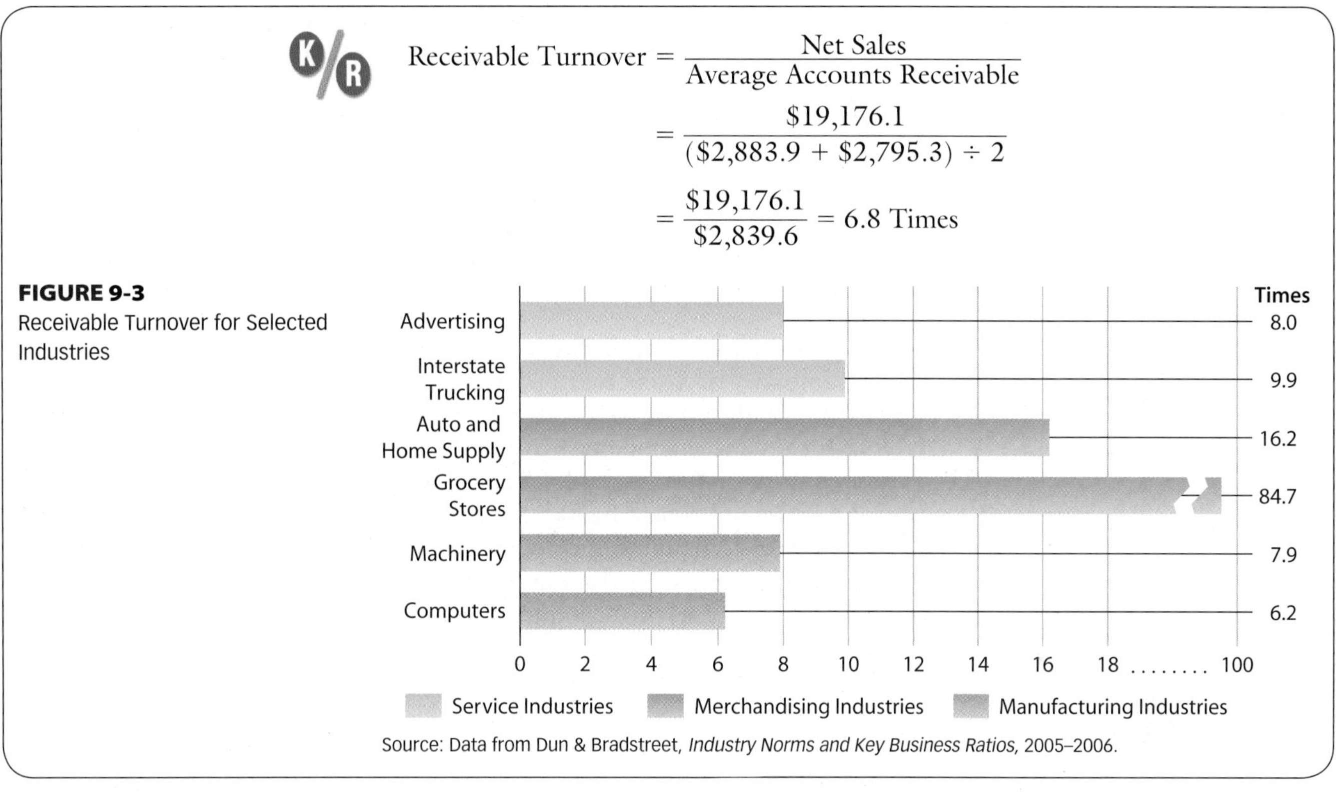

$$\text{Receivable Turnover} = \frac{\text{Net Sales}}{\text{Average Accounts Receivable}}$$

$$= \frac{\$19,176.1}{(\$2,883.9 + \$2,795.3) \div 2}$$

$$= \frac{\$19,176.1}{\$2,839.6} = 6.8 \text{ Times}$$

FIGURE 9-3
Receivable Turnover for Selected Industries

Source: Data from Dun & Bradstreet, *Industry Norms and Key Business Ratios*, 2005–2006.

To find days' sales uncollected, the number of days in the accounting period, in this case a year, is divided by the receivable turnover, as follows:

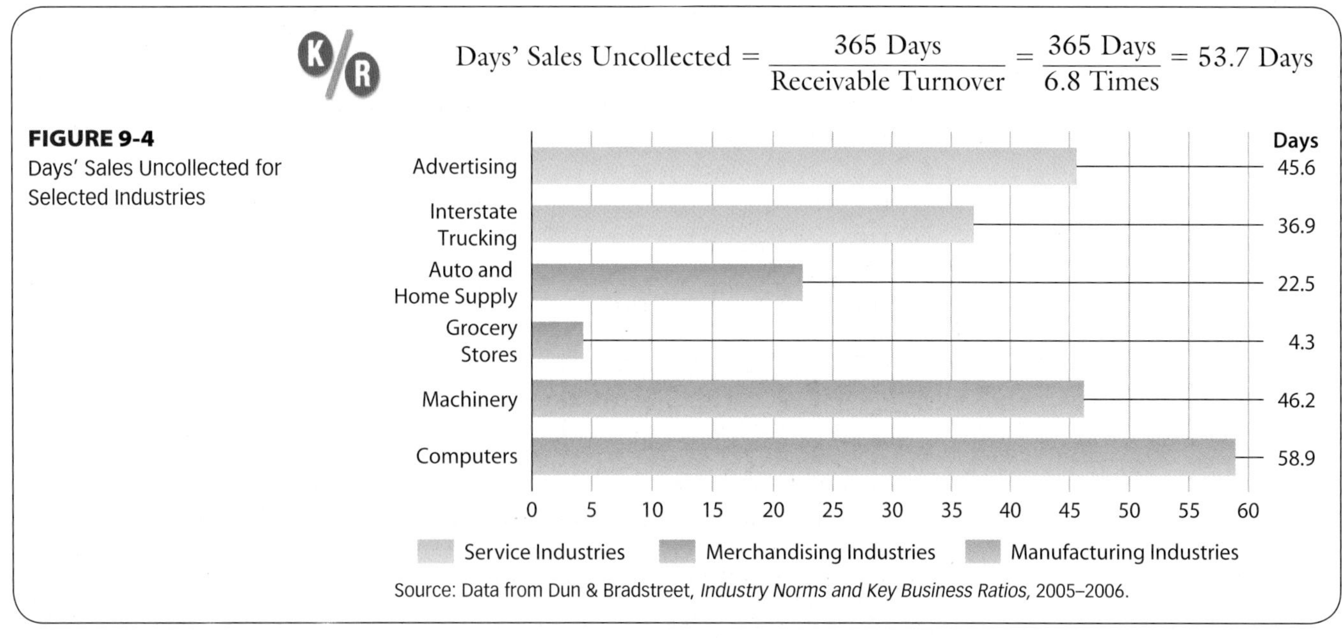

$$\text{Days' Sales Uncollected} = \frac{365 \text{ Days}}{\text{Receivable Turnover}} = \frac{365 \text{ Days}}{6.8 \text{ Times}} = 53.7 \text{ Days}$$

FIGURE 9-4
Days' Sales Uncollected for Selected Industries

Source: Data from Dun & Bradstreet, *Industry Norms and Key Business Ratios*, 2005–2006.

> **Study Note**
>
> For many businesses with seasonal sales activity, such as **Nordstrom, Dillard's, Marshall Field's**, and **Macy's**, the fourth quarter produces more than 25 percent of annual sales. For these businesses, receivables are highest at the balance sheet date, resulting in an artificially low receivable turnover and high days' sales uncollected.

Thus, Nike turned its receivables 6.8 times a year, or an average of every 53.7 days. A turnover period of this length is not unusual among apparel companies because their credit terms allow retail outlets time to sell products before paying for them. When the days' sales uncollected is added to the days' inventory on hand of 83.0 days computed in Chapter 8, Nike must provide financing for a total of 136.7 days (83.0 + 53.7) or more than four months.

As Figure 9-3 shows, the receivable turnover ratio varies substantially from industry to industry. Because grocery stores have few receivables, they have a very quick turnover. The turnover in interstate trucking is 10.7 times because the typical credit terms in that industry are 30 days. The turnover in the machinery and computer industries is lower because those industries tend to have longer credit terms.

Figure 9-4 shows the days' sales uncollected for the industries listed in Figure 9-3. Grocery stores, which have the lowest ratio (4.0 days) require the least amount of receivables financing; the computer industry, with days' sales uncollected of 58.9 days, requires the most.

Financing Receivables

Financial flexibility is important to most companies. Companies that have significant amounts of assets tied up in accounts receivable may be unwilling or unable to wait until they collect cash from their receivables. Many corporations have set up finance companies to help their customers pay for the purchase of their products. For example, **Ford** has set up Ford Motor Credit Company (FMCC) and **Sears** has set up Sears Roebuck Acceptance Corporation (SRAC). Other companies borrow funds by pledging their accounts receivable as collateral. If a company does not pay back its loan, the creditor can take the collateral (in this case, the accounts receivable) and convert it to cash to satisfy the loan.

> **Study Note**
>
> A company that factors its receivables will have a better receivable turnover and days' sales uncollected than a company that does not factor them.

Companies can also raise funds by selling or transferring accounts receivable to another entity, called a **factor**, as illustrated in Figure 9-5. The sale or transfer of accounts receivable, called **factoring**, can be done with or without recourse. *With recourse* means that the seller of the receivables is liable to the factor (i.e., the purchaser) if a receivable cannot be collected. *Without recourse* means that the factor bears any losses from unpaid accounts. A company's acceptance of credit cards like Visa, MasterCard, or American Express is an example of factoring without recourse because the issuers of the cards accept the risk of nonpayment.

The factor, of course, charges a fee for its service. The fee for sales with recourse is usually about 2 percent of the accounts receivable. The fee is higher

FIGURE 9-5
How Factoring Works

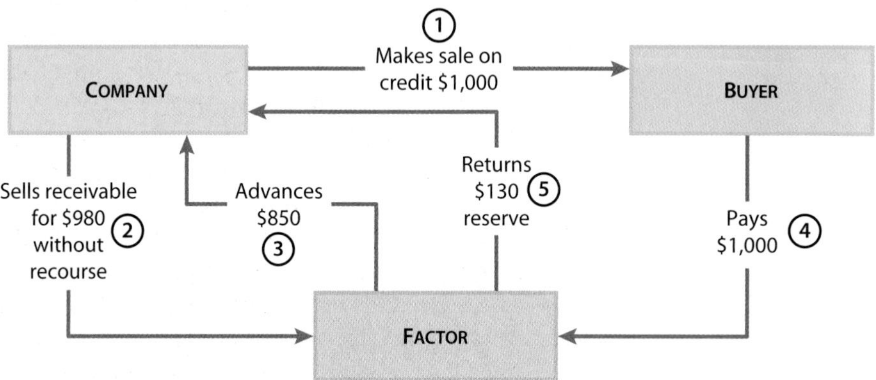

Note: Factor will keep $130 reserve if buyer does not pay.

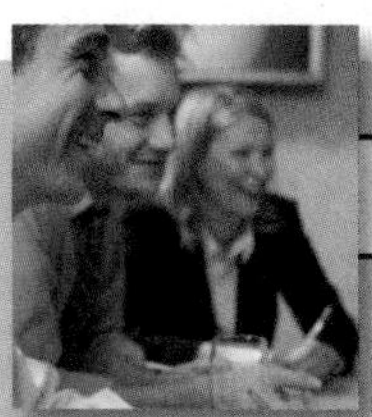

FOCUS ON BUSINESS PRACTICE

How Do Powerful Buyers Cause Problems for Small Suppliers?

Big buyers often have significant power over small suppliers, and their cash management decisions can cause severe cash flow problems for the little companies that depend on them. For instance, in an effort to control costs and optimize cash flow, **Ameritech Corp.** told 70,000 suppliers that it would begin paying its bills in 45 days instead of 30. Other large companies routinely take 90 days or more to pay. Some small suppliers are so anxious to get the big companies' business that they fail to realize the implications of the deals they make until it is too late. When **Earthly Elements, Inc.**, accepted a $10,000 order for dried floral gifts from a national home shopping network, its management was ecstatic because the deal increased sales by 25 percent. But in four months, the resulting cash crunch forced the company to close down. When the shopping network finally paid for the order six months later, it was too late to revive Earthly Elements.[4]

for sales without recourse because the factor's risk is greater. In accounting terminology, a seller of receivables with recourse is said to be contingently liable. A **contingent liability** is a potential liability that can develop into a real liability if a particular event occurs. In this case, the event would be a customer's nonpayment of a receivable. A contingent liability generally requires disclosure in the notes to the financial statements.

Another way for a company to generate cash from its receivables is through a process called securitization. Under **securitization**, a company groups its receivables in batches and sells them at a discount to companies and investors. When the receivables are paid, the buyers get the full amount; their profit depends on the amount of the discount. **Circuit City** tried to avoid bankruptcy by selling all its receivables without recourse, which means that after selling them, it had no further liability, even if no customers were to pay. If Circuit City sold its receivables with recourse and a customer did not pay, it would have had to make good on the debt.[5] However, by selling without recourse, it had to accept a lower price for its receivables. This strategy did not prevent it from going bankrupt.

A form of securitization that has caused huge problems in the real estate market in recent years is subprime loans (home loans to individuals with poor credit ratings and low incomes). These loans are batched together and sold in units. Although subprime loans (home loans to individuals with poor credit ratings and low incomes) represent only a small portion of the mortgage loan market, they have caused huge problems in the real estate market in recent years. These loans are a form of securitization in that they are batched together and sold in units as safe investments, when in fact they are quite risky. As just one of many examples, when people by the thousands were unable to keep up with their mortgage payments, the investments were marked down to their fair value. This loss of value led to the demise of such venerable firms as Lehman Brothers, the sale of Merrill Lynch, and ultimately to a massive government bailout.[6]

Another method of financing receivables is to sell promissory notes, held as notes receivable, to a financial lender, usually a bank. This practice is called **discounting** because the bank derives its profit by deducting the interest from the maturity value of the note. The holder of the note (usually the payee) endorses the note and turns it over to the bank. The bank expects to collect the maturity value of the note (principal plus interest) on the maturity date, but it also has recourse against the note's endorser.

For example, if Company X holds a $20,000 note from Company Z and the note will pay $1,200 in interest, a bank may be willing to buy the note for $19,200. If Company Z pays, the bank will receive $21,200 at maturity and realize a $2,000 profit. If it fails to pay, Company X is liable to the bank for payment. In the meantime, Company X has a contingent liability in the amount of the discounted note plus interest that it must disclose in the notes to its financial statements.

Ethics and Estimates in Accounting for Receivables

As we have noted, companies extend credit to customers because they expect it will increase their sales and earnings, but they know they will always have some credit customers who cannot or will not pay. The accounts of such customers are called **uncollectible accounts**, or *bad debts*, and they are expenses of selling on credit. To match these expenses, or losses, to the revenues they help generate, they should be recognized at the time credit sales are made.

Of course, at the time a company makes credit sales, it cannot identify which customers will not pay their bills, nor can it predict the exact amount of money it will lose. Therefore, to adhere to the matching rule, it must estimate losses from uncollectible accounts. The estimate becomes an expense in the fiscal year in which the sales are made.

Because the amount of uncollectible accounts can only be estimated and the exact amount will not be known until later, a company's earnings can be easily manipulated. Earnings can be overstated by underestimating the amount of losses from uncollectible accounts, and they can be understated by overestimating the amount of the losses. Misstatements of earnings can occur simply because of a bad estimate. But, as we have noted elsewhere, they can be deliberately made to meet analysts' estimates of earnings, reduce income taxes, or meet benchmarks for bonuses.

Among the many examples of unethical or questionable practices in dealing with uncollectible accounts are the following:

- **WorldCom** (now **MCI**) increased revenues and hid losses by continuing to bill customers for service for years after the customers had quit paying.
- The policy of **Household International**, a large personal finance company, seems to be flexible about when to declare loans delinquent. As a result, the company can vary its estimates of uncollectible accounts from year to year.[7]
- By making large allowances for estimated uncollectible accounts and then gradually reducing them, **Bank One** improved its earnings over several years.[8]
- **HealthSouth** manipulated its income by varying its estimates of the difference between what it charged patients and what it could collect from insurance companies.[9]

Companies with high ethical standards try to be accurate in their estimates of uncollectible accounts, and they disclose the basis of their estimates. For example, **Nike**'s management describes its estimates as follows:

> We make ongoing estimates relating to the collectibility of our accounts receivables and maintain an allowance for estimated losses resulting from the inability of our customers to make required payments. In determining the amount of the allowance, we consider our historical level of credit losses and make judgments about the creditworthiness of significant customers based on ongoing credit evaluations. Since we cannot predict future changes in the financial stability of our customers, actual future losses from uncollectible accounts may differ from our estimates.[10]

Santorini Company has cash of $20,000, net accounts receivable of $60,000, and net sales of $500,000. Last year's net accounts receivable were $40,000. Compute the following ratios: receivable turnover and days' sales uncollected.

SOLUTION

$$\text{Receivable Turnover} = \frac{\text{Net Sales}}{\text{Average Accounts Receivable}}$$

$$= \frac{\$500{,}000}{(\$60{,}000 + \$40{,}000) \div 2}$$

$$= \frac{\$500{,}000}{\$50{,}000} = 10.0 \text{ Times}$$

$$\text{Days' Sales Uncollected} = \frac{365 \text{ Days}}{\text{Receivable Turnover}} = \frac{365 \text{ Days}}{10.0 \text{ Times}} = 36.5 \text{ Days}$$

Cash Equivalents and Cash Control

LO2 Define *cash equivalents,* and explain methods of controlling cash, including bank reconciliations.

Cash Equivalents

As we noted earlier, cash is the asset most readily available to pay debts, but at times a company may have more cash on hand than it needs to pay its debts. Excess cash should not remain idle, especially during periods of high interest rates. Management may decide to invest the excess cash in short-term interest-bearing accounts or certificates of deposit (CDs) at banks and other financial institutions, in government securities (such as U.S. Treasury notes), or in other securities. If these investments have a term of 90 days or less when they are purchased, they are called **cash equivalents** because the funds revert to cash so quickly they are treated as cash on the balance sheet.

Nike describes its treatment of cash and cash equivalents as follows:

> Cash and equivalents represent cash and short-term, highly liquid investments with maturities of three months or less at date of purchase. The carrying amounts reflected in the consolidated balance sheet for cash and equivalents approximate fair value.[11]

According to a recent survey of 600 large U.S. corporations, 6 percent use the term *cash* as the balance sheet caption, and 89 percent use either *cash and cash equivalents* or *cash and equivalents.* The rest either combine cash with marketable securities or have no cash.[12]

> **Study Note**
>
> The statement of cash flows explains the change in the balance of cash and cash equivalents from one accounting period to the next.

Fair Value of Cash and Cash Equivalents

Cash and cash equivalents are financial instruments that are valued at fair value. In most cases, the amount recorded in the records approximates fair value, and most businesses and other entities consider cash equivalents to be very safe investments. Companies often invest these funds in money market funds to earn interest with cash when they don't need cash for current operations. Money market funds usually invest in very safe securities, such as commercial paper, which is short-term debt of other entities. Although money market funds are not guaranteed, investors do not expect losses on these investments. However, in recent years a few of these funds invested in batches of subprime mortgages in an attempt to earn a little higher interest rate. The result has been traumatic for all parties. **Bank of America**, for instance, shut down its $34 billion Columbia Strategic Cash Portfolio money market fund when investors pulled out $21 billion because the fund was losing so much money from investing in subprime loans.[13]

Cash Control Methods

In an earlier chapter, we discussed the concept of internal control and how it applies to cash transactions. Here, we address three additional ways of controlling cash: imprest systems; banking services, including electronic funds transfer; and bank reconciliations.

Imprest Systems Most companies need to keep some currency and coins on hand. Currency and coins are needed for cash registers, for paying expenses that are impractical to pay by check, and for situations that require cash advances—for example, when sales representatives need cash for travel expenses. One way to control a cash fund and cash advances is by using an **imprest system**.

A common form of imprest system is a petty cash fund, which is established at a fixed amount. A receipt documents each cash payment made from the fund. The fund is periodically reimbursed, based on the documented expenditures, by the exact amount necessary to restore its original cash balance. The person responsible for the petty cash fund must always be able to account for its contents by showing that total cash and receipts equal the original fixed amount.

Banking Services All businesses rely on banks to control cash receipts and cash disbursements. Banks serve as safe depositories for cash, negotiable instruments, and other valuable business documents, such as stocks and bonds. The checking accounts that banks provide improve control by minimizing the amount of currency a company needs to keep on hand and by supplying permanent records of all cash payments. Banks also serve as agents in a variety of transactions, such as the collection and payment of certain kinds of debts and the exchange of foreign currencies.

Electronic funds transfer (EFT) is a method of conducting business transactions that does not involve the actual transfer of cash. With EFT, a company electronically transfers cash from its bank to another company's bank. For the banks, the electronic transfer is simply a bookkeeping entry. Companies today rely heavily on this method of payment. **Wal-Mart**, for example, makes 75 percent of its payments to suppliers through EFT.

> **Study Note**
>
> Periodically, banks detect individuals who are *kiting*. Kiting is the illegal issuing of checks when there is insufficient money to cover them. Before one kited check clears the bank, a kited check from another account is deposited to cover it, making an endless circle.

Because of EFT and other electronic banking services, we are rapidly becoming a cashless society. Automated teller machines (ATMs) allow bank customers to make deposits, withdraw cash, transfer funds among accounts, and pay bills. Large consumer banks like **Citibank**, **Chase**, and **Bank of America** process hundreds of thousands of ATM transactions each week. Many banks also give customers the option of paying bills online, over the telephone, and with *debit cards*. In 2007, debit cards accounted for more than 1 trillion transactions.[14] When a customer makes a retail purchase using a debit card, the amount of the purchase is deducted directly from the buyer's bank account. The bank usually documents debit card transactions for the retailer, but the retailer must develop new internal controls to ensure that the transactions are recorded properly and that unauthorized transfers do not occur. It is expected that within a few years, a majority of all retail activity will be handled electronically.

Bank Reconciliations

> **Study Note**
> The ending balance on a company's bank statement does not represent the amount of cash that should appear on its balance sheet. At the balance sheet date, deposits may be in transit to the bank, and some checks may be outstanding. That is why companies must prepare a bank reconciliation.

Rarely does the balance of a company's Cash account exactly equal the cash balance on its bank statement. The bank may not yet have recorded certain transactions that appear in the company's records, and the company may not yet have recorded certain bank transactions. A bank reconciliation is therefore a necessary step in internal control. A **bank reconciliation** is the process of accounting for the difference between the balance on a company's bank statement and the balance in its Cash account. This process involves making additions to and subtractions from both balances to arrive at the adjusted cash balance.

The following are the transactions that most commonly appear in a company's records but not on its bank statement:

1. ***Outstanding checks:*** These are checks that a company has issued and recorded but that do not yet appear on its bank statement.
2. ***Deposits in transit:*** These are deposits a company has sent to its bank but that the bank did not receive in time to enter on the bank statement.

Transactions that may appear on the bank statement but not in the company's records include the following:

1. ***Service charges (SC):*** Banks often charge a fee, or service charge, for the use of a checking account. Many banks base the service charge on a number of factors, such as the average balance of the account during the month or the number of checks drawn.
2. ***NSF (nonsufficient funds) checks:*** An NSF check is a check that a company has deposited but that is not paid when the bank presents it to the issuer's bank. The bank charges the company's account and returns the check so that the company can try to collect the amount due. If the bank has deducted the NSF check on the bank statement but the company has not deducted it from its book balance, an adjustment must be made in the bank reconciliation. The company usually reclassifies the NSF check from Cash to Accounts Receivable because it must now collect from the person or company that wrote the check.
3. ***Miscellaneous debits and credits:*** Banks also charge for other services, such as stopping payment on checks and printing checks. The bank notifies the depositor of each deduction by including a debit memorandum with the monthly statement. A bank also sometimes serves as an agent in collecting on promissory notes for the depositor. When it does, it includes a credit memorandum in the bank statement, along with a debit memorandum for the service charge.
4. ***Interest income:*** Banks commonly pay interest on a company's average balance. Accounts that pay interest are sometimes called NOW or money market accounts.

> **Study Note**
> A credit memorandum means that an amount was *added* to the bank balance; a debit memorandum means that an amount was *deducted.*

An error by either the bank or the depositor will, of course, require immediate correction.

To illustrate the preparation of a bank reconciliation, suppose that Terry Services Company's bank statement for August shows a balance of $1,735.53 on August 31 and that on the same date, the company's records show a cash balance of $1,207.95. The purpose of a bank reconciliation is to identify the items that make up the difference between these amounts and to determine the correct cash balance. Exhibit 9-1 shows Terry Services Company's bank reconciliation for August. The circled numbers in the exhibit refer to the following:

1. The bank has not recorded a deposit in the amount of $138.00 that the company mailed to the bank on August 31.

Study Note

Bank reconciliations perform an important function in internal control. If carried out by someone who does not have access to the bank account, they provide an independent check on the person or persons who do have that access.

2. The bank has not paid the five checks that the company issued in July and August: Even though the July 14 check was deducted in the July 30 reconciliation, it must be deducted again in each subsequent month in which it remains outstanding.

3. The company incorrectly recorded a $150 deposit from cash sales as $165.00. On August 6, the bank received the deposit and corrected the amount.

4. Among the returned checks was a credit memorandum showing that the bank had collected a promissory note from K. Diaz in the amount of $140.00, plus $10.00 in interest on the note. A debit memorandum was also enclosed for the $2.50 collection fee. The company had not entered these amounts in its records.

5. Also returned with the bank statement was an NSF check for $64.07 that the company had received from a customer named Austin Chase. The NSF check was not reflected in the company's records.

6. A debit memorandum was enclosed for the regular monthly service charge of $6.25. The company had not yet recorded this charge.

7. Interest earned on the company's average balance was $7.81.

As you can see in Exhibit 9-1, starting from their separate balances, both the bank and book amounts are adjusted to the amount of $1,277.94. This adjusted

EXHIBIT 9-1
Bank Reconciliation

Terry Services Company
Bank Reconciliation
August 31, 2011

Balance per bank, August 31		$ 1,735.53
①Add deposit of August 31 in transit		138.00
		$ 1,873.53
②Less outstanding checks:		
No. 551, issued on July 14	$ 75.00	
No. 576, issued on Aug. 30	20.34	
No. 578, issued on Aug. 31	250.00	
No. 579, issued on Aug. 31	185.00	
No. 580, issued on Aug. 31	65.25	595.59
Adjusted bank balance, August 31		**$1,277.94**
Balance per books, August 31		$ 1,207.95
Add:		
④Note receivable collected by bank	$140.00	
④Interest income on note	10.00	
⑦Interest income	7.81	157.81
		$ 1,365.76
Less:		
③Overstatement of deposit of August 6	$ 15.00	
④Collection fee	2.50	
⑤NSF check of Austin Chase	64.07	
⑥Service charge	6.25	87.82
Adjusted book balance, August 31		**$1,277.94**

Study Note

It is possible to place an item in the wrong section of a bank reconciliation and still have it balance. The *correct* adjusted balance must be obtained.

balance is the amount of cash the company owns on August 31 and thus is the amount that should appear on its August 31 balance sheet.

When outstanding checks are presented to the bank for payment and the bank receives and records the deposit in transit, the bank balance will automatically become correct. However, the company must update its book balance by recording all the items reported by the bank. Thus, Terry Services Company would record an increase (debit) in Cash with the following items:

- Decrease (credit) in Notes Receivable, $140.00
- Increase (credit) in Interest Income, $10.00 (interest on note)
- Increase (credit) in Interest Income, $7.81 (interest on average bank balance)

The company would record a reduction (credit) in Cash with these items:

- Decrease (debit) in Sales, $15.00 (error in recording deposit)
- Increase (debit) in Accounts Receivable, $64.07 (return of NSF check)
- Increase (debit) in Bank Service Charges, $8.75 ($6.25 + $2.50)

As the use of electronic funds transfer, automatic payments, and debit cards increases, the items that most businesses will have to deal with in their bank reconciliations will undoubtedly grow.

STOP & APPLY >

At year end, Sunjin Company had currency and coins in cash registers of $1,100, money orders from customers of $2,000, deposits in checking accounts of $12,000, U.S. Treasury bills due in 80 days of $50,000, certificates of deposit at the bank that mature in six months of $200,000, and U.S. Treasury bonds due in one year of $100,000. Calculate the amount of cash and cash equivalents that will be shown on the company's year-end balance sheet.

SOLUTION

Currency and coins	$ 1,100
Money orders	2,000
Checking accounts	12,000
U.S.Treasury bills (due in 80 days)	50,000
Cash and Cash equivalents	$65,100

The certificates of deposit and U.S. Treasury Bonds mature in more than 90 days and thus are not cash equivalents.

Uncollectible Accounts

LO3 Apply the allowance method of accounting for uncollectible accounts.

Some companies recognize a loss at the time they determine that an account is uncollectible by reducing Accounts Receivable and increasing Uncollectible Accounts Expense. Federal regulations require companies to use this method of recognizing a loss—called the **direct charge-off method**—in computing taxable income. Although small companies may use this method for all purposes, companies that follow generally accepted accounting principles do not use it in their financial statements. The reason they do not is that a direct charge-off is usually recorded in a different accounting period from the one in which the sale takes place, and the method therefore does not conform to the matching rule. Companies that follow GAAP use the allowance method.

The Allowance Method

> **Study Note**
> The allowance method relies on an estimate of uncollectible accounts, but unlike the direct charge-off method, it is in accord with the matching rule.

Under the **allowance method**, losses from bad debts are matched against the sales they help to produce. As mentioned earlier, when management extends credit to increase sales, it knows it will incur some losses from uncollectible accounts. Losses from credit sales should be recognized at the time the sales are made so that they are matched to the revenues they help generate. Of course, at the time a company makes credit sales, management cannot identify which customers will not pay their debts, nor can it predict the exact amount of money the company will lose. Therefore, to observe the matching rule, losses from uncollectible accounts must be estimated, and the estimate becomes an expense in the period in which the sales are made.

For example, suppose that Sharon Sales Company made most of its sales on credit during its first year of operation, 2011. At the end of the year, accounts receivable amounted to $200,000. On December 31, 2011, management reviewed the collectible status of the accounts receivable. Approximately $12,000 of the $200,000 of accounts receivable were estimated to be uncollectible. The following adjusting entry would be made on December 31 of that year:

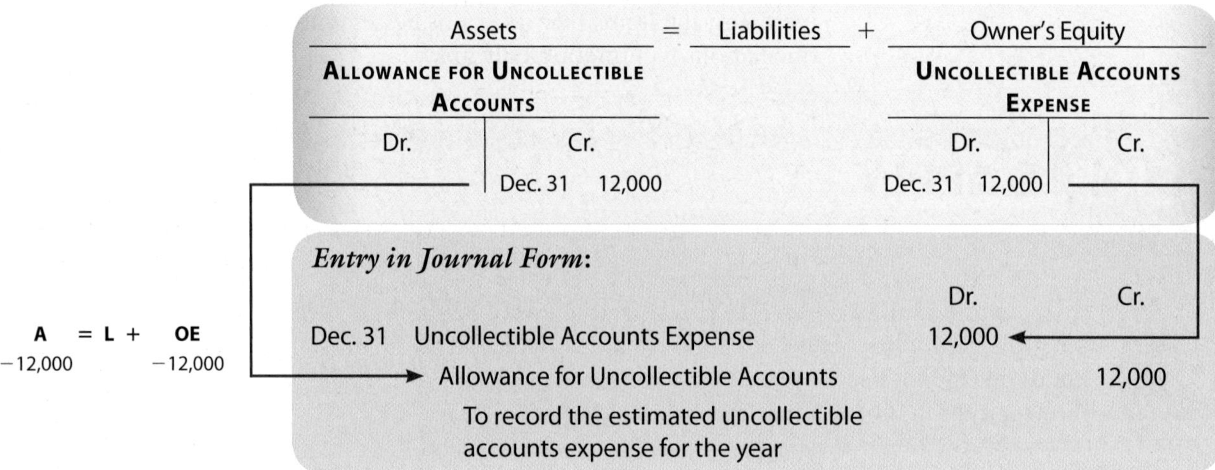

Disclosure of Uncollectible Accounts

> **Study Note**
> Allowance for Uncollectible Accounts reduces the gross accounts receivable to the amount estimated to be collectible (net realizable value). The purpose of another contra account, Accumulated Depreciation, is *not* to reduce the gross plant and equipment accounts to realizable value. Rather, its purpose is to show how much of the cost of the plant and equipment has been allocated as an expense to previous accounting periods.

Uncollectible Accounts Expense appears on the income statement as an operating expense. **Allowance for Uncollectible Accounts** appears on the balance sheet as a contra account that is deducted from accounts receivable. It reduces the accounts receivable to the amount expected to be collected in cash, as follows:

Current assets:		
Cash		$ 20,000
Short-term investments		30,000
Accounts receivable	$200,000	
Less allowance for uncollectible accounts	12,000	188,000
Inventory		112,000
Total current assets		$350,000

Accounts receivable may also be shown on the balance sheet as follows:

Accounts receivable (net of allowance for uncollectible accounts of $12,000)	$188,000

Study Note

The allowance account is necessary because the specific uncollectible accounts will not be identified until later.

Or accounts receivable may be shown at "net," with the amount of the allowance for uncollectible accounts identified in a note to the financial statements. For most companies, the "net" amount of accounts receivable approximates fair value. Fair value disclosures are not required for accounts receivable but 341 of 600 large companies made this disclosure voluntarily. Of those, 325, or 95 percent, indicated that the net accounts receivable approximated fair value.[15]

The allowance account often has other titles, such as *Allowance for Doubtful Accounts* and *Allowance for Bad Debts.* Once in a while, the older phrase *Reserve for Bad Debts* will be seen, but in modern practice it should not be used. *Bad Debts Expense* is a title often used for Uncollectible Accounts Expense.

Estimating Uncollectible Accounts Expense

Study Note

The accountant looks at both local and national economic conditions in determining the estimated uncollectible accounts expense.

As noted, expected losses from uncollectible accounts must be estimated. Of course, estimates can vary widely. If management takes an optimistic view and projects a small loss from uncollectible accounts, the resulting net accounts receivable will be larger than if management takes a pessimistic view. The net income will also be larger under the optimistic view because the estimated expense will be smaller. The company's accountant makes an estimate based on past experience and current economic conditions. For example, losses from uncollectible accounts are normally expected to be greater in a recession than during a period of economic growth. The final decision, made by management, on the amount of the expense will depend on objective information, such as the accountant's analyses, and on certain qualitative factors, such as how investors, bankers, creditors, and others view the performance of the debtor company. Regardless of the qualitative considerations, the estimated losses from uncollectible accounts should be realistic.

Two common methods of estimating uncollectible accounts expense are the percentage of net sales method and the accounts receivable aging method.

Percentage of Net Sales Method The **percentage of net sales method** asks the question, How much of this year's *net sales* will not be collected? The answer determines the amount of uncollectible accounts expense for the year.

FOCUS ON BUSINESS PRACTICE

Cash Collections Can Be Hard to Estimate

Companies must not only sell goods and services; they must also generate cash flows by collecting on those sales. When there are changes in the economy, some companies make big mistakes in estimating the amount of accounts they will collect. For example, when the dot-com bubble burst in the early 2000s, companies like **Nortel Networks**, **Cisco Systems**, and **Lucent Technologies** increased their estimates of allowances for uncollectible accounts—actions that eliminated previously reported earnings and caused the companies' stock prices to fall.[16] However, it turned out that these companies had overestimated how bad the losses would be. In later years, they reduced their allowances for credit losses, thereby increasing their reported earnings.[17]

Study Note

Unlike the direct charge-off method, the percentage of net sales method matches revenues with expenses.

For example, the following balances represent Shivar Company's ending figures for 2012:

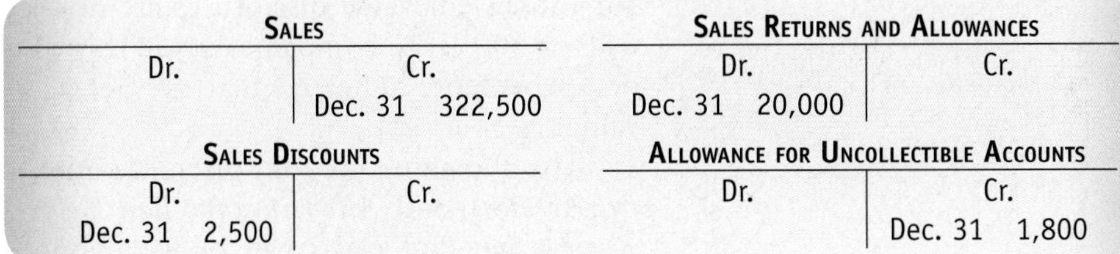

The following are Shivar's actual losses from uncollectible accounts for the past three years:

Year	*Net Sales*	*Losses from Uncollectible Accounts*	*Percentage*
2009	$260,000	$ 5,100	1.96
2010	297,500	6,950	2.34
2011	292,500	4,950	1.69
Total	$850,000	$17,000	2.00

Credit sales often constitute most of a company's sales. If a company has substantial cash sales, it should use only its net credit sales in estimating uncollectible accounts. Shivar's management believes that its uncollectible accounts will continue to average about 2 percent of net sales. The uncollectible accounts expense for the year 2012 is therefore estimated as follows:

$$0.02 \times (\$322{,}500 - \$20{,}000 - \$2{,}500) = 0.02 \times \$300{,}000 = \$6{,}000$$

The following entry would be made to record the estimate:

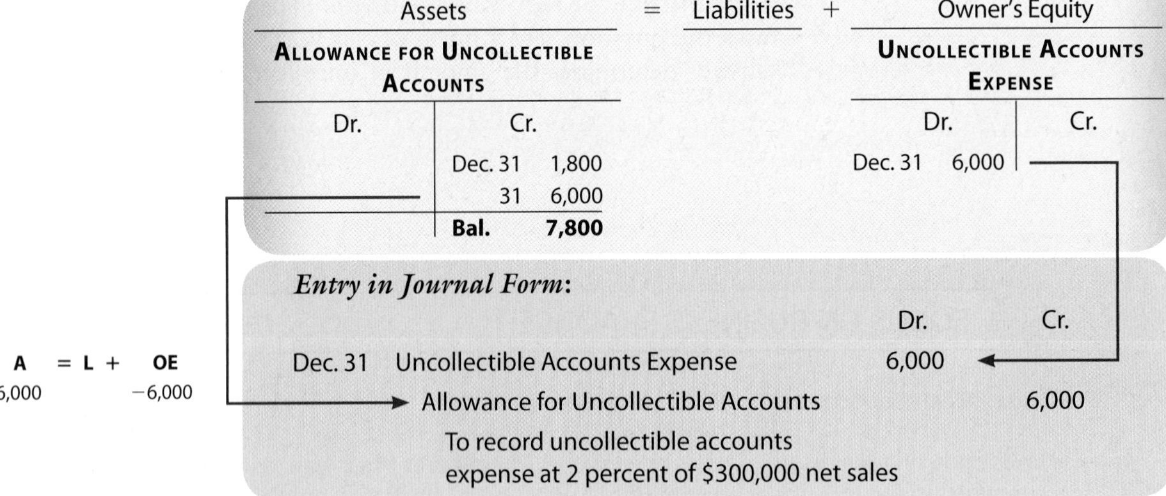

A	= L +	OE
−6,000		−6,000

Note that the Allowance for Uncollectible Accounts now has a balance of $7,800. The balance consists of the $6,000 estimated uncollectible accounts receivable from 2012 sales and the $1,800 estimated uncollectible accounts receivable from previous years.

> **Study Note**
> An aging of accounts receivable is an important tool in cash management because it helps to determine what amounts are likely to be collected in the months ahead.

Accounts Receivable Aging Method The **accounts receivable aging method** asks the question, How much of the *ending balance of accounts receivable* will not be collected? With this method, the ending balance of Allowance for Uncollectible Accounts is determined directly through an analysis of accounts receivable. The difference between the amount determined to be uncollectible and the actual balance of Allowance for Uncollectible Accounts is the expense for the period. In theory, this method should produce the same result as the percentage of net sales method, but in practice it rarely does.

The **aging of accounts receivable** is the process of listing each customer's receivable account according to the due date of the account. If the customer's account is past due, there is a possibility that the account will not be paid. And that possibility increases as the account extends further beyond the due date. The aging of accounts receivable helps management evaluate its credit and collection policies and alerts it to possible problems.

Exhibit 9-2 illustrates the aging of accounts receivable for Gomez Company. Each account receivable is classified as being not yet due or as being 1–30 days, 31–60 days, 61–90 days, or over 90 days past due. Based on past experience, the estimated percentage for each category is determined and multiplied by the amount in each category to determine the estimated, or target, balance of Allowance for Uncollectible Accounts. In total, it is estimated that $4,918 of the $88,800 in accounts receivable will not be collected.

Once the target balance for Allowance for Uncollectible Accounts has been found, it is necessary to determine the amount of the adjustment. The amount depends on the current balance of the allowance account. Let us assume two cases for the December 31 balance of Gomez Company's Allowance for Uncollectible Accounts: (1) a credit balance of $1,600 and (2) a debit balance of $1,600.

EXHIBIT 9-2 Analysis of Accounts Receivable by Age

Gomez Company
Analysis of Accounts Receivable by Age
December 31, 2011

Customer	Total	Not Yet Due	1–30 Days Past Due	31–60 Days Past Due	61–90 Days Past Due	Over 90 Days Past Due
K. Wu	$ 300		$ 300			
R. List	800			$ 800		
B. Smith	2,000	$ 1,800	200			
T. Vigo	500				$ 500	
Others	85,200	42,000	28,000	7,600	4,400	$3,200
Totals	$88,800	$43,800	$28,500	$8,400	$4,900	$3,200
Estimated percentage uncollectible		1.0	2.0	10.0	30.0	50.0
Allowance for Uncollectible Accounts	$ 4,918	$ 438	$ 570	$ 840	$1,470	$1,600

In the first case, an adjustment of $3,318 is needed to bring the balance of the allowance account to a $4,918 credit balance:

Targeted balance for allowance for uncollectible accounts	$4,918
Less current credit balance of allowance for uncollectible accounts	1,600
Uncollectible accounts expense	$3,318

The uncollectible accounts expense is recorded as follows:

A = L + OE
−3,318 −3,318

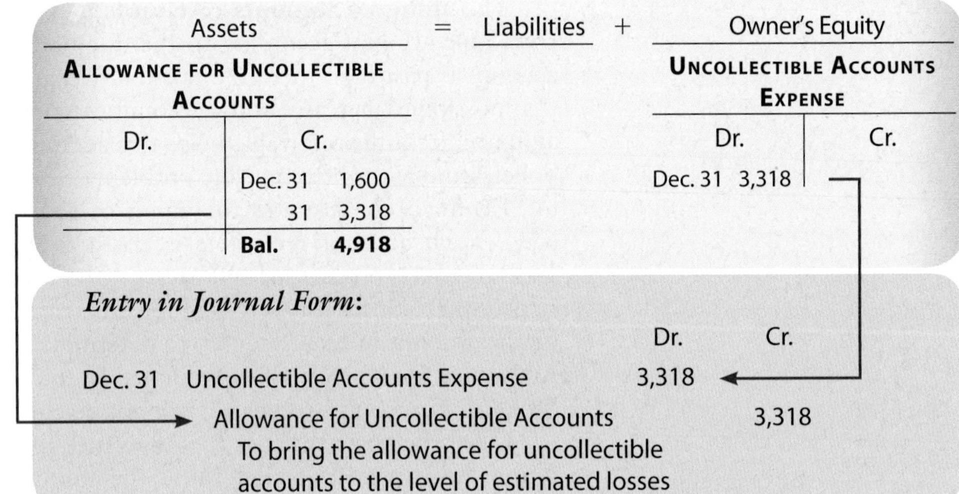

Note that the resulting balance of Allowance for Uncollectible Accounts is $4,918.

In the second case, because Allowance for Uncollectible Accounts has a debit balance of $1,600, the estimated uncollectible accounts expense for the year will have to be $6,518 to reach the targeted balance of $4,918. This calculation is as follows:

Study Note

When the write-offs in an accounting period exceed the amount of the allowance, a debit balance in the Allowance for Uncollectible Accounts account results.

Targeted balance for allowance for uncollectible accounts	$ 4,918
Plus current debit balance of allowance for uncollectible accounts	1,600
Uncollectible accounts expense	$6,518

The uncollectible accounts expense is recorded as follows:

A = L + OE
−6,518 −6,518

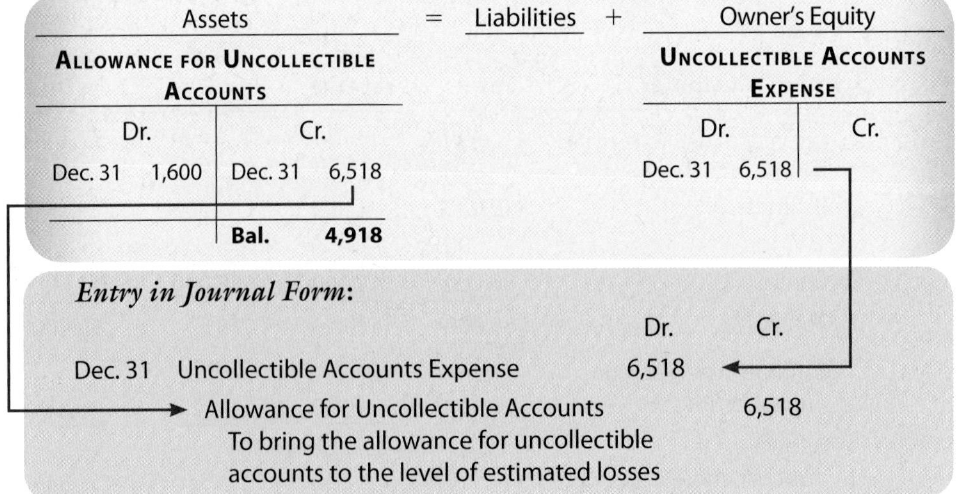

Note that after this entry, Allowance for Uncollectible Accounts has a credit balance of $4,918.

Study Note

Describing the aging method as the balance sheet method emphasizes that the computation is based on ending accounts receivable rather than on net sales for the period.

Comparison of the Two Methods Both the percentage of net sales method and the accounts receivable aging method estimate the uncollectible accounts expense in accordance with the matching rule, but as shown in Figure 9-6, they do so in different ways. The percentage of net sales method is an income statement approach. It assumes that a certain proportion of sales will not be collected, and this proportion is the *amount of Uncollectible Accounts Expense* for the accounting period. The accounts receivable aging method is a balance sheet approach. It assumes that a certain proportion of accounts receivable outstanding will not be collected. This proportion is the *targeted balance of the Allowance for Uncollectible Accounts account.* The expense for the accounting period is the difference between the targeted balance and the current balance of the allowance account.

Writing Off Uncollectible Accounts

Regardless of the method used to estimate uncollectible accounts, the total of accounts receivable written off in an accounting period will rarely equal the estimated uncollectible amount. The allowance account will show a credit balance when the total of accounts written off is less than the estimated uncollectible amount. It will show a debit balance when the total of accounts written off is greater than the estimated uncollectible amount.

Study Note

When writing off an individual account, debit Allowance for Uncollectible Accounts, not Uncollectible Accounts Expense.

When it becomes clear that a specific account receivable will not be collected, the amount should be written off to Allowance for Uncollectible Accounts. Remember that the uncollectible amount was already accounted for as an expense when the allowance was established. For example, assume that

FIGURE 9-6
Two Methods of Estimating Uncollectible Accounts

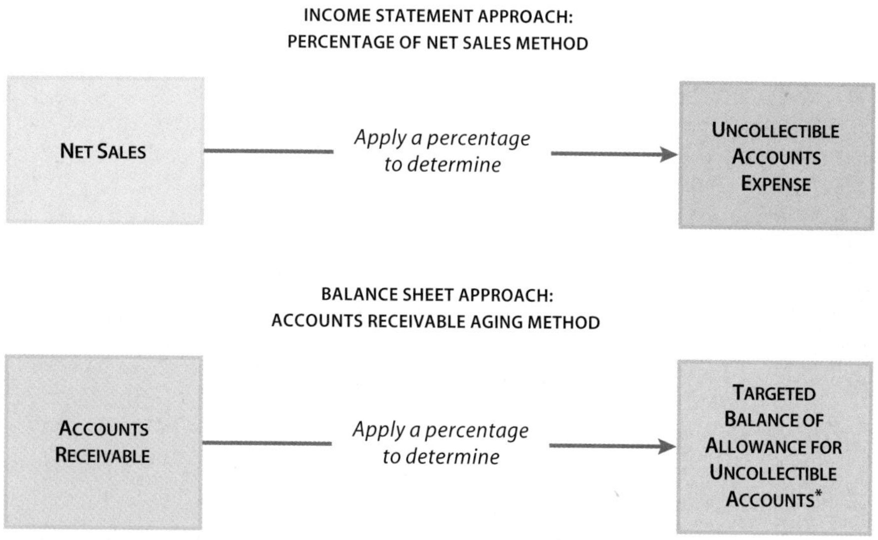

**Add current debit balance or subtract current credit balance to determine uncollectible accounts expense.*

on January 15, 2012, T. Vigo, who owes Gomez Company $500, is declared bankrupt by a federal court. The entry to *write off* this account is as follows:

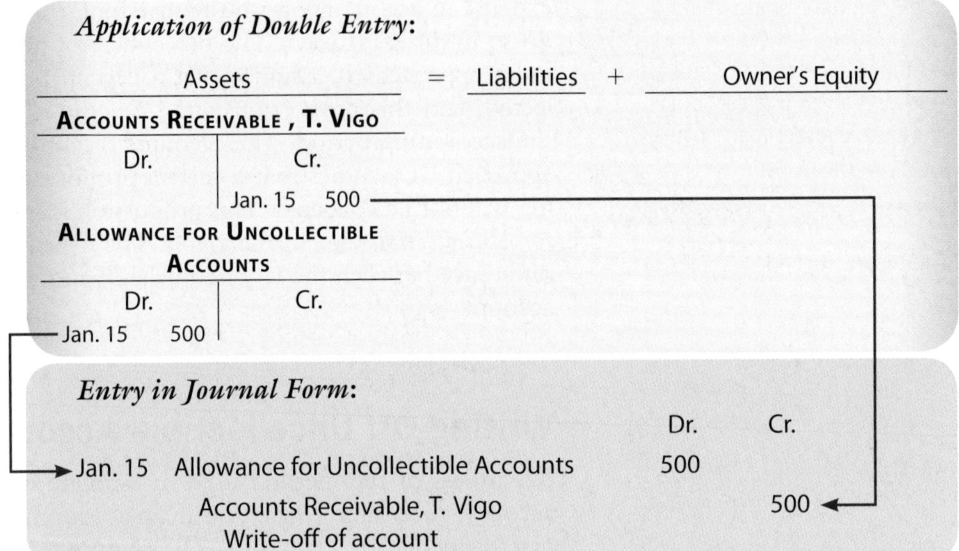

A = L + OE
+500
−500

Although the write-off removes the uncollectible amount from Accounts Receivable, it does not affect the estimated net realizable value of accounts receivable. It simply reduces T. Vigo's account to zero and reduces Allowance for Uncollectible Accounts by $500, as shown below:

	Balances Before Write-off	*Balances After Write-off*
Accounts receivable	$88,800	$88,300
Less allowance for uncollectible accounts	4,918	4,418
Estimated net realizable value of accounts receivable	$83,882	$83,882

Occasionally, a customer whose account has been written off as uncollectible will later be able to pay some or all of the amount owed. When that happens, two entries must be made: one to reverse the earlier write-off (which is now incorrect) and another to show the collection of the account.

STOP & APPLY >

Jazz Instruments Co., sells its merchandise on credit. In the company's last fiscal year, which ended July 31, it had net sales of $7,000,000. At the end of the fiscal year, it had Accounts Receivable of $1,800,000 and a credit balance in Allowance for Uncollectible Accounts of $11,200. In the past, the company has been unable to collect on approximately 1 percent of its net sales. An aging analysis of accounts receivable has indicated that $80,000 of current receivables is uncollectible.

1. Calculate the amount of uncollectible accounts expense, and use T accounts to determine the resulting balance of Allowance for Uncollectible Accounts under the percentage of net sales method and the accounts receivable aging method.
2. How would your answers change if Allowance for Uncollectible Accounts had a debit balance of $11,200 instead of a credit balance?

(continued)

SOLUTION

1. Percentage of net sales method:

ALLOWANCE FOR UNCOLLECTIBLE ACCOUNTS

Dr.	Cr.		
	July 31		11,200
	31	UA Exp.	70,000*
	July 31	**Bal.**	**81,200**

*Uncollectible Accounts Expense = $7,000,000 × 0.01

Aging Method:

ALLOWANCE FOR UNCOLLECTIBLE ACCOUNTS

Dr.	Cr.		
	July 31		11,200
	31	UA Exp.	68,800*
	July 31	**Bal.**	**80,000**

*Uncollectible Accounts Expense = $80,000 − $11,200

2. Under the percentage of net sales method, the amount of the expense is the same in **1** and **2** but the ending balance will be $58,800 ($70,000 − $11,200). Under the accounts receivable aging method, the ending balance is the same, but the amount of the expense will be $91,200 ($80,000 + $11,200).

Notes Receivable

LO4 Define *promissory note,* and make common calculations for promissory notes receivable.

A **promissory note** is an unconditional promise to pay a definite sum of money on demand or at a future date. The person or company that signs the note and thereby promises to pay is the *maker* of the note. The entity to whom payment is to be made is the *payee.*

The promissory note shown in Figure 9-7 is an unconditional promise by the maker, Samuel Mason, to pay a definite sum—or principal ($1,000)—to the payee, Cook County Bank & Trust, on August 18, 2011. As you can see, this promissory note is dated May 20, 2011 and bears an interest rate of 8 percent.

A payee includes all the promissory notes it holds that are due in less than one year in **notes receivable** in the current assets section of its balance sheet. A maker includes them in **notes payable** in the current liabilities section of its balance sheet. Since notes receivable and notes payable are financial instruments, companies may voluntarily disclose their fair value. In most cases, fair value approximates the amount in the account records, but sometimes the adjustments to fair value are significant, such as in the recent cases of subprime loans gone bad.

Study Note

Notes receivable and notes payable are distinguished from accounts receivable and accounts payable because the latter were not created by a formal promissory note.

The nature of a company's business generally determines how frequently it receives promissory notes from customers. Firms that sell durable goods of high value, such as farm machinery and automobiles, often accept promissory notes. Among the advantages of these notes are that they produce interest income and represent a stronger legal claim against a debtor than do accounts receivable. In addition, selling—or discounting—promissory notes to banks is a common financing method. Almost all companies occasionally accept promissory notes, and many companies obtain them in settlement of past-due accounts.

FIGURE 9-7 A Promissory Note

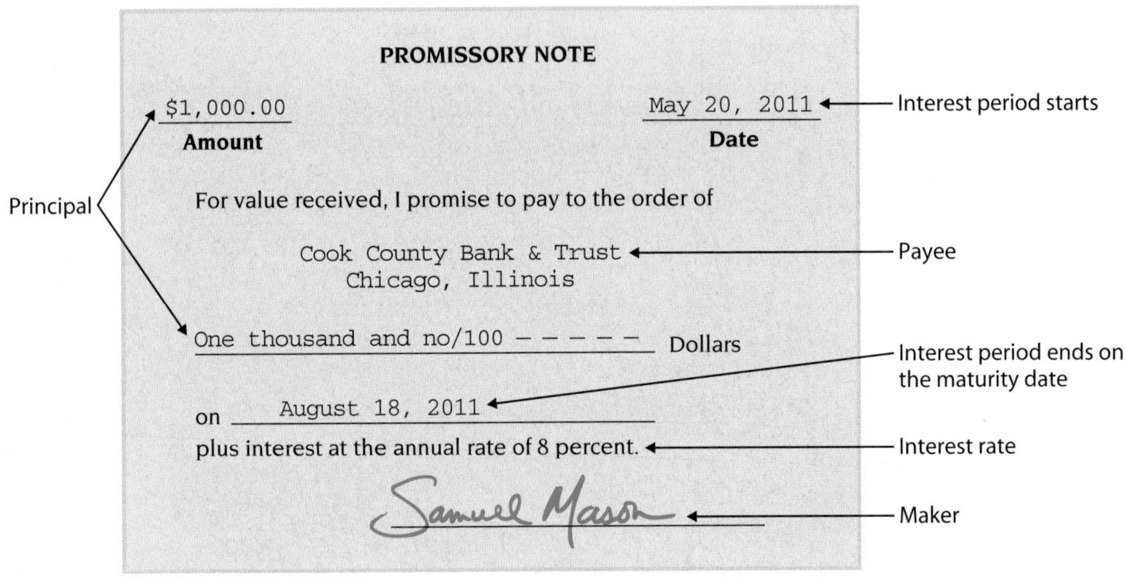

PROMISSORY NOTE

$1,000.00 — **Amount**

May 20, 2011 — **Date**

For value received, I promise to pay to the order of

Cook County Bank & Trust
Chicago, Illinois

One thousand and no/100 - - - - - Dollars

on August 18, 2011

plus interest at the annual rate of 8 percent.

Samuel Mason

Maturity Date

The **maturity date** is the date on which a promissory note must be paid. This date must be stated on the note or be determinable from the facts stated on the note. The following are among the most common statements of maturity date:

1. A specific date, such as "November 14, 2011"
2. A specific number of months after the date of the note, such as "three months after November 14, 2011"
3. A specific number of days after the date of the note, such as "60 days after November 14, 2011"

The maturity date is obvious when a specific date is stated. And when the maturity date is a number of months from the date of the note, one simply uses the same day in the appropriate future month. For example, a note dated January 20 that is due in two months would be due on March 20.

When the maturity date is a specific number of days from the date of the note, however, the exact maturity date must be determined. In computing the maturity date, it is important to exclude the date of the note. For example, a note dated May 20 and due in 90 days would be due on August 18, determined as follows:

Days remaining in May (31−20)	11
Days in June	30
Days in July	31
Days in August	18
Total days	90

Automobile manufacturers like Toyota, whose assembly line is pictured here, often accept promissory notes, which are unconditional promises to pay a definite sum of money on demand or at a future date. These notes produce interest income and represent a stronger legal claim against a debtor than do accounts receivable. In addition, firms commonly raise money by selling—or discounting—promissory notes to banks.

Courtesy of Ricardo Azoury/ iStockphoto.com.

Study Note

Another way to compute the duration of notes is to begin with the interest period, as in this example:

90	Interest period
−11	days remaining in May (31 − 20)
79	
−30	days in June
49	
−31	days in July
18	due date in August

Duration of a Note

The **duration of a note** is the time between a promissory note's issue date and its maturity date. Knowing the exact number of days in the duration of a note is important because interest is calculated on that basis. Identifying the duration is easy when the maturity date is stated as a specific number of days from the date of the note because the two numbers are the same. However, when the maturity date is stated as a specific date, the exact number of days must be determined. Assume that a note issued on May 10 matures on August 10. The duration of the note is 92 days:

Days remaining in May (31−10)	21
Days in June	30
Days in July	31
Days in August	10
Total days	92

Interest and Interest Rate

Interest is the cost of borrowing money or the return on lending money, depending on whether one is the borrower or the lender. The amount of interest is based on three factors: the principal (the amount of money borrowed or lent), the rate of interest, and the loan's length of time. The formula used in computing interest is as follows:

$$\text{Principal} \times \text{Rate of Interest} \times \text{Time} = \text{Interest}$$

Interest rates are usually stated on an annual basis. For example, the interest on a one-year, 8 percent, \$1,000 note would be \$80 (\$1,000 × 8/100 × 1 = \$80). If the term, or time period, of the note is three months instead of a year, the interest charge would be \$20 (\$1,000 × 8/100 × 3/12 = \$20).

When the term of a note is expressed in days, the exact number of days must be used in computing the interest. Thus, if the term of the note described above was 45 days, the interest would be \$9.86, computed as follows: \$1,000 × 8/100 × 45/365 = \$9.86.

Maturity Value

The **maturity value** is the total proceeds of a promissory note—face value plus interest—at the maturity date. The maturity value of a 90-day, 8 percent, \$1,000 note is computed as follows:

$$
\begin{aligned}
\text{Maturity Value} &= \text{Principal} + \text{Interest} \\
&= \$1{,}000 + (\$1{,}000 \times 8/100 \times 90/365) \\
&= \$1{,}000 + \$19.73 \\
&= \$1{,}019.73
\end{aligned}
$$

There are also so-called non-interest-bearing notes. The maturity value is the face value, or principal amount. In this case, the principal includes an implied interest cost.

Accrued Interest

A promissory note received in one accounting period may not be due until a later period. The interest on a note accrues by a small amount each day of the note's duration. As we described in an earlier chapter, the matching rule requires that the accrued interest be apportioned to the periods in which it belongs. For example, assume that the \$1,000, 90-day, 8 percent note discussed above was received on August 31 and that the fiscal year ended on September 30. In this case, 30 days interest, or \$6.58 (\$1,000 × 8/100 × 30/365 = \$6.58), would be earned in the fiscal year that ends on September 30. An adjusting entry would be made to record the interest receivable as an asset and the interest income as revenue. The remainder of the interest income, \$13.15 (\$1,000 × 8/100 × 60/365), would be recorded as income, and the interest receivable (\$6.58) would be shown as received when the note is paid. Note that all the cash for the interest is received when the note is paid, but the interest income is apportioned to two fiscal years.

Dishonored Note

When the maker of a note does not pay the note at maturity, it is said to be a **dishonored note**. The holder, or payee, of a dishonored note should make an entry to transfer the total amount due (including interest income) from Notes Receivable to an account receivable from the debtor. Two objectives are accomplished by transferring a dishonored note into an Accounts Receivable account. First, it leaves only notes that have not matured and are presumably negotiable and collectible in the Notes Receivable account. Second, it establishes a record in the borrower's accounts receivable account that the customer has dishonored a note receivable. Such information may be helpful in deciding whether to extend credit to the customer in the future.

STOP & APPLY >

Assume that on December 1, 2011, a company receives a 90-day, 8 percent, $5,000 note and that the company prepares financial statements monthly.

1. What is the maturity date of the note?
2. How much interest will be earned on the note if it is paid when due?
3. What is the maturity value of the note?
4. If the company's fiscal year ends on December 31, describe the adjusting entry that would be made, including the amount.
5. How much interest will be earned on this note in 2012?

SOLUTION

1. Maturity date is March 1, 2012, determined as follows:

Days remaining in December (31−1)	30
Days in January	31
Days in February	28
Days in March	1
Total days	90

2. Interest: $5,000 × 8/100 × 90/365 = $98.63
3. Maturity value: $5,000 × $98.63 = $5,098.63
4. An adjusting entry to accrue 30 days of interest income in the amount of $32.88 ($5,000 × 8/100 × 30/365) would be needed.
5. Interest earned in 2012: $65.75 ($98.63 − $32.88)

▸ PENTE COMPUTER COMPANY: REVIEW PROBLEM

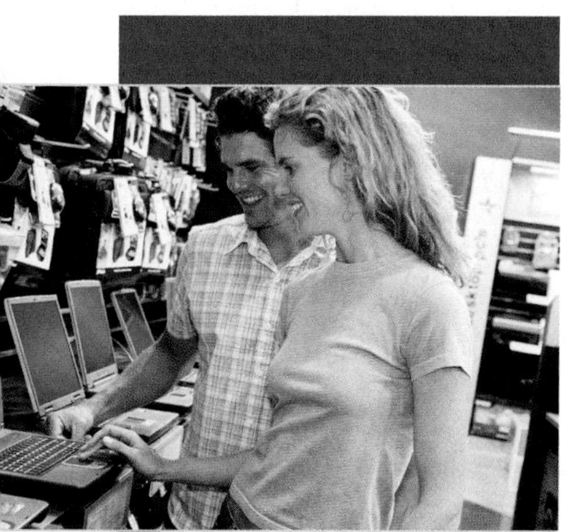

Aging and Net Sales Method Contrasted and Receivables Ratios
LO1 LO3

In this chapter's Decision Point, we posed the following questions:

- How can Pente Computer Company manage its cash needs?
- How can the company reduce the level of uncollectible accounts and increase the likelihood that accounts receivable will be paid on time?
- How can the company evaluate the effectiveness of its credit policies and the level of its accounts receivable?

During the months when sales are at their peak, Pente Computer Company may have excess cash available that it can invest in a way that earns a return but still permits ready access to cash. At other times, it may have to arrange for short-term borrowing. To ensure that it can borrow funds when it needs to, the company must maintain good relations with its bank.

To reduce the level of its uncollectible accounts and increase the likelihood that accounts receivable will be paid on time, Pente should set credit policies and have a credit department that administers the policies when screening customers who are applying for credit.

To evaluate the effectiveness of the company's credit policies and the level of its accounts receivable, management can compare the current year's receivable turnover and days' sales uncollected with those ratios in previous years.

The following data (in thousands) are from Pente's records for 2009 and 2010. Use these data to complete the requirements below.

	2010	2009
Cash	$ 100	$ 300
Accounts receivable	800	650
Allowance for doubtful accounts	(42)	(30)
Net sales	2,400	1,800

Required

1. Compute Uncollectible Accounts Expense for 2010, and determine the ending balance of Allowance for Uncollectible Accounts and Accounts Receivable, Net, under (a) the percentage of net sales method and (b) the accounts receivable aging method, assuming year-end uncollectible accounts to be $76,000.
2. Compute the receivable turnover and days' sales uncollected using the data from the accounts receivable aging method in requirement **1** and assuming that the prior year's net accounts receivable were $706,000.
3. User insight: Why do the two methods in requirement **1** produce different results? What are the implications of the result in requirement **2**?

Answers to Review Problem

1. Uncollectible Accounts Expense and ending account balances
   a. Percentage of net sales method:

      Uncollectible Accounts Expense = 1.5 percent × $2,400,000 = $36,000

      Allowance for Uncollectible Accounts = $36,000 + $42,000 = $78,000

      Accounts Receivable, Net = $800,000 − $78,000 = $722,000

   b. Accounts receivable aging method:

      Uncollectible Accounts Expense = $76,000 − $30,000 = $46,000

      Allowance for Uncollectible Accounts = $76,000

      Accounts Receivable, Net = $800,000 − $76,000 = $724,000

2. Receivable turnover and days' sales uncollected

$$\text{Receivable Turnover} = \frac{\text{Net Sales}}{\text{Average Accounts Receivable}} = \frac{\$2{,}400{,}000}{(\$724{,}000 + \$620{,}000) \div 2}$$

$$= \frac{\$2{,}400{,}000}{\$672{,}000}$$

$$= 3.6 \text{ times}$$

$$\text{Days' Sales Uncollected} = \frac{365 \text{ days}}{\text{Receivable Turnover}} = \frac{365 \text{ days}}{3.6 \text{ times}} = 101.4 \text{ days}$$

3. Both methods are estimates and thus are likely to give different results. Ideally, the results are similar. It takes Pente 101.4 days on average to collect its sales. This is almost four months, which means the company must manage its cash and borrowings carefully or revise its credit terms.

LO1 Identify and explain the management and ethical issues related to cash and receivables.

The management of cash and receivables is critical to maintaining adequate liquidity. In dealing with these assets, management must (1) consider the need for short-term investing and borrowing as the business's balance of cash fluctuates during seasonal cycles, (2) establish credit policies that balance the need for sales with the ability to collect, (3) evaluate the level of receivables using receivable turnover and days' sales uncollected, (4) assess the need to increase cash flows through the financing of receivables, and (5) understand the importance of ethics in estimating credit losses.

LO2 Define *cash equivalents*, and explain methods of controlling cash, including bank reconciliations.

Cash equivalents are investments that have a term of 90 days or less. Cash and cash equivalents are financial instruments that are valued at fair value. Methods of controlling cash include imprest systems; banking services, including electronic funds transfer; and bank reconciliations. A bank reconciliation accounts for the difference between the balance on a company's bank statement and the balance in its Cash account. It involves adjusting for outstanding checks, deposits in transit, service charges, NSF checks, miscellaneous debits and credits, and interest income.

LO3 Apply the allowance method of accounting for uncollectible accounts.

Because of the time lag between credit sales and the time accounts are judged uncollectible, the allowance method is used to match the amount of uncollectible accounts against revenues in any given period. Uncollectible accounts expense is estimated by using either the percentage of net sales method or the accounts receivable aging method. When the first method is used, bad debts are judged to be a certain percentage of sales during the period. When the second method is used, certain percentages are applied to groups of accounts receivable that have been arranged by due dates.

Allowance for Uncollectible Accounts is a contra-asset account to Accounts Receivable. The estimate of uncollectible accounts is debited to Uncollectible Accounts Expense and credited to the allowance account. When an individual account is determined to be uncollectible, it is removed from Accounts Receivable by debiting the allowance account and crediting Accounts Receivable. If the written-off account is later collected, the earlier entry is reversed and the collection is recorded in the normal way.

LO4 Define *promissory note*, and make common calculations for promissory notes receivable.

A promissory note is an unconditional promise to pay a definite sum of money on demand or at a future date. Companies that sell durable goods of high value, such as farm machinery and automobiles, often accept promissory notes. Selling these notes to banks is a common financing method. In accounting for promissory notes, it is important to know how to calculate the maturity date, duration of a note, interest and interest rate, and maturity value.

REVIEW of Concepts and Terminology

The following concepts and terms were introduced in this chapter:

Key Ratios

CHAPTER ASSIGNMENTS

BUILDING Your Basic Knowledge and Skills

Short Exercises

LO1 **Management Issues**

SE 1. Indicate whether each of the following actions is related to (a) managing cash needs, (b) setting credit policies, (c) financing receivables, or (d) ethically reporting receivables:

1. Selling accounts receivable to a factor
2. Borrowing funds for short-term needs during slow periods
3. Conducting thorough checks of new customers' ability to pay
4. Making every effort to reflect possible future losses accurately

LO1 **Short-Term Liquidity Ratios**

SE 2. Graff Company has cash of $40,000, net accounts receivable of $90,000, and net sales of $720,000. Last year's net accounts receivable were $70,000. Compute the following ratios: (a) receivable turnover and (b) days' sales uncollected.

LO2 **Cash and Cash Equivalents**

SE 3. Compute the amount of cash and cash equivalents on Car Wash Company's balance sheet if, on the balance sheet date, it has currency and coins on hand of $125, deposits in checking accounts of $750, U.S. Treasury bills due in 80 days of $7,500, and U.S. Treasury bonds due in 200 days of $12,500.

LO2 **Bank Reconciliation**

SE 4. Prepare a bank reconciliation from the following information:

a. Balance per bank statement as of June 30, $4,862.77
b. Balance per books as of June 30, $2,479.48
c. Deposits in transit, $654.24
d. Outstanding checks, $3,028.89
e. Interest on average balance, $8.64

LO3 **Percentage of Net Sales Method**

SE 5. At the end of October, Zion Company's management estimates the uncollectible accounts expense to be 1 percent of net sales of $1,500,000. Prepare the entry to record the uncollectible accounts expense, assuming the Allowance for Uncollectible Accounts has a debit balance of $7,000.

LO3 **Accounts Receivable Aging Method**

SE 6. An aging analysis on June 30 of the accounts receivable of Sung Corporation indicates that uncollectible accounts amount to $86,000. Prepare the entry to record uncollectible accounts expense under each of the following independent assumptions:

a. Allowance for Uncollectible Accounts has a credit balance of $18,000 before adjustment.
b. Allowance for Uncollectible Accounts has a debit balance of $14,000 before adjustment.

LO3 **Write-off of Accounts Receivable**

SE 7. Windy Corporation, which uses the allowance method, has accounts receivable of $50,800 and an allowance for uncollectible accounts of $9,800. An account receivable from Tom Novak of $4,400 is deemed to be uncollectible and is written off. What is the amount of net accounts receivable before and after the write-off?

LO4 **Notes Receivable Calculations**

SE 8. On August 25, Champion Company received a 90-day, 9 percent note in settlement of an account receivable in the amount of $20,000. Determine the maturity date, amount of interest on the note, and maturity value.

Exercises

LO1 LO2 **Discussion Questions**

E 1. Develop a brief answer to each of the following questions:

1. Name some businesses whose needs for cash fluctuate during the year. Name some whose needs for cash are relatively stable over the year.
2. Why is it advantageous for a company to finance its receivables?
3. To increase its sales, a company decides to increase its credit terms from 15 to 30 days. What effect will this change in policy have on receivable turnover and days' sales uncollected?
4. How might the receivable turnover and days' sales uncollected reveal that management is consistently underestimating the amount of losses from uncollectible accounts? Is this action ethical?

LO3 LO4 **Discussion Questions**

E 2. Develop a brief answer to each of the following questions:

1. What accounting rule is violated by the direct charge-off method of recognizing uncollectible accounts? Why?
2. In what ways is Allowance for Uncollectible Accounts similar to Accumulated Depreciation? In what ways is it different?
3. Under what circumstances would an accrual of interest income on an interest-bearing note receivable not be required at the end of an accounting period?

LO1 **Management Issues**

E 3. Indicate whether each of the following actions is primarily related to (a) managing cash needs, (b) setting credit policies, (c) financing receivables, or (d) ethically reporting accounts receivable:

1. Buying a U.S. Treasury bill with cash that is not needed for a few months
2. Comparing receivable turnovers for two years
3. Setting a policy that allows customers to buy on credit
4. Selling notes receivable to a financing company
5. Making careful estimates of losses from uncollectible accounts
6. Borrowing funds for short-term needs in a period when sales are low
7. Changing the terms for credit sales in an effort to reduce the days' sales uncollected
8. Revising estimated credit losses in a timely manner when conditions change
9. Establishing a department whose responsibility is to approve customers' credit

LO1 **Short-Term Liquidity Ratios**

E 4. Using the following data from Lopez Corporation's financial statements, compute the receivable turnover and the days' sales uncollected:

Current assets	
Cash	$ 35,000
Short-term investments	85,000
Notes receivable	120,000
Accounts receivable, net	200,000
Inventory	250,000
Prepaid assets	25,000
Total current assets	$ 715,000
Current liabilities	
Notes payable	$ 300,000
Accounts payable	75,000
Accrued liabilities	10,000
Total current liabilities	$ 385,000
Net sales	$1,600,000
Last year's accounts receivable, net	$ 180,000

LO2 **Cash and Cash Equivalents**

E 5. At year end, Lam Company had currency and coins in cash registers of $2,800, money orders from customers of $5,000, deposits in checking accounts of $32,000, U.S. Treasury bills due in 80 days of $90,000, certificates of deposit at the bank that mature in six months of $100,000, and U.S. Treasury bonds due in one year of $50,000. Calculate the amount of cash and cash equivalents that will be shown on the company's year-end balance sheet.

LO2 **Bank Reconciliation**

E 6. Prepare a bank reconciliation from the following information:

a. Balance per bank statement as of May 31, $17,755.44
b. Balance per books as of May 31, $12,211.94
c. Deposits in transit, $2,254.81
d. Outstanding checks, $7,818.16
e. Bank service charge, $19.85

LO3 **Percentage of Net Sales Method**

E 7. At the end of the year, Emil Enterprises estimates the uncollectible accounts expense to be 0.8 percent of net sales of $7,575,000. The current credit balance of Allowance for Uncollectible Accounts is $12,900. Prepare the entry to record the uncollectible accounts expense. What is the balance of Allowance for Uncollectible Accounts after this adjustment?

LO3 **Accounts Receivable Aging Method**

E 8. The Accounts Receivable account of Samson Company shows a debit balance of $52,000 at the end of the year. An aging analysis of the individual accounts indicates estimated uncollectible accounts to be $3,350.

Prepare the entry to record the uncollectible accounts expense under each of the following independent assumptions: (a) Allowance for Uncollectible Accounts has a credit balance of $400 before adjustment, and (b) Allowance for Uncollectible Accounts has a debit balance of $400 before adjustment. What is the balance of Allowance for Uncollectible Accounts after each of these adjustments?

LO3 Aging Method and Net Sales Method Contrasted

E 9. At the beginning of 2011, the balances for Accounts Receivable and Allowance for Uncollectible Accounts were $430,000 and $31,400 (credit), respectively. During the year, credit sales were $3,200,000 and collections on account were $2,950,000. In addition, $35,000 in uncollectible accounts was written off.

Using T accounts, determine the year-end balances of Accounts Receivable and Allowance for Uncollectible Accounts. Then prepare the year-end adjusting entry to record the uncollectible accounts expense under each of the following conditions. Also show the year-end balance sheet presentation of accounts receivable and allowance for uncollectible accounts.

a. Management estimates the percentage of uncollectible credit sales to be 1.4 percent of total credit sales.
b. Based on an aging of accounts receivable, management estimates the end-of-year uncollectible accounts receivable to be $38,700.

Post the results of each of the entries to the T account for Allowance for Uncollectible Accounts.

LO3 Aging Method and Net Sales Method Contrasted

E 10. During 2010, Omega Company had net sales of $11,400,000. Most of the sales were on credit. At the end of 2010, the balance of Accounts Receivable was $1,400,000 and Allowance for Uncollectible Accounts had a debit balance of $48,000. Omega Company's management uses two methods of estimating uncollectible accounts expense: the percentage of net sales method and the accounts receivable aging method. The percentage of uncollectible sales is 1.5 percent of net sales, and based on an aging of accounts receivable, the end-of-year uncollectible accounts total $140,000.

Prepare the end-of-year adjusting entry to record the uncollectible accounts expense under each method. What will the balance of Allowance for Uncollectible Accounts be after each adjustment? Why are the results different? Which method is likely to be more reliable? Why?

LO3 Aging Method and Net Sales Method Contrasted

E 11. The First Fence Company sells merchandise on credit. During the fiscal year ended July 31, the company had net sales of $1,150,000. At the end of the year, it had Accounts Receivable of $300,000 and a debit balance in Allowance for Uncollectible Accounts of $1,700. In the past, approximately 1.4 percent of net sales have proved to be uncollectible. Also, an aging analysis of accounts receivable reveals that $15,000 of the receivables appears to be uncollectible.

Prepare entries in journal form to record uncollectible accounts expense using (a) the percentage of net sales method and (b) the accounts receivable aging method. What is the resulting balance of Allowance for Uncollectible Accounts under each method? How would your answers under each method change if Allowance for Uncollectible Accounts had a credit balance of $1,700 instead of a debit balance? Why do the methods result in different balances?

LO3 Write-off of Accounts Receivable

E 12. Colby Company, which uses the allowance method, has Accounts Receivable of $65,000 and an allowance for uncollectible accounts of $6,400 (credit). The company sold merchandise to Irma Hegerman for $7,200 and later received $2,400 from Hegerman. The rest of the amount due from Hegerman had to be written off as uncollectible. Using T accounts, show the beginning balances and the effects of the Hegerman transactions on Accounts Receivable and Allowance for Uncollectible Accounts. What is the amount of net accounts receivable before and after the write-off?

LO4 **Interest Computations**

E 13. Determine the interest on the following notes:

a. $77,520 at 10 percent for 90 days
b. $54,400 at 12 percent for 60 days
c. $61,200 at 9 percent for 30 days
d. $102,000 at 15 percent for 120 days
e. $36,720 at 6 percent for 60 days

LO4 **Notes Receivable Calculations**

E 14. Determine the maturity date, interest at maturity, and maturity value for a 90-day, 10 percent, $36,000 note from Archer Corporation dated February 15.

LO4 **Notes Receivable Calculations**

E 15. Determine the maturity date, interest in 2010 and 2011, and maturity value for a 90-day, 12 percent, $30,000 note from a customer dated December 1, 2010, assuming a December 31 year end.

LO4 **Notes Receivable Calculations**

E 16. Determine the maturity date, interest at maturity, and maturity value for each of the following notes:

a. A 60-day, 10 percent, $4,800 note dated January 5 received from A. Gal for granting a time extension on a past-due account.
b. A 60-day, 12 percent, $3,000 note dated March 9 received from T. Kawa for granting a time extension on a past-due account.

Problems

LO2 **Bank Reconciliation**

P 1. The following information is available for Unique Globe, as of May 31, 2011:

a. Cash on the books as of May 31 amounted to $43,784.16. Cash on the bank statement for the same date was $53,451.46.
b. A deposit of $5,220.94, representing cash receipts of May 31, did not appear on the bank statement.
c. Outstanding checks totaled $3,936.80.
d. A check for $1,920.00 returned with the statement was recorded incorrectly in the check register as $1,380.00. The check was for a cash purchase of merchandise.
e. The bank service charge for May amounted to $30.
f. The bank collected $12,200.00 for Unique Globe, on a note. The face value of the note was $12,000.00.
g. An NSF check for $178.56 from a customer, Eve Lay, was returned with the statement.
h. The bank mistakenly charged to the company account a check for $750.00 drawn by another company.
i. The bank reported that it had credited the account for $250.00 in interest on the average balance for May.

Required

1. Prepare a bank reconciliation for Unique Globe, Inc., as of May 31, 2011.
2. Prepare the entries in journal form necessary to adjust the accounts.
3. What amount of cash should appear on Unique Globe's balance sheet as of May 31?

User insight ▶ 4. Why is a bank reconciliation considered an important control over cash?

LO1 LO3 **Methods of Estimating Uncollectible Accounts and Receivables Analysis**

P 2. Moore Company had an Accounts Receivable balance of $640,000 and a credit balance in Allowance for Uncollectible Accounts of $33,400 at January 1, 2011. During the year, the company recorded the following transactions:

a. Sales on account, $2,104,000
b. Sales returns and allowances by credit customers, $106,800
c. Collections from customers, $1,986,000
d. Worthless accounts written off, $39,600

The company's past history indicates that 2.5 percent of its net credit sales will not be collected.

Required

1. Prepare T accounts for Accounts Receivable and Allowance for Uncollectible Accounts. Enter the beginning balances, and show the effects on these accounts of the items listed above, summarizing the year's activity. Determine the ending balance of each account.
2. Compute Uncollectible Accounts Expense and determine the ending balance of Allowance for Uncollectible Accounts under (a) the percentage of net sales method and (b) the accounts receivable aging method, assuming an aging of the accounts receivable shows that $48,000 may be uncollectible.
3. Compute the receivable turnover and days' sales uncollected, using the data from the accounts receivable aging method in requirement 2.

User insight ▶ 4. How do you explain that the two methods used in requirement 2 result in different amounts for Uncollectible Accounts Expense? What rationale underlies each method?

LO3 **Accounts Receivable Aging Method**

P 3. The Ciao Style Store uses the accounts receivable aging method to estimate uncollectible accounts. On February 1, 2010, the balance of the Accounts Receivable account was a debit of $442,341, and the balance of Allowance for Uncollectible Accounts was a credit of $43,700. During the year, the store had sales on account of $3,722,000, sales returns and allowances of $60,000, worthless accounts written off of $44,300, and collections from customers of $3,211,000. As part of the end-of-year (January 31, 2011) procedures, an aging analysis of accounts receivable is prepared. The analysis, which is partially complete, is as follows:

Customer Account	Total	Not Yet Due	1–30 Days Past Due	31–60 Days Past Due	61–90 Days Past Due	Over 90 Days Past Due
Balance Forward	$793,791	$438,933	$149,614	$106,400	$57,442	$41,402

To finish the analysis, the following accounts need to be classified:

Account	Amount	Due Date
J. Kras	$11,077	Jan. 15
T. Lopez	9,314	Feb. 15 (next fiscal year)
L. Zapal	8,664	Dec. 20
R. Caputo	780	Oct. 1
E. Rago	14,710	Jan. 4
S. Smith	6,316	Nov. 15
A. Quinn	4,389	Mar. 1 (next fiscal year)
	$55,250	

From past experience, the company has found that the following rates are realistic for estimating uncollectible accounts:

Time	Percentage Considered Uncollectible
Not yet due	2
1–30 days past due	5
31–60 days past due	15
61–90 days past due	25
Over 90 days past due	50

Required

1. Complete the aging analysis of accounts receivable.
2. Compute the end-of-year balances (before adjustments) of Accounts Receivable and Allowance for Uncollectible Accounts.
3. Prepare an analysis computing the estimated uncollectible accounts.
4. How much is Ciao Style Store's estimated uncollectible accounts expense for the year? (Round the adjustment to the nearest whole dollar.)

User insight ▶ 5. What role do estimates play in applying the aging analysis? What factors might affect these estimates?

LO4 **Notes Receivable Calculations**

P 4. Rich Importing Company engaged in the following transactions involving promissory notes:

May 3	Sold engines to Kabel Company for $30,000 in exchange for a 90-day, 11 percent promissory note.
16	Sold engines to Vu Company for $16,000 in exchange for a 60-day, 12 percent note.
31	Sold engines to Vu Company for $15,000 in exchange for a 90-day, 10 percent note.

Required

1. For each of the notes, determine the (a) maturity date, (b) interest on the note, and (c) maturity value.
2. Assume that the fiscal year for Rich Importing Company ends on June 30. How much interest income should be recorded on that date?

User insight ▶ 3. What are the effects of the transactions in May on cash flows for the year ended June 30?

Alternate Problems

LO2 **Bank Reconciliation**

P 5. The following information is available for Prime Company as of April 30, 2011:

a. Cash on the books as of April 30 amounted to $113,175.28. Cash on the bank statement for the same date was $140,717.08.

b. A deposit of $14,349.84, representing cash receipts of April 30, did not appear on the bank statement.
c. Outstanding checks totaled $7,302.64.
d. A check for $2,420.00 returned with the statement was recorded as $2,024.00. The check was for advertising.
e. The bank service charge for April amounted to $35.00.
f. The bank collected $36,300.00 for Prime Company on a note. The face value of the note was $36,000.00
g. An NSF check for $1,140.00 from a customer, Tom Jones, was returned with the statement.
h. The bank mistakenly deducted a check for $700.00 that was drawn by Tiger Corporation.
i. The bank reported a credit of $560.00 for interest on the average balance.

Required

1. Prepare a bank reconciliation for Prime Company as of April 30, 2011.
2. Prepare the necessary entries in journal form from the reconciliation.
3. State the amount of cash that should appear on Prime Company's balance sheet as of April 30.
4. User insight ▶ Why is a bank reconciliation a necessary internal control?

LO1 LO3 Methods of Estimating Uncollectible Accounts and Receivables Analysis

P 6. On December 31 of last year, the balance sheet of Korab Company had Accounts Receivable of $149,000 and a credit balance in Allowance for Uncollectible Accounts of $10,150. During the current year, Korab Company's records included the following selected activities: (a) sales on account, $597,500; (b) sales returns and allowances, $36,500; (c) collections from customers, $575,000; and (d) accounts written off as worthless, $8,000. In the past, 1.6 percent of Korab Company's net sales have been uncollectible.

Required

1. Prepare T accounts for Accounts Receivable and Allowance for Uncollectible Accounts. Enter the beginning balances, and show the effects on these accounts of the items listed above, summarizing the year's activity. Determine the ending balance of each account.
2. Compute Uncollectible Accounts Expense and determine the ending balance of Allowance for Uncollectible Accounts under (a) the percentage of net sales method and (b) the accounts receivable aging method. Assume that an aging of the accounts receivable shows that $10,000 may be uncollectible.
3. Compute the receivable turnover and days' sales uncollected, using the data from the accounts receivable aging method in requirement 2.
4. User insight ▶ How do you explain that the two methods used in requirement 2 result in different amounts for Uncollectible Accounts Expense? What rationale underlies each method?

LO3 Accounts Receivable Aging Method

P 7. Garcia Company uses the accounts receivable aging method to estimate uncollectible accounts. At the beginning of the year, the balance of the Accounts Receivable account was a debit of $90,430, and the balance of Allowance for Uncollectible Accounts was a credit of $8,100. During the year, the company had sales on account of $475,000, sales returns and allowances of $6,200, worthless accounts written off of $8,800, and collections from customers of $452,730. At the end of year (December 31, 2011), a junior accountant for Garcia Company was preparing an aging analysis of accounts receivable. At the top of page 6 of the report, the following totals appeared:

Customer Account	Total	Not Yet Due	1–30 Days Past Due	31–60 Days Past Due	61–90 Days Past Due	Over 90 Days Past Due
Balance Forward	$89,640	$49,030	$24,110	$9,210	$3,990	$3,300

To finish the analysis, the following accounts need to be classified:

Account	Amount	Due Date
B. Smith	$ 930	Jan. 14 (next year)
L. Wing	645	Dec. 24
A. Rak	1,850	Sept. 28
T. Cat	2,205	Aug. 16
M. Nut	350	Dec. 14
S. Prince	1,785	Jan. 23 (next year)
J. Wind	295	Nov. 5
	$8,060	

From past experience, the company has found that the following rates are realistic for estimating uncollectible accounts:

Time	Percentage Considered Uncollectible
Not yet due	2
1–30 days past due	5
31–60 days past due	15
61–90 days past due	25
Over 90 days past due	50

Required

1. Complete the aging analysis of accounts receivable.
2. Compute the end-of-year balances (before adjustments) of Accounts Receivable and Allowance for Uncollectible Accounts.
3. Prepare an analysis computing the estimated uncollectible accounts.
4. Calculate Garcia Company's estimated uncollectible accounts expense for the year (round the amount to the nearest whole dollar).

User insight ▶ 5. What role do estimates play in applying the aging analysis? What factors might affect these estimates?

LO4 **Notes Receivable Calculations**

P 8. Abraham Importing Company engaged in the following transactions involving promissory notes:

May 3	Sold engines to Anton Company for $60,000 in exchange for a 90-day, 12 percent promissory note.
16	Sold engines to Yu Company for $32,000 in exchange for a 60-day, 13 percent note.
31	Sold engines to Yu Company for $30,000 in exchange for a 90-day, 11 percent note.

Required

1. For each of the notes, determine the (a) maturity date, (b) interest on the note, and (c) maturity value.
2. Assume that the fiscal year for Abraham Importing Company ends on June 30. How much interest income should be recorded on that date?

User insight ▶ 3. What are the effects of the transactions in May on cash flows for the year ended June 30?

ENHANCING Your Knowledge, Skills, and Critical Thinking

LO1 **Role of Credit Sales**

C 1. **Mitsubishi Corp.**, a broadly diversified Japanese corporation, instituted a credit plan called Three Diamonds for customers who buy its major electronic products, such as large-screen televisions and videotape recorders, from specified retail dealers.[18] Under the plan, approved customers who make purchases in July of one year do not have to make any payments until September of the next year. Nor do they have to pay interest during the intervening months. Mitsubishi pays the dealer the full amount less a small fee, sends the customer a Mitsubishi credit card, and collects from the customer at the specified time.

What was Mitsubishi's motivation for establishing such generous credit terms? What costs are involved? What are the accounting implications?

LO1 LO3 **Role of Estimates in Accounting for Receivables**

C 2. **CompuCredit** is a credit card issuer in Atlanta. It prides itself on making credit cards available to almost anybody in a matter of seconds over the Internet. The cost to the consumer is an interest rate of 28 percent, about double that of companies that provide cards only to customers with good credit. Despite its high interest rate, CompuCredit has been successful, reporting 1.9 million accounts and an income of approximately $100 million. To calculate its income, the company estimates that 10 percent of its $1.3 billion in accounts receivable will not be paid; the industry average is 7 percent. Some analysts have been critical of CompuCredit for being too optimistic in its projections of losses.[19]

Why are estimates necessary in accounting for receivables? If CompuCredit were to use the same estimate of losses as other companies in its industry, what would its income have been for the year? How would one determine if CompuCredit's estimate of losses is reasonable?

LO1 **Receivables Financing**

C 3. Bernhardt Appliances, Inc., located in central Ohio, is a small manufacturer of washing machines and dryers. Bernhardt sells most of its appliances to large, established discount retail companies that market the appliances under their own names. Bernhardt sells the appliances on trade credit terms of n/60. If a customer wants a longer term, however, Bernhardt will accept a note with a term of up to nine months. At present, the company is having cash flow troubles and needs $10 million immediately. Its cash balance is $400,000, its accounts receivable balance is $4.6 million, and its notes receivable balance is $7.4 million.

How might Bernhardt Appliance's management use its accounts receivable and notes receivable to raise the cash it needs? What are the company's prospects for raising the needed cash?

LO1 LO3 **Ethics and Uncollectible Accounts**

C 4. Caldwell Interiors, a successful retail furniture company, is located in an affluent suburb where a major insurance company has just announced a restructuring that will lay off 4,000 employees. Caldwell Interiors sells quality furniture, usually on credit. Accounts Receivable is one of its major assets. Although the company's annual uncollectible accounts losses are not out of line, they represent a sizable amount. The company depends on bank loans for its financing. Sales and net income have declined in the past year, and some customers are falling behind in paying their accounts.

Abby Caldwell, the owner of the business, knows that the bank's loan officer likes to see a steady performance. She has therefore instructed the company's controller to underestimate the uncollectible accounts this year to show a small growth in earnings. Caldwell believes this action is justified because earnings in future years will average out the losses, and since the company has a history of success, she believes the adjustments are meaningless accounting measures anyway.

Are Caldwell's actions ethical? Would any parties be harmed by her actions? How important is it to try to be accurate in estimating losses from uncollectible accounts?

LO1 LO2 LO3

Cash and Receivables

CASH FLOW

C 5. Refer to **CVS Corporation**'s annual report in the Supplement to Chapter 5 to answer the following questions:

1. What amount of cash and cash equivalents did CVS Corporation have in 2008? Do you suppose most of that amount is cash in the bank or cash equivalents?
2. What customers represent the main source of CVS's accounts receivable, and how much is CVS's allowance for uncollectible accounts?

LO1

Accounts Receivable Analysis

C 6. Refer to the **CVS** annual report in the Supplement to Chapter 5 and to the following data (in millions) for **Walgreens**: net sales, $59,034.0 and $53,762.0 for 2008 and 2007, respectively; accounts receivable, net, $2,527.0 and $2,236.5 for 2008 and 2007, respectively.

1. Compute receivable turnover and days' sales uncollected for 2008 and 2007 for CVS and Walgreens. Accounts Receivable in 2006 were $2,381.7 million for CVS and $2,062.7 million for Walgreens.
2. Do you discern any differences in the two companies' credit policies? Explain your answer.

CHAPTER

10 Current Liabilities and Fair Value Accounting

Making a Statement

INCOME STATEMENT

Revenues

– Expenses

= Net Income

STATEMENT OF OWNER'S EQUITY

Beginning Balance

+ Net Income

– Withdrawals

= Ending Balance

BALANCE SHEET

Assets	**Liabilities**
	Owner's Equity

A = L + OE

STATEMENT OF CASH FLOWS

Operating activities
+ Investing activities
+ Financing activities
= Change in Cash
+ Beginning Balance
= Ending Cash Balance

Measurement of unearned revenues and accrued expenses impacts the amount of current liabilities on the balance sheet and revenues and expenses on the income statement.

Although some current liabilities, such as accounts payable, are recorded when a company makes a purchase, others accrue during an accounting period and are not recorded until adjusting entries are made at the end of the period. In addition, the value of some accruals must be estimated. If accrued liabilities are not recognized and valued properly, both liabilities and expenses will be understated on the financial statements, making the company's performance look better than it actually is.

LEARNING OBJECTIVES

LO1 Identify the management issues related to current liabilities. (pp. 432–436)

LO2 Identify, compute, and record definitely determinable and estimated current liabilities. (pp. 436–447)

LO3 Distinguish *contingent liabilities* from *commitments*. (pp. 447–448)

LO4 Identify the valuation approaches to fair value accounting, and define *time value of money* and *interest* and apply them to present values. (pp. 448–453)

LO5 Apply present value to simple valuation situations. (pp. 453–455)

DECISION POINT ▸ A USER'S FOCUS MEGGIE'S FITNESS CENTER

- ▸ How should Meggie Jones identify and account for all her company's current liabilities?
- ▸ How should she evaluate her company's liquidity?

In January 2009, Meggie Jones started a business called Meggie's Fitness Center. In addition to offering exercise classes, the center sells nutritional supplements. Meggie has limited experience in running a business, but she knows that it is extremely important for a company, especially a new company, to manage its liabilities so that it has enough cash on hand to pay debts when they come due and that without a sufficient inflow of cash to do that, a company is likely to fail.

Meggie is also well aware that incurring liabilities is a necessary part of doing business. When she started her business, Meggie signed over a promissory note to her bank for $16,000. To help operate the business, she hired two exercise instructors to whom she pays monthly salaries, and she has incurred debt in maintaining an inventory of nutritional supplements. Because she has not yet filed any tax reports for her business, other liabilities include taxes owed to both the federal and state governments, as well as $3,600 in annual property taxes that the business owes the city government.

As the company is approaching the end of its second fiscal year, Meggie is anxious to figure out what the company currently owes the government and other parties and to assess its liquidity. After reading this chapter, you will know how Meggie should identify, compute, and record her company's current liabilities. You will also be familiar with the key measures used in evaluating liquidity.

Management Issues Related to Current Liabilities

Current liabilities require careful management of liquidity and cash flows, as well as close monitoring of accounts payable. In reporting on current liabilities, managers must understand how they should be recognized, valued, classified, and disclosed.

LO1 Identify the management issues related to current liabilities.

Managing Liquidity and Cash Flows

The primary reason a company incurs current liabilities is to meet its needs for cash during the operating cycle. As explained in Chapter 6, the operating cycle is the length of time it takes to purchase inventory, sell the inventory, and collect the resulting receivable. Most current liabilities arise in support of this cycle, as when accounts payable arise from purchases of inventory, accrued expenses arise from operating costs, and unearned revenues arise from customers' advance payments. Companies incur short-term debt to raise cash during periods of inventory buildup or while waiting for collection of receivables. They use the cash to pay the portion of long-term debt that is currently due and to pay liabilities arising from operations.

Failure to manage the cash flows related to current liabilities can have serious consequences for a business. For instance, if suppliers are not paid on time, they may withhold shipments that are vital to a company's operations. Continued failure to pay current liabilities can lead to bankruptcy. To evaluate a company's ability to pay its current liabilities, analysts often use two measures of liquidity—working capital and the current ratio, both of which we defined in an earlier chapter. Current liabilities are a key component of both these measures. They typically equal from 25 to 50 percent of total assets.

As shown below (in millions), **Nike**'s short-term liquidity as measured by working capital and the current ratio was positive in 2008 and improved somewhat in 2009.

	Current Assets	–	Current Liabilities	=	Working Capital	Current Ratio*
2008	$8,839.3	–	$3,321.5	=	$5,517.8	2.66
2009	$9,734.0	–	$3,277.0	=	$6,457.0	2.97

The increase in Nike's working capital and current ratio from 2008 to 2009 was caused primarily by a large increase in cash and short-term investments. Overall, Nike is in a strong current situation and exercises very good management of its cash flow.

Evaluating Accounts Payable

Another consideration in managing liquidity and cash flows is the time suppliers give a company to pay for purchases. Measures commonly used to assess a company's ability to pay within a certain time frame are **payables turnover** and **days' payable**. Payables turnover is the number of times, on average, that a company pays its accounts payable in an accounting period. Days' payable shows how long, on average, a company takes to pay its accounts payables.

*Current assets divided by current liabilities.

FOCUS ON BUSINESS PRACTICE

Debt Problems Can Plague Even Well-Known Companies

In a Wall Street horror story that illustrates the importance of managing current liabilities, **Xerox Corporation**, one of the most storied names in American business, found itself combating rumors that it was facing bankruptcy. Following a statement by Xerox's CEO that the company's financial model was "unsustainable," management was forced to defend the company's liquidity by saying it had adequate funds to continue operations. But in a report filed with the SEC, management acknowledged that it had tapped into its $7 billion line of bank credit for more than $3 billion to pay off short-term debt that was coming due. Unable to secure more money from any other source to pay these debts, Xerox had no choice but to turn to the line of credit from its bank. Had it run out, the company might well have gone bankrupt.[1] Fortunately, Xerox was able to restructure its line of credit to stay in business.

To measure payables turnover for **Nike**, we must first calculate purchases by adjusting cost of goods sold for the change in inventory. An increase in inventory means purchases were more than cost of goods sold; a decrease means purchases were less than cost of goods sold. Nike's cost of goods sold in 2009 was $10,571.7 million, and its inventory decreased by $81.4 million. Its payables turnover is computed as follows (in millions):

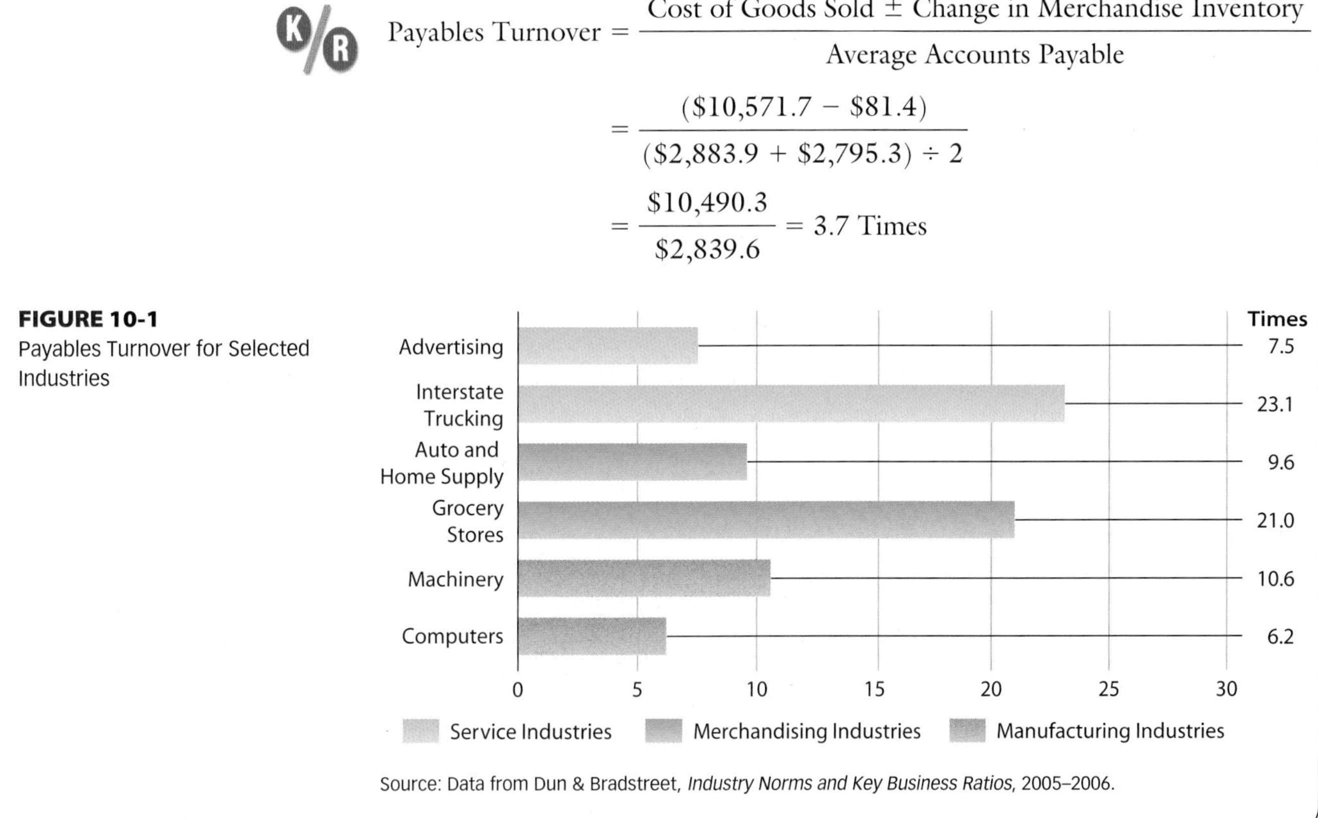

$$\text{Payables Turnover} = \frac{\text{Cost of Goods Sold} \pm \text{Change in Merchandise Inventory}}{\text{Average Accounts Payable}}$$

$$= \frac{(\$10{,}571.7 - \$81.4)}{(\$2{,}883.9 + \$2{,}795.3) \div 2}$$

$$= \frac{\$10{,}490.3}{\$2{,}839.6} = 3.7 \text{ Times}$$

FIGURE 10-1
Payables Turnover for Selected Industries

Source: Data from Dun & Bradstreet, *Industry Norms and Key Business Ratios*, 2005–2006.

To find the days' payable, the number of days in the accounting period is divided by the payables turnover:

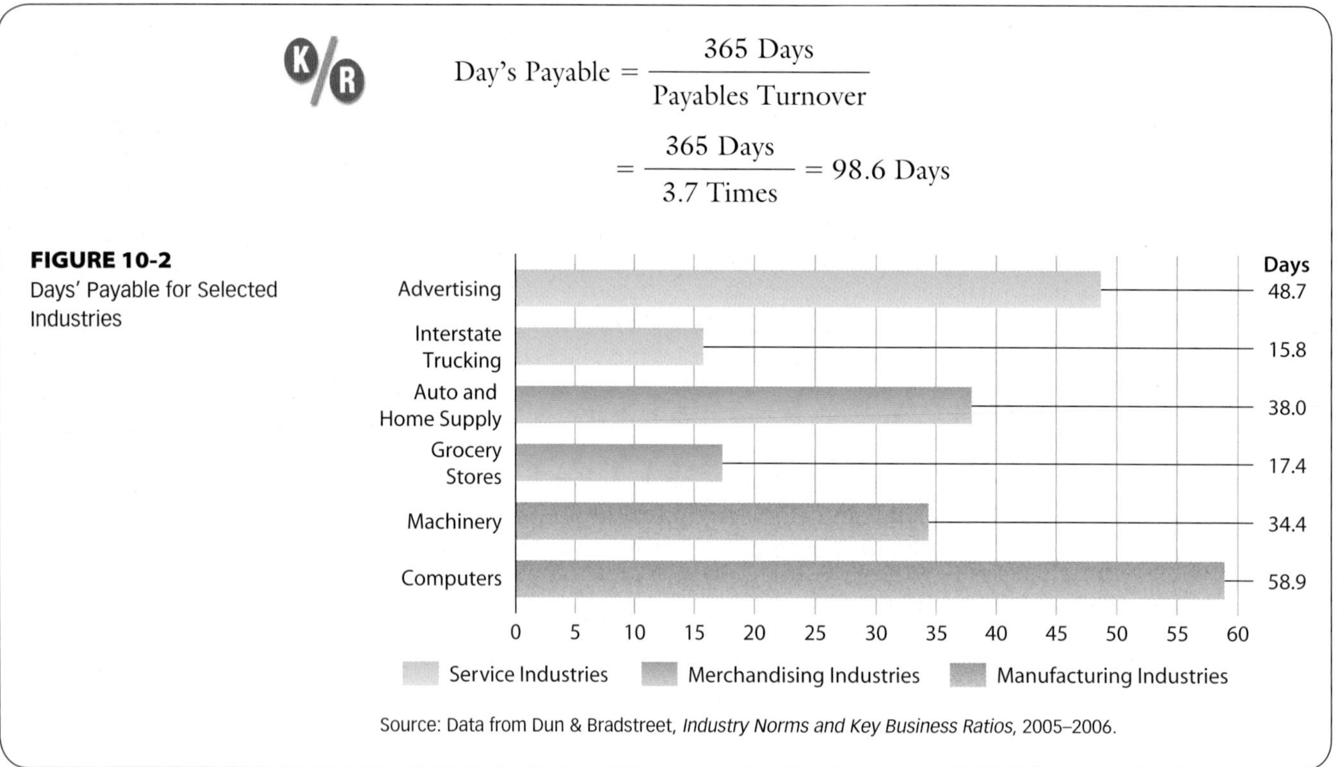

FIGURE 10-2
Days' Payable for Selected Industries

Source: Data from Dun & Bradstreet, *Industry Norms and Key Business Ratios,* 2005–2006.

The payables turnover of 3.7 times and days' payable of 98.6 days indicate that the credit terms Nike receives from its suppliers are excellent and help offset the long inventory days' on hand and days' receivable outstanding calculated in prior chapters, thus, giving a full picture of Nike's operating cycle and liquidity. Nike's financing period is only 38.1 days (83.0 days' inventory on hand + 53.7 days' sales uncollected − 98.6 days' payable). Nike's suppliers are providing most of the financing of its operating cycle.

In other industries, credit terms and product costs are not nearly as favorable. As you can see in Figures 10-1 and 10-2, companies in other industries have higher payables turnover and lower days' payable than Nike.

Reporting Liabilities

In deciding whether to buy stock in a company or lend money to it, investors and creditors must evaluate not only the company's current liabilities but its future obligations as well. In doing so, they have to rely on the integrity of the company's financial statements.

Ethical reporting of liabilities requires that they be properly recognized, valued, classified, and disclosed. In one notable case involving unethical reporting of liabilities, the CEO and other employees of **Nortel Networks Corporation**, a Canadian manufacturer of telecommunications equipment, understated accrued liabilities (and corresponding expenses) in order to report a profit and obtain salary bonuses. After all accrued liabilities had been identified, it was evident that the company was in fact losing money. The board of directors of the corporation fired all who had been involved.[2]

Recognition Timing is important in the recognition of liabilities. Failure to record a liability in an accounting period very often goes along with failure to record an expense. The two errors lead to an understatement of expense and an overstatement of income.

Generally accepted accounting principles require that a liability be recorded when an obligation occurs. This rule is harder to apply than it might appear. When a transaction obligates a company to make future payments, a liability arises and is recognized, as when goods are bought on credit. However, some current liabilities are not the result of direct transactions. One of the key reasons for making adjusting entries at the end of an accounting period is to recognize unrecorded liabilities that accrue during the period. Accrued liabilities include salaries payable and interest payable. Other liabilities that can only be estimated, such as taxes payable, must also be recognized through adjusting entries.

Agreements for future transactions do not have to be recognized. For instance, **Microsoft** might agree to pay an executive $250,000 a year for a period of three years, or it might agree to buy an unspecified amount of advertising at a certain price over the next five years. Such contracts, though they are definite commitments, are not considered liabilities because they are for future—not past—transactions. Because there is no current obligation, no liability is recognized, but they would be mentioned in the notes to the financial statements and SEC filings if material.

Valuation On the balance sheet, a liability is generally valued at the amount of money needed to pay the debt or at the fair market value of the goods or services to be delivered. The amount of most liabilities is definitely known. For example, **Amazon.com** sells a large number of gift certificates that are redeemable in the future. The amount of the liability (unearned revenue) is known, but the exact timing is not known.

> **Study Note**
>
> Disclosure of the fair value and the bases for estimating the fair value of short-term notes payable, loans payable, and other short-term debt are required unless it is not practical to estimate the value. Guidance for determining fair value is covered later in this chapter.

Some companies, however, must estimate future liabilities. For example, an automobile dealer that sells a car with a one-year warranty must provide parts and service during the year. The obligation is definite because the sale has occurred, but the amount of the obligation can only be estimated. Such estimates are usually based on past experience and anticipated changes in the business environment.

Classification As you may recall from our discussion of classified balance sheets in an earlier chapter, **current liabilities** are debts and obligations that a company expects to satisfy within one year or within its normal operating cycle, whichever is longer. These liabilities are normally paid out of current assets or with cash generated by operations. **Long-term liabilities** are liabilities due beyond one year or beyond the normal operating cycle. For example, Meggie's Fitness Center may incur long-term liabilities to finance its expansion to a new larger location, among other objectives. The distinction between current and long-term liabilities is important because it affects the evaluation of a company's liquidity.

Disclosure A company may have to include additional explanation of some liability accounts in the notes to its financial statements. For example, if a company's Notes Payable account is large, it should disclose the balances, maturity dates, interest rates, and other features of the debts in an explanatory note. Any special credit arrangements should also be disclosed. For example, in a note to its financial statements, **Hershey Foods Corporation**, the famous candy company, discloses the rationale for its credit arrangements:

Borrowing Arrangements

> We maintain debt levels we consider prudent based on our cash flow, interest coverage ratio and percentage of debt to capital. We use debt financing to lower our overall cost of capital, which increases our return on stockholders' equity.[3]

Unused lines of credit allow a company to borrow on short notice up to the credit limit, with little or no negotiation. Thus, the type of disclosure in Hershey's note is helpful in assessing whether a company has additional borrowing power.

STOP & APPLY >

Jackie's Cookie Company has current assets of $30,000 and current liabilities of $20,000, of which accounts payable are $15,000. Jackie's cost of goods sold is $125,000, its merchandise inventory increased by $5,000, and accounts payable were $11,000 the prior year. Calculate Jackie's working capital, payables turnover, and days' payable.

SOLUTION

Working Capital = Current Assets − Current Liabilities
= $30,000 − $20,000
= $10,000

$$\text{Payables Turnover} = \frac{\text{Cost of Goods Sold} \pm \text{Change in Inventory}}{\text{Average Accounts Payable}}$$

$$= \frac{\$125{,}000 + \$5{,}000}{(\$15{,}000 + \$11{,}000) \div 2} = \frac{\$130{,}000}{\$13{,}000}$$

= 10 Times

Days' Payable = 365 Days ÷ Payables Turnover

$$= \frac{365 \text{ Days}}{10 \text{ Times}} = 36.5 \text{ Days}$$

Common Types of Current Liabilities

LO2 Identify, compute, and record definitely determinable and estimated current liabilities.

As noted earlier, a company incurs current liabilities to meet its needs for cash during the operating cycle. These liabilities fall into two major groups: definitely determinable liabilities and estimated liabilities.

Definitely Determinable Liabilities

Current liabilities that are set by contract or statute and that can be measured exactly are called **definitely determinable liabilities**. The problems in accounting for these liabilities are to determine their existence and amount and to see that they are recorded properly. The most common definitely determinable liabilities are described below.

Accounts Payable Accounts payable (sometimes called *trade accounts payable*) are short-term obligations to suppliers for goods and services. The amount in the Accounts Payable account is generally supported by an accounts payable subsidiary ledger, which contains an individual account for each person or company to which money is owed.

> **Study Note**
> On the balance sheet, the order of presentation for current liabilities is not as strict as for current assets. Generally, accounts payable or notes payable appear first, and the rest of current liabilities follow.

Bank Loans and Commercial Paper Management often establishes a **line of credit** with a bank. This arrangement allows the company to borrow funds when they are needed to finance current operations. In a note to its financial statements, **Goodyear Tire & Rubber Company** describes its lines of credit as follows: "In aggregate, we had credit arrangements of $8,208 million available at December 31, 2006, of which $533 million were unused."[4]

Although a company signs a promissory note for the full amount of a line of credit, it has great flexibility in using the available funds. It can increase its borrowing up to the limit when it needs cash and reduce the amount borrowed when it generates enough cash of its own. Both the amount borrowed and the interest rate charged by the bank may change daily. The bank may require the company to meet certain financial goals (such as maintaining specific profit margins, current ratios, or debt to equity ratios) to retain its line of credit.

Companies with excellent credit ratings can borrow short-term funds by issuing **commercial paper**, which are unsecured loans (i.e., loans not backed up by any specific assets) that are sold to the public, usually through professionally managed investment firms. Highly rated companies rely heavily on commercial paper to raise short-term funds, but they can quickly lose access to this means of borrowing if their credit rating drops. Because of disappointing operating results in recent years, well-known companies like **DaimlerChrysler**, **Lucent Technologies**, and **Motorola** have lost some or all of their ability to issue commercial paper.

> **Study Note**
> Only the used portion of a line of credit is recognized as a liability in the financial statements.

The portion of a line of credit currently borrowed and the amount of commercial paper issued are usually combined with notes payable in the current liabilities section of the balance sheet. Details are disclosed in a note to the financial statements.

Notes Payable Short-term notes payable are obligations represented by promissory notes. A company may sign promissory notes to obtain bank loans, pay suppliers for goods and services, or secure credit from other sources.

Interest is usually stated separately on the face of the note, as shown in Figure 10-3. The entries to record the note in Figure 10-3 follow.

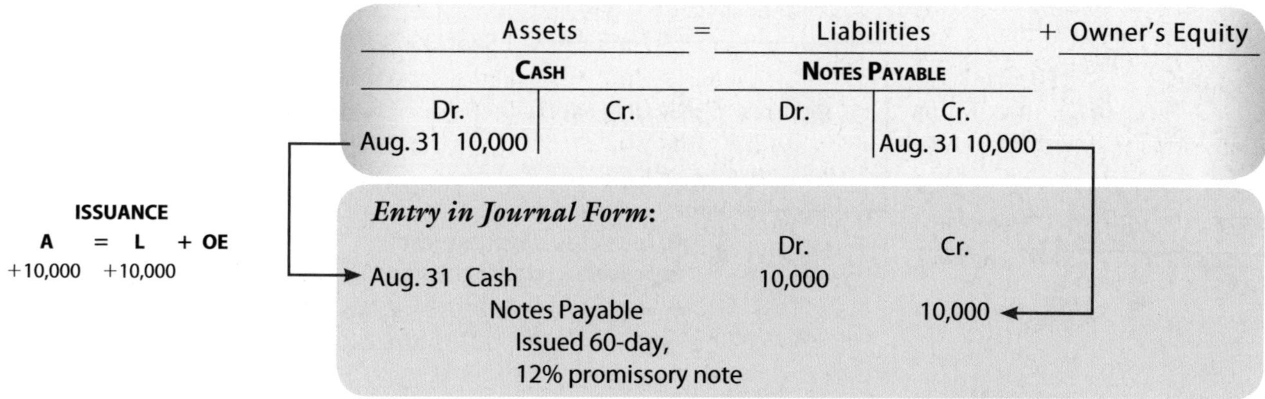

FIGURE 10-3
Promissory Note

Chicago, Illinois August 31, 2011

Sixty days after date I promise to pay First Federal Bank the sum of $10,000 with interest at the rate of 12% per annum.

Sandra Caron
Caron Corporation

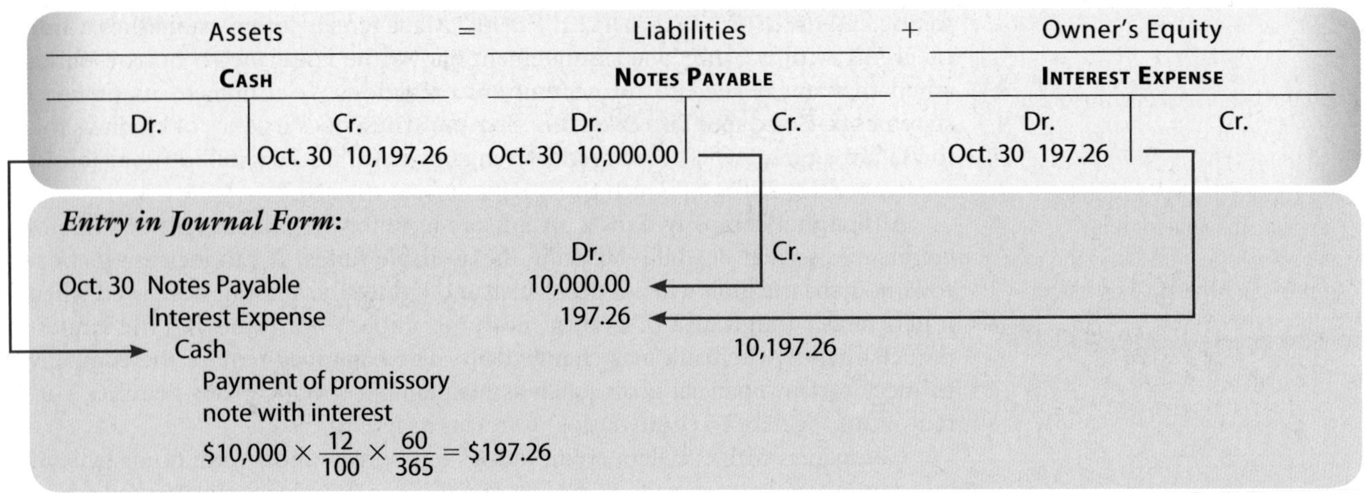

PAYMENT

A	=	L	+	OE
−10,197.26		−10,000.00		−197.26

Accrued Liabilities As we noted earlier, a key reason for making adjusting entries at the end of an accounting period is to recognize liabilities that are not already in the accounting records. This practice applies to any type of liability. As you will see, accrued liabilities (also called *accrued expenses*) can include estimated liabilities.

Here, we focus on interest payable, a definitely determinable liability. Interest accrues daily on interest-bearing notes. In accordance with the matching rule, an adjusting entry is made at the end of each accounting period to record the interest obligation up to that point. For example, if the accounting period of the maker of the note in Figure 10-3 ends on September 30, or 30 days after the issuance of the 60-day note, the adjusting entry would be as follows:

A	=	L	+	OE
		+98.63		−98.63

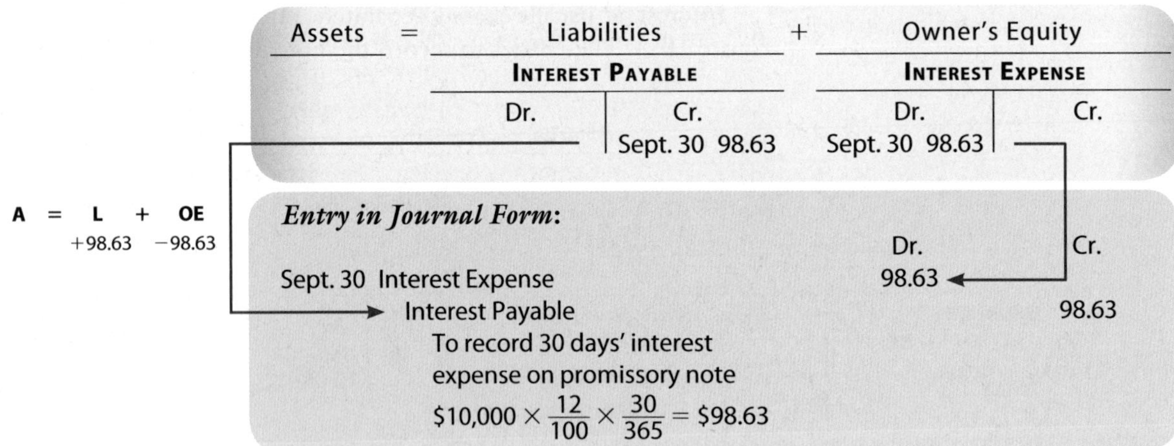

Dividends Payable As you know, cash dividends are a distribution of earnings to a corporation's stockholders, and a corporation's board of directors has the sole authority to declare them. The corporation has no liability for dividends until the date of declaration. The time between that date and the date of payment of dividends is usually short. During this brief interval, the dividends declared are considered current liabilities of the corporation.

Sales and Excise Taxes Payable Most states and many cities levy a sales tax on retail transactions, and the federal government imposes an excise tax on some products, such as gasoline. A merchant that sells goods subject to these taxes must collect the taxes and forward them periodically to the appropriate government agency. Until the merchant remits the amount it has collected to the government, that amount represents a current liability.

For example, suppose a merchant makes a $200 sale that is subject to a 5 percent sales tax and a 10 percent excise tax. If the sale takes place on June 1, the entry to record it is as follows:

A	=	L	+	OE
+230		+10		+200
		+20		

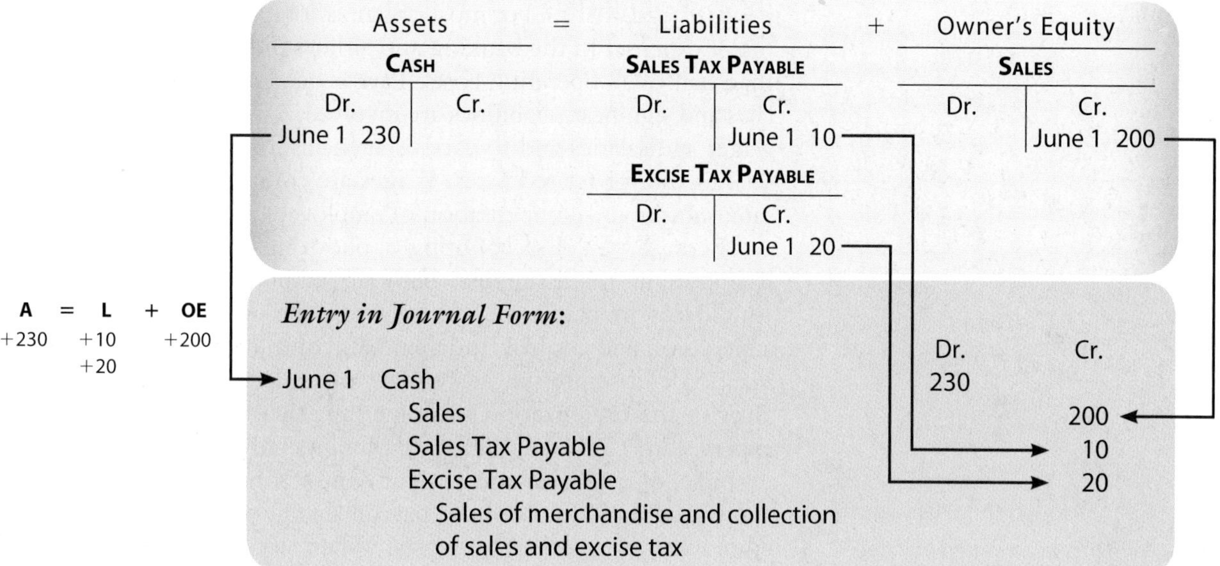

The sale is properly recorded at $200, and the taxes collected are recorded as liabilities to be remitted to the appropriate government agencies.

Companies that have a physical presence in many cities and states require a complex accounting system for sales taxes because the rates vary from state to state and city to city. For Internet companies, the sales tax situation is simpler. For example, **Amazon.com** is an Internet company without a physical presence in most states and thus does not always have to collect sales tax from its customers, so its sales tax situation is simpler. This situation may change in the future, but so far Congress has exempted most Internet sales from sales tax.

FOCUS ON BUSINESS PRACTICE

Small Businesses Offer Benefits, Too

A survey of small businesses in the Midwest focused on the employee benefits that these companies offer. The graph at the right presents the results. As you can see, 77 percent of respondents provided both paid vacation and health/medical benefits, and 23 percent even offered their employees tuition reimbursement.[5]

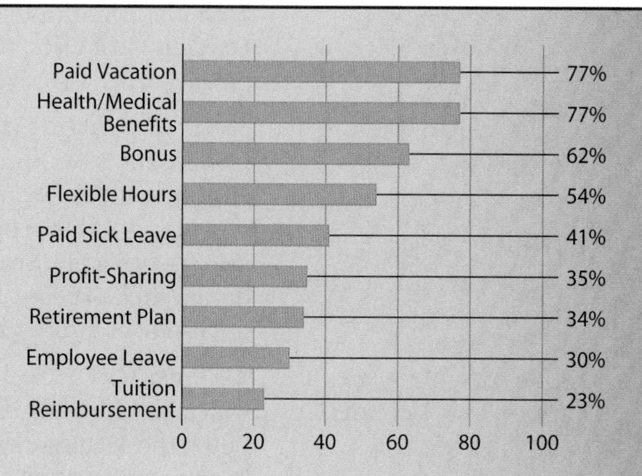

Current Portion of Long-Term Debt If a portion of long-term debt is due within the next year and is to be paid from current assets, that portion is classified as a current liability. It is common for companies to have portions of long-term debt, such as notes or mortgages, due in the next year. No journal entry is necessary when this is the case. The total debt is simply reclassified or divided into two categories—short-term and long-term—when the company prepares its balance sheet and other financial statements.

Payroll Liabilities For most organizations, the cost of labor and payroll taxes is a major expense. In the banking and airlines industries, payroll costs represent more than half of all operating costs. Payroll accounting is important because complex laws and significant liabilities are involved. The employer is liable to employees for wages and salaries and to various agencies for amounts withheld from wages and salaries and for related taxes. **Wages** are compensation of employees at an hourly rate; **salaries** are compensation of employees at a monthly or yearly rate.

Because payroll accounting applies only to an organization's employees, it is important to distinguish between employees and independent contractors. Employees are paid a wage or salary by the organization and are under its direct supervision and control. Independent contractors are not employees of the organization and so are not accounted for under the payroll system. They offer services to the organization for a fee, but they are not under its direct control or supervision. Certified public accountants, advertising agencies, and lawyers, for example, often act as independent contractors.

Study Note

In many organizations, a large portion of the cost of labor is not reflected in employees' regular paychecks. Vacation pay, sick pay, personal days, health insurance, life insurance, and pensions are some of the additional costs that may be negotiated between employers and employees.

Figure 10-4 shows how payroll liabilities relate to employee earnings and employer taxes and other costs. When accounting for payroll liabilities, it is important to keep the following in mind:

- The amount payable to employees is less than the amount of their earnings. This occurs because employers are required by law or are requested by employees to withhold certain amounts from wages and send them directly to government agencies or other organizations.
- An employer's total liabilities exceed employees' earnings because the employer must pay additional taxes and make other contributions (e.g., for pensions and medical care) that increase the cost and liabilities.

The most common withholdings, taxes, and other payroll costs are described below.

Federal Income Taxes Employers are required to withhold federal income taxes from employees' paychecks and pay them to the United States Treasury. These taxes are collected each time an employee is paid.

State and Local Income Taxes Most states and some local governments levy income taxes. In most cases, the procedures for withholding are similar to those for federal income taxes.

Social Security (FICA) Tax The Social Security program (the Federal Insurance Contribution Act) provides retirement and disability benefits and survivor's benefits. About 90 percent of the people working in the United States fall under the provisions of this program. The 2009 Social Security tax rate of 6.2 percent was paid by *both* employee and employer on the first $106,800 earned by an employee during the calendar year. Both the rate and the base to which it applies are subject to change in future years.

Study Note

The employee pays all federal, state, and local taxes on income. The employer and employee share FICA and Medicare taxes. The employer bears FUTA and state unemployment taxes.

Medicare Tax A major extension of the Social Security program is Medicare, which provides hospitalization and medical insurance for persons over age 65. In 2009, the Medicare tax rate was 1.45 percent of gross income, with no limit, paid by *both* employee and employer.

FIGURE 10-4
Illustration of Payroll Costs

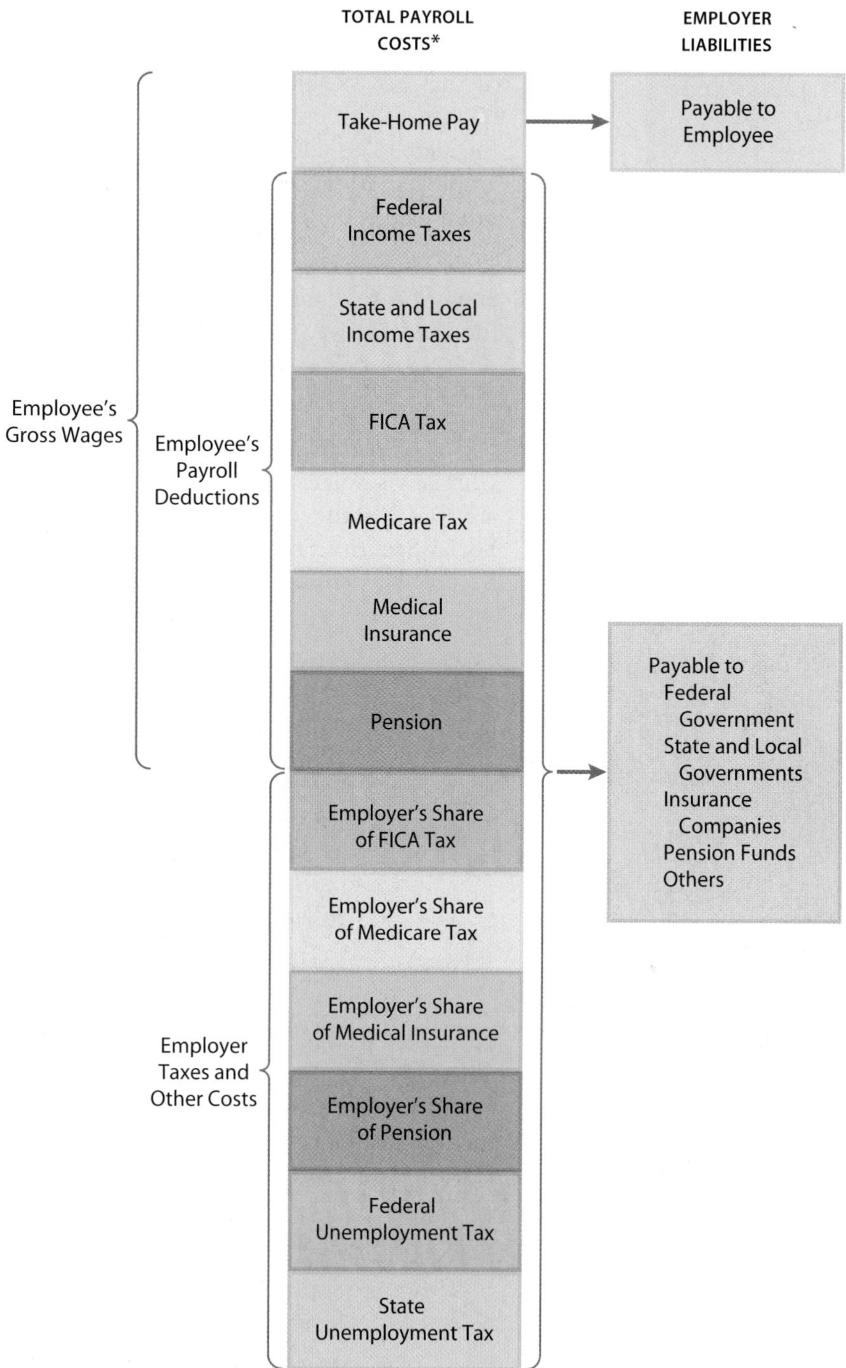

Boxes are not proportional to amounts.

Medical Insurance Many organizations provide medical benefits to employees. Often, the employee contributes a portion of the cost through withholdings from income and the employer pays the rest—usually a greater amount—to the insurance company.

Pension Contributions Many organizations also provide pension benefits to employees. A portion of the pension contribution is withheld from the employee's income, and the organization pays the rest of the amount into the pension fund.

Federal Unemployment Insurance (FUTA) Tax This tax pays for programs for unemployed workers. It is paid *only* by employers and recently was 6.2 percent of the first $7,000 earned by each employee (this amount may vary from state to state). The employer is allowed a credit for unemployment taxes it pays to the state. The maximum credit is 5.4 percent of the first $7,000 earned by each employee. Most states set their rate at this maximum. Thus, the FUTA tax most often paid is 0.8 percent (6.2 percent − 5.4 percent) of the taxable wages.

State Unemployment Insurance Tax State unemployment programs provide compensation to eligible unemployed workers. The compensation is paid out of the fund provided by the 5.4 percent of the first $7,000 (or whatever amount the state sets) earned by each employee. In some states, employers with favorable employment records may be entitled to pay less than 5.4 percent.

To illustrate the recording of a payroll, suppose that on February 15, a company's wages for employees are $65,000 and withholdings for employees are $10,800 for federal income taxes, $2,400 for state income taxes, $4,030 for Social Security tax, $942 for Medicare tax, $1,800 for medical insurance, and $2,600 for pension contributions. The entry to record this payroll is as follows:

A =	L +	OE
	+10,800	−65,000
	+2,400	
	+4,030	
	+942	
	+1,800	
	+2,600	
	+42,428	

		Debit	Credit
Feb. 15	Wages Expense	65,000	
	Employees' Federal Income Taxes Payable		10,800
	Employees' State Income Taxes Payable		2,400
	Social Security Tax Payable		4,030
	Medicare Tax Payable		942
	Medical Insurance Premiums Payable		1,800
	Pension Contributions Payable		2,600
	Wages Payable		42,428
	To record the payroll		

Note that although the employees earned $65,000, their take-home pay was only $42,428.

Using the same data but assuming that the employer pays 80 percent of the medical insurance premiums and half of the pension contributions, the employer's taxes and benefit costs would be recorded as follows:

A =	L +	OE
	+4,030	−18,802
	+942	
	+7,200	
	+2,600	
	+520	
	+3,510	

		Debit	Credit
Feb. 15	Payroll Taxes and Benefits Expense	18,802	
	Social Security Tax Payable		4,030
	Medicare Tax Payable		942
	Medical Insurance Premiums Payable		7,200
	Pension Contributions Payable		2,600
	Federal Unemployment Tax Payable		520
	State Unemployment Tax Payable		3,510
	To record payroll taxes and other costs		

Note that the payroll taxes and benefits expense increase the total cost of the payroll to $83,802 ($18,802 + $65,000), which exceeds the amount earned by employees by almost 29 percent. This is a typical situation.

Unearned Revenues **Unearned revenues** are advance payments for goods or services that a company must provide in a future accounting period. It then recognizes the revenue over the period in which it provides the products or services. Assume that Meggie's Fitness Center receives the cash from a customer in advance for a one-year membership in the fitness center. The following entry would be made:

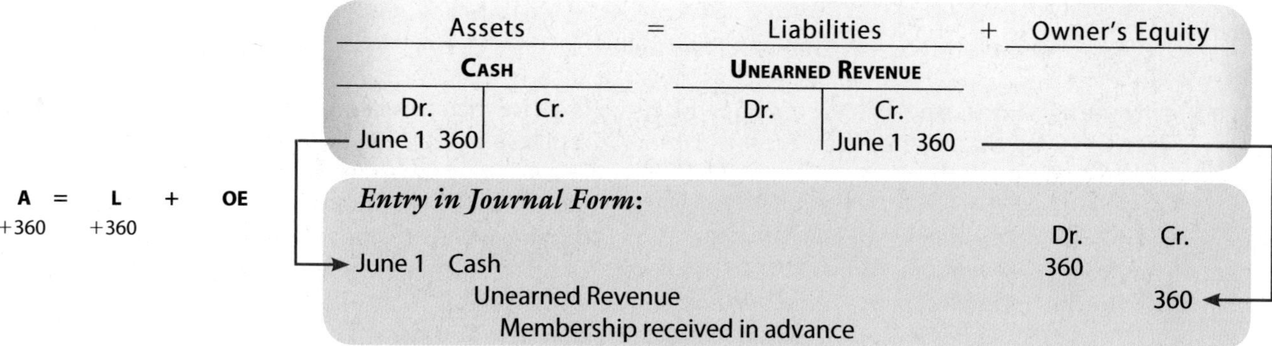

A	=	L	+	OE
+360		+360		

Meggie has a liability of $360 that will slowly be reduced over the year as it provides the service. After the first month, the company records the recognition of revenue as follows:

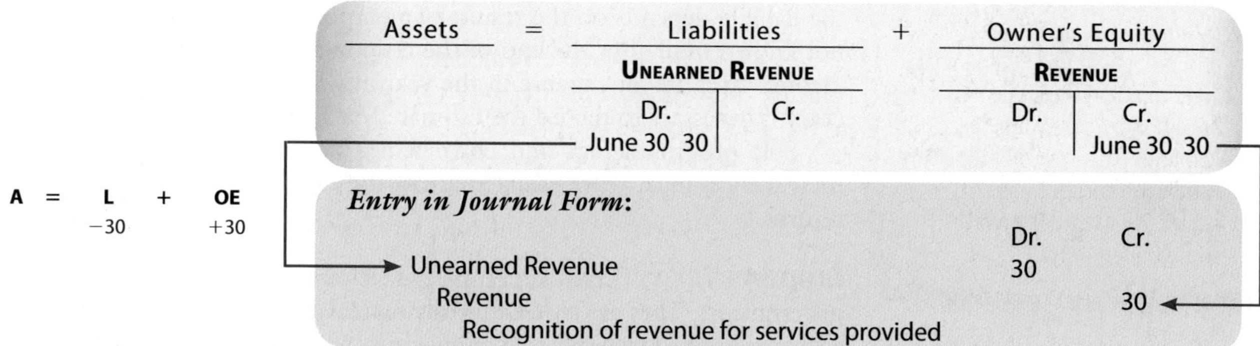

A	=	L	+	OE
		−30		+30

Many businesses, including repair companies, construction companies, and special-order firms, ask for a deposit before they will begin work. Until they deliver the goods or services, these deposits are current liabilities.

Estimated Liabilities

Estimated liabilities are definite debts or obligations whose exact dollar amount cannot be known until a later date. Because there is no doubt that a legal obligation exists, the primary accounting problem is to estimate and record the amount of the liability. Examples of estimated liabilities follow.

FOCUS ON BUSINESS PRACTICE

Those Little Coupons Can Add Up

Many companies promote their products by issuing coupons that offer "cents off" or other enticements. Because four out of five shoppers use coupons, companies are forced by competition to distribute them. The total value of unredeemed coupons, each of which represents a potential liability for the issuing company, is staggering. *PROMO Magazine* estimates that almost 300 billion coupons are issued annually. Of course, the liability depends on how many coupons will actually be redeemed. *PROMO* estimates that number at approximately 3.6 billion, or about 1.2 percent. Thus, a big advertiser that puts a cents-off coupon in Sunday papers to reach 60 million people can be faced with liability for 720,000 coupons. The total value of coupons redeemed each year is estimated at more than $3.6 billion.[6]

FOCUS ON BUSINESS PRACTICE

What Is the Cost of Frequent Flyer Miles?

In the early 1980s, **American Airlines** developed a frequent flyer program that awards free trips and other bonuses to customers based on the number of miles they fly on the airline. Since then, many other airlines have instituted similar programs, and it is estimated that 40 million people now participate in them. Today, U.S. airlines have more than 4 trillion "free miles" outstanding, and 8 percent of passengers travel on "free" tickets. Estimated liabilities for these tickets have become an important consideration in evaluating an airline's financial position. Complicating the estimate is that almost half the miles have been earned through purchases from hotels, car rental and telephone companies, Internet service providers like **AOL**, and bank credit cards.[7]

Study Note

Estimated liabilities are recorded and presented on the financial statements in the same way as definitely determinable liabilities. The only difference is that the computation of estimated liabilities involves some uncertainty.

Income Taxes Payable The federal government, most state governments, and some cities and towns levy a tax on a corporation's income. The amount of the liability depends on the results of a corporation's operations, which are often not known until after the end of the corporation's fiscal year. However, because income taxes are an expense in the year in which income is earned, an adjusting entry is necessary to record the estimated tax liability.

Sole proprietorships and partnerships do *not* pay income taxes. However, their owners must report their share of the firm's income on their individual tax returns.

Property Taxes Payable Property taxes are a main source of revenue for local governments. They are levied annually on real property, such as land and buildings, and on personal property, such as inventory and equipment. Because the fiscal years of local governments rarely correspond to a company's fiscal year, it is necessary to estimate the amount of property taxes that applies to each month of the year.

Promotional Costs You are no doubt familiar with the coupons and rebates that are part of many companies' marketing programs and with the frequent flyer programs that airlines have been offering for more than 20 years. Companies usually record the costs of these programs as a reduction in sales (a contra-sales account) rather than as an expense with a corresponding current liability. As **Hershey Foods Corporation** acknowledges in its annual report, promotional costs are hard to estimate:

> Accrued liabilities requiring the most difficult or subjective judgments include liabilities associated with marketing promotion programs.... We recognize the costs of marketing promotion programs as a reduction to net sales with a corresponding accrued liability based on estimates at the time of revenue recognition.... We determine the amount of the accrued liability by analysis of programs offered; historical trends; expectations regarding customer and consumer participation; sales and payment trends; and experience... with previously offered programs.[8]

Hershey accrues over $600 million in promotional costs each year and reports that its estimates are usually accurate within about 4 percent, or $24 million.

Product Warranty Liability When a firm sells a product or service with a warranty, it has a liability for the length of the warranty. The warranty is a feature of the product and is included in the selling price; its cost should therefore be

Study Note
Recording a product warranty expense in the period of the sale is an application of the matching rule.

debited to an expense account in the period of the sale. Based on past experience, it should be possible to estimate the amount the warranty will cost in the future. Some products will require little warranty service; others may require much. Thus, there will be an average cost per product.

For example, suppose a muffler company like **Midas** guarantees that it will replace free of charge any muffler it sells that fails during the time the buyer owns the car. The company charges a small service fee for replacing the muffler. In the past, 6 percent of the mufflers sold have been returned for replacement under the warranty. The average cost of a muffler is $50. If the company sold 700 mufflers during July, the accrued liability would be recorded as an adjustment at the end of July, as shown below:

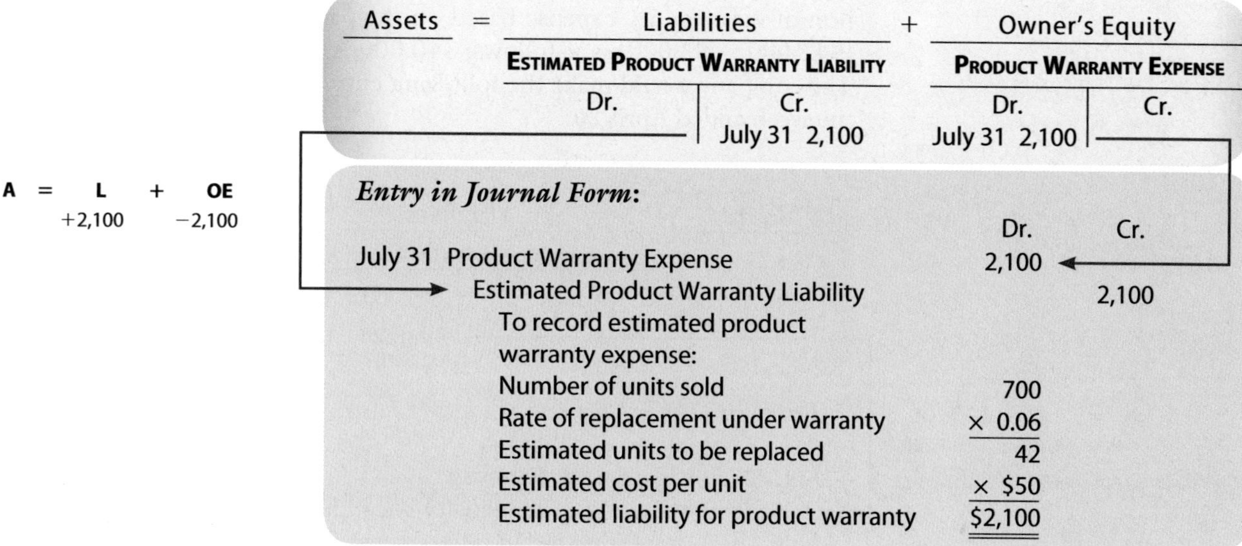

A	=	L	+	OE
		+2,100		−2,100

When a muffler is returned for replacement under the warranty, the cost of the muffler is charged against the Estimated Product Warranty Liability account. For example, suppose that on December 5, a customer returns with a defective muffler, which cost $60, and pays a $30 service fee to have it replaced. The entry is as follows:

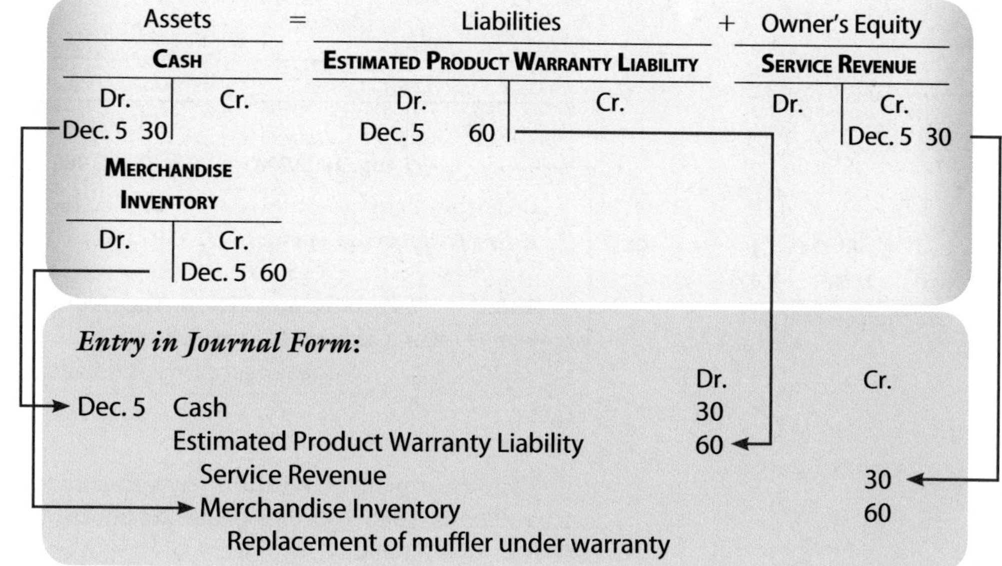

A	=	L	+	OE
+30		−60		+30
−60				

Vacation Pay Liability In most companies, employees accrue paid vacation as they work during the year. For example, an employee may earn 2 weeks of paid vacation for each 50 weeks of work. Thus, the person is paid 52 weeks' salary for 50 weeks' work. The cost of the 2 weeks' vacation should be allocated as an expense over the whole year so that month-to-month costs will not be distorted. The vacation pay represents 4 percent (two weeks' vacation divided by 50 weeks) of a worker's pay. Every week worked earns the employee a small fraction of vacation pay, which is 4 percent of total annual salary.

Suppose that a company has a vacation policy of 2 weeks of paid vacation for each 50 weeks of work. It also has a payroll of $42,000 and paid $2,000 of that amount to employees on vacation for the week ended April 20. Because of turnover and rules regarding term of employment, the company assumes that only 75 percent of employees will ultimately collect vacation pay. The computation of vacation pay expense based on the payroll of employees not on vacation ($42,000 − $2,000) is as follows: $40,000 × 4 percent × 75 percent = $1,200. The company would make the following entry to record vacation pay expense for the week ended April 20:

A = L + OE
+1,200 −1,200

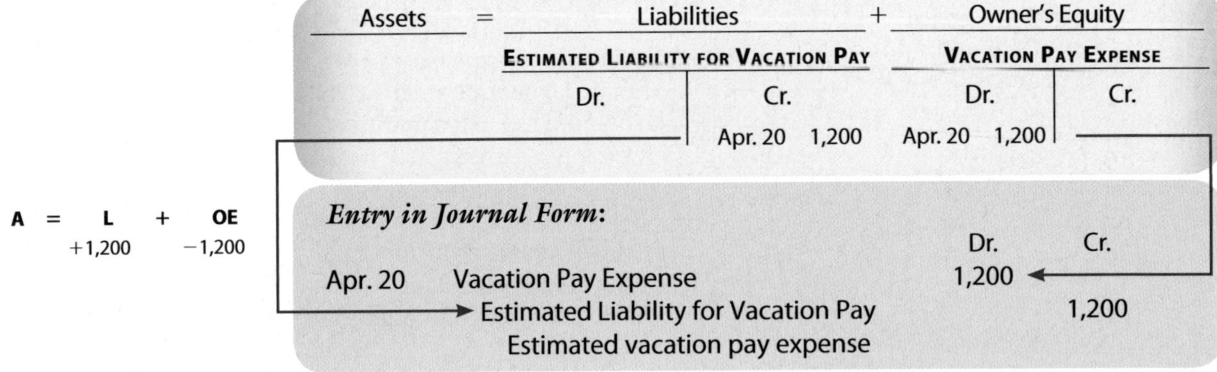

At the time employees receive their vacation pay, an entry is made debiting Estimated Liability for Vacation Pay and crediting Cash or Wages Payable. This entry records the $2,000 paid to employees on vacation during August:

A* = L + OE
−2,000 −2,000
*Assumes cash paid.

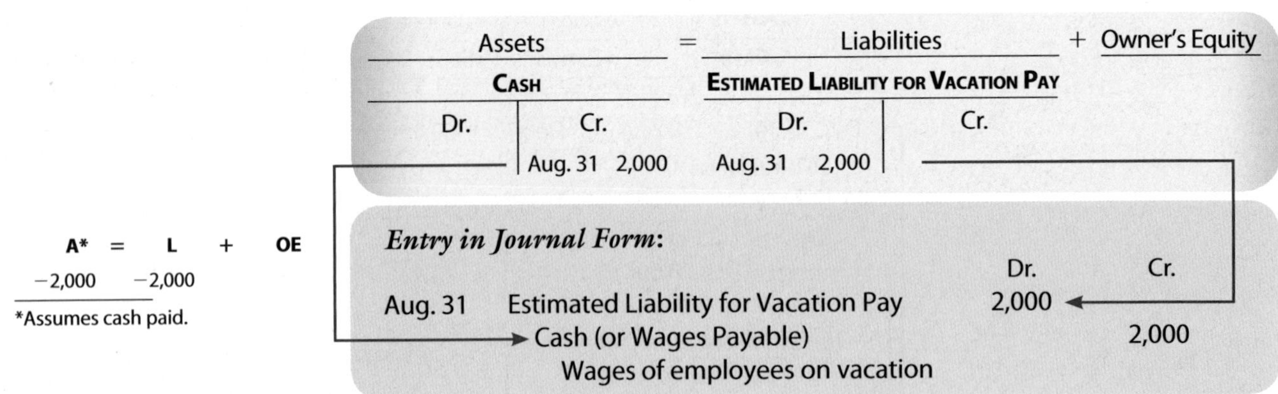

The treatment of vacation pay presented here can also be applied to other payroll costs, such as bonus plans and contributions to pension plans.

STOP & APPLY >

Identify each of the following as either (1) a definitely determinable liability or (2) an estimated liability:

______	a. Bank loan	______	f. Vacation pay liability
______	b. Dividends payable	______	g. Notes payable
______	c. Product warranty liabilities	______	h. Property taxes payable
______	d. Interest payable	______	i. Commercial paper
______	e. Income taxes payable	______	j. Gift certificate liability

SOLUTION

a. 1; b. 1; c. 2; d. 1; e. 2; f. 2; g. 1; h. 2; i. 1; j. 1

Contingent Liabilities and Commitments

LO3 Distinguish *contingent liabilities* from *commitments.*

The FASB requires companies to disclose in a note to their financial statements any contingent liabilities and commitments they may have. A **contingent liability** is not an *existing* obligation. Rather, it is a *potential* liability because it depends on a future event arising out of a past transaction. Contingent liabilities often involve lawsuits, income tax disputes, discounted notes receivable, guarantees of debt, and failure to follow government regulations. For instance, a construction company that built a bridge may have been sued by the state for using poor materials. The past transaction is the building of the bridge under contract. The future event is the outcome of the lawsuit, which is not yet known.

The FASB has established two conditions for determining when a contingency should be entered in the accounting records:

1. The liability must be probable.
2. The liability can be reasonably estimated.[9]

Study Note

Contingencies are recorded when they are probable and can be reasonably estimated.

Estimated liabilities like the income tax, warranty, and vacation pay liabilities that we have described meet those conditions. They are therefore accrued in the accounting records.

In a survey of 600 large companies, the most common types of contingencies reported were litigation, which can involve many different issues, and environmental concerns, such as toxic waste cleanup.[10] In a note to its financial statements, **Microsoft** describes contingent liabilities in the area of lawsuits involving potential infringement of European competition law, antitrust and overcharge actions, patent and intellectual property claims, and others. Microsoft's management states:

> While we intend to vigorously defend these matters, there exists the possibility of adverse outcomes that we estimate could be up to $4.15 billion in aggregate beyond recorded amounts.[11]

A **commitment** is a legal obligation that does not meet the technical requirements for recognition as a liability and so is not recorded. The most common examples are purchase agreements and leases. For example, Microsoft also reports in its notes to the financial statements construction commitments in the amount of $821 million and purchase commitments in the amount of $1,824 million.[12] Knowledge of these amounts is very important for planning cash flows in the coming year.

Indicate whether each of the following is (a) a contingent liability or (b) a commitment:

1. A tax dispute with the IRS
2. A long-term lease agreement
3. An agreement to purchase goods in the future
4. A potential lawsuit over a defective product

SOLUTION

1. a; 2. b; 3. b; 4. a

Valuation Approaches to Fair Value Accounting

LO4 Identify the valuation approaches to fair value accounting, and define *time value of money* and *interest* and apply them to present values.

Recall that *fair value* is the price for which an asset or liability could be sold. As pointed out previously, the concept of fair value applies to financial assets, such as cash equivalents, accounts receivable, and investments, and to liabilities, such as accounts payable and short-term loans. Fair value is also applicable to determining whether tangible assets such as inventories and long-term assets have sustained a permanent decline in value below their cost. The FASB identifies three approaches to measurement of fair value:[13]

- ***Market approach.*** When available, external market transactions involving identical or comparable assets or liabilities are ideal. For example, the market approach is good for valuing investments and liabilities for which there is a ready market. However, a ready market is not always available. For example, there may not be a market for special-purpose equipment. In these cases, other approaches must be used.
- ***Income (or cash flow) approach.*** The income approach, as defined by the FASB, converts future cash flows to a single present value. This approach is based on management's best determination of the future cash amounts generated by an asset or payments that will be made for a liability. It is based on internally generated information, which should be reasonable for the circumstances.
- ***Cost approach.*** The cost approach is based on the amount that currently would be required to replace an asset. For example, inventory is usually valued at lower of cost or market, where market is the replacement cost. For a plant asset, the replacement cost of a new asset must be adjusted to take into account the asset's age, condition, depreciation, and obsolescence.

Complicating factors may arise in applying the market and cost approaches, but conceptually they are relatively straightforward. The income or cash flow approach requires knowledge of interest and the time value of money, and present value techniques, as presented in the following sections.

Interest and the Time Value of Money

"Time is money" is a common expression. It derives from the concept of the **time value of money**, which refers to the costs or benefits derived from holding or not holding money over time. **Interest** is the cost of using money for a specific period.

The interest associated with the time value of money is an important consideration in any kind of business decision. For example, if you sell a bicycle for \$100 and hold that amount for one year without putting it in a savings account, you have forgone the interest that the money would have earned. However, if you accept a note payable instead of cash and add the interest to the price of the bicycle, you will not forgo the interest that the cash could have earned.

Simple interest is the interest cost for one or more periods when the principal sum—the amount on which interest is computed—stays the same from period to period. **Compound interest** is the interest cost for two or more periods when after each period, the interest earned in that period is added to the amount on which interest is computed in future periods. In other words, the principal sum is increased at the end of each period by the interest earned in that period. The following two examples illustrate these concepts:

Study Note

In business, compound interest is the most useful concept of interest because it helps decision makers choose among alternative courses of action.

Example of Simple Interest Willy Wang accepts an 8 percent, $15,000 note due in 90 days. How much will he receive at that time? The interest is calculated as follows:

$$\begin{aligned}\text{Interest} &= \text{Principal} \times \text{Rate} \times \text{Time}\\ &= \$15{,}000.00 \times 8/100 \times 90/365\\ &= \$295.89\end{aligned}$$

Therefore, the total that Wang will receive is $15,295.89, calculated as follows:

$$\begin{aligned}\text{Total} &= \text{Principal} + \text{Interest}\\ &= \$15{,}000.00 + \$295.89\\ &= \$15{,}295.89\end{aligned}$$

Example of Compound Interest Terry Soma deposits $10,000 in an account that pays 6 percent interest. She expects to leave the principal and accumulated interest in the account for three years. How much will the account total at the end of three years? Assume that the interest is paid at the end of the year and is added to the principal at that time, and that this total in turn earns interest. The amount at the end of three years is computed as follows:

Year	*Principal Amount at Beginning of Year*	*Annual Amount of Interest (Col. 2 × 6%)*	*Accumulated Amount at End of Year (Col. 2 + Col. 3)*
1	$10,000.00	$600.00	$10,600.00
2	10,600.00	636.00	11,236.00
3	11,236.00	674.16	11,910.16

At the end of three years, Soma will have $11,910.16 in her account. Note that the amount of interest increases each year by the interest rate times the interest of the previous year. For example, between year 1 and year 2, the interest increased by $36, which equals 6 percent times $600. The final amount of $11,910.16 is referred to as the **future value**, which is the amount an investment ($10,000 in this case) will be worth at a future date if invested at compound interest.

Study Note

Present value is a method of valuing future cash flows. Financial analysts commonly compute present value to determine the value of potential investments.

Calculating Present Value

Suppose you had the choice of receiving $100 today or one year from today. No doubt, you would choose to receive it today. Why? If you have the money today you can put it in a savings account to earn interest so you will have more than $100 a year from today. In other words, an amount to be received in the future

(future value) is not worth as much today as an amount received today (present value). **Present value** is the amount that must be invested today at a given rate of interest to produce a given future value. Thus, present value and future value are closely related.

For example, suppose Kelly Fontaine needs $10,000 one year from now. How much does she have to invest today to achieve that goal if the interest rate is 5 percent? From earlier examples, we can establish the following equation:

Present Value × (1.0 + Interest Rate)	= Future Value
Present Value × 1.05	= $10,000.00
Present Value	= $10,000.00 ÷ 1.05
Present Value	= $9,523.81

To achieve a future value of $10,000, Fontaine must invest a present value of $9,523.81. Interest of 5 percent on $9,523.81 for one year equals $476.19, and these two amounts added together equal $10,000.

Present Value of a Single Sum Due in the Future When more than one period is involved, the calculation of present value is more complicated. For example, suppose Ron More wants to be sure of having $8,000 at the end of three years. How much must he invest today in a 5 percent savings account to achieve this goal? We can compute the present value of $8,000 at compound interest of 5 percent for three years by adapting the above equation:

Year	*Amount at End of Year*		*Divide by*		*Present Value at Beginning of Year*
3	$8,000.00	÷	1.05	=	$7,619.05
2	7,619.05	÷	1.05	=	7,256.24
1	7,256.24	÷	1.05	=	6,910.70

Ron More must invest $6,910.70 today to achieve a value of $8,000 in three years.

We can simplify the calculation by using the appropriate table. In Table 10-1, the point at which the 5 percent column and the row for period 3 intersect shows a factor of 0.864. This factor, when multiplied by $1, gives the present value of $1 to be received three years from now at 5 percent interest. Thus, we solve the problem as follows:

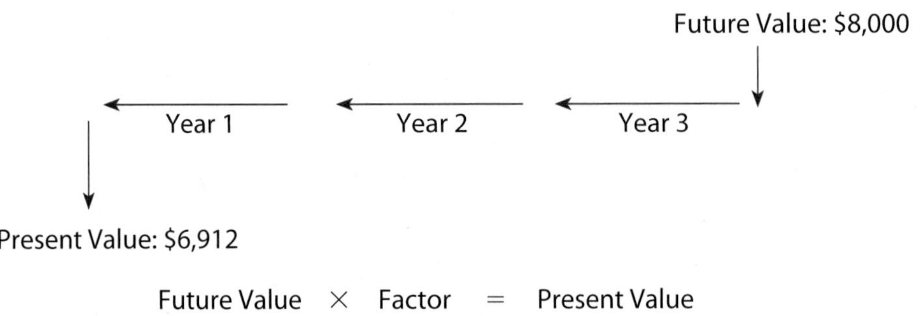

Future Value	×	Factor	=	Present Value
$8,000	×	0.864	=	$6,912

Except for a rounding difference of $1.30, this result is the same as our earlier one.

Present Value of an Ordinary Annuity It is often necessary to compute the present value of a series of receipts or payments equally spaced over time—in other words, the present value of an **ordinary annuity.** For example, suppose Vickie Long has sold a piece of property and is to receive $18,000 in three equal annual payments of $6,000 beginning one year from today. What is the present value of this sale if the current interest rate is 5 percent?

Using Table 10-1, we can compute the present value by calculating a separate value for each of the three payments and summing the results, as follows:

Future Receipts (Annuity)				*Present Value Factor at 5 Percent (from Table 10-1)*		*Present Value*
Year 1	*Year 2*	*Year 3*				
$6,000			×	0.952	=	$ 5,712
	$6,000		×	0.907	=	5,442
		$6,000	×	0.864	=	5,184
Total Present Value						$16,338

The present value of the sale is $16,338. Thus, there is an implied interest cost (given the 5 percent rate) of $1,662 associated with the payment plan that allows the purchaser to pay in three installments.

We can make this calculation more easily by using Table 10-2. The point at which the 5 percent column intersects the row for period 3 shows a factor of 2.723. When multiplied by $1, this factor gives the present value of a series of three $1 payments (spaced one year apart) at compound interest of 5 percent. Thus, we solve the problem as follows:

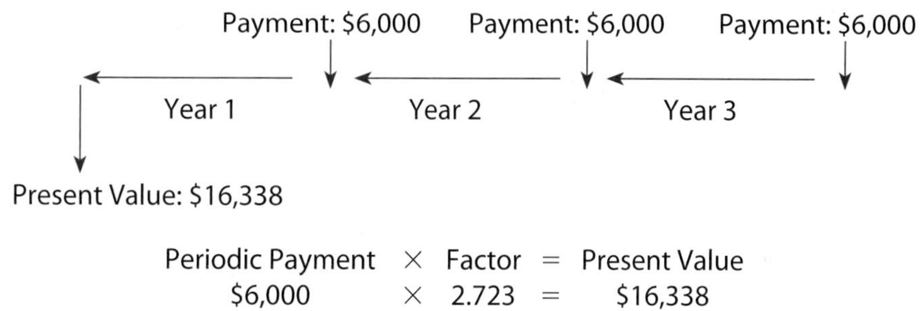

Periodic Payment	×	Factor	=	Present Value
$6,000	×	2.723	=	$16,338

This result is the same as the one we computed earlier.

TABLE 10-1 Present Value of $1 to Be Received at the End of a Given Number of Periods

Period	1%	2%	3%	4%	5%	6%	7%	8%	9%	10%
1	0.990	0.980	0.971	0.962	0.952	0.943	0.935	0.926	0.917	0.909
2	0.980	0.961	0.943	0.925	0.907	0.890	0.873	0.857	0.842	0.826
3	0.971	0.942	0.915	0.889	0.864	0.840	0.816	0.794	0.772	0.751
4	0.961	0.924	0.888	0.855	0.823	0.792	0.763	0.735	0.708	0.683
5	0.951	0.906	0.863	0.822	0.784	0.747	0.713	0.681	0.650	0.621
6	0.942	0.888	0.837	0.790	0.746	0.705	0.666	0.630	0.596	0.564
7	0.933	0.871	0.813	0.760	0.711	0.665	0.623	0.583	0.547	0.513
8	0.923	0.853	0.789	0.731	0.677	0.627	0.582	0.540	0.502	0.467
9	0.914	0.837	0.766	0.703	0.645	0.592	0.544	0.500	0.460	0.424
10	0.905	0.820	0.744	0.676	0.614	0.558	0.508	0.463	0.422	0.386

TABLE 10-2 Present Value of an Ordinary $1 Annuity Received in Each Period for a Given Number of Periods

Period	1%	2%	3%	4%	5%	6%	7%	8%	9%	10%
1	0.990	0.980	0.971	0.962	0.952	0.943	0.935	0.926	0.917	0.909
2	1.970	1.942	1.913	1.886	1.859	1.833	1.808	1.783	1.759	1.736
3	2.941	2.884	2.829	2.775	2.723	2.673	2.624	2.577	2.531	2.487
4	3.902	3.808	3.717	3.630	3.546	3.465	3.387	3.312	3.240	3.170
5	4.853	4.713	4.580	4.452	4.329	4.212	4.100	3.993	3.890	3.791
6	5.795	5.601	5.417	5.242	5.076	4.917	4.767	4.623	4.486	4.355
7	6.728	6.472	6.230	6.002	5.786	5.582	5.389	5.206	5.033	4.868
8	7.652	7.325	7.020	6.733	6.463	6.210	5.971	5.747	5.535	5.335
9	8.566	8.162	7.786	7.435	7.108	6.802	6.515	6.247	5.995	5.759
10	9.471	8.983	8.530	8.111	7.722	7.360	7.024	6.710	6.418	6.145

Study Note

The interest rate used when compounding interest for less than one year is the annual rate divided by the number of periods in a year.

Time Periods As in all our examples, the compounding period is in most cases one year, and the interest rate is stated on an annual basis. However, the left-hand column in Tables 10-1 and 10-2 refers not to years but to periods. This wording accommodates compounding periods of less than one year. Savings accounts that record interest quarterly and bonds that pay interest semiannually are cases in which the compounding period is less than one year. To use the tables in these cases, it is necessary to (1) divide the annual interest rate by the number of periods in the year and (2) multiply the number of periods in one year by the number of years.

For example, suppose we want to compute the present value of a $6,000 payment that is to be received in two years, assuming an annual interest rate of 8 percent. The compounding period is semiannual. Before using Table 10-1 in this computation, we must compute the interest rate that applies to each compounding period and the total number of compounding periods. First, the interest rate to use is 4 percent (8% annual rate ÷ 2 periods per year). Second, the total number of compounding periods is 4 (2 periods per year × 2 years). From Table 10-1, therefore, the present value of the payment is computed as follows:

Principal	×	Factor	=	Present Value
$6,000	×	0.855	=	$5,130

The present value of the payment is $5,130. This procedure is used anytime the corresponding period is less than one year. For example, a monthly compounding requires dividing the annual interest rate by 12 and multiplying the number of years by 12 to use the tables.

This method of determining the interest rate and the number of periods when the compounding period is less than one year can be used with Tables 10-1 and 10-2.

Use Tables 10-1 and 10-2 to determine the present value of (1) a single payment of $10,000 at 5 percent for 10 years, (2) 10 annual payments of $1,000 at 5 percent, (3) a single payment of $10,000 at 7 percent for 5 years, and (4) 10 annual payments of $1,000 at 9 percent.

SOLUTION

1. From Table 10-1: $10,000 × 0.614 = $6,140
2. From Table 10-2: $1,000 × 7.722 = $7,722
3. From Table 10-1: $10,000 × 0.713 = $7,130
4. From Table 10-2: $1,000 × 6.418 = $6,418

Applications Using Present Value

LO5 Apply the present value to simple valuation situations.

The concept of present value is widely used in business decision making and financial reporting. As mentioned above, the FASB has made it the foundation of its approach in determining the fair value of assets and liabilities when a ready market price is not available. For example, the value of a long-term note receivable or payable can be determined by calculating the present value of the future interest payments.

The Office of the Chief Accountant of the SEC has issued guidance on how to apply fair value accounting.[14] For instance, it says that management's internal assumptions about expected cash flows may be used to measure fair value and that market quotes may be used when they are from an orderly, active market as opposed to a distressed, inactive market. Thus, **Microsoft** may determine the expected present value of the future cash flows of an investment by using its internal cash flow projections and a market rate of interest. By comparing the result to the current value of the investment, Microsoft can determine if an adjustment needs to be made to record a gain or loss.

In the sections that follow, we illustrate two simple, useful applications of present value, which will be helpful in understanding the uses of present value in subsequent chapters.

Valuing an Asset

An asset is something that will provide future benefits to the company that owns it. Usually, the purchase price of an asset represents the present value of those future benefits. It is possible to evaluate a proposed purchase price by comparing it with the present value of the asset to the company.

For example, Mike Yeboah is thinking of buying a new machine that will reduce his annual labor cost by $1,400 per year. The machine will last eight years. The interest rate that Yeboah assumes for making managerial decisions is 10 percent. What is the maximum amount (present value) that Yeboah should pay for the machine?

The present value of the machine to Yeboah is equal to the present value of an ordinary annuity of $1,400 per year for eight years at compound interest of 10 percent. Using the factor from Table 10-2, we compute the value as follows:

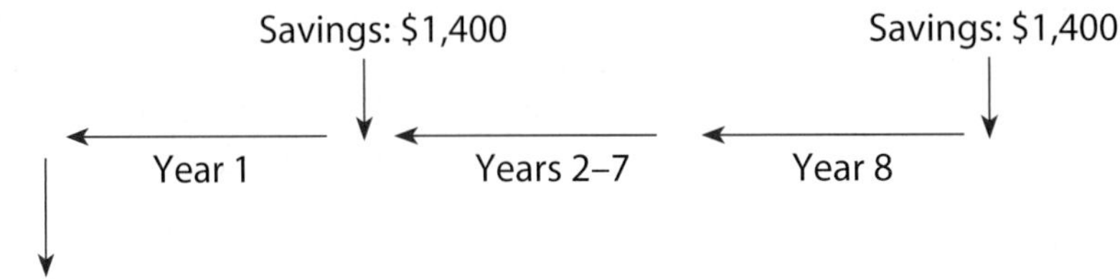

Present Value: $7,469

Periodic Savings	×	Factor	=	Present Value
$1,400	×	5.335	=	$7,469

Yeboah should not pay more than $7,469 for the machine because this amount equals the present value of the benefits he would receive from owning it.

Deferred Payment

To encourage buyers to make a purchase, sellers sometimes agree to defer payment for a sale. This practice is common among companies that sell agricultural equipment; to accommodate farmers who often need new equipment in the spring but cannot pay for it until they sell their crops in the fall, these companies are willing to defer payment.

Suppose Field Helpers Corporation sells a tractor to Sasha Ptak for $100,000 on February 1 and agrees to take payment ten months later, on December 1.

Companies that sell agricultural equipment like these combine harvesters often agree to defer payment for a sale. This practice is common because farmers often need new equipment in the spring but cannot pay for it until they sell their crops in the fall. Deferred payment is a useful application of the time value of money.

Courtesy of istockphoto.com.

When such an agreement is made, the future payment includes not only the selling price but also an implied (imputed) interest cost. If the prevailing annual interest rate for such transactions is 12 percent compounded monthly, the actual price of the tractor would be the present value of the future payment, computed using the factor from Table 10-1 (10 periods, 1 percent [12 percent divided by 12 months]), as follows:

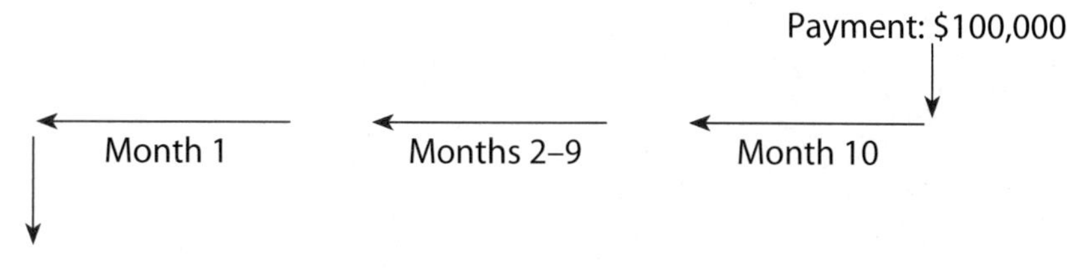

Present Value: $90,500

Future Payment	×	Factor	=	Present Value
$100,000	×	0.905	=	$90,500

Ptak records the present value, $90,500, in his purchase records, and Field Helpers Corporation records it in its sales records. The balance consists of interest expense or interest income.

Other Applications

There are many other applications of present value in accounting, including computing imputed interest on non-interest-bearing notes, accounting for installment notes, valuing a bond, and recording lease obligations. Present value is also applied in accounting for pension obligations; valuing debt; depreciating property, plant, and equipment; making capital expenditure decisions; and generally in accounting for any item in which time is a factor.

& APPLY >

Jerry owns a restaurant and has the opportunity to buy a high-quality espresso coffee machine for $5,000. After carefully studying projected costs and revenues, Jerry estimates that the machine will produce a net cash flow of $1,600 annually and will last for five years. He determines that an interest rate of 10 percent is an adequate return on investment for his business.

Calculate the present value of the machine to Jerry. Based on your calculation, do you think a decision to purchase the machine would be wise?

SOLUTION

Calculation of the present value:

Annual cash flow	$ 1,600.00
Factor from Table 10-2 (5 years at 10%)	× 3.791
Present value of net cash flows	$ 6,065.60
Less purchase price	−5,000.00
Net present value	$ 1,065.60

The present value of the net cash flows from the machine exceeds the purchase price. Thus, the investment will return more than 10 percent to Jerry's business. A decision to purchase the machine would therefore be wise.

▶ MEGGIE'S FITNESS CENTER: REVIEW PROBLEM

In the Decision Point at the beginning of the chapter, we noted that Meggie Jones, owner of Meggie's Fitness Center, was anxious to assess her company's status at the end of its first year of operations. We posed the following questions:

- How should Meggie Jones identify and account for all her company's current liabilities?
- How should she evaluate her company's liquidity?

Current Liabilities and Liquidity Analysis
LO1 LO2

Meggie compiled the following list (as of December 31, 2010):

K/R

Unpaid invoices for nutritional supplements	$12,000
Sales of nutritional supplements (excluding sales tax)	57,000
Cost of nutritional supplements sold	33,600
Exercise instructors' salaries	22,800
Exercise revenues	81,400
Promissory note	16,000
Property taxes	3,600
Current assets	40,000
Nutritional supplements inventory (12/31/10)	27,000
Nutritional supplements inventory (12/31/09)	21,000

In addition to the items on this list, Meggie's Fitness Center sold gift certificates in the amount of $700 that have not been redeemed. It also deducted $1,374 from its two employees' salaries for federal income taxes owed to the government. The current Social Security tax is 6.2 percent of maximum earnings of $102,000 for each employees and the current Medicare tax is 1.45 percent (no maximum earnings). The FUTA tax is 5.4 percent to the state and 0.8 percent to the federal government on the first $7,000 earned by each employee; both employees earned more than $7,000. Meggie has not filed a sales tax report to the state (6 percent of supplements sales).

Required

1. Given these facts, determine the company's current liabilities as of December 31, 2010.
2. User insight: Your analysis of the company's current liabilities has been based on documents that the owner showed you. What liabilities may be missing from your analysis?
3. User insight: Evaluate the company's liquidity by calculating working capital, payables turnover, and days' payable. Comment on the results. (Assume average accounts payable were the same as year-end accounts payable.)

Answers to Review Problem

1. The current liabilities of Meggie's Fitness Center as of December 31, 2010, are as follows:

	A	B	C	D	E	F	G
1	Accounts payable		$12,000.00				
2	Notes payable		16,000.00				
3	Property taxes payable		3,600.00				
4	Sales tax payable	($57,000 × 0.06)	3,420.00				
5	Social Security tax payable	($22,800 × 0.062)	1,413.60				
6	Medicare tax payable	($22,800 × 0.0145)	330.60				
7	State unemployment tax payable	($22,800 × 0.054)	1,231.20				
8	Federal unemployment tax payable	($22,800 × 0.008)	182.40				
9	Employees' federal income taxes payable		1,374.00				
10	Unearned revenues		700.00				
11	Total current liabilities		$40,251.80				

2. The company may have current liabilities for which you have not seen any documentary evidence. For instance, invoices for accounts payable could be missing. In addition, the company may have accrued liabilities, such as vacation pay for its two employees, which would require establishing an estimated liability. If the promissory note to Lee's bank is interest-bearing, it also would require an adjustment to accrue interest payable, and the company could have other loans outstanding for which you have not seen documentary evidence. Moreover, it may have to pay penalties and interest to the federal and state governments because of its failure to remit tax payments on a timely basis. City and state income tax withholding for the employees could be another overlooked liability.

3. Liquidity ratios computed and evaluated:

	A	B	C
1	Working Capital	=	Current Assets – Current Liabilities
3		=	$40,000.00 – $40,251.80
5		=	($251.80)
6			
7	Payables	=	Cost of Goods Sold +/– Change in Merchandise Inventory
8	Turnover		Average Accounts Payable
10		=	$33,600 + $6,000
11			$12,000
13		=	$39,600
14			$12,000
16		=	3.3 times
17			
18	Days' Payable	=	365 days
19			Payables Turnover
21		=	365 days
22			3.3 times
24		=	110.6 days

Meggie's Fitness Center has a negative working capital of $251.80, its payables turnover is only 3.3 times, and it takes an average of 110.6 days to pay its accounts payable. Its liquidity is therefore highly questionable. Many of its current assets are inventory, which it must sell to generate cash, and it must pay most of its current liabilities sooner than the 110.6 days would indicate.

STOP & REVIEW >

LO1 Identify the management issues related to current liabilities.

Current liabilities are an important consideration in managing a company's liquidity and cash flows. Key measures of liquidity are working capital, payables turnover, and days' payable. Liabilities result from past transactions and should be recognized at the time a transaction obligates a company to make future payments. They are valued at the amount of money necessary to satisfy the obligation or at the fair value of the goods or services to be delivered. Liabilities are classified as current or long-term. Supplemental disclosure is required when the nature or details of the obligations would help in understanding the liability.

LO2 Identify, compute, and record definitely determinable and estimated current liabilities.

The two major categories of current liabilities are definitely determinable liabilities and estimated liabilities. Definitely determinable liabilities can be measured exactly. They include accounts payable, bank loans and commercial paper, notes payable, accrued liabilities, dividends payable, sales and excise taxes payable, the current portion of long-term debt, payroll liabilities, and unearned revenues.

Estimated liabilities definitely exist, but their amounts are uncertain and must be estimated. They include liabilities for income taxes, property taxes, promotional costs, product warranties, and vacation pay.

LO3 Distinguish *contingent liabilities* from *commitments*.

A contingent liability is a potential liability that arises from a past transaction and is dependent on a future event. Contingent liabilities often involve lawsuits, income tax disputes, discounted notes receivable, guarantees of debt, and failure to follow government regulations. A commitment is a legal obligation, such as a purchase agreement, that is not recorded as a liability.

LO4 Identify the valuation approaches to fair value accounting, and define *time value of money* and *interest* and apply them to present values.

Three approaches to measurement of fair value are market, income (or cash flow), and cost. The time value of money refers to the costs or benefits derived from holding or not holding money over time.

Interest is the cost of using money for a specific period. In the computation of simple interest, the amount on which the interest is computed stays the same from period to period. In the computation of compound interest, the interest for a period is added to the principal amount before the interest for the next period is computed.

Future value is the amount an investment will be worth at a future date if invested at compound interest. Present value is the amount that must be invested today at a given rate of interest to produce a given future value.

An ordinary annuity is a series of equal payments made at the end of equal intervals of time, with compound interest on the payments. The present value of an ordinary annuity is the present value of a series of payments. Calculations of present values are simplified by using the appropriate tables, which appear in an appendix to this book.

LO5 Apply present value to simple valuation situations.

Present value is commonly used in determining fair value and may be used in determining the value of an asset, in computing the present value of deferred payments, in establishing a fund for loan repayment, and in numerous other accounting situations in which time is a factor.

REVIEW of Concepts and Terminology

The following concepts and terms were introduced in this chapter:

Commercial paper 437 (LO2)

Commitment 447 (LO3)

Compound interest 449 (LO4)

Contingent liability 447 (LO3)

Current liabilities 435 (LO1)

Definitely determinable liabilities 436 (LO2)

Estimated liabilities 443 (LO2)

Future value 449 (LO4)

Interest 448 (LO4)

Line of credit 437 (LO2)

Long-term liabilities 435 (LO1)

Ordinary annuity 450 (LO4)

Present value 450 (LO4)

Salaries 440 (LO2)

Simple interest 449 (LO4)

Time value of money 448 (LO4)

Unearned revenues 442 (LO2)

Wages 440 (LO2)

Key Ratios

Days' payable 432 (LO1)

Payables turnover 432 (LO1)

CHAPTER ASSIGNMENTS

BUILDING Your Basic Knowledge and Skills

Short Exercises

LO1 **Issues in Accounting for Liabilities**

SE 1. Indicate whether each of the following actions relates to (a) managing liquidity and cash flow, (b) recognition of liabilities, (c) valuation of liabilities, (d) classification of liabilities, or (e) disclosure of liabilities:

1. Determining that a liability will be paid in less than one year
2. Estimating the amount of a liability
3. Providing information about when liabilities are due and their interest rates
4. Determining when a liability arises
5. Assessing working capital and payables turnover

LO1 **Measuring Short-Term Liquidity**

SE 2. Robinson Company has current assets of $65,000 and current liabilities of $40,000, of which accounts payable are $35,000. Robinson's cost of goods sold is $230,000, its merchandise inventory increased by $10,000, and accounts payable were $25,000 the prior year. Calculate Robinson's working capital, payables turnover, and days' payable.

LO2 LO3 **Types of Liabilities**

SE 3. Indicate whether each of the following is (a) a definitely determinable liability, (b) an estimated liability, (c) a commitment, or (d) a contingent liability:

1. Dividends payable
2. Pending litigation
3. Income taxes payable
4. Current portion of long-term debt
5. Vacation pay liability
6. Guaranteed loans of another company
7. Purchase agreement

LO2 **Interest Expense on Note Payable**

SE 4. On the last day of August, Avenue Company borrowed $240,000 on a bank note for 60 days at 12 percent interest. Assume that interest is stated separately. Prepare the following entries in journal form: (1) August 31, recording of note; and (2) October 30, payment of note plus interest.

LO2 **Payroll Expenses**

SE 5. The following payroll totals for the month of April are from the payroll register of Young Corporation: salaries, $223,000; federal income taxes withheld, $31,440; Social Security tax withheld, $13,826; Medicare tax withheld, $3,234; medical insurance deductions, $6,580; and salaries subject to unemployment taxes, $156,600.

Determine the total and components of (1) the monthly payroll and (2) employer payroll expenses, assuming Social Security and Medicare taxes equal to the amounts for employees, a federal unemployment insurance tax of

0.8 percent, a state unemployment tax of 5.4 percent, and medical insurance premiums for which the employer pays 80 percent of the cost.

LO2 **Product Warranty Liability**

SE 6. Harper Corp. manufactures and sells travel clocks. Each clock costs $12.50 to produce and sells for $25. In addition, each clock carries a warranty that provides for free replacement if it fails during the two years following the sale. In the past, 5 percent of the clocks sold have had to be replaced under the warranty. During October, Harper sold 52,000 clocks, and 2,800 clocks were replaced under the warranty. Prepare entries in journal form to record the estimated liability for product warranties during the month and the clocks replaced under warranty during the month.

Note: Tables 1 and 2 in the appendix on present value tables may be used where appropriate to solve **SE 7, SE 8**, and **SE 9**.

LO4 **Simple and Compound Interest**

SE 7. Ursus Motors, Inc., receives a one-year note that carries a 12 percent annual interest rate on $6,000 for the sale of a used car. Compute the maturity value under each of the following assumptions: (1) Simple interest is charged. (2) The interest is compounded semiannually.

LO4 **Present Value Calculations**

SE 8. Find the present value of (1) a single payment of $24,000 at 6 percent for 12 years, (2) 12 annual payments of $2,000 at 6 percent, (3) a single payment of $5,000 at 9 percent for five years, and (4) five annual payments of $5,000 at 9 percent.

LO4 LO5 **Valuing an Asset for the Purpose of Making a Purchasing Decision**

SE 9. Hogan Whitner owns a machine shop and has the opportunity to purchase a new machine for $30,000. After carefully studying projected costs and revenues, Whitner estimates that the new machine will produce a net cash flow of $7,200 annually and will last for eight years. Whitner believes that an interest rate of 10 percent is adequate for his business.

Calculate the present value of the machine to Whitner. Does the purchase appear to be a smart business decision?

Exercises

LO1 LO2 LO3 **Discussion Questions**

E1. Develop a brief answer to each of the following questions:

1. Nimish Banks, a star college basketball player, received a contract from the Midwest Blazers to play professional basketball. The contract calls for a salary of $420,000 a year for four years, dependent on his making the team in each of those years. Should this contract be considered a liability and recorded on the books of the basketball team? Why or why not?
2. Is increasing payables turnover good or bad for a company? Why or why not?
3. Do adjusting entries involving estimated liabilities and accruals ever affect cash flows?
4. When would a commitment be recognized in the accounting records?

LO4 Discussion Questions

E 2. Develop a brief answer to each of the following questions:

1. Is a friend who borrows money from you for three years and agrees to pay you interest after each year paying you simple or compound interest?
2. Ordinary annuities assume that the first payment is made at the end of each year. In a transaction, who is better off in this arrangement, the payer or the receiver? Why?
3. Why is present value one of the most useful concepts in making business decisions?

LO1 Issues in Accounting for Liabilities

E 3. Indicate whether each of the following actions relates to (a) managing liquidity and cash flows, (b) recognition of liabilities, (c) valuation of liabilities, (d) classification of liabilities, or (e) disclosure of liabilities:

1. Setting a liability at the fair market value of goods to be delivered
2. Relating the payment date of a liability to the length of the operating cycle
3. Recording a liability in accordance with the matching rule
4. Providing information about financial instruments on the balance sheet
5. Estimating the amount of "cents-off" coupons that will be redeemed
6. Categorizing a liability as long-term debt
7. Measuring working capital
8. Comparing days' payable with last year

LO1 Measuring Short-Term Liquidity

E 4. In 2010, Hagler Company had current assets of $310,000 and current liabilities of $200,000, of which accounts payable were $130,000. Cost of goods sold was $850,000, merchandise inventory increased by $80,000, and accounts payable were $110,000 in the prior year. In 2011, Hagler had current assets of $420,000 and current liabilities of $320,000, of which accounts payable were $150,000. Cost of goods sold was $950,000, and merchandise inventory decreased by $30,000. Calculate Hagler's working capital, payables turnover, and days' payable for 2010 and 2011. Assess Hagler's liquidity and cash flows in relation to the change in payables turnover from 2010 to 2011.

LO2 Interest Expense on Note Payable

E 5. On the last day of October, Wicker Company borrows $120,000 on a bank note for 60 days at 11 percent interest. Interest is not included in the face amount. Prepare the following entries in journal form: (1) October 31, recording of note; (2) November 30, accrual of interest expense; and (3) December 30, payment of note plus interest.

LO2 Sales and Excise Taxes

E 6. Web Design Services billed its customers a total of $490,200 for the month of August, including 9 percent federal excise tax and 5 percent sales tax.

1. Determine the proper amount of service revenue to report for the month.
2. Prepare an entry in journal form to record the revenue and related liabilities for the month.

LO2 Payroll Expenses

E 7. At the end of October, the payroll register for Global Tool Corporation contained the following totals: wages, $742,000; federal income taxes withheld,

$189,768; state income taxes withheld, $31,272; Social Security tax withheld, $46,004; Medicare tax withheld, $10,759; medical insurance deductions, $25,740; and wages subject to unemployment taxes, $114,480.

Determine the total and components of the (1) monthly payroll and (2) employer payroll expenses, assuming Social Security and Medicare taxes equal to the amount for employees, a federal unemployment insurance tax of 0.8 percent, a state unemployment tax of 5.4 percent, and medical insurance premiums for which the employer pays 80 percent of the cost.

LO2 Product Warranty Liability

E 8. Sanchez Company manufactures and sells electronic games. Each game costs $50 to produce, sells for $90, and carries a warranty that provides for free replacement if it fails during the two years following the sale. In the past, 7 percent of the games sold had to be replaced under the warranty. During July, Sanchez sold 6,500 games, and 700 games were replaced under the warranty.

1. Prepare an entry in journal form to record the estimated liability for product warranties during the month.
2. Prepare an entry in journal form to record the games replaced under warranty during the month.

LO2 Vacation Pay Liability

E 9. Angel Corporation gives three weeks' paid vacation to each employee who has worked at the company for one year. Based on studies of employee turnover and previous experience, management estimates that 65 percent of the employees will qualify for vacation pay this year.

1. Assume that Angel's July payroll is $150,000, of which $10,000 is paid to employees on vacation. Figure the estimated employee vacation benefit for the month.
2. Prepare an entry in journal form to record the employee benefit for July.
3. Prepare an entry in journal form to record the pay to employees on vacation.

Note: Tables 1 and 2 in the appendix on present value tables may be used where appropriate to solve **E 10** through **E 16.**

LO4 LO5 Determining an Advance Payment

E 10. Tracy Collins is contemplating paying five years' rent in advance. Her annual rent is $25,200. Calculate the single sum that would have to be paid now for the advance rent if we assume compound interest of 8 percent.

LO4 Present Value Calculations

E 11. Find the present value of (1) a single payment of $24,000 at 6 percent for 12 years, (2) 12 annual payments of $2,000 at 6 percent, (3) a single payment of $5,000 at 9 percent for five years, and (4) 5 annual payments of $5,000 at 9 percent.

LO4 LO5 Present Value of a Lump-Sum Contract

E 12. A contract calls for a lump-sum payment of $15,000. Find the present value of the contract, assuming that (1) the payment is due in five years and the current interest rate is 9 percent; (2) the payment is due in ten years and the current interest rate is 9 percent; (3) the payment is due in five years and the current interest rate is 5 percent; and (4) the payment is due in ten years and the current interest rate is 5 percent.

LO4 LO5 **Present Value of an Annuity Contract**

E 13. A contract calls for annual payments of $1,200. Find the present value of the contract, assuming that (1) the number of payments is 7 and the current interest rate is 6 percent; (2) the number of payments is 14 and the current interest rate is 6 percent; (3) the number of payments is 7 and the current interest rate is 8 percent; and (4) the number of payments is 14 and the current interest rate is 8 percent.

LO4 LO5 **Valuing an Asset for the Purpose of Making a Purchasing Decision**

E 14. Robert Baka owns a service station and has the opportunity to purchase a car-wash machine for $30,000. After carefully studying projected costs and revenues, Baka estimates that the car-wash machine will produce a net cash flow of $5,200 annually and will last for eight years. He determines that an interest rate of 14 percent is adequate for his business. Calculate the present value of the machine to Baka. Does the purchase appear to be a smart business decision?

LO4 LO5 **Deferred Payment**

E 15. Antwone Equipment Corporation sold a precision tool machine with computer controls to Trudeau Corporation for $200,000 on January 2 and agreed to take payment nine months later on October 2. Assuming that the prevailing annual interest rate for such a transaction is 16 percent compounded quarterly, what is the actual sale (purchase) price of the machine tool?

LO4 LO5 **Negotiating the Sale of a Business**

E 16. Eva Prokop is attempting to sell her business to Joseph Khan 2. The company has assets of $3,600,000, liabilities of $3,200,000, and owner's equity of $400,000. Both parties agree that the proper rate of return to expect is 12 percent; however, they differ on other assumptions. Prokop believes that the business will generate at least $400,000 per year of cash flows for 20 years. Khan thinks that $320,000 in cash flows per year is more reasonable and that only 10 years in the future should be considered. Using Table 2 in the appendix on present value tables, determine the range for negotiation by computing the present value of Prokop's offer to sell and of Khan's offer to buy.

Problems

LO1 LO2 LO3 **Identification of Current Liabilities, Contingencies, and Commitments**

P 1. Listed below are common types of current liabilities, contingencies, and commitments:

a. Accounts payable
b. Bank loans and commercial paper
c. Notes payable
d. Dividends payable
e. Sales and excise taxes payable
f. Current portion of long-term debt
g. Payroll liabilities
h. Unearned revenues
i. Income taxes payable
j. Property taxes payable
k. Promotional costs
l. Product warranty liability
m. Vacation pay liability
n. Contingent liability
o. Commitment

Required

1. For each of the following statements, identify the category above to which it gives rise or with which it is most closely associated:

    1. A company agrees to replace parts of a product if they fail.
    2. An employee earns one day off for each month worked.
    3. A company signs a contract to lease a building for five years.
    4. A company puts discount coupons in the newspaper.
    5. A company agrees to pay insurance costs for employees.
    6. A portion of a mortgage on a building is due this year.
    7. The board of directors declares a dividend.
    8. A company has trade payables.
    9. A company has a pending lawsuit against it.
    10. A company arranges for a line of credit.
    11. A company signs a note due in 60 days.
    12. A company operates in a state that has a sales tax.
    13. A company earns a profit that is taxable.
    14. A company owns buildings that are subject to property taxes.

User insight ▶ 2. Of the items listed from **a** to **o** above, which ones would you not expect to see listed on the balance sheet with a dollar amount? Of those items that would be listed on the balance sheet with a dollar amount, which ones would you consider to involve the most judgment or discretion on the part of management?

LO2 Notes Payable and Wages Payable

P 2. Part A: State Mill Company, whose fiscal year ends December 31, completed the following transactions involving notes payable:

2010	
Nov. 25	Purchased a new loading cart by issuing a 60-day 10 percent note for $86,400.
Dec. 31	Made the end-of-year adjusting entry to accrue interest expense.
2011	
Jan. 24	Paid off the loading cart note.

Required

1. Prepare entries in journal form for State Mill Company's notes payable transactions.

User insight ▶ 2. When notes payable appears on the balance sheet, what other current liability would you look for to be associated with the notes? What would it mean if this other current liability did not appear?

Part B: At the end of October, the payroll register for State Mill Company contained the following totals: wages, $185,500; federal income taxes withheld, $47,442; state income taxes withheld, $7,818; Social Security tax withheld, $11,501; Medicare tax withheld, $2,690; medical insurance deductions, $6,400; and wages subject to unemployment taxes, $114,480.

Required

Prepare entries in journal form to record the (1) monthly payroll and (2) employer payroll expenses, assuming Social Security and Medicare taxes equal to the amount for employees, a federal unemployment insurance tax of 0.8 percent, a state unemployment tax of 5.4 percent, and medical insurance premiums for which the employer pays 80 percent of the cost.

LO2 **Product Warranty Liability**

P 3. The Smart Way Products Company manufactures and sells wireless video cell phones, which it guarantees for five years. If a cell phone fails, it is replaced free, but the customer is charged a service fee for handling. In the past, management has found that only 3 percent of the cell phones sold required replacement under the warranty. The average cell phone costs the company $120. At the beginning of September, the account for estimated liability for product warranties had a credit balance of $104,000. During September, 250 cell phones were returned under the warranty. The company collected $4,930 of service fees for handling. During the month, the company sold 2,800 cell phones.

Required

1. Prepare entries in journal form to record (a) the cost of cell phones replaced under warranty and (b) the estimated liability for product warranties for cell phones sold during the month.
2. Compute the balance of the Estimated Product Warranty Liability account at the end of the month.

User insight ▶

3. If the company's product warranty liability is underestimated, what are the effects on current and future years' income?

LO1 **Identification and Evaluation of Current Liabilities**

P 4. Tony Garcia opened a small dryer repair shop, Garcia Repair Shop, on January 2, 2010. The shop also sells a limited number of dryer parts. In January 2011, Garcia realized he had never filed any tax reports for his business and therefore probably owes a considerable amount of taxes. Since he has limited experience in running a business, he has brought you all his business records, including a checkbook, canceled checks, deposit slips, suppliers' invoices, a notice of annual property taxes of $2,310 due to the city, and a promissory note to his father-in-law for $2,500. He wants you to determine what his business owes the government and other parties.

You analyze all his records and determine the following as of December 31, 2010:

Unpaid invoices for dryer parts	$ 9,000
Parts sales (excluding sales tax)	44,270
Cost of parts sold	31,125
Workers' salaries	18,200
Repair revenues	60,300
Current assets	16,300
Dryer parts inventory	11,750

You learn that the company has deducted $476 from the two employees' salaries for federal income taxes owed to the government. The current Social Security tax is 6.2 percent on maximum earnings of $102,000 for each employee, and the current Medicare tax is 1.45 percent (no maximum earnings). The FUTA tax is 5.4 percent to the state and .8 percent to the federal government on the first $7,000 earned by each employee, and each employee earned more than $7,000. Garcia has not filed a sales tax report to the state (5 percent of sales).

Required

1. Given these limited facts, determine Garcia Repair Shop's current liabilities as of December 31, 2010.

User insight ▶

2. What additional information would you want from Garcia to satisfy yourself that all current liabilities have been identified?

User insight ▶ 3. Evaluate Garcia's liquidity by calculating working capital, payables turnover, and days' payable. Comment on the results. (Assume average accounts payable were the same as year-end accounts payable.)

LO4 LO5

Applications of Present Value

P 5. Andy Corporation's management took the following actions, which went into effect on January 2, 2010. Each action involved an application of present value.

a. Andy Corporation enters into a purchase agreement that calls for a payment of $500,000 three years from now.
b. Bought out the contract of a member of top management for a payment of $50,000 per year for four years beginning January 2, 2011.

Required

1. Assuming an annual interest rate of 10 percent and using Tables 1 and 2 in the appendix of present value tables, answer the following questions:
   a. In action **a,** what is the present value of the liability for the purchase agreement?
   b. In action **b,** what is the cost (present value) of the buyout?

User insight ▶ 2. Many businesses analyze present value extensively when making decisions about investing in long-term assets. Why is this type of analysis particularly appropriate for such decisions?

Alternate Problems

LO2

Notes Payable and Wages Payable

P 6. Part A: Nazir Corporation, whose fiscal year ended June 30, 2011, completed the following transactions involving notes payable:

May 21	Obtained a 60-day extension on an $18,000 trade account payable owed to a supplier by signing a 60-day $18,000 note. Interest is in addition to the face value, at the rate of 14 percent.
June 30	Made the end-of-year adjusting entry to accrue interest expense.
July 20	Paid off the note plus interest due the supplier.

Required

1. Prepare entries in journal form for the notes payable transactions.

User insight ▶ 2. When notes payable appears on the balance sheet, what other current liability would you look for to be associated with the notes? What would it mean if this other current liability did not appear?

Part B: The payroll register for Nazir Corporation contained the following totals at the end of July: wages, $139,125; federal income taxes withheld, $35,582; state income taxes withheld, $5,863; Social Security tax withheld, $8,626; Medicare tax withheld, $2,017; medical insurance deductions, $4,800; and wages subject to unemployment taxes, $85,860.

Required

Prepare entries in journal form to record the (1) monthly payroll and (2) employer payroll expenses, assuming Social Security and Medicare taxes equal to the amount for employees, a federal unemployment insurance tax of 0.8 percent, a state unemployment tax of 5.4 percent, and medical insurance premiums for which the employer pays 80 percent of the cost.

LO2

Product Warranty Liability

P 7. Telemix Company is engaged in the retail sale of high-definition televisions (HDTVs). Each HDTV has a 24-month warranty on parts. If a repair under warranty is required, a charge for the labor is made. Management has found that 20 percent of the HDTVs sold require some work before the warranty expires. Furthermore, the average cost of replacement parts has been $60 per repair. At the beginning of January, the account for the estimated liability for product warranties had a credit balance of $14,300. During January, 146 HDTVs were returned under the warranty. The cost of the parts used in repairing the HDTVs was $8,760, and $9,442 was collected as service revenue for the labor involved. During January, the month before the Super Bowl, Telemix Company sold 450 new HDTVs.

Required

1. Prepare entries in journal form to record each of the following: (a) the warranty work completed during the month, including related revenue; (b) the estimated liability for product warranties for HDTVs sold during the month.
2. Compute the balance of the Estimated Product Warranty Liability account at the end of the month.

User insight ▶

3. If the company's product warranty liability is overestimated, what are the effects on current and future years' income?

LO4 LO5

Applications of Present Value

P 8. The management of K&S, Inc., took the following actions that went into effect on January 2, 2010. Each action involved an application of present value.

a. Asked for another fund to be established by a single payment to accumulate to $75,000 in four years.
b. Approved the purchase of a parcel of land for future plant expansion. Payments are to start January 2, 2011, at $50,000 per year for five years.

Required

1. Assuming an annual interest rate of 8 percent and using Tables 1 and 2 in the appendix of present value tables, answer the following questions:
   a. In action **a**, how much will need to be deposited initially to accumulate the desired amount?
   b. In action **b**, what is the purchase price (present value) of the land?

User insight ▶

2. What is the fundamental reason present value analysis is a useful tool in making business decisions?

LO1

Identification and Evaluation of Current Liabilities

P 9. Jose Hernandez opened a small motorcycle repair shop, Hernandez Cycle Repair, on January 2, 2011. The shop also sells a limited number of motorcycle parts. In January 2012, Hernandez realized he had never filed any tax reports for his business and therefore probably owes a considerable amount of taxes. Since he has limited experience in running a business, he has brought you all his business records, including a checkbook, canceled checks, deposit slips, suppliers' invoices, a notice of annual property taxes of $4,620 due to the city, and a promissory note to his father-in-law for $5,000. He wants you to determine what his business owes the government and other parties.

You analyze all his records and determine the following as of December 31, 2011:

Unpaid invoices for motorcycle parts	$ 18,000
Parts sales (excluding sales tax)	88,540
Cost of parts sold	62,250
Workers' salaries	20,400
Repair revenues	120,600
Current assets	32,600
Motorcycle parts inventory	23,500

You learn that the company has deducted $952 from the two employees' salaries for federal income taxes owed to the government. The current Social Security tax is 6.2 percent on maximum earnings of $102,000 for each employee, and the current Medicare tax is 1.45 percent (no maximum earnings). The FUTA tax is 5.4 percent to the state and 0.8 percent to the federal government on the first $7,000 earned by each employee, and each employee earned more than $7,000. Hernandez has not filed a sales tax report to the state (5 percent of sales).

Required

1. Given these limited facts, determine Hernandez Cycle Repair's current liabilities as of December 31, 2011.

User insight ▶ 2. What additional information would you want from Hernandez to satisfy yourself that all current liabilities have been identified?

User insight ▶ 3. Evaluate Hernandez's liquidity by calculating working capital, payables turnover, and days' payable. Comment on the results. (Assume average accounts payable were the same as year-end accounts payable.)

ENHANCING Your Knowledge, Skills, and Critical Thinking

LO2 Frequent Flyer Plan

C 1. JetGreen Airways instituted a frequent flyer program in which passengers accumulate points toward a free flight based on the number of miles they fly on the airline. One point was awarded for each mile flown, with a minimum of 750 miles being given for any flight. Because of competition in 2010, the company began a bonus plan in which passengers received triple the normal mileage points. In the past, about 1.5 percent of passenger miles were flown by passengers who had converted points to free flights. With the triple mileage program, JetGreen expects that a 2.5 percent rate will be more appropriate for future years.

During 2010, the company had passenger revenues of $966.3 million and passenger transportation operating expenses of $802.8 million before depreciation and amortization. Operating income was $86.1 million. What is the appropriate rate to use to estimate free miles? What would be the effect of the estimated liability for free travel by frequent fliers on 2010 net income? Describe several ways to estimate the amount of this liability. Be prepared to discuss the arguments for and against recognizing this liability.

LO4 LO5 **Time Value of Money**

C 2. In its "Year-End Countdown Sale," a local **Cadillac** auto dealer advertised "0% interest for 60 months!"[15] What role does the time value of money play in this promotion? Assuming that Cadillac is able to borrow funds at 8 percent interest, what is the cost to Cadillac of every customer who takes advantage of this offer? If you were able to borrow to pay cash for this car, which rate would be more relevant in determining how much you might offer for the car—the rate at which you borrow money or the rate at which Cadillac borrows money?

LO2 **Nature and Recognition of an Estimated Liability**

C 3. The decision to recognize and record a liability is sometimes a matter of judgment. People who use **General Motors** credit cards earn rebates toward the purchase or lease of GM vehicles in relation to the amount of purchases they make with their cards. General Motors chooses to treat these outstanding rebates as a commitment in the notes to its financial statements:

> GM sponsors a credit card program...which offers rebates that can be applied primarily against the purchase or lease of GM vehicles. The amount of rebates available to qualified cardholders (net of deferred program income) was $4.9 billion and $4.7 billion at December 31, 2006, and 2005, respectively.[16]

Using the two criteria established by the FASB for recording a contingency, explain GM's reasoning in treating this liability as a commitment in the notes, where it will likely receive less attention by analysts, rather than including it on the income statement as an expense and on the balance sheet as an estimated liability. Do you agree with this position? (**Hint:** Apply the matching rule.)

LO2 LO5 **Nature and Recognition of an Estimated Liability**

C 4. Assume that you work for Theater-At-Home, Inc., a retail company that sells basement movie projection systems for $10,000. Your boss is considering two types of promotions:

1. Offering customers a $1,000 coupon that they can apply to future purchases, including the purchase of annual maintenance.
2. Offering credit terms that allow payments of $2,000 down and $2,000 per year for four years starting one year after the purchase. Theater-At-Home would have to borrow money at 7 percent interest to finance these credit arrangements.

Divide the class into groups. After discussing the relative merits of these two plans, including their implications for accounting and the time value of money, each group should decide on the best alternative. The groups may recommend changes in the plans. A representative of each group should report the group's findings to the class.

LO1 LO3 **Short-Term Liabilities and Seasonality; Commitments and Contingencies**

C 5. Refer to the quarterly financial report near the end of the notes to the financial statements in **CVS**'s annual report. Is CVS's a seasonal business? Would you expect short-term borrowings and accounts payable to be unusually high or unusually low at the balance sheet date of December 31, 2008?

Read CVS's note on commitments and contingencies. What commitments and contingencies does the company have? Why is it important to consider this information in connection with payables analysis?

LO1 **Payables Analysis**

C 6. Refer to **CVS**'s financial statements in the Supplement to Chapter 5 and to the following data for **Walgreens**:

	2008	2007	2006
Cost of goods sold	$42,391	$38,518	$34,240
Accounts payable	4,289	3,734	4,039
Increase in merchandise inventories	412	676	376

Compute the payables turnover and days' payable for CVS and Walgreens for the past two years.

In 2006, CVS had accounts payable of $3,411.6 million, and its merchandise inventory increased by $448.0 in 2007. Which company do you think makes the most use of creditors for financing the needs of the operating cycle? Has the trend changed?

CHAPTER

11 Long-Term Assets

Making a Statement

INCOME STATEMENT

Revenues

– Expenses

= Net Income

STATEMENT OF OWNER'S EQUITY

Beginning Balance

+ Net Income

– Withdrawals

= Ending Balance

BALANCE SHEET

Assets	**Liabilities**
	Owner's Equity

A = L + OE

STATEMENT OF CASH FLOWS

Operating activities

+ Investing activities

+ Financing activities

= Change in Cash

+ Beginning Balance

= Ending Cash Balance

Purchase, use, and disposal of long-term assets affect all financial statements.

Long-term assets include tangible assets, such as land, buildings, and equipment; natural resources, such as timberland and oil fields; and intangible assets, such as patents and copyrights. These assets represent a company's strategic commitments well into the future. The judgments related to their acquisition, operation, and disposal and to the allocation of their costs will affect a company's performance for years to come. Investors and creditors rely on accurate and full reporting of the assumptions and judgments that underlie the measurement of long-term assets.

LEARNING OBJECTIVES

LO1 Define *long-term assets*, and explain the management issues related to them. (pp. 474–479)

LO2 Distinguish between *capital expenditures* and *revenue expenditures*, and account for the cost of property, plant, and equipment. (pp. 479–483)

LO3 Compute depreciation under the straight-line, production, and declining-balance methods. (pp. 483–490)

LO4 Account for the disposal of depreciable assets. (pp. 490–494)

LO5 Identify the issues related to accounting for natural resources, and compute depletion. (pp. 494–496)

LO6 Identify the issues related to accounting for intangible assets, including research and development costs and goodwill. (pp. 497–501)

DECISION POINT ▸ A USER'S FOCUS CAMPUS CLEANERS

To provide goods and services to customers, businesses need tangible long-term assets, such as buildings, machines, or trucks. Among the issues involved in accounting for long-term assets is how to allocate their costs over their expected useful lives. For instance, suppose that on January 2, 2010, Campus Cleaners pays $29,000 for a small van that it will use in making deliveries to its customers. The company expects that the van will be driven a total of 150,000 miles over a 5-year period and that at the end of that time, it will be worth $2,000. The table that follows shows the estimated mileage in each of the 5 years that the van is expected to be in use. Campus Cleaners can allocate the cost of the van over the 5 years based on mileage. However, the company has a choice to make because, as you will learn in this chapter, there are three common ways of allocating the cost of a tangible long-term asset over accounting periods.

Years	*Miles*
2010	30,000
2011	52,500
2012	45,000
2013	15,000
2014	7,500
Total	150,000

- ▸ What long-term assets other than a delivery van might Campus Cleaners have, and how should it account for them?
- ▸ What are the three common methods of calculating depreciation on tangible long-term assets, and how do the patterns of depreciation that they produce differ?

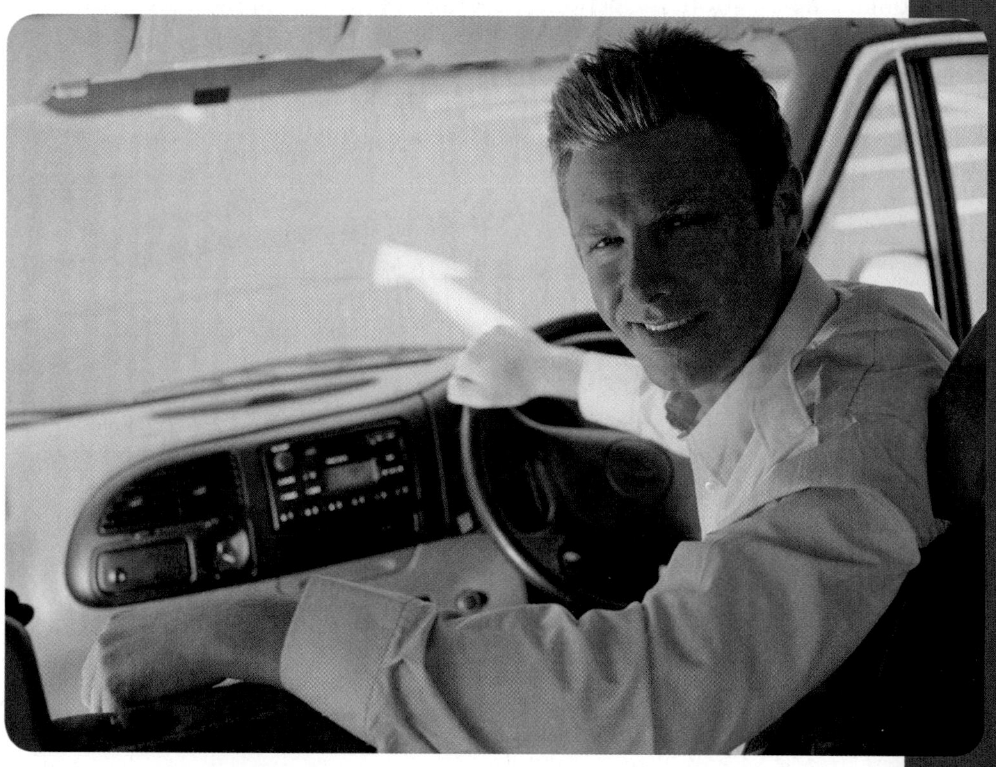

Management Issues Related to Long-Term Assets

LO1 Define *long-term assets,* and explain the management issues related to them.

Long-term assets were once called *fixed assets,* but this term has fallen out of favor because it implies that the assets last forever, which they do not. Long-term assets have the following characteristics:

- **They have a useful life of more than one year.** This distinguishes them from current assets, which a company expects to use up or convert to cash within 1 year or during its operating cycle, whichever is longer. They also differ from current assets in that they support the operating cycle, rather than being part of it. Although there is no strict rule for defining the useful life of a long-term asset, the most common criterion is that the asset be capable of repeated use for at least a year. Included in this category is equipment used only in peak or emergency periods, such as electric generators.
- **They are used in the operation of a business.** Assets not used in the normal course of business, such as land held for speculative reasons or buildings no longer used in ordinary business operations, should be classified as long-term investments, not as long-term assets.
- **They are not intended for resale to customers.** An asset that a company intends to resell to customers should be classified as inventory—not as a long-term asset—no matter how durable it is. For example, a printing press that a manufacturer offers for sale is part of the manufacturer's inventory, but it is a long-term asset for a printing company that buys it to use in its operations.

Study Note

A computer that a company uses in an office is a long-term plant asset. An identical computer that a company sells to customers is considered inventory.

Figure 11-1 shows the relative importance of long-term assets in various industries. Figure 11-2 shows how long-term assets are classified and defines the methods of accounting for them. Plant assets, which are **tangible assets**, are accounted for through **depreciation**. (Although land is a tangible asset, it is not depreciated because it has an unlimited life.) **Natural resources**, which are also tangible assets, are accounted for through **depletion**. Most **intangible assets** are accounted for through **amortization**, the periodic allocation of the cost of the asset to the periods it benefits. However, some intangible assets, including goodwill, are not subject to amortization if their fair value is below the carrying value.

Carrying value (also called *book value*) is the unexpired part of an asset's cost (see Figure 11-3). Long-term assets are generally reported at carrying

FIGURE 11-1
Long-Term Assets as a Percentage of Total Assets for Selected Industries

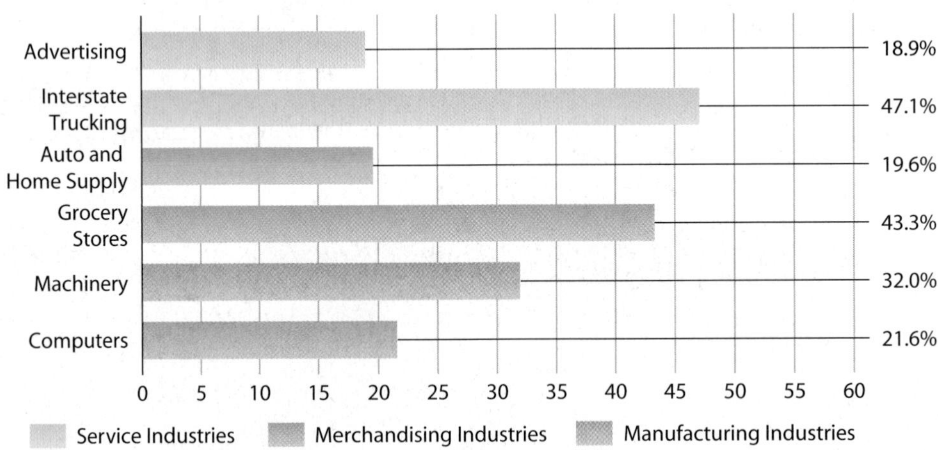

Source: Data from Dun & Bradstreet, *Industry Norms and Key Business Ratios,* 2005–2006.

FIGURE 11-2 Classification of Long-Term Assets and Methods of Accounting for Them

BALANCE SHEET Long-Term Assets		INCOME STATEMENT Expenses
	**Tangible Assets:** long-term assets that have physical substance Land Plant, Buildings, Equipment (plant assets)	Land is not expensed because it has an unlimited life. **Depreciation:** periodic allocation of the cost of a tangible long-lived asset (other than land and natural resources) over its estimated useful life
	**Natural Resources:** long-term assets purchased for the economic value that can be taken from the land and used up, as with ore, lumber, oil, and gas or other resources contained in the land Mines Timberland Oil and Gas Fields	**Depletion:** exhaustion of a natural resource through mining, cutting, pumping, or other extraction, and the way in which the cost is allocated
	**Intangible Assets:** long-term assets that have no physical substance but have a value based on rights or advantages accruing to the owner Patents, Copyrights, Software, Trademarks, Licenses, Brands, Franchises, Leaseholds, Noncompete Covenants, Customer Lists, Goodwill	**Amortization:** periodic allocation of the cost of an intangible asset to the periods it benefits

value. If a long-term asset loses some or all of its potential to generate revenue before the end of its useful life, it is deemed *impaired*, and its carrying value is reduced.

> **Study Note**
>
> For an asset to be classified as property, plant, and equipment, it must be "put in use," which means it is available for its intended purpose. An emergency generator is "put in use" when it is available for emergencies, even if it is never used.

All long-term assets are subject to an annual impairment evaluation. **Asset impairment** occurs when the carrying value of a long-term asset exceeds its fair value.[1] *Fair value* is the amount for which the asset could be bought or sold in a current transaction. For example, if the sum of the expected cash flows from an asset is less than its carrying value, the asset would be impaired. Reducing carrying value to fair value, as measured by the present value of future cash flows, is an application of conservatism. A reduction in carrying value as the result of

FIGURE 11-3 Carrying Value of Long-Term Assets on the Balance Sheet

Plant Assets	Natural Resources	Intangible Assets
Less Accumulated Depreciation	Less Accumulated Depletion	Less Accumulated Amortization
Carrying Value	Carrying Value	Carrying Value

> **Study Note**
> To be classified as intangible, an asset must lack physical substance, be long-term, and represent a legal right or advantage.

impairment is recorded as a loss. When the market prices used to establish fair value are not available, the amount of an impairment must be estimated from the best available information.

In 2004, **Apple Computer** recognized losses of $5.5 million in asset impairments, but it recognized none in subsequent years. A few years earlier, in the midst of an economic slowdown in the telecommunications industry, **WorldCom** recorded asset impairments that totaled $79.8 billion, the largest impairment write-down in history. Since then, other telecommunications companies, including **AT&T** and **Qwest Communications**, have taken large impairment write-downs. Due to these companies' declining revenues, the carrying value of some of their long-term assets no longer exceeded the cash flows that they were meant to help generate.[2] Because of the write-downs, these companies reported large operating losses.

Taking a large write-down in a bad year is often called "taking a big bath" because it "cleans" future years of the bad year's costs and thus can help a company return to a profitable status. In other words, by taking the largest possible loss on a long-term asset in a bad year, companies hope to reduce the costs of depreciation or amortization on the asset in subsequent years.[3]

In the next few pages, we discuss the management issues related to long-term assets—how management decides whether it will acquire them, how it will finance them, and how it will account for them.

Acquiring Long-Term Assets

The decision to acquire a long-term asset is a complex process. For example, **Apple**'s decision to invest capital in establishing its own retail stores throughout the country required very careful analysis. Methods of evaluating data to make rational decisions about acquiring long-term assets are grouped under a topic called capital budgeting, which is usually covered as a managerial accounting topic. However, an awareness of the general nature of the problem is helpful in understanding the management issues related to long-term assets.

To illustrate an acquisition decision, suppose that Apple's management is considering the purchase of a $100,000 customer-relations software package. Management estimates that the new software will save net cash flows of $40,000 per year for four years, the usual life of new software, and that the software will be worth $20,000 at the end of that period. These data are shown in Table 11-1. To put the cash flows on a comparable basis, it is helpful to use present value tables, such as Tables 1 and 2 in the appendix on present value tables. If the interest rate set by management as a desirable return is 10 percent compounded annually, the purchase decision would be evaluated as follows:

		Present Value
Acquisition cost	Present value factor = 1.000 1.000 × $100,000	($100,000)
Net annual savings in cash flows	Present value factor = 3.170 (Table 2: 4 periods, 10%) 3.170 × $40,000	126,800
Disposal price	Present value factor = .683 (Table 1: 4 periods, 10%) 0.683 × $20,000	13,660
Net present value		$ 40,460

TABLE 11-1
Illustration of an Acquisition Decision

	Year 1	Year 2	Year 3	Year 4
Acquisition cost	($100,000)			
Net annual savings in cash flows	40,000	$40,000	$40,000	$40,000
Disposal price				20,000
Net cash flows	($ 60,000)	$40,000	$40,000	$60,000

As long as the net present value is positive, Apple will earn at least 10 percent on the investment. In this case, the return is greater than 10 percent because the net present value is a positive $40,460. Moreover, the net present value is large relative to the investment. Based on this analysis, it appears that Apple's management should make the decision to purchase. However, in making its decision, it should take other important considerations into account, including the costs of training personnel to use the software. It should also allow for the possibility that because of unforeseen circumstances, the savings may not be as great as expected.

Information about acquisitions of long-term assets appears in the investing activities section of the statement of cash flows. In referring to this section of its 2007 annual report, Apple's management makes the following statement:

> The company's total capital expenditures were $822 million during fiscal 2007.... The company currently anticipates it will utilize approximately $1.1 billion for capital expenditures during 2008, approximately $400 million for further expansion of the Company's Retail segment and [the remainder] utilized to support normal replacement of existing capital assets.

Financing Long-Term Assets

When management decides to acquire a long-term asset, it must also decide how to finance the purchase. Many financing arrangements are based on the life of the asset. For example, an automobile loan generally spans 4 or 5 years, whereas a mortgage on a house may span 30 years. For a major long-term acquisition, a company may issue stock, long-term notes, or bonds. Some companies are profitable enough to pay for long-term assets out of cash flows from operations. A good place to study a company's investing and financing activities is its statement of cash flows, and a good measure of its ability to finance long-term assets is free cash flow.

Free cash flow is the amount of cash that remains after deducting the funds a company must commit to continue operating at its planned level. The commitments to be covered include current or continuing operations, interest, income taxes, dividends, and net capital expenditures (purchases of plant assets minus sales of plant assets). If a company fails to pay for current or continuing operations, interest, and income taxes, its creditors and the government can take legal action. Although the payment of dividends is not strictly required, dividends normally represent a commitment to stockholders. If they are reduced or eliminated, stockholders will be unhappy, and the price of the company's stock will fall. Net capital expenditures represent management's plans for the future.

A positive free cash flow means that a company has met all its cash commitments and has cash available to reduce debt or to expand its operations. A negative free cash flow means that it will have to sell investments, borrow money, or issue stock in the short term to continue at its planned level. If free cash flow remains negative for several years, a company may not be able to raise cash by issuing stock or bonds.

> **Study Note**
> The computation of free cash flow uses *net capital expenditures* in place of *purchases of plant assets + sales of plant assets* when plant assets are small or immaterial.

Using data from **Apple**'s statement of cash flows in its 2007 annual report, we can compute the company's free cash flow as follows (in millions):

$$\begin{aligned}\text{Free Cash Flow} &= \text{Net Cash Flows from Operating Activities} - \text{Dividends}\\ &\quad - \text{Purchases of Plant Assets} + \text{Sales of Plant Assets}\\ &= \$5{,}470 - \$0 - \$735 + \$0\\ &= \$4{,}735\end{aligned}$$

This analysis confirms Apple's strong financial position. Its cash flow from operating activities far exceeds its net capital expenditures of $735 million. A factor that contributes to its positive free cash flow of $4,735 million is that the company pays no dividends. The financing activities section of Apple's statement of cash flows also indicates that the company, rather than incurring debt for expansion, actually made net investments of $2,312 million.

Applying the Matching Rule

When a company records an expenditure as a long-term asset, it is deferring an expense until a later period. Thus, the current period's profitability looks better than it would if the expenditure had been expensed immediately. Management has considerable latitude in making the judgments and estimates necessary to account for all types and aspects of long-term assets. Sometimes, this latitude is used unwisely and unethically. For example, in the infamous **WorldCom** accounting fraud, management ordered that certain expenditures which should have been recorded as operating expenses be capitalized as long-term assets and written off over several years. The result was an overstatement of income by about $10 billion, which ultimately led to the second largest bankruptcy in history of U.S. business.

To avoid fraudulent reporting of long-term assets, a company's management must apply the matching rule in resolving two important issues. The first is how much of the total cost of a long-term asset to allocate to expense in the current accounting period. The second is how much to retain on the balance sheet as an asset that will benefit future periods. To resolve these issues, management must answer four important questions about the acquisition, use, and disposal of each long-term asset (see Figure 11-4):

FIGURE 11-4
Issues in Accounting for Long-Term Assets

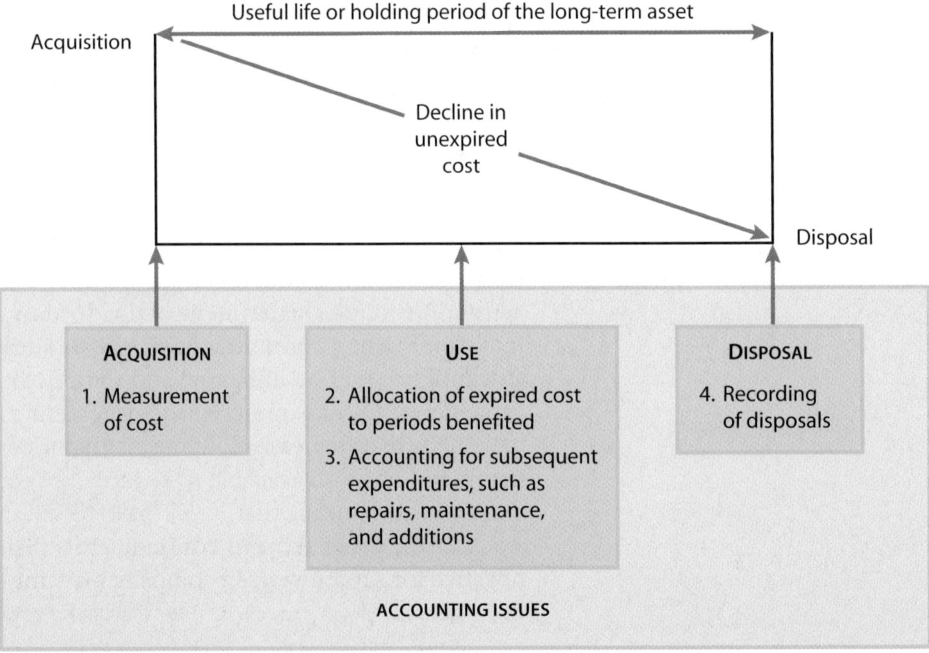

1. How is the cost of the long-term asset determined?
2. How should the expired portion of the cost of the long-term asset be allocated against revenues over time?
3. How should subsequent expenditures, such as repairs and additions, be treated?
4. How should disposal of the long-term asset be recorded?

Management's answers to these questions can be found in the company's annual report under management's discussion and analysis and in the notes to the financial statements.

STOP & APPLY >

Corus Company had net cash flows from operating activities during the past year of $133,000. During the year, the company expended $61,000 for property, plant, and equipment; sold property, plant, and equipment for $14,000; and paid dividends of $20,000. Calculate the company's free cash flow. What does the result tell you about the company?

SOLUTION

Net cash flows from operating activities	$133,000
Purchases of property, plant, and equipment	(61,000)
Sales of property, plant, and equipment	14,000
Dividends	(20,000)
Free cash flow	$ 66,000

Corus's operations provide sufficient cash flows to fund its current expansion and dividends without raising additional capital through borrowing or owner investments.

Acquisition Cost of Property, Plant, and Equipment

LO2 Distinguish between *capital expenditures* and *revenue expenditures*, and account for the cost of property, plant, and equipment.

Expenditure refers to a payment or an obligation to make a future payment for an asset, such as a truck, or for a service, such as a repair. Expenditures are classified as capital expenditures or revenue expenditures.

- A **capital expenditure** is an expenditure for the purchase or expansion of a long-term asset. Capital expenditures are recorded in asset accounts because they benefit several future accounting periods.
- A **revenue expenditure** is an expenditure made for the ordinary repairs and maintenance needed to keep a long-term asset in good operating condition. For example, trucks, machines, and other equipment require periodic tune-ups and routine repairs. Expenditures of this type are recorded in expense accounts because their benefits are realized in the current period.

Capital expenditures include outlays for plant assets, natural resources, and intangible assets. They also include expenditures for the following:

- **Additions**, which are enlargements to the physical layout of a plant asset. For example, if a new wing is added to a building, the benefits from the expenditure will be received over several years, and the amount paid should be debited to an asset account.

- **Betterments**, which are improvements to a plant asset but that do not add to the plant's physical layout. Installation of an air-conditioning system is an example. Because betterments provide benefits over a period of years, their costs should be debited to an asset account.
- **Extraordinary repairs**, which are repairs that significantly enhance a plant asset's estimated useful life or residual value. For example, a complete overhaul of a building's heating and cooling system may extend the system's useful life by five years. Extraordinary repairs are typically recorded by reducing the Accumulated Depreciation account; the assumption in doing so is that some of the depreciation previously recorded on the asset has now been eliminated. The effect of the reduction is to increase the asset's carrying value by the cost of the extraordinary repair. The new carrying value should be depreciated over the asset's new estimated useful life.

The distinction between capital and revenue expenditures is important in applying the matching rule. For example, if the purchase of a machine that will benefit a company for several years is mistakenly recorded as a revenue expenditure, the total cost of the machine becomes an expense on the income statement in the current period. As a result, current net income will be reported at a lower amount (understated), and in future periods, net income will be reported at a higher amount (overstated). If, on the other hand, a revenue expenditure, such as the routine overhaul of a piece of machinery, is charged to an asset account, the expense of the current period will be understated. Current net income will be overstated by the same amount, and the net income of future periods will be understated.

General Approach to Acquisition Costs

The acquisition cost of property, plant, and equipment includes all expenditures reasonable and necessary to get an asset in place and ready for use. For example, the cost of installing and testing a machine is a legitimate cost of acquiring the machine. However, if the machine is damaged during installation, the cost of repairs is an operating expense, not an acquisition cost.

> **Study Note**
> Expenditures necessary to prepare an asset for its intended use are a cost of the asset.

Acquisition cost is easiest to determine when a purchase is made for cash. In that case, the cost of the asset is equal to the cash paid for it plus expenditures for freight, insurance while in transit, installation, and other necessary related costs. Expenditures for freight, insurance while in transit, and installation are included in the cost of the asset because they are necessary if the asset is to function. In accordance with the matching rule, these expenditures are allocated over the asset's useful life rather than charged as expenses in the current period.

Any interest charges incurred in purchasing an asset are not a cost of the asset; they are a cost of borrowing the money to buy the asset and are therefore an operating expense. An exception to this rule is that interest costs incurred during the construction of an asset are properly included as a cost of the asset.[4]

As a matter of practicality, many companies establish policies that define when an expenditure should be recorded as an expense or as an asset. For example, small expenditures for items that qualify as long-term assets may be treated as expenses because the amounts involved are not material in relation to net income. Thus, although a wastebasket may last for years, it would be recorded as supplies expense rather than as a depreciable asset.

Specific Applications

In the sections that follow, we discuss some of the problems of determining the cost of long-term plant assets.

Study Note

Many costs may be incurred to prepare land for its intended use and condition. All such costs are a cost of the land.

Study Note

The costs of tearing down existing buildings can be major. Companies may spend millions of dollars imploding buildings so they can remove them and build new ones.

Land The purchase price of land should be debited to the Land account. Other expenditures that should be debited to the Land account include commissions to real estate agents; lawyers' fees; accrued taxes paid by the purchaser; costs of preparing the land to build on, such as the costs of tearing down old buildings and grading the land; and assessments for local improvements, such as putting in streets and sewage systems. The cost of landscaping is usually debited to the Land account because such improvements are relatively permanent. Land is not subject to depreciation because it has an unlimited useful life.

Let us assume that a company buys land for a new retail operation. The net purchase price is $340,000. The company also pays brokerage fees of $12,000, legal fees of $4,000, $20,000 to have an old building on the site torn down, and $2,000 to have the site graded. It receives $8,000 in salvage from the old building. The cost of the land is $370,000, calculated as follows:

Net purchase price		$340,000
Brokerage fees		12,000
Legal fees		4,000
Tearing down old building	$20,000	
Less salvage	8,000	12,000
Grading		2,000
Total cost		$370,000

Land Improvements Some improvements to real estate, such as driveways, parking lots, and fences, have a limited life and thus are subject to depreciation. They should be recorded in an account called Land Improvements rather than in the Land account.

Buildings When a company buys a building, the cost includes the purchase price and all repairs and other expenditures required to put the building in usable

Like other costs involved in preparing land for use, the cost of implosion is debited to the Land account. Other expenditures debited to the Land account include the purchase price of the land, brokerage and legal fees involved in the purchase, taxes paid by the purchaser, and landscaping.

Courtesy of Ariel Bravy, 2009/Used under license from shutterstock.com.

condition. When a company uses a contractor to construct a building, the cost includes the net contract price plus other expenditures necessary to put the building in usable condition. When a company constructs its own building, the cost includes all reasonable and necessary expenditures, including the costs of materials, labor, part of the overhead and other indirect costs, architects' fees, insurance during construction, interest on construction loans during the period of construction, lawyers' fees, and building permits. Because buildings have a limited useful life, they are subject to depreciation.

Leasehold Improvements Improvements to leased property that become the property of the lessor (the owner of the property) at the end of the lease are called **leasehold improvements**. For example, a tenant's installation of light fixtures, carpets, or walls would be considered a leasehold improvement. These improvements are usually classified as tangible assets in the property, plant, and equipment section of the balance sheet. Sometimes, they are included in the intangible assets section; the theory in reporting them as intangibles is that because they revert to the lessor at the end of the lease, they are more of a right than a tangible asset. The cost of a leasehold improvement is depreciated or amortized over the remaining term of the lease or the useful life of the improvement, whichever is shorter.

Leasehold improvements are fairly common in large businesses. A study of large companies showed that 22 percent report leasehold improvements. The percentage is likely to be much higher for small businesses because they generally operate in leased premises.[5]

Study Note

The wiring and plumbing of a dental chair are included in the cost of the asset because they are a necessary cost of preparing the asset for use.

Equipment The cost of equipment includes all expenditures connected with purchasing the equipment and preparing it for use. Among these expenditures are the invoice price less cash discounts; freight, including insurance; excise taxes and tariffs; buying expenses; installation costs; and test runs to ready the equipment for operation. Equipment is subject to depreciation.

Group Purchases Companies sometimes purchase land and other assets for a lump sum. Because land has an unlimited life and is a nondepreciable asset, it must have a separate ledger account, and the lump-sum purchase price must be apportioned between the land and the other assets. For example, suppose a company buys a building and the land on which it is situated for a lump sum of $170,000. The company can apportion the costs by determining what it would have paid for the building and for the land if it had purchased them separately and applying the appropriate percentages to the lump-sum price. Assume that appraisals yield estimates of $20,000 for the land and $180,000 for the building if purchased separately. In that case, 10 percent of the lump-sum price, or $17,000, would be allocated to the land, and 90 percent, or $153,000, would be allocated to the building, as follows:

	Appraisal	*Percentage*	*Apportionment*
Land	$ 20,000	10% ($ 20,000 ÷ $200,000)	$ 17,000 ($170,000 × 10%)
Building	180,000	90% ($180,000 ÷ $200,000)	153,000 ($170,000 × 90%)
Totals	$200,000	100%	$170,000

Match each term below with the corresponding action in the list that follows by writing the appropriate numbers in the blanks:

1. Addition
2. Betterment
3. Extraordinary repair
4. Land
5. Land improvement
6. Leasehold improvement
7. Buildings
8. Equipment
9. Not a capital expenditure

____ a. Purchase of a computer

____ b. Purchase of a lighting system for a parking lot

____ c. Repainting of an existing building

____ d. Installation of a new roof that extends an existing building's useful life

____ e. Construction of a foundation for a new building

____ f. Erection of a new storage facility at the back of an existing building

____ g. Installation of partitions and shelves in a leased space

____ h. Clearing of land in preparation for construction of a new building

____ i. Installation of a new heating system in an existing building

SOLUTION

a. 8; b. 5; c. 9; d. 3; e. 7; f. 1; g. 6; h. 4; i. 2

Depreciation

LO3 Compute depreciation under the straight-line, production, and declining-balance methods.

As we noted earlier, *depreciation* is the periodic allocation of the cost of a tangible asset (other than land and natural resources) over the asset's estimated useful life. In accounting for depreciation, it is important to keep the following points in mind:

- **All tangible assets except land have a limited useful life, and the costs of these assets must be distributed as expenses over the years they benefit.** Physical deterioration and obsolescence are the major factors in limiting a depreciable asset's useful life.
  - **Physical deterioration** results from use and from exposure to the elements, such as wind and sun. Periodic repairs and a sound maintenance policy may keep buildings and equipment in good operating order and extract the maximum useful life from them, but every machine or building must at some point be discarded. Repairs do not eliminate the need for depreciation.
  - **Obsolescence** refers to the process of going out of date. Because of fast-changing technology and fast-changing demands, machinery and even buildings often become obsolete before they wear out.

  Accountants do not distinguish between physical deterioration and obsolescence because they are interested in the length of an asset's useful life, not in what limits its useful life.
- **Depreciation refers to the allocation of the cost of a plant asset to the periods that benefit from the asset, not to the asset's physical deterioration or decrease in market value.** The term *depreciation* describes the gradual conversion of the cost of the asset into an expense.

Study Note

A computer may be functioning as well as it did on the day it was purchased four years ago, but because much faster, more efficient computers have become available, the old computer is now obsolete.

Study Note

Depreciation is the allocation of the acquisition cost of a plant asset, and any similarity between undepreciated cost and current market value is pure coincidence.

- **Depreciation is not a process of valuation.** Accounting records are not indicators of changing price levels; they are kept in accordance with the cost principle. Because of an advantageous purchase price and market conditions, the value of a building may increase. Nevertheless, because depreciation is a process of allocation, not valuation, depreciation on the building must continue to be recorded. Eventually, the building will wear out or become obsolete regardless of interim fluctuations in market value.

Factors in Computing Depreciation

Four factors affect the computation of depreciation:

1. **Cost.** As explained earlier, cost is the net purchase price of an asset plus all reasonable and necessary expenditures to get it in place and ready for use.
2. **Residual value. Residual value** is the portion of an asset's acquisition cost that a company expects to recover when it disposes of the asset. Other terms used to describe residual value are *salvage value*, *disposal value*, and *trade-in value.*
3. **Depreciable cost. Depreciable cost** is an asset's cost less its residual value. For example, a truck that cost $24,000 and that has a residual value of $6,000 would have a depreciable cost of $18,000. Depreciable cost must be allocated over the useful life of the asset.
4. **Estimated useful life. Estimated useful life** is the total number of service units expected from a long-term asset. Service units may be measured in terms of the years an asset is expected to be used, the units it is expected to produce, the miles it is expected to be driven, or similar measures. In computing an asset's estimated useful life, an accountant should consider all relevant information, including past experience with similar assets, the asset's present condition, the company's repair and maintenance policy, and current technological and industry trends.

Study Note

It is depreciable cost, not acquisition cost, that is allocated over a plant asset's useful life.

Depreciation is recorded at the end of an accounting period with an adjusting entry that takes the following form:

A	= L +	OE
−XXX		−XXX

		Dr.	Cr.
Dec. 31	Depreciation Expense—Asset Name	XXX	
	Accumulated Depreciation—Asset Name		XXX
	To record depreciation for the period		

Methods of Computing Depreciation

Many methods are used to allocate the cost of plant assets to accounting periods through depreciation. Each is appropriate in certain circumstances. The most common methods are the straight-line method, the production method, and an accelerated method known as the declining-balance method.

Straight-Line Method When the **straight-line method** is used to calculate depreciation, the asset's depreciable cost is spread evenly over the estimated useful life of the asset. The straight-line method is based on the assumption that depreciation depends only on the passage of time. The depreciation expense for each period is computed by dividing the depreciable cost (cost of the depreciating asset less its estimated residual value) by the number of accounting periods in the asset's estimated useful life. The rate of depreciation is the same in each year.

FOCUS ON BUSINESS PRACTICE

How Long Is the Useful Life of an Airplane?

Most airlines depreciate their planes over an estimated useful life of 10 to 20 years. But how long will a properly maintained plane really last? Western Airlines paid $3.3 million for a new Boeing 737 in July 1968. More than 78,000 flights and 30 years later, this aircraft was still flying for Vanguard Airlines, a no-frills airline. Among the other airlines that have owned this plane are **Piedmont, Delta,** and **US Airways.** Virtually every part of the plane has been replaced over the years. **Boeing** believes the plane could theoretically make double the number of flights before it is retired.

The useful lives of many types of assets can be extended indefinitely if the assets are correctly maintained, but proper accounting in accordance with the matching rule requires depreciation over a "reasonable" useful life. Each airline that owned the plane would have accounted for the plane in this way.

Study Note

Residual value and useful life are, at best, educated guesses.

Suppose, for example, that a delivery truck cost $20,000 and has an estimated residual value of $2,000 at the end of its estimated useful life of five years. Under the straight-line method, the annual depreciation would be $3,600, calculated as follows:

$$\frac{\text{Cost} - \text{Residual Value}}{\text{Estimated Useful Life}} = \frac{\$20{,}000 - \$2{,}000}{5 \text{ years}} = \$3{,}600 \text{ per year}$$

Table 11-2 shows the depreciation schedule for the five years. Note that in addition to annual depreciation's being the same each year, the accumulated depreciation increases uniformly and the carrying value decreases uniformly until it reaches the estimated residual value.

Study Note

The production method is appropriate when a company has widely fluctuating rates of production. For example, carpet mills often close during the first 2 weeks in July but may run double shifts in September. With the production method, depreciation would be in direct relation to a mill's units of output.

Production Method The **production method** is based on the assumption that depreciation is solely the result of use and that the passage of time plays no role in the process. If we assume that the delivery truck in the previous example has an estimated useful life of 90,000 miles, the depreciation cost per mile would be determined as follows:

$$\frac{\text{Cost} - \text{Residual Value}}{\text{Estimated Units of Useful Life}} = \frac{\$20{,}000 - \$2{,}000}{90{,}000} = \$0.20 \text{ per mile}$$

If the truck was driven 20,000 miles in the first year, 30,000 miles in the second, 10,000 miles in the third, 20,000 miles in the fourth, and 10,000 miles in the fifth, the depreciation schedule for the truck would be as shown in Table 11-3. As you can see, the amount of depreciation each year is directly related to the units

TABLE 11-2
Depreciation Schedule, Straight-Line Method

	Cost	Annual Depreciation	Accumulated Depreciation	Carrying Value
Date of purchase	$20,000	—	—	$20,000
End of first year	20,000	$3,600	$ 3,600	16,400
End of second year	20,000	3,600	7,200	12,800
End of third year	20,000	3,600	10,800	9,200
End of fourth year	20,000	3,600	14,400	5,600
End of fifth year	20,000	3,600	18,000	2,000

TABLE 11-3
Depreciation Schedule, Production Method

	Cost	Miles	Annual Depreciation	Accumulated Depreciation	Carrying Value
Date of purchase	$20,000	—	—	—	$20,000
End of first year	20,000	20,000	$4,000	$ 4,000	16,000
End of second year	20,000	30,000	6,000	10,000	10,000
End of third year	20,000	10,000	2,000	12,000	8,000
End of fourth year	20,000	20,000	4,000	16,000	4,000
End of fifth year	20,000	10,000	2,000	18,000	2,000

of use. The accumulated depreciation increases annually in direct relation to these units, and the carrying value decreases each year until it reaches the estimated residual value.

The production method should be used only when the output of an asset over its useful life can be estimated with reasonable accuracy. In addition, the unit used to measure the estimated useful life of an asset should be appropriate for the asset. For example, the number of items produced may be an appropriate measure for one machine, but the number of hours of use may be a better measure for another.

Study Note

Accelerated depreciation is appropriate for assets that provide the greatest benefits in their early years. Under an accelerated method, depreciation charges will be highest in years when revenue generation from the asset is highest.

Declining-Balance Method An **accelerated method** of depreciation results in relatively large amounts of depreciation in the early years of an asset's life and smaller amounts in later years. This type of method, which is based on the passage of time, assumes that many plant assets are most efficient when new and so provide the greatest benefits in their first years. It is consistent with the matching rule to allocate more depreciation to an asset in its earlier years than to later ones if the benefits it provides in its early years are greater than those it provides later on.

Fast-changing technologies often cause equipment to become obsolescent and lose service value rapidly. In such cases, using an accelerated method is appropriate because it allocates more depreciation to earlier years than to later ones. Another argument in favor of using an accelerated method is that repair expense is likely to increase as an asset ages. Thus, the total of repair and depreciation expense will remain fairly constant over the years. This result naturally assumes that the services received from the asset are roughly equal from year to year.

The **declining-balance method** is the most common accelerated method of depreciation. With this method, depreciation is computed by applying a fixed rate to the carrying value (the declining balance) of a tangible long-term asset. It therefore results in higher depreciation charges in the early years of the asset's life. Although any fixed rate can be used, the most common rate is a percentage equal to twice the straight-line depreciation percentage. When twice the straight-line rate is used, the method is usually called the **double-declining-balance method**.

In our example of the straight-line method, the delivery truck had an estimated useful life of five years, and the annual depreciation rate for the truck was therefore 20 percent (100 percent ÷ 5 years). Under the double-declining-balance method, the fixed rate would be 40 percent (2 × 20 percent). This fixed rate is applied to the carrying value that remains at the end

TABLE 11-4
Depreciation Schedule, Double-Declining-Balance Method

	Cost	Annual Depreciation	Accumulated Depreciation	Carrying Value
Date of purchase	$20,000	—	—	$20,000
End of first year	20,000	(40% × $20,000) = $8,000	$ 8,000	12,000
End of second year	20,000	(40% × $12,000) = 4,800	12,800	7,200
End of third year	20,000	(40% × $ 7,200) = 2,880	15,680	4,320
End of fourth year	20,000	(40% × $ 4,320) = 1,728	17,408	2,592
End of fifth year	20,000	592*		2,000

*Depreciation is limited to the amount necessary to reduce carrying value to residual value: $2,592 (previous carrying value) − $2,000 (residual value) = $592.

Study Note
The double-declining-balance method is the only method presented here in which the residual value is not deducted before beginning the depreciation calculation.

of each year. With this method, the depreciation schedule would be as shown in Table 11-4.

Note that the fixed rate is always applied to the carrying value at the end of the previous year. Depreciation is greatest in the first year and declines each year after that. The depreciation in the last year is limited to the amount necessary to reduce carrying value to residual value.

Comparison of the Three Methods Figure 11-5 compares yearly depreciation and carrying value under the three methods. The graph on the left shows yearly depreciation. As you can see, straight-line depreciation is uniform at $3,600 per year over the 5-year period. The double-declining-balance method begins at $8,000 and decreases each year to amounts that are less than straight-line (ultimately, $592). The production method does not generate a regular pattern because of the random fluctuation of the depreciation from year to year.

The graph on the right side of Figure 11-5 shows the carrying value under the three methods. Each method starts in the same place (cost of $20,000) and ends at the same place (residual value of $2,000). However, the patterns of carrying value during the asset's useful life differ. For instance, the carrying value under the straight-line method is always greater than under the double-declining-balance method, except at the beginning and end of the asset's useful life.

FIGURE 11-5
Graphic Comparison of Three Methods of Determining Depreciation

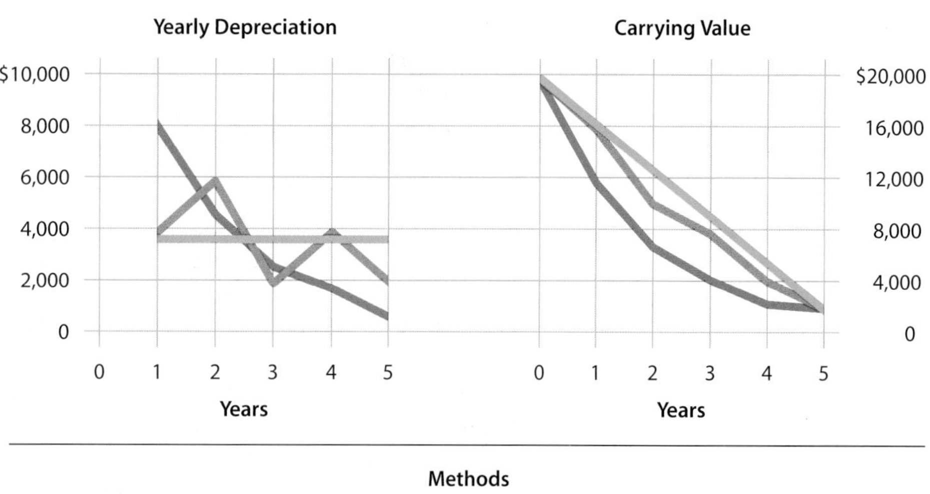

FOCUS ON BUSINESS PRACTICE

Accelerated Methods Save Money!

As shown in Figure 11-6, an AICPA study of 600 large companies found that the overwhelming majority used the straight-line method of depreciation for financial reporting. Only about 8 percent used some type of accelerated method, and 4 percent used the production method. These figures tend to be misleading about the importance of accelerated depreciation methods, however, especially when it comes to income taxes. Federal income tax laws allow either the straight-line method or an accelerated method, and for tax purposes, about 75 percent of the 600 companies studied preferred an accelerated method. Companies use different methods of depreciation for good reason. The straight-line method can be advantageous for financial reporting because it can produce the highest net income, and an accelerated method can be beneficial for tax purposes because it can result in lower income taxes.

Special Issues in Depreciation

Other issues in depreciating assets include group depreciation, depreciation for partial years, revision of depreciation rates, and accelerated cost recovery for tax purposes.

Group Depreciation The estimated useful life of an asset is the average length of time assets of the same type are expected to last. For example, the average useful life of a particular type of machine may be six years, but some machines in this category may last only two or three years, while others may last eight or nine years or longer. For this reason, and for convenience, large companies group similar assets, such as machines, trucks, and pieces of office equipment, to calculate depreciation. This method, called **group depreciation**, is widely used in all fields of industry and business. A survey of large businesses indicated that 65 percent used group depreciation for all or part of their plant assets.[6]

Depreciation for Partial Years To simplify our examples of depreciation, we have assumed that plant assets were purchased at the beginning or end of an accounting period. Usually, however, businesses buy assets when they are needed and sell or discard them when they are no longer needed or useful. The time of year is normally not a factor in the decision. Thus, it is often necessary to calculate depreciation for partial years. Some companies compute depreciation to the nearest month. Others use the half-year convention, in which one-half year of depreciation is taken in the year the asset is purchased and one-half year is taken in the year the asset is sold.

FIGURE 11-6
Depreciation Methods Used by 600 Large Companies for Financial Reporting

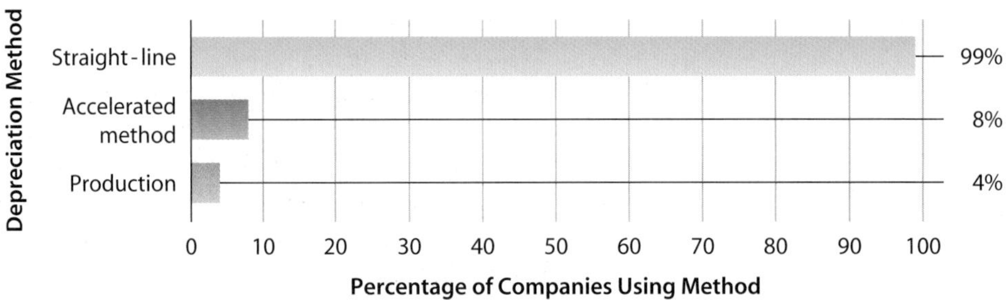

Revision of Depreciation Rates Because a depreciation rate is based on an estimate of an asset's useful life, the periodic depreciation charge is seldom precise. It is sometimes very inadequate or excessive. Such a situation may result from an underestimate or overestimate of the asset's useful life or from a wrong estimate of its residual value. What should a company do when it discovers that a piece of equipment that it has used for several years will last a shorter—or longer—time than originally estimated? Sometimes, it is necessary to revise the estimate of useful life so that the periodic depreciation expense increases or decreases. Then, to reflect the revised situation, the remaining depreciable cost of the asset is spread over the remaining years of useful life.

With this technique, the annual depreciation expense is increased or decreased to reduce the asset's carrying value to its residual value at the end of its remaining useful life. For example, suppose a delivery truck cost $14,000 and has a residual value of $2,000. At the time of the purchase, the truck was expected to last six years, and it was depreciated on the straight-line basis. However, after two years of intensive use, it is determined that the truck will last only two more years, but its residual value at the end of the two years will still be $2,000. In other words, at the end of the second year, the truck's estimated useful life is reduced from six years to four years. At that time, the asset account and its related accumulated depreciation account would be as follows:

Delivery Truck

Dr.		Cr.
Cost	14,000	

Accumulated Depreciation—Delivery Truck

Dr.	Cr.	
	Depreciation, Year 1	2,000
	Depreciation, Year 2	2,000

The remaining depreciable cost is computed as follows:

$$\text{Cost} - \text{Depreciation Already Taken} - \text{Residual Value}$$

$$\$14{,}000 - \$4{,}000 - \$2{,}000 = \$8{,}000$$

The new annual periodic depreciation charge is computed by dividing the remaining depreciable cost of $8,000 by the remaining useful life of two years. Therefore, the new periodic depreciation charge is $4,000. This method of revising depreciation is used widely in industry. It is also supported by *Opinion No. 9* and *Opinion No. 20* of the Accounting Principles Board of the AICPA.

Study Note

For financial reporting purposes, the objective is to measure performance accurately. For tax purposes, the objective is to minimize tax liability.

Special Rules for Tax Purposes Over the years, to encourage businesses to invest in new plant and equipment, Congress has revised the federal income tax law to provide an economic stimulus to the economy. For instance, for tax purposes the law allows rapid write-offs of plant assets through accelerated depreciation, which differs considerably from the depreciation methods most companies use for financial reporting. Tax methods of depreciation are usually not acceptable for financial reporting because the periods over which deductions may be taken are often shorter than the assets' estimated useful lives. The most recent change in the federal income tax law—the **Economic Stimulus Act of 2008**—allows a small company to expense the first $250,000 of equipment expenditures rather than record them as assets and depreciate them over their useful lives. Also, for assets that are subject to depreciation, there is a bonus first-year deduction. These laws are quite complex and are the subject of more advanced courses.

STOP & APPLY >

On January 13, 2010, Chen Company purchased a company car for $47,500. Chen expects the car to last five years or 120,000 miles, with an estimated residual value of $7,500 at the end of that time. During 2011, the car is driven 24,000 miles. Chen's year-end is December 31. Compute the depreciation for 2011 under each of the following methods: (1) straight-line, (2) production, and (3) double-declining-balance.

SOLUTION

Depreciation computed:

(1) Straight-line method: ($47,500 − $7,500) ÷ 5 years = $8,000

(2) Production method: ($47,500 − $7,500) ÷ 120,000 miles = $0.3333 per mile

24,000 miles × $0.3333 = $8,000*

(3) Double-declining-balance method: (1 ÷ 5) × 2 = 0.40

2010: $47,500 × 0.40 = $19,000

2011: ($47,500 − $19,000) × 0.40 = $11,400

*Rounded

Disposal of Depreciable Assets

LO4 Account for the disposal of depreciable assets.

When plant assets are no longer useful because they have physically deteriorated or become obsolete, a company can dispose of them by discarding them, selling them for cash, or trading them in on the purchase of a new asset. Regardless of how a company disposes of a plant asset, it must record depreciation expense for the partial year up to the date of disposal. This step is required because the company used the asset until that date and, under the matching rule, the accounting period should receive the proper allocation of depreciation expense.

In the next sections, we show how a company records each type of disposal. As our example, we assume that KOT Company purchases a machine on January 2, 2009, for $13,000 and plans to depreciate it on a straight-line basis over an estimated useful life of eight years. The machine's residual value at the end of eight years is estimated to be $600. On December 31, 2014, the balances of the relevant accounts are as follows:

Study Note

When it disposes of an asset, a company must bring the depreciation up to date and remove all evidence of ownership of the asset, including the contra account Accumulated Depreciation.

MACHINERY	
Dr.	Cr.
13,000	

ACCUMULATED DEPRECIATION—MACHINERY	
Dr.	Cr.
	9,300

On January 2, 2015, management disposes of the asset.

Discarded Plant Assets

A plant asset rarely lasts exactly as long as its estimated life. If it lasts longer than its estimated life, it is not depreciated past the point at which its carrying value equals its residual value. The purpose of depreciation is to spread the depreciable cost of an asset over its estimated life. Thus, the total accumulated depreciation should never exceed the total depreciable cost. If an asset remains in use beyond the end of its estimated life, its cost and accumulated depreciation remain in the ledger accounts. Proper records will thus be available for maintaining control over plant assets. If the residual value is zero, the carrying value of a fully depreciated asset is zero until the asset is disposed of. If such an asset is discarded, no gain or loss results.

In our example, however, the discarded equipment has a carrying value of $3,700 at the time of its disposal. The carrying value is computed from the T accounts above as machinery of $13,000 less accumulated depreciation of $9,300. A loss equal to the carrying value should be recorded when the machine is discarded, as follows:

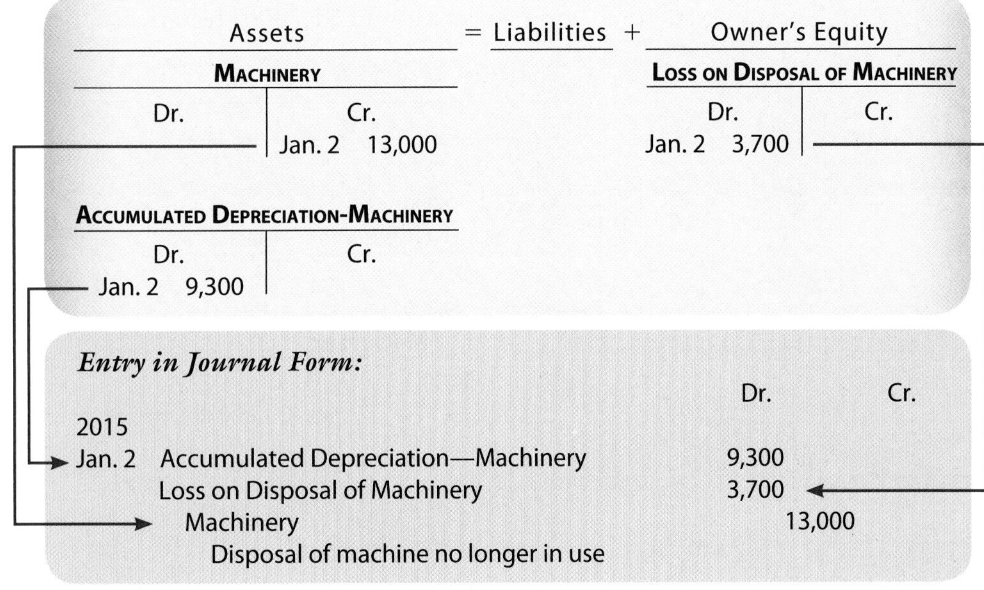

A	= L +	OE
+9,300		−3,700
−13,000		

Gains and losses on disposals of plant assets are classified as other revenues and expenses on the income statement.

Study Note

When an asset is discarded or sold for cash, the gain or loss equals cash received minus the carrying value.

Plant Assets Sold for Cash

The entry to record a plant asset sold for cash is similar to the one just illustrated, except that the receipt of cash should also be recorded. The following entries show how to record the sale of a machine under three assumptions about the selling price. In the first case, the $3,700 cash received is exactly equal to the $3,700 carrying value of the machine; therefore, no gain or loss occurs:

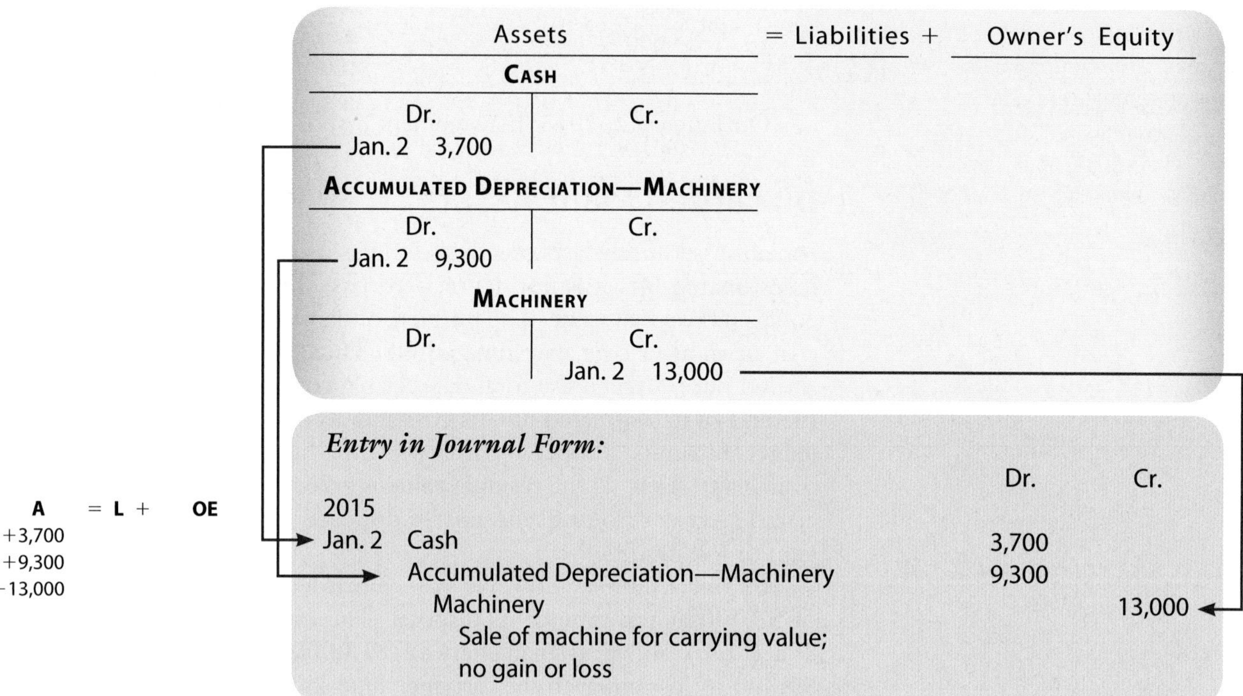

In the second case, the $2,000 cash received is less than the carrying value of $3,700, so a loss of $1,700 is recorded:

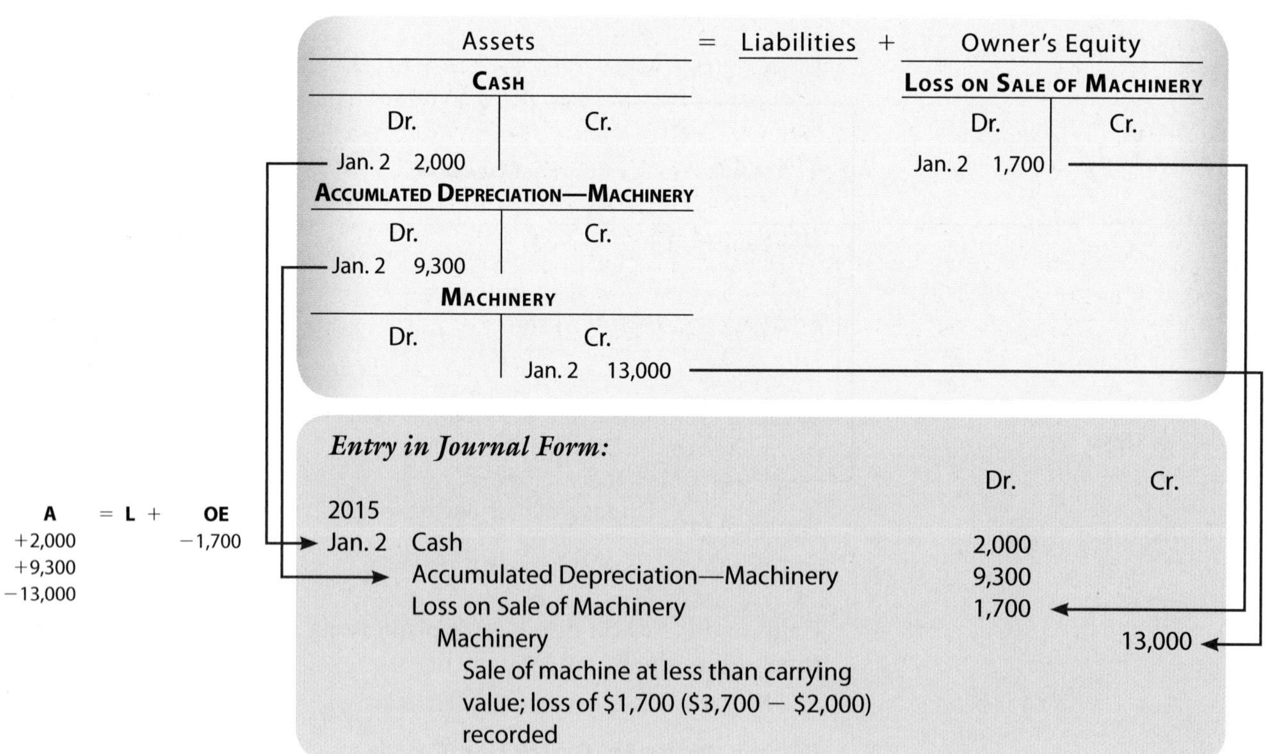

In the third case, the $4,000 cash received exceeds the carrying value of $3,700, so a gain of $300 is recorded:

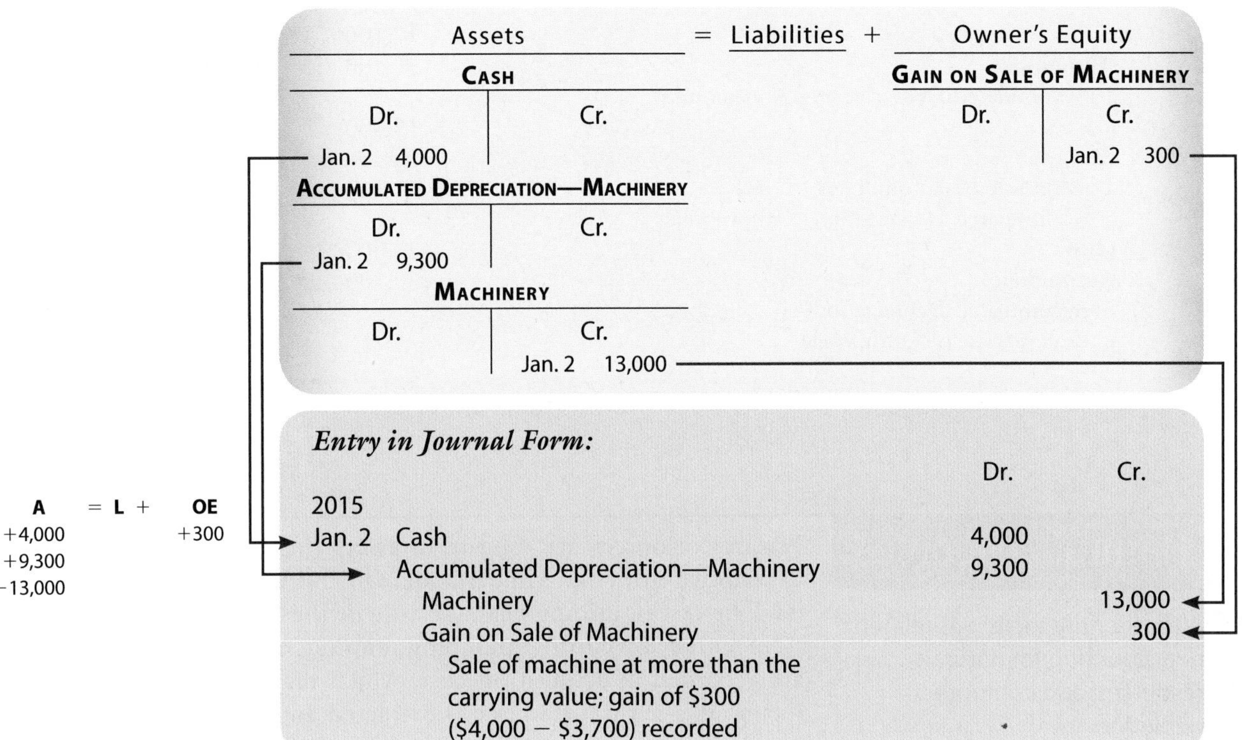

Exchanges of Plant Assets

As we have noted, businesses can dispose of plant assets by trading them in on the purchase of other plant assets. Exchanges may involve similar assets, such as an old machine traded in on a newer model, or dissimilar assets, such as a cement mixer traded in on a truck. In either case, the purchase price is reduced by the amount of the trade-in allowance.

Basically, accounting for exchanges of plant assets is similar to accounting for sales of plant assets for cash. If the trade-in allowance is greater than the asset's carrying value, the company realizes a gain. If the allowance is less, it suffers a loss. (Some special rules apply and are addressed in more advanced courses.)

Chen Company sold a car, that cost $47,500 and on which $30,400 of accumulated depreciation had been recorded, on January 2, the first day of business of the current year. For each of the following assumptions, prepare the entry in journal form (without explanation) for the disposal. (1) The car was sold for $17,100 cash. (2) The car was sold for $15,000 cash. (3) The car was sold for $20,000 cash.

(continued)

SOLUTION

	Dr.	Cr.
(1) Cash	17,100	
Automobile	30,400	
Accumulated Depreciation—Automobile		47,500
(2) Cash	15,000	
Automobile	30,400	
Loss on Sale of Automobile	2,100	
Accumulated Depreciation—Automobile		47,500
(3) Cash	20,000	
Automobile	30,400	
Accumulated Depreciation—Automobile		47,500
Gain on Sale of Automobile		2,900

Natural Resources

LO5 Identify the issues related to accounting for natural resources, and compute depletion.

Natural resources are long-term assets that appear on a balance sheet with descriptive titles like Timberlands, Oil and Gas Reserves, and Mineral Deposits. The distinguishing characteristic of these assets is that they are converted to inventory by cutting, pumping, mining, or other extraction methods. They are recorded at acquisition cost, which may include some costs of development. As a natural resource is extracted and converted to inventory, its asset account must be proportionally reduced. For example, the carrying value of oil reserves on the balance sheet is reduced by the proportional cost of the barrels pumped during the period. As a result, the original cost of the oil reserves is gradually reduced, and depletion is recognized in the amount of the decrease.

Depletion

Depletion refers not only to the exhaustion of a natural resource but also to the proportional allocation of the cost of a natural resource to the units extracted. The way in which the cost of a natural resource is allocated closely resembles the production method of calculating depreciation. When a natural resource is purchased or developed, the total units that will be available, such as barrels of oil, tons of coal, or board-feet of lumber, must be estimated. The depletion cost per unit is determined by dividing the cost of the natural resource (less residual value, if any) by the estimated number of units available. The amount of the depletion cost for each accounting period is then computed by multiplying the depletion cost per unit by the number of units extracted and sold.

For example, suppose a mine was purchased for $3,600,000 and that it has an estimated residual value of $600,000 and contains an estimated 3,000,000 tons of coal. The depletion charge per ton of coal is $1, calculated as follows:

$$\frac{\$3{,}600{,}000 - \$600{,}000}{3{,}000{,}000 \text{ tons}} = \$1 \text{ per ton}$$

Thus, if 230,000 tons of coal are mined and sold during the first year, the depletion charge for the year is $230,000. This charge would be recorded as follows:

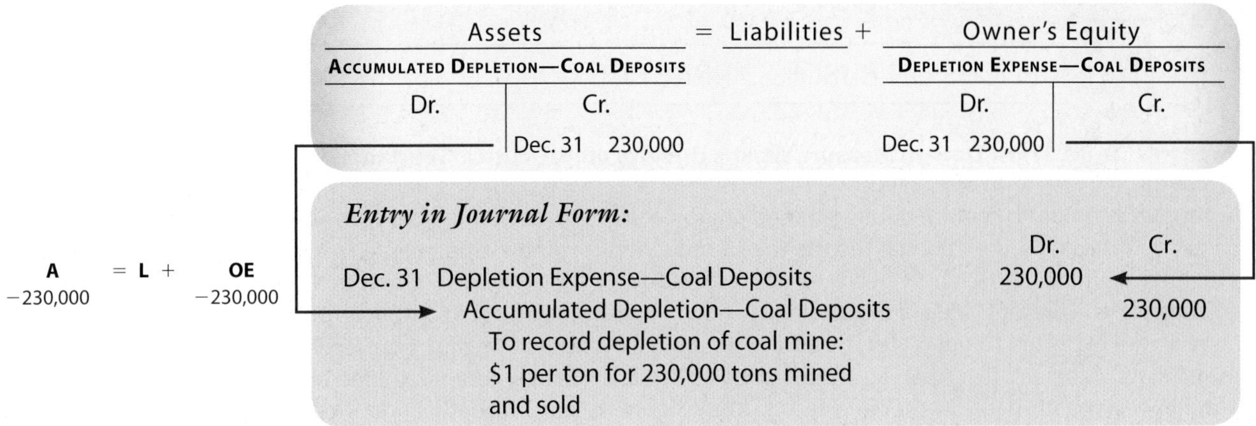

On the balance sheet, data for the mine would be presented as follows:

Coal deposits	$3,600,000	
Less accumulated depletion	230,000	$3,370,000

Sometimes, a natural resource is not sold in the year it is extracted. It is important to note that it would then be recorded as a depletion *expense* in the year it is *sold*. The part not sold is considered inventory.

Depreciation of Related Plant Assets

The extraction of natural resources generally requires special on-site buildings and equipment (e.g., conveyors, drills, and pumps). The useful life of these plant assets may be longer than the estimated time it will take to deplete the resources. However, a company may plan to abandon these assets after all the resources have been extracted because they no longer serve a useful purpose. In this case, they should be depreciated on the same basis as the depletion.

> **Study Note**
> A company may abandon equipment that is still in good working condition because of the expense involved in dismantling the equipment and moving it to another site.

For example, if machinery with a useful life of ten years is installed on an oil field that is expected to be depleted in eight years, the machinery should be depreciated over the eight-year period, using the production method. That way, each year's depreciation will be proportional to the year's depletion. If one-sixth of the oil field's total reserves is pumped in one year, then the depreciation should be one-sixth of the machinery's cost.

If the useful life of a long-term plant asset is less than the expected life of the resource, the shorter life should be used to compute depreciation. In such cases, or when an asset will not be abandoned after all reserves have been depleted, other depreciation methods, such as straight-line or declining-balance, are appropriate.

Development and Exploration Costs in the Oil and Gas Industry

The costs of exploring and developing oil and gas resources can be accounted for under one of two methods. Under **successful efforts accounting**, the cost of successful exploration—for example, producing an oil well—is a cost of the resource. It should be recorded as an asset and depleted over the estimated life of the resource. The cost of an unsuccessful exploration—such as the cost of a dry well—is written off immediately as a loss. Because of these immediate write-offs, successful efforts accounting is considered the more conservative method and is used by most large oil companies.

FOCUS ON BUSINESS PRACTICE

How Do You Measure What's Underground? With a Good Guess.

Accounting standards require publicly traded energy companies to disclose in their annual reports their production activities, estimates of their proven oil and gas reserves, and estimates of the present value of the future cash flows those reserves are expected to generate. The figures are not easy to estimate. After all, the reserves are often miles underground or beneath deep water. As a result, these figures are considered "supplementary" and not reliable enough to be audited independently. Nevertheless, it appears that some companies, including **Royal Dutch/Shell Group**, have overestimated their reserves and thus overestimated their future prospects. Apparently, some managers at Royal Dutch/Shell Group receive bonuses based on the amount of new reserves added to the annual report. When the company recently announced that it was reducing its reported reserves by 20 percent, the price of its stock dropped.[7]

On the other hand, smaller, independent oil companies argue that the cost of dry wells is part of the overall cost of the systematic development of an oil field and is thus a part of the cost of producing wells. Under the **full-costing method,** all costs, including the cost of dry wells, are recorded as assets and depleted over the estimated life of the producing resources. This method tends to improve a company's earnings performance in its early years.

The Financial Accounting Standards Board permits the use of either method.[8]

STOP & APPLY >

Ouyang Mining Company paid $8,800,000 for land containing an estimated 40 million tons of ore. The land without the ore is estimated to be worth $2,000,000. The company spent $1,380,000 to erect buildings on the site and $2,400,000 on installing equipment. The buildings have an estimated useful life of 30 years, and the equipment has an estimated useful life of 10 years. Because of the remote location, neither the buildings nor the equipment has a residual value. The company expects that it can mine all the usable ore in 10 years. During its first year of operation, it mined and sold 2,800,000 tons of ore.

1. Compute the depletion charge per ton.
2. Compute the depletion expense that Ouyang Mining should record for its first year of operation.
3. Determine the depreciation expense for the year for the buildings, making it proportional to the depletion.
4. Determine the depreciation expense for the year for the equipment under two alternatives: (a) making the expense proportional to the depletion, and (b) using the straight-line method.

SOLUTION

1. $\dfrac{\$8{,}800{,}000 - \$2{,}000{,}000}{40{,}000{,}000 \text{ tons}} = \$0.17 \text{ per ton}$

2. 2,800,000 tons × $0.17 per ton = $476,000

3. $\dfrac{2{,}800{,}000 \text{ tons}}{40{,}000{,}000 \text{ tons}} \times \$1{,}380{,}000 = \$96{,}600$

4. a. $\dfrac{2{,}800{,}000 \text{ tons}}{40{,}000{,}000 \text{ tons}} \times \$2{,}400{,}000 = \$168{,}000$

b. $\dfrac{\$2{,}400{,}000}{10 \text{ years}} \times 1 \text{ year} = \$240{,}000$

Intangible Assets

LO6 Identify the issues related to accounting for intangible assets, including research and development costs and goodwill.

An intangible asset is both long term and nonphysical. Its value comes from the long-term rights or advantages it affords its owner. Table 11-5 describes the most common types of intangible assets—goodwill, trademarks and brand names, copyrights, patents, franchises and licenses, leaseholds, software, noncompete covenants, and customer lists—and their accounting treatment. Like intangible assets, some current assets—for example, accounts receivable and certain prepaid expenses—have no physical substance, but because current assets are short term, they are not classified as intangible assets.

TABLE 11-5 Accounting for Intangible Assets

Type	Description	Usual Accounting Treatment
	Subject to Amortization and Annual Impairment Test	
Copyright	An exclusive right granted by the federal government to reproduce and sell literary, musical, and other artistic materials and computer programs for a period of the author's life plus 70 years.	Record at acquisition cost, and amortize over the asset's useful life, which is often much shorter than its legal life. For example, the cost of paperback rights to a popular novel would typically be amortized over a useful life of 2 to 4 years.
Patent	An exclusive right granted by the federal government for a period of 20 years to make a particular product or use a specific process. A design may be granted a patent for 14 years.	The cost of successfully defending a patent in a patent infringement suit is added to the acquisition cost of the patent. Amortize over the asset's useful life, which may be less than its legal life.
Leasehold	A right to occupy land or buildings under a long-term rental contract. For example, if Company A sells its right to use a retail location to Company B for 10 years, Company B has purchased a leasehold.	Company B debits Leasehold for the amount of the purchase price and amortizes it over the life of the leasehold (10 years).
Software	Capitalized costs of computer programs developed for sale, lease, or internal use.	Record the amount of capitalizable production costs, and amortize over the estimated economic life of the product.
Noncompete covenant	A contract limiting the rights of others to compete in a specific industry or line of business for a specified period.	Record at acquisition cost, and amortize over the contract period.
Customer list	A list of customers or subscribers.	Debit Customer Lists for amount paid, and amortize over the asset's expected life.
	Subject to Annual Impairment Test Only	
Goodwill	The excess of the amount paid for a business over the fair market value of the business's net assets.	Debit Goodwill for the acquisition cost, and review impairment annually.
Trademark, Brand name	A registered symbol or name that can be used only by its owner to identify a product or service.	Debit Trademark or Brand Name for the acquisition cost, and amortize it over a reasonable life.
Franchise, License	A right to an exclusive territory or market, or the right to use a formula, technique, process, or design.	Debit Franchise or License for the acquisition cost, and amortize it over a reasonable life, not to exceed 40 years.

Source: Accounting for Intangible Assets: From "Accounting Trends & Techniques" (New York: AICPA, 2007).

FIGURE 11-7
Intangible Assets Reported by 600 Large Companies

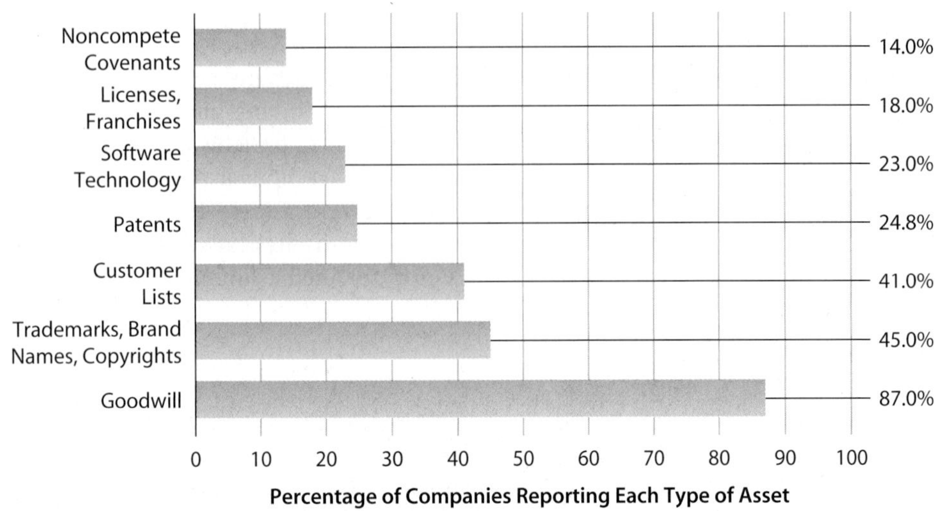

Source: Data from American Institute of Certified Public Accountants, *Accounting Trends & Techniques* (New York: AICPA, 2007).

Figure 11-7 shows the percentage of companies that report the various types of intangible assets. For some companies, intangible assets make up a substantial portion of total assets. For example, **Apple Computer**'s goodwill, other acquired intangible assets, and capitalized software costs amounted to $420 million in 2007. How these assets are accounted for has a major effect on Apple's performance.

The purchase of an intangible asset is a special kind of capital expenditure. Such assets are accounted for at acquisition cost—that is, the amount that a company paid for them. Some intangible assets, such as goodwill and trademarks, may be acquired at little or no cost. Even though these assets may have great value and be needed for profitable operations, a company should include them on its balance sheet only if it purchased them from another party at a price established in the marketplace. When a company develops its own intangible assets, it should record the costs of development as expenses. An exception is the cost of internally developed computer software after a working prototype of the software has been developed.

Purchased intangible assets are recorded at cost, or at fair value when purchased as part of a group of assets. The useful life of an intangible asset is the

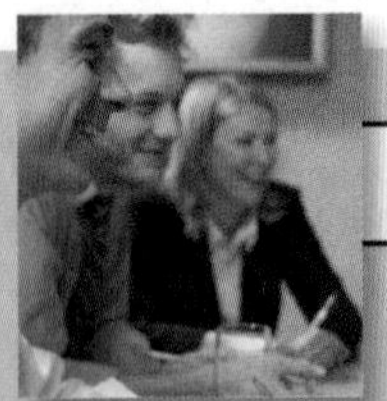

FOCUS ON BUSINESS PRACTICE

Who's Number-One in Brands?

Brands are intangible assets that often do not appear on a company's balance sheet because rather than purchasing them, the company has developed them over time. A report attempted to value brands by the discounted present value of future cash flows.[9] According to the report, the 10 most valuable brands in the world were as follows:

Coca-Cola	**Nokia**
Microsoft	**Toyota**
IBM	**Disney**
GE	**McDonald's**
Intel	**Mercedes-Benz**

Coca-Cola's brand was valued at almost $67 billion, whereas the Mercedes-Benz brand was valued at $22 billion.

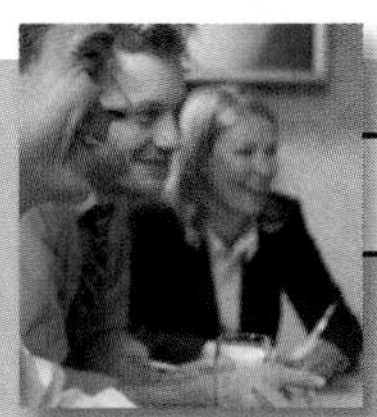

FOCUS ON BUSINESS PRACTICE

Should a Customer List Be Amortized?

One of the most valuable intangible assets some companies have is a list of customers. The Internal Revenue Service has argued that a customer list has an *indefinite useful life* and therefore cannot be used to provide tax deductions through amortization, but the U.S. Supreme Court has upheld the right to amortize the value of a customer list, arguing that it has a *limited useful life*. This ruling has benefited businesses that purchase everything from bank deposits to pharmacy prescription files. For example, **The New York Times Company**, a major newspaper, has spent $221 million on subscriber lists and amortized them to the extent of $196 million, leaving a carrying value of $25 million.[10]

period over which the asset is expected to contribute to future cash flows of the entity. The useful life may be definite or indefinite.[11]

- **Definite useful life.** A definite useful life means the useful life is subject to a legal limit or can be reasonably estimated. Examples include patents, copyrights, and leaseholds. Often the estimated useful lives of these assets are less than their legal limits. The cost of an intangible asset with a definite useful life should be allocated to expense through periodic amortization over its useful life in the same way that a building is depreciated.
- **Indefinite useful life.** An indefinite useful life means that the useful life of the asset is not limited by legal, regulatory, contractual, competitive, economic, or other factors. This definition does not imply that these assets last forever. Examples can include trademarks and brands. The costs of intangible assets with an indefinite life are not amortized as long as circumstances continue to support an indefinite life.

Study Note

The cost of mailing lists may be recorded as an asset because the mailing lists will be used over and over and will benefit future accounting periods.

All intangible assets, whether definite or indefinite, are subject to an annual impairment test to determine if the assets justify their value on the balance sheet. If it is determined that they have lost some or all of their value in producing future cash flows, they should be written down to their fair value or to zero if they have no fair value. The amount of the write-down is shown on the income statement as an impairment charge (deduction) in determining income from operations.

To illustrate these procedures, suppose Water Bottling Company purchases a patent on a unique bottle cap for $36,000. The purchase would be recorded with an entry of $36,000 to the asset account Patents. (Note that if the company developed the bottle cap internally instead of purchasing the patent, the costs of developing the cap—such as researchers' salaries and the costs of supplies and equipment used in testing—would be expensed as incurred.) Although the patent for the bottle cap will last for 20 years, Water determines that it will sell the product that uses the cap for only six years.

The entry to record the annual amortization expense would be for $6,000 ($36,000 ÷ 6 years). The Patents account is reduced directly by the amount of the amortization expense. This is in contrast to the treatment of other long-term asset accounts, for which depreciation or depletion is accumulated in separate contra accounts.

If the patent becomes worthless before it is fully amortized, the remaining carrying value is written off as a loss by removing it from the Patents account.

Research and Development Costs

Most successful companies carry out research and development (R&D) activities, often within a separate department. Among these activities are development of new products, testing of existing and proposed products, and pure research. The costs of these activities are substantial for many companies. In a recent year, **General Motors** spent $6.6 billion, or about 4 percent of its revenues, on R&D.[12] R&D costs can be even greater in high-tech fields like pharmaceuticals. For example, **Abbott Laboratories** recently spent $2.3 billion, or 10.2 percent of its revenues, on R&D.[13]

The Financial Accounting Standards Board requires that all R&D costs be treated as revenue expenditures and charged to expense in the period in which they are incurred.[14] The reasoning behind this requirement is that it is too hard to trace specific costs to specific profitable developments. Also, the costs of research and development are continuous and necessary for the success of a business and so should be treated as current expenses. To support this conclusion, the FASB cited studies showing that 30 to 90 percent of all new products fail and that 75 percent of new-product expenses go to unsuccessful products. Thus, their costs do not represent future benefits.

Computer Software Costs

The costs that companies incur in developing computer software for sale or lease or for their own internal use are considered research and development costs until the product has proved technologically feasible. Thus, costs incurred before that point should be charged to expense as they are incurred. A product is deemed technologically feasible when a detailed working program has been designed. Once that occurs, all software production costs are recorded as assets and are amortized over the software's estimated economic life using the straight-line method. Capitalized software costs are becoming more prevalent and, as shown in Figure 11-7, appear on 21 percent of 600 large companies' balance sheets. If at any time a company cannot expect to realize from the software the amount of the unamortized costs on the balance sheet, the asset should be written down to the amount expected to be realized.[15]

Goodwill

Goodwill means different things to different people. Generally, it refers to a company's good reputation. From an accounting standpoint, goodwill exists when a purchaser pays more for a business than the fair market value of the business's net assets. In other words, the purchaser would pay less if it bought the assets separately. Most businesses are worth more as going concerns than as collections of assets.

When the purchase price of a business is more than the fair market value of its physical assets, the business must have intangible assets. If it does not have patents, copyrights, trademarks, or other identifiable intangible assets of value, the excess payment is assumed to be for goodwill. Goodwill reflects all the factors that allow a company to earn a higher-than-market rate of return on its assets, including customer satisfaction, good management, manufacturing efficiency, the advantages of having a monopoly, good locations, and good employee relations. The payment above and beyond the fair market value of the tangible assets and other specific intangible assets is properly recorded in the Goodwill account.

The FASB requires that purchased goodwill be reported as a separate line item on the balance sheet and that it be reviewed annually for impairment. If the fair value of goodwill is less than its carrying value on the balance sheet, goodwill

FOCUS ON BUSINESS PRACTICE

Wake up, Goodwill Is Growing!

As Figure 11-7 shows, 87 percent of 600 large companies separately report goodwill as an asset. Because much of the growth of these companies has come through purchasing other companies, goodwill as a percentage of total assets has also grown. As the table at the right shows, the amount of goodwill can be material.[16]

	Goodwill (in billions)	Percentage of Total Assets
General Mills	\$6,835	38%
Heinz	\$2,835	28%
Cisco Systems	\$9,298	21%

is considered impaired. In that case, it is reduced to its fair value, and the impairment charge is reported on the income statement. A company can perform the fair value measurement for each reporting unit at any time as long as the measurement date is consistent from year to year.[17]

A company should record goodwill only when it acquires a controlling interest in another business. The amount to be recorded as goodwill can be determined by writing the identifiable net assets up to their fair market values at the time of purchase and subtracting the total from the purchase price. For example, suppose a company pays \$11,400,000 to purchase another business. If the net assets of the business (total assets − total liabilities) are fairly valued at \$10,000,000, then the amount of the goodwill is \$1,400,000 (\$11,400,000 − \$10,000,000).

STOP & APPLY >

For each of the following intangible assets, indicate (a) if the asset is to be amortized over its useful life or (b) if the asset is not amortized but only subject to annual impairment test:

1. Goodwill
2. Copyright
3. Brand name
4. Patent
5. Trademark

SOLUTION

1. b; 2. a; 3. b; 4. a; 5. b

▸ CAMPUS CLEANERS: REVIEW PROBLEM

Comparison of Depreciation Methods
LO3 LO4

In the Decision Point at the beginning of this chapter, we pointed out that Campus Cleaners had a choice to make about which depreciation method it would use in allocating the cost of its delivery van over a 5-year period. We asked these questions:

- What long-term assets other than a delivery van might Campus Cleaners have, and how should it account for them?
- What are the three common methods of calculating depreciation on tangible long-term assets, and how do the patterns of depreciation that they produce differ?

In addition to its delivery van, Campus Cleaners' tangible long-term assets might include land, buildings, and equipment, as well as leasehold improvements if it operates out of a rented space. All these assets would be accounted for through depreciation. Campus Cleaners might also have intangible assets, such as a trademark, which would be accounted for through amortization. In accounting for its delivery van, Campus Cleaners would have to determine the purchase price, useful life, residual value, and costs of repairs, maintenance, and other expenses incurred in operating the van. The company could use any one of the three common methods of calculating depreciation to allocate the cost of the van to the accounting periods in which the van serves customers.

Required

1. Compute the depreciation expense and carrying value of the delivery van for 2010 to 2014 using the following methods: (a) straight-line, (b) production, and (c) double-declining balance.
2. Assuming the straight-line method is used and that the delivery van is sold for $5,000 on December 31, 2014, show the entry in journal form to record the sale.
3. User insight: What conclusions can you draw from the patterns of yearly depreciation?

Answers to Review Problem

1. Depreciation computed:

	A	B	C	D	E	F	G
1	Depreciation Method	Year	Computation	Depreciation	Carrying Value		
2	a. Straight-line	2010	$27,000 ÷ 5	$5,400	$23,600		
3		2011	27,000 ÷ 5	5,400	18,200		
4		2012	27,000 ÷ 5	5,400	12,800		
5		2013	27,000 ÷ 5	5,400	7,400		
6		2014	27,000 ÷ 5	5,400	2,000		
7							
8	b. Production	2010	$27,000 × 30,000	$5,400	$23,600		
9			150,000				
10							
11		2011	27,000 × 52,500	9,450	14,150		
12			150,000				
13							
14		2012	27,000 × 45,000	8,100	6,050		
15			150,000				
16							
17		2013	27,000 × 15,000	2,700	3,350		
18			150,000				
19							
20		2014	27,000 × 7,500	1,350	2,000		
21			150,000				
22							
23	c. Double - declining - balance	2010	$29,000 × 0.40	$11,600	$17,400		
24		2011	17,400 × 0.40	6,960	10,440		
25		2012	10,440 × 0.40	4,176	6,264		
26		2013	6,264 × 0.40	2,506	3,758		
27		2014	$3,758 − $2,000	1,758*	2,000		
28							
29	* Remaining depreciation to reduce carrying value to residual value ($3,758 −$2,000)						
30							

2. Sale recorded on December 31, 2014:

	A	B	C	D
1	Dec. 31	Cash	5,000	
2		Accumulated Depreciation—Delivery Van	27,000	
3		Delivery Van		29,000
4		Gain on Sale of Delivery Van		3,000
5		Sale of delivery van		

3. The pattern of depreciation for the straight-line method differs significantly from the pattern for the double-declining-balance method. In the earlier years, the amount of depreciation under the double-declining-balance method is significantly greater than the amount under the straight-line method. In the later years, the opposite is true. The carrying value under the straight-line method is greater than under the double-declining-balance method at the end of all years except the fifth year. Depreciation under the production method differs from depreciation under the other methods in that it follows no regular pattern. It varies with the amount of use. Consequently, depreciation is greatest in 2011 and 2012, which are the years of greatest use. Use declined significantly in the last two years.

LO1 Define *long-term assets*, and explain the management issues related to them.

Long-term assets have a useful life of more than one year, are used in the operation of a business, and are not intended for resale. They can be tangible or intangible. In the former category are land, plant assets, and natural resources. In the latter are patents, trademarks, franchises, and other rights, as well as goodwill. The management issues related to long-term assets include decisions about whether to acquire the assets, how to finance them, and how to account for them.

LO2 Distinguish between *capital expenditures* and *revenue expenditures*, and account for the cost of property, plant, and equipment.

Capital expenditures are recorded as assets, whereas revenue expenditures are recorded as expenses of the current period. Capital expenditures include not only outlays for plant assets, natural resources, and intangible assets, but also expenditures for additions, betterments, and extraordinary repairs that increase an asset's residual value or extend its useful life. Revenue expenditures are made for ordinary repairs and maintenance. The error of classifying a capital expenditure as a revenue expenditure, or vice versa, has an important effect on net income.

The acquisition cost of property, plant, and equipment includes all expenditures reasonable and necessary to get the asset in place and ready for use. Among these expenditures are purchase price, installation cost, freight charges, and insurance during transit. The acquisition cost of a plant asset is allocated over the asset's useful life.

LO3 Compute depreciation under the straight-line, production, and declining-balance methods.

Depreciation—the periodic allocation of the cost of a plant asset over its estimated useful life—is commonly computed by using the straight-line method, the production method, or an accelerated method. The straight-line method is related directly to the passage of time, whereas the production method is related directly to use or output. An accelerated method, which results in relatively large amounts of depreciation in earlier years and reduced amounts in later years, is based on the assumption that plant assets provide greater economic benefits in their earlier years than in later ones. The most common accelerated method is the declining-balance method.

LO4 Account for the disposal of depreciable assets.

A company can dispose of a long-term plant asset by discarding or selling it or exchanging it for another asset. Regardless of the way in which a company disposes of such an asset, it must record depreciation up to the date of disposal. To record the disposal, it must remove the carrying value from the asset account and the depreciation to date from the accumulated depreciation account. When a company sells a depreciable long-term asset at a price that differs from its carrying value, it should report the gain or loss on its income statement. In recording exchanges of similar plant assets, a gain or loss may arise.

LO5 Identify the issues related to accounting for natural resources, and compute depletion.

Natural resources are depletable assets that are converted to inventory by cutting, pumping, mining, or other forms of extraction. They are recorded at cost as long-term assets. As natural resources are sold, their costs are allocated as expenses through depletion charges. The depletion charge is based on the ratio of the resource extracted to the total estimated resource. A major issue related to this subject is accounting for oil and gas reserves.

LO6 Identify the issues related to accounting for intangible assets, including research and development costs and goodwill.

The purchase of an intangible asset should be treated as a capital expenditure and recorded at acquisition cost. All intangible assets are subject to annual tests for impairment of value. Intangible assets with a definite life are also amortized annually. The FASB requires that research and development costs be treated as revenue expenditures and charged as expenses in the periods of expenditure. Software costs are treated as research and development costs and expensed until a feasible working program is developed, after which time the costs may be capitalized and amortized over a reasonable estimated life. Goodwill is the excess of the amount paid for a business over the fair market value of the net assets and is usually related to the business's superior earning potential. It should be recorded only when a company purchases an entire business, and it should be reviewed annually for possible impairment.

REVIEW of Concepts and Terminology

The following concepts and terms were introduced in this chapter:

Accelerated method 486 (LO3)

Additions 479 (LO2)

Amortization 475 (LO1)

Asset impairment 475 (LO1)

Betterments 480 (LO2)

Brand name 497 (LO6)

Capital expenditure 479 (LO2)

Carrying value 474 (LO1)

Copyright 497 (LO6)

Customer list 497 (LO6)

Declining-balance method 486 (LO3)

Depletion 475 (LO1)

Depreciable cost 484 (LO3)

Depreciation 475 (LO1)

Double-declining-balance method 486 (LO3)

Economic Stimulus Act of 2008 489 (LO3)

Estimated useful life 484 (LO3)

Expenditure 479 (LO2)

Extraordinary repairs 480 (LO2)

Franchise 497 (LO6)

Free cash flow 477 (LO1)

Full-costing method 496 (LO5)

Goodwill 497 (LO6)

Group depreciation 488 (LO3)

Intangible assets 475 (LO1)

Leasehold 497 (LO6)

Leasehold improvements 482 (LO2)

License 497 (LO6)

Long-term assets 474 (LO1)

Natural resources 475 (LO1)

Noncompete covenant 497 (LO6)

Obsolescence 483 (LO3)

Patent 497 (LO6)

Physical deterioration 483 (LO3)

Production method 485 (LO3)

Residual value 484 (LO3)

Revenue expenditure 479 (LO2)

Software 497 (LO6)

Straight-line method 484 (LO3)

Successful efforts accounting 495 (LO5)

Tangible assets 479 (LO1)

Trademark 497 (LO6)

CHAPTER ASSIGNMENTS

BUILDING Your Basic Knowledge and Skills

Short Exercises

LO1 **Management Issues**

SE 1. Indicate whether each of the following actions is primarily related to (a) acquisition of long-term assets, (b) evaluating the adequacy of financing of long-term assets, or (c) applying the matching rule to long-term assets.

1. Deciding between common stock and long-term notes for the raising of funds
2. Relating the acquisition cost of a long-term asset to the cash flows generated by the asset
3. Determining how long an asset will benefit the company
4. Deciding to use cash flows from operations to purchase long-term assets
5. Determining how much an asset will sell for when it is no longer useful to the company
6. Calculating free cash flow

LO1 **Free Cash Flow**

SE 2. Rak Corporation had cash flows from operating activities during the past year of $97,000. During the year, the company expended $12,500 for dividends; expended $79,000 for property, plant, and equipment; and sold property, plant, and equipment for $6,000. Calculate the company's free cash flow. What does the result tell you about the company?

LO2 **Determining Cost of Long-Term Assets**

SE 3. Smith Auto purchased a neighboring lot for a new building and parking lot. Indicate whether each of the following expenditures is properly charged to (a) Land, (b) Land Improvements, or (c) Buildings.

1. Paving costs
2. Architects' fee for building design
3. Cost of clearing the property
4. Cost of the property
5. Building construction costs
6. Lights around the property
7. Building permit
8. Interest on the construction loan

LO2 **Group Purchase**

SE 4. Lian Company purchased property with a warehouse and parking lot for $1,500,000. An appraiser valued the components of the property if purchased separately as follows:

Land	$ 400,000
Land improvements	200,000
Building	1,000,000
Total	$1,600,000

Determine the cost to be assigned to each component.

LO3 **Straight-Line Method**

SE 5. Kelly's Fitness Center purchased a new step machine for $16,500. The apparatus is expected to last four years and have a residual value of $1,500. What will the depreciation expense be for each year under the straight-line method?

LO3 Production Method

SE 6. Assume that the step machine in **SE 5** has an estimated useful life of 10,000 hours and was used for 2,400 hours in year 1, 2,000 hours in year 2, 2,200 hours in year 3, and 1,400 hours in year 4. How much would depreciation expense be in each year?

LO3 Double-Declining-Balance Method

SE 7. Assume that the step machine in **SE 5** is depreciated using the double-declining-balance method. How much would depreciation expense be in each year?

LO4 Disposal of Plant Assets: No Trade-In

SE 8. Alarico Printing owned a piece of equipment that cost $16,200 and on which it had recorded $9,000 of accumulated depreciation. The company disposed of the equipment on January 2, the first day of business of the current year.

1. Calculate the carrying value of the equipment.
2. Calculate the gain or loss on the disposal under each of the following assumptions:
   a. The equipment was discarded as having no value.
   b. The equipment was sold for $3,000 cash.
   c. The equipment was sold for $8,000 cash.

LO5 Natural Resources

SE 9. Narda Company purchased land containing an estimated 4,000,000 tons of ore for $16,000,000. The land will be worth $2,400,000 without the ore after 8 years of active mining. Although the equipment needed for the mining will have a useful life of 20 years, it is not expected to be usable and will have no value after the mining on this site is complete. Compute the depletion charge per ton and the amount of depletion expense for the first year of operation, assuming that 600,000 tons of ore are mined and sold. Also, compute the first-year depreciation on the mining equipment using the production method, assuming a cost of $19,200,000 with no residual value.

LO6 Intangible Assets: Computer Software

SE 10. Danya Company has created a new software application for PCs. Its costs during research and development were $250,000. Its costs after the working program was developed were $175,000. Although the company's copyright may be amortized over 40 years, management believes that the product will be viable for only 5 years. How should the costs be accounted for? At what value will the software appear on the balance sheet after 1 year?

Exercises

LO1 LO2 LO3 Discussion Questions

E 1. Develop a brief answer for each of the following questions:

1. Is carrying value ever the same as market value?
2. What major advantage does a company that has positive free cash flow have over a company that has negative free cash flow?
3. What incentive does a company have to allocate more of a group purchase price to land than to building?
4. Which depreciation method would best reflect the risk of obsolescence from rapid technological changes?

LO4 LO5 LO6

Discussion Questions

E 2. Develop a brief answer for each of the following questions:

1. When would the disposal of a long-term asset result in no gain or loss?
2. When would annual depletion not equal depletion expense?
3. Why would a firm amortize a patent over fewer years than the patent's life?
4. Why would a company spend millions of dollars on goodwill?

LO1

Management Issues

E 3. Indicate whether each of the following actions is primarily related to (a) acquisition of long-term assets, (b) evaluating the financing of long-term assets, or (c) applying the matching rule to long-term assets.

1. Deciding to use the production method of depreciation
2. Allocating costs on a group purchase
3. Determining the total units a machine will produce
4. Deciding to borrow funds to purchase equipment
5. Estimating the savings a new machine will produce and comparing that amount to cost
6. Examining the trend of free cash flow over several years
7. Deciding whether to rent or buy a piece of equipment

LO1

Purchase Decision—Present Value Analysis

E 4. Management is considering the purchase of a new machine for a cost of \$12,000. It is estimated that the machine will generate positive net cash flows of \$3,000 per year for five years and will have a disposal price at the end of that time of \$1,000. Assuming an interest rate of 9 percent, determine if management should purchase the machine. Use Tables 1 and 2 in the appendix on present value tables to determine the net present value of the new machine.

LO1

Free Cash Flow

E 5. Zedek Corporation had net cash flows from operating activities during the past year of \$216,000. During the year, the company expended \$462,000 for property, plant, and equipment; sold property, plant, and equipment for \$54,000; and paid dividends of \$50,000. Calculate the company's free cash flow. What does the result tell you about the company?

LO2

Special Types of Capital Expenditures

E 6. Tell whether each of the following transactions related to an office building is a revenue expenditure (RE) or a capital expenditure (CE). In addition, indicate whether each transaction is an ordinary repair (OR), an extraordinary repair (ER), an addition (A), a betterment (B), or none of these (N).

1. The hallways and ceilings in the building are repainted at a cost of \$6,250.
2. The hallways, which have tile floors, are carpeted at a cost of \$28,000.
3. A new wing is added to the building at a cost of \$105,470.
4. Furniture is purchased for the entrance to the building at a cost of \$13,250.
5. The air-conditioning system is overhauled at a cost of \$21,153. The overhaul extends the useful life of the air-conditioning system by 10 years.
6. A cleaning firm is paid \$150 per week to clean the newly installed carpets.

LO2

Determining Cost of Long-Term Assets

E 7. Colletta Manufacturing purchased land next to its factory to be used as a parking lot. The expenditures incurred by the company were as follows: purchase price, \$600,000; broker's fees, \$48,000; title search and other fees, \$4,400; demolition of a cottage on the property, \$16,000; general grading of property, \$8,400; paving parking lots, \$80,000; lighting for parking lots, \$64,000; and signs for parking lots, $12,800. Determine the amounts that should be debited to the Land account and the Land Improvements account.

LO2 **Group Purchase**

E 8. Joanna Mak purchased a car wash for $480,000. If purchased separately, the land would have cost $120,000, the building $270,000, and the equipment $210,000. Determine the amount that should be recorded in the new business's records for land, building, and equipment.

LO2 LO3 **Cost of Long-Term Asset and Depreciation**

E 9. Nick Santiago purchased a used tractor for $35,000. Before the tractor could be used, it required new tires, which cost $2,200, and an overhaul, which cost $2,800. Its first tank of fuel cost $150. The tractor is expected to last six years and have a residual value of $4,000. Determine the cost and depreciable cost of the tractor and calculate the first year's depreciation under the straight-line method.

LO3 **Depreciation Methods**

E 10. On January 13, 2010, Silverio Oil Company purchased a drilling truck for $45,000. Silverio expects the truck to last five years or 200,000 miles, with an estimated residual value of $7,500 at the end of that time. During 2011, the truck is driven 48,000 miles. Silverio's year end is December 31. Compute the depreciation for 2011 under each of the following methods: (1) straight-line, (2) production, and (3) double-declining-balance. Using the amount computed in (3), prepare the entry in journal form to record depreciation expense for the second year, and show how the Drilling Truck account would appear on the balance sheet.

LO3 **Double-Declining-Balance Method**

E 11. Stop Burglar Alarm Systems Company purchased a computer for $2,240. It has an estimated useful life of four years and an estimated residual value of $240. Compute the depreciation charge for each of the four years using the double-declining-balance method.

LO3 **Revision of Depreciation Rates**

E 12. Hope Hospital purchased a special X-ray machine. The machine, which cost $311,560, was expected to last ten years, with an estimated residual value of $31,560. After two years of operation (and depreciation charges using the straight-line method), it became evident that the X-ray machine would last a total of only seven years. The estimated residual value, however, would remain the same. Given this information, determine the new depreciation charge for the third year on the basis of the revised estimated useful life.

LO4 **Disposal of Plant Assets**

E 13. A piece of equipment that cost $32,400 and on which $18,000 of accumulated depreciation had been recorded was disposed of on January 2, the first day of business of the current year. For each of the following assumptions, compute the gain or loss on the disposal.

1. The equipment was discarded as having no value.
2. The equipment was sold for $6,000 cash.
3. The equipment was sold for $18,000 cash.

LO4 Disposal of Plant Assets

E 14. Samson Company purchased a computer on January 2, 2009, at a cost of $1,250. The computer is expected to have a useful life of five years and a residual value of $125. Assume that the computer is disposed of on July 1, 2012. Record the depreciation expense for half a year and the disposal under each of the following assumptions:

1. The computer is discarded.
2. The computer is sold for $200.
3. The computer is sold for $550.

LO5 Natural Resource Depletion and Depreciation of Related Plant Assets

E 15. Nelson Company purchased land containing an estimated 2.5 million tons of ore for a cost of $4,400,000. The land without the ore is estimated to be worth $250,000. During its first year of operation, the company mined and sold 375,000 tons of ore. Compute the depletion charge per ton. Compute the depletion expense that Nelson should record for the year.

LO6 Amortization of Copyrights and Trademarks

E 16. The following exercise is about amortizing copyrights and trademarks.

1. Fulton Publishing Company purchased the copyright to a basic computer textbook for $80,000. The usual life of a textbook is about four years. However, the copyright will remain in effect for another 50 years. Calculate the annual amortization of the copyright.
2. Sloan Company purchased a trademark from a well-known supermarket for $640,000. The management of the company argued that the trademark's useful life was indefinite. Explain how the cost should be accounted for.

LO6 Accounting for a Patent

E 17. At the beginning of the fiscal year, Andy Company purchased for $2,060,000 a patent that applies to the manufacture of a unique tamper-proof lid for medicine bottles. Andy incurred legal costs of $900,000 in successfully defending use of the lid by a competitor. Andy estimated that the patent would be valuable for at least ten years.

During the first two years of operations, Andy Company successfully marketed the lid. At the beginning of the third year, a study appeared in a consumer magazine showing that children could in fact remove the lid. As a result, all orders for the lids were canceled, and the patent was rendered worthless.

Prepare entries in journal form to record the following: (a) purchase of the patent; (b) successful defense of the patent; (c) amortization expense for the first year; and (d) write-off of the patent as worthless.

Problems

LO1 LO2 Identification of Long-Term Assets Terminology

P 1. Listed below are common terms associated with long-term assets:

a. Tangible assets
b. Natural resources
c. Intangible assets
d. Additions
e. Betterments
f. Extraordinary repair
g. Depreciation
h. Depletion
i. Amortization
j. Revenue expenditure
k. Free cash flow

Required

1. For each of the following statements, identify the term listed above with which it is associated. (If two terms apply, choose the one that is most closely associated.)
    1. Periodic cost associated with intangible assets
    2. Cost of constructing a new wing on a building
    3. A measure of funds available for expansion
    4. A group of assets encompassing property, plant, and equipment
    5. Cost associated with enhancing a building but not expanding it
    6. Periodic cost associated with tangible assets
    7. A group of assets that gain their value from contracts or rights
    8. Cost of normal repairs to a building
    9. Assets whose value derives from what can be extracted from them
    10. Periodic cost associated with natural resources
    11. Cost of a repair that extends the useful life of a building

User insight ▶ 2. Assuming the company uses cash for all its expenditures, which of the items listed above would you expect to see on the income statement? Which ones would not result in an outlay of cash?

LO2 Determining Cost of Assets

P 2. Siber Computers constructed a new training center in 2010. You have been hired to manage the training center. A review of the accounting records shows the following expenditures debited to an asset account called Training Center:

Attorney's fee, land acquisition	$ 35,200
Cost of land	597,000
Architect's fee, building design	102,000
Building	1,025,000
Parking lot and sidewalk	135,600
Electrical wiring, building	168,000
Landscaping	55,000
Cost of surveying land	8,900
Training equipment, tables, and chairs	136,400
Installation of training equipment	65,600
Cost of grading the land	14,000
Cost of changes in building to soundproof rooms	58,700
Total account balance	$2,401,400

During the center's construction, an employee of Siber Computers worked full-time overseeing the project. He spent two months on the purchase and preparation of the site, six months on the construction, one month on land improvements, and one month on equipment installation and training-room furniture purchase and setup. His salary of $72,000 during this ten-month period was charged to Administrative Expense. The training center was placed in operation on November 1.

Required

1. Prepare a schedule with the following four column (account) headings: Land, Land Improvements, Building, and Equipment. Place each of the above expenditures in the appropriate column. Total the columns.

User insight ▶ 2. What impact does the classification of the items among several accounts have on evaluating the profitability performance of the company?

LO3 LO4 Comparison of Depreciation Methods

P 3. Ivan Manufacturing Company purchased a robot for $360,000 at the beginning of year 1. The robot has an estimated useful life of four years and an estimated residual value of $30,000. The robot, which should last 20,000 hours, was operated 6,000 hours in year 1; 8,000 hours in year 2; 4,000 hours in year 3; and 2,000 hours in year 4.

Required

1. Compute the annual depreciation and carrying value for the robot for each year assuming the following depreciation methods: (a) straight-line, (b) production, and (c) double-declining-balance.
2. If the robot is sold for $375,000 after year 2, what would be the amount of gain or loss under each method?

User insight ▶

3. What conclusions can you draw from the patterns of yearly depreciation and carrying value in requirement 1? Do the three methods differ in their effect on the company's profitability? Do they differ in their effect on the company's operating cash flows? Explain.

LO3 LO4 Comparison of Depreciation Methods

P 4. Roman's Construction Company purchased a new crane for $721,000 at the beginning of year 1. The crane has an estimated residual value of $70,000 and an estimated useful life of six years. The crane is expected to last 20,000 hours. It was used 3,600 hours in year 1; 4,000 hours in year 2; 5,000 hours in year 3; 3,000 hours in year 4; 2,400 hours in year 5; and 2,000 hours in year 6.

Required

1. Compute the annual depreciation and carrying value for the new crane for each of the six years (round to the nearest dollar where necessary) under each of the following methods: (a) straight-line, (b) production, and (c) double-declining-balance.
2. If the crane is sold for $500,000 after year 3, what would be the amount of gain or loss under each method?

User insight ▶

3. Do the three methods differ in their effect on the company's profitability? Do they differ in their effect on the company's operating cash flows? Explain.

LO5 Natural Resource Depletion and Depreciation of Related Plant Assets

P 5. Kulig Company purchased land containing an estimated 10 million tons of ore for a cost of $3,300,000. The land without the ore is estimated to be worth $600,000. The company expects that all the usable ore can be mined in 10 years. Buildings costing $300,000 with an estimated useful life of 20 years were erected on the site. Equipment costing $360,000 with an estimated useful life of 10 years was installed. Because of the remote location, neither the buildings nor the equipment has an estimated residual value. During its first year of operation, the company mined and sold 450,000 tons of ore.

Required

1. Compute the depletion charge per ton.
2. Compute the depletion expense that Kulig should record for the year.
3. Determine the depreciation expense for the year for the buildings, making it proportional to the depletion.
4. Determine the depreciation expense for the year for the equipment under two alternatives: (a) making the expense proportional to the depletion and (b) using the straight-line method.

User insight ▶ 5. Suppose the company mined and sold 250,000 tons of ore (instead of 450,000) during the first year. Would the change in the results in requirement 2 or 3 affect earnings or cash flows? Explain.

Alternate Problems

LO2 Determining Cost of Assets

P 6. Global Company was formed on January 1, 2010, and began constructing a new plant. At the end of 2010, its auditor discovered that all expenditures involving long-term assets had been debited to an account called Fixed Assets. An analysis of the Fixed Assets account, which had a year-end balance of $2,659,732, disclosed that it contained the following items:

Cost of land	$ 320,600
Surveying costs	4,100
Transfer of title and other fees required by the county	920
Broker's fees for land	21,144
Attorney's fees associated with land acquisition	7,048
Cost of removing timber from land	49,600
Cost of grading land	4,200
Cost of digging building foundation	35,100
Architect's fee for building and land improvements (80 percent building)	67,200
Cost of building construction	715,000
Cost of sidewalks	11,400
Cost of parking lots	54,400
Cost of lighting for grounds	80,300
Cost of landscaping	11,800
Cost of machinery	993,000
Shipping cost on machinery	55,300
Cost of installing machinery	176,200
Cost of testing machinery	21,600
Cost of changes in building to comply with safety regulations pertaining to machinery	12,540
Cost of repairing building that was damaged in the installation of machinery	8,900
Cost of medical bill for injury received by employee while installing machinery	2,560
Cost of water damage to building during heavy rains prior to opening the plant for operation	6,820
Account balance	$2,659,732

Global Company sold the timber it cleared from the land to a firewood dealer for $7,000. This amount was credited to Miscellaneous Income.

During the construction period, two of Global's supervisors devoted full time to the construction project. Their annual salaries were $51,000 and $39,000, respectively. They spent two months on the purchase and preparation of the land, six months on the construction of the building (approximately one-sixth of which was devoted to improvements on the grounds), and one month on machinery installation. When the plant began operation on October 1, the supervisors returned to their regular duties. Their salaries were debited to Factory Salaries Expense.

Required

1. Prepare a schedule with the following column headings: Land, Land Improvements, Buildings, Machinery, and Expense. Place each of the above expenditures in the appropriate column. Negative amounts should be shown in parentheses. Total the columns.

User insight ▶ 2. What impact does the classification of the items among several accounts have on evaluating the profitability performance of the company?

LO3 LO4 **Comparison of Depreciation Methods**

P 7. Relax Designs, Inc. purchased a computerized blueprint printer that will assist in the design and display of plans for factory layouts. The cost of the printer was $45,000, and its expected useful life is four years. The company can probably sell the printer for $5,000 at the end of four years. The printer is expected to last 6,000 hours. It was used 1,200 hours in year 1; 1,800 hours in year 2; 2,400 hours in year 3; and 600 hours in year 4.

Required

1. Compute the annual depreciation and carrying value for the new blueprint printer for each of the four years (round to the nearest dollar where necessary) under each of the following methods: (a) straight-line, (b) production, and (c) double-declining-balance.
2. If the printer is sold for $24,000 after year 2, what would be the gain or loss under each method?

User insight ▶ 3. What conclusions can you draw from the patterns of yearly depreciation and carrying value in requirement 1? Do the three methods differ in their impact on profitability? Do they differ in their effect on the company's operating cash flows? Explain.

LO5 **Natural Resource Depletion and Depreciation of Related Plant Assets**

P 8. Fuentez Mining Company purchased land containing an estimated 20 million tons of ore for a cost of $8,800,000. The land without the ore is estimated to be worth $1,600,000. The company expects that all the usable ore can be mined in 10 years. Buildings costing $800,000 with an estimated useful life of 30 years were erected on the site. Equipment costing $960,000 with an estimated useful life of 10 years was installed. Because of the remote location, neither the buildings nor the equipment has an estimated residual value. During its first year of operation, the company mined and sold 1,600,000 tons of ore.

Required

1. Compute the depletion charge per ton.
2. Compute the depletion expense that Fuentez Mining should record for the year.
3. Determine the depreciation expense for the year for the buildings, making it proportional to the depletion.
4. Determine the depreciation expense for the year for the equipment under two alternatives: (a) making the expense proportional to the depletion and (b) using the straight-line method.

User insight ▶ 5. Suppose the company mined and sold 2,000,000 tons of ore (instead of 1,600,000) during the first year. Would the change in the results in requirements **2** or **3** affect earnings or cash flows? Explain.

LO3 LO4 **Comparison of Depreciation Methods**

P 9. Myles Construction Company purchased a new crane for $360,500 at the beginning of year 1. The crane has an estimated residual value of $35,000 and an estimated useful life of six years. The crane is expected to last 10,000 hours.

It was used 1,800 hours in year 1; 2,000 hours in year 2; 2,500 hours in year 3; 1,500 hours in year 4; 1,200 hours in year 5; and 1,000 hours in year 6.

Required

1. Compute the annual depreciation and carrying value for the new crane for each of the six years (round to the nearest dollar where necessary) under each of the following methods: (a) straight-line, (b) production, and (c) double-declining-balance.
2. If the crane is sold for $250,000 after year 3, what would be the amount of gain or loss under each method?

User insight ▶ 3. Do the three methods differ in their effect on the company's profitability? Do they differ in their effect on the company's operating cash flows? Explain.

ENHANCING Your Knowledge, Skills, and Critical Thinking

LO1 Effect of Change in Estimates

C 1. The airline industry was hit particularly hard after the 9/11 attacks on the World Trade Center in 2001. In 2002, **Southwest Airlines**, one of the healthier airline companies, made a decision to lengthen the useful lives of its aircraft from 22 to 27 years. Shortly thereafter, following Southwest's leadership, other airlines made the same move.[18] What advantage, if any, can the airlines gain by making this change in estimate? Will it change earnings or cash flows and, if it does, will the change be favorable or negative?

Some people argue that the useful lives and depreciation of airplanes are irrelevant. They claim that because of the extensive maintenance and testing airline companies are required by law to perform, the planes theoretically can be in service for an indefinite future period. What is wrong with this argument?

LO1 Impairment Test

C 2. The annual report for **Costco Wholesale Corporation**, the large discount company, contains the following statement:

> The company periodically evaluates the realizability of long-lived assets for impairment when [circumstances] may indicate the carrying amount of the asset may not be recoverable.[19]

What does the concept of impairment mean in accounting? What effect does impairment have on profitability and cash flows? Why would the concept of impairment be referred to as a conservative accounting approach?

LO6 Brands

C 3. Hilton Hotels Corporation and **Marriott International** provide hospitality services. Hilton Hotels' well-known brands include Hilton, Doubletree, Hampton Inn, Embassy Suites, Red Lion Hotels and Inns, and Homewood Suites. Marriott also owns or manages properties with recognizable brand names, such as Marriott Hotels, Resorts and Suites; Ritz-Carlton; Renaissance Hotels; Residence Inn; Courtyard; and Fairfield Inn.

On its balance sheet, Hilton Hotels Corporation includes brands (net of amortization) of $1.7 billion, or 19.5 percent of total assets. Marriott International, however, does not list brands among its intangible assets.[20] What principles of accounting for intangibles would cause Hilton to record brands as an asset while Marriott does not? How will these differences in accounting for brands generally affect the net income and *return on assets* of these two competitors?

LO2 **Ethics and Allocation of Acquisition Costs**

C 4. Raintree Company has purchased land and a warehouse for $18,000,000. The warehouse is expected to last 20 years and to have a residual value equal to 10 percent of its cost. The chief financial officer (CFO) and the controller are discussing the allocation of the purchase price. The CFO believes that the largest amount possible should be assigned to the land because this action will improve reported net income in the future. Depreciation expense will be lower because land is not depreciated. He suggests allocating one-third, or $6,000,000, of the cost to the land. This results in depreciation expense each year of $540,000 [($12,000,000 − $1,200,000) ÷ 20 years].

The controller disagrees. She argues that the smallest amount possible, say one-fifth of the purchase price, should be allocated to the land, thereby saving income taxes, since the depreciation, which is tax-deductible, will be greater. Under this plan, annual depreciation would be $648,000 [($14,400,000 − $1,440,000) ÷ 20 years]. The annual tax savings at a 30 percent tax rate is $32,400 [($648,000 − $540,000) × 0.30]. How would each decision affect the company's cash flows? Ethically, how should the purchase cost be allocated? Who will be affected by the decision?

LO1 LO2 LO3 LO6 **Long-Term Assets**

C 5. To answer the following questions, refer to **CVS Corporation**'s annual report in the Supplement to Chapter 5. Examine the balance sheets and the summary of significant accounting policies on property and equipment in the notes to the financial statements.

1. What percentage of total assets in the most recent year was property and equipment, net? Identify the major categories of CVS's property and equipment. Which is the most significant type of property and equipment? What are leasehold improvements? How significant are these items, and what are their effects on the earnings of the company?
2. Continue with the summary of significant accounting policies item on property and equipment in the CVS annual report. What method of depreciation does CVS use? How long does management estimate its buildings will last as compared with furniture and equipment? What does this say about the company's need to remodel its stores?
3. Refer to the note on impairment of long-lived assets in the summary of significant accounting policies in CVS Corporation's annual report. How does the company determine if it has impaired assets?

LO1 **Long-Term Assets and Free Cash Flows**

C 6. Refer to the annual report of **CVS Corporation** and to the financial statements of **Southwest Airlines Co.** in the Supplement to Chapter 5 to answer the following questions:

1. Prepare a table that shows the net amount each company spent on property and equipment (from the statement of cash flows), the total property and equipment (from the balance sheet), and the percentage of the first figure to the second for each of the past two years. Which company grew its property and equipment at a faster rate?
2. Calculate free cash flow for each company for the past two years. What conclusions can you draw about the need for each company to raise funds from debt and equity and the ability of each company to grow?

CHAPTER

12 Contributed Capital

Making a Statement

INCOME STATEMENT

Revenues

– Expenses

= Net Income

STATEMENT OF RETAINED EARNINGS

Beginning Balance

+ Net Income

– Dividends

= Ending Balance

BALANCE SHEET

Assets	**Liabilities**
	Stockholders' Equity

A = L + OE

STATEMENT OF CASH FLOWS

Operating activities
+ Investing activities
+ Financing activities
= Change in Cash
+ Beginning Balance
= Ending Cash Balance

Most stock transactions only impact the balance sheet and the statement of cash flows.

In this chapter, we make the transition from the sole proprietorship form of business to the corporate form. We accomplish this objective by focusing on long-term equity financing—that is, on the capital that stockholders invest in a corporation. The issues involved in equity financing include the type of stock a corporation issues, the dividends that it pays, and the treasury stock that it purchases. These issues can significantly affect return on equity and other measures of profitability on which management's compensation is based. Thus, ethics is a major concern. Management's decisions must be based not on personal gain, but on the value created for the corporation's owners.

LEARNING OBJECTIVES

LO1 Identify and explain the management issues related to contributed capital. (pp. 520–528)

LO2 Identify the components of stockholders' equity. (pp. 528–531)

LO3 Identify the characteristics of preferred stock. (pp. 531–534)

LO4 Account for the issuance of stock for cash and other assets. (pp. 534–538)

LO5 Account for treasury stock. (pp. 539–543)

DECISION POINT ▸ A USER'S FOCUS GAMMON, INC.

In 2010, a group of investors in Arizona formed a corporation called Gammon, Inc. The corporation's state charter authorized it to issue 2 million shares of $1 par value common stock and 50,000 shares of 4 percent, $20 par value cumulative and convertible preferred stock. Gammon's **initial public offering (IPO)** (i.e., its first sale of stock to the public) occurred on February 1, 2010, when it issued 200,000 shares of common stock for $250,000 and thereby realized its first influx of contributed capital.

During its first year of operations, Gammon engaged in a number of other transactions involving common stock, as well as transactions involving preferred stock, treasury stock, and dividends. In this chapter, you will learn how to account for these transactions. You will also learn why corporations are the dominant form of business in the U.S. economy and how a corporation's owners—its stockholders—can evaluate the return on their investments.

- ▸ Why might Gammon's founders have chosen to form a corporation rather than a partnership?
- ▸ How should a corporation account for its stock transactions and dividends?
- ▸ What measures should stockholders use to evaluate the return on their investments?

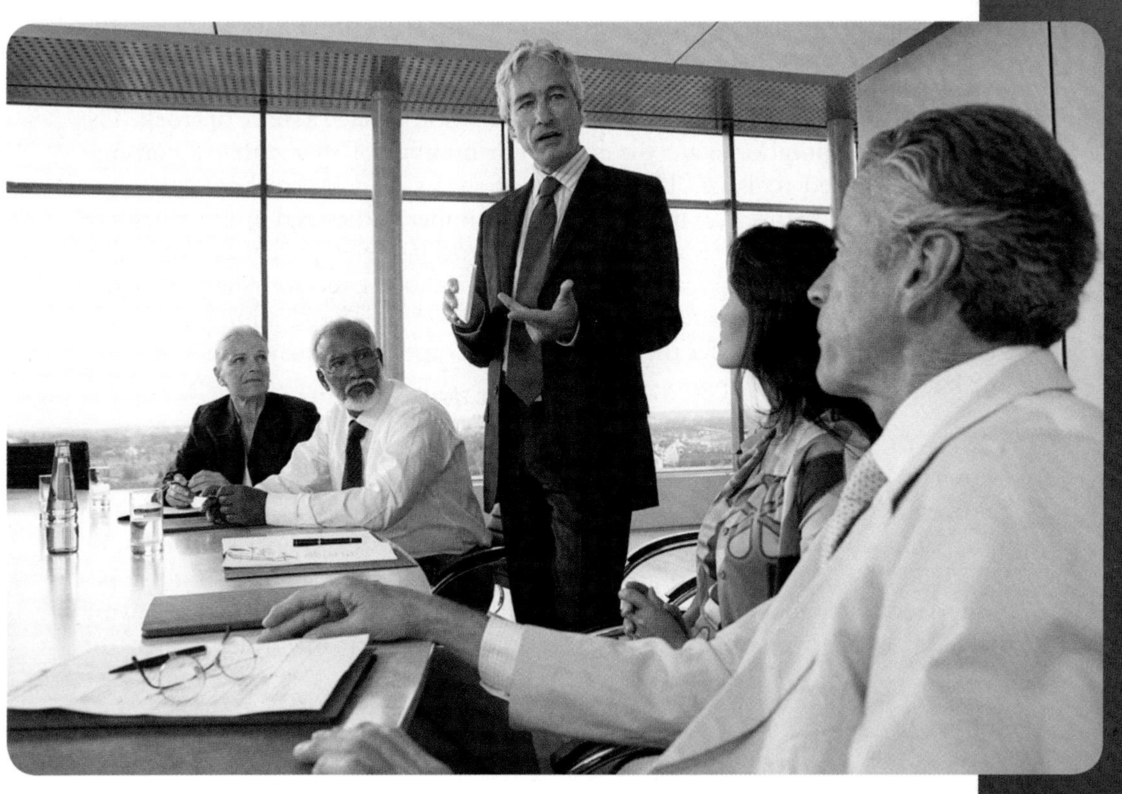

Management Issues Related to Contributed Capital

LO1 Identify and explain the management issues related to contributed capital.

In Chapter 1, we defined a *corporation* as a business unit chartered by the state and legally separate from its owners—that is, its stockholders. *Contributed capital,* which refers to stockholders' investments in a corporation, is a major means of financing a corporation. Managing contributed capital requires an understanding of the corporate organization, its advantages and disadvantages, and the issues involved in equity financing. It also requires familiarity with dividend policies, with how to use return on equity to evaluate performance, and with stock option plans.

The Corporate Form of Business

The corporate form of business is well suited to today's trends toward large organizations, international trade, and professional management. Although fewer in number than sole proprietorships and partnerships, corporations dominate the U.S. economy, in part because of their ability to raise large amounts of capital. In 2004, the amount of new capital that corporations raised was $2,859 billion. Even though 2008 was a down year for markets, the amount of new capital raised by corporations exceeded $4 trillion of which about 90 percent was from bond issues and 10 percent from stock issues.[1]

To form a corporation, most states require persons (called incorporators) to sign an application and file it with the proper state official. This application contains the **articles of incorporation**. If approved by the state, these articles, which form the company charter, become a contract between the state and the incorporators. The company is then authorized to do business as a corporation.

The authority to manage a corporation is delegated by its stockholders to a board of directors and by the board of directors to the corporation's officers (see Figure 12-1). That is, the stockholders elect a board of directors, which sets corporate policies and chooses the corporation's officers, who in turn carry out the corporate policies in their management of the business.

Stockholders A unit of ownership in a corporation is called a **share of stock.** The articles of incorporation state the maximum number of shares that a corporation is authorized to issue. The number of shares held by stockholders is the outstanding stock; this may be less than the number authorized in the articles of incorporation. To invest in a corporation, a stockholder transfers cash or other resources to the corporation. In return, the stockholder receives shares of stock representing a proportionate share of ownership in the corporation. Afterward, the stockholder may transfer the shares at will. Corporations may have more than one kind of stock.

Board of Directors As noted, a corporation's board of directors decides on major business policies. Among the board's specific duties are authorizing contracts, setting executive salaries, and arranging major loans with banks. The declaration of dividends is also an important function of the board of directors. **Dividends** are distributions of resources, generally in the form of cash, to stockholders, and only the board of directors has the authority to declare them. Paying dividends is one way of rewarding stockholders for their investment when the

FIGURE 12-1
The Corporate Organization

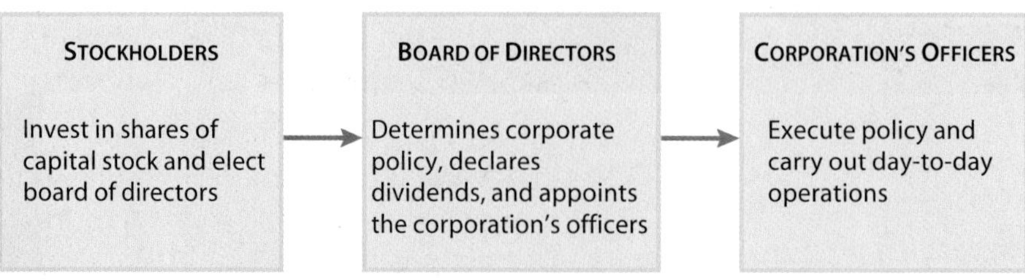

corporation has been successful in earning a profit. (The other way is through a rise in the market value of the stock.) There is usually a delay of two or three weeks between the time the board declares a dividend and the date of the actual payment.

The composition of the board of directors varies from company to company, but generally it includes several officers of the corporation and several outsiders. The outsiders are called *independent directors* because they do not directly participate in managing the business.

Corporation's Officers The corporate officers, appointed by the board of directors to carry out corporate polices and run day-to-day operations, consist of the operating officers—generally the president, or chief executive officer; vice presidents; chief financial officer; and chief operating officer. Besides being responsible for running the business, they have the duty of reporting the financial results of their administration to the board of directors and the stockholders. Though they must, at a minimum, make a comprehensive annual report, they generally report more often. The annual report of large public corporations are available to the public. Excerpts from many of them appear throughout this book.

Advantages and Disadvantages of Incorporation

Managers of a corporation must be familiar with the advantages and disadvantages of this form of business. Some of the advantages are as follows:

- ***Separate legal entity***: As a separate legal entity, a corporation can buy and sell property, sue other parties, enter into contracts, hire and fire employees, and be taxed.
- ***Limited liability***: Because a corporation is a legal entity, separate from its owners, its creditors can satisfy their claims only against the assets of the corporation, not against the personal property of the corporation's owners. Because the owners are not responsible for the corporation's debts, their liability is limited to the amount of their investment. In contrast, the personal property of sole proprietors and partners generally is available to creditors.
- ***Ease of capital generation***: It is fairly easy for a corporation to raise capital because shares of ownership in the business are available to a great number of potential investors for a small amount of money. As a result, a single corporation can have many owners.
- ***Ease of transfer of ownership***: A share of stock, a unit of ownership in a corporation, is easily transferable. A stockholder can normally buy and sell shares without affecting the corporation's activities or needing the approval of other owners.
- ***Lack of mutual agency***: Mutual agency is not a characteristic of corporations. If a stockholder tries to enter into a contract for the corporation, the corporation is not bound by the contract. But in a partnership, because of mutual agency, all the partners can be bound by one partner's actions.
- ***Continuous existence***: Because a corporation is a separate legal entity, an owner's death, incapacity, or withdrawal does not affect the life of the corporation. A corporation's life is set by its charter and regulated by state laws.
- ***Centralized authority and responsibility***: The board of directors represents the stockholders and delegates the responsibility and authority for the day-to-day operation of the corporation to a single person, usually the president. Operating power is not divided among the many owners of the business. The

president may delegate authority over certain segments of the business to others, but he or she is held accountable to the board of directors. If the board is dissatisfied with the performance of the president, it can replace that person.

- *Professional management*: Large corporations have many owners, most of whom are unequipped to make timely decisions about business operations. So, management and ownership are usually separate. This allows a corporation to hire the best talent available to manage the business.

The disadvantages of corporations include the following:

- *Government regulation*: Corporations must meet the requirements of state laws. As "creatures of the state," they are subject to greater state control and regulation than are other forms of business. They must file many reports with the state in which they are chartered. Publicly held corporations must also file reports with the Securities and Exchange Commission and with the stock exchanges on which they are listed. Meeting these requirements is very costly.
- *Taxation*: A major disadvantage of the corporate form of business is **double taxation.** Because a corporation is a separate legal entity, its earnings are subject to federal and state income taxes, which may be as much as 35 percent of corporate earnings. If any of the corporation's after-tax earnings are paid out as dividends, the earnings are taxed again as income to the stockholders. In contrast, the earnings of sole proprietorships and partnerships are taxed only once, as personal income to the owners.
- *Limited liability*: Although limited liability is an advantage of incorporation, it can also be a disadvantage. Limited liability restricts the ability of a small corporation to borrow money. Because creditors can lay claim only to the assets of a corporation, they may limit their loans to the level secured by those assets or require stockholders to guarantee the loans personally.
- *Separation of ownership and control*: Just as limited liability can be a drawback of incorporation, so can the separation of ownership and control. Management sometimes makes decisions that are not good for the corporation as a whole. Poor communication can also make it hard for stockholders to exercise control over the corporation or even to recognize that management's decisions are harmful.

Study Note

Among the agencies that regulate corporations are the Public Company Accounting Oversight Board (PCAOB), Securities and Exchange Commission (SEC), the Occupational Safety and Health Administration (OSHA), the Federal Trade Commission (FTC), the Environmental Protection Agency (EPA), the Nuclear Regulatory Commission (NRC), the Equal Employment Opportunity Commission (EEOC), the Interstate Commerce Commission (ICC), the National Transportation Safety Board (NTSB), the Federal Aviation Administration (FAA), and the Federal Communications Commission (FCC).

Study Note

Lenders to a small corporation may require the corporation's officers to sign a promissory note, which makes them personally liable for the debt.

Equity Financing

Equity financing is accomplished through the issuance of stock to investors in exchange for assets, usually cash. Once the stock has been issued to them, the stockholders can transfer their ownership at will. When they do, they must sign their **stock certificates,** documents showing the number of shares that they own, and send them to the corporation's secretary. In large corporations that are listed on the stock exchanges, stockholders' records are hard to maintain. Such companies can have millions of shares of stock, thousands of which change ownership every day. Therefore, they often appoint independent registrars and transfer agents (usually banks and trust companies) to help perform the secretary's duties. The outside agents are responsible for transferring the corporation's stock, maintaining stockholders' records, preparing a list of stockholders for stockholders' meetings, and paying dividends.

Par value and *legal capital* are important terms in equity financing:

- **Par value** is an arbitrary amount assigned to each share of stock. It must be recorded in the capital stock accounts, and it constitutes a corporation's legal capital.

- **Legal capital** is the number of shares issued times the par value. It is the minimum amount that a corporation can report as contributed capital.

Par value usually bears little if any relationship to the shares' market value or book value. For example, the Internet search company **Google** sold its common stock for $85 per share in its initial public offering, but the market value is now much higher and its par value per share is only $0.001. Google's legal capital is only about $315,000 (315 million shares × $0.001) even though the total market value of its shares exceeds $180 billion.

To help with its initial public offering (IPO), a corporation often uses an **underwriter**—an intermediary between the corporation and the investing public. For a fee—usually less than 1 percent of the selling price—the underwriter guarantees the sale of the stock. The corporation records the amount of the net proceeds of the offering—what the public paid less the underwriter's fees, legal and printing expenses, and any other direct costs of the offering—in its capital stock and additional paid-in capital accounts. Because of the size of its IPO, Google used a group of investment banks headed by two well-known investment bankers, **Morgan Stanley** and **Credit Suisse First Boston**.

The costs of forming a corporation are called **start-up and organization costs**. These costs, which are incurred before a corporation begins operations, include state incorporation fees and attorneys' fees for drawing up the articles of incorporation. They also include the cost of printing stock certificates, accountants' fees for registering the firm's initial stock, and other expenditures necessary for the formation of the corporation. Because Google's IPO was so large, the fees of the lawyers, accountants, and underwriters who helped arrange the IPO amounted to millions of dollars.

Study Note

Start-up and organization costs are expensed when incurred.

Theoretically, start-up and organization costs benefit the entire life of a corporation. For that reason, a case can be made for recording them as intangible assets and amortizing them over the life of the corporation. However, a corporation's life normally is not known, so accountants expense start-up and organization costs as they are incurred.

Advantages of Equity Financing Financing a business by issuing common stock has several advantages:

- It is less risky than financing with debts because a company does not pay dividends on common stock unless the board of directors decides to pay them. In contrast, if a company does not pay interest on bonds, it can be forced into bankruptcy.
- When a company does not pay a cash dividend, it can plow the cash generated by profitable operations back into the company's operations. **Google**, for instance, does not currently pay any dividends, and its issuance of common stock provides it with funds for expansion.
- K/R A company can use the proceeds of a common stock issue to maintain or improve its debt to equity ratio.

Disadvantages of Equity Financing Issuing common stock also has certain disadvantages:

- Unlike interest on bonds, dividends paid on stock are not tax-deductible.
- When a corporation issues more stock, it dilutes its ownership. Thus, the current stockholders must yield some control to the new stockholders.

Dividend Policies

A corporation's board of directors has sole authority to declare dividends, but senior managers, who usually serve as members of the board, influence dividend policies. Receiving dividends is one of two ways in which stockholders can earn a return on their investment in a corporation. The other way is to sell their shares for more than they paid for them.

Although a corporation may have sufficient cash and retained earnings to pay a dividend, its board of directors may not declare one for several reasons. The corporation may need the cash for expansion; it may want to improve its overall financial position by liquidating debt; or it may be facing major uncertainties, such as a pending lawsuit or strike or a projected decline in the economy, which makes it prudent to preserve resources.

A corporation pays dividends quarterly, semiannually, annually, or at other times declared by its board of directors. Most states do not allow a corporation to declare a dividend that exceeds its retained earnings. When a corporation does declare a dividend that exceeds retained earnings, it is, in essence, returning to the stockholders part of their contributed capital. This is called a liquidating dividend. A corporation usually pays a **liquidating dividend** only when it is going out of business or reducing its operations.

Having sufficient retained earnings in itself does not justify the declaration of a dividend. If a corporation does not have cash or other assets readily available for distribution, it might have to borrow money to pay the dividend—an action most boards of directors want to avoid.

Dividend Dates Three important dates are associated with dividends:

> **Study Note**
> Entries for dividends are made only on the declaration date and the payment date.

- The **declaration date** is the date on which the board of directors formally declares that the corporation is going to pay a dividend. Because the legal obligation to pay the dividend arises at this time, a liability for Dividends Payable is recorded and the Dividends account is debited on this date. In the accounting process, Retained Earnings will be reduced by the total dividends declared during the period.

- The **record date** is the date on which ownership of stock, and therefore the right to receive a dividend, is determined. Persons who own the stock on the record date will receive the dividend. No entry is made on this date. Between the record date and the date of payment, the stock is said to be **ex-dividend.** If the owner on the date of record sells the shares of stock before the date of payment, the right to the dividend remains with that person; it does not transfer with the shares to the second owner.

- The **payment date** is the date on which the dividend is paid to the stockholders of record. On this date, the Dividends Payable account is eliminated, and the Cash account is reduced.

Because an accounting period may end between the record date and the payment date, dividends declared during the period may exceed the amount paid for dividends. For example, in Figure 12-2, the accounting period ends on December 31. The declaration date for the dividends is December 21, the record date is December 31, and the payment date is January 11. In this case, the statement of retained earnings for the accounting period will show a reduction to Retained Earnings in the amount of dividends declared, but the statement of cash flows will not show the dividends because the cash has not yet been paid out.

FIGURE 12-2
Dividend Dates

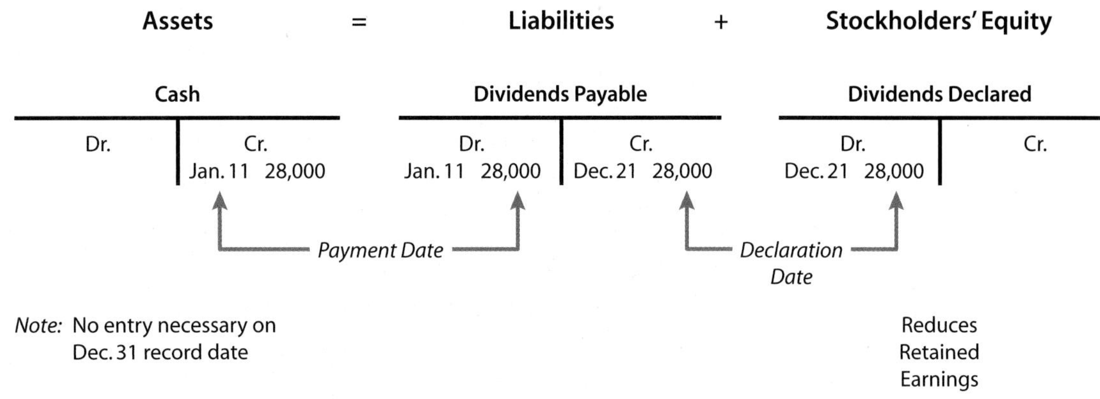

Evaluating Dividend Policies To evaluate the amount of dividends they receive, investors use the **dividends yield** ratio. Dividends yield is computed by dividing the dividends per share by the market price per share. **Microsoft**'s history of dividend payments provides an interesting example. Having built up a large cash balance through its years of profitable operations, Microsoft increased its annual dividend to \$4.5 billion (\$0.52 per share) in 2009.[2] Using Microsoft's regular annual dividend as a more realistic measure of what investors can expect in the future, its dividends yield is computed as follows:

$$\text{Dividends Yield} = \frac{\text{Dividends per Share}}{\text{Market Price per Share}} = \frac{\$0.52}{\$28} = 1.8\%$$

Because the yield on corporate bonds exceeds 5 percent, Microsoft shareholders must expect some of their return to come from increases in the price of the shares.

Companies usually pay dividends only when they have had profitable operations. For example, **Apple Computer** began paying dividends in 1987, but it stopped those payments in 1996 to conserve cash after it suffered large operating losses in 1995. However, factors other than earnings affect the decision to pay dividends. Among them are the following:

- ***Industry policies*:** A company may change its dividend policy to bring it into line with the prevailing policy in its industry. For example, despite positive earnings, **AT&T Corporation** slashed its dividends by 83 percent. This action put AT&T's policy more in line with the policies of its peers in the telecommunications industry, most of which do not pay dividends.[3]

- ***Volatility of earnings*:** If a company has years of good earnings followed by years of poor earnings, it may want to keep dividends low to avoid giving a false impression of sustained high earnings. For example, for years, **General Motors** paid a fairly low but stable dividend but declared a bonus dividend in especially good years.

- ***Effect on cash flows*:** A company may not pay dividends because its operations do not generate enough cash to do so or because it wants to invest cash in future operations. **Abbott Laboratories** increases its dividends per share each year to reward its stockholders but also keeps back a portion of its earnings to spend for other purposes, such as researching and developing new drugs that will generate revenue in the future. In a recent year, for example, the company paid \$1.44 per share dividend on earnings per share of \$3.16.[4]

Recently, because of a 15 percent reduction in the tax rate on dividends, attitudes toward dividends have changed. Many firms have either increased their dividends or started to pay dividends for the first time. The special dividend by Microsoft mentioned earlier is a good example of this effect.

Using Return on Equity to Measure Performance

Return on equity is the most important ratio associated with stockholders' equity. It is also a common measure of management's performance. For instance, when *BusinessWeek* and *Forbes* rate companies on their success, return on equity is the major basis of their evaluations. In addition, the compensation of top executives is often tied to return on equity benchmarks.

Google's return on equity in 2008 is computed as follows:[5]

$$\text{Return on Equity} = \frac{\text{Net Income}}{\text{Average Stockholders' Equity}}$$

$$= \frac{\$4{,}226{,}858}{(\$28{,}238{,}862 + \$22{,}689{,}679) \div 2}$$

$$= \frac{\$4{,}226{,}858}{\$25{,}464{,}271}$$

$$= 16.6\%$$

Google's healthy return on equity of 16.6 percent depends, of course, on the amount of net income the company earns. But it also depends on the level of stockholders' equity, which in turn depends on management decisions about the amount of stock the company sells to the public. As more shares are sold, stockholders' equity increases, and as a result, return on equity decreases. Management can keep stockholders' equity at a minimum by financing the business with cash flows from operations and by issuing debt instead of stock. But, issuing bonds and other types of debt increases a firm's risk because the interest and principal of the debt must be paid on time.

Management can also reduce the number of shares in the hands of the public by buying back the company's shares on the open market. The cost of these shares, which are called **treasury stock,** has the effect of reducing stockholders' equity and thereby increasing return on equity. Many companies follow this practice instead of paying or increasing dividends. Their reason for doing so is that it puts money into the hands of stockholders in the form of market price appreciation without creating a commitment to higher dividends in the future. For instance, in 2009, **Microsoft** purchased $9.4 billion of its common stock on the open market.[6] Microsoft's stock repurchases will improve the company's return on equity, increase its earnings per share, and lower its price/earnings ratio.

The **price/earnings (P/E) ratio** is a measure of investors' confidence in a company's future. It is calculated by dividing the market price per share by the earnings per share. The price/earnings ratio will vary as market price per share fluctuates daily and the amount of earnings per share changes. Using the annual earnings per share from Microsoft's most recent income statement, its P/E ratio can be calculated as follows:

$$\text{Price/Earnings (P/E) Ratio} = \frac{\text{Market Price per Share}}{\text{Earnings per Share}} = \frac{\$27.87}{\$1.62} = 17.2 \text{ times}$$

Because the market price is 17.2 times earnings, investors are paying a good price in relation to earnings. They do so in the expectation that this software company will continue to be successful.

Stock Options as Compensation

More than 97 percent of public companies encourage employees to invest in their common stock through **stock option plans**.[7] Most such plans give employees the right to purchase stock in the future at a fixed price. Some companies offer stock option plans only to management personnel, but others, including **Google**, make them available to all employees. Because the market value of a company's stock is tied to a company's performance, these plans are a means of both motivating and compensating employees. As the market value of the stock goes up, the difference between the option price and the market price grows, which increases the amount of compensation. Another key benefit of stock option plans is that compensation expense is tax-deductible.

On the date stock options are granted, the fair value of the options must be estimated. The amount in excess of the exercise price is recorded as compensation expense over the grant period.[8] For example, suppose that on July 1, 2010, a company grants its top executives the option to purchase 100,000 shares of common stock at $15 per share. The fair value of the option must be estimated on that date to determine compensation expense. Any one of several methods of estimating the fair value of options at the grant date may be used; they are dealt with in more advanced courses. Later, when the market price is $25 per share, one of the firm's vice presidents exercises her option and purchases 2,000 shares. Although the vice president has a gain of $20,000 (the $50,000 market value less the $30,000 option price), no compensation expense is recorded. The company receives only the option price, not the current market value.

In one example of how firms value stock options, Google recognized $1.1 billion of stock-based compensation expense in 2008. This amount represented about 7.4 percent of the company's total expenses and almost 26.5 percent of the net income. Management used a well-known statistical method to estimate the option values.[9]

Cash Flow Information

The best source of information concerning cash flows related to stock transactions and dividends is the financing activities section of the statement of cash flows. For instance, **Microsoft**'s cash flows from these activities are clearly revealed in this partial section of the company's statement of cash flows (in millions):

	2009	**2008**
Financing Activities		
Common stock issued	$ 579	$ 3,494
Common stock repurchased	(9,353)	(12,533)
Common stock cash dividend	**(4,468)**	**(3,805)**

Note the increasing amounts of common stock repurchased (treasury stock) and the increasing amounts of dividends from year to year. Both actions are a reflection of the company's success.

FOCUS ON BUSINESS PRACTICE

Politics and Accounting Don't Mix

The FASB has long held that stock options should be treated as an expense, but in trying to pass this rule, it has encountered heavy opposition from the technology industry, which is the largest user of stock options. Leaders of the technology industry have maintained that expensing stock options would hurt their companies' profits and growth. The FASB argued that stock options are a form of compensation and therefore have value. The U.S. Congress got involved and pressured the FASB to back down, using the companies' reasoning that stock options essentially have no value and thus are not an expense on the income statement, although they should be mentioned in a note to the financial statements. What was happening was that many stock options were granted, and companies granting them were very loose in how they accounted for them. Many of the stock transactions were backdated so that the exercise price would be most advantageous to the executives who were benefiting. The SEC has more than 100 ongoing criminal investigations of backdating practices. Estimates are that between 1994 to 2005, when the FASB finally ruled that all publicly traded companies must expense stock options, $246 billion of options compensation expense had been ignored, overstating reported earnings by 7 percent.[10]

STOP & APPLY >

Indicate whether each of the following is related to (a) advantages of the corporate form of business, (b) disadvantages of corporations, (c) dividend policies, (d) performance evaluation, or (e) stock options:

1. U.S. tax policies
2. Return on equity
3. Separate legal entity
4. Employee's right to purchase shares at a given price
5. Ease of ownership transfer
6. Distributing cash to stockholders
7. Need to deal with government regulation

SOLUTION

1. b; 2. d; 3. a; 4. e; 5. a; 6. c; 7. b

Components of Stockholders' Equity

LO2 Identify the components of stockholders' equity.

In a corporation's balance sheet, the owners' claims to the business are called *stockholders' equity*. As shown in Exhibit 12-1, this section of a corporate balance sheet usually has at least three components.

- ***Contributed capital***: the stockholders' investments in the corporation.
- ***Retained earnings***: the earnings of the corporation since its inception, less any losses, dividends, or transfers to contributed capital. Retained earnings are reinvested in the business. They are not a pool of funds to be distributed to the stockholders; instead, they represent the stockholders' claim to assets resulting from profitable operations.
- ***Treasury stock***: shares of its own stock that the corporation has bought back on the open market. The cost of these shares is treated not as an investment, but as a reduction in stockholders' equity. By buying back the shares, the corporation reduces the ownership of the business.

EXHIBIT 12-1
Stockholders' Equity Section of a Balance Sheet

Stockholders' Equity		
Contributed capital		
Preferred stock, $50 par value, 2,000 shares authorized, issued, and outstanding		$100,000
Common stock, $5 par value, 60,000 shares authorized, 40,000 shares issued, 36,000 shares outstanding	$200,000	
Additional paid-in capital	100,000	300,000
Total contributed capital		$400,000
Retained earnings		120,000
Total contributed capital and retained earnings		$520,000
Less treasury stock–common (4,000 shares at cost)		40,000
Total stockholders' equity		$480,000

A category called "other items" may also appear in a company's stockholders' equity section. We discuss these items in a later chapter.

A corporation can issue two types of stock:

- **Common stock** is the basic form of stock that a corporation issues; that is, if a corporation issues only one type of stock, it is common stock. Because shares of common stock carry voting rights, they generally provide their owners with the means of controlling the corporation. Common stock is also called **residual equity,** which means that if the corporation is liquidated, the claims of all creditors and usually those of preferred stockholders rank ahead of the claims of common stockholders.
- To attract investors whose goals differ from those of common stockholders, a corporation may also issue preferred stock. **Preferred stock** gives its owners preference over common stockholders, usually in terms of receiving dividends and in terms of claims to assets if the corporation is liquidated. (We describe these preferences in more detail later in the chapter.)

FOCUS ON BUSINESS PRACTICE

Are You a First-Class or Second-Class Stockholder?

When companies go public, insiders—usually the founders of the company or top management—often get first-class shares with extra votes, while outsiders get second-class shares with fewer votes. The class A and class B shares of **Adolph Coors Company**, the large brewing firm, are an extreme example. The company's class B shares, owned by the public, have no votes except in the case of a merger. Its class A shares, held by the Coors family trust, have all the votes on other issues.

Google also has two classes of common shares. Both classes are identical except that each class B share is entitled to ten votes and each class A share is entitled to only one vote. Class A shares are the ones that Google offered to the public in its IPO. As a result, Class B holders control 78 percent of the company.[11]

Shareholder advocates denounce the class division of shares as undemocratic. They maintain that this practice gives a privileged few shareholders all or most of the control of a company and that it denies other shareholders voting power consistent with the risk they are taking. Defenders of the practice argue that it shields top executives from the market's obsession with short-term results and allows them to make better long-term decisions. They also point out that many investors don't care about voting rights as long as the stock performs well.

FIGURE 12-3
Relationship of Authorized Shares to Unissued, Issued, Outstanding, and Treasury Shares

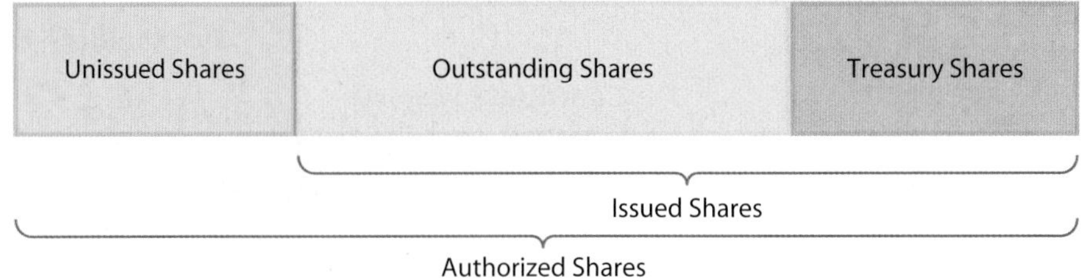

In keeping with the convention of full disclosure, the stockholders' equity section of a corporate balance sheet gives a great deal of information about the corporation's stock. Under contributed capital, it lists the kinds of stock; their par value; and the number of shares authorized, issued, and outstanding.

- **Authorized shares** are the maximum number of shares that a corporation's state charter allows it to issue. Most corporations are authorized to issue more shares than they need to issue at the time they are formed. Thus, they are able to raise more capital in the future by issuing additional shares. When a corporation issues all of its authorized shares, it cannot issue more without a change in its state charter.
- **Issued shares** are those that a corporation sells or otherwise transfers to stockholders. The owners of a corporation's issued shares own 100 percent of the business. Unissued shares have no rights or privileges until they are issued.
- **Outstanding shares** are shares that a corporation has issued and that are still in circulation. Treasury stock is not outstanding because it consists of shares that a corporation has issued but that it has bought back and thereby put out of circulation. Thus, a corporation can have more shares issued than are currently outstanding.

Figure 12-3 shows the relationship of authorized shares to issued, unissued, outstanding, and treasury shares. In this regard, **Google** is an interesting example. The company has 9 billion authorized shares of stock and only about 309 million shares issued. With its excess of authorized shares, Google obviously has plenty of flexibility for future stock transactions.

The following data are from the records of Garcia Corporation on December 31, 2011:

	Balance
Preferred stock, $100 par value, 6 percent noncumulative, 5,000 shares authorized, issued, and outstanding	$500,000
Common stock, $2 par value, 100,000 shares authorized, 90,000 shares issued, and 85,000 shares outstanding	180,000
Additional paid-in capital	489,000
Retained earnings	172,500
Treasury stock–common (5,000 shares, at cost)	110,000

Prepare a stockholders' equity section for Garcia Corporation's balance sheet.

(continued)

SOLUTION

Garcia Corporation
Balance Sheet
December 31, 2011
Stockholders' Equity

Contributed capital		
Preferred stock, $100 par value, 6 percent noncumulative, 5,000 shares authorized, issued, and outstanding		$ 500,000
Common stock, $2 par value, 100,000 shares authorized, 90,000 shares issued, 85,000 shares outstanding	$180,000	
Additional paid-in capital	489,000	669,000
Total contributed capital		$1,169,000
Retained earnings		172,500
Total contributed capital and retained earnings		$1,341,500
Less treasury stock–common (5,000 shares at cost)		110,000
Total stockholders' equity		$1,231,500

Preferred Stock

LO3 Identify the characteristics of preferred stock.

Most preferred stock has one or more of the following characteristics: preference as to dividends, preference as to assets if a corporation is liquidated, convertibility, and a callable option. A corporation may offer several different classes of preferred stock, each with distinctive characteristics to attract different investors.

Study Note

Preferred stock has many different characteristics. They are rarely exactly the same from company to company.

Preference as to Dividends

Preferred stockholders ordinarily must receive a certain amount of dividends before common stockholders receive anything. The amount that preferred stockholders must be paid before common stockholders can be paid is usually stated in dollars per share or as a percentage of the par value of the preferred shares. For example, a company might pay an annual dividend of $4 per share on preferred stock, or it might issue preferred stock at $50 par value and pay an annual dividend of 8 percent of par value, which would also be $4 per share.

Preferred stockholders have no guarantee of ever receiving dividends. A company must have earnings and its board of directors must declare dividends on preferred stock before any liability arises. The consequences of not granting an annual dividend on preferred stock vary according to whether the stock is noncumulative or cumulative:

- If the stock is **noncumulative preferred stock** and the board of directors fails to declare a dividend on it in any given year, the company is under no obligation to make up the missed dividend in future years.
- If the stock is **cumulative preferred stock**, the dividend amount per share accumulates from year to year, and the company must pay the whole amount before it pays any dividends on common stock.

Dividends not paid in the year they are due are called **dividends in arrears**. For example, suppose that a corporation has 20,000 shares of $100 par value, 5 percent cumulative preferred stock outstanding. If the corporation pays no dividends in 2011, preferred dividends in arrears at the end of the year would amount to $100,000 (20,000 shares × $100 × 0.05 = $100,000). If the corporation's board declares dividends in 2012, the corporation must pay preferred stockholders the dividends in arrears plus their current year's dividends before paying any dividends on common stock.

Dividends in arrears are not recognized as liabilities because no liability exists until the board of directors declares a dividend. A corporation cannot be sure it is going to make a profit, so, of course, it cannot promise dividends to stockholders. However, if it has dividends in arrears, it should report the amount either in the body of its financial statements or in a note to its financial statements.

The following note is typical of one that might appear in a company's annual report:

> On December 31, 2010, the company was in arrears by $37,851,000 ($1.25 per share) on dividends to its preferred stockholders. The company must pay all dividends in arrears to preferred stockholders before paying any dividends to common stockholders.

Suppose that on January 1, 2011, a corporation issued 20,000 shares of $10 par value, 6 percent cumulative preferred stock and 100,000 shares of common stock. Operations in 2011 produced income of only $8,000. However, in the same year, the corporation's board of directors declared a $6,000 cash dividend to the preferred stockholders. Thus, the dividend picture at the end of 2011 was as follows:

2011 dividends due preferred stockholders ($200,000 × 0.06)	$12,000
Less 2011 dividends declared to preferred stockholders	6,000
2011 preferred stock dividends in arrears	$ 6,000

Now suppose that in 2012, the corporation earns income of $60,000 and wants to pay dividends to both the preferred and the common stockholders. Because the preferred stock is cumulative, the corporation must pay the $6,000 in arrears on the preferred stock, plus the current year's dividends on the preferred stock, before it can distribute a dividend to the common stockholders. If the corporation's board of directors now declares a $24,000 dividend to be distributed to preferred and common stockholders, the distribution would be as follows:

2012 declaration of dividends	$24,000
Less 2011 preferred stock dividends in arrears	6,000
Amount available for 2012 dividends	$18,000
Less 2012 dividends due preferred stockholders ($200,000 × 0.06)	12,000
Remainder available to common stockholders	$ 6,000

Preference as to Assets

Preferred stockholders often have preference in terms of their claims to a corporation's assets if the corporation is liquidated. If a corporation does go out of business, these preferred stockholders have a right to receive the par value of their stock or a larger stated liquidation value per share before the common stockholders receive any share of the corporation's assets. This preference can also extend to any dividends in arrears owed to the preferred stockholders.

Study Note

When preferred stockholders convert their shares to common stock, they gain voting rights but lose the dividend and liquidation preference. Conversion back to preferred stock is not an option.

Convertible Preferred Stock

Like all preferred stockholders, owners of **convertible preferred stock** are more likely than common stockholders to receive regular dividends. In addition, they can exchange their shares of preferred stock for shares of common stock at a ratio stated in the company's preferred stock contract. If the market value of the company's common stock increases, the conversion feature is attractive to stockholders because it allows them to share in the increase by converting their stock to common stock.

Suppose, for instance, that a company issues 1,000 shares of 8 percent, $100 par value convertible preferred stock for $100 per share. Each share of stock can be converted to five shares of the company's common stock at any time. The market value of the common stock at the time the company issues the convertible preferred stock is $15 per share. In the past, an owner of the common stock could expect dividends of about $1 per share per year. The owner of one share of preferred stock, on the other hand, now holds an investment that has a market value of about $75 and is also more likely than a common stockholder to receive dividends.

Now suppose that in the next several years, the corporation's earnings increase, the dividends paid to common stockholders increase to $3 per share, and the market value of a share of common stock increases from $15 to $30. Preferred stockholders can convert each of their preferred shares to five common shares, thereby increasing their dividends from $8 on each preferred share to $15 ($3 on each of five common shares). Moreover, the market value of each share of preferred stock will be close to the $150 value of the five shares of common stock because each share can be converted to five shares of common stock.

Callable Preferred Stock

Most preferred stock is **callable preferred stock**—that is, the issuing corporation can redeem or retire it at a price stated in the preferred stock contract. An owner of nonconvertible preferred stock must surrender it to the issuing corporation when asked to do so. If the preferred stock is convertible, the stockholder can either surrender the stock to the corporation or convert it to common stock when the corporation calls the stock. The *call price*, or redemption price, is usually higher than the stock's par value. For example, preferred stock that has a $100 par value might be callable at $103 per share.

When preferred stock is called and surrendered, the stockholder is entitled to the following:

- The par value of the stock
- The call premium
- Any dividends in arrears
- The current period's dividend prorated by the proportion of the year to the call date

FOCUS ON BUSINESS PRACTICE

How Does a Stock Become a Debt?

Some companies have used the flexibility of preferred stocks to create a type of stock that is similar to debt. Usually, stocks do not have maturity dates, and companies do not buy them back except at the option of management. However, **CMS Energy**, **Time Warner**, **Xerox**, and other companies have issued preferred stock that is "mandatorily redeemable." This means that the issuing companies are required to buy back the stock at fixed future dates or under predetermined conditions. Thus, these special preferred stocks are similar to bonds in that they have a fixed maturity date. In addition, in much the same way as bonds require periodic interest payments at a fixed rate, these stocks require an annual dividend payment, also at a fixed rate. Even though companies list these stocks in the stockholders' equity section of their balance sheets, the astute analyst will treat them as debt when calculating a company's debt to equity ratio.[12]

A corporation may decide to call its preferred stock for any of the following reasons:

- It may want to force conversion of the preferred stock to common stock because the dividend that it pays on preferred shares is higher than the dividend that it pays on the equivalent number of common shares.
- It may be able to replace the outstanding preferred stock with a preferred stock at a lower dividend rate or with long-term debt, which can have a lower after-tax cost.
- It may simply be profitable enough to retire the preferred stock.

STOP & APPLY >

Sung Corporation has 2,000 shares of $100 par value, 7 percent cumulative preferred stock outstanding and 200,000 shares of $1 par value common stock outstanding. In the corporation's first three years of operation, its board of directors declared cash dividends as follows:

2010, none
2011, $20,000
2012, $30,000

Determine the total cash dividends paid to the preferred and common stockholders during each of the three years.

SOLUTION

2010:	None	
2011:	Preferred dividends in arrears (2,000 shares × $100 × 0.07)	$14,000
	Current year remainder to preferred ($20,000 − $14,000)	6,000
	Total to preferred stockholders	$20,000
2012:	Preferred dividends in arrears ($14,000 − $6,000)	$ 8,000
	Current year to preferred (2,000 shares × $100 × 0.07)	14,000
	Total to preferred stockholders	$22,000
	Total to common stockholders ($30,000 − $22,000)	8,000
	Total dividends in 2012	$30,000

Issuance of Common Stock

LO4 Account for the issuance of stock for cash and other assets.

A share of capital stock may be either par or no-par. The value of par stock is stated in the corporate charter and must be printed on each stock certificate. It can be $0.01, $1, $5, $100, or any other amount established by the organizers of the corporation. For instance, the par value of **Google**'s common stock is $0.001. The par values of common stocks tend to be lower than those of preferred stocks.

As noted earlier, par value is the amount per share that is recorded in a corporation's capital stock accounts, and it constitutes a corporation's legal capital. A corporation cannot declare a dividend that would cause stockholders' equity to fall below the firm's legal capital. Par value is thus a minimum cushion of capital that protects a corporation's creditors. Any amount in excess of par value that a corporation receives from a stock issue is recorded in its Additional Paid-in Capital account and represents a portion of its contributed capital.

No-par stock is capital stock that does not have a par value. A corporation may issue stock without a par value for several reasons. For one thing, rather than

> **Study Note**
> Legal capital is the minimum amount a corporation can report as contributed capital. To protect creditors, a corporation cannot declare a dividend that would reduce capital below the amount of legal capital.

recognizing par value as an arbitrary figure, investors may confuse it with the stock's market value. For another, most states do not allow a stock issue below par value, and this limits a corporation's flexibility in obtaining capital.

State laws often require corporations to place a **stated value** on each share of stock that they issue, but even when this is not required, a corporation's board of directors may do so as a matter of convenience. The stated value can be any value set by the board unless the state specifies a minimum amount, which is sometimes the case. The stated value can be set before or after the shares are issued if the state law is not specific.

Par Value Stock

When a corporation issues par value stock, the appropriate capital stock account (usually Common Stock or Preferred Stock) is credited for the par value regardless of whether the proceeds are more or less than the par value.

When a corporation issues stock at a price greater than par value, as is usually the case, the proceeds in excess of par are credited to an account called Additional Paid-in Capital. For example, suppose Norek Corporation is authorized to issue 10,000 shares of $10 par value common stock and that it issues 5,000 shares at $12 each on January 1, 2011. The T accounts and entry to record the issuance of the stock at the price in excess of par value would be as follows:

A	= L +	SE
+60,000		+50,000
		+10,000

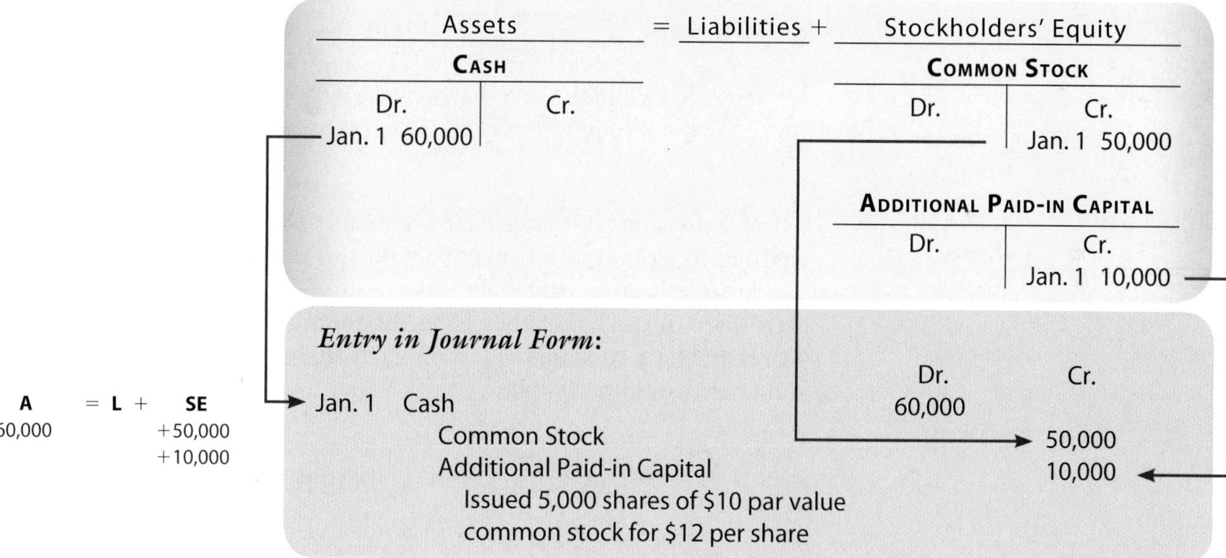

Cash is debited for the proceeds of $60,000 (5,000 shares × $12), and Common Stock is credited for the total par value of $50,000 (5,000 shares × $10). Additional Paid-in Capital is credited for the difference of $10,000 (5,000 shares × $2).

The amount in excess of par value is part of Norek Corporation's contributed capital and will be included in the stockholders' equity section of its balance sheet. Immediately after the stock issue, this section of Norek's balance sheet would appear as follows:

Contributed capital	
Common stock, $10 par value, 10,000 shares authorized, 5,000 shares issued and outstanding	$50,000
Additional paid-in capital	10,000
Total contributed capital	$60,000
Retained earnings	—
Total stockholders' equity	$60,000

If a corporation issues stock for less than par value, an account called Discount on Capital Stock is debited for the difference. The issuance of stock at a discount rarely occurs; it is illegal in many states.

No-Par Stock

Study Note

When no-par stock has a stated value, the stated value serves the same purpose as par value in that it represents the minimum legal capital.

Most states require that all or part of the proceeds from a corporation's issuance of no-par stock be designated as legal capital, which cannot be used unless the corporation is liquidated. The purpose of this requirement is to protect the corporation's assets for creditors.

Suppose that on January 1, 2011, Norek Corporation issues 5,000 shares of no-par common stock at $15 per share. The $75,000 (5,000 shares × $15) in proceeds would be recorded as follows:

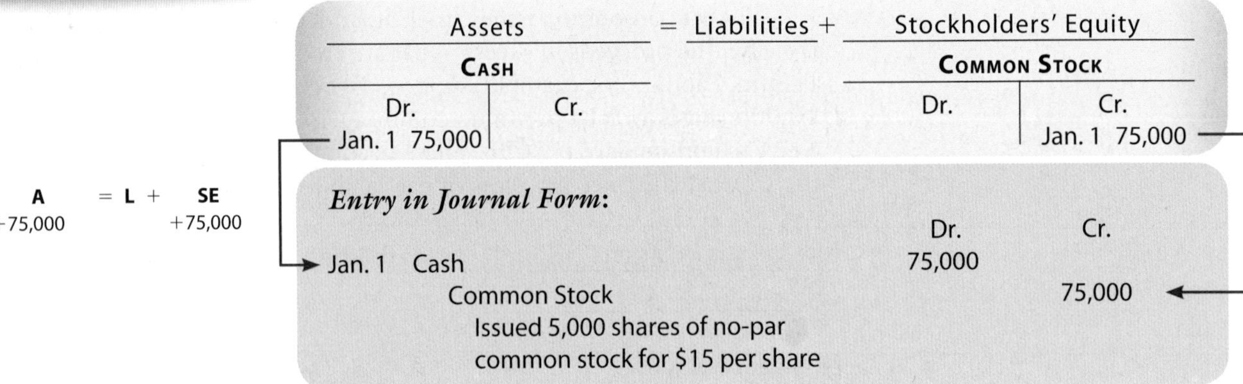

A	= L +	SE
+75,000		+75,000

Because the stock does not have a stated or par value, all proceeds of the issue are credited to Common Stock and are part of the company's legal capital.

As noted earlier, state laws may require corporations to put a stated value on each share of stock that they issue. Assuming the same facts as above except that Norek puts a $10 stated value on each share of its no-par stock, the T account and entry would be as follows:

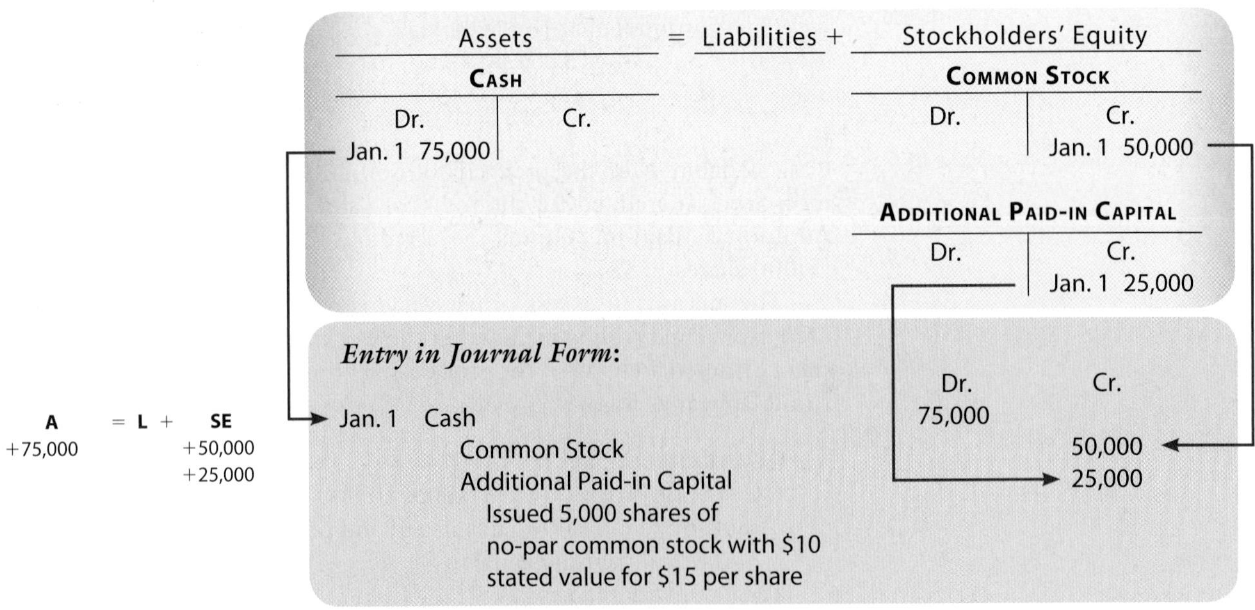

A	= L +	SE
+75,000		+50,000
		+25,000

Notice that the legal capital credited to Common Stock is the stated value decided by Norek's board of directors. Also note that the Additional Paid-in Capital account is credited for $25,000, which is the difference between the proceeds ($75,000) and the total stated value ($50,000).

Issuance of Stock for Noncash Assets

A corporation may issue stock in return for assets or services other than cash. Transactions of this kind usually involve a corporation's exchange of stock for land or buildings or for the services of attorneys and others who help organize the corporation. In such cases, the problem is to determine the dollar amount at which the exchange should be recorded.

A corporation's board of directors has the right to determine the fair market value of the assets or services that the corporation receives in exchange for its stock. Generally, such a transaction is recorded at the fair market value of the stock that the corporation is giving up. If the stock's fair market value cannot be determined, the fair market value of the assets or services received can be used.

Study Note

In establishing the fair market value of property that a corporation exchanges for stock, a board of directors cannot be arbitrary; it must use all the information at its disposal.

For example, suppose that when Norek Corporation was formed on January 1, 2011, its attorney agreed to accept 200 shares of its $10 par value common stock for services rendered. At that time, the market value of the stock could not be determined. However, for similar services, the attorney would have charged Norek $3,000. The T account and entry to record this noncash transaction is as follows:

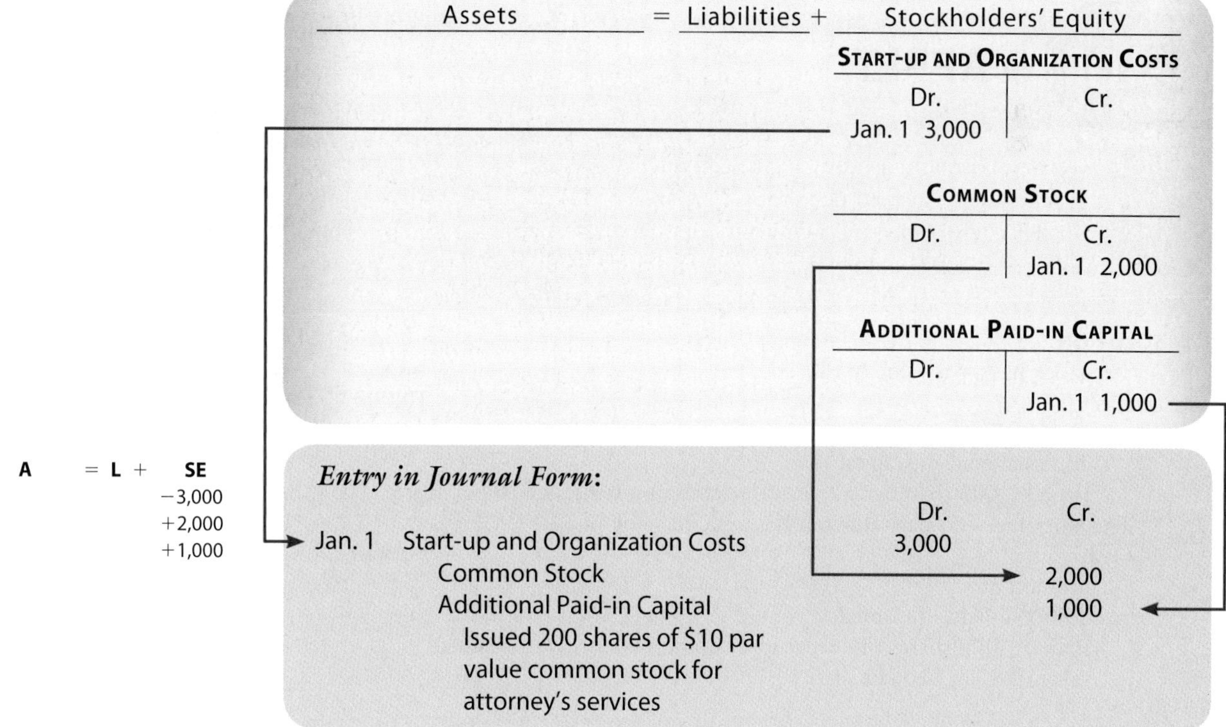

A	= L +	SE
		−3,000
		+2,000
		+1,000

Entry in Journal Form:

		Dr.	Cr.
Jan. 1	Start-up and Organization Costs	3,000	
	Common Stock		2,000
	Additional Paid-in Capital		1,000
	Issued 200 shares of $10 par value common stock for attorney's services		

Now suppose that two years later, Norek Corporation exchanged 500 shares of its $10 par value common stock for a piece of land. At the time of the exchange, Norek's stock was selling on the market for $16 per share. The following T account and entry records this exchange:

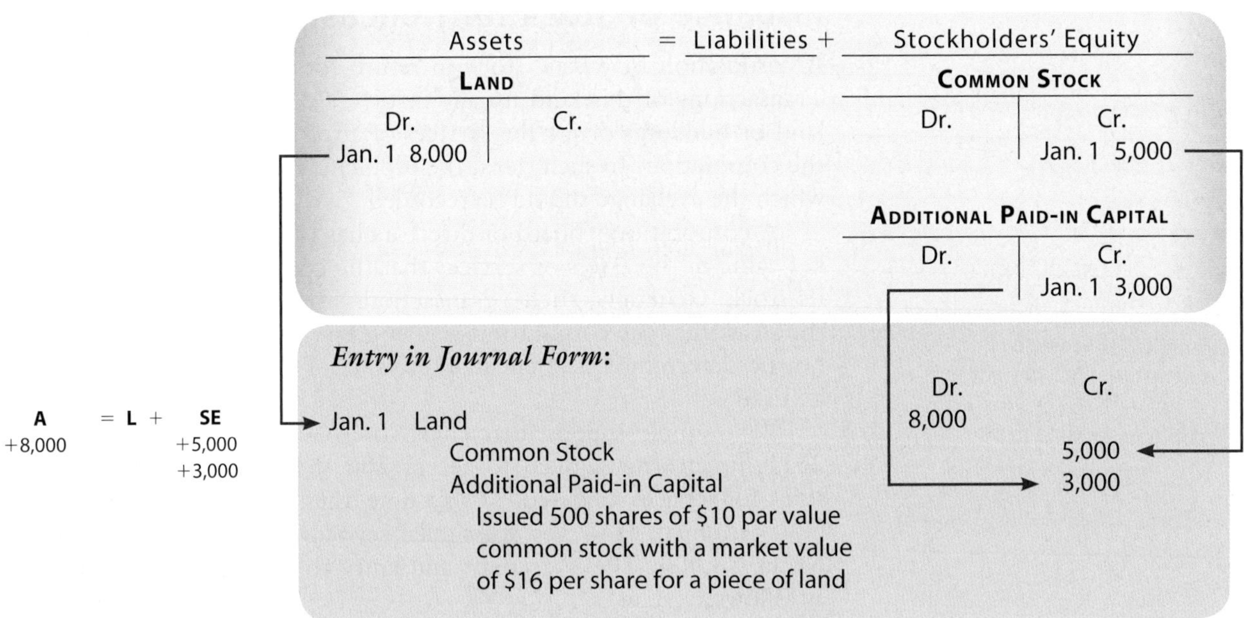

Entry in Journal Form:

		Dr.	Cr.
Jan. 1	Land	8,000	
	Common Stock		5,000
	Additional Paid-in Capital		3,000
	Issued 500 shares of $10 par value common stock with a market value of $16 per share for a piece of land		

A	= L +	SE
+8,000		+5,000
		+3,000

STOP & APPLY >

Arena Company is authorized to issue 10,000 shares of common stock. The company sold 1,000 shares at $10 per share. Prepare entries in journal form to record the sale of stock for cash under each of the following independent alternatives: (1) The stock has a par value of $2, and (2) the stock has no-par value but a stated value of $1 per share.

SOLUTION

	Dr.	Cr.
1. The stock has a par value of $2.		
Cash	10,000	
Common Stock		2,000
Additional Paid-in Capital		8,000
Issued 1,000 shares of $2 par value common stock at $10 per share		
2. The stock has a no-par value but has a stated value of $1.		
Cash	10,000	
Common Stock		1,000
Additional Paid-in Capital		9,000
Issued 1,000 shares of no-par value common stock with a stated value of $1 at $10 per share		

Accounting for Treasury Stock

LO5 Account for treasury stock.

> **Study Note**
> Treasury stock is not the same as unissued stock. Treasury stock represents shares that have been issued but are no longer outstanding. Unissued shares, on the other hand, have never been in circulation.

As we noted earlier, treasury stock is stock that the issuing company has reacquired, usually by purchasing shares on the open market. Although repurchasing its own stock can be a severe drain on a corporation's cash, it is common practice. In a recent year, 386, or 64 percent, of 600 large companies held treasury stock.[13]

Among the reasons a company may want to buy back its own stock are the following:

- It may want stock to distribute to employees through stock option plans.
- It may be trying to maintain a favorable market for its stock.
- It may want to increase its earnings per share or stock price per share.
- It may want to have additional shares of stock available for purchasing other companies.
- It may want to prevent a hostile takeover.

A purchase of treasury stock reduces a company's assets and stockholders' equity. It is not considered a purchase of assets, as the purchase of shares in another company would be. A company can hold treasury shares for an indefinite period or reissue or retire them. Treasury shares have no rights until they are reissued. Like unissued shares, they do not have voting rights, rights to dividends, or rights to assets during liquidation of the company. However, there is one major difference between unissued shares and treasury shares. A share of stock issued at par value or greater and that was reacquired as treasury stock can be reissued at less than par value without negative results.

Purchase of Treasury Stock

When treasury stock is purchased, it is recorded at cost. The par value, stated value, or original issue price of the stock is ignored. As noted above, the purchase reduces both a firm's assets and its stockholders' equity. For example, suppose that on September 15, Amber Corporation purchases 2,000 shares of its common stock on the market at a price of $50 per share. The purchase would be recorded as follows:

A	= L +	SE
−100,000		−100,000

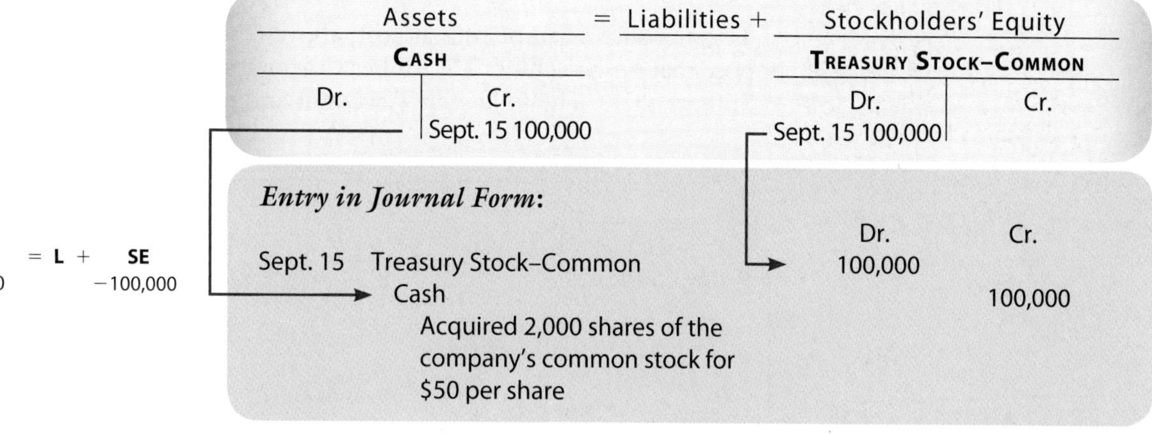

Entry in Journal Form:

		Dr.	Cr.
Sept. 15	Treasury Stock–Common	100,000	
	Cash		100,000
	Acquired 2,000 shares of the company's common stock for $50 per share		

FOCUS ON BUSINESS PRACTICE

Are Share Buybacks Really Good?

Corporate America sets new records for share buybacks every year: $10 billion in 1991; $123 billion in 2000; $197 billion in 2004; and an estimated $500 billion in 2007. **Home Depot, Inc., Wal-Mart, Inc., General Electric, Johnson & Johnson**, and **Microsoft**, along with many other companies, spent billions to boost their stock prices—but to no avail. The stated aim is to boost stock prices and earnings per share by reducing the supply of stock in public hands.

According to renowned investor Warren Buffett and others, share buybacks are ill-advised. Many of the purchases in 2007, for example, occurred when the market was experiencing record highs. Also, what is often not stated publicly is that many shares do not stay out of public hands because the companies recycle the stock into generous stock options for management and thus do not achieve the stated goal of reducing outstanding shares. Estimates are that perhaps half of the stock purchased is little more than a "backdoor compensation" for employees. Furthermore, many companies have borrowed money to repurchase stock, thereby increasing their debt to equity ratios. These companies later suffered reductions in their credit ratings and severe declines in their stock prices.[14]

Study Note

Because treasury stock reduces stockholders' equity—the denominator of the return on equity ratio—the return on equity will increase when treasury shares are purchased even though there is no increase in earnings.

The stockholders' equity section of Amber's balance sheet shows the cost of the treasury stock as a deduction from the total of contributed capital and retained earnings:

Contributed capital	
Common stock, $5 par value, 200,000 shares authorized, 60,000 shares issued, 58,000 shares outstanding	$ 300,000
Additional paid-in capital	60,000
Total contributed capital	$ 360,000
Retained earnings	1,800,000
Total contributed capital and retained earnings	$2,160,000
Less treasury stock–common (2,000 shares at cost)	100,000
Total stockholders' equity	$2,060,000

Notice that the number of shares issued, and therefore the legal capital, has not changed. However, the number of shares outstanding has decreased as a result of the transaction.

Sale of Treasury Stock

Treasury shares can be sold at cost, above cost, or below cost. For example, suppose that on November 15, Amber Corporation sells its 2,000 treasury shares for $50 per share. The following T account and entry records the transaction:

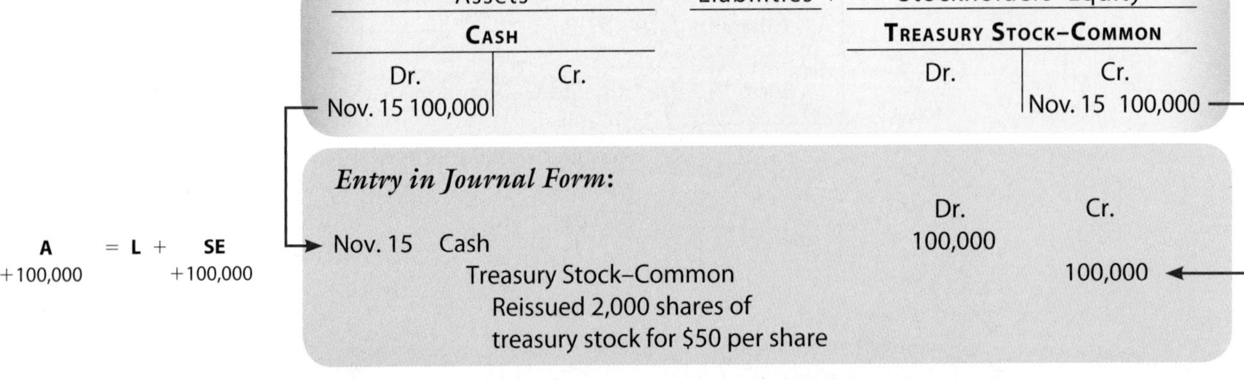

When treasury shares are sold for an amount greater than their cost, the excess of the sales price over cost should be credited to Paid-in Capital, Treasury Stock. No gain should be recorded.

For instance, suppose that on November 15, Amber Corporation sells its 2,000 treasury shares for $60 per share. The T account and entry for the reissue would be as follows:

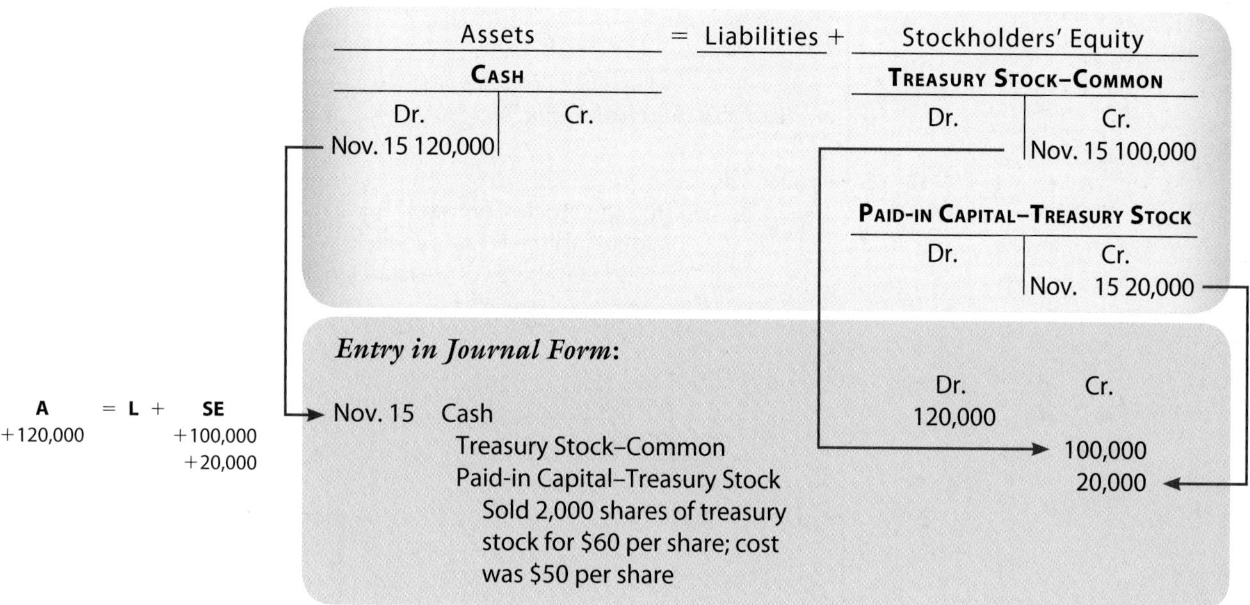

A	= L +	SE
+120,000		+100,000
		+20,000

Study Note

Gains and losses on the reissue of treasury stock are never recognized as such. Instead, the Retained Earnings and Paid-in Capital, Treasury Stock accounts are used.

When treasury shares are sold below their cost, the difference is deducted from Paid-in Capital, Treasury Stock. If this account does not exist or if its balance is insufficient to cover the excess of cost over the reissue price, Retained Earnings absorbs the excess. No loss is recorded.

For example, suppose that on September 15, Amber bought 2,000 shares of its common stock on the market at a price of $50 per share. On October 15, the company sold 800 shares for $60 per share, and on December 15, it sold the remaining 1,200 shares for $42 per share. The T accounts and entries for these three transactions are as follows:

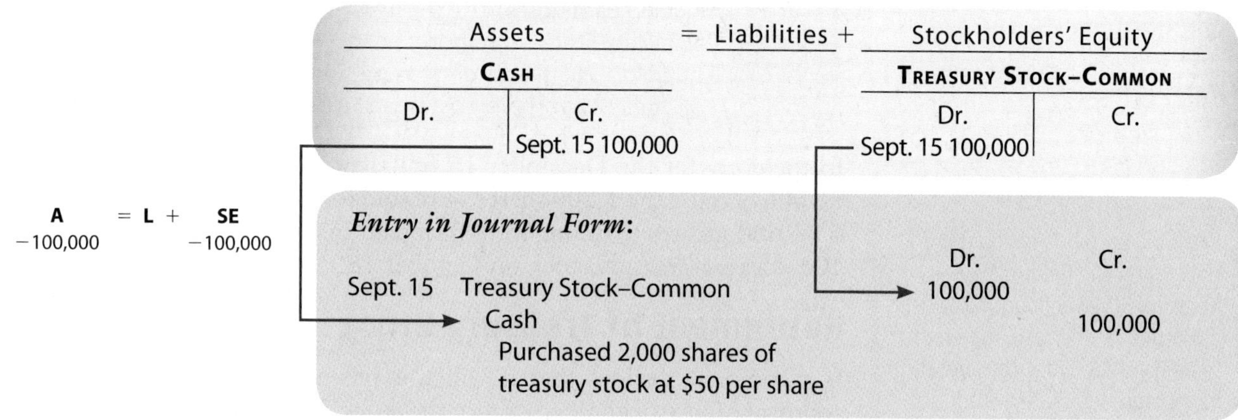

A	= L +	SE
−100,000		−100,000

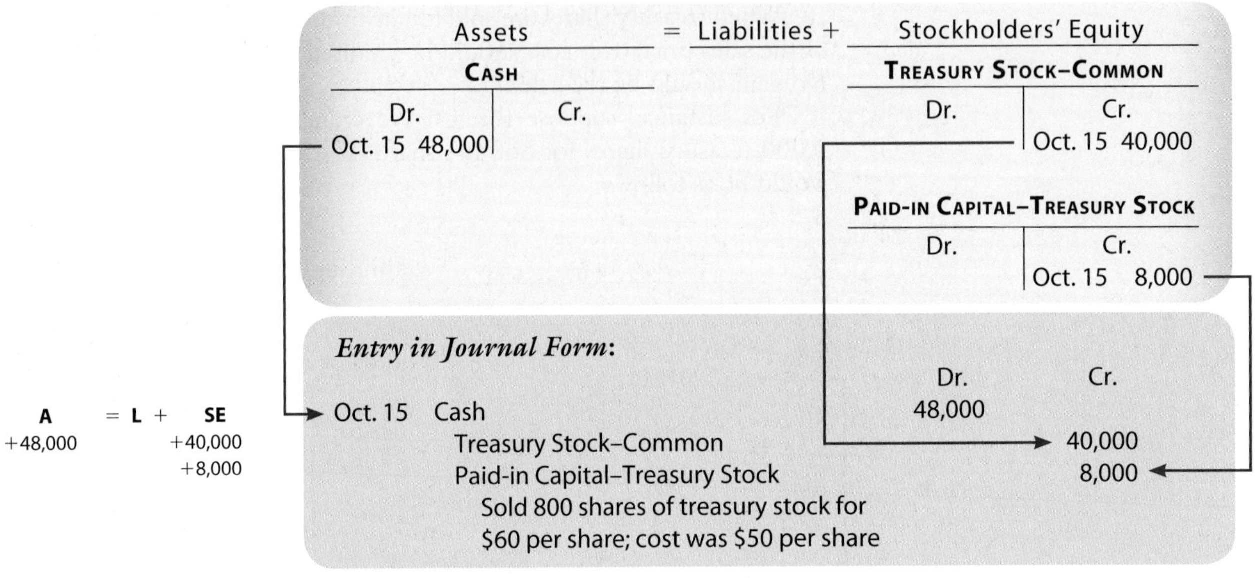

A	= L +	SE
+48,000		+40,000
		+8,000

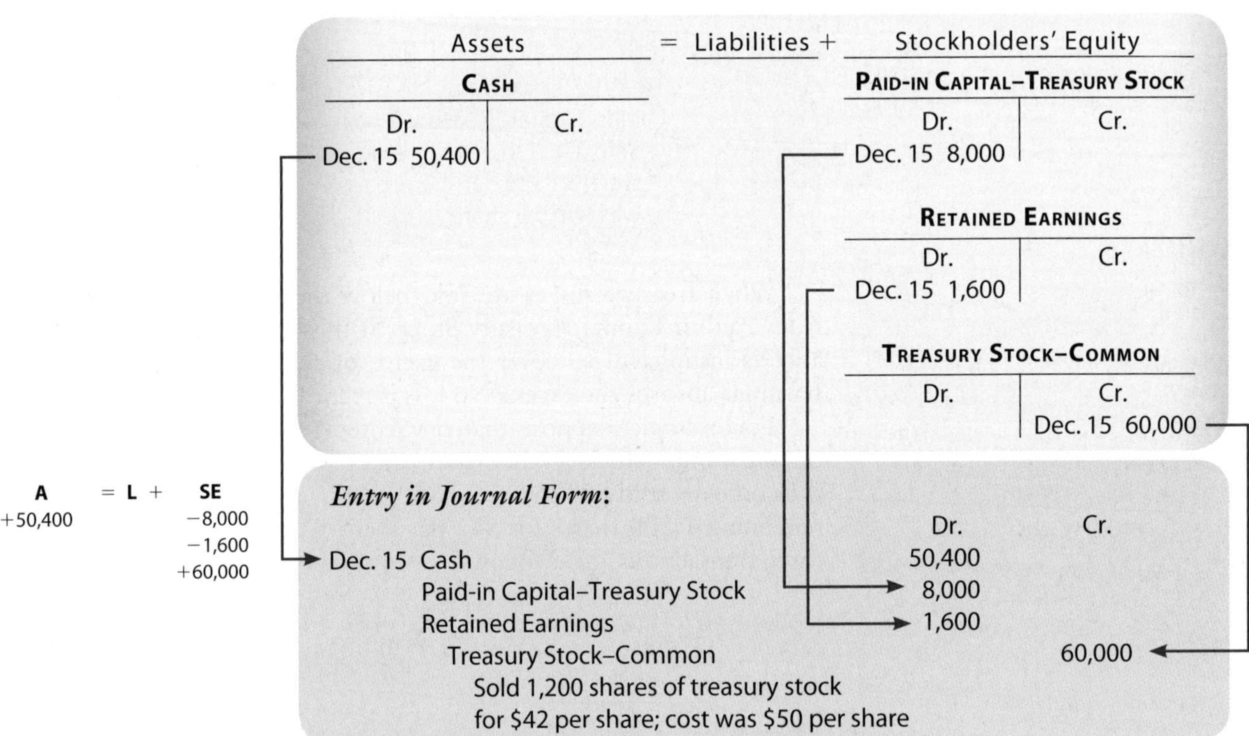

A	= L +	SE
+50,400		−8,000
		−1,600
		+60,000

In the entry for the December 15 transaction, Retained Earnings is debited for $1,600 because the 1,200 shares were sold for $9,600 less than cost. That amount is $1,600 greater than the $8,000 of paid-in capital generated by the sale of the 400 shares of treasury stock on October 15.

> **Study Note**
>
> Retained Earnings is debited only when the Paid-in Capital, Treasury Stock account has been depleted. In this case, the credit balance of $8,000 is completely exhausted before Retained Earnings absorbs the excess.

Retirement of Treasury Stock

If a company decides that it will not reissue treasury stock, it can, with the approval of its stockholders, retire the stock. When shares of stock are retired, all items related to those shares are removed from the associated capital accounts. If the cost of buying back the treasury stock is less than the company received when it issued the stock, the difference is recorded in Paid-in Capital, Retirement of Stock. If the reacquisition cost is more than was received when the stock was first issued, the difference is a reduction in stockholders' equity and is debited to Retained Earnings. For instance, suppose that on November 15, Amber

Corporation decides to retire the 2,000 shares of stock that it bought back for $100,000. If the $5 par value common stock was originally issued at $6 per share, this entry would record the retirement:

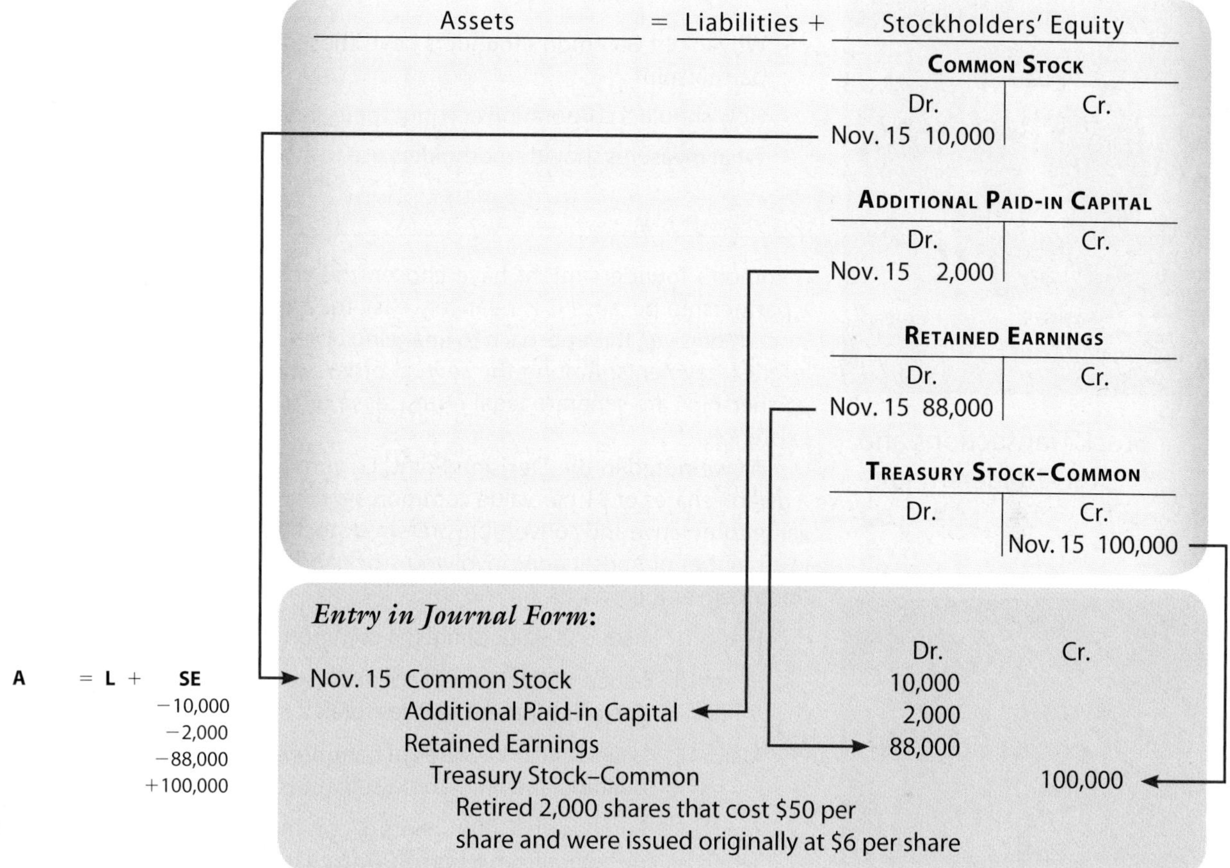

STOP & APPLY >

Prepare in journal form the entries necessary to record the following stock transactions of the Paulo Company during 2011:

May 1 Purchased 5,000 shares of its own $1 par value common stock for $10 per share, the current market price.

17 Sold 1,000 shares of treasury stock purchased on May 1 for $11 per share.

SOLUTION

	Dr.	Cr.
May 1		
Treasury Stock	50,000	
Cash		50,000
Purchased 5,000 shares of Paulo Company's common stock at $10 per share		
May 17		
Cash	11,000	
Treasury Stock		10,000
Paid-in Capital, Treasury Stock		1,000
Sold 1,000 shares of treasury stock for $11 per share		

▸ GAMMON, INC.: REVIEW PROBLEM

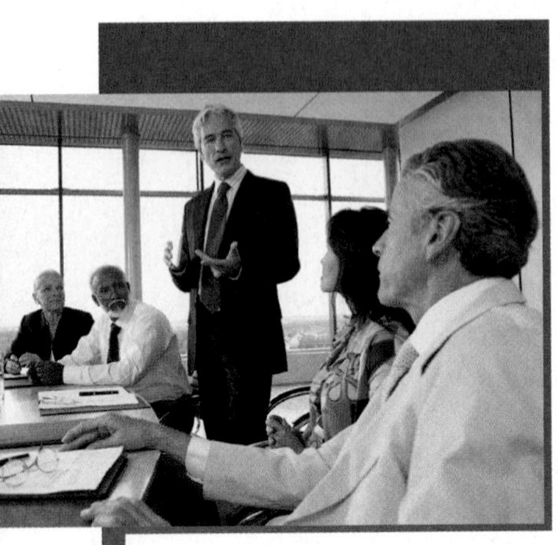

Stock Transactions and Stockholders' Equity
LO1 LO2
LO4

In the Decision Point at the beginning of the chapter, we posed these questions:

- Why might Gammon's founders have chosen to form a corporation rather than a partnership?
- How should a corporation account for its stock transactions and dividends?
- What measures should stockholders use to evaluate the return on their investments?

Gammon's founders might have chosen the corporate form of business rather than a partnership because it is relatively easy for a corporation to raise capital by issuing stock. Moreover, this approach to financing does not burden a company with debts and interest payments. Among the several other advantages that corporations have over partnerships are separate legal entity, ease of transfer of ownership, and continuous existence.

As we noted in the Decision Point, Gammon's state charter authorized it to issue 2 million shares of $1 par value common stock and 50,000 shares of 4 percent, $20 par value cumulative and convertible preferred stock. We also noted that Gammon engaged in a number of transactions involving stock and dividends during 2010. These transactions were as follows:

Feb. 1	Issued 200,000 shares of common stock for $250,000.
15	Issued 6,000 shares of common stock for accounting and legal services. The bills for these services totaled $7,200.
Mar. 15	Issued 240,000 shares of common stock to Tom Lee in exchange for a building and land appraised at $200,000 and $50,000, respectively.
Apr. 2	Purchased 40,000 shares of common stock for the treasury at $1.25 per share from a person who changed her mind about investing in the company.
July 1	Issued 50,000 shares of preferred stock for $1,000,000.
Sept. 30	Sold 20,000 of the shares in the treasury for $1.50 per share.
Dec. 31	Fisher's board of directors declared dividends of $49,820 payable on January 15, 2011, to stockholders of record on January 7. Dividends included preferred stock dividends of $20,000 for one-half year.

For the period ended December 31, 2010, Gammon reported net income of $80,000 and earnings per common share of $0.14. At December 31, the market price per common share was $1.60.

Required

1. Record Gammon's stock transactions in T accounts.
2. Prepare the stockholders' equity section of Gammon's balance sheet as of December 31, 2010. (**Hint:** Use net income and dividends to calculate retained earnings.)
3. Calculate Gammon's dividends yield on common stock, price/earnings ratio of common stock, and return on equity.

Answers to Review Problem

1. Entries in T accounts:

Assets = **Liabilities** + **Stockholders' Equity**

Cash

Feb.	1	250,000	Apr.	2	50,000
July	1	1,000,000			
Sept.	30	30,000			

Building

Mar.	15	200,000			

Land

Mar.	15	50,000			

Dividends Payable

			Dec.	31	49,820

Preferred Stock

			July	1	1,000,000

Common Stock

			Feb.	1	200,000
				15	6,000
			Mar.	15	240,000
			Bal.		446,000

Additional Paid-in Capital

			Feb.	1	50,000
				15	1,200
			Mar.	15	10,000
			Bal.		61,200

Paid-in Capital–Treasury Stock

			Sept.	30	5,000

Dividends

Dec.	31	49,820			

Treasury Stock

Apr.	2	50,000	Sept.	30	25,000
Bal.		25,000			

Start-up and Organization Costs

Feb.	15	7,200			

2. Stockholders' equity section of the balance sheet:

Gammon Inc.
Balance Sheet
December 31, 2010

Stockholders' Equity

Contributed capital		
Preferred stock, 4 percent cumulative convertible, $20 par value, 50,000 shares authorized, issued, and outstanding		$1,000,000
Common stock, $1 par value, 2,000,000 shares authorized, 446,000 shares issued, and 426,000 shares outstanding		446,000
Additional paid-in capital	$61,200	
Paid-in capital, treasury stock	5,000	66,200
Total contributed capital		$1,512,200
Retained earnings		30,180*
Total contributed capital and retained earnings		$1,542,380
Less treasury stock (20,000 shares, at cost)		25,000
Total stockholders' equity		$1,517,380

*Retained Earning = Net Income – Cash Dividends Declared
Retained Earnings = $80,000 – $49,820 = $30,180

3. Dividends yield on common stock, price/earnings ratio of common stock, and return on equity:

$$\text{Dividends per Share} = \frac{\text{Common Stock Dividend}}{\text{Common Shares Outstanding}} = \frac{\$29{,}820}{426{,}000} = \$0.07$$

$$\text{Dividends Yield} = \frac{\text{Dividends per Share}}{\text{Market Price per Share}} = \frac{\$0.07}{\$1.60} = 4.4\%$$

$$\text{Price/Earnings Ratio} = \frac{\text{Market Price per Share}}{\text{Earnings per Share}} = \frac{\$1.60}{\$0.14} = 11.4 \text{ times}$$

The opening balance of stockholders' equity on February 1, 2010, was $250,000.

$$\text{Return on Equity} = \frac{\text{Net Income}}{\text{Average Stockholders' Equity}}$$

$$= \frac{\$80{,}000}{(\$1{,}517{,}380 + \$250{,}000) \div 2}$$

$$= \frac{\$80{,}000}{\$883{,}690}$$

$$= 9.1\%$$

LO1 Identify and explain the management issues related to contributed capital.

Contributed capital is a critical component in corporate financing. Managing contributed capital requires an understanding of the advantages and disadvantages of the corporate form of business and of the issues involved in using equity financing. Managers must also know how to determine dividend policies and how to evaluate these policies using dividends yield, return on equity, and the price/earnings ratio. The liability for payment of dividends arises on the date the board of directors declares a dividend. The declaration is recorded with a debit to Dividends and a credit to Dividends Payable. The record date—the date on which ownership of the stock, and thus of the right to receive a dividend, is determined—requires no entry. On the payment date, the Dividends Payable account is eliminated, and the Cash account is reduced. Another issue involved in managing contributed capital is using stock options as compensation.

LO2 Identify the components of stockholders' equity.

The stockholders' equity section of a corporate balance sheet usually has at least three components: contributed capital, retained earnings, and treasury stock. Contributed capital consists of money raised through stock issues. A corporation can issue two types of stock: common stock and preferred stock. Common stockholders have voting rights; they also share in the earnings of the corporation. Preferred stockholders usually have preference over common stockholders in one or more areas. Retained earnings are reinvested in the corporation; they represent stockholders' claims to assets resulting from profitable operations. Treasury stock is stock that the issuing corporation has reacquired. It is treated as a deduction from stockholders' equity.

LO3 Identify the characteristics of preferred stock.

Preferred stock generally gives its owners first right to dividend payments. Only after these stockholders have been paid can common stockholders receive any portion of a dividend. If the preferred stock is cumulative and dividends are in arrears, a corporation must pay the amount in arrears to preferred stockholders before it pays any dividends to common stockholders. Preferred stockholders also usually have preference over common stockholders in terms of their claims to corporate assets if the corporation is liquidated. In addition, preferred stock may be convertible to common stock, and it is often callable at the option of the corporation.

LO4 Account for the issuance of stock for cash and other assets.

Corporations normally issue their stock in exchange for cash or other assets. Most states require corporations to issue stock at a minimum value called *legal capital.* Legal capital is represented by the stock's par or stated value.

When stock is issued for cash at par or stated value, Cash is debited and Common Stock or Preferred Stock is credited. When stock is sold at an amount greater than par or stated value, the excess is recorded in Additional Paid-in Capital.

When stock is issued for noncash assets, the general rule is to record the stock at its market value. If this value cannot be determined, the fair market value of the asset received is used to record the transaction.

LO5 Account for treasury stock.

Treasury stock is stock that the issuing company has reacquired. A company may buy back its own stock for several reasons, including a desire to create stock option plans, maintain a favorable market for the stock, increase earnings per share, or purchase other companies. Treasury stock is recorded at cost and is deducted from stockholders' equity. It can be reissued or retired. It is similar to unissued stock in that it does not have rights until it is reissued.

REVIEW of Concepts and Terminology

The following concepts and terms were introduced in this chapter:

Key Ratios

CHAPTER ASSIGNMENTS

BUILDING Your Basic Knowledge and Skills

Short Exercises

LO1 **Management Issues**

SE 1. Indicate whether each of the following actions is related to (a) managing under the corporate form of business, (b) using equity financing, (c) determining dividend policies, (d) evaluating performance using return on equity, or (e) issuing stock options:

1. Considering whether to make a distribution to stockholders
2. Controlling day-to-day operations
3. Determining whether to issue preferred or common stock
4. Compensating management based on the company's meeting or exceeding the targeted return on equity
5. Compensating employees by giving them the right to purchase shares at a given price
6. Transferring shares without the approval of other owners

LO1 **Advantages and Disadvantages of a Corporation**

SE 2. Identify whether each of the following characteristics is an advantage or a disadvantage of the corporate form of business:

1. Ease of transfer of ownership
2. Taxation
3. Separate legal entity
4. Lack of mutual agency
5. Government regulation
6. Continuous existence

LO1 **Effect of Start-up and Organization Costs**

SE 3. At the beginning of 2011, Patel Company incurred the following start-up and organization costs: (1) attorneys' fees with a market value of $20,000, paid with 12,000 shares of $1 par value common stock, and (2) incorporation fees of $12,000. Calculate total start-up and organization costs. What will be the effect of these costs on the income statement and balance sheet?

LO1 **Exercise of Stock Options**

SE 4. On June 6, Aretha Dafoe exercised her option to purchase 20,000 shares of Shalom Company $1 par value common stock at an option price of $8. The market price per share was $8 on the grant date and $36 on the exercise date. (1) When must the fair value of the option be estimated? (2) Is the market price of the stock on the exercise date most relevant to Dafoe or to Shalom Company?

LO2 **Stockholders' Equity**

SE 5. Prepare the stockholders' equity section of Fina Corporation's balance sheet from the following accounts and balances on December 31, 2011:

Common Stock, $10 par value, 30,000 shares authorized, 20,000 shares issued, and 19,500 shares outstanding	$200,000
Additional Paid-in Capital	100,000
Retained Earnings	15,000
Treasury Stock, Common (500 shares, at cost)	7,500

LO1 **Cash Dividends**

SE 6. Tone Corporation has authorized 200,000 shares of $1 par value common stock, of which 160,000 are issued and 140,000 are outstanding. On May 15, the board of directors declared a cash dividend of $0.20 per share, payable on June 15 to stockholders of record on June 1. Prepare the entries in T accounts, as necessary, for each of the three dates.

LO3 **Preferred Stock Dividends with Dividends in Arrears**

SE 7. The Ferris Corporation has 2,000 shares of $100, 8 percent cumulative preferred stock outstanding and 40,000 shares of $1 par value common stock outstanding. In the company's first three years of operation, its board of directors paid cash dividends as follows: 2010, none; 2011, $40,000; and 2012, $80,000. Determine the total cash dividends and dividends per share paid to the preferred and common stockholders during each of the three years.

LO4 **Issuance of Stock**

SE 8. Rattich Company is authorized to issue 50,000 shares of common stock. The company sold 2,500 shares at $12 per share. Prepare entries in journal form to record the sale of stock for cash under each of the following independent alternatives: (1) The stock has a par value of $5, and (2) the stock has no par value but a stated value of $1 per share.

LO4 **Issuance of Stock for Noncash Assets**

SE 9. Embossing Corporation issued 32,000 shares of its $1 par value common stock in exchange for land that had a fair market value of $200,000. Prepare in journal form the entries necessary to record the issuance of the stock for the land under each of these conditions: (1) The stock was selling for $7 per share on the day of the transaction; (2) management attempted to place a value on the common stock but could not do so.

LO5 **Treasury Stock Transactions**

SE 10. Prepare in journal form the entries necessary to record the following stock transactions of the Seoul Company during 2011:

Oct.	1	Purchased 2,000 shares of its own $2 par value common stock for $20 per share, the current market price.
	17	Sold 500 shares of treasury stock purchased on October 1 for $25 per share.

LO5 **Retirement of Treasury Stock**

SE 11. On October 28, 2011, the Seoul Company (**SE 10**) retired the remaining 1,500 shares of treasury stock. The shares were originally issued at $5 per share. Prepare the necessary entry in journal form.

Exercises

LO1 LO2 **Discussion Questions**

E 1. Develop brief answers to each of the following questions:

1. Why are most large companies established as corporations rather than as partnerships?
2. Why do many companies like to give stock options as compensation?
3. If an investor sells shares after the declaration date but before the date of record, does the seller still receive the dividend?
4. Why does a company usually not want to issue all its authorized shares?

LO3 LO4 LO5 **Discussion Questions**

E 2. Develop brief answers to each of the following questions:

1. Why would a company want to issue callable preferred stock?
2. What arguments can you give for treating preferred stock as debt rather than equity when carrying out financial analysis?
3. What relevance does par value or stated value have to a financial ratio, such as return on equity or debt to equity?
4. Why is treasury stock not considered an investment or an asset?

LO1 **Dividends Yield and Price/Earnings Ratio**

E 3. In 2011, Rainbow Corporation earned $8.80 per share and paid a dividend of $4.00 per share. At year end, the price of its stock was $132 per share. Calculate the dividends yield and the price/earnings ratio.

LO2 **Stockholders' Equity**

E 4. The following accounts and balances are from the records of Stuard Corporation on December 31, 2011:

Preferred Stock, $100 par value, 9 percent cumulative, 10,000 shares authorized, 3,000 shares issued and outstanding	$300,000
Common Stock, $12 par value, 45,000 shares authorized, 15,000 shares issued, and 14,250 shares outstanding	180,000
Additional Paid-in Capital	97,000
Retained Earnings	11,500
Treasury Stock, Common (750 shares, at cost)	15,000

Prepare the stockholders' equity section of Stuard Corporation's balance sheet as of December 31, 2011.

LO2 LO3 **Characteristics of Common and Preferred Stock**

E 5. Indicate whether each of the following characteristics is more closely associated with common stock (C) or preferred stock (P):

1. Often receives dividends at a set rate
2. Is considered the residual equity of a company
3. Can be callable
4. Can be convertible
5. More likely to have dividends that vary in amount from year to year
6. Can be entitled to receive dividends not paid in past years
7. Likely to have full voting rights
8. Receives assets first in liquidation
9. Generally receives dividends before other classes of stock

LO2 LO4 **Stock Entries Using T Accounts; Stockholders' Equity**

E 6. Shark School Supply Corporation was organized in 2011. It was authorized to issue 200,000 shares of no-par common stock with a stated value of $5 per share, and 40,000 shares of $100 par value, 6 percent noncumulative preferred stock. On March 1, the company issued 60,000 shares of its common stock for $15 per share and 8,000 shares of its preferred stock for $100 per share.

1. Record the issuance of the stock in T accounts.
2. Prepare the stockholders' equity section of Shark School Supply Corporation's balance sheet as it would appear immediately after the company issued the common and preferred stock.

LO1 Cash Dividends

E 7. Pine Corporation secured authorization from the state for 100,000 shares of $10 par value common stock. It has 40,000 shares issued and 35,000 shares outstanding. On June 5, the board of directors declared a $0.25 per share cash dividend to be paid on June 25 to stockholders of record on June 15. Prepare entries in T accounts to record these events.

LO1 LO5 Cash Dividends

E 8. Avena Corporation has 250,000 authorized shares of $1 par value common stock, of which 100,000 are issued, including 10,000 shares of treasury stock. On October 15, the corporation's board of directors declared a cash dividend of $0.50 per share payable on November 15 to stockholders of record on November 1. Prepare entries in T accounts for each of the three dates.

LO3 Cash Dividends with Dividends in Arrears

E 9. Ghana Corporation has 10,000 shares of its $100 par value, 7 percent cumulative preferred stock outstanding and 50,000 shares of its $1 par value common stock outstanding. In Ghana's first four years of operation, its board of directors paid cash dividends as follows: 2009, none; 2010, $120,000; 2011, $140,000; 2012, $140,000. Determine the dividends per share and total cash dividends paid to the preferred and common stockholders during each of the four years.

LO3 Cash Dividends on Preferred and Common Stock

E 10. Dylan Corporation pays dividends at the end of each year. The dividends that it paid for 2010, 2011, and 2012 were $80,000, $60,000, and $180,000, respectively. Calculate the total amount of dividends Dylan Corporation paid in each of these years to its common and preferred stockholders under both of the following capital structures: (1) 20,000 shares of $100 par, 6 percent noncumulative preferred stock and 60,000 shares of $10 par common stock; (2) 10,000 shares of $100 par, 7 percent cumulative preferred stock and 60,000 shares of $10 par common stock. Dylan Corporation had no dividends in arrears at the beginning of 2010.

LO4 Issuance of Stock

E 11. Powet Net Company is authorized to issue 50,000 shares of common stock. On August 1, the company issued 2,500 shares at $25 per share. Prepare entries in journal form to record the issuance of stock for cash under each of the following alternatives:

1. The stock has a par value of $25.
2. The stock has a par value of $10.
3. The stock has no par value.
4. The stock has a stated value of $1 per share.

LO4 Issuance of Stock for Noncash Assets

E 12. On July 1, 2011, Kosa, a new corporation, issued 20,000 shares of its common stock to finance a corporate headquarters building. The building has a fair market value of $600,000 and a book value of $400,000. Because Kosa is a new corporation, it is not possible to establish a market value for its common stock. Record the issuance of stock for the building, assuming the following conditions: (1) the par value of the stock is $10 per share; (2) the stock is no-par stock; and (3) the stock has a stated value of $4 per share.

LO5 **Treasury Stock Transactions**

E 13. Record in T accounts the following stock transactions of Pigua Corporation, which represent all the company's treasury stock transactions during 2011:

May	5	Purchased 1,600 shares of its own $2 par value common stock for $40 per share, the current market price.
	17	Sold 600 shares of treasury stock purchased on May 5 for $44 per share.
	21	Sold 400 shares of treasury stock purchased on May 5 for $40 per share.
	28	Sold the remaining 600 shares of treasury stock purchased on May 5 for $38 per share.

LO5 **Treasury Stock Transactions Including Retirement**

E 14. Record in T accounts the following stock transactions of Lopez Corporation, which represent all its treasury stock transactions for the year:

June	1	Purchased 2,000 shares of its own $15 par value common stock for $35 per share, the current market price.
	10	Sold 500 shares of treasury stock purchased on June 1 for $40 per share.
	20	Sold 700 shares of treasury stock purchased on June 1 for $29 per share.
	30	Retired the remaining shares purchased on June 1. The original issue price was $21 per share.

Problems

LO1 LO2 LO4 **Common Stock Transactions and Stockholders' Equity**

P 1. On March 1, 2011, Dora Corporation began operations with a charter from the state that authorized 50,000 shares of $4 par value common stock. Over the next quarter, the firm engaged in the transactions that follow.

Mar.	1	Issued 15,000 shares of common stock, $100,000.
	2	Paid fees associated with obtaining the charter and starting up and organizing the corporation, $12,000.
Apr.	10	Issued 6,500 shares of common stock, $65,000.
	15	Purchased 2,500 shares of common stock, $25,000
May	31	The board of directors declared a $0.20 per share cash dividend to be paid on June 15 to shareholders of record on June 10.

Required

1. Record the above transactions in T accounts.
2. Prepare the stockholders' equity section of Dora Corporation's balance sheet on May 31, 2011. Net income earned during the first quarter was $15,000.

User insight ▶ 3. What effect, if any, will the cash dividend declaration on May 31 have on Dora Corporation's net income, retained earnings, and cash flows?

LO1 LO3 **Preferred and Common Stock Dividends and Dividends Yield**

P 2. The Rago Corporation had the following stock outstanding from 2009 through 2012:

Preferred stock: $100 par value, 8 percent cumulative, 5,000 shares authorized, issued, and outstanding

Common stock: $10 par value, 100,000 shares authorized, issued, and outstanding

The company paid $30,000, $30,000, $94,000, and $130,000 in dividends during 2009, 2010, 2011, and 2012, respectively. The market price per common share was $7.25 and $8.00 per share at the end of years 2011 and 2012, respectively.

Required

1. Determine the dividends per share and the total dividends paid to common stockholders and preferred stockholders in 2009, 2010, 2011, and 2012.
2. Perform the same computations, with the assumption that the preferred stock was noncumulative.
3. Calculate the 2011 and 2012 dividends yield for common stock, using the dividends per share computed in requirement **2**.

User insight ▶

4. How are cumulative preferred stock and noncumulative preferred stock similar to long-term bonds? How do they differ from long-term bonds?

LO1 LO2 LO3 LO4 LO5

KA KLOOSTER & ALLEN

Comprehensive Stockholders' Equity Transactions

P 3. In January 2010, Janas Corporation was organized and authorized to issue 1,000,000 shares of no-par common stock and 25,000 shares of 5 percent, $50 par value, noncumulative preferred stock. The stock-related transactions for the first year's operations were as follows:

		Account			
		Debited		Credited	
		Account Number	Dollar Amount	Account Number	Dollar Amount
Jan. 19	Sold 7,500 shares of common stock for $15,750. State law requires a minimum of $1 stated value per share.	110	$15,750	310 312	$7,500 $8,250
21	Issued 2,500 shares of common stock to attorneys and accountants for services valued at $5,500 and provided during the organization of the corporation.				
Feb. 7	Issued 15,000 shares of common stock for a building that had an appraised value of $39,000.				
Mar. 22	Purchased 5,000 shares of its common stock at $3 per share.				
July 15	Issued 2,500 shares of common stock to employees under a stock option plan that allows any employee to buy shares at the current market price, which is now $3 per share.				

Aug.	1	Sold 1,250 shares of treasury stock for $4 per share.				
Sept.	1	Declared a cash dividend of $0.15 per common share to be paid on September 25 to stockholders of record on September 15.				
	15	Date of record for cash dividends.				
	25	Paid cash dividends to stockholders of record on September 15.				
Oct.	30	Issued 2,000 shares of common stock for a piece of land. The stock was selling for $3 per share, and the land had a fair market value of $6,000.				
Dec.	15	Issued 1,100 shares of preferred stock for $50 per share.				

Required

1. For each of the above transactions, enter in the blanks provided the account numbers and dollar amounts (as shown in the example) for the account(s) debited and credited. The account numbers are listed below.

110 Cash	312 Additional Paid-in Capital
120 Land	313 Paid-in Capital, Treasury Stock
121 Building	340 Retained Earnings
220 Dividends Payable	341 Dividends
305 Preferred Stock	350 Treasury Stock, Common
310 Common Stock	510 Start-up and Organization Costs

User insight ▶ 2. Why is the stockholders' equity section of the balance sheet an important consideration in analyzing the performance of a company?

LO1 LO2 LO3 LO4 LO5

Comprehensive Stockholders' Equity Transactions and Stockholders' Equity

P 4. Kras, Inc., was organized and authorized to issue 50,000 shares of $100 par value, 9 percent preferred stock and 50,000 shares of no-par, $5 stated value common stock on July 1, 2011. Stock-related transactions for Kras are as follows:

July	1	Issued 10,000 shares of common stock at $11 per share.
	1	Issued 500 shares of common stock at $11 per share for services rendered in connection with the organization of the company.
	2	Issued 1,000 shares of preferred stock at par value for cash.
	10	Issued 2,500 shares of common stock for land on which the asking price was $35,000. Market value of the stock was $12. Management wishes to record the land at the market value of the stock.

Aug. 2 Purchased 1,500 shares of its common stock at $13 per share.
10 Declared a cash dividend for one month on the outstanding preferred stock and $0.02 per share on common stock outstanding, payable on August 22 to stockholders of record on August 12.
12 Date of record for cash dividends.
22 Paid cash dividends.

Required

1. Record the transactions in journal form.
2. Prepare the stockholders' equity section of the balance sheet as it would appear on August 31, 2011. Net income for July was zero and August was $11,500.
3. (User insight ▶) Calculate dividends yield, price/earnings ratio, and return on equity. Assume earnings per common share are $1.00 and market price per common share is $20. For beginning stockholders' equity, use the balance after the July transactions.
4. (User insight ▶) Discuss the results in requirement **3**, including the effect on investors' returns and the company's profitability as it relates to stockholders' equity.

LO1 LO5 **Treasury Stock**

P 5. The Rolek Company was involved in the following treasury stock transactions during 2010:

a. Purchased 40,000 shares of its $1 par value common stock on the market for $2.50 per share.
b. Purchased 8,000 shares of its $1 par value common stock on the market for $2.80 per share.
c. Sold 22,000 shares purchased in **a** for $65,500.
d. Sold the other 18,000 shares purchased in **a** for $36,000.
e. Sold 3,000 of the remaining shares of treasury stock for $1.60 per share.
f. Retired all the remaining shares of treasury stock. All shares originally were issued at $1.50 per share.

Required

1. Record the treasury stock transactions in T accounts.
2. (User insight ▶) What is the reasoning behind treating the purchase of treasury stock as a reduction in stockholders' equity as opposed to treating it as an investment asset?

Alternate Problems

LO1 LO2 LO4 LO5 **Common Stock Transactions and Stockholders' Equity**

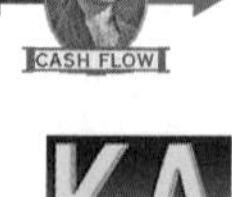

P 6. Glass Corporation began operations on September 1, 2011. The corporation's charter authorized 150,000 shares of $8 par value common stock. Glass Corporation engaged in the following transactions during its first quarter:

Sept. 1 Issued 25,000 shares of common stock, $250,000.
1 Paid an attorney $16,000 to help start up and organize the corporation and obtain a corporate charter from the state.
Oct. 2 Issued 40,000 shares of common stock, $480,000.
15 Purchased 5,000 shares of common stock for $75,000.
Nov. 30 Declared a cash dividend of $0.40 per share to be paid on December 15 to stockholders of record on December 10.

Required

1. Prepare entries in T accounts to record the above transactions.
2. Prepare the stockholders' equity section of Glass Corporation's balance sheet on November 30, 2011. Net income for the quarter was $40,000.

User insight ▶ 3. What effect, if any, will the cash dividend declaration on November 30 have on net income, retained earnings, and cash flows?

LO1 LO3

Preferred and Common Stock Dividends and Dividends Yield

P 7. The Vegas Corporation had both common stock and preferred stock outstanding from 2010 through 2012. Information about each stock for the three years is as follows:

Type	Par Value	Shares Outstanding	Other
Preferred	$100	20,000	7% cumulative
Common	20	300,000	

The company paid $70,000, $400,000, and $550,000 in dividends for 2010 through 2012, respectively. The market price per common share was $15 and $17 per share at the end of years 2011 and 2012, respectively.

Required

1. Determine the dividends per share and total dividends paid to the common and preferred stockholders each year.
2. Assuming that the preferred stock was noncumulative, repeat the computations performed in requirement **1**.
3. Calculate the 2011 and 2012 dividends yield for common stock using dividends per share computed in requirement **2**.

User insight ▶ 4. How are cumulative preferred stock and noncumulative preferred stock similar to long-term bonds? How do they differ from long-term bonds?

LO1 LO2 LO3 LO4 LO5

Comprehensive Stockholders' Equity Transactions and Financial Ratios

P 8. Stavski Plastics Corporation was chartered in the Commonwealth of Massachusetts. The company was authorized to issue 10,000 shares of $100 par value, 6 percent preferred stock and 50,000 shares of no-par common stock. The common stock has a $2 stated value. The stock-related transactions for the quarter ended October 31, 2011, were as follows:

Aug.	3	Issued 10,000 shares of common stock at $22 per share.
	15	Issued 8,000 shares of common stock for land. Asking price for the land was $100,000. Common stock's market value was $12 per share. Management wishes to record the land at the market value of the stock.
	22	Issued 5,000 shares of preferred stock for $500,000.
Oct.	4	Issued 5,000 shares of common stock for $60,000.
	10	Purchased 2,500 shares of common stock for the treasury for $6,500.
	15	Declared a quarterly cash dividend on the outstanding preferred stock and $0.10 per share on common stock outstanding, payable on October 31 to stockholders of record on October 25.
	25	Date of record for cash dividends.
	31	Paid the cash dividends declared on October 15.

Required

1. Record transactions for the quarter ended October 31, 2011, in T accounts.
2. Prepare the stockholders' equity section of the balance sheet as of October 31, 2011. Net income for the quarter was $23,000.

User insight ▶ 3. Calculate dividends yield, price/earnings ratio, and return on equity. Assume earnings per common share are $1.97 and market price per common share is $25. For beginning stockholders' equity, use the balance after the August transactions.

User insight ▶ 4. Discuss the results in requirement **3**, including the effect on investors' returns and the firm's profitability as it relates to stockholders' equity.

LO1 LO2 LO3 LO4 LO5

Comprehensive Stockholders' Equity Transactions

P 9. In January 2011, Jones Corporation was organized and authorized to issue 2,000,000 shares of no-par common stock and 50,000 shares of 5 percent, $50 par value, noncumulative preferred stock. The stock-related transactions for the first year's operations were as follows:

		Account			
		Debited		Credited	
Date	Transaction	Account Number	Dollar Amount	Account Number	Dollar Amount
Jan. 19	Sold 15,000 shares of common stock for $31,500. State law requires a minimum of $1 stated value per share.	110	$31,500	310 312	$15,000 $16,500
21	Issued 5,000 shares of common stock to attorneys and accountants for services valued at $11,000 and provided during the organization of the corporation.				
Feb. 7	Issued 30,000 shares of common stock for a building that had an appraised value of $78,000.				
Mar. 22	Purchased 10,000 shares of its common stock at $3 per share.				
July 15	Issued 5,000 shares of common stock to employees under a stock option plan that allows any employee to buy shares at the current market price, which is now $3 per share.				
Aug. 1	Sold 2,500 shares of treasury stock for $4 per share.				

Sept. 1	Declared a cash dividend of $0.15 per common share to be paid on September 25 to stockholders of record on September 15.	___	___	___	___
15	Date of record for cash dividends.	___	___	___	___
25	Paid cash dividends to stockholders of record on September 15.	___	___	___	___
Oct. 30	Issued 4,000 shares of common stock for a piece of land. The stock was selling for $3 per share, and the land had a fair market value of $12,000.	___	___	___	___
Dec. 15	Issued 2,200 shares of preferred stock for $50 per share.	___	___	___	___

Required

1. For each of the above transactions, enter in the blanks provided the account numbers and dollar amounts (as shown in the example) for the account(s) debited and credited. The account numbers are listed below.

110 Cash	312 Additional Paid-in Capital
120 Land	313 Paid-in Capital, Treasury Stock
121 Building	340 Retained Earnings
220 Dividends Payable	341 Dividends
305 Preferred Stock	350 Treasury Stock, Common
310 Common Stock	510 Start-up and Organization Costs

User insight ▶ 2. Why is the stockholders' equity section of the balance sheet an important consideration in analyzing the performance of a company?

LO1 LO5 **Treasury Stock**

P 10. The Spivak Company was involved in the following treasury stock transactions during 2011:

a. Purchased 80,000 shares of its $1 par value common stock on the market for $2.50 per share.
b. Purchased 16,000 shares of its $1 par value common stock on the market for $2.80 per share.
c. Sold 44,000 shares purchased in **a** for $131,000.
d. Sold the other 36,000 shares purchased in **a** for $72,000.
e. Sold 6,000 of the remaining shares of treasury stock for $1.60 per share.
f. Retired all the remaining shares of treasury stock. All shares originally were issued at $1.50 per share.

Required

1. Record the treasury stock transactions in T accounts.

User insight ▶ 2. What is the reasoning behind treating the purchase of treasury stock as a reduction in stockholders' equity as opposed to treating it as an investment asset?

ENHANCING Your Knowledge, Skills, and Critical Thinking

LO1 Reasons for Issuing Common Stock

C 1. DreamWorks Animation, led by billionaire Microsoft founder Paul Allen, went public in a recent year with its class A common stock at $28 per share, raising $650 million. By the end of the first day, it was up 27 percent to $38 per share, giving the company a value of almost $1 billion. This initial enthusiasm did not last. By the end of 2007, the price was only around $25 per share.[15] As a growing company that has produced such animated hits as *Shrek* and *Shrek II*, DreamWorks could have borrowed significant funds by issuing long-term debt. What are some advantages of issuing common stock as opposed to bonds? What are some disadvantages?

LO5 Purposes of Treasury Stock

C 2. Many companies in recent years have bought back their common stock. For example, **IBM**, with large cash holdings, spent almost $18 billion over three years repurchasing its stock.[16] What are the reasons companies buy back their own shares? What is the effect of common stock buybacks on earnings per share, return on equity, return on assets, debt to equity, and the current ratio?

LO4 Effect of Stock Issue

C 3. When **Google, Inc.** went public with an IPO, it used an auction system that allowed everyone to participate rather than allocating shares of stock to a few insiders.[17] The company's IPO drew widespread attention. Announcements of the IPO would have been similar to the following:

22,500,000 Shares

GOOGLE, INC.

$0.001 Par Value Common Stock

Price $85 a share

The gross proceeds of the IPO before issue costs were $1.9 billion.

Shown below is a portion of the stockholders' equity section of the balance sheet adapted from Google's annual report, which was issued prior to this stock offering:

Stockholders' Equity

(Dollar amounts in thousands)

Common Stock, $0.001 par value, 700,000,000 shares authorized; 161,000,000 shares issued and outstanding	$ 161
Additional paid-in capital	725,219
Retained earnings	191,352

1. Assume that the net proceeds to Google after issue costs were $1.8 billion. Record the stock issuance on Google's accounting records in journal form.
2. Prepare the portion of the stockholders' equity section of the balance sheet shown above after the issue of the common stock, based on the information given. Round all answers to the nearest thousand.
3. Based on your answer in **2**, did Google have to increase its authorized shares to undertake this stock issue?
4. What amount per share did Google receive and how much did Google's underwriters receive to help in issuing the stock? What do underwriters do to earn their fee?

LO1 LO5 **Treasury Stock or Dividends?**

C 4. In your class, divide into small groups. Assume the president of a small company that has been profitable for several years but has not paid a dividend has hired your group. The company has built up a cash reserve. It has 20 stockholders, but the president owns 40 percent of the company's shares. Several of the stockholders with smaller numbers of shares would like to sell their shares, but there is no ready market. The president of the company has asked your group to determine whether it would be better to recommend to the board of directors that they pay a dividend to all stockholders or whether they should buy out the smaller stockholders to hold shares in the treasury and possibly retire them. In your group, decide which recommendation you will make to the president. Develop a series of points to support your argument. Participate in a class debate among teams who have chosen opposing positions.

LO2 LO5 **Stockholders' Equity**

C 5. Refer to the **CVS Corporation** annual report in the Supplement to Chapter 5 to answer the following questions:

1. What type of capital stock does CVS have? What is the par value? How many shares were authorized, issued, and outstanding at the end of fiscal 2008?
2. What is the dividends yield (use average price of stock in last quarter) for CVS and its relationship to the investors' total return? Does the company rely mostly on stock or on earnings for its stockholders' equity? (CVS's fourth quarter of 2008 high and low market prices were $34.90 and $23.19, respectively).
3. Does the company have a stock option plan? To whom do the stock options apply? Do employees have significant stock options? Given the market price of the stock shown in the report, do these options represent significant value to the employees?

LO1 LO5 **Return on Equity, Treasury Stock, and Dividends Policy**

C 6. Refer to the annual report of **CVS Corporation** and the financial statements of **Southwest Airlines Co.** in the Supplement to Chapter 5.

1. Compute the return on equity for both companies for fiscal 2008 and 2007. Total stockholders' equity for CVS and Southwest in 2006 was $9,917.6 million and $6,449 million, respectively.
2. Did either company purchase treasury stock during these years? How will the purchase of treasury stock affect return on equity and earnings per share?
3. Did either company issue stock during these years? What are the details?
4. Compare the dividend policy of the two companies.

CHAPTER

13 Long-Term Liabilities

Making a Statement

INCOME STATEMENT

Revenues

– Expenses

= Net Income

STATEMENT OF RETAINED EARNINGS

Beginning Balance

+ Net Income

– Dividends

= Ending Balance

BALANCE SHEET

Assets	Liabilities
	Stockholders' Equity

A = L + OE

STATEMENT OF CASH FLOWS

Operating activities
+ Investing activities
+ Financing activities
= Change in Cash
+ Beginning Balance
= Ending Cash Balance

Long-term liability transactions can impact all financial statements.

Long-term liabilities can be an attractive means of financing the expansion of a business. By incurring long-term debt to fund growth, a company may be able to earn a return that exceeds the interest it pays on the debt. When it does, it increases earnings for stockholders—that is, return on equity. Many companies reward top managers with bonuses for improving return on equity. This incentive provides a temptation to incur too much debt, which increases a company's financial risk. Thus, in deciding on an appropriate level of debt, as in so many other management issues, ethics is a major concern.

LEARNING OBJECTIVES

LO1 Identify the management issues related to long-term debt. (pp. 564–572)

LO2 Describe the features of a bond issue and the major characteristics of bonds. (pp. 573–575)

LO3 Record bonds issued at face value and at a discount or premium. (pp. 575–579)

LO4 Use present values to determine the value of bonds. (pp. 579–581)

LO5 Amortize bond discounts and bond premiums using the straight-line and effective interest methods. (pp. 581–589)

SUPPLEMENTAL OBJECTIVES

SO6 Account for the retirement of bonds and the conversion of bonds into stock. (pp. 590–592)

SO7 Record bonds issued between interest dates and year-end adjustments. (pp. 592–595)

DECISION POINT ▸ A USER'S FOCUS WILSON MANUFACTURING COMPANY

Wilson Manufacturing Company wants to expand its metal window division, but it does not have enough long-term capital to finance the project. As indicated in the data from Wilson's balance sheets that appear below, the company has until now been able to rely on the issuance of capital stock to take care of its financing needs. (Note the increase in stockholders' equity between 2009 and 2010.) Not included in the balance sheets are annual payments of $100,000 that Wilson makes on long-term leases of various properties.

	2010	2009
Total current liabilities	$1,000,000	$ 800,000
Long-term debt	0	0
Total stockholders' equity	3,200,000	3,000,000
Total liabilities and stockholders' equity	$4,200,000	$3,800,000

Wilson's management is now considering how to finance expansion of the metal window division. Several options are available, among them the issuance of long-term bonds. In making its decision, management will have to assess how much debt the company should carry and how much risk it is undertaking by assuming long-term debt.

- ▸ What should Wilson consider in deciding to issue long-term debt?
- ▸ How does one evaluate whether a company has too much debt?
- ▸ How are long-term bonds accounted for in Wilson's records?

Management Issues Related to Issuing Long-Term Debt

LO1 Identify the management issues related to long-term debt.

Profitable operations and short-term credit seldom provide sufficient cash for a growing business. Growth usually requires investment in long-term assets and in research and development and other activities that will produce income in future years. To finance these assets and activities, a company needs funds that will be available for long periods. Two key sources of long-term funds are the issuance of capital stock and the issuance of long-term debt. The management issues related to long-term debt financing are whether to take on long-term debt, how much long-term debt to carry, and what types of long-term debt to incur.

Deciding to Issue Long-Term Debt

A key decision for management is whether to rely solely on stockholders' equity—capital stock issued and retained earnings—for long-term funds or to rely partially on long-term debt. Some companies, such as **Microsoft** and **Apple Computer**, do not issue long-term debt, but like **CVS** and **Southwest Airlines**, most companies find it useful to do so.

Because long-term debt must be paid at maturity and usually requires periodic payments of interest, issuing common stock has two advantages over issuing long-term debt: (1) It does not have to be paid back, and (2) a company normally pays dividends on common stock only if it earns sufficient income. Issuing long-term debt, however, has the following advantages over issuing common stock

- **No loss of stockholder control.** When a corporation issues long-term debt, common stockholders do not relinquish any of their control over the company because bondholders and other creditors do not have voting rights. But when a corporation issues additional shares of common stock, the votes of the new stockholders may force current stockholders and management to give up some control.
- **Tax effects.** The interest on debt is tax-deductible, whereas dividends on common stock are not. For example, if a corporation pays \$100,000 in interest and its income tax rate is 30 percent, its net cost will be \$70,000 because it will save \$30,000 on income taxes. To pay \$100,000 in dividends on common stock, the corporation would have to earn \$142,857 before income taxes [\$100,000 ÷ (1 − 0.30)].
- **Financial leverage.** If a corporation earns more from the funds it raises by incurring long-term debt than it pays in interest on the debt, the excess will increase its earnings for the stockholders. This concept is called **financial leverage**, or *trading on equity*. For example, if a company earns 12 percent on a \$1,000,000 investment financed by long-term 10 percent notes, it will earn \$20,000 before income taxes (\$120,000 − \$100,000). The debt to equity ratio, explained on the following page, is considered an overall measure of a company's financial leverage.

Despite these advantages, debt financing is not always in a company's best interest. It may entail the following:

- **Financial risk.** A high level of debt exposes a company to financial risk. A company whose plans for earnings do not pan out, whose operations are subject to the ups and downs of the economy, or whose cash flow is weak may be unable to pay the principal amount of its debt at the maturity date or even to make periodic interest payments. Creditors can then force the company into bankruptcy—something that has occurred often in the heavily debt-financed airline industry. **TWA**, **Continental Airlines**, and **United Airlines** filed for bankruptcy protection because they could not make payments on their long-term debt and other liabilities. (While in bankruptcy, they restructured their debt and interest payments: **TWA** sold off its assets; **Continental** and **United** survived to come out of bankruptcy.)

- **Negative financial leverage.** Financial leverage can work against a company if the earnings from its investments do not exceed its interest payments. For example, many small Internet companies failed in recent years because they relied too heavily on debt financing before developing sufficient resources to ensure their survival.

Evaluating Long-Term Debt

The amount of long-term debt that companies carry varies widely. For many companies, it is less than 1.0 times stockholders' equity. However, as Figure 13-1 shows, the average debt to equity for selected industries often exceeds 1.0 times stockholders' equity. The range is from 77.7 to 192.7 times stockholders' equity.

To assess how much debt to carry, managers compute the debt to equity ratio. Using data from Wilson Manufacturing Company presented in the Decision Point, we can compute its debt to equity ratio in 2010 as follows (in thousands):

$$\text{Debt to Equity Ratio} = \frac{\text{Total Liabilities}}{\text{Total Stockholders' Equity}}$$

$$= \frac{\$1,000}{\$3,200} = 0.31 \text{ Times}$$

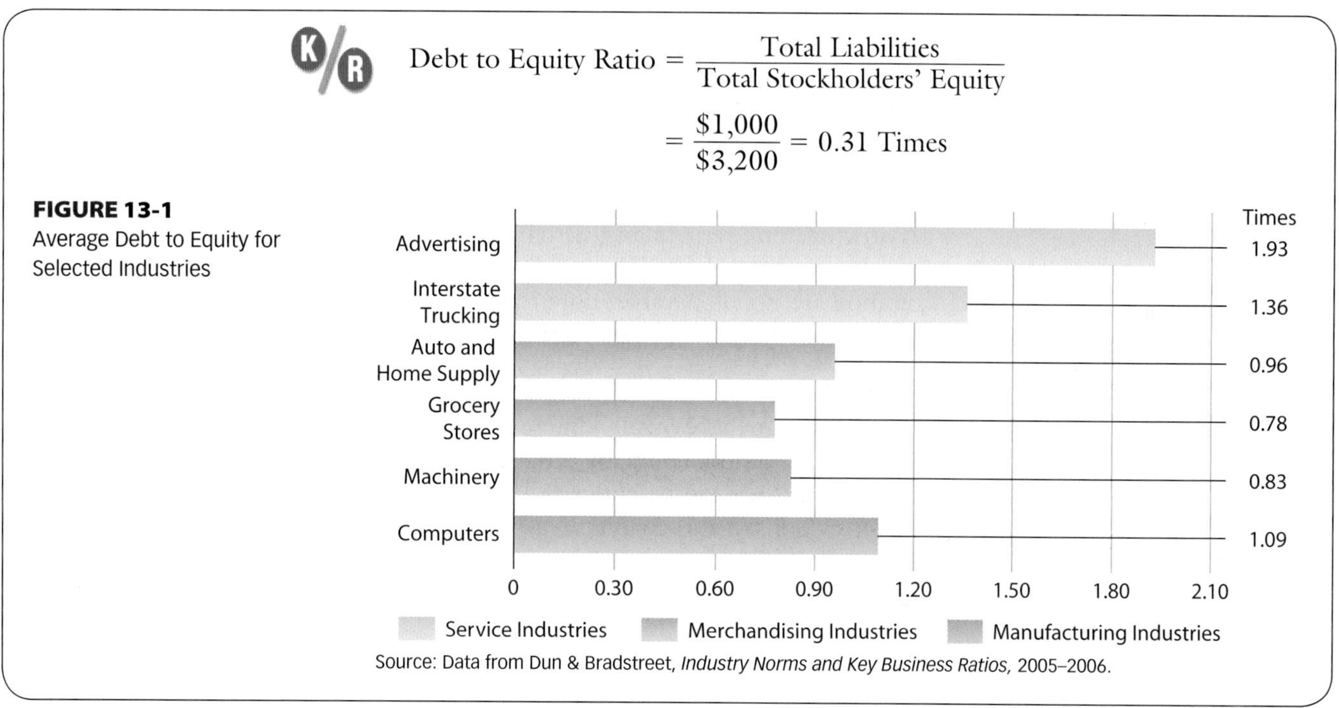

FIGURE 13-1
Average Debt to Equity for Selected Industries

Source: Data from Dun & Bradstreet, *Industry Norms and Key Business Ratios*, 2005–2006.

A debt to equity ratio of 0.31 times is relatively low, but it does not tell the whole story. As we noted in the Decision Point, Wilson also has long-term leases on various properties, which require annual payments of $100,000. Wilson structures these leases in such a way that they do not appear as liabilities on the balance sheet. This practice is called **off-balance-sheet financing** and, as used by Wilson, is entirely legal. The leases are, however, long-term commitments of cash payments and so have the effect of long-term liabilities.

Financial leverage—using long-term debt to fund investments or operations that increase return on equity—is advantageous as long as a company is able to make timely interest payments and repay the debt at maturity. Because failure to do so can force a company into bankruptcy, companies must assess the financial risk involved. A common measure of how much risk a company undertakes by assuming long-term debt is the **interest coverage ratio**. It measures the degree of protection a company has from default on interest payments. Most analysts want to see an interest coverage ratio of at least three or four times. Lower interest coverage would mean the company is at risk from a downturn in the economy.

Wilson's 2010 income statement shows that the company had income before income taxes of $250 million and interest expense of $50 million. Using these figures, we can compute Wilson's interest coverage ratio as follows:

$$\text{Interest Coverage Ratio} = \frac{\text{Income Before Income Taxes} + \text{Interest Expense}}{\text{Interest Expense}}$$

$$= \frac{\$250{,}000 + \$50{,}000}{\$50{,}000}$$

$$= \frac{\$300{,}000}{\$50{,}000}$$

$$= 6.0 \text{ Times}$$

Wilson's strong interest coverage ratio of 6.0 times shows that it is in no danger of being unable to make interest payments. However, in computing this ratio, management will add the company's off-balance-sheet rent expense of $100,000 to its interest expense. This procedure decreases the interest coverage ratio to about 2.7 times. Although still adequate to cover interest payments, the adjusted coverage ratio is far less robust, which demonstrates the significant effect that off-balance-sheet financing for leases can have on a company's financial situation.

Types of Long-Term Debt

To structure long-term financing to the best advantage of their companies, managers must know the characteristics of the various types of long-term debt. The most common are bonds payable, notes payable, mortgages payable, long-term leases, pension liabilities, other post-retirement benefits, and deferred income taxes.

Bonds Payable Long-term bonds are the most common type of long-term debt. They can have many different characteristics, including the amount of interest, whether the company can elect to repay them before their maturity date, and whether they can be converted to common stock. We cover bonds in detail in later sections of this chapter.

Notes Payable Long-term notes payable, those that come due in more than one year, are also very common. They differ from bonds mainly in the way the

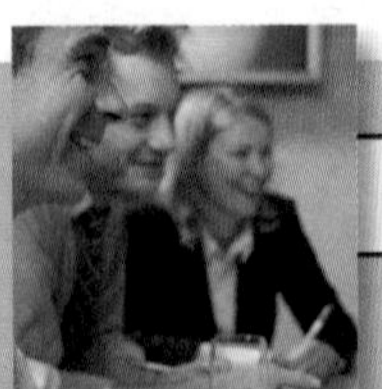

FOCUS ON BUSINESS PRACTICE

How Does Debt Affect a Company's Ability to Borrow?

Credit ratings by agencies like Standard & Poor's reflect the fact that the greater a company's debt, the greater its financial risk. Standard & Poor's rates companies from AAA (best) to CCC (worst) based on various factors, including a company's debt to equity ratio, as shown to the right.

RATING	AAA	AA	A	BBB	BB	B	CCC
Debt/Equity Ratio*	4.5	34.1	42.9	47.9	59.8	76.0	75.7

These ratings affect not only how much a company can borrow but also what the interest will cost. The lower its rating, the more a company must pay in interest, and vice versa.

*Averages of companies with similar ratings.

TABLE 13-1
Monthly Payment Schedule on a $100,000, 9 Percent Mortgage

	A	B	C	D	E
Payment Date	Unpaid Balance at Beginning of Period	Monthly Payment	Interest for 1 Month at 1% on Unpaid Balance* (0.75% × A)	Reduction in Debt (B − C)	Unpaid Balance at End of Period (A − D)
June 1					$100,000
July 1	$100,000	$1,200	$750	$450	99,550
Aug. 1	99,550	1,200	747	453	99,097
Sept. 1	99,097	1,200	743	457	98,640

*Rounded to the nearest dollar.

contract with the creditor is structured. A long-term note is a promissory note that represents a loan from a bank or other creditor, whereas a bond is a more complex financial instrument that usually involves debt to many creditors. Analysts often do not distinguish between long-term notes and bonds because they have similar effects on the financial statements.

Mortgages Payable A **mortgage** is a long-term debt secured by real property. It is usually paid in equal monthly installments. Each monthly payment includes interest on the debt and a reduction in the debt. Table 13-1 shows the first three monthly payments on a $100,000, 9 percent mortgage. The mortgage was obtained on June 1, and the monthly payments are $1,200. The T accounts and entry to record the July 1 payment would be as follows:

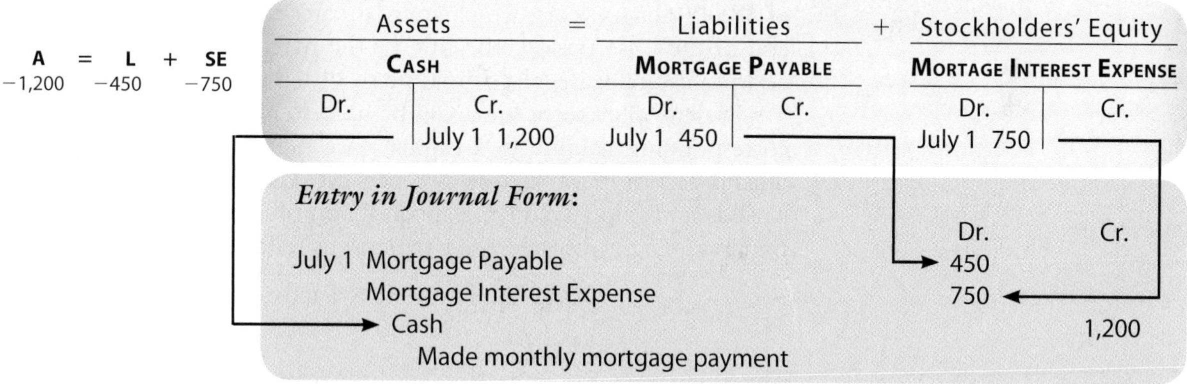

Notice from the entry and from Table 13-1 that the July 1 payment represents interest expense of $750 ($\$100{,}000 \times 0.09 \times \frac{1}{12}$) and a reduction in the debt of $450 ($1,200 − $750). Therefore, the July payment reduces the unpaid balance to $99,550. August's interest expense is slightly less than July's because of the decrease in the debt.

Long-Term Leases A company can obtain an operating asset in three ways:

1. By borrowing money and buying the asset
2. By renting the asset on a short-term lease
3. By obtaining the asset on a long-term lease

The first two methods do not create accounting problems. When a company uses the first method, it records the asset and liability at the amount paid, and the asset is subject to periodic depreciation.

When a company uses the second method, the lease is short in relation to the useful life of the asset, and the risks of ownership remain with the lessor. This type of agreement is called an **operating lease**. Payments on operating leases are properly treated as rent expense.

The third method is one of the fastest-growing ways of financing plant assets in the United States today. A long-term lease on a plant asset has several advantages. It requires no immediate cash payment, the rental payment is deducted in full for tax purposes, and it costs less than a short-term lease. Acquiring the use of plant assets under long-term leases does create several accounting challenges, however.

Study Note

Under a capital lease, the lessee should record depreciation, using any allowable method.

Long-term leases may be carefully structured, as they are by companies like **CVS**, so that they can be accounted for as operating leases. Accounting standards require, however, that a long-term lease be treated as a **capital lease** when it meets the following conditions:

- It cannot be canceled.
- Its duration is about the same as the useful life of the asset.
- It stipulates that the lessee has the option to buy the asset at a nominal price at the end of the lease.

Study Note

A capital lease is in substance an installment purchase, and the leased asset and related liability must be recognized at their present value.

A capital lease is thus more like a purchase or sale on installment than a rental. The lessee in a capital lease should record an asset, depreciation on the asset, and a long-term liability equal to the present value of the total lease payments during the lease term.[1] Much like a mortgage payment, each lease payment consists partly of interest expense and partly of repayment of debt.

Suppose, for example, that Polany Manufacturing Company enters into a long-term lease July 1 for a machine. The lease terms call for an annual payment of $8,000 for six years, which approximates the useful life of the machine. At the end of the lease period, the title to the machine passes to Polany. This lease is clearly a capital lease and should be recorded as an asset and a liability.

Present value techniques can be used to place a value on the asset and on the corresponding liability in a capital lease. Suppose Polany's interest cost on the unpaid part of its obligation is 8 percent. Using the factor for 8 percent and six periods in Table 13-2 in the appendix on present values tables, we can compute the present value of the lease payments as follows:

$$\text{Periodic Payment} \times \text{Factor} = \text{Present Value}$$
$$\$8{,}000 \times 4.623 = \$36{,}984$$

The T accounts and entry to record the lease is as follows:

A	=	L	+	SE
+36,984		+36,984		

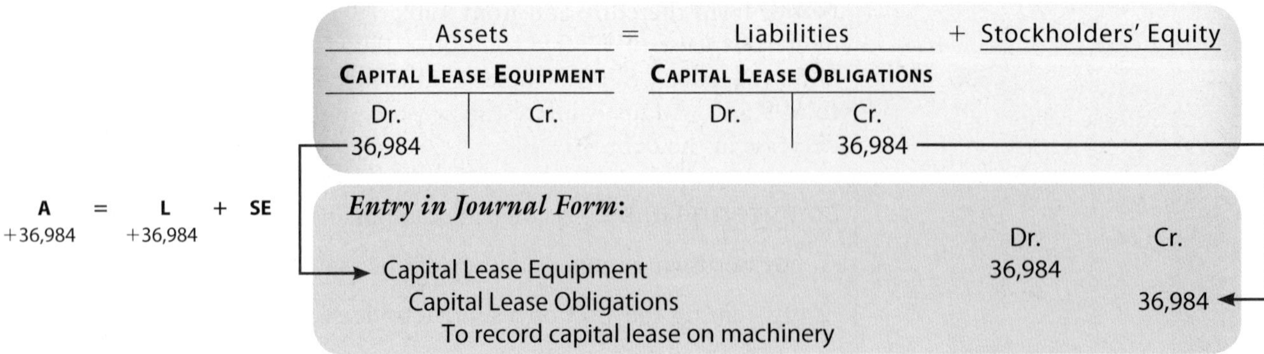

Capital Lease Equipment is classified as a long-term asset. Capital Lease Obligations is classified as a long-term liability.

TABLE 13-2
Payment Schedule on an 8 Percent Capital Lease

Year	A Lease Payment	B Interest (8%) on Unpaid Obligation* (D × 8%)	C Reduction of Lease Obligation (A – B)	D Balance of Lease Obligation (D – C)
Beginning				$36,984
1	$ 8,000	$ 2,959	$ 5,041	31,943
2	8,000	2,555	5,445	26,498
3	8,000	2,120	5,880	20,618
4	8,000	1,649	6,351	14,267
5	8,000	1,141	6,859	7,408
6	8,000	592[†]	7,408	—
	$48,000	$11,016	$36,984	

*Rounded to the nearest dollar.

[†]The last year's interest equals $592 ($8,000 – $7,408); it does not exactly equal $593 ($7,408 × $\frac{8}{100}$ × 1) because of the cumulative effect of rounding.

Each year, Polany must record depreciation on the leased asset. Using straight-line depreciation, a six-year life, and no residual value, the following T accounts and entry would record the depreciation:

A	=	L	+	SE
+6,164				+6,164

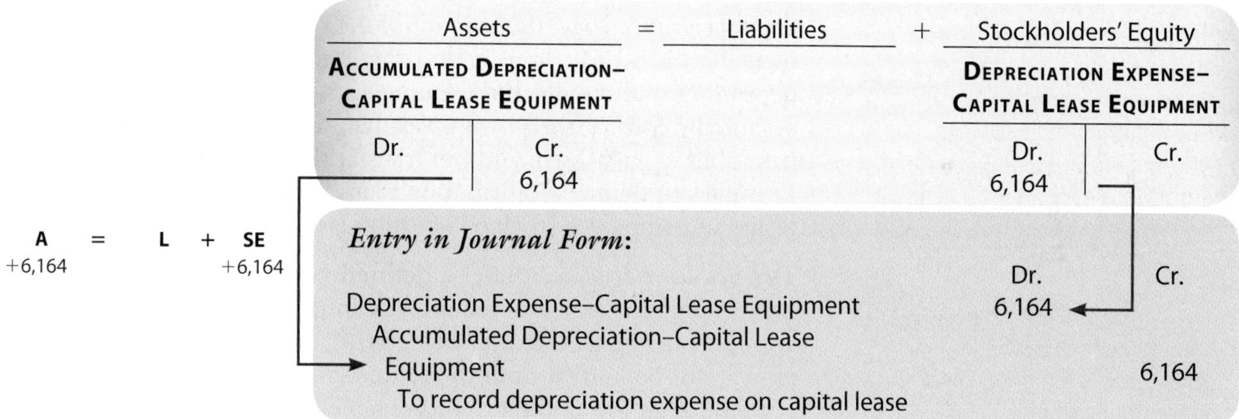

Assets	=	Liabilities	+	Stockholders' Equity

Accumulated Depreciation–Capital Lease Equipment

Dr.	Cr.
	6,164

Depreciation Expense–Capital Lease Equipment

Dr.	Cr.
6,164	

Entry in Journal Form:

	Dr.	Cr.
Depreciation Expense–Capital Lease Equipment	6,164	
Accumulated Depreciation–Capital Lease Equipment		6,164
To record depreciation expense on capital lease		

The interest expense for each year is computed by multiplying the interest rate (8 percent) by the amount of the remaining lease obligation. Table 13-2 shows these calculations. Using the data in the table, the first lease payment would be recorded as follows:

A	=	L	+	SE
−8,000		−5,041		−2,959

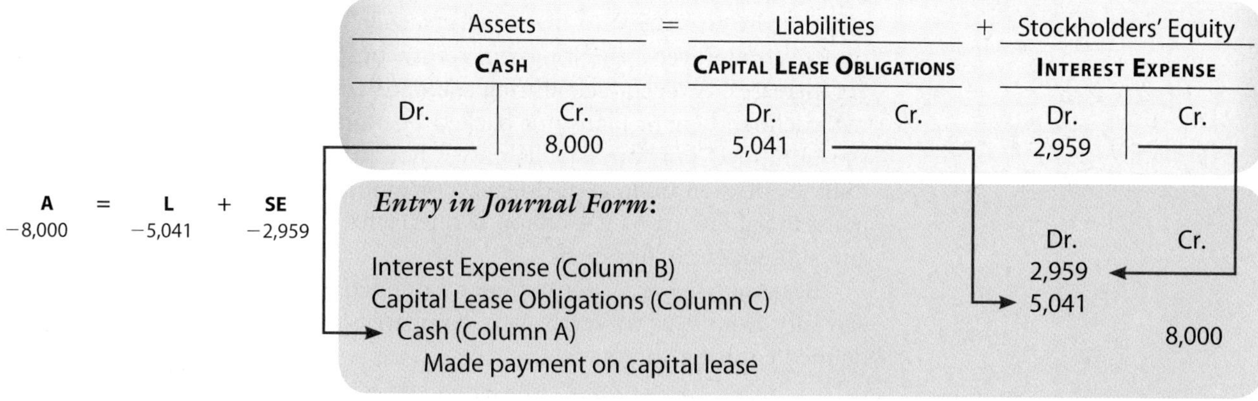

Assets	=	Liabilities	+	Stockholders' Equity

Cash

Dr.	Cr.
	8,000

Capital Lease Obligations

Dr.	Cr.
5,041	

Interest Expense

Dr.	Cr.
2,959	

Entry in Journal Form:

	Dr.	Cr.
Interest Expense (Column B)	2,959	
Capital Lease Obligations (Column C)	5,041	
Cash (Column A)		8,000
Made payment on capital lease		

This example suggests why companies are motivated to engage in off-balance-sheet financing for leases. By structuring long-term leases so that they can be accounted for as operating leases, companies avoid recording them on the balance sheet as long-term assets and liabilities. This practice, which, as we have noted, is legal, not only improves the debt to equity ratio by showing less debt on the balance sheet; it also improves the return on assets by reducing the total assets.

Pension Liabilities Most employees of medium-sized and large companies are covered by a **pension plan,** a contract that requires a company to pay benefits to its employees after they retire. Some companies pay the full cost of the pension plan, but in many companies, employees share the cost by contributing part of their salaries or wages. The contributions from employer and employees are usually paid into a **pension fund,** which is invested on behalf of the employees and from which benefits are paid to retirees. Pension benefits typically consist of monthly payments to retired employees and other payments upon disability or death.

Employers whose pension plans do not have sufficient assets to cover the present value of their pension obligations must record the amount of the shortfall as a liability on their balance sheets. If a pension plan has sufficient assets to cover its obligations, no balance sheet reporting is required or permitted.

There are two kinds of pension plans:

> **Study Note**
> Companies prefer defined contribution plans because the employees assume the risk that their pension assets will earn a sufficient return to meet their retirement needs.

- ***Defined contribution plan.*** Under a **defined contribution plan**, the employer makes a fixed annual contribution, usually a percentage of the employee's gross pay; the amount of the contribution is specified in an agreement between the company and the employees. Retirement payments vary depending on how much the employee's retirement account earns. Employees usually control their own investment accounts, can make additional contributions of their own, and can transfer the funds if they leave the company. Examples of defined contribution plans include 401(k) plans, profit-sharing plans, and employee stock ownership plans (ESOPs).

> **Study Note**
> Accounting for a defined benefit plan is far more complex than accounting for a defined contribution plan. Fortunately, accountants can rely on the calculations of professional actuaries, whose expertise includes the mathematics of pension plans.

- ***Defined benefit plan.*** Under a **defined benefit plan**, the employer contributes an amount annually required to fund estimated future pension liability arising from employment in the current year. The exact amount of the liability will not be known until the retirement and death of the current employees. Although the amount of future benefits is fixed, the annual contributions vary depending on assumptions about how much the pension fund will earn.

Annual pension expense under a defined contribution plan is simple and predictable. Pension expense equals the fixed amount of the annual contribution. In contrast, annual expense under a defined benefit plan is one of the most complex topics in accounting. The intricacies are reserved for advanced courses, but in concept, the procedure is simple. Computation of the annual expense takes into account the estimation of many factors, such as the average remaining service life of active employees, the long-run return on pension plan assets, and future salary increases. A recent accounting standard requires companies and other entities with defined benefit plans not backed by a fund sufficient to pay them to record the unfunded portion as a liability.[2] For many companies this can amount to millions or even billions of dollars. For example, **General Motors Corporation**'s pension liability of $11.4 billion is one factor that led to its government bailout and subsequent bankruptcy.[3]

Because pension expense under a defined benefit plan is not predictable and can vary from year to year, many companies are adopting the more predictable defined contribution plans.

FOCUS ON BUSINESS PRACTICE

Post-Retirement Liabilities Affect Everyone

The rule requiring recognition of unfunded pension plans as liabilities impacts even government entities. Most government entities have defined benefit pension plans and provide post-retirement medical benefits. As a result, states, school districts, and municipalities are all encountering previously ignored pension and health care liabilities. For example, a series of evasive tactics in San Diego led to a $1.1 billion shortfall, which almost caused the city to declare bankruptcy.[4] The state of New Jersey actually stopped setting aside funds to pay for health care in order to give a tax cut. No one added up the cost until the new accounting rule required it. The estimated cost to provide the health care promised to New Jersey's current and future retirees is $58 billion, or twice the state's annual budget.[5] These cases, while extreme, are not unusual. Citizens across the country will face tax increases to pay for these liabilities.

Study Note

Other post-retirement benefits should be expensed as the employee earns them, not when they are paid after the employee retires. This practice conforms to the matching rule.

Other Post-Retirement Benefits Many companies provide retired employees not only with pensions but also with health care and other benefits. In the past, these **other post-retirement benefits** were accounted for on a cash basis—that is, they were expensed when the benefits were paid, after an employee had retired. More recent accounting standards hold that employees earn these benefits during their employment and that, in accordance with the matching rule, they should be estimated and accrued during the time the employee is working.[6]

The estimates must take into account assumptions about retirement age, mortality, and, most significantly, future trends in health care benefits. Like pension benefits, such future benefits should be discounted to the current period. A field test conducted by the Financial Executives Research Foundation determined that the change to accrual accounting increased post-retirement benefits by two to seven times the amount recognized on a cash basis.

Deferred Income Taxes Among the long-term liabilities on the balance sheets of many companies, including **Southwest Airlines**, is an account called Deferred Income Taxes. **Deferred income taxes** are the result of using different accounting methods to calculate income taxes on the income statement and income tax

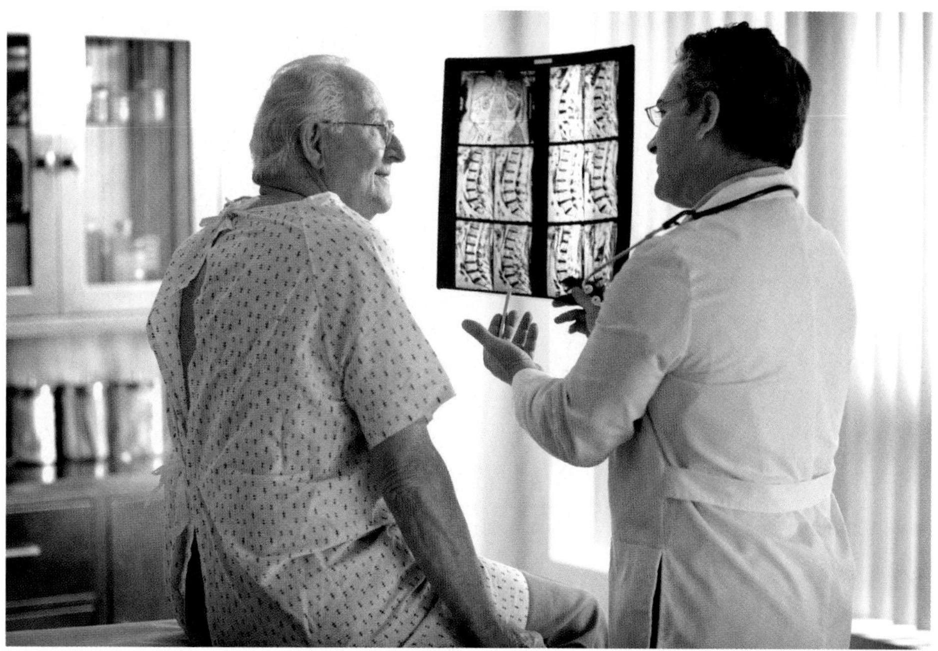

Post-retirement benefits, such as health care, are a type of long-term debt for the company that provides them. Recent accounting standards hold that employees earn these benefits during their employment and that the benefits should therefore be estimated and accrued while the employee is working.

Courtesy of Steve Cole/iStockphoto.com.

liability on the income tax return. For instance, companies often use straight-line depreciation for financial reporting and an accelerated method to calculate income tax liability. Because straight-line depreciation is less than accelerated depreciation in the early years of an asset's life, the presumption is that the income taxes will eventually have to be paid. Thus, the difference is listed as a long-term liability, deferred income taxes. Because companies try to manage their affairs to minimize income taxes paid, deferred income taxes can become quite large. In Southwest Airlines' case, they amount to about $1.9 billion or almost 20 percent of total liabilities.[7] We cover deferred income taxes in greater detail in a later chapter.

Cash Flow Information

The best source of information concerning cash flows about short-term and long-term debt is the financing activities section of the statement of cash flows. For instance, cash flows from these activities are clearly revealed in this partial section of **McDonald Corporation**'s statement of cash flows (in millions):[8]

Financing Activities	*2008*	*2007*	*2006*
Net short-term borrowings	$ 266.7	$ 101.3	$ 34.5
Long-term financing issuances	3,477.5	2,116.8	1.9
Long-term financing repayments	(2,698.5)	(1,645.5)	(2,301.1)

Note that McDonald's has little short-term borrowing and that the company's cash outflows for long-term borrowing exceeded cash inflows for long-term borrowing by $1,049 million for all three years.

STOP & APPLY >

Each type of long-term liability below is closely related to one of the statements in the list that follows. Write the number of the liability next to the statement to which it applies.

1. Bonds payable
2. Long-term notes payable
3. Mortgage payable
4. Long-term lease
5. Pension liabilities
6. Other post-retirement benefits
7. Deferred income taxes

____ a. Cost of health care after employees' retirement

____ b. The most common type of long-term debt

____ c. The result of differences between accounting income and taxable income

____ d. Debt that is secured by real estate

____ e. Promissory note that is due in more than one year

____ f. May be based on a percentage of employees' wages or on future benefits

____ g. Can be similar in form to an installment purchase

SOLUTION

a. 6; b. 1; c. 7; d. 3; e. 2; f. 5; g. 4

The Nature of Bonds

LO2 Describe the features of a bond issue and the major characteristics of bonds.

A **bond** is a security, usually long term, representing money that a corporation borrows from the investing public. (Federal, state, and local governments also issue bonds to raise money, as do foreign countries.) A bond entails a promise to repay the amount borrowed, called the *principal*, on a specified date and to pay interest at a specified rate at specified times—usually semiannually. In contrast to stockholders, who are the owners of a corporation, bondholders are a corporation's creditors.

When a public corporation decides to issue bonds, it must submit the appropriate legal documents to the Securities and Exchange Commission for permission to borrow the funds. The SEC reviews the corporation's financial health and the specific terms of the **bond indenture,** which is a contract that defines the rights, privileges, and limitations of the bondholders. The bond indenture generally describes such things as the maturity date of the bonds, interest payment dates, and the interest rate. It may also cover repayment plans and restrictions. Once the bond issue is approved, the corporation has a limited time in which to issue the authorized bonds. As evidence of its debt to the bondholders, the corporation provides each of them with a **bond certificate.**

Study Note
An investor who purchases debt securities, such as bonds or notes, is a creditor of the organization, not an owner.

Bond Issue: Prices and Interest Rates

A **bond issue** is the total value of bonds issued at one time. For example, a \$1,000,000 bond issue could consist of a thousand \$1,000 bonds. The prices of bonds are stated in terms of a percentage of the face value, or principal, of the bonds. A bond issue quoted at 103½ means that a \$1,000 bond costs \$1,035 (\$1,000 × 1.035). When a bond sells at exactly 100, it is said to sell at face (or par) value. When it sells below 100, it is said to sell at a discount; above 100, at a premium. For instance, a \$1,000 bond quoted at 87.62 would be selling at a discount and would cost the buyer \$876.20.

Study Note
When bonds with an interest rate different from the market rate are issued, they sell at a discount or premium. The discount or premium acts as an equalizing factor.

Face Interest Rate and Market Interest Rate Two interest rates relevant to bond prices are the face interest rate and the market interest rate:

- The **face interest rate** is the fixed rate of interest paid to bondholders based on the face value of the bonds. The rate and amount are fixed over the life of the bond. To allow time to file with the SEC, publicize the bond issue, and print the bond certificates, a company must decide in advance what the face interest rate will be. Most companies try to set the face interest rate as close as possible to the market interest rate.
- The **market interest rate** is the rate of interest paid in the market on bonds of similar risk.* It is also called the *effective interest rate*. The market interest rate fluctuates daily. Because a company has no control over it, the market interest rate often differs from the face interest rate on the issue date.

Study Note
A bond sells at face value when the face interest rate of the bond is identical to the market interest rate for similar bonds on the date of issue.

Discounts and Premiums If the market interest rate fluctuates from the face interest rate before the issue date, the issue price of bonds will not equal their face value. This fluctuation in market interest rate causes the bonds to sell at either a discount or a premium:

- A **discount** equals the excess of the face value over the issue price. The issue price will be less than the face value when the market interest rate is higher than the face interest rate.

*At the time this chapter was written, the market interest rates on corporate bonds were volatile. Therefore, we use a variety of interest rates in our examples.

- A **premium** equals the excess of the issue price over the face value. The issue price will be more than the face value when the market interest rate is lower than the face interest rate.

Discounts or premiums are contra and adjunct accounts, respectively, that are subtracted from or added to bonds payable on the balance sheet.

Characteristics of Bonds

A bond indenture can be written to fit an organization's financing needs. As a result, the bonds issued in today's financial markets have many different features. We describe several of the more important features in the following paragraphs.

Study Note

Do not confuse the terms *indenture* and *debenture*. They sound alike, but an indenture is a bond contract, whereas a debenture is an unsecured bond. A debenture bond of a stable company actually might be a less risky investment than a secured bond of an unstable company.

Unsecured and Secured Bonds Bonds can be either unsecured or secured. **Unsecured bonds** (also called *debenture bonds*) are issued on the basis of a corporation's general credit. **Secured bonds** carry a pledge of certain corporate assets as a guarantee of repayment. A pledged asset may be a specific asset, such as a truck, or a general category of asset, such as property, plant, and equipment.

Term and Serial Bonds When all the bonds of an issue mature at the same time, they are called **term bonds**. For instance, a company may decide to issue $1,000,000 worth of bonds, all due 20 years from the date of issue.

When the bonds of an issue mature on different dates, they are called **serial bonds**. For example, suppose a $1,000,000 bond issue calls for paying $200,000 of the principal every five years. This arrangement means that after the first $200,000 payment is made, $800,000 of the bonds would remain outstanding for the next five years, $600,000 for the next five years, and so on. A company may issue serial bonds to ease the task of retiring its debt—that is, paying off what it owes on the bonds.

Study Note

An advantage of issuing serial bonds is that the organization retires the bonds over a period of years, rather than all at once.

Callable and Convertible Bonds When bonds are callable and convertible, a company may be able to retire them before their maturity dates. When a company does retire a bond issue before its maturity date, it is called **early extinguishment of debt**. Doing so can be to a company's advantage.

Callable bonds give the issuer the right to buy back and retire the bonds before maturity at a specified **call price**, which is usually above face value. Callable bonds give a company flexibility in financing its operations. For example, if bond interest rates drop, the company can call the bonds and reissue debt at a lower interest rate. A company might also call its bonds if it has earned enough to pay off the debt, if the reason for having the debt no longer exists, or if it wants to restructure its debt to equity ratio. The bond indenture states the time period and the prices at which the bonds can be redeemed.

Convertible bonds allow the bondholder to exchange a bond for a specified number of shares of common stock. The face value of a convertible bond when issued is greater than the market value of the shares to which it can be converted. However, if the market price of the common stock rises above a certain level, the value of the bond rises in relation to the value of the common stock. Even if the stock price does not rise, the investor still holds the bond and receives both the periodic interest payments and the face value at the maturity date.

One advantage of issuing convertible bonds is that the interest rate is usually lower because investors are willing to give up some current interest in the hope that the value of the stock will increase and the value of the bonds will therefore also increase. In addition, if the bonds are both callable and convertible and the market value of the stock rises to a level at which the bond is worth more than face value, management can avoid repaying the bonds by calling them for redemption, thereby forcing the bondholders to convert their bonds into common stock. The bondholders will agree to convert because no gain or loss results from the transaction.

Registered and Coupon Bonds **Registered bonds** are issued in the names of the bondholders. The issuing organization keeps a record of the bondholders' names and addresses and pays them interest by check on the interest payment date. Most bonds today are registered. **Coupon bonds** are not registered with the organization. Instead, they bear coupons stating the amount of interest due and the payment date. The bondholder removes the coupons from the bonds on the interest payment dates and presents them at a bank for collection.

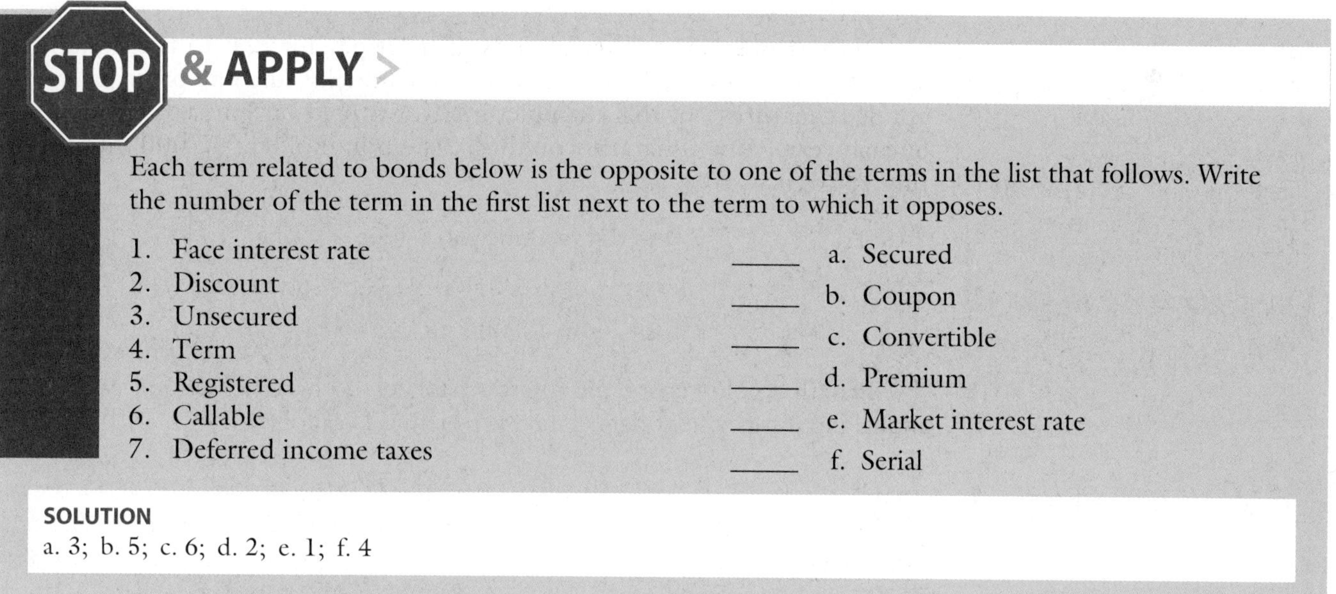

STOP & APPLY >

Each term related to bonds below is the opposite to one of the terms in the list that follows. Write the number of the term in the first list next to the term to which it opposes.

1. Face interest rate	____ a. Secured
2. Discount	____ b. Coupon
3. Unsecured	____ c. Convertible
4. Term	____ d. Premium
5. Registered	____ e. Market interest rate
6. Callable	____ f. Serial
7. Deferred income taxes	

SOLUTION

a. 3; b. 5; c. 6; d. 2; e. 1; f. 4

Accounting for the Issuance of Bonds

LO3 Record bonds issued at face value and at a discount or premium.

When the board of directors of a public corporation decides to issue bonds, the company must submit the appropriate legal documents to the Securities and Exchange Commission for authorization to borrow the funds. It is not necessary to make an entry to record the authorization of a bond issue. However, most companies disclose the authorization in the notes to their financial statements. The note lists the number and value of bonds authorized, the interest rate, the interest payment dates, and the life of the bonds. In the sections that follow, we show how to record bonds issued at face value, at a discount, and at a premium.

Bonds Issued at Face Value

Suppose Bharath Corporation issues $200,000 of 7 percent, five-year bonds on January 1, 2010, at face value. The bond indenture states that interest is to be paid on January 1 and July 1 of each year. The T accounts and entry to record the bond issue is as follows:

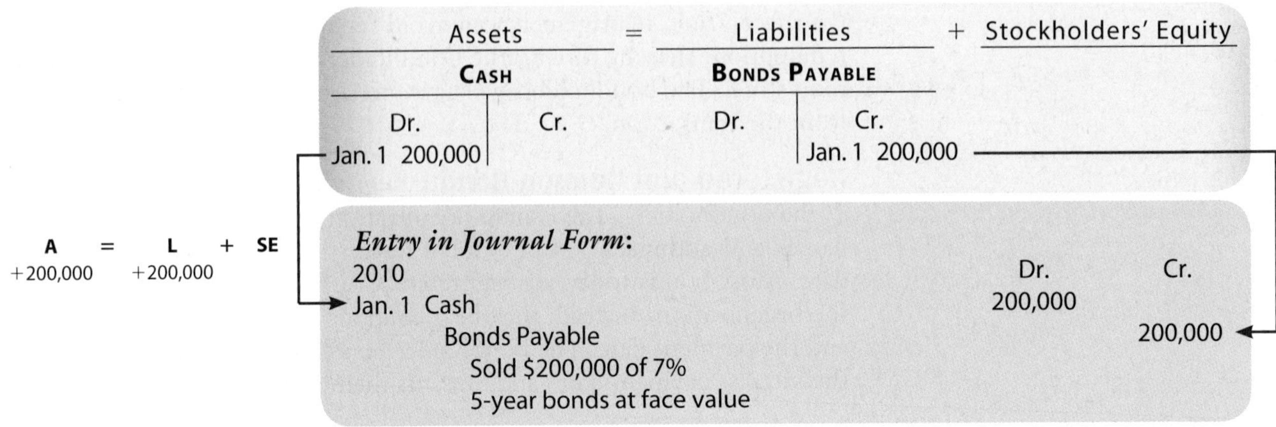

Study Note

When calculating semiannual interest, do not use the annual rate (7 percent in this case). Rather, use half the annual rate.

Once a corporation issues bonds, it must pay interest to the bondholders over the life of the bonds, usually semiannually, and the principal of the bonds at maturity. In this example, interest is paid on January 1 and July 1 of each year. Thus, Bharath would owe the bondholders $7,000 interest on July 1, 2010:

$$\begin{aligned}\text{Interest} &= \text{Principal} \times \text{Rate} \times \text{Time}\\ &= \$200{,}000 \times \frac{7}{100} \times 6/12 \text{ year}\\ &= \$7{,}000\end{aligned}$$

Bharath would record the interest paid to the bondholders on each semiannual interest payment date (January 1 or July 1) as follows:

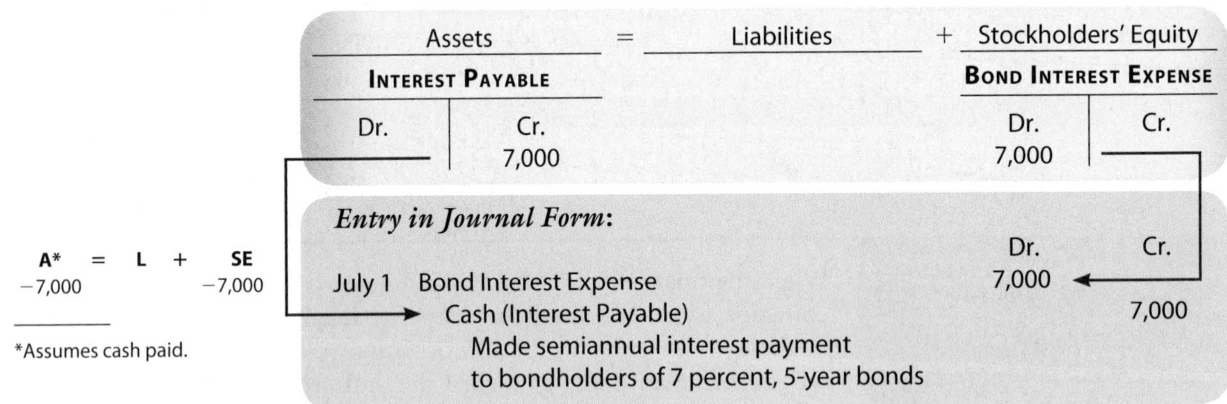

Bonds Issued at a Discount

Suppose Bharath Corporation issues $200,000 of 7 percent, five-year bonds at 95.9445 on January 1, 2010, when the market interest rate is 8 percent. In this case, the bonds are being issued at a discount because the market interest rate exceeds the face interest rate. The following T accounts and entry records the issuance of the bonds at a discount:

FOCUS ON BUSINESS PRACTICE

100-Year Bonds Are Not for Everyone

In 1993, interest rates on long-term debt were at historically low levels, which induced some companies to attempt to lock in those low costs for long periods. One of the most aggressive companies in that regard was **The Walt Disney Company**, which issued $150 million of 100-year bonds at a yield of only 7.5 percent. It was the first time since 1954 that 100-year bonds had been issued. Among the others that followed Walt Disney's lead by issuing 100-year bonds were the **Coca-Cola Company, Columbia HCA Healthcare, Bell South, IBM**, and even the People's Republic of China. Some analysts wondered if even Mickey Mouse could survive 100 years. Investors who purchase such bonds take a financial risk because if interest rates rise, which is always likely, the market value of the bonds will decrease.[9]

A	=	L	+	SE
+191,889		−8,111		
		+200,000		

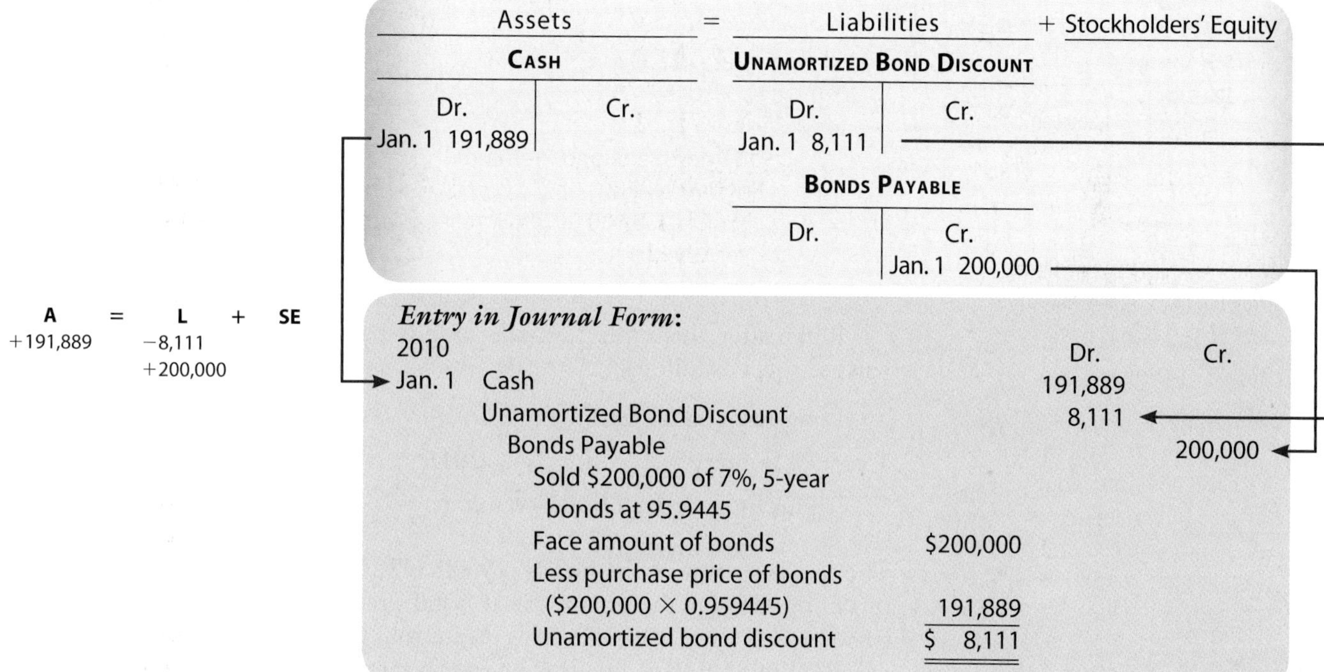

Entry in Journal Form:

2010		Dr.	Cr.
Jan. 1	Cash	191,889	
	Unamortized Bond Discount	8,111	
	Bonds Payable		200,000
	Sold $200,000 of 7%, 5-year bonds at 95.9445		

Face amount of bonds	$200,000
Less purchase price of bonds ($200,000 × 0.959445)	191,889
Unamortized bond discount	$ 8,111

In this entry, Cash is debited for the amount received ($191,889), Bonds Payable is credited for the face amount ($200,000) of the bond liability, and the difference ($8,111) is debited to Unamortized Bond Discount. If a balance sheet is prepared right after the bonds are issued at a discount, the liability for bonds payable is reported as follows:

Long-term liabilities		
7% bonds payable, due 1/1/2015	$200,000	
Less unamortized bond discount	8,111	$191,889

Unamortized Bond Discount is a contra-liability account. Its balance is deducted from the face amount of the bonds to arrive at the carrying value, or present value, of the bonds. The bond discount is described as unamortized because it will be amortized (written off) over the life of the bonds.

Bonds Issued at a Premium

When bonds have a face interest rate above the market rate for similar investments, they are issued at a price above the face value, or at a premium. For example, suppose Bharath Corporation issues $200,000 of 7 percent, five-year bonds for $208,530 on January 1, 2010, when the market interest rate is 6 percent. This means that investors will purchase the bonds at 104.265 percent of their face value. The issuance would be recorded as follows:

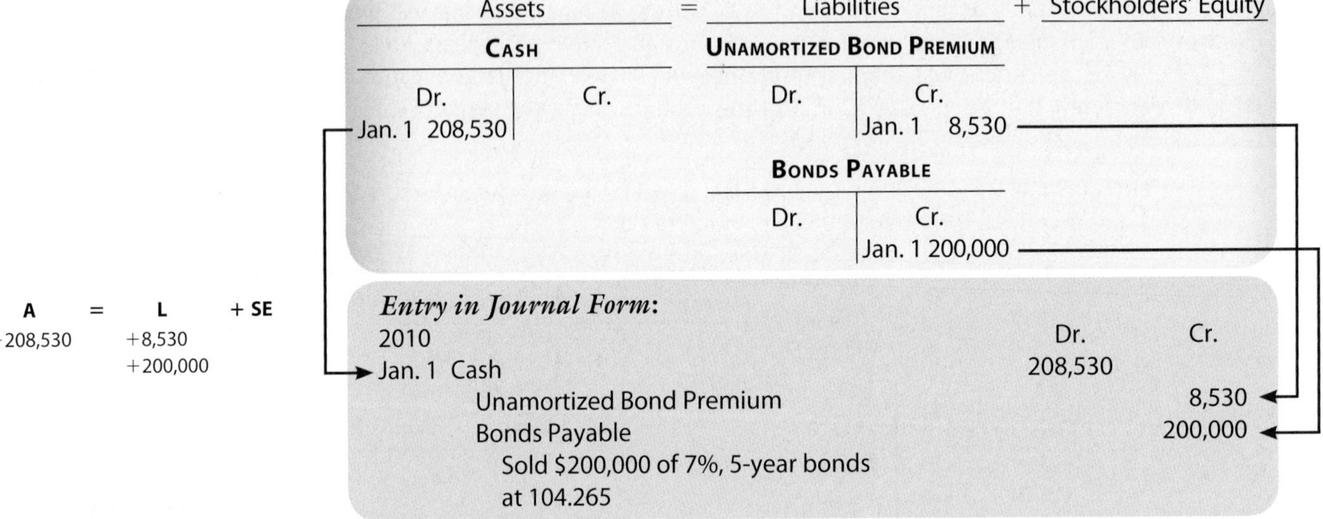

A	=	L	+ SE
+208,530		+8,530	
		+200,000	

Entry in Journal Form:

2010		Dr.	Cr.
Jan. 1	Cash	208,530	
	Unamortized Bond Premium		8,530
	Bonds Payable		200,000
	Sold $200,000 of 7%, 5-year bonds at 104.265		

Right after this entry is made, bonds payable would be presented on the balance sheet as follows:

Long-term liabilities		
7% bonds payable, due 1/1/2015	$200,000	
Plus unamortized bond premium	8,530	$208,530

Study Note

The carrying amount is always the face value of the bonds less the unamortized discount or plus the unamortized premium. The carrying amount always approaches the face value over the life of the bond.

The carrying value of the bonds payable is $208,530, which equals the face value of the bonds plus the unamortized bond premium. The cash received from the bond issue is also $208,530. This means that the purchasers were willing to pay a premium of $8,530 to buy these bonds because their face interest rate was higher than the market interest rate.

Bond Issue Costs

The costs of issuing bonds can amount to as much as 5 percent of a bond issue. These costs often include the fees of underwriters, whom corporations hire to take care of the details of marketing a bond issue. Because the issue costs benefit the whole life of a bond issue, it makes sense to spread them over that period. It is generally accepted practice to establish a separate account for these costs and to amortize them over the life of the bonds.

Because issue costs decrease the amount of money a company receives from a bond issue, they have the effect of raising the discount or lowering the premium on the issue. Thus, bond issue costs can be spread over the life of the bonds through the amortization of a discount or premium. This method simplifies recordkeeping. In the rest of our discussion, we assume that all bond issue costs increase the discounts or decrease the premiums on bond issues.

STOP & APPLY >

Gill Foods is planning to issue $1,000,000 in long-term bonds. Depending on market conditions, Gill's CPA advises that the bonds could be issued at (a) 99, (b) 100, or (b) 101. Calculate the amount that Gill would receive under each alternative and indicate whether it is at face value, a discount or a premium and the amount of each.

SOLUTION

(a) $1,000,000 × 0.99 = $990,000; a discount of $10,000
(b) $1,000,000 × 1.00 = $1,000,000; at face value; no discount or premium
(c) $1,000,000 × 1.01 = $1,010,000; a premium of $10,000

Using Present Value to Value a Bond

LO4 Use present values to determine the value of bonds.

A bond's value is based on the present value of two components of cash flow: a series of fixed interest payments, and a single payment at maturity. The amount of interest a bond pays is fixed over its life. However, the market interest rate varies from day to day. Thus, the amount investors are willing to pay for a bond varies as well.

Case 1: Market Rate Above Face Rate

Suppose a bond has a face value of $20,000 and pays fixed interest of $700 every six months (a 7 percent annual rate). The bond is due in five years. If the market interest rate today is 10 percent, what is the present value of the bond?

To answer this question, we use Table 2 in the appendix on present value tables to calculate the present value of the periodic interest payments of $700, and we use Table 1 in the same appendix to calculate the present value of the single payment of $20,000 at maturity. Because interest payments are made every six months, the compounding period is half a year. Thus, we have to convert the annual rate to a semiannual rate of 5 percent (10 percent divided by two six-month periods per year) and use ten periods (five years multiplied by two six-month periods per year). With this information, we can compute the present value of the bond as follows:

Present value of 10 periodic payments at 5%: $700 × 7.722 (from Table 2 in the appendix)	$ 5,405.40
Present value of a single payment at the end of 10 periods at 5%: $20,000 × 0.614 (from Table 1 in the appendix):	12,280.00
Present value of $20,000 bond	$17,685.40

The market interest rate has increased so much since the bond was issued—from 7 percent to 10 percent—that the value of the bond today is only $17,685.40. That amount is all investors would be willing to pay at this time for a bond that provides income of $700 every six months and a return of the $20,000 principal in five years.

Case 2: Market Rate Below Face Rate

Figure 13-2 illustrates both of these examples—that is, when the market rate is above the face rate (Case 1) and when the market rate is below the face rate (Case 2). If the market interest rate on the bond described on page 579 falls below the face interest rate, say to 6 percent (3 percent semiannually), the present value of the bond will be greater than the face value of $20,000:

Present value of 10 periodic payments at 3%: $700 × 8.530 (from Table 2 in the appendix)	$ 5,971.00
Present value of a single payment at the end of 10 periods at 3%: $20,000 × 0.744 (from Table 1 in the appendix)	14,880.00
Present value of $20,000 bond	$20,851.00

FIGURE 13-2 Using Present Value to Value a $20,000, 7 Percent, Five-Year Bond

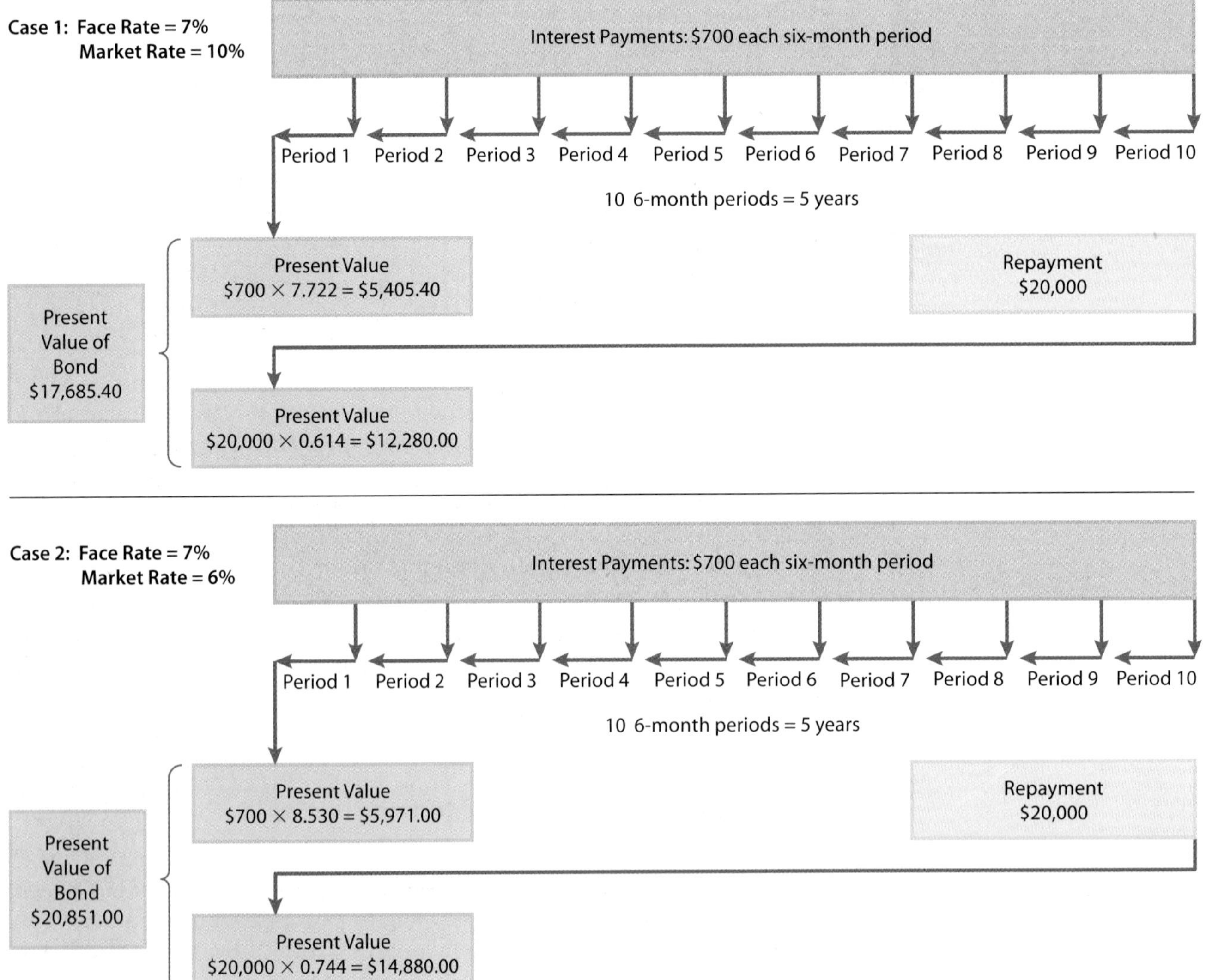

Tyler Company's $900,000 bond issue pays semiannual interest of $16,000 and is due in 20 years. Assume that the market interest rate is 6 percent. Calculate the amount that Tyler will receive. (Calculate the present value of each bond issue and sum.)

SOLUTION

Present value of 40 periodic payments of 3% (from Table 2*):
$16,000 × 23.115* = $369,840

Present value of a single payment at the end of 20 years (40 periods) at 3% (from Table 1*):
$500,000 × 0.307** = 153,500
Total value of the bond issue $523,340

Total amount that Tyler will receive:
$369,840 + $523,340 = $893,180

*From Table 2 in the appendix on present value tables
**From Table 1 in the appendix on present value tables

Amortization of Bond Discounts and Premiums

LO5 Amortize bond discounts and bond premiums using the straight-line and effective interest methods.

A bond discount or premium represents the amount by which the total interest cost is higher or lower than the total interest payments. To record interest expense properly and ensure that the carrying value of bonds payable at maturity equals face value, it is necessary to systematically reduce the bond discount or premium—that is, to amortize them—over the life of the bonds. This is accomplished by using either the straight-line method or the effective interest method.

Amortizing a Bond Discount

In one of our earlier examples, Bharath Corporation issued $200,000 of five-year bonds at a time when the market interest rate of 8 percent exceeded the face interest rate of 7 percent. The bonds sold for $191,889, resulting in an unamortized bond discount of $8,111.

Because a bond discount affects interest expense in each year of a bond issue, the bond discount should be amortized over the life of the bond issue. In this way, the unamortized bond discount will decrease gradually over time, and the carrying value of the bond issue (face value less unamortized discount) will gradually increase. By the maturity date, the carrying value of the bond issue will equal its face value, and the unamortized bond discount will be zero.

In the following sections, we calculate Bharath Corporation's total interest cost and amortize its bond discount using the straight-line and the effective interest methods.

Study Note

A bond discount is a component of interest cost because it represents the amount in excess of the issue price that a corporation must pay on the maturity date.

Calculating Total Interest Cost When a corporation issues bonds at a discount, the market (or effective) interest rate that it pays is greater than the face interest rate on the bonds. The reason is that the interest cost is the stated interest payments *plus* the amount of the bond discount. That is, although the company does not receive the full face value of the bonds on issue, it still must pay back the full face value at maturity. The difference between the issue price and the face value must be added to the total interest payments to arrive at the actual interest expense.

The full cost to Bharath Corporation of issuing its bonds at a discount is as follows:

Cash to be paid to bondholders	
Face value at maturity	$200,000
Interest payments ($200,000 × 0.07 × 5 years)	70,000
Total cash paid to bondholders	$270,000
Less cash received from bondholders	191,889
Total interest cost	$ 78,111

Or, alternatively:

Interest payments ($200,000 × 0.07 × 5 years)	$ 70,000
Bond discount	8,111
Total interest cost	$ 78,111

The total interest cost of $78,111 is made up of $70,000 in interest payments and the $8,111 bond discount. Thus, the bond discount increases the interest paid on the bonds from the face interest rate to the market interest rate. The market (or effective) interest rate is the real interest cost of the bond over its life.

To have each year's interest expense reflect the market interest rate, the discount must be allocated over the remaining life of the bonds as an increase in the interest expense each period. Thus, interest expense for each period will exceed the actual payment of interest by the amount of the bond discount amortized over the period. This process of allocation is called *amortization of the bond discount.*

Study Note

The discount on a zero coupon bond represents the interest that will be paid (in its entirety) on the maturity date.

Some bonds do not require periodic interest payments. These bonds, called **zero coupon bonds**, are simply a promise to pay a fixed amount at the maturity date. They are issued at a large discount because the only interest that the buyer earns or the issuer pays is the discount. For example, a five-year, $200,000 zero coupon bond issued when the market rate is 10 percent, compounded semiannually, would sell for only $122,800. That amount is the present value of a single payment of $200,000 at the end of five years. The discount of $77,200 ($200,000 − $122,800) is the total interest cost, which is amortized over the life of the bond.

Straight-Line Method The **straight-line method** equalizes amortization of a bond discount for each interest period. Using our example of Bharath Corporation, the interest payment dates of the bond issue are January 1 and July 1 of each year, and the bonds mature in five years. With the straight-line method, the amount of the bond discount amortized and the interest expense for each semiannual period are calculated in four steps:

1. Total Interest Payments = Interest Payments per Year × Life of Bonds
$$= 2 \times 5 = 10$$

2. Amortization of Bond Discount per Interest Period $= \dfrac{\text{Bond Discount}}{\text{Total Interest Payments}}$
$$= \frac{\$8{,}111}{10}$$
$$= \$811^*$$

3. Cash Interest Payment = Face Value × Face Interest Rate × Time
$$= \$200{,}000 \times 0.07 \times 6/12 = \$7{,}000$$

4. Interest Expense per Interest Period = Interest Payment + Amortization of Bond Discount
= \$7,000 + \$811 = \$7,811

On July 1, 2010, the first semiannual interest date, the T accounts and entry would be:

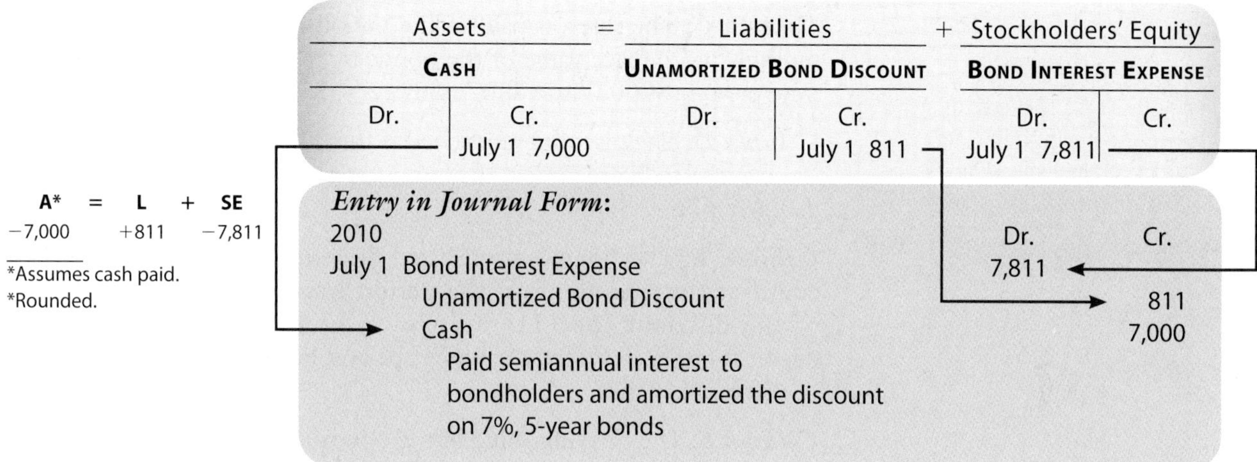

Notice that the bond interest expense is \$7,811, but the amount paid to the bondholders is the \$7,000 face interest payment. The difference of \$811 is the credit to Unamortized Bond Discount. This lowers the debit balance of Unamortized Bond Discount and raises the carrying value of the bonds payable by \$811 each interest period. If no changes occur in the bond issue, this entry will be made every six months for the life of the bonds. When the bond issue matures, the Unamortized Bond Discount account will have a zero balance, and the carrying value of the bonds will be \$200,000—exactly equal to the amount due the bondholders.

Although the straight-line method has long been used, it has a certain weakness. When it is used to amortize a discount, the carrying value goes up each period, but the bond interest expense stays the same; thus, the rate of interest falls over time. Conversely, when this method is used to amortize a premium, the rate of interest rises over time. The Accounting Principles Board therefore holds that the straight-line method should be used only when it does not lead to a material difference from the effective interest method.[10] A material difference is one that affects the evaluation of a company.

Effective Interest Method When the **effective interest method** is used to compute the interest and amortization of a bond discount, a constant interest rate is applied to the carrying value of the bonds at the beginning of each interest period. This constant rate is the market rate (i.e., the effective rate) at the time the bonds were issued. The amount amortized each period is the difference between the interest computed by using the market rate and the actual interest paid to bondholders.

As an example, we use the same facts we used earlier—a \$200,000 bond issue at 7 percent, with a five-year maturity and interest to be paid twice a year. The market rate at the time the bonds were issued was 8 percent, so the bonds sold for \$191,889, a discount of \$8,111. Table 13-3 shows the interest and amortization of the bond discount.

The amounts in the table for period 1 were computed as follows:

Column A: The carrying value of the bonds is their face value less the unamortized bond discount ($200,000 − $8,111 = $191,889).

Column B: The interest expense to be recorded is the effective interest. It is found by multiplying the carrying value of the bonds by the market interest rate for one-half year ($191,889 × 0.08 × 6/12 = $7,676).

Column C: The interest paid in the period is a constant amount computed by multiplying the face value of the bonds by their face interest rate by the interest time period ($200,000 × 0.07 × 6/12 = $7,000).

Study Note

Whether a bond is sold at a discount or a premium, its carrying value will equal its face value on the maturity date.

Column D: The discount amortized is the difference between the effective interest expense to be recorded and the interest to be paid on the interest payment date ($7,676 − $7,000 = $676).

Column E: The unamortized bond discount is the balance of the bond discount at the beginning of the period less the current period amortization of the discount ($8,111 − $676 = $7,435). The unamortized discount decreases in each interest payment period because it is amortized as a portion of interest expense.

Column F: The carrying value of the bonds at the end of the period is the carrying value at the beginning of the period plus the amortization during the period ($191,889 + $676 = $192,565). Notice that the sum of the carrying value and the unamortized discount (column F + column E) always equals the face value of the bonds ($192,565 + $7,435 = $200,000).

The entry to record the interest expense is exactly like the one when the straight-line method is used. However, the amounts debited and credited to the

TABLE 13-3 Interest and Amortization of a Bond Discount: Effective Interest Method

	A	B	C	D	E	F
Semiannual Interest Period	Carrying Value at Beginning of Period	Semiannual Interest Expense at 8% to Be Recorded* (4% × A)	Semiannual Interest Payment to Bondholders (3 1/2% × $200,000)	Amortization of Bond Discount (B − C)	Unamortized Bond Discount at End of Period (E − D)	Carrying Value at End of Period (A + D)
0					$8,111	$191,889
1	$191,889	$7,676	$7,000	$676	7,435	192,565
2	192,565	7,703	7,000	703	6,732	193,268
3	193,268	7,731	7,000	731	6,001	193,999
4	193,999	7,760	7,000	760	5,241	194,759
5	194,758	7,790	7,000	790	4,451	195,549
6	195,548	7,822	7,000	822	3,629	196,371
7	196,370	7,855	7,000	855	2,774	197,226
8	197,225	7,889	7,000	889	1,885	198,115
9	198,114	7,925	7,000	925	960	199,040
10	199,038	7,960†	7,000	960	—	200,000

*Rounded to the nearest dollar.

various accounts are different. Using the effective interest method, the T accounts and entry for July 1, 2010, would be as follows:

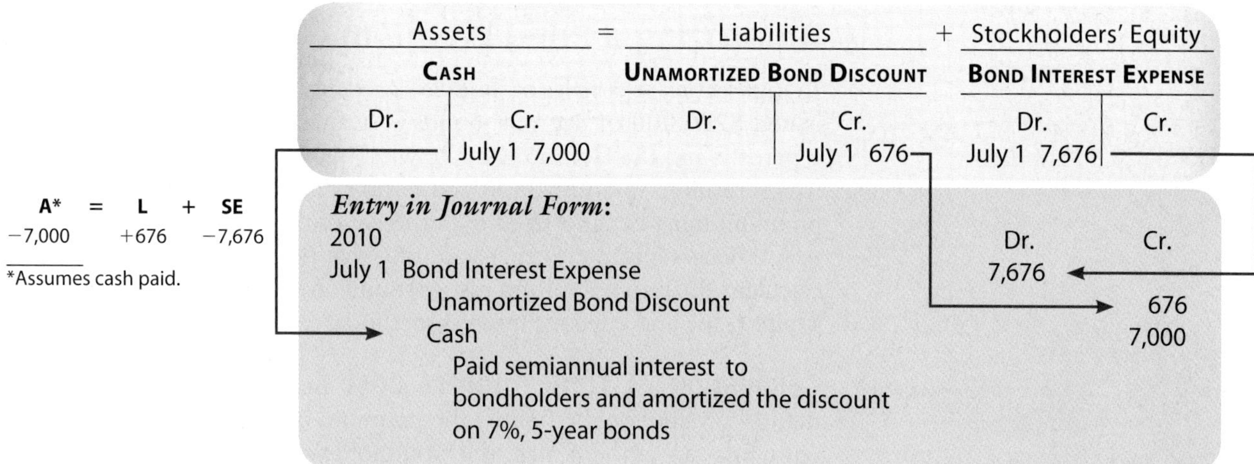

A*	=	L	+	SE
−7,000		+676		−7,676

*Assumes cash paid.

Study Note

The bond interest expense recorded exceeds the amount of interest paid because of the amortization of the bond discount. The matching rule dictates that the discount be amortized over the life of the bond.

Although an interest and amortization table is useful because it can be prepared in advance for all periods, it is not necessary to have one to determine the amortization of a discount for any one interest payment period. It is necessary only to multiply the carrying value by the effective interest rate and subtract the interest payment from the result. For example, the amount of discount to be amortized in the seventh interest payment period is $855, calculated as follows: ($196,370 × 0.04) − $7,000.

Figure 13-3, which is based on the data in Table 13-3, shows how the effective interest method affects the amortization of a bond discount. Notice that the carrying value (the issue price) is initially less than the face value, but that it gradually increases toward face value over the life of the bond issue. Notice also that interest expense exceeds interest payments by the amount of the bond discount amortized.

FIGURE 13-3
Carrying Value and Interest Expense—Bonds Issued at a Discount

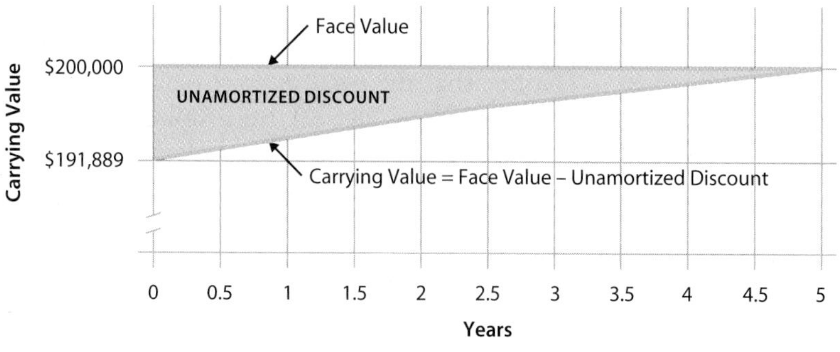

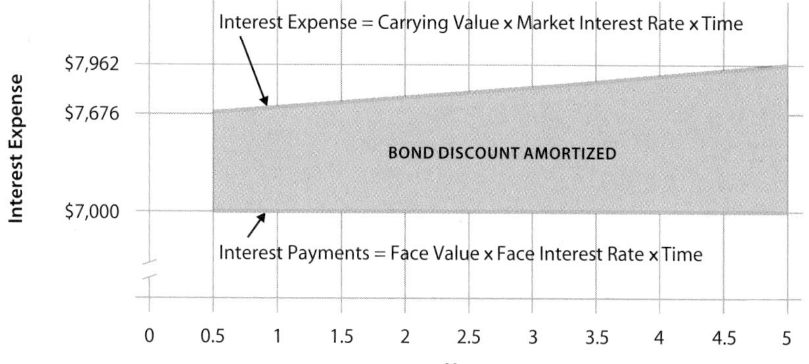

Study Note

The bond interest *increases* each period because the carrying value of the bonds (the principal on which the interest is calculated) increases each period.

Interest expense increases gradually over the life of the bond because it is based on the gradually increasing carrying value (multiplied by the market interest rate).

Amortizing a Bond Premium

In our earlier example of bonds issued at a premium, Bharath Corporation issued $200,000 of five-year bonds at a time when the market interest rate was 6 percent and the face interest rate was 7 percent. The bonds sold for $208,530, which resulted in an unamortized bond premium of $8,530. Like a discount, a premium must be amortized over the life of the bonds so that it can be matched to its effects on interest expense during that period. In the following sections, we calculate Bharath's total interest cost and amortize its bond premium using the straight-line and effective interest methods.

Study Note

A bond premium is deducted from interest payments in calculating total interest because a bond premium represents an amount over the face value of a bond that the corporation never has to return to the bondholders. In effect, it reduces the higher-than-market interest the corporation is paying on the bond.

Calculation of Total Interest Cost Because the bondholders paid more than face value for the bonds, the premium of $8,530 ($208,530 − $200,000) represents an amount that the bondholders will not receive at maturity. The premium is in effect a reduction, in advance, of the total interest paid on the bonds over the life of the bond issue. The total interest cost over the issue's life can be computed as follows:

Cash to be paid to bondholders	
Face value at maturity	$200,000
Interest payments ($200,000 × 0.07 × 5 years)	70,000
Total cash paid to bondholders	$270,000
Less cash received from bondholders	208,530
Total interest cost	$ 61,470

Alternatively, the total interest cost can be computed as follows:

Interest payments ($200,000 × 0.07 × 5 years)	$ 70,000
Less bond premium	8,530
Total interest cost	$ 61,470

Notice that the total interest payments of $70,000 exceed the total interest cost of $61,470 by $8,530, the amount of the bond premium.

Straight-Line Method Under the straight-line method, the bond premium is spread evenly over the life of the bond issue. As with bond discounts, the amount of the bond premium amortized and the interest expense for each semiannual period are computed in four steps:

1. $$\text{Total Interest Payments} = \text{Interest Payments per Year} \times \text{Life of Bonds} = 2 \times 5 = 10$$

2. $$\text{Amortization of Bond Premium per Interest Period} = \frac{\text{Bond Premium}}{\text{Total Interest Payments}} = \frac{\$8{,}530}{10} = \$853$$

3. $$\text{Cash Interest Payment} = \text{Face Value} \times \text{Face Interest Rate} \times \text{Time} = \$200{,}000 \times 0.07 \times 6/12 = \$7{,}000$$

4. $$\text{Interest Expense per Interest Period} = \text{Interest Payment} - \text{Amortization of Bond Premium} = \$7{,}000 - \$853 = \$6{,}147$$

On July 1, 2010, the first semiannual interest date, the T accounts and entry would be like this:

A*	=	L	+	SE
−7,000		−853		−6,147

*Assumes cash paid.

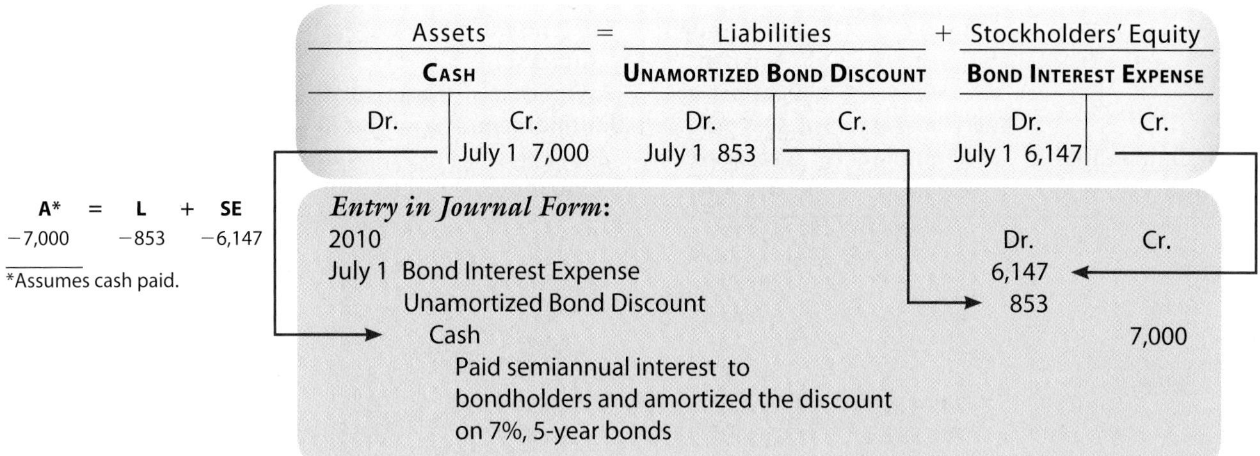

Study Note

The bond interest expense recorded is less than the amount of the interest paid because of the amortization of the bond premium. The matching rule dictates that the premium be amortized over the life of the bond.

Note that the bond interest expense is $6,147, but the amount that bondholders receive is the $7,000 face interest payment. The difference of $853 is the debit to Unamortized Bond Premium. This lowers the credit balance of the Unamortized Bond Premium account and the carrying value of the bonds payable by $853 each interest period. If the bond issue remains unchanged, the same entry will be made on every semiannual interest date over the life of the bond issue. When the bond issue matures, the balance in the Unamortized Bond Premium account will be zero, and the carrying value of the bonds payable will be $200,000—exactly equal to the amount due the bondholders.

As noted earlier, the straight-line method should be used only when it does not lead to a material difference from the effective interest method.

Effective Interest Method Under the straight-line method, the effective interest rate changes constantly, even though the interest expense is fixed, because the effective interest rate is determined by comparing the fixed interest expense with a carrying value that changes as a result of amortizing the discount or premium. To apply a fixed interest rate over the life of the bonds based on the actual market rate at the time of the bond issue, one must use the effective interest method. With this method, the interest expense decreases slightly each period (see Table 13-4, column B) because the amount of the bond premium amortized increases slightly (column D). This occurs because a fixed rate is applied each period to the gradually decreasing carrying value (column A). The first interest payment is recorded as follows:

A*	=	L	+	SE
−7,000		−744		−6,256

*Assumes cash paid.

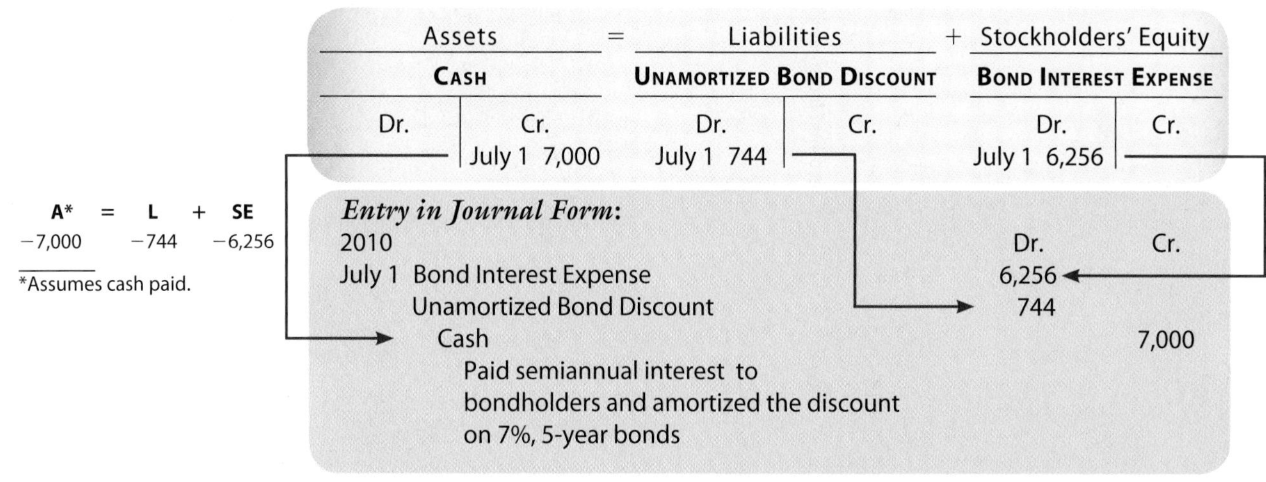

TABLE 13-4 Interest and Amortization of a Bond Premium: Effective Interest Method

	A	B	C	D	E	F
Semiannual Interest Period	Carrying Value at Beginning of Period	Semiannual Interest Expense at 6% to Be Recorded* (3% × A)	Semiannual Interest Payment to Bondholders (3 1/2% × $200,000)	Amortization of Bond Premium (C − B)	Unamortized Bond Premium at End of Period (E − D)	Carrying Value at End of Period (A − D)
0					$8,530	$208,530
1	$208,530	$6,256	$7,000	$744	7,786	207,786
2	207,786	6,234	7,000	766	7,020	207,020
3	207,020	6,211	7,000	789	6,231	206,231
4	206,231	6,187	7,000	813	5,418	205,418
5	205,418	6,163	7,000	837	4,581	204,581
6	204,581	6,137	7,000	863	3,718	203,718
7	203,718	6,112	7,000	888	2,830	202,830
8	202,830	6,085	7,000	915	1,915	201,915
9	201,915	6,057	7,000	943	972	200,972
10	200,972	6,028†	7,000	972	—	200,000

*Rounded to the nearest dollar.

†Last period's interest expense equals $6,028 ($7,000 − $972); it is actually equal to $6,029 ($200,972 × 0.03) but the difference is because of the cumulative effect of rounding.

FIGURE 13-4
Carrying Value and Interest Expense—Bonds Issued at a Premium

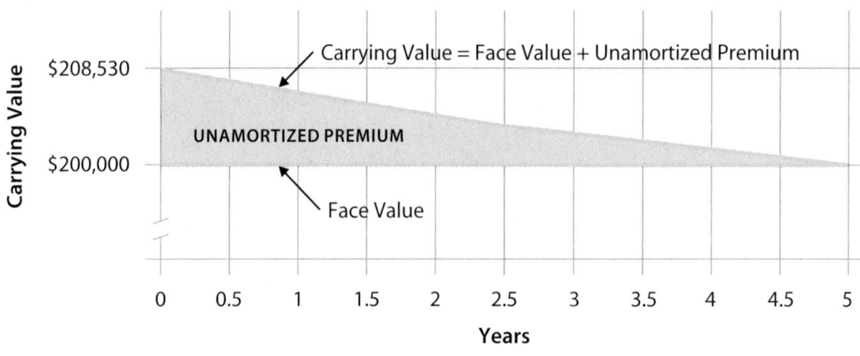

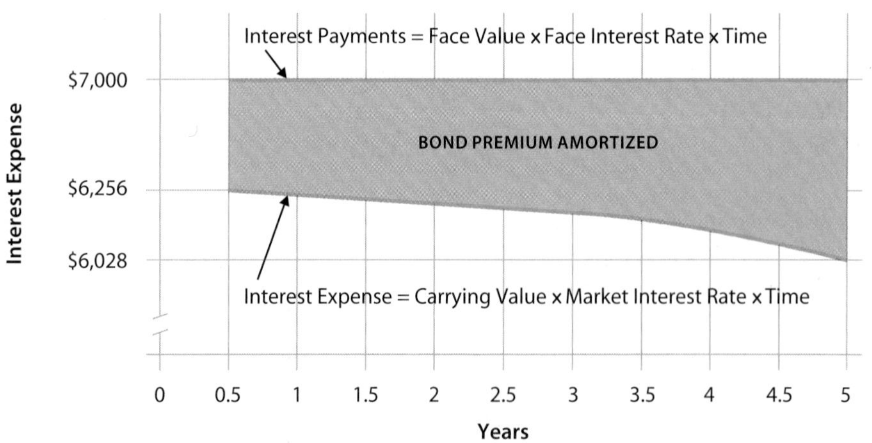

Note that the unamortized bond premium (column E) decreases gradually to zero as the carrying value decreases to the face value (column F). To find the amount of premium amortized in any one interest payment period, subtract the effective interest expense (the carrying value times the effective interest rate, column B) from the interest payment (column C). In semiannual interest period 5, for example, the amortization of premium is $837, which is calculated in the following manner: $7,000 − ($205,418 × 0.03).

Figure 13-4, which is based on the data in Table 13-4, shows how the effective interest method affects the amortization of a bond premium. Notice that the carrying value (issue price) is initially greater than the face value, but that it gradually decreases toward the face value over the life of the bond issue. Notice also that interest payments exceed interest expense by the amount of the premium amortized. Interest expense decreases gradually over the life of the bond because it is based on the gradually decreasing carrying value (multiplied by the market interest rate).

STOP & APPLY >

On June 1, Lazo Corporation issues $4,000,000 of 8 percent, 20-year bonds at 97. Interest is payable semiannually, on May 31 and November 30. Lazo's fiscal year ends on November 30.

1. Using the straight-line method of amortization, prepare entries in journal form for June 1 and November 30.
2. Using the effective interest method and assuming the same facts as above except that the market rate of interest is 9 percent, prepare the entry in journal form for November 30.

SOLUTION

1. Straight-line method

		Dr.	Cr.
June 1	Cash	3,880,000	
	Unamortized Bond Discount	120,000	
	Bonds Payable		4,000,000
	Issue of $4,000,000 of 8%, 20-year bonds at 97		
	$4,000,000 × 0.97 = $3,880,000		
Nov. 30	Bond Interest Expense	163,000	
	Unamortized Bond Discount		3,000
	Cash		160,000
	Paid bondholders semiannual interest and amortized the discount on 8%, 20-year bonds		
	$120,000 ÷ 40 periods = $3,000		
	$4,000,000 × 0.04 = $160,000		

2. Effective interest method

		Dr.	Cr.
Nov. 30	Bond Interest Expense	174,600	
	Unamortized Bond Discount		14,600
	Cash		160,000
	Paid bondholders semiannual interest and amortized the discount on 8%, 20-year bonds		
	$3,880,000 × 0.045 = $174,600		
	$4,000,000 × 0.04 = $160,000		

Retirement of Bonds

SO6 Account for the retirement of bonds and the conversion of bonds into stock.

Usually, companies pay bonds when they are due—on the maturity date. However, as we noted in our earlier discussion of callable and convertible bonds, retiring a bond issue before its maturity date can be to a company's advantage. For example, when interest rates drop, many companies refinance their bonds at the lower rate, much like homeowners who refinance their mortgage loans when interest rates go down. Even though companies usually pay a premium for early extinguishment of bond debt, what they save on interest can make the refinancing cost-effective.

Calling Bonds

Let's suppose that Bharath Corporation can call, or retire, at 105 the $200,000 of bonds it issued at a premium (104.265) on January 1, 2010, and that it decides to do so on July 1, 2013. The retirement thus takes place on the seventh interest payment date. Assume that the entry for the required interest payment and the amortization of the premium has been made. The T accounts and entry to record the retirement of the bonds is as follows:

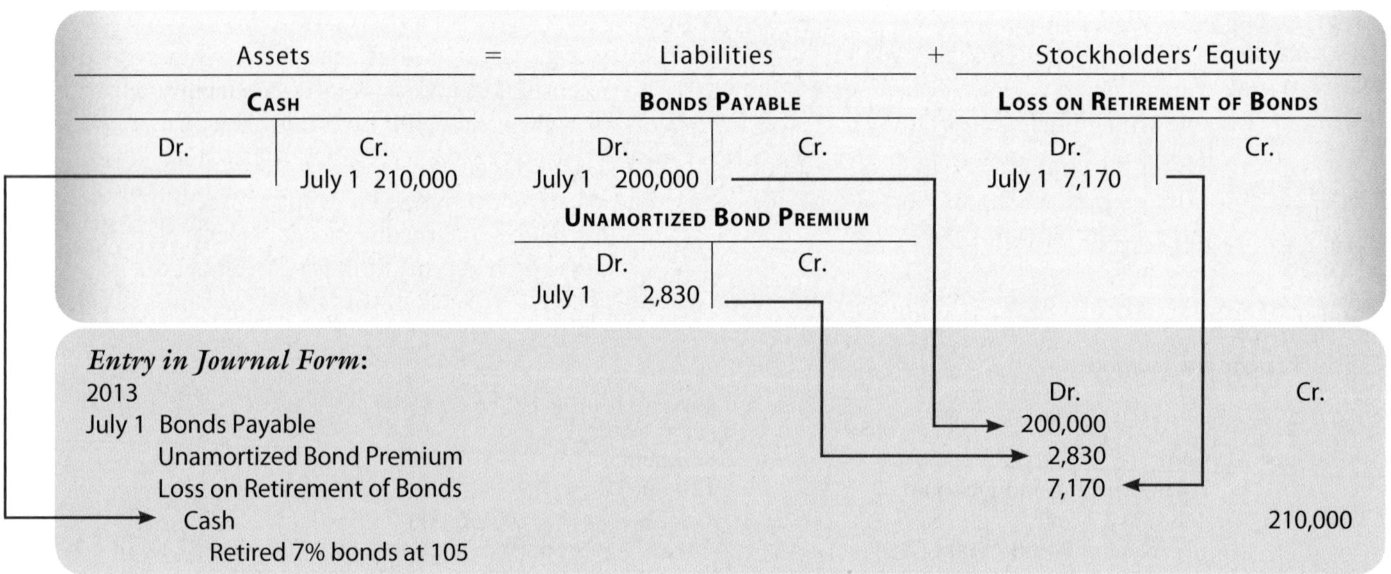

A	=	L	+	SE
−210,000		−200,000		−7,170
		−2,830		

In this entry, the cash paid is the face value times the call price ($200,000 × 1.05 = $210,000). The unamortized bond premium can be found in column E of Table 13-4. The loss on retirement of bonds occurs because the call price of the bonds is greater than the carrying value ($210,000 − $202,830 = $7,170).

Sometimes, a rise in the market interest rate can cause the market value of bonds to fall considerably below their face value. If it has the cash to do so, the company may find it advantageous to purchase the bonds on the open market and retire them, rather than wait and pay them off at face value. A gain is recognized for the difference between the purchase price of the bonds and the carrying value of the retired bonds.

For example, suppose that because of a rise in interest rates, Bharath Corporation is able to purchase the $200,000 bond issue on the open market at 85. The T accounts and entry would be as follows:

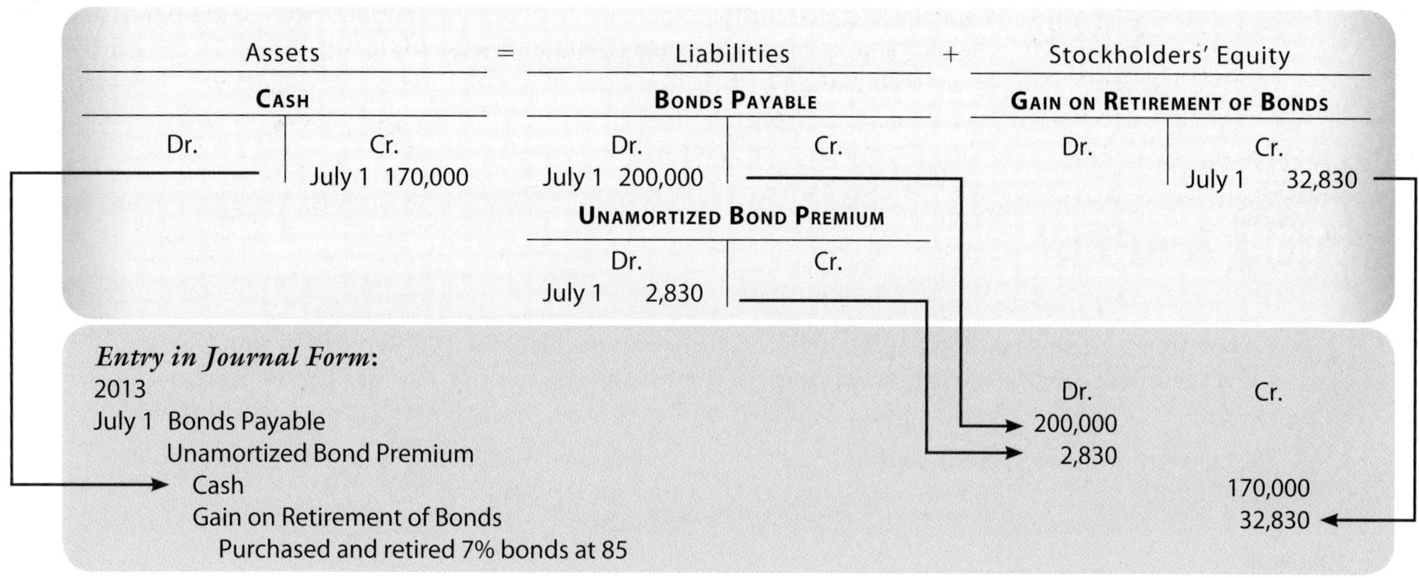

A	=	L	+	SE
−170,000		−200,000		+32,830
		−2,830		

Converting Bonds

When a bondholder converts bonds to common stock, the company records the common stock at the carrying value of the bonds. The bond liability and the unamortized discount or premium are written off the books. For this reason, no gain or loss on the transaction is recorded. For example, suppose Bharath Corporation does not call its bonds on July 1, 2013. Instead, the corporation's bondholders decide to convert all their bonds to $8 par value common stock under a convertible provision of 40 shares of common stock for each $1,000 bond. The T accounts and entry would be as follows:

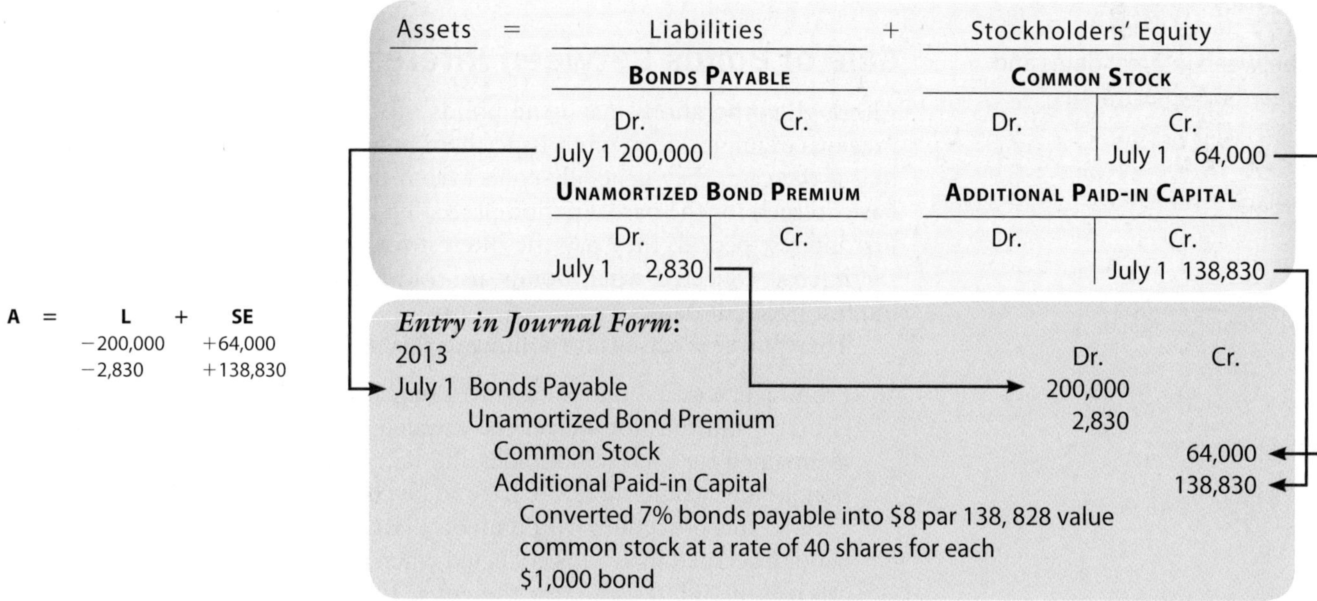

A	=	L	+	SE
		−200,000		+64,000
		−2,830		+138,830

The unamortized bond premium is found in column E of Table 13-4. At a rate of 40 shares for each $1,000 bond, 8,000 shares will be issued, with a total par value of $64,000 (8,000 × $8). The Common Stock account is credited for the amount of the par value of the stock issued. In addition, Additional Paid-in

Capital is credited for the difference between the carrying value of the bonds and the par value of the stock issued ($202,830 − $64,000 = $138,830). No gain or loss is recorded.

Schiff Stores has outstanding $100,000 of 7 percent bonds callable at 103. On July 1, immediately after recording the payment of the semiannual interest and the amortization of the premium, the unamortized bond premium equaled $2,500. On that date, all of the bonds were called and retired.

a. How much cash must be paid to retire the bonds?

b. Is there a gain or loss on retirement, and if so, how much is it?

SOLUTION

(1) Amount paid: $100,000 × 1.03 = $103,000

(2) There is a loss on retirement of $500, computed as follows:
Cash paid − Book value: $103,000 − ($100,000 + $2,500) = $500

Other Bonds Payable Issues

SO7 Record bonds issued between interest dates and year-end adjustments.

Among the other issues involved in accounting for bonds payable are the sale of bonds between interest payment dates and the year-end accrual of bond interest expense.

Sale of Bonds Between Interest Dates

Although corporations may issue bonds on an interest payment date, as in our previous examples, they often issue them between interest payment dates. When that is the case, they generally collect from the investors the interest that would have accrued for the partial period preceding the issue date, and at the end of the first interest period, they pay the interest for the entire period. In other words, the interest collected when bonds are sold is returned to investors on the next interest payment date.

There are two reasons for following this procedure:

1. From a practical standpoint, if a company issued bonds on several different days and did not collect the accrued interest, records would have to be maintained for each bondholder and date of purchase. The interest due each bondholder would therefore have to be computed for a different time period. Clearly, this procedure would involve large bookkeeping costs. On the other hand, if accrued interest is collected when the bonds are sold, the corporation can pay the interest due for the entire period on the interest payment date, thereby eliminating the extra computations and costs.

2. When accrued interest is collected in advance, the amount is subtracted from the full interest paid on the interest payment date. Thus, the resulting interest expense represents the amount for the time the money was borrowed.

For example, suppose Bharath Corporation sold $200,000 of 7 percent, five-year bonds for face value on May 1, 2010, rather than on January 1, 2010. The T accounts and entry to record the sale of the bonds is as follows:

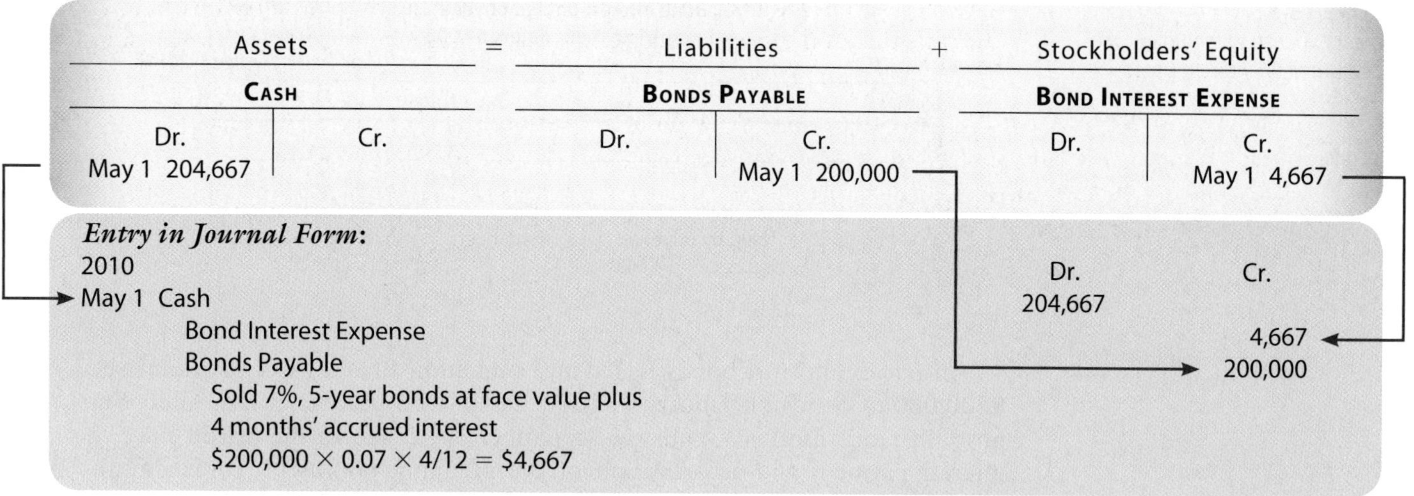

A	=	L	+	SE
+204,667		+200,000		+4,667

Cash is debited for the amount received, $204,667 (the face value of $200,000 plus four months' accrued interest of $4,667). Bond Interest Expense is credited for the $4,667 of accrued interest, and Bonds Payable is credited for the face value of $200,000.

When the first semiannual interest payment date arrives, this T account and entry is made:

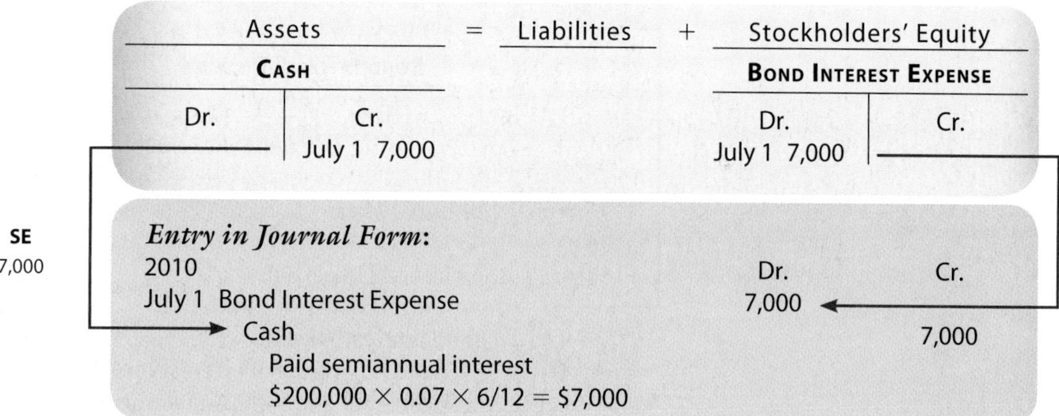

A*	=	L	+	SE
−7,000				−7,000

*Assumes cash paid.

Notice that the entire half-year interest is debited to Bond Interest Expense and credited to Cash because the corporation pays bond interest every six months, in full six-month amounts. Figure 13-5 illustrates this process. The actual interest expense for the two months that the bonds were outstanding is $2,333. This amount is the net balance of the $7,000 debit to Bond Interest Expense on July 1 less the $4,667 credit to Bond Interest Expense on May 1. You can see these steps clearly in the following T account:

BOND INTEREST EXPENSE

Dr.		Cr.	
Bal.	0	May 1	4,667
July 1	7,000		
Bal.	**2,333**		

Year-End Accrual of Bond Interest Expense

Bond interest payment dates rarely correspond with a company's fiscal year. Therefore, an adjustment must be made to accrue the interest expense on the bonds from the last interest payment date to the end of the fiscal year. In addition, any discount or premium on the bonds must be amortized for the partial period.

Study Note

Remember that adjusting entries never affect cash.

FIGURE 13-5
Interest Expense When Bonds Are Issued Between Interest Dates

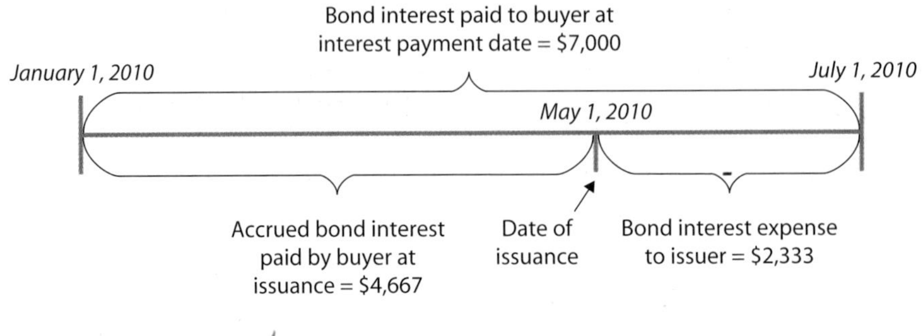

In our example of bonds issued at a premium, Bharath Corporation issued $200,000 of bonds on January 1, 2010, at 104.265 percent of face value. Suppose Bharath's fiscal year ends on September 30, 2010. In the period since the interest payment and amortization of the premium on July 1, three months' worth of interest has accrued. Under the effective interest method, the following adjusting T account and entry would be made:

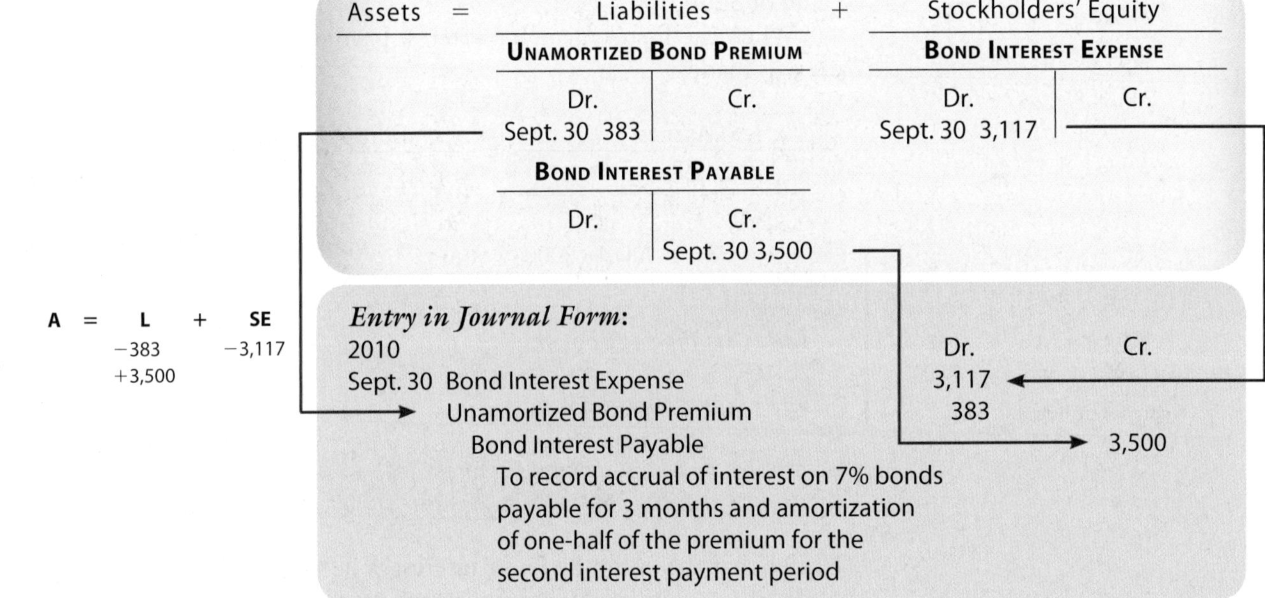

A	=	L	+	SE
		−383		−3,117
		+3,500		

Entry in Journal Form:

2010		Dr.	Cr.
Sept. 30	Bond Interest Expense	3,117	
	Unamortized Bond Premium	383	
	Bond Interest Payable		3,500
	To record accrual of interest on 7% bonds payable for 3 months and amortization of one-half of the premium for the second interest payment period		

This entry covers one-half of the second interest period. Unamortized Bond Premium is debited for $383, which is one-half of $766, the amortization of the premium for the second period from Table 13-4. Bond Interest Payable is credited for $3,500, three months' interest on the face value of the bonds ($200,000 × 0.07 × 3/12). The net debit figure of $3,117 ($3,500 − $383) is the bond interest expense for the three-month period.

On the interest payment date of January 1, 2011, the entry to pay the bondholders and amortize the premium is as follows:

Study Note

The matching rule dictates that both the accrued interest and the amortization of a premium or discount be recorded at year end.

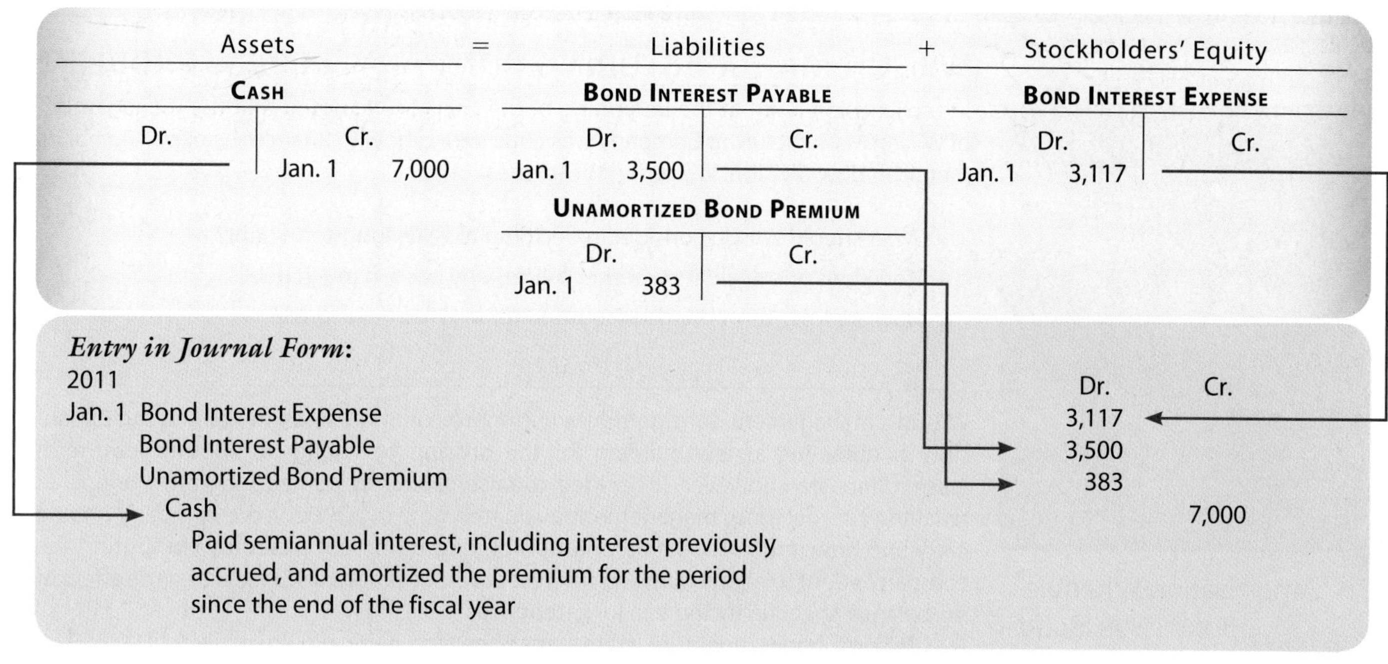

A	=	L	+ SE
−7,000		−3,500	−3,117
		−383	

One-half ($3,500) of the amount paid ($7,000) was accrued on September 30. Unamortized Bond Premium is debited for $383, the remaining amount to be amortized for the period ($766 − $383). The resulting bond interest expense is the amount that applies to the three-month period from October 1 to December 31.

Bond discounts are recorded at year end in the same way as bond premiums. The difference is that the amortization of a bond discount increases interest expense instead of decreasing it.

STOP & APPLY >

Hardin Associates is authorized to issue $1,000,000 in bonds on January 1. The bonds carry a face interest rate of 8 percent, which is to be paid on January 1 and July 1. Prepare entries in journal form for (a) the issue of the bonds on April 1 at 100 and (b) the interest payment on July 1. (c) How much was the total interest expense for the first six months of the year?

SOLUTION

(a) April 1	Cash	1,020,000	
	Bonds Payable		1,000,000
	Bond Interest Expense		20,000
	Issuance of 8 percent bonds		
(b) July 1	Bond Interest Expense	40,000	
	Cash		40,000
	Interest payment		

(c) Total interest expense: $40,000 − $20,000 = $20,000

▸ WILSON MANUFACTURING COMPANY: REVIEW PROBLEM

In the Decision Point at the beginning of the chapter, we noted that the management of Wilson Manufacturing Company was considering how to finance the expansion of its metal window division. We posed these questions:

- What should Wilson consider in deciding to issue long-term debt?
- How does one evaluate whether a company has too much debt?
- How are long-term bonds accounted for in Wilson's records?

Amortization Schedule, Bond Issue, Bond Retirement, Bond Conversion, and Debt Analysis
LO1 LO3
LO5 SO6

Wilson's management considered issuing more common stock to finance the expansion or obtaining a new building for the division by taking on another long-term lease. Ultimately, however, it decided to raise capital by issuing long-term bonds. In reaching this decision, management evaluated how much debt the company should carry and how much risk the assumption of long-term debt posed by computing the company's debt to equity ratio and interest coverage ratio. It also calculated the effect of off-balance-sheet financing of a long-term lease.

Wilson's bond indenture stated that the company would issue $2,500,000 of 8 percent, five-year bonds on January 1, 2011, and would pay interest semiannually on June 30 and December 31 in each of the five years. It also stated that the bonds would be callable at 104 and that each $1,000 bond would be convertible to 30 shares of $10 par value common stock.

Wilson sold the bonds on January 1, 2011, at 96 because the market rate of interest for similar investments was 9 percent. It decided to amortize the bond discount by using the effective interest method. On July 1, 2013, management called and retired half the bonds, and investors converted the other half to common stock.

Required

1. Prepare an interest and amortization schedule for the first five interest periods.
2. Prepare entries in journal form to record the sale of the bonds, the first two interest payments, the bond retirement, and the bond conversion.
3. User insight: Using the figures presented for Wilson in the Decision Point and recalling that the company had income before income taxes of $250 million and interest expense of $50 million, compute its debt to equity ratio and interest coverage ratio in the first year of the bond issue. What is your assessment of Wilson's level of debt?

Answers to Review Problem

1. Schedule for the first five interest periods:

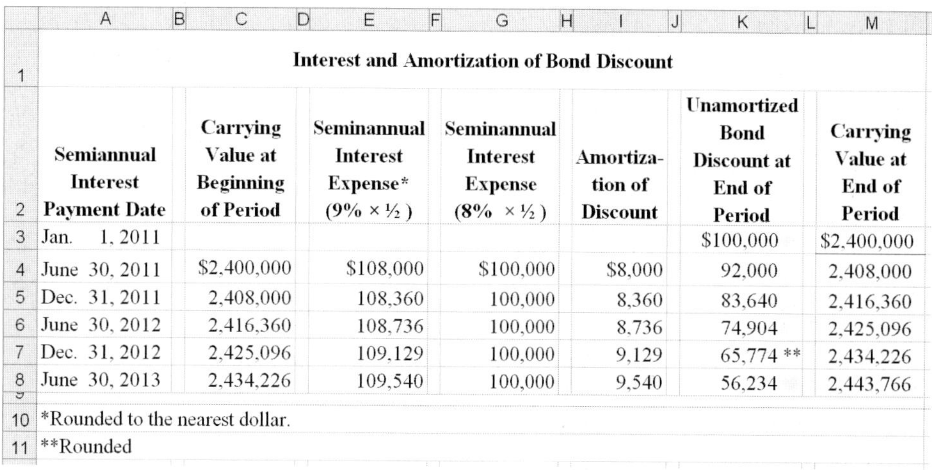

Semiannual Interest Payment Date	Carrying Value at Beginning of Period	Seminannual Interest Expense* (9% × ½)	Seminannual Interest Expense (8% × ½)	Amortiza-tion of Discount	Unamortized Bond Discount at End of Period	Carrying Value at End of Period
Interest and Amortization of Bond Discount						
Jan. 1, 2011					$100,000	$2,400,000
June 30, 2011	$2,400,000	$108,000	$100,000	$8,000	92,000	2,408,000
Dec. 31, 2011	2,408,000	108,360	100,000	8,360	83,640	2,416,360
June 30, 2012	2,416,360	108,736	100,000	8,736	74,904	2,425,096
Dec. 31, 2012	2,425,096	109,129	100,000	9,129	65,774 **	2,434,226
June 30, 2013	2,434,226	109,540	100,000	9,540	56,234	2,443,766

*Rounded to the nearest dollar.
**Rounded

2. Entries in journal form:

			Debit	Credit
2011				
Jan.	1	Cash	2,400,000	
		Unamortized Bond Discount	100,000	
		Bonds Payable		2,500,000
		Sold $2,500,000 of 8%, 5-year bonds at 96		
June	30	Bond Interest Expense	108,000	
		Unamortized Bond Discount		8,000
		Cash		100,000
		Paid semiannual interest and amortized the discount on 8%, 5-year bonds		
Dec.	31	Bond Interest Expense	108,360	
		Unamortized Bond Discount		8,360
		Cash		100,000
		Paid semiannual interest and amortize the discount on 8%, 5-year bonds		
2013				
July	1	Bonds Payable	1,250,000	
		Loss on Retirement of Bonds	78,118	
		Unamortized Bond Discount		28,118
		Cash		1,300,000
		Called $1,250,000 of 8% bonds and retired them at 104		
		($56,235 × 1/2 = $28,118*)		
		Bonds Payable	1,250,000	
		Unamortized Bond Discount		28,117
		Common Stock		375,000
		Additional Paid-in Capital		846,883
		Converted $1,250,000 of 8% bonds into common stock		
		1,250 × 30 shares = 37,500 shares		
		37,500 shares × $10 = $375,000		
		$56,235 − $28,118 = $28,117		
		$1,250,000 − ($28,117 + $375,000) = $846,883		

3. Ratios computed subsequent to bond issue:

$$\text{Debt to Equity Ratio} = \frac{\text{(Total Liabilities + Bond Issue less Discount)}}{\text{Stockholders' Equity}}$$

$$= \frac{\$1{,}000{,}000 + \$2{,}400{,}000}{\$3{,}200{,}000}$$

$$= \frac{\$3{,}400{,}000}{\$3{,}200{,}000}$$

$$= 1.06 \text{ Times}$$

$$\text{Interest Coverage} = \frac{\text{Income Before Income Taxes + Interest Expense + Bond Interest Expense}}{\text{Interest Expense + Bond Interest Expense}}$$

$$= \frac{\$250{,}000 + \$50{,}000 + \$216{,}360}{\$50{,}000 + \$216{,}360}$$

$$= \frac{\$516{,}360}{\$266{,}360}$$

$$= 1.94 \text{ Times}$$

The increased debt will represent more risk, especially since Wilson has long-term lease obligations.

LO1 Identify the management issues related to long-term debt.

Long-term debt is used to finance assets and business activities, such as research and development, that will produce income in future years. The management issues related to long-term debt are whether to take on long-term debt, how much debt to carry, and what types of debt to incur. The advantages of issuing long-term debt are that common stockholders do not relinquish any control, interest on debt is tax-deductible, and financial leverage can increase earnings. The disadvantages are that interest and principal must be paid on time and financial leverage can work against a company if an investment is not successful. The level of debt can be evaluated using the debt to equity ratio and the interest coverage ratio. Common types of long-term debt are bonds, notes, mortgages, long-term leases, pension liabilities, other post-retirement benefits, and deferred income taxes.

LO2 Describe the features of a bond issue and the major characteristics of bonds.

A bond is a security that represents money borrowed from the investing public. When a corporation issues bonds, it enters into a contract, called a bond indenture, with the bondholders. The bond indenture defines the terms of the bond issue. A bond issue is the total value of bonds issued at one time. The prices of bonds are stated in terms of a percentage of the face value, or principal, of the bonds. The face interest rate is the fixed rate of interest paid to bondholders based on the face value. The market interest rate is the rate of interest paid in the market on bonds of similar risk. If the market rate fluctuates from the face interest rate before the bond issue date, the bonds will sell at either a discount or a premium.

A corporation can issue several types of bonds, each having different characteristics. For example, a bond issue may or may not require security (secured versus unsecured bonds). It may be payable at a single time (term bonds) or at several times (serial bonds). And the holder may receive interest automatically (registered bonds) or may have to return coupons to receive interest payable (coupon bonds). Bonds may also be callable and convertible.

LO3 Record bonds issued at face value and at a discount or premium.

Bondholders pay face value for bonds when the interest rate on the bonds approximates the market rate for similar investments. The issuing corporation records the bond issue at face value as a long-term liability in the Bonds Payable account. Bonds are issued at a discount when their face interest rate is lower than the market rate for similar investments. The difference between the face value and the issue price is debited to Unamortized Bond Discount. Bonds are issued at a premium when their face interest rate is greater than the market interest rate on similar investments. The difference between the issue price and the face value is credited to Unamortized Bond Premium.

LO4 Use present values to determine the value of bonds.

The value of a bond is determined by summing the present values of (1) the series of fixed interest payments of the bond issue and (2) the single payment of the face value at maturity. Tables 1 and 2 in the appendix on present value tables should be used in making these computations.

LO5 Amortize bond discounts and bond premiums using the straight-line and effective interest methods.

The straight-line method allocates a fixed portion of a bond discount or premium each interest period to adjust the interest payment to interest expense. The effective interest method, which is used when the effects of amortization are material, applies a constant rate of interest to the carrying value of the bonds. To find interest and the amortization of discounts or premiums, the effective interest rate is applied to the carrying value of the bonds (face value minus the discount or plus the premium) at the beginning of the interest period. The amount of the discount or premium to be amortized is the difference between the interest figured by using the effective rate and that obtained by using the face rate. The results of using the effective interest method on bonds issued at a discount or a premium are summarized below and compared with issuance at face value:

	Bonds Issued at		
	Face Value	Discount	Premium
Trend in carrying value over bond term	Constant	Increasing	Decreasing
Trend in interest expense over bond term	Constant	Increasing	Decreasing
Interest expense versus interest payments	Interest expense = interest payments	Interest expense > interest payments	Interest expense < interest payments
Classification of bond discount or premium	Not applicable	Contra-liability (deducted from Bonds Payable)	Adjunct-liability (added to Bonds Payable)

Supplemental Objectives

SO6 Account for the retirement of bonds and the conversion of bonds into stock.

Callable bonds can be retired before maturity at the option of the issuing corporation. The call price is usually an amount greater than the face value of the bonds, in which case the corporation recognizes a loss on the retirement of the bonds. Sometimes, a rise in the market interest rate causes the market value of the bonds to fall below face value. If a company purchases its bonds on the open market at a price below carrying value, it recognizes a gain on the transaction.

Convertible bonds allow the bondholder to convert bonds to the issuing corporation's common stock. When bondholders exercise this option, the common stock issued is recorded at the carrying value of the bonds being converted. No gain or loss is recognized.

SO7 Record bonds issued between interest dates and year-end adjustments.

When bonds are sold between the interest payment dates, the issuing corporation collects from investors the interest that has accrued since the last interest payment date. When the next interest payment date arrives, the corporation pays the bondholders interest for the entire interest period.

When the end of a corporation's fiscal year does not fall on an interest payment date, the corporation must accrue bond interest expense from the last interest payment date to the end of its fiscal year. This accrual results in the inclusion of the interest expense in the year it is incurred.

REVIEW of Concepts and Terminology

The following concepts and terms were introduced in this chapter:

Bond 573 (LO2)

Bond certificate 573 (LO2)

Bond indenture 573 (LO2)

Bond issue 573 (LO2)

Callable bonds 574 (LO2)

Call price 574 (LO2)

Capital lease 568 (LO1)

Convertible bonds 574 (LO2)

Coupon bonds 575 (LO2)

Deferred income taxes 571 (LO1)

Defined benefit plan 570 (LO1)

Defined contribution plan 570 (LO1)

Discount 573 (LO2)

Early extinguishment of debt 574 (LO2)

Effective interest method 583 (LO5)

Face interest rate 573 (LO2)

Financial leverage 564 (LO1)

Market interest rate 573 (LO2)

Mortgage 567 (LO1)

Off-balance-sheet financing 565 (LO1)

Operating lease 568 (LO1)

Other post-retirement benefits 571 (LO1)

Pension fund 570 (LO1)

Pension plan 570 (LO1)

Premium 574 (LO2)

Registered bonds 575 (LO2)

Secured bonds 574 (LO2)

Serial bonds 574 (LO2)

Straight-line method 582 (LO5)

Term bonds 574 (LO2)

Unsecured bonds 574 (LO2)

Zero coupon bonds 582 (LO5)

Key Ratio

Interest coverage ratio 566 (LO1)

CHAPTER ASSIGNMENTS

BUILDING Your Basic Knowledge and Skills

Short Exercises

LO1 **Bond Versus Common Stock Financing**

SE 1. Indicate whether each of the following is an advantage or a disadvantage of using long-term bond financing rather than issuing common stock.

1. Interest paid on bonds is tax deductible.
2. Investments are sometimes not as successful as planned.
3. Financial leverage can have a negative effect when investments do not earn as much as the interest payments on the related debt.
4. Bondholders do not have voting rights in a corporation.
5. Positive financial leverage may be achieved.

LO1 **Types of Long-Term Liabilities**

SE 2. Place the number of the liability next to the statement to which it applies.

1. Bonds payable
2. Long-term notes payable
3. Mortgage payable
4. Long-term lease
5. Pension liabilities
6. Other post-retirement benefits
7. Deferred income taxes

___ a. May result in a capital lease
___ b. Differences in income taxes on accounting income and taxable income
___ c. The most popular form of long-term financing
___ d. Often used to purchase land and buildings
___ e. Often used interchangeably with bonds payable
___ f. Future health care costs are a major component
___ g. May include 401(k), ESOPs, or profit-sharing

LO1 **Mortgage Payable**

SE 3. Karib Corporation purchased a building by signing a $150,000 long-term mortgage with monthly payments of $1,200. The mortgage carries an interest rate of 8 percent. Prepare a monthly payment schedule showing the monthly payment, the interest for the month, the reduction in debt, and the unpaid balance for the first three months. (Round to the nearest dollar.)

LO4 **Valuing Bonds Using Present Value**

SE 4. Rogers Paints, Inc., is considering the sale of two bond issues. Choice A is a $600,000 bond issue that pays semiannual interest of $32,000 and is due in 20 years. Choice B is a $600,000 bond issue that pays semiannual interest of $30,000 and is due in 15 years. Assume that the market interest rate for each bond is 12 percent. Calculate the amount that Rogers Paints will receive if both bond issues occur. (Calculate the present value of each bond issue and sum.)

LO3 LO5 **Straight-Line Method**

SE 5. On April 1, 2010, Morimoto Corporation issued $8,000,000 in 8 percent, five-year bonds at 98. The semiannual interest payment dates are April 1 and October 1. Prepare entries in journal form for the issue of the bonds by Morimoto on April 1, 2010, and the first two interest payments on October 1, 2010, and April 1, 2011. Use the straight-line method and ignore year-end accruals.

LO3 LO5 SO7

Effective Interest Method

SE 6. On March 1, 2011, Fast Freight Company sold $400,000 of its 9 percent, 20-year bonds at 109.9. The semiannual interest payment dates are March 1 and September 1. The market interest rate is 8 percent. The firm's fiscal year ends August 31. Prepare entries in journal form to record the sale of the bonds on March 1, the accrual of interest and amortization of premium on August 31, and the first interest payment on September 1. Use the effective interest method to amortize the premium.

SO6

Bond Retirement

SE 7. The Silk Corporation has outstanding $200,000 of 8 percent bonds callable at 104. On December 1, immediately after the payment of the semiannual interest and the amortization of the bond discount were recorded, the unamortized bond discount equaled $5,250. On that date, $120,000 of the bonds were called and retired. Prepare the entry in journal form to record the retirement of the bonds on December 1.

SO6

Bond Conversion

SE 8. The Tramot Corporation has $2,000,000 of 6 percent bonds outstanding. There is $40,000 of unamortized discount remaining on the bonds after the March 1, 2011, semiannual interest payment. The bonds are convertible at the rate of 20 shares of $10 par value common stock for each $1,000 bond. On March 1, 2011, bondholders presented $1,200,000 of the bonds for conversion. Prepare the entry in journal form to record the conversion of the bonds.

SO7

Bond Issue Between Interest Dates

SE 9. Downey Corporation sold $400,000 of 9 percent, 10-year bonds for face value on September 1, 2011. The issue date of the bonds was May 1, 2011. The company's fiscal year ends on December 31, and this is its only bond issue. Record the sale of the bonds on September 1 and the first semiannual interest payment on November 1, 2011. What is the bond interest expense for the year ended December 31, 2011?

LO3 LO5 SO7

Year-End Accrual of Bond Interest

SE 10. On October 1, 2010, Tender Corporation issued $500,000 of 9 percent bonds at 96. The bonds are dated October 1 and pay interest semiannually. The market rate of interest is 10 percent, and the company's year end is December 31. Prepare the entries in journal form to record the issuance of the bonds, the accrual of the interest on December 31, 2010, and the payment of the first semiannual interest on April 1, 2011. Assume the company uses the effective interest method to amortize the bond discount.

Exercises

LO1 LO2 SO6

Discussion Questions

K/R

E 1. Develop brief answers to each of the following questions:

1. How does a lender assess the risk that a borrower may default—that is, not pay interest and principal when due?
2. If a company with a high debt to equity ratio wants to increase its debt when the economy is weak, what kind of bond might it issue?
3. Why might a company lease a long-term asset rather than buy it and issue long-term bonds?
4. Why are callable and convertible bonds considered to add to management's future flexibility in financing a business?

LO3 LO4 LO5 SO7

Discussion Questions

E 2. Develop brief answers to each of the following questions:

1. What determines whether bonds are issued at a discount, premium, or face value?
2. Why does the market price of a bond vary over time?
3. When is it acceptable to use the straight-line method to amortize a bond discount or premium?
4. Why must the accrual of bond interest be recorded at the end of an accounting period?

LO1

Interest Coverage Ratio

E 3. Compute the interest coverage ratios for 2010 and 2011 from the partial income statements of Chimney Corporation that appear below. State whether the ratio improved or worsened over time.

	2011	2010
Income from operations	$23,890	$18,460
Interest expense	5,800	3,300
Income before income taxes	$18,090	$15,160
Income taxes	5,400	4,500
Net income	$12,690	$10,660

LO1

Mortgage Payable

E 4. Victory Corporation purchased a building by signing a $150,000 long-term mortgage with monthly payments of $2,000. The mortgage carries an interest rate of 12 percent.

1. Prepare a monthly payment schedule showing the monthly payment, the interest for the month, the reduction in debt, and the unpaid balance for the first three months. (Round to the nearest dollar.)
2. Prepare entries in journal form to record the purchase and the first two monthly payments.

LO1

Recording Lease Obligations

E 5. Tapas Corporation has leased a piece of equipment that has a useful life of 12 years. The terms of the lease are payments of $43,000 per year for 12 years. Tapas currently is able to borrow money at a long-term interest rate of 8 percent. (Round answers to the nearest dollar.)

1. Calculate the present value of the lease.
2. Prepare the entry in journal form to record the lease agreement.
3. Prepare the entry in journal form to record depreciation of the equipment for the first year using the straight-line method.
4. Prepare the entries in journal form to record the lease payments for the first two years.

LO4

Valuing Bonds Using Present Value

E 6. Avanti, Inc., is considering the sale of two bond issues. Choice A is a $800,000 bond issue that pays semiannual interest of $64,000 and is due in 20 years. Choice B is a $800,000 bond issue that pays semiannual interest of $60,000 and is due in 15 years. Assume that the market interest rate for each bond is 8 percent. Calculate the amount that Avanti, Inc., will receive if both bond issues are made. (**Hint**: Calculate the present value of each bond issue and sum.)

LO4 Valuing Bonds Using Present Value

E 7. Use the present value tables in the appendix on present value tables to calculate the issue price of a $300,000 bond issue in each of the following independent cases. Assume interest is paid semiannually.

a. A 10-year, 8 percent bond issue; the market interest rate is 10 percent.
b. A 10-year, 8 percent bond issue; the market interest rate is 6 percent.
c. A 10-year, 10 percent bond issue; the market interest rate is 8 percent.
d. A 20-year, 10 percent bond issue; the market interest rate is 12 percent.
e. A 20-year, 10 percent bond issue; the market interest rate is 6 percent.

LO4 Zero Coupon Bonds

E 8. The state of Ohio needs to raise $25,000,000 for highway repairs. Officials are considering issuing zero coupon bonds, which do not require periodic interest payments. The current market interest rate for the bonds is 8 percent. What face value of bonds must be issued to raise the needed funds, assuming the bonds will be due in 30 years and compounded annually? How would your answer change if the bonds were due in 50 years? How would both answers change if the market interest rate were 6 percent instead of 8 percent?

LO3 LO5 Straight-Line Method

E 9. DNA Corporation issued $4,000,000 in 8 percent, 10-year bonds on February 1, 2010, at 115. Semiannual interest payment dates are January 31 and July 31. Use the straight-line method and ignore year-end accruals.

1. With regard to the bond issue on February 1, 2010:
   a. How much cash is received?
   b. How much is Bonds Payable?
   c. What is the difference between **a** and **b** called and how much is it?
2. With regard to the bond interest payment on July 31, 2010:
   a. How much cash is paid in interest?
   b. How much is the amortization?
   c. How much is interest expense?
3. With regard to the bond interest payment on January 31, 2011:
   a. How much cash is paid in interest?
   b. How much is the amortization?
   c. How much is interest expense?

LO3 LO5 Straight-Line Method

E 10. Nina Corporation issued $8,000,000 in 6 percent, five-year bonds on March 1, 2010, at 92. The semiannual interest payment dates are September 1 and March 1. Prepare entries in journal form for the issue of the bonds by Nina on March 1, 2010, and the first two interest payments on September 1, 2010, and March 1, 2011. Use the straight-line method and ignore year-end accruals.

LO3 LO5 Effective Interest Method

E 11. The Smart Company sold $500,000 of 8 percent, 20-year bonds on April 1, 2011, at 105. The semiannual interest payment dates are March 31 and September 30. The market interest rate is 7.5 percent. The company's fiscal year ends September 30. Use the effective interest method to calculate the amortization.

1. With regard to the bond issue on April 1, 2011:
   a. How much cash is received?
   b. How much is Bonds Payable?
   c. What is the difference between **a** and **b** called and how much is it?

2. With regard to the bond interest payment on September 30, 2011:
   a. How much cash is paid in interest?
   b. How much is the amortization?
   c. How much is interest expense?
3. With regard to the bond interest payment on March 31, 2012:
   a. How much cash is paid in interest?
   b. How much is the amortization?
   c. How much is interest expense?

LO3 LO5 **Effective Interest Method**

E 12. On March 1, 2010, Knap Corporation issued $1,200,000 of 6 percent, five-year bonds. The semiannual interest payment dates are February 28 and August 31. Because the market rate for similar investments was 7 percent, the bonds had to be issued at a discount. The discount on the issuance of the bonds was $49,900. The company's fiscal year ends February 28. Prepare entries in journal form to record the bond issue on March 1, 2010, the payment of interest, and the amortization of the discount on August 31, 2010 and on February 28, 2011. Use the effective interest method. (Round answers to the nearest dollar.)

SO6 **Bond Retirement**

E 13. The Rondo Corporation has outstanding $400,000 of 8 percent bonds callable at 104. On September 1, immediately after recording the payment of the semiannual interest and the amortization of the discount, the unamortized bond discount equaled $10,500. On that date, $240,000 of the bonds was called and retired.

1. How much cash must be paid to retire the bonds?
2. Is there a gain or loss on retirement, and if so, how much is it?

SO6 **Bond Conversion**

E 14. The Jolly Corporation has $400,000 of 6 percent bonds outstanding. There is $20,000 of unamortized discount remaining on these bonds after the July 1, 2011, semiannual interest payment. The bonds are convertible at the rate of 20 shares of $5 par value common stock for each $1,000 bond. On July 1, 2011, bondholders presented $300,000 of the bonds for conversion.

1. Is there a gain or loss on conversion, and if so, how much is it?
2. How many shares of common stock are issued in exchange for the bonds?
3. In dollar amounts, how does this transaction affect the total liabilities and the total stockholders' equity of the company? In your answer, show the effects on four accounts.

LO5 SO7 **Effective Interest Method and Interest Accrual**

E 15. The long-term debt section of the Midwest Corporation's balance sheet at the end of its fiscal year, December 31, 2010, is as follows:

Long-term liabilities		
Bonds payable—8%, interest payable		
1/1 and 7/1, due 12/31/16	$250,000	
Less unamortized bond discount	20,000	$230,000

Using the effective interest method, prepare entries in journal form relevant to the interest payments on July 1, 2011, December 31, 2011, and January 1, 2012. Assume a market interest rate of 10 percent.

LO4 SO6 **Time Value of Money and Early Extinguishment of Debt**

E 16. Anna's, Inc., has a $350,000, 4 percent bond issue that was issued a number of years ago at face value. There are now 10 years left on the bond issue, and the market interest rate is 8 percent. Interest is paid semiannually. The company purchases the bonds on the open market at the calculated current market value and retires the bonds.

1. Using present value tables, calculate the current market value of the bond issue.
2. Is there a gain or loss on retirement of the bonds, and if so, how much is it?

LO3 SO7 **Bond Issue on and Between Interest Dates**

E 17. Jigar Tech, Inc., is authorized to issue $1,800,000 in bonds on June 1. The bonds carry a face interest rate of 9 percent, which is to be paid on June 1 and December 1. Prepare entries in journal form for the issue of the bonds by Jigar Tech, Inc., under the assumptions that (a) the bonds are issued on September 1 at 100 and (b) the bonds are issued on June 1 at 105.

SO7 **Bond Issue Between Interest Dates**

E 18. Arif Corporation sold $400,000 of 12 percent, 10-year bonds at face value on September 1, 2011. The issue date of the bonds was May 1, 2011.

1. Record the sale of the bonds on September 1 and the first semiannual interest payment on November 1, 2011.
2. The company's fiscal year ends on December 31, and this is its only bond issue. What is the bond interest expense for the year ended December 31, 2011?

LO3 LO5 SO7 **Year-End Accrual of Bond Interest**

E 19. Hinali Corporation issued $1,000,000 of 7 percent bonds on October 1, 2010, at 96. The bonds are dated October 1 and pay interest semiannually. The market interest rate is 8 percent, and Hinali's fiscal year ends on December 31. Prepare the entries in journal form to record the issuance of the bonds, the accrual of the interest on December 31, 2010, and the first semiannual interest payment on April 1, 2011. Assume the company uses the effective interest method to amortize the bond discount.

Problems

LO1 **Lease Versus Purchase**

P 1. Shen Corporation can either lease or buy a small garage next to its business that will provide parking for its customers. The company can lease the building for a period of 12 years, which approximates the useful life of the facility and thus qualifies as a capital lease. The terms of the lease are payments of $12,000 per year for 12 years. Shen currently is able to borrow money at a long-term interest rate of 9 percent. The company can purchase the building by signing an $80,000 long-term mortgage with monthly payments of $1,000. The mortgage also carries an interest rate of 9 percent.

Required

1. With regard to the lease option,
    a. Calculate the present value of the lease. (Round answers to the nearest dollar.)
    b. Prepare the entry in journal form to record the lease agreement.
    c. Prepare the entry in journal form to record depreciation of the building for the first year using the straight-line method.
    d. Prepare the entries in journal form to record the lease payments for the first two years.
2. With regard to the purchase option,
    a. Prepare a monthly payment schedule showing the monthly payment, the interest for the month, the reduction in debt, and the unpaid balance for the first three months. (Round to the nearest dollar.)

b. Prepare entries in journal form to record the purchase and the first two monthly payments.

User insight ▶ 3. Based on your calculations, which option seems to be best? Aside from cost, name an advantage and a disadvantage of each option.

LO1 LO2 LO3

Bond Terminology

P 2. Listed below are common terms associated with bonds:

a. Bond certificate
b. Bond issue
c. Bond indenture
d. Unsecured bonds
e. Debenture bonds
f. Secured bonds
g. Term bonds
h. Serial bonds
i. Registered bonds
j. Coupon bonds
k. Callable bonds
l. Convertible bonds
m. Face interest rate
n. Market interest rate
o. Effective interest rate
p. Bond premium
q. Bond discount

Required

1. For each of the following statements, identify the category above with which it is associated. (If two statements apply, choose the category with which it is most closely associated.)

   1. Occurs when bonds are sold at more than face value
   2. Rate of interest that will vary depending on economic conditions
   3. Bonds that may be exchanged for common stock
   4. Bonds that are not registered
   5. A bond issue in which all bonds are due on the same date
   6. Occurs when bonds are sold at less than face value
   7. Rate of interest that will be paid regardless of market conditions
   8. Bonds that may be retired at management's option
   9. A document that is evidence of a company's debt
   10. Same as market rate of interest
   11. Bonds for which the company knows who owns them
   12. A bond issue for which bonds are due at different dates
   13. The total value of bonds issued at one time
   14. Bonds whose payment involves a pledge of certain assets
   15. Same as debenture bonds
   16. Contains the terms of the bond issue
   17. Bonds issued on the general credit of the company

User insight ▶ 2. What effect will a decrease in interest rates below the face interest rate and before a bond is issued have on the cash received from the bond issue? What effect will the decrease have on interest expense? What effect will the decrease have on the amount of cash paid for interest?

LO3 LO5 SO6

Bond Basics—Straight-Line Method, Retirement and Conversion

P 3. Murcia Corporation has $4,000,000 of 8 percent, 25-year bonds dated May 1, 2011, with interest payable on April 30 and October 31. The company's fiscal year ends on December 31, and it uses the straight-line method to amortize bond premiums or discounts. The bonds are callable after 10 years at 103 or convertible into 40 shares of $10 par value common stock.

Required

1. Assume the bonds are issued at 103.5 on May 1, 2011.
   a. How much cash is received?
   b. How much is Bonds Payable?

c. What is the difference between **a** and **b** called, and how much is it?
d. With regard to the bond interest payment on October 31, 2011:
(1) How much cash is paid in interest?
(2) How much is the amortization?
(3) How much is interest expense?

2. Assume the bonds are issued at 96.5 on May 1, 2011.
a. How much cash is received?
b. How much is Bonds Payable?
c. What is the difference between **a** and **b** called, and how much is it?
d. With regard to the bond interest payment on October 31, 2011:
(1) How much cash is paid in interest?
(2) How much is the amortization?
(3) How much is interest expense?

3. Assume the issue price in requirement **1** and that the bonds are called and retired 10 years later.
a. How much cash will have to be paid to retire the bonds?
b. Is there a gain or loss on the retirement, and if so, how much is it?

4. Assume the issue price in requirement **2** and that the bonds are converted to common stock 10 years later.
a. Is there a gain or loss on conversion, and if so, how much is it?
b. How many shares of common stock are issued in exchange for the bonds?
c. In dollar amounts, how does this transaction affect the total liabilities and the total stockholders' equity of the company? In your answer, show the effects on four accounts.

User insight ▶ 5. Assume that after 10 years market interest rates have dropped significantly and that the price of the company's common stock has risen significantly. Also assume that management wants to improve its credit rating by reducing its debt to equity ratio and that it needs what cash it currently has for expansion. Would management prefer the approach and result in requirement **3** or **4**? Explain your answer. What would be a disadvantage of the approach you chose?

LO3 LO5

Bond Transactions—Effective Interest Method

P 4. Dygat Corporation has $10,000,000 of 9 percent, 20-year bonds dated June 1, 2010 with interest payment dates of May 31 and November 30. The company's fiscal year ends November 30. It uses the effective interest method to amortize bond premiums or discounts.

Required

1. Assume the bonds are issued at 109.9 on June 1 to yield an effective interest rate of 8 percent. Prepare entries in journal form for June 1, 2010, November 30, 2010, and May 31, 2011. (Round amounts to the nearest dollar.)
2. Assume the bonds are issued at 91.4 on June 1 to yield an effective interest rate of 10 percent. Prepare entries in journal form for June 1, 2010, November 30, 2010, and May 31, 2011. (Round amounts to the nearest dollar.)

User insight ▶ 3. Explain the role that market interest rates play in causing a premium in requirement **1** and a discount in requirement **2**.

LO3 LO5 SO7

Bonds Issued at a Discount and a Premium—Effective Interest Method

P 5. Johnson Corporation issued bonds twice during 2010. The transactions were as follows:

2010
Jan. 1 Issued $1,000,000 of 7.5 percent, 10-year bonds dated January 1, 2010, with interest payable on June 30 and December 31. The

bonds were sold at 96.6, resulting in an effective interest rate of 8 percent.

Apr.	1	Issued $2,000,000 of 8.5 percent, 10-year bonds dated April 1, 2010, with interest payable on March 31 and September 30. The bonds were sold at 103.4, resulting in an effective interest rate of 8 percent.
June	30	Paid semiannual interest on the January 1 issue and amortized the discount, using the effective interest method.
Sept.	30	Paid semiannual interest on the April 1 issue and amortized the premium, using the effective interest method.
Dec.	31	Paid semiannual interest on the January 1 issue and amortized the discount, using the effective interest method.
	31	Made an end-of-year adjusting entry to accrue interest on the April 1 issue and to amortize half the premium applicable to the second interest period.
2011		
Mar.	31	Paid semiannual interest on the April 1 issue and amortized the premium applicable to the second half of the second interest period.

Required

1. Prepare entries in journal form to record the bond transactions. (Round amounts to the nearest dollar.)

User insight ▶

2. Describe the effect of the above transactions on profitability and liquidity by answering the following questions.
   a. What is the total interest expense in 2010 for each of the bond issues?
   b. What is the total cash paid in 2010 for each of the bond issues?
   c. What differences, if any, do you observe, and how do you explain them?

Alternate Problems

LO3 LO5 SO6

Bond Basics—Straight-line Method, Retirement, and Conversion

P 6. Golden Corporation has $20,000,000 of 7 percent, 20-year bonds dated June 1, 2010, with interest payment dates of May 31 and November 30. After 10 years, the bonds are callable at 104, and each $1,000 bond is convertible into 25 shares of $20 par value common stock. The company's fiscal year ends on December 31. It uses the straight-line method to amortize bond premiums or discounts.

Required

1. Assume the bonds are issued at 103 on June 1, 2010.
   a. How much cash is received?
   b. How much is Bonds Payable?
   c. What is the difference between **a** and **b** called, and how much is it?
   d. With regard to the bond interest payment on November 30, 2010:
      (1) How much cash is paid in interest?
      (2) How much is the amortization?
      (3) How much is interest expense?
2. Assume the bonds are issued at 97 on June 1, 2010.
   a. How much cash is received?
   b. How much is Bonds Payable?
   c. What is the difference between **a** and **b** called, and how much is it?
   d. With regard to the bond interest payment on November 30, 2010:

(1) How much cash is paid in interest?
(2) How much is the amortization?
(3) How much is interest expense?

3. Assume the issue price in requirement **1** and that the bonds are called and retired 10 years later.
   a. How much cash will have to be paid to retire the bonds?
   b. Is there a gain or loss on the retirement, and if so, how much is it?
4. Assume the issue price in requirement **2** and that the bonds are converted to common stock 10 years later.
   a. Is there a gain or loss on the conversion, and if so, how much is it?
   b. How many shares of common stock are issued in exchange for the bonds?
   c. In dollar amounts, how does this transaction affect the total liabilities and the total stockholders' equity of the company? In your answer, show the effects on four accounts.

User insight ▶ 5. Assume that after 10 years, market interest rates have dropped significantly and that the price on the company's common stock has risen significantly. Also assume that management wants to improve its credit rating by reducing its debt to equity ratio and that it needs what cash it has for expansion. Which approach would management prefer—the approach and result in requirement **3** or **4**? Explain your answer. What would be a disadvantage of the approach you chose?

LO3 LO5 **Bond Transactions—Effective Interest Method**

P 7. Jose Corporation has $4,000,000 of 9 percent, 25-year bonds dated March 1, 2010, with interest payable on February 28 and August 31. The company's fiscal year end is February 28. It uses the effective interest method to amortize bond premiums or discounts. (Round amounts to the nearest dollar.)

Required

1. Assume the bonds are issued at 110.7 on March 1, 2010, to yield an effective interest rate of 8 percent. Prepare entries in journal form for March 1, 2010, August 31, 2010, and February 28, 2011.
2. Assume the bonds are issued at 90.87 on March 1, 2010, to yield an effective interest rate of 10 percent. Prepare entries in journal form for March 1, 2010, August 31, 2010, and February 28, 2011.

User insight ▶ 3. Explain the role that market interest rates play in causing a premium in requirement **1** and a discount in requirement **2**.

LO3 LO5 SO7 **Bonds Issued at a Discount and a Premium—Effective Interest Method**

P 8. Rago Corporation issued bonds twice during 2010. A summary of the transactions involving the bonds follows.

2010		
Jan.	1	Issued $3,000,000 of 7 percent, 10-year bonds dated January 1, 2010, with interest payable on June 30 and December 31. The bonds were sold at 107.4, resulting in an effective interest rate of 6 percent.
Mar.	1	Issued $2,000,000 of 7.5 percent, 10-year bonds dated March 1, 2010, with interest payable March 1 and September 1. The bonds were sold at 96.6, resulting in an effective interest rate of 8 percent.
June	30	Paid semiannual interest on the January 1 issue and amortized the premium, using the effective interest method.

Sept. 1 Paid semiannual interest on the March 1 issue and amortized the discount, using the effective interest method.

Dec. 31 Paid semiannual interest on the January 1 issue and amortized the premium, using the effective interest method.

31 Made an end-of-year adjusting entry to accrue interest on the March 1 issue and to amortize two-thirds of the discount applicable to the second interest period.

2011

Mar. 1 Paid semiannual interest on the March 1 issue and amortized the remainder of the discount applicable to the second interest period.

Required

1. Prepare entries in journal form to record the bond transactions. (Round amounts to the nearest dollar.)

User insight ▶

2. Describe the effect on profitability and liquidity by answering the following questions.
   a. What is the total interest expense in 2010 for each of the bond issues?
   b. What is the total cash paid in 2010 for each of the bond issues?
   c. What differences, if any, do you observe and how do you explain them?

ENHANCING Your Knowledge, Skills, and Critical Thinking

LO1

Effect of Long-Term Leases

C 1. Many companies use long-term leases to finance long-term assets. Although these leases are similar to mortgage payments, they are structured in such a way that they qualify as operating leases. As a result, the lease commitments do not appear on the companies' balance sheets.

In a recent year, **Continental Airlines** had almost $15 billion in total operating lease commitments, of which $1.5 billion was due in the current year. Further, the airline had total assets of $12.686 billion and total liabilities of $12.581 billion. Because of heavy losses in previous years, its stockholders' equity was only $0.105 billion.[11]

What effect do these types of leases have on the balance sheet? Why would the use of these long-term leases make a company's debt to equity ratio, interest coverage ratio, and free cash flow look better than they really are? What is a capital lease? How does the application of capital lease accounting provide insight into a company's financial health?

LO2 SO6

Bond Issue

C 2. Eastman Kodak, the photography company, issued a $1 billion bond issue. Even though the company's credit rating was low, the bond issue was well received by the investment community because the company offered attractive terms. The offering comprised $500 million of 10-year unsecured notes and $500 million of 30-year convertible bonds. The convertibles were callable after seven years and would be convertible into common stock about 40 to 45 percent higher than the current price.[12]

What are unsecured notes? Why would they carry a relatively high interest rate? What are convertible securities? Why are they good for the investor and for the company? Why would they carry a relatively low interest rate? What does *callable* mean? What advantage does this feature give the company?

LO2 SO3 **Bond Interest Rates and Market Prices**

C 3. **Dow Chemical** is one of the largest chemical companies in the world. Among its long-term liabilities was a bond due in 2011 that carried a face interest rate of 6.125 percent.[13] This bond sold on the New York Stock Exchange at 104 5/8. Did this bond sell at a discount or a premium? Assuming the bond was originally issued at face value, did interest rates rise or decline after the date of issue? Would you have expected the market rate of interest on this bond to be more or less than 6.125 percent? Did the current market price affect either the amount that the company paid in semiannual interest or the amount of interest expense for the same period? Explain your answers.

LO2 **Characteristics of Convertible Debt**

C 4. **Amazon.com, Inc.**, gained renown as an online marketplace for books, records, and other products. Although the increase in its stock price was initially meteoric, only recently has the company begun to earn a profit. To support its enormous growth, Amazon.com issued $500,000,000 in 6.845 percent convertible notes due in 2010 at face value. Interest is payable on February 1 and August 1. The notes are convertible into common stock at a price of $112 per share, which at the time of issue was above the market price. The market value of Amazon.com's common stock has been quite volatile, from $39 to $95 in 2007.[14]

What reasons can you suggest for Amazon.com's management choosing notes that are convertible into common stock rather than simply issuing nonconvertible notes or issuing common stock directly? Are there any disadvantages to this approach? If the price of the company's common stock goes to $100 per share, what would be the total theoretical value of the notes? If the holders of the notes were to elect to convert the notes into common stock, what would be the effect on the company's debt to equity ratio, and what would be the effect on the percentage ownership of the company by other stockholders?

LO1 **Business Practice, Long-Term Debt, Leases, and Pensions**

C 5. To answer the following questions, refer to the financial statements and the notes to the financial statements in **CVS Corporation**'s annual report in the Supplement to Chapter 5:

1. Is it the practice of CVS to own or lease most of its buildings?
2. Does CVS lease property predominantly under capital leases or under operating leases? How much was rental expense for operating leases in 2008?
3. Does CVS have a defined benefit pension plan? Does it offer post-retirement benefits?

LO1 **Use of Debt Financing**

C 6. Refer to the annual report of **CVS Corporation** and the financial statements of **Southwest Airlines Co.** in the Supplement to Chapter 5. Calculate the debt to equity ratio and the interest coverage ratio for both companies' two most recent years. Find the note to the financial statements that contains information on leases and lease commitments by CVS. Southwest's lease expenses were $469 million and $527 million in 2007 and 2008, respectively, and total lease commitments for future years were $2,032 million. What effect do the total lease commitments and lease expense have on your assessment of the ratios you calculated? Evaluate and comment on the relative performance of the two companies with regard to debt financing. Which company has more risk of not being able to meet its interest obligations? How does leasing affect the analysis? Explain.

CHAPTER

15 The Statement of Cash Flows

Making a Statement

INCOME STATEMENT

Revenues

– Expenses

= Net Income

STATEMENT OF RETAINED EARNINGS

Beginning Balance

+ Net Income

– Dividends

= Ending Balance

BALANCE SHEET

Assets	Liabilities
	Stockholders' Equity

A = L + OE

STATEMENT OF CASH FLOWS

Operating activities

+ Investing activities

+ Financing activities

= Change in Cash

+ Beginning Balance

= Ending Cash Balance

The statement of cash flows explains the changes in cash on the balance sheet.

Cash flows are the lifeblood of a business. They enable a company to pay expenses, debts, employees' wages, and taxes, and to invest in the assets it needs for its operations. Without sufficient cash flows, a company cannot grow and prosper. Because of the importance of cash flows, one must be alert to the possibility that items may be incorrectly classified in a statement of cash flows and that the statement may not fully disclose all pertinent information. This chapter identifies the classifications used in a statement of cash flows and explains how to analyze the statement.

LEARNING OBJECTIVES

LO1 Describe the principal purposes and uses of the statement of cash flows, and identify its components. (pp. 658–663)

LO2 Analyze the statement of cash flows. (pp. 663–667)

LO3 Use the indirect method to determine cash flows from operating activities. (pp. 668–674)

LO4 Determine cash flows from investing activities. (pp. 674–677)

LO5 Determine cash flows from financing activities. (pp. 678–681)

DECISION POINT ▸ A USER'S FOCUS LOPATA CORPORATION

- ▸ Why were Lopata Corporation's operating cash flows less than its net income, and why did its cash and cash equivalents decline during the year?
- ▸ What measures do managers, stockholders, and potential investors use to evaluate the strength of a company's cash flows and liquidity?

Lopata Corporation is a distributor of accessories for cell phones, iPods, iPhones, and other small electronic devices. Lopata's managers have just finished preparing the company's financial statements for 2011. Although they are satisfied with net sales for the year—$825,000—they are concerned because cash flows from operating activities are less than net income ($58,300 vs. $82,200) and because cash and cash equivalents decreased by $8,000 during the year. They have also noted that the company has recently been having difficulty paying its bills on time.

Strong cash flows are critical to achieving and maintaining liquidity. If Lopata Corporation's cash flows are insufficient to maintain current operations or finance future growth, the company will have to sell investments, borrow funds, or issue stock. On the other hand, if its cash flows are strong, Lopata can use excess cash to reduce debt, thereby lowering its debt to equity ratio and improving its financial position. That, in turn, can increase the market value of its stock, which will increase stockholders' value.

Lopata's statement of cash flows will provide the company's managers, as well as its stockholders and potential investors, with information that is essential to evaluating the strength of the company's cash flows and liquidity.

Overview of the Statement of Cash Flows

LO1 Describe the principal purposes and uses of the statement of cash flows, and identify its components.

CASH FLOW

Study Note

Money market accounts, commercial paper (short-term notes), and U.S. Treasury bills are considered cash equivalents because they are highly liquid, temporary (90 days or less) holding places for cash not currently needed to operate the business.

The **statement of cash flows** shows how a company's operating, investing, and financing activities have affected cash during an accounting period. It explains the net increase (or decrease) in cash during the period. For purposes of preparing this statement, **cash** is defined as including both cash and cash equivalents. **Cash equivalents** are investments that can be quickly converted to cash; they have a maturity of 90 days or less when they are purchased. They include money market accounts, commercial paper, and U.S. Treasury bills. A company invests in cash equivalents to earn interest on cash that would otherwise be temporarily idle.

Suppose, for example, that a company has $1,000,000 that it will not need for 30 days. To earn a return on this amount, the company could place the cash in an account that earns interest (such as a money market account), lend the cash to another corporation by purchasing that corporation's short-term notes (commercial paper), or purchase a short-term obligation of the U.S. government (a Treasury bill).

Because cash includes cash equivalents, transfers between the Cash account and cash equivalents are not treated as cash receipts or cash payments. On the statement of cash flows, cash equivalents are combined with the Cash account. Cash equivalents should not be confused with short-term investments, or marketable securities. These items are not combined with the Cash account on the statement of cash flows; rather, purchases of marketable securities are treated as cash outflows, and sales of marketable securities are treated as cash inflows.

Purposes of the Statement of Cash Flows

The primary purpose of the statement of cash flows is to provide information about a company's cash receipts and cash payments during an accounting period. A secondary purpose is to provide information about a company's operating, investing, and financing activities during the accounting period. Some information about those activities may be inferred from other financial statements, but the statement of cash flows summarizes *all* transactions that affect cash.

Uses of the Statement of Cash Flows

The statement of cash flows is useful to management, as well as to investors and creditors.

- Management uses the statement of cash flows to assess liquidity, to determine dividend policy, and to evaluate the effects of major policy decisions involving investments and financing. Examples include determining if short-term financing is needed to pay current liabilities, deciding whether to raise or lower dividends, and planning for investing and financing needs.
- Investors and creditors use the statement to assess a company's ability to manage cash flows, to generate positive future cash flows, to pay its liabilities, to pay dividends and interest, and to anticipate its need for additional financing.

Classification of Cash Flows

The statement of cash flows has three major classifications: operating, investing, and financing activities. The components of these activities are illustrated in Figure 15-1 and summarized below.

1. **Operating activities** involve the cash inflows and outflows from activities that enter into the determination of net income. Cash inflows in this

category include cash receipts from the sale of goods and services and from the sale of *trading securities*. Trading securities are a type of marketable security that a company buys and sells for the purpose of making a profit in the near term. Cash inflows also include interest and dividends received on loans and investments. Cash outflows include cash payments for wages, inventory, expenses, interest, taxes, and the purchase of trading securities. In effect, accrual-based income from the income statement is changed to reflect cash flows.

2. **Investing activities** involve the acquisition and sale of property, plant, and equipment and other long-term assets, including long-term investments. They also involve the acquisition and sale of short-term marketable

FIGURE 15-1 Classification of Cash Inflows and Cash Outflows

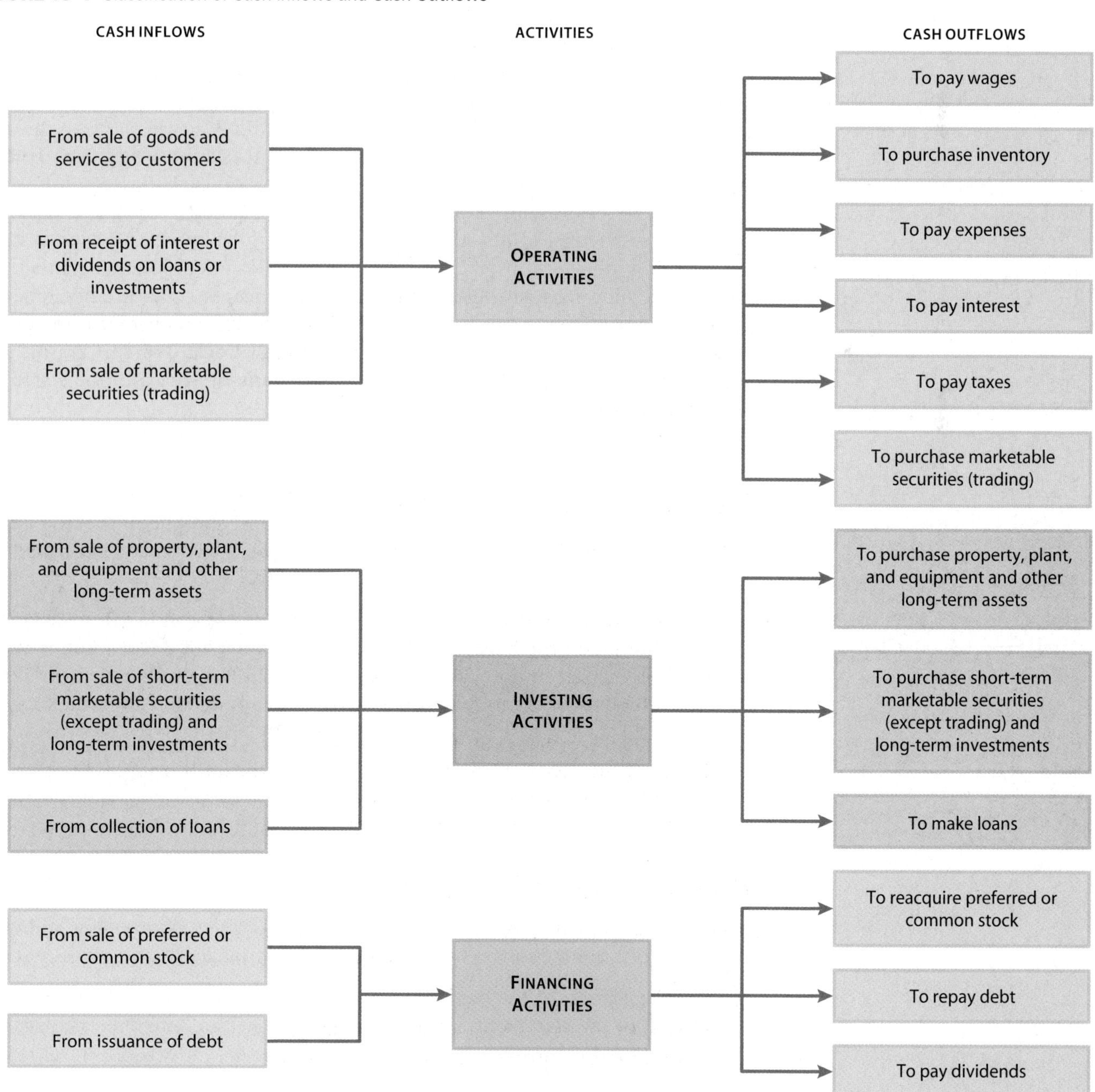

> **Study Note**
>
> Operating activities involve the day-to-day sale of goods and services, investing activities involve long-term assets and investments, and financing activities deal with stockholders' equity accounts and debt (borrowing).

securities, other than trading securities, and the making and collecting of loans. Cash inflows include the cash received from selling marketable securities and long-term assets and from collecting on loans. Cash outflows include the cash expended on purchasing these securities and assets and the cash lent to borrowers.

3. **Financing activities** involve obtaining resources from stockholders and providing them with a return on their investments and obtaining resources from creditors and repaying the amounts borrowed or otherwise settling the obligations. Cash inflows include the proceeds from stock issues and from short- and long-term borrowing. Cash outflows include the repayments of loans (excluding interest) and payments to owners, including cash dividends. Treasury stock transactions are also considered financing activities. Repayments of accounts payable or accrued liabilities are not considered repayments of loans; they are classified as cash outflows under operating activities.

Required Disclosure of Noncash Investing and Financing Transactions

Companies occasionally engage in significant **noncash investing and financing transactions**. These transactions involve only long-term assets, long-term liabilities, or stockholders' equity. For instance, a company might exchange a long-term asset for a long-term liability, settle a debt by issuing capital stock, or take out a long-term mortgage to purchase real estate. Noncash transactions represent significant investing and financing activities, but they are not reflected on the statement of cash flows because they do not affect current cash inflows or outflows. They will, however, affect future cash flows. For this reason, it is required that they be disclosed in a separate schedule or as part of the statement of cash flows.

Format of the Statement of Cash Flows

Amazon.com is the largest online retailer in the world and one of the 500 largest companies in the United States. Exhibit 15-1 shows the company's consolidated statements of cash flows for 2008, 2007, and 2006.

- The first section of the statement of cash flows is cash flows from operating activities. When the indirect method is used to prepare this section, it begins with net income and ends with cash flows from operating activities. This is the method most commonly used; we discuss it in detail later in the chapter.
- The second section, cash flows from investing activities, shows cash transactions involving capital expenditures (for property and equipment) and loans. Cash outflows for capital expenditures are usually shown separately from cash inflows from their disposal. However, when the inflows are not material, some companies combine these two lines to show the net amount of outflow as Amazon.com does.
- The third section, cash flows from financing activities, shows debt and common stock transactions, as well as payments for dividends and treasury stock.
- A reconciliation of the beginning and ending balances of cash appears at the bottom of the statement. These cash balances will tie into the cash balances of the balance sheets.

EXHIBIT 15-1 Consolidated Statement of Cash Flows

Amazon.com, Inc.
Consolidated Statements of Cash Flows

	For the Years Ended		
(In millions)	**2008**	**2007**	**2006**
Operating Activities			
Net income	$ 645	$ 476	$ 190
Adjustments to reconcile net income to net cash from operating activities:			
Depreciation and amortization	287	246	205
Stock-based compensation	275	185	101
Deferred income taxes	(5)	(99)	22
Excess tax benefits from stock-based compensation	(159)	(257)	(102)
Other	(60)	22	2
Changes in operating assets and liabilities:			
Inventories	(232)	(303)	(282)
Accounts receivable, net and other	(218)	(255)	(103)
Accounts payable	812	928	402
Accrued expenses and other	247	429	241
Additions to unearned revenue and other	105	33	26
Net cash provided by operating activities	$1,697	$ 1,405	$ 702
Investing Activities			
Purchases of fixed assets, including software and website development	$ (333)	$ (224)	($ 216)
Acquisitions, net of cash received and other	(494)	(75)	(32)
Sales and maturities of marketable securities and other investments	1,305	1,271	1,845
Purchases of marketable securities and other investments	(1,677)	(930)	(1,930)
Net cash provided by (used in) investing activities	($1,199)	$ 42	($ 333)
Financing Activities			
Proceeds from exercises of stock options	$ 11	$ 91	$ 35
Excess tax benefits from exercises of stock options	159	257	102
Common stock repurchased (Treasury stock)	(100)	(248)	(252)
Proceeds from long-term debt and other	87	24	98
Repayments of long-term debt and capital lease obligations	(355)	(74)	(383)
Net cash provided by (used in) financing activities	($ 198)	$ 50	($ 400)
Foreign-currency effect on cash and cash equivalents	$ (70)	$ 20	$ 40
Net (Decrease) Increase in Cash and Cash Equivalents	$ 230	$ 1,517	$ 9
Cash and Cash Equivalents, beginning of year	2,539	1,022	1,013
Cash and Cash Equivalents, end of year	$2,769	$ 2,539	$1,022

Source: Amazon.com, Inc., *Annual Report*, 2008 (adapted).

FOCUS ON BUSINESS PRACTICE 

How Universal Is the Statement of Cash Flows?

Despite the importance of the statement of cash flows in assessing the liquidity of companies in the United States, there has been considerable variation in its use and format in other countries. For example, in many countries, the statement shows the change in working capital rather than the change in cash and cash equivalents. Although the European Union's principal directives for financial reporting do not address the statement of cash flows, international accounting standards require it, and international financial markets expect it to be presented. As a result, most multinational companies include the statement in their financial reports. Most European countries adopted the statement of cash flows when the European Union adopted international accounting standards.

Ethical Considerations and the Statement of Cash Flows

Although cash inflows and outflows are not as subject to manipulation as earnings are, managers are acutely aware of users' emphasis on cash flows from operations as an important measure of performance. Thus, an incentive exists to overstate these cash flows.

In earlier chapters, we cited an egregious example of earnings management. As you may recall, by treating operating expenses of about $10 billion over several years as purchases of equipment, **WorldCom** reduced reported expenses and improved reported earnings. In addition, by classifying payments of operating expenses as investments on the statement of cash flows, it was able to show an improvement in cash flows from operations. The inclusion of the expenditures in the investing activities section did not draw special attention because the company normally had large capital expenditures.

Another way a company can show an apparent improvement in its performance is through lack of transparency, or lack of full disclosure, in its financial statements. For instance, securitization—the sale of batches of accounts receivable—is clearly a means of financing, and the proceeds from it should be shown in the financing section of the statement of cash flows. However, because the accounting standards are somewhat vague about where these proceeds should go, some companies net the proceeds against the accounts receivable in the operating section of the statement and bury the explanation in the notes to the financial statements. By doing so, they make collections of receivables in the operating activities section look better than they actually were. It is not illegal to do this, but from an ethical standpoint, it obscures the company's true performance.

STOP & APPLY >

Filip Corporation engaged in the transactions listed below. Identify each transaction as (a) an operating activity, (b) an investing activity, (c) a financing activity, (d) a noncash transaction, or (e) not on the statement of cash flows. (Assume the indirect method is used.)

1. Purchased office equipment, a long-term investment.
2. Decreased accounts receivable.
3. Sold land at cost.
4. Issued long-term bonds for plant assets.
5. Increased inventory.

(continued)

6. Issued common stock.
7. Repurchased common stock.
8. Issued notes payable.
9. Increased income taxes payable.
10. Purchased a 60-day Treasury bill.
11. Purchased a long-term investment.
12. Declared and paid a cash dividend.

SOLUTION

1. b; 2. a; 3. b; 4. d; 5. a; 6. c; 7. c; 8. c; 9. a; 10. e (cash equivalent); 11. b; 12. c

Analyzing Cash Flows

LO2 Analyze the statement of cash flows.

Like the analysis of other financial statements, an analysis of the statement of cash flows can reveal significant relationships. Two areas on which analysts focus when examining a company's statement of cash flows are cash-generating efficiency and free cash flow.

Can a Company Have Too Much Cash?

Before the bull market ended in 2007, many companies had accumulated large amounts of cash. **Exxon Mobil**, **Microsoft**, and **Cisco Systems**, for example, had amassed more than $100 billion in cash. At that time, the average large company in the United States had 7 percent of its assets in cash.

Increased cash can be a benefit or a potential risk. Many companies put their cash to good use. Of course they are wise to have cash on hand for emergencies. They may also invest in productive assets, conduct research and development, pay off debt, buy back stock, or pay dividends. Sometimes, however, shareholders suffer when executives are too conservative and keep the money in low-paying money market accounts or make unwise acquisitions. For the user of financial statements, the lesson is that it is important to look closely at the components of the statement of cash flows to see how management is spending its cash.[1]

Cash-Generating Efficiency

Managers accustomed to evaluating income statements usually focus on the bottom-line result. While the level of cash at the bottom of the statement of cash flows is certainly an important consideration, such information can be obtained from the balance sheet. The focal point of cash flow analysis is on cash inflows and outflows from operating activities. These cash flows are used in ratios that measure **cash-generating efficiency,** which is a company's ability to generate cash from its current or continuing operations. The ratios that analysts use to compute cash-generating efficiency are cash flow yield, cash flows to sales, and cash flows to assets.

In this section, we compute these ratios for **Amazon.com** in 2008 using data for net income and net cash flows from Exhibit 15-1 and the following information from Amazon.com's 2008 annual report (all dollar amounts are in millions).

	2008	2007	2006
Net Sales	$19,166	$14,835	$10,711
Total Assets	8,314	6,485	4,363

Cash flow yield is the ratio of net cash flows from operating activities to net income:

K/R

$$\text{Cash Flow Yield} = \frac{\text{Net Cash Flows from Operating Activities}}{\text{Net Income}}$$

$$= \frac{\$1{,}697}{\$645}$$

$$= 2.6 \text{ Times*}$$

For most companies, the cash flow yield should exceed 1.0. In 2008, Amazon.com performed much better than this minimum. With a cash flow yield of 2.6 times, Amazon.com generated about $2.60 of cash for every dollar of net income.

The cash flow yield needs to be examined carefully. Keep in mind, for instance, that a firm with significant depreciable assets should have a cash flow yield greater than 1.0 because depreciation expense is added back to net income to arrive at cash flows from operating activities. If special items, such as discontinued operations, appear on the income statement and are material, income from continuing operations should be used as the denominator. Also, an artificially high cash flow yield may result if a firm has very low net income, which is the denominator in the ratio.

Cash flows to sales is the ratio of net cash flows from operating activities to sales:

K/R

$$\text{Cash Flows to Sales} = \frac{\text{Net Cash Flows from Operating Activities}}{\text{Sales}}$$

$$= \frac{\$1{,}697}{\$19{,}166}$$

$$= 8.9\%\text{*}$$

Thus, Amazon.com generated positive cash flows to sales of 8.9 percent in 2008. Another way to state this result is that every dollar of sales generates 8.9 cents in cash.

Cash flows to assets is the ratio of net cash flows from operating activities to average total assets:

K/R

$$\text{Cash Flows to Assets} = \frac{\text{Net Cash Flows from Operating Activities}}{\text{Average Total Assets}}$$

$$= \frac{\$1{,}697}{(\$8{,}314 + \$6{,}485) \div 2}$$

$$= 22.9\%\text{*}$$

At 22.9 percent, Amazon.com's cash flows to assets ratio indicates that for every dollar of assets, the company generates almost 23 cents. This excellent result is higher than its cash flows to sales ratio because of its good asset turnover ratio (sales ÷ average total assets) of 2.6 times (22.9% ÷ 8.9%). Cash flows to sales and cash flows to assets are closely related to the profitability measures of profit margin and return on assets. They exceed those measures by the amount of the cash flow yield ratio because cash flow yield is the ratio of net cash flows from operating activities to net income.

---

*Rounded.

Asking the Right Questions About the Statement of Cash Flows

Most readers of financial statements are accustomed to looking at the "bottom line" to get an overview of a company's financial status. They look at total assets on the balance sheet and net income on the income statement. However, the statement of cash flows requires a different approach because the bottom line of cash on hand does not tell the reader very much; changes in the components of the statement during the year are far more revealing.

In interpreting a statement of cash flows, it pays to know the right questions to ask. To illustrate, let's use **Amazon.com** as an example.

- In our discussion of cash flow yield, we saw that Amazon.com generated about $2.60 of cash from operating activities for every dollar of net income in 2007. What are the primary reasons that cash flows from operating activities differed from net income?

For Amazon.com, the largest positive items in 2008 were accounts payable and depreciation. They are added to net income for different reasons. Accounts payable represents an increase in the amount owed to creditors, whereas depreciation represents a noncash expense that is deducted in arriving at net income. Amazon.com's two largest negative items were increases in inventories and receivables. As a growing company, Amazon.com was managing its operating cycle by generating cash from creditors to pay for increases in inventories and receivables.

- Amazon.com had a use of almost $1.2 billion in cash in 2008 due to purchases of fixed assets, acquisitions. What were its most important investing activities other than capital expenditures?

The company managed its investing activities by purchasing fixed assets, making acquisitions, and making active use of investments in marketable securities and other investments. Due to the company's success in generating cash flows from operations, it was able to purchase more marketable securities and other investments than it sold during the year.

- Amazon.com's financing activities show a relatively small use of cash of about $200 million. How did the company manage its financing activities during that fiscal year?

Exercise of stock options and the tax effects of stock-based compensation provided funds to buy back treasury stock and pay off some long-term debt. Because of its good cash flow from operations, Amazon.com did not need long-term financing.

Free Cash Flow

As we noted in an earlier chapter, **free cash flow** is the amount of cash that remains after deducting the funds a company must commit to continue operating at its planned level. If free cash flow is positive, it means that the company has met all of its planned cash commitments and has cash available to reduce debt or to expand. A negative free cash flow means that the company will have to sell investments, borrow money, or issue stock in the short term to continue at its planned level; if a company's free cash flow remains negative for several years, it may not be able to raise cash by issuing stocks or bonds. On the statement of cash flows, cash commitments for current and continuing operations, interest, and income taxes are incorporated in cash flows from current operations.

FOCUS ON BUSINESS PRACTICE

Cash Flows Tell All

In early 2001, the telecommunications industry began one of the biggest market crashes in history. Could it have been predicted? The capital expenditures that telecommunications firms must make for equipment, such as cable lines and computers, are sizable. When the capital expenditures (a negative component of free cash flow) of 41 telecommunications companies are compared with their cash flows from sales over the six years preceding the crash, an interesting pattern emerges. In the first three years, both capital expenditures and cash flows from sales were about 20 percent of sales. In other words, operations were generating enough cash flows to cover capital expenditures. Although cash flows from sales in the next three years stayed at about 20 percent of sales, free cash flows turned very negative, and almost half of capital expenditures had to be financed by debt instead of operations, making these companies more vulnerable to the downturn in the economy that occurred in 2001[2] and especially in 2008. The predictive reliability of free cash flow was confirmed in a later study that showed that of 100 different measures, stock price to free cash flow was the best predictor of future increases in stock price.[3]

Study Note

The computation for free cash flow sometimes uses *net capital expenditures* in place of *purchases of plant assets + sales of plant assets.*

Amazon.com has a stated primary financial objective of "long-term sustainable growth in free cash flow."[4] The company definitely achieved this objective in 2008. Its free cash flow for this year is computed as follows (in millions):

Free Cash Flow = Net Cash Flows from Operating Activities − Dividends − Purchases of Plant Assets + Sales of Plant Assets

= $1,697 − $0 − $333 + $0

= $1,364

Purchases of plant assets (capital expenditures) and sales (dispositions) of plant assets, if any, appear in the investing activities section of the statement of cash flows. Dividends, if any, appear in the financing activities section.

Construction firms must make large capital expenditures for plant assets, such as the equipment shown here. These expenditures are a negative component of free cash flow, which is the amount of cash that remains after deducting the funds a company needs to operate at its planned level. In 2007, negative free cash flows forced a number of construction firms to rely heavily on debt to finance their capital expenditures, thus increasing their vulnerability to the economic downturn of 2008.

Courtesy R, 2009/Used under license from Shutterstock.com.

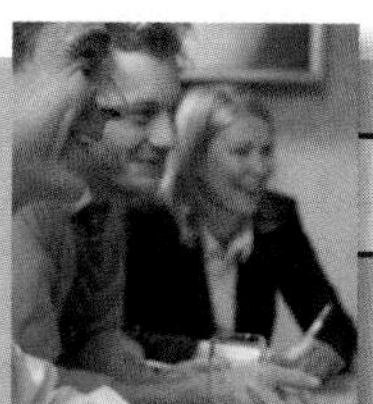

FOCUS ON BUSINESS PRACTICE

What Do You Mean, "Free Cash Flow"?

Because the statement of cash flows has been around for less than 25 years, no generally accepted analyses have yet been developed. For example, the term *free cash flow* is commonly used in the business press, but there is no agreement on its definition. An article in *Forbes* defines *free cash flow* as "cash available after paying out capital expenditures and dividends, but *before taxes and interest*" [emphasis added].[5] An article in *The Wall Street Journal* defines it as "operating income less maintenance-level capital expenditures."[6] The definition with which we are most in agreement is the one used in *BusinessWeek:* free cash flow is net cash flows from operating activities less net capital expenditures and dividends. This "measures truly discretionary funds—company money that an owner could pocket without harming the business."[7]

Amazon.com is a growing company and does not have material sales of plant assets and does not pay dividends. The company's positive free cash flow of $1,364 million was due primarily to its strong operating cash flow of $1,697 million. Consequently, the company does not have to borrow money to expand.

Because cash flows can vary from year to year, analysts should look at trends in cash flow measures over several years. It is also important to consider the effect of seasonality on a company's sales. Because Amazon.com's sales peak toward the end of the year, the cash situation at that time may not be representative of the rest of the year. For example, Amazon.com's management states that

> Our cash, cash equivalents, and marketable securities balances typically reach their highest level [at the end of each year.] This operating cycle results in a corresponding increase in accounts payable at December 31. Our accounts payable balance generally declines during the first three months of the year, resulting in a corresponding decline in our cash . . ."[8]

& APPLY >

In 2011, Monfort Corporation had year-end assets of $2,400,000, sales of $2,000,000, net income of $400,000, net cash flows from operating activities of $360,000, dividends of $100,000, purchases of plant assets of $200,000, and sales of plant assets of $40,000. In 2010, year-end assets were $2,200,000. Calculate cash flow yield, cash flows to sales, cash flows to assets, and free cash flow.

SOLUTION

$$\text{Cash Flow Yield} = \frac{\$360{,}000}{\$400{,}000} = 0.9 \text{ Times}$$

$$\text{Cash Flows to Sales} = \frac{\$360{,}000}{\$2{,}000{,}000} = 0.18, \text{ or } 18\%$$

$$\text{Cash Flows to Assets} = \frac{\$360{,}000}{(\$2{,}400{,}000 + \$2{,}200{,}000) \div 2} = 0.16, \text{ or } 16\% \text{ (rounded)}$$

$$\text{Free Cash Flow} = \$360{,}000 - \$100{,}000 - \$200{,}000 + \$40{,}000 = \$100{,}000$$

Operating Activities

LO3 Use the indirect method to determine cash flows from operating activities.

To demonstrate the preparation of the statement of cash flows, we will work through an example step-by-step. The data for this example are presented in Exhibit 15-2, which shows Laguna Corporation's income statement for 2010, and in Exhibit 15-3, which shows Laguna's balance sheets for December 31, 2010 and 2009. Exhibit 15-3 shows the balance sheet accounts that we use for analysis and whether the change in each account is an increase or a decrease.

The first step in preparing the statement of cash flows is to determine cash flows from operating activities. The income statement indicates how successful a company has been in earning an income from its operating activities, but because that statement is prepared on an accrual basis, it does not reflect the inflow and outflow of cash related to operating activities. Revenues are recorded even though the company may not yet have received the cash, and expenses are recorded even though the company may not yet have expended the cash. Thus, to ascertain cash flows from operations, the figures on the income statement must be converted from an accrual basis to a cash basis.

There are two methods of accomplishing this:

- The **direct method** adjusts each item on the income statement from the accrual basis to the cash basis. The result is a statement that begins with cash receipts from sales and interest and deducts cash payments for purchases, operating expenses, interest payments, and income taxes to arrive at net cash flows from operating activities.
- The **indirect method** does not require the adjustment of each item on the income statement. It lists only the adjustments necessary to convert net income to cash flows from operations.

Study Note

The direct and indirect methods relate only to the operating activities section of the statement of cash flows. They are both acceptable for financial reporting purposes.

The direct and indirect methods always produce the same net figure. The average person finds the direct method easier to understand because its presentation of operating cash flows is more straightforward than that of the indirect method. However, the indirect method is the overwhelming choice of most companies and accountants. A survey of large companies shows that 99 percent use this method.[9]

EXHIBIT 15-2
Income Statement

Laguna Corporation
Income Statement
For the Year Ended December 31, 2010

Sales		$698,000
Cost of goods sold		520,000
Gross margin		$178,000
Operating expenses (including depreciation expense of $37,000)		147,000
Operating income		$ 31,000
Other income (expenses)		
Interest expense	($23,000)	
Interest income	6,000	
Gain on sale of investments	12,000	
Loss on sale of plant assets	(3,000)	(8,000)
Income before income taxes		$ 23,000
Income taxes expense		7,000
Net income		$ 16,000

EXHIBIT 15-3 Comparative Balance Sheets Showing Changes in Accounts

Laguna Corporation
Comparative Balance Sheets
December 31, 2010 and 2009

	2010	2009	Change	Increase or Decrease
Assets				
Current assets				
Cash	$ 46,000	$ 15,000	$ 31,000	Increase
Accounts receivable (net)	47,000	55,000	(8,000)	Decrease
Inventory	144,000	110,000	34,000	Increase
Prepaid expenses	1,000	5,000	(4,000)	Decrease
Total current assets	$ 238,000	$185,000	$ 53,000	
Investments	$ 115,000	$127,000	($ 12,000)	Decrease
Plant assets	$ 715,000	$505,000	$210,000	Increase
Less accumulated depreciation	(103,000)	(68,000)	(35,000)	Increase
Total plant assets	$ 612,000	$437,000	$175,000	
Total assets	$ 965,000	$749,000	$216,000	
Liabilities				
Current liabilities				
Accounts payable	$ 50,000	$ 43,000	$ 7,000	Increase
Accrued liabilities	12,000	9,000	3,000	Increase
Income taxes payable	3,000	5,000	(2,000)	Decrease
Total current liabilities	$ 65,000	$ 57,000	$ 8,000	
Long-term liabilities				
Bonds payable	295,000	245,000	50,000	Increase
Total liabilities	$ 360,000	$302,000	$ 58,000	
Stockholders' Equity				
Common stock, $5 par value	$ 276,000	$200,000	$ 76,000	Increase
Additional paid-in capital	214,000	115,000	99,000	Increase
Retained earnings	140,000	132,000	8,000	Increase
Treasury stock	(25,000)	0	(25,000)	Increase
Total stockholders' equity	$ 605,000	$447,000	$158,000	
Total liabilities and stockholders' equity	$ 965,000	$749,000	$216,000	

From an analyst's perspective, the indirect method is superior to the direct method because it begins with net income and derives cash flows from operations; the analyst can readily identify the factors that cause cash flows from operations. From a company's standpoint, the indirect method is easier and less expensive to prepare. For these reasons, we use the indirect method in our example.

As Figure 15-2 shows, the indirect method focuses on adjusting items on the income statement to reconcile net income to net cash flows from operating

FIGURE 15-2 Indirect Method of Determining Net Cash Flows from Operating Activities

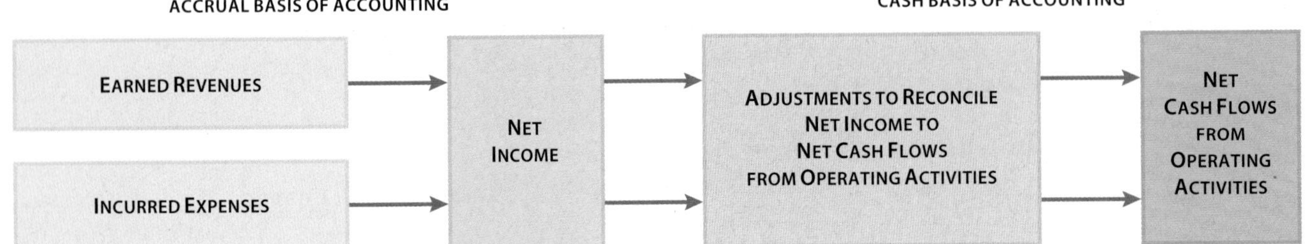

activities. These items include depreciation, amortization, and depletion; gains and losses; and changes in the balances of current asset and current liability accounts. The schedule in Exhibit 15-4 shows the reconciliation of Laguna Corporation's net income to net cash flows from operating activities. We discuss each adjustment in the sections that follow.

Depreciation

> **Study Note**
> Operating expenses on the income statement include depreciation expense, which does not require a cash outlay.

The investing activities section of the statement of cash flows shows the cash payments that the company made for plant assets, intangible assets, and natural resources during the accounting period. Depreciation expense, amortization expense, and depletion expense for these assets appear on the income statement as allocations of the costs of the original purchases to the current accounting period. The amount of these expenses can usually be found in the income statement or in a note to the financial statements. As you can see in Exhibit 15-2, Laguna Corporation's income statement discloses depreciation expense of $37,000, which would have been recorded as follows:

A	= L +	SE
−37,000		−37,000

Entry in Journal Form:

	Dr.	Cr.
Depreciation Expense	37,000	
Accumulated Depreciation		37,000
To record annual depreciation on plant assets		

Even though depreciation expense appears on the income statement, it involves no outlay of cash and so does not affect cash flows in the current period. Thus, to arrive at cash flows from operations on the statement of cash flows,

FOCUS ON BUSINESS PRACTICE IFRS

The Direct Method May Become More Important

At present, the direct method of preparing the operating section of the statement of cash flows is not important, but this may change if the International Accounting Standards Board (IASB) has its way. As mentioned earlier in the text, 99 percent of public companies in the United States presently use the indirect method to show the operating activities section of the statement of cash flows. However, in the interest of converging U.S. GAAP with international financial reporting standards (IFRS), the IASB is promoting the use of the direct method, even though it is more costly for companies to prepare. IFRS will continue to require a reconciliation of net income and net cash flows from operating activities similar to what is now done in the indirect method. **CVS**'s statement of cash flows, as shown in the Supplement to Chapter 5, is one of the few U.S. companies to use the direct method with reconciliation. Thus, its approach is very similar to what all companies may do if IFRS are adopted in the United States.

EXHIBIT 15-4
Schedule of Cash Flows from Operating Activities: Indirect Method

Laguna Corporation
Schedule of Cash Flows from Operating Activities
For the Year Ended December 31, 2010

Cash flows from operating activities		
Net income		$16,000
Adjustments to reconcile net income to net cash flows from operating activities		
Depreciation	$ 37,000	
Gain on sale of investments	(12,000)	
Loss on sale of plant assets	3,000	
Changes in current assets and current liabilities		
Decrease in accounts receivable	8,000	
Increase in inventory	(34,000)	
Decrease in prepaid expenses	4,000	
Increase in accounts payable	7,000	
Increase in accrued liabilities	3,000	
Decrease in income taxes payable	(2,000)	14,000
Net cash flows from operating activities		$30,000

an adjustment is needed to increase net income by the amount of depreciation expense shown on the income statement.

Gains and Losses

Study Note

Gains and losses by themselves do not represent cash flows; they are merely bookkeeping adjustments. For example, when a long-term asset is sold, it is the proceeds (cash received), not the gain or loss, that constitute cash flow.

Like depreciation expense, gains and losses that appear on the income statement do not affect cash flows from operating activities and need to be removed from this section of the statement of cash flows. The cash receipts generated by the disposal of the assets that resulted in the gains or losses are included in the investing activities section of the statement of cash flows. Thus, to reconcile net income to cash flows from operating activities (and prevent double counting), gains and losses must be removed from net income.

For example, on its income statement, Laguna Corporation shows a $12,000 gain on the sale of investments. This amount is subtracted from net income to reconcile net income to net cash flows from operating activities. The reason for doing this is that the $12,000 is included in the investing activities section of the statement of cash flows as part of the cash from the sale of the investment. Because the gain has already been included in the calculation of net income, the $12,000 gain must be subtracted to prevent double counting.

Laguna's income statement also shows a $3,000 loss on the sale of plant assets. This loss is already reflected in the sale of plant assets in the investing activities section of the statement of cash flows. Thus, the $3,000 is added to net income to reconcile net income to net cash flows from operating activities.

Changes in Current Assets

Decreases in current assets other than cash have positive effects on cash flows, and increases in current assets have negative effects on cash flows. A decrease in a current asset frees up invested cash, thereby increasing cash flow. An increase in a current asset consumes cash, thereby decreasing cash flow. For example, look at Laguna Corporation's income statement and balance sheets in Exhibits 15-2 and 15-3. Note that net sales in 2010 were $698,000 and that Accounts Receivable decreased by $8,000. Thus, collections were $8,000 more than sales recorded for the year, and the total cash received from sales was $706,000 ($698,000 + $8,000 = $706,000). The effect on Accounts Receivable can be illustrated as follows:

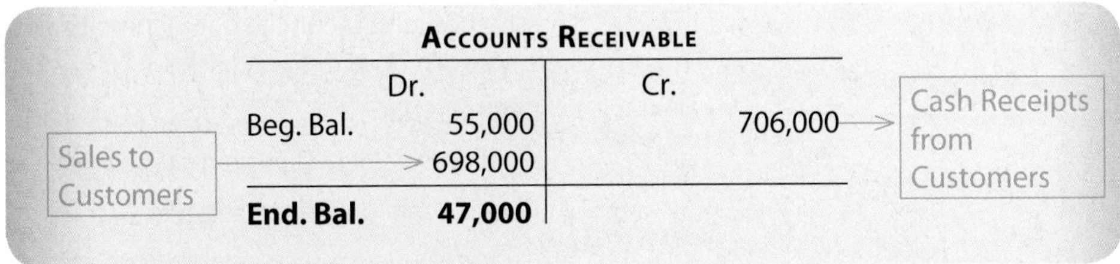

To reconcile net income to net cash flows from operating activities, the $8,000 decrease in accounts receivable is added to net income.

Inventory can be analyzed in the same way. For example, Exhibit 15-3 shows that Laguna's Inventory account increased by $34,000 between 2009 and 2010. This means that Laguna expended $34,000 more in cash for purchases than it included in cost of goods sold on its income statement. Because of this expenditure, net income is higher than net cash flows from operating activities, so $34,000 must be deducted from net income. By the same logic, the decrease of $4,000 in prepaid expenses shown on the balance sheets must be added to net income to reconcile net income to net cash flows from operating activities.

Changes in Current Liabilities

The effect that changes in current liabilities have on cash flows is the opposite of the effect of changes in current assets. An increase in a current liability represents a postponement of a cash payment, which frees up cash and increases cash flow in the current period. A decrease in a current liability consumes cash, which decreases cash flow. To reconcile net income to net cash flows from operating activities, increases in current liabilities are added to net income, and decreases are deducted. For example, Exhibit 15-3 shows that from 2009 to 2010, Laguna's accounts payable increased by $7,000. This means that Laguna paid $7,000 less to creditors than the amount indicated in the cost of goods sold on its income statement. The following T account illustrates this relationship:

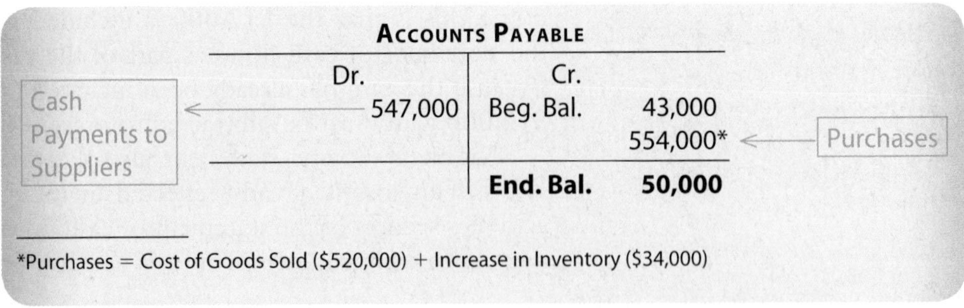

Thus, $7,000 must be added to net income to reconcile net income to net cash flows from operating activities. By the same logic, the increase of $3,000 in accrued liabilities shown on the balance sheets must be added to net income, and the decrease of $2,000 in income taxes payable must be deducted from net income.

Schedule of Cash Flows from Operating Activities

In summary, Exhibit 15-4 shows that by using the indirect method, net income of $16,000 has been adjusted by reconciling items totaling $14,000 to arrive at net cash flows from operating activities of $30,000. This means that although Laguna's net income was $16,000, the company actually had net cash flows of $30,000 available from operating activities to use for purchasing assets, reducing debts, and paying dividends.

The treatment of income statement items that do not affect cash flows can be summarized as follows:

	Add to or Deduct from Net Income
Depreciation expense	Add
Amortization expense	Add
Depletion expense	Add
Losses	Add
Gains	Deduct

The following summarizes the adjustments for increases and decreases in current assets and current liabilities:

	Add to Net Income	*Deduct from Net Income*
Current assets		
Accounts receivable (net)	Decrease	Increase
Inventory	Decrease	Increase
Prepaid expenses	Decrease	Increase
Current liabilities		
Accounts payable	Increase	Decrease
Accrued liabilities	Increase	Decrease
Income taxes payable	Increase	Decrease

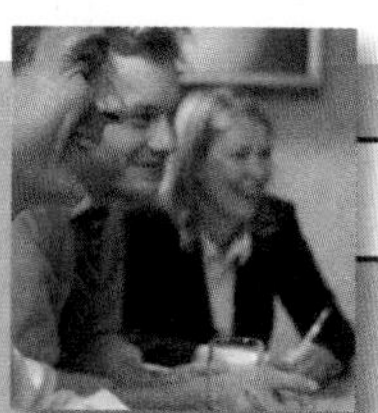

FOCUS ON BUSINESS PRACTICE

What Is EBITDA, and Is It Any Good?

Some companies and analysts like to use EBITDA (an acronym for Earnings Before Interest, Taxes, Depreciation, and Amortization) as a short-cut measure of cash flows from operations. But recent events have caused many analysts to reconsider this measure of performance. For instance, when **WorldCom** transferred $3.8 billion from expenses to capital expenditures in one year, it touted its EBITDA; at the time, the firm was, in fact, nearly bankrupt. The demise of **Vivendi**, the big French company that imploded when it did not have enough cash to pay its debts and that also touted its EBITDA, is another reason that analysts have had second thoughts about relying on this measure of performance.

Some analysts are now saying that EBITDA is "to a great extent misleading" and that it "is a confusing metric.... Some take it for a proxy for profits and some take it for a proxy for cash flow, and it's neither."[10] Cash flows from operations and free cash flow, both of which take into account interest, taxes, and depreciation, are better and more comprehensive measures of a company's cash-generating efficiency.

For the year ended June 30, 2011, Hoffer Corporation's net income was $7,400. Its depreciation expense was $2,000. During the year, its Accounts Receivable increased by $4,400, Inventories increased by $7,000, Prepaid Rent decreased by $1,400, Accounts Payable increased by $14,000, Salaries Payable increased by $1,000, and Income Taxes Payable decreased by $600. The company also had a gain on the sale of investments of $1,800. Use the indirect method to prepare a schedule of cash flows from operating activities.

SOLUTION

Hoffer Corporation
Schedule of Cash Flows from Operating Activities
For the Year Ended June 30, 2011

Cash flows from operating activities		
Net income		$ 7,400
Adjustments to reconcile net income to net cash flows from operating activities		
Depreciation	$ 2,000	
Gain on sale of investments	(1,800)	
Changes in current assets and current liabilities		
Increase in accounts receivable	(4,400)	
Increase in inventories	(7,000)	
Decrease in prepaid rent	1,400	
Increase in accounts payable	14,000	
Increase in salaries payable	1,000	
Decrease in income taxes payable	(600)	4,600
Net cash flows from operating activities		$12,000

Investing Activities

LO4 Determine cash flows from investing activities.

To determine cash flows from investing activities, accounts involving cash receipts and cash payments from investing activities are examined individually. The objective is to explain the change in each account balance from one year to the next.

Although investing activities center on the long-term assets shown on the balance sheet, they also include any short-term investments shown under current assets on the balance sheet and any investment gains and losses on the income statement. The balance sheets in Exhibit 15-3 show that Laguna had no short-term investments and that its long-term assets consisted of investments and plant assets. The income statement in Exhibit 15-2 shows that Laguna had a gain on the sale of investments and a loss on the sale of plant assets.

The following transactions pertain to Laguna's investing activities in 2010:

1. Purchased investments in the amount of $78,000.
2. Sold for $102,000 investments that cost $90,000.
3. Purchased plant assets in the amount of $120,000.
4. Sold for $5,000 plant assets that cost $10,000 and that had accumulated depreciation of $2,000.
5. Issued $100,000 of bonds at face value in a noncash exchange for plant assets.

Study Note

Investing activities involve long-term assets and short- and long-term investments. Inflows and outflows of cash are shown in the investing activities section of the statement of cash flows.

In the following sections, we analyze the accounts related to investing activities to determine their effects on Laguna's cash flows.

Investments

Our objective in this section is to explain Laguna Corporation's $12,000 decrease in investments. We do this by analyzing the increases and decreases in Laguna's Investments account to determine their effects on the Cash account.

Item **1** in the list of Laguna's transactions states that its purchases of investments totaled $78,000 during 2010. This transaction, which caused a $78,000 decrease in cash flows, is recorded as follows:

A	=	L	+	SE
+78,000				
−78,000				

	Dr.	Cr.
Investments	78,000	
Cash		78,000
Purchase of investments		

Item **2** states that Laguna sold for $102,000 investments that cost $90,000. This transaction resulted in a gain of $12,000. It is recorded as follows:

A	=	L	+	SE
+102,000				+12,000
−90,000				

	Dr.	Cr.
Cash	102,000	
Investments		90,000
Gain on Sale of Investments		12,000
Sale of investments for a gain		

Study Note

The $102,000 price obtained, not the $12,000 gained, constitutes the cash flow.

The effect of this transaction is a $102,000 increase in cash flows. Note that the gain on the sale is included in the $102,000. This is the reason we excluded it in computing cash flows from operations. If it had been included in that section, it would have been counted twice. We have now explained the $12,000 decrease in the Investments account during 2010, as illustrated in the following T account:

Investments

Dr.		Cr.	
Beg. Bal.	127,000	Sales	90,000
Purchases	78,000		
End. Bal.	**115,000**		

The cash flow effects of these transactions are shown in the investing activities section of the statement of cash flows as follows:

Purchase of investments	($ 78,000)
Sale of investments	102,000

Notice that purchases and sales are listed separately as cash outflows and inflows to give readers of the statement a complete view of investing activity. However, some companies prefer to list them as a single net amount. If Laguna Corporation had short-term investments or marketable securities, the analysis of cash flows would be the same.

Plant Assets

For plant assets, we have to explain changes in both the Plant Assets account and the related Accumulated Depreciation account. Exhibit 15-3 shows that from 2009 to 2010, Laguna Corporation's plant assets increased by $210,000 and that accumulated depreciation increased by $35,000.

Item **3** in the list of Laguna's transactions in 2010 states that the company purchased plant assets totaling $120,000. The following entry records this cash outflow:

A	=	L	+	SE
+120,000				
−120,000				

	Dr.	Cr.
Plant Assets	120,000	
Cash		120,000
Purchase of plant assets		

Item **4** states that Laguna Corporation sold for $5,000 plant assets that cost $10,000 and that had accumulated depreciation of $2,000. Thus, this transaction resulted in a loss of $3,000. The entry to record it is as follows:

A	=	L	+	SE
+5,000				−3,000
+2,000				
−10,000				

	Dr.	Cr.
Cash	5,000	
Accumulated Depreciation	2,000	
Loss on Sale of Plant Assets	3,000	
Plant Assets		10,000
Sale of plant assets at a loss		

Study Note

Even though Laguna had a loss on the sale of plant assets, it realized a positive cash flow of $5,000, which will be reported in the investing activities section of its statement of cash flows. When the indirect method is used, the loss is eliminated with an "add-back" to net income.

Note that in this transaction, the positive cash flow is equal to the amount of cash received, $5,000. The loss on the sale of plant assets is included in the investing activities section of the statement of cash flows and excluded from the operating activities section by adjusting net income for the amount of the loss. The amount of a loss or gain on the sale of an asset is determined by the amount of cash received and does not represent a cash outflow or inflow.

The investing activities section of Laguna's statement of cash flows reports the firm's purchase and sale of plant assets as follows:

Purchase of plant assets	($120,000)
Sale of plant assets	5,000

Cash outflows and cash inflows are listed separately here, but companies sometimes combine them into a single net amount, as they do the purchase and sale of investments.

Item **5** in the list of Laguna's transactions is a noncash exchange that affects two long-term accounts, Plant Assets and Bonds Payable. It is recorded as follows:

A	=	L	+	SE
+100,000		+100,000		

	Dr.	Cr.
Plant Assets	100,000	
Bonds Payable		100,000
Issued bonds at face value for plant assets		

Although this transaction does not involve an inflow or outflow of cash, it is a significant transaction involving both an investing activity (the purchase of plant assets) and a financing activity (the issue of bonds payable). Because one purpose of the statement of cash flows is to show important investing and financing activities, the transaction is listed at the bottom of the statement of cash flows or in a separate schedule, as follows:

Schedule of Noncash Investing and Financing Transactions

Issue of bonds payable for plant assets	$100,000

We have now accounted for all the changes related to Laguna's plant asset accounts. The following T accounts summarize these changes:

PLANT ASSETS

Dr.		Cr.	
Beg. Bal.	505,000	Sales	10,000
Cash Purchase	120,000		
Noncash Purchase	100,000		
End. Bal.	**715,000**		

ACCUMULATED DEPRECIATION

Dr.		Cr.	
Sale	2,000	Beg. Bal.	68,000
		Dep. Exp.	37,000
		End. Bal.	**103,000**

Had the balance sheet included specific plant asset accounts (e.g., Equipment and the related accumulated depreciation account) or other long-term asset accounts (e.g., Intangibles), the analysis would have been the same.

& APPLY >

The following T accounts show Matiz Company's plant assets and accumulated depreciation at the end of 2011:

PLANT ASSETS

Dr.		Cr.	
Beg. Bal.	65,000	Disposals	23,000
Purchases	33,600		
End. Bal.	**75,600**		

ACCUMULATED DEPRECIATION

Dr.		Cr.	
Disposals	14,700	Beg. Bal.	34,500
		Depreciation	10,200
		End. Bal.	**30,000**

Matiz's income statement shows a gain on the sale of plant assets of $4,400. Compute the amounts that should be shown as cash flows from investing activities, and show how they should appear on Matiz's 2011 statement of cash flows.

SOLUTION

Cash flows from investing activities:

Purchase of plant assets	($33,600)
Sale of plant assets	12,700

The T accounts show total purchases of plant assets of $33,600, which is an outflow of cash, and disposal of plant assets that cost $23,000 and that had accumulated depreciation of $14,700. The income statement shows a $4,400 gain on the sale of the plant assets. The cash inflow from the disposal was as follows:

Plant assets	$23,000
Less accumulated depreciation	14,700
Book value	$ 8,300
Add gain on sale	4,400
Cash inflow from sale of plant assets	$12,700

Because the gain on the sale is included in the $12,700 in the investing activities section of the statement of cash flows, it should be deducted from net income in the operating activities section.

Financing Activities

LO5 Determine cash flows from financing activities.

Determining cash flows from financing activities is very similar to determining cash flows from investing activities, but the accounts analyzed relate to short-term borrowings, long-term liabilities, and stockholders' equity. Because Laguna Corporation does not have short-term borrowings, we deal only with long-term liabilities and stockholders' equity accounts.

The following transactions pertain to Laguna's financing activities in 2010:

1. Issued $100,000 of bonds at face value in a noncash exchange for plant assets.
2. Repaid $50,000 of bonds at face value at maturity.
3. Issued 15,200 shares of $5 par value common stock for $175,000.
4. Paid cash dividends in the amount of $8,000.
5. Purchased treasury stock for $25,000.

Bonds Payable

Exhibit 15-3 shows that Laguna's Bonds Payable account increased by $50,000 in 2010. Both items **1** and **2** in the list above affect this account. We analyzed item **1** in connection with plant assets, but it also pertains to the Bonds Payable account. As we noted, this transaction is reported on the schedule of noncash investing and financing transactions. Item **2** results in a cash outflow, which is recorded as follows:

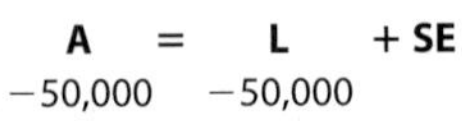

	Dr.	Cr.
Bonds Payable	50,000	
Cash		50,000
Repayment of bonds at face value at maturity		

This appears in the financing activities section of the statement of cash flows as follows:

Repayment of bonds ($50,000)

The following T account explains the change in Bonds Payable:

BONDS PAYABLE

Dr.		Cr.	
Repayment	50,000	Beg. Bal.	245,000
		Noncash Issue	100,000
		End. Bal.	**295,000**

If Laguna Corporation had any notes payable, the analysis would be the same.

Common Stock

Like the Plant Assets account and its related account, accounts related to stockholders' equity should be analyzed together. For example, the Additional Paid-in Capital account should be examined along with the Common Stock account. In 2010, Laguna's Common Stock account increased by $76,000, and its Additional Paid-in Capital account increased by $99,000. Item **3** in the list of Laguna's transactions, which states that the company issued 15,200 shares of $5 par

FOCUS ON BUSINESS PRACTICE

How Much Cash Does a Company Need?

Some kinds of industries are more vulnerable to downturns in the economy than others. Historically, because of the amount of debt they carry and their large interest and loan payments, companies in the airline and automotive industries have been hard hit by economic downturns. But research has shown that high-tech companies with large amounts of intangible assets are also hard hit. Biotechnology, pharmaceutical, and computer hardware and software companies can lose up to 80 percent of their value in times of financial stress. In contrast, companies with large amounts of tangible assets, such as oil companies and railroads, can lose as little as 10 percent. To survive during economic downturns, it is very important for high-tech companies to use their cash-generating efficiency to build cash reserves. It makes sense for these companies to hoard cash and not pay dividends to the extent that companies in other industries do.[11]

value common stock for $175,000, explains these increases. The entry to record the cash inflow is as follows:

A	= L +	SE
+175,000		+76,000
		+99,000

	Dr.	Cr.
Cash	175,000	
Common Stock		76,000
Additional Paid-in Capital		99,000
Issued 15,200 shares of $5 par value common stock		

This appears in the financing activities section of the statement of cash flows as:

Issuance of common stock	$175,000

The following analysis of this transaction is all that is needed to explain the changes in the two accounts during 2010:

Common Stock

Dr.	Cr.	
	Beg. Bal.	200,000
	Issue	76,000
	End. Bal.	**276,000**

Additional Paid-in Capital

Dr.	Cr.	
	Beg. Bal.	115,000
	Issue	99,000
	End. Bal.	**214,000**

Retained Earnings

At this point, we have dealt with several items that affect retained earnings. The only item affecting Laguna's retained earnings that we have not considered is the payment of $8,000 in cash dividends (item **4** in the list of Laguna's transactions). At the time it declared the dividend, Laguna would have debited its Cash Dividends account. After paying the dividend, it would have closed the Cash Dividends account to Retained Earnings and recorded the closing with the following entry:

A	= L +	SE
		−8,000
		+8,000

	Dr.	Cr.
Retained Earnings	8,000	
Cash Dividends		8,000
To close the Cash Dividends account		

Study Note

It is dividends paid, not dividends declared, that appear on the statement of cash flows.

Cash dividends would be displayed in the financing activities section of Laguna's statement of cash flows as follows:

Payment of dividends	($8,000)

The following T account shows the change in the Retained Earnings account:

RETAINED EARNINGS

Dr.		Cr.	
Cash Dividends	8,000	Beg. Bal.	132,000
		Net Income	16,000
		End. Bal.	**140,000**

EXHIBIT 15-5
Statement of Cash Flows: Indirect Method

Laguna Corporation
Statement of Cash Flows
For the Year Ended December 31, 2010

Cash flows from operating activities		
Net income		$ 16,000
Adjustments to reconcile net income to net cash flows from operating activities		
Depreciation	$ 37,000	
Gain on sale of investments	(12,000)	
Loss on sale of plant assets	3,000	
Changes in current assets and current liabilities		
Decrease in accounts receivable	8,000	
Increase in inventory	(34,000)	
Decrease in prepaid expenses	4,000	
Increase in accounts payable	7,000	
Increase in accrued liabilities	3,000	
Decrease in income taxes payable	(2,000)	14,000
Net cash flows from operating activities		$ 30,000
Cash flows from investing activities		
Purchase of investments	($ 78,000)	
Sale of investments	102,000	
Purchase of plant assets	(120,000)	
Sale of plant assets	5,000	
Net cash flows from investing activities		(91,000)
Cash flows from financing activities		
Repayment of bonds	($ 50,000)	
Issuance of common stock	175,000	
Payment of dividends	(8,000)	
Purchase of treasury stock	(25,000)	
Net cash flows from financing activities		92,000
Net increase in cash		$ 31,000
Cash at beginning of year		15,000
Cash at end of year		$ 46,000

Schedule of Noncash Investing and Financing Transactions

Issue of bonds payable for plant assets	$100,000

Treasury Stock

As we noted in the chapter on contributed capital, many companies buy back their own stock on the open market. These buybacks use cash, as this entry shows:

A	=	L	+	SE
−25,000				−25,000

	Dr.	Cr.
Treasury Stock	25,000	
Cash		25,000
Purchased treasury stock		

Study Note

The purchase of treasury stock qualifies as a financing activity, but it is also a cash outflow.

This use of cash is classified in the statement of cash flows as a financing activity:

Purchase of treasury stock	($25,000)

The T account for this transaction is as follows:

Treasury Stock

Dr.		Cr.
Purchase	25,000	

We have now analyzed all Laguna Corporation's income statement items, explained all balance sheet changes, and taken all additional information into account. Exhibit 15-5 shows how our data are assembled in Laguna's statement of cash flows.

STOP & APPLY >

During 2011, F & K Company issued $1,000,000 in long-term bonds at par, repaid $200,000 of notes payable at face value, issued notes payable of $40,000 for equipment, paid interest of $40,000, paid dividends of $25,000, and repurchased common stock in the amount of $50,000. Prepare the cash flows from financing activities section of the statement of cash flows.

SOLUTION

Cash flows from financing activities	
Issuance of long-term bonds	$1,000,000
Repayment of notes payable	(200,000)
Payment of dividends	(25,000)
Purchase of treasury stock	(50,000)
Net cash flows from financing activities	$ 725,000

Note: Interest is an operating activity. The exchange of the notes payable for equipment is a noncash investing and financing transaction.

▸ LOPATA CORPORATION: REVIEW PROBLEM

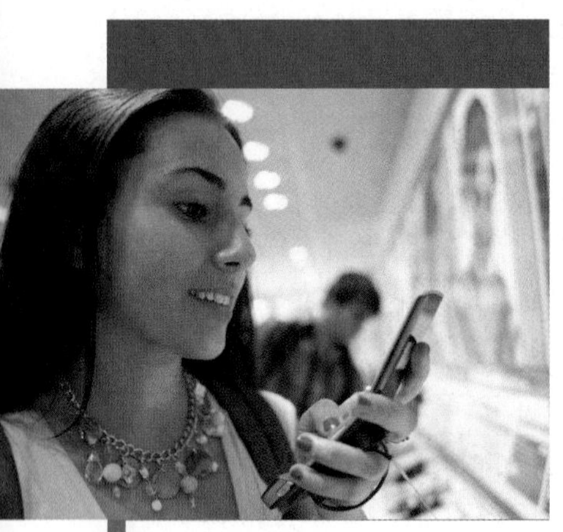

As we pointed out in this chapter's Decision Point, the managers of Lopata Corporation were concerned because in 2011, cash flows from operating activities were less than net income, cash and cash equivalents declined during the year, and the company was having trouble paying its bills on time. We asked the following questions:

- Why were Lopata Corporation's operating cash flows less than its net income, and why did its cash and cash equivalents decline during the year?
- What measures do managers, stockholders, and potential investors use to evaluate the strength of a company's cash flows and liquidity?

Statement of Cash Flows and Its Analysis

LO2 LO3 LO4 LO5

Lopata Corporation's income statement for 2011 appears below. Its comparative balance sheets for 2011 and 2010 follow. The company's records for 2011 provide this additional information:

a. Sold long-term investments that cost $35,000 for a gain of $6,250; made other long-term investments in the amount of $10,000.

b. Purchased 5 acres of land to build a parking lot for $12,500.

c. Sold equipment that cost $18,750 and that had accumulated depreciation of $12,650 at a loss of $1,150; purchased new equipment for $15,000.

d. Repaid notes payable in the amount of $50,000; borrowed $15,000 by signing new notes payable.

e. Converted $50,000 of bonds payable into 3,000 shares of common stock.

f. Reduced the Mortgage Payable account by $10,000.

g. Declared and paid cash dividends of $25,000.

h. Purchased treasury stock for $5,000.

	A	B	C
1	**Lopata Corporation**		
2	**Income Statement**		
3	**For the Year Ended December 31, 2011**		
4			
5	Net sales		$825,000
6	Cost of goods sold		460,000
7	Gross margin		$365,000
8	Operating expenses (including depreciation		
9	expense of $6,000 on buildings and		
10	$11,550 on equipment and amortization		
11	expense of $2,400)		235,000
12	Operating income		$130,000
13	Other income		
14	Interest expense	($27,500)	
15	Dividend income	1,700	
16	Gain on sale of investments	6,250	
17	Loss on disposal of equipment	(1,150)	(20,700)
18	Income before income taxes		$109,300
19	Income taxes expense		26,100
20	Net income		$ 83,200

	A	B	C	D	E
1	Lopata Corporation				
2	Comparative Balance Sheets				
3	December 31, 2011 and 2010				
4					
5		2011	2010	Change	Increase or Decrease
6	Assets				
7	Cash	$ 52,925	$ 60,925	($ 8,000)	Decrease
8	Accounts receivable (net)	148,000	157,250	(9,250)	Decrease
9	Inventory	161,000	150,500	10,500	Increase
10	Prepaid expenses	3,900	2,900	1,000	Increase
11	Long-term investments	18,000	43,000	(25,000)	Decrease
12	Land	75,000	62,500	12,500	Increase
13	Buildings	231,000	231,000	—	—
14	Accumulated depreciation–buildings	(45,500)	(39,500)	(6,000)	Increase
15	Equipment	79,865	83,615	(3,750)	Decrease
16	Accumulated depreciation–equipment	(21,700)	(22,800)	1,100	Decrease
17	Intangible assets	9,600	12,000	(2,400)	Decrease
18	Total assets	$712,090	$741,390	($29,300)	
19					
20	Liabilities and Stockholders' Equity				
21	Accounts payable	$ 66,875	$116,875	($50,000)	Decrease
22	Notes payable (current)	37,850	72,850	(35,000)	Decrease
23	Accrued liabilities	2,500	—	2,500	Increase
24	Income taxes payable	10,000	—	10,000	Increase
25	Bonds payable	105,000	155,000	(50,000)	Decrease
26	Mortgage payable	165,000	175,000	(10,000)	Decrease
27	Common stock, $10 par value	200,000	170,000	30,000	Increase
28	Additional paid-in capital	45,000	25,000	20,000	Increase
29	Retained earnings	104,865	46,665	58,200	Increase
30	Treasury stock	(25,000)	(20,000)	(5,000)	Increase
31	Total liabilities and stockholders' equity	$712,090	$741,390	($29,300)	

Required

1. Using the indirect method, prepare a statement of cash flows for Lopata Corporation for the year ended December 31, 2011.

2. User insight: Using data from Lopata's statement of cash flows, income statement, and comparative balance sheets, compute the company's cash flow yield, cash flows to sales, cash flows to assets, and free cash flow for 2011. What do your results indicate about the company's cash-generating efficiency? What do they indicate about Lopata's need to sell investments, issue stock, or borrow money to maintain current operations or finance future growth?

3. User insight: What is the apparent cause of Lopata's operating cash flow problem and the decline in its cash and cash equivalents?

Answers to Review Problem

1. Statement of cash flows using the indirect method:

	A	B	C
1	**Lopata Corporation**		
2	**Statement of Cash Flows**		
3	**For the Year Ended December 31, 2011**		
4			
5	**Cash flows from operating activities**		
6	Net income		$83,200
7	Adjustments to reconcile net income to net cash flows from operating activities		
8	Depreciation expense, buildings	$ 6,000	
9	Depreciation expense, equipment	11,550	
10	Amortization expense, intangible assets	2,400	
11	Gain on sale of investments	(6,250)	
12	Loss on disposal of equipment	1,150	
13	Changes in current assets and current liabilities		
14	Decrease in accounts receivable	9,250	
15	Increase in inventory	(10,500)	
16	Increase in prepaid expenses	(1,000)	
17	Decrease in accounts payable	(50,000)	
18	Increase in accrued liabilities	2,500	
19	Increase in income taxes payable	10,000	(24,900)
20	Net cash flows from operating activities		$58,300
21	**Cash flows from investing activities**		
22	Sale of long-term investments	$41,250 [a]	
23	Purchase of long-term investments	(10,000)	
24	Purchase of land	(12,500)	
25	Sale of equipment	4,950 [b]	
26	Purchase of equipment	(15,000)	
27	Net cash flows from investing activities		8,700
28	**Cash flows from financing activities**		
29	Repayment of notes payable	($50,000)	
30	Issuance of notes payable	15,000	
31	Reduction in mortgage	(10,000)	
32	Dividends paid	(25,000)	
33	Purchase of treasury stock	(5,000)	
34	Net cash flows from financing activities		(75,000)
35	Net (decrease) in cash		($ 8,000)
36	Cash at beginning of year		60,925
37	Cash at end of year		$52,925
38			
39	**Schedule of Noncash Investing and Financing Transactions**		
40	Conversion of bonds payable into common stock		$50,000
41			
42	[a] $35,000 + $6,250 (gain) = $41,250		
43	[b] $18,750 − $12,650 = $6,100 (book value) − $1,150 (loss) = $4,950		

2. Cash flow yield, cash flows to sales, cash flows to assets, and free cash flow for 2011:

$$\text{Cash Flow Yield} = \frac{\$58{,}300}{\$83{,}200} = 0.7 \text{ Times*}$$

$$\text{Cash Flows to Sales} = \frac{\$58{,}300}{\$825{,}000} = 7.1\%*$$

$$\text{Cash Flows to Assets} = \frac{\$58{,}300}{(\$712{,}090 + \$741{,}390) \div 2} = 8.0\%*$$

$$\text{Free Cash Flow} = \$58{,}300 - \$25{,}000 - \$12{,}500 - \$15{,}000 + \$4{,}950 = \$10{,}750$$

Lopata should generate at least $1 of net cash flows from operations for each $1 of net income. However, its cash flow yield shows that it generated only 70 cents for each $1 of net income. Judging from this result alone, Lopata's cash-generating efficiency is weak, and it seems likely that the company will have to sell investments, borrow money, or issue stock to maintain current operations or finance future growth.

3. The operating activities section of Lopata's statement of cash flows shows that the company reduced its accounts payable by $50,000. This one item more than offset the effects of all the other items and accounts for Lopata's operating cash flow problem and the decline in its cash and cash equivalents. Either Lopata unnecessarily paid its creditors a large amount, or its creditors have changed their terms. In the aftermath of the recession of the last few years, it has not been unusual for creditors to give less favorable terms as credit from banks has tightened.

*Rounded.

& REVIEW >

LO1 Describe the principal purposes and uses of the statement of cash flows, and identify its components.

The statement of cash flows shows how a company's operating, investing, and financing activities have affected cash during an accounting period. For the statement of cash flows, *cash* is defined as including both cash and cash equivalents. The primary purpose of the statement is to provide information about a firm's cash receipts and cash payments during an accounting period. A secondary purpose is to provide information about a firm's operating, investing, and financing activities. Management uses the statement to assess liquidity, determine dividend policy, and plan investing and financing activities. Investors and creditors use it to assess the company's cash-generating ability.

The statement of cash flows has three major classifications: (1) operating activities, which involve the cash effects of transactions and other events that enter into the determination of net income; (2) investing activities, which involve the acquisition and sale of marketable securities and long-term assets and the making and collecting of loans; and (3) financing activities, which involve obtaining resources from stockholders and creditors and providing the former with a return on their investments and the latter with repayment. Noncash investing and financing transactions are also important because they affect future cash flows; these exchanges of long-term assets or liabilities are of interest to potential investors and creditors.

LO2 Analyze the statement of cash flows.

In examining a firm's statement of cash flows, analysts tend to focus on cash-generating efficiency and free cash flow. Cash-generating efficiency is a firm's ability to generate cash from its current or continuing operations. The ratios used to measure cash-generating efficiency are cash flow yield, cash flows to sales, and cash flows to assets. Free cash flow is the cash that remains after deducting the funds a firm must commit to continue operating at its planned level. These commitments include current and continuing operations, interest, income taxes, dividends, and capital expenditures.

LO3 Use the indirect method to determine cash flows from operating activities.

The indirect method adjusts net income for all items in the income statement that do not have cash flow effects (such as depreciation, amortization, and gains and losses on sales of assets) and for changes in current assets and current liabilities that affect operating cash flows. Generally, increases in current assets have a negative effect on cash flows, and decreases have a positive effect. Conversely, increases in current liabilities have a positive effect on cash flows, and decreases have a negative effect.

LO4 Determine cash flows from investing activities.

Investing activities involve the acquisition and sale of property, plant, and equipment and other long-term assets, including long-term investments. They also involve the acquisition and sale of short-term marketable securities, other than trading securities, and the making and collecting of loans. Cash flows from investing activities are determined by analyzing the cash flow effects of changes in each account related to investing activities. The effects of gains and losses reported on the income statement must also be considered.

LO5 Determine cash flows from financing activities.

Determining cash flows from financing activities is almost identical to determining cash flows from investing activities. The difference is that the accounts analyzed relate to short-term borrowings, long-term liabilities, and stockholders' equity. After the changes in the balance sheet accounts from one accounting period to the next have been explained, all the cash flow effects should have been identified.

REVIEW of Concepts and Terminology

The following concepts and terms were introduced in this chapter:

Cash 658 (LO1)

Cash equivalents 658 (LO1)

Cash-generating efficiency 663 (LO2)

Direct method 668 (LO3)

Financing activities 660 (LO1)

Free cash flow 665 (LO2)

Indirect method 668 (LO3)

Investing activities 659 (LO1)

Noncash investing and financing transactions 660 (LO1)

Operating activities 658 (LO1)

Statement of cash flows 658 (LO1)

Key Ratios

Cash flows to assets 664 (LO2)

Cash flows to sales 664 (LO2)

Cash flow yield 664 (LO2)

CHAPTER ASSIGNMENTS

BUILDING Your Basic Knowledge and Skills

Short Exercises

LO1 **Classification of Cash Flow Transactions**

SE 1. The list that follows itemizes Furlong Corporation's transactions. Identify each as (a) an operating activity, (b) an investing activity, (c) a financing activity, (d) a noncash transaction, or (e) none of the above.

1. Sold land.
2. Declared and paid a cash dividend.
3. Paid interest.
4. Issued common stock for plant assets.
5. Issued preferred stock.
6. Borrowed cash on a bank loan.

LO2 **Cash-Generating Efficiency Ratios and Free Cash Flow**

SE 2. In 2011, Ross Corporation had year-end assets of $550,000, sales of $790,000, net income of $90,000, net cash flows from operating activities of $180,000, purchases of plant assets of $120,000, and sales of plant assets of $20,000, and it paid dividends of $40,000. In 2010, year-end assets were $500,000. Calculate the cash-generating efficiency ratios of cash flow yield, cash flows to sales, and cash flows to assets. Also calculate free cash flow.

LO2 **Cash-Generating Efficiency Ratios and Free Cash Flow**

SE 3. Examine the cash flow measures in requirement **2** of the review problem in this chapter. Discuss the meaning of these ratios.

LO3 **Computing Cash Flows from Operating Activities: Indirect Method**

SE 4. Wachowski Corporation had a net income of $33,000 during 2010. During the year, the company had depreciation expense of $14,000. Accounts Receivable increased by $11,000, and Accounts Payable increased by $5,000. Those were the company's only current assets and current liabilities. Use the indirect method to determine net cash flows from operating activities.

LO3 **Computing Cash Flows from Operating Activities: Indirect Method**

SE 5. During 2010, Minh Corporation had a net income of $144,000. Included on its income statement were depreciation expense of $16,000 and amortization expense of $1,800. During the year, Accounts Receivable decreased by $8,200, Inventories increased by $5,400, Prepaid Expenses decreased by $1,000, Accounts Payable decreased by $14,000, and Accrued Liabilities decreased by $1,700. Use the indirect method to determine net cash flows from operating activities.

LO4 **Cash Flows from Investing Activities and Noncash Transactions**

SE 6. During 2010, Howard Company purchased land for $375,000. It paid $125,000 in cash and signed a $250,000 mortgage for the rest. The company also sold for $95,000 cash a building that originally cost $90,000, on which it had $70,000 of accumulated depreciation, making a gain of $75,000. Prepare the cash flows from investing activities section and the schedule of noncash investing and financing transactions of the statement of cash flows.

LO5 **Cash Flows from Financing Activities**

SE 7. During 2010, Arizona Company issued $500,000 in long-term bonds at 96, repaid $75,000 of bonds at face value, paid interest of $40,000, and paid dividends of $25,000. Prepare the cash flows from the financing activities section of the statement of cash flows.

LO1 LO3 LO4 LO5

Identifying Components of the Statement of Cash Flows

SE 8. Assuming the indirect method is used to prepare the statement of cash flows, tell whether each of the following items would appear (a) in cash flows from operating activities, (b) in cash flows from investing activities, (c) in cash flows from financing activities, (d) in the schedule of noncash investing and financing transactions, or (e) not on the statement of cash flows at all:

1. Dividends paid
2. Cash receipts from sales
3. Decrease in accounts receivable
4. Sale of plant assets
5. Gain on sale of investments
6. Issue of stock for plant assets
7. Issue of common stock
8. Net income

Exercises

LO1 LO2

Discussion Questions

E 1. Develop brief answers to each of the following questions:

1. Which statement is more useful—the income statement or the statement of cash flows?
2. How would you respond to someone who says that the most important item on the statement of cash flows is the change in the cash balance for the year?
3. If a company's cash flow yield is less than 1.0, would its cash flows to sales and cash flows to assets be greater or less than profit margin and return on assets, respectively?

LO3 LO4 LO5

Discussion Questions

E 2. Develop brief answers to each of the following questions:

1. If a company has positive earnings, can cash flows from operating activities ever be negative?
2. Which adjustments to net income in the operating activities section of the statement of cash flows are directly related to cash flows in other sections?
3. In computing free cash flow, what is an argument for treating the purchases of treasury stock like dividend payments?

LO1

Classification of Cash Flow Transactions

E 3. Koral Corporation engaged in the transactions listed below. Identify each transaction as (a) an operating activity, (b) an investing activity, (c) a financing activity, (d) a noncash transaction, or (e) not on the statement of cash flows. (Assume the indirect method is used.)

1. Declared and paid a cash dividend.
2. Purchased a long-term investment.
3. Increased accounts receivable.
4. Paid interest.
5. Sold equipment at a loss.
6. Issued long-term bonds for plant assets.
7. Increased dividends receivable.
8. Issued common stock.
9. Declared and issued a stock dividend.
10. Repaid notes payable.
11. Decreased wages payable.
12. Purchased a 60-day Treasury bill.
13. Purchased land.

LO2

Cash-Generating Efficiency Ratios and Free Cash Flow

E 4. In 2011, Heart Corporation had year-end assets of $1,200,000, sales of $1,650,000, net income of $140,000, net cash flows from operating activities of $195,000, dividends of $60,000, purchases of plant assets of $250,000, and sales of plant assets of $45,000. In 2010, year-end assets were $1,050,000. Calculate free cash flow and the cash-generating efficiency ratios of cash flow yield, cash flows to sales, and cash flows to assets.

LO3 Cash Flows from Operating Activities: Indirect Method

E 5. The condensed single-step income statement for the year ended December 31, 2012, of Sunderland Chemical Company, a distributor of farm fertilizers and herbicides, appears as follows:

Sales		$13,000,000
Less: Cost of goods sold	$7,600,000	
Operating expenses (including depreciation of $820,000.	3,800,000	
Income taxes expense	400,000	11,800,000
Net income		$ 1,200,000

Selected accounts from Sunderland Chemical Company's balance sheets for 2012 and 2011 are as follows:

	2012	2011
Accounts receivable	$2,400,000	$1,700,000
Inventory	840,000	1,020,000
Prepaid expenses	260,000	180,000
Accounts payable	960,000	720,000
Accrued liabilities	60,000	100,000
Income taxes payable	140,000	120,000

Present in good form a schedule of cash flows from operating activities using the indirect method.

LO3 Computing Cash Flows from Operating Activities: Indirect Method

E 6. During 2010, Diaz Corporation had net income of $41,000. Included on its income statement were depreciation expense of $2,300 and amortization expense of $300. During the year, Accounts Receivable increased by $3,400, Inventories decreased by $1,900, Prepaid Expenses decreased by $200, Accounts Payable increased by $5,000, and Accrued Liabilities decreased by $450. Determine net cash flows from operating activities using the indirect method.

LO3 Preparing a Schedule of Cash Flows from Operating Activities: Indirect Method

E 7. For the year ended June 30, 2011, net income for Silk Corporation was $7,400. Depreciation expense was $2,000. During the year, Accounts Receivable increased by $4,400, Inventories increased by $7,000, Prepaid Rent decreased by $1,400, Accounts Payable increased by $14,000, Salaries Payable increased by $1,000, and Income Taxes Payable decreased by $600. Use the indirect method to prepare a schedule of cash flows from operating activities.

LO4 Computing Cash Flows from Investing Activities: Investments

E 8. CUD Company's T account for long-term available-for-sale investments at the end of 2010 is as follows:

Investments

Dr.		Cr.	
Beg. Bal.	152,000	Sales	156,000
Purchases	232,000		
End. Bal.	**228,000**		

In addition, CUD Company's income statement shows a loss on the sale of investments of $26,000. Compute the amounts to be shown as cash flows from investing activities, and show how they are to appear in the statement of cash flows.

LO4 Computing Cash Flows from Investing Activities: Plant Assets

E 9. The T accounts for plant assets and accumulated depreciation for CUD Company at the end of 2010 are as follows:

Plant Assets				Accumulated Depreciation			
Dr.		Cr.		Dr.		Cr.	
Beg. Bal.	260,000	Disposals	92,000	Disposals	58,800	Beg. Bal.	138,000
Purchases	134,400					Depreciation	40,800
End. Bal.	**302,400**					**End. Bal.**	**120,000**

In addition, CUD Company's income statement shows a gain on sale of plant assets of $17,600. Compute the amounts to be shown as cash flows from investing activities, and show how they are to appear on the statement of cash flows.

LO5 Determining Cash Flows from Financing Activities: Notes Payable

E 10. All transactions involving Notes Payable and related accounts of Pearl Company during 2010 are as follows:

	Dr.	Cr.
Cash	18,000	
Notes Payable		18,000
Bank loan		

	Dr.	Cr.
Patent	30,000	
Notes Payable		30,000
Purchase of patent by issuing note payable		

	Dr.	Cr.
Notes Payable	5,000	
Interest Expense	500	
Cash		5,500
Repayment of note payable at maturity		

Determine the amounts of the transactions affecting financing activities and show how they are to appear on the statement of cash flows for 2010.

LO3 LO4 LO5 Preparing the Statement of Cash Flows: Indirect Method

E 11. Olbrot Corporation's income statement for the year ended June 30, 2012, and its comparative balance sheets for June 30, 2012 and 2011 appear below and on the following page.

Olbrot Corporation
Income Statement
For the Year Ended June 30, 2012

Sales	$244,000
Cost of goods sold	148,100
Gross margin	$ 95,900
Operating expenses	45,000
Operating income	$ 50,900
Interest expense	2,800
Income before income taxes	$ 48,100
Income taxes expense	12,300
Net income	$ 35,800

Olbrot Corporation
Comparative Balance Sheets
June 30, 2012 and 2011

	2012	2011
Assets		
Cash	$139,800	$ 25,000
Accounts receivable (net)	42,000	52,000
Inventory	86,800	96,800
Prepaid expenses	6,400	5,200
Furniture	110,000	120,000
Accumulated depreciation–furniture	(18,000)	(10,000)
Total assets	$367,000	$289,000
Liabilities and Stockholders' Equity		
Accounts payable	$ 26,000	$ 28,000
Income taxes payable	2,400	3,600
Notes payable (long-term)	74,000	70,000
Common stock, $10 par value	230,000	180,000
Retained earnings	34,600	7,400
Total liabilities and stockholders' equity	$367,000	$289,000

Olbrot issued a $44,000 note payable for purchase of furniture; sold at carrying value furniture that cost $54,000 with accumulated depreciation of $30,600; recorded depreciation on the furniture for the year, $38,600; repaid a note in the amount of $40,000; issued $50,000 of common stock at par value; and paid dividends of $8,600. Prepare Olbrot's statement of cash flows for the year 2012 using the indirect method.

Problems

LO1 Classification of Cash Flow Transactions

P 1. Analyze each transaction listed in the table that follows and place X's in the appropriate columns to indicate the transaction's classification and its effect on cash flows using the indirect method.

	Cash Flow Classification				Effect on Cash Flows		
Transaction	**Operating Activity**	**Investing Activity**	**Financing Activity**	**Noncash Transaction**	**Increase**	**Decrease**	**No Effect**
1. Paid a cash dividend.							
2. Decreased accounts receivable.							
3. Increased inventory.							
4. Incurred a net loss.							
5. Declared and issued a stock dividend.							
6. Retired long-term debt with cash.							
7. Sold available-for-sale securities at a loss.							

(continued)

Transaction	Cash Flow Classification				Effect on Cash Flows		
	Operating Activity	Investing Activity	Financing Activity	Noncash Transaction	Increase	Decrease	No Effect
8. Issued stock for equipment.							
9. Decreased prepaid insurance.							
10. Purchased treasury stock with cash.							
11. Retired a fully depreciated truck (no gain or loss).							
12. Increased interest payable.							
13. Decreased dividends receivable on investment.							
14. Sold treasury stock.							
15. Increased income taxes payable.							
16. Transferred cash to money market account.							
17. Purchased land and building with a mortgage.							

LO1 LO2 **Interpreting and Analyzing the Statement of Cash Flows**

P 2. The comparative statements of cash flows for Executive Style Corporation, a manufacturer of high-quality suits for men, appear on the next page. To expand its markets and familiarity with its brand, the company attempted a new strategic diversification in 2011 by acquiring a chain of retail men's stores in outlet malls. Its plan was to expand in malls around the country, but department stores viewed the action as infringing on their territory.

Required

Evaluate the success of the company's strategy by answering the questions that follow.

1. What are the primary reasons cash flows from operating activities differ from net income? What is the effect on the acquisition in 2009? What conclusions can you draw from the changes in 2010?
2. Compute free cash flow for both years. What was the total cost of the acquisition? Was the company able to finance expansion in 2009 by generating internal cash flow? What was the situation in 2010?
3. User insight ▶ What are the most significant financing activities in 2009? How did the company finance the acquisition? Do you think this is a good strategy? What other issues might you question in financing activities?
4. User insight ▶ Based on results in 2010, what actions was the company forced to take and what is your overall assessment of the company's diversification strategy?

Executive Style Corporation
Statement of Cash Flows
For the Years Ended December 31, 2011 and 2010

(In thousands)	2011	2010
Cash flows from operating activities		
Net income (loss)	($ 21,545)	$ 38,015
Adjustments to reconcile net income to net cash flows from operating activities		
Depreciation	35,219	25,018
Loss on closure of retail outlets	35,000	
Changes in current assets and current liabilities		
Decrease (increase) in accounts receivable	50,000	(44,803)
Decrease (increase) in inventory	60,407	(51,145)
Decrease (increase) in prepaid expenses	1,367	2,246
Increase (decrease) in accounts payable	30,579	1,266
Increase (decrease) in accrued liabilities	1,500	(2,788)
Increase (decrease) in income taxes payable	(8,300)	(6,281)
	$205,772	($ 76,487)
Net cash flows from operating activities	$184,227	($ 38,472)
Cash flows from investing activities		
Capital expenditures, net	($ 16,145)	($ 33,112)
Purchase of Retail Division, cash portion	—	(201,000)
Net cash flows from investing activities	($ 16,145)	($234,112)
Cash flows from financing activities		
Increase (decrease) in notes payable to banks	($123,500)	$228,400
Reduction in long-term debt	(9,238)	(10,811)
Payment of dividends	(22,924)	(19,973)
Purchase of treasury stock	—	(12,500)
Net cash flows from financing activities	($155,662)	$185,116
Net increase (decrease) in cash	$ 12,420	($ 87,468)
Cash at beginning of year	16,032	103,500
Cash at end of year	$ 28,452	$ 16,032

Schedule of Noncash Investing and Financing Transactions

Issue of bonds payable for retail acquisition		$ 50,000

LO2 LO3 LO4 LO5

Statement of Cash Flows: Indirect Method

P 3. The comparative balance sheets for Alvin Arts, Inc., for December 31, 2011 and 2009 appear on the opposite page. Additional information about Alvin Arts's operations during 2010 is as follows: (a) net income, $28,000; (b) building and equipment depreciation expense amounts, $15,000 and $3,000, respectively; (c) equipment that cost $13,500 with accumulated depreciation of $12,500 sold at a gain of $5,300; (d) equipment purchases, $12,500; (e) patent amortization, $3,000; purchase of patent, $1,000; (f) funds borrowed by issuing notes payable, $25,000; notes payable repaid, $15,000; (g) land and building purchased for $162,000 by signing a mortgage for the total cost; (h) 1,500 shares of $20 par value common stock issued for a total of $50,000; and (i) paid cash dividends, $9,000.

Alvin Arts, Inc.
Comparative Balance Sheets
December 31, 2010 and 2009

	2010	2009
Assets		
Cash	$ 94,560	$ 27,360
Accounts receivable (net)	102,430	75,430
Inventory	112,890	137,890
Prepaid expenses	—	20,000
Land	25,000	—
Building	137,000	—
Accumulated depreciation–building	(15,000)	—
Equipment	33,000	34,000
Accumulated depreciation–equipment	(14,500)	(24,000)
Patents	4,000	6,000
Total assets	$479,380	$276,680
Liabilities and Stockholders' Equity		
Accounts payable	$ 10,750	$ 36,750
Notes payable (current)	10,000	—
Accrued liabilities	—	12,300
Mortgage payable	162,000	—
Common stock, $10 par value	180,000	150,000
Additional paid-in capital	57,200	37,200
Retained earnings	59,430	40,430
Total liabilities and stockholders' equity	$479,380	$276,680

Required

1. Using the indirect method, prepare a statement of cash flows for Alvin Arts, Inc.

User insight ▶ 2. Why did Alvin Arts have an increase in cash of $67,200 when it recorded net income of only $28,000? Discuss and interpret.

User insight ▶ 3. Compute and assess cash flow yield and free cash flow for 2010. What is your assessment of Alvin's cash-generating ability?

LO2 LO3 LO4 LO5

Statement of Cash Flows: Indirect Method

P 4. The comparative balance sheets for Lopez Tools, Inc., for December 31, 2010 and 2009, are at the top of the next page. During 2010, the company had net income of $48,000 and building and equipment depreciation expenses of $40,000 and $30,000, respectively. It amortized intangible assets in the amount of $10,000; purchased investments for $58,000; sold investments for $75,000, on which it recorded a gain of $17,000; issued $120,000 of long-term bonds at face value; purchased land and a warehouse through a $160,000 mortgage; paid $20,000 to reduce the mortgage; borrowed $30,000 by issuing notes payable; repaid notes payable in the amount of $90,000; declared and paid cash dividends in the amount of $18,000; and purchased treasury stock in the amount of $10,000.

Lopez Tools, Inc.
Comparative Balance Sheets
December 31, 2010 and 2009

	2010	2009
Assets		
Cash	$ 128,800	$ 152,800
Accounts receivable (net)	369,400	379,400
Inventory	480,000	400,000
Prepaid expenses	7,400	13,400
Long-term investments	220,000	220,000
Land	180,600	160,600
Building	600,000	460,000
Accumulated depreciation–building	(120,000)	(80,000)
Equipment	240,000	240,000
Accumulated depreciation–equipment	(58,000)	(28,000)
Intangible assets	10,000	20,000
Total assets	$2,058,200	$1,938,200
Liabilities and Stockholders' Equity		
Accounts payable	$ 235,400	$ 330,400
Notes payable (current)	20,000	80,000
Accrued liabilities	5,400	10,400
Mortgage payable	540,000	400,000
Bonds payable	500,000	380,000
Common stock	650,000	650,000
Additional paid-in capital	40,000	40,000
Retained earnings	127,400	97,400
Treasury stock	(60,000)	(50,000)
Total liabilities and stockholders' equity	$2,058,200	$1,938,200

Required

1. Using the indirect method, prepare a statement of cash flows for Lopez Tools, Inc.

User insight ▶ 2. Why did Lopez Tools experience a decrease in cash in a year in which it had a net income of $48,000? Discuss and interpret.

User insight ▶ 3. Compute and assess cash flow yield and free cash flow for 2010. Why is each of these measures important in assessing cash-generating ability?

LO2 LO3 LO4 LO5

Statement of Cash Flows: Indirect Method

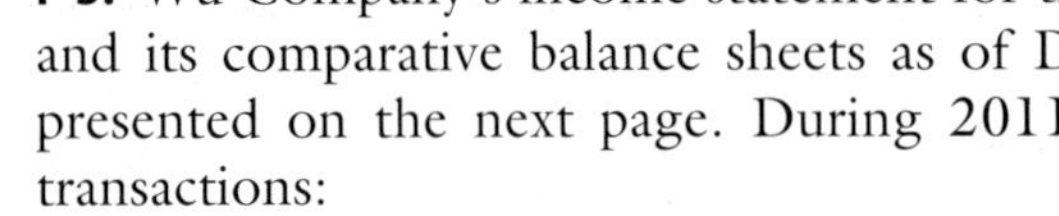

P 5. Wu Company's income statement for the year ended December 31, 2011, and its comparative balance sheets as of December 31, 2011 and 2010, are presented on the next page. During 2011, Wu Company engaged in these transactions:

a. Sold at a gain of $7,000 furniture and fixtures that cost $35,600, on which it had accumulated depreciation of $28,800.
b. Purchased furniture and fixtures in the amount of $39,600.
c. Paid a $20,000 note payable and borrowed $40,000 on a new note.
d. Converted bonds payable in the amount of $100,000 into 4,000 shares of common stock.
e. Declared and paid $6,000 in cash dividends.

Wu Company
Income Statement
For the Year Ended December 31, 2011

Sales		$1,609,000
Cost of goods sold		1,127,800
Gross margin		$ 481,200
Operating expenses (including depreciation expense of $46,800)		449,400
Income from operations		$ 31,800
Other income (expenses)		
Gain on sale of furniture and fixtures	$ 7,000	
Interest expense	(23,200)	(16,200)
Income before income taxes		$ 15,600
Income taxes expense		4,600
Net income		$ 11,000

Wu Company
Comparative Balance Sheets
December 31, 2011 and 2010

	2011	2010
Assets		
Cash	$164,800	$ 50,000
Accounts receivable (net)	165,200	200,000
Merchandise inventory	350,000	450,000
Prepaid rent	2,000	3,000
Furniture and fixtures	148,000	144,000
Accumulated depreciation–furniture and fixtures	(42,000)	(24,000)
Total assets	$788,000	$823,000
Liabilities and Stockholders' Equity		
Accounts payable	$143,400	$200,400
Income taxes payable	1,400	4,400
Notes payable (long-term)	40,000	20,000
Bonds payable	100,000	200,000
Common stock, $20 par value	240,000	200,000
Additional paid-in capital	181,440	121,440
Retained earnings	81,760	76,760
Total liabilities and stockholders' equity	$788,000	$823,000

Required

1. Using the indirect method, prepare a statement of cash flows for Wu Company. Include a supporting schedule of noncash investing transactions and financing transactions.

User insight ▶ 2. What are the primary reasons for Wu Company's large increase in cash from 2010 to 2011, despite its low net income?

User insight ▶ 3. Compute and assess cash flow yield and free cash flow for 2011. Compare and contrast what these two performance measures tell you about Wu Company's cash-generating ability.

Alternate Problems

LO1 **Classification of Cash Flow Transactions**

P 6. Analyze each transaction listed in the table that follows and place X's in the appropriate columns to indicate the transaction's classification and its effect on cash flows using the indirect method.

	Cash Flow Classification				Effect on Cash Flows		
Transaction	**Operating Activity**	**Investing Activity**	**Financing Activity**	**Noncash Transaction**	**Increase**	**Decrease**	**No Effect**
1. Increased accounts payable.							
2. Decreased inventory.							
3. Increased prepaid insurance.							
4. Earned a net income.							
5. Declared and paid a cash dividend.							
6. Issued stock for cash.							
7. Retired long-term debt by issuing stock.							
8. Purchased a long-term investment with cash.							
9. Sold trading securities at a gain.							
10. Sold a machine at a loss.							
11. Retired fully depreciated equipment.							
12. Decreased interest payable.							
13. Purchased available-for-sale securities (long-term).							
14. Decreased dividends receivable.							
15. Decreased accounts receivable.							
16. Converted bonds to common stock.							
17. Purchased 90-day Treasury bill.							

LO2 LO3 LO4 LO5 **Statement of Cash Flows: Indirect Method**

P 7. Ortega Corporation's income statement for the year ended June 30, 2011, and its comparative balance sheets as of June 30, 2011 and 2010, appear on the next page. During 2011, the corporation sold at a loss of $4,000 equipment that cost $24,000, on which it had accumulated depreciation of $17,000. It also purchased land and a building for $100,000 through an increase of $100,000 in Mortgage Payable; made a $20,000 payment on the mortgage; repaid $80,000 in notes but borrowed an additional $30,000 through the issuance of a new note payable; and declared and paid a $60,000 cash dividend.

Ortega Corporation
Income Statement
For the Year Ended June 30, 2011

Sales		$4,040,900
Cost of goods sold		3,656,300
Gross margin		$ 384,600
Operating expenses (including depreciation expense of $60,000)		189,200
Income from operations		$ 195,400
Other income (expenses)		
Loss on sale of equipment	($ 4,000)	
Interest expense	(37,600)	(41,600)
Income before income taxes		$ 153,800
Income taxes expense		34,200
Net income		$ 119,600

Ortega Corporation
Comparative Balance Sheets
June 30, 2011 and 2010

	2011	2010
Assets		
Cash	$ 167,000	$ 20,000
Accounts receivable (net)	100,000	120,000
Inventory	180,000	220,000
Prepaid expenses	600	1,000
Property, plant, and equipment	628,000	552,000
Accumulated depreciation–property, plant, and equipment	(183,000)	(140,000)
Total assets	$ 892,600	$ 773,000
Liabilities and Stockholders' Equity		
Accounts payable	$ 64,000	$ 42,000
Notes payable (due in 90 days)	30,000	80,000
Income taxes payable	26,000	18,000
Mortgage payable	360,000	280,000
Common stock, $5 par value	200,000	200,000
Retained earnings	212,600	153,000
Total liabilities and stockholders' equity	$ 892,600	$ 773,000

Required

1. Using the indirect method, prepare a statement of cash flows. Include a supporting schedule of noncash investing and financing transactions.

User insight ▶ 2. What are the primary reasons for Ortega Corporation's large increase in cash from 2010 to 2011?

User insight ▶ 3. Compute and assess cash flow yield and free cash flow for 2011. How would you assess the corporation's cash-generating ability?

LO2 LO3 LO4 LO5

Statement of Cash Flows: Indirect Method

P 8. The comparative balance sheets for Sharma Fabrics, Inc., for December 31, 2011 and 2010, appear on the next page. Additional information about Sharma Fabrics' operations during 2011 is as follows: (a) net income, $56,000; (b) building and equipment depreciation expense amounts, $30,000 and $6,000, respectively; (c) equipment that cost $27,000 with accumulated depreciation of $25,000 sold at a gain of $10,600; (d) equipment purchases, $25,000; (e) patent amortization, $6,000; purchase of patent, $2,000; (f) funds borrowed by issuing notes payable, $50,000; notes payable repaid, $30,000; (g) land and building purchased for $324,000 by signing a mortgage for the total cost; (h) 3,000 shares of $20 par value common stock issued for a total of $100,000; and (i) paid cash dividend, $18,000.

Sharma Fabrics, Inc.
Comparative Balance Sheets
December 31, 2011 and 2010

	2011	2010
Assets		
Cash	$189,120	$ 54,720
Accounts receivable (net)	204,860	150,860
Inventory	225,780	275,780
Prepaid expenses	—	40,000
Land	50,000	—
Building	274,000	—
Accumulated depreciation–building	(30,000)	—
Equipment	66,000	68,000
Accumulated depreciation–equipment	(29,000)	(48,000)
Patents	8,000	12,000
Total assets	$958,760	$553,360
Liabilities and Stockholders' Equity		
Accounts payable	$ 21,500	$ 73,500
Notes payable (current)	20,000	—
Accrued liabilities	—	24,600
Mortgage payable	324,000	—
Common stock, $10 par value	360,000	300,000
Additional paid-in capital	114,400	74,400
Retained earnings	118,860	80,860
Total liabilities and stockholders' equity	$958,760	$553,360

Required

1. Using the indirect method, prepare a statement of cash flows for Sharma Fabrics, Inc.

User insight ▶ 2. Why did Sharma Fabrics have an increase in cash of $134,400 when it recorded net income of only $56,000? Discuss and interpret.

User insight ▶ 3. Compute and assess cash flow yield and free cash flow for 2011. What is your assessment of Sharma's cash-generating ability?

LO2 LO3 LO4 LO5

Statement of Cash Flows: Indirect Method

P 9. The comparative balance sheets for Karidis Ceramics, Inc., for December 31, 2012 and 2011, are presented on the next page. During 2012, the company had net income of $96,000 and building and equipment depreciation expenses of $80,000 and $60,000, respectively. It amortized intangible assets in the amount of $20,000; purchased investments for $116,000; sold investments for $150,000, on which it recorded a gain of $34,000; issued $240,000 of long-term bonds at face value; purchased land and a warehouse through a $320,000 mortgage; paid $40,000 to reduce the mortgage; borrowed $60,000 by issuing notes payable; repaid notes payable in the amount of $180,000; declared and paid cash dividends in the amount of $36,000; and purchased treasury stock in the amount of $20,000.

Karidis Ceramics, Inc.
Comparative Balance Sheets
December 31, 2012 and 2011

	2012	2011
Assets		
Cash	$ 257,600	$ 305,600
Accounts receivable (net)	738,800	758,800
Inventory	960,000	800,000
Prepaid expenses	14,800	26,800
Long-term investments	440,000	440,000
Land	361,200	321,200
Building	1,200,000	920,000
Accumulated depreciation–building	(240,000)	(160,000)
Equipment	480,000	480,000
Accumulated depreciation–equipment	(116,000)	(56,000)
Intangible assets	20,000	40,000
Total assets	$4,116,400	$3,876,400
Liabilities and Stockholders' Equity		
Accounts payable	$ 470,800	$ 660,800
Notes payable (current)	40,000	160,000
Accrued liabilities	10,800	20,800
Mortgage payable	1,080,000	800,000
Bonds payable	1,000,000	760,000
Common stock	1,300,000	1,300,000
Additional paid-in capital	80,000	80,000
Retained earnings	254,800	194,800
Treasury stock	(120,000)	(100,000)
Total liabilities and stockholders' equity	$4,116,400	$3,876,400

Required

1. Using the indirect method, prepare a statement of cash flows for Karidis Ceramics, Inc.

User insight ▶ 2. Why did Karidis Ceramics experience a decrease in cash in a year in which it had a net income of $96,000? Discuss and interpret.

User insight ▶ 3. Compute and assess cash flow yield and free cash flow for 2012. Why is each of these measures important in assessing cash-generating ability?

LO2 LO3 LO4 LO5

Statement of Cash Flows: Indirect Method

P 10. O'Brien Corporation's income statement for the year ended December 31, 2012, and its comparative balance sheets as of December 31, 2012 and 2011, are presented on the next page. During 2012, O'Brien Corporation engaged in these transactions:

a. Sold at a gain of $3,500 furniture and fixtures that cost $17,800, on which it had accumulated depreciation of $14,400.
b. Purchased furniture and fixtures in the amount of $19,800.
c. Paid a $10,000 note payable and borrowed $20,000 on a new note.

d. Converted bonds payable in the amount of $50,000 into 2,000 shares of common stock.
e. Declared and paid $3,000 in cash dividends.

O'Brien Corporation
Income Statement
For the Year Ended December 31, 2012

Sales		$804,500
Cost of goods sold		563,900
Gross margin		$240,600
Operating expenses (including depreciation expense of $23,400)		224,700
Income from operations		$ 15,900
Other income (expenses)		
Gain on sale of furniture and fixtures	$ 3,500	
Interest expense	(11,600)	(8,100)
Income before income taxes		$ 7,800
Income taxes expense		2,300
Net income		$ 5,500

O'Brien Corporation
Comparative Balance Sheets
December 31, 2012 and 2011

	2012	2011
Assets		
Cash	$ 82,400	$ 25,000
Accounts receivable (net)	82,600	100,000
Merchandise inventory	175,000	225,000
Prepaid rent	1,000	1,500
Furniture and fixtures	74,000	72,000
Accumulated depreciation–furniture and fixtures	(21,000)	(12,000)
Total assets	$394,000	$411,500
Liabilities and Stockholders' Equity		
Accounts payable	$ 71,700	$100,200
Income taxes payable	700	2,200
Notes payable (long-term)	20,000	10,000
Bonds payable	50,000	100,000
Common stock, $20 par value	120,000	100,000
Additional paid-in capital	90,720	60,720
Retained earnings	40,880	38,380
Total liabilities and stockholders' equity	$394,000	$411,500

Required

1. Using the indirect method, prepare a statement of cash flows for O'Brien Corporation. Include a supporting schedule of noncash investing transactions and financing transactions.

User insight ▶ 2. What are the primary reasons for O'Brien Corporation's large increase in cash from 2011 to 2012, despite its low net income?

User insight ▶ 3. Compute and assess cash flow yield and free cash flow for 2012. Compare and contrast what these two performance measures tell you about O'Brien's cash-generating ability.

ENHANCING Your Knowledge, Skills, and Critical Thinking

LO1 LO3 **EBITDA and the Statement of Cash Flows**

C 1. When **Fleetwood Enterprises, Inc.**, a large producer of recreational vehicles and manufactured housing, warned that it might not be able to generate enough cash to satisfy debt requirements and could be in default of a loan agreement, its cash flow, defined in the financial press as "EBITDA" (earnings before interest, taxes, depreciation, and amortization), was a negative \$2.7 million. The company would have had to generate \$17.7 million in the next accounting period to comply with the loan terms.[12] To what section of the statement of cash flows does EBITDA most closely relate? Is EBITDA a good approximation for this section of the statement of cash flows? Explain your answer, which should include an identification of the major differences between EBITDA and the section of the statement of cash flows you chose.

LO2 **Anatomy of a Disaster**

C 2. On October 16, 2001, Kenneth Lay, chairman and CEO of **Enron Corporation**, announced the company's earnings for the first nine months of 2001 as follows:

> Our 26 percent increase in recurring earnings per diluted share shows the very strong results of our core wholesale and retail energy businesses and our natural gas pipelines. The continued excellent prospects in these businesses and Enron's leading market position make us very confident in our strong earnings outlook.[13]

Less than six months later, the company filed for the biggest bankruptcy in U.S. history. Its stock dropped to less than \$1 per share, and a major financial scandal was underway.

Presented on the next page is Enron's statement of cash flows for the first nine months of 2001 and 2000 (restated to correct the previous accounting errors). Assume you report to an investment analyst who has asked you to analyze this statement for clues as to why the company went under.

1. For the two time periods shown, compute the cash-generating efficiency ratios of cash flow yield, cash flows to sales (Enron's revenues were \$133,762 million in 2001 and \$55,494 million in 2000), and cash flows to assets (use total assets of \$61,783 million for 2001 and \$64,926 million for 2000). Also compute free cash flows for the two years.
2. Prepare a memorandum to the investment analyst that assesses Enron's cash-generating efficiency in light of the chairman's remarks and that evaluates its available free cash flow, taking into account its financing activities. Identify significant changes in Enron's operating items and any special operating items that should be considered. Include your computations as an attachment.

LO2 **Ethics and Cash Flow Classifications**

C 3. Specialty Metals, Inc., a fast-growing company that makes metals for equipment manufacturers, has an \$800,000 line of credit at its bank. One section in the credit agreement says that the ratio of cash flows from operations to interest expense must exceed 3.0. If this ratio falls below 3.0, the company must reduce the balance outstanding on its line of credit to one-half the total line if the funds borrowed against the line of credit exceed one-half of the total line.

After the end of the fiscal year, the company's controller informs the president: "We will not meet the ratio requirements on our line of credit in 2010

Enron Corporation
Statement of Cash Flows
For the Nine Months Ended September 30, 2001 and 2000

(In millions)	**2001**	**2000**
Cash Flows from Operating Activities		
Reconciliation of net income to net cash provided by operating activities		
Net income	$ 225	$ 797
Cumulative effect of accounting changes, net of tax	(19)	0
Depreciation, depletion and amortization	746	617
Deferred income taxes	(134)	8
Gains on sales of non-trading assets	(49)	(135)
Investment losses	768	0
Changes in components of working capital		
Receivables	987	(3,363)
Inventories	1	339
Payables	(1,764)	2,899
Other	464	(455)
Trading investments		
Net margin deposit activity	(2,349)	541
Other trading activities	173	(555)
Other, net	198	(566)
Net Cash Provided by (Used in) Operating Activities	$ (753)	$ 127
Cash Flows from Investing Activities		
Capital expenditures	$(1,584)	$(1,539)
Equity investments	(1,172)	(858)
Proceeds from sales of non-trading investments	1,711	222
Acquisition of subsidiary stock	0	(485)
Business acquisitions, net of cash acquired	(82)	(773)
Other investing activities	(239)	(147)
Net Cash Used in Investing Activities	$(1,366)	$(3,580)
Cash Flows from Financing Activities		
Issuance of long-term debt	$ 4,060	$ 2,725
Repayment of long-term debt	(3,903)	(579)
Net increase in short-term borrowings	2,365	1,694
Issuance of common stock	199	182
Net redemption of company-obligated preferred securities of subsidiaries	0	(95)
Dividends paid	(394)	(396)
Net (acquisition) disposition of treasury stock	(398)	354
Other financing activities	(49)	(12)
Net Cash Provided by Financing Activities	$ 1,880	$ 3,873
Increase (Decrease) in Cash and Cash Equivalents	$ (239)	$ 420
Cash and Cash Equivalents, Beginning of Period	1,240	333
Cash and Cash Equivalents, End of Period	$ 1,001	$ 753

Source: Adapted from Enron Corporation, SEC filings, 2001.

because interest expense was $1.2 million and cash flows from operations were $3.2 million. Also, we have borrowed 100 percent of our line of credit. We do not have the cash to reduce the credit line by $400,000."

The president says, "This is a serious situation. To pay our ongoing bills, we need our bank to increase our line of credit, not decrease it. What can we do?"

"Do you recall the $500,000 two-year note payable for equipment?" replied the controller. "It is now classified as 'Proceeds from Notes Payable' in cash flows provided from financing activities in the statement of cash flows. If we move it to cash flows from operations and call it 'Increase in Payables,' it would increase cash flows from operations to $3.7 million and put us over the limit."

"Well, do it," ordered the president. "It surely doesn't make any difference where it is on the statement. It is an increase in both places. It would be much worse for our company in the long term if we failed to meet this ratio requirement."

What is your opinion of the controller and president's reasoning? Is the president's order ethical? Who benefits and who is harmed if the controller follows the president's order? What are management's alternatives? What would you do?

LO1 LO2 **Alternative Uses of Cash**

C 4. Perhaps because of hard times in their start-up years, companies in the high-tech sector of American industry seem more prone than those in other sectors to building up cash reserves. For example, companies like **Cisco Systems**, **Intel**, **Dell**, and **Oracle** have amassed large cash balances.[14]

Assume you work for a company in the high-tech industry that has built up a substantial amount of cash. The company is still growing through development of new products, has some debt, and has never paid a dividend or bought treasury stock. The company is doing better than most companies in the current financial crisis but the company's stock price is lagging. Outline at least four strategies for using the company's cash to improve the company's financial outlook.

LO1 **Analysis of the Statement of Cash Flows**

C 5. Refer to the statement of cash flows in the **CVS Corporation** annual report in the Supplement to Chapter 5 to answer the following questions:

1. Does CVS use the indirect method of reporting cash flows from operating activities? Other than net earnings, what are the most important factors affecting the company's cash flows from operating activities? Explain the trend of each of these factors.
2. Based on the cash flows from investing activities, in 2007 and 2008, would you say that CVS is a contracting or an expanding company? Explain.
3. Has CVS used external financing during 2007 and 2008? If so, where did it come from?

LO1 LO2 LO3 LO4 LO5 **Cash Flows Analysis**

C 6. Refer to the annual report of **CVS Corporation** and the financial statements of **Southwest Airlines** in the Supplement to Chapter 5. Calculate for two years each company's cash flow yield, cash flows to sales, cash flows to assets, and free cash flow. At the end of 2006, Southwest's total assets were $13,460 million and CVS's total assets were $20,574.1 million.

Discuss and compare the trends of the cash-generating ability of CVS and Southwest. Comment on each company's change in cash and cash equivalents over the two-year period.

APPENDIX

Accounting for Investments

Many companies invest in the stock or debt securities of other firms. They may do so for several reasons. A company may temporarily have excess funds on which it can earn a return, or investments may be an integral part of its business, as in the case of a bank. A company may also invest in other firms for the purpose of partnering with or controlling them.

Management Issues Related to Investments

The issues of recognition, valuation, classification, and disclosure apply to accounting for investments.

Recognition Recognition of investments as assets follows the general rule for recording transactions that we described earlier in the text. Purchases of investments are recorded on the date on which they are made, and sales of investments are reported on the date of sale. At the time of the transaction, there is either a transfer of funds or a definite obligation to pay. Income from investments is reported as other income on the income statement. Any gains or losses on investments are also reported on the income statement. Gains and losses appear as adjustments in the operating activities section of the statement of cash flows. The cash amounts of purchases and sales of investments appear in the investing activities section of the statement of cash flows.

Valuation Like other purchase transactions, investments are valued according to the *cost principle*—that is, they are valued in terms of their cost at the time they are purchased. The cost, or purchase price, includes any commissions or fees. However, after the purchase, the value of investments on the balance sheet is adjusted to reflect subsequent conditions. These conditions may reflect changes in the market value or fair value of the investments, changes caused by the passage of time (as in amortization), or changes in the operations of the investee companies. Long-term investments must be evaluated annually for any impairment or decline in value that is more than temporary. If such an impairment exists, a loss on the investment must be recorded.

IFRS

Under a new accounting standard, the goal of which is to bring U.S. standards more in line with international financial reporting standards, companies may elect to measure investments at fair value. Recall that *fair value* is defined as the *exchange price* associated with an actual or potential business transaction between market participants. This option applies to all types of investments except in the case of a subsidiary that is consolidated into the statements of the parent company. Generally, companies can elect the investment to which to apply fair value, but having done so, they cannot change the use of fair value in the future. Fair value can be determined when there is a ready market for the security, but determination is more problematic when a ready market does not exist. In the latter case, the fair value must be estimated through a method such as net present value.[1]

Classification Investments in debt and equity securities are classified as either short-term or long-term. *Short-term investments*, also called *marketable securities*, have a maturity of more than 90 days but are intended to be held only until cash is needed for current operations. (As we pointed out in an earlier chapter, investments with a maturity of *less* than 90 days are classified as cash equivalents.) Long-term investments are intended to be held for more than one year. *Long-term investments* are reported in the investments section of the balance sheet, not in the current assets section. Although long-term investments may be just as marketable as short-term assets, management intends to hold them for an indefinite time.

Short-term and long-term investments must be further classified as trading securities, available-for-sale securities, or held-to-maturity securities.[2]

- *Trading securities* are debt or equity securities bought and held principally for the purpose of being sold in the near term.
- *Available-for-sale securities* are debt or equity securities that do not meet the criteria for either trading or held-to-maturity securities. They may be short-term or long-term depending on what management intends to do with them.
- *Held-to-maturity securities* are debt securities that management intends to hold until their maturity date.

Figure 1 illustrates the classification of short-term and long-term investments. Table 1 shows the relationship between the percentage of ownership in a company's stock and the investing company's level of control, as well as the classifications and accounting treatments of these stock investments. These classifications are important because each one requires a different accounting treatment.

FIGURE 1
Classification of Investments

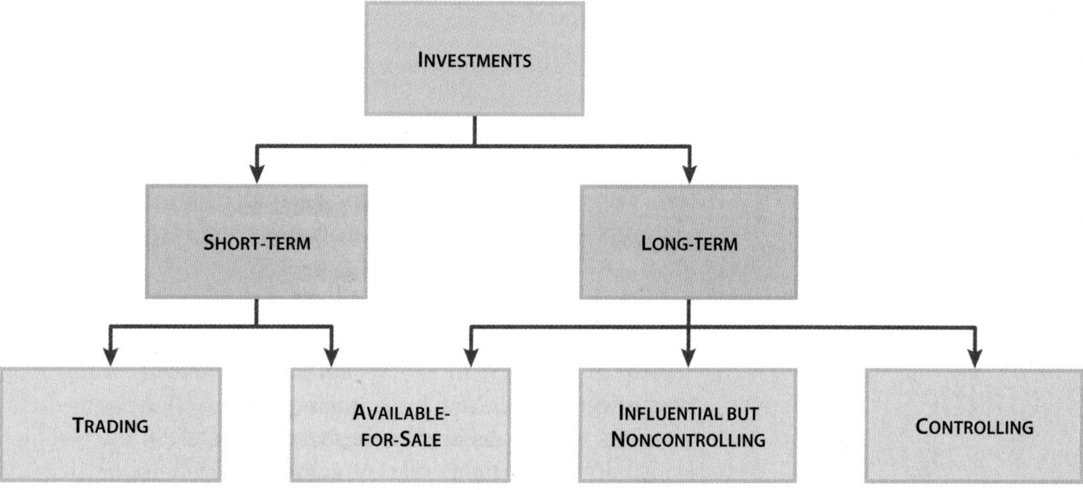

TABLE 1
Accounting for Equity Investments

Level of Control	Percentage of Ownership	Classification	Accounting Treatment
Noninfluential and noncontrolling	Less than 20%	Short-term investments—trading securities	Recorded at cost initially; cost adjusted after purchase for changes in market value; unrealized gains and losses reported on income statement
		Short-term or long-term investments—available-for-sale securities	Recorded at cost initially; cost adjusted for changes in market value with unrealized gains and losses to stockholders' equity
Influential but noncontrolling	Between 20% and 50%	Long-term investments	Equity method: recorded at cost initially; cost subsequently adjusted for investor's share of net income or loss and for dividends received
Controlling	More than 50%	Long-term investments	Financial statements consolidated

In general, the percentage of ownership in another company's stock has the following effects:

- ***Noninfluential and noncontrolling investment:*** A firm that owns less than 20 percent of the stock of another company has no influence on the other company's operations.
- ***Influential but noncontrolling investment:*** A firm that owns between 20 to 50 percent of another company's stock can exercise *significant influence* over that company's operating and financial policies, even though it holds 50 percent or less of the voting stock. Indications of significant influence include representation on the board of directors, participation in policymaking, exchange of managerial personnel, and technological dependency between the two companies.
- ***Controlling investment:*** A firm that owns more than 50 percent of another company's stock.

Disclosure Companies provide detailed information about their investments and the manner in which they account for them in the notes to their financial statements. Such disclosures help users assess the impact of the investments.

Trading Securities

Trading securities are always short-term investments and are frequently bought and sold to generate profits on short-term changes in their prices. They are classified as current assets on the balance sheet and are valued at fair value, which is usually the same as market value. An increase or decrease in the fair value of a company's total trading portfolio (the group of securities it holds for trading purposes) is included in net income in the accounting period in which the increase or decrease occurs.

For example, suppose Jackson Company buys 10,000 shares of **IBM** for $900,000 ($90 per share) and 10,000 shares of **Microsoft** for $300,000 ($30 per share) on October 25, 2010. The purchase is made for trading purposes—that is, Jackson's management intends to realize a gain by holding the shares for only a short period. The entry in journal form to record the investment at cost is as follows:

Purchase

A	= L	+ OE
+1,200,000		
−1,200,000		

2010			
Oct. 25	Short-Term Investments	1,200,000	
	Cash		1,200,000
	Investment in stocks for trading ($900,000 + $300,000 = $1,200,000)		

Assume that at year end, IBM's stock price has decreased to $80 per share and Microsoft's has risen to $32 per share. The trading portfolio is now valued at $1,120,000:

Security	*Market Value*	*Cost*	*Gain (Loss)*
IBM (10,000 shares)	$ 800,000	$ 900,000	
Microsoft (10,000 shares)	320,000	300,000	
Totals	$1,120,000	$1,200,000	($80,000)

Because the current fair value of the portfolio is $80,000 less than the original cost of $1,200,000, the following adjusting entry is needed:

Year-End Adjustment

A	= L	+ OE
−80,000		−80,000

2010			
Dec. 31	Unrealized Loss on Investments	80,000	
	Allowance to Adjust Short-Term Investments to Market		80,000
	Recognition of unrealized loss on trading portfolio		

Study Note

The Allowance to Adjust Short-Term Investments to Market account is never changed when securities are sold. It changes only when an adjusting entry is made at year end.

The unrealized loss will appear on the income statement as a reduction in income. The loss is unrealized because the securities have not been sold; if unrealized gains occur, they are treated the same way. The Allowance to Adjust Short-Term Investments to Market account appears on the balance sheet as a contra-asset, as follows:

Short-term investments (at cost)	$1,200,000
Less allowance to adjust short-term investments to market	80,000
Short-term investments (at market)	$1,120,000

or, more simply,

Short-term investments (at market value, cost is $1,200,000)	$1,120,000

If Jackson sells its 10,000 shares of Microsoft for $35 per share on March 2, 2011, a realized gain on trading securities is recorded as follows:

Sale

A	=	L	+	OE
+350,000				+50,000
−300,000				

2011			
Mar. 2	Cash	350,000	
	Short-Term Investments		300,000
	Realized Gain on Sale of Investments		50,000
	Sale of 10,000 shares of Microsoft for $35 per share; cost was $30 per share		

The realized gain will appear on the income statement. Note that the realized gain is unaffected by the adjustment for the unrealized loss at the end of 2010. The two transactions are treated independently. If the stock had been sold for less than cost, a realized loss on investments would have been recorded. Realized losses also appear on the income statement.

Now let's assume that during 2011, Jackson buys 4,000 shares of **Apple Computer** at $32 per share and has no transactions involving its shares of IBM. Also assume that by December 31, 2011, the price of IBM's stock has risen to $95 per share, or $5 per share more than the original cost, and that Apple's stock price has fallen to $29, or $3 less than the original cost. We can now analyze Jackson's trading portfolio as follows:

Security	*Market Value*	*Cost*	*Gain (Loss)*
IBM (10,000 shares)	$ 950,000	$ 900,000	
Apple (4,000 shares)	116,000	128,000	
Totals	$1,066,000	$1,028,000	$38,000

The market value of Jackson's trading portfolio now exceeds the cost by $38,000 ($1,066,000 − $1,028,000). This amount represents the targeted ending balance for the Allowance to Adjust Short-Term Investments to Market account. Recall that at the end of 2010, that account had a credit balance of $80,000, meaning that the market value of the trading portfolio was less than the cost. Because no entries are made to the account during 2011, it retains its balance until adjusting entries are made at the end of the year. The adjustment for 2011 must be $118,000—enough to result in a debit balance of $38,000 in the allowance account:

Year-End Adjustment

A	=	L	+	OE
+118,000				+118,000

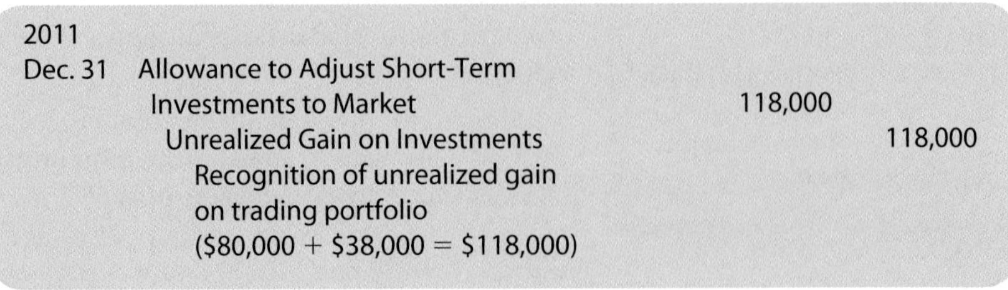

2011			
Dec. 31	Allowance to Adjust Short-Term Investments to Market	118,000	
	Unrealized Gain on Investments		118,000
	Recognition of unrealized gain on trading portfolio ($80,000 + $38,000 = $118,000)		

The 2011 ending balance of Jackson's allowance account can be determined as follows:

Allowance to Adjust Short-Term Investments to Market

Dec. 31, 2011 Adj.	118,000	Dec. 31, 2010 Bal.	80,000
Dec. 31, 2011 Bal.	38,000		

The balance sheet presentation of short-term investments is as follows:

Short-term investments (at cost)	$1,028,000
Plus allowance to adjust short-term investments to market	38,000
Short-term investments (at market)	$1,066,000

or, more simply,

Short-term investments (at market value, cost is $1,028,000)	$1,066,000

If the company also has held-to-maturity securities that will mature within one year, they are included in short-term investments at cost adjusted for the effects of interest.

Available-for-Sale Securities

Short-term available-for-sale securities are accounted for in the same way as trading securities with two exceptions: (1) An unrealized gain or loss is reported as a special item in the stockholders' equity section of the balance sheet, not as a gain or loss on the income statement; (2) if a decline in the value of a security is considered permanent, it is charged as a loss on the income statement.

Long-Term Investments in Equity Securities

As indicated in Table 1, the accounting treatment of long-term investments in equity securities, such as common stock, depends on the extent to which the investing company can exercise control over the other company.

Noninfluential and Noncontrolling Investment As noted earlier, available-for-sale securities are debt or equity securities that cannot be classified as trading or held-to-maturity securities. When long-term equity securities are involved, a further criterion for classifying them as available for sale is that they be noninfluential and noncontrolling investments of less than 20 percent of the voting stock. Accounting for long-term available-for-sale securities requires using the *cost-adjusted-to-market method*. With this method, the securities are initially recorded at cost and are thereafter adjusted periodically for changes in market value by using an allowance account.[3]

Available-for-sale securities are classified as long-term if management intends to hold them for more than one year. When accounting for long-term available-for-sale securities, the unrealized gain or loss resulting from the adjustment is not reported on the income statement. Instead, the gain or loss is reported as a special item in the stockholders' equity section of the balance sheet and in the disclosure of comprehensive income.

At the end of each accounting period, the total cost and the total market value of these long-term stock investments must be determined. If the total market value is less than the total cost, the difference must be credited to a contra-asset account called Allowance to Adjust Long-Term Investments to Market. Because of the long-term nature of the investment, the debit part of the entry, which represents a decrease in value below cost, is treated as a temporary decrease and does not appear as a loss on the income statement. It is shown in a contra-stockholders' equity account called Unrealized Loss on Long-Term Investments.* Thus, both of these accounts are balance sheet accounts. If the market value exceeds the cost, the allowance account is added to Long-Term Investments, and the unrealized gain appears as an addition to stockholders' equity.

*If the decrease in market value of a long-term investment is deemed permanent or if the investment is deemed impaired, the decline or impairment is recorded by debiting a loss account on the income statement instead of the Unrealized Loss account.

When a company sells its long-term investments in stock, the difference between the sale price and the cost of the stock is recorded and reported as a realized gain or loss on the income statement. Dividend income from such investments is recorded by a debit to Cash and a credit to Dividend Income. For example, assume the following facts about the long-term stock investments of Nardini Corporation:

June 1, 2010	Paid cash for the following long-term investments: 10,000 shares of Herald Corporation common stock (representing 2 percent of outstanding stock) at $25 per share; 5,000 shares of Taza Corporation common stock (representing 3 percent of outstanding stock) at $15 per share.
Dec. 31, 2010	Quoted market prices at year end: Herald common stock, $21; Taza common stock, $17
Apr. 1, 2011	Change in policy required the sale of 2,000 shares of Herald common stock at $23.
July 1, 2011	Received cash dividend from Taza equal to $0.20 per share.
Dec. 31, 2011	Quoted market prices at year end: Herald common stock, $24; Taza common stock, $13.

Study Note

Nardini's sale of stock on April 1, 2011, was the result of a *change in policy*. This illustrates that intent is often the only difference between long-term investments and short-term investments.

Entries to record these transactions are as follows:

Investment

A	= L +	OE
+325,000		
−325,000		

2010			
June 1	Long-Term Investments	325,000	
	Cash		325,000
	Investments in Herald common stock (10,000 shares × $25 = $250,000) and Taza common stock (5,000 shares × $15 = $75,000)		

Year-End Adjustment

A	= L +	OE
−30,000		−30,000

2010			
Dec. 31	Unrealized Loss on Long-Term Investments	30,000	
	Allowance to Adjust Long-Term Investments to Market		30,000
	To record reduction of long-term investment to market		

This adjustment involves the following computations:

Company	*Shares*	*Market Price*	*Total Market*	*Total Cost*
Herald	10,000	$21	$210,000	$250,000
Taza	5,000	17	85,000	75,000
			$295,000	$325,000

Total Cost − Total Market Value = $325,000 − $295,000 = $30,000

Other entries are as follows:

Sale

A	= L +	OE
+46,000		−4,000
−50,000		

2011			
Apr. 1	Cash	46,000	
	Realized Loss on Sale of Investments	4,000	
	Long-Term Investments		50,000
	Sale of 2,000 shares of Herald common stock 2,000 × $23 = $46,000 2,000 × $25 = 50,000 Loss $ 4,000		

Dividend Received

A	= L +	OE
+1,000		+1,000

2011			
July 1	Cash	1,000	
	Dividend Income		1,000
	Receipt of cash dividend from Taza stock 5,000 × $0.20 = $1,000		

Year-End Adjustment

A	= L +	OE
+12,000		+12,000

2011			
Dec. 31	Allowance to Adjust Long-Term Investment to Market	12,000	
	Unrealized Loss on Long-Term Investments		12,000
	To record the adjustment in long-term investment so it is reported at market		

The adjustment equals the previous balance ($30,000 from the December 31, 2010, entry) minus the new balance ($18,000), or $12,000. The new balance of $18,000 is the difference at the present time between the total market value and the total cost of all investments. It is figured as follows:

Company	*Shares*	*Market Price*	*Total Market*	*Total Cost*
Herald	8,000	$24	$192,000	$200,000
Taza	5,000	13	65,000	75,000
			$257,000	$275,000

Total Cost − Total Market Value = $275,000 − $257,000 = $18,000

The Allowance to Adjust Long-Term Investments to Market and the Unrealized Loss on Long-Term Investments are reciprocal contra accounts, each with the same dollar balance, as shown by the effects of these transactions on the T accounts:

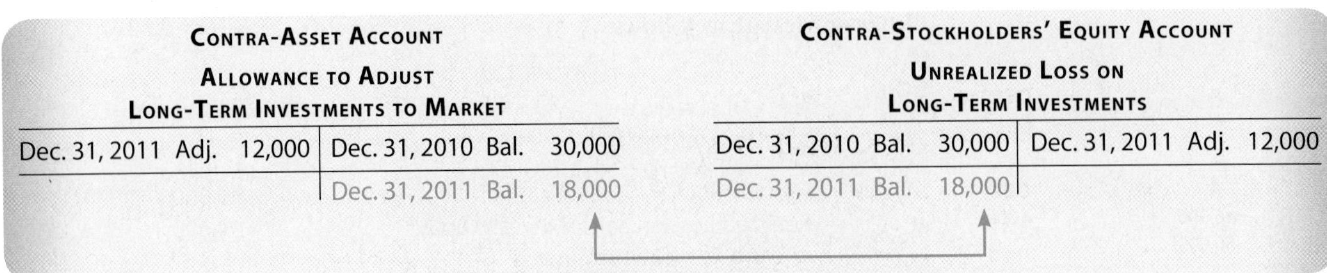

The Allowance account reduces long-term investments by the amount by which the cost of the investments exceeds market; the Unrealized Loss account reduces stockholders' equity by a similar amount. The opposite effects will exist if market value exceeds cost, resulting in an unrealized gain.

Influential but Noncontrolling Investment As we have noted, ownership of 20 percent or more of a company's voting stock is considered sufficient to influence the company's operations. When that is the case, the *equity method* should be used to account for the stock investment. The equity method presumes that an investment of 20 percent or more is not a passive investment and that the investor should therefore share proportionately in the success or failure of the company. The three main features of this method are as follows:

1. The investor records the original purchase of the stock at cost.
2. The investor records its share of the company's periodic net income as an increase in the Investment account, with a corresponding credit to an income account. Similarly, it records its share of a periodic loss as a decrease in the Investment account, with a corresponding debit to a loss account.
3. When the investor receives a cash dividend, the asset account Cash is increased, and the Investment account is decreased.

To illustrate the equity method, suppose that on January 1 of the current year, ITO Corporation acquired 40 percent of Quay Corporation's voting common stock for $180,000. With this share of ownership, ITO can exert significant influence over Quay's operations. During the year, Quay reported net income of $80,000 and paid cash dividends of $20,000. ITO recorded these transactions as follows:

Investment

A	=	L	+	OE
+180,000				
−180,000				

	Debit	Credit
Investment in Quay Corporation	180,000	
Cash		180,000
Investments in Quay Corporation common stock		

Recognition of Income

A	=	L	+	OE
+32,000				+32,000

	Debit	Credit
Investment in Quay Corporation	32,000	
Income, Quay Corporation Investment		32,000
Recognition of 40% of income reported by Quay Corporation		
40% × $80,000 = $32,000		

Receipt of Cash Dividend

A	=	L	+	OE
+8,000				
−8,000				

Cash	8,000	
Investment in Quay Corporation		8,000
Cash dividend from Quay Corporation 40% × \$20,000 = \$8,000		

The balance of the Investment in Quay Corporation account after these transactions is \$204,000, as shown here:

INVESTMENT IN QUAY CORPORATION

Investment	180,000	Dividend Received	8,000
Share of Income	32,000		
Bal.	204,000		

The share of income is reported as a separate line item on the income statement as a part of income from operations. The dividends received affect cash flows from operating activities on the statement of cash flows. The reported income (\$32,000) exceeds the cash received by \$24,000.

Controlling Investment When a controlling interest exists—usually when one company owns more than 50 percent of the voting stock of another company—consolidated financial statements are required. The investing company is the *parent company*; the other company is a *subsidiary*. Because a parent company and its subsidiaries are separate legal entities, each prepares separate financial statements. However, because of their special relationship, they are viewed for external financial reporting purposes as a single economic entity. For this reason, the FASB requires that they combine their financial statements into a single set of statements called *consolidated financial statements*. The concepts and procedures related to the preparation of consolidated financial statements are the subject of more advanced courses.

Investments in Debt Securities

As noted in previous chapters, debt securities are considered financial instruments because they are claims that will be paid in cash. When a company purchases debt securities, it records them at cost plus any commissions and fees. Like investments in equity securities, short-term investments in debt securities are valued at fair value at the end of the accounting period and are accounted for as trading securities or available-for-sale securities. However, the accounting treatment is different if they qualify as held-to-maturity securities.

Held-to-Maturity Securities As we noted earlier, held-to-maturity securities are debt securities that management intends to hold to their maturity date. Such securities are recorded at cost and are valued on the balance sheet at cost adjusted for the effects of interest. For example, suppose that on December 1, 2010, Webber Company pays \$97,000 for U.S. Treasury bills, which are short-term debt of the federal government. The bills will mature in 120 days at \$100,000. Webber would make the following entry:

A	=	L	+	OE
+97,000				
−97,000				

2010			
Dec. 1	Short-Term Investments	97,000	
	Cash		97,000
	Purchase of U.S. Treasury bills that mature in 120 days		

At Webber's year end on December 31, the entry to accrue the interest income earned to date would be as follows:

A	=	L	+	OE
+750				+750

2010			
Dec. 31	Short-Term Investments	750	
	Interest Income		750
	Accrual of interest on U.S. Treasury bills \$3,000 × 30/120 = \$750		

On December 31, the U.S. Treasury bills would be shown on the balance sheet as a short-term investment at their amortized cost of \$97,750 (\$97,000 + \$750). When Webber receives the maturity value on March 31, 2011, the entry is as follows:

A	=	L	+	OE
+100,000				+2,250
−97,750				

2011			
Mar. 31	Cash	100,000	
	Short-Term Investments		97,750
	Interest Income		2,250
	Receipt of cash at maturity of U.S. Treasury bills and recognition of related income		

Long-Term Investments in Bonds

Like all investments, investments in bonds are recorded at cost, which, in this case, is the price of the bonds plus the broker's commission. When bonds are purchased between interest payment dates, the purchaser must also pay an amount equal to the interest that has accrued on the bonds since the last interest payment date. Then, on the next interest payment date, the purchaser receives an interest payment for the whole period. The payment for accrued interest should be recorded as a debit to Interest Income, which will be offset by a credit to Interest Income when the semiannual interest is received.

Subsequent accounting for a corporation's long-term bond investments depends on the classification of the bonds. If the company plans to hold the bonds until they are paid off on their maturity date, they are considered held-to-maturity securities. Except in industries like insurance and banking, it is unusual for companies to buy the bonds of other companies with the express purpose of holding them until they mature, which can be in 10 to 30 years. Thus, most long-term bond investments are classified as available-for-sale securities, meaning that the company plans to sell them at some point before their maturity date. Such bonds are accounted for at fair value, much as equity or stock investments are; fair value is usually the market value. When bonds are intended to be held to maturity, they are accounted for not at fair value but at cost, adjusted for the amortization of their discount or premium. The procedure is similar to accounting for long-term bond liabilities, except that separate accounts for discounts and premiums are not used.

STOP & REVIEW >

- What is the role of fair value in accounting for investments?
- What is the difference between trading securities, available-for-sale securities, and held-to-maturity securities?
- Why are the level and percentage of ownership important in accounting for equity investments?
- How are trading securities valued at the balance sheet date?
- What are unrealized gains and losses on trading securities? On what statement are they reported?
- How does accounting for available-for-sale securities differ from accounting for trading securities?
- At what value are held-to-maturity securities shown on the balance sheet?

Problems

Trading Securities

P 1. Omar Corporation, which has begun investing in trading securities, engaged in the following transactions:

Jan. 6 Purchased 7,000 shares of Quaker Oats stock, $30 per share.
Feb. 15 Purchased 9,000 shares of EG&G, $22 per share.

At year end on June 30, Quaker Oats was trading at $40 per share, and EG&G was trading at $18 per share.

Record the entries in journal form for the purchases. Then record the necessary year-end adjusting entry. (Include a schedule of the trading portfolio cost and market in the explanation.) Also record the entry for the sale of all the EG&G shares on August 20 for $16 per share. Is the last entry affected by the June 30 adjustment?

Methods of Accounting for Long-Term Investments

P 2. Teague Corporation has the following long-term investments:

1. 60 percent of the common stock of Ariel Corporation
2. 13 percent of the common stock of Copper, Inc.
3. 50 percent of the nonvoting preferred stock of Staffordshire Corporation
4. 100 percent of the common stock of its financing subsidiary, EQ, Inc.
5. 35 percent of the common stock of the French company Rue de le Brasseur
6. 70 percent of the common stock of the Canadian company Nova Scotia Cannery

For each of these investments, tell which of the following methods should be used for external financial reporting, and why:

a. Cost-adjusted-to-market method
b. Equity method
c. Consolidation of parent and subsidiary financial statements

Long-Term Investments

P 3. Fulco Corporation has the following portfolio of long-term available-for-sale securities at year end, December 31, 2011:

Company	Percentage of Voting Stock Held	Cost	Year-End Market Value
A Corporation	4	$ 80,000	$ 95,000
B Corporation	12	375,000	275,000
C Corporation	5	30,000	55,000
Total		$485,000	$425,000

Both the Unrealized Loss on Long-Term Investments account and the Allowance to Adjust Long-Term Investments to Market account currently have a balance of $40,000 from the last accounting period. Prepare T accounts with a beginning balance for each of these accounts. Record the effects of the above information on the accounts, and determine the ending balances.

Long-Term Investments: Cost-Adjusted-to-Market and Equity Methods

P 4. On January 1, Rourke Corporation purchased, as long-term investments, 8 percent of the voting stock of Taglia Corporation for $250,000 and 45 percent of the voting stock of Curry Corporation for $2 million. During the year, Taglia Corporation had earnings of $100,000 and paid dividends of $40,000. Curry Corporation had earnings of $300,000 and paid dividends of $200,000. The market value did not change for either investment during the year. Which of these investments should be accounted for using the cost-adjusted-to-market method? Which should be accounted for using the equity method? At what amount should each investment be carried on the balance sheet at year end? Give a reason for each choice.

Held-to-Maturity Securities

P 5. Dale Company experiences heavy sales in the summer and early fall, after which time it has excess cash to invest until the next spring. On November 1, 2011, the company invested $194,000 in U.S. Treasury bills. The bills mature in 180 days at $200,000. Prepare entries in journal form to record the purchase on November 1; the adjustment to accrue interest on December 31, which is the end of the fiscal year; and the receipt of cash at the maturity date of April 30.

Comprehensive Accounting for Investments

P 6. Gulf Coast Corporation is a successful oil and gas exploration business in the southwestern United States. At the beginning of 2011, the company made investments in three companies that perform services in the oil and gas industry. The details of each of these investments follow.

Gulf Coast purchased 100,000 shares of Marsh Service Corporation at a cost of $16 per share. Marsh has 1.5 million shares outstanding and during 2011 paid dividends of $0.80 per share on earnings of $1.60 per share. At the end of the year, Marsh's shares were selling for $24 per share.

Gulf Coast also purchased 2 million shares of Crescent Drilling Company at $8 per share. Crescent has 10 million shares outstanding. In 2011, Crescent paid a dividend of $0.40 per share on earnings of $0.80 per share. During the year, the president of Gulf Coast was appointed to Crescent's board of directors. At the end of the year, Crescent's stock was selling for $12 per share.

In another action, Gulf Coast purchased 1 million shares of Logan Oil Field Supplies Company's 5 million outstanding shares at $12 per share. The president of Gulf Coast sought membership on Logan's board of directors but was rebuffed when a majority of shareholders stated they did not want to be associated with Gulf Coast. Logan paid a dividend of $0.80 per share and reported a net income of only $0.40 per share for the year. By the end of the year, its stock price had dropped to $4 per share.

Required

1. For each investment, make entries in journal form for (a) initial investment, (b) receipt of cash dividend, and (c) recognition of income (if appropriate).
2. What adjusting entry (if any) is required at the end of the year?
3. Assuming that Gulf Coast sells its investment in Logan after the first of the year for $6 per share, what entry would be made?
4. Assuming no other transactions occur and that the market value of Gulf Coast's investment in Marsh exceeds cost by $2,400,000 at the end of the second year, what adjusting entry (if any) would be required?
5. What principal factors were considered in determining how to account for Gulf Coast's investments? Should they be shown on the balance sheet as short-term or long-term investments? What factors affect this decision?

User insight ▶ (item 5)

Long-Term Investments: Equity Method

P 7. Rylander Corporation owns 35 percent of the voting stock of Waters Corporation. The Investment account on Rylander's books as of January 1, 2011, was $720,000. During 2011, Waters reported the following quarterly earnings and dividends:

Quarter	Earnings	Dividends Paid
1	$160,000	$100,000
2	240,000	100,000
3	120,000	100,000
4	(80,000)	100,000
	$440,000	$400,000

Because of the percentage of voting shares Rylander owns, it can exercise significant influence over the operations of Waters Corporation. Therefore, Rylander Corporation must account for the investment using the equity method.

Required

1. Prepare a T account for Rylander Corporation's investment in Waters, and enter the beginning balance, the relevant entries for the year in total, and the ending balance.
2. What is the effect and placement of the entries in requirement **1** on Rylander Corporation's earnings as reported on the income statement?
3. What is the effect and placement of the entries in requirement **1** on the statement of cash flows?
4. How would the effects on the statements differ if Rylander's ownership represented only a 15 percent share of Waters?

User insight ▶ (items 2, 3, 4)

APPENDIX

B Present Value Tables

TABLE 1 Present Value of $1 to Be Received at the End of a Given Number of Time Periods

Periods	1%	2%	3%	4%	5%	6%	7%	8%	9%	10%	12%
1	0.990	0.980	0.971	0.962	0.952	0.943	0.935	0.926	0.917	0.909	0.893
2	0.980	0.961	0.943	0.925	0.907	0.890	0.873	0.857	0.842	0.826	0.797
3	0.971	0.942	0.915	0.889	0.864	0.840	0.816	0.794	0.772	0.751	0.712
4	0.961	0.924	0.888	0.855	0.823	0.792	0.763	0.735	0.708	0.683	0.636
5	0.951	0.906	0.883	0.822	0.784	0.747	0.713	0.681	0.650	0.621	0.567
6	0.942	0.888	0.837	0.790	0.746	0.705	0.666	0.630	0.596	0.564	0.507
7	0.933	0.871	0.813	0.760	0.711	0.665	0.623	0.583	0.547	0.513	0.452
8	0.923	0.853	0.789	0.731	0.677	0.627	0.582	0.540	0.502	0.467	0.404
9	0.914	0.837	0.766	0.703	0.645	0.592	0.544	0.500	0.460	0.424	0.361
10	0.905	0.820	0.744	0.676	0.614	0.558	0.508	0.463	0.422	0.386	0.322
11	0.896	0.804	0.722	0.650	0.585	0.527	0.475	0.429	0.388	0.350	0.287
12	0.887	0.788	0.701	0.625	0.557	0.497	0.444	0.397	0.356	0.319	0.257
13	0.879	0.773	0.681	0.601	0.530	0.469	0.415	0.368	0.326	0.290	0.229
14	0.870	0.758	0.661	0.577	0.505	0.442	0.388	0.340	0.299	0.263	0.205
15	0.861	0.743	0.642	0.555	0.481	0.417	0.362	0.315	0.275	0.239	0.183
16	0.853	0.728	0.623	0.534	0.458	0.394	0.339	0.292	0.252	0.218	0.163
17	0.844	0.714	0.605	0.513	0.436	0.371	0.317	0.270	0.231	0.198	0.146
18	0.836	0.700	0.587	0.494	0.416	0.350	0.296	0.250	0.212	0.180	0.130
19	0.828	0.686	0.570	0.475	0.396	0.331	0.277	0.232	0.194	0.164	0.116
20	0.820	0.673	0.554	0.456	0.377	0.312	0.258	0.215	0.178	0.149	0.104
21	0.811	0.660	0.538	0.439	0.359	0.294	0.242	0.199	0.164	0.135	0.093
22	0.803	0.647	0.522	0.422	0.342	0.278	0.226	0.184	0.150	0.123	0.083
23	0.795	0.634	0.507	0.406	0.326	0.262	0.211	0.170	0.138	0.112	0.074
24	0.788	0.622	0.492	0.390	0.310	0.247	0.197	0.158	0.126	0.102	0.066
25	0.780	0.610	0.478	0.375	0.295	0.233	0.184	0.146	0.116	0.092	0.059
26	0.772	0.598	0.464	0.361	0.281	0.220	0.172	0.135	0.106	0.084	0.053
27	0.764	0.586	0.450	0.347	0.268	0.207	0.161	0.125	0.098	0.076	0.047
28	0.757	0.574	0.437	0.333	0.255	0.196	0.150	0.116	0.090	0.069	0.042
29	0.749	0.563	0.424	0.321	0.243	0.185	0.141	0.107	0.082	0.063	0.037
30	0.742	0.552	0.412	0.308	0.231	0.174	0.131	0.099	0.075	0.057	0.033
40	0.672	0.453	0.307	0.208	0.142	0.097	0.067	0.046	0.032	0.022	0.011
50	0.608	0.372	0.228	0.141	0.087	0.054	0.034	0.021	0.013	0.009	0.003

Table 1 is used to compute the value today of a single amount of cash to be received sometime in the future. To use Table 1, you must first know (1) the time period in years until funds will be received, (2) the stated annual rate of interest, and (3) the dollar amount to be received at the end of the time period.

Example—Table 1. What is the present value of \$30,000 to be received 25 years from now, assuming a 14 percent interest rate? From Table 1, the required multiplier is 0.038, and the answer is:

$$\$30{,}000 \times 0.038 = \$1{,}140$$

The factor values for Table 1 are:

$$\text{PV Factor} = (1 + r)^{-n}$$

14%	15%	16%	18%	20%	25%	30%	35%	40%	45%	50%	Periods
0.877	0.870	0.862	0.847	0.833	0.800	0.769	0.741	0.714	0.690	0.667	1
0.769	0.756	0.743	0.718	0.694	0.640	0.592	0.549	0.510	0.476	0.444	2
0.675	0.658	0.641	0.609	0.579	0.512	0.455	0.406	0.364	0.328	0.296	3
0.592	0.572	0.552	0.516	0.482	0.410	0.350	0.301	0.260	0.226	0.198	4
0.519	0.497	0.476	0.437	0.402	0.328	0.269	0.223	0.186	0.156	0.132	5
0.456	0.432	0.410	0.370	0.335	0.262	0.207	0.165	0.133	0.108	0.088	6
0.400	0.376	0.354	0.314	0.279	0.210	0.159	0.122	0.095	0.074	0.059	7
0.351	0.327	0.305	0.266	0.233	0.168	0.123	0.091	0.068	0.051	0.039	8
0.308	0.284	0.263	0.225	0.194	0.134	0.094	0.067	0.048	0.035	0.026	9
0.270	0.247	0.227	0.191	0.162	0.107	0.073	0.050	0.035	0.024	0.017	10
0.237	0.215	0.195	0.162	0.135	0.086	0.056	0.037	0.025	0.017	0.012	11
0.208	0.187	0.168	0.137	0.112	0.069	0.043	0.027	0.018	0.012	0.008	12
0.182	0.163	0.145	0.116	0.093	0.055	0.033	0.020	0.013	0.008	0.005	13
0.160	0.141	0.125	0.099	0.078	0.044	0.025	0.015	0.009	0.006	0.003	14
0.140	0.123	0.108	0.084	0.065	0.035	0.020	0.011	0.006	0.004	0.002	15
0.123	0.107	0.093	0.071	0.054	0.028	0.015	0.008	0.005	0.003	0.002	16
0.108	0.093	0.080	0.060	0.045	0.023	0.012	0.006	0.003	0.002	0.001	17
0.095	0.081	0.069	0.051	0.038	0.018	0.009	0.005	0.002	0.001	0.001	18
0.083	0.070	0.060	0.043	0.031	0.014	0.007	0.003	0.002	0.001		19
0.073	0.061	0.051	0.037	0.026	0.012	0.005	0.002	0.001	0.001		20
0.064	0.053	0.044	0.031	0.022	0.009	0.004	0.002	0.001			21
0.056	0.046	0.038	0.026	0.018	0.007	0.003	0.001	0.001			22
0.049	0.040	0.033	0.022	0.015	0.006	0.002	0.001				23
0.043	0.035	0.028	0.019	0.013	0.005	0.002	0.001				24
0.038	0.030	0.024	0.016	0.010	0.004	0.001	0.001				25
0.033	0.026	0.021	0.014	0.009	0.003	0.001					26
0.029	0.023	0.018	0.011	0.007	0.002	0.001					27
0.026	0.020	0.016	0.010	0.006	0.002	0.001					28
0.022	0.017	0.014	0.008	0.005	0.002						29
0.020	0.015	0.012	0.007	0.004	0.001						30
0.005	0.004	0.003	0.001	0.001							40
0.001	0.001	0.001									50

TABLE 2 Present Value of $1 Received Each Period for a Given Number of Time Periods

Periods	1%	2%	3%	4%	5%	6%	7%	8%	9%	10%	12%
1	0.990	0.980	0.971	0.962	0.952	0.943	0.935	0.926	0.917	0.909	0.893
2	1.970	1.942	1.913	1.886	1.859	1.833	1.808	1.783	1.759	1.736	1.690
3	2.941	2.884	2.829	2.775	2.723	2.673	2.624	2.577	2.531	2.487	2.402
4	3.902	3.808	3.717	3.630	3.546	3.465	3.387	3.312	3.240	3.170	3.037
5	4.853	4.713	4.580	4.452	4.329	4.212	4.100	3.993	3.890	3.791	3.605
6	5.795	5.601	5.417	5.242	5.076	4.917	4.767	4.623	4.486	4.355	4.111
7	6.728	6.472	6.230	6.002	5.786	5.582	5.389	5.206	5.033	4.868	4.564
8	7.652	7.325	7.020	6.733	6.463	6.210	5.971	5.747	5.535	5.335	4.968
9	8.566	8.162	7.786	7.435	7.108	6.802	6.515	6.247	5.995	5.759	5.328
10	9.471	8.983	8.530	8.111	7.722	7.360	7.024	6.710	6.418	6.145	5.650
11	10.368	9.787	9.253	8.760	8.306	7.887	7.499	7.139	6.805	6.495	5.938
12	11.255	10.575	9.954	9.385	8.863	8.384	7.943	7.536	7.161	6.814	6.194
13	12.134	11.348	10.635	9.986	9.394	8.853	8.358	7.904	7.487	7.103	6.424
14	13.004	12.106	11.296	10.563	9.899	9.295	8.745	8.244	7.786	7.367	6.628
15	13.865	12.849	11.938	11.118	10.380	9.712	9.108	8.559	8.061	7.606	6.811
16	14.718	13.578	12.561	11.652	10.838	10.106	9.447	8.851	8.313	7.824	6.974
17	15.562	14.292	13.166	12.166	11.274	10.477	9.763	9.122	8.544	8.022	7.120
18	16.398	14.992	13.754	12.659	11.690	10.828	10.059	9.372	8.756	8.201	7.250
19	17.226	15.678	14.324	13.134	12.085	11.158	10.336	9.604	8.950	8.365	7.366
20	18.046	16.351	14.878	13.590	12.462	11.470	10.594	9.818	9.129	8.514	7.469
21	18.857	17.011	15.415	14.029	12.821	11.764	10.836	10.017	9.292	8.649	7.562
22	19.660	17.658	15.937	14.451	13.163	12.042	11.061	10.201	9.442	8.772	7.645
23	20.456	18.292	16.444	14.857	13.489	12.303	11.272	10.371	9.580	8.883	7.718
24	21.243	18.914	16.936	15.247	13.799	12.550	11.469	10.529	9.707	8.985	7.784
25	22.023	19.523	17.413	15.622	14.094	12.783	11.654	10.675	9.823	9.077	7.843
26	22.795	20.121	17.877	15.983	14.375	13.003	11.826	10.810	9.929	9.161	7.896
27	23.560	20.707	18.327	16.330	14.643	13.211	11.987	10.935	10.027	9.237	7.943
28	24.316	21.281	18.764	16.663	14.898	13.406	12.137	11.051	10.116	9.307	7.984
29	25.066	21.844	19.189	16.984	15.141	13.591	12.278	11.158	10.198	9.370	8.022
30	25.808	22.396	19.600	17.292	15.373	13.765	12.409	11.258	10.274	9.427	8.055
40	32.835	27.355	23.115	19.793	17.159	15.046	13.332	11.925	10.757	9.779	8.244
50	39.196	31.424	25.730	21.482	18.256	15.762	13.801	12.234	10.962	9.915	8.305

Table 2 is used to compute the present value of a *series* of *equal* annual cash flows.

Example—Table 2. Arthur Howard won a contest on January 1, 2010, in which the prize was $30,000, payable in 15 annual installments of $2,000 each December 31, beginning in 2010. Assuming a 9 percent interest rate, what is the present value of Howard's prize on January 1, 2010? From Table 2, the required multiplier is 8.061, and the answer is:

$$\$2{,}000 \times 8.061 = \$16{,}122$$

The factor values for Table 2 are:

$$\text{PVa Factor} = \frac{1 - (1 + r)^{-n}}{r}$$

14%	15%	16%	18%	20%	25%	30%	35%	40%	45%	50%	Periods
0.877	0.870	0.862	0.847	0.833	0.800	0.769	0.741	0.714	0.690	0.667	1
1.647	1.626	1.605	1.566	1.528	1.440	1.361	1.289	1.224	1.165	1.111	2
2.322	2.283	2.246	2.174	2.106	1.952	1.816	1.696	1.589	1.493	1.407	3
2.914	2.855	2.798	2.690	2.589	2.362	2.166	1.997	1.849	1.720	1.605	4
3.433	3.352	3.274	3.127	2.991	2.689	2.436	2.220	2.035	1.876	1.737	5
3.889	3.784	3.685	3.498	3.326	2.951	2.643	2.385	2.168	1.983	1.824	6
4.288	4.160	4.039	3.812	3.605	3.161	2.802	2.508	2.263	2.057	1.883	7
4.639	4.487	4.344	4.078	3.837	3.329	2.925	2.598	2.331	2.109	1.922	8
4.946	4.772	4.607	4.303	4.031	3.463	3.019	2.665	2.379	2.144	1.948	9
5.216	5.019	4.833	4.494	4.192	3.571	3.092	2.715	2.414	2.168	1.965	10
5.453	5.234	5.029	4.656	4.327	3.656	3.147	2.752	2.438	2.185	1.977	11
5.660	5.421	5.197	4.793	4.439	3.725	3.190	2.779	2.456	2.197	1.985	12
5.842	5.583	5.342	4.910	4.533	3.780	3.223	2.799	2.469	2.204	1.990	13
6.002	5.724	5.468	5.008	4.611	3.824	3.249	2.814	2.478	2.210	1.993	14
6.142	5.847	5.575	5.092	4.675	3.859	3.268	2.825	2.484	2.214	1.995	15
6.265	5.954	5.669	5.162	4.730	3.887	3.283	2.834	2.489	2.216	1.997	16
6.373	6.047	5.749	5.222	4.775	3.910	3.295	2.840	2.492	2.218	1.998	17
6.467	6.128	5.818	5.273	4.812	3.928	3.304	2.844	2.494	2.219	1.999	18
6.550	6.198	5.877	5.316	4.844	3.942	3.311	2.848	2.496	2.220	1.999	19
6.623	6.259	5.929	5.353	4.870	3.954	3.316	2.850	2.497	2.221	1.999	20
6.687	6.312	5.973	5.384	4.891	3.963	3.320	2.852	2.498	2.221	2.000	21
6.743	6.359	6.011	5.410	4.909	3.970	3.323	2.853	2.498	2.222	2.000	22
6.792	6.399	6.044	5.432	4.925	3.976	3.325	2.854	2.499	2.222	2.000	23
6.835	6.434	6.073	5.451	4.973	3.981	3.327	2.855	2.499	2.222	2.000	24
6.873	6.464	6.097	5.467	4.948	3.985	3.329	2.856	2.499	2.222	2.000	25
6.906	6.491	6.118	5.480	4.956	3.988	3.330	2.856	2.500	2.222	2.000	26
6.935	6.514	6.136	5.492	4.964	3.990	3.331	2.856	2.500	2.222	2.000	27
6.961	6.534	6.152	5.502	4.970	3.992	3.331	2.857	2.500	2.222	2.000	28
6.983	6.551	6.166	5.510	4.975	3.994	3.332	2.857	2.500	2.222	2.000	29
7.003	6.566	6.177	5.517	4.979	3.995	3.332	2.857	2.500	2.222	2.000	30
7.105	6.642	6.234	5.548	4.997	3.999	3.333	2.857	2.500	2.222	2.000	40
7.133	6.661	6.246	5.554	4.999	4.000	3.333	2.857	2.500	2.222	2.000	50

Table 2 is the columnar sum of Table 1. Table 2 applies to *ordinary annuities,* in which the first cash flow occurs one time period beyond the date for which the present value is computed.

An *annuity due* is a series of equal cash flows for N time periods, but the first payment occurs immediately. The present value of the first payment equals the face value of the cash flow; Table 2 then is used to measure the present value of N − 1 remaining cash flows.

Example—Table 2. Determine the present value on January 1, 2010, of 20 lease payments; each payment of $10,000 is due on January 1, beginning in 2010. Assume an interest rate of 8 percent.

Present Value = Immediate Payment + Present Value of 19 Subsequent Payments at 8%
= $10,000 + ($10,000 × 9.604) = $106,040

ENDNOTES

Chapter 1

1. *Statement of Financial Accounting Concepts No. 1,* "Objectives of Financial Reporting by Business Enterprises" (Norwalk, Conn.: Financial Accounting Standards Board, 1978), par. 9.
2. Ibid.
3. CVS Corporation, *Annual Report,* 2008.
4. Ibid.
5. Christopher D. Ittner, David F. Larcker, and Madhav V. Rajan, "The Choice of Performance Measures in Annual Bonus Contracts," *The Accounting Review,* April 1997.
6. National Commission on Fraudulent Financial Reporting, *Report of the National Commission on Fraudulent Financial Reporting* (Washington, D.C.: 1987), p. 2.
7. Target Corporation, Form 10-K, 2008.
8. "Gallup Poll Shows the Public's Opinion of Accounting Profession Is Improving," http://www.picpa.org, August 24, 2005.
9. Robert Johnson, "The New CFO," *Crain's Chicago Business,* July 19, 2004.
10. *Accounting Principles Board Statement No. 4,* "Basic Concepts and Accounting Principles Underlying Financial Statements of Business Enterprises" (New York: AICPA, 1970), par. 138.
11. Securities and Exchange Commission, *Roadmap for the Potential Use of Financial Statements Prepared in Accordance with International Financial Reporting Standards by US Issuers,* August 2008.
12. *Statement Number 1C,* "Standards of Ethical Conduct for Management Accountants" (Montvale, N.J.: Institute of Management Accountants, 1983; revised 1997).
13. Curtis C. Verschoor, "Corporate Performance Is Closely Tied to a Strong Ethical Commitment," *Journal of Business and Society,* Winter 1999; Verschoor, "Does Superior Governance Still Lead to Better Financial Performance?" *Strategic Finance,* October 2004.
14. Costco Wholesale Corporation, *Annual Report,* 2006.
15. Southwest Airlines Co., *Annual Report,* 1996.

Chapter 2

1. The Boeing Company, *Annual Report,* 2008.
2. *Statement of Financial Accounting Standards No. 157,* "Fair Value Measurements" (Norwalk, Conn.: Financial Accounting Standards Board, 2007).
3. Intel Corporation, *Annual Report,* 2008.
4. The Boeing Company, *Annual Report,* 2008.
5. Gary McWilliams, "EDS Accounting Change Cuts Past Earnings by $2.24 Billion," *The Wall Street Journal,* October 28, 2003.
6. Nike, Inc., *Annual Report,* 2008.

Chapter 3

1. Netflix, Inc., *Annual Report,* 2008.
2. "Microsoft Settles with SEC," *CBSNews.com,* June 5, 2002.
3. Christofer Lawson and Don Clark, "Dell to Restate 4 Years of Results," *The Wall Street Journal, August 17, 2007.*
4. Securities and Exchange Commission, *Staff Accounting Bulletin No. 10,* 1999.
5. Ken Brown, "Wall Street Plays Numbers Games with Savings, Despite Reforms," *The Wall Street Journal,* July 22, 2003.
6. Netflix, Inc., *Annual Report,* 2008.
7. Ibid.

Chapter 4

1. Adapted from Robert Half International, Inc., *Annual Report,* 2005.

Chapter 5

1. *Statement of Financial Accounting Concepts No. 1,* "Objectives of Financial Reporting by Business Enterprises" (Norwalk, Conn.: Financial Accounting Standards Board, 1978), pars. 32–54.
2. *Statement of Financial Accounting Concepts No. 2,* "Qualitative Characteristics of Accounting Information" (Norwalk, Conn.: Financial Accounting Standards Board, 1980), par. 20.
3. L. Todd Johnson, "Relevance and Reliability," *The FASB Report,* February 28, 2005.
4. Dell Computer Corporation, Form 10-K for the Fiscal Year Ended February 3, 2006.
5. "Ex-Chief of WorldCom Is Found Guilty in $11 Billion Fraud," *The New York Times,* March 16, 2005.
6. *Accounting Principles Board, Opinion No. 20,* "Accounting Changes" (New York: AICPA, 1971), par. 17.
7. Securities and Exchange Commission, *Staff Accounting Bulletin No. 99,* 1999.
8. http://www.fasb.org, July 12, 2008.
9. Ray J. Groves, "Here's the Annual Report. Got a Few Hours?" *The Wall Street Journal Europe,* August 26–27, 1994.
10. Roger Lowenstein, "Investors Will Fish for Footnotes in Abbreviated' Annual Reports," *The Wall Street Journal,* September 14, 1995.
11. Securities and Exchange Commission, *Staff Accounting Bulletin No. 99,* 1999.
12. Roger Lowenstein, "The 20% Club' Is No Longer Exclusive," *The Wall Street Journal,* May 4, 1995.
13. Albertson's Inc., *Annual Report,* 2008; Great Atlantic & Pacific Tea Company, *Annual Report,* 2008.

Chapter 6

1. Jathon Sapsford, "As Cash Fades, America Becomes a Plastic Nation," *The Wall Street Journal,* July 23, 2004.
2. Helen Leggatt, "Growth Forecast for 2009 On-line Retail Sales," *BizReport,* January 30, 2009.
3. Joel Millman, "Here's What Happens to Many Lovely Gifts After Santa Rides Off," *The Wall Street Journal,* December 26, 2001.
4. Matthew Rose, "Magazine Revenue at Newsstands Falls in Worst Year Ever," *The Wall Street Journal,* May 15, 2001.

Chapter 7

1. Committee of Sponsoring Organizations of the Treadway Commission (COSO), *Internal Control—Integrated Framework, 1985–2005.*
2. Costco Wholesale Corporation, *Annual Report,* 2008.
3. Jonathan Weil, "Accounting Scheme Was Straightforward but Hard to Detect," *The Wall Street Journal,* July 23, 2004.
4. Costco Wholesale Corporation, *Annual Report,* 2008.

5. *Professional Standards,* vol. 1, Sec. AU 325.16.
6. KPMG Peat Marwick, "1998 Fraud Survey," 1998.
7. Elizabeth Woyke, "Attention Shoplifters," *BusinessWeek,* September 11, 2006.
8. Amy Merrick, "Starbucks Accuses Employee, Husband of Embezzling $3.7 Million from Firm," *The Wall Street Journal,* November 20, 2000.

Chapter 8

1. Toyota Motor Corporation, *Annual Report,* 2008.
2. Gary McWilliams, "Whirlwind on the Web," *BusinessWeek,* April 7, 1997.
3. Karen Lundebaard, "Bumpy Ride," *The Wall Street Journal,* May 21, 2001.
4. "Cisco's Numbers Confound Some," *International Herald Tribune,* April 19, 2001.
5. "Kmart Posts $67 Million Loss Due to Markdowns," *The Wall Street Journal,* November 10, 2000.
6. American Institute of Certified Public Accountants, *Accounting Trends & Techniques* (New York: AICPA, 2008).
7. Toyota Motor Corporation., *Annual Report,* 2008.
8. Ernst & Young, *U.S. GAAP vs. IFRS: The Basics,* 2007.
9. American Institute of Certified Public Accountants, *Accounting Trends & Techniques* (New York: AICPA, 2007).
10. American Institute of Certified Public Accountants, *Accounting Trends & Techniques* (New York: AICPA, 2008).

Chapter 9

1. Peter Coy and Michael Arndt, "Up a Creek with Lots of Cash," *BusinessWeek,* November 12, 2001.
2. "So Much for Detroit's Cash Cushion," *BusinessWeek,* November 5, 2001.
3. Jesse Drucker, "Sprint Expects Loss of Subscribers," *The Wall Street Journal,* September 24, 2002.
4. Michael Selz, "Big Customers' Late Bills Choke Small Suppliers," *The Wall Street Journal,* June 22, 1994.
5. Circuit City Stores, Inc., *Annual Report,* 2005.
6. Deborah Solomon and Damian Paletta, "U.S. Drafts Sweeping Plans to Fight Crisis as Turmoil Worsens in Credit Markets," *The Wall Street Journal,* September 19, 2008.
7. Heather Timmons, "Do Household's Numbers Add Up?" *BusinessWeek,* December 10, 2001.
8. Steve Daniels, "Bank One Reserves Feed Earnings," *Crain's Chicago Business,* December 15, 2003.
9. Jonathon Weil, "Accounting Scheme Was Straightforward but Hard to Detect," *The Wall Street Journal,* March 20, 2003.
10. Nike, Inc., *Annual Report,* 2009.
11. Ibid.
12. American Institute of Certified Public Accountants, *Accounting Trends & Techniques* (New York: AICPA, 2007).
13. Tom Lauricella, Shefali Anand, and Valerie Bauerlein, "A $34 Billion Cash Fund to Close Up," *The Wall Street Journal,* December 11, 2007.
14. Jathon Sapsford, "As Cash Fades, America Becomes a Plastic Nation," *The Wall Street Journal,* July 23, 2004.
15. American Institute of Certified Public Accountants, *Accounting Trends & Techniques* (New York: AICPA, 2007).
16. "Bad Loans Rattle Telecom Vendors," *BusinessWeek,* February 19, 2001.
17. Scott Thurm, "Better Debt Bolsters Bottom Lines," *The Wall Street Journal,* August 18, 2003.
18. Information based on promotional brochures of Mitsubishi Corp.
19. Elizabeth McDonald, "Unhatched Chickens," *Forbes,* February 19, 2001.

Chapter 10

1. Pamela L. Moore, "How Xerox Ran Short of Black Ink," *BusinessWeek,* October 30, 2000.
2. Mark Heinzel, Deborah Solomon, and Joann S. Lublin, "Nortel Board Fires CEO and Others," *The Wall Street Journal,* April 29, 2004.
3. Hershey Foods Corporation, *Annual Report,* 2006.
4. Goodyear Tire & Rubber Company, *Annual Report,* 2006.
5. Andersen Enterprise Group, cited in *Crain's Chicago Business,* July 5, 1999.
6. Promomagazine.com, July 6, 2005.
7. Scott McCartney, "Your Free Flight to Mars Is Hobbling the Airline Industry," *The Wall Street Journal,* February 4, 2004.
8. Hershey Foods Corporation, *Annual Report,* 2007.
9. *Statement of Financial Accounting Standards No. 5,* "Accounting for Contingencies" (Norwalk, Conn.: Financial Accounting Standards Board, 1975).
10. American Institute of Certified Public Accountants, *Accounting Trends & Techniques* (New York: AICPA, 2007).
11. Microsoft, *Annual Report,* 2007.
12. American Institute of Certified Public Accountants, *Accounting Trends & Techniques* (New York: AICPA, 2007).
13. *Statement of Financial Accounting Concepts No. 7,* "Using Cash Flow Information and Present Value in Accounting Measurement" (Norwalk, Conn.: Financial Accounting Standards Board, 2000).
14. "Clarifications on Fair-Value Accounting," U.S. Securities and Exchange Commission, *Release 2008-234,* October 1, 2008.
15. Advertisement, *Chicago Tribune,* November 8, 2002.
16. General Motors Corporation, *Annual Report,* 2006.

Chapter 11

1. *Statement of Financial Accounting Standards No. 144,* "Accounting for the Impairment or Disposal of Long-Lived Assets" (Norwalk, Conn.: Financial Accounting Standards Board, 2001).
2. Sharon Young, "Large Telecom Firms, After WorldCom Moves, Consider Writedowns," *The Wall Street Journal,* March 18, 2003.
3. Edward J. Riedl, "An Examination of Long-lived Asset Impairments," *The Accounting Review,* Vol. 79, No. 3, pp. 823–852.
4. *Statement of Financial Accounting Standards No. 34,* "Capitalization of Interest Cost" (Norwalk, Conn.: Financial Accounting Standards Board, 1979), pars. 9–11.
5. American Institute of Certified Public Accountants, *Accounting Trends & Techniques* (New York: AICPA, 2007).
6. Ibid.
7. Jonathan Weil, "Oil Reserves Can Sure Be Slick," *The Wall Street Journal,* March 11, 2004.
8. *Statement of Financial Accounting Standards No. 25,* "Suspension of Certain Accounting Requirements for Oil and Gas Producing Companies" (Norwalk, Conn.: Financial Accounting Standards Board, 1979).
9. "The Top 100 Brands," *BusinessWeek,* August 5, 2002.
10. The New York Times Company, *Annual Report,* 2006.
11. *Statement of Financial Accounting Standards No. 142,* "Goodwill and Other Intangible Assets" (Norwalk, Conn.: Financial Accounting Standards Board, 2001), pars. 11–17.
12. General Motors Corporation, *Annual Report,* 2005.
13. Abbott Laboratories, *Annual Report,* 2005.

14. *Statement of Financial Accounting Standards No. 2,* "Accounting for Research and Development Costs" (Norwalk, Conn.: Financial Accounting Standards Board, 1974), par. 12.
15. *Statement of Financial Accounting Standards No. 86,* "Accounting for the Costs of Computer Software to Be Sold, Leased, or Otherwise Marketed" (Norwalk, Conn.: Financial Accounting Standards Board, 1985).
16. General Mills, Inc., *Annual Report,* 2007; H.J. Heinz Company, *Annual Report,* 2007; Tribune Company, *Annual Report,* 2007.
17. *Statement of Financial Accounting Standards No. 142,* "Goodwill and Other Intangible Assets" (Norwalk, Conn.: Financial Accounting Standards Board, 2001), pars. 11–17.
18. Southwest Airlines Co., *Annual Report,* 2002.
19. Costco Wholesale Corporation, *Annual Report,* 2007.
20. Hilton Hotels Corporation, *Annual Report,* 2006; Marriott International, Inc., *Annual Report,* 2006.

Chapter 12

1. "Stock and Bond Market Shrivels," Wall Street Journal Digital Network, January 2, 2009.
2. Microsoft Corporation, *Annual Report,* 2009.
3. Deborah Solomon, "AT&T Slashes Dividends 83%, Cuts Forecasts," *The Wall Street Journal,* December 21, 2002.
4. Abbott Laboratories, *Annual Report,* 2008.
5. Google, Inc., *Form S-1* (Registration Statement), 2007.
6. Microsoft Corporation, *Annual Report,* 2009.
7. American Institute of Certified Public Accountants, *Accounting Trends & Techniques* (New York: AICPA, 2007).
8. *Statement of Accounting Standards No. 123,* "Stock-Based Payments" (Norwalk, Conn.: Financial Accounting Standards Board, 1995; amended 2004).
9. Google, Inc., *Form S-1* (Registration Statement), 2009.
10. Jonathan Weil, "FASB Unveils Expensing Plan on Option Pay," *The Wall Street Journal,* April 1, 2004.
11. Joseph Weber, "One Share, Many Votes," *BusinessWeek,* March 29, 2004; Google, Inc., *Form S-1* (Registration Statement), 2004.
12. Michael Rapaport and Jonathan Weil, "More Truth-in-Labeling for Accounting Carries Liabilities," *The Wall Street Journal,* August 23, 2003.
13. American Institute of Certified Public Accountants, *Accounting Trends & Techniques* (New York: AICPA, 2007).
14. David Henry, "The Dirty Little Secret about Buybacks," *BusinessWeek,* January 23, 2006; Peter A. McKay and Justin Lahart, "Boom in Buybacks Helps Lift Stocks to Record Heights," *The Wall Street Journal,* July 18, 2007.
15. Mariss Marr, "Dreamworks Shares Rise 38% on First Day," *The Wall Street Journal,* October 10, 2004; *Yahoo Finance,* December 26, 2007.
16. IBM Corporation, *Annual Report,* 2006.
17. Google, Inc., *Form S-1* (Registration Statement), 2004.

Chapter 13

1. *Statement of Financial Accounting Standards No. 13,* "Accounting for Leases" (Norwalk, Conn.: Financial Accounting Standards Board, 1976), par. 10.
2. *Statement of Financial Accounting Standards No. 158,* "Employers' Accounting for Defined Benefit Pension and Other Postretirement Plans" (Norwalk, Conn.: Financial Accounting Standards Board, 2007).
3. General Motors, *Annual Report,* 2007.
4. Deborah Soloman, "After Pension Fund Debacle, San Diego Mired in Probes," *The Wall Street Journal,* October 10, 2005.
5. Mary Williams Walsh, "$53 Billion Shortfall for New Jersey Retiree Care," *The New York Times,* July 25, 2007.
6. *Statement of Financial Accounting Standards No. 106,* "Employers' Accounting for Postretirement Benefits Other than Pensions" (Norwalk, Conn.: Financial Accounting Standards Board, 1990).
7. Southwest Airlines, *Annual Report,* 2008.
8. McDonald's, Inc., *Annual Report,* 2008.
9. Bill Barnhart, "Bond Bellwether," *Chicago Tribune,* December 4, 1996.
10. Accounting Principles Board, *Opinion No. 21,* "Interest on Receivables and Payables" (New York: AICPA, 1971), par. 15.
11. Continental Airlines, *Annual Report,* 2008.
12. Tom Sullivan and Sonia Ryst, "Kodak $1 Billion Issue Draws Crowds," *The Wall Street Journal,* October 8, 2003.
13. Adapted from quotations in *The Wall Street Journal Online,* December 18, 2007.
14. Amazon.com, *Annual Report,* 2007.

Chapter 14

1. Cited in *The Week in Review* (Deloitte Haskins & Sells), February 28, 1985.
2. "Up to the Minute, Down to the Wire," *Twentieth Century Mutual Funds Newsletter,* 1996.
3. "After Charge for Licensing, McDonald's Posts a Record Loss," *The New York Times,* July 25, 2007; Christina Cheddar Berk, "Campbell's Profit Jumps 31 Percent," *The Wall Street Journal,* November 22, 2005.
4. Elizabeth MacDonald, "Pro Forma Puff Jobs," *Forbes,* December 9, 2002.
5. Barbara A. Lougee and Carol A. Marquardt, "Earnings Informativeness and Strategic Disclosure: An Empirical Examination of Pro Forma Earnings," *The Accounting Review,* July 2004.
6. American Institute of Certified Public Accountants, *Accounting Trends & Techniques* (New York: AICPA, 2007).
7. *Statement of Financial Reporting Standards No. 145,* "Rescission and Revision of Various Statements" (Norwalk, Conn.: Financial Accounting Standards Board, 2002).
8. *Statement of Financial Accounting Standards No. 109,* "Accounting for Income Taxes" (Norwalk, Conn.: Financial Accounting Standards Board, 1992).
9. American Institute of Certified Public Accountants, *Accounting Trends & Techniques* (New York: AICPA, 2007).
10. Accounting Principles Board, *Opinion No. 30,* "Reporting the Results of Operations" (New York: AICPA, 1973), par. 20.
11. *Statement of Financial Accounting Standards No. 128,* "Earnings per Share and the Disclosure of Information About Capital Structure" (Norwalk, Conn.: Financial Accounting Standards Board, 1997).
12. *Statement of Financial Accounting Standards No. 130,* "Reporting Comprehensive Income" (Norwalk, Conn.: Financial Accounting Standards Board, 1997).
13. American Institute of Certified Public Accountants, *Accounting Trends & Techniques* (New York: AICPA, 2007).
14. American Institute of Certified Public Accountants, *Accounting Research Bulletin No. 43* (New York: AICPA, 1953), chap. 7, sec. B, par. 10.
15. Ibid., par. 13.
16. Nike, *Annual Report,* 2007.

17. Robert O'Brien, "Tech's Chill Fails to Stem Stock Splits," *The Wall Street Journal,* June 8, 2000.
18. YahooFinance.com, 2007.
19. "Technology Firms Post Strong Earnings but Stock Prices Decline Sharply," *The Wall Street Journal,* January 21, 1988; Donald R. Seace, "Industrials Plunge 57.2 Points—Technology Stocks' Woes Cited," *The Wall Street Journal,* January 21, 1988.

Chapter 15

1. Ian McDonald, "Cash Dilemma: How to Spend It," *The Wall Street Journal,* May 24, 2006; Ian McDonald, "Companies Are Rolling in Cash, Too Bad," *The Wall Street Journal,* August 20, 2006.
2. "Deadweight on the Markets," *BusinessWeek,* February 19, 2001.
3. "Free Cash Flow Standouts," *Upside Newsletter,* October 3, 2001.
4. Amazom.com, *Form 10-K,* 2008.
5. Gary Slutsker, "Look at the Birdie and Say: 'Cash Flow,'" *Forbes,* October 25, 1993.
6. Jonathan Clements, "Yacktman Fund Is Bloodied but Unbowed," *The Wall Street Journal,* November 8, 1993.
7. Jeffery Laderman, "Earnings, Schmearnings—Look at the Cash," *BusinessWeek,* July 24, 1989.
8. Amazom.com, *Form 10-K,* 2008.
9. American Institute of Certified Public Accountants, *Accounting Trends & Techniques* (New York: AICPA, 2006).
10. Martin Peers and Robin Sidel, "WorldCom Causes Analysts to Evaluate EBITDA's Role," *The Wall Street Journal,* July 15, 2002.
11. Richard Passov, "How Much Cash Does Your Company Need?" *Harvard Business Review,* November 2003.
12. "Cash Flow Shortfall in Quarter May Lead to Default on Loan," *The Wall Street Journal,* September 4, 2001.
13. Enron Corporation, *Press Release,* October 16, 2001.
14. Dean Foust, "So Much Cash, So Few Dividends," *BusinessWeek,* January 20, 2003.

Chapter 16

1. David Henry, "The Numbers Game," *BusinessWeek,* May 14, 2001.
2. Jonathan Weil, "Pro Forma in Earnings Reports? . . . As If," *The Wall Street Journal,* April 24, 2003.
3. *Statement of Financial Accounting Standards No. 131,* "Segment Disclosures" (Norwalk, Conn.: Financial Accounting Standards Board, 1997).
4. Starbucks Corporation, *Annual Report,* 2008.
5. Ibid.
6. Ibid.
7. Target Corporation, *Proxy Statement,* May 18, 2005.
8. Starbucks Corporation, *Annual Report,* 2008.
9. Lee Hawkins, Jr., "S&P Cuts Rating on GM and Ford to Junk Status," *The Wall Street Journal,* May 6, 2005.

Chapter 17

1. "Nokia Unveils Plans for Chinese Centre," *Financial Times London,* May 9, 2000.

Appendix A

1. *Statement of Financial Accounting Standards No. 157,* "Fair Value Measurements" (Norwalk, Conn.: Financial Accounting Standards Board, 2007). *Statement of Financial Accounting Standards No. 159,* "The Fair Value Option for Financial Assets and Financial Liabilities" (Norwalk, Conn.: Financial Accounting Standards Board, 2007).
2. *Statement of Financial Accounting Standards No. 115,* "Accounting for Certain Investments in Debt and Equity Securities" (Norwalk, Conn.: Financial Accounting Standards Board, 1993).
3. Ibid.

COMPANY NAME INDEX

SUBJECT INDEX